WORLD
OF
LANGUAGE

DISCOVER
A
WHOLE
NEW
WORLD

SILVER BURDETT & GINN

learning through language...

Silver Burdett & Ginn World of Language leads your students to new discoveries. About their language. About themselves. About the world around them. Quality literature, a variety of writing opportunities, and meaningful connections open a whole new world of learning!

Welcome to a whole new world.

TABLE OF CONTENTS

WORLD OF LANGUAGE

We believe

that language inspires the journey. And that *real* books by *real* writers spark interest along the way. **World of Language** gives your children the opportunity to delight in words, in sounds, in the sheer pleasure of using language.

We believe that meaningful connections guide the journey. By connecting the known to the new and the language arts to other curriculum areas, **World of Language** creates understanding, nurtures knowledge, and fosters growth.

We believe that new discoveries are found along the journey. **World of Language** is personalized–its world is the child's world. **World of Language** is teachable– the logical, flexible, two-part organization empowers you to teach according to your needs and the needs of your students.

Step into a whole new world.

SILVER BURDETT & GINN

**A program
for every
teaching
style.**

A TEACHER'S EDITION TAILOR-MADE FOR YOU

World of Language is designed to meet the various needs of all the students in your classroom, to meet your school or district objectives, and to accommodate your individual teaching style.

Flexibility

Each unit in **World of Language** has a major flexibility option. Every one opens with a Writer's Warm-up where students write in their journals. This activity promotes writing fluency and introduces students to the unit theme, which is reflected throughout the activities and the high-quality literature selection.

Start with Part 1...

Following the Writer's Warm-up, you may choose to start the unit activities with either Part 1 or Part 2 of the unit. Teachers who believe that their students need the concrete experiences of language awareness lessons prior to engaging in the writing process should begin with Part 1. This section emphasizes grammar, mechanics, and usage by using students' journal writing as a springboard.

Or Start with Part 2...

For teachers who believe that exposure to the best children's literature and writing fluency should be stressed first and that language awareness should be taught using the students' own writing, turn directly to Part 2. This self-contained section emphasizes the integration of all the language arts through reading and responding to literature and through a writing process activity.

Whether you begin with Part 1 or Part 2, a diagnostic language awareness test is provided for each unit so that prescriptive teaching of grammar may be accomplished, depending on your students' special needs. Because either Part 1 or 2 may come first, each section of the unit can stand alone; however, both sections are unified by the prevailing theme, which is always related to the literature selection in the unit. The grammar lessons are not taught in isolation but are tied into the students' own writing and the unit theme. ◇

UNIT 6

TWO-PART *flexibility*

Unit 6 Overview

books ON UNIT THEME

OVERVIEW

USING LANGUAGE TO DESCRIBE

EASY

The Big Snow by Berta and Elmer Hader. Macmillan. This beautifully illustrated book shows how the birds and wild animals who live along the Hudson River prepare for the winter and the big snow. **Caldecott Medal.**

The Birth of a Pond by John Hamberger. Coward. The process of how a people-made pond is created is described in simple text and accompanied by detailed wildlife illustrations.

AVERAGE

The Ugly Duckling by Marianna Mayer. Macmillan. This version of the favorite Hans Christian Andersen tale is told in highly descriptive language. Magnificent full-color paintings by the award-winning artist Thomas Locker accompany each page of text.

Year on Muskrat Marsh by Berniece Freschet. Scribner. This descriptive chronicle of a year in a marshland shows how the changing seasons affect the life of its many inhabitants.

CHALLENGING

From Pond to Prairie: The Changing World of a Pond and Its Life by Laurence Pringle. Macmillan. The author describes the evolution of a pond from a barren water hole to a world teeming with life to a marsh and finally a prairie.

Mysteries of Migration by Robert M. McClung. Garrard. This book describes the migration patterns of various birds, mammals, fish, frogs, and insects.

READ-ALOUDS

The Wind in the Willows by Kenneth Grahame. Scribner. This is an illustrated edition of the classic fantasy adventure about a mole and friends who live on a riverbank.

A Time to Fly Free by Stephanie S. Tolan. Scribner. Josh meets Old Rafferty, who helps injured birds on the Virginia waterways, and learns a lot about birds and about himself.

270

1. Two-Part Organization designed to help you best meet the needs of *your* class. You may begin with Part 1 or Part 2—whichever works best for you.

2. Books on Unit Theme offer additional reading suggestions. Easy, average, challenging, and read-aloud selections give students the opportunity to go beyond the basal.

3. Unit Opener, reduced from the Pupil Edition for ease of reference.

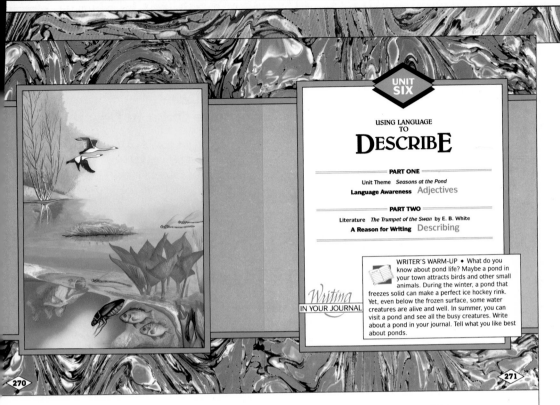

start with
WRITING IN YOUR JOURNAL

Writer's Warm-up is designed to help students activate prior knowledge of the unit theme, ''Season at the Pond.'' Whether you begin instruction with Part 1 or Part 2, encourage students to focus attention on the illustration on page 270 of their textbooks. Encourage them to discuss what they see. Then have a volunteer read aloud the **Writer's Warm-up** on page 271. Have students write their thoughts in their journals. You may wish to tell them that they will refer to this writing in the first lesson of Part 1, in the Grammar-Writing Connection, and in the Curriculum Connection.

THEN START WITH
part 1

Language Awareness: Sentences developmental lessons focus on the concept of adjectives. Each lesson is carefully constructed not only to help students learn the concept well but also to help build interest and background knowledge for the thinking, reading, and writing they will do in Part 2. The last lesson in Part 1 is a Vocabulary lesson with which students learn how to use suffixes. The Grammar-Writing Connection that follows serves as a bridge to Part 2, encouraging students to work together to apply their new language skills at the sentence level of writing.

...OR WITH
part 2

A Reason for Writing: Researching is the focus of Part 2. First students learn a thinking strategy for describing. Then they read and respond to a literature selection on which they may model their own writing. Developmental composition lessons, including ''An Oral Description,'' a speaking and listening lesson, all reflect the literature and culminate in the Writing Process lesson. There a ''Grammar Check,'' a ''Word Choice'' hint, and proofreading strategies help you focus on single traits for remediation or instruction through the lessons in Part 1. The unit ends with Curriculum Connection and Books to Enjoy, which help students discover how their new skills apply to writing across the curriculum.

EGORIES	People	Communications/ Fine Arts	Expressions	Business/World of Work	Imagination	Social Studies	Environments	Science
HEMES	UNIT 1 Hobbies	UNIT 4 Artists at Work	UNIT 3 Nature	UNIT 5 Early Days of Education	UNIT 7 Fables	UNIT 2 Colonial America	UNIT 6 Seasons at the Pond	UNIT 8 The Ocean

4. *Start With* is how you begin teaching the unit. Whether you choose to begin with Part 1 or Part 2 you will always start with a writing activity.

5. *Then Start With… or With* is a reminder where you have the option to gear your teaching to your needs and to the needs of your class.

6. Unit Theme Bar shows you at a glance the theme of every unit.

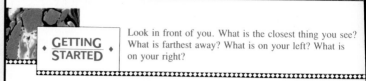

UNIT 6
Writing

■ Easy ■ Average ■ Challenging

OBJECTIVES
To use space order to organize
details in a paragraph
To write a paragraph in correct
space order

ASSIGNMENT GUIDE
BASIC   Practice A
                Practice B
ADVANCED   Practice C

All should do the Apply activity.

RESOURCES
■ Reteaching Master 52
■ Practice Master 52

TEACHING
THE LESSON

1. Getting Started
Oral Language Focus attention on
this oral activity, encouraging all to
participate. You may wish to have volunteers describe what they see in each
direction from different places in the
classroom or in the schoolyard.

2. Developing the Lesson
Guide students through the explanation of space order in descriptions,
emphasizing the examples and the
summary. Lead students through the
Guided Practice. Identify those who
would benefit from reteaching. Assign
independent Practice A–C.

3. Closing the Lesson
After students complete the Apply activity, you may wish to call on volunteers to read their paragraphs aloud.
Encourage students to discuss how
other parts of the classroom, such as
the library and cloakroom, are organized. Point out to students that learning how to use space order will help
them organize details for place
descriptions.

298

◆ GETTING STARTED ◆

Look in front of you. What is the closest thing you see?
What is farthest away? What is on your left? What is
on your right?

WRITING ◆
Space Order in Descriptions

Read this paragraph from *The Trumpet of the Swan.* How
does the author help us picture the scene?

> Louis liked Boston the minute he saw it from the sky. Far
> beneath him was a river. Near the river was a park. In the
> park was a lake. In the lake was an island. On the shore was
> dock. Tied to the dock was a boat shaped like a swan. The
> place looked ideal. There was even a very fine hotel nearby.

E.B. White used space order to help you see where
everything was. *Space order* means "the way things are
arranged in space." The words that are underlined show spa
order. They show where the river, park, lake, island, dock,
boat, and hotel are located. Do you see how the description
matches the map?

> **Summary** ◆ **Space order** is one way to arrange details
> in a paragraph. Space order often works well when you
> are describing a place.

298   WRITING: Space Order

ESSENTIAL LANGUAGE SKILLS
This lesson provides opportunities to:

LISTENING ◆ listen for specific information ◆
listen and respond to orally presented language for
the purpose of gathering information and making
judgments

SPEAKING ◆ communicate specific information
to an audience ◆ make organized oral presentations ◆ respond appropriately to questions from
teachers and peers

READING ◆ accuratley comprehend the details in
a reading selection ◆ draw conclusions from facts
given ◆ read and follow written directions

WRITING ◆ arrange information in sequentia
order ◆ identify audience and purpose ◆ writ
short stories and plays ◆ organize information re
lated to a single topic

LANGUAGE ◆ produce a variety of sentenc
patterns ◆ recognize and use options for wor
order ◆ understand the conventions of usage an
mechanics

---

7. Key objectives, assignment guide, and
additional resources
are boxed for easy reference
at the beginning of the
lesson.

8. Step-by-step lesson
organization with
specific teaching
strategies helps you guide
your students through the
lesson.

9. Essential Language
Skills show you at a
glance how to meet
your teaching objectives and
plan your lesson.

ed Practice

what order you would arrange details that describe
n below. Choose *top to bottom*, *bottom to top*, *left to*
front to back.

to bottom; bottom to top
ns in a stack
to right
rds in a sentence

3. front to back
rows on an airplane
4. top to bottom
a baseball batting order

tice

what order you would arrange details that describe each
n below? Write *top to bottom*, *bottom to top*, *left to*
*, *near to far*, or *front to back* to show the order.

front to back
chapters in a book
left to right
books on a shelf
top to bottom; bottom to top
a totem pole

8. left to right
players sitting on a bench
9. near to far
a highway disappearing
into the distance

te a paragraph. Begin with the topic sentence below.
n write the three details in correct space order.
rrect sentence order: 11, 12, 10
pic Sentence: Four boats were heading toward the dock.

. A swan boat was behind the sailboat.
. A rowboat was in front of all the other boats.
. A motorboat was between the rowboat and a sailboat.

Louis landed at your playground, what would he see?
aw a picture of it. Then write a paragraph to describe
Use space order to organize the details. For example,
scribe the scene from left to right or from near to far.
swers will vary.

ly ◆ Think and Write

ribing Your Space ◆ Write a paragraph that
es where you sit in your classroom. Are the desks in
If so, how many rows? How many desks are in each
Which row are you in? Which desk? Who sits in front
? Behind you? On your left? On your right?

✎ **Remember**
to use space order
as one way of
organizing details
for a description.

WRITING: Space Order   **299**

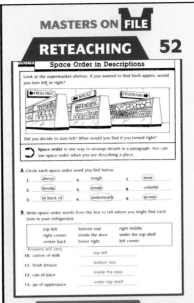

MASTERS ON **FILE**

RETEACHING   52

Space Order in Descriptions

Look at the supermarket shelves. If you wanted to find fresh apples, would
you turn left or right?

FRESH FRUIT   BREAD   FROZEN FOOD

Did you decide to turn left? What would you find if you turned right?

↩ **Space order** is one way to arrange details in a paragraph. You can
use space order when you are describing a place.

A. Circle each space order word you find below.

1. above   4. tough   7. near
2. beside   5. inside   8. colorful
3. in back of   6. underneath   9. across

B. Write space order words from the box to tell where you might find each
item in your refrigerator.

top left	bottom rear	right middle
right corner	inside the door	under the top shelf
center back	lower right	left corner

Answers will vary.
10. carton of milk   top left
11. fresh lettuce   bottom rear
12. can of juice   inside the door
13. jar of applesauce   under top shelf

PRACTICE   52

Space Order in Descriptions

↩ Space order is one way to arrange details in a paragraph. Space
order often works well when you are describing a place.

A. Answer the questions with space order words. Answers will vary.

1. Are the pencils on the left or right side?   right side
2. Are the elastics in the front or the back?   back
3. Where are the paper clips and elastics?   left side
4. Where is the paper kept?   middle

B. Write a place name from the box next to the space order words.

| football game | bookshelves | coat closet |
| classroom | city street | department store |

Answers will vary.
5. left, right, across   city street
6. top, bottom, middle   bookshelves
7. high, low, beside   coat closet
8. near, far, inside   football game

WRITE IT
On a separate paper, use space order words to write a paragraph telling
how to go from your house to the nearest store.   Answers will vary.

◀▥▥ **TEACHING OPTIONS** ▥▥▶

RETEACHING

Different Modality Explain that space
der words can help students draw a map
any room. Draw a large outline of the
ssroom on the chalkboard. Label the
es and corners as the nearest student
nds in a corresponding position in the
m. Help students brainstorm and list
ace-order words that tell you where to
aw each object the map should include.
en have students use their lists to draw
d label maps of their favorite rooms.

CLASS ENRICHMENT

A Cooperative Activity Have students
work in small groups to research and write
one paragraph about everything that is
over, under, and beside them, from base-
ments and subways to chimneys and stars
and trees and stores. Remind them to use
space-order words to generate ideas. Have
groups share their paragraphs and use
them to plan and paint a class mural.

CHALLENGE

An Independent Extension Have students use space-order words to write a description of a well-organized bedroom
where everything is easy to find. Help them
prepare by discussing some creative ways
to store things, such as sports equipment
and toys in underutilized spaces, perhaps
the top half of a room. Students might suggest suspending nets from the ceiling for
bats and balls or hanging toys on doors.
Have them share and discuss their work.

299

10. Lesson-related
Reteaching and
Practice Masters are
displayed on the teacher page
to help you select the assignments that best meet your
students' individual needs.

11. Additional teaching
options, color-coded
for easy scanning,
allow you to redevelop the
lesson concept, provide class
enrichment, or extend the
lesson content.

12. Teaching Options
provide students with
opportunities to use a
variety of modalities, to
participate in cooperative
activities and to engage in
independent extensions.

Discover *WORLD OF LANGUAGE* and discover a whole new world of writing.

Welcome to **World of Language** where your students learn to write through a variety of writing opportunities. They write about the theme-related content, the high-interest literary selections, and a wide range of school subjects. Students learn to put their thoughts in order, to develop concepts, to make facts come alive. They're guided by eight reasons for writing and inspired by examples of how top-quality writers have written for each reason. Students link prior knowledge to new experiences as they use the five stages of the writing process. Through each writing experience they become better thinkers, readers, listeners, and speakers. But most importantly, your students learn about themselves and grow in self-confidence. After all, learning is what writing is all about!

Writing activates learning.

Why Johnny can write!

AN INTERVIEW WITH DR. MARIAN DAVIES TOTH

Why is the teaching of writing gaining attention in the media, the press, and professional educational publications?

Research has taught us that writing improves reading comprehension, and we have discovered that writing enhances learning in every academic discipline. We have learned how to teach the writing process, which virtually any student can use to write more fluently and effectively.

We used to believe that all writing tasks were very much the same. Does this belief influence writing instruction today?

We know now that writing tasks differ. As a basis for discussion, we can use James Britton's definitions of three kinds of writing: *expressive*, *transactional*, and *poetic*.

Expressive writing captures thoughts while ideas are still forming. Journal entries and personal letters are familiar expressive writing forms.

Transactional writing gets things done in the world. We use it for contracts, research reports, and business letters.

Poetic writing produces short stories, plays, novels, and poetry.

How does expressive writing help students learn?

Expressive writing allows students to try out new ideas and to experiment with ideas on paper. When everyone in class *writes* a response to a question, every student has something to say and class discussions are more alive and dynamic. Writing can activate social, active, and interactive learning.

Why is it necessary for students to experience a wide variety of writing assignments?

Teachers realize that writing is thinking and that students benefit from using writing to learn in all of their subjects.

Writing stimulates a processing of information and fosters creative thinking. Students connect facts in different ways and writing binds the new information to the known.

How does World of Language meet the students' need for a wide variety of writings?

World of Language provides a comprehensive writing program within a frame of units. Each of the units in every text meets a need to use a function of language. For example, students have practice with poetic writing in the narrating, creating, and imagining units. Transactional writing experiences are introduced with writing to research, writing to persuade, and writing to explain. Students meet expressive writings in the unit openers, in the creative writing activity in the Part 2 opener, in the response to literature sections, and in the writing across the curriculum feature.

Dr. Marian Davies Toth is an authority on the writing process. She serves as a consultant to schools nationwide and is an author of *World of Language* and *World of Reading*.

For years we have heard that Johnny can't write. Do you think American students can learn how to make writing work for them personally?

Johnny *can* write. As a matter of fact, the National Assessment of Educational Progress indicates that children's writing in the primary grades is improving. Now, more than ever before, the teaching and learning of writing can be rewarding and enjoyable.

How has the whole language movement changed the way we teach writing?

In the past we merely assigned writing. Now we teach it as a process, through a series of five steps: prewriting, writing, revising, proofreading, and publishing. Plus, we stress the connection between oral and written language and encourage writing *fluency* instead of the creation of a "perfect" product.

Do all students write in a linear pattern from step 1 through step 5 with no turning back?

No, most students write recursively. Often, students pause in revision, returning to prewriting and gathering more information. Frequently, children stop during proofreading and take more time for revision. One of the best features of the writing process is that it allows students to use the new ideas that flow into their minds while they are creating and improving manuscripts.

All of us do not compose in exactly the same way. Nearly all of us, however, spend some time getting ready to write, writing, revising, proofreading, and sharing our work.

Our text helps teachers guide students through each of these important steps. It helps students realize that working through a writing process produces clear thinking and meaningful manuscripts.

World of Language urges students to work with their peers. Why is partnering advantageous?

Partnering helps with the management of the writing process. When students work in pairs, they have an opportunity to test the meaning of the words on the first draft. By sharing their writing, students soon discover if the words say what was intended. Revisions and text changes occur as a result of conversation about the written manuscript; consequently, the writing improves.

When students work on drafts together, the teacher receives manuscripts that have already gone through one revision. Working together builds students' commitment to the writing process. Students acquire social skills as they reinforce and extend their writing skills.

From your experience, what factors contribute most to a student's success in writing?

Fluency, frequency, and teacher attitude are the factors that make a difference. In my opinion, the teacher's supportive attitude toward the students' ideas is what changes poor writers into fine authors. In addition, students must have opportunities to write frequently and acquire a writing fluency that equals their speaking fluency.

Writing is a powerful tool for learning. It helps students become courageous, independent, and resourceful. Most important of all, every time students write, they think. They are helped to develop the wide range of thinking skills they will need as problem solvers and decision makers in the 21st century. ◇

5-Step Writing Process
in Part 2 of every unit

Beyond the Writing Process

◆ **Journal Writing** is spontaneous, impromptu writing that one does for oneself. **World of Language** encourages the use of a journal in four specific exercises in each unit.

◆ **Creative Writing** motivates the imagination and stimulates exciting discovery of new ideas. In **World of Language** students think and write creatively in response to examples of fine art, specific writing process lessons, and to writing applications.

◆ **Writing to Learn** is a short, spur-of-the-moment writing exercise that occurs twice in every unit of **World of Language**.

◆ **Writing in Response to Literature** in **World of Language** is informal writing that gives students the opportunity to pause and respond to literature.

◆ **Applied Writing** is an opportunity for students to *practice* writing throughout **World of Language** using a newly learned grammar or composition skill.

◆ **Writing Across the Curriculum,** in **World of Language**, gives students the opportunity to write about topics of interest to them and helps them continue to polish their writing skills at the same time.

● **Eight Reasons for Writing** one in each unit

◆ Narrating ◆ Informing ◆ Creating ◆ Researching
◆ Describing ◆ Persuading ◆ Imagining ◆ Classifying

Discover WORLD OF LANGUAGE and discover a whole new world of literature.

World of Language actively involves your students in a world of experience. Through quality literature, which is the foundation of every unit and every unit theme, your students visit places near and far, make many new friends, and participate in familiar and unfamiliar events. As reading stimulates and focuses thinking, students discover how much they already know and build on their prior knowledge to become better writers. As readers, your students gain prior knowledge that gives them something to write about. As writers, they use what they read as inspiration for their own work. In **World of Language** your students write to become more sensitive readers. They read to become more effective writers.

WORLD OF LANGUAGE

SILVER BURDETT & GINN

BY DR. THEODORE CLYMER

Great literature captures the heart.

10 ways

10 WAYS TO RECOGNIZE GREAT CHILDREN'S LITERATURE

Great literature, everyone agrees, is the foundation of a successful language arts program. But what makes a particular story or poem worthy of the label?

Great literature for young readers lends insight into their own lives, as well as those of others, and gives children a new way of looking at the world. The language is rich and fresh. It delights, informs, surprises. It instructs even as it entertains. It helps a child find a secure place in a complex world.

As we selected works of prose and poetry for **World of Language**, we established ten guidelines to ensure a standard of literary excellence throughout our program. As you choose children's literature for your own students, we hope you find these guidelines helpful.

1. Great literature captures the heart.

Reading involves thinking and feeling. The stories that are remembered long after they are read, the stories that are read over and over again, the stories that reveal something new with each reading—these are literature of merit. These are the stories that touch the heart. These are the stories that introduce children to a lifetime of reading.

2. Great literature elicits high praise from adults and children.

Several important awards honor excellence in literature for children and young adults. These include the Newbery and Caldecott awards, the Pulitzer prize, and the American Library Association notables. We have chosen selections from the ranks of this honored literature, including *Owl Moon* by Jane Yolen, "A Curve in the River" from *More Stories Julian Tells* by Ann Cameron, *Volcano* by Patricia Lauber, *The House of Dries Drear* by Virginia Hamilton, and *The Yearling* by Marjorie Kinnan Rawlings.

Dr. Theodore Clymer is Director of the Institute for Reading Research, Carmel, California. He is founding editor of the *Reading Research Quarterly* and is an authority on children's literature. Dr. Clymer is an author of *World of Reading*.

3. Great literature meets the reader's needs and growth level.

As children grow and mature, their needs clearly change. In the early primary levels, adjusting to school routine or learning to take turns might feel strange and new. At other levels, peer approval is a vital concern. As students change, literature selections should reflect the kinds of challenges they encounter.

At the end of every section in this program, you'll find a useful feature, Reader's Response, that helps make the connection between the story and each youngster's life. It invites children to share personal reactions to the selections and form opinions based on their own experience.

4. Great literature stimulates thought and imagination.

A great selection tends to raise more questions than it answers. In a nonfiction piece on Mars, for example, a reader will learn a great deal about that planet. This new knowledge will lead to questions about other planets and the solar system. If a character in a work of fiction solves a problem in a new or unusual way, the student discovers a new way of looking at the world. This literary quality helps develop readers who are active and independent.

5. Great literature carries an important message.

Great literature has something important to say to a reader. It helps a reader discover how people think about and respond to life's everyday challenges. The message may be a pointed one, as in Aesop's fable "The Crow and the Pitcher," or a subtle one, as in Patricia MacLachlan's *Through Grandpa's Eyes*.

6. Great literature acquaints a reader with many literary genres.

Folktales, realistic fiction, autobiography, poetry, and essay are just a few of the genres that a student should encounter in any language program. Each style has its own characteristics and special way of telling a story. In this program, you'll find selections as varied as *The Midnight Fox, Anne Frank: The Diary of a Young Girl,* "The Jabberwocky," and John F. Kennedy's "Letter to Peter Galbraith."

Literature Checklist

- ◆ *Is an award-winning or recognized work*
- ◆ *Stimulates thought and imagination*
- ◆ *Develops cultural literacy*
- ◆ *Expands the reader's world*
- ◆ *Fosters a lifelong love of reading*

---

7. Great literature adds to a reader's store of information.

Great literature should represent a world of knowledge and experience. We have organized each level of our program into eight thematic units — Imagination, Expression, Environment, People, Science, Social Studies, Business/World of Work, and Communications/Fine Arts. Each theme springs directly from the literature featured in the unit and is reflected in every lesson of the unit. These organizational devices help students make important inferences from their readings.

8. Great literature introduces the reader to great authors.

Getting to know authors and understanding that they are people with issues and experiences similar to one's own helps readers to understand the world of writing. In addition, an extensive interview with one author is available on audio cassette for each grade level.

9. Great literature contributes to a reader's cultural literacy.

In order for children to thrive in today's world, they need to encounter a range of experience that includes all of the areas of human activity and provides a basis for understanding our commonality. Our program seeks to broaden your students' experience with a variety of selections from stories like *The Paper Crane* and *Sacagawea* to "Sky-Bright Axe" from *American Tall Tales* and "The Littlest Sculptor."

10. Great literature develops a life-long love of reading.

Great literature leads to more great literature. It follows that as children read stories and books they love, they will want to read more. A number of helpful program features provide opportunities for children to read beyond the text. Books to Enjoy, at the end of every unit, suggests additional titles on the same theme or by the same author that students can explore on their own. Read Aloud, found in the teacher pages at the beginning of each unit, introduces fresh new literature selections. Teacher pages also provide lists for further reading on the unit theme and suggested books that tie into the literary selection. ◇

BY DAVID N. PERKINS

Language is basic to thinking.

Thinking

THINKING—EMPOWERING READERS

Organized Thinking and Thinking Organizers

Considerable research on writing, reading, and other thought-demanding activities shows that success depends in large part on organized thinking. Although all students think, not all think in the kinds of organized patterns that help them to retain information, build understandings, or find and take creative opportunities when they write. The thinking patterns that many students need to use are not very complex or limiting. Rather, they liberate the mind from narrowness.

To build understandings and to find and follow through on creative opportunities, students need to consider many possibilities beyond the obvious ones that they think of first. When they face difficulties, they need to focus their attention on defining the problem instead of rushing ahead to find solutions to the wrong problem. Students who have difficulty "working through" a problem need *thinking organizers*—strategies that offer better patterns of organization for thinking and learning. Students who already know how to work through a problem can expand their mental reach even farther with thinking organizers.

Graphic Organizers in World of Language

The thinking strand in **World of Language** addresses students' fundamental need for thinking organizers, emphasizing a carefully chosen and systematically practiced set of *graphic organizers*—diagrams and charts that help youngsters guide their thinking. Graphic organizers help children who may have language difficulties with strategies expressed entirely in words. They also help teachers to teach thinking.

Most fundamentally, graphic organizers make patterns of thinking visible and concrete for students. By working through ideas on paper with the help of graphic organizers, students can see their thoughts unfolding before them in organized patterns. Students have the opportunity to make these patterns their own, adapting them to their personal needs and styles and internalizing them. Graphic organizers help students to become more metacognitive—more aware of and reflective about their own thinking processes. ◇

Why are my stepsisters so mean? I'm determined to be happy anyway!

Dr. David Perkins is the Director of Project Zero (Research in Thinking Skills and Cognitive Behavior) at Harvard University and is a consultant on the teaching of thinking. Dr. Perkins is an author of *World of Language*.

Prior Knowledge

THE BRIDGE TO NEW LEARNING

Developing comprehension helps bridge the gap between what is known and what is new. It opens students to new learning by reassuring them that the concepts are within their grasp. It gives them a reference point for assimilating new material and adds greater meaning to the new content.

Activating prior knowledge is therefore essential in introducing new concepts to all students — no matter what their ability level. That is why **World of Language** has been meticulously constructed to build on a child's existing knowledge *every step of the way*. In its strong thematic content, as well as its organization and unit activities, **World of Language** helps gear children for success by thoroughly preparing them for each new learning experience.

Strong unit themes enhance meaning

Each child brings to the classroom a rich storehouse of knowledge about the world. To tap this reservoir of information and experience, and thereby provide the bridge to new learning, each **World of Language** unit is organized around a single, specific theme — a theme inspired by the literature selection in that unit.

The theme, whether it is people and wildlife, hobbies, or seasons at the pond, furnishes the subject matter for all the lessons in the unit. In a unit on farm life, featuring an excerpt from *The Midnight Fox*, for example, practice sentences might give fascinating facts about foxes. Students, in turn, may use these facts later as they respond to the Apply: Think and Write section that ends each of these lessons. Later, in the unit's writing process lesson, students have the opportunity to combine prior and new knowledge in writing on a topic related to the theme.

Providing a theme ensures that each child will be bringing some personal knowledge to that topic. Each child will feel more comfortable with it from the very outset, be more confident, and will feel involved immediately.

Moreover, by activating and building on prior knowledge, this strong thematic base makes the content much more meaningful. In one teacher's words, "These are sentences that go somewhere... there is meaning on every page."

Each lesson is a stepping stone to the next

In **World of Language** each lesson leads to the next, increasing a child's knowledge, interest, and confidence along the way. Just as unit lessons build on a common, unifying theme, each lesson in a unit builds upon the last to take students to higher and higher levels of learning and understanding.

Assisted by the unit theme, the lessons in Part One of each unit progress from language awareness skills to vocabulary development to the Grammar-Writing Connection, a feature which provides a logical, smooth transition to applying the language skills just learned. In Part Two, a critical thinking lesson sets the stage for literature appreciation, while the Reading-Writing Connection helps students make the leap from reading exceptional literature to creating their own original writing.

When each lesson leads to the next in this manner, students are then receptive to literature and the writing process *because they have been so well prepared*. And by activating and augmenting their

Tapping experience enhances meaning.

own knowledge at every turn, the program enables students to approach literature and writing easily, enjoyably, and successfully.

Activities that activate prior knowledge are built into the program

Throughout **World of Language**, exercises that trigger existing knowledge and draw students into the lesson have been built right into the program.

Each unit, for example, begins with a Writing in Your Journal activity that asks students to reflect on their own experiences with the unit topic, thus opening them to the new learning which follows.

Similarly, each language awareness lesson begins with Getting Started, an oral exercise involving the entire class that helps students discover that they already know a great deal about the concept at hand.

Preceding each unit's literature selection, a host of prereading and vocabulary development activities awaken interest and pave the way for greater understanding of the reading that follows. In addition, the Dictionary of Knowledge found in The Writer's Reference Book at the end of every text supplies students with additional background information.

With **World of Language**, students take a fascinating step-by-step journey to greater language proficiency. It is a journey that is built on the knowledge and experiences they bring to each lesson and which builds on itself each step of the way. The result is a program that teaches language in the context of students' lives, better preparing them to appreciate literature and writing and to succeed in the language arts. ◇

***WORLD OF LANGUAGE* Activates Prior Knowledge Through:**

- ***Strong unit themes that enhance meaning and provide springboards to learning***
- ***Writing in Your Journal unit openers that invite students to reflect on and record their own knowledge and experience on the unit theme***
- ***Lessons that build on each other, taking the student to continually higher levels of learning***
- ***Getting Started lesson openers that help students discover what they already know about the topic at hand***
- ***Prereading and vocabulary development activities that set the stage for literature appreciation***
- ***The Dictionary of Knowledge, which supplies additional background on literature topics***
- ***Prewriting activities that build a solid prior-knowledge foundation for the writing process lesson***

BY NANCY N. RAGNO

Connections

LEARNING, LANGUAGE, AND LIFE: MAKING CONNECTIONS

The language arts are unique. They hold a place in the curriculum and in life unlike that of any other subject our children will study — for language cannot be separated from learning. Language cannot be separated from life. Of all subjects in the curriculum, language alone is basic to thinking. Because of this, the language arts are at the core of the curriculum. *Listening, speaking, reading, writing* — language is the connection.

The way to become fluent in language is to *use* language. That is how we first learn language, and it remains the easiest and most efficient way to develop language facility and the ability to communicate clearly. As we planned and developed **World of Language**, our chief goal was to actively engage children in *using* language as they will in life, for real purposes and real audiences. In order to achieve this, we built on the following three connections that are fundamental to language arts.

Language is linked with learning. Language and learning go hand in hand, since language is indispensable to thinking. The tools of language — *listening, speaking, reading, writing* — are the tools of learning *across the curriculum*.

The language arts are integrated. They enhance one another. Readers become better writers; writers become better readers. Reading and writing,

in turn, have their roots in oral language. This means that when children use one mode of language, they reinforce others. It also means that the language arts are best taught by an *integrated approach*, not by an isolated skills approach.

Language is linked with life. Language is the bond that joins us with the outside world and with others. It is also our means of connecting with our inner world, of discovering who we are. Language is a bridge in time, the vehicle for transmitting culture. Through it we remember the past, and it is through language that we shall transmit our legacy to the future. Language is our human heritage. Thus language teaching should not be isolated from life, but should relate directly to life and to the experiences of our children.

Integrating the Language Arts

World of Language reflects the uses of language in the real world. Listening, speaking, reading, and writing are taught not as isolated skills, but in an integrated manner. This interrelationship is evident throughout each unit and lesson, but particularly emphasized in two features found in each unit, the Grammar-Writing Connection and the Reading-Writing Connection.

In the Grammar-Writing Connection children are shown how to use a unit's grammar instruction to improve their writing. The Reading-Writing Connection helps students use outstanding literature as a model for their own writing.

Nancy Nickell Ragno has an extensive background in reading and has many years of experience as an editor. She is an author of *World of Language*.

Language, learning, and life are intertwined.

In addition to these two recurring unit features, each developmental lesson — including those on grammar, mechanics, and usage — begins with speaking/listening activities and ends with a writing exercise. The result is a program that enables students to discover how listening, speaking, reading, and writing all contribute to one another.

Language & Life: Connecting with Others and with Ourselves

There are, finally, many important ways in which children use language to connect with others and to connect with themselves in **World of Language.** Methods of communicating with others include discussion, learning through group activities and exercises, peer conferencing, and writing or speaking.

Numerous opportunities are presented for using language to learn about oneself through thinking, writing, and exploring one's imagination and creativity.

Language, learning, and life — the three are intertwined. **World of Language** builds on those connections to make language learning easier, more effective, and more "real." At the same time, we sincerely hope that you and your children will thoroughly enjoy your journey through **World of Language** and that as a result your children will come to appreciate an additional reason for using language. That is, to delight in words, in wordplay, in all the sounds of language — to experience the sheer pleasure of using language. ◇

Discover *WORLD OF LANGUAGE* and discover the world.

In *World of Language* your students journey across the curriculum to discover the fascinating worlds of science, social studies, health science, art, and music. Through literature inspired unit themes, to the Grammar-Writing and Reading-Writing Connections, as well as the Curriculum Connection, your students learn language by *using* language. They build on prior knowledge and learn even more. They become better readers and writers. They learn to think critically and creatively. And as they connect with others—through discussion, peer conferencing, and sharing—they learn to become better speakers and listeners. In *World of Language* your students grow beyond the basics. They explore their creativity, learn about themselves, their peers, and the world around them. But best of all, they grow to become successful students and contributing members of a literate community.

System

Pluto

Neptune

WORLD
OF
LANGUAGE

SILVER BURDETT & GINN

Cooperative Learning

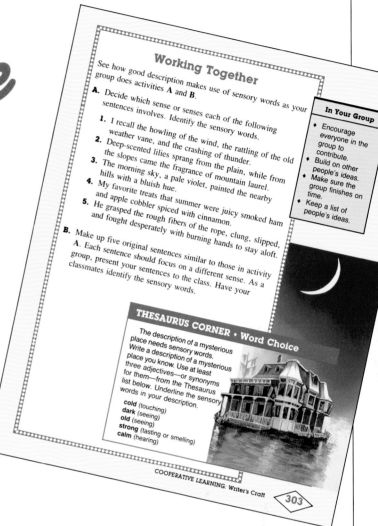

WHY COOPERATIVE LEARNING IS CATCHING ON

Cooperative learning is one of the instructional strategies generating a lot of excitement among educators. Teachers, guided by research and their own classroom experience, are increasingly turning to it to increase academic achievement, develop thinking and problem-solving skills, and boost long-term retention. Cooperative learning can also improve self-esteem and attitudes toward school.

How is cooperative learning different from traditional group activities?

Both involve a small group of children working together to reach a common goal. But in cooperative learning, the group is heterogeneous and activities are designed to make members interdependent in the most positive way. That is, children will attain their goal only if every group member achieves individual goals. So in addition to the familiar social goals of group projects, cooperative learning allows students to actively help each other learn. This involves verbal, face-to-face interaction as students work out a common understanding.

What is the teacher's role?

The teacher acts as a consultant, setting academic and collaborative objectives, helping children choose tasks, providing materials, supporting and assessing group interaction, and guiding children in monitoring their own progress. The teacher also provides an opportunity for closure, which includes discussion by students about their group's performance. ◇

Evaluation Checklist

◆ *Provides meaningful group activities tied to the unit theme*

◆ *Provides opportunities for students to evaluate group tasks*

◆ *Cooperative learning opportunities in every developmental lesson*

BY PATRICIA A. EDWARDS

You, the teacher, play a powerful role.

At Risk

TEACHING LANGUAGE ARTS TO CHILDREN AT RISK

Over the years, a number of terms have been used to describe children who are not doing well in our schools. They include "culturally deprived," "culturally handicapped," "disadvantaged," "underprivileged," and even "disaffected." Recently, these children have acquired yet another label: CHILDREN AT RISK. But no matter what the terminology, the challenge remains the same: how to effectively teach them.

Because children "at risk" very often have deficits in both oral and written language, and because language is the foundation for all learning, these children are of special concern to language arts teachers. In the next few paragraphs I suggest ways in which you, the classroom teacher, can be instrumental in fostering the success of these children, and how **World of Language** can assist you in that goal.

Patricia A. Edwards is a Senior Researcher at the University of Illinois. As an assistant professor of curriculum and instruction at Louisiana State University, she developed a very successful early reading program.

Keep your expectations high

As the teacher, you are the most important factor in your classroom, and a positive attitude toward these students and their ability to acquire English skills is a key ingredient in their success — and yours. It is, therefore, of paramount importance for you to have high expectations for *all* your students.

If children know that we truly believe they have potential and that we are going to try everything within our power to tap that potential, it will help build their self-esteem and spark a willingness to try. It is up to you, and it will make all the difference.

Create a no-risk literacy environment

Speaking and writing are risk-taking activities for all children, and even more "risky" for those with poor language development. For these children to feel comfortable enough to experiment with language, it is

essential to create a secure, supportive environment in the classroom.

As Barbara Shade has pointed out, there are several important steps you can take to achieve this. First, accept each "at-risk" child as he or she is today, with an emphasis on what the child *CAN* do. By accepting a child's efforts to read and write, you will encourage further risk taking on his or her part. Second, present content in a way that is meaningful and relevant for your students. Tap their prior knowledge and experience. And third, establish positive communication patterns and an atmosphere of cooperation.

By following the above suggestions, you will be on your way to creating a no-risk literacy environment where thinking, speaking, listening, reading, and writing are highly valued activities. An environment of this type will allow your students to experiment with language, and thereby allow you to be sensitive to individual students who have difficulty reading and writing.

Create opportunities for all students to participate

Active participation is the key to language skills acquisition because children learn to write by writing, read by reading, and speak and listen through participation. **World of Language** offers valuable support in this area by providing a myriad of activities and ways that encourage students "at risk" to participate in each lesson. From the whole-class oral exercise that opens each lesson, to partnering and cooperative learning activities featured in every unit, to suggestions for role-playing and games, to high-interest reading lists that ignite student imagination and curiosity, the program specifically involves all students.

And by being observant of and sensitive to the differences in your students as they participate, you can help them build on what they already know and use their base of knowledge as a springboard to further learning.

Recognize and reward student progress

It is vitally important to acknowledge the achievements of children "at risk." Students take pleasure and acquire confidence when they have tangible proof of their improvement in English. Keeping samples of your students' writings, recording their accomplishments, showering their work with positive reinforcers, rather than just marking errors, all provide students with prized signposts marking their personal progress in the language arts.

As a teacher you play a powerful role in the linguistic development of your students. In the case of children "at risk" that role is all the more crucial because of the special learning problems these children face. By making that extra effort, by taking that extra step, you will help ensure that your classroom is a place that promotes language acquisition and literacy learning for all your students. ◇

WORLD OF LANGUAGE
Helps You Help
Children At Risk:

◆ *Suggests ways to activate a student's prior knowledge and introduce concepts in meaningful ways*

◆ *Explores different modalities, from manipulatives to role-playing*

◆ *Promotes student participation through partnering and cooperative learning exercises*

◆ *Includes high-interest projects that stimulate student imagination and invention*

◆ *Presents tools and strategies for promoting critical and creative thought*

◆ *Proposes ways to encourage positive student attitudes*

◆ *Lists further reading opportunities*

BY BETTY GRAY

Self-evaluation fosters growth.

Evaluation

EVALUATION AS AN INTEGRAL PART OF THE WRITING PROCESS

Appropriate and timely evaluation can give young writers needed feedback for overcoming problems with *work in progress*. It can help them focus more clearly on what they want to say and pinpoint the areas that need improvement. That is why **World of Language** incorporates evaluation techniques that bring the most out of students and foster their growth as writers.

In **World of Language** teacher evaluation as well as carefully directed peer and self-evaluation have been *integrated into the writing process*. Designed to provide fledgling writers with the positive encouragement they need to succeed — and to furnish teachers with a host of supplemental resources — this three-part approach includes:

Expedient Teacher Evaluation: Most language arts teachers inevitably equate teaching writing with mountains of papers. However, this need not be the case. **World of Language** supplies teachers with samples of and guidelines for an array of methods for evaluating writing performance, including general impression marking, focused holistic scoring, and primary trait scoring. These methods enable teachers

to quickly evaluate writing on specific criteria and offer students the immediate feedback they need.

Guided Peer Evaluation: Drawing upon the latest research findings on teaching writing, **World of Language** features peer evaluation in the revision stage of each writing process lesson. To assist teachers, helpful hints and specific questions are included in each of these lessons. In addition, a guide for peer evaluation can be found in the test booklet that accompanies the program. The guide includes questions that help students give specific, constructive feedback to their peers.

Student Self-Evaluation: An essential element of the writing process, self-evaluation can help lead each student toward greater self-reliance and independence as a writer. The **World of Language** program addresses this important area, furnishing students with forms for commenting on and evaluating their own writing, for establishing their own goals for improvement, and for keeping a record of that improvement.

In order to grow in their writing ability, students need the feedback of evaluation. Evaluation can be valuable, and it is the goal of **World of Language** to provide that opportunity for each writer by presenting lessons that make peer as well as teacher evaluation an integral part of the writing process. ◆

Betty G. Gray is a high school teacher in Spring, Texas. She is also Past President of Texas Joint Council of Teachers of English and was selected as Texas Teacher of the Year, 1988. Betty G. Gray is an author of *World of Language*.

A language arts program tailor-made for you and your students.

Pacing

*O*nly you can determine the best pace of instruction for your class. **World of Language** makes pacing decisions easy with manageable bite-size lessons that easily fit into the busiest school day. The amount of time you spend on each lesson is a matter of your personal emphasis on composition, literature, oral language, and grammar.

However you choose to organize your instruction, the end result will be a language arts program tailor-made for your students and a teacher's edition tailor-made for you!

Flexibility Options

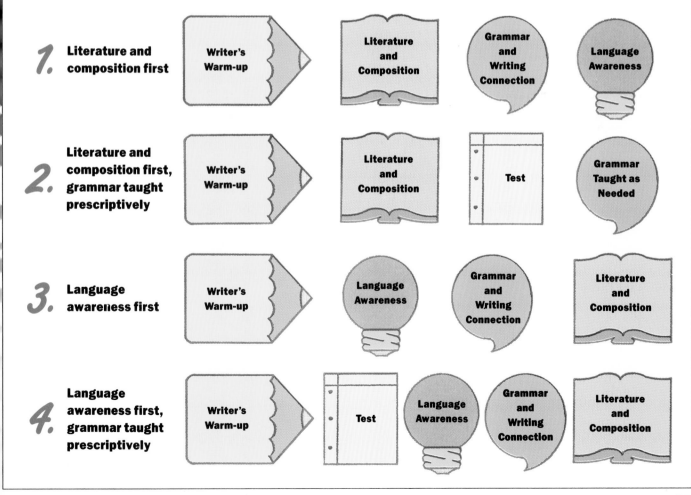

1. **Literature and composition first** — Writer's Warm-up → Literature and Composition → Grammar and Writing Connection → Language Awareness

2. **Literature and composition first, grammar taught prescriptively** — Writer's Warm-up → Literature and Composition → Test → Grammar Taught as Needed

3. **Language awareness first** — Writer's Warm-up → Language Awareness → Grammar and Writing Connection → Literature and Composition

4. **Language awareness first, grammar taught prescriptively** — Writer's Warm-up → Test → Language Awareness → Grammar and Writing Connection → Literature and Composition

Scope & Sequence

GRAMMAR

Sentences

Sentences	K	1	2	3	4	5	6	7	8
Definition	♦	♦	♦	♦	♦	♦	♦	♦	♦
Word order in sentences		♦	♦	♦					

Sentence Parts

Sentence Parts	K	1	2	3	4	5	6	7	8
Complete subject	♦	♦	♦	♦	♦	♦	♦	♦	♦
Complete predicate			♦	♦	♦	♦	♦	♦	♦
Simple subject				♦	♦	♦	♦	♦	♦
Simple predicate				♦	♦	♦	♦	♦	♦
Compound subject				♦	♦	♦	♦	♦	♦
Compound predicate				♦	♦	♦	♦	♦	♦
Predicate adjective				♦	♦	♦	♦	♦	♦
Understood subject					♦	♦	♦	♦	♦
Direct object					♦	♦	♦	♦	♦
Predicate nominative							♦	♦	♦
Indirect object								♦	♦
Independent clause								♦	♦
Subordinate clause								♦	♦

Sentence Types

Sentence Types	K	1	2	3	4	5	6	7	8
Simple	♦	♦	♦	♦	♦	♦	♦	♦	♦
Declarative	♦	♦	♦	♦	♦	♦	♦	♦	♦
Interrogative	♦	♦	♦	♦	♦	♦	♦	♦	♦
Exclamatory			♦	♦	♦	♦	♦	♦	♦
Imperative			♦	♦	♦	♦	♦	♦	♦
Compound					♦	♦	♦	♦	♦
Complex								♦	♦

Sentence Errors

Sentence Errors	K	1	2	3	4	5	6	7	8
Run-on sentence						♦	♦	♦	♦
Sentence fragment							♦	♦	♦

Working with Sentence Structure

Working with Sentence Structure	K	1	2	3	4	5	6	7	8
Sentence combining/ sentence expansion			♦	♦	♦	♦	♦	♦	♦
Diagraming sentences						♦	♦	♦	♦

PARTS OF SPEECH

Nouns	K	1	2	3	4	5	6	7	8
Definition	♦	♦	♦	♦	♦	♦	♦	♦	♦
Common noun	♦	♦	♦	♦	♦	♦	♦	♦	♦
Proper noun	♦	♦	♦	♦	♦	♦	♦	♦	♦
Singular noun	♦	♦	♦	♦	♦	♦	♦	♦	♦
Plural noun	♦	♦	♦	♦	♦	♦	♦	♦	♦
Possessive noun			♦	♦	♦	♦	♦	♦	♦
Collective noun								♦	♦
Used as other parts of speech								♦	♦
Gerunds								♦	♦
Gerund phrases									♦
Infinitives as nouns								♦	♦
Infinitive phrases as nouns									♦
Used as phrase or clause									♦

Verbs	K	1	2	3	4	5	6	7	8
Definition		♦	♦	♦	♦	♦	♦	♦	♦
Action verb	♦	♦	♦	♦	♦	♦	♦	♦	♦
Linking verb	♦	♦	♦	♦	♦	♦	♦	♦	♦
State-of-being verb						♦	♦	♦	♦
Present tense	♦	♦	♦	♦	♦	♦	♦	♦	♦
Past tense	♦	♦	♦	♦	♦	♦	♦	♦	♦
Irregular verb		♦	♦	♦	♦	♦	♦	♦	♦
Main verb and helping verb				♦	♦	♦	♦	♦	♦
Future tense					♦	♦	♦	♦	♦
Principal parts, regular verbs						♦	♦	♦	♦
Participle						♦	♦	♦	♦
Present perfect, past perfect, and future perfect tense								♦	♦
Verb phrase								♦	♦
Transitive and intransitive								♦	♦
Gerund								♦	♦
Infinitive								♦	♦
Active and passive voice								♦	♦
Progressive form									♦

Pronouns	K	1	2	3	4	5	6	7	8
Definition	♦	♦	♦	♦	♦	♦	♦	♦	♦
Subject pronoun	♦	♦	♦	♦	♦	♦	♦	♦	♦
Object pronoun	♦	♦	♦	♦	♦	♦	♦	♦	♦
Possessive pronoun			♦	♦	♦	♦	♦	♦	♦
Pronoun antecedents							♦	♦	♦
Demonstrative pronoun								♦	♦
Indefinite pronoun								♦	♦
Reflexive pronoun								♦	♦
Intensive pronoun								♦	♦
Interrogative pronoun								♦	♦
Relative pronoun									♦

Adjectives	K	1	2	3	4	5	6	7	8
Definition	♦	♦	♦	♦	♦	♦	♦	♦	♦
Comparative and superlative forms	♦	♦	♦	♦	♦	♦	♦	♦	♦
Articles *a, an, the*		♦	♦	♦	♦	♦	♦	♦	♦
Predicate adjective				♦	♦	♦	♦	♦	♦
Adjective phrase							♦	♦	♦
Proper adjective							♦	♦	♦
Demonstrative adjective							♦	♦	♦
Used as other parts of speech								♦	♦
Participles as adjectives								♦	♦
Participial phrases									♦
Infinitives as adjectives								♦	♦
Infinitive phrases as adjectives									♦
Clause used as adjective									♦

Adverbs	K	1	2	3	4	5	6	7	8
Definition	♦	♦	♦	♦	♦	♦	♦	♦	♦
Comparative and superlative forms					♦	♦	♦	♦	♦
Adverb phrase								♦	♦
Infinitives as adverbs								♦	♦
Infinitive phrases as adverbs									♦
Clause used as adverb									♦

USAGE

Prepositions

	K	1	2	3	4	5	6	7	8
Definition						♦	♦	♦	♦
Prepositional phrase						♦	♦	♦	♦
Object of preposition						♦	♦	♦	♦
Prepositional phrase as adjective							♦	♦	♦
Prepositional phrase as adverb							♦	♦	♦

Conjunctions

	K	1	2	3	4	5	6	7	8
Definition						♦	♦	♦	♦
Coordinating conjunction								♦	♦
Correlative conjunction								♦	♦
Subordinating conjunction								♦	♦

Interjections

	K	1	2	3	4	5	6	7	8
Definition						♦	♦	♦	♦

Words Commonly Misused

	K	1	2	3	4	5	6	7	8
Homophones	♦	♦	♦	♦	♦	♦	♦	♦	♦
Pronouns and contractions						♦	♦	♦	♦
Prepositions						♦	♦	♦	♦

Noun and Pronoun Usage

	K	1	2	3	4	5	6	7	8
Using subject and object pronouns	♦	♦	♦	♦	♦	♦	♦	♦	♦
Naming self last	♦	♦	♦	♦	♦	♦			
Confusion of possessive and plural noun forms							♦	♦	♦
Agreement of pronouns and antecedents							♦	♦	♦
Using reflexive pronouns								♦	♦
Needless pronoun insertion or shift								♦	♦

Adjective and Adverb Usage

	K	1	2	3	4	5	6	7	8
Using *a, an*		♦	♦	♦	♦	♦			
Adjectives: comparative and superlative forms			♦	♦	♦	♦	♦	♦	
Adverbs: comparative and superlative forms				♦	♦	♦	♦	♦	
Double negatives				♦	♦	♦	♦	♦	
Adjective/adverb confusion						♦	♦	♦	♦
Misplaced modifier									♦

Verb Usage

	K	1	2	3	4	5	6	7	8
Subject/verb agreement	♦	♦	♦	♦	♦	♦	♦	♦	♦
Using irregular verbs	♦	♦	♦	♦	♦	♦	♦	♦	♦
Unnecessary change of tense			♦	♦	♦	♦	♦	♦	♦
Troublesome verb pairs						♦	♦	♦	♦

MECHANICS

Capitalization

	K	1	2	3	4	5	6	7	8
First word of sentence	♦	♦	♦	♦	♦	♦	♦	♦	♦
Proper nouns		♦	♦	♦	♦	♦	♦	♦	♦
Pronoun *I*		♦	♦	♦	♦	♦		♦	♦
Titles and initials		♦	♦	♦	♦	♦	♦	♦	♦
Titles of written works			♦	♦	♦	♦	♦	♦	♦
Greeting and closing of letter		♦	♦	♦	♦	♦	♦	♦	♦
Abbreviations			♦	♦	♦	♦	♦	♦	♦
First word of direct quotations					♦	♦	♦	♦	♦
Proper adjectives							♦	♦	♦

PUNCTUATION

Period

	K	1	2	3	4	5	6	7	8
At end of declarative and imperative sentences	♦	♦	♦	♦	♦	♦	♦	♦	♦
With abbreviations and initials		♦	♦	♦	♦	♦	♦	♦	♦

Question Mark

	K	1	2	3	4	5	6	7	8
	♦	♦	♦	♦	♦	♦	♦	♦	♦

Exclamation Mark

	K	1	2	3	4	5	6	7	8
			♦	♦	♦	♦	♦	♦	♦

Comma

	K	1	2	3	4	5	6	7	8
In dates			♦	♦	♦	♦	♦	♦	♦
After greeting and closing of letter			♦	♦	♦	♦	♦	♦	♦
To separate city and state or country			♦	♦	♦	♦	♦	♦	♦
With introductory words, phrases, clauses					♦	♦	♦	♦	♦
With nouns of direct address			♦	♦	♦	♦	♦	♦	♦
With items in a series				♦	♦	♦	♦	♦	♦
In compound sentences					♦	♦	♦	♦	♦
With quotations					♦	♦	♦	♦	♦
When writing last name first						♦	♦	♦	
With appositives								♦	♦
With interrupters								♦	♦
In complex sentences								♦	♦
With nonessential participial phrase									♦

Quotation Marks

	K	1	2	3	4	5	6	7	8
Direct quotations				♦	♦	♦	♦	♦	♦
Titles of written works				♦	♦			♦	♦

Italics and Underlining

	K	1	2	3	4	5	6	7	8
					♦	♦	♦	♦	♦

Apostrophe

	K	1	2	3	4	5	6	7	8
Contractions			♦	♦	♦	♦	♦	♦	♦
Possessives				♦	♦	♦	♦	♦	♦

Semicolon

	K	1	2	3	4	5	6	7	8
								♦	♦

Colon and Hyphen

	K	1	2	3	4	5	6	7	8
					♦	♦	♦	♦	♦

Indenting

	K	1	2	3	4	5	6	7	8
			♦	♦	♦	♦	♦	♦	♦

SPELLING

	K	1	2	3	4	5	6	7	8
Plural forms of nouns		♦	♦	♦	♦	♦	♦	♦	♦
Verbs in present and past tense		♦	♦	♦	♦	♦	♦	♦	♦
Spelling rules			♦	♦	♦	♦	♦	♦	♦
Words often written		♦	♦	♦	♦	♦	♦	♦	♦
Possessive forms					♦	♦	♦	♦	♦
Writing out numbers								♦	♦

HANDWRITING

	K	1	2	3	4	5	6	7	8
	♦	♦	♦						

VOCABULARY

	K	1	2	3	4	5	6	7	8
Compounds		♦	♦	♦	♦	♦	♦	♦	♦
Synonyms		♦	♦	♦	♦	♦	♦	♦	♦
Antonyms		♦	♦	♦	♦	♦	♦	♦	♦
Prefixes			♦	♦	♦	♦	♦	♦	♦
Suffixes			♦	♦	♦	♦	♦	♦	♦
Homophones			♦	♦	♦	♦	♦	♦	♦
Contractions			♦	♦	♦	♦	♦	♦	♦
Using context clues		♦	♦	♦	♦	♦	♦	♦	♦
Homographs				♦	♦	♦	♦	♦	♦
Base and root words					♦			♦	♦
Connotation and denotation							♦	♦	♦
Etymologies/history of English language						♦	♦	♦	♦
Idiomatic expression								♦	♦
Formal and informal language								♦	♦
Shades of meaning								♦	♦

SPEAKING

	K	1	2	3	4	5	6	7	8
Discussions and conversations	♦	♦	♦	♦	♦	♦	♦	♦	♦
Telling a story	♦	♦	♦	♦	♦	♦	♦	♦	♦
Using the telephone	♦	♦	♦				♦		
Choral reading	♦	♦	♦	♦	♦	♦	♦		
Dramatization, improvisation, pantomime	♦	♦	♦	♦	♦	♦	♦	♦	
Oral reading	♦	♦	♦	♦	♦	♦	♦	♦	♦
Giving directions	♦	♦	♦	♦	♦	♦	♦		
Giving opinions and persuasive talks	♦	♦	♦	♦	♦	♦	♦	♦	♦
Peer conferencing	♦	♦	♦	♦	♦	♦	♦	♦	
Oral reports and informative talks			♦	♦	♦	♦	♦	♦	
Interviews and surveys			♦	♦	♦	♦	♦	♦	♦
To give descriptive details		♦	♦	♦	♦	♦	♦	♦	
Sharing opinions				♦	♦	♦	♦	♦	♦
Voice and speech techniques				♦	♦	♦	♦	♦	♦
To give comparison and contrast				♦	♦				♦

Genres	K	1	2	3	4	5	6	7	8
Poetry (also finger plays, nursery rhymes, and songs)	♦	♦	♦	♦	♦	♦	♦	♦	♦
Wordless picture story/story	♦	♦	♦	♦	♦				
Play		♦	♦						
Short story								♦	
Fable/myth/tall tale/folklore		♦	♦	♦	♦	♦	♦	♦	♦
Essay/article				♦	♦	♦	♦	♦	♦
Personal narrative			♦	♦	♦	♦	♦	♦	♦
Literary letter		♦	♦	♦					
Literary diary/journal									♦
Responding to literature	♦	♦	♦	♦	♦	♦	♦	♦	♦
Appreciation of literature	♦	♦	♦	♦	♦	♦	♦	♦	♦

Other Forms/Genres

	K	1	2	3	4	5	6	7	8
Stories and narratives	♦	♦	♦	♦	♦	♦	♦	♦	♦
Poems	♦	♦	♦	♦	♦	♦	♦	♦	♦
Journals			♦	♦	♦	♦	♦	♦	♦
Writing to learn			♦	♦	♦	♦	♦	♦	♦

Writing Process

	K	1	2	3	4	5	6	7	8
Building foundation for writing process	♦	♦							
Steps in writing process (prewriting, writing, revising, proofreading, publishing)			♦	♦	♦	♦	♦	♦	♦
Identifying purpose			♦	♦	♦	♦	♦	♦	♦
Identifying audience			♦	♦	♦	♦	♦	♦	♦
Improving word choice			♦	♦	♦	♦	♦	♦	♦
Revising and proofreading marks			♦	♦	♦	♦	♦	♦	♦
Peer conferencing			♦	♦	♦	♦	♦	♦	♦
Sharing writing products			♦	♦	♦	♦	♦	♦	♦
Receiving response to writing			♦	♦	♦	♦	♦	♦	♦

LITERATURE

Genres	K	1	2	3	4	5	6	7	8
Poetry (also finger plays, nursery rhymes, and songs)						♦		♦	♦
Short story						♦			
Novel excerpt						♦		♦	♦
Fable/myth/tall tale/folklore						♦		♦	♦
Essay/article									♦
Personal narrative						♦		♦	♦
Nonfiction						♦		♦	♦
Literary diary/journal								♦	♦
Appreciation of literature						♦		♦	♦

Literary Elements and Devices

	K	1	2	3	4	5	6	7	8
Plot, character, setting	♦	♦	♦	♦	♦	♦	♦	♦	♦
Speaker (point-of-view)			♦	♦	♦	♦	♦	♦	♦
Exaggeration			♦						
Forms of poetry (couplet, tercet, haiku, limerick, ballad)			♦	♦	♦	♦	♦	♦	♦
Poetic voice (lyric, dramatic, narrative)	♦	♦	♦	♦	♦	♦	♦	♦	♦
Figures of speech (simile, metaphor, personification)					♦	♦		♦	♦
Sound devices (onomatopoeia, alliteration, assonance, consonance, rhyme, repetition)	♦	♦	♦	♦	♦	♦	♦	♦	♦
Sensory words	♦	♦	♦	♦	♦	♦	♦	♦	♦
Dialogue					♦	♦	♦	♦	♦

THINKING SKILLS

Critical Thinking

	K	1	2	3	4	5	6	7	8
Compare/contrast				♦			♦	♦	
Drawing conclusions			♦		♦				♦
Observing			♦	♦	♦	♦			
Problem solving	♦						♦	♦	
Sequencing	♦					♦			♦

Creative Thinking

	K	1	2	3	4	5	6	7	8
Elaborating					♦		♦	♦	
Supposing	♦					♦			♦
Point of view					♦	♦	♦	♦	
Predicting		♦	♦	♦					
Wondering			♦	♦					♦

WRITING

Fine Arts

	K	1	2	3	4	5	6	7	8
			♦	♦	♦	♦	♦	♦	♦

Pictures

	K	1	2	3	4	5	6	7	8
Drawing a picture to tell a story	♦	♦							
Drawing a picture for a response	♦	♦	♦						

Sentences

	K	1	2	3	4	5	6	7	8
Writing sentences	♦	♦	♦	♦	♦	♦	♦	♦	♦
Sentence combining and expansion			♦	♦	♦	♦	♦	♦	♦
Clincher sentences								♦	♦

Paragraphs

	K	1	2	3	4	5	6	7	8
Definition			♦	♦	♦	♦	♦	♦	♦
Topic sentence			♦	♦	♦	♦	♦	♦	♦
Detail (supporting) sentences			♦	♦	♦	♦	♦	♦	♦
Order of ideas in paragraphs			♦	♦	♦	♦	♦	♦	♦
Informative and explanatory			♦	♦	♦	♦	♦	♦	♦
Descriptive			♦	♦	♦	♦	♦	♦	♦
Narrative			♦	♦	♦	♦	♦	♦	♦
Persuasive				♦	♦	♦	♦	♦	♦
Comparison/contrast				♦	♦	♦	♦	♦	♦
Paragraph unity								♦	♦
Methods of developing paragraphs							♦	♦	♦
Clincher sentence								♦	♦

Other Expository Forms

	K	1	2	3	4	5	6	7	8
Book reports and media reviews	♦	♦	♦	♦	♦	♦	♦	♦	♦
Research reports			♦	♦	♦	♦	♦	♦	♦
Summaries				♦	♦	♦	♦	♦	♦
Newspaper/magazine articles and editorials						♦	♦	♦	♦

Letters

	K	1	2	3	4	5	6	7	8
Friendly letters		♦	♦	♦	♦	♦	♦	♦	♦
Thank-you notes/invitations		♦	♦	♦	♦	♦	♦	♦	♦
Envelopes		♦	♦	♦	♦	♦	♦	♦	♦
Business letters					♦	♦	♦	♦	♦

LISTENING

	K	1	2	3	4	5	6	7	8
To appreciate literature	♦	♦	♦	♦	♦	♦	♦	♦	♦
For rhyme, rhythm, and other poetic sound devices	♦	♦	♦	♦	♦	♦	♦	♦	♦
In discussions and conversations		♦	♦	♦	♦	♦	♦	♦	♦
For main idea or details		♦	♦	♦	♦	♦	♦	♦	♦
On telephone		♦	♦	♦			♦		
For sequence		♦	♦	♦	♦	♦	♦	♦	♦
To answer questions/ interviews		♦	♦	♦	♦	♦	♦		♦
To follow directions		♦	♦	♦	♦	♦	♦	♦	♦
Manners and techniques		♦	♦	♦	♦	♦	♦	♦	♦
Peer conferencing		♦	♦	♦	♦	♦	♦	♦	♦
For context clues			♦	♦	♦	♦		♦	♦
For fact vs opinion				♦	♦	♦	♦	♦	♦
Active listening				♦	♦	♦	♦	♦	♦
Critical listening				♦	♦	♦	♦	♦	♦

STUDY SKILLS

	K	1	2	3	4	5	6	7	8
Using alphabetical order	♦	♦	♦	♦	♦	♦	♦	♦	♦
Using the library	♦	♦	♦	♦	♦	♦	♦	♦	♦
Recognizing author and title	♦	♦	♦	♦	♦	♦	♦	♦	♦
Using a thesaurus	♦	♦	♦	♦	♦	♦	♦	♦	♦
Organizing information and classifying	♦	♦	♦	♦	♦	♦	♦	♦	♦
Reading pictures	♦	♦	♦	♦	♦	♦	♦	♦	♦
Parts of a book		♦	♦	♦	♦	♦	♦	♦	♦
Following written directions		♦	♦	♦	♦	♦	♦	♦	♦
Spelling rules		♦	♦	♦	♦	♦	♦	♦	♦
Using the dictionary for spelling, pronunciation, meaning		♦	♦	♦	♦	♦	♦	♦	♦
Using and locating words in the dictionary			♦	♦	♦	♦	♦	♦	♦
Choosing/narrowing a topic			♦	♦	♦	♦	♦	♦	♦
Using an encyclopedia				♦	♦	♦	♦	♦	♦
Summarizing				♦	♦	♦	♦	♦	♦
Taking tests				♦	♦	♦	♦	♦	♦
Taking notes				♦	♦	♦	♦	♦	♦
Using an atlas, almanac, newspaper, *Reader's Guide*				♦	♦	♦	♦	♦	♦
Study tips/habits				♦	♦	♦	♦	♦	
Outlining					♦	♦	♦	♦	♦
Using the library's card catalogue or computer listing					♦	♦	♦	♦	♦
Paraphrasing								♦	♦

Enjoy the journey...

SILVER BURDETT & GINN

10-89-292 (A282)
ISBN 0-382-16429

WORLD OF LANGUAGE

SILVER BURDETT & GINN

Marian Davies Toth   Nancy Nickell Ragno   Betty G. Gray

Contributing Author — Primary   Elfrieda Hiebert
Contributing Author — Vocabulary   Richard E. Hodges
Contributing Author — Poetry   Myra Cohn Livingston

Consulting Author — Thinking Skills   David N. Perkins

SILVER BURDETT & GINN
MORRISTOWN, NJ   NEEDHAM, MA
Atlanta, GA   Cincinnati, OH   Dallas, TX   Menlo Park, CA   Deerfield, IL

USING THE COVER

The cover illustration was inspired by the literature *The Midnight Fox* by Betsy Byars that begins on page 24 in Unit 1.

Explain to students that the fox is a quick, skillful hunter. It has keen hearing and an excellent sense of smell. It depends especially on these two senses in locating prey. Foxes sometimes stand on their hind legs to get a better view in tall grass.

Explain to students that the qualities that make the fox an excellent hunter have inspired many folktales and fables. You may wish to read to the class the Aesop fable *The Fox and the Grapes,* The Native American *Fox Boy and His Shadow,* or the Chinese folktale *The Fox's Daughter.* Students may wish to use oral composition to develop their own story with the fox as a character.

Acknowledgments

Contributing artists: Doron Ben-Ami, Alex Bloch, Tom Cardamone Associates, Heidi Chang, Eldon Doty, Carol Inouye

Picture credits: Photographs on the following pages are by Ken Karp for Silver Burdett & Ginn: 3D, 3F, 59D, 59F, 115D, 115F, 175D, 175F, 233D, 233F, 283D, 283F, 339D, 339F, 387D, 387F, T512–T527.

Permissions: We wish to thank the following authors, publishers, agents, corporations, and individuals for their permission to reprint copyrighted materials. Page 3A: Excerpt from *Farmer Boy* by Laura Ingalls Wilder. Copyright 1933 by Harper & Bros. Reprinted by permission of Harper & Row, Publishers, Inc. Page 59A: Excerpt from *Grandmother Brown's Hundred Years* by Harriet Connor Brown. Copyright © 1929. Used by permission. Page 115A: "Pecos Bill Becomes a Coyote" from *Pecos Bill, The Greatest Cowboy of All Time* by James Cloyd Bowman. Copyright © 1937, 1964 by Albert Whitman & Co. Used by permission of Albert Whitman & Co. Page 175A: Quotes from *Grandma Moses: My Life's History* by Anna Mary Robertson Moses. Copyright © 1952 (renewed 1970) by Grandma Moses Properties, Co., New York. Used by permission. Page 283A: Excerpt from *The 21 Balloons* by William Pene DuBois. Copyright © 1975 by William Pene DuBois. Reprinted by permission of Viking Penguin, Inc. Page 339A: "Beech" from *One at a Time* by David McCord. Copyright © 1965, 1966 by David McCord. Reprinted by permission of Little, Brown & Co., Inc. "Silver" reprinted by permission of the Literary Trustees of Walter de la Mare and The Society of Authors as their representative. "The Wind" by Padraic Colum (copyright holder cannot be located). Page 387A: Excerpt from *Beaver Valley* by Walter D. Edmonds. Copyright © 1971 by Walter D. Edmonds. Reprinted by permission of Harold Ober Associates, Inc. Every effort has been made to locate the authors. If errors have occurred, the publisher can be notified and corrections will be made.

Acknowledgments

Cover: Allen Davis

Contributing Writers: Sandra Breuer, Judy Brim, Wendy Davis, Bernie Brodsky, Anne Maley, Marcia Miller, Gerry Tomlinson

Contributing artists: E. Albanese, Lori Bernero, Tom Bobroski, Lisa Bonforte, Paul Birling, Helen Davie, Bert Dodson, Susan David, Michele Epstein, Liane Fried, Dennis Hockerman, Robert Jackson, Pam Johnson, Lainie Johnson, John Killgrew, Gary Lippincott, Karen Loccisano, Richard Loehle, Peter McCaffrey, Diana Magnusen, Darcy May, Yoshi Miyake, Loughran O'Connor, Jordi Penalva, Brian Pinkney, David Rickman, Sandy Rabinowitz, Larry Raymond, Sally Schaedler, Pat Soper, Sandra Speidel, Deb Troyer, Gary Undercuffler.

Handwriting samples: Michele Epstein

Picture credits: All photographs by Silver Burdett & Ginn (SB&G) unless otherwise noted. **Introduction:** 5: Kamyar Samoul **Unit 1** 4: John Colwell/Grant Heilman Photography. 5: Animals Animals/© Charles Palek. 6: Grant Heilman/Grant Heilman Photography. 7: Earth Scenes/© Dr. Nigel Smith. 12: Grant Heilman/Grant Heilman Photography. 14: © David R. Frazier/Photo Researchers, Inc. 15: Larry Lefever/Grant Heilman Photography. 17: Thomas Zimmerman/FPG International. 20: Angel E. Allende. 42: Dan De Wilde for SB&G. 47: Jacket illustration by Lloyd Bloom from *Arthur, for the Very First Time* by Patricia Maclachlan, illustrated by Lloyd Bloom. Illustration copyright © 1980 by Lloyd Bloom. Reprinted by permission of Harper & Row, Publishers, Inc. **Unit 2** 60: Art Resource. 65: *Pete-Repete*, painted and carved on birch by Judy Kensley McKie, 1981. Courtesy Pritam & Eames Furniture Gallery, East Hampton, New York. 67: Photographed by Mark Sexton, courtesy of The Essex Institute, Salem, MA. 71: Glass vase by Louis C. Tiffany, at Smithsonian Institution, photographed by Aldo TuTino/Art Resource. 76: The Corning Museum of Glass, Corning, New York. 81: *t.* R. Duchaine/The Stock Market of NY. 87: Karl Kummels/Shostal Associates. 91: Robert Frerck/Odyssey Productions. 93: Larry Lefever/Grant Heilman Photography. 98: Dan De Wilde for SB&G. 102: Chris Jones/The Stock Market of NY. 103: *t.* Model a Monster by Colin Caket. Courtesy Bland Ford Press, Cassell plc, distributed in the US by Sterling Publishing Company, Inc., NY. **Unit 3** 133: Henley & Savage/The Stock Market of NY. 138: From the collection of the Museum of African American Art, Palmer C. Hayden collection. Gift of Miriam A. Hayden. 156: Dan De Wilde for SB&G. 161: Illustrations by Richard Powers from *American Tall Tales* by Adrienne Stoutenberg. Copyright © 1966 by The Viking Press, Inc. All rights reserved. Reprinted by permission of Viking Penguin, Inc. **Unit 4** 179: Charles Krebs/The Stock Market of NY. 183: *t.* Ernest Haas/Magnum; *b.* Mitch Epstein. 185: University Art Museum, University of Minnesota, Minneapolis/Purchase. 187: Hampton University Archival & Museum Collection, Hampton University, Hampton, Virginia. 192: ARS New York/ADAGP. Photo by Cathlyn Melloan/TSW-Click/Chicago. 198: *l.* Jim Pickerell; *r.* Courtesy of the Illinois State Historical Library. 202: Louise Nevelson, *Royal Tide 1*, 1960, wood painted gold, 96" x 40" x 8". Private collection of Jean Lipman, photo courtesy of The Pace Gallery. 203: The State

Historical Society of Wisconsin. 207: Courtesy of Hampton University Art Museum, Hampton, Virginia. 208: Courtesy of The State Historical Society of Wisconsin. 214: Dan De Wilde for SB&G. 218: Courtesy of Mr. August A. Busch, Jr. 219: Illustration by Donna Diamond from *Dorothea Lange: Life Through the Camera* by Milton Meltzer. Illustrations copyright © 1985 by Donna Diamond. All rights reserved. Reprinted by permission of Viking Penguin, Inc. **Unit 5** 233: NASA. 241: Ken Reagan/Camera 5. 246: Quilt, *Spacious Skies*. Charlotte Warr-Anderson, Kearns, Utah. Cotton with some polyester blends. 1985–1986. 72" x 71½". Collection of the Museum of American Folk Art; Museum of American Folk Art: The Scotchgard Collection of contemporary quilts (1986.14.2.) 257. Grace Moore. 268: Dan De Wilde for SB&G. 273: *t.* Photo by NASA from *To Space and Back* by Sally Ride and Susan Okie, courtesy William Morrow & Company, Inc./Publishers. **Unit 6** 282, 285: United States Department of the Interior, U.S. Geological Survey, David A. Johnston Cascades Volcano Observatory, Vancouver, Washington. 288: Steve Vidler/Four by Five. 289: *t.* W. Stoy/Bruce Coleman; *b.* Dennis Oda/Gamma Liaison. 296: Nicholas Devore III/Bruce Coleman. 298: Virginia Museum of Fine Arts, Richmond, Virginia. Giraudon/Art Resource. 302–306: United States Department of the Interior, U.S. Geological Survey, David A. Johnston Cascades Volcano Observatory, Vancouver, Washington. 309: Ed Cooper/Shostal Associates. 311: Renee Pauli/Shostal Associates. 313: Ed Cooper/Shostal Associates. 315: Stella Snead/Bruce Coleman. 316: Animals Animals/© E.R. Degginger. 317: Phil Degginger. 322: Dan De Wilde for SB&G. 327: Text Copyright © 1981 by Isaac Asimov, illustrations Copyright © 1981 by David Wool. 318: United States Department of the Interior, U.S. Geological Survey, David A. Johnston Cascades Volcano Observatory, Vancouver, Washington. **Unit 7** 340: Roy Morsch/The Stock Market of NY 342: James Ranklev/Shostal Associates. 349: Animals Animals/© John Chellman. 352: © The Metropolitan Museum of Art, bequest of Loula D. Lasker. New York City, 1961 (59.206). 372: Dan De Wilde for SB&G. 377: *t.* Jacket art from *A Visit to William Blake's Inn* by Nancy Willard, illustration copyright © 1981 by Alice Provensen and Martin Provensen, reproduced by permission of Harcourt Brace Jovanovich, Inc. **Unit 8** 389: Animals Animals/© G.L. Kogyman. 395: Bill Hurter/Leo deWys, Inc. 397: Animals Animals/© J.C. Stevenson. 404: Courtesy of Kennedy Galleries, Inc., New York. 414: Hans Pfletschinger/Peter Arnold, Inc. 415: *l.* © Toni Angermayer/Photo Researchers, Inc; *r.* Addison Geary/Stock, Boston. 417: *l.* Hans Reinhard/Bruce Coleman; *r.* Runk/Schoenberger/Grant Heilman Photography. 419: *l.* The Granger Collection; *r.* Owen Franken/Stock, Boston. 424: Dan De Wilde for SB&G. 428: C.C. Lockwood/Bruce Coleman. 429: *t.* Illustration from *Do Animals Dream?* by Joyce Pope. Copyright © 1986 by Marshall Editions, Ltd. All rights reserved. Reprinted by permission of Viking Penguin, Inc. **Dictionary** 457: *l.* Jim Alinder; *r.* Brown Brothers. 458: *l.* National Portrait Gallery, Smithsonian Institution, Washington, D.C.; *r.* State Preservation Board, Texas Capitol. Photo courtesy of the Archives Division, Texas State Library. 459: *l.* Fred Hirschmann; *r.* Greenwillow. 460: *l.* Ira Wyman for SB&G; *r. Lewis and Clark at Three Forks* (detail) by E.S. Paxson, completed 1912. Courtesy of the Montana Historical Society. 461: W.E. Ruth/Bruce Coleman; 462: *l.* Sam Sweezy/The Stock Market of NY; *r.* C.B. & D.W. Frith/Bruce Coleman. 463: David Stoecklein/West Stock, Inc. 465: *l.* William Ferguson; *r.* Copyright © 1973, Laura Ingalls Wilder Memorial Library. Every effort has been made to locate the original sources. If any errors have occurred the publisher can be notified and corrections will be made.

Acknowledgments continued on page 442

◆ CONTENTS ◆

INTRODUCTORY UNIT

UNIT 1

USING LANGUAGE TO NARRATE

UNIT 2

USING LANGUAGE TO INFORM

PART ONE

LANGUAGE AWARENESS ♦ NOUNS

THEME

...dicrafts

PART TWO

A REASON FOR WRITING ♦ INFORMING

...ERATURE

...andicrafts"
by
...icia Fent Ross

UNIT 3

USING LANGUAGE TO IMAGINE

UNIT 4

USING LANGUAGE TO PERSUADE

THEME

Visual Arts

LITERATURE

"The Littlest
Sculptor" by
Joan Zeier

UNIT 5

USING LANGUAGE TO DESCRIBE

UNIT 6

USING LANGUAGE TO RESEARCH

PART ONE

LANGUAGE AWARENESS ♦ ADVERBS

THEME

lcanoes

PART TWO

A REASON FOR WRITING ♦ RESEARCHING

TERATURE

Volcano
by
atricia Lauber

ix

UNIT 7

USING LANGUAGE TO CREATE

PART ONE

LANGUAGE AWARENESS ♦ PREPOSITIONS

UNIT THEME

Nature

PART TWO

A REASON FOR WRITING ♦ CREATING

LITERATURE

Poetry

x

UNIT 8

USING LANGUAGE TO CLASSIFY

THEME

al Habitats

TERATURE

"Two of a
Kind"
by
Ron Hirschi

WRITER'S REFERENCE BOOK

AWARD
· LITERATURE ·
WINNING

AWARD
WINNING
AUTHOR

The Midnight Fox
by Betsy Byars

AWARD
WINNING
AUTHOR

Zeely
by Virginia Hamilton

NEWBERY
HONOR
1987

Volcano
by Patricia Lauber

INTRODUCTORY UNIT

OBJECTIVES
To become aware of oneself as a writer

To become familiar with five stages of the writing process

Literature in Your World

After students read "Literature in Your World," you may wish to tell them about some of the books and stories you have enjoyed, including nursery rhymes, simple folktales, and books you particularly liked when you were their age. Share with students some of the feelings and insights literature has given you. Then encourage students to talk about stories they have read and enjoyed, and to identify some of the feelings they have experienced in response to these books. These feelings may have included suspense, surprise, delight, joy, and sadness. Lead students to see that literature can give us new understandings of ourselves and others and of our world.

LITERATURE

from
Zeel...
by Virginia Ha...

250

LITERATURE

from
The Midnight Fox
by Betsy Byars

In all his life, Tom had never spent longer, slower days than the first three days on his Aunt Millie's farm. He had fought going to the farm in the first place. He didn't get along with animals or enjoy the outdoors. He had only agreed to go, finally, so that his parents could take a summer trip to Europe.

Now Tom missed his parents and his friend Petie Burkis. Most of all, though, he missed doing his own, unplanned things every day. He felt completely useless on the farm, where everything had been well-planned without him. He was going to have a miserable summer, he feared, with nothing to look forward to but his daily trip to the mailbox. Then, everything changed. Here is Tom's story of what happened.

24   LITERATURE: Story

WORLD OF LANGUAGE

Introductory Unit

Literature in Your World

In the *World of Language* literature plays a key role. Why is it so important? What can literature mean for you in your world?

Literature unlocks your imagination. It opens your mind to the world of ideas. Through literature you can enter any time and any place. You can experience many different adventures, meet people you would never meet, share ideas with the greatest minds. Literature is indeed a key. It is a key to expanding your world. It is the key to enriching your world of language.

Writing in Your World

Writing begins with you. Writing is a way for you to connect with the world outside you. When you write, you write *to* someone. You write for your readers, and you write to be read. Writing is also a way for you to connect with your inner world, your world of thoughts, feelings, and dreams. Sometimes you write for others, and sometimes you write just for yourself.

Writing is creating, and you are the creator. Writing is thinking, and writing is discovering what you think. Writing is a way of finding out about your world, and writing is a way to change it! That is a powerful thought. Writing is powerful — a powerful tool in your world and in the wonderful world of language.

Introduction 1

Writing in Your World

Help students to understand that writing is a pathway to thinking. When they write, they collect and express their thoughts about a topic. They decide which items are more important than others, and in what order the items should appear. In their final drafts, they communicate these ideas to an audience of readers. After students read "Writing in Your World," tell them that the goal of the writing lessons that appear throughout the WORLD OF LANGUAGE is to improve their writing so that they can use this powerful tool effectively in school and other areas of their lives— to make them good communicators.

What Is a Writer?

Have students discuss the kinds of writing explained in **What Is a Writer?** You may wish to have them tell about times that they have used each kind of writing.

Then have students read "Journal Writing." Explain to them that they will be keeping a journal that they will use in various ways throughout the year. You may wish to share with them some of the suggestions for journal writing made in WORLD OF LANGUAGE. These include writing ideas about a theme, writing observations and descriptions that may become part of a writing lesson, and writing personal notes about reading and about events.

You may wish to have students make their own journals by folding and stapling paper into a notebook. Students can personalize their journals by decorating the covers using art paper, markers, fabric, or snapshots.

For students who make journal writing a habit, writing may become less mysterious and forbidding. It is a way for students to find their own natural writing process or style. Many may find that journal writing is an enjoyable and important outlet for their feelings and ideas.

Journal writing is usually not graded. However, try to read student journals and respond to them once a week or so. A small note from you, such as "Interesting!" or "I like the smell of breakfast cooking, too," will encourage them to continue to think and write.

What Is a Writer?

A writer is anyone who writes. *You* are a writer. *You* are a writer whenever you jot down a message, write a letter, create a story, or outline a report. You do many kinds of writing, and you write for many reasons. Here are three kinds of writing. You will try them this year.

Writing to Inform ♦ Writing can help you get something done in the world. You might write a business letter, for example, to someone to let them know about a particular problem.

Writing to Create ♦ You can use your imagination to write a poem, a play, or a story.

Writing to Express Yourself ♦ You can use writing to express what you think or feel. Expressive writing is writing to explore your ideas, plans, and impressions. It is a kind of talking to yourself.

Writing for yourself is a very important kind of writing It deserves a special place, for it will be special to you. A journal can be that ideal place.

Journal Writing

A journal is a writer's best friend. Carry one with you and you're always prepared to
- capture an idea by jotting it down
- practice and experiment with all kinds of writing
- think things through and explain things to yourself
- note what you think about books, movies, music
- record your impressions — your first day at school, a new friend, a painting, a puppy, for instance

A journal can be a special notebook or a section of another notebook. It can be a notebook you make yourself by stapling paper in a folder. Once you have your journal, you can begin to use it as other writers do. You will find many opportunities and ideas for journal writing throughout this book.

ntroducing the Writing Process

Sometimes you want to write something, make it really good, polish it, and then share it with other people. What the best way to go about doing this? Focus on the *rocess of writing*. Take time to think, plan, get ideas, ake changes. Do not expect to write a perfect paper e first time. Take time to go through the writing process.

The writing process breaks writing into steps. For each ep there are lots of *strategies* — ways of working — that ou can learn. There are ways to get ideas and organize eas. There are hints for how to get started and how to eep going. There are strategies for improving your riting and sharing it.

hink, Read, Speak, Listen, Write

At the end of each unit, you will use the writing process r writing something that you will publish, or share with thers. You will be well-prepared for this, because first ou will have a series of lessons to get you started.

A **Thinking Skills** lesson will give you a strategy to use in reading and writing.
A **Literature** lesson will provide you with a model for your writing.
A **Speaking and Listening** lesson will show you how to use oral language correctly.
Writing skills lessons will show you how to do the kinds of writing you will do in the Writing Process lessons.
Two **Connection** lessons will show you how to apply the skills you learned in the unit directly to your writing.

Introducing the Writing Process

Explain that the writing process is a way of approaching writing that can help make writing easier and more natural. Guide students through the textbook page. Emphasize that the strategies described in each stage are suggestions. You may wish to point out to students that they will find the strategies that work best for them by trying many different ones, and that different strategies may work best for different types of writing.

You may also wish to reassure students that before they begin a Writing Process lesson, a number of other lessons will have helped them prepare for it. "Think, Read, Speak, Listen, Write" tells students about the types of lessons they will find in the WORLD OF LANGUAGE. Knowing what is in store for them, students will approach learning with self-confidence and enthusiasm.

INTRODUCTORY UNIT

Using the Writing Process

This is an introductory lesson designed to guide students through the stages of the Writing Process and introduce them to some strategies for success. Students learn that the stages Prewriting, Writing, Revising, Proofreading, and Publishing are meant to be used with flexibility. Writers go back and forth between stages. They write, revise, and often tell or show each other their ideas during prewriting.

They continue to generate brand-new ideas during writing and revising. Writers even revise and rewrite their work after it has been published.

Even though students are introduced to the writing process stages in a linear way, this order is only a general guide.

1. PREWRITING

Guide students through the explanation of Prewriting, pointing out that it is the stage in which writers choose a topic and gather ideas and information to use in their writing. "Prewriting Ideas" spells out a way to observe and describe an object using all five senses. You may wish to model the strategy by having students choose an object. Then make a chart on the chalkboard of the five senses and have volunteers add words to the chart to tell how the object looks, sounds, feels, smells, and maybe tastes. You may wish to point out that there are no right or wrong answers—people's descriptions of the same object may differ because people perceive things in different ways. One person might describe an apple as sweet, another as crunchy, another as red, and another as round.

Using the Writing Process

Write a Description

At the end of each unit, you will use the writing process for writing you will publish, or share with others. On the next four pages you will have a preview of the five stages of the writing process and will try each one. These stages are: *prewriting, writing, revising, proofreading,* and *publishing.*

Writers often start with prewriting and end by publishing. They may, however, go back and forth among the other stages or do two or more stages at once. As you become more familiar with the stages, you will feel more comfortable moving back and forth. With each stage there is an activity. When you have done all five activities, you will have written a description.

Read the Writer's Hint now. For your description your *purpose* is to describe an object so accurately your audience can "see" it; your *audience* is your classmates.

1 Prewriting ♦ Getting ready to write

Have you ever said, "I don't know what to write about" or "I don't have any ideas"? Welcome to the writers' club! Most writers feel that way before they start writing. How can you get the ideas you need? There are lots of ways. For example, you can brainstorm, draw an idea cluster, keep a journal, or do an interview.

PREWRITING IDEA

Using Your Senses: Sight

Choose an object to describe, something you can see in your classroom or outside through the window. Don't tell anyone what you choose.

Observe the object carefully for several minutes. What do you see? Take notes about your observations. Jot down words that describe size, shape, and color.

Write down everything you notice. First write down the main points — the things you probably notice first. Then look for small details. It is the little details that make your object unique.

Your notes will be your reminders of what you observed and thought. They can be just words if you wish.

Writing ♦ Putting your ideas on paper

You have decided what to write about. You have gathered some ideas. Now you are facing a blank page. It's time to start writing, but sometimes you don't know how to get started. Often, once you start, you don't know how to keep going.

The important thing is just to start writing. Don't worry if your ideas are out of order or if you make spelling errors. You will be able to improve your writing when you revise and proofread.

2. WRITING

Before students write their first drafts, guide them through the explanation, emphasizing that at this stage their task is to get ideas on paper. Be sure students understand that during writing they need only to generate a first draft. It is a time in which ideas that were explored in Prewriting begin to take shape. During Writing, writers do not have to worry about spelling or punctuation. That will come later, in the Proofreading stage.

"Writing Ideas" is designed to help students get started. You may wish to model the strategy by writing a question and an ending statement for the object chosen in Prewriting. Remind students that they can stop writing at any time and return to prewriting if they need to gather more details or change to another topic.

WRITING IDEA

Starting with a Question

Put your prewriting notes in front of you before you begin writing your description. How can you begin? You might begin with a question such as *Have you ever really looked at the oak tree outside our window?* After you start, use your notes to tell what the object looks like. Tell the main things you noticed and the interesting details. Do not try to include *everything* you jotted down, though. Pick and choose. Write on every other line to give yourself room to make changes later. Finally, add an ending sentence, such as *The oak tree is probably the oldest tree in our schoolyard.*

Introduction 5

INTRODUCTORY UNIT

3. REVISING

During Revising a writer discovers whether the writing says what was intended. Help students understand that during the revising stage the writer's task is to make any necessary changes in the draft to be sure that it communicates ideas effectively. Students are to read their drafts and ask themselves if they have clearly conveyed their meaning and if they have said it in a way that is interesting. During Revising writers are not to concern themselves with spelling, capitalization, and punctuation; instead they are to concentrate on what they want to say and how they want to say it.

"Revising Idea" explains two important ways to approach the revising stage: writers read to themselves and read to partners. You may wish to emphasize that students need not make actual changes during the first reading. This is the time to think about whether their meaning is clear.

Remind students that sharing a draft is like performing a dress rehearsal before a friendly audience. Thoughtful feedback is valuable. Emphasize that partners need to think carefully and sensitively about their responses to the questions, *What part did you like best?* and *Is there anything you would like to hear more details about?* You might also wish them to answer the question, *What might be added to the description that would make the image clear to anyone reading it?*

Then explain to writers that they are to use their partners' suggestions only if they feel the ideas will help improve the writing. As writers make changes based on readers' responses and on their own thinking, they gain more control and understanding of their writing.

3 Revising ◆ Making changes to improve your writing

Reading to yourself is an important revising strategy. First think about your *purpose*. Did you stick to your purpose of describing an object? Or did you forget to describe and start telling a story? Also think about your *audience*. Were you writing for your classmates? Will they understand what you wrote?

Another revising strategy is sharing with a partner. Read your writing aloud. Ask your partner to make suggestions and ask questions. Think about your partner's suggestions. Then make the changes *you* feel are important.

REVISING IDEA

Read to Yourself and Read to a Partner

First read your description to yourself. Think about your purpose and audience. Did you really create a picture of what you are describing? Make changes to improve your description. You can cross out words and write in new words. You can draw arrows to show where to move words or sentences. Your writing may look very messy at this point. That is all right.

Next read your description to a partner. Ask, "What part did you like the best? What would you like to know more about?" Listen to the answers. Then make the changes you think will improve your description.

Introduction 6

Proofreading ♦ Looking for and fixing errors

After you have made sure your writing says what you want it to say, proofread for correctness. Check capital letters and punctuation, indenting, and spelling. Then make a clean copy in your best handwriting. A correct copy is a courtesy to your reader.

PROOFREADING IDEA

One Thing at a Time

It's hard to look for every kind of error at once. Check for one thing at a time. First check indenting, then capitalization, then punctuation. Check your spelling last.

Publishing ♦ Sharing your writing with others

There are many ways to share your writing. You may read it aloud to others. You may record it with a tape recorder or post it on a bulletin board. One of the best parts of writing is hearing or seeing your audience's response.

PUBLISHING IDEA

A Guessing Game

Take turns reading your descriptions aloud to each other. For extra fun, play a guessing game. In place of the name of your object, say "thingamajig." For example,

Have you ever really looked at the thingamajig outside our window? See if you have described your object so well that your classmates can guess what it is.

4. PROOFREADING

Tell students that Proofreading is a time to look for and correct errors in punctuation, spelling, capitalization, and mechanics. Emphasize that making their writing clear and correct is a courtesy to the reader. "Proofreading Idea" explains how to look for different kinds of errors one at a time, which can help students spot errors more easily than if they tried to check for everything in one reading. After students have corrected their errors, they are to make a neat, clean copy of their writing.

5. PUBLISHING

Publishing comes when writing is shared with an audience. It means going public and celebrating authorship. Publishing is also the time when a writer notes readers' responses. "Publishing Idea" suggests making readers' responses a game of trying to guess the identity of the object being described. Students can share their writing orally or by displaying it. In either case, allow time for the audience to respond. (If the descriptions are displayed, you may wish to provide a sheet of paper next to each description on which students can write what they believe the object is.)

Encourage students to offer praise for their classmates' writing that is particularly effective.

OVERVIEW

TWO-PART

flexibility

USING LANGUAGE TO NARRATE

Unit 1 Overview

books

ON UNIT THEME

EASY

📖 **Farming the Land: Modern Farmers and Their Machines** by Jerry Bushey. Carolrhoda. Clear photographs and text show the equipment and skills involved in operating a large, modern farm during a typical growing season.

📖 **Sugaring Time** by Kathryn Lasky. Macmillan. In descriptive prose and photographs, this book depicts a Vermont family making maple syrup on their farm. **Newbery Honor Book.**

AVERAGE

📖 **Arthur, for the Very First Time** by Patricia MacLachlan. Harper. Also available with Silver Burdett & Ginn's World of Books Classroom Library. A ten-year-old boy has new experiences on a farm. **Golden Kite Award, American Library Association Notable Children's Book.**

📖 **Farm Animals** by Dorothy Hinshaw Patent. Holiday. This well-researched book describes the variety of animal life found on American farms.

CHALLENGING

📖 **Joel: Growing Up a Farm Man** by Patricia and Jack Demuth. Dodd. This photo essay about a boy on his family farm in Illinois shows many aspects of farm life. **Society of Midland Authors Book Award.**

📖 **A Prairie Boy's Winter** by William Kurelek. Houghton. The author-illustrator recalls a prairie farm in winter during the 1930s. **New York Times Best Illustrated Children's Book.**

READ-ALOUDS

📖 **Rascal: A Memoir of a Better Era** by Sterling North. Dutton. The author recalls his childhood adventures with a raccoon. **Newbery Honor Book.**

📖 **A Gathering of Days: A New England Girl's Journal, 1830–1832** by Joan Blos. Scribner. This historical novel tells about life on a New England farm. **Newbery Medal.**

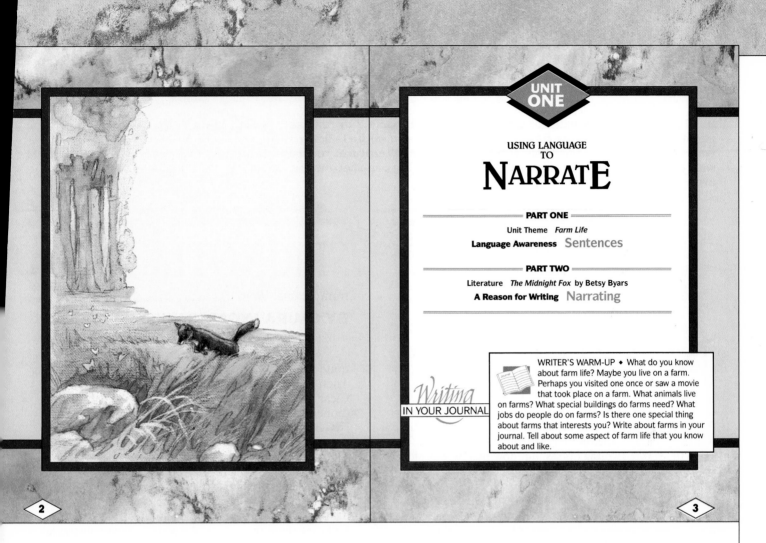

UNIT ONE

USING LANGUAGE TO
NARRATE

=== PART ONE ===

Unit Theme *Farm Life*

Language Awareness Sentences

=== PART TWO ===

Literature *The Midnight Fox* by Betsy Byars

A Reason for Writing Narrating

Writing
IN YOUR JOURNAL

WRITER'S WARM-UP ♦ What do you know about farm life? Maybe you live on a farm. Perhaps you visited one once or saw a movie that took place on a farm. What animals live on farms? What special buildings do farms need? What jobs do people do on farms? Is there one special thing about farms that interests you? Write about farms in your journal. Tell about some aspect of farm life that you know about and like.

start with WRITING IN YOUR JOURNAL

Writers' Warm-up is designed to help students activate prior knowledge of the unit theme, "Farm Life." Whether you begin instruction with Part 1 or Part 2, encourage students to focus attention on the illustration on page 2 of their textbook. Encourage them to discuss what they see. Then have a volunteer read aloud the **Writers' Warm-up** on page 3. Have students write their thoughts in their journals. You may wish to tell them that they will refer to this writing in the first lesson of Part 1, in the Grammar-Writing Connection, and in the Curriculum Connection.

THEN START WITH *part 1*

Language Awareness: Sentences Developmental lessons focus on the concept of sentences. Each lesson is carefully constructed not only to help students learn the concept well but also to help build interest and background knowledge for the thinking, reading, and writing they will do in Part 2. The last lesson in Part 1 is a vocabulary lesson with which students learn how to use a thesaurus. The Grammar-Writing Connection that follows serves as a bridge to Part 2, encouraging students to work together to apply their new language skills at the sentence level of writing.

...OR WITH *part 2*

A Reason for Writing: Narrating is the focus of Part 2. First, students learn a thinking strategy for narrating. Then they read and respond to a selection of literature on which they may model their writing. Developmental composition lessons, including "Telling an Anecdote," a speaking and listening lesson, all reflect the literature and culminate in the Writing Process lesson. There a "Grammar Check," a "Word Choice" hint, and proofreading strategies help you focus on single traits for remediation or instruction through the lessons in Part 1. The unit ends with Curriculum Connection and Books to Enjoy, which help students discover how their new skills apply to writing across the curriculum.

THEME BAR

CATEGORIES	Environments	Business/World of Work	Imagination	Communications/ Fine Arts	People	Science	Expressions	Social Studies
THEMES	UNIT 1 Farm Life	UNIT 2 Handicrafts	UNIT 3 Tall Tales	UNIT 4 The Visual Arts	UNIT 5 Lasting Impressions	UNIT 6 Volcanoes	UNIT 7 Nature	UNIT 8 Animal Habitats
PACING	1 month	1 month	1 month	1 month	1 month	1 month	1 month	1 month

Build background knowledge of the unit theme, "Farm Life," by reading aloud this selection to your class. At the same time you will be building your students' knowledge of our rich heritage of fine literature. You may wish to use the "Notes for Listening" on the following page before and after reading aloud.

SPRINGTIME

from *Farmer Boy*

BY LAURA INGALLS WILDER

Now breakfast was eaten before dawn and the sun was rising beyond the dewy meadows when Almanzo drove his team from the barns.

He had to stand on a box to lift the heavy collars onto the horses' shoulders and to slip the bridles over their ears, but he knew how to drive. He had learned when he was little. Father wouldn't let him touch the colts, nor drive the spirited young horses, but now that he was old enough to work in the fields he could drive the old, gentle work-team, Bess and Beauty.

They knew how to plow without stepping on corn, or making the furrows crooked. They knew how to harrow, and to turn at the end of the field. Almanzo would have enjoyed driving them more if they hadn't known so much. He hitched them to the harrow. Last fall the fields had been plowed and covered with manure; now the lumpy soil must be harrowed.

Bess and Beauty stepped out willingly, not too fast, yet fast enough to harrow well. They liked to work in the springtime, after the long winter of standing in their stalls. Back and forth across the field they pulled the harrow, while Almanzo walked behind it, holding the reins. At the end of the row he turned the team around and set the harrow so that its teeth barely overlapped the strip already harrowed. Then he slapped the reins on the horses' rumps, shouted "Giddap!" and away they went again.

All over the countryside other boys were harrowing, too, turning up the moist earth to the sunshine. Far to the north the St. Lawrence River was a silver streak at the edge of the sky. The woods were clouds of delicate green. Birds hopped twittering on the stone fences, and squirrels frisked. Almanzo walked whistling behind his team.

When he harrowed the whole field across one way, then he harrowed it across the other way. The harrow's sharp teeth combed again and again through the earth, breaking up the lumps. All the soil must be made mellow and fine and smooth.

By and by Almanzo was too hungry to whistle. He grew hungrier and hungrier. It seemed that noon would never come. He wondered how many miles he'd walked. And still the sun seemed to stand still, the shadows seemed not to change at all. He was starving.

At last the sun stood overhead, the shadows were quite gone. Almanzo harrowed another row, and another. Then at last he heard the horns blowing, far and near. Clear and joyful came the sound of Mother's big tin dinner-horn.

Bess and Beauty pricked up theirs ears and stepped more briskly. At the edge of the field toward the house they stopped. Almanzo unfastened the traces and looped them up, and leaving the harrow in the field, he climbed onto Beauty's broad back.

He rode down to the pumphouse and let the horses drink. He put them in their stall, took off their bridles, and gave them their grain. A good horseman always takes care of his horses before he eats or rests. But Almanzo hurried.

How good dinner was! And how he ate! Father heaped his plate again and again, and Mother smiled and gave him two pieces of pie.

He felt better when he went back to work, but the afternoon seemed much longer than the morning. He was tired when he rode down to the barns at sunset, to do the chores. At supper he was drowsy, and as soon as he had eaten he climbed upstairs and went to bed. It was so good to stretch out on the soft bed. Before he could pull up the coverlet he fell fast asleep.

In just a minute Mother's candle-light shone on the stairs and she was calling. Another day had begun.

There was no time to lose, no time to waste in rest or play. The life of the earth comes up with a rush in the springtime. All the wild seeds of weed and thistle, the sprouts of vine and bush and tree, are trying to take the fields. Farmers must fight them with harrow and plow and hoe; they must plant the good seeds quickly.

Almanzo was a little soldier in this great battle. From dawn to dark he worked, from dark to dawn he slept, then he was up again and working.

He harrowed the potato field till the soil was smooth and mellow and every little sprouting weed was killed. Then he helped Royal take the seed potatoes from the bin in the cellar and cut them into pieces, leaving two or three eyes on each piece.

Potato plants have blossoms and seeds, but no one knows what kind of potato will grow from a potato seed.

All the potatoes of one kind that have ever been grown have come from one potato. A potato is not a seed; it is part of a potato plant's root. Cut it up and plant it, and it will always make more potatoes just like itself.

Every potato has several little dents in it, that look like eyes. From these eyes the little roots grow down into the soil, and little leaves push up toward the sun. They eat up the piece of potato while they are small, before they are strong enough to take their food from the earth and the air.

Father was marking the field. The marker was a log with a row of wooden pegs driven into it, three and a half feet apart. One horse drew the log crosswise behind him, and the pegs made little furrows. Father marked the field lengthwise and crosswise, so the furrows made little squares. Then the planting began.

Father and Royal took their hoes, and Alice and Almanzo carried pails full of pieces of potato. Almanzo went in front of Royal and Alice went in front of Father, down the rows.

At the corner of each square, where the furrows crossed, Almanzo dropped one piece of potato. He must drop it exactly in the corner, so that the rows would be straight and could be plowed. Royal covered it with dirt and patted it firm with the hoe. Behind Alice, Father covered the pieces of potato that she dropped.

Planting potatoes was fun. A good smell came from the fresh earth and from the clover fields. Alice was pretty and gay, with the breeze blowing her curls and setting her hoopskirts swaying. Father was jolly, and they all talked while they worked.

Almanzo and Alice tried to drop potatoes so fast that they'd have a minute at the end of a row, to look for birds' nests or chase a lizard into the stone fence. But Father and Royal were never far behind. Father said:

"Hustle along there, son, hustle along!" So they hustled, and when they were far enough ahead Almanzo plucked a grass-stem and made it whistle between his thumbs. Alice tried, but she could not do that. She could pucker her mouth and whistle. Royal teased her.

"Whistling girls and crowing hens
Always come to some bad ends."

Back and forth across the field they went, all morning, all afternoon, for three days. Then the potatoes were planted.

Then Father <u>sowed</u> the grain. He sowed a field of wheat for white bread, a field of rye for rye bread, and a field of oats mixed with Canada peas, to feed the horses and cows next winter.

While Father sowed the grain, Almanzo followed him over the fields with Bess and Beauty, harrowing the seeds into the earth. Almanzo could not sow grain yet; he must practice a long time before he could spread the seeds evenly. That is hard to do.

The heavy sack of grain hung from a strap over Father's left shoulder. As he walked, he took handfuls of grain from the sack. With a sweep of his arm and a bend of his wrist he let the little grains fly from his fingers. The sweep of his arm kept time with his steps, and when Father finished sowing a field every inch of ground had its evenly scattered seeds, nowhere too many or too few.

When all the grain was sowed, Almanzo and Alice planted the carrots. They had sacks full of the little, red, round carrot seeds hanging from their shoulders, like Father's big seed-sack. Father had marked the carrot field lengthwise, with a marker whose teeth were only eighteen inches apart. Almanzo and Alice, with the carrot seeds, went up and down the long field, straddling the little furrows.

Now the weather was so warm that they could go barefooted. Their bare feet felt good in the air and the soft dirt. They dribbled the carrot seed into the furrows, and with their feet they pushed the dirt over the seeds and pressed it down. ◇

	LESSON TITLE	STUDENT TEXT				TEACHING RESOURCES		
		Student Lesson	Unit Review	Cumulative Review	Extra Practice	Reteaching Master	Practice Master	Testing Program
1 DAY	Unit Opener							
1 DAY	Writing Sentences	4–5			50, 51	1	1	
1 DAY	Four Kinds of Sentences	6–7	48	106, 222, 330, 432	50, 52	2	2	T532
1 DAY	Complete Subjects and Complete Predicates	8–9	48	106, 222, 330, 432	50, 53	3	3	T532
1 DAY	Simple Subjects	10–11	48	106, 222, 330, 432	50, 54	4	4	T532
1 DAY	Simple Predicates	12–13	48	106, 222, 330, 432	50, 56	5	5	T532
1 DAY	Subjects in Imperative Sentences	14–15	48	106, 222, 330, 432	50, 57	6	6	T532
1 DAY	VOCABULARY ◆ Using the Thesaurus	16–17	48			7	7	T532
1 DAY	GRAMMAR-WRITING CONNECTION ◆ How to Combine Sentences	18–19						

PART 1

THINK

1 DAY	CRITICAL THINKING ◆ A Strategy for Narrating	22–23	See also pages 29, 40, 46					

READ

1 DAY	LITERATURE ◆ *The Midnight Fox* by Betsy Byars	24–29				Audio Library 2		

SPEAK/LISTEN

1 DAY	SPEAKING AND LISTENING ◆ Telling an Anecdote	30–31				Video Library		

WRITE

1 DAY	WRITING ◆ Character, Setting, and Plot	32–33	49			8	8	T532
1 DAY	WRITING ◆ Quotations	34–35	49			9	9	T532
1 DAY	READING-WRITING CONNECTION ◆ Focus on the Narrator	36–37						

WRITING PROCESS ◆ Prewriting • Writing • Revising • Proofreading • Publishing

4–5 DAYS	WRITING PROCESS ◆ Writing a Personal Narrative	38–45				Spelling Connection Transparencies		T552
1 DAY	CURRICULUM CONNECTION ◆ Writing for Science	46				Writing Across the Curriculum Guide		

PART 2

Unit 1 Planning and Pacing Guide

Teacher Resource File
Reteaching Masters 1–9
Practice Masters 1–9
Evaluation and Testing Program, including Unit Pretest, Posttest, and Picture Prompt Writing Samples
Parent Letters in English and Spanish
Classroom Theme Posters
Writing Across the Curriculum Teacher Guide
Integrated Language Arts Projects with Masters (see pages T511–T529)
Spelling Connection, Teacher Edition
Writing Process Transparencies
Audio Library 1: Read-Alouds and Sing-Alouds

Also available:
Achieving English Proficiency Guide and Activities
Spelling Connection, Pupil Edition
Student Resource Books
Student Writing Portfolios
Professional Handbook
WORLD OF BOOKS Classroom Library

Multi-Modal Materials
Audio Library 1: Read-Alouds and Sing-Alouds
Audio Library 2: Listening to Literature
Video Library
Revising and Proofreading Transparencies
Fine Arts Transparencies with Viewing Booklet
Writing Process Transparencies
Writing Process Computer Program

LANGUAGE *game*

Who Am I?

Objective: To use correct end punctuation
Materials: Index cards, chalkboard

Write the following sample on the chalkboard, excluding the items in parentheses:

(.) I work with clay.   (.) Please sit still.
(?) Who will model for me?   (!) How pleased you will be with my sculpture!
                             (Sculptor)

Divide the class into four or five groups. Each group chooses a specific identifying role, such as police officer, principal, farmer, lawyer, or sculptor. Each group must compose four types of sentences about the role, using correct end punctuation marks. The sentences can be displayed without identifying the role or the punctuation. Then the class can guess what type of person would say those sentences and add the correct end punctuation.

Multi-Modal Activities

BULLETIN BOARD *idea*

You may wish to use a bulletin board as a springboard for discussing the unit theme, or you may prefer to have students create a bulletin board as they move through the unit. Encourage students to explore what farm life might be like. Have students look through old newspapers and magazines to find pictures of farm animals, farm buildings, fields of crops, and so on. If possible allow students to work in groups to create one part of a farm display, such as a stable of horses, bales of hay, saddles and other riding equipment, buckets of feed, and pails of water. Encourage discussion of the layout of the farm and what is needed to make it complete. You may wish to label the display *Our Class Farm*.

MEETING INDIVIDUAL NEEDS

Students with different learning styles will all benefit from a natural approach to language learning, including frequent and varied use of oral language in the classroom.

Students "At Risk"

The following suggestions can help you help the students in your classroom who may be considered "at risk."

Activate Prior Knowledge

The "Getting Started" at the top of every developmental lesson in the Student Textbook is a whole-class oral activity that acts as the anticipatory set to the lesson. Encourage your low achievers, slow learners and readers, and others who may be considered at risk to participate in the activity. Use it as a highly motivating instructional technique. It helps students discover that they already know a good deal about the concept to be studied, and it encourages them to be open to new learning by reassuring them that the concept is within their reach. As the Getting Started activity sets the stage for learners to succeed, it also helps them clearly focus their attention on the concept to be explored and learned.

Limited English Proficiency

Teachers whose classes contain students with limited English proficiency may find the following activities helpful in developing students' skills in grammar and composition.

Question and Answer Chart

Display pictures from magazines or books that depict people, places, and things associated with farm life, such as a farmer, a cowhand, a barn, and a cow. On the chalkboard begin a farm life chart such as the one on this page.

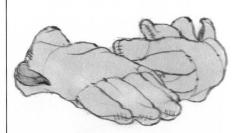

Point to the first picture you displayed and elicit declarative sentences by asking questions such as : *Where does a farmer work? What does a farmer do? When does a farmer work? What do you picture when you hear the word* farmer? Record students' responses under the appropriate heading on the chart. Repeat this procedure with the remaining pictures. When the chart is completed, review the process of forming interrogative sentences by demonstrating how the heads at the top of the chart can be turned into questions. Suggest another person, place, or thing, such as a cow, and have students use the headings to ask questions about that aspect of farm life: *Where might you see a cow? What is a cow? When might you see a cow? What do you picture when you hear the word* cow?

Everyday Commands

Point out to students that people often give directions, or commands, to each other or to pets and other animals. For example, a student may say to another student: *Hand me the chalk*. That same student may say to a pet: *Stay* or *Heel*. Then display the farm life pictures from the previous activity. Have students brainstorm directions that they might

hear if they were living on a farm. Record their responses on the chalkboard. If a student responds with a declarative or interrogative sentence, accept that answer but write it in another column on the chalkboard. Then discuss with students why that sentence is not a direction or a command. Elicit imperative sentences such as the following as students work together on this activity:

Farm Life Commands
Help me fix the tractor.
Call the animal doctor.
Set the alarm for four-thirty.
Drive the truck to the barn.

Personal Narrative

Help students brainstorm about products that come from the farm, such as meat, cereal, milk, and cotton. Record these products on the chalkboard. Discuss how each item is produced. Then write the following questions below the products and read them aloud.

1. Which farm product did you use this week?
2. Where did you get this product?
3. Who gave you this product?
4. How did you use this product?
5. Why is this product important to you?

Have students think about each question. Then have them use the questions to tell about an event in which they used a farm product.

Person, Place, Thing	Where	What	When	Feat
farmer	*farm*	*plant*		

Gifted and Talented Students

To enable gifted and talented students to work at their own pace and to explore the content further, you may wish to use one or more of these activities.

Sentences to Order

Have students work as individuals or in small groups to make up different kinds of sentences. Each student or group should choose an aspect of farm life and make up different types of sentences about it. You may wish to give them an assignment or have them decide what the requirements are; for example, three declarative, two interrogative, one imperative, and one exclamatory sentence.

Students should brainstorm things they might want to say about farm life and then decide which type of sentence to use for each thought. Have students or groups exchange papers and evaluate whether each sentence was correctly identified and punctuated.

When they have completed other assignments, students can work together again, giving themselves similar "assignments" to apply to other topics.

Subjects and Predicates

Have students work in pairs or small groups to write interesting or outlandish subjects and predicates. An equal number of subjects and predicates should be written on individual cards, and placed in two piles. Then allow students to play with the sentence parts, each choosing a combination that makes a wacky but grammatically sensible statement.

Have each student write a short humorous essay or paragraph, using the wacky sentence as a springboard or topic sentence. Have students share their work by reading aloud or posting their paragraphs on a bulletin board.

As a more difficult task, group members can take turns putting together sentences that tell a group story.

Changing Sentences

Have students work with the sentences they created in the first activity or create new sentences of four kinds, each labeled *declarative, interrogative, imperative,* or *exclamatory.* Have them rewrite each sentence in one or more different sentence forms and label the variations. Then have students exchange papers and compare their sentences to see if they can make any generalizations. For example, when changing declarative sentences to the interrogative form, they will note a change in word order and the use of words such as *what, where, when,* and *why.*

Have students make a chart or poster of their generalizations. They should test the statements using sentences from a variety of sources. They may add to the chart as they learn more about sentences and writing.

Meeting Individual Needs

UNIT 1/LESSON 1

OBJECTIVES
To identify and write complete sentences

ASSIGNMENT GUIDE

BASIC　　　Practice A
　↓　　　　Practice B
ADVANCED　Practice C

All should do the Apply activity.

RESOURCES
■ Reteaching Master 1
■ Practice Master 1
■■■ Extra Practice, pp. 50, 51
Unit 1 Pretest, p. T532

TEACHING THE LESSON

1. Getting Started
Oral Language Focus attention on this oral activity, encouraging all to participate. You may wish to suggest that students give information using sensory details that describe how each animal looks, sounds, and acts. Encourage students to give specific rather than general details, such as *a hoofed animal* rather than *a four-legged animal*.

2. Developing the Lesson
Guide students through the explanation of a sentence, emphasizing the examples and the summary. Using the examples, you may wish to point out that each complete sentence both names a person or thing and tells something about that person or thing. Lead students through the **Guided Practice**. Identify those who would benefit from reteaching. Assign independent Practice A–C.

3. Closing the Lesson
After students complete the Apply activity, have volunteers read samples of their original incomplete sentences and then tell how they made the sentences complete. Point out that writing complete sentences will help students express their thoughts more clearly.

GETTING STARTED

Choose an animal of the woods, fields, or farm. Without naming the animal, give some information about it. The first person to guess your animal tells about the next mystery animal.

1 Writing Sentences

When you exchange thoughts and ideas, you speak and write in sentences. A sentence goes somewhere and does something. It is complete when it finishes the thought it begins. A group of words that does not complete its thought is not a sentence. For example, *Does only part of the job* is not a sentence. *It does only part of the job* is a sentence.

Read each group of words below. The first group in each set is not a complete sentence. The second group of words is a sentence.

1. a. A fox.
   b. A fox ran into the forest.
2. a. Watched it.
   b. Mei Ling watched it.
3. a. About foxes on the farm.
   b. Luis wrote a report about foxes on the farm.

> **Summary** ◆ A **sentence** is a group of words that expresses a complete thought. When you write, make sure each of your sentences is complete. This will help your reader understand what you mean.

Guided Practice

Tell whether each group of words below is or is not a sentence.

1. Foxes look like small dogs. *sentence*
2. Foxes have bushy tails and sharp snouts. *sentence*
3. A fox and her pups. *not a sentence*
4. Foxes live in dens. *sentence*
5. Underground, among rocks, or in a hollow log. *not a sentence*
6. A fox may appear suddenly. *sentence*

4　GRAMMAR and WRITING: Identifying Sentences

ESSENTIAL LANGUAGE SKILLS
This lesson provides opportunities to:

LISTENING ◆ follow the logical organization of an oral presentation ◆ select from an oral presentation the information needed

SPEAKING ◆ use a variety of words to express feelings and ideas ◆ make organized oral presentations

READING ◆ relate experiences with appropriate vocabulary in complete sentences ◆ evaluate and make judgments ◆ follow a set of directions

WRITING ◆ use ideas and information from sources other than personal experiences for writing ◆ apply the conventions of writing to produce effective communication

LANGUAGE ◆ use the fundamentals of grammar, punctuation, and spelling

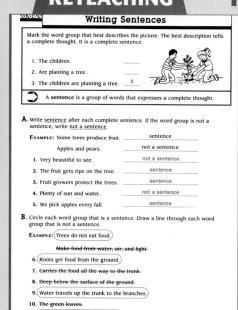

Practice

A. Decide whether each group of words expresses a complete thought. Write *sentence* or *not a sentence*.

7. An adult fox is about twenty-five inches long. sentence
8. Weighs about ten pounds. not a sentence
9. Living in family groups while young are growing. not a sentence
10. Foxes can be playful. sentence
11. Foxes have a keen sense of smell. sentence
12. Hunts mostly at night. not a sentence
13. Foxes communicate through growls and barks. sentence
14. Lives up to fourteen years. not a sentence
15. The red fox is common in the northern United States. sentence
16. Eats mice, birds, lizards, and rabbits. not a sentence

B. Write the group of words in each pair that is a sentence.

17. **a.** In late winter or early spring.
    b. A female fox gives birth to her pups. sentence
18. **a.** The male and female foxes bring food to the young. sentence
    b. Leading enemies away from the den.
19. **a.** The pups or cubs wrestle with each other. sentence
    b. Jumps on insects and parents' tails.
20. **a.** Showing the young how to stalk or chase prey.
    b. The adults bring live mice for the pups to pounce on. sentence
21. **a.** May wander far from the area in which they were born.
    b. The pups start to live on their own in late summer. sentence

C. Add words to make each group of words a sentence. Answers will vary. Possible answers follow.

22. A sleek red fox _was standing_ near the fence.
23. The cows in the pasture _ambled_ toward the barn.
24. _The speedy fox_ splashed across the shallow stream.
25. The tall golden grass _quivered_ in the breeze.
26. _I strolled_ near the side of the farmhouse.

Apply • Think and Write

From Your Writing ♦ Read what you wrote for the Writer's Warm-up. Did you express yourself in complete sentences? Rewrite any incomplete sentences you find.

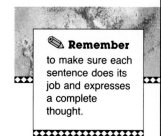

✎ Remember to make sure each sentence does its job and expresses a complete thought.

GRAMMAR and WRITING: Identifying Sentences **5**

◀ TEACHING OPTIONS ▶

RETEACHING

A Different Modality Write the four sentences below on cardboard strips. Cut each sentence in two between the subject and the predicate. Mix the strips and have students form complete sentences.

1. Concord/is the capital of New Hampshire.
2. The State House/is made of stone.
3. The Merrimack River / flows through Concord.
4. Our family/visits each summer.

CLASS ENRICHMENT

A Cooperative Activity Have partners list five titles of novels, songs, or poems at least two of which should be complete sentences, such as "I Hear America Singing." You may wish to have students use anthologies or the card catalog in the school library to find titles. Have partners read aloud their list and then ask classmates to identify each title that expresses a complete thought.

CHALLENGE

An Independent Extension Distribute newspaper headlines you have clipped. Have students turn them into complete sentences. You may prefer to write on the chalkboard the following titles as headlines.
Example: Yesterday's snow was a big surprise.

1. Surprise Snow　　5. Hot Weather
2. River Rising　　　6. President's Plan
3. Alive and Well　　7. Final Game Today
4. Traffic Delays　　8. Bank Robbery

UNIT 1/LESSON 2

OBJECTIVES
To identify and write declarative, interrogative, imperative, and exclamatory sentences
To use correct end punctuation for declarative, interrogative, imperative, and exclamatory sentences

ASSIGNMENT GUIDE
BASIC   Practice A
↓   Practice B
ADVANCED   Practice C

All should do the Apply activity.

RESOURCES
■ Reteaching Master 2
■ Practice Master 2
■ ■ ■ Extra Practice, pp. 50, 52

TEACHING THE LESSON

1. Getting Started
Oral Language Focus attention on this oral activity, encouraging all to participate. You may wish to model the three kinds of sentences, such as *Today a severe thunderstorm may hit our area; Will a severe thunderstorm hit our area today?; What a severe thunderstorm hit our area today!*

2. Developing the Lesson
Guide students through the explanation of the four kinds of sentences, emphasizing the examples and the summary. Using the examples, you may wish to demonstrate how voice tone changes when a person makes a statement, asks a question, gives a command, or expresses strong feeling. Tell students that end punctuation helps readers know how a sentence is meant to be read, just as voice tone helps listeners distinguish the kinds of sentences being spoken. Lead students through the **Guided Practice.** Identify those who would benefit from reteaching. Assign independent Practice A–C.

3. Closing the Lesson
After students complete the Apply activity, encourage volunteers to read aloud their four kinds of sentences. Point out to students that knowing how to use the four kinds of sentences can help make their writing and speaking more interesting.

6

How many different ways can you think of to complete the sentence so that it tells something, asks something, or shows stro— feeling: _____ *a severe thunderstorm* _____ (.) (?) (!)

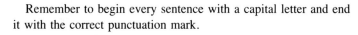

2 Four Kinds of Sentences

There are four kinds of sentences. All begin with capital letters.

Four Kinds of Sentences	
Declarative A declarative sentence makes a statement. It ends with a period (.).	Rice is a popular food.
Interrogative An interrogative sentence asks a question. It ends with a question mark (**?**).	Are there many rice farmers in America?
Imperative An imperative sentence gives a command or makes a request. It ends with a period (.).	Begin harvesting the wheat tomorrow.
Exclamatory An exclamatory sentence expresses strong feeling. It ends with an exclamation mark (**!**).	How beautiful the waving wheat looks!

Remember to begin every sentence with a capital letter and end it with the correct punctuation mark.

> **Summary** ◆ A **declarative sentence** makes a statement. An **interrogative sentence** asks a question. An **imperative sentence** gives a command or makes a request. An **exclamatory sentence** expresses strong feeling.

Guided Practice

Tell which kind of sentence each of the following is.

declarative
1. Rice is used in cereals.

interrogative
3. How much wheat will you plant?

exclamatory
2. What a day for plowing!

imperative
4. Attach the plow to the tractor.

6   GRAMMAR and MECHANICS: Kinds of Sentences

ESSENTIAL LANGUAGE SKILLS
This lesson provides opportunities to:

LISTENING ◆ employ active listening in a variety of situations

SPEAKING ◆ use a variety of words to express feelings and ideas

READING ◆ evaluate and make judgments ◆ follow a set of directions

WRITING ◆ apply the conventions of punctuation and capitalization

LANGUAGE ◆ produce a variety of sentence patterns ◆ use the fundamentals of grammar, punctuation, and spelling

ractice

For each sentence below, write *declarative*, *interrogative*, *imperative*, or *exclamatory*.

5. Rice is the primary food for half the people of the world. declarative
6. Is rice a grain? interrogative
7. Rice is often grown in flooded fields. declarative
8. Plant the rice in the muddy ground. imperative
9. What an incredible sight that rice field is! exclamatory
10. Does a rice field need a constant supply of water? interrogative
11. Harvesting begins when the golden heads of rice bend down. declarative
12. Leave the cut rice stalks in the sun to dry. imperative

Write each sentence, using capital letters and end punctuation correctly.

13. wheat is a grasslike cereal grain W .
14. how tall those wheat plants are H !
15. do leaves grow from the stalk of a wheat plant D ?
16. about 30,000 different kinds of wheat are grown A .
17. what a large number of varieties that is W !
18. is much wheat grown in the United States I ?
19. wheat is ready for harvest when it is dry and hard W .
20. transfer the harvested wheat to the grain elevator T .

C. Rewrite each sentence. Change it to the kind named in parentheses ( ). Answers may vary. Possible answers follow.

21. Is the soil plowed before wheat seeds are planted?
    (declarative) The soil is plowed before wheat seeds are planted.
22. Machines are used to plant the wheat. (interrogative) Are machines used to plant the wheat?
23. Do you sometimes add nitrogen to the soil? (imperative) Add nitrogen to the soil.
24. The endless fields of golden wheat are beautiful.
    (exclamatory) How beautiful are the endless fields of golden wheat!

Apply • Think and Write

Sentence Variety • Pretend that you are about to enjoy a bowl of cereal made of rice or wheat. Using all four kinds of sentences, write about the cereal.

> ✏ **Remember**
> to use different kinds of sentences to express your ideas.

GRAMMAR and MECHANICS: Kinds of Sentences **7**

RETEACHING 2

Four Kinds of Sentences

Read the sentences below. Circle the end punctuation in each one.
1. There are two lions in the cage.   3. How fierce that lion looks!
2. Do only lions and horses have manes?   4. Stay back from the wall.

A **declarative sentence** makes a statement. It ends with a period (.). An **interrogative sentence** asks a question. It ends with a question mark (?). An **imperative sentence** gives a command or makes a request. It ends with a period (.). An **exclamatory sentence** expresses strong feeling. It ends with an exclamation mark (!). All sentences begin with a capital letter.

A. Circle the end punctuation in each sentence. Then write declarative, interrogative, imperative, or exclamatory.

EXAMPLE: Zoos are fun places to visit.   declarative

1. I have a wonderful idea.   declarative
2. Meet me at the bus stop.   imperative
3. Isn't this a perfect day for a trip?   interrogative
4. How smart you are to bring a camera!   exclamatory

B. Write the correct punctuation mark at the end of each sentence. Circle any letter that should be capitalized. Then write each sentence correctly.

EXAMPLE: please hand me the camera ___ .
         Please hand me the camera.

5. how exciting it is to see a baby panda ___ !
   How exciting it is to see a baby panda!
6. in which countries are pandas found ___ ?
   In which countries are pandas found?
7. the pandas are eating bamboo stalks ___ .
   The pandas are eating bamboo stalks.
8. please take some pictures of the pandas ___ .
   Please take some pictures of the pandas.

PRACTICE 2

Four Kinds of Sentences

A **declarative sentence** makes a statement. An **interrogative** sentence asks a question. An **imperative sentence** gives a command or makes a request. An **exclamatory sentence** expresses strong feeling.

A. Write the correct punctuation mark at the end of each sentence. Then identify each sentence as declarative, interrogative, imperative, or exclamatory.

1. How many different kinds of birds are there ___ ?   interrogative
2. Find out if all birds can fly ___   imperative
3. Flying birds have light bodies and strong wings ___   declarative
4. Is an ostrich light enough to fly ___ ?   interrogative
5. Look at this picture of an ostrich ___   imperative
6. What a funny-looking bird it is ___ !   exclamatory
7. An ostrich is often heavier than an adult human ___   declarative

B. Write each sentence. Use capital letters and end punctuation correctly.

8. a bird's wing feathers are used for flying
   A bird's wing feathers are used for flying.
9. are birds' tail feathers important for flying
   Are birds' tail feathers important for flying?
10. read this article for more information about birds
    Read this article for more information about birds.
11. how important those tail feathers are for steering and balance
    How important those tail feathers are for steering and balance!
12. feathers also keep birds warm
    Feathers also keep birds warm.

WRITE IT
Write about the birds in your state. Include all four kinds of sentences. Write on a separate sheet of paper. Answers will vary.

◀|||| TEACHING OPTIONS ||||▶

RETEACHING

A Different Modality Write the following four sentences on the chalkboard: *Wasn't that Maple Avenue? That was my stop! Please stop the bus. I live on that street.* Have volunteers circle the end punctuation mark in each sentence. Then have students write, in turn, the sentence that makes a request, and expresses strong feeling.

CLASS ENRICHMENT

A Cooperative Activity Have each student make four sentence puzzles on cardboard strips, such as *Declarative/I'm glad you can help me. Interrogative/Have you read the first problem? Imperative/Please check my work. Exclamatory/How difficult the problem is!* Have volunteers cut the strips between the labels and the sentences. Then have students work in pairs to combine strips correctly.

CHALLENGE

An Independent Extension Have students write and then label four kinds of sentences for each topic. Encourage students to check each other's labels.

Example: belonging to a math club
         The Math Club meets now. declarative
         Do you want to come? interrogative
         Join the Math Club. imperative
         What fun the meetings are! exclamatory

1. belonging to a math club
2. going on a trip
3. entering a contest

7

UNIT 1/LESSON 3

OBJECTIVES
To identify the complete subject and complete predicate in sentences

ASSIGNMENT GUIDE

BASIC   Practice A
             Practice B
ADVANCED   Practice C

All should do the Apply activity.

RESOURCES
■ Reteaching Master 3
■ Practice Master 3
■ ■ ■ Extra Practice, pp. 50, 54

TEACHING THE LESSON

1. Getting Started
Oral Language Focus attention on this oral activity, encouraging all to participate. You may wish to have students supply two responses, one logical and the other silly. Have students give logical sentences first. Then provide an example of a silly sentence, such as *Carmen Ruiz conquers raspberries*. Encourage all students to supply a silly sentence.

2. Developing the Lesson
Guide students through the explanation of complete subjects and complete predicates, emphasizing the examples and the summary. You may wish to give more examples of one-word complete subjects and one-word complete predicates, such as *Birds fly. Babies crawl. People work.* Lead students through the **Guided Practice.** Identify those who would benefit from reteaching. Assign independent Practice A–C.

3. Closing the Lesson
After students complete the Apply activity, you may wish to encourage them to use their sentences in a real letter to a friend. Point out that knowing how to identify subjects and predicates can help them be sure their ideas have been expressed completely and clearly.

GETTING STARTED

Play "Who-Does-What?" Begin a sentence with your first and last names. Use words that begin with your initials to finish the sentence. For example: *Carmen Ruiz collects rocks*.

3 Complete Subjects and Complete Predicates

Think about what a sentence needs in order to do its job of expressing a complete thought. It needs certain parts, just like a machine. Every sentence has two main parts. The complete subject names someone or something. The complete predicate tells what the subject is or does.

Read the sentences below. The part in blue is the complete subject. The part in green is the complete predicate.

1. Insects   can be harmful to farm plants.
2. Some insects   help.
3. The potato beetle   is a harmful insect.
4. Farmers in some areas   lose their crops through insects.

The complete subject may have only one word as in **1** above. The complete subjects in **2**, **3**, and **4** have more than one word. The complete predicate may also have one word or many words.

> **Summary** ♦ The **complete subject** is all the words in the subject part of a sentence. The subject part names someone or something. The **complete predicate** is all the words in the predicate part of a sentence. The predicate part tells what the subject is or does.

Guided Practice

Name each complete subject and complete predicate.

comp. subj.   comp. pred.
1. Insects | are small animals.
comp. subj.   comp. pred.
2. All insects | have six legs.
   comp. subj.   comp. pred.
3. Millions of kinds of insects | live throughout the world.
   comp. subj.   comp. pred.
4. The bodies of dead insects | enrich the soil.
comp. subj.   comp. pred.
5. Insects | help many plants produce seeds through pollination.

8   GRAMMAR: Complete Subjects and Complete Predicates

ESSENTIAL LANGUAGE SKILLS
This lesson provides opportunities to:

LISTENING ♦ listen to appreciate the sound device of alliteration ♦ follow the logical organization of an oral presentation ♦ select from an oral presentation the information needed

SPEAKING ♦ use a variety of words to express feelings and ideas ♦ make organized oral presentations

READING ♦ use context to understand the meaning of words ♦ evaluate and make judgments ♦ follow a set of directions

WRITING ♦ use ideas and information from sources other than personal experiences for writing

LANGUAGE ♦ use parts of speech correctly ♦ use the fundamentals of grammar, punctuation, and spelling

ractice

Read each sentence. Then write the complete subject of each.

6. Many insects are helpful to farmers.
7. Bees pollinate farmers' crops.
8. The bees on our farm make delicious honey.
9. Predators are animals that eat other animals.
10. Some helpful insects are predators.
11. The ladybug eats several kinds of crop-destroying insects.
12. Other insects on the farm are parasites.
13. These insects live on or in the bodies of harmful insects.
14. A certain kind of wasp lays eggs in harmful caterpillars.
15. The young wasps feed on the caterpillars and kill them.

B. Write each sentence. Underline the complete subject once. Underline the complete predicate twice.

16. The corn earworm destroys corn crops.
17. The caterpillar of the cabbage butterfly damages cauliflower.
18. Wheat crops are hurt by maggots.
19. Gypsy moth caterpillars strip the leaves from many trees.
20. Harmful insects cause billions of dollars in crop damage.

C. Add a complete subject or a complete predicate to each group of words below. Write the complete sentence.
Answers will vary. Possible answers follow.
EXAMPLE: _____ wrote a report about harmful insects.
ANSWER: Tom wrote a report about harmful insects.

21. Scientists examined the damage insects caused to the crops.
22. The study of insects will help us learn how to control them.
23. Some farmers have very few problems with insects.
24. A bee flew very close to my face.
25. A thick, furry caterpillar is crawling up my arm.

Apply • Think and Write

Telling a Story • Imagine that you have spent a week on a farm. Write a story about your stay. Be sure to include your chores as well as any special events that occurred on the farm.

GRAMMAR: Complete Subjects and Complete Predicates **9**

✏ **Remember**
that every sentence has two main parts—a subject and a predicate.

RETEACHING 3
Complete Subjects and Predicates

Imagine that you are a detective. Read the sentence to find out who did what.

Subject	Predicate
The young boy	walked quietly into the room.

Who walked quietly into the room? Write all the words in the subject part of the sentence.

The young boy

What did the young boy do? Write all the words in the predicate part of the sentence.

walked quietly into the room

> The **complete subject** is all the words in the subject part of a sentence. The subject part names someone or something. It may have one word or many words. The **complete predicate** is all the words in the predicate part of a sentence. The predicate part tells what the subject is or does. It may have one word or many words.

A. Circle the complete subject in each sentence. Write each complete subject under the heading **Who Did It?**

	Who Did It?
EXAMPLE: Sherlock Holmes solved many mysteries.	Sherlock Holmes
1. People asked him to solve many mysteries.	People
2. The police came to him for help.	The police
3. Doctor Watson helped Holmes with his work.	Doctor Watson
4. Holmes had many adventures.	Holmes

B. Circle the complete predicate in each sentence. Write each complete predicate under the heading **What Did They Do?**

	What Did They Do?
EXAMPLE: The crime victims counted on Holmes.	counted on Holmes
5. Two men looked for clues.	looked for clues
6. The criminals hid from Holmes.	hid from Holmes
7. Criminals could not trick him.	could not trick him

PRACTICE 3
Complete Subjects and Predicates

> The **complete subject** is all the words in the subject part of a sentence. The subject part names someone or something. The **complete predicate** is all the words in the predicate part of a sentence. The predicate part tells what the subject is or does.

A. Decide if the underlined part is the complete subject or the complete predicate. Circle the correct answer.

1. Pearl oysters are different from clams. — (subject) predicate
2. People may find a small pearl in an ordinary oyster. — subject (predicate)
3. These pearls are not worth very much. — (subject) predicate
4. Pearl oysters grow in warm southern seas. — subject (predicate)
5. Pearl divers look for pearls under water. — subject (predicate)
6. People all over the world prize pearls. — (subject) predicate

B. Underline the complete subject and circle the complete predicate.

7. Oysters are useful sea creatures.
8. Fishermen grow oysters as a sea crop.
9. Most oysters live in the quiet, shallow waters of bays.
10. Hole-boring snails are enemies of oysters.
11. Oysters live in many parts of the world.
12. Many oysters make pearls.
13. The shells are very beautiful.
14. Some people eat raw oysters.
15. Oysters breathe with gills.
16. Some oysters live more than twenty years.

WRITE IT
On a separate sheet of paper, write about the things that live in the sea. Be sure to use a complete subject and complete predicate in each sentence.
Answers will vary.

◄‖‖‖ TEACHING OPTIONS ‖‖‖►

RETEACHING

A Different Modality Ask a student to do a simple action, such as *stand*. Ask a volunteer to say aloud in a sentence what the student did (*Kathy stood up*). Using the definitions in the lesson summary, identify, write on the chalkboard, and label the "complete subject" (*Kathy*) and "complete predicate" (*stood up*). Ask a volunteer to write the two parts together and label it "complete sentence." Repeat this activity using different sentences.

CLASS ENRICHMENT

A Cooperative Activity Have students write a class story about wacky pets. Begin by putting the first two sentences of the story on the chalkboard: *Our pet giraffe likes soccer. Other animals play too.* Ask volunteers to write additional declarative sentences on the chalkboard, adding to the story. When the story is complete, have students take turns identifying the complete subjects and complete predicates.

CHALLENGE

An Independent Extension Have students work in pairs. Have each set of partners write as many sentences as they can using the subject and predicate from this sentence: *Most hippos rest after lunch.* They might form sentences such as the following: *Most hippos are fat. Most hippos live in zoos. Most hippos need dentists. I rest after lunch. My teachers rest after lunch. Some wicked witches rest after lunch.*

■ Easy ■ Average ■ Challenging

OBJECTIVES
To identify simple subjects in sentences

ASSIGNMENT GUIDE
BASIC	Practice A
↓	Practice B
ADVANCED	Practice C

All should do the Apply activity.

RESOURCES
■ Reteaching Master 4
■ Practice Master 4
■ ■ ■ Extra Practice, pp. 50, 55

TEACHING THE LESSON

1. Getting Started
Oral Language Focus attention on this oral activity, encouraging all to participate. You may wish to model for the class, naming a food in the subject part of a sentence, such as *Kiwis are great for dessert. Carrots are crunchy. Cheese makes me sneeze.*

2. Developing the Lesson
Guide students through the explanation of simple subjects, emphasizing the examples and the summary. You may wish to point out to students that a simple subject can also be the complete subject of a sentence. Lead students through the **Guided Practice**. Identify those who would benefit from reteaching. Assign independent Practice A–C.

3. Closing the Lesson
After students complete the Apply activity, encourage volunteers to share their sentences aloud. Point out that using precise words as simple subjects can help make meaning clear in written as well as spoken language.

◆ GETTING STARTED ◆

What foods do you like in each category below?
dairy products   fruits   meats   vegetables
Use the names of those foods in the subjects of sentences.

4 Simple Subjects

Remember that the complete subject is all the words in the subject part of a sentence. The most important word in the complete subject is called the simple subject.

Read the sentences below. The complete subject of each sentence is shown in blue. The simple subject is underlined.

1. Livestock are farm animals.
2. Some farmers raise livestock.
3. The chickens on a farm provide eggs and meat.
4. Susie Thompson visited a nearby farm.
5. She fed the chickens.

Look at the sentences again. Notice that most of the time the simple subject is one word. Sometimes it is more than one word. In sentence **4** the simple subject is two words because it is a person's full name.

> **Summary** ◆ The **simple subject** is the main word in the complete subject. When you write, choose an exact word as a simple subject to make your meaning clear.

Guided Practice

A line has been drawn between the complete subject and the complete predicate of each sentence. Name the simple subject in each sentence.

1. Livestock | provide food and other valuable products.
2. Some specialized farms | raise only livestock.
3. The farmers on a specialized farm | may raise only one kind of animal.
4. Kevin Johnson | owns a cattle ranch.
5. The sprawling ranch | is over 10,000 acres in size.

10   GRAMMAR: Simple Subjects

ESSENTIAL LANGUAGE SKILLS
This lesson provides opportunities to:

LISTENING ◆ follow the logical organization of an oral presentation ◆ select from an oral presentation the information needed

SPEAKING ◆ use a variety of words to express feelings and ideas ◆ make organized oral presentations

READING ◆ use context to understand the meaning of words ◆ evaluate and make judgments ◆ follow a set of directions

WRITING ◆ use ideas and information from sources other than personal experiences for writing ◆ use chronological and spatial order and order of importance

LANGUAGE ◆ use the fundamentals of grammar, punctuation, and spelling

ractice

. Read each sentence below. A line has been drawn between the complete subject and the complete predicate. Write each complete subject. Draw a line under the simple subject.

6. Many <u>farmers</u> in the United States | raise chickens.
7. <u>Chickens</u> on a farm | may live in wire cages.
8. A <u>rooster</u> | is an adult male chicken.
9. A <u>hen</u> | is a mature female chicken.
10. Over 240 <u>eggs</u> | may be laid by a hen in a year.
11. Many <u>farmers</u> | buy pullets from other farms.
12. A <u>pullet</u> | is a female chicken less than a year old.
13. Some <u>farms</u> | raise chickens to produce meat.
14. Special <u>feed</u> | makes chickens gain weight quickly.
15. The <u>age</u> of a chicken | determines how it should be cooked.

B. Write the simple subject of each sentence.

16. <u>Cattle</u> are very important farm animals.
17. Many different <u>meats</u> come from cattle.
18. The <u>milk</u> from cows is a very nutritious food.
19. Some <u>farmers</u> milk their cows by hand.
20. Most large <u>farms</u> use electric milking machines.

C. The sentences below are each missing a simple subject. Choose one of the following words to complete each sentence.

yogurt   step   truck   milk   technicians

21. Cow's <u>milk</u> contains carbohydrates, fats, minerals, proteins, and vitamins.
22. <u>Yogurt</u> is one of many foods made from milk.
23. A <u>truck</u> takes milk from the farm to the processing plant.
24. Laboratory <u>technicians</u> check the taste and appearance of milk.
25. The final <u>step</u> in the processing of milk is packaging.

Apply • Think and Write

Restating Facts • Write at least five sentences that state facts you learned in this lesson about livestock farming. Use your own words, and use a variety of simple subjects.

✎ **Remember**
to use precise simple subjects to make your meaning clear.

GRAMMAR: Simple Subjects   **11**

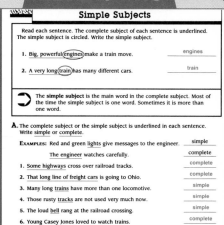

MASTERS ON FILE

RETEACHING   4

Simple Subjects

Read each sentence. The complete subject of each sentence is underlined. The simple subject is circled. Write the simple subject.

1. Big, powerful (engines) make a train move.   engines
2. A very long (train) has many different cars.   train

The **simple subject** is the main word in the complete subject. Most of the time the simple subject is one word. Sometimes it is more than one word.

A. The complete subject or the simple subject is underlined in each sentence. Write simple or complete.

EXAMPLES: Red and green lights give messages to the engineer.   simple
The engineer watches carefully.   complete

1. Some highways cross over railroad tracks.   complete
2. That long line of freight cars is going to Ohio.   complete
3. Many long trains have more than one locomotive.   simple
4. Those rusty tracks are not used very much now.   simple
5. The loud bell rang at the railroad crossing.   simple
6. Young Casey Jones loved to watch trains.   complete

B. The complete subject in each sentence is underlined. Cross out all the underlined words except the simple subject.

EXAMPLE: A huge black train roared down the tracks.

7. The very loud whistle scared the cows.
8. The early workers built many bridges.
9. Old wooden bridges are still being used.
10. New bridges usually are made of steel and concrete.
11. A long dark tunnel goes right through the mountain.

PRACTICE   4

Simple Subjects

The **simple subject** is the main word in the complete subject.

A. Underline the simple subject in each sentence. Then write each simple subject in the spaces. The boxed letters will complete this sentence: The diver wore pajamas to the _____ oyster bed _____

1. The great oceans are still mysteries.   o c e a n s
2. Huge rays glide through the water.   r a y s
3. Hungry sharks search for food all the time.   s h a r k s
4. The scary octopus is really very shy.   o c t o p u s
5. Large eels often are caught in nets.   e e l s
6. The graceful porpoise is a friendly animal.   p o r p o i s e
7. The strange-looking lobster is very tasty.   l o b s t e r
8. The shell of a clam is used for protection.   s h e l l
9. The scared squid squirts ink.   s q u i d

B. Draw a line between the complete subject and the complete predicate. Then write each simple subject on the line.

10. Many strange creatures live in the depths of the sea.   creatures
11. Brave scientists gather information in submarines.   scientists
12. Special submarines have cameras and lights.   submarines
13. Very bright lights help scientists in deep water.   lights
14. These daring explorers take many photographs.   explorers
15. Sensitive underwater cameras are used by scuba divers, too.   cameras
16. A simple snorkel helps many swimmers.   snorkel

WRITE IT
On a separate sheet of paper, write about the kinds of fish you might see in an aquarium. Use clear simple subjects in your sentences. Answers will vary.

◀|||| TEACHING OPTIONS ||||▶

RETEACHING

A Different Modality Write on the chalkboard: *The large green cabinet between the door and the chalkboard is used often.* Have students identify the complete subject. Then point to the word *chalkboard* and ask *Is this what the sentence is about?* (no) Erase the word. Continue with each word until only the simple subject and complete predicate remain. Tell students that *what* or *who* a sentence is about is the simple subject.

CLASS ENRICHMENT

A Cooperative Activity Have students write ten sentences on a topic of interest to them, such as music or soccer. Then have students make a chart on their papers with the headings *Complete Subject* and *Simple Subject*, completing the chart with information from their sentences. Have partners work together to check each other's work.

CHALLENGE

An Independent Extension Have students choose five of the words below to use as simple subjects in complete sentences. Encourage them to include colorful details. You may wish to have students use a dictionary for word meaning.

1. adobe   6. karate   11. moccasin
2. arroyo   7. kimono   12. pueblo
3. cocoa   8. lagoon   13. sombrero
4. corral   9. lariat   14. veranda
5. hogan   10. mango   15. yucca

11

UNIT 1/LESSON 5

OBJECTIVES
To identify simple predicates in sentences

ASSIGNMENT GUIDE
BASIC   Practice A
          Practice B
ADVANCED   Practice C

All should do the Apply activity.

RESOURCES
■ Reteaching Master 5
■ Practice Master 5
■ ■ ■ Extra Practice, pp. 50, 56

TEACHING THE LESSON

1. Getting Started
Oral Language Focus attention on this oral activity, encouraging all to participate. You may wish to develop a semantic map on the chalkboard. Have students brainstorm names of animals, such as *ant, alligator, bear, bat, cow, chicken, colt.* Model a sample sentence, such as *A hungry cow eats.*

2. Developing the Lesson
Guide students through the explanation of simple predicates, emphasizing the examples and the summary. Lead students through the **Guided Practice.** Identfiy those who would benefit from reteaching. Assign independent Practice A–C.

3. Closing the Lesson
After students complete the Apply activity, have them exchange papers to compare their sentences. Have them underline the simple predicates in each sentence. Point out that knowing about simple predicates can help them create sentences that make action seem real.

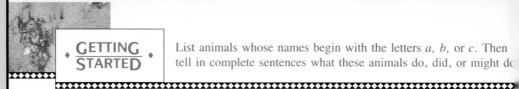

◆ GETTING STARTED ◆

List animals whose names begin with the letters *a, b,* or *c.* Then tell in complete sentences what these animals do, did, or might do

5 Simple Predicates

You have learned that the complete predicate is all the words in the predicate part of a sentence. The simple predicate is the most important word or words in this part. The simple predicate is the word or words that show action.

Bob's class was writing about various plants and animals that are found on farms. The students used exact action words to make the action seem real. Here are some of the sentences they wrote. The complete predicate of each sentence is shown in green. The simple predicate is underlined.

1. The rooster <u>crows.</u>
2. The Holstein cow <u>swished</u> its tail.
3. The wheat <u>is waving</u> rhythmically in the wind.
4. The horse <u>had trotted</u> toward me.

In sentences **1** and **2,** the simple predicate is one word. In sentences **3** and **4,** the simple predicate is more than one word.

> **Summary** ◆ The **simple predicate** is the main word or words in the complete predicate. When you write, use exact action words as simple predicates to make the action seem real.

Guided Practice

Here are some more sentences Bob's class wrote. A line has been drawn between the complete subject and the complete predicate. Name the simple predicate.

1. A ripe red apple │ <u>plopped</u> to the ground.
2. My pony │ <u>snorted</u> in disgust.
3. The bright yellow sunflowers │ <u>were bursting</u> with seeds.
4. The lamb with the thick fleece │ <u>nuzzled</u> my fingers.
5. My aunt's farmhand │ <u>had scattered</u> feed for the hungry chickens.

ESSENTIAL LANGUAGE SKILLS
This lesson provides opportunities to:

LISTENING ◆ follow the logical organization of an oral presentation ◆ select from an oral presentation the information needed

SPEAKING ◆ use a variety of words to express feelings and ideas ◆ make organized oral presentations

READING ◆ use context to understand the meaning of words ◆ understand content area vocabulary ◆ evaluate and make judgments ◆ follow a set of directions

WRITING ◆ use ideas and information from sources other than personal experiences for writing ◆ use chronological and spatial order and order of importance

LANGUAGE ◆ use the fundamentals of grammar, punctuation, and spelling

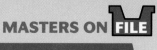
ractice

. Read each sentence below. A line has been drawn between the complete subject and the complete predicate. Write each complete predicate. Draw a line under the simple predicate.

6. Some farms | produce both crops and livestock.
7. They | are called mixed farms.
8. Mixed farms | grow crops and livestock for their region.
9. Cattle and peanuts | are produced on farms in the South.
10. A midwestern mixed farm | raises hogs, cattle, and grain.
11. Hogs | provide much meat for American consumption.
12. Belts and shoes | are made from hog's skin.
13. Hogs | wallow in mud on hot days.
14. Hogs | have a keen sense of smell.
15. A very young hog | is called a pig.

B. Write the simple predicate of each sentence.

16. A peanut plant grows about two and one-half feet high.
17. A peanut belongs to the pea family.
18. The peanuts themselves develop in pods underground.
19. George Washington Carver, an American botanist, made over 300 products from the peanut.
20. Manufacturers grind roasted peanuts for peanut butter.

C. The sentences are each missing a simple predicate. Choose one of the following simple predicates to complete each sentence.
Answers will vary. Suggested answers follow.

| sweetens | are located | stretch | thrive | is harvested |

21. Pineapples thrive in Hawaii.
22. Many potato farms are located in California, Idaho, and Maine.
23. A large tomato crop is harvested in New Jersey each year.
24. The fresh scent of citrus fruits sweetens the Florida breeze.
25. America's rich farmlands stretch from coast to coast.

Apply • Think and Write

Dictionary of Knowledge ◆ George Washington Carver was an American botanist. Read about him in the Dictionary of Knowledge. Write some sentences about his discoveries.

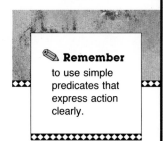

✏️ **Remember**
to use simple predicates that express action clearly.

GRAMMAR: Simple Predicates **13**

◀║║ TEACHING OPTIONS ║║▶

RETEACHING

A Different Modality Make paper strips with complete predicates written on them. Fold each strip so that you can fold the words that are not part of the simple predicate behind the simple predicate. Say complete subjects, such as *The deer.* Have students form a sentence using the compete predicate and then a sentence using only the simple predicate.

| ran ⋮ into the woods |

CLASS ENRICHMENT

A Cooperative Activity Have students write a new simple predicate for each sentence below. When they are finished, have them exchange papers to write new simple subjects.

1. We spotted a small striped snake.
2. The snake slithered along the path.
3. A dog chased after the snake.
4. Someone was calling the dog.
5. The snake disappeared in the grass.

CHALLENGE

An Independent Extension. Have students write complete sentences about five interesting actions, such as mountain climbers struggling up the Alps. Tell them to use a clear simple subject and exact action words in the predicate of each sentence. Then have students exchange sentences with a partner and identify each complete subject, complete predicate, simple subject, and simple predicate.

■ Easy ■ Average ■ Challenging

OBJECTIVES
To identify *you* (understood) as the subject of imperative sentences

ASSIGNMENT GUIDE
BASIC   Practice A
⬇
ADVANCED   Practice B

All should do the Apply activity.

RESOURCES
■ Reteaching Master 6
■ Practice Master 6
■ ■ ■ Extra Practice, pp. 50, 57

TEACHING THE LESSON

1. Getting Started
Oral Language Focus attention on this oral activity, encouraging all to participate. You may wish to call on one student to supply a simple predicate, such as *leap.* Then have volunteers take turns supplying the rest of the command, such as *Leap to the top of the Empire State Building. Leap across the Mississippi River.* Encourage imaginative responses.

2. Developing the Lesson
Guide students through the explanation of subjects in imperative sentences, emphasizing the examples and the summary. You may wish to review the definitions of imperative and declarative sentences: An imperative sentence gives a command or makes a request. A declarative sentence makes a statement. Lead students through the **Guided Practice.** Identify those who would benefit from reteaching. Assign independent Practice A and B.

3. Closing the Lesson
After students complete the Apply activity, you may wish to have volunteers read their sentences aloud. Ask classmates to identify each sentence as declarative or imperative. Point out to students that knowing about the understood *you* as the subject of imperative sentences can help them identify commands and requests, as well as help them make their own commands and requests as clear as possible.

♦ GETTING STARTED ♦

Think of commands that would be impossible to obey, such as "Drain all the water from the seas."

6 Subjects in Imperative Sentences

You have learned that the subject part of a sentence names someone or something. In a declarative sentence the subject usually comes first.

■ Some farmers | face many problems.

In the declarative sentence above, the complete subject is *Some farmers* and the simple subject is *farmers*.

In imperative sentences the simple subject is always the word *you*. However, the word *you* is not usually stated. We say that it is "understood." In each of the two imperative sentences below, the subject is *you* (understood).

■ *(You)* | Turn on the water.
■ *(You)* | Turn on the irrigation system.

Read the two imperative sentences above again. Notice that the second one gives more exact information and is easier to understand. Always make a command or request as clear as possible.

> **Summary** ♦ *You* (understood) is the subject of an imperative sentence. When you write an imperative sentence, make the command or request as clear as possible.

Guided Practice

Name the subject in each sentence below. Some of the sentences are imperative.

1. The layer of fertile soil is very thin.
2. Plow across the slope. You
3. This soil does not have enough nutrients.
4. Apply the fertilizer. You

14   GRAMMAR: Subjects in Imperative Sentences

ESSENTIAL LANGUAGE SKILLS
This lesson provides opportunities to:

LISTENING ♦ follow the logical organization of an oral presentation

SPEAKING ♦ use a variety of words to express feelings and ideas ♦ make organized oral presentations

READING ♦ relate experiences with appropriate vocabulary in complete sentences ♦ draw logical conclusions ♦ evaluate and make judgments ♦ follow a set of directions

WRITING ♦ arrange information to accomplish a specific purpose

LANGUAGE ♦ produce a variety of sentence patterns ♦ use the fundamentals of grammar, punctuation, and spelling

Practice

[1.] Write each sentence. Underline the simple subject. Write (*You*) if the subject is understood.

   EXAMPLE: Plant alfalfa in this field instead of corn.
   ANSWER: (*You*) Plant alfalfa in this field instead of corn.

   5. <u>Erosion</u> wears away soil and rock.
   6. <u>Rainwater</u> washes away the soil on farms.
(You) **7.** Plant grass between each row of corn.
(You) **8.** Build terraces, or wide, flat rows, up that entire slope.
   9. <u>Wind</u> can blow away topsoil.
(You)**10.** Plant a row of trees for a windbreak.
  11. <u>Fields</u> at plowing time are scattered with dead stalks and leaves from the previous crop.
(You)**12.** Plow the field with the old plant matter.
(You)**13.** Use this method of tilling for erosion control.
  14. <u>Conservation</u> of the soil saves farmland from destruction.

B. Write each sentence. Write *declarative* or *imperative* to show the kind of sentence. Underline the simple subject in each declarative sentence. Write (*You*) for each imperative sentence.

  15. <u>Plants</u> need seventeen nutrients for proper growth. declarative
  16. Analyze the nutrients in the soil. imperative (You)
  17. Some <u>fertilizers</u> supply potassium to plants. declarative
  18. <u>Farmers</u> in very dry areas irrigate, or water, their crops. declarative
  19. Install a sprinkler irrigation system in the cornfield. imperative (You)
  20. Turn on the water immediately. imperative (You)
  21. Some <u>animals</u> harm farm crops. declarative
  22. Spray the crops with pesticide. imperative (You)
  23. <u>Mice</u> are eating the grain in storage. declarative
  24. <u>Bring</u> in some foxes for control of the mice. imperative (You)

Apply ◆ Think and Write

Problems and Solutions ◆ Imagine that you own a farm. Write three declarative sentences and three imperative sentences. In each declarative sentence, state a problem on the farm. In each imperative sentence, provide a solution to the problem.

✎ **Remember**
to state your commands and requests clearly.

GRAMMAR: Subjects in Imperative Sentences **15**

◀||| TEACHING OPTIONS |||▶

RETEACHING

A Different Modality Remind students that in a command or request, the subject of a sentence is *you*, although often the word is not spoken or written. Have a volunteer give you a command that you may carry out, such as *Stand on your toes.* Write the command on the chalkboard and have students tell the subject of the imperative sentence (*you*). You may wish to repeat with several other commands.

CLASS ENRICHMENT

A Cooperative Activity Have students work in small groups to write instructions on how to play a game, either a real one or an invented one. Have students write declarative sentences that tell about the equipment, the number of players, and the object of the game. Then have them write imperative sentences that give the rules of the game. You may wish to have each group proofread its work to make sure it is correct.

CHALLENGE

An Independent Extension Have students cut out ads from newspapers and magazines. Ask them to find and underline imperative sentences. Encourage students to draw conclusions about why imperative sentences often are found in ads. Have them share their conclusions with the rest of the class. (*Advertisers want to urge readers to try, buy, and use their products.*)

UNIT 1
Vocabulary

■ Easy ■ Average ■ Challenging

OBJECTIVES
To recognize that a thesaurus contains lists of synonyms and antonyms
To use thesaurus entries to replace given words with appropriate synonyms

ASSIGNMENT GUIDE
BASIC   Practice A

ADVANCED   Practice B

All should do the Language Corner.

RESOURCES
■ Reteaching Master 7
■ Practice Master 7

TEACHING THE LESSON

1. Getting Started
Oral Language Focus attention on this oral activity, encouraging all to participate. As each animal is named, you may wish to ask students to tell other words that describe how that animal moves.

2. Developing the Lesson
Guide students through the explanation of using a thesaurus, emphasizing the definition and the examples. Tell students they may have to use a dictionary to find the meanings in some thesaurus entries. Guide students through Building Your Vocabulary. Identify those who would benefit from reteaching. Assign independent Practice A and B.

3. Closing the Lesson
After students complete the Practice exercises, tell them to choose a word they wrote in their notebooks. Then have them find a synonym that better fits the meaning of their sentence. Point out to students that using a thesaurus when they write can help them use words that fit their meaning more exactly.

Language Corner You may wish to have students discuss how easy or difficult it is for them to recognize whether or not a word can be read forward and backward.

16

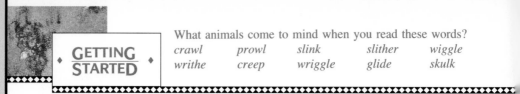

◆ **GETTING STARTED** ◆

What animals come to mind when you read these words?

crawl	*prowl*	*slink*	*slither*	*wiggle*
writhe	*creep*	*wriggle*	*glide*	*skulk*

VOCABULARY ◆
Using the Thesaurus

The word *thesaurus* comes from a Greek word meaning "a treasure," and a thesaurus is truly a treasury of words. Like a dictionary, a **thesaurus** lists entry words in alphabetical order. A list of synonyms, or words with similar meanings, is given for each entry word. Antonyms, or words with opposite meanings, are also listed for many of the entry words. You will learn more about synonyms and antonyms in Unit 7.

A thesaurus is a valuable tool for writers. It helps them choose the best word to fit their meaning. You will find a thesaurus beginning on page 466 of this book. Study the thesaurus entry below for the word *tell*.

	Part of Speech Definition
Entry Word	**tell** (v)—to express in words; to say; to give an account of; to relate.
Example Sentence	Tell me what you think of it.
	advise—to give advice to; to counsel; to offer an opinion to. Would you advise me about what to get my mother for a birthday present?
	communicate—to give news or information by speaking or writing; to telephone; to write. Have you communicated recently with your sister in New Mexico?
	inform—to supply with facts, knowledge, or news; to tell. I was not informed of the change in plans until today.
Synonyms	*instruct*—to teach; to train; to give knowledge to; to give orders or directions to. I was instructed to hand out the drawing materials.
	narrate—to tell the story of; to relate. He will narrate the well-known story, which has been set to music.
	report—to tell of something seen, done, heard, or read; to state or announce. Allison reported the results of her science experiment to us.
Cross-reference	See also *say* (v).
Antonym	ANTONYM: **listen**

16   VOCABULARY and STUDY SKILLS: Thesaurus

ESSENTIAL LANGUAGE SKILLS

This lesson provides opportunities to:

LISTENING ◆ employ active listening in a variety of situations

SPEAKING ◆ use a variety of words to express feelings and ideas

READING ◆ understand content area vocabulary ◆ evaluate and make judgments ◆ follow a set of directions

WRITING ◆ use the thesaurus as a means to expand vocabulary

LANGUAGE ◆ understand the conventions of usage and mechanics

Building Your Vocabulary

Use the thesaurus entry on page 16 to answer these questions.

1. What word is opposite in meaning to *tell*? **listen**
2. What other word can you look up for more synonyms of *tell*? **say**
3. What part of speech are *tell* and its synonyms? **verbs**

Practice

A. Write each sentence. Complete it with a synonym for *tell*. Use a
different synonym in each sentence. **Answers may vary. Possible answers follow.**

1. Undersea telephone lines were put in so that the two countries
   could __communicate__.
2. Carl tried to __instruct__ the child on how to use the computer.
3. __Inform__ me about the animals that live in the tide pool.
4. The actor will __narrate__ the story "Peter and the Wolf."
5. Did Ana __advise__ you to get up early because the trip would
   be long?

B. Use the Thesaurus to find the synonyms for *rough* that fit best
in these sentences. Use a different synonym for each sentence.
Answers may vary. Possible answers follow.

6. A sea urchin has __bristly__ spines covering its shell.
7. The landscape of the Nevada desert was rocky and __rugged__.
8. __Harsh__ sounds of machinery echoed through the factory.
9. The auto mechanic's hands were strong and __coarse__.
10. After the accident there were many __jagged__ scraps of metal
    and glass lying about.

LANGUAGE CORNER • Reversal Words

Some words say one thing
when you read them forward and
another thing when you read them
backward. For example, *stab* read
backward is *bats*.

Can you decode the following
sentence? *Tap was net keels
spools.*
Pat saw ten sleek sloops.

RETEACHING 7

Using the Thesaurus

A thesaurus contains lists of synonyms and antonyms. Synonyms are words
that have almost the same meaning. Antonyms are words that have opposite
meanings. Read the thesaurus entry below. Circle the entry word good.

good (adj.)—1 having high quality; superior. A good rocking chair lasts a long
time. 2. as it ought to be; right; proper; agreeable. Doing what is good
sometimes takes courage. 3 clever, skillful. He always tells a good joke.

beneficial—producing good; helpful.
excellent—very good; better than others.
honest—not lying; not stealing or cheating; truthful.
pleasant—giving pleasure; agreeable.
proficient—well advanced in an art, science, or subject; skilled.

ANTONYMS: awful, bad, disagreeable, dishonest, incompetent, worthless

A. Write an answer to each question. Use the thesaurus entry above to help you.
Answers will vary. Possible answers follow.
   EXAMPLE: What is one definition of good? __having high quality__

1. What part of speech is good? __adjective__
2. What are two synonyms for good? __beneficial, excellent__
3. What is one antonym for good? __awful__

B. Complete each sentence. Write a synonym for good. Answers will vary.
   EXAMPLE: The new student has been doing __excellent__ work in this
   class.

4. People like Mary because she has a very __pleasant__ nature.
5. We want to hire a __proficient__ worker who will not make mistakes.
6. A really __honest__ person will not cheat anyone.
7. Our principal makes many __beneficial__ suggestions.
8. I know of a __pleasant__ spot for fishing.
9. Dr. Wilkes had some __beneficial__ advice for us.
10. The stranger had a rough but __honest__ look on his face.
11. Ahmed gave the teacher an __excellent__ reply.

PRACTICE 7

Using the Thesaurus

A. Write an answer to each question. Use the thesaurus entry to help you.
Answers may vary. Possible answers follow.
beautiful (adj.)—very pleasing to see or hear; delighting the mind or the senses.
That is a beautiful painting.

attractive—pleasing; winning attention and liking.
dazzling—brilliantly shining; splendid.
glorious—having great beauty; splendid; magnificent.
handsome—pleasing or impressive in appearance.
lovely—beautiful in mind, appearance, or character; delightful.
pretty—pleasing by delicacy or grace.
ANTONYMS: ugly, unattractive

1. What is one definition of beautiful? __very pleasing to see or hear__
2. What part of speech is beautiful? __adjective__
3. What are two synonyms for beautiful? __attractive, dazzling__
4. What is one antonym for beautiful? __ugly__

B. Read the paragraph below. Each time the word beautiful appears, replace it
with a synonym from the thesaurus entry. Use each synonym only once.
Answers will vary.
   When Fritz woke up, he discovered that it was a truly beautiful morning.
The sun was just rising, and beautiful golden rays of light sparkled on the
water. The sunlight shone on a beautiful ship tied nearby. The sun's rays
transformed the ship's color from white to golden yellow. A sailor who wore a
beautiful sweater cleaned the deck. On the dock, a man and his beautiful
daughter stopped to admire the ship. Fritz photographed the whole beautiful
scene with his camera.

   When Fritz woke up, he discovered that it was a truly glorious morning.
   The sun was just rising, and dazzling golden rays of light sparkled on the
   water. The sunlight shone on a handsome ship tied nearby. The sun's rays
   transformed the ship's color from white to golden yellow. A sailor who
   wore an attractive sweater cleaned the deck. On the dock, a man and his
   pretty daughter stopped to admire the ship. Fritz photographed the whole
   lovely scene with his camera.

◀▏▏▏ TEACHING OPTIONS ▏▏▏▶

RETEACHING

A Different Modality Ask a volunteer to
supply a word that describes size, such as
large or *little*. Help students find the word
in the Student Textbook's thesaurus. Discuss how the words in this entry are similar
and how they are different. Point out any
antonyms listed in this entry. Help students
understand that a thesaurus lists synonyms
and antonyms and can be used by writers
to help them choose the word that best fits
their meaning.

CLASS ENRICHMENT

A Cooperative Activity Have students
work in pairs. Tell them to choose a paragraph from their Writer's Notebook. Have
the pairs work together, using the Student
Textbook's thesaurus to see how they can
improve the paragraphs they wrote by
choosing words that better fit the meaning
of their sentences.

CHALLENGE

An Independent Extension Have students use a thesaurus to find and list other
reversal words. You may wish to tell them
that such words are called *palindromes*.
When they have found enough words, have
them use the words to write a coded message that makes sense when the words are
read backward.

Grammar-Writing Connection

How to Combine Sentences

Point out to students that they can use the grammar skills they learned in Unit 1 to help them develop good writing techniques. Explain that in this Grammar-Writing Connection, students will use what they know about subjects, predicates, and writing sentences to learn how to combine sentences.

You may wish to guide students through the explanation of how to combine subjects and predicates, stressing the examples. Then have students apply the information by completing the activity at the bottom of the first page. Students may work in small groups or with partners to combine each pair of sentences orally, or they may combine the sentences in writing as an independent activity.

Help students to understand that combining sentences is an effective way to improve writing and that it can make their writing less repetitious, clearer, and more interesting.

GRAMMAR
◆ **CONNECTION** ◆
WRITING

How to Combine Sentences

Would a singer sing the same song more than once at a concert? Probably not, because most people would not want to hear the same thing twice. For a similar reason, you should avoid repeating words in your writing. One way to do this is by combining, or joining, sentences that repeat words. Read the examples below.

1. Sheldon hiked ten miles through a rugged canyon. Marty hiked ten miles through a rugged canyon.
2. Sheldon and Marty hiked ten miles through a rugged canyon.

In example **1**, both sentences tell about people who did the same thing. Example **2** was made by combining the two subjects, *Sheldon* and *Marty*, with the word *and*. The two sentences that share the same predicate are combined into one strong sentence.

You can also use the word *and* to combine two sentences that share the same subject. Which word is shared in the two sentences in example **3**? Leah

3. Leah wrote to the state park. Leah applied for a job.
4. Leah wrote to the state park and applied for a job.

Read the two sentences in example **5**. The understood subject of both sentences is *you*. What word is added to combine the predicates in example **6** to make one strong sentence? and

5. Look at this picture. Tell me if these are moose or elk.
6. Look at this picture and tell me if these are moose or elk.

The Grammar Game ◆ Match them up! Choose a sentence from the left to combine with a sentence from the right.

Put the cassette in the case and give it to Marsha.
Put the cassette in the case.   Rick fixed the door handle.
Rick washed the car and fixed the door handle.
Rick washed the car.   Her friend entered the race.
My cousin and her friend entered the race.
My cousin entered the race.   Give it to Marsha.

 18 COOPERATIVE LEARNING: Combining Sentences

ESSENTIAL LANGUAGE SKILLS

This lesson provides opportunities to:

LISTENING ◆ select from an oral presentation the information needed

SPEAKING ◆ use a variety of words to express feelings and ideas ◆ make organized oral presentations

READING ◆ evaluate and make judgments ◆ follow a set of directions

WRITING ◆ adapt information to accomplish a specific purpose with a particular audience

LANGUAGE ◆ produce a variety of sentence patterns

Working Together

As your group does activities **A** and **B**, you will avoid repeating words by using the word *and* to combine sentences.

In Your Group

♦ Be sure everyone understands the directions.

♦ Encourage everyone to share ideas.

♦ Agree or disagree in a pleasant way.

♦ Help the group reach agreement.

A. Complete each pair of sentences with a group member's name. Then combine the sentences, using the word *and*. Can your group create its own sentences to combine? How many can you add?

cones and makes
1. ____ collects pine cones. ____ makes table decorations.
puppets and puts
2. ____ designs puppets. ____ puts on shows for young children.
insects and hangs
3. ____ builds model insects. ____ hangs them from the ceiling.
birds and feeds
4. ____ loves wild birds. ____ feeds them every winter.
music and has
5. ____ enjoys music. ____ has a wonderful record collection.

B. Combine each pair of sentences. Make sure each group member writes at least one sentence. Then arrange the combined sentences into a paragraph. Paragraphs may vary. Possible sentence order is shown.

2. A rooster crowed and woke me up.
6. A rooster crowed. A rooster woke me up.
1. The sun and the clouds brought color to the morning sky.
7. The sun brought color to the morning sky. The clouds brought color to the morning sky.
3. Ducks quacked and waddled to the edge of the pond.
8. Ducks quacked. Ducks waddled to the edge of the pond.
5. I yawned and stretched and finally got out of bed.
9. I yawned and stretched. I finally got out of bed.
4. Then the gray colt kicked up its heels and trotted towards its mother.
10. Then the gray colt kicked up its heels. The gray colt trotted towards its mother.

WRITERS' CORNER ♦ Stringy Sentences

Be careful not to use *and* or *and so* to string together too many sentences. Stringy sentences are hard to read and understand.

STRINGY: **We went to the movies last night, and everyone in town was there, and so we waited in line for over thirty minutes, and we were lucky to find seats together.**

IMPROVED: **We went to the movies last night, and everyone in town was there. We waited in line for over thirty minutes. We were lucky to find seats together.**

Read what you wrote for the Writer's Warm-up. Did you use any stringy sentences? If you did, can you improve them?

COOPERATIVE LEARNING: Combining Sentences ◁ 19 ▷

Working Together

The Working Together activities involve students in cooperative learning work groups. This is an opportunity to pair strong writers with students whose skills are weaker. Working together, they can all experience success.

Divide the class into small groups and have students read In Your Group. Encourage them to discuss why each task is important. Have them tell what might happen if the group does not follow through on each task. *(If everyone does not understand the directions, we will not be able to work together successfully. If we do not let everyone share ideas, we might miss some ideas that could be helpful. If we do not agree or disagree in a pleasant way, our ideas may not be listened to. If we cannot reach agreement, we cannot complete the activities successfully.)*

Before students begin activities A and B, you may wish to have each group appoint a member to record their sentences. You also may wish to have groups appoint a timekeeper. Then set a time limit of ten or fifteen minutes. After each activity is completed, have the groups compare the sentences they wrote.

Writers' Corner

The Writers' Corner provides students with the opportunity to extend the Grammar-Writing Connection, helping them to develop the skills necessary to review and revise their own writing. Discuss the introductory sentences with students. Then have them work as a class or in pairs to discuss the two examples. Have students read aloud each example and identify the changes that were made. Have them tell how those changes made the improved example "sound better." Then have students apply the subject and predicate combining techniques from this Grammar-Writing Connection to the sentences they wrote about farm life for the Writers' Warm-up. Encourage students to rewrite their sentences if necessary. Discuss with them how combining subjects and predicates strengthened their sentences, improving the flow of their writing and the clarity of their ideas.

O V E R V I E W

TWO-PART

flexibility

USING LANGUAGE TO NARRATE

Unit 1 Overview

books

FOR EXTENDED READING

EASY

▮ **On the Trail of the Fox** by Claudia Schnieper. Carolrhoda. This absorbing account of the daily life of a pair of red foxes and their growing pups is highlighted by striking color photographs.

AVERAGE

▮ **The Winged Colt of Casa Mia** by Betsy Byars. Viking. In this fantasy Charles visits the ranch of his Uncle Coot and encounters a colt with supernatural abilities.

CHALLENGING

▮ **A Family of Foxes** by Eilis Dillon. Funk. The efforts of a group of boys help a family of foxes survive on the island where they have been washed ashore.

READ-ALOUD

▮ **Carrots and Miggle** by Ardath Mayhar. Atheneum. This descriptive novel about life on a dairy farm in east Texas is highlighted by the arrival of a distant cousin from Europe.

OXCART IN SUGAR CANE FIELD
painting by Angel E. Allende.

UNIT
ONE

USING LANGUAGE
TO
NARRATE

═══════ PART TWO ═══════

Literature   *The Midnight Fox* by Betsy Byars
A Reason for Writing Narrating

CREATIVE
Writing

FINE ARTS ◆ This painting by Angel E. Allende shows an oxcart in a field of sugar cane. The oxcart is waiting there, but there are no workers. Where do you think the workers are? Have they gone home for the day? Are they eating lunch? Imagine that you are one of the workers who work in this field. Write an entry for this day in your journal. Tell about the work you did and what you did after work. Tell about the ox and how it helped you.

CREATIVE WRITING

Fine Arts gives your students a chance to express themselves creatively in writing. After students observe the illustration on page 20 for a moment or two, have a volunteer read aloud the Fine Arts paragraph on page 21. Have students write their reactions in their journals. Then encourage a discussion of their ideas.

 VIEWING

See the **Fine Arts Transparencies with Viewing Booklet** and the **Video Library**.

THEN START WITH
part 2

A Reason for Writing: Narrating is the focus of Part 2. First students learn a thinking strategy for narrating. Then they read and respond to a selection of literature on which they may model their own writing. Developmental composition lessons, including ''Telling an Anecdote,'' a speaking and listening lesson, help students learn to use language correctly to narrate. All the lessons reflect the literature. All culminate in the Writing Process lesson. The unit ends with the Curriculum Connection and Books to Enjoy, which help students discover how their new language skills apply to writing across the curriculum and to their own lives.

◆ If you began with grammar instruction, you may wish to remind students of the unit theme, Farm Life. Tell them that the information they gathered through the thematic lessons helped them prepare for reading the literature, *The Midnight Fox* by Betsy Byars.

◆ If you are beginning with Part 2, use the lessons in Part 1 for remediation or instruction. For grammar, spelling, and mechanics instructional guidance, you may wish to refer to the end-of-text Glossary and Index, as well as to the *Spelling Connection* booklet; the full-color *Revising and Proofreading Transparencies;* and the Unit Pretest, Posttest, and Writing Samples.

THEME BAR							
CATEGORIES	Environments	Business/World of Work	Imagination	Communications/ Fine Arts	People	Science	Expressions	Social Studies
THEMES	UNIT 1 Farm Life	UNIT 2 Handicrafts	UNIT 3 Tall Tales	UNIT 4 The Visual Arts	UNIT 5 Lasting Impressions	UNIT 6 Volcanoes	UNIT 7 Nature	UNIT 8 Animal Habitats
PACING	1 month	1 month	1 month	1 month	1 month	1 month	1 month	1 month

UNIT 1
Critical Thinking

■ Easy ■ Average ■ Challenging

OBJECTIVES
To use an observation chart as a
strategy for narrating

TEACHING
THE LESSON

1. Getting Started
Oral Language Introduce the thinking skill, observing, by asking students
to imagine a one-person band. Say:
*The person is playing a drum, harmon-
ica, fiddle, and cymbals at the same
time. You can't wait to tell your friends.
What details would you want to remember?* Ask volunteers to tell which
senses might be important in observing details about a one-player band
(e.g., sight, hearing) before asking
others to suggest details (e.g., *thump-
ing, scratchy sounds; the player was
beating the drum with his foot*). Explain that noticing details is called
observing.

   Metacognition Help students become aware of their own thinking
(think metacognitively) by asking follow-up questions when they respond
(e.g., *Have you ever seen a one-person
band? How did you remember the details? If you haven't seen one, how did
you imagine the details?*). Encourage
students to be aware of their own and
other students' thinking strategies.
Explain that in this lesson they will
learn about one strategy for observing.

2. Developing the Lesson
Guide students through the introduction to narrating (the kind of literature
and writing they will deal with in this
unit) and its connection to observing.
Lead them through Learning the Strategy, emphasizing the model observation chart. Identify those who would
benefit from reteaching. Assign Using
the Strategy A and B.

3. Closing the Lesson
Metacognition Applying the Strategy is a metacognitive activity in which
students consider *how* they think
(question 1) and *when* they think
(question 2).
   Question 1: Encourage students to
share how they thought up the subheads for their charts in Using the

---

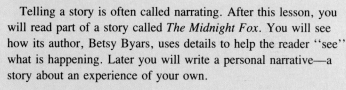

CRITICAL THINKING ◆
A Strategy for Narrating

AN OBSERVATION CHART

   Telling a story is often called narrating. After this lesson, you
will read part of a story called *The Midnight Fox*. You will see
how its author, Betsy Byars, uses details to help the reader "see"
what is happening. Later you will write a personal narrative—a
story about an experience of your own.

   In *The Midnight Fox* the storyteller, Tom, uses the words *I* and
me to narrate an experience he had. Here is part of *The Midnight
Fox* in which Tom tells about meeting a black fox. What details in
these two sentences make the fox seem real?

> Her head was cocked to one side, her tail curled up, her front
> left foot raised. In all my life I never saw anything like that fox
> standing there with her pale golden eyes on me and this great
> black fur being blown by the wind.

   A writer who observes carefully can include information that
makes a story come to life. When you observe, you look for and
pay special attention to details.

◆ Learning the Strategy

   You observe details all day long. For example, suppose you are
in the park and see a great spot for flying your new kite. You want
to be able to go there again. What details would help you
remember where it was? Maybe you want to be a one-person band.
What details would you need to imitate? Perhaps you are going to
a World Series game. It is so exciting that you want to write a
story about it for your school newspaper.

 22   CRITICAL THINKING: Observing

ESSENTIAL LANGUAGE SKILLS
This lesson provides opportunities to:

LISTENING ◆ employ active listening in a variety
of situations

SPEAKING ◆ use a variety of words to express
feelings and ideas

READING ◆ evaluate and make judgments ◆
follow a set of directions ◆ use graphic sources of
information, such as tables and lists, charts and
graphs

WRITING ◆ adapt information to accomplish a
specific purpose with a particular audience

LANGUAGE ◆ use the fundamentals of grammar,
punctuation, and spelling

Making an observation chart is a strategy that can help you remember details. For example, an observation chart about the World Series game could help you record details to use in the story you want to write. It might look like this.

Topic —

Subtopics —

A World Series Game			
What I Saw	40,000 fans two home runs pennants	a sea of people the winners jumping up and down	
What I Heard	people shouting The Star-Spangled Banner Take Me Out to the Ball Game	the crack of the bat hitting the ball	
What I Felt	excited about being there thrilled when my team won	upset when my team struck out	

— Details

Using the Strategy

A. Observe your left shoe. Then make an observation chart about it. Write ''My Left Shoe'' as the topic. Think of subtopics you like such as ''How It Looks,'' ''How It Feels,'' and ''Where It Has Been.'' Record details for each heading. You might use your chart to help you tell someone a story about your shoe.

B. *The Midnight Fox* takes place on a farm. Before you read the story, think about what you know about farms. Organize your ideas in an observation chart. Write the topic, ''Farms.'' Then decide on subtopics such as ''What I Might See,'' ''What I Might Hear,'' and ''What I Might Feel.'' Record details for each subtopic. As you read *The Midnight Fox*, notice what Tom observes on the farm. Is the farm in the story like farms you have heard about or observed?

Applying the Strategy

◆ How did you decide which subtopics to include in your observation charts? Why might these headings be different the next time you make an observation chart?

◆ When might it be helpful to you to record observations in your journal?

CRITICAL THINKING: Observing 23

Strategy A (e.g., *I just looked at my shoe and started to write topics it made me think of. I thought of the five senses. I thought about times when I wear it.*) Discuss why subtopics may change (e.g., *Different things would be important about, say, a shoe and a flower. You might have a different purpose for making the chart so you'd have descriptive heads for writing a description, scientific heads for a science project*).

Question 2: Encourage a variety of responses (e.g., *I'd record observations if I were going to write a description. I'd record observations to help me figure out how something works. I'd record observations about how someone else did something like a fancy dive so I could do it, too*).

Looking Ahead
The thinking strategy introduced in this lesson, an observation chart, is used in Using the Strategy B as a prereading strategy to help students anticipate the literature, *The Midnight Fox*. It will appear three more times in this unit and again in Unit 8.

OBSERVATION CHART			
Strategy for Narrating	Writing to Learn	Prewriting	Writing Across the Curriculum
23	29	40	46

Strategy for Classifying	Writing to Learn	Prewriting	Writing Across the Curriculum
407	411	422	428

Although the observation chart strategy is repeated in each presentation, the context in which it is used changes. Students will thus be given the opportunity to discover how the strategy can help them in reading, in writing across the curriculum, and in their daily lives.

◀▥▥ **TEACHING OPTIONS** ▥▥▶

RETEACHING

A Different Modality Suggest the topic *thunderstorm*. Post the headings *What I Might See, What I Might Hear, What I Might Feel* on tagboard in different corners of the room. Have students write on big pieces of paper details about a thunderstorm such as *lightning flashes; upset about canceled ballgame; people running for shelter; loud, rumbling noises*. Have the students tape their detail under the appropriate heading. Discuss the choices.

CLASS ENRICHMENT

A Cooperative Activity Choose a place such as a park, the lunchroom, or the principal's office. Form small groups. Have them visit the place or close their eyes and imagine they are there, then cooperate to make an observation chart about it. Be sure that each group member contributes details. Have groups share their charts and explain how they thought of their subheads and details. Help them to appreciate the variety of strategies different groups used.

CHALLENGE

An Independent Extension Have students imagine that they are time travelers from the future who are observing a present-day object of their choice, such as a paperclip or a pizza. Have them make an observation chart with details they will use to write a report about this object to the future society they came from. Students may enjoy making futuristic costumes or props to use while reading their reports to ''the governing body of the future'' (the class).

UNIT 1
Literature

OBJECTIVES
To appreciate fiction
To read and respond to personal narrative
To use a thinking strategy

VOCABULARY STRATEGIES

Developing Concepts and Teaching Vocabulary

Preteach the following words from the story. Use the Dictionary of Knowledge at the back of the book to provide definitions of base words and context sentences.

demolish, stationery, quiver(ed)

Write the vocabulary words on the chalkboard and call on a volunteer to pronounce them. Have students use the words *demolished* and *quivered* in sentences. Then discuss with students the difference between the homophones *stationary* (not moving) and *stationery* (writing paper).

GUIDING COMPREHENSION

Building Background

The first half of this unit includes information especially chosen to build background for *The Midnight Fox*. If you started the unit with grammar instruction, you may wish to have a class discussion on the unit theme, **Farm Life**, based on the information in those lessons.

If you started the unit with composition instruction, you may wish to build students' knowledge of farm life by asking: *What do you know about farm life? What are some crops that are grown on farms? What are some kinds of animals living on farms?* (Students may recall that wheat, corn, fruits, and vegetables are grown on farms. Besides the animals living on farms, such as pigs, cows, and chickens, wild animals such as foxes, hedgehogs, and raccoons are usually found in the countryside nearby.)

LITERATURE

from

The Midnight Fox
by Betsy Byars

In all his life, Tom had never spent longer, slower days than the first three days on his Aunt Millie's farm. He had fought going to the farm in the first place. He didn't get along with animals or enjoy the outdoors. He had only agreed to go, finally, so that his parents could take a summer trip to Europe.

Now Tom missed his parents and his friend Petie Burkis. Most of all, though, he missed doing his own, unplanned things every day. He felt completely useless on the farm, where everything had been well-planned without him. He was going to have a miserable summer, he feared, with nothing to look forward to but his daily trip to the mailbox. Then, everything changed. Here is Tom's story of what happened.

24 ◇ LITERATURE: Story

ESSENTIAL LANGUAGE SKILLS
This lesson provides opportunities to:

LISTENING ◆ employ active listening in a variety of situations

SPEAKING ◆ use a variety of words to express feelings and ideas

READING ◆ relate experiences with appropriate vocabulary in complete sentences ◆ identify an implied main idea of a longer selection ◆ understand cause-and-effect relationships ◆ evaluate and make judgments ◆ respond to various forms of literature ◆ describe the time and setting of a story

WRITING ◆ use ideas and information from sources other than personal experiences for writing

LANGUAGE ◆ use the fundamentals of grammar, punctuation, and spelling

The one highlight of my day was to go down to the mailbox for the mail. This was the only thing I did all day that was of any use. Then, too, the honking of the mail truck would give me the feeling that there was a letter of great importance waiting for me in the box. I could hardly hurry down the road fast enough. Anyone watching me from behind would probably have seen only a cloud of dust, my feet would pound so fast. So far, the only mail I had received was a post card from my mom with a picture of the Statue of Liberty on it telling me how excited and happy she was.

This Thursday morning when I went to the mailbox there was a letter to me from Petie Burkis and I was never so glad to see anything in my life. I ripped it open and completely destroyed the envelope I was in such a hurry. And I thought that when I was a hundred years old, sitting in a chair with a rug over my knees, and my mail was brought in on a silver tray, if there was a letter from Petie Burkis on that tray, I would snatch it up and rip it open just like this. I could hardly get it unfolded— Petie folds his letters up small—I was so excited.

Dear Tom,

There is nothing much happening here. I went to the playground Saturday after you left, and you know that steep bank by the swings? Well, I fell all the way down that. Here's the story—

BOY FALLS DOWN BANK
WHILE GIRL ONLOOKERS CHEER

Today Petie Burkis fell down the bank at Harley Playground. It is reported that some ill-mannered girls at the park for a picnic cheered and laughed at the sight of the young, <u>demolished</u> boy. The brave youngster left the park unaided.

Not much else happened. Do you get Chiller Theater? There was a real good movie on Saturday night about mushroom men.

Write me a letter,
Petie Burkis

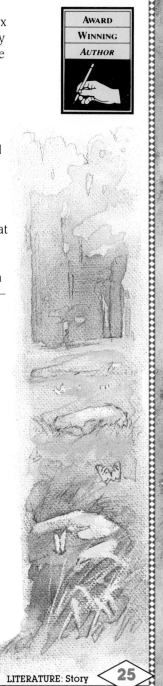

AWARD
WINNING
AUTHOR

LITERATURE: Story **25**

SUMMARY

In this selection from *The Midnight Fox*, Tom, the narrator, is bored spending the summer on his aunt and uncle's farm. The highlight of his vacation comes when he receives a letter from a friend back home. But just as he finishes writing back to Petie, something truly exciting happens to him: Tom sees a black fox leaping across the field. The black fox comes closer, giving Tom a very special look at her—an "awesome" experience.

ABOUT THE AUTHOR

Born and raised in Charlotte, North Carolina, BETSY BYARS (1928–) began her writing career while raising four children in Morgantown, West Virginia. It was with the publication of *The Midnight Fox* in 1968 that her work began to receive attention. Since then she has received wide critical acclaim for such titles as *The Summer of the Swans*, winner of the **Newbery Medal** in 1971, and *The Night Swimmers*, an **American Book Award** winner in 1980.

Developing a Purpose for Reading

Option 1: Have students set their own purpose for reading. Then have them read the story introduction and study the illustrations. Ask students to complete sentences about the story that begin: *I wonder . . .* To complete the sentences, have students consider the story title, introduction, and the vocabulary words. Remind students to recall what they know about farm life before writing. When the "I wonder" sentences are completed, have volunteers share their sentences with the class. Suggest that students set their own reading purpose by reviewing their sentences and underlining the most important information they would like to learn from the story.

Option 2: If you wish to set a reading purpose for everyone, have students pay special attention to what they learn about the feelings of the narrator. Have them ask themselves: *What does Tom tell me about how he is feeling?*

GUIDED READING

Please note that opportunities for students' personal responses to the selection are offered in the Reader's Response question and the Selection Follow-up at the end of this lesson.

Page 24 *What is the setting of this story?* (a farm where there are chickens, pigs, and a flower garden) RECALL: SETTING/PLACE

Page 26 *Where did Tom go to write a letter to Petie? Why?* (He went to a nice place over the hill by the creek because he thought it was the best place on the farm.) INFER: CAUSE/EFFECT

Page 26 *Tom describes his thoughts about a butterfly contest and writes to Petie about a movie he is planning. What does this tell you about Tom's character?* (Tom is a boy with an active imagination.) ANALYZE: CHARACTER

I went in and gave the rest of the mail to Aunt Millie, who said, "Well, let's see what the government's sending us today," and then I got my box of <u>stationery</u> and went outside.

There was a very nice place over the hill by the creek. There were trees so big I couldn't get my arms around them, and soft grass and rocks to sit on. They were planning to let the cows into this field later on, and then it wouldn't be as nice, but now it was the best place on the farm.

Incidentally, anyone interested in butterflies would have gone crazy. There must have been a million in that one field. I had thought about there being a contest—a butterfly contest and hundreds of people would come from all over the country to catch butterflies. I had thought about it so much that I could almost see this real fat lady from Maine running all over the field with about a hundred butterfly nets and a fruit jar under her arm.

Anyway, I sat down and wrote Petie a letter.

Dear Petie,

I do not know whether we get Chiller Theater or not. Since there is no TV set here, it is very difficult to know what we could get if we had one.

My farm chores are feeding the pigs, feeding the chickens, weeding the flowers, getting the mail, things like that. I have a lot of time to myself and I am planning a movie about a planet that collides with Earth, and this planet and Earth become fused together, and the people of Earth are terrified of the planet, because it is very weird-looking and they have heard these terrible moanlike cries coming from the depths of it. That's all so far.

Write me a letter,
Tom

I had just finished writing this letter and was waiting for a minute to see if I would think of anything to add when I looked up and saw the black fox.

26 ▷ LITERATURE: Story

I did not believe it for a minute. It was like my eyes were playing a trick or something, because I was just sort of staring across this field, thinking about my letter, and then in the distance, where the grass was very green, I saw a fox leaping over the crest of the field. The grass moved and the fox sprang toward the movement, and then, seeing that it was just the wind that had caused the grass to move, she ran straight for the grove of trees where I was sitting.

It was so great that I wanted it to start over again, like you can turn movie film back and see yourself repeat some fine thing you have done, and I wanted to see the fox leaping over the grass again. In all my life I have never been so excited.

I did not move at all, but I could hear the paper in my hand shaking, and my heart seemed to have moved up in my body and got stuck in my throat.

The fox came straight toward the grove of trees. She wasn't afraid, and I knew she had not seen me against the tree. I stayed absolutely still even though I felt like jumping up and screaming, "Aunt Millie! Uncle Fred! Come see this. It's a fox, *a fox!*"

Her steps as she crossed the field were lighter and quicker than a cat's. As she came closer I could see that her black fur was tipped with white. It was as if it were midnight and the moon were shining on her fur, frosting it. The wind parted her fur as it changed directions. Suddenly she stopped. She was ten feet away now, and with the changing of the wind she had got my scent. She looked right at me.

I did not move for a moment and neither did she. Her head was cocked to one side, her tail curled up, her front left foot raised. In all my life I never saw anything like that fox standing there with her pale golden eyes on me and this great black fur being blown by the wind.

Suddenly her nose quivered. It was such a slight movement I almost didn't see it, and then her mouth opened and I could see the pink tip of her tongue. She turned. She still was not afraid, but with a bound that was lighter than the wind—it was as if she was being blown away over the field—she was gone.

LITERATURE: Story ◇ **27** ◇

GUIDED READING

Page 27 *What made seeing the fox so special?* (What excited Tom most when he first saw the fox was the black color of her fur. Also, Tom was seeing the fox in the wild, not in the zoo, and the fox came close enough so that Tom could see the tip of her pink tongue.)
ANALYZE: MAIN IDEA

STRATEGIC READING

Page 27 Read aloud the three paragraphs beginning "The fox came straight toward . . ." Ask students to picture in their minds the scene Tom is describing. Ask volunteers to tell about the scene in their own words. If students have difficulty visualizing, you may wish to suggest that they reread the paragraphs and use the thinking strategy of making an observation chart about what they learn about the fox. METACOGNITION: SUMMARIZING AND DETAILS

Returning to the Reading Purpose

Option 1: Those students who have written ''I wonder'' sentences may wish to review them to determine which ones were answered.

Option 2: If you have established a common reading purpose, review it and ask volunteers to summarize what they learned about Tom and his feelings.

READER'S RESPONSE

Would you like to see the fox? Why or why not? (Before having students respond, you may wish to encourage them to think about and share with the class their experiences with animals outside of a zoo.)

STORY MAP

You may want to have students make a story map for this excerpt from *The Midnight Fox* similar to the one below.

Characters:	Tom, a black fox
Setting:	a farm
	recent times

↓

Problem: Tom is bored spending the summer on his Aunt Millie's farm.

Event 1: Tom receives a letter from his friend Petie.

↓

Event 2: He goes to a field on the farm and writes a letter to Petie.

↓

Event 3: Tom spots a black fox leaping through the grass across the field.

↓

Event 4: The fox comes closer, and Tom gets a special look at her before she runs away.

Resolution: Seeing the fox is a very special, exciting experience for Tom.

Still I didn't move. I couldn't. I couldn't believe that I had really seen the fox.

I had seen foxes before in zoos, but I was always in such a great hurry to get on to the good stuff that I was saying stupid things like, "I want to see the go-rilllllllas," and not once had I ever really looked at a fox. Still, I could never remember seeing a black fox, not even in a zoo.

Also, there was a great deal of difference between seeing an animal in the zoo in front of painted fake rocks and trees and seeing one natural and free in the woods. It was like seeing a kite on the floor and then, later, seeing one up in the sky where it was supposed to be, pulling at the wind.

I started to pick up my pencil and write as quickly as I could, "P.S. Today I saw a black fox." But I didn't. This was the most exciting thing that had happened to me, and "P.S. Today I saw a black fox" made it nothing. "So what else is happening?" Petie Burkis would probably write back. I folded my letter, put it in an envelope, and sat there.

I thought about this old newspaper that my dad had had in his desk drawer for years. It was orange and the headline was just one word, very big, the letters about twelve inches high. WAR! And I mean it was awesome to see that word like that, because you knew it was a word that was going to change your whole life, the whole world even. And everytime I would see that newspaper, even though I wasn't even born when it was printed, I couldn't say anything for a minute or two.

Well, this was the way I felt right then about the black fox. I thought about a newspaper with just one word for a headline, very big, very black letters, twelve inches high. FOX! And even that did not show how awesome it had really been to me.

Library Link ◆ *If you would like to read more about Tom and the fox, read* The Midnight Fox *by Betsy Byars.*

Reader's Response

Would you like to see the fox? Why or why not?

28 LITERATURE: Story

HIGHLIGHTING LITERATURE

Page 28 Point out how Tom's feeling of excitement at seeing the fox is described. First, Tom says that he wanted to be able to start again, "like you can turn movie film back and see yourself repeat some fine thing you have done. . . ." Then he describes how his hand shakes and his heart seems to get stuck in his throat. Encourage students to describe times they have been very excited.

The Midnight Fox

Responding to Literature

1. What animal would you like to see face to face? Tell where you would be and what you would do.

2. Tom and Petie made up headlines for exciting things that happened to them. What exciting thing might happen to you? Make up a headline. Tell the story that would go with the headline.

3. With a partner, discuss a sequel to this episode. Tell what might happen if Tom and the fox were to meet again. Together, share your ending with the class. As a class, decide which ending is the favorite.

Writing to Learn

Think and Observe ✦ Select an animal that you know well. Take a few minutes to observe it carefully. Collect details in an observation chart like the one below.

black fox	
What I See	black fur tipped with white, pale golden eyes, pink tongue, quivering nose, cat-like steps
What I Hear	soft breathing, no other sound
What I Feel	afraid I will chase it off

Observation Chart

Write ✦ Compose a brief description of your animal. Include the details that you noted while you were observing.

LITERATURE: Story ◆ 29

WRITING TO LEARN

Have students apply the thinking strategy of making an observation chart to show what they know about the animal they choose. You may wish to suggest that they choose an animal they are familiar with. Then have students complete the Write activity by using the information from their observation charts in the description they write. Have volunteers read aloud their descriptions.

SELECTION FOLLOW-UP

You may wish to incorporate any or all of the following discussion questions and activities in your follow-up to the literature selection, *The Midnight Fox.*

RESPONDING TO LITERATURE

Encourage students to use their personal experiences as well as what they learned from the selection to discuss these questions. The questions are designed to encourage students to think of and respond to the selection as a whole. Explain to students that although they may use details from the selection to support their opinions, the questions have no right or wrong answers. Encourage them to express a variety of points of view. You may wish to have students respond as a class, in groups, or with partners.

1. *What animal would you like to see face to face? Tell where you would be and what you would do.* (Students' answers will depend on their personal experiences with animals and what animals they have read about. Encourage them to think about one particular animal they know only through books or television and have them describe what it might feel like to encounter this animal face to face.)

2. *Tom and Petie made up headlines for exciting things that happened to them. What exciting thing might happen to you? Make up a headline. Tell the story that would go with the headline.* (You may wish to have students practice forming headlines as a class for events in stories they have read before having them make up headlines for exciting things they think may happen to them.)

3. *With a partner discuss a sequel to this episode. Tell what might happen if Tom and the fox were to meet again. Together, share your ending with the class. As a class decide which ending is the favorite.* (Before students decide on what they think will happen next, encourage them to try to put themselves in Tom's place and think about what excites him and stirs his imagination.)

 World of Language Audio Library

A recording of this selection is available in the **Audio Library.**

UNIT 1
Speaking/Listening

■ Easy ■ Average ■ Challenging

OBJECTIVES
To recognize that a speaker's expression can make a story amusing
To use guidelines for telling and listening to an anecdote

ASSIGNMENT GUIDE
BASIC   Practice A

↓

ADVANCED   Practice B

All should do the Apply activity.

RESOURCES
■ World of Language Video Library

TEACHING THE LESSON

1. Getting Started
Oral Language Focus attention on this oral activity, encouraging all to participate. You may wish to discuss with students what first graders are like and what they might consider funny. If any of the students have younger brothers or sisters, you may wish to have them share with the class what they know about their younger siblings' interests.

2. Developing the Lesson
Guide students through a discussion of the lesson, emphasizing the guidelines for telling an anecdote and being an active listener. Have volunteers give examples of stories that young children would like. Then lead students through the **Guided Practice**. Identify those who would benefit from reteaching. Assign independent Practice A and B.

3. Closing the Lesson
After students complete the Apply activity, call on individuals to read their anecdotes aloud. Then have students work in small groups to discuss how they might improve their anecdotes and their delivery. Point out that learning to tell anecdotes in an amusing or dramatic way can help make them the kind of speakers that others enjoy hearing.

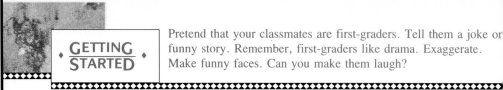

GETTING STARTED ♦ Pretend that your classmates are first-graders. Tell them a joke or funny story. Remember, first-graders like drama. Exaggerate. Make funny faces. Can you make them laugh?

SPEAKING and LISTENING ♦
Telling an Anecdote

Tom is capturing Petie's interest with an anecdote. An anecdote is a short, interesting story about someone. You can use anecdotes to tell someone what happened in an amusing or dramatic fashion.

Keep your audience in mind. When telling an anecdote to adults use words and a style different from those you use when speaking to children. Here are speaking and listening guides to help you.

Telling an Anecdote	1. Make sure to tell all of the important details and to tell them in order. 2. Practice telling your story at least twice—the second time in front of a mirror. If possible, record your voice. 3. Look at your audience. Be confident. Smile! 4. Make sure everyone can hear you. Speak clearly. 5. Be dramatic! Use your face, your voice, and your body to show how you feel. Use your voice to build suspense. Use sound words, such as *Bam*! *Crash*! *Zzzzzip*!
Being an Active Listener	1. Be polite. Show by your face that you are interested. 2. As you listen to an anecdote, try to predict its ending. 3. Keep the order of events straight in your mind. 4. Listen to be prepared to ask questions. 5. Listen and watch to see how the speaker dramatizes the story.

Summary ♦ An **anecdote** is a short, interesting story about someone. When telling an anecdote, give all of the important details in the right order. Listen to an anecdote with interest.

30   SPEAKING and LISTENING: Anecdotes

ESSENTIAL LANGUAGE SKILLS
This lesson provides opportunities to:

LISTENING ♦ employ active listening in a variety of situations

SPEAKING ♦ engage in creative dramatic activities and nonverbal communication ♦ present stories, anecdotes, and plays for entertainment

READING ♦ identify an implied main idea of a longer selection

WRITING ♦ use ideas and information from sources other than personal experiences for writing ♦ adapt information to accomplish a specific purpose with a particular audience

LANGUAGE ♦ use the fundamentals of grammar, punctuation, and spelling

Guided Practice

The sentence below is from *The Midnight Fox*.

I could hardly hurry down the road fast enough.

Say the sentence four times. Be dramatic and show these feelings.

1. amusement **2.** fear **3.** anger **4.** excitement

Practice

A. Say these sentences from *The Midnight Fox* as if they were a part of an anecdote. Be dramatic. Say each in a way that shows how you feel.

5. I want to see the go-rilllllllas! (angry)
6. I want to see the go-rillllllas! (pleading)
7. The headline was just one word . . . .WAR! (amazed)
8. The headline was just one word . . . .WAR! (nervous)
9. Today I saw a black fox. (matter-of-fact)
10. Today I saw a black fox. (overjoyed)

B. Tell an anecdote to a partner. Before you tell it, jot down notes to make sure you tell all of the details in order. Try to build suspense. When you tell your story, stop just before the end and ask your listener what might happen next. Anecdotes will vary.

Apply ◆ Think and Write

Dictionary of Knowledge ◆ Anecdotes are often used in speeches to amuse the audience or to make a point. Read the entry about speech-making techniques in the Dictionary of Knowledge. Then write an anecdote you might use to begin or end a speech.

✎ **Remember**
to tell anecdotes in an amusing or dramatic way.

SPEAKING and LISTENING: Anecdotes **31**

🖵 **World of Language Video Library**

You may wish to refer to the *Video Library* to teach this lesson.

EVALUATION PROGRAM

See Evaluation and Testing Program, pp. C9–C11.

Speaking and Listening Checklist Masters

◀▥▥ TEACHING OPTIONS ▥▥▶

RETEACHING

A Different Modality To help students practice following the guidelines from the lesson, have them tell and retell a simple story that is familiar to them, such as "The Three Little Pigs" or "The Three Billy-Goats Gruff." Give students practice telling the story in small groups until they are sure of themselves. Remind the storytellers and listeners to follow the specific guidelines for "Telling an Anecdote" in the chart in the lesson.

CLASS ENRICHMENT

A Cooperative Activity Have students work in pairs to make a booklet of their favorite class anecdotes. You may wish to have one partner underline the parts of their story that is to receive the most emphasis and have the other partner draw appropriate illustrations for the underlined parts. If possible give them the opportunity to share some of their favorites with another class.

CHALLENGE

An Independent Extension Have students read a book of jokes or humorous stories in the library and choose the joke or story they like best to retell to the class. You may wish to have them select the most appropriate story to tell to a first grader, a teacher, a parent, or another relative.

UNIT 1
Writing

■ Easy ■ Average ■ Challenging

OBJECTIVES
To recognize the three elements of a story: character, setting, and plot

ASSIGNMENT GUIDE
BASIC   Practice A
          ↓   Practice B
ADVANCED   Practice C

All should do the Apply activity.

RESOURCES
■ Reteaching Master 8
■ Practice Master 8

TEACHING THE LESSON

1. Getting Started
Oral Language Focus attention on this oral activity, encouraging all to participate. If the first story comes to an end quickly, you may wish to start another with *I was really surprised when I opened the front door of my house.*

2. Developing the Lesson
Guide students through the explanation of character, setting, and plot, emphasizing the examples and the summary. Lead students through the **Guided Practice.** Identify those who would benefit from reteaching. Assign independent Practice A–C.

3. Closing the Lesson
After students complete the Apply activity, encourage volunteers to share their solutions with the class. You may wish to have individual students prepare their solutions with appropriate illustrations for a bulletin board display. Point out to students that knowing about character, setting, and plot will help them create stories that capture their readers' imaginations.

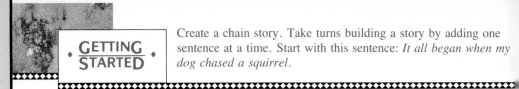

♦ GETTING STARTED ♦

Create a chain story. Take turns building a story by adding one sentence at a time. Start with this sentence: *It all began when my dog chased a squirrel.*

WRITING ♦
Character, Setting, and Plot

No two stories are exactly alike. Yet most stories contain the same three parts: character, setting, and plot. The parts of a story are explained below.

The Parts of a Story

1. You need one or more characters—people, animals, or imaginary creatures. Create characters to interest your readers.
2. Put your characters in a setting—a time and a place. The setting is a background for the characters and the action.
3. Add a plot—action and events. A plot has a beginning, a middle, and an end. It usually tells events in time order, or the order in which they happened.
4. Remember to add an interesting title.

Here are some examples of the parts of a story.

A character: Uncle Giorgio; Rumpelstiltskin; Wilbur
A setting: (time) a March morning; sunrise; June 21, 1865
                (place) a fox's den; an empty house; the Alamo
A plot: (beginning) The main character faces a problem.
              (middle) Action, suspense, and excitement build.
              (end) The character solves the problem.

Summary ♦ The three main parts of a story are **character**, **setting**, and **plot**. They work together to capture a reader's interest.

Guided Practice

Tell whether each of these is an example of character, setting, or plot.

1. *setting*   The road was dusty.
2. *character*   Tom was often lonely.
3. *plot*   The fox ran toward him.
4. *setting*   It was a lazy, hazy day.
5. *plot*   The fox stopped just ten feet away.

ESSENTIAL LANGUAGE SKILLS
This lesson provides opportunities to:

LISTENING ♦ employ active listening in a variety of situations

SPEAKING ♦ use a variety of words to express feelings and ideas

READING ♦ understand content area vocabulary ♦ evaluate and make judgments ♦ follow a set of directions

WRITING ♦ generate ideas using a variety of strategies, such as brainstorming, clustering, mapping, question and answer

LANGUAGE ♦ use the fundamentals of grammar, punctuation, and spelling

Practice

A. Read these sentences about *The Midnight Fox*. Write *character*, *setting*, or *plot* to show what each one illustrates.

6. There must have been a million butterflies in the field! setting
7. I have a lot of time to myself and am planning a movie. plot
8. I was so excited that I could hardly unfold the letter! character
9. It was a fox, and she was running straight toward me. plot
10. There were big trees and soft grass and rocks to sit on. setting

B. Answer these questions about a book you recently read.
Answers will vary.

11. What is the title of the book, and who is the main character?
12. Where does the story take place?
13. What problem does the main character face?
14. What is the most important event in the story?
15. How does the story end?

C. Make up three story parts of your own. Follow the example below.
Answers will vary.

Characters: Alicia, a ten-year-old
Felipe, her four-year-old brother

Setting: A farm in Kansas
A stormy summer afternoon

Plot: Felipe is afraid of storms.
Alicia helps him to be brave.

Apply ◆ Think and Write

A Problem and Solution ◆ Put yourself in this plot: You are trapped on a planet in outer space. How will you escape? What will you do? Write a solution.

✏️ **Remember**
to make character, setting, and plot work together when you write a story.

WRITING: Elements of a Story **33**

RETEACHING 8

Character, Setting, and Plot

The parts of a story are listed below. Draw an arrow to each example.
1. Character —— Miss Muffet
2. Setting —— long ago on a farm
3. Plot —— First, she is eating. Then, a spider sits beside her. Last, it frightens her away.

The three main parts of a story are **character, setting,** and **plot.** Characters can be people, animals, or imaginary creatures. Setting is the time and place. Plot is the action and events.

Write character, setting, or plot to show what each sentence describes.

EXAMPLE: It was afternoon in the woods near Don and Kim's house. ___setting___

1. The sun was shining. ___setting___
2. Don and Kim were brother and sister. ___character___
3. Kim's front tire went flat. ___plot___
4. Don fixed the flat tire. ___plot___
5. Don was confident. ___character___
6. Kim and Don wore sneakers. ___character___
7. Kim pedaled hard and reached the top of the hill first. ___plot___
8. The afternoon air turned frosty. ___setting___
9. Sunlight shined through the trees. ___setting___
10. It began to snow. ___setting___
11. Kim enjoyed windy, snowy days. ___character___
12. They drank hot chocolate when they got home. ___plot___
13. Their mother hugged them and made a fire in the fireplace. ___plot___
14. The house felt cozy and warm. ___setting___

PRACTICE 8

Character, Setting, and Plot

The three main parts of a story are **character, setting,** and **plot.**

A. Write character, setting, or plot to show what each sentence describes.
1. It was a bright, hot summer day at the beach. ___setting___
2. Maria was a clever, quiet girl. ___character___
3. Fong never missed a chance to show off. ___character___
4. The river dipped and rushed between its banks. ___setting___
5. The fire fighters put out the fire before it spread. ___plot___
6. The air was thin and cold at the mountaintop. ___setting___
7. The lights went out and the treasure map disappeared. ___plot___
8. No dog was braver or more loyal than Stanley. ___character___
9. The pilot saw the signal fire and landed. ___plot___
10. It was a dark and stormy night. ___setting___

B. The story below is missing details about the characters, setting, and plot. Complete the story by writing the missing information. Answers will vary.

Once upon a time in a land called _____ (setting),
there lived a _____ (character) and his _____ (character).
They had almost everything they could want except for _____ (plot)
One day they decided to solve this problem, so they _____ (plot)
_____
_____
_____

◀||| TEACHING OPTIONS |||▶

RETEACHING

A Different Modality Write on the chalkboard: <u>Characters</u> (people, animals, imaginary creatures), <u>Setting</u> (time and place), and <u>Plot</u> (action and events). Give students examples of story parts, using stories that are familiar to them. Then have students suggest other examples and write them under the appropriate heading. Encourage students to continue the lists by taking turns writing an entry under each heading.

CLASS ENRICHMENT

A Cooperative Activity Divide the class into groups of three. Have one student describe two or more imaginary characters, the next student describe a setting, and the third student supply a plot. Have the group discuss its story parts and revise them, if necessary, so the parts work together. You may wish to have each group write a story paragraph using its chosen story parts.

CHALLENGE

An Independent Extension Have students brainstorm and write story parts for a farm setting, a colonial times setting, and a futuristic setting. Have them choose one of the sets of story parts to use as the basis for writing a story paragraph of their own.

UNIT 1
Writing

■ Easy ■ Average ■ Challenging

OBJECTIVES
To punctuate and capitalize quotations correctly, including divided quotations
To avoid overuse of the verb *said*

ASSIGNMENT GUIDE
BASIC   Practice A
⬇   Practice B
ADVANCED Practice C

All should do the Apply activity.

RESOURCES
■ Reteaching Master 9
■ Practice Master 9

TEACHING THE LESSON

1. Getting Started
Oral Language Focus attention on this oral activity, encouraging all to participate. You may wish to have volunteers suggest other tongue-twister quotations, such as "Surely, she should serve soup," said Shirley.

2. Developing the Lesson
Guide students through the explanation of quotations, emphasizing the examples and the summary. You may wish to present two sentences, such as *Johnny said that he wanted to join us. Johnny said, "I'd like to join you."* Explain to students that the sentences express the same idea, but that the second sentence gives Johnny's exact words. Lead students through the **Guided Practice.** Identify those who would benefit from reteaching. Assign independent Practice A–C.

3. Closing the Lesson
After students complete the Apply activity, encourage volunteers to read their quotations aloud. You may wish to have groups of students prepare a bulletin board display of rewrites and the cartoons. Point out to students that knowing how to punctuate quotations correctly will help them show their readers the exact words of a speaker.

34

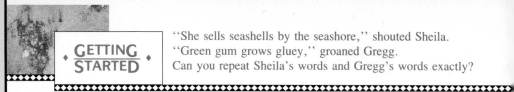

◆ **GETTING STARTED** ◆

"She sells seashells by the seashore," shouted Sheila.
"Green gum grows gluey," groaned Gregg.
Can you repeat Sheila's words and Gregg's words exactly?

WRITING ◆
Quotations

When you repeat someone's exact words, the repeated words are a <u>quotation</u>. When you write, quotation marks (" ") help identify and set off a quotation. Here are two ways to write a quotation.

■ Mike commented, "Today I saw a frog with red markings."
■ "I've never heard of a frog with red markings," said Amy.

The first word of a quotation begins with a capital letter. A comma separates the quotation from the words that tell who spoke.

If a quotation is a question, it ends with a question mark.

■ "Did you do anything special today?" asked Uncle Bill.

An **interjection** is a word that expresses feeling or emotion. It is usually followed by an exclamation mark. The two quotations below express strong feelings. The first quotation contains an interjec

■ "Wow!" yelled Mike.   "That's great!" cried Amy.

Sometimes a quotation is divided into two parts. If the two parts make one sentence, use commas to separate the quotation from the words that tell who spoke.

■ "Aunt Jane," said Mike, "let me help you."

If a divided quotation is two separate sentences, use a period after the words that tell who spoke. Begin the second sentence with a capital letter.

■ "Dave is outside," Mike whispered. "He's my best friend."

Don't overuse the word *said*. Use a variety of verbs. You might try *replied, snickered, wailed, begged,* or *added.*

> **Summary** ◆ Use **quotation marks** (" ") to show the exact words of a speaker.

34   WRITING and MECHANICS: Quotations

ESSENTIAL LANGUAGE SKILLS
This lesson provides opportunities to:

LISTENING ◆ employ active listening in a variety of situations

SPEAKING ◆ use a variety of words to express feelings and ideas

READING ◆ understand content area vocabulary ◆ evaluate and make judgments ◆ follow a set of directions

WRITING ◆ adapt information to accomplish a specific purpose with a particular audience

LANGUAGE ◆ use the fundamentals of grammar, punctuation, and spelling

Guided Practice

Read these quotations that might have been said by the characters of *The Midnight Fox*. Tell where quotation marks should be added.

1. Tom grumbled, "I'm not used to things here on the farm."
2. "I'm afraid," complained Tom, "that I'm a little bored."
3. "May I drive the tractor?" asked Tom.
4. "Gracious!" replied Uncle Fred. "You're just a kid."

Practice

A. Write each sentence. Place quotation marks where they belong.

5. "Did you bring the stale bread?" asked Tommy.
6. "Of course," Jeffrey answered. "It's in this bag."
7. "Let's go down to the lake," Susie urged.
8. "Wait!" Jeffrey shouted. "I'm not running there!"
9. Susie yelled, "It's not far from here."
10. "I know," replied Jeffrey, "but I don't want to scare them."
11. "Look," exclaimed Tommy. "There they are!"
12. "Oh!" whispered Susie. "I count six of them."
13. "Yes," said Jeffrey. "There are six baby ducks."
14. "Look how they follow the mother duck," added Tommy.

B. Write the sentences correctly. Add the necessary punctuation. Use capital letters where they are needed.

15. "Give me some bread to feed them," pleaded Susie.
16. "Wait a minute," answered Jeffrey. "let me open the bag."
17. "Wow!" said Tommy. "look at them eat." (or !")
18. "If you ask me," added Susie, "they look like they're starving."

C. **19–23.** Suppose you were discussing the ducks with Susie. Write five quotations from your conversation. Be sure to include all the necessary punctuation marks and capital letters.
Answers will vary.

Apply ◆ Think and Write

Writing Conversation ◆ Look at the conversation "balloons" of a comic strip. Rewrite one of the cartoon conversations, using quotation marks. Use lively verbs to tell how the characters speak.

✏️ **Remember** to use interesting verbs to tell how the speaker said the words of a quotation.

WRITING and MECHANICS: Quotations **35**

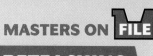

RETEACHING 9
Quotations

Quotation marks (" ") help identify and set off the exact words of a speaker. Circle the speaker's exact words in each sentence below.

1. Wai remarked, "This is an interesting book."
2. "Can you find one like it for me?" asked Lin.
3. "Yes," said the librarian, "I think I can."
4. "Wow!" cried Lin. "Thank you very much."

Use quotation marks (" ") to show the exact words of a speaker. Don't overuse the word *said*. Vary the verbs that tell who spoke.

Write each sentence correctly. Add the necessary punctuation. Use capital letters where needed.

EXAMPLE: Mr. Part said "the new computers have arrived"
Mr. Part said, "The new computers have arrived."

1. "can we begin using them today" asked Lee
   "Can we begin using them today?" asked Lee.

2. Mr. Part replied "first we must connect them and test them"
   Mr. Part replied, "First we must connect them and test them."

3. "maybe" he said "some of you can help me"
   "Maybe," he said, "some of you can help me."

4. "I will open the boxes" Josie said "I am good at that"
   "I will open the boxes," Josie said. "I am good at that."

5. "be sure that you do not drop anything" warned Mr. Part
   "Be sure that you do not drop anything," warned Mr. Part.

6. Lee asked "should I read the instruction booklet"
   Lee asked, "Should I read the instruction booklet?"

7. "I think" replied Mr. Part "that is an excellent idea"
   "I think," replied Mr. Part, "that is an excellent idea."

PRACTICE 9
Quotations

Use quotation marks (" ") to show the exact words of a speaker.

A. Write each sentence. Add the necessary punctuation.

1. Did you bring your new camera? asked Judy.
   "Did you bring your new camera?" asked July.

2. I brought the camera, Olga replied, and two rolls of film.
   "I brought the camera," Olga replied, "and two rolls of film."

3. They also sell film at the museum store, commented Judy.
   "They also sell film at the museum store," commented Judy.

4. We can put the pictures on the bulletin board, suggested Ramon.
   "We can put the pictures on the bulletin board," suggested Ramon.

5. That is an excellent idea for a project, Olga remarked.
   "That is an excellent idea for a project," Olga remarked.

B. Unscramble each set of words to write a sentence with quotations. Add punctuation marks and capital letters where needed. Answers may vary. Possible answers follow.

6. asked class a our going is Raphael on trip
   "Is our class going on a trip?" asked Raphael.

7. will Ms. Smith yes replied museum going to we
   "Yes," replied Ms. Smith, "we will be going to the museum."

8. many the see Jane at interesting museum things commented to are
   "There are many interesting things to see at the museum,"
   commented Jane.

9. cried boy great sounds this like trip Raphael
   "Boy!" cried Raphael. "This sounds like a great trip."

   "I wish we could leave right now," Amy said.

◀▥▥▥ TEACHING OPTIONS ▥▥▥▶

RETEACHING

A Different Modality Discuss favorite books and movies with students and record quotations from the discussion on the chalkboard. Use the quotations to illustrate the correct form for divided quotations, interjections, and so forth. You may wish to model sentences, such as *Jan commented*, *"That is my favorite book." "Wow!" said Nat. "It was great!" "Did you see the movie?" asked Nancy.* Have students tell you how each quote is punctuated.

CLASS ENRICHMENT

A Cooperative Activity Have groups of students discuss something of interest to them, such as a favorite novel, hobby, or TV show. You may wish to have one person in the group record the exact words of the others. Then have each group write a conversation, using quotation marks and other punctuation, and a variety of verbs other than *said*. You may wish to suggest the following verbs: *observed, argued, commented, whispered,* and *explained.*

CHALLENGE

An Independent Extension Have students write a one-page story about a sporting event they would like to see. Encourage them to include vivid dialogue and a variety of verbs. You may wish to have students involve at least two characters, for example, *"Run to third," yelled the coach. "I can't," shouted Elizabeth. "I just missed second base!"* Remind them to use quotation marks and other punctuation correctly.

35

Reading–Writing Connection

OBJECTIVES
To distinguish between first- and third-person point of view
To work together to use first-person point of view to narrate a story
To use the Thesaurus to improve word choice

Focus on the Narrator

Review the Unit 1 literature selection, *The Midnight Fox,* with students and have them recall how Betsy Byars used the first-person point of view to let Tom tell his own story. Then point out to students that they can use this selection to help them learn how to use first-person and third-person points of view to tell a story of their own.

You may wish to guide students through the introductory paragraphs, stressing the examples. Then have students read the first-person and third-person sentences on their own. Discuss how the wording in each sentence differs. Point out how the first-person point of view makes the reader feel involved in the scene with the main character.

Next have students apply the information in the Reading-Writing Connection by discussing the question at the bottom of the page. As students respond to the question, guide them to recognize that although *I* and *me* are used to tell the main character's point of view, *he, she, they,* and *them* are also needed for the main character to tell about the other characters.

Focus on the Narrator

Every story has a narrator. When you read a story or when you write one, you must ask yourself these questions: Who is telling this story? Is the story being told by one of the characters? Or is it being told by the author? The answers to these questions are important. You need to know the story's **point of view**.

Nearly all stories are in the first-person or third-person point of view. Notice how these points of view differ.

First Person	Third Person
The story is told by a character in the story who refers to himself or herself as *I* or *me*.	The story is told by the writer, who refers to the main character as *he* or *she*.
I stared at the black fox.	*He stared at the black fox.*

A writer chooses point of view carefully, for that choice shapes the story. In *The Midnight Fox*, which you read earlier, Betsy Byars writes in the first person. She wants to have Tom tell his own story. We see events unfold through Tom's point of view. We share his thoughts, his feelings, his observations.

First-person point of view makes us feel that we are on the scene with the main character. We really get to know that character. The drawback of this point of view is that it is limiting. The writer can tell us *only* the main character's thoughts. If an event occurs where the main character is not present, the first-person narrator cannot report directly.

The Writer's Voice ◆ The key words for identifying first-person point of view are *I* and *me*. The key words for identifying third-person point of view are *he* and *she*. However, the words *he* and *she* (as well as *they* and *them*) also appear in first-person narration. Why?

◆ 36 ◆ COOPERATIVE LEARNING: Writer's Craft

ESSENTIAL LANGUAGE SKILLS
This lesson provides opportunities to:

LISTENING ◆ select from an oral presentation the information needed

SPEAKING ◆ use a variety of words to express feelings and ideas

READING ◆ relate experiences with appropriate vocabulary in complete sentences ◆ recall specific facts and details that support the main idea and/or conclusion ◆ draw logical conclusions ◆ evaluate and make judgments ◆ follow a set of directions ◆ recognize differences in first- and third-person point of view ◆ explain and relate to the feelings and emotions of characters

WRITING ◆ adapt information to accomplish a specific purpose with a particular audience ◆ participate in writing conferences

LANGUAGE ◆ understand the conventions of usage and mechanics

Working Together

Point of view can be either first person or third person. Remember this as you work with your group on activities **A** and **B**.

A. Each sentence is written in the first-person point of view. Change each one into third person.

EXAMPLE: I remembered having seen foxes in zoos.

ANSWER: He remembered having seen foxes in zoos.

Answers will vary. Possible answers follow.

1. So far I had received just a post card from my mom. he his
2. When I went to the mailbox, there was a letter for me. he him
3. I was in such a hurry that I ripped open the envelope. He   he
4. I thought about being a hundred years old. He
5. Would they bring me my mail on a silver tray? him   his

B. Have your group pretend to be the black fox in *The Midnight Fox*. The fox will be a first-person narrator. Write a short report of your (the fox's) meeting with Tom. Follow the events in Betsy Byars's story, but add details of your own. Try to have everyone contribute ideas. Make the fox seem as real as possible.

Answers will vary.

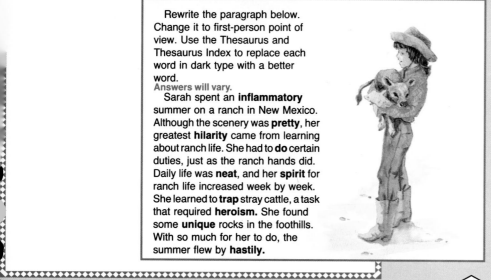

THESAURUS CORNER • Word Choice

Rewrite the paragraph below. Change it to first-person point of view. Use the Thesaurus and Thesaurus Index to replace each word in dark type with a better word.

Answers will vary.

Sarah spent an **inflammatory** summer on a ranch in New Mexico. Although the scenery was **pretty**, her greatest **hilarity** came from learning about ranch life. She had to **do** certain duties, just as the ranch hands did. Daily life was **neat**, and her **spirit** for ranch life increased week by week. She learned to **trap** stray cattle, a task that required **heroism.** She found some **unique** rocks in the foothills. With so much for her to do, the summer flew by **hastily.**

COOPERATIVE LEARNING: Writer's Craft ⟨37⟩

Working Together

The Working Together activities provide opportunities for students to work together in cooperative learning groups. You may wish to pair strong writers with students whose skills are weaker so that all students may experience success in writing.

Divide the class into small groups and have students read In Your Group. Encourage them to discuss what might happen if the group does not follow through on each task. *(If we do not encourage everyone to share ideas, we might miss out on important ideas. If we do not help the group reach agreement, we will not be able to complete the activities successfully. If we do not show appreciation for everyone's contribution, people may be reluctant to contribute. If we do not record the group's ideas, we may forget important points.)*

You may wish to have each group appoint a recorder and a timekeeper. Then set a time limit of ten or fifteen minutes. After students complete activity A, encourage groups to compare the sentences they wrote. After students complete activity B, call on a member of each group to read aloud their paragraph. Have the rest of the class listen to determine whether or not the first-person point of view was followed and to note the details that were added to the story.

Thesaurus Corner

The Thesaurus Corner provides students with the opportunity to extend the Reading-Writing Connection by using the Thesaurus in the back of their textbooks. After students have rewritten the paragraph, call on individuals to read their paragraphs aloud. Encourage students to compare their paragraphs and tell why the synonyms add to the feeling of being on the scene that is conveyed by the first-person point of view. Have students save their paragraphs for use later in the Writing Process lesson. Point out that learning about choosing synonyms that convey an impression of being on the scene can help students develop their ability to use the first-person point of view in their writing.

OBJECTIVES

To write a personal narrative

To use five stages of the writing process: prewriting, writing, revising, proofreading, and publishing

RESOURCES

Writing Process Transparencies 1–4

Revising and Proofreading Transparencies

Spelling Connection

Writing Sample Tests, p. T552

INTRODUCTION

Connecting to Literature Have a volunteer read the lesson introduction aloud. Remind students that the literature selection, *The Midnight Fox,* is a personal narrative. Have students point out the elements in the selection that show that it is a personal narrative. (The story is told from one person's point of view, a boy named Tom. Tom says *I* and *me* when he talks about himself. He tells how he felt when he got a letter from his friend Petie Burkis and how he felt when he saw the black fox in the field.) Explain to students that they will be writing their own personal narrative.

Purpose and Audience Ask students if they have ever told or written a story that was a personal narrative, or a story about yourself. Have volunteers describe those stories. (Students may describe personal narratives they wrote in letters or in their journals. They may describe personal narratives told to friends, family, or classmates.)

Have students consider the questions: *What is my purpose?* (To tell about an experience I had with an animal) *Who is my audience?* (My classmates) Have students discuss what they believe they need to consider when they write for other fifth-graders. Encourage a diversity of responses.

WRITING PROCESS
NARRATING

Writing a Personal Narrative

A story is often called a narrative. A person's own story is a personal narrative. The point of view of a personal narrative is fir[?] person. The writer uses the words *I* and *me*.

In *The Midnight Fox*, Tom narrates his exciting adventure a black fox. No one else can te[?] the story exactly the way Tom First-person point of view helps see through Tom's eyes. It help[?] share his thoughts and feelings.

Know Your Purpose and Audience

You may never have met a black fox. However, you have probably had some experience with an animal. In this lesson you will write a personal narrative. Your purpose will be to tell about an experience you had with an animal.

Your audience will be your classmates. Later, you and your classmates can read your personal narratives to each other. You can also display your narratives on a story net.

What's — MY PURPOSE

Who's — MY AUDIENCE

38   WRITING PROCESS: Personal Narrative

ESSENTIAL LANGUAGE SKILLS
This lesson provides opportunities to:

LISTENING ◆ listen for specific information ◆ select from an oral presentation the information needed

SPEAKING ◆ make organized oral presentations ◆ adapt content and formality of oral language to fit purpose and audience

READING ◆ recall facts and details that support the main idea ◆ draw conclusions ◆ synthesize ideas and information ◆ follow a set of directions

WRITING ◆ select and narrow a topic for a specific purpose ◆ generate ideas using a variety of strategies, such as brainstorming, clustering, free writing ◆ participate in writing conferences

LANGUAGE ◆ use language for narrating ◆ use the fundamentals of grammar, punctuation, and spelling

Prewriting

Prewriting is getting ready to write. First choose a topic for your personal narrative. Then gather ideas about your topic.

Choose Your Topic ◆ Perhaps you were riding your bike and saw a deer. Maybe you found a lost cat or watched a seal at an aquarium. Make a list of animals and circle your choice.

Think About It

Close your eyes and try to visualize animals you have met. Try saying "animal, animal, animal" to yourself until a picture comes to mind. Then look at your list. Which animal did you see most clearly? Which was the most memorable? That is your choice.

Talk About It

Discuss animal encounters with your classmates. Recall times when you were at a zoo, a park, or in a woods. You might have seen a horse pulling a carriage on a city street, even. Make a list of places where you might have seen animals.

Topic Ideas

a deer near bushes
a lost cat
a seal at the aquarium
a giraffe at the zoo
a robin in a nest

WRITING PROCESS: Personal Narrative ◇39◇

Pacing

A five-day pacing guide follows, but the writing process can take longer if students want to spend several days on prewriting, revising, or preparing for publishing.

Day 1—Prewriting   Day 3—Revising
Day 2—Writing   Day 4—Proofreading
        Day 5—Publishing

Evaluation

Process Check questions at the end of each stage of the writing process help you to keep track of students' progress.

Holistic Evaluation Guidelines may be found in the teaching notes on page 45. They offer criteria for average, above-average, and below-average compositions.

Possible responses are overprinted on this reduced fac-simile only. Use Writing Process Transparencies to inter-act with your students on the ideas that interest them.

WRITING PROCESS

1. PREWRITING

Guide students through the explanation of Prewriting, pointing out that Prewriting is the stage in which writers choose a topic and gather ideas and information to use in their writing.

MODELING THE WRITING PROCESS

If you feel students need instruction before they begin, you may wish to model this stage of the process. Tell students you want to find a topic for a personal narrative. Have students help you begin to work through the thinking process by naming memorable animals that they have met. List four or five animals on the chalkboard or use *Writing Process Transparency 1*. Then have students tell where and when they saw each animal and what happened during each encounter.

Let students hear how you might go about selecting the best topic for a personal narrative. Review the "Animal Encounters" list you made, giving reasons why each encounter may or may not be a good topic to write about. Encourage students to help you. (Possible discussion: Parrots are funny and unusual animals. My audience might enjoy learning about how a parrot frightened me. Watching a shark at the aquarium one day might not provide enough activity for a narrative.) Circle the name of the animal that everyone agrees would make the best topic.

Writing Process Transparency 1*

Animals, Animals, Animals	
Animal	Where Seen/What Happened
1. squirrel	park/I gave it nuts to eat.
2. horse	farm/I petted it and talked to it.
3. parrot	friend's house/It frightened me. Then it made me laugh.
4. shark	aquarium/I watched it swim in its tank.

WRITING PROCESS

Choose Your Strategy   Before inviting students to choose a prewriting strategy that will help them gather information for their personal narratives, guide them through the explanations of both strategies. Then have students choose a strategy they feel will help them get started.

As a variation on the first strategy, a Conversation, you may suggest that students who are listening to a partner's story might write down details about the story and give them to their partners. For the second strategy, an Observation Chart, you may wish to have students read aloud their charts in small groups in order to compare what they wrote.

You may wish to remind students that they have learned about using an Observation Chart as a strategy for observing in the Critical Thinking lesson on pages 22–23.

Choose Your Strategy ◆ Here are two strategies that could help you remember details about your animal. Read both. Then decide which strategy you will use.

PREWRITING IDEAS

CHOICE ONE

A Conversation

One way to recall details is to have a conversation with a partner. Tell each other a story about your experience with an animal. Be sure that you tell the complete story about what happened. After your conversation, jot down the details you told.

Model

riding my bike home
saw a deer near bushes
Deer: big, beautiful,
smooth hide, tan,
stared at me
Me: excited, held my
breath

CHOICE TWO

An Observation Chart

An observation chart is another way to gather details. First, visualize the animal. Let your experience with it run like a movie in your mind. What did you see? What did you hear? How did you feel? Write the details.

Model

Meeting a Deer	
What I Saw	a doe, sleek hide, huge eyes, still as a statue
What I Heard	a faint rustling, then silence
What I Felt	surprised, excited, as if in a dream

PROCESS CHECK   At the completion of the Prewriting stage, students should be able to answer *yes* to these questions:
- Do I have a topic I like for a personal narrative?
- Do I have prewriting notes or a chart on which I have written details for my article?

Teacher to Teacher

Use your own experiences to help students get started in developing a topic. You might say, for instance, "Once, when I was out in the wind, my hat blew off. I had to chase it. What has happened to you on a windy day?" Then encourage students to discuss their experiences. You might wish to write their contributions on the chalkboard to serve as a pool of ideas and images. By nudging students' memories and imaginations you can help them create imagery for their own writing.

Writing

Place your conversation notes or observation chart in front of you. Then begin to write your personal narrative. Here are ways to begin.

♦ Did I ever tell you about the time I found a _____?
♦ I couldn't believe my eyes when I saw the _____.
♦ "Be careful of stray animals," Mom told me, but _____.

Remember that a story includes characters, a plot, and a setting. In your narrative, you and the animal will be characters. The plot will be what happened. The setting will be where it happened. Use *I* and *me* for first person point of view.

The main thing is to keep writing till you finish your story. Don't worry about mistakes. You can correct them later.

Sample First Draft ♦

I couldn't believe my eyes! I had taken a new shortcut, and suddenly I found a deer munching leafs. It had a smooth, tan hide and was taller than my bike. It was eating from the tall bushes next to the parking lot. I rode my bike closer. The deer looked up.

I said, "hello, you beautiful creature." I expected the deer to bolt, but it didn't it just stared at me with its Large brown eyes. Quietly, I got off my bike and placed it on the ground. When I looked up, the deer was gone.

WRITING PROCESS: Personal Narrative 〈41〉

2. WRITING

Before students write their first drafts, guide them through the explanation of Writing, emphasizing that at this stage the most important task is to get all their ideas on paper.

Help students include ideas in their narratives that describe what they thought and felt during their encounter with the animal.

MODELING THE WRITING PROCESS

If you feel students need instruction before they begin this stage of the process, you may wish to ask them to think about the topic circled on *Writing Process Transparency 1*. Have them help you create detail sentences that might be used in a personal narrative about that topic. Remind students that a personal narrative includes details about setting, plot, and character. Write the detail sentences on the chalkboard or on *Writing Process Transparency 2*. Then read aloud what you wrote and work with students to create a sentence that might be used to begin the narrative (e.g., *Something unusual happened to me at my friend's house. It was the strangest animal I have ever seen. Did I ever tell you about the time I was frightened by my friend's parrot?*)

Writing Process Transparency 2*

Writing a Personal Narrative
Setting: I was at my friend's house. The house was very still and quiet. My friend was upstairs.
Plot: I heard someone say hello. I was frightened. The voice came from my friend's parrot.
Character: The parrot was green. It had a long tail and a large beak. It had a loud, gruff voice.

PROCESS CHECK At the completion of the Writing stage, students should be able to answer *yes* to these questions:
• Do I have a complete first draft?
• Have I included details about character, plot, and setting?
• Have I used *I* and *me* to tell a first-person point of view?

*Possible responses are overprinted on this reduced facsimile only. Use Writing Process Transparencies *to interact with your students on the ideas that interest them.*

3. REVISING

Help students understand that during Revising writers make their drafts communicate ideas more clearly and effectively to an audience. During Revising writers are not to concern themselves with errors in spelling, capitalization, and punctuation; instead they should concentrate on the quality and effectiveness of their ideas.

I D E A B A N K

Grammar Connection

If you started the unit with Part 2, you may wish to include grammar instruction at this time.

Option 1 ◆ If you wish to begin grammar instruction related to the Grammar Check in this lesson, then refer to Part 1 of this unit.

Option 2 ◆ If you wish to begin grammar instruction *not* related to the Grammar Check in this lesson, then refer to the end-of-book Glossary or Index.

First Read to Yourself You may wish to emphasize that students need not make actual changes during the first reading. This is a time to think about whether their writing is clear and says what they mean it to say.

Remind students to check to make sure that they have used the words *I* and *me* to tell their stories. Ask whether they have included their thoughts and feelings in their narratives.

Then Share with a Partner Suggest that writers' partners offer three responses, at least one positive, and that they accompany any critical responses with suggestions for improvement. Be sure writers ask the Focus question: *Did you understand how I felt about the experience?*

Emphasize that partners need to be constructive and say what they really think. Point out that even though students are to be honest about their opinions, they should make their comments in a sensitive way. Then explain to writers that they should use their partners' suggestions only if they feel the suggestions will help improve their writing.

3 Revising

Revising is making changes to improve your writing. How can you know if you need to make changes? Here is a strategy that may help you decide.

REVISING IDEA

FIRST   Read to Yourself

Review your purpose. Did you write a personal narrative about an experience with an animal? Think about your audience. Will they see what you saw? Hear what you heard? Feel what you felt? Decide which part of your story you like best.

Focus: Have you used first person point of view to make your readers see your story through your eyes?

THEN   Share with a Partner

Ask a classmate to be your first audience. Read your narrative aloud and ask for honest opinions. Below are some guidelines that may help you both.

The Writer

Guidelines: Read aloud to your partner slowly and clearly. Listen to your partner, then make the changes *you* think are important.

Sample questions:
• Did you understand what happened?
• **Focus question:** Did you understand how I felt about the experience?

The Writer's Partner

Guidelines: Be honest. Say what you really think. Be kind. Make your comments politely.

Sample responses:
• What did you do when ____?
• How did you feel when ____?

---

42   WRITING PROCESS: Personal Narrative

Teacher to Teacher

Make sure that young writers write regularly, at least three or four times a week, and that they have enough time to become involved in the process. Organize specific writing sessions by starting with group brainstorming or clustering. As students begin their first drafts, circulate around the room and confer with those who need help. Create periodic publishing sessions in which students who are ready may share their work.

WRITING AS A RECURSIVE PROCESS

Connecting Grammar to the Writing Process

Writing is a recursive process. In other words, good writers will often go back and forth among steps. Depending on the individual styles of your students, some may choose to correct grammar at Step Three, Revising; others may prefer to fix grammar or usage errors at Step Four, Proofreading. Ideally, this should be a decision made by the writer. Remind students, however, that once they have completed their proofreading, all the grammar errors should be corrected.

Revising Model ◆ Look at this sample that is being revised.
The marks show the changes the writer wants to make.

Revising Marks

cross out	—
add	∧
move	↻

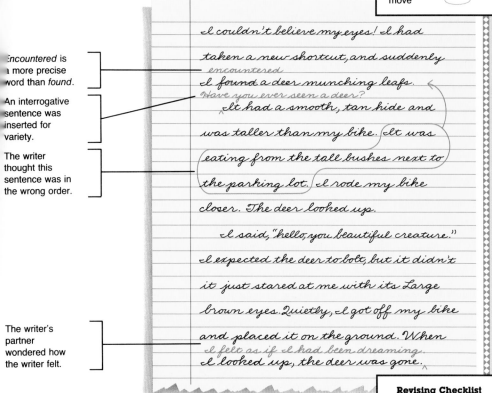

Encountered is a more precise word than *found*.

An interrogative sentence was inserted for variety.

The writer thought this sentence was in the wrong order.

The writer's partner wondered how the writer felt.

I couldn't believe my eyes! I had taken a new shortcut, and suddenly
~~I found~~ a deer munching leafs. *encountered*
Have you ever seen a deer?
It had a smooth, tan hide and was taller than my bike. It was eating from the tall bushes next to the parking lot. I rode my bike closer. The deer looked up.
I said, "hello, you beautiful creature."
I expected the deer to bolt, but it didn't it just stared at me with its Large brown eyes. Quietly, I got off my bike and placed it on the ground. When *I felt as if I had been dreaming.* I looked up, the deer was gone.

Read the revised draft above the way the writer has decided it *should* be. Then revise your own personal narrative.

Revising Checklist

☐ **Purpose:** Did I write a personal narrative about my experience with an animal?

☐ **Audience:** Will my classmates understand what happened and how I felt?

☐ **Focus:** Did I use first person point of view?

Grammar Check ◆ Your writing may be more interesting if you use interrogative, imperative, or exclamatory sentences for variety.

Word Choice ◆ Do you want to use a more precise word for a word like *found*? A thesaurus can help you improve your word choice.

WRITING PROCESS: Personal Narrative ◇ 43

Revising Model Guide students through the model, noting the reasons for changes and the revision marks. Point out to students that on the model the revising marks are in blue. Encourage the class to discuss the changes in the model. Ask them to consider whether or not the changes made the writing clearer so that the reader will now understand what happened and how the writer felt.

MODELING THE WRITING PROCESS

If you feel students need instruction before they begin this stage of the process, you may wish to present *Writing Process Transparency 3*. Have students read the draft silently, or have a volunteer read it aloud. Then ask whether anything needs to be changed. Work through the thinking process to help students give reasons for the changes. Have them tell you how to mark the changes on the draft. (Students might add a sentence to explain more fully how the writer felt, change sentence order in the second paragraph for clarity, add a more precise word such as *beak,* and add an interrogative sentence for variety.) Remind students that at this time they are revising for meaning. They will correct spelling and punctuation later when they proofread.

Writing Process Transparency 3*

Strange Noises

Something unusual happened to me at my freind's house. I was waiting for my freind, Jim, to come *It made me feel uneasy.* downstairs His house was so still and quiet! Suddenly a loud, gruff voice called out, "Hello! Hello!" I jumped. *There was* "Who's there?" I asked. no answer. I peeked into the Kitchen. It shook its long tail feathers and opened its *beak* large mouth. There in a cage sat a brite green parrot. "Hello!" it squawked then I began to laff . *Who would have thought a parrot could sound so frightening?*

PROCESS CHECK At the completion of the Revising stage, students should be able to answer *yes* to the following questions:
• Do I have a complete draft with revising marks that show changes I plan to make?
• Has my draft been reviewed by another writer?

Possible responses are overprinted on this reduced facsimile only. Use Writing Process Transparencies *to interact with your students on the ideas that interest them.*

4. PROOFREADING

Guide students through the explanation of proofreading and review the Proofreading Model. Point out to students that on the model the proofreading marks are in red. Tell them that proofreading helps to eliminate errors such as incorrect spelling or run-on sentences that may distract or confuse their readers.

Review the Proofreading Strategy, Proofreading Marks, and the Proofreading Checklist with students. Then invite students to use the checklist and proofread their own personal narratives.

MODELING THE WRITING PROCESS

If you feel students need instruction before they begin this stage of the process, you may wish to use *Writing Process Transparency 4*. Create a "window" by cutting a piece of paper as directed on textbook page 44. Go through the transparency word by word, having students identify words they think are misspelled.

Then have volunteers read each item on the Proofreading Checklist and answer the question or suggest a correction. Mark students' corrections on the transparency.

Writing Process Transparency 4*

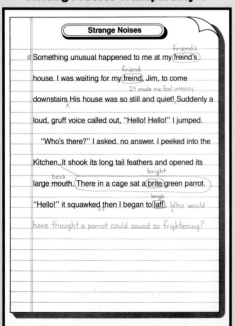

---

4 Proofreading

Proofreading is looking for and fixing errors.

Proofreading Model ◆ Here is the sample draft of the narrative. Notice that red proofreading marks have been added.

Proofreading Marks	
capital letter	=
small letter	/
indent paragraph	¶
check spelling	⬭

I couldn't believe my eyes! I had taken a new shortcut, and suddenly encountered I found a deer munching leafs. Have you ever seen a deer? It had a smooth, tan hide and was taller than my bike. It was eating from the tall bushes next to the parking lot. I rode my bike closer. The deer looked up.

I said, "hello, you beautiful creature." I expected the deer to bolt, but it didn't, it just stared at me with its Large brown eyes. Quietly, I got off my bike and placed it on the ground. When I felt as if I had been dreaming. I looked up, the deer was gone.

Proofreading Checklist

- ☐ Did I spell words correctly?
- ☐ Did I indent paragraphs?
- ☐ Did I use capital letters correctly?
- ☐ Did I use correct marks at the end of sentences?
- ☐ Did I use my best handwriting?

PROOFREADING IDEA

Spelling Check

To catch spelling errors, try reading through a window. Cut a small rectangle in the middle of a piece of paper. Read one word at a time as you move the window along your paper.

Now proofread your personal narrative, add a title, and make a neat copy.

44   WRITING PROCESS: Personal Narrative

PROCESS CHECK At the completion of the Proofreading stage, students should be able to answer *yes* to the following questions:
- Do I have a complete draft with proofreading marks that show changes I plan to make?
- Have I used the proofreading marks shown in the lesson?

Possible responses are overprinted on this reduced facsimile only. Use Writing Process Transparencies *to interact with your students on the ideas that interest them.*

EVALUATION PROGRAM

See Evaluation and Testing Program, pp. C1–C8.

Masters are available for the following:
  Self Evaluation Checklist
  Personal Goals for Writing
  Peer Response
  Teacher Response

  Holistic Evaluation Guides
  Analytic Evaluation Guides

Publishing

Publishing is sharing your writing with others. Try one of the ideas below for sharing your personal narrative.

Meeting a Deer

I couldn't believe my eyes! I had taken a new shortcut, and suddenly I encountered a deer munching leaves. It was eating from the tall bushes next to the parking lot. Have you ever seen a deer? It had a smooth, tan hide and was taller than my bike. I rode my bike closer. The deer looked up. I said, "Hello, you beautiful creature." I expected the deer to bolt, but it didn't. It just stared at me with its large brown eyes. Quietly, I got off my bike and placed it on the ground. When I looked up, the deer was gone. I felt as if I had been dreaming.

PUBLISHING IDEAS

Share Aloud	Share in Writing
Draw pictures of the animals featured in your personal narratives. Mount them on a bulletin board. Read your personal narratives aloud. Ask your classmates to identify the picture that matches your story.	Arrange netting across one wall. Mount your narratives on the story net. Place small pieces of paper and paper clips near the netting. Invite readers to write comments and clip their notes to the narratives.

WRITING PROCESS: Personal Narrative ◁ 45 ▷

IDEA BANK

Spelling and Mechanics Connection

You may wish to include spelling or mechanics at this time.

Spelling ◆ If you wish to include spelling instruction with this lesson, then refer to the Spelling Guide on pages 490–492, the Index, or the *Spelling Connection* booklet.

Mechanics ◆ If you wish to include mechanics instruction with this lesson, then refer to the Glossary, the Index, or the *Revising and Proofreading Transparencies.*

5. PUBLISHING

Oral Sharing If students choose to share their writing orally, invite the class to discuss each personal narrative after it is read aloud. Encourage students to make constructive, positive comments and to explain why they feel as they do.

Written Sharing If students choose to share their writing by displaying it, set aside a specific time when students may read each other's narratives and respond to them. You also may wish to have the class invite other students or parents to their classroom to read the personal narratives on display.

Holistic Evaluation Guidelines

A personal narrative of **average** quality will:
. tell what happened to the writer during an encounter with an animal
. express the writer's feelings
. recall events in an orderly manner

A personal narrative of **above-average** quality may:
. use language that is more specific
. begin or end in an unusual way

A personal narrative of **below-average** quality may:
. have events presented illogically
. give scanty or incomplete information

PROCESS CHECK At the completion of the Publishing stage, students should be able to answer *yes* to these questions:
• Have I shared my writing with an audience?
• Have readers shared reactions with me?
• Have I thought about what I especially liked in this writing? Or about what was particularly difficult?
• Have I thought about what I would like to work on the next time I write?

Encourage students to keep a log or journal of their own and their readers' reactions.

Curriculum Connection

OBJECTIVES
To practice a thinking strategy for writing across the curriculum
To write a journal entry

Writing Across the Curriculum

Explain to students that scientists observe and then record in an organized way what they see. Tell students they will use an observation chart to help them find out and write about an animal.

You may wish to remind students that they have used an observation chart as a strategy for narrating in the Critical Thinking lesson, in their response to the literature selection, and in the Writing Process lesson.

Writing to Learn

To help students get started, have them name some animals that would be interesting to find out about. Write the names on the chalkboard.

> You may wish to have students with limited English proficiency describe animals that interest them and provide the animals' English names.

Help students use their science books or books from their classroom library to find information about the animals of their choice.

Writing in Your Journal

When they have finished writing, have students read their earlier journal entries. Encourage them to discuss what they have learned about the theme and to observe how their writing has changed or improved.

Remind students that their journals have many purposes. Besides paragraphs and stories, they can write questions, story ideas, or thoughts and reflections on a subject. Journals also may be used to support student self-evaluation throughout the program.

Writing Across the Curriculum Science

In this unit you wrote about a personal encounter with an animal. Scientists do that, too. Scientists first learn about an animal by observing it. Then they are able to write about what they saw. You can use an observation chart when you are studying about an animal in a class.

Writing to Learn

Think and Observe ◆ Find information about an animal that interests you in your science book. Make an observation chart about the animal based on the information you read. Record details about the animal's color, size, or shape. Record other information such as number of legs, body covering, or special abilities.

Observation Chart

Write ◆ Use the information from your chart to write about the animal. Tell whether you would like to see one someday, or if you would like one for a pet.

Writing in Your Journal

In the Writer's Warm-up you wrote about an aspect of farm life that interested you. Throughout this unit you've learned a lot more about foxes and other animals. You've also learned about how farms work. Browse back through the pages. What did you learn that you didn't know about before? Choose an aspect of farm life you learned about in this unit and write about it in your journal.

ESSENTIAL LANGUAGE SKILLS
This lesson provides opportunities to:

LISTENING ◆ employ active listening in a variety of situations ◆ follow the logical organization of an oral presentation

SPEAKING ◆ express ideas clearly and effectively ◆ contribute to class and small group discussions

READING ◆ locate and utilize desired information in reference sources ◆ evaluate and make judgments ◆ use graphic sources for information, such as lists, tables, charts, graphs ◆ select books for individual needs and interests

WRITING ◆ adapt information to accomplish a specific purpose with a particular audience ◆ expand topics by collecting information from a variety of sources ◆ keep journals, logs, or notebooks to express feelings, record ideas, discover new knowledge, and free the imagination

LANGUAGE ◆ use language for describing ◆ use the fundamentals of grammar, punctuation, and spelling

Read More About It

The Summer of the Swans *by Betsy Byars*
Betsy Byars has given us many stories just as good as *The Midnight Fox*. In this book, Sarah tells us about her feelings for her retarded brother, Peter.

Newbery Award

Arthur, For the Very First Time
by Patricia MacLachlan
Arthur learns a lot about handling grownups the summer he spends on a farm. His Great Aunt Elda and his Great Uncle Wrisby seem to live in a scattered way.

Sounder *by William Armstrong*
The dog Sounder had the neck and shoulders of a bulldog and the melodious bay of a hound. The boy loved the dog almost as much as he loved his father. When the sheriff's shotgun wounds Sounder, the dog crawls off and bays no more.

Newbery Award

Book Report Idea Postcard

Did you ever read a story that took you right along for the ride? The next time you give a book report, give it as though you were along for the ride.

Create a Giant Postcard ◆ On
one side, draw a picture of a scene from the story. On the other side, tell about the story as though you were there. Address the postcard to other readers, and be sure to tell why you liked the "trip."

I will never forget the day I woke up on the beach of a desert island. How had I gotten there? Who were these strange, mean-looking people coming toward me? Read about my adventures in *The First Two Lives of Lukas-Kasha* by Lloyd Alexander.

The Fifth...
Central Sch...
234 Main...
Grand Br...

Books to Enjoy **47**

WORLD OF **BOOKS**
CLASSROOM LIBRARIE**S**
is a collection of high-quality children's literature available with this program.

Books
to Enjoy

OBJECTIVES
To appreciate a variety of literature
To share a book through a creative activity

Read More About It
Call students' attention to Read More About It and discuss theme-related books. Point out that the books listed here contain stories about farm life and about children's relationships with animals. Encourage students to mention other titles that deal with these topics. Encourage students to examine pictures and jacket illustrations of books in the classroom to find books they will enjoy reading.

Book Report Idea
You may wish to have students use the book report form provided in the back of their textbook. Book Report Idea presents a lively alternative way for interested students to share books they have read.

You may wish to share the reports with the class or in small groups. Have students post their "postcards" with the picture side showing. Students may guess about characters and events from a "postcard" picture, and then turn the card to find out more about the book from the reader who wrote the report.

Integrated Language Arts Project
The Integrated Language Arts Project on pages T512–T513 may be used with this unit.

REVIEW OR TEST
You may wish to use the Unit Review as a review of the unit skills before administering the Unit Posttest, or you may wish to use the Unit Review in lieu of the Unit Posttest.

REVIEW PROCEDURES
The lesson pages that are reviewed are listed beside the heading of each segment. You may wish to choose one of the procedures listed below for using the pages with the Unit Review exercises.

Review/Evaluate Have students restudy the lesson pages before doing the Unit Review exercises.

Open-Book Review Allow students to refer to the lesson pages if they need to while they are doing the Unit Review exercises.

Evaluate/Review Have students do the Unit Review exercises, then turn to the lesson pages to restudy concepts for which incorrect responses are given.

ADDITIONAL REVIEW AND PRACTICE
For additional review and practice, turn to the Extra Practice pages at the end of the unit.

UNIT REVIEW

Unit 1

Sentences   *Pages 6–15*

A. Write each sentence. Then write *declarative, interrogative, imperative,* or *exclamatory* to show what kind of sentence it is.

   1. Give me that book. *imperative*
   2. How cold it is today! *exclamatory*
   3. Will I see you at the party? *interrogative*
   4. John rarely watches television. *declarative*
   5. Lucy is going to the gym. *declarative*
   6. Is Frank catching a cold? *interrogative*
   7. That girl can really run! *exclamatory*
   8. Please help me with this problem. *imperative*
   9. Harriet is my second cousin. *declarative*
  10. Did Linda paint that picture? *interrogative*

B. Write each sentence. Underline the complete subject once. Underline the complete predicate twice.

  11. Charles is taking voice lessons.
  12. The girl in the television commercial wore a green dress.
  13. My father likes mystery stories.
  14. The boy next door won a prize.
  15. Diana Sims works here after school.
  16. The tall, blond man is my uncle.
  17. The white cat had kittens.
  18. Our history class wrote a play about the Revolutionary War.
  19. The voters elected a new mayor.
  20. Paul and I played golf on Friday.

C. Write the simple subject of each sentence. Write (*You*) if the subject is understood.

  21. My visit to the city was wonderful.
  22. Follow these directions carefully. *(You)*
  23. The tiny bird chirped merrily.
  24. Take me to the zoo with you. *(You)*
  25. Nancy is a marvelous storyteller.
  26. That portrait is by Rembrandt.
  27. Bring the coleslaw to the picnic. *(You)*
  28. Carry this heavy package, please. *(You)*
  29. A shiny new bicycle sped past us.

D. Write the simple predicate of each sentence.

  30. We are going to a movie.
  31. Cynthia has won the last two races.
  32. Four dogs were running in the yard.
  33. The puppy barked at the stranger.
  34. A leaf fluttered to the ground.
  35. Lifeguards have saved many lives on this beach.
  36. An elderly man was humming a tune.
  37. The river will overflow its banks.
  38. The library closes in five minutes.

Thesaurus   *pages 16–17*

E. Read the thesaurus entry. Then answer each question.

enormous (adj)—larger than normal in size or force. The enormous cat approached the house.
gigantic—huge in size
mammoth—huge in size and bulk
ANTONYMS: tiny, puny

  39. What are two synonyms for *enormous?* gigantic, mammoth
  40. What are two antonyms for *enormous?* tiny, puny

48   Unit Review

Character, Setting, and Plot
pages 32–33

F. Read the following paragraph. Then write answers to the questions.

Mark Twain's *The Adventures of Tom Sawyer* is about a young boy growing up in a small town. Tom's Aunt Polly assigns him the chore of "whitewashing" a fence—painting it white. Tom hates this chore. Even so, he makes a start at it. Another boy comes along and teases Tom for having to do the job. Tom manages to convince his friend that whitewashing a fence is an honor and a privilege. The other boy asks if he can do some of the work. Tom pretends to be unwilling but lets his friend do the whitewashing. Other boys come along. Each of them gets the "privilege" of whitewashing the fence. By the end of the day, the job is done. Tom has performed almost none of the work himself. Even more, he has been able to persuade his friends to pay for the privilege. He is richer after the chore is finished than when it began.

(Wording of certain answers may vary.)

41. Where does the story take place? In a small town

42. Who is the main character of the story? Tom Sawyer

43. Who are the other characters? Tom's Aunt Polly and the other boys

44. How does the story begin? Aunt Polly tells Tom to paint the fence.

45. What happens in the middle of the story? Tom talks the other boys into painting the fence for him.

46. How does the story end? Tom has done little of the work himself.

47. What do you learn about the main character? Tom is very clever and persuasive.

48. What do you learn about the other characters? They are easily persuaded.

Quotations *pages 34–35*

G. Write each sentence correctly. Add quotation marks where they belong. Add capital letters and punctuation marks where they are needed.

49. "Wow, Joe exclaimed. That is certainly a surprise!"

50. Aunt Betty asked, What did you do in school today?"

51. "Look out, Perry yelled. Here they come again!"

52. "I understand," said Mrs. Torres, "what you are trying to say."

53. "I think I know the answer," Stu said thoughtfully.

54. "Why not, Bernice suggested, bring your little brother to the picnic?"

55. "Golly, Shirley said. That was fun!"

56. My mother warned, Wipe your feet before you come into the house."

57. "We all know," said Faith, how the movie ends."

58. "If you try, Mr. Bacon urged, I know you will do a good job."

59. "Can someone please help me carry these books? asked Frank.

60. Donna whispered, This place frightens me."

61. "Watch out, yelled Melvin. That tree is about to fall!"

62. "I know," said Kathy, "that this path is the shortest way home."

63. "It's much faster than the main road," agreed her brother Ernie.

64. "Look, cried Kathy. There's a blue jay!"

65. "Is that a woodpecker up in that tree?" asked Ernie.

66. "I believe it is, answered his big sister.

Unit Review **49**

Language Puzzlers

Unit
1

OBJECTIVES
To solve language puzzles based on skills taught in the unit

ANSWERS

Sports Chain
1. annoyed
2. sent
3. owes or owed
4. Erase
5. outran (preceding subject: *You*)
6. answered
7. checked
8. returned
9. arrived
10. amazed

Secret Messages
We have found the treasure box. Wait until you see what is in it! Can you get here tonight? Do not tell anyone.

LANGUAGE PUZZLERS
Unit 1 Challenge

Sports Chain

The clue to this sports puzzle is a chain of letters. The last two letters of each subject are the first two letters of the verb in the following sentence. Also, the last two letters of the subject in the last sentence are the first two letters of the verb in the first sentence. (Hint: Remember that *You* is the understood subject of an imperative sentence.)

1. The crowd's noise _ _ _ _ _ _ _ the golfers.
2. The new snow _ _ _ _ skiers to the slopes.
3. My brother _ _ _ _ me a new pair of sneakers.
4. _ _ _ _ _ the scoreboard.
5. Joan _ _ _ _ _ _ the other racers.
6. The coach _ _ _ _ _ _ _ _ my question sharply.
7. The umpire _ _ _ _ _ _ _ the lineup.
8. The tennis star _ _ _ _ _ _ _ _ the serve.
9. The visiting team _ _ _ _ _ _ _ this morning.
10. The team captain's plan _ _ _ _ _ _ us.

Secret Messages

Here is a system for sending secret messages. First a sentence is broken into five-letter groups.

Pat arrives by train on Monday.
Patar / rives / bytra / inonM / onday.

Then each group is written backward without punctuation or capitalization.

ratap sevir artyb mnoni yadno

Write the secret message hidden in the four lines below. (Hint: Each line is a sentence.) Be sure to insert punctuation and capital letters.

vahew nuofe tehtd usaer xober
utiaw ylitn eesuo itahw tinis
oynac htegu otere thgin
tonod allet enoyn

50 Language Puzzlers

50

Unit 1 Extra Practice

1 Writing Sentences
p. 4

A. Write *sentence* or *not a sentence* for each group of words below.

1. Writing began with pictures.
2. On rocks and on the walls of caves.
3. Ancient people recorded many things.
4. Drew pictures of people and animals.
5. Three thousand years ago in the Middle East.
6. Scratched lines on wet clay.
7. This writing is called cuneiform.
8. During that time in Egypt, only certain people were allowed to write.
9. Drawn on papyrus or carved on stone.
10. Chinese writing began as a kind of picture writing.
11. Scratched on bone, bronze, or stone.
12. Changed very little in the last 3,000 years.
13. Today the Chinese write on paper with a brush and ink.
14. More than 40,000 separate signs are used in Chinese.
15. These signs are sometimes called pictographs.
16. Different pictographs for new words.
17. A difficult task for Chinese students.
18. The sign for *sun* behind the sign for *tree*.
19. This combination means "east."

B. Write the group of words in each pair that is a sentence.

20. **a.** Sitting in the library.
    b. Jana worked on her report every day.
21. **a.** She needed more pictures for her report.
    b. The librarian at the main desk.
22. **a.** After reading Jana's first draft.
    b. Over the weekend she made some changes.
23. **a.** Saw an A+ the top of her paper.
    b. Jana got an A+ on her report.
24. **a.** Jana's teacher put the report on the bulletin board.
    b. With slight changes and using more pictures.

Extra Practice **51**

OBJECTIVES
To practice skills taught in the unit

ANSWERS
Writing Sentences

A. 1. sentence
    2. not a sentence
    3. sentence
    4. not a sentence
    5. not a sentence
    6. not a sentence
    7. sentence
    8. sentence
    9. not a sentence
    10. sentence
    11. not a sentence
    12. not a sentence
    13. sentence
    14. sentence
    15. sentence
    16. not a sentence
    17. not a sentence
    18. not a sentence
    19. sentence

B. 20. **b.** Jana worked on her report every day.
   21. **a.** She needed more pictures for her report.
   22. **b.** Over the weekend she made some changes.
   23. **b.** Jana got an A+ on her report.
   24. **a.** Jana's teacher put the report on the bulletin board.

Extra Practice and Challenge
For those students who need additional grammar practice have them refer to these pages. **The practice exercises progress in difficulty from Easy to Average. Practice A is Easy. Practice B is Average.** Difficult concepts requiring more practice have additional Exercises C and D at the Average level.
We do not recommend these exercises for students who have mastered the skill in the basic lesson. Those students should do the **Challenge** word puzzles on page 50.

Extra Practice

Four Kinds of Sentences

A.
1. declarative
2. declarative
3. declarative
4. interrogative
5. declarative
6. interrogative
7. declarative
8. interrogative
9. declarative
10. interrogative
11. declarative
12. interrogative
13. declarative
14. interrogative
15. declarative
16. interrogative
17. declarative
18. declarative
19. interrogative

B.
20. How many Native American foods can you name?
21. Peppers, corn, and tomatoes were first grown in America.
22. Bananas are native to South America.
23. Are pineapples originally from Hawaii?
24. What did Europeans eat for Christmas dinner before 1492?
25. The turkey should be our national bird.
26. Is anything more American than pumpkin pie?
27. When were jack-o'-lanterns first made?
28. The colonists brought apples to America.
29. Did they bring blueberries, too?
30. Was Thomas Jefferson the first president to eat a tomato?

---

2 Four Kinds of Sentences
p.

A. Write each sentence. Then write *declarative* or *interrogative* to show what kind of sentence it is.

1. Many foods of today were first found in the New World.
2. Potatoes come from Peru.
3. Chocolate was a favorite food of the Aztecs in Mexico.
4. How many kinds of squash did Native Americans grow?
5. Wild rice is a special kind of plant.
6. Does anyone know the origin of the hot dog?
7. Yams were brought to America from Africa.
8. What kind of corn is used to make hominy?
9. Alligator pear is another name for avocado.
10. Where were peanuts first grown?
11. Spanish explorers brought peanuts to Africa and Spain in the sixteenth century.
12. Did you know that the peanut is a member of the pea fam[...]
13. Tomatoes were once thought to be poisonous.
14. Are the tomato and the potato related?
15. French gardeners grew potatoes for their blossoms.
16. When did people begin to eat vegetables that were found in the New World?
17. Corn and beans were eaten by the Pilgrims.
18. Peppers are called chilies by the people of Mexico.
19. What would pizza taste like without tomatoes?

B. Write each declarative and interrogative sentence. Begin the sentence correctly. Use correct punctuation at the end.

20. how many Native American foods can you name
21. peppers, corn, and tomatoes were first grown in America
22. bananas are native to South America
23. are pineapples originally from Hawaii
24. what did Europeans eat for Christmas dinner before 1492
25. the turkey should be our national bird
26. is anything more American than pumpkin pie
27. when were jack-o'-lanterns first made
28. the colonists brought apples to America
29. did they bring blueberries, too
30. was Thomas Jefferson the first president to eat a tomato

. Write each sentence. Then write *imperative* or *exclamatory* to show what kind of sentence it is.

31. Look at that strange mask.
32. What a great disguise that is!
33. You really fooled me!
34. Put your costume on quickly.
35. Please tie my shoes for me.
36. How dark it is outside!
37. Please help me fix this crown.
38. You look great in that helmet!
39. Try some of this yellow paint on your mask.
40. I can hardly wait for Alan's party to begin!
41. Meet me there at five o'clock.
42. Watch out for the tub of apples in the basement.
43. What a weird noise that is!
44. Don't be afraid to go down those stairs.
45. That is the most terrifying sound I have ever heard!
46. Let Paula go ahead of you then.
47. Absolutely nothing frightens her!
48. How strange everything looks down here!
49. Please wait for me to catch up with you.
50. Be careful in the dark.
51. How scary this is!

. Write each imperative and exclamatory sentence. Begin each sentence correctly. Use a period or an exclamation mark at the end.

52. that sounded just like an owl screeching
53. please be careful over there
54. sit down next to me on the bench
55. there's a cat peering in that window
56. reach into this bowl
57. something cold and slimy is in there
58. how awful it feels
59. please say what this is
60. turn the lights on
61. please look in the bowl
62. what a relief it is to see cold spaghetti
63. don't scare us again like that
64. how exciting this party is

Extra Practice

C. 31. imperative
32. exclamatory
33. exclamatory
34. imperative
35. imperative
36. exclamatory
37. imperative
38. exclamatory
39. imperative
40. exclamatory
41. imperative
42. imperative
43. exclamatory
44. imperative
45. exclamatory
46. imperative
47. exclamatory
48. exclamatory
49. imperative
50. imperative
51. exclamatory

D. 52. That sounded just like an owl screeching!
53. Please be careful over there.
54. Sit down next to me on the bench.
55. There's a cat peering in that window!
56. Reach into this bowl.
57. Something cold and slimy is in there!
58. How awful it feels!
59. Please say what this is.
60. Turn the lights on.
61. Please look in the bowl.
62. What a relief it is to see cold spaghetti!
63. Don't scare us again like that!
64. How exciting this party is!

Extra Practice and Challenge

For those students who need additional grammar practice have them refer to these pages. **The practice exercises progress in difficulty from Easy to Average. Practice A is Easy. Practice B is Average.** Difficult concepts requiring more practice have additional Exercises C and D at the Average level.
We do not recommend these exercises for students who have mastered the skill in the basic lesson. Those students should do the **Challenge** word puzzles on page 50.

Complete Subjects and Complete Predicates

A. 1. Caves <u>may have been the first human dwellings</u>.
   2. <u>Simple mud houses</u> <u>were a later development</u>.
   3. <u>Castles of stone and iron</u> <u>kept off attackers</u>.
   4. <u>A houseboat</u> <u>provides shelter and transportation</u>.
   5. <u>The White House</u> <u>is a home as well as a national monument</u>.
   6. <u>Cave dwellers</u> <u>painted animal pictures on the walls of caves</u>.
   7. <u>Snow houses</u> <u>can be quite warm</u>.
   8. <u>The Pueblos of New Mexico</u> <u>built homes of clay</u>.
   9. <u>Settlers in Nebraska</u> <u>built sod houses</u>.
   10. <u>People in ancient Egypt</u> <u>lived in mud and brick houses</u>.
   11. <u>Tribes of wandering shepherds</u> <u>made tents of skin</u>.
   12. <u>Tepees</u> <u>sheltered Native Americans on the Great Plains</u>.
   13. <u>Glass houses</u> <u>make good use of solar energy</u>.
   14. <u>The dwelling place of the future</u> <u>may be a space station</u>.
   15. <u>Stone cottages with tile roofs</u> <u>are common in Ireland</u>.
   16. <u>Woven grass</u> <u>kept the rain out of Hawaiian homes long ago</u>.
   17. <u>A tree house</u> <u>is a temporary dwelling</u>.
   18. <u>Some people</u> <u>like to live in log houses</u>.

B. Answers will vary. The following are possible answers.
   19. The carpenter built two new doors.
   20. The attic is on the top floor.
   21. The house next door has just been painted.
   22. The old brick house needs a new roof.
   23. Jonah lives in a twelve-story building.
   24. Two new apartment houses were built on our street.
   25. Three bears lived in a cottage in the woods.
   26. The lighthouse stood on a rocky island.
   27. A log cabin is a place to live.
   28. Our neighbors live in a trailer home.

3 Complete Subjects and Complete Predicates

p. 8

A. Write each sentence. Underline the complete subject once. Underline the complete predicate twice.

   1. Caves may have been the first human dwellings.
   2. Simple mud houses were a later development.
   3. Castles of stone and iron kept off attackers.
   4. A houseboat provides shelter and transportation.
   5. The White House is a home as well as a national monume
   6. Cave dwellers painted animal pictures on the walls of cav
   7. Snow houses can be quite warm.
   8. The Pueblos of New Mexico built homes of clay.
   9. Settlers in Nebraska built sod houses.
   10. People in ancient Egypt lived in mud and brick houses.
   11. Tribes of wandering shepherds made tents of skin.
   12. Tepees sheltered Native Americans on the Great Plains.
   13. Glass houses make good use of solar energy.
   14. The dwelling place of the future may be a space station.
   15. Stone cottages with tile roofs are common in Ireland.
   16. Woven grass kept the rain out of Hawaiian homes long ago
   17. A tree house is a temporary dwelling.
   18. Some people like to live in log houses.

B. Add a complete subject or a complete predicate to each group of words below. Write the complete sentence.

   EXAMPLE: _____ were made of wood.
   ANSWER: The stairs were made of wood.

   19. The carpenter _____ .
   20. _____ is on the top floor.
   21. _____ has just been painted.
   22. The old brick house _____ .
   23. _____ lives in a twelve-story building.
   24. Two new apartment houses _____ .
   25. _____ lived in a cottage in the woods.
   26. _____ stood on a rocky island.
   27. A log cabin _____ .
   28. Our neighbors _____ .

Simple Subjects

p. 10

Read each sentence below. A line has been drawn between the complete subject and the complete predicate. Write the complete subject. Draw a line under the simple subject.

1. School | is very exciting this year.
2. Every school in town | has a computer.
3. My English class | goes to the computer lab twice a week.
4. Luís Ramos | used the computer today.
5. He | made this design.
6. Our whole class | was surprised.
7. A strange machine | sat on the desk.
8. The first lesson on the computer | was easy.
9. Leroy Johnson | showed us what to do.
10. Computers | can solve problems quickly.
11. Scientists | use special computers for difficult problems.
12. Ordinary people | can use computers easily.
13. Every computer | has a memory.
14. Information | is stored in the memory.
15. The computer's memory | contains instructions.
16. The instructions | are in a special language.
17. The words in this language | look like English.
18. Some meanings | are different, though.
19. Special commands | tell the computer when to count.
20. A touch of the finger | stops the machine.

B. Write the simple subject of each sentence.

21. This button turns on the machine.
22. An arrow on the screen lights up.
23. The keys on the right make the arrow move.
24. A student types letters on the keyboard.
25. Words appear on the screen.
26. Emma's friends in the class want to work with the computer.
27. The class uses the computer for writing.
28. Some programs will correct misspelled words.
29. Two students draw pictures with the computer.
30. The computer in Mrs. Walker's class can talk.
31. Sarah Easton hopes to have a computer of her own.
32. My brother uses a computer in his college classes.

Extra Practice **55**

Simple Subjects

A.
1. <u>School</u>
2. Every <u>school</u> in town
3. My English <u>class</u>
4. <u>Luís Ramos</u>
5. <u>He</u>
6. Our whole <u>class</u>
7. A strange <u>machine</u>
8. The first <u>lesson</u> on the computer
9. <u>Leroy Johnson</u>
10. <u>Computers</u>
11. <u>Scientists</u>
12. Ordinary <u>people</u>
13. Every <u>computer</u>
14. <u>Information</u>
15. The computer's <u>memory</u>
16. The <u>instructions</u>
17. The <u>words</u> in this language
18. Some <u>meanings</u>
19. Special <u>commands</u>
20. A <u>touch</u> of the finger

B.
21. button
22. arrow
23. keys
24. student
25. Words
26. friends
27. class
28. programs
29. students
30. computer
31. Sarah Easton
32. brother

Extra Practice and Challenge

For those students who need additional grammar practice have them refer to these pages. **The practice exercises progress in difficulty from Easy to Average. Practice A is Easy. Practice B is Average.** Difficult concepts requiring more practice have additional Exercises C and D at the Average level.
We do not recommend these exercises for students who have mastered the skill in the basic lesson. Those students should do the **Challenge** word puzzles on page 50.

Extra Practice

p. 12

Simple Predicates

A.
1. <u>bounce</u>
2. <u>played</u> ringball
3. <u>was throwing</u> mostly fastballs
4. <u>had lost</u> most of its air
5. <u>was invented</u> in Scotland
6. <u>lost</u> his glasses
7. <u>practices</u> every day for six hours
8. <u>has made</u> three fouls in just the first half of the game
9. <u>is playing</u> again this year
10. <u>are played</u> today
11. <u>develop</u> skills for daily use
12. <u>is growing</u> more popular than ever
13. <u>requires</u> speed and practice
14. <u>teach</u> confidence to sailors and swimmers
15. <u>cools</u> the body
16. <u>has saved</u> many lives
17. <u>makes</u> fingers nimble
18. <u>helps</u> your heart and lungs
19. <u>have proved</u> useful in many ways

B.
20. has made
21. had called
22. threw
23. was trying
24. has broken
25. scored
26. prevented
27. cleared
28. won
29. likes
30. competes

5 Simple Predicates

A. Read each sentence below. A line has been drawn between the complete subject and the complete predicate. Write each complete predicate. Draw a line under the simple predicate.

1. Balls | bounce.
2. The Aztecs | played ringball.
3. The pitcher, a left-hander, | was throwing mostly fastballs.
4. The soccer ball in the garage | had lost most of its air.
5. The game of golf | was invented in Scotland.
6. The surprised umpire | lost his glasses.
7. Sally Jo, a champion rodeo rider, | practices every day for six hours.
8. The player in the red shirt | has made three fouls in just the first half of the game.
9. The winner of last year's prize | is playing again this year.
10. Many different sports | are played today.
11. Some sports | develop skills for daily use.
12. Soccer | is growing more popular than ever.
13. Baseball | requires speed and practice.
14. Water sports | teach confidence to sailors and swimmers.
15. A swim on a hot day | cools the body.
16. The ability to float | has saved many lives.
17. Practice with jacks | makes fingers nimble.
18. Exercise in the open air | helps your heart and lungs.
19. Sports | have proved useful in many ways.

B. Write the simple predicate of each sentence.

20. Our team has made another touchdown.
21. The quarterback had called a new play.
22. The new shortstop threw the ball to second.
23. She was trying for a double play.
24. Ellen, our best hitter, has broken her wrist.
25. Julio scored several goals a game.
26. The great goalie prevented the other team from scoring.
27. The large chestnut horse cleared the first fence easily.
28. Marcy Jackson, a new young rider, won the blue ribbon.
29. Lee likes water sports.
30. He competes in swimming races.

Subjects in Imperative Sentences

p. 14

Write each sentence. Underline the simple subject. Write (*You*) if the subject is understood.

EXAMPLE: Start feeding in September.

ANSWER: (You) Start feeding in September.

1. A large red bird flew to the feeder.
2. Watch the birds from the window.
3. Fill the bird feeder every day.
4. The nuthatch walks down the side of the tree.
5. Mix peanut butter and oatmeal together.
6. Birds with short, stubby beaks crack seeds.
7. Throw stale bread covered with bacon grease on the ground.
8. One interesting hobby is bird-watching.
9. Birds of all kinds can be seen in the park.
10. Borrow a pair of field glasses.
11. Look for finches in the pine trees.
12. Your own backyard is a good place for bird-watching.
13. Robins look for worms in the ground.
14. A thrush in a nearby park brightens the day with song.
15. Get some books about birds from the library.
16. Ask the librarian for more information about birds.
17. Set up a bird-feeding station near the kitchen window.

B. Write each sentence. Then write *declarative* or *imperative* to show what kind of sentence it is. Underline the simple subject in each declarative sentence. Write (*You*) for each imperative sentence.

18. Different birds eat different kinds of food.
19. Supply a variety of foods.
20. The bright red cardinal likes sunflower seeds.
21. Mix fats with peanut butter.
22. Keep the squirrels away.
23. Hummingbirds will sip nectar and sugar water.
24. Put the food on the ground.
25. Some birds eat only from the ground.
26. A hungry jay will drive away other birds.

Extra Practice

Subjects in Imperative Sentences

A.
1. bird
2. (You)
3. (You)
4. nuthatch
5. (You)
6. Birds
7. (You)
8. hobby
9. Birds
10. (You)
11. (You)
12. backyard
13. Robins
14. thrush
15. (You)
16. (You)
17. (You)

B.
18. declarative, birds
19. imperative, (You)
20. declarative, cardinal
21. imperative, (You)
22. imperative, (You)
23. declarative, Hummingbirds
24. imperative, (You)
25. declarative, birds
26. declarative, jay

Extra Practice and Challenge

For those students who need additional grammar practice have them refer to these pages. **The practice exercises progress in difficulty from Easy to Average. Practice A is Easy. Practice B is Average.** Difficult concepts requiring more practice have additional Exercises C and D at the Average level. We do not recommend these exercises for students who have mastered the skill in the basic lesson. Those students should do the **Challenge** word puzzles on page 50.

UNIT 2

OVERVIEW

TWO-PART
flexibility

Unit 2
Overview

books
ON UNIT THEME

USING LANGUAGE TO INFORM

EASY

📖 **The Pennsylvania Dutch: Craftsmen and Farmers** by Eva Deutsch Costabel. Atheneum. The author introduces the reader to the life of a typical Pennsylvania Dutch farming family in colonial times.

📖 **The Basket Maker and the Spinner** by Beatrice Siegel. Walker. The ancient arts of basket weaving and spinning are described through the stories of a Native American and a colonial settler.

AVERAGE

📖 **Hammocks, Hassocks and Hideaways** by Timothy Fisher. Addison. This book gives instructions for making various items of furniture.

📖 **23 Varieties of Ethnic Art and How to Make Each One** by Jean and Cle Kinney. Atheneum. This guide explains the contributions to American culture of many different ethnic groups and provides instructions for making their folk art.

CHALLENGING

📖 **Dollmaker** by Kathryn Lasky. Scribner. Photographs and text illustrate the entire process—from mold to costuming—by which a master dollmaker of Boston makes a sculpted-head portrait doll.

📖 **The Long Ago Lake** by Marne Wilkins. Sierra. The author shares her childhood summers in the Wisconsin Lakes district and the nature lessons she and her family learned.

READ-ALOUDS

📖 **People Who Make Things: How American Craftsmen Live and Work** by Carolyn Meyer. Atheneum. Each of the eight chapters of this book presents a different craft and examines the lives of people who are currently practicing it.

📖 **My Journals and Sketchbooks** by Robinson Crusoe. Harcourt. This book presents Crusoe's record of survival as if it were written and illustrated by Crusoe.

UNIT TWO

USING LANGUAGE TO
INFORM

—— PART ONE ——

Unit Theme *Handicrafts*

Language Awareness Nouns

—— PART TWO ——

Literature "Handicrafts" by Patricia Fent Ross

A Reason for Writing Informing

Writing

IN YOUR JOURNAL

WRITER'S WARM-UP ◆ What do you know about handicrafts? Have you ever worked with clay to make a mug or a bowl? Perhaps you have woven a simple potholder or a place mat. Maybe you have carved a toy boat from soap or wood. You may have visited a crafts demonstration at a museum or a hobby shop. You might own a handmade object that you got as a gift. Write in your journal about handicrafts. Tell what you like about them and what makes them special.

start with
WRITING IN YOUR JOURNAL

Writers' Warm-up is designed to help students activate prior knowledge of the unit theme, "Handicrafts." Whether you begin instruction with Part 1 or Part 2, encourage students to focus attention on the illustration on page 58 of their textbooks. Encourage them to discuss what they see. Then have a volunteer read aloud the **Writers' Warm-up** on page 59. Have students write their thoughts in their journals. You may wish to tell them that they will refer to this writing in the first lesson of Part 1, in the Grammar-Writing Connection, and in the Curriculum Connection.

THEN START WITH
part 1

Language Awareness: Nouns Developmental lessons focus on the concept of nouns. Each lesson is carefully constructed not only to help students learn the concept well but also to help build interest and background knowledge for the thinking, reading, and writing they will do in Part 2. The last lesson in Part 1 is a vocabulary lesson with which students learn context clues. The Grammar-Writing Connection that follows serves as a bridge to Part 2, encouraging students to work together to apply their new language skills at the sentence level of writing.

...OR WITH
part 2

A Reason for Writing: Informing is the focus of Part 2. First, students learn a thinking strategy for informing. Then they read and respond to a selection of nonfiction on which they may model their writing. Developmental composition lessons, including "Directions," a speaking and listening lesson, all reflect the literature and culminate in the Writing Process lesson. There a "Grammar Check," a "Word Choice" hint, and proofreading strategies help you focus on single traits for remediation or instruction through the lessons in Part 1. The unit ends with Curriculum Connection and Books to Enjoy, which help students discover how their new skills apply to writing across the curriculum.

THEME BAR

CATEGORIES	Environments	Business/World of Work	Imagination	Communications/ Fine Arts	People	Science	Expressions	Social Studies
THEMES	UNIT 1 Farm Life	UNIT 2 Handicrafts	UNIT 3 Tall Tales	UNIT 4 The Visual Arts	UNIT 5 Lasting Impressions	UNIT 6 Volcanoes	UNIT 7 Nature	UNIT 8 Animal Habitats
PACING	1 month	1 month	1 month	1 month	1 month	1 month	1 month	1 month

Build background knowledge of the unit theme, "Handicrafts," by reading aloud this selection to your class.

A Girl in Old Ohio

from *Grandmother Brown's Hundred Years*

BY HARRIET CONNOR BROWN

We were always glad to get back to our own father's dear old home. Nowhere else did we have the same conveniences. We did most of our work there in the summer kitchen. That was where we had the big brick oven. We used to fire it twice a week and do a sight o' baking all at once. We'd make a hot fire in the oven, and then, when the bricks were thoroughly heated, we'd scrape out all the coals with a big iron scraper, dump the coals into the fireplace, and shove in the roasts and fowls, the pies and bread. At other times we'd use the open fireplace. It wasn't nearly so difficult to work by as people think. When we went to keeping house in 1845, Dan'l and I, he bought me a little iron stove, a new thing in those days. It was no good, and would only bake things on one side. I soon went back to cooking at an open fireplace.

You know the look of <u>andirons</u>, crane, spit, reflectors. Our heavy iron vessels were swung from chains. When we wanted to lift the iron lids off, we'd have to reach in with a hook and swing them off. They had a <u>flange</u> around the edge. Many of our dishes were baked in Dutch ovens on the hearth. We used to bake Indian pone—that is, bread made of rye and corn meal—that way. We would set it off in a corner of the hearth covered with coals and ashes, and there it would bake slowly all night long. In the morning the crust would be thick but soft—oh, so good.

For roasting meat we had reflectors. Some joints we roasted in our big iron kettles with a bit of water. And others we put on three-legged gridirons which could be turned. These had a little fluted place for the gravy to run down. Chickens we could split down the back and lay on the gridiron with a plate and flatirons on top to hold them down. Oh, how different, how different, is everything now, <u>encumbered</u> with conveniences!

The difference between those who were naturally clean and orderly and those who were not was perhaps more marked in those days than it is now. It was so easy, for instance, since we had no screens, to let the flies spoil everything. My mother just wouldn't have it so. We weren't allowed to bring apples into the house in summer, because apples attract flies. If any of us dropped a speck of butter or cream on the floor, she had to run at once for a cloth to wipe it up. Our kitchen floor was of ash, and Ma was very proud of keeping it white. In the summer kitchen the floor was of brick, and it was expected to be spotless also. At mealtime someone stood and fanned to keep the flies away while the others ate. When Sister Libbie went to housekeeping, she had little round-topped screens for every dish on her table. That was considered quite stylish. Ma used to set some tall thing in the centre of her table, spread a cloth over it, and slip food under until we were ready to sit down. As soon as the meal was finished, all curtains had to be pulled down and the flies driven from the darkened room.

Our dishes for common use were white with blue edges. The finer ones were a figured blue. I remember, also, a large blue soup tureen with a cover and a blue, long-handled ladle, all very handsome.

Our forks were two-tined. They weren't much good for holding some things. But if we used our knives for conveying food to our mouths it had to be done with the back of the knife towards the face. We had no napkins. We used our handkerchiefs. Tablecloths were made of cotton diaper especially woven for the purpose. The first white bedspread I ever had was made of two widths of that same cotton whitened on the grass.

In warm weather we washed outdoors under the quince bushes. We used our well water. It was so soft, it was just beautiful. We'd draw a barrel of water, put one shovel of ashes into it, and it would just suds up like soft water, so white and clean. We used soft soap, of course. Our starch was of two kinds—either made from a dough of flour worked round and round until it was smooth and fine or made from grated potato cooked to the right consistency.

Ma put us girls to work early. It was taken as a matter of course that we should learn all kinds of housework. I know that before I was seven years old I used to wash the dishes. But our mother had village girls to help her also. I remember one Ann Fierce who was with us for years, but it seems to me that Sister Libbie and I usually did the washing. There was need of many hands to get all the work done. It required more knowledge to do the things for everyday living than is the case nowadays. If one wants light now, all one has to do is pull a string or push a button. Then, we had to pick up a coal with tongs, hold it against a candle, and blow. And one had to make the candles, perhaps.

I remember the first matches that I ever saw. Someone handed me a little bunch of them, fastened together at the bottom in a solid block of wood about a half inch square. "Lucifer matches" they called them. I tore one off and set the whole thing afire.

We did not make our candles at home, but got them usually from Uncle Dean, who made candles for the town. I used to love to watch him and Aunt Maria at work dipping candles—she with the hot tallow in a big kettle on the hearth, he with stillyards beside him, weighing carefully. Occasionally we had some sperm candles made of fine whale tallow. Besides candles, people sometimes burned sperm or whale oil in little lamps that looked like square-topped candlesticks. In the square top was a place for a bowl that would hold perhaps a half pint of oil.

Even without candle making, there was certainly a plenty to do to keep life going in those days. Baking, washing, ironing, sewing, kept us busy. Not to mention the spinning and weaving that had to be done before cloth was available for the seamstress.

My mother used to spin. She made beautiful fine thread. She taught Sister Libbie how to spin, but decided, before my turn came, that spinning was doomed to become a lost art, and that I might be better employed in some other way. I used to love to watch her at the spinning wheel. She had two wheels, lovely big ones. She used a wheel boy to turn her wheel. I can just close my eyes and see Ma standing over there spinning a thread as far as from here to the bed—say, twelve feet long.

My mother and her sister had some beautiful woolen cloth of their own spinning and weaving. Part of the thread was made with the open, part with the crossed, band. They colored it with butternut bark, but the two kinds would never color alike, so that part of it was a light and part a dark brown. They wove it into a plaid and had it pressed, and then they made fine dresses out of it to wear to church. I remember, too, that my mother raised flax, spun it into linen, wove it into cloth—colored blue in the yarn—made it up into a dress for me which she embroidered in white above the hem. I wish I had kept that dress to show my children the beautiful work of their grandmother.

Ma used to use Aunt Betsy's loom sometimes. When I was eight years old, she wove me a plaid dress of which I was very proud. I remember the pattern: eight threads of brown, then one of red, one of blue, one of red, then brown again, both in the warp and in the woof. It made the prettiest flannel, and that dress lasted me for years.

Women made their own designs for cloth as well as for dresses in those days. If a woman had taste, she had a chance to show it in her weaving. But, oh, it was hard work. You never saw warping bars, did you? Clumsy things, long as a bed. On them work was prepared for the loom. You had to draw each thread through a reed. I used to love to watch my mother weaving, her shuttle holding the spool with yarn shooting through the warp, then back the other way. When she had woven as far as she could reach, she would bend below the loom and wind the woven cloth into a roll beneath. Blankets made at home used to last a long time. Homespun things were good.

We had all the things that were really necessary for our comfort in those days, and we had quite as much leisure as people have now. ◇

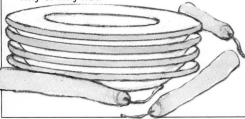

	LESSON TITLE	STUDENT TEXT				TEACHING RESOURCES		
		Student Lesson	Unit Review	Cumulative Review	Extra Practice	Reteaching Master	Practice Master	Testing Program
PART 1	1 DAY Unit Opener							
	1 DAY Writing with Nouns	60–61	104	107, 223	108, 109	10	10	
	1 DAY Singular and Plural Nouns	62–63	104	107, 223	108, 110	11	11	T534
	1 DAY Common and Proper Nouns	64–65	104	107, 223	108,110	12	12	
	1 DAY Capitalizing Proper Nouns	66–67	104	107, 223, 330, 433	108, 111	13	13	T534
	1 DAY Abbreviations	68–69	104	107, 223, 330, 433	108, 112	14	14	T534
	1 DAY Possessive Nouns	70–71	105	107, 223	108, 113	15	15	T534
	1 DAY VOCABULARY ◆ Context Clues	72–73	105			16	16	T534
	1 DAY GRAMMAR-WRITING CONNECTION ◆ How to Revise Sentences with Nouns	74–75						
PART 2	▶ **THINK**							
	1 DAY CRITICAL THINKING ◆ A Strategy for Informing	78–79	See also pages 83, 96, 102					
	▶ **READ**							
	1 DAY LITERATURE ◆ *Handicrafts* by Patricia Fent Ross	80–81	Audio Library 2					
	▶ **SPEAK/LISTEN**							
	1 DAY SPEAKING AND LISTENING ◆ Directions	84–85	Video Library					
	▶ **WRITE**							
	1 DAY WRITING ◆ A Paragraph	86–87	105			17	17	
	1 DAY WRITING ◆ Topic Sentence and Supporting Sentences	88–89	105			18	18	T534
	1 DAY WRITING ◆ Using Commas	90–91	105	330, 433		19	19	T534
	1 DAY READING-WRITING CONNECTION ◆ Focus on Sequence	92–93						T534
	▶ **WRITING PROCESS** ◆ Prewriting • Writing • Revising • Proofreading • Publishing							
	4–5 DAYS WRITING PROCESS ◆ Writing a How-to Article	94–101				Spelling Connection Transparencies		T552
	1 DAY CURRICULUM CONNECTION ◆ Writing for Art	102				Writing Across the Curriculum Guide		

Teacher Resource File

Reteaching Masters 10–19
Practice Masters 10–19
Evaluation and Testing Program, including Unit Pretest, Posttest, and Picture Prompt Writing Samples
Parent Letters in English and Spanish
Classroom Theme Posters
Writing Across the Curriculum Teacher Guide
Integrated Language Arts Projects with Masters (see pages T511–T529)
Spelling Connection, Teacher Edition
Writing Process Transparencies
Audio Library 1: Read-Alouds and Sing-Alouds

Also available:

Achieving English Proficiency Guide and Activities
Spelling Connection, Pupil Edition
Student Resource Books
Student Writing Portfolios
Professional Handbook
WORLD OF BOOKS Classroom Library

Multi-Modal Materials

Audio Library 1: Read-Alouds and Sing-Alouds
Audio Library 2: Listening to Literature
Video Library
Revising and Proofreading Transparencies
Fine Arts Transparencies with Viewing Booklet
Writing Process Transparencies
Writing Process Computer Program

Unit 2 Planning and Pacing Guide

LANGUAGE *game*

Proper Noun Play-Off

Objective: To use proper nouns
Materials: Pieces of chalk, list of general topics

You may wish to distribute this list of general topics:

states	lakes	composers	book characters	mountains	languages
landmarks	streets	holidays	U.S. presidents	inventors	countries
schools	cities	explorers	first names	teachers	famous animals

Divide the class into two or three teams and have students line up in relay-race style. Mark off the chalkboard into as many sections as there are teams. Each team member will have one minute to write on the chalkboard as many different proper nouns as possible within the category named. The team that compiles the longest list is a winner. You may wish to continue the relay until all players have written proper nouns for at least two categories.

Multi-Modal Activities

BULLETIN BOARD *idea*

You may wish to use a bulletin board as a springboard for discussing the unit theme, or you may prefer to have students create a bulletin board as they move through the unit. Encourage students to share information about their own handicrafts by having them provide drawings or photos of themselves showing them either in the process of making something or with something they have completed. Allow space for one-line captions explaining each handicraft. You may wish to include a picture of yourself with something you have made. Encourage students to share photos or drawings they have made, whether it is as small as a bookmark or as large as a tree house. You may wish to set aside time for a question-and-answer period in which students answer classmates' questions about the handicrafts. You may wish to label the bulletin board *Handicrafts by Class*.

Students with different learning styles will all benefit from a natural approach to language learning, including frequent and varied use of oral language in the classroom.

Students "At Risk"

The following suggestions can help you help the students in your classroom who may be considered "at risk."

Explore Different Modalities

Introduce concepts as concretely as possible. Consider using the Reteaching option offered in your Teacher Edition with every developmental lesson. This feature includes directions for the explicit use of illustrations, photographs, and diagrams, as well as individual and small-group activities such as role-playing, games, and the direct manipulation of materials—all helping students to relate to the concept in ways different from the textbook presentation.

Notice, too, the Reteaching Masters. These masters offer easy-level practice of each lesson's basic concept by first leading students in a unique, interactive way to create their own models for success.

Limited English Proficiency

Teachers whose classes contain students with limited English proficiency may find the following activities helpful in developing students' skills in grammar and composition.

Noun Chart

Display pictures from magazines or books that depict artists and their handicrafts, such as potter—pottery; weaver—blankets; woodworker—furniture.

On the chalkboard begin a handicrafts chart such as the one below.

Point to the first picture you displayed and ask such questions as: *Who is this person? What is the person weaving? What do you call two or more of these products? Where might the weaving take place? In what particular place might the weaving take place?* Record students' responses under the appropriate heading on the chart. Repeat this procedure with the remaining pictures. Tell students to be as realistic as possible in their responses but emphasize that you will accept any reasonable responses, such as a made-up name for a particular person. Encourage discussion of *Who?* and *Where?* to elicit both common and proper nouns.

Word Web

Tell students that making a word web can help to create ideas. Have students choose the noun *person, place, thing,* or *idea* as the core word of their web. Then have them think of a related noun, such as *friend,* and write that in the web. Have them continue by thinking of yet another related noun, such as *Pat Corwin,* and continue to add words until either they run out of ideas or you say their time is up. Encourage students to use both common and proper nouns and singular and plural nouns. When students have completed their word webs, have them group according to their core word and compare their webs.

A partially completed word web might look like the following:

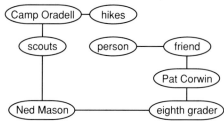

A How-to

To focus on sequence words, have students discuss directions for completing a simple craft, such as painting a water-color, making a collage, or cutting geometric shapes. You may wish to write sequence words such as the following on the chalkboard to help students: *first, second, then, next, last.* Have students discuss materials and the steps they would follow. Encourage them to make sure the steps are logical and that nothing important is missing. Then have a volunteer act as scribe. You may wish to have a volunteer read aloud the directions.

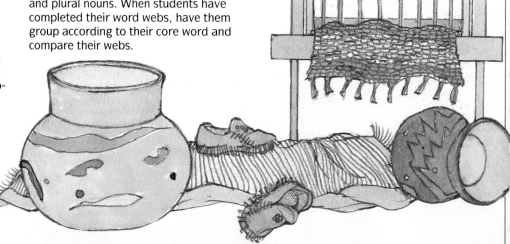

General Person	Particular Person	1 Product	2 or More Products	General Place	Particular Place
weaver	Ana Montez	rug	rugs	a reservation	Arizona

Gifted and Talented Students

To enable gifted and talented students to work at their own pace and to explore the content further, you may wish to use one or more of these activities.

Word Web

Have students work as individuals or in small groups to create a word web for the noun *business.* Each student or group should use the word as the core word, finding other nouns related to it and to each other. You may wish to give students an assignment or have them decide on the requirements, such as three singular nouns, two plural nouns, two proper nouns, and one abbreviation.

Have students exchange papers and evaluate whether or not each word is a noun and whether requirements have been met.

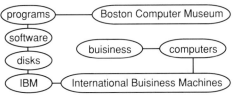

When students have completed other assigments, you may wish to have them create a word web for the noun *handicrafts,* following the procedure above.

Using Nouns Creatively

Have students work in pairs or small groups to find a two- or three-paragraph article in a children's magazine. Have students copy the article, deleting all the nouns and putting in write-on blanks instead. Then have pairs or groups exchange papers to fill in the blanks. Encourage students to be creative, but remind them that their sentences must be grammatically correct.

You may wish to have pairs or groups complete their article twice, first in a serious way and then in a humorous way. Then have students compare their revised articles with the originals.

Have pairs or groups share their articles and the originals by having one member read them aloud or by posting the articles, along with the originals, on a bulletin board.

Changing Sentences

Have students work with a sentence you supply or with a sentence they create. Have them rewrite the sentence using as many different nouns as possible. Encourage students to use

singular and plural nouns and common and proper nouns. You may wish to supply this sentence: *The children picked blueberries from the bushes.* Students may suggest such variations as: *Farmer Brown picked strawberries from the plants. The squirrel picked an acorn from the tree. The receptionist picked messages from the desk. A helicopter picked the hikers from Mount Washington. Dr. Garcia picked instruments from the tray.*

Have students share their original sentence along with its variations by reading them aloud. Encourage listeners to try to add to the variations.

Meeting Individual Needs

■ Easy ■ Average ■ Challenging

OBJECTIVES
To identify nouns
To use nouns in writing

ASSIGNMENT GUIDE
BASIC	Practice A
⬇	Practice B
ADVANCED	Practice C

All should do the Apply activity.

RESOURCES
■ Reteaching Master 10
■ Practice Master 10
■ ■ ■ Extra Practice, pp. 108, 109
Unit 2 Pretest, p. T534

TEACHING THE LESSON

1. Getting Started
Oral Language Focus attention on this oral activity, encouraging all to participate. You may wish to have students close their eyes for a moment to picture the things they brought with them to school that day.

2. Developing the Lesson
Guide students through the explanation of writing with nouns, emphasizing the examples and the summary. You may wish to emphasize nouns that name ideas. Provide more examples, such as *joy, freedom, friendship, hope, anger, fear, excitement,* and *greatness.* Lead students through the **Guided Practice.** Identify those who would benefit from reteaching. Assign independent Practice A–C.

3. Closing the Lesson
After students complete the Apply activity, have volunteers read aloud the nouns they listed under each heading. You may wish to have other students form short sentences, using each noun. Point out to students that using nouns can help create clear word pictures in their speaking and writing.

Think of words that name things you might bring to school. The things might be ordinary, like a pencil, or unusual, like a centipede.

1 Writing with Nouns

In order to speak and write, we have to use naming words. Without such words, we would have blank spaces in our communication. We would say

■ The _____ shaped the _____ with his _____ .

instead of

■ The <u>man</u> shaped the <u>clay</u> with his <u>hands</u>.

Man, clay, and *hands* are nouns—words that name. A noun can name a person, a place, or a thing. We can see or touch all of these. A noun can also name an idea, something we cannot see or touch.

Examples of Nouns		
Persons	Freddie	potter	weaver
Places	town	beach	Japan
Things	plate	chair	blanket
Ideas	honesty	skill	beauty

Summary ◆ A **noun** names a person, place, thing, or idea. Use nouns to give information when you speak and write.

Guided Practice

Each sentence below has three nouns. Read the sentences. Name the nouns.

1. <u>Ralph</u> is reading a <u>book</u> about <u>handicrafts</u>.
2. <u>Potters</u> in ancient <u>Greece</u> made <u>vases</u>.
3. Such <u>objects</u> were valued for their <u>usefulness</u> and <u>beauty</u>.
4. <u>Handicrafters</u> use <u>tools</u> in their <u>trades</u>.

ESSENTIAL LANGUAGE SKILLS
This lesson provides opportunities to:

LISTENING ◆ employ active listening in a variety of situations ◆ follow the logical organization of an oral presentation

SPEAKING ◆ use a variety of words to express feelings and ideas

READING ◆ use context to understand the meanings of words ◆ follow a set of directions ◆ understand content area vocabulary

WRITING ◆ apply conventions of capitalization and punctuation ◆ generate ideas using a variety of strategies

LANGUAGE ◆ use the fundamentals of grammar, spelling, and punctuation

Practice

A. Write the nouns you find in each sentence.

5. Yoshi is learning about making cloth.
6. Her mother owns a loom.
7. Her sister will use dye to add colors.
8. In America, weavers have produced beautiful objects.
9. Their skill has earned great respect.
10. Blankets woven by the Navajo now hang in museums.
11. The warmth of the colors brightens many homes.
12. Yoshi has studied the work of the weavers of the Southwest.
13. These workers still practice their craft.
14. Their products are national treasures.

B. Use the nouns below to complete the paragraph. Write the completed paragraph.

cloth	Yoshi	Native American	blanket	airplane
loom	Arizona	reservation	color	sister

(**15.** _Yoshi_) and her (**16.** _sister_) traveled on an (**17.** airplane) to (**18.** Arizona). They visited a vast (**19.** _reservation_). There they saw a (**20.** _Native American_) weaving a (**21.** blanket) on her (**22.** _loom_). The (**23.** color) of the (**24.** cloth) was beautiful.

C. Use the model below to write five sentences of your own. Notice how using different nouns gives a totally different meaning to each sentence. **Answers will vary.**

25–29. The _____ made a _____ for the _____ .

Apply ◆ Think and Write

From Your Writing ◆ Read what you wrote for the Writer's Warm-up. List the nouns you used in four categories: persons, places, things, and ideas.

✎ **Remember**
that nouns help to create a clear word picture for your reader.

Writing with Nouns

Complete the sentence. Write one word for each picture.

The _____ rowed a _____ in the _____ .
(noun)　　　　(noun)　　　　(noun)

↻ A **noun** names a person, place, thing, or idea. Nouns name things we can see or touch. Nouns also name ideas, such as *honesty, skill,* and *beauty.*

A. Circle the nouns in each sentence. The number in parentheses ( ) after the sentence tells how many nouns are in the sentence.

EXAMPLE: (Emilio) visited (Newfoundland) in (Canada). (3)

1. The island has an interesting history. (2)
2. The Vikings were early explorers of the land. (3)
3. One group built a settlement on the island in the tenth century. (4)
4. The settlers stayed for only a few years. (2)

B. Complete each sentence with a noun from the box. Use the noun that best fits the sentence.

EXAMPLE: _____John Cabot_____ explored the eastern coast of Canada.

coast	Canada	fish	John Cabot

5. _____John Cabot_____ claimed Newfoundland and other areas for England.
6. Cabot told stories about amazing numbers of fish off the _____coast_____ of Newfoundland.
7. Travelers to _____Canada_____ found some of the best fishing banks in the world.
8. A fishing bank is a shallow part of the ocean that has many _____fish_____.

Writing with Nouns

↻ A **noun** names a person, place, thing, or idea.

A. Circle the nouns in each sentence.

1. Canada is the northern neighbor of the United States.
2. The country has two official languages.
3. Both French and English are spoken there.
4. Many different people form the population.
5. Important products include wheat and iron.
6. Wheat is grown on the prairies.
7. The mountains are rich in minerals.
8. There are many rivers and lakes.
9. Waterfalls help produce electricity.
10. Montreal is the largest city.
11. Montreal is named for a high mountain.

B. Find the nouns in the paragraph. List them below.

Canada is the second largest country in the world. Only the Soviet Union is larger in area. The Pacific Ocean is on the west. The Atlantic Ocean is on the east. The United States shares the southern boundary. It is the longest border without posts for defense in the world.

12. Canada	17. Pacific Ocean	22. boundary
13. country	18. west	23. border
14. world	19. Atlantic Ocean	24. posts
15. Soviet Union	20. east	25. defense
16. area	21. United States	26. world

WRITE IT
Write sentences about a place of interest to you. Use nouns. Write on a separate sheet of paper. Answers will vary.

◀‖‖ TEACHING OPTIONS ‖‖▶

RETEACHING

A Different Modality Distribute to each student a short list of nouns that includes persons, places, things, and ideas. Write on the chalkboard the headings *Persons, Places, Things,* and *Ideas.* Have volunteers write each noun under the correct heading. You may wish to help students by writing the first noun in each column, such as *secretary, Indiana, radio,* and *truth.*

CLASS ENRICHMENT

A Cooperative Activity Have each student clip a newspaper or magazine picture they like. Then have small groups work together to write noun captions for their pictures. Tell them to try to include all four kinds of nouns—nouns that name persons, places, things, and ideas (e.g., *clown, circus, costume, humor*). Have volunteers share their work with the class.

CHALLENGE

An Independent Extension Have students write a sentence that includes each pair of words. Tell them to be sure to use each one as a noun.

Example: Most plants have leaves.

1. plants, leaves
2. water, diver
3. speaker, meeting
4. puzzle, solution
5. scientist, success
6. laboratory, test
7. reporter, news
8. seats, auditorium
9. student, question
10. result, discussion

■ Easy ■ Average ■ Challenging

OBJECTIVES
To identify singular and plural nouns
To form plural nouns ending in -s, -es, and -ies
To form irregular plural nouns

ASSIGNMENT GUIDE
BASIC   Practice A
↓   Practice B
ADVANCED Practice C

All should do the Apply activity.

RESOURCES
■ Reteaching Master 11
■ Practice Master 11
■ ■ ■ Extra Practice, pp. 108, 110

TEACHING THE LESSON

1. Getting Started
Oral Language Focus attention on this oral activity, encouraging all to participate. You may wish to model an example of your own, such as *I would like to have one cat. I would not like to have five caterpillars.* You may then wish to have one volunteer supply a sentence and another supply a matching *have not* sentence.

2. Developing the Lesson
Guide students through the explanation of singular and plural nouns, emphasizing the examples and the summary. Lead students through the **Guided Practice.** Identify those who would benefit from reteaching. Assign independent Practice A–C.

3. Closing the Lesson
After students complete the Apply activity, have volunteers read their work to the class. Encourage students to identify the plural nouns and to tell whether they were formed by adding -s, -es, or -ies. Point out to students that they should proofread their written work to check for correct spelling of plural nouns.

◆ GETTING STARTED ◆

Follow the examples below to play "To Have or Have Not."
I would like to have two hamsters.
I would not like to have forty-seven snakes.

2 Singular and Plural Nouns

Nouns can name one thing or more than one thing. In other words, nouns can be singular or plural. Most nouns add an ending in the plural. Some nouns change their spelling. A few nouns are the same in the singular and the plural.

Here are the singular and plural forms of some nouns.

Singular	Plural
girl tiger mirror	girls tigers mirrors
bush lunch dress tax	bushes lunches dresses taxes
lady baby country	ladies babies countries
boy valley turkey	boys valleys turkeys
leaf wolf knife	leaves wolves knives
foot tooth man	feet teeth men
salmon deer moose	salmon deer moose

Summary ◆ A **singular noun** names one person, place, thing, or idea. A **plural noun** names more than one person, place, thing, or idea. When you write, pay special attention to the spelling of plural nouns.

Guided Practice

Tell whether each of these nouns is singular or plural.

1. dogs *plu.*
2. monkey *sing.*
3. tooth *sing.*
4. village *sing.*
5. men *plu.*
6. country *sing.*
7. feet *plu.*
8. tool *sing.*
9. leaves *plu.*
10. dishes *plu.*
11. cousin *sing.*
12. kites *plu.*

ESSENTIAL LANGUAGE SKILLS
This lesson provides opportunities to:

LISTENING ◆ follow the logical organization of an oral presentation ◆ select from an oral presentation the information needed

SPEAKING ◆ speak expressively by varying volume, rate, and intonation ◆ speak before an audience to communicate specific information

READING ◆ follow a set of directions ◆ accurately comprehend the details in a reading selection ◆ locate and utilize desired information in reference sources

WRITING ◆ proofread for spelling, capitalization, and punctuation ◆ generate ideas using a variety of strategies

LANGUAGE ◆ use the fundamentals of grammar, punctuation, and spelling ◆ produce a variety of sentence patterns

Practice

. Write the underlined noun in each sentence. Then write *singular* if the noun is singular. Write *plural* if it is plural.

13. <u>Items</u> made of baked clay are called pottery. *plu.*
14. There are different <u>methods</u> of making pottery. *plu.*
15. Some pottery is made in <u>factories</u>. *plu.*
16. A <u>potter</u> led us on a guided tour. *sing.*
17. Our class visited such a <u>place</u>. *sing.*
18. We examined <u>wheels</u> used by potters. *plu.*
19. We watched several <u>men</u> packing the finished items. *plu.*
20. These people put the bowls and vases into <u>boxes</u>. *plu.*
21. One vase had a red <u>strawberry</u> painted on it. *sing.*
22. Another was formed in the shape of a <u>shoe</u>. *sing.*
23. My fondest <u>wish</u> is to become a potter. *sing.*
24. I would make beautiful <u>bowls</u>. *plu.*
25. I would decorate each one with a <u>picture</u>. *sing.*
26. <u>Butterflies</u> are my favorite decorations. *plu.*

B. Write the plural of each of these nouns.

27. hand — hands
28. city — cities
29. tray — trays
30. man — men
31. cherry — cherries
32. church — churches
33. foot — feet
34. deer — deer
35. ostrich — ostriches
36. donkey — donkeys
37. life — lives
38. salmon — salmon
39. tooth — teeth
40. army — armies
41. brush — brushes

C. Write four sentences of your own, using the plural forms of the words below.
Sentences will vary. Plural forms are listed.

42. box — boxes
43. leaf — leaves
44. woman — women
45. moose — moose

Apply • Think and Write

Dictionary of Knowledge ◆ Read about pottery in the Dictionary of Knowledge. Then write several sentences about the art of making pottery. Use plural nouns in your writing.

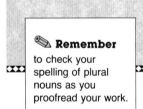
🖉 **Remember**
to check your spelling of plural nouns as you proofread your work.

GRAMMAR and SPELLING: Singular Nouns and Plural Nouns **63**

◀◀|||| TEACHING OPTIONS ||||▶

RETEACHING

A Different Modality Write singular and their matching plural nouns on separate strips of paper. Label the reverse side of each *singular* or *plural*. Separate the strips into two piles. Have volunteers read a "singular" strip and then find and read aloud its "plural" equivalent. Have them compare the two spellings and describe how the plural is formed. You may want to make a poster similar to the chart in the lesson for display on the bulletin board.

CLASS ENRICHMENT

A Cooperative Activity Write a list of singular nouns on the chalkboard, such as *man, woman, baby, bench, swing, sandwich, knife, puppy, foot,* and *bush.* Have students work in small groups to write a story paragraph using as many of the nouns in plural form as possible. Have a group recorder underline plural nouns. You may wish to have a volunteer from each group write the plural nouns on the chalkboard as another member reads the story aloud.

CHALLENGE

An Independent Extension Have students write original sentences using five nouns from the list below as singular nouns and then as plural nouns.

1. tooth
2. wharf
3. elf
4. calf
5. ceremony
6. woman
7. mongoose
8. cabbage
9. genius
10. batch
11. caboose
12. ax
13. navy
14. mystery
15. hedge

OBJECTIVES
To identify common and proper nouns

ASSIGNMENT GUIDE
BASIC   Practice A
⬇   Practice B
ADVANCED   Practice C

All should do the Apply activity.

RESOURCES
■ Reteaching Master 12
■ Practice Master 12
■ ■ ■ Extra Practice, pp. 108, 110

TEACHING THE LESSON

1. Getting Started
Oral Language Focus attention on this oral activity, encouraging all to participate. You may wish to tell students that the things they take to an island must begin with the first letter of their first name and their last name. Model a response of your own using your initials. Then have volunteers respond until all students tell what they could take.

2. Developing the Lesson
Guide students through the explanation of common and proper nouns, emphasizing the examples and the summary. You may wish to point out to students that only important words in proper nouns are capitalized. Tell them a word such as *of* is not an important word and therefore is not capitalized. Provide more examples, such as *Isle of Man* and *Statue of Liberty*. Lead students through the **Guided Practice.** Identify those who would benefit from reteaching. Assign independent Practice A–C.

3. Closing the Lesson
After students complete the Apply activity, have volunteers read their work aloud. Have the whole class raise their hands when they hear a proper noun. Point out to students that correctly using common and proper nouns can help them give more exact information to their readers and listeners.

◆ GETTING STARTED ◆

If he went to an island, Marty Torres could take a melon and a turtle. Cindy Evans could take a cat and eggs. Figure out what you could take to an island.

3 Common and Proper Nouns

What is the difference between these two sentences?

A <u>girl</u> visited a <u>museum</u> in a <u>city</u>.
<u>Linda</u> visited the <u>American Craft Museum</u> in <u>New York</u>.

The first sentence uses general naming words to refer to a person, a thing, and a place. The second sentence names a particular person, a particular thing, and a particular place. The words *girl*, *museum*, and *city* are common nouns. The proper noun *Linda* names a particular person. The proper noun *American Craft Museum* names a particular thing. The proper noun *New York* names a particular place. Notice that a proper noun can be more than one word.

When you speak and write, you sometimes want to be as specific as possible. You might use the proper noun *Baltimore* instead of the common noun *city*. You might use *Aunt Lucy* instead of *relative*, and *Walters Art Gallery* instead of *gallery*.

> **Summary** ◆ A **common noun** is the general name for a person, place, or thing. A **proper noun** names a particular person, place, or thing. Use proper nouns to make your writing more specific.

Guided Practice

Tell whether the underlined nouns are common or proper.

1. Ms. <u>Ashe</u> [prop.] showed us <u>pictures</u> [com.] of handmade <u>furniture</u> [com.].
2. <u>Linda</u> [prop.] admired a beautiful <u>table</u> [com.] made in <u>Italy</u> [prop.].
3. The <u>antique</u> [com.] was sold to a <u>collector</u> [com.] in <u>Chicago</u> [prop.].
4. He gave the <u>piece</u> [com.] to the <u>Art Institute of Chicago</u> [prop.] on <u>Michigan Boulevard</u> [prop.].
5. <u>Nathan</u> [prop.] saw a <u>collection</u> [com.] of handmade <u>items</u> [com.] in the <u>Cranfield Library</u> [prop.].

64   GRAMMAR: Common Nouns and Proper Nouns

ESSENTIAL LANGUAGE SKILLS

This lesson provides opportunities to:

LISTENING ◆ follow the logical organization of an oral presentation ◆ select from an oral presentation the information needed

SPEAKING ◆ speak expressively by varying volume, rate, and intonation ◆ speak before an audience to communicate specific information

READING ◆ follow a set of directions ◆ understand content area vocabulary

WRITING ◆ form cursive letters legibly ◆ use correct spelling, capitalization, and punctuation

LANGUAGE ◆ use the fundamentals of grammar, punctuation, and spelling ◆ produce a variety of sentence patterns

Practice

A. Write each underlined noun. Then write *common* or *proper* to show what kind of noun it is.

  6. Woodworkers are people who make things from wood.

  7. My uncle, David Johnson, makes furniture.

  8. Uncle David designs and assembles cabinets and desks.

  9. He lives near New Orleans in Louisiana.

10. The Mississippi River is not far from his home.

11. Mrs. Baxter told Karen about the materials she uses.

12. Oak is a hardwood, and pine is a softwood.

13. Mayor Jesse Roe gave handmade shelves to the Scott School.

14. My cousin in Georgia carves her initials in her work.

15. Kristen made a checkerboard, a birdhouse, and a bookcase.

B. Write the sentences. Draw one line under the common nouns. Draw two lines under the proper nouns.

16. Much furniture is made by machines.

17. Some woodworkers, such as John Dunnigan, make tables by hand.

18. Judy Kensley McKie has created an unusual table.

19. This piece features two carved animals.

20. Museums and galleries in places such as Los Angeles display furniture.

21. Gary and Sue took a bus to the Metropolitan Museum of Art in New York City.

22. Gary enjoyed the ride through the Lincoln Tunnel.

23. In Manhattan, skyscrapers soared into the sky.

24. The museum had an exhibit of furniture.

25. The displays included many handmade items.

C. **26–28.** Write three sentences about wooden toys or other objects. Use at least one proper noun in each sentence.
Sentences will vary.

Apply • Think and Write

Planning a Trip ◆ Be an armchair traveler. Write about a museum you would like to visit. Include the names of people you would like to take along.

GRAMMAR: Common Nouns and Proper Nouns   **65**

"Pete & Repete"—painted and carved on birch by Judy Kensley McKie, 1981. Courtesy Pritam & Eames Furniture Gallery, East Hampton, New York

✏️ **Remember**
that you can use both common and proper nouns to give information.

RETEACHING   12
Common and Proper Nouns

Read the travel stickers. The common nouns are circled. The proper nouns are underlined. Write the common nouns and proper nouns in the chart.

Common Nouns	Proper Nouns
mountain	Lake Ontario
lake	Rocky Mountains

We found the mountain. Visit beautiful Lake Ontario. I climbed the Rocky Mountains. Follow me to the lake.

A **common noun** is the general name for a person, place, or thing. A **proper noun** names a particular person, place, or thing. A proper noun can be more than one word.

A. Underline each common noun. Circle each proper noun.

EXAMPLE: His favorite painter is Paul Gauguin.

1. My family drove to Washington.
2. A famous president is Abraham Lincoln.
3. Lake Louise is a beautiful place.
4. I took a trip to Arizona.
5. She fished last year at Alexandria Bay.

B. Complete each sentence with a common noun. Use the word or words in parentheses ( ) as a guide. Answers will vary. Possible answers follow.

EXAMPLE: Sean loves to watch _baseball_. (sport)

6. Joyce has a _snake_ in her backyard. (animal)
7. Manuel ate _spaghetti_ at the picnic. (food)
8. Chim Van went to the _bank_ on Tuesday. (place)
9. Elton saw a _man_ enter the room. (person)
10. Carla plays the _trumpet_ in the band. (musical instrument)

PRACTICE   12
Common and Proper Nouns

A **common noun** is the general name for a person, place, or thing. A **proper noun** names a particular person, place, or thing.

A. Circle the common nouns. Underline the proper nouns.

1. The Vikings sailed across the ocean from Iceland to Canada.
2. The new land was named Vinland by Leif Ericson.
3. Christopher Columbus looked for a new route to India.
4. Columbus made four voyages to the islands of the Caribbean Sea.
5. The country of Brazil was claimed by Pedro Cabral for Portugal.
6. The people of Brazil speak Portuguese.
7. Amerigo Vespucci was a skilled sailor from Italy.
8. Ponce de León landed in Florida.

B. Rewrite each sentence. Change the underlined words to a proper noun. Answers will vary. Possible answers follow.

9. The bus went to the city.
   The bus went to Cleveland.

10. The baseball player hit a home run.
   Thomas hit a home run.

11. The rock star sang the girl's favorite song.
   Michael Jackson sang the girl's favorite song.

12. My neighbor collects stamps from another country.
   Mrs. Figaroa collects stamps from Puerto Rico.

13. I love to hear the stories my relative tells.
   I love to hear the stories Aunt Alice tells.

WRITE IT
On separate paper, write about a place you would like to explore with a friend. Use both common and proper nouns. Answers will vary.

◀◀|||| TEACHING OPTIONS ||||▶▶

RETEACHING

A Different Modality Write a student's name on the chalkboard under the heading *Proper Nouns*. Beside the name, write *student* under the heading *Common Nouns*. Explain that the name is a proper noun because it refers to a particular person and that *student* is a common noun because it is a general naming word. Help students add other proper and common nouns under the appropriate headings.

CLASS ENRICHMENT

A Cooperative Activity Have small groups of students work together to make noun puzzles. Have group members list common nouns on the left side of a sheet of chart paper and then write appropriate proper nouns on the right side of the paper, such as *river—Snake River*. Then have each group cut the list apart, mix and trade pieces with another group, and reconstruct the list so that each proper noun matches its common noun in the puzzle.

CHALLENGE

An Independent Extension Using the list below, have students write a proper noun for each common noun and then use both in an original sentence.

Example: I was born in the month of May.

1. month   6. magazine
2. friend   7. country
3. city   8. park
4. street   9. inventor
5. mountain 10. bridge

■ Easy ■ Average ■ Challenging

OBJECTIVES
To capitalize proper nouns correctly

ASSIGNMENT GUIDE
BASIC — Practice A
↓ — Practice B
ADVANCED — Practice C

All should do the Apply activity.

RESOURCES
■ Reteaching Master 13
■ Practice Master 13
■■■ Extra Practice, pp. 108, 111

TEACHING THE LESSON

1. Getting Started
Oral Language Focus attention on this oral activity, encouraging all to participate. You may wish to have students focus on their own first and last names, such as *sandy* (gritty feel), *Sandy* (Sandra); *sue* (bring to court), *Sue* (Susan); *cliff* (steep slope), *Cliff* (Clifford); *ray* (beam of light), *Ray* (Raymond or Rafael); *pat* (touch), *Pat* (Patrick or Patricia); *bob* (move up and down), *Bob* (Robert). Provide other examples, such as *mars* (damages), *Mars* (planet); *ford* (to cross), *Ford* (make of car); *may* (permission), *May* (month); *miss* (error), *Miss* (title); *navy* (color), *Navy* (armed force); *crow* (bird), *Crow* (Native American).

2. Developing the Lesson
Guide students through the explanation of capitalizing proper nouns, emphasizing the examples and the summary. Lead students through the **Guided Practice**. Identify those who would benefit from reteaching. Assign independent Practice A–C.

3. Closing the Lesson
After students complete the Apply activity, encourage them to share their sampler sentences with the class. You may wish to have volunteers write their sentences with appropriate illustrations on construction paper for a bulletin board display. Point out to students that capitalizing proper nouns makes it clear that they intend to use a particular name rather than a general one.

66

What is the difference between *turkey* and *Turkey*? Between *china* and *China*? Think of other words whose meanings change when the words are capitalized.

4 Capitalizing Proper Nouns

When you write a proper noun, always begin it with a capital letter. Many proper nouns consist of more than one word. In that case, capitalize each important word.

The chart below gives some rules and examples for capitalizing proper nouns.

Capitalizing Proper Nouns	
Rule	**Examples**
1. Capitalize the names of people and pets.	Pedro Garcia, Ms. Adams, Fido, the Franklins, Americans
2. Capitalize every important word in the names of particular places and things.	New England, Madison Avenue, Museum of Modern Art, Texas, San Diego, Statue of Liberty, Gulf of Mexico, Holland Tunnel
3. Capitalize the names of months, days, and holidays.	January, May, Thursday, Fourth of July, Labor Day

Summary ◆ When you write, use capital letters to begin the important words in proper nouns.

Guided Practice

Name the proper nouns in each sentence below. Tell which letters should be capitalized.

1. Last july, several students traveled with roland washington to chicago, illinois.
2. The students visited the sears tower on wacker drive.
3. At the art institute of chicago, the group saw fine needlework done by americans.

66   MECHANICS: Capitalizing Proper Nouns

ESSENTIAL LANGUAGE SKILLS
This lesson provides opportunities to:

LISTENING ◆ listen actively and attentively

SPEAKING ◆ participate in group discussions ◆ speak expressively by varying volume, rate, and intonation ◆ speak before an audience to communicate information

READING ◆ follow a set of directions ◆ understand content area vocabulary

WRITING ◆ form cursive letters legibly ◆ select and narrow a topic for a specific purpose ◆ apply conventions of punctuation and capitalization

LANGUAGE ◆ use the fundamentals of grammar, punctuation, and spelling ◆ produce a variety of sentence patterns

Practice

Write each sentence. Capitalize the proper nouns.

4. I hope uncle joe is making a quilt for my birthday
in october.

5. He is a georgian, and he lives near stone mountain.

6. On friday, manuel cruz showed the davises
a book about handicrafters.

7. The whole family liked the sampler by sarah stone
of salem, massachusetts.

8. The needlework that catherine wheeler did is beautiful.

9. A fine coverlet was embroidered by prudence
geer punderson.

10. She lived in preston, connecticut.

11. The coverlet is owned by the connecticut
historical society.

12. Have you seen this linen sampler by patty coggeshall?

13. Needleworkers such as mary comstock have left
a rich heritage for americans.

B. Write a proper noun for each common noun
below. Then use the proper noun in a sentence.
Proper nouns and sentences will vary.

14. lake	**17.** mountain	**20.** street
15. state	**18.** country	**21.** bridge
16. pet	**19.** holiday	**22.** month

C. **23–28.** Write three common
nouns and three proper
nouns for the animal
in the picture.

Answers will vary. Possible
answers are kitten, pet, cat,
Puff, Catkins, and Tiger

Apply • Think and Write

A Proper-Noun Sampler ♦ Imagine that you are going to
embroider onto a sampler some sentences about your friends. Write
the sentences. Include your friends' full names.

Sampler by Mary Hollingsworth, 1665.
Courtesy of the Essex Institute, Salem,
Massachusetts

> **✎ Remember**
> to be sure to use
> capital letters for
> proper nouns.

MECHANICS: Capitalizing Proper Nouns   **67**

◀||| TEACHING OPTIONS |||▶

RETEACHING

A Different Modality Review the rules
of capitalizing proper nouns. Using the
chart in the lesson, help students make personalized charts to illustrate the rules, using
their own names, names of friends and relatives, and names of pets to illustrate the
first rule; the names of their street, town,
and school to illustrate the second rule; and
the name of the month they were born and
their favorite holidays to illustrate the third
rule.

CLASS ENRICHMENT

A Cooperative Activity Have students
write five or six sentences about a vacation
they would like to take. Have them include
the name of a state, a city, a person, and a
month or day of the week. Then have small
groups of students work together to list all
the proper names they used and categorize
the nouns according to the rules in the lesson's chart.

CHALLENGE

An Independent Extension Have students make a list of common nouns that can
be proper nouns when part of a particular
name, such as *avenue* and *Fifth Avenue*;
fourth and *Fourth of July*; *mountain* and
Stone Mountain. Have students write a
sentence for each common noun and a sentence for each proper noun.

Example: We live on the avenue.
Fifth Avenue is a famous street in New
York.

67

■ Easy ■ Average ■ Challenging

OBJECTIVES
To write abbreviations correctly

ASSIGNMENT GUIDE
BASIC   Practice A
                 Practice B
ADVANCED   Practice C

All should do the Apply activity.

RESOURCES
■ Reteaching Master 14
■ Practice Master 14
■ ■ ■ Extra Practice, pp. 108, 112

TEACHING THE LESSON

1. Getting Started
Oral Language Focus attention on this oral activity, encouraging all to participate. You may wish to have volunteers say aloud names of other adults and other places to meet them. As students make suggestions, write the names on the chalkboard, using the appropriate abbreviations.

2. Developing the Lesson
Guide students through the explanation of abbreviations, emphasizing the examples and the summary. You may wish to tell students that the colon is used in messages to replace words such as *as follows*. You may also wish to tell students that a dictionary is a good source for the definition of any abbreviation. Lead students through the **Guided Practice**. Identify those who would benefit from reteaching. Assign independent Practice A–C.

3. Closing the Lesson
After students complete the Apply activity, you may wish to have volunteers prepare a bulletin board display of their World Travel Agency forms. Point out to students that correctly writing abbreviations and initials will ensure that readers understand their messages and lists.

◆ GETTING STARTED ◆

Follow this example to answer the questions that follow:
reminder: meet Mr. Lopez, 672 Main St.
What other adults might you meet? Where else might you meet them?

5 Abbreviations

In the following message, the letters in red are abbreviations, or shortened forms of words. The letters in blue are initials, or the first letters of names.

■ Ms. M. G. Dolan: departs for Mexico, 8:00 P.M. , Mon. , Jan. 2

Most abbreviations may be used only in special types of writing, such as messages and lists. Only titles with names (*Mr.*, *Ms.*, *Mrs.*, *Sr.*, *Jr.*, *Dr.*) and *A.M.* and *P.M.* may be used in sentences. Initials may be used in any writing. Here are some abbreviations.

Abbreviation	Explanation	Abbreviation	Explanation
Mr.	Mister (a man)	St.	Street
Ms.	a woman	Ave.	Avenue
Mrs.	a married woman	Blvd.	Boulevard
Sr.	Senior (older)	Dr.	Drive
Jr.	Junior (younger)	Rd.	Road
Dr.	Doctor	Rte.	Route
A.M.	before noon	P.M.	after noon

Mon.	Tues.	Wed.	Thurs.	Fri.	Sat.	Sun.
Jan.	Feb.	Mar.	Apr.	Aug.	Sept.	Oct.	Nov.	Dec.

Summary ◆ An **abbreviation** is a shortened form of a word. Many abbreviations begin with a capital letter and end with a period. An **initial** is the first letter of a name. It is written with a capital letter and followed by a period.

Guided Practice

Explain the abbreviations and initials in each group of words.
Initials are underlined.
1. Dr. Felicia S. Iglesias — Doctor
2. 427 Jackson Blvd. — Boulevard
3. 3:15 P.M., Tues., Aug. 19 — after noon, Tuesday, August
4. Rte. 15 and Drexler Rd. — Route, Road

68   MECHANICS: Abbreviations

ESSENTIAL LANGUAGE SKILLS
This lesson provides opportunities to:

LISTENING ◆ listen actively and attentively ◆ listen for specific information

SPEAKING ◆ speak before an audience to communicate information

READING ◆ use context to understand the meaning of words ◆ follow a set of directions ◆ read for specific details

WRITING ◆ apply increasingly complex conventions of punctuation and capitalization

LANGUAGE ◆ use the fundamentals of grammar, punctuation, and spelling

Practice

Each group of words below is written incorrectly. Write each group correctly, using capital letters and periods.

    Mr.   D.

5. mr Juan d Blanco

           Ave.

6. 57 Westmont ave

    Dr.   R.

7. dr Susan r Clayton

    Ms.

8. ms Lien Chang

          A.M. Mon. Mar.

9. 10:30 am, mon, mar 9

    Mr. D. J.   Jr.

10. mr d j Warren, jr

B. The messages below contain initials and abbreviations written incorrectly. Write each message. Correct all mistakes.

     A.M.   Dr.

11. 10:30 am: dental appointment with dr Davis

             Wed.   P.M.

12. band practice: wed at 3:15 pm

     Mrs.   Jan.

13. mrs Clement: called jan 16

                                 Ms.   F.

14. speaker about Mexican Handicrafts: ms Carmen f Acuna

                                     Dr.

15. location: Central Library on Kent dr

                              Blvd.   St.

16. Central Library entrance: between Culver blvd and Elm st

    Mon. Oct.   P.M.   M. L.

17. mon, oct 29, 5:30 pm: meet m l

C. You know that some abbreviations can be used in sentences. Find the words that can be abbreviated in the sentences below. Write the sentences with the abbreviation.

    Mr.

18. Mister Harvey took us to the Mexican Gallery of Art.

                                   Dr.

19. We went on a guided tour led by Doctor Roberto Sanchez.

                      A.M.

20. The tour began at 10:30 before noon.

                    Jr.

21. Jonathan Marks, Junior, enjoyed the handicrafts exhibit.

Apply • Think and Write

Giving Information ◆ You are taking a trip. Copy the travel agency form, and fill it out. Use abbreviations where possible.

World Travel Agency

Name _____

Street _____

City _____ State _____ Zip _____

Destination _____ Departure date _____

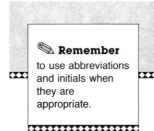

✏️ **Remember**
to use abbreviations and initials when they are appropriate.

MECHANICS: Abbreviations   **69**

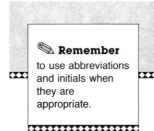

◀▥▥ TEACHING OPTIONS ▥▥▶

RETEACHING

A Different Modality On a strip of chart paper, write *Avenue* in large letters. On another strip of paper, write *Ave.* in similar letters. Ask students to tell which one is shorter. Explain that the two mean the same, but that the abbreviation is shorter and easier to write. You may wish to work through the chart of common abbreviations in the lesson, emphasizing that abbreviations usually begin with a capital letter and end with a period.

CLASS ENRICHMENT

A Cooperative Activity Have pairs of students work together to write an invitation and a guest list to an imaginary party. Tell students to use abbreviations for the day, month, time, and place on the invitation. Have them write names on the guest lists with abbreviated titles and initials for first and middle names. Tell them that addresses with abbreviations are to be written for each name.

CHALLENGE

An Independent Extension Have students use a dictionary to find and write the explanation for each abbreviation.

1. m.p.h.   miles per hour
2. R.F.D.   Rural Free Delivery
3. P.O.   Post Office
4. Gov.   Governor
5. D.C.   District of Columbia
6. Pl.   place
7. Sen.   Senator

UNIT 2/LESSON 6

■ Easy ■ Average ■ Challenging

OBJECTIVES
To form singular possessive nouns
To form plural possessive nouns

ASSIGNMENT GUIDE
BASIC   Practice A
⬇   Practice B
ADVANCED   Practice C

All should do the Apply activity.

RESOURCES
■ Reteaching Master 15
■ Practice Master 15
■ ■ ■ Extra Practice, pp. 108, 113

TEACHING THE LESSON

1. Getting Started
Oral Language Focus attention on this oral activity, encouraging all to participate. You may wish to encourage students who provide the first sentence to speak slowly and clearly. Have volunteers provide the first sentence. Suggest that partners work together to explain aloud the relationships.

2. Developing the Lesson
Guide students through the explanation of possessive nouns, emphasizing the examples and the summary. You may wish to tell students that the use of apostrophes with possessive nouns helps readers distinguish them from plural nouns in written material. Write the following sentences on the chalkboard to illustrate: *Is that a boy's shirt? Will all the boys stand up?* Lead students through the **Guided Practice**. Identify those who would benefit from reteaching. Assign independent Practice A–C.

3. Closing the Lesson
After students complete the Apply activity, have volunteers read their sentences to the class. Each time students read a possessive noun you may wish to have them write its correct form on the chalkboard. Point out to students that writing possessive nouns correctly will help them make their meaning clear.

70

◆ GETTING STARTED ◆

Have fun with sentences that show relationships. You might say, "Fluffy is Teena's brother's daughter's cat." Then a partner can try to explain, "Fluffy belongs to the daughter of the brother of Teena." Try it.

6 Possessive Nouns

You have learned that a noun names a person, a place, a thing, or an idea. The underlined word in each sentence below is a possessive noun. The possessive form of a noun shows that the person or thing named owns something.

1. The <u>girl's</u> mother is a potter.
2. The <u>vases'</u> colors are vibrant and beautiful.
3. I admire those <u>women's</u> creations.

In sentence **1** the possessive noun is singular. In sentences **2** and **3** the possessive nouns are plural.

The chart below lists the rules for forming possessive nouns. You write an apostrophe and *s* or only an apostrophe.

To form the possessive of	Add	Examples
a singular noun	's	girl's aunt, James's smile
a plural noun ending in -s	'	vases' colors, boys' hats
a plural noun not ending in -s	's	women's creations, moose's hoofs, men's jobs

> **Summary** ◆ A **possessive noun** shows ownership. When you write, be careful to form possessive nouns correctly.

Guided Practice

Name the possessive noun in each sentence below. Tell whether it is singular or plural.

1. The weavers' craft requires much skill.
2. Sara's aunts make handwoven rugs.
3. Her aunts' rugs have pictures on them.

70   GRAMMAR and MECHANICS: Possessive Nouns

ESSENTIAL LANGUAGE SKILLS
This lesson provides opportunities to:

LANGUAGE ◆ follow the logical organization of an oral presentation ◆ select from an oral presentation the information needed

SPEAKING ◆ speak slowly and clearly ◆ speak before an audience to communicate specific information

READING ◆ understand content vocabulary ◆ follow a set of directions ◆ read for specific information

WRITING ◆ apply increasingly complex conventions of punctuation and capitalization ◆ join sentences to form a paragraph

LANGUAGE ◆ use the fundamentals of grammar, punctuation, and spelling ◆ produce a variety of sentence patterns

---

70

Practice

Write the sentences. Draw one line under each possessive noun that is singular. Draw two lines under each possessive noun that is plural.

4. Thomas's uncle Nathan is a glassblower.
5. Many glassblowers' works are on display in the Chen Gallery.
6. Karen Chen, the gallery's owner, shook Nathan's hand.
7. Ms. Chen's greeting was warm and friendly.
8. She led him to the exhibitors' displays.
9. She said, "Your elegant vases show an artist's touch."
10. The man's smile lit up the gallery.
11. Then she took him to a room with children's handicrafts.
12. The young handicrafters' rag-doll exhibit was popular.
13. The youngsters' wonderful dolls received much praise.

B. Write the possessive form of each noun below.

14.	calf	18.	guests	22.	people
	calf's		guests'		people's
15.	cousin	19.	women	23.	canaries
	cousin's		women's		canaries'
16.	exhibitor	20.	deer	24.	mouse
	exhibitor's		deer's		mouse's
17.	potters	21.	weavers	25.	coaches
	potters'		weavers'		coaches'

C. Write each sentence. Choose the possessive noun in parentheses ( ) that correctly completes the sentence.

26. With my (mothers', mother's) help, I am learning to knit.
27. A (knitters', knitter's) basic stitches are the knit and the purl.
28. My two (brothers, brothers') sweaters were hard to make.
29. Knitted goods are sold at (men's, mens') clothing stores.
30. My (family's, families') preference is for handmade sweaters.

Apply • Think and Write

Craft Sale Information ♦ Imagine that you and your friends went to a sidewalk craft sale. Write several sentences telling about the things people were buying and selling. Use singular and plural possessive nouns in your writing.

✏️ **Remember**
that possessive nouns show that something belongs to someone.

GRAMMAR and MECHANICS: Possessive Nouns **71**

◀‖‖‖ TEACHING OPTIONS ‖‖‖▶

RETEACHING	**CLASS ENRICHMENT**	**CHALLENGE**
A Different Modality On the chalkboard illustrate several singular possessive nouns in phrases such as *the nose of the antelope* and *the antelope's nose*. Guide students to draw the conclusion that their meaning is the same. Be sure students recognize and understand the apostrophe. Explain that the possessive of a noun is usually formed by writing an apostrophe and s. Continue with plural possessive nouns, such as *classes'*, *men's*, *mice's*, and *babies'*.	**A Cooperative Activity** Have small groups of students work together to write a list of items they would like to sell and a list of items they would like to buy at an imaginary sale. Have students include a possessive noun to describe each item (*girls' jeans, men's ties*). Encourage students to include humorous items, such as *bears' socks* and *hummingbird's parachutes*. Encourage the groups to share their work with one another.	**An Independent Extension** Have students use a dictionary to discover the meanings of four nouns. Have them write plural possessive nouns in sentences that tell what each person would own. Example: The choreographers' dance shoes were new. 1. choreographers' 5. conductors' 2. archaeologists' 6. geniuses' 3. announcers' 7. apprentices' 4. blacksmiths' 8. senators'

■ Easy ■ Average ■ Challenging

OBJECTIVES
To use context clues to determine the meaning of an unfamiliar word or phrase

ASSIGNMENT GUIDE

BASIC   Practice A
↓   Practice B
ADVANCED   Practice C

All should do the Language Corner.

RESOURCES
■ Reteaching Master 16
■ Practice Master 16

TEACHING THE LESSON

1. Getting Started
Oral Language Focus attention on this oral activity, encouraging all to participate. As volunteers say their ideas on the meanings of the underlined words, you may wish to ask students how they deduced the correct definitions.

2. Developing the Lesson
Guide students through the explanation of context clues, emphasizing the definition and the examples. You may wish to tell students that context clues may appear in the same sentence with the unknown word or in sentences before or after that with the unknown word. Guide students through Building Your Vocabulary. Identify those who would benefit from reteaching. Assign independent Practice A–C.

3. Closing the Lesson
After students complete the Practice exercises, tell them to watch for unknown words in their reading during the rest of the day. Tell them to write in their notebooks the unknown words and any context clues that helped them understand the unknown word. Point out to students that using context clues to understand unknown words can save them trips to the dictionary.

Language Corner You may wish to have students discuss how they created their tongue twisters.

◆ GETTING STARTED ◆   What do you think the underlined words in the following sentences mean? *The clay pots were thrown on a potter's wheel. A smooth, shiny coating of glaze was then put on the crockery.*

VOCABULARY ◆
Context Clues

When you read, you often come across unfamiliar words. Sometimes the **context**, or the words that surround an unknown word, will give you clues to the word's meaning. Such clues are called **context clues**. These clues can help you understand an unknown word when you are not able to use a dictionary.

The chart below gives examples of different kinds of context clues.

Kinds of Clues	Example
A *synonym*, or word with almost the same meaning	Most textiles, or *cloths*, were originally woven on a loom.
A *definition* of the new word	Weaving is *the art of making fabric out of thread.*
Further information about the new word's meaning	A satin weave is *very smooth, soft, and shiny.*

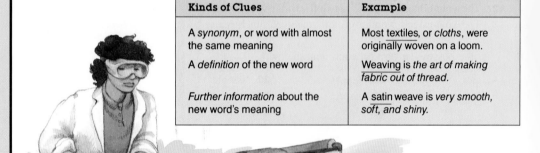

Building Your Vocabulary

Determine the meaning of each underlined word in the sentences below.  Answers will vary. Possible answers follow.

1. A <u>dowel</u> held the two pieces of wood together. This wooden pin is used in place of a metal screw or nail. a wooden pin used to join pieces of
2. The woman <u>pared</u> the wood with a chisel. Thin shavings of the wood fell to the floor. carved
3. Pottery is baked in a <u>kiln</u>, which dries out any moisture and produces a hardened product. an oven for baking pottery

72   VOCABULARY: Context Clues

ESSENTIAL LANGUAGE SKILLS
This lesson provides opportunities to:

LISTENING ◆ listen actively and attentively ◆ listen to appreciate the sound device of alliteration

SPEAKING ◆ respond appropriately to questions from teachers and peers ◆ use oral language for a variety of purposes

READING ◆ use context to understand the meaning of words ◆ evaluate and make judgments ◆ use graphic sources for information, such as tables and lists, charts and graphs ◆ read and follow printed directions

WRITING ◆ adapt information to accomplish a specific purpose with a particular audience

LANGUAGE ◆ use language for personal expression ◆ recognize ways in which language can be used to influence others

Practice

A. Write *definition*, *further information*, or *synonym* to name the context clue given for each underlined word.

definition
1. Twine, which is a strong cord, is made by weaving together several strands of string.
synonym
2. Strands of hair can be woven to form plaits, or braids.
3. Wood slats can be woven together to form a trellis, which vines can grow on.
further information
synonym
4. Cotton is often spun, or twisted, into thread.
definition
5. Yarn—that is, spun thread—is often used for weaving.

B. A *nonce word* is a word made up for a special occasion. Below are several nonce words. Use context to guess their meanings. Then write the meanings. **Answers will vary. Possible answers follow.**

trouble
6. James is in dirple because he came in late.
jogs, runs
7. Doris gets up every morning at six and trushes for two miles at a fast pace.
ice cream
8. His favorite dessert is triffium. He especially likes chocolate
ice cream
or vanilla triffium sundaes.
laughed
9. We squaked so loud that we woke our neighbors. It was the funniest program we had ever watched.
gallon
10. Dad asked me to buy a sursip, or four quarts, of milk.

C. 11–15. Make up five nonce words of your own. Then use them in sentences that show their meanings. See if your classmates can guess the meanings of your words.

LANGUAGE CORNER ◆ Alliteration

Can you say quickly three times "Sheep shun sunshine?" Tongue twisters like this use **alliteration**, the repeated use of beginning sounds.

Create some tongue twisters for your classmates to try.

VOCABULARY: Context Clues **73**

MASTERS ON FILE

RETEACHING 16

Context Clues

A context clue helps you to understand the meaning of an unfamiliar word. Draw a line to match each kind of context clue with its example.

Kind of Context Clue	Example
synonym	A minstrel is a traveling musician.
definition	A spring bouquet may include tulips and daffodils.
further information	We wrote the data, or information, in our books.

A. Read each sentence. Write the word or words that give you a clue to the meaning of the underlined word.

EXAMPLE: The marsh, or low wet land, was cold and damp. Answers may vary.
low wet land   Possible answers follow.

1. The king will banish, or send away from the kingdom, all criminals.
send away from the kingdom

2. Granite is a hard stone that does not wear away quickly.
a hard stone

3. They enjoyed the excursion so much that they were sorry when the trip ended.
trip

4. This legislature is a good law-making body.
law-making body

B. Read each sentence. Write the meaning of the underlined word.

EXAMPLE: The man's parka, or hooded jacket, was very warm. Answers may vary.
a hooded jacket   Possible answers follow.

5. He made a noose and hooked the loop of rope to the boat.
loop of rope

6. Tom trained his dog to retrieve, or bring back, a stick he threw.
to bring back

PRACTICE 16

Context Clues

A. Circle the context clue that tells the meaning of each underlined word.

1. Juan saw his favorite steed, a spotted horse.
2. As it cantered, Juan admired its easy gallop.
3. Juan stared at the overcast sky and grumbled at the clouds.
4. He stowed a raincoat in a bag. Then he packed a hat, too.
5. Juan took a running jump and vaulted into the saddle.
6. He pondered his route. He thought about it a great deal.
7. Finally he decided to ramble, or roam, near the river.

B. Write the meaning of each underlined word. Use context clues. Answers will vary. Possible answers follow.
8. He was not usually sullen, but today he felt gloomy.
gloomy

9. Sometimes a remedy, or cure, takes a long time to work. cure

10. The rain soon penetrated my jacket. It soaked right through! soaked right through

11. Sue was employed, or hired, by her uncle. hired

12. Bill established his lemonade stand last summer. He started it with Ned. started

13. The spire, or tower, rose twenty feet. tower

14. Betty sprouted two inches this fall. She never grew so fast before. grew

15. He wants to install an elevator, but it would be difficult to put one in. put in

16. A trip abroad is a trip overseas. overseas

17. Li thrashed, or tossed restlessly, all night. tossed restlessly

◀||| TEACHING OPTIONS |||▶

RETEACHING

A Different Modality Write *gannet* on the chalkboard. Ask students if they know the meaning of this word. Then write: *You can see gannets, terns, sea gulls, and other sea birds along the coast of Florida.* Now ask students if they have a better idea of what *gannet* means and ask volunteers for suggestions. Point out that the words *sea gulls* and *other sea birds* gave them clues to the word's meaning and that such clues are called *context clues*.

CLASS ENRICHMENT

A Cooperative Activity Have each student find an unfamiliar word and its definition in a dictionary. Then have each student write a sentence, underlining the chosen word and giving context clues to the word's meaning. Have partners exchange papers and guess the meaning of their partner's word. You may wish to have students read their sentences to the class and have the class figure out the meanings of the mystery words from the context clues.

CHALLENGE

An Independent Extension Have students write seven tongue twisters. Have them choose five different consonants and two different vowels. Have them practice saying their tongue twisters quickly. Then have students discuss which tongue twisters were easier to say than others and why they think this is so.

Grammar-Writing Connection

How to Revise Sentences with Nouns

Point out to students that they can use the grammar skills they learned in Unit 2 to help them develop good writing techniques. Explain that in this Grammar-Writing Connection, students will use what they know about singular and plural nouns, common and proper nouns, and possessive nouns to learn how to revise sentences with nouns.

You may wish to guide students through the explanation of how to use exact nouns, stressing the example. Then have students apply the information by completing the activity at the bottom of the first page. Students may work in small groups or with partners to choose exact nouns for each general noun orally, or they may write the exact nouns as an independent activity.

Help students to understand that using exact nouns is an effective way to improve writing by adding important details and exact information that will help readers create clear pictures in their minds. Point out that exact nouns can make their writing clearer and more interesting.

How to Revise Sentences with Nouns

You have been using nouns in sentences to name persons, places, and things. The nouns you choose can make a difference in your writing. Exact nouns can give a reader important details and information. For example, which of the sentences below gives you more information?

1. The mechanic asked Tanya for a tool.
2. The mechanic asked Tanya for a wrench.

Both sentences tell us what the mechanic asked for. Sentence **2**, however, tells us exactly what the mechanic wanted. The noun *wrench* is more exact than the general, or vague, noun *tool*. Some other exact nouns for *tool* are *pliers, saw, chisel,* and *hammer*. Asking for a specific tool can make a difference if you must pound in a nail or turn off the water in a hurry.

Look for chances to use exact nouns in your writing. They can make the difference between a vague sentence and a specific one.

The Grammar Game ◆ Check your noun knowledge from A to Z! As quickly as you can, think of exact nouns for each word or group of words below. **Answers will vary.**

athlete	furniture	laborer	sport
bird	game	machine	store
body of water	hobby	noise	tree
career	home	occasion	vegetable
dog	insect	place	world
event	jewelry	relative	zoo animal

Compare lists with a classmate. Did you write any of the same exact nouns?

ESSENTIAL LANGUAGE SKILLS

This lesson provides opportunities to:

LISTENING ◆ select from an oral presentation the information needed

SPEAKING ◆ use a variety of words to express feelings and ideas ◆ use questions to draw others into a conversation

READING ◆ understand content area vocabulary ◆ evaluate and make judgments ◆ follow a set of directions

WRITING ◆ adapt information to accomplish a specific purpose with a particular audience ◆ participate in writing conferences

LANGUAGE ◆ select a usage level appropriate for a given audience or purpose ◆ use clear and interesting words to express thoughts

Working Together

Work as a group on activities **A** and **B**. Choose exact nouns to add details and information to your writing.

A. Draw this "Word Wheel." Each group member should choose an exact noun to add information to each spoke of the wheel. Then draw the wheel again, this time writing general nouns in each spoke.

food — animal — method of transportation — musical instrument — entertainer — occupation — building — item of clothing

In Your Group

• Ask questions to get people talking.

• Build on other people's ideas.

• Keep the group on the subject.

• Help the group finish on time.

B. How well do you know your group members? Each of you should complete the paragraph by using the most exact nouns. (Don't let anyone see what you wrote!) Then mix up the papers and have the group figure out who wrote each one.   **Answers will vary.**

I almost never leave my house without my ____ . I'm most comfortable wearing ____ and ____ . I could eat ____ seven days a week. I love to go to ____ . I hope to work as a ____ someday. I think the person who invented the ____ is the greatest of them all.

WRITERS' CORNER • Fuzzy Sentences

Don't get lazy when you speak or write! Avoid using too many vague nouns in your sentences. Fuzzy, unclear sentences are dull and confusing to read. Can you tell what is happening in the fuzzy sentence below?

FUZZY: Bring me that thing so I can finish these things and go to the thing.

IMPROVED: Bring me that pan so I can finish these dishes and go to the movies.

Read what you wrote for the Writer's Warm-up. Did you use any fuzzy sentences? If you did, can you improve them?

Working Together

The Working Together activities involve students in cooperative learning work groups. This is an opportunity to pair strong writers with students whose skills are weaker. Working together, they can all experience success.

Divide the class into small groups and have students read In Your Group. Encourage them to discuss why each task is important. Have them tell what might happen if the group does not follow through on each task. *(If we do not get everyone's ideas, we may miss some ideas that could be helpful. If we do not build on other people's ideas, we are not using information effectively. If we do not keep on the subject, we will waste time and may not be able to complete the activities. If we do not help the group finish on time, our work possibly will be late.)*

Before students begin activities A and B, you may wish to have each group appoint a member to record group members' responses. You also may wish to have groups appoint a timekeeper. Then set a limit of ten or fifteen minutes. After each activity is completed, have the groups compare the exact nouns they wrote.

Writers' Corner

The Writers' Corner provides students with the opportunity to extend the Grammar-Writing Connection, helping them to develop the skills necessary to review and revise their own writing. Discuss the introductory sentences with students. Then have them work as a class or in pairs to discuss the two examples. Have students read aloud each example and identify the changes that were made. Have them tell how those changes made the improved example "sound better." Then have students apply the using exact nouns techniques from this Grammar-Writing Connection to the sentences they wrote about handicrafts for the Writers' Warm-up. Encourage students to rewrite their sentences if necessary. Discuss with them how using exact nouns improved their sentences, making their ideas clearer and more specific.

OVERVIEW

USING LANGUAGE TO INFORM

Unit 2 Overview

books FOR EXTENDED READING

EASY

The Art of the Southwest Indians by Shirley Glubok. Macmillan. Photographs and text re-create the unique arts and crafts of Native American peoples of the Southwest, including sand paintings, rock paintings, decorated pottery, and silver and turquoise jewelry.

AVERAGE

The Weaver's Gift by Kathryn Lasky. Warne. Drawing the reader into the weaver's world with a poetic text and vivid photographs, this book describes the steps involved in weaving, beginning with the birth of a lamb and covering the shearing, dyeing, spinning, and weaving of wool to make a soft blanket. **Boston Globe-Horn Book Award.**

CHALLENGING

Ceramics: From Clay to Kiln by Harvey Weiss. Young Scott. This how-to book gives instructions for all the steps involved in making pottery and is enhanced by photographs of ceramic masterpieces from ancient to modern times.

READ-ALOUD

Cabin on a Ridge by Howard Simon. Follett. In this autobiography an artist recounts his five years spent in a mountain cabin and talks about the people and the surroundings that became the subject of his art.

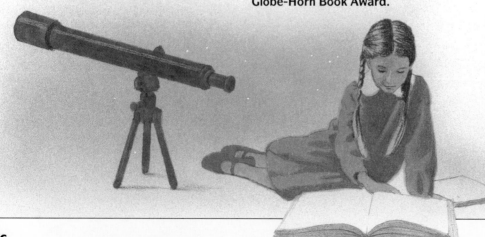

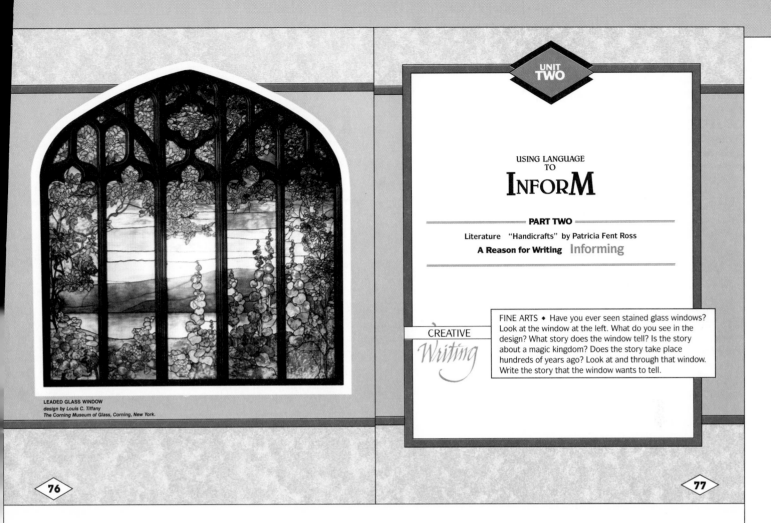

LEADED GLASS WINDOW
design by Louis C. Tiffany
The Corning Museum of Glass, Corning, New York.

UNIT TWO

USING LANGUAGE
TO
INFORM

PART TWO
Literature   "Handicrafts" by Patricia Fent Ross
A Reason for Writing Informing

CREATIVE
Writing

FINE ARTS ◆ Have you ever seen stained glass windows? Look at the window at the left. What do you see in the design? What story does the window tell? Is the story about a magic kingdom? Does the story take place hundreds of years ago? Look at and through that window. Write the story that the window wants to tell.

start with CREATIVE WRITING

Fine Arts gives your students a chance to express themselves creatively in writing. After students observe the illustration on page 76 for a moment or two, have a volunteer read aloud the Fine Arts paragraph on page 77. Have students write their reactions in their journals. Then encourage a discussion of their ideas.

VIEWING

See the **Fine Arts Transparencies with Viewing Booklet** and the **Video Library**.

THEN START WITH *part 2*

A Reason for Writing: Informing is the focus of Part 2. First students learn a thinking strategy for informing. Then they read and respond to a selection of nonfiction on which they may model their own writing. Developmental composition lessons, including "Directions," a speaking and listening lesson, help students learn to use language correctly to inform. All the lessons reflect the literature. All culminate in the Writing Process lesson. The unit ends with the Curriculum Connection and Books to Enjoy, which help students discover how their new language skills apply to writing across the curriculum and to their own lives.

◆ If you began with grammar instruction, you may wish to remind students of the unit theme, Handicrafts. Tell them that the information they gathered through the thematic lessons helped them prepare for reading the literature, *Handicrafts* by Patricia Fent Ross.

◆ If you are beginning with Part 2, use the lessons in Part 1 for remediation or instruction. For grammar, spelling, and mechanics instructional guidance, you may wish to refer to the end-of-text Glossary and Index, as well as to the *Spelling Connection* booklet; the full-color *Revising and Proofreading Transparencies;* and the Unit Pretest, Posttest, and Writing Samples.

THEME BAR

CATEGORIES	Environments	Business/World of Work	Imagination	Communications/ Fine Arts	People	Science	Expressions	Social Studies
THEMES	UNIT 1 Farm Life	UNIT 2 Handicrafts	UNIT 3 Tall Tales	UNIT 4 The Visual Arts	UNIT 5 Lasting Impressions	UNIT 6 Volcanoes	UNIT 7 Nature	UNIT 8 Animal Habitats
PACING	1 month	1 month	1 month	1 month	1 month	1 month	1 month	1 month

UNIT 2
Critical Thinking

OBJECTIVES
To use an order circle as a strategy
for informing

TEACHING THE LESSON

1. Getting Started
Oral Language Introduce the thinking skill, sequencing or putting things in order, by asking students to suppose they are looking through dresser drawers for a favorite T-shirt. Say: *You can't find it because the drawers are a mess. What could you do to make your shirts easy to find?* (e.g., *Put all of one kind of shirt together. Put all the same color together*). Explain that putting things in order is called *sequencing;* being able to figure out what kind of order to put things in is an important thinking skill.

    Metacognition Help students become aware of their own thinking (think metacognitively) by asking follow-up questions when they respond (e.g., *How did you come up with that answer?* or *Would it be possible to do it another way?*). Encourage students to be aware of their own and other students' thinking strategies and to appreciate that thinking strategies are as different as the people who use them. Explain that in this lesson they will learn about one possible strategy for putting things in order.

2. Developing the Lesson
Guide students through the introduction to informing (the kind of literature and writing they will deal with in this unit) and its connection to putting things in order. Lead them through Learning the Strategy, emphasizing the model order circle. Identify those who would benefit from reteaching. Assign Using the Strategy A and B.

3. Closing the Lesson
Metacognition Applying the Strategy is a metacognitive activity in which students consider *how* they think (question 1) and *when* they think (question 2).

    Question 1: Encourage students to think of a variety of ways of organizing dresser drawers. Ask whether they

CRITICAL THINKING ◆
A Strategy for Informing

AN ORDER CIRCLE

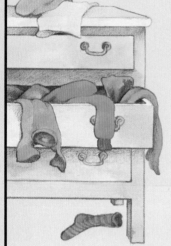

    When you write to inform, you give important facts about a topic. Sometimes you give step-by-step directions for how to do something. After this lesson, you will read an article called "Handicrafts." In it the author gives directions for making pictures with yarn. Later you will write a how-to article about something you can do well.

    "Handicrafts" is more than a how-to article. It also gives general information about Mexican villagers' crafts.

> One of the reasons the villagers still work at their crafts is that
> . . . Mexicans have a great respect for tradition . . . . A more
> important reason is that they love beauty, and they like to
> create things that are beautiful.

    The author gives two reasons why the villagers work at their crafts. A less important reason is first, a more important reason second. Putting information in order helps readers understand and remember it.

◆ Learning the Strategy

    There are many times when putting things in order is important. Suppose you decided to organize your dresser drawers. You might put your clothes in the drawers according to color. What is another way? Imagine you are describing to someone a beautiful lake where you went camping. In what order would you give the details? Suppose you have to write a report about the life of Christopher Columbus. In what order would you organize the facts? Do you think there might be another good way?

 78   CRITICAL THINKING: Sequencing

ESSENTIAL LANGUAGE SKILLS
This lesson provides opportunities to:

LISTENING ◆ listen actively and attentively ◆ follow the logical organization of an oral presentation

SPEAKING ◆ use a variety of words to express feelings and ideas

READING ◆ evaluate and make judgments ◆ follow a set of directions ◆ use graphic sources of information, such as tables and lists, charts and graphs

WRITING ◆ write and compose for a variety of purposes ◆ generate ideas using graphic organizers

LANGUAGE ◆ use language for informing

An order circle, like the one shown below, can help you. Inside the circle write what you want to put in order. On the arrows write some kinds of order. Decide which kind of order works best for what you plan to organize.

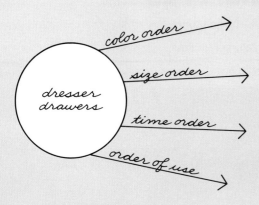

Using the Strategy

A. Use an order circle to help organize your desk. What kinds of order could you use? Which would work best? Write *my desk* inside an order circle. Write some kinds of order on the arrows. Decide which kind of order would work best. Is there another order that might work better?

B. In "Handicrafts" the author tells how to make yarn pictures. In what kind of order might the steps be given? Write *making yarn pictures* inside an order circle. Write some kinds of order on the arrows. Decide which kind of order the author will use to present the steps. Then read to find out if you were right.

Applying the Strategy

♦ How did you decide how to organize your desk? How many possible ways do you think there are?

♦ When have you had to put things in order during the past week? What kind of order did you use?

CRITICAL THINKING: Sequencing 79

found the order circle helpful in thinking through kinds of order and also to share any personal strategies they might prefer to use. For instance, some students may say they figure out how to order things by putting them in a pile and then making groups. Others may prefer to make lists. Reassure them that an order circle is only one possible strategy for deciding on a kind of order, that they should use what works for them.

Question 2: Encourage a variety of responses by asking students to think of things they have put in order at home and at school, concrete things like objects and abstract things like study schedules.

Looking Ahead

The thinking strategy introduced in this lesson, an order circle, is used in Using the Strategy B as a prereading strategy to help students anticipate the literature, "Handicrafts." It will appear three more times in this unit and again in Unit 6.

ORDER CIRCLE			
Strategy for Informing	Writing to Learn	Prewriting	Writing Across the Curriculum
79	83	96	102

Strategy for Researching	Writing to Learn	Prewriting	Writing Across the Curriculum
301	307	320	326

Although the order circle strategy is repeated in each presentation, the context in which it is used changes. Students will thus be given the opportunity to discover how the strategy can help them in reading, in writing across the curriculum, and in their daily lives.

◄|||| TEACHING OPTIONS ||||►

RETEACHING

A Different Modality On a table put some books of varying sizes and colors such as reds, blues, and browns. On the chalkboard draw an order circle with arrows labeled *size order, color order, time order, order of use, alphabetical order.* Have volunteers arrange the books in size order, then color order. Discuss how they might be arranged in time order (e.g. by copyright or subject matter era), order of use, or alphabetical order.

CLASS ENRICHMENT

A Cooperative Activity Form small groups and have them choose the dishes that would comprise a favorite meal. Ask them to imagine they are to write a paper on how to make the meal. Have them discuss what must be done and what steps followed. Have them make an order wheel and use it to help them decide on the best order for organizing the notes and writing the paper. Encourage them to consider many kinds of order.

CHALLENGE

An Independent Extension Have students choose any group of objects they like, such as seashells, kitchen utensils, coins, houses. Have them display or describe the objects in at least three different orders by drawing pictures, arranging photographs, making a list, or writing a description. Encourage imaginative kinds of order (e.g., seashells by color, by size, by shape, by kind of animal they came from, by date or place they were found).

UNIT 2
Literature

OBJECTIVES
To appreciate nonfiction
To read and respond to directions
To use a thinking strategy

VOCABULARY STRATEGIES

Developing Concepts and Teaching Vocabulary

Preteach the following words from the story. Use the Dictionary of Knowledge at the back of the book to provide definitions of base words and context sentences.

lacquer (ed), gourd

Discuss with students the idea that different fields, such as sports or the arts, have specialized vocabularies that are used to discuss them. Illustrate the concept by saying words—such as *base, bunt, outfield,* and *catcher*—that relate to baseball. Then write the vocabulary words on the chalkboard and identify them as words connected with Mexican handicrafts. Ask students if they have ever seen *gourds* at Halloween time and have them describe them. Then ask students if they have ever *lacquered* wood or another material. Ask: *How did the lacquer make the wood look?* (shiny)

GUIDING COMPREHENSION

Building Background

The first half of this unit includes information especially chosen to build background for *Handicrafts*. If you started the unit with grammar instruction, you may wish to have a class discussion on handicrafts, based on the information in those lessons.

   If you started the unit with composition instruction, you may wish to build students' knowledge of handicrafts by asking: *Have you ever made a bracelet or belt for yourself or someone else? Have you ever made a pot or bowl in art class? What is important to remember about following directions? What types of handicrafts do you know and admire?* (Students may recall that

LITERATURE
Handicrafts
from Mexico
By Patricia Fent Ross

80   LITERATURE: Nonfiction

ESSENTIAL LANGUAGE SKILLS

This lesson provides opportunities to:

LISTENING ◆ listen for specific information ◆ listen actively and attentively

SPEAKING ◆ use oral language for a variety of purposes ◆ use a set of reasons to persuade a group

READING ◆ understand content area vocabulary ◆ understand cause-and-effect relationships ◆ evaluate and make judgments ◆ respond to various forms of literature

WRITING ◆ use chronological and spatial order and order of importance

LANGUAGE ◆ use language to inform

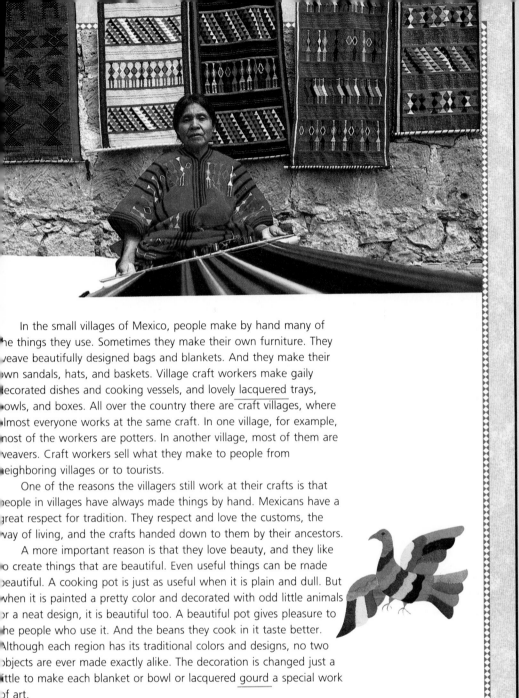

In the small villages of Mexico, people make by hand many of the things they use. Sometimes they make their own furniture. They weave beautifully designed bags and blankets. And they make their own sandals, hats, and baskets. Village craft workers make gaily decorated dishes and cooking vessels, and lovely lacquered trays, bowls, and boxes. All over the country there are craft villages, where almost everyone works at the same craft. In one village, for example, most of the workers are potters. In another village, most of them are weavers. Craft workers sell what they make to people from neighboring villages or to tourists.

One of the reasons the villagers still work at their crafts is that people in villages have always made things by hand. Mexicans have a great respect for tradition. They respect and love the customs, the way of living, and the crafts handed down to them by their ancestors.

A more important reason is that they love beauty, and they like to create things that are beautiful. Even useful things can be made beautiful. A cooking pot is just as useful when it is plain and dull. But when it is painted a pretty color and decorated with odd little animals or a neat design, it is beautiful too. A beautiful pot gives pleasure to the people who use it. And the beans they cook in it taste better. Although each region has its traditional colors and designs, no two objects are ever made exactly alike. The decoration is changed just a little to make each blanket or bowl or lacquered gourd a special work of art.

LITERATURE: Nonfiction ◇ 81 ◇

practical and are made by people all over the world. They probably know that directions need to be followed step by step with careful attention to details.) You may wish to share with students that all through history people have been making practical items such as blankets, pots, and clothes more beautiful by embellishing them with decoration and color.

Developing a Purpose for Reading

Option 1: Have students set their own purpose for reading. Then have them read the story introduction and study the illustrations. On the chalkboard write *I expect . . .* and have students complete the sentence telling what they expect they might learn in the following articles. Remind students to recall what they know about handicrafts before writing. When the sentences are written, have volunteers share their sentences with the class. Suggest that students read the articles to find how many of their questions are answered.

Option 2: If you wish to set a reading purpose for everyone, have students pay special attention to what is unique about Mexican handicrafts and about yarn paintings. Have them ask themselves: *What are Mexican handicrafts like? How is a yarn painting different from other kinds of painting?*

GUIDED READING

Please note that opportunities for students' personal responses to the selection are offered in the Reader's Response question and the Selection Follow-up at the end of this lesson.

Page 80 *What are some of the things the people in small Mexican villages make by hand?* (They make sandals, hats, baskets, bags, blankets, and so forth.) RECALL: DETAILS

Page 81 *Why do villagers still make things by hand?* (They respect tradition and love the customs, way of living, and crafts handed down by their ancestors. They also love beauty and enjoy creating beautiful things.) INFER: CAUSE/EFFECT

SUMMARY

"Handicrafts," an excerpt from a social studies textbook, gives students the opportunity to experience reading in the content areas. The selection introduces the handmade goods made by craft workers—potters and weavers—in villages throughout Mexico. It describes the crafts they make and tells about the Mexican respect for tradition and love of beautiful things. "How to Make a Yarn Painting" is a how-to piece about Mexican-style yarn painting.

ABOUT THE AUTHOR

PATRICIA FENT ROSS is the author of "Handicrafts." Her article can be found in *Mexico,* published by the Fideler Company in 1982.

Page 82 *How is a yarn painting different from other paintings?* (The color and design are made with yarn instead of paint.) INFER: DETAILS

Page 82 *Why do you think it is important not to use too much glue when making a yarn painting?* (It takes only a small amount, and too much will be messy and may damage the painting.) ANALYZE: CAUSE/EFFECT

Returning to the Reading Purpose

Option 1: Those students who have written "I expect" sentences may wish to review them to determine which of their questions were answered.

Option 2: If you have established a common reading purpose, review it and ask volunteers to tell what they learned about Mexican handicrafts and yarn paintings from these articles.

READER'S RESPONSE

What handicraft would you like to know how to make? Tell why. (You may wish to provide time for volunteers to tell about the handicrafts they know how to make or ones they have admired at craft shows or museums.)

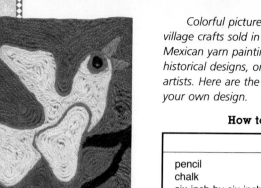

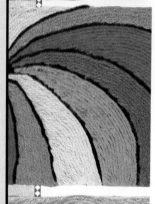

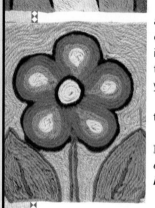

Colorful pictures "painted" with yarn are one of the village crafts sold in marketplaces in modern Mexico. These Mexican yarn paintings may picture animals and flowers, historical designs, or any other subjects that interest the artists. Here are the directions for making a yarn painting of your own design.

How to Make a Yarn Painting

You will need	
pencil	paper
chalk	white glue
six-inch by six-inch cardboard	yarn

The first step in making a yarn painting is to plan your design carefully. Sketch a simple design on a piece of paper. Plan which colors of yarn you will use.

Next, use chalk to lightly copy your sketch onto the cardboard square. The chalk can be rubbed off later if it is not completely covered by yarn.

Begin outlining your design with a dark color of yarn. Cover a small part of your outline with beads of glue. It takes only a small amount, so be careful not to use too much. Lightly press a piece of yarn onto the glue. Continue outlining your design in this way.

When your outline is complete, fill in the rest of the design with a lighter color of yarn. Continue putting glue on small sections and covering them with yarn. Applying the yarn in one direction might improve the appearance of your finished painting. You might choose to apply the yarn up and down, side to side, or round and round until your outline is filled.

Last, you may wish to glue a small loop of yarn to the back of the painting. Then you can hang it up for others to enjoy.

Library Link ♦ *If you would like to learn more about the country of Mexico, read* Mexico, *in the American Neighbors series, by Patricia Fent Ross.*

 Reader's Response

What handicraft would you like to know how to make? Tell why.

82 LITERATURE: Nonfiction

STRATEGIC READING

Page 82 Point out to students the difference between the way the information about Mexican handicrafts and a yarn painting is presented. The information about the yarn painting is presented as a recipe. It begins with a list of materials and then tells what to do first, second, and so forth. The information about Mexican handicrafts begins with a general description and ends with the most important reason people make things by hand.

HIGHLIGHTING LITERATURE

Page 82 Ask students to think of one or two questions that might be used to test someone's understanding of what they have read. You may then have students work in pairs to ask and answer each other's questions. You may wish to suggest that they pay special attention to what is most important, less important, and so forth. METACOGNITION: ASKING QUESTIONS

Handicrafts

 ## Responding to Literature

1. Hundreds of years ago, potters fashioned bowls on wheels that they turned by hand. Many artists make bowls in the same way today. Those artists could use machines to do their work. Why do you think they prefer to work in the old ways?

2. Many people have respect for tradition. Cooking and stuffing a Thanksgiving turkey is an example of a tradition that many American families enjoy. Tell about your favorite tradition. What makes it special to you?

3. You know that a weaver is a person who weaves fabric or rugs. A weaver uses tools such as yarn and a loom. Many people use tools in their work. What tools do these workers use?

carpenter   auto mechanic   chef   journalist

Writing to Learn

Think and Order ◆ An order circle helps you decide how something should be arranged. Plan information to tell how to do something. Make an order circle like the one below. Choose the order you will use to present your information.

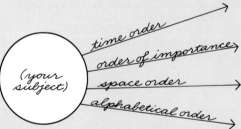

Order Circle

Write ◆ Use the order you chose. Write your information in that order.

LITERATURE: Nonfiction   83

 World of Language Audio Library

A recording of this selection is available in the **Audio Library.**

WRITING TO LEARN

Have students apply the thinking strategy of making an order circle as described in Think and Order. Then have them complete the Write activity by writing their information in the order they choose. Have volunteers share with the class their instructions on how to create a handicraft.

SELECTION FOLLOW-UP

You may wish to incorporate any or all of the following discussion questions and activities in your follow-up to the literature selection, *Handicrafts.*

RESPONDING TO LITERATURE

Encourage students to use their personal experiences as well as what they learned from the selection to discuss these questions. The questions are designed to encourage students to think of and respond to the selection as a whole. Explain to students that although they may use details from the selection to support their opinions, the questions have no right or wrong answers. Encourage them to express a variety of points of view. You may wish to have students respond as a class, in groups, or with partners.

1. *Hundreds of years ago, potters fashioned bowls on wheels that they turned by hand. Many artists make bowls in the same way today. Those artists could use machines to do their work. Why do you think they prefer to work in the old ways?* (To give students a point of view for the discussion, ask them about the satisfaction they felt when they made something by hand.)

2. *Many people have respect for tradition. Cooking and stuffing a Thanksgiving turkey is an example of a tradition that many American families enjoy. Tell about your favorite tradition. What makes it special to you?* (Students may wish to share their feelings about favorite holidays. You may wish to tell them that the basis for some of these holiday traditions go back hundreds and sometimes thousands of years. People enjoy following traditions because they give them a connection with their pasts and their ancestors.)

3. *You know that a weaver is a person who weaves fabric or rugs. A weaver uses tools such as yarn and a loom. Many people use tools in their work. What tools do these workers use: carpenter, auto mechanic, chef, journalist?* (Students probably know that carpenters use such tools as hammers, saws, and nails; auto mechanics have special sets of wrenches; chefs have utensils similar to those used in their own kitchens to cook; and journalists use paper, pencils, telephones, and computers.)

UNIT 2
Speaking/Listening

■ Easy ■ Average ■ Challenging

OBJECTIVES
To recognize that directions give information
To use guidelines for giving, listening to, and following directions

ASSIGNMENT GUIDE
BASIC   Practice A

↓

ADVANCED   Practice B

All should do the Apply activity.

RESOURCES
■ World of Language Video Library

TEACHING THE LESSON

1. Getting Started
Oral Language Focus attention on this oral activity, encouraging all to participate. You may wish to suggest different shapes for students to describe, such as a circle, square, rectangle, or triangle.

2. Developing the Lesson
Guide students through a discussion of the lesson, emphasizing the guidelines for giving and following directions. Have volunteers tell what would happen if any of the guidelines for giving directions were not followed. You may wish to ask questions, such as: *What would happen if you did not give the steps in the correct order?* Then lead students through the **Guided Practice**. Identify those who would benefit from reteaching. Assign independent Practice A and B.

To allow students to practice their speaking and listening skills, you may wish to provide as much class time as possible for oral discussion throughout this lesson.

3. Closing the Lesson
After students complete the Apply activity, call on individuals to read aloud their directions for locating and recognizing Ursa Major. Point out that knowing how to give and following directions will help students enjoy learning and teaching new things.

♦ GETTING STARTED ♦

Picture a shape in your mind. Without revealing what the shape is, tell your listeners how to draw it. How many of them can draw the shape?

SPEAKING and LISTENING ♦
Directions

In the past, people learned the handicrafts of their ancestors by listening and watching. They followed the directions of their elders as they learned to make pottery, to weave, and to decorate tools and everyday objects. Knowing how to give and how to follow directions is just as important today as it was then. We still give oral directions to teach someone else what we know. We listen to directions to find out how to do something new. We observe, too, although we now often turn to "how-to" books or television programs.

Here are some guidelines to help you give and follow oral directions. These same guidelines might well have been followed by your ancestors as they learned and taught their handicrafts to their children.

Giving Directions	1. Look directly at your listeners and speak clearly. 2. Tell what materials, if any, are needed. 3. Explain every step in its correct order, giving details so that your listeners can picture each step. 4. Use gestures, drawings, or objects to help you. 5. Ask if there are any questions.
Following Directions	1. Look directly at the speaker and listen closely. 2. Show that you understand; for example, nod your head. 3. Picture each step in your mind. 4. Repeat the directions to yourself or to the speaker. 5. Ask the speaker to explain anything you do not understand.

Summary ♦ Give complete directions and explain the steps in order. Listen closely to directions to picture each step and to remember the steps in order.

84   SPEAKING and LISTENING: Directions

ESSENTIAL LANGUAGE SKILLS
This lesson provides opportunities to:

LISTENING ♦ listen for specific information ♦ follow oral directions ♦ follow the logical organization of an oral presentation ♦ select from an oral presentation the information needed

SPEAKING ♦ participate in group discussions ♦ speak expressively by varying volume, rate, and intonation ♦ speak before an audience to communicate specific information ♦ make organized oral presentations

READING ♦ follow a set of directions ♦ accurately comprehend the details in a reading selection ♦ locate and utilize desired information in reference sources

WRITING ♦ apply conventions of punctuation and capitalization ♦ write and compose for a variety of purposes

LANGUAGE ♦ use modifiers correctly ♦ produce a variety of sentence patterns

You may wish to use the *Video Library* to teach this lesson.

Guided Practice

The pictures on this page show how to make a yarn doll. Study the pictures. Then take turns giving and listening to directions on how to make it.

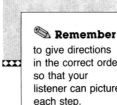

A.
8"

B.
2"

C.

D.
3"

E.

Practice

A. Work with a partner. Choose one of the ideas below. Take turns giving clear and complete directions. Make notes for yourself if you wish. As a listener, picture each step in your mind. Ask questions about anything you do not understand.
Answers will vary.
  1. Explain how to mix paints to make different colors.
  2. Tell how to make a colorful bookmark.
  3. Tell how to check a book out of the library.
  4. Explain the safe way to use swings on the playground.
  5. Explain how to use the telephone.

B. With a partner, take turns giving and following directions. Choose one of the ideas below, and give step-by-step directions for that task. To find out whether your directions are clear and complete, ask your partner to do *only* what you say.
Answers will vary.
  6. how to sharpen a pencil
  7. how to zip a jacket
  8. how to draw an automobile
  9. how make a paper-bag book cover
  10. how to find a word in a dictionary

Apply ◆ Think and Write

Dictionary of Knowledge ◆ Have you ever heard of Ursa Major? Look it up in the Dictionary of Knowledge. Write a set of directions telling how to locate and recognize Ursa Major in the night sky. Then you will be able to tell someone else how to locate this constellation.

✎ **Remember**
to give directions in the correct order so that your listener can picture each step.

SPEAKING and LISTENING: Directions **85**

EVALUATION PROGRAM

See Evaluation and Testing Program, pp. C9–C11.

Speaking and Listening Checklist Masters

◀║║ TEACHING OPTIONS ║║▶

RETEACHING

A Different Modality Have students reverse the Guided Practice activity. Instead of looking at pictures that show how to do something, have them draw pictures that show how to do one other activity they choose, such as *How to Bathe a Dog, How to Make a Bed,* or *How to Tie a Bow.* Have volunteers explain their pictures.

CLASS ENRICHMENT

A Cooperative Activity Provide pairs of students with colored paper, scissors, and glue. Allow each pair to choose two or three additional items from a box of supplies (e.g., sparkles, yarn, buttons, wire). Have each pair work together to decide on something to make with their materials, make it, then write and illustrate directions for making it. Post creations and directions together.

CHALLENGE

An Independent Extension Have students investigate the art of origami in the library and learn how to make one or more origami figures. You may wish to have them write directions for one of their figures, using their own words and including illustrations when appropriate. Alternatively, allow them to do the activity with any other craft they choose to read about.

UNIT 2
Writing

■ Easy ■ Average ■ Challenging

OBJECTIVES
To identify a paragraph as a group of sentences about one main idea
To write sentences in paragraph form

ASSIGNMENT GUIDE
BASIC   Practice A

⬇

ADVANCED   Practice B

All should do the Apply activity.

RESOURCES
■ Reteaching Master 17
■ Practice Master 17

TEACHING THE LESSON

1. Getting Started
Oral Language Focus attention on this oral activity, encouraging all to participate. You may wish to choose a picture in the textbook and tell its main idea, allowing two volunteers to give details about it. Write the main idea and details on the chalkboard and label them appropriately.

2. Developing the Lesson
Guide students through the explanation of a paragraph, emphasizing the example and the summary. You may wish to tell students that writers sometimes leave an extra blank line between paragraphs. Then lead students through the **Guided Practice**. Identify those who would benefit from reteaching. Assign independent Practice A–B.

3. Closing the Lesson
After students complete the Apply activity, have volunteers read aloud their paragraphs. You may wish to have classmates identify the main idea of each paragraph as it is read. Point out to students that knowing what paragraphs are and writing them correctly will help them be sure their meaning is clear to their readers.

Play "What's the Big Idea?" Choose a picture in this book and te its main idea in a sentence. Whoever finds the picture first and gives two details about it gives the next main idea.

WRITING ◆
A Paragraph

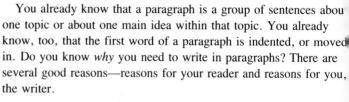

You already know that a paragraph is a group of sentences abou one topic or about one main idea within that topic. You already know, too, that the first word of a paragraph is indented, or moved in. Do you know *why* you need to write in paragraphs? There are several good reasons—reasons for your reader and reasons for you, the writer.

Let us consider your reader first. Pick up a book and find a page without pictures. Now imagine that page without paragraphs. Would you want to read it? You would probably look at it and think, "Give me a break!" That is exactly what a new paragraph gives the reader—a mental break.

More importantly, though, paragraphs signal major ideas. A new paragraph tells the reader, "You have just come to the end of one main idea. Now the author is going to discuss another."

What does writing paragraphs do for you, the writer? As you write a paragraph, you have to focus on your main idea. All of the sentences in the paragraph must relate to the main idea. The paragraph gives you writing power, because it helps to make your meaning clear. Notice how the paragraph below focuses your attention on its main idea.

> One of the reasons the villagers still work at their crafts is that people in villages have always made things by hand. Mexicans have a great respect for tradition. They respect and love the customs, the way of living, and the crafts handed down to them by their ancestors.

Summary ◆ A **paragraph** is a group of sentences that tell about one main idea. When you write a paragraph, indent the first word.

86   WRITING: Paragraphs

ESSENTIAL LANGUAGE SKILLS
This lesson provides opportunities to:

LISTENING ◆ distinguish between main and supporting ideas in an oral message ◆ select from an oral presentation the information needed

SPEAKING ◆ make organized oral presentations ◆ speak before an audience to communicate information

READING ◆ determine the main idea of a reading selection ◆ recall specific facts and ideas that support a main idea ◆ follow a set of directions ◆ arrange events in sequential order

WRITING ◆ select and narrow a topic for a specific purpose ◆ apply conventions of punctuation and capitalization ◆ join sentences to form a paragraph

LANGUAGE ◆ use the fundamentals of grammar, spelling, and punctuation ◆ produce a variety of sentence patterns

Guided Practice

Some of the sentences below belong together in a paragraph. Others do not. Tell which sentences belong in the paragraph. *3, 5*

1. The history of handicrafts is as old as history itself.
2. Handicrafts can help disabled people develop stronger muscles.
3. The first handicrafts developed as people made useful objects.
4. Hobbies are not necessarily the same thing as handicrafts.
5. Basketry, weaving, and pottery were among the first handicrafts.

Practice

A. Decide which sentences below belong in a paragraph about making quilts. For each sentence, write *yes* or *no*.

6. Three layers of fabric are used to make a quilt. yes
7. Quilts are a popular item in antique stores. no
8. People appreciate the warmth of a fine down quilt. no
9. Pieces of cloth can be sewn together to make a quilt top. yes
10. The quilter needs thread, scissors, and special needles. yes

B. Decide which three sentences below tell about the main idea. Then use the main idea and the three sentences to write a paragraph. Start with the main idea. Paragraph includes sentences 12, 14, 15.

MAIN IDEA: Papier-mâché craft is inexpensive and fun.

11. Working in stained glass is an expensive handicraft.
12. This material is made from paper, water, and paste.
13. Professional jewelry designers work with papier-mâché.
14. Papier-mâché is used like clay to model almost anything.
15. Jewelry, masks, and puppets are just a few things you can make from papier-mâché.

Apply ♦ Think and Write

An Informative Photo ♦ Write a paragraph about the photograph on this page. It shows a jewelry maker at work. Think of a main idea first and use it to decide what you will say.

✎ **Remember**
that a paragraph focuses on a single main idea.

WRITING: Paragraphs **87**

RETEACHING 17
Paragraphs

Read the paragraph. The sentence that tells the main idea is underlined. Circle the indented word.

Insects use feelers, or antennae, to sense things. The antennae help insects smell and feel. Sometimes they help them taste and hear, too!

➥ A **paragraph** is a group of sentences that tells about one main idea. The first word in the paragraph is indented. It is a signal to the reader that the sentences are about a new idea.

A. Write yes beside each sentence that belongs in a paragraph about starfish. Write no beside each sentence that does not belong.

EXAMPLE: The body of a starfish is covered with spines. __yes__

1. It has five arms that come out from its center part. yes
2. Sand dollars are round and have spiny skin. no
3. The underside of each arm has rows of tiny tube feet. yes
4. The tube feet enable the starfish to walk on the ocean floor. yes

B. Draw a line through each sentence that does not belong in the paragraph. The first one is done for you.

It is not necessary to be afraid of spiders. Few of them are harmful. ~~Many people fear snakes.~~ In fact, many spiders are useful because they kill harmful insects. ~~A daddy longlegs is not a true spider.~~

C. Write each sentence you did not cross out in Exercise A to form a paragraph. The first sentence is done for you.

It is not necessary to be afraid of spiders. Few of them are harmful.

In fact, many spiders are useful because they kill harmful insects.

PRACTICE 17
Paragraphs

➥ A **paragraph** is a group of sentences that tells about one main idea. When you write a paragraph, indent the first word.

A. Write yes beside each sentence that belongs in a paragraph about James Weldon Johnson. Write no if a sentence does not belong.

1. James Weldon Johnson had many talents and interests. yes
2. He was active in the civil rights movement. yes
3. Martin Luther King, Jr., was active in the civil rights movement. no
4. Johnson was a poet. yes
5. In 1900 he wrote a poem in honor of Abraham Lincoln's birthday. yes
6. Not all poems rhyme. no
7. Many poems tell long stories. no
8. Johnson's brother set the words to music. yes
9. Their work became the song "Lift Ev'ry Voice and Sing." yes
10. Scott Joplin was a talented music composer. no

B. Use the sentences with yes after them in Exercise A to write a paragraph about James Weldon Johnson. Write the sentences in paragraph form, leaving out the numbers. Be sure to indent the first word of the paragraph.

James Weldon Johnson had many talents and interests. He was active in the civil rights movement. Johnson was a poet. In 1900 he wrote a poem in honor of Abraham Lincoln's birthday. Johnson's brother set the words to music. Their work became the song "Lift Ev'ry Voice and Sing."

WRITE IT
Write a paragraph on a separate sheet of paper. Use your favorite song as your main idea. Then write details that tell why it is your favorite song. *Answers will vary.*

◀▥▥ TEACHING OPTIONS ▥▥▶

RETEACHING

A Different Modality Choose a topic, such as *Pets,* and use it as the focus of a semantic map. Have students brainstorm categories for the map relating to pets, such as *Kinds of Pets* and *Benefits of Owning a Pet.* Have students choose one category and brainstorm ideas relating to it. Have them help you develop a paragraph on the chalkboard, using their list. Encourage discussion and evaluation of each idea included in the paragraph.

CLASS ENRICHMENT

A Cooperative Activity Have small groups of students work together to choose a topic, such as *Computers in the Classroom and How We Use Them.* Tell them to write a main idea sentence and details about their topic. When they are finished, have group members check to see that each detail tells about the main idea and then use them to compose a paragraph. You may wish to have the recorder in each group read its paragraph to the class.

CHALLENGE

An Independent Extension Have students analyze three paragraphs from their social studies or science textbook. Tell them to write a main idea sentence from each paragraph and then list the details. You may wish to have students exchange papers with a partner and then work together to check their work.

UNIT 2
Writing

■ Easy ■ Average ■ Challenging

OBJECTIVES
To identify the topic sentence and the supporting sentences in a paragraph
To write complete paragraphs by supplying topic and supporting sentences

ASSIGNMENT GUIDE
BASIC   Practice A
↓   Practice B
ADVANCED   Practice C

All should do the Apply activity.

RESOURCES
■ Reteaching Master 18
■ Practice Master 18

TEACHING THE LESSON

1. Getting Started
Oral Language Focus attention on this oral activity, encouraging all to participate. You may wish to write the main ideas and their details on the chalkboard as students respond. Encourage imaginative responses, such as *Many kinds of life are found in the ocean* (main idea). *Plants grow on the ocean floor* (detail). *Fish and aquatic mammals live in the water* (detail).

2. Developing the Lesson
Guide students through the explanation of a topic sentence and supporting sentences, emphasizing the examples and the summary. Lead students through the **Guided Practice**. Identify those who would benefit from reteaching. Assign independent Practice A–C.

3. Closing the Lesson
After students complete the Apply activity, have volunteers read aloud the paragraphs they wrote. Encourage a discussion that evaluates the placement of each topic sentence. Point out to students that knowing how to state the main idea in a topic sentence can help both them and their readers focus on the most important ideas.

List some main ideas about your classroom, such as *Our classroom is a creative place*. Take turns giving details that explain one of those main ideas.

WRITING ◆ Topic Sentence and Supporting Sentences

Every paragraph has a main idea. Some paragraphs put that main idea into words. If a paragraph puts that idea into words, it is stated in a topic sentence. The topic sentence often comes first, since it is helpful to let the reader know the topic of the paragraph right away. The other sentences in the paragraph are supporting sentences. They support the main idea by telling more about it or by giving details about it. Here is an example. Notice that the supporting sentences are arranged in a logical order.

Topic sentence
Supporting sentences

> All over Mexico there are craft villages. Almost everyone works at the same craft. In one village, for example, most of the people may be potters. In another they may be weavers, and in still another they may be jewelry makers.

A topic sentence does not have to come first. Often it comes last. Then the supporting sentences lead up to the main idea, as in this example.

Supporting sentences
Topic sentence

> In one Mexican village most of the people are potters. In another they are weavers. In still another they are jewelry makers. Such villages are common. All over Mexico there are craft villages.

When the purpose of your writing is to give information, you may wish to begin or end a paragraph with a topic sentence. It helps both you and your reader focus on the most important idea.

> **Summary ◆** The **topic sentence** states the main idea of a paragraph. **Supporting sentences** develop the main idea. Topic sentences are especially useful in informative writing.

88 WRITING: Topic Sentence and Supporting Sentences

ESSENTIAL LANGUAGE SKILLS
This lesson provides opportunities to:

LISTENING ◆ listen actively and attentively ◆ follow oral directions

SPEAKING ◆ speak before an audience to communicate information

READING ◆ arrange events in sequential order ◆ determine the main idea of a reading selection ◆ recall specific facts and ideas that support a main idea

WRITING ◆ apply conventions of punctuation and capitalization ◆ join sentences to form a paragraph ◆ participate in writing conferences

LANGUAGE ◆ use the fundamentals of grammar, punctuation, and spelling ◆ produce a variety of sentence patterns

Guided Practice

Put these sentences in order, starting with the topic sentence. Then arrange the supporting sentences in a logical order.
Sentence order should be 2, 3, 1, 5, 4.

1. There may be many that look alike.
2. Pottery is made by craftspeople and in factories.
3. Inexpensive mugs, for example, are generally mass-produced.
4. Some pieces of pottery have become valuable.
5. A potter, however, is more likely to make a one-of-a-kind piece considered a work of art.

Practice

A. Use the sentences below to write a paragraph. Find the topic sentence and write it first. Then complete the paragraph by writing the supporting sentences. Write them in an order that makes sense.
Sentence order should be 7, 9, 6, 8.

6. By folding and curving the paper, you get a new effect.
7. Paper sculpture is fun to try.
8. The curved paper looks three-dimensional.
9. Begin by folding and curving a flat piece of paper.

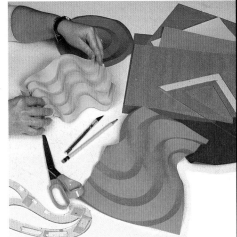

B. Write two supporting sentences for each topic sentence below.
Sentences will vary but must give supporting details.

10. You can make many beautiful things from seashells.
11. Papier-mâché can be used instead of clay.

C. Write a topic sentence and two or more supporting sentences for each of these topics. Sentences will vary. Topic sentence must state the main idea. Supporting sentences must provide details.

12. a handicraft you would like to try
13. why people enjoy handicrafts

Apply • Think and Write

A Paragraph • Will everything be made by machines in the future? Write a paragraph that tells about handicrafts in the year 2500. Begin or end your paragraph with a topic sentence.

✎ **Remember**
to state the main idea of your paragraph in a topic sentence.

WRITING: Topic Sentence and Supporting Sentences **89**

MASTERS ON FILE

RETEACHING 18

Topic and Supporting Sentences

Read the paragraph below. The first sentence tells the main idea, or topic. The other sentences give details about the main idea. They are called supporting sentences. Underline the supporting sentences.

There are many pictures and paintings of Abraham Lincoln. They usually show him with a full beard. In most pictures his expression looks serious.

Every paragraph has a main idea. The **topic sentence** states the main idea of a paragraph. **Supporting sentences** develop the main idea.

A. The sentences below are in scrambled order. Find the topic sentence and write topic next to it. Write supporting next to each supporting sentence.

EXAMPLE: He traveled from Virginia to New York.　supporting

1. A large, cheering crowd watched as he was sworn into office.　supporting
2. He stood on a balcony above Wall Street.　supporting
3. George Washington became our first president on April 30, 1789.　topic
4. The people heard him promise to defend the United States.　supporting
5. This ceremony marked the start of his presidency.　supporting
6. He proceeded to become a great president.　supporting

B. Use sentences 1–6 in Exercise A to write a paragraph. Write the topic sentence first. Then complete the paragraph by writing the supporting sentences. Write them in an order that makes sense.　Answers will vary. Possible answer follows.

George Washington became our first president on April 30, 1789. He stood on a balcony above Wall Street. A large, cheering crowd watched as he was sworn into office. The people heard him promise to defend the United States. This ceremony marked the start of his presidency.

He proceeded to become a great president.

PRACTICE 18

Topic and Supporting Sentences

A **topic sentence** states the main idea of the paragraph. **Supporting sentences** develop the main idea.

A. Use the sentences below to write a paragraph. Find and write the topic sentence first. Complete the paragraph by writing the supporting sentences in an order that makes sense.

1. Other sources of energy include wind and water.
2. One major source of energy is the burning of fossil fuels.
3. A high standard of living depends on a plentiful supply of energy.
4. Atomic power adds to our supply of energy, too.　Answers will vary. Possible answer follows.

A high standard of living depends on a plentiful supply of energy. One major source of energy is the burning of fossil fuels. Other sources of energy include wind and water. Atomic power adds to our supply of energy, too.

B. Use the ideas in the box to write a topic sentence and supporting sentences.

Personal Energy		
exercise	rest	energy for daily activities
proper diet		enough sleep

Answers will vary. Possible answer follows.

There are several ways you can make sure you have enough energy for your daily activities. First, you should get the right kind of exercise. Second, you should rest during the day and get enough sleep at night. Third, you should eat a proper diet.

WRITE IT
Write a paragraph that tells what you do to get enough energy. Underline your topic sentence. Write on a separate sheet of paper.　Answers will vary.

◀‖‖ TEACHING OPTIONS ‖‖▶

RETEACHING

A Different Modality On cardboard strips, write each sentence of a four- or five-sentence paragraph from a social studies or science textbook. Star the topic sentence. Explain that it tells the main idea of the paragraph and that a topic sentence may appear anywhere in a paragraph. Have students take turns manipulating the sentence order. Encourage discussion of the placement of the topic sentence and the supporting sentences.

CLASS ENRICHMENT

A Cooperative Activity Have small groups of students work together to compose a paragraph about a real or an imaginary person. Have each group write a topic sentence, underline it, and then write supporting sentences. Then have the group recorder read aloud their paragraph, omitting the topic sentence. Have classmates suggest a topic sentence and then compare it to the original one.

CHALLENGE

An Independent Extension Have students write a paragraph about their favorite sport, with at least two supporting sentences for their topic sentence. Encourage them to try to place their topic sentence both at the beginning and end of the paragraph.

UNIT 2
Writing

OBJECTIVES
To use commas correctly (in a series; after *yes, no, well*; direct address; last name written first)

ASSIGNMENT GUIDE
BASIC   Practice A
   ↓   Practice B
ADVANCED   Practice C

All should do the Apply activity.

RESOURCES
■ Reteaching Master 19
■ Practice Master 19

TEACHING THE LESSON

1. Getting Started
Oral Language Focus attention on this oral activity, encouraging all to participate. Help students to recognize that there are two correct responses for each name listed: Benjamin Franklin and Franklin, Benjamin; Thomas Jefferson and Jefferson, Thomas. You may wish to encourage students to name other people who have two "first" names, such as John Glenn, Matthew Perry, John Henry, Patrick Henry, Jesse James, Susan B. Anthony, and Frederick Douglass.

2. Developing the Lesson
Guide students through the explanation of using commas, emphasizing the examples and the summary. Lead students through the **Guided Practice.** Identify those who would benefit from reteaching. Assign independent Practice A–C.

3. Closing the Lesson
After students complete the Apply activity, have volunteers display their charts. Encourage discussion of how a listing by last name first can help a reader. *(More than one student may have the same first name; the last name immediately makes clear who is meant; it is used when alphabetizing names.)* Point out to students that using commas correctly can help to make their meaning clear and their writing easier to understand.

I was an early American statesman and scientist. Find my name.
Benjamin Franklin   Franklin, Benjamin   Benjamin, Franklin
I was the third American president. Find my name.
Jefferson, Thomas   Thomas Jefferson   Thomas, Jefferson

WRITING ♦
Using Commas

A comma can tell a reader where to pause. Correctly placed commas help to make your meaning clear.

> Please buy paper towels, tuna salad, and limes.
> Please buy paper, towels, tuna, salad, and limes.

Four different uses for commas are shown below.

When to Use a Comma	Examples
1. To separate words in a series of three or more items (No comma is used after the last item.)	Beth gathered, sorted, and polished the stones.
2. To set off *yes, no,* or *well* at the beginning of a sentence	Yes, I have seen rock art. No, I haven't tried it myself.
3. To set off the name of someone directly spoken to	José, gather some small rocks. I think, Lou, we have enough.
4. To separate a last name from a first name when the last name is written first	Jackson, Lou Kwan, Beth Laredo, José

Summary ♦ Use commas for the purposes shown in the chart. Commas used correctly make your meaning clear and your writing easier to understand.

Guided Practice

Tell where commas belong in these sentences.

1. Who borrowed the book on wood handicrafts Mr. O'Dowd?
2. Well the name on the card says "Dixon Cara."
3. I found the book to be interesting informative and detailed.

ESSENTIAL LANGUAGE SKILLS
This lesson provides opportunities to:

LISTENING ♦ listen for specific information ♦ listen actively and attentively

SPEAKING ♦ respond appropriately to questions from teachers and peers ♦ use oral language for a variety of purposes

READING ♦ evaluate and make judgments ♦ follow a set of directions ♦ use graphic sources for information, such as tables and lists, charts and graphs

WRITING ♦ apply increasingly complex conventions of punctuation and capitalization

LANGUAGE ♦ use the fundamentals of grammar, punctuation, and spelling

ractice

Write each item below, using commas where they are needed.

4. frosty,cool,and refreshing
5. apples,lemons,and melons
6. cutting,pasting,and painting
7. Mrs. Kliban,Ms. Bannerji,and my cousin
8. Schofield,Patrick

Write the sentences. Use commas where they are needed.

9. Ancient Greek mosaics decorated walls,floors,and ceilings.
10. Josh,some Greek mosaics are over two thousand years old.
11. How did the Greeks get the stones to stick,Molly?
12. Well,they didn't have the modern,efficient,and long-lasting glue that we have.
13. They usually used cement or plaster,Roger.
14. Yes,but we don't have those supplies in school.
15. No,Evan,but Mr. O'Dowd says that white glue will work fine.
16. What can we use for a suitable,firm,and sturdy background?
17. We could use heavy cardboard,plastic trays,or a piece of slate.
18. Let's get our supplies,roll up our sleeves,and begin.

. Write sentences with commas to answer the questions below.

EXAMPLE: Can you follow directions well?

ANSWER: Yes, I can follow directions well.

Answers will vary.
19. What four foods do you consider healthful?
20. How does your name look if you write your last name first?
21. What are the names of three people you admire?

Apply ◆ Think and Write

Chart ◆ Pretend that your class will take part in a handicrafts how. Make a chart that lists at least eight students in your class. .ist their full names, last name first. Beside each name, write the andicraft that person will work on for the show.

✏️ **Remember**
that commas help to make your meaning clear.

WRITING and MECHANICS: Commas **91**

RETEACHING 19

Commas

Each sentence shows a different way to use a comma. Circle each comma.
1. Tanya, go home please.
2. Then, Ray, you follow her.
3. Yes, we will go right now.
4. Well, I need to make a list.
5. Dora, Amy, and Tony will come.
6. Hernandez, Dora   Sella, Sandra
   Johnson, Andy   Timmons, Mary
   Salerno, Tony   Vega, Dan

A **comma** can tell a reader where to pause.
• Use a comma to separate words in a series of three or more items.
• Use a comma to set off yes, no, or well at the beginning of a sentence.
• Use a comma to set off the name of someone directly spoken to.
• Use a comma to separate a last name from a first name when the last name is written first.

A. Add commas where they are needed.
EXAMPLE: Well, I hope to become an astronaut one day.
1. Jenny tell me about Sally Ride.
2. Well she was the first American woman in space.
3. An astronaut's life must be fascinating exciting and sometimes scary.
4. This article Mike tells about life aboard a space shuttle.
5. Yes I would miss my family on a space voyage.
6. Well you could use the communication system to relay messages.
7. How much food water and equipment can fit in a spacecraft?
8. Gina let's go to the library.
9. Come with us Ben.
10. Let's find out more about space travel astronauts and moonwalks.

B. Write a sentence to answer each question.
EXAMPLE: What are the names of three of your classmates?
    John, Kate, and Tina are three of my classmates.
    Answers will vary. Possible answers follow.
11. What are three of your favorite sports?
    Soccer, baseball, and swimming are three of my favorite sports.
12. Which birds live in your town or city?
    Crows, sparrows, and pigeons live in my town.

PRACTICE 19

Commas

• Use a comma to separate words in a series of three or more items.
• Use a comma to set off yes, no, or well at the beginning of a sentence.
• Use a comma to set off the name of someone directly spoken to.
• Use a comma to separate a last name from a first name when the last name is written first.

A. Add commas where they are needed.
1. Yes John Glenn was the first American to orbit the earth.
2. Kim who is your favorite hero?
3. Well I think Thomas Edison and his inventions helped the most people.
4. Yes I think someone like Charles Lindbergh is a true hero.
5. Pecos Bill Paul Bunyan and Calamity Jane are my favorite folk heroes.
6. John Henry was strong hardworking and brave.
7. Was he a real person Jill?
8. No I don't think so.

B. Write a complete sentence for each direction. Answers will vary. Possible answers follow.
9. Name three states you would like to visit.
   I would like to visit Florida, Texas, and California.
10. Name three breakfast foods.
    Three breakfast foods are eggs, pancakes, and cereal.
11. Name the four seasons.
    The four seasons are spring, summer, fall, and winter.
12. Name three of your favorite vegetables.
    Corn, carrots, and beets are my favorite vegetables.
13. Name three kinds of transportation.
    Planes, trains, and cars are three kinds of transportation.

WRITE IT
Write sentences that name your favorite three foods in each food group. Use commas where they are needed. Write on a separate sheet of paper. Answers will vary.

◀▌▌▌ TEACHING OPTIONS ▐▐▐▶

RETEACHING

A Different Modality Explain that commas can help writers make their meaning clear. Write the following sentence pairs on the chalkboard and have volunteers tell how the commas change the meaning.

1. The books are for Sara Diego and Lee.
   The books are for Sara, Diego, and Lee.
2. No one knows the answer.
   No, one knows the answer.
3. Kim the cat wants to go out.
   Kim, the cat wants to go out.

CLASS ENRICHMENT

A Cooperative Activity Have students work with a partner to interview each other about a subject of mutual interest, such as pastimes or hobbies. Have students use yes, no, well, or the partner's first name at the beginning of each sentence as they write the interview. Have students follow this format:

Diego, do you like mysteries?
Yes, but I like sports stories better.

CHALLENGE

An Independent Extension Have students write: Do punctuation marks help make meaning clear? Then have them write a sentence using the name of three classmates. Next have them write an alphabetical list of their classmates' names. Then have them write questions using each name at the beginning and end of their sentences. When students finish, have them answer the first question they wrote.

Reading–Writing Connection

OBJECTIVES
To identify and use order words to show sequence
To work together to write a paragraph that shows a sequence of events
To use the Thesaurus to improve word choice

Focus on Sequence

Review the Unit 2 literature selection, *Handicrafts*, with students and have them describe the sequence of reasons, from the least important to the most important. Have students read the words in the article that show this order *(One of the reasons; A more important reason)*. Then point out to students that they can use this selection to help them learn how to use sequence in their writing to show time order or order of importance.

You may wish to guide students through the introductory paragraphs, stressing the words that give clues to time order or order of importance. Discuss the importance of time order in a set of directions and the purpose of placing reasons in a certain order. *(Steps in a process must be followed in order; reasons may be placed in an order from the least important to the most important so that the reader/listener will remember the most important reason, the one that is read/heard last.)*

Next, have students apply the information in the Reading-Writing Connection by discussing the questions at the bottom of the page. As students respond to the first question, you may wish to list their responses on the chalkboard. For question 2 you may wish to have volunteers act out simple three-step directions, such as *Stand up. Clap hands while standing. Sit down.* Have students discuss what happens if steps are not followed in order. You may wish to have volunteers add clue words to the steps to make the order clear.

Focus on Sequence

You have probably heard the expression "First things first." That is excellent advice to follow whenever you write directions or explain something in time order. In fact, you might add "Second things second, third things third," and so on. When it comes to directions or time order, **sequence** is very important.

Sequence comes from a Latin word meaning "to follow." The numbers *1, 2, 3, 4* follow each other in a numerical sequence. The letters *A, B, C, D* follow each other in an alphabetical sequence. In a set of directions or in a time-order paragraph, the steps follow each other in a chronological, or time, sequence.

◆ FIRST: The first time-order step may use the word *first.*
◆ SECOND: Sometimes the words *second, third*, and so on, are used. More often the writer switches to *then* or *next.*
◆ THEN: The words *then, next*, and *after that* are all-purpose time-order words. They may appear more than once in an explanation.
◆ FINALLY: The words *finally* and *last* are common in conclusions.

Sequence is often based on chronology, but not always. Sometimes it is based on order of importance, as in the article "Handicrafts," which you read earlier. That article is developed with reasons, not chronological steps. In "Handicrafts" the order is from the least important to the most important reason.

◆ *One of the reasons…*
◆ *A more important reason…*

> **The Writer's Voice** ◆ Words like *first, then*, and *finally* show chronological order. What are some other words and expressions that show chronological order? (Think about dates and hours.) Answers will vary.
>
> Why is it so important to get the sequence correct in writing directions?
> Often, steps must be followed in a certain order for the desired results to be obtained.

 92 COOPERATIVE LEARNING: Writer's Craft

ESSENTIAL LANGUAGE SKILLS
This lesson provides opportunities to:

LISTENING ◆ listen for specific information, such as main idea, details, answers to questions

SPEAKING ◆ participate in group discussions ◆ respond appropriately to questions from teachers and peers ◆ use a set of reasons to persuade a group

READING ◆ understand content area vocabulary ◆ arrange events in sequential order when sequence is not stated ◆ understand cause-and-effect relationships ◆ follow a set of directions

WRITING ◆ use chronological and spatial order and order of importance ◆ generate ideas using a variety of strategies, such as brainstorming, clustering, free writing ◆ use the thesaurus as a means to expand vocabulary

LANGUAGE ◆ use language for informing ◆ use the fundamentals of grammar, punctuation, and spelling

Working Together

When you write, you must arrange ideas in a logical order. The sequence may or may not be chronological. Work with your group or activities **A** and **B**.

Arrange the sentences below in a logical order. Look for time-order words that provide clues.   4   6   2   1   5   3

1. Each rider covered seventy miles on seven horses.
2. After ten miles he switched to a fresh horse at a pony express station and kept riding.
3. While he rested, other riders galloped on with the mail.
4. Pony express riders rode their horses at breakneck speed between St. Joseph, Missouri, and San Francisco, California.
5. The exhausted rider then rested for the return trip.
6. First a rider raced at full gallop for ten miles.

B. Discuss possible topics for a paragraph. Decide on one of the topics. Then make a list of at least five points to be covered in the paragraph. Arrange the points in a logical order. This can be chronological order or order of importance. Be ready to present the paragraph plan in class and to explain it.

THESAURUS CORNER • Word Choice

Twelve of the main entry words in the Thesaurus are nouns. Write them down. Then write a good paragraph based on one of the nouns. For instance, you might write on a funny *accident* or a *story* from last summer. In your paragraph, try to use at least three synonyms for the noun you have chosen. Make sure your sentences are in a logical order.

COOPERATIVE LEARNING: Writer's Craft   93

Working Together

The Working Together activities provide opportunities for students to work together in cooperative learning groups. You may wish to pair strong writers with students whose skills are weaker so that all students may experience success in writing.

Divide the class into small groups and have students read In Your Group. Encourage them to discuss why each task is important. Have them tell what might happen if the group does not follow through on each of the tasks. *(If we do not contribute ideas, the discussion will reach a dead end. If we do not invite others to talk, we will not benefit from their ideas. If we do not help the group reach agreement, we may be unable to complete the activity. If we do not keep a list ideas, we may forget important points that were discussed.)*

You may wish to have each group appoint a timekeeper and a recorder. Then set a time limit of ten or fifteen minutes. After students complete activity A, encourage groups to discuss how they decided on order. After students complete activity B, call on a member of each group to read aloud the paragraph plan and to explain it. Have the rest of the class listen to determine whether the points were arranged in chronological order or order of importance.

Thesaurus Corner

The Thesaurus Corner provides students with the opportunity to extend the Reading-Writing Connection by using the Thesaurus in the back of the textbook. If necessary, remind them how a thesarus is used. After students have written their paragraphs, call on individuals to read them aloud. Encourage students to compare and discuss their use of synonyms and logical order. Have students save their paragraphs for use later in the Writing Process lesson. Point out that learning about logical order can help students develop their ability to present information clearly and accurately when writing and speaking.

UNIT 2

OBJECTIVES

To write a how-to article

To use five stages of the writing process: prewriting, writing, revising, proofreading, and publishing

RESOURCES

Writing Process Transparencies 5–8

Revising and Proofreading Transparencies

Spelling Connection

Writing Sample Tests, p. T552

INTRODUCTION

Connecting to Literature Have a volunteer read the lesson introduction aloud. Remind them of the literature selection, *Handicrafts,* which gives directions for making a yarn picture. Then have students recall and summarize those directions. (First, plan the design by sketching it. Next, copy your sketch onto a cardboard square. Then outline and fill in the design with yarn. Last, glue a loop of yarn to hang the picture if you wish.) Point out that the directions were given in steps that were clear, orderly, and easy to understand. Explain to students that they will soon be writing a how-to article of their own.

Purpose and Audience Ask students to give their own definition of a how-to article. (A written explanation of how to make something or how to do something) Ask students when they have used how-to articles to help them in their own lives. (Students may have used how-to articles to help them learn games, sports, or school-related activities. They may also have used how-to articles to learn how to make model airplanes, beaded jewelry, or origami.)

Have students consider the questions: *What is my purpose?* (To explain how to do something) *Who is my audience?* (My classmates) Have students discuss what they believe they need to consider when they write for other fifth-graders. Encourage a diversity of responses.

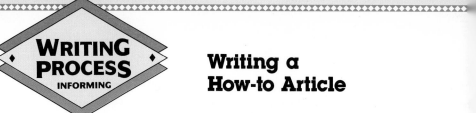

WRITING PROCESS
INFORMING

Writing a How-to Article

A how-to article, as its title suggests, explains how to do something. An example in "Handicrafts" was the part that told how to make yarn pictures. If you followed the directions, you could make a yarn picture yourself.

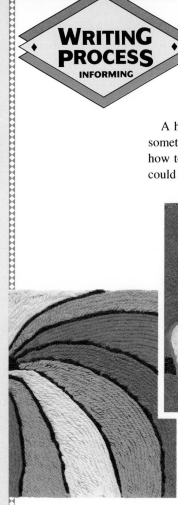

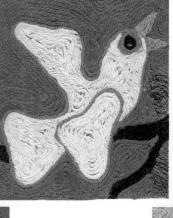

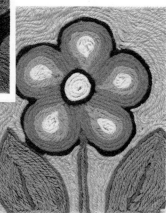

What's MY PURPOSE

Who's MY AUDIENCE

Know Your Purpose and Audience

In this lesson you will write a how-to article. Your purpose will be to explain how to do something.

Your audience will be your classmates. Later you can share your article with an oral presentation or a comic strip.

◆ 94 ◆   WRITING PROCESS: How-to Article

ESSENTIAL LANGUAGE SKILLS
This lesson provides opportunities to:

LISTENING ◆ listen for specific information ◆ select from an oral presentation the information needed

SPEAKING ◆ read aloud a variety of written materials ◆ make organized oral presentations ◆ explain processes

READING ◆ read for specific details or information ◆ synthesize ideas and information ◆ follow a set of directions ◆ interpret and use information presented graphically, such as charts, tables, and diagrams

WRITING ◆ select and narrow a topic for a specific purpose ◆ use chronological and spatial order and order of importance ◆ adapt information to accomplish a specific purpose with a particular audience ◆ participate in writing conferences

LANGUAGE ◆ use language for informing ◆ use the fundamentals of grammar, punctuation, and spelling

Prewriting

To get ready to write, first choose your topic. That is, decide what you will explain how to do. Then gather ideas about your topic.

Choose Your Topic ♦ Make a list of things you can do well. Then look over your list. Which topic would be most fun to write about? Circle your choice.

Think About It

You can do many things. Which would you choose for your topic? Think about which idea would be the most fun to explain. Which could you explain most clearly? Which would your classmates find most interesting? Circle your favorite.

Talk About It

Work with a group of three or four. Discuss things you know how to do. Take turns saying, "I know how to _____." Then make your list. Help others by reminding them of things you know they can do well.

Topic Ideas

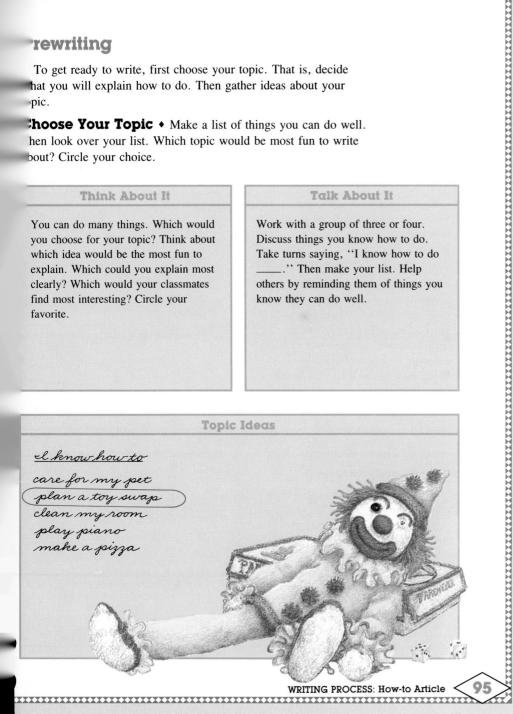

I know how to
care for my pet
plan a toy swap
clean my room
play piano
make a pizza

WRITING PROCESS: How-to Article 95

1. PREWRITING

Guide students through the explanation of Prewriting, pointing out that Prewriting is the stage in which writers choose a topic and gather ideas and information to use in their writing.

MODELING THE WRITING PROCESS

If you feel students need instruction before they begin, you may wish to model this stage of the process. Tell students you want to find a suitable topic for a how-to article. Emphasize the importance of choosing a topic one can do well. Have students help you name a variety of possible topics, such as learning to play baseball, bake bread, knit, or start a stamp collection. Stop when you have four or five topics. Write each topic on the chalkboard or use Writing Process Transparency 5.

Let students hear how you might go about selecting the best topic to write about in a how-to article. As you speak, encourage students to help you. Write on the chart the reasons why each topic may or may not be a good topic to write about. (Possible discussion: Topic 1 is interesting to most fifth-graders, my audience, but it may have too many rules to explain. Topics 2 and 3 may not interest most of my audience, and Topic 3 is hard to explain. Topic 4 is good because I know a lot about it.)

Writing Process Transparency 5*

"I Know How to _____" List	
Topic	Reasons why topic is good/poor
1. play baseball	interesting to audience many rules to explain
2. bake bread	may not interest audience
3. knit	may not interest audience hard to explain
4. collect stamps	I know a lot about this interesting to audience

Pacing

Children write better, just as adults do, if they have time to think — to let ideas and fresh insights develop between prewriting and writing, writing and revising. A five-day pacing guide follows, but the writing process may take longer.

Day 1—Prewriting   Day 3—Revising
Day 2—Writing   Day 4—Proofreading
     Day 5—Publishing

Evaluation

Process Check questions at the end of each stage of the writing process help you to keep track of students' progress.

Holistic Evaluation Guidelines may be found in the teaching notes on page 101. They offer criteria for average, above-average, and below-average compositions.

*Possible responses are overprinted on this reduced facsimile only. Use Writing Process Transparencies to interact with your students on the ideas that interest them.

Choose Your Strategy

Before inviting students to choose a prewriting strategy that will help them gather information for their how-to articles, guide them through the explanations of both strategies. Then have students choose a strategy they feel will help them get started.

As a variation on the first strategy, an Order Circle, you may wish to have students work in pairs to determine which type of order will work best when writing about their topics.

page 96

You may wish to remind students that they have learned about using an Order Circle as a strategy for sequencing in the Critical Thinking lesson on pages 78–79.

IDEA BANK

Prewriting Ideas

Always encourage young writers to try new ways to discover ideas they want to write about. Reassure them, though, that it is appropriate to use the strategies that work best for them. You may wish to remind them of the prewriting ideas already introduced in their textbooks:
- A Conversation, page 40
- An Observation Chart, page 40
- An Order Circle, page 96
- A Clock Graph, page 96

Choose Your Strategy ♦ Here are two strategies that can help you gather ideas for your how-to article. Read both. Then decide which strategy you will use.

PREWRITING IDEAS

CHOICE ONE

An Order Circle

Write your topic inside an order circle. Write some kinds of order on arrows. How will you arrange your how-to directions? Look at your order circle and decide which kind of order will work best.

You might try a kind of order named below. Time order tells what to do first, next, and last. Order of use tells what materials to use first, next, and last. Order of importance starts with the most important step, and ends with the least. Space order tells what happens in one place, then another.

Model

a toy swap → time order / order of use / order of importance / space order

CHOICE TWO

A Clock Graph

Work with a partner to make a clock graph. Draw a large clock shape. Then explain your activity to your partner. Ask your partner to write the steps around the clock graph as you talk. What if you tell a step out of order? Help your partner write it in the right place on the graph. When you are sure the steps are in the right order, number them.

Model

1. Check with parents.
2. Look through old toys.
3. Set aside toys to swap.
4. Make posters.
5. Put toys out on swap day.

PROCESS CHECK At the completion of the Prewriting stage, students should be able to answer *yes* to these questions:
- Do I have a topic I like for a how-to article?
- Do I have a circle or a graph on which I have written directions for my article?
- Have I decided on the best way to order the directions in my article?

Teacher to Teacher

Use classroom interaction to help students find subjects that have power and meaning for them. Encourage students to brainstorm ideas for the Writing Process topic by freely sharing ideas and experiences. Write all contributions on chart paper or on the chalkboard. Later students can examine the ideas critically and make a choice. Brainstorming creates a pool of ideas and arouses students' enthusiasm and energy.

Writing

Look over your order wheel or clock graph. Then begin to write your how-to article. Here are some ways you might start.

- Would you like to learn how to _____?
- _____ can be a lot of fun to do.

Now write the directions in the order you have chosen to use. For clarity, use order words like *first*, *next*, *then*, and *last*.

Sample First Draft ◆

Planning a toy swap can be fun. Look through your old toys games and activitys. Set aside the ones you'll offer in the swap. Next make posters to advertise the swap. Decorate the posters with drawings of things you plan to swap. Hang up the posters around your Neighborhood. Finally, on the day of the swap, put your toys and games on a table. Soon you'll have a pile of "new" toys and games to play with. First get your parents permission make sure that they don't object to your swapping your toys and games.

---

2. WRITING

Before students write their first drafts, guide them through the explanation of Writing, emphasizing that at this stage the most important task is to get all their ideas on paper.

Encourage students to use an opening sentence that will capture the interest of their audience. Remind them to use order words for clarity.

MODELING THE WRITING PROCESS

If you feel students need instruction before they begin this stage of the process, you may wish to ask them to think about the topic on *Writing Process Transparency 5* that they liked best. Have them help you create directions that might be used in a how-to article based on that topic. Stress that directions should be put in an order that makes sense. Write the directions on the chalkboard or on *Writing Process Transparency 6*. Then read aloud what you wrote and work with students to determine whether or not the order of the directions needs to be changed. Encourage students to think about how to rearrange the directions so they follow a logical sequence.

Writing Process Transparency 6*

Writing a How-to Article
Starting a stamp collection **can be fun.**
1. Look for stamps on letters and packages.
2. Remove stamps by soaking them in warm water.
3. Dry the stamps between two paper towels.
4. Arrange stamps by size, color, or design.
5. Place stamps in stamp album or labeled envelope.

PROCESS CHECK At the completion of the Writing stage, students should be able to answer *yes* to these questions:
- Do I have a complete first draft?
- Have I written my article in an order that makes my directions clear?
- Have I used order words for clarity?

*Possible responses are overprinted on this reduced facsimile only. Use Writing Process Transparencies *to interact with your students on the ideas that interest them.*

97

WRITING PROCESS

3. REVISING

Help students understand that during Revising writers make their drafts communicate ideas more clearly and effectively to an audience.

I D E A   B A N K

Grammar Connection

You may wish to remind students of the Grammar Checks already introduced in their textbooks:
- Use a variety of sentence types, p. 43
- Use exact nouns, p. 99

Option 1 ◆ If you wish to begin grammar instruction related to the Grammar Check in this lesson, then refer to Part 1 of this unit.

Option 2 ◆ If you wish to begin grammar instruction *not* related to the Grammar Check in this lesson, then refer to the end-of-book Glossary or Index.

First Read to Yourself   You may wish to emphasize that students need not make actual changes during the first reading. This is a time to think about whether their writing is clear and says what they mean it to say.

Remind students to check to make sure that they have written an article that is enjoyable to read, not just a list of directions. Ask whether they have included an opening sentence as well as order words to make their directions easy to follow.

Then Share with a Partner   Suggest that writers' partners offer three responses, at least one positive, and that they accompany any critical responses with suggestions for improvement. Be sure writers ask the Focus question: *Is the order of directions clear?*

Emphasize that partners need to think carefully and sensitively about their responses. Point out that although constructive feedback is valuable, criticism must be made in a way that is friendly and helpful.

Then explain to writers that they should use their partners' suggestions only if they feel the suggestions will help improve their writing.

---

3 Revising

Now you have written your how-to article. Would you like to improve it? This idea for revising may help you.

REVISING IDEA

FIRST   Read to Yourself

As you read, review your purpose. Did you write a how-to article? Did you explain how to do something? Consider your audience. Would your classmates be able to follow the steps?

Focus: Is the order of directions clear? Put a caret (ˆ) where you want to add order words like *first*, *next*, *then*, and *last*.

THEN   Share with a Partner

Ask a partner to read your article aloud to you. Listen for parts you would like to improve. These guidelines may help you.

The Writer

Guidelines: Listen as if you were hearing your writing for the first time. Ask for your partner's ideas.

Sample questions:
- Did I give enough information?
- Could you follow my directions?
- **Focus question:** Is the order of the steps clear?

The Writer's Partner

Guidelines: Read the article aloud clearly. Then give honest, helpful suggestions.

Sample responses:
- Could you explain more about _____?
- I think this step should come before _____.

98   WRITING PROCESS: How-to Article

Teacher to Teacher

At the Writing stage, the writers' task is to put ideas down on paper in any way he or she can. Each writer has a personal style. One person may write in short bursts; another may work painstakingly, one sentence at a time. When students believe they are finished, or feel they have run short of ideas, a conference with you or with a peer can help them go further. Reading work to a listener who asks questions and gives responses grants a writer focus and fresh inspiration.

WRITING AS A RECURSIVE PROCESS

Connecting Grammar to the Writing Process

Writing is a recursive process. In other words, good writers will often go back and forth among steps. Depending on the individual styles of your students, some may choose to correct grammar at Step Three, Revising; others may prefer to fix grammar or usage errors at Step Four, Proofreading. Ideally, this should be a decision made by the writer. Remind students, however, that once they have completed their proofreading, all the grammar errors should be corrected.

Revising Model ◆ Look at this sample how-to article that is being revised. The marks show changes the writer wants to make.

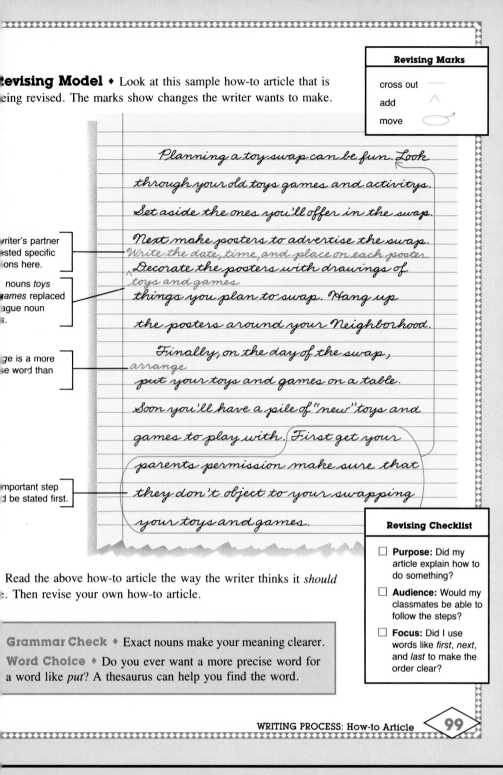

Revising Marks

cross out	—
add	∧
move	↶

writer's partner
ested specific
ons here.

nouns *toys*
games replaced
ague noun
s.

ge is a more
se word than

mportant step
d be stated first.

Planning a toy swap can be fun. Look

through your old toys games and activitys.

Set aside the ones you'll offer in the swap.

Next make posters to advertise the swap.
Write the date, time, and place on each poster.
Decorate the posters with drawings of
toys and games
things you plan to swap. Hang up

the posters around your Neighborhood.

Finally, on the day of the swap,
arrange
put your toys and games on a table.

Soon you'll have a pile of "new" toys and

games to play with. First get your

parents permission make sure that

they don't object to your swapping

your toys and games.

Read the above how-to article the way the writer thinks it *should* . Then revise your own how-to article.

Grammar Check ◆ Exact nouns make your meaning clearer.

Word Choice ◆ Do you ever want a more precise word for a word like *put*? A thesaurus can help you find the word.

Revising Checklist

☐ **Purpose:** Did my article explain how to do something?

☐ **Audience:** Would my classmates be able to follow the steps?

☐ **Focus:** Did I use words like *first*, *next*, and *last* to make the order clear?

Revising Model Guide students through the model, noting the reasons for changes and the revision marks. Point out to students that on the model the revising marks are in blue. Encourage the class to discuss the changes in the model. Ask them to consider whether or not the changes made the writing clearer so that the reader will now understand what the writer intended to say.

MODELING THE WRITING PROCESS

If you feel students need instruction before they begin this stage of the process, you may wish to present *Writing Process Transparency 7*. Have students read the draft silently, or have a volunteer read it aloud. Then ask whether there is anything that needs to be changed. Have students give a reason for each change they suggest and tell how to mark the change on the draft. (Students might use the exact nouns *letters* and *packages* instead of *things,* add more specific directions about removing the stamps, rearrange the second paragraph so that the directions are in order, and use the more precise word *arrange* instead of *put.*) Remind students that at this time they are revising for meaning. They will correct spelling and punctuation later when they proofread.

Writing Process Transparency 7*

How to Collect Stamps

Starting a stamp collection can be fun. First look for
letters and packages
interesting stamps on things that have been sent to you
by soaking them in warm water.
Next remove the stamps. Dri the stamps between two

paper towels.

Last of all, place the stamps in a stamp album if you,

don't have a stamp album, you can label envelopes for

the stamps. Tell what kind of stamps are in each
arrange   arrange
envelope. Then put the Stamps in order. You can put

them according to size color or evan design.

PROCESS CHECK At the completion of the Revising stage, students should be able to answer *yes* to the following questions:
• Do I have a complete draft with revising marks that show changes I plan to make?
• Has my draft been reviewed by another writer?

Possible responses are overprinted on this reduced facsimile only. Use Writing Process Transparencies to interact with your students on the ideas that interest them.

99

WRITING PROCESS

4. PROOFREADING

Guide students through the explanation of proofreading and review the Proofreading Model. Point out to students that on the model the proofreading marks are in red. Tell them that proofreading helps to eliminate errors such as incorrect spelling or run-on sentences that may distract or confuse their readers.

Review the Proofreading Strategy, Proofreading Marks, and the Proofreading Checklist with students. Then invite students to use the checklist and proofread their own how-to articles.

MODELING THE WRITING PROCESS

If you feel students need instruction before they begin this stage of the process, you may wish to use *Writing Process Transparency 8*. Create a "window" by cutting a piece of paper as directed on textbook page 44. Go through the transparency word by word, having students identify words they think are misspelled.

Then have volunteers read each item on the Proofreading Checklist and answer the question or suggest a correction. Mark students' corrections on the transparency.

Writing Process Transparency 8*

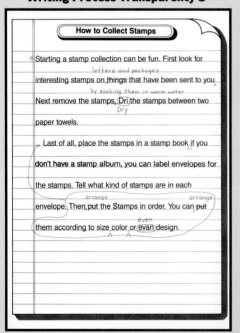

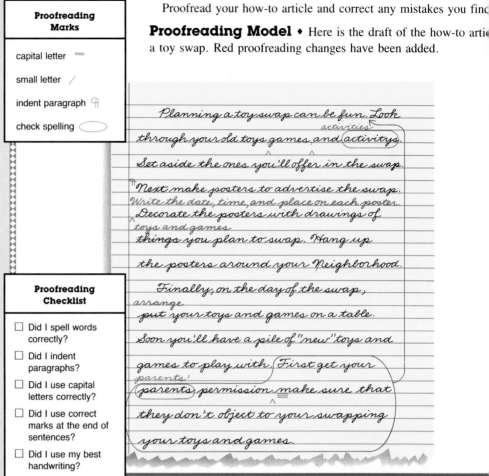

4 Proofreading

Proofread your how-to article and correct any mistakes you find

Proofreading Model ◆ Here is the draft of the how-to artic a toy swap. Red proofreading changes have been added.

PROOFREADING IDEA

Handwriting Check

Check your handwriting for poorly formed letters. Do some letters look like others? Handwriting charts in your classroom or spelling book can help you correct bad handwriting habits.

Now proofread your how-to article, add a title, and make a nea copy.

PROCESS CHECK At the completion of the Proofreading stage, students should be able to answer *yes* to the following questions:
- Do I have a complete draft with proofreading marks that show changes I plan to make?
- Have I used the proofreading marks shown in the lesson?

Possible responses are overprinted on this reduced facsimile only. Use Writing Process Transparencies to interact with your students on the ideas that interest them.

EVALUATION PROGRAM

See Evaluation and Testing Program, pp. C1–C8.

Masters are available for the following:
Self Evaluation Checklist
Personal Goals for Writing
Peer Response
Teacher Response

Holistic Evaluation Guides
Analytic Evaluation Guides

Publishing

Try one of these ways of sharing your how-to article.

A Toy Swap

Planning a toy swap can be fun. First, get your parents' permission. Make sure that they don't object to your swapping your toys and games. Look through your old toys, games, and activities. Set aside the ones you'll offer in the swap.

Next make posters to advertise the swap. Write the date, time, and place on each poster. Decorate the posters with drawings of toys and games you plan to swap. Hang up the posters around your neighborhood.

Finally, on the day of the swap, arrange your toys and games on a table. Soon you'll have a pile of "new" toys and games to play with.

PUBLISHING IDEAS

Share Aloud	Share in Writing
Read your article to a small group of classmates. Use a visual aid, such as a chart of steps or a clock graph. If you can, demonstrate the activity. Ask members of your audience to tell what part of your activity they would enjoy most.	Draw comic-strip instructions for your activity. Show one step in each frame. Display your comic strip beside your how-to article. Ask classmates to suggest a title for the comic strip.

Holistic Evaluation Guidelines

A how-to article of **average** quality will:
1. tell readers how to make something or how to do something
2. state directions in an orderly way
3. use order words

A how-to article of **above-average** quality may:
1. use language that is more descriptive
2. make the process exciting

A how-to article of **below-average** quality may:
1. have steps presented in an illogical order
2. give scanty or incomplete information

PROCESS CHECK

At the completion of the Publishing stage, students should be able to answer *yes* to these questions:

• Have I shared my writing with an audience?
• Have readers shared reactions with me?
• Have I thought about what I especially liked about this writing? Or about what was particularly difficult?
• Have I thought about what I would like to work on the next time I write?

Encourage students to keep a log or journal of their own and their readers' reactions.

I D E A   B A N K

Spelling and Mechanics Connection

You may wish to remind students of Proofreading ideas already introduced in their textbooks:
• Read through a window, p. 44
• Check for poorly formed letters, p. 100

Spelling ◆ If you wish to include spelling instruction with this lesson, then refer to the Spelling Guide on pages 490–492, the Index, or the *Spelling Connection* booklet.

Mechanics ◆ If you wish to include mechanics instruction with this lesson, then refer to the Glossary, the Index, or the *Revising and Proofreading Transparencies*.

5. PUBLISHING

Oral Sharing If students choose to share their writing orally in small groups, invite group discussion after sharing. Encourage students to make constructive comments and explain why they feel the way they do. You also may wish to invite members of each group to choose a favorite among the articles they heard and follow the directions in their free time at school or at home.

Written Sharing If students choose to share their writing by displaying it with a set of comic-strip instructions, set aside a specific time during class when students may read each other's comic strips and articles and respond to them. You may also wish to have students assemble their comic strips and articles together to form a class "How-to Book." Students may share the book with parents or with students from other classes.

Curriculum Connection

OBJECTIVES
To practice a thinking strategy for writing across the curriculum
To write a journal entry

Writing Across the Curriculum

Explain to students that museum and art gallery directors arrange exhibits in an order that helps viewers see important things about the art. Tell students they will use an order circle to help them organize an art exhibit.

You may wish to remind students that they have used an order circle as a strategy for informing in the Critical Thinking lesson, in their response to the literature selection, and in the Writing Process lesson.

Writing to Learn

To help students get started, have them name familiar kinds of pottery, furniture, and quilts and the times and places in which these items might have been crafted. Write students' responses on the chalkboard.

> You may wish to have students with limited English proficiency describe furniture that interests them and provide the English names.

Help students use their social studies books or books from their classroom library to find information about the handicrafts of their choice.

Writing in Your Journal

When they have finished writing, have students read their earlier journal entries. Encourage them to discuss what they have learned about the theme, and to observe how their writing has changed or improved.

Remind students that their journals have many purposes. Besides paragraphs and stories, they can write questions, story ideas, or thoughts and reflections on a subject. Suggest to them that entries in their journals may provide ideas for later writing.

102

 ## Writing Across the Curriculum   Art

Recently you wrote a how-to article. You used an order circle to help you choose the best order for your information. Another way to present information is by setting up an exhibit. When you visit a museum or an art gallery, you may notice that the items are arranged in a certain order. The arrangement helps you see important things about the art. It helps you compare and contrast different pieces. An order circle can be a tool for determining how to arrange an art exhibit.

Writing to Learn

Think and Plan ◆ Imagine that you have been asked to arrange an exhibit of pottery, furniture, and quilts in your school auditorium. These items come from every state in the country. Some items are very old, others are new. Use an order circle to help you decide how to organize your art exhibit.

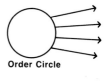
Order Circle

Write ◆ Draw a plan that shows how you would arrange your exhibit. Add labels and explain why you have chosen this arrangement.

 ## Writing in Your Journal

In the Writer's Warm-up, you wrote about crafts. Then you read about weaving, pottery, and furniture making. What other crafts have you read about? In your journal, write about an interesting craft. Tell why you might like to master i

---

ESSENTIAL LANGUAGE SKILLS
This lesson provides opportunities to:

LISTENING ◆ listen actively and attentively ◆ follow the logical organization of an oral presentation

SPEAKING ◆ respond appropriately to questions from teachers and peers

READING ◆ recall specific facts and details that support a main idea ◆ evaluate and make judgments ◆ use graphic sources for information, such as charts and graphs, tables and lists, pictures and diagrams ◆ select books for individual needs and interests

WRITING ◆ select and narrow a topic for a specific purpose ◆ keep journals, logs, or notebooks to express feelings, record ideas, discover new knowledge, and free the imagination ◆ generate ideas using graphic organizers

LANGUAGE ◆ use language for personal expression ◆ use the fundamentals of grammar, punctuation, and spelling

Read More About It

The Weaver's Gift *by Kathryn Lasky*
Spend a year with Carolyn and Milton Frye on their sheep farm. The Fryes raise sheep and shear them each year. Carolyn cleans the wool and spins it into yarn. Then she weaves the yarn into blankets.

Model a Monster *by Colin Caket*
Learn how to model your favorite prehistoric animals. The step-by-step directions in this book are easy to follow. The author includes facts about the dinosaurs you will make.

Book Report Idea   Bookmark

A handmade bookmark can tell about a book while it marks a page. Share a book in a new and useful way.

Create a Bookmark ✦ Begin with a strip of oaktag, assorted markers, and some colored yarn. Cut the oaktag into a long shape suggested by the book you read. Fasten a tail of yarn to one end. Write the book's title and the author's name on the front of the bookmark. To catch the interest of possible readers, copy a short, interesting passage from the book on the back. Share the bookmarks by hanging them from their tails in a book-review display.

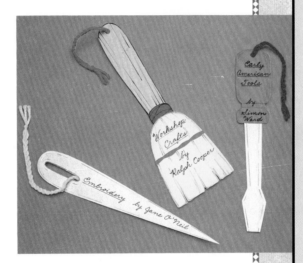

Books to Enjoy 〈103〉

WORLD OF BOOKS
CLASSROOM LIBRARIES
is a collection of high-quality children's literature available with this program.

OBJECTIVES
To appreciate a variety of literature
To share a book through a creative activity

Read More About It

Call students' attention to Read More About It and discuss theme-related books. Point out that the books listed here contain stories about handicrafts and include information about handicrafts used for both work and play. Encourage students to mention other titles that deal with these topics. Encourage students to examine pictures and jacket illustrations of books in the classroom to find books they will enjoy reading.

Book Report Idea

You may wish to have students use the book report form provided in the back of their textbooks. Book Report Idea presents a lively alternative way for interested students to share books they have read.

You may wish to share the reports with the class or in small groups. Have students exchange bookmarks with the illustrated side showing. Students may guess about characters and events from the illustrated side before reading the passage on the back of the bookmark. Allow those who have read the books to add their comments to the backs of the bookmarks before hanging them in a book review display.

Integrated Language Arts Project

The **Integrated Language Arts Project** on pages T514–T515 may be used with this unit.

REVIEW OR TEST
You may wish to use the Unit Review as
a review of the unit skills before administering the Unit Posttest, or you may
wish to use the Unit Review in lieu of
the Unit Posttest.

REVIEW PROCEDURES
The lesson pages that are reviewed are
listed beside the heading of each segment. You may wish to choose one of
the procedures listed below for using
the pages with the Unit Review
exercises.

Review/Evaluate Have students restudy the lesson pages before doing
the Unit Review exercises.

Open-Book Review Allow students
to refer to the lesson pages if they
need to while they are doing the Unit
Review exercises.

Evaluate/Review Have students do
the Unit Review exercises, then turn to
the lesson pages to restudy concepts
for which incorrect responses are
given.

ADDITIONAL REVIEW AND PRACTICE
For additional review and practice,
turn to the Extra Practice pages at the
end of the unit.

UNIT REVIEW

Unit 2

Nouns   *pages 60–65*

A. Write the plural form of each noun.

1. pet — pets
2. ox — oxen
3. wife — wives
4. pie — pies
5. deer — deer
6. foot — feet
7. city — cities
8. penny — pennies
9. shelf — shelves
10. woman — women
11. dress — dresses
12. country — countries
13. village — villages
14. sheep — sheep
15. goose — geese
16. monkey — monkeys
17. berry — berries
18. man — men
19. hat — hats
20. boy — boys
21. wish — wishes
22. box — boxes
23. glass — glasses
24. leaf — leaves
25. tooth — teeth
26. lady — ladies

B. Read each noun. If it is a common
noun, write *common*. If it is a proper
noun, write *proper*.

27. Pittsburgh — proper
28. theater — common
29. month — common
30. February — proper
31. trees — common
32. Lake Erie — proper
33. ostrich — common
34. Bronx Zoo — proper
35. Mars — proper
36. Delaware — proper
37. mayor — common
38. Thanksgiving — proper
39. polar bear — common
40. Abraham Lincoln — proper
41. marching band — common
42. public library — common
43. Pacific Ocean — proper
44. encyclopedia — common
45. Samuel Houston — proper
46. train station — common
47. soccer field — common
48. Davis Boulevard — proper

104   Unit Review

Capital Letters and Periods
pages 66–69

C. Write each sentence. Capitalize the
proper nouns.

49. The chongs went to san fransisco la
october.
50. They visited their relatives on geary
boulevard.
51. Mrs. chong and her daughter rose had
a picnic in golden gate park.
52. Her son lee fed the animals at the zoo.
53. The entire family ate lunch at a
restaurant on union square.
54. Then they went to the san francisco
museum of modern art.
55. Lee chong admired a painting by john
sloan.
56. Later the chongs rode on a cable car
down to fisherman's wharf.
57. They gazed across san francisco bay
toward alcatraz island.
58. At the end of the week, the chongs
returned to boston, massachusetts.

D. Write the sentences. Abbreviate the
underlined words.

59. Harold Walker, Junior, is running for
mayor.
60. Doctor Jeanne Klein is my aunt.
61. She lives on Jackson Boulevard.
62. Her birthday is October 29.
63. Our music teacher is Mister Brody.
64. The big game will take place on
Friday afternoon.
65. The band will march up Washington
Street.
66. On Saturday, everybody will rest.

Apostrophes *pages 70–71*

. Write the possessive form of each
oun.

7. girls girls'   **72.** friend friend's
8. child child's   **73.** people people's
9. Sally Sally's   **74.** building building's
0. men men's   **75.** Charles Charles's
1. mice mice's   **76.** deer deer's

Paragraphs *pages 86–87*

. Decide which sentences below belong
n a paragraph about stamp collecting. For
ach sentence, write *yes* or *no*.

7. People of all ages collect stamps. yes
8. Some people prefer to collect rare
coins. no
79. A stamp album will protect your
stamps from damage. yes
0. Stamps from foreign countries are
often interesting. yes
1. The cost of mailing a letter keeps
increasing. no

**Topic Sentences and Supporting
Sentences** *pages 88–89*

. Use the sentences below to write a
paragraph. Find the topic sentence
nd write it first. Then complete the
paragraph by writing the supporting
entences in an order that makes sense.

2. First, purchase a model plane kit. 2
3. Let the glue dry. 5
4. Building a model plane can be fun. 1
5. Glue the plane parts together. 4
6. Finally, paint the assembled plane. 6
7. Gather the parts of the plane. 3

Commas *pages 90–91*

H. Write the sentences. Add commas
where they are needed.

88. The kittens romped, quarreled, and
finally went to sleep.
89. Bonnie, Jared, and Ellen are bringing
the food.
90. No, that is an incorrect answer.
91. Her name is listed in the book's
index as *Bloomer, Amelia*.
92. Tom, give me the pencil.
93. Yes, she is my sister.
94. We studied, rested, then studied some
more.
95. Look in the phone book under
Sanchez, Pedro.
96. Well, I am certainly disappointed in
you!
97. Fred, meet my uncle and aunt.
98. The small dog barked, wagged its
tail, and ran up to greet me.
99. Sidney Rowe, I am surprised at you!
100. We need butter, eggs, and two cups of
flour for this recipe.
101. No, Henrietta, that is not a portrait of
my father.
102. Mr. Phelan, Ms. Boggs, and I are
rehearsing for the play.
103. Will you please tell me, Perry, what
you have done all day.
104. The Nolans, the Chens, and the
Goldbergs were all at the picnic.
105. No, madam, I am not the person who
rang your doorbell.
106. Bradley, have you seen my pet
lizard?
107. Everyone knows that the American
flag is red, white, and blue.

Unit Review **105**

Cumulative Review

CUMULATIVE REVIEW

The Cumulative Review reviews basic skills from the first through the present unit. The lesson pages that are reviewed are listed beside the heading for each segment. You may wish to have students restudy the lesson pages listed before assigning the Cumulative Review exercises.

ADDITIONAL REVIEW AND PRACTICE

For additional review and practice of skills, you may wish to assign the appropriate Extra Practice pages found at the end of each unit.

◆ CUMULATIVE ◆ REVIEW

Unit 1: Sentences *pages 6–15*

A. Write the declarative, interrogative, imperative, and exclamatory sentences. Begin each sentence correctly. Use correct punctuation at the end.

1. what a lovely dress!
2. is that a robin on the windowsill?
3. bring your cousin to the party.
4. how exciting this movie is!
5. here is my drawing.
6. will you give me your advice?
7. tell me what you think.
8. what a rainy day this is!
9. when will it stop raining?
10. tomorrow is supposed to be sunny and warm.
11. do you know my music teacher?
12. the supermarket is located next to the bank.
13. please bring me that book.
14. she is my best friend.
15. why can't you sit still?
16. the dog sniffed the tree.
17. turn off that television set.
18. did you see an enormous turtle crawl by here?
19. your turtle is over there.
20. what a huge creature he is!
21. how much does it cost to feed him?
22. his food is not that expensive.
23. he eats mostly leafy vegetables.
24. does he have a name?
25. his name is Max.

B. Write the complete subject of each sentence. Underline the simple subject. Write (*You*) if the subject is understood. Simple subjects are underlined twice.

26. The kitten in the middle is mine.
27. The boys are brushing their teeth.
28. Look at that beautiful rainbow! (You)
29. That bunch of purple grapes looks delicious.
30. Ask me a question. (You)
31. The timid puppy hid behind a tree.
32. Put your notebook on the desk. (You)
33. The best players on the team are Ben and Gerry.
34. Take off those dirty shoes. (You)
35. The huge, black bear slept soundly.
36. Three students in my class received perfect scores on the test.
37. The big toe on my left foot aches.
38. The prices in that store are high.

C. Write the complete predicate of each sentence. Underline the simple predicate. Simple predicates are underlined twice.

39. I am studying for my math test.
40. The boys ran up and down the hall.
41. Kelvin is going with us.
42. Mia has done all her chores.
43. The roses look beautiful!
44. Ms. Romano was driving her new car.
45. We have learned our parts for the class play.
46. Susie threw the basketball to her friend.
47. Tom loves mystery stories.
48. Our team has won the tennis match.
49. Jeremy and Terri will visit their grandparents next week.
50. Debbie worked hard on her project.

Unit 2: Nouns   *pages 60–65*

D. Write each sentence. Underline the nouns in each sentence.

51. Our <u>class</u> visited a <u>museum</u> of <u>art</u>.
52. There is a beautiful <u>fountain</u> near the <u>entrance</u> to the <u>building</u>.
53. <u>Joan</u> admired a <u>painting</u> by <u>Vincent van Gogh</u>.
54. <u>Mr. Watts</u> led us to a <u>group</u> of <u>statues</u> by <u>Michelangelo</u>.
55. <u>Steve</u> and <u>Liza</u> stood gazing for <u>minutes</u> at a <u>mural</u> by <u>Diego Rivera</u>.
56. A <u>room</u> near the <u>entrance</u> displays <u>prints</u> by many famous <u>artists</u>.
57. A large <u>case</u> made of <u>glass</u> holds a <u>collection</u> of old <u>coins</u>.
58. <u>Tina</u> bought several <u>postcards</u> with <u>pictures</u> of famous <u>works</u> of <u>art</u>.
59. After several <u>hours</u> the <u>students</u> returned to <u>school</u>.
60. <u>Jennie</u>, <u>Sam</u>, <u>Tony</u>, and <u>Melissa</u> wanted to go again.

E. Write the plural form of each noun.

61. mouse — *mice*
62. woman — *women*
63. deer — *deer*
64. glass — *glasses*
65. child — *children*
66. inch — *inches*
67. foot — *feet*
68. life — *lives*
69. baby — *babies*
70. holiday — *holidays*

F. Write *common* or *proper* for each noun.

71. cow — *common*
72. Houston — *proper*
73. bicycle — *common*
74. envelope — *common*
75. Ms. Wong — *proper*
76. country — *common*
77. Ben Franklin — *proper*
78. Great Salt Lake — *proper*
79. tennis court — *common*
80. Pennsylvania — *proper*

Unit 2: Capital Letters and Periods   *pages 66–69*

G. Write each sentence. Capitalize the proper nouns.

81. I read a biography of *T*homas *J*efferson.
82. He was a great *A*merican.
83. This statesman wrote the *D*eclaration of *I*ndependence.
84. He was born on *A*pril 13, 1743, in *A*lbemarle *C*ounty, *V*irginia.
85. In 1772 he married *M*artha *W*ayles *S*kelton, the daughter of a lawyer.
86. In 1801, *J*efferson was elected *p*resident of the *u*nited *S*tates.
87. One of his greatest achievements was the *L*ouisiana *P*urchase.
88. This land deal with *F*rance doubled the size of the *u*nited *S*tates.
89. In 1826, *J*efferson died at *M*onticello, his *V*irginia home.

H. Write the sentences. Abbreviate the underlined words.

90. <u>Mister</u> Russo is a wonderful dancer. — *Mr.*
91. We went fishing on <u>Sunday</u> morning. — *Sun.*
92. Please finish the work by <u>April</u> 15. — *Apr.*
93. <u>Doctor</u> Harper is my dentist. — *Dr.*
94. Her office is located on <u>Route</u> 27. — *Rte.*

Unit 2: Apostrophes   *pages 70–71*

I. Write the possessive form of each noun.

95. women — *women's*
96. singer — *singer's*
97. Otis — *Otis's*
98. books — *books'*
99. sheep — *sheep's*
100. brother — *brother's*
101. foxes — *foxes'*
102. cows — *cows'*
103. tiger — *tiger's*
104. actresses — *actresses'*

Language Puzzlers

Unit 2

OBJECTIVES
To solve language puzzles based on skills taught in the unit

ANSWERS

Story Ad-Libs
Answers will vary.

A Noun Scramble
1. South Carolina
2. San Antonio
3. Memorial Day
4. Chinese
5. American Kennel Club
6. North America
7. Great Dane
8. September
9. Atlantic Ocean
10. *New York Times*

LANGUAGE PUZZLERS

Unit 2 Challenge

Story Ad-Libs

Complete this science-fiction story with the kinds of nouns named in ( ). Then write an exciting ending of your own.

On June 6, 2989, an earthling named (proper) set out for a vacation on the planet (proper). For the trip she borrowed her (possessive) spacemobile and packed a (common) and a (common). She also brought her (possessive) (common).

When she got to the other planet, she was surprised to find that the houses were made of (common). She decided to stay at the (proper), which was very near (proper).

At dinner that night she met (proper), who was the (common) of (proper). He warned her not to go to (proper) because there was a dangerous (common) there...

A Noun Scramble

Unscramble each set of letters. (Hint: The unscrambled words contain capital letters.)

1. a state: untcosailohra
2. a city: ooaannnist
3. a holiday: oerdmiyamla
4. a language: iesnhce
5. a club: mcnknecaearienlubl
6. a continent: rhmaotirenac
7. a dog breed: aengtdare
8. a month: emrsbetep
9. a body of water: ntliatoacneca
10. a newspaper: rkwoytnmseie

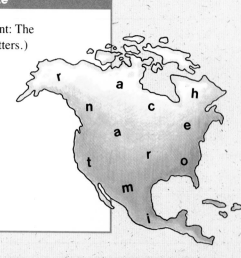

Unit 2 Extra Practice

Writing with Nouns
p. 60

A. Write the following sentences. Underline all the nouns in each sentence.

1. The class studied life in ancient Greece.
2. The students saw statues in a museum.
3. Ancient Greeks studied mathematics and music.
4. This report is about their houses and their cities.
5. The Greeks liked sunshine.
6. Ancient Greeks lived in plain and simple houses.
7. The warm weather made the garden a popular place.
8. Families worked and played under the trees.
9. Many people lived in cities.
10. Towns were planned with great thoughtfulness.
11. The adults met their friends at the open markets.
12. Temples and theaters were also important buildings.
13. Tim showed a picture of a theater to the class.
14. Wide streets led into town.
15. Walls surrounded the city for safety.

B. Write the following sentences. Complete each sentence with one of the nouns below. Use the noun that best fits the sentence.

chairs   clothes   beds   writers   windows
nails   house   comforts tables   heat

16. Many _____ have left descriptions of ancient Greece.
17. The Greeks enjoyed many of the _____ of life.
18. Each room in a Greek _____ had a different use.
19. Some rooms contained _____ for sleeping.
20. Some clothing was hung on _____ in the walls.
21. Other _____ were stored in chests.
22. Greeks did not sit on _____ to eat their meals.
23. Instead, their _____ were placed beside couches.
24. Their _____ was supplied by charcoal stoves.
25. The _____ were left open for fresh air.

Extra Practice **109**

OBJECTIVES
To practice skills taught in the unit

ANSWERS
Writing with Nouns
A. 1. class, life, Greece
   2. students, statues, museum
   3. Greeks, mathematics, music
   4. report, houses, cities
   5. Greeks, sunshine
   6. Greeks, houses
   7. weather, garden, place
   8. Families, trees
   9. people, cities
   10. Towns, thoughtfulness
   11. adults, friends, markets
   12. Temples, theaters, buildings
   13. Tim, picture, theater, class
   14. streets, town
   15. Walls, city, safety

B. 16. writers
   17. comforts
   18. house
   19. beds
   20. nails
   21. clothes
   22. chairs
   23. tables
   24. heat
   25. windows

Extra Practice and Challenge

For those students who need additional grammar practice have them refer to these pages. **The practice exercises progress in difficulty from Easy to Average. Practice A is Easy. Practice B is Average.** Difficult concepts requiring more practice have additional Exercises C and D at the Average level.
We do not recommend these exercises for students who have mastered the skill in the basic lesson. Those students should do the **Challenge** word puzzles on page 108.

Extra Practice

Singular and Plural Nouns

A.
1. singular
2. singular
3. plural
4. singular
5. singular
6. plural
7. plural
8. singular
9. plural
10. singular

B.
11. singular
12. plural
13. plural
14. singular
15. plural
16. plural
17. plural
18. plural
19. singular
20. singular

C.
21. axes
22. armies
23. glasses
24. moose
25. turkeys
26. geese
27. villages
28. ostriches
29. shelves
30. bats

Common and Proper Nouns

A.
1. Death Valley (proper), desert (common), America (proper)
2. Sequoia National Park (proper), desert (common)
3. General Sherman Tree (proper), tree (common), state (common)
4. churches (common), missions (common), Carmel (proper), San Luis Obispo (proper)
5. Father Junipero Serra (proper), chapels (common), missions (common)

2 Singular and Plural Nouns   *p. 6.*

A. Write whether each of these nouns is singular or plural.

1. wish   3. monkeys   5. dash   7. knives   9. women
2. toy   4. box   6. feet   8. rake   10. kite

B. Write the underlined noun in each sentence. Then write *singular* if the noun is singular. Write *plural* if it is plural.

11. The smallest <u>muscle</u> is in the ear.
12. The tallest <u>women</u> are over seven feet tall.
13. One cat had a litter of thirteen <u>kittens</u>.
14. What is the largest <u>ruby</u> in the world?
15. Are the most expensive <u>dresses</u> from Paris?
16. What <u>holidays</u> are celebrated by the most people?
17. These <u>sheep</u> have the longest horns in the world.
18. What country has the greatest number of <u>wolves</u>?
19. The largest <u>flag</u> in the world is in the United States.
20. This <u>mouse</u> weighs less than an ounce.

C. Write the plural of each of these nouns.

21. ax   26. goose
22. army   27. village
23. glass   28. ostrich
24. moose   29. shelf
25. turkey   30. bat

3 Common and Proper Nouns   *p. 64*

A. In each sentence below, the nouns are underlined. Write each noun. Then write *common* or *proper* to show what kind of noun it is.

1. <u>Death Valley</u> is the lowest, hottest <u>desert</u> in <u>America</u>.
2. <u>Sequoia National Park</u> is not far from this <u>desert</u>.
3. The <u>General Sherman Tree</u> is the largest <u>tree</u> in the <u>state</u>.
4. Many beautiful <u>churches</u> and <u>missions</u> are found between <u>Carmel</u> and <u>San Luis Obispo</u>.
5. <u>Father Junipero Serra</u> built <u>chapels</u> at the <u>missions</u>.

Write each sentence. Draw one line under the common nouns.
Draw two lines under the proper nouns.

6. Grapes for raisins are grown in the valleys.
7. People seeking gold hurried to Sutter's Creek.
8. Now tourists visit Sutter's Mill on the creek.
9. Another favorite attraction is Yosemite National Park.
10. Many movies are made in Hollywood.
11. Giant redwood trees grow in Muir Woods National Monument.
12. The highest peak in the Sierra Nevada is Mount Whitney.
13. Lake Tahoe is a beautiful place for a vacation.
14. Disneyland charms adults as well as children.
15. The Sacramento is the longest river in California.
16. The Golden Gate Bridge is a famous landmark.
17. Fisherman's Wharf is a popular area in San Francisco.
18. Many seals live on the rocks along the coast.
19. San Diego is a large city near Mexico.

4 Capitalizing Proper Nouns

p. 66

A. Write each sentence. Capitalize the proper nouns.

1. The town of plymouth is in massachusetts.
2. Many people visit the town each november.
3. They remember the first thanksgiving.
4. Actors dress up as pilgrims for the dinner.
5. Some visitors cross main street to look at plymouth rock.
6. It is on the shore at the edge of cape cod bay.
7. At a little store alicia and laura bought postcards.
8. On the way home they visited the thornton burgess museum.
9. They saw some glass plates with pictures of peter rabbit and joe otter.

Write a proper noun for each common noun below.

10. state
11. lake
12. president
13. school
14. holiday
15. city
16. bridge
17. river
18. street
19. pet

Extra Practice

B. 6. Grapes, raisins, valleys
7. People, gold, Sutter's Creek
8. tourists, Sutter's Mill, creek
9. attraction, Yosemite National Park
10. movies, Hollywood
11. trees, Muir Woods National Monument
12. peak, Sierra Nevada, Mount Whitney
13. Lake Tahoe, place, vacation
14. Disneyland, adults, children
15. Sacramento, river, California
16. Golden Gate Bridge, landmark
17. Fisherman's Wharf, area, San Francisco
18. seals, rocks, coast
19. San Diego, city, Mexico

Capitalizing Proper Nouns
A. 1. Plymouth, Massachusetts
2. November
3. Thanksgiving
4. Pilgrims
5. Main Street, Plymouth Rock
6. Cape Cod Bay
7. Alicia, Laura
8. Thornton Burgess Museum
9. Peter Rabbit, Joe Otter

B. Answers will vary. The following are possible answers.
10. California
11. Lake Michigan
12. Abraham Lincoln
13. Maplewood Elementary School
14. Columbus Day
15. San Diego
16. Golden Gate Bridge
17. Colorado River
18. Center Street
19. Rover

Extra Practice and Challenge

For those students who need additional grammar practice have them refer to these pages. **The practice exercises progress in difficulty from Easy to Average. Practice A is Easy. Practice B is Average.** Difficult concepts requiring more practice have additional Exercises C and D at the Average level.
We do not recommend these exercises for students who have mastered the skill in the basic lesson. Those students should do the **Challenge** word puzzles on page 108.

Extra Practice

p. 68

C.
20. Harrisons, Florida
21. Park Hotel, Everglades National Park
22. Friday, Key West, Gulf of Mexico
23. Audubon House, Whitehead Street
24. Disney World, Orlando
25. Logan Airport, Boston

Abbreviations

A.
1. Mrs. Gelardi's
2. 9 A.M.
3. Oliver Mayo, Jr.
4. Garden St.
5. Dr. Giddings
6. 4 P.M.
7. M. A. Cruz
8. Dec. 21
9. Ms. Ling's
10. Apr. 3

B.
11. Dr. Romero
12. Mon. night
13. Jan. 11
14. 15 Valley Rd.
15. Mr. Chang
16. George Young, Sr.
17. Central Blvd.
18. this Sat.
19. Rte. 3
20. Feb. 1

C. Capitalize the proper nouns in each sentence below.

20. The harrisons flew to florida last week.
21. The park hotel is in everglades national park.
22. On friday we'll drive to key west on the gulf of mexico.
23. The audubon house is on whitehead street.
24. They will visit disney world in orlando.
25. The whole family will fly back to logan airport in boston.

5 Abbreviations

A. Each message below contains initials or an abbreviation written incorrectly. Write each message. Make the abbreviation or initials correct.

1. The students in mrs Gelardi's class have a bulletin board.
2. They collect their messages at 9 am every day.
3. Oliver Mayo, jr, sent Akiko a note.
4. Meet me at the Garden st door after school.
5. One message says, "Hear dr Giddings speak today."
6. Public debate will start at 4 pm in the auditorium.
7. Writer m a cruz will speak to the science fiction book club.
8. Winter vacation begins on dec 21.
9. We have invited ms Ling's class to our play.
10. They will take a field trip on apr 3.

B. Each sentence or message below contains a word that can be abbreviated. Write the sentence or message using the correct abbreviation.

11. The following messages have been left for Doctor Romero.
12. Martha Potts cannot be here Monday night.
13. She would like an appointment for January 11 instead.
14. The patient at 15 Valley Road called.
15. Please telephone Mister Chang immediately.
16. George Young, Senior, called yesterday.
17. The hospital on Central Boulevard has room for him.
18. You have a conference this Saturday at the medical school.
19. You can get there quickly on Route 3.
20. Please fill out this form before February 1.

C. Explain the initials and abbreviations in the messages below.

21. Meet T. J. at 126 Brewer St.   **24.** Nov. 19: Adam's birthday
22. Club meeting Fri., 3 P.M.   **25.** Call Mr. Warshawsky
23. R. L. to dentist Thurs.   **26.** B. K.'s home: 11 Elm Dr.

6 Possessive Nouns

p. 70

A. Write the sentences. Draw one line under each possessive noun that is singular. Draw two lines under each possessive noun that is plural.

1. Martina's grandmother came to visit.
2. Her stories always kept the children's interest.
3. The stories' last words were always proverbs.
4. The fox's tail will show no matter how hard he tries to hide it.
5. Fools' names, like their faces, are often seen in public places.
6. You cannot hold two cows' tails at once.
7. The chicken hawk's prayer does not catch the chicken.
8. People's purses will never be bare
If they know when to buy, to spend, and to spare.
9. Beware of a wolf in sheep's clothing.
10. A friend's frown is better than a fool's smile.
11. Poor folks' wisdom goes for little.
12. In a fiddler's house all are dancers.
13. Merchants' goods are bought and sold.

B. Write the possessive form of each noun given.

14. flower	**25.** navy
15. officers	**26.** carpenters
16. tribe	**27.** canary
17. men	**28.** wife
18. hotel	**29.** nephew
19. neighbors	**30.** man
20. niece	**31.** worker
21. coaches	**32.** lions
22. chimpanzee	**33.** mouse
23. actors	**34.** child
24. leader	**35.** puppy

Extra Practice

C. **21.** T. J. (initials), St. (Street)
     22. Fri. (Friday), P.M. (after noon)
     23. R. L. (initials), Thurs. (Thursday)
     24. Nov. (November)
     25. Mr. (Mister)
     26. B. K. (initials), Dr. (Drive)

Possessive Nouns
A.   **1.** Martina's
     2. children's
     3. stories'
     4. fox's
     5. Fools'
     6. cows'
     7. hawk's
     8. People's
     9. sheep's
     10. friend's, fool's
     11. folks'
     12. fiddler's
     13. Merchants'

B. **14.** flower's
     15. officers'
     16. tribe's
     17. men's
     18. hotel's
     19. neighbors'
     20. niece's
     21. coaches'
     22. chimpanzee's
     23. actors'
     24. leader's
     25. navy's
     26. carpenters'
     27. canary's
     28. wife's
     29. nephew's
     30. man's
     31. worker's
     32. lions'
     33. mouse's
     34. child's
     35. puppy's

Extra Practice and Challenge

For those students who need additional grammar practice have them refer to these pages. **The practice exercises progress in difficulty from Easy to Average. Practice A is Easy. Practice B is Average.** Difficult concepts requiring more practice have additional Exercises C and D at the Average level.
We do not recommend these exercises for students who have mastered the skill in the basic lesson. Those students should do the **Challenge** word puzzles on page 108.

UNIT 3

OVERVIEW

USING LANGUAGE TO IMAGINE

TWO-PART *flexibility*

Unit 3 Overview

books ON UNIT THEME

EASY

📘 **If You Say So, Claude** by Joan Lowery Nixon. Viking. In this hilarious tall tale from Texas, Shirley and Claude set out to find a new home. Also recommended is the sequel, *Beats Me, Claude*.

📘 **Cloudy With a Chance of Meatballs** by Judi Barrett. Atheneum. In the land of Chewandswallow, bad weather comes, bringing big problems. **IRA/CBC Children's Choice, New York Times Best Illustrated Children's Book.**

AVERAGE

📘 **Jim Bridger's Alarm Clock, and Other Tall Tales** by Sid Fleischman. Dutton. Three humorous tales tell about an army scout who discovered the great Salt Lake, the Petrified Forest, and an unusual mountain.

📘 **Homer Price** by Robert McCloskey. Viking. This modern classic features six hilarious tales about the dilemmas of a small-town boy. **American Library Association Notable Children's Book, Young Reader's Choice Award.**

CHALLENGING

📘 **Ellen Grae** by Vera and Bill Cleaver. Norton. Eleven-year-old Ellen, who is known for her amusing tall tales, finally reports the truth and no one believes her.

📘 **By the Great Horn Spoon!** by Sid Fleischman. Little. In this comical tall tale, Jack and his aunt's butler, Praiseworthy, stow away on a ship bound for California and the Gold Rush of 1849. **George C. Stone Award.**

READ-ALOUDS

📘 **The Phantom Tollbooth** by Norton Juster. Random. In this modern classic, Milo passes through a tollbooth that admits him to fantasylands where logic, language, and science are turned upside down. **George C. Stone Award.**

📘 **Grandfather Tales** by Richard Chase. Houghton. This collection of traditional tales gathered from the American South is imbued with authentic dialect.

UNIT THREE

USING LANGUAGE TO IMAGINE

PART ONE

Unit Theme *Tall Tales*

Language Awareness Verbs

PART TWO

Literature ''Sky-Bright Axe'' by Adrien Stoutenburg

A Reason for Writing Imagining

Writing
IN YOUR JOURNAL

WRITER'S WARM-UP ◆ What do you know about the world of American tall tales? Perhaps you have heard or read stories about some tall-tale characters, such as Paul Bunyan or Pecos Bill. Some of the wild and woolly characters of America's past have even starred in cartoons or films you may have seen. Why do people find tall tales funny? What parts of tall tales may be based on facts? Write in your journal. Tell what you already know about tall tales.

start with WRITING IN YOUR JOURNAL

Writers' Warm-up is designed to help students activate prior knowledge of the unit theme, ''Tall Tales.'' Whether you begin instruction with Part 1 or Part 2, encourage students to focus attention on the illustration on page 114 of their textbooks. Encourage them to discuss what they see. Then have a volunteer read aloud the **Writers' Warm-up** on page 115. Have students write their thoughts in their journals. You may wish to tell them that they will refer to this writing in the first lesson of Part 1, in the Grammar-Writing Connection, and in the Curriculum Connection.

THEN START WITH *part 1*

Language Awareness: Verbs Developmental lessons focus on the concept of verbs. Each lesson is carefully constructed not only to help students learn the concept well but also to help build interest and background knowledge for the thinking, reading, and writing they will do in Part 2. The last lesson in Part 1 is a vocabulary lesson with which students learn how to use prefixes. The Grammar-Writing Connection that follows serves as a bridge to Part 2, encouraging students to work together to apply their new language skills at the sentence level of writing.

...OR WITH *part 2*

A Reason for Writing: Imagining is the focus of Part 2. First students learn a thinking strategy for imagining. Then they read and respond to a selection of literature on which they may model their writing. Developmental composition lessons, including ''Exaggeration,'' a speaking and listening lesson, all reflect the literature and culminate in the Writing Process lesson. There a ''Grammar Check,'' a ''Word Choice'' hint, and proofreading strategies help you focus on single traits for remediation or instruction through the lessons in Part 1. The unit ends with Curriculum Connection and Books to Enjoy, which help students discover how their new skills apply to writing across the curriculum.

THEME BAR

CATEGORIES	Environments	Business/World of Work	Imagination	Communications/ Fine Arts	People	Science	Expressions	Social Studies
THEMES	UNIT 1 Farm Life	UNIT 2 Handicrafts	UNIT 3 Tall Tales	UNIT 4 The Visual Arts	UNIT 5 Lasting Impressions	UNIT 6 Volcanoes	UNIT 7 Nature	UNIT 8 Animal Habitats
PACING	1 month	1 month	1 month	1 month	1 month	1 month	1 month	1 month

Build background knowledge of the unit theme, "Tall Tales," by reading aloud this selection to your class. At the same time you will be building your students' knowledge of our rich heritage of fine literature. You may wish to use the "Notes for Listening" on the following page before and after reading aloud.

from *Pecos Bill*

BY JAMES BOWMAN

Pecos Bill had the strangest and most exciting experience any boy ever had. He became a member of a pack of wild Coyotes, and until he was a grown man, believed that his name was Cropear, and that he was a full-blooded Coyote. Later he discovered that he was a human being and very shortly thereafter became the greatest cowboy of all time. This is how it all came about.

Pecos Bill's family was migrating westward through Texas in the early days, in an old covered wagon with wheels made from cross sections of a sycamore log. His father and mother were riding in the front seat, and his father was driving a wall-eyed, spavined roan horse and a red and white spotted milch cow hitched side by side. The eighteen children in the back of the wagon were making such a medley of noises that their mother said it wasn't possible even to hear thunder.

Just as the wagon was rattling down to the ford across the Pecos River, the rear left wheel bounced over a great piece of rock, and Bill, his red hair bristling like porcupine quills, rolled out of the rear of the wagon, and landed, up to his neck, in a pile of loose sand. He was only four years old at the time, and he lay dazed until the wagon had crossed the river and had disappeared into the sage brush. It wasn't until his mother rounded up the family for the noonday meal that Bill was missed. The last anyone remembered seeing him was just before they had forded the river.

The mother and eight or ten of the older children hurried back to the river and hunted everywhere, but they could find no trace of the lost boy. When evening came, they were forced to go back to the covered wagon, and later, to continue their journey without him. Ever after, when they thought of Bill, they remembered the river, and so they naturally came to speak of him as Pecos Bill.

What had happened to Bill was this. He had strayed off into the mesquite, and a few hours later was found by a wise old Coyote, who was the undisputed leader of the Loyal and Approved Packs of the Pecos and Rio Grande Valleys. He was, in fact, the Granddaddy of the entire race of Coyotes, and so his followers, out of affection to him, called him Grandy.

When he accidentally met Bill, Grandy was curious, but shy. He sniffed and he yelped, and he ran this way and that, the better to get the scent, and to make sure there was no danger. After a while he came quite near, sat up on his haunches, and waited to see what the boy would do. Bill trotted up to Grandy and began running his hands through the long, shaggy hair.

"What a nice old doggie you are," he repeated again and again.

"Yes, and what a nice Cropear you are," yelped Grandy joyously.

And so, ever after, the Coyotes called the child Cropear.

Grandy became his teacher and schooled him in the knowledge that had been handed down through thousands of generations of the Pack's life. He taught Cropear the many signal calls, and the code of right and wrong, and the gentle art of loyalty to the leader. He also trained him to leap long distances and to dance; and to flip-flop and to twirl his body so fast that the eye could not follow his movements. And most important of all, he instructed him in the silent, rigid pose of invisibility, so that he could see all that was going on around him without being seen.

And as Cropear grew tall and strong, he became the pet of the Pack. The Coyote were always bringing him what they thought he would like to eat, and were ever showing him the many secrets of the fine art of hunting.

Grandy took pains to introduce Cropear to each of the animals and made every one of them promise he would not harm the growing man-child. "Au-g-gh!" growled the Mountain Lion, "I will be as careful as I can. But be sure to tell your child to be careful, too!"

"Gr-r-rr!" growled the fierce Grizzly Bear, "I have crunched many a marrow bone, but I will not harm your boy. Gr-r-rr!"

But when Grandy talked things over with me the Bull Rattlesnake, he was met with the defiance of hissing rattles. "Nobody will ever make me promise to protect anybody or anything! S-s-s-s-ss! I'll do just as I please!"

"Be careful of your wicked tongue," warned Grandy, "or you'll be very sorry."

But when Grandy met the Wouser, things were even worse. The Wouser was a cross between the Mountain Lion and the Grizzly Bear, and was ten times larger than either. Besides that, he was the nastiest creature in the world. "I can only give you fair warning," yowled the Wouser, "and if you prize your man-child, as you say you do, you will have to keep him out of harm's way!" And as the Wouser continued, he stalked back and forth, lashing his tail and gnashing his jaws, and acting as if he were ready to snap somebody's head off.

So it happened that all the animals, save only the Bull Rattlesnake and the Wouser, promised to help Cropear bear a charmed life so that no harm should come near him. And by good fortune, the boy was never sick. The vigorous exercise and the fresh air and the constant sunlight helped him to become the healthiest, strongest, most active boy in the world.

All this time Cropear was growing up in the belief that he was a full-blooded Coyote. Long before he had grown to manhood, he learned to understand the language of every creeping, hopping, walking, and flying creature; and, boylike, he began to amuse himself by mimicking every animal of his acquaintance. He soon learned to trill and warble like a Mocking Bird, and to growl like a Grizzly Bear.

By the time Cropear had become a man, he could run with the fleetest of the Coyotes. At night, he squatted on his launches in the circle and barked and yipped and howled sadly, according to the best tradition of the Pack.

The Loyal and Approved Packs were proud, indeed, that they had made a man-child into a Noble Coyote, the equal of the best both in the hunt and in the inner circle where the laws and customs of the Pack were unfolded. They were prouder still that they had taught him to believe that the Human Race, to a greater extent than any other race of animals, was *inhuman*. Just what the Human Race was, Cropear never knew, however. For Grandy kept him far away even from the cowboys' trails.

As the years passed, the fame of Cropear spread widely, for the proud Coyotes could not help bragging about him to everybody they met, and the other animals began to envy the clever Pack that had made the man-child into a Coyote. Naturally enough, Cropear became the chief surgeon of the Pack. When a cactus thorn or a porcupine quill lodged in the foot or imbedded itself in the muzzle of any of his brethren, Cropear, with his supple human hand, pulled it out.

Thus the years ran through their ceaseless glass, and the shadow of time lengthened among the Pack. Grandy, for all his wisdom, grew too feeble to follow the trail, too heavy and slow to pull down the alert, bounding pronghorn, or to nip the heels of the fleeting Buffalo Calf. His teeth loosened so that he could no longer tear the savory meat from the bone, or crunch out the juicy marrow.

Then one day Grandy went out alone to hunt and did not return; and everyone knew that he had gone down the long, long trail that has no turning.

But there was no longer need for anyone to help Cropear. He was sturdy and supple, swift as a bird in flight. Often he got the better of the Pack in the hunt and outwitted his brother Coyotes every day. Many of them began to wonder if they had done such a wise thing after all in making Cropear a member of their Pack. ◇

Introducing the Selection

Relate to theme Tell students that the unit theme is "Tall Tales." Encourage them to discuss what makes a tale a tall tale. Elicit that a tall tale uses exaggeration to entertain.

Discuss word meanings Explain to students that in "Pecos Bill Becomes a Coyote," they will hear new words that they may not understand. Pronounce the words below and write them on the chalkboard. Give students the meaning of each word and tell them that knowing the words will help them understand the selection.

spavined lame
roan reddish-brown
mesquite a spiny shrub or small tree found in the Southwest
defiance open opposition to someone or something

Listening to the Selection

Set a purpose Tell students they are going to listen to an excerpt from *Pecos Bill* by James Bowman. Have students listen for the exaggeration that makes this a tall tale.

Starting with Literature

Discussing the Selection

Return to purpose After you have read the selection, discuss with students the exaggerated abilities of Pecos Bill, the main character. Have students tell what Pecos Bill could do that ordinary people could not and then make a more general statement, such as: *Pecos Bill had all the physical abilities of both humans and animals.*

UNIT 3 PLANNING AND PACING GUIDE

		LESSON TITLE	STUDENT TEXT				TEACHING RESOURCES		
			Student Lesson	Unit Review	Cumulative Review	Extra Practice	Reteaching Master	Practice Master	Testing Program
PART 1	1 DAY	Unit Opener							
PART 1	1 DAY	Writing with Action Verbs	116–117	162	224, 331, 433	164, 165	20	20	T536
PART 1	1 DAY	Linking Verbs	118–119	162	224, 331, 433	164, 166	21	21	T536
PART 1	1 DAY	Main Verbs and Helping Verbs	120–121	162	224, 331, 433	164, 167	22	22	T536
PART 1	1 DAY	Verbs with Direct Objects	122–123	162	224, 331, 433	164, 168	23	23	T536
PART 1	1 DAY	Tenses of Verbs	124–125	162	224, 331, 433	164, 169	24	24	T536
PART 1	1 DAY	Using the Present Tense	126–127	162	224, 331, 433	164, 170	25	25	T536
PART 1	1 DAY	Using Irregular Verbs	128–131	162	224, 331, 433	164, 171	26, 27	26, 27	T536
PART 1	1 DAY	Using Troublesome Verb Pairs	132–133	162	224, 331, 433	164, 173	28	28	T536
PART 1	1 DAY	VOCABULARY ◆ Prefixes	134–135	163			29	29	T536
PART 1	1 DAY	GRAMMAR-WRITING CONNECTION ◆ How to Revise Sentences with Verbs	136–137						
PART 2		**THINK**							
PART 2	1 DAY	CREATIVE THINKING ◆ A Strategy for Imagining	140–141	See also pages 145, 154, 160					
PART 2		**READ**							
PART 2	1 DAY	LITERATURE ◆ *Sky-Bright Axe* by Adrien Stoutenberg	142–145				Audio Library 2		
PART 2		**SPEAK/LISTEN**							
PART 2	1 DAY	SPEAKING AND LISTENING ◆ Exaggeration	146–147				Video Library		
PART 2		**WRITE**							
PART 2	1 DAY	WRITING ◆ Similes and Metaphors	148–149				30	30	
PART 2	1 DAY	READING-WRITING CONNECTION ◆ Focus on Tall Tales	150–151						
PART 2		**WRITING PROCESS** ◆ Prewriting • Writing • Revising • Proofreading • Publishing							
PART 2	4–5 DAYS	WRITING PROCESS ◆ Writing a Tall Tale	152–159				Spelling Connection Transparencies		T553
PART 2	1 DAY	CURRICULUM CONNECTION ◆ Writing for Mathematics	160				Writing Across the Curriculum Guide		

Unit 3 Planning and Pacing Guide

Teacher Resource File

Reteaching Masters 20–30
Practice Masters 20–30
Evaluation and Testing Program, including Unit Pretest, Posttest, and Picture Prompt Writing Samples
Parent Letters in English and Spanish
Classroom Theme Posters
Writing Across the Curriculum Teacher Guide
Integrated Language Arts Projects with Masters (see pages T511–T529)
Spelling Connection, Teacher Edition
Writing Process Transparencies
Audio Library 1: Read-Alouds and Sing-Alouds

Also available:

Achieving English Proficiency Guide and Activities
Spelling Connection, Pupil Edition
Student Resource Books
Student Writing Portfolios
Professional Handbook
WORLD OF BOOKS Classroom Library

Multi-Modal Materials

Audio Library 1: Read-Alouds and Sing-Alouds
Audio Library 2: Listening to Literature
Video Library
Revising and Proofreading Transparencies
Fine Arts Transparencies with Viewing Booklet
Writing Process Transparencies
Writing Process Computer Program

LANGUAGE *game*

Spin, Spun, Has Spun

Objective: To use irregular verbs

Materials: Spinner, empty box, small slips of paper
Write each of the following verbs on a slip of paper:

choose	think	bring	find	eat	swim	run	drink	come	write
speak	break	catch	say	see	ring	do	sing	give	go

Place the slips of paper in a box. Construct a spinner to indicate *Past, Present,* and *Past Participle.* Divide the class into two teams, each with a captain. The first player on a team chooses a verb. That player then spins the spinner to find out what tense to use in constructing a sentence for the verb picked. The captain of the other team hears the sentence and judges its correct use. If a player is correct, the second player on that team continues the game. If a player is incorrect, the first player on the other team gets a turn. The first team whose members successfully construct sentences wins the game.

Multi-Modal Activities

BULLETIN BOARD *idea*

You may wish to use a bulletin board as a springboard for discussing the unit theme, or you may prefer to have students create a bulletin board as they move through the unit. Encourage students to use their imaginations to create tall-tale characters. Have them make a bulletin board semantic map to create a series of exaggerations suitable for a tall-tale character. For example, under the heading *Hair,* students may suggest *wriggling snakes, cactus thorns,* or *puffy clouds.* Have students list similar exaggerated characteristics under such headings as *Eyes, Teeth,* and *Strength.* You may wish to have individual students draw one item under each heading to create a picture of a tall-tale character. Mount students' pictures around the semantic map under the heading *Tall-Tale Characters.*

Students with different learning styles will all benefit from a natural approach to language learning, including frequent and varied use of oral language in the classroom.

Students "At Risk"

The following suggestions can help you help the students in your classroom who may be considered "at risk."

Assign Learning Partners

Consider pairing students, especially those with different learning styles and levels of achievement. Partnering can help alleviate a learner's sense of aloneness. It also can (1) encourage students to feel responsible for their own learning; (2) empower them with the perception that people can deal with challenges, situations, and themselves in different, acceptable, and productive ways; and (3) help them focus on and re-inforce their strengths.

Take advantage of the partnering and cooperative learning opportunities offered in the Student Textbook in many "Apply" activities, as well as on the "Working" Together pages of the Grammar-Writing Connection and Reading-Writing Connection. See also the "Class Enrichment" teaching options offered with every developmental lesson in the Teacher Edition.

Limited English Proficiency

Teachers whose classes contain students with limited English proficiency may find the following activities helpful in developing students' skills in grammar and composition.

Verb Chart

Collect ten to fifteen different small objects and spread them out on a table. You may wish to use these objects:

comb	paper clip	letter opener
soap	button	marble
eraser	spoon	ball
pencil	rubber band	ruler

Help students identify each item and say what it does, such as: *A comb combs. Soap cleans.* Have students suggest as many action verbs as possible to describe what each item does.

Then explain that each verb can describe what happened in the past, is happening now, or will happen. On the chalkboard draw an action chart such as the one below:

Action Chart

Object	Present Tense	Past Tense	Future Tense
A comb	combs	combed	will comb

Point to one object at a time and help students complete the chart as they describe the actions for each object.

When the chart is complete, you may wish to continue the activity by having students add direct objects for as many action verbs as possible. See example below.

Tall-Tale Actions

On the chalkboard begin a chart such as the one below.

Action Chart

Present	Past	Past Participle
eat	ate	(has, have, had) eaten
fly	flew	(has, have, had) flown
ride	rode	(has, have, had) ridden
see	saw	(has, have, had) seen
speak	spoke	(has, have, had) spoken

Complete the chart with as many of the irregular verbs as you wish. Review the verb forms with students. Then tell them to use the verb forms to create sentences that might appear in a tall tale, such as *The moon eats cheese. The moon ate cheese. The moon has eaten cheese.* You may wish to have students take turns supplying either one or all three sentences for a verb. Encourage students to use exaggeration effectively as they create their sentences.

Action Charts

Object	Present Tense	Past Tense	Future Tense	Direct Object
a comb	combs	combed	will comb	hair

Gifted and Talented Students

To enable gifted and talented students to work at their own pace and to explore the content further, you may wish to use one or more of these activities.

Constructing Sentences with Verbs

Have students work as individuals or in small groups to write sentences with action verbs and linking verbs. Have each student or group create a character, setting, or plot for a tall tale and make up sentences about it. You way wish to give students an assignment, or have them decide in advance what the requirements are (for example, three sentences with action verbs and two with linking verbs).

You may wish to model this example:

     AV
The giant roared in anger. A huge
   AV   **LV**
mountain blocked his path. He was too
          AV
lazy to walk around it. He pounded

the mountain with his huge fists.
    LV
Soon the mountain was flat.

After you have allowed time for students to complete their writing, have students or groups exchange papers and identify the action verbs and linking verbs.Encourage discussion of how students differentiated between action verbs and linking verbs. (Action verbs show action. Linking verbs show being.)

Creating Similes and Metaphors

Have students create comparisons—similes and metaphors—from verbs in the irregular verb lists in the Student Textbook. Encourage students to use exaggeration to write at least five comparisons suitable for a tall tale, such as *The feather duster flew like a tornado across the furniture.* Encourage students to use both the past and the past participle forms of the verbs (e.g., *The feather duster had flown like a tornado across the furniture*).

Have students share their work by reading aloud or illustrating their comparisons and posting them on a tall-tale bulletin board display.

Portraying and Identifying Actions

Have students work as individuals or in small groups to choose five irregular verbs to act out for classmates. Encourage students to be creative planning their portrayals. You may wish to allow students to use simple props, if they wish, to depict their actions. If classmates are unable to guess an action, allow the actor or actors to plan new portrayals until each action is clear.

At the end of the activity, you may wish to have volunteers write on the chalkboard descriptions of the actions using both the past and the past participle forms of each verb, such as *Sara wrote a math problem on the chalkboard; Sara has written a math problem on the chalkboard.*

Meeting Individual Needs

UNIT 3/LESSON 1

OBJECTIVES
To identify action verbs
To use action verbs in writing

ASSIGNMENT GUIDE
BASIC   Practice A

ADVANCED   Practice B

All should do the Apply activity.

RESOURCES
■ Reteaching Master 20
■ Practice Master 20
■■■ Extra Practice, pp. 164, 165
Unit 3 Pretest, p. T536

TEACHING THE LESSON

1. Getting Started
Oral Language Focus attention on this oral activity, encouraging all to participate. As volunteers say aloud words, you may wish to write the list on the chalkboard. (Encourage students to use the most descriptive and exact words possible.) You may wish to extend the activity by asking them for words that tell the way people sit (*slump, sprawl*) and drink (*sip, gulp*).

2. Developing the Lesson
Guide students through the explanation of writing with action verbs, emphasizing the examples and the summary. Lead students through the **Guided Practice**. Identify those who would benefit from reteaching. Assign independent Practice A and B.

3. Closing the Lesson
After students complete the Apply activity, you may wish to encourage them to start and keep in their journals a log of colorful, exact verbs and their definitions. You also may wish to encourage students to use a thesaurus to discover more exact verbs for general verbs they find. Point out to students that using more colorful action verbs will make their writing come alive for their readers.

116

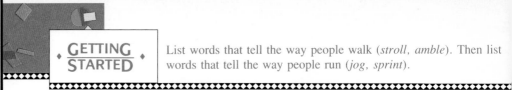

List words that tell the way people walk (*stroll, amble*). Then list words that tell the way people run (*jog, sprint*).

1 Writing with Action Verbs

You have learned that you need both a subject and a predicate to form a complete sentence. You have also learned to identify the simple predicate—the main word or words in the predicate. The simple predicate is often an action verb. An action verb tells what the subject of the sentence does.

Read the sentences below. The underlined word in each sentence is an action verb.

Pecos Bill rides the wild stallion.
The stallion snorts.
It rears and bucks.
The horse flies like the wind.

The verb *rides* tells what Pecos Bill does. The verbs *snorts*, *rears*, *bucks*, and *flies* tell what the wild stallion does. Here are some more verbs that can be used to tell about a horse's actions.

■ twist   leap   whinny   gallop   halt

What action verbs can you add to this list?

> **Summary** ◆ An **action verb** shows action. When you write, use vivid action verbs that make the action clear.

Guided Practice

Name the action verb in each sentence.

1. People read tall tales.
2. Tall tales spark readers' imaginations.
3. Sometimes readers laugh at these adventures.
4. Many tales told of Pecos Bill, the world's greatest cowboy.
5. Pecos Bill romped throughout the West.

116   GRAMMAR and WRITING: Action Verbs

ESSENTIAL LANGUAGE SKILLS
This lesson provides opportunities to:

LISTENING ◆ employ active listening in a variety of situations

SPEAKING ◆ participate in group discussions ◆ speak clearly to a group

READING ◆ follow a set of written directions ◆ use context clues to determine meaning

WRITING ◆ keep journals, logs, or notebooks to record ideas and free the imagination

LANGUAGE ◆ demonstrate use of language for personal expression ◆ use clear and interesting words to express thoughts

Practice

A. The sentences below tell about Pecos Bill. Write the action verb you find in each sentence.

6. Today people tell tales about Pecos Bill.
7. One day he fell from his family's covered wagon.
8. A coyote found him.
9. For years, Bill lived among the coyotes.
10. He learned the coyote's ways.
11. He howled like a coyote.
12. As an adult, he started the biggest ranch in the West.
13. During a drought he dug the Rio Grande for water.
14. He named his horse Widow Maker.

B. Write the sentences. Use an action verb to complete each sentence. Answers will vary. Possible answers follow.

EXAMPLE: Pecos Bill _____ the ranchers how to tame horses.
ANSWER: Pecos Bill teaches the ranchers how to tame horses.

15. The rancher _rides_ her dark brown horse.
16. She _ties_ a rope on the fence post.
17. The cattle _wander_ across the pasture.
18. The ranchers _sweat_ in the scorching heat.
19. They _work_ for hours without a drink of water.
20. The ranchers _eat_ lunch at twelve noon.
21. Dark billowy clouds _appear_ in the distance.
22. All of the ranchers _hope_ for rain.
23. Everyone _hears_ a low rumble of thunder.
24. A horse _swishes_ its tail.
25. Some giant raindrops _plop_ on the ground.
26. Lightning _flashes_ brilliantly.
27. A blast of thunder _booms_ loudly.

Apply ♦ Think and Write

From Your Writing ♦ Read what you wrote for the Writer's Warm-up. List the action verbs you used. If some of the verbs were not exact, replace them with more exact verbs.

✎ Remember
to use lively verbs that appeal to a reader's imagination.

GRAMMAR and WRITING: Action Verbs **117**

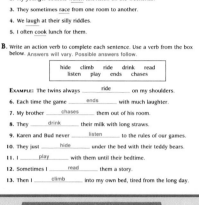

◄⫴⫴ TEACHING OPTIONS ⫴⫴►

RETEACHING

A Different Modality Remind students that an action verb shows what the subject of the sentence does. Write the following sentences on the chalkboard: *Patty ran to the video store. Patty dashed to the video store.* Have volunteers read the sentences and identify the action verbs. Point out that the verb in the second sentence is a vivid verb that makes the action clear and interesting.

CLASS ENRICHMENT

A Cooperative Activity Have students write brief paragraphs about a favorite sport or game they enjoy playing. Encourage them to use colorful, exact verbs in their sentences. Then have them exchange papers, read each other's paragraphs, and work together to underline each action verb they find. You may wish to have partners choose the most vivid verbs from each paper and write them on the chalkboard.

CHALLENGE

An Independent Extension Have students design a game of "Simon Says," using a thesaurus to help them choose vivid verbs. Model an example, such as , instead of saying *Simon says frown*, the vivid verb version might be *Simon Says scowl*. Have students write ten commands for their vivid verb version of "Simon Says."

UNIT 3/LESSON 2

OBJECTIVES
To identify linking verbs

ASSIGNMENT GUIDE
BASIC   Practice A
    ⬇   Practice B
ADVANCED   Practice C

All should do the Apply activity.

RESOURCES
■ Reteaching Master 21
■ Practice Master 21
■ ■ ■ Extra Practice, pp. 164, 166

TEACHING THE LESSON

1. Getting Started
Oral Language Focus attention on this oral activity, encouraging all to participate. You may wish to have students take turns telling something they do and why they are able to do it, or you may wish to have small groups of students work together to suggest pairs of sentences. Use the following as models: *I scoot home every day. / I am hungry. She paddles her canoe slowly. / She is tired.*

2. Developing the Lesson
Guide students through the explanation of linking verbs, emphasizing the examples and the summary. You may wish to give students examples of sentences using the linking verbs *look* (Orchids look delicate), *seem* (The hot days seem endless), *taste* (Apples taste tart), *feel* (The sun feels warm), and *smell* (The stew smells good). Lead students through the **Guided Practice**. Identify those who would benefit from reteaching. Assign independent Practice A–C.

3. Closing the Lesson
After students complete the Apply activity, have them copy their paragraphs on chart paper for a bulletin board display. You may wish to have students include appropriate illustrations in the display. Point out that being able to use linking verbs correctly will help them write sentences that clearly relate subjects to ideas in the predicates.

GETTING STARTED

Tell something you do. Tell why you are able to do it.
EXAMPLE: *I play basketball.*
I am in good physical condition.

2 Linking Verbs

A verb can show action by telling what the subject does.

■ Slue Foot Sue <u>rides</u> a huge catfish.

A verb can also show being, as in the sentences below.

1. She <u>is</u> a brave woman.
2. This catfish <u>was</u> the biggest in the West.

In sentence **1** the verb *is* links, or connects, the subject *she* with the word *woman*. In sentence **2** the verb *was* connects the subject *catfish* with the word *biggest*. Both *is* and *was* are forms of *be*, the most common linking verb.

Using the Forms of *Be*		
Use *am/was*	with *I*	I am/I was
Use *is/was*	with *she, he, it,* and singular nouns	She is Slue Foot Sue was
Use *are/were*	with *we, you, they,* and plural nouns	They are The ranchers were

Other linking verbs are *seem, feel, taste, smell,* and *look.*

> **Summary** ◆ A **linking verb** shows being. A linking verb connects the subject with a word or words in the predicate.

Guided Practice

Name the linking verb in each sentence. Name the words in the subject and the predicate that the linking verb connects.
Connected words are shaded.
1. My favorite dish <u>is</u> catfish.
2. You <u>seem</u> surprised by that.
3. Catfish <u>taste</u> delicious.
4. It <u>was</u> a fine meal.

118   GRAMMAR and USAGE: Linking Verbs

ESSENTIAL LANGUAGE SKILLS
This lesson provides opportunities to:

LISTENING ◆ employ active listening in a variety of situations

SPEAKING ◆ participate in group discussions ◆ express ideas clearly and effectively

READING ◆ follow a set of directions ◆ locate and utilize desired information in reference sources

WRITING ◆ relate experiences with appropriate vocabulary in complete sentences ◆ apply conventions of punctuation and spelling ◆ join related sentences to form a paragraph

LANGUAGE ◆ produce a variety of sentence patterns ◆ use the fundamentals of grammar, spelling, and punctuation ◆ use correct forms of irregular verbs

Practice

A. Write each sentence. Underline the linking verb. Use an arrow to connect the words that the linking verb links.
Connected words are shaded.

EXAMPLE: Slue Foot Sue was a special friend of Pecos Bill.

ANSWER: Slue Foot Sue was a special friend of Pecos Bill.

5. Sue <u>seemed</u> afraid of nothing.
6. Sue <u>was</u> ready for anything.
7. "Sue <u>is</u> a good match for me," said Pecos Bill.
8. The catfish <u>were</u> her servants.
9. She <u>looked</u> extremely graceful.
10. "You <u>are</u> light on your feet," said Bill.
11. Sue <u>felt</u> embarrassed by that remark.
12. "I <u>am</u> sorry," Bill apologized.
13. Her smile <u>felt</u> warm like the sun.
14. They <u>were</u> friends forever.

B. Write the sentences. Choose the correct form of *be* to complete each sentence.

15. Tena ____ a reader of tall tales. (<u>is</u>, are)
16. Tales about heroes ____ her favorites. (is, <u>are</u>)
17. Tena ____ a rancher's daughter. (<u>is</u>, are)
18. Horses ____ her childhood friends. (was, <u>were</u>)
19. I ____ an eager listener when she tells stories. (<u>am</u>, are)

C. **20–24.** Write five sentences with linking verbs. Use forms of *be* and other linking verbs. Use these models.
Sentences will vary.

She <u>is</u> the best roper on this ranch.
The freshly mown hay <u>smells</u> sweet.

Apply ◆ Think and Write

Dictionary of Knowledge ◆ Slue Foot Sue and Pecos Bill were not real people. Read about Daniel Boone, a real-life hero, in the Dictionary of Knowledge. Using a variety of linking verbs, write a paragraph about this frontiersman.

> ✏️ **Remember**
> that linking verbs relate the subject to an idea in the predicate.

GRAMMAR and USAGE: Linking Verbs **119**

RETEACHING 21

Linking Verbs

Read the chart. Then underline the verbs in the example sentences.

Forms of be

I	am, was	1. I <u>am</u> sure.
she, he, it, and singular nouns	is, was	2. He <u>is</u> certain.
we, you, they, and plural nouns	are, were	3. They <u>are</u> positive.

A **linking verb** shows being. Forms of the verb <u>be</u> are the most common linking verbs. Other linking verbs are <u>seem</u>, <u>feel</u>, <u>taste</u>, <u>smell</u>, <u>look</u>.

A. Underline the linking verb in each sentence.

EXAMPLE: Everything <u>seems</u> great at the fair.

1. Those shiny apples <u>look</u> delicious.
2. The cherry pies <u>smell</u> wonderful, too.
3. The peaches <u>taste</u> sweet and sour at the same time.
4. I <u>was</u> at the fair last year, too.
5. The cows <u>look</u> so big and healthy.
6. The sheep <u>seem</u> heavier than last year.
7. That chicken <u>looks</u> fit and trim.
8. They <u>are</u> the best in the whole show.
9. His goat <u>is</u> the one with the white tail.

B. Complete each sentence with a linking verb.

EXAMPLE: They ___were___ happy at the fair.

10. We ___are___ full and content.
11. I ___was___ tired after the fair.
12. A fair ___is___ an interesting place in many ways.

PRACTICE 21

Linking Verbs

A **linking verb** shows being. Use a linking verb to connect the subject with a word or words in the predicate.

A. Underline the linking verb and the two words each one connects. Then write each underlined word in the correct column below. The first is done for you.

1. My <u>mother</u> <u>is</u> a wonderful <u>gardener</u>.
2. Her flower <u>garden</u> <u>looks</u> <u>beautiful</u>.
3. The <u>yard</u> <u>smells</u> <u>sweet</u> in the summer months.
4. My mother's favorite <u>flowers</u> <u>are</u> <u>roses</u>.
5. The <u>daisy</u> <u>is</u> <u>best</u> in my opinion.

Subject	Linking Verb	Word in the Predicate
1. mother	is	gardener
2. garden	looks	beautiful
3. yard	smells	sweet
4. flowers	are	roses
5. daisy	is	best

B. Write the correct linking verb in each sentence. Choose from the words in parentheses ( ).

6. Corn ___is___ a valuable crop grown in the United States. (is, are)
7. The explorer ___was___ surprised at the sight of corn. (was, were)
8. Sweet corn and flour corn ___were___ two common types. (was, were)
9. Corn flakes ___are___ a popular breakfast food. (is, are)
10. I ___am___ sure everyone has eaten some form of corn. (am, are)

WRITE IT
Write sentences about fruits and vegetables you like to eat. Use linking verbs in your sentences. Write on a separate sheet of paper. Answers will vary.

◀▥▥ TEACHING OPTIONS ▥▥▶

RETEACHING

A Different Modality Illustrate on the chalkboard that linking verbs show being and that they connect the subject of a sentence with a word or words in the predicate that tell about the subject:

Pat is clever. Pat = clever.

Cheetahs are fleet. Cheetahs = fleet.

CLASS ENRICHMENT

A Cooperative Activity Have small groups of students work together to write riddles. Have them describe a classroom item in sentences with linking verbs in their riddles (e.g., *What is thick, feels heavy, has many pages, and is filled with definitions?* Answer: *dictionary*). Have each group read its riddles aloud and ask the class to guess what is being described.

CHALLENGE

An Independent Extension Have students clip magazine pictures of scenes in the country or city. Have them each write two paragraphs about the photographs. Tell them to use linking verbs in the first paragraph to describe the scene and action verbs in the second paragraph to describe an action in the scene (e.g., *The street looks crowded. The buildings are tall. I feel small beside them*).

■ Easy ■ Average ■ Challenging

OBJECTIVES
To identify main verbs and helping verbs

ASSIGNMENT GUIDE
BASIC   Practice A
↓   Practice B
ADVANCED   Practice C

All should do the Apply activity.

RESOURCES
■ Reteaching Master 22
■ Practice Master 22
■ ■ ■ Extra Practice, pp. 164, 167

TEACHING THE LESSON

1. Getting Started
Oral Language Focus attention on this oral activity, encouraging all to participate. You may wish to write on the chalkboard the example sentences from the text as a model for students. Provide models of your own that follow the example instructions, such as *Yesterday I clanged the train's bell. Tomorrow I will ride in the caboose.*

2. Developing the Lesson
Guide students through the explanation of main verbs and helping verbs, emphasizing the examples and the summary. You may wish to point out to students that forms of the verb *be* can be used as both linking verbs and helping verbs. Lead students through the **Guided Practice.** Identify those who would benefit from reteaching. Assign independent Practice A–C.

3. Closing the Lesson
After students complete the Apply activity, have volunteers read aloud the sentence that tells the best ''whopper.'' Point out to students that carefully choosing helping verbs will help them express action clearly.

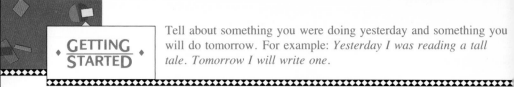

♦ GETTING STARTED ♦

Tell about something you were doing yesterday and something you will do tomorrow. For example: *Yesterday I was reading a tall tale. Tomorrow I will write one.*

3 Main Verbs and Helping Verbs

In each of the following sentences, the simple predicate is more than one word.

Sophia <u>is</u> <u>writing</u> a report on Slue Foot Sue.
She <u>has</u> <u>read</u> several books about Sue and Pecos Bill.
We <u>will</u> <u>hear</u> her report tomorrow.

In these sentences, *is*, *has*, and *will* are **helping verbs**. They work with the main verbs *writing*, *read*, and *hear*. The **main verb** is the most important verb in the predicate. The chart shows you how to use helping verbs with main verbs.

Using Helping Verbs	
When you use the helping verb *am, is, are, was,* or *were*, the main verb often ends in *-ing*.	I am <u>reading</u>. You are <u>reading</u>. They were <u>reading</u>.
When you use the helping verb *has, have,* or *had*, the main verb often ends in *-ed*.	He has <u>finished</u>. We have <u>finished</u>. They had <u>finished</u>.
When you use the helping verb *will*, the main verb is unchanged.	She will <u>present</u> a report. You will <u>present</u> a report. I will <u>present</u> a report.

Summary ♦ A helping verb works with the main verb.

Guided Practice

Tell whether the underlined word in each sentence is a main verb or a helping verb.

1. The wedding day <u>was</u> (HV) approaching fast.
2. Slue Foot Sue had <u>wanted</u> (MV) to ride Bill's horse, Widow Maker.
3. The guests <u>will</u> (HV) see Sue ride Widow Maker on that day.

120   GRAMMAR: Main Verbs and Helping Verbs

ESSENTIAL LANGUAGE SKILLS
This lesson provides opportunities to:

LISTENING ♦ listen for specific information ♦ employ active listening in a variety of situations

SPEAKING ♦ participate in storytelling and creative dramatics ♦ speak expressively by varying volume, rate, and intonation ♦ read aloud a variety of written materials

READING ♦ follow a set of directions ♦ distinguish reality from fantasy ♦ recognize literary forms and explain how they differ ♦ understand figurative language

WRITING ♦ write short stories, plays, essays, or poems ♦ apply conventions of punctuation and capitalization ♦ use dialogue effectively

LANGUAGE ♦ use correct forms of irregular verbs ♦ produce a variety of sentence patterns ♦ use the fundamentals of grammar, punctuation, and spelling

Practice

A. Write each sentence. Draw one line under the main verb. Draw two lines under the helping verb.

4. Sophia will tell us about Slue Foot Sue's wedding day.
5. Pecos Bill had courted Sue for many months.
6. On their wedding day she was staring at Widow Maker with great curiosity.
7. Widow Maker had pranced up and down the corral.
8. Sue was approaching the horse.
9. The guests were watching Sue closely.
10. Sue has mounted Widow Maker.
11. Will Slue Foot Sue ride Widow Maker?
12. The horse is bucking fiercely.
13. Sue is bouncing up and down on Widow Maker.
14. Widow Maker has thrown her.
15. Sue has bounced all the way to the moon!
16. Will Pecos Bill save Slue Foot Sue?

B. Write the sentences. Use the helping verbs *am, are, has, have,* and *will* to complete the sentences.

17. Pecos Bill __has__ rescued Sue with his lasso.
18. The cowhands __are__ cheering wildly.
19. Bill and Sue __have__ found true love.
20. They __will__ live happily ever after.
21. I __am__ enjoying the tales about Slue Foot Sue.

C. **22–26.** Write five sentences using these helping verbs with the correct forms of these main verbs.
Sentences will vary.
Helping verbs: are, was, has, had, will
Main verbs: ride, rope, bounce, buck, study

EXAMPLE: Slue Foot Sue will ride tomorrow.

Apply ◆ Think and Write

Personal Tall Tales ◆ Write some "whoppers," or tall tales, about yourself. Use main verbs and helping verbs in your sentences. For example: *Someday I will jump to the moon.*

✏ **Remember**
to choose helping verbs carefully to express action clearly.

RETEACHING 22

Main Verbs and Helping Verbs

The verbs in the sentences are underlined. Notice that the verb has is a main verb in sentence 1. The verb has is a helping verb in sentence 2.

1. Jane has a chess book.
2. Jane has read a chess book.

In which sentence is has the only verb? __1__
In which sentence is has used with another verb? __2__

A **helping verb** works with the main verb. The main verb is the most important verb in the predicate.

A. A word is underlined in each sentence. Write *main verb* or *helping verb* to describe each one.

EXAMPLE: They have started the competition.   helping verb

1. Many players have arrived today.   helping verb
2. Six judges are speaking about the rules.   main verb
3. This contest has caused much excitement.   helping verb
4. We will sit in the first row.   helping verb
5. Li and Nikki are practicing their moves.   helping verb
6. They will become famous chess players.   main verb

B. Complete each sentence. Use the helping verb *are, have,* or *will.*

EXAMPLE: Li and Nikki __are__ performing today.

7. They __have__ practiced for several months.
8. Their team __will__ do a good job today.
9. I __have__ watched them for two years.
10. Other teams __have__ found them unbeatable.
11. They __will__ win the new competition.
12. All the teams __are__ wearing colorful shirts.
13. The judges __have__ recorded all the scores.

PRACTICE 22

Main Verbs and Helping Verbs

A **helping verb** works with the main verb.

A. The simple predicate is underlined in each sentence. Write each underlined word in the correct place in the chart below. The first one is done for you.

1. Doug and Bobby have delivered newspapers for one year.
2. Doug is folding the papers correctly.
3. Bobby will listen for the weather report.
4. The boys are planning a collection on Friday.
5. They have earned almost enough money for new bicycles.
6. They will buy them in the spring.

	Helping Verb	Main Verb
1.	have	delivered
2.	is	folding
3.	will	listen
4.	are	planning
5.	have	earned
6.	will	buy

B. Write the helping verb *are, has, have, is,* or *will* to complete each sentence.

7. My older brother and sister __will__ deliver papers tomorrow.
8. They __are__ counting on Nicole's help.
9. She __has__ helped them before.
10. The fifth grader __is__ hoping for a route of her own.
11. Tom and Marie __have__ promised to help her get the job.

WRITE IT
Describe the jobs you do to help your family. Write sentences with main verbs and helping verbs. Write on a separate sheet of paper. Answers will vary.

◀|||| TEACHING OPTIONS ||||▶

RETEACHING

A Different Modality Write several sentences such as the following on the chalkboard: *The bird will fly into the tree.* Point out that two words often form a verb, one that shows action and one that helps. Add students' examples to the others on the chalkboard by asking students to tell what they did yesterday or plan to do tomorrow. Point out that a helping verb always comes before the main verb.

CLASS ENRICHMENT

A Cooperative Activity Have groups write on chart paper humorous sentences with helping verbs. Have the first student in a group provide the subject, the second provide a helping verb, the third provide a main verb, and so on. When a sentence has been completed, have the group recorder start a new sentence. Encourage students to use past and future tense with questions, such as *What happened before that? What happened after that?*

CHALLENGE

An Independent Extension Have students underline the helping verb and then write the correct form of the main verb.

1. We are __making__ pancakes. (make)
2. The cook will __flip__ them as high as the treetops. (flip)
3. We were __hoping__ for giant muffins. (hope)
4. Have you __eaten__ giant cookies? (eat)

121

UNIT 3/LESSON 4

■ Easy ■ Average ■ Challenging

OBJECTIVES
To identify direct objects

ASSIGNMENT GUIDE
BASIC　　　Practice A
⬇　　　　Practice B
ADVANCED　Practice C

All should do the Apply activity.

RESOURCES
■ Reteaching Master 23
■ Practice Master 23
■■■ Extra Practice, pp. 164, 168

TEACHING THE LESSON

1. Getting Started
Oral Language Focus attention on this oral activity, encouraging all to participate. You may wish to help students get started by asking them what a *glort* might do to specific things you suggest, such as *mountains, houses, trailers,* and *roads.* Encourage imaginative responses, such as *A glort leaps mountains every Sunday. A glort eats houses for breakfast.*

2. Developing the Lesson
Guide students through the explanation of verbs with direct objects, emphasizing the examples and the summary. You may wish to remind them that a direct object comes after an action verb and not after a linking verb. Lead students through the **Guided Practice.** Identify those who would benefit from reteaching. Assign independent Practice A–C.

3. Closing the Lesson
After students complete the Apply activity, you may wish to have them share their riddles with the class and have volunteers solve them. Point out to students that using direct objects after action verbs will add more information to their sentences.

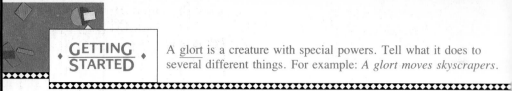

GETTING STARTED A *glort* is a creature with special powers. Tell what it does to several different things. For example: *A glort moves skyscrapers.*

4 Verbs with Direct Objects

Like a verb, a direct object is part of the complete predicate. A direct object comes after an action verb and is often a noun. It answers the question *whom* or *what.*

In the sentences below, the underlined nouns are direct objects.

> Railroad workers tell tales about John Henry.　(tell what?)
>
> They sing songs about the steel-driving man.　(sing what?)
>
> The railroad workers cheered John Henry.　(cheered whom?)

If you want to find the direct object in a sentence, ask "whom?" or "what?" after the verb.

In the sentences below, the underlined nouns are direct objects. They receive the action of the verbs *hammered* and *remembered.* What question does each direct object below answer?

> John Henry hammered huge spikes.　what?
>
> People remembered the steel-driving man.　whom?

> **Summary** ✦ The **direct object** receives the action of the verb. Direct objects answer the questions *whom* or *what.*

Guided Practice

Read these sentences about John Henry. Name the action verb and the direct object in each sentence.

1. John Henry dug a tunnel through a mountain.
2. He used a twelve-pound hammer.
3. He drove steel for many hours without a break.
4. The other railroad workers admired John.
5. People still praise his work in song and story.

122　GRAMMAR: Direct Objects

ESSENTIAL LANGUAGE SKILLS
This lesson provides opportunities to:

LISTENING ◆ listen for specific information ◆ distinguish relevant statements from irrelevant statements

SPEAKING ◆ respond appropriately to questions from teachers and peers ◆ read aloud a variety of written materials

READING ◆ draw logical conclusions ◆ use context clues for word identification ◆ follow a set of directions

WRITING ◆ write and compose for a variety of purposes ◆ apply conventions of punctuation and capitalization

LANGUAGE ◆ produce a variety of sentence patterns ◆ use language for imagining

Practice

A. Write each sentence. Draw one line under the action verb. Draw two lines under the direct object.

6. A black cloud covered the moon.
7. Thunder pounded the earth like a hammer.
8. The thunder announced the birth of a great hero.
9. As a baby, John Henry ate food in huge quantities.
10. His parents put his meals on seven tables.
11. As a child, he picked cotton.
12. When grown up, he married Polly Ann.
13. She helped her husband with his railroad work.
14. His hammer drove spikes deep into the rock.
15. Later he used two hammers at the same time.

B. Write the direct object of each sentence. Then write *what* or *whom* to show what question the direct object answers.

16. One day a man brought a special drill to the boss. *(what)*
17. Steam powered the new machine. *(what)*
18. The machine did not scare John Henry. *(whom)*
19. He did more work than the steam drill. *(what)*
20. The race with the drill killed this amazing worker. *(whom)*

C. Choose for each sentence a direct object from the following list of nouns. Write each sentence.

work	death	sound	John Henry

21. John Henry did the ___ of ten men. *(work)*
22. The railroad tunnel workers mourned his ___ . *(death)*
23. No one forgot ___ . *(John Henry)*
24. Railroad workers still hear the ___ of his pounding hammer. *(sound)*

Apply • Think and Write

Objects in Action • Write a verb riddle about an object. Tell what the object does. Use a direct object in your riddle. Then ask a classmate to read and solve your riddle. For example: *It hides the sun. It brings the rain. What is it?* (a cloud)

> ✎ **Remember**
> that using direct objects after action verbs adds more information to your sentences.

GRAMMAR: Direct Objects **123**

◀◀◀‖‖‖ TEACHING OPTIONS ‖‖‖▶▶▶

RETEACHING

A Different Modality Write on the chalkboard: *I hit the ball. The crowd applauded me.* Explain that the word that answers the question "Whom?" or "What?" is the direct object. Ask: *What did I hit?* (ball) *Whom did the crowd applaud?* (me) On the chalkboard write the headings *Whom?* and *What?* Have students identify each direct object in sentences, such as *A storm surprised Joe.* Then have them write the word under the correct heading.

CLASS ENRICHMENT

A Cooperative Activity Have students work in small groups to search through newspaper articles or favorite short stories for examples of sentences with action verbs and direct objects. You may wish to assign one student in each group the job of scribe. Have volunteers from each group read their example sentences aloud and then have the class identify the direct objects and tell whether the direct objects answer the questions "Whom?" or "What?"

CHALLENGE

An Independent Extension Have students fill in the chart below and then compose complete sentences.
Possible answers follow.

	Subject	Action Verb	Direct Object
1.	Amy	plays	jacks
2.	batter	hits	ball
3.	audience	watches	show
4.	horse	jumps	hill

123

■ Easy ■ Average ■ Challenging

OBJECTIVES
To identify the present, past, and future tenses of regular verbs

ASSIGNMENT GUIDE
BASIC   Practice A

             Practice B

ADVANCED   Practice C

All should do the Apply activity.

RESOURCES
■ Reteaching Master 24

■ Practice Master 24

■ ■ ■ Extra Practice, pp. 164, 169

TEACHING THE LESSON

1. Getting Started
Oral Language Focus attention on this oral activity, encouraging all to participate. You may wish to have students close their eyes as they envision a past and a future. Encourage students to concentrate on their actions rather than on their feelings as they tell about their experiences on the time machine. You may wish to use model sentences, such as *I raced from the fossil cave. I will dance on a space voyage to Mars.*

2. Developing the Lesson
Guide students through the explanation of tenses of verbs, emphasizing the examples and the summary. Lead students through the **Guided Practice**. Identify those who would benefit from reteaching. Assign independent Practice A–C.

3. Closing the Lesson
After students complete the Apply activity, have volunteers read aloud their sentences. You may wish to have them say each verb and its tense. Point out to students that being able to identify correct verb tenses can help them make clear when actions take place.

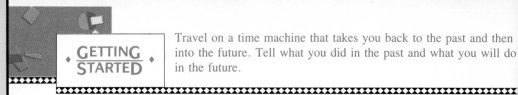

Travel on a time machine that takes you back to the past and then into the future. Tell what you did in the past and what you will do in the future.

5 Tenses of Verbs

The form of a verb shows when the action takes place.

1. Mr. Scott <u>directs</u> the play.
2. The class <u>learned</u> the script.
3. Lois Chu <u>will perform</u> the role of Molly Pitcher.

In sentence **1** the verb is in the present tense: *directs*. In sentence **2** the verb is in the past tense: *learned*. In sentence **3** the verb is in the future tense: *will perform*.

A verb in the **present tense** shows action that happens now.

■ They <u>work</u>.   She <u>studies</u>.   We <u>stop</u>.

A verb in the **past tense** shows action that already happened.

■ They <u>worked</u>.   She <u>studied</u>.   We <u>stopped</u>.

A verb in the **future tense** shows action that will happen. The future tense is usually formed with the helping verb *will* or *shall*.

■ They <u>will work</u>.   She <u>will study</u>.   We <u>will stop</u>.

Sometimes the spelling of a verb changes when you write its form in the present or past tense. Notice how *study* changes to *studies* and *studied*. The verb *stop* changes to *stopped*.

> **Summary** ♦ The tense of a verb shows the time of the action.

Guided Practice

The verbs in the sentences are underlined. Tell whether each verb is in the present, past, or future tense.

1. The stage crew <u>carried</u> the props to the stage. past
2. Rosa and Carl <u>paint</u> a cardboard cannon. pres.
3. The actors <u>will perform</u> the play tonight. fut.

124   GRAMMAR: Verbs in the Present, Past, and Future Tenses

ESSENTIAL LANGUAGE SKILLS
This lesson provides opportunities to:

LISTENING ♦ listen actively and attentively ♦ follow the logical organization of an oral presentation ♦ listen for specific information

SPEAKING ♦ speak expressively by varying volume, rate, and intonation ♦ make organized oral presentations ♦ participate in storytelling and creative dramatics

READING ♦ draw logical conclusions ♦ follow a set of directions ♦ read for specific information

WRITING ♦ join related ideas to form a paragraph ♦ relate experiences with appropriate vocabulary in complete sentences ♦ apply conventions of capitalization and punctuation ♦ maintain a consistent and appropriate voice throughout a written work ♦ write short stories, plays, essays, or poems

LISTENING ♦ produce a variety of sentence patterns ♦ use the fundamentals of grammar, spelling, and punctuation ♦ use language for imagining

Practice

A. Write the verb in each sentence. Then write *present*, *past*, or *future* to show what tense it is.

4. In her costume, Lois Chu resembles Molly Pitcher. <u>pres.</u>
5. Lois will make a fine heroine. <u>fut.</u>
6. Songs and stories about Molly created an American legend. <u>past</u>
7. Molly Pitcher worked as a servant in Carlisle, Pennsylvania. <u>past</u>
8. She married John Casper Hays, a barber. <u>past</u>
9. Just before the Revolutionary War, he joined the army. <u>past</u>
10. Molly traveled with her husband to the battlefields. <u>past</u>
11. Our play about the battle of Monmouth will thrill you. <u>fut.</u>
12. The soldiers fight bravely. <u>pres.</u>
13. Molly helps them during the battle. <u>pres.</u>

B. Each underlined verb below is in the present tense. Write each sentence. Change the verb to the tense shown in parentheses ( ).

EXAMPLE: Molly Pitcher earns her nickname in a battle. (past)
ANSWER: Molly Pitcher earned her nickname in a battle.

14. Molly carries pitchers of water to the soldiers in battle. (past) <u>carried</u>
15. She pours the water quickly. (past) <u>poured</u>
16. The water relieves the soldiers' thirst. (past) <u>relieved</u>
17. Molly's husband drops to the ground from heatstroke. (past) <u>dropped</u>
18. Molly fills his place during the battle. (past) <u>filled</u>
19. The legend of Molly Pitcher lives forever. (future) <u>will live</u>
20. Americans remember her always. (future) <u>will remember</u>

C. **21–23.** Write three sentences, one for each of the following verbs: *perform, act, rehearse*. Write one sentence in the past tense, one in the present tense, and one in the future tense.
Sentences will vary.

Apply ♦ Think and Write

Imagining Fame ♦ Write sentences telling how you might become an American legend. Tell what you have done, what you are doing, and what you will do to make yourself famous.

✎ **Remember**
to use appropriate verb tenses to tell when the action takes place.

GRAMMAR: Verbs in the Present, Past, and Future Tenses **125**

RETEACHING 24

Tenses of Verbs

The action verb in each sentence is underlined. Draw a line to match each sentence with the word that tells when the action takes place.

1. The team practices in the gym. ——— past
2. They won a game last night. ——— present
3. The coach will discuss it with them. ——— future

↪ The **tense** of a verb shows the time of the action. The future tense usually is formed with the helping verb *will* or *shall*.

A. The verb in each sentence is underlined. Circle its tense.

EXAMPLE: Jennie will hang the net. present (future)

1. The players tap the ball back and forth. (present) past
2. One player hits the ball too hard. (present) future
3. The coach will talk to her about it later. past (future)
4. I hope she learned from her mistake. (past) future
5. Someone loudly blows a whistle. future (present)
6. The two captains of the teams will shake hands. (future) present
7. She will toss a coin in the air. (future) present
8. The spectators in the stands cheer for their team. (present) past
9. The long game ended with a tie score. (past) present

B. Rewrite each sentence. Use the tense shown in the parentheses ( ) to help change the underlined verb.

EXAMPLE: Ivan plays a new position. (future tense)
Ivan will play a new position.

10. The coach wants him at third base. (past tense)
The coach wanted him at third base.

11. He watches Ivan very carefully during the game. (future tense)
He will watch Ivan very carefully during the game.

PRACTICE 24

Tenses of Verbs

↪ The **tense** of a verb shows the time of the action.

A. Rewrite the paragraph. Change each verb to the past tense and underline it.

The crew prepares the powerful car for the big race. One man rolls two new tires to another worker. They remove the old tires from the special wheels. Then they attach the new ones. Meanwhile other crew members check the engine and brakes. A special team fills the large tank in the car with fuel. The crew chief times the car with a watch. He studies its movement. The car stops many laps later.

The crew <u>prepared</u> the powerful car for the big race. One man <u>rolled</u> two new tires to another worker. They <u>removed</u> the old tires from the special wheels. Then they <u>attached</u> the new ones. Meanwhile other crew members <u>checked</u> the engine and brakes. A special team <u>filled</u> the large tank with fuel. The crew chief <u>timed</u> the car with a watch. He <u>studied</u> its movement. The car <u>stopped</u> many laps later.

B. Rewrite the paragraph in Exercise A in the future tense. Underline each verb.

The crew <u>will prepare</u> the powerful car for the big race. One man <u>will roll</u> two new tires to another worker. They <u>will remove</u> the old tires from the special wheels. Then they <u>will attach</u> the new ones. Meanwhile other crew members <u>will check</u> the engine and brakes. A special team <u>will fill</u> the large tank in the car with fuel. The crew chief <u>will time</u> the car with a watch. He <u>will study</u> its movement. The car <u>will stop</u> many laps later.

WRITE IT
On a separate sheet of paper, write about a sports competition. Describe what happens before, during, and after the event. Use verbs in the past, present, and future tenses. Answers will vary.

◀◀‖‖ TEACHING OPTIONS ‖‖▶

RETEACHING

A Different Modality Explain that the present tense of a verb shows action that is happening now, the past tense shows action that happened, and the future tense shows action that will happen. Write the three tenses of several regular verbs on separate index cards and label the reverse sides *present, past,* or *future*. Have students use it in a sentence and then list the verb on the chalkboard under the heading *Present Tense, Past Tense,* or *Future Tense*.

CLASS ENRICHMENT

A Cooperative Activity Have students work in small groups to choose from a book a paragraph that describes a historic event using the past tense. Have them copy the paragraph on large chart paper. Then tell them to imagine that they are living in that particular time and to rewrite the paragraph in the present tense. You may wish to have groups share both versions of their paragraphs with the class.

CHALLENGE

An Independent Extension Have students use three verbs from the list below in sentences about the present. Then have them rewrite their sentences, first telling about the past and then about the future.

1. disappear   4. thrash   7. operate
2. explode   5. anchor   8. somersault
3. gulp   6. strain   9. wobble

UNIT 3/LESSON 6

■ Easy ■ Average ■ Challenging

OBJECTIVES
To use the present tense of verbs correctly

ASSIGNMENT GUIDE
BASIC   Practice A
↓   Practice B
ADVANCED   Practice C

All should do the Apply activity.

RESOURCES
■ Reteaching Master 25
■ Practice Master 25
■ ■ ■ Extra Practice, pp. 164, 170

TEACHING THE LESSON

1. Getting Started
Oral Language Focus attention on this oral activity, encouraging all to participate. You may wish to have students brainstorm their ideas about activities in colonial days or offer model sentences, such as *One child sits quietly in the schoolhouse. Ten children learn candlemaking.* Write students' responses on the chalkboard before having volunteers take turns telling what one child does and then what ten children do.

2. Developing the Lesson
Guide students through the explanation of using the present tense, emphasizing the examples and the summary. You may wish to point out to them that *-s* or *-es* is added to most verbs to show present tense with singular subjects; however, *-s* or *-es* is not added to the verb when the subject is *I* or *you.* Lead students through the **Guided Practice.** Identify those who would benefit from reteaching. Assign independent Practice A–C.

3. Closing the Lesson
After students complete the Apply activity, have volunteers read their sentences to the class. You may wish to have classmates identify the present-tense verbs after each sentence is read. Point out to students that using subjects and verbs that agree in their writing will help them make their meaning clear.

126

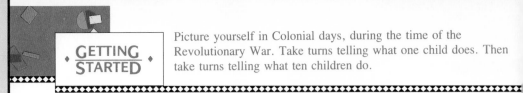

GETTING STARTED

Picture yourself in Colonial days, during the time of the Revolutionary War. Take turns telling what one child does. Then take turns telling what ten children do.

6 Using the Present Tense

When you studied linking verbs, you learned that certain forms of *be* are used with certain subjects.

> I am an admirer of Tempe Wick.
> Historians are unsure of the facts about her and her horse.

A subject and verb are said to agree when the correct form of the verb is used. For example, *am* agrees with the subject *I. Are* agrees with the subject *historians.*

Action verbs must also agree with their subjects. This means you have to know when to use *-s* or *-es* in the present tense.

Using the Present Tense
With a singular noun, use *-s* or *-es*.
Carl listens to the Tempe Wick story. Carl studies it.
With a plural noun, do not use *-s* or *-es*.
People listen to the Tempe Wick story. People study it.
With *she, he,* or *it,* use *-s* or *-es*.
She admires Tempe Wick. She teaches the legend.
With *I, you, we,* or *they,* do not use *-s* or *-es*.
We admire Tempe Wick. We teach the legend.

Summary ♦ A verb in the present tense needs to agree with the subject of the sentence. When you are proofreading, check for agreement between each subject and its verb.

Guided Practice

Name the form of the verb in parentheses ( ) that correctly completes each sentence.

1. We (know, knows) Tempe Wick was a real person.
2. Her house still (stand, stands).
3. Tourists (visit, visits) Tempe Wick's house.

126   USAGE: Subject-Verb Agreement

ESSENTIAL LANGUAGE SKILLS
This lesson provides opportunities to:

LISTENING ♦ listen for specific information ♦ listen actively and attentively

SPEAKING ♦ speak expressively by varying volume, rate, and intonation ♦ read aloud from a variety of written materials ♦ make organized oral presentations

READING ♦ draw logical conclusions ♦ follow a set of directions ♦ distinguish reality from fantasy

WRITING ♦ join related sentences to form a paragraph ♦ relate experiences with appropriate vocabulary in complete sentences ♦ apply conventions of capitalization and punctuation

LANGUAGE ♦ produce a variety of sentence patterns ♦ use the fundamentals of grammar, spelling, and punctuation ♦ use language for imagining

Practice

A. Write each sentence. Use the correct form of the verb in parentheses ( ).

4. People (<u>remember</u>, remembers) Tempe Wick for her courage.
5. Her story (take, <u>takes</u>) place during the Revolutionary War.
6. The Wick house (stand, <u>stands</u>) near Morristown, New Jersey.
7. Historians (<u>tell</u>, tells) about soldiers rebelling against George Washington.
8. Carl (know, <u>knows</u>) that the soldiers got little food.
9. When Tempe Wick heard a cannon shot, she thought, "I (<u>sense</u>, senses) trouble."
10. Her horse, Bonny, (play, <u>plays</u>) an important part in the legend.
11. People (<u>believe</u>, believes) the soldiers wanted the horse.
12. We (<u>think</u>, thinks) Tempe Wick resisted them.
13. The legend (teach, <u>teaches</u>) the meaning of courage.

B. Write each sentence. Use the correct present-tense form of the verb in parentheses ( ).

14. The story of Betsy Ross <u>survives</u> as another American legend. (survive)
15. The story <u>says</u> she sewed the first American flag. (say)
16. According to legend, George Washington <u>visits</u> her. (visit)
17. He <u>asks</u> her to make a flag with a certain design. (ask)
18. She <u>sews</u> the flag with stars and stripes. (sew)
19. Historians <u>think</u> the story may not be true. (think)
20. Still, people <u>write</u> about her because of this legend. (write)

C. 21–23. Write three sentences in the present tense. At least one of your subjects should be singular, and at least one should be plural.

Apply ◆ Think and Write

A Present-Day Legend ◆ Write at least five sentences about a real person who you think could become a legend. Use present-tense verbs.

✎ **Remember**
that subjects and verbs need to agree.

USAGE: Subject-Verb Agreement **127**

MASTERS ON **FILE**

RETEACHING 25

Using the Present Tense

The verb in each sentence is underlined. Write singular or plural for each subject.
1. Seth *shows* his report to friends. ____ singular
2. Friends *show* their reports to Seth. ____ plural

Notice that singular and plural subjects use different verb forms in the present tense.

➲ A verb in the present tense needs to agree with the subject of the sentence. Add *-s* or *-es* to the verb when the subject is a singular noun or the pronoun *he, she,* or *it.*

A. Each subject is underlined. Write each present-tense verb.

EXAMPLE: The *horse* runs quickly. ____ runs
1. The Pony Express *rider* mounts his horse. ____ mounts
2. The other *horses* loudly stamp their feet. ____ stamp
3. The mail *agent* gives the bundle to the rider. ____ gives
4. *He* places the package in his leather pouch. ____ places

B. Complete each sentence. Write the present-tense form of the verb in parentheses ( ).

EXAMPLE: The Pony Express no longer ____ delivers ____ mail. (deliver)
5. Modern trains ____ carry ____ mail quickly and safely. (carry)
6. A plane ____ delivers ____ mail rapidly over long distances. (deliver)
7. A mail truck ____ comes ____ to my house every afternoon. (come)
8. In some places horses still ____ bring ____ the mail. (bring)
9. A mail carrier ____ drives ____ through snow, sleet, and hail. (drive)
10. My mother ____ receives ____ mail almost every day. (receive)
11. She ____ reads ____ her mail immediately. (read)
12. She ____ writes ____ to her brother in Texas once a month. (write)
13. He ____ answers ____ her letters very quickly. (answer)

PRACTICE 25

Using the Present Tense

➲ A verb in the present tense needs to agree with the subject of the sentence.

A. Complete the puzzle. Write the correct present-tense form of each verb in parentheses ( ).

Across
1. The sailors (call) out.
3. The captain (recognize) the ship.
5. The captain (know) the way.
6. Two ships (sail) by.

Down
1. Several sailors (clean) the deck.
2. The captain (give) an order.
4. Water (spill) over the deck.

Crossword: C A L L / R E C O G N I Z E S / K N O W S / S A I L (with G, L, A, V, E, S, P, I, L, L, S)

B. Write the correct form of a verb in the present tense. Answers will vary. Possible answers follow.
7. A large whale ____ swims ____ in the water.
8. Many of the sailors ____ take ____ pictures of the whale.
9. Seagulls ____ land ____ in the water near the ship.
10. The whale ____ shoots ____ a spray of water into the air.
11. Two more whales ____ rise ____ from the ocean depths.
12. One sailor ____ captures ____ the sight with his movie camera.
13. The whales ____ slap ____ their tails on the water.
14. The smiling captain ____ blows ____ the ship's loud horn.

WRITE IT
Look around you. On a separate sheet of paper, describe what you see. Use present-tense verbs in your sentences. Answers will vary.

◀‖‖ TEACHING OPTIONS ‖‖▶

RETEACHING

A Different Modality Write on the chalkboard sentences with singular and plural nouns and pronouns as subjects and present-tense verbs, such as: *She floats like a feather. You reach for the stars. The bird soars to the sky.* Show how present-tense verbs agree with the subject of the sentence. Have students identify each subject as singular or plural and have them underline the *-s* or *-es* in the verb used with the singular pronouns *he, she,* and *it.*

CLASS ENRICHMENT

A Cooperative Activity Have students work in small groups to compose a series of sentences telling about their favorite cartoon characters. Have students write two sentences for each character, such as *Snoopy likes children. Snoopy belongs to Charlie Brown.* Have group members proofread each other's work for subject-verb agreement. You may wish to have volunteers choose their favorite sentence to share aloud with the class.

CHALLENGE

An Independent Extension Have students write a paragraph about a recent game or special event, using only the present tense. Have them pretend to be radio announcers describing the action as it happens, with sentences such as *Sloan slides into first base. The first baseman steps on his thumb. Sloan looks dazed. He rises. He waves his hat to the cheering crowd.* You may wish to have students read their paragraphs aloud in dramatic fashion.

127

UNIT 3 / LESSON 7

■ Easy ■ Average ■ Challenging

OBJECTIVES
To identify and use the past and past participle forms of irregular verbs

ASSIGNMENT GUIDE
BASIC	Practice A
⬇	Practice B
ADVANCED	Practice C

All should do the Apply activity.

RESOURCES
■ Reteaching Master 26
■ Practice Master 26
■ ■ ■ Extra Practice, pp. 164, 171

TEACHING THE LESSON

1. Getting Started
Oral Language Focus attention on this oral activity, encouraging all to participate. You may wish to point out to students that the word *yesterday* is a clue word that tells that the action took place in the past. You may wish to have volunteers say each of the verbs *ride, fall,* and *fly* after they say sentences such as *Yesterday the camels rode quickly toward the lake. Yesterday Boris flew on a pelican.*

2. Developing the Lesson
Guide students through the explanation of using irregular verbs, emphasizing the examples and the summary. You may wish to tell students that the past forms of irregular verbs are shown in a dictionary. Lead students through the **Guided Practice**. Identify those who would benefit from reteaching. Assign independent Practice A–C.

3. Closing the Lesson
After students complete the Apply activity, have volunteers read their sentences aloud. You may wish to have classmates identify the irregular verbs after each sentence is read. Point out to students that in order to express themselves clearly, it is important that they use the past forms of irregular verbs correctly.

GETTING STARTED

Think of animals you could train and ride. Use forms of the verbs *train, ride, fall,* and *fly* in sentences about these animals. Begin each sentence with the word *yesterday*.

7 Using Irregular Verbs

You have learned that the past tense of most verbs is formed by adding *-ed*. Verbs that do not follow this rule are called **irregular verbs.**

The forms of some common irregular verbs appear below. The **past participle** is the form used with the helping verb *has*, *have*, or *had*.

Present	Past	Past Participle
come	came	(has, have, had) come
do	did	(has, have, had) done
eat	ate	(has, have, had) eaten
fall	fell	(has, have, had) fallen
fly	flew	(has, have, had) flown
give	gave	(has, have, had) given
go	went	(has, have, had) gone
grow	grew	(has, have, had) grown
ride	rode	(has, have, had) ridden
run	ran	(has, have, had) run
see	saw	(has, have, had) seen
take	took	(has, have, had) taken
wear	wore	(has, have, had) worn
write	wrote	(has, have, had) written

Summary ◆ Irregular verbs do not form the past and past participle by adding *-ed*. When you write, use forms of irregular verbs carefully.

Guided Practice

Name the past and past participle of each verb. Use the helping verb *has* with each past participle. See the chart for answers.

1. give   **2.** run   **3.** come   **4.** do   **5.** see

128   USAGE: Irregular Verbs

ESSENTIAL LANGUAGE SKILLS
This lesson provides opportunities to:

LISTENING ◆ listen for specific information ◆ listen actively and attentively

SPEAKING ◆ speak expressively by varying volume, rate, and intonation ◆ participate in storytelling and creative dramatics ◆ read aloud a variety of written materials

READING ◆ follow a set of directions ◆ distinguish reality from fantasy

WRITING ◆ join related sentences to form a paragraph ◆ write and compose for a variety of purposes ◆ apply conventions of punctuation and capitalization

LANGUAGE ◆ use correct forms of irregular verbs ◆ produce a variety of sentence patterns ◆ use the fundamentals of grammar, spelling, and punctuation

Practice

A. Write each sentence. Use the past tense of the verb in parentheses ( ).

6. Authors (write) tall tales about animals as well as people. *wrote*
7. Some legendary animals (eat) enormous amounts of food. *ate*
8. Others (do) amazing stunts. *did*
9. Some (ride) with the speed of the wind. *rode*
10. Other imaginary animals (grow) to an enormous size. *grew*
11. Writers told about horses that (fly). *flew*
12. I never (see) a flying horse myself. *saw*
13. Pecos Bill (give) his horse the name Widow Maker. *gave*
14. This horse (run) like streaked lightning. *ran*
15. Still, Widow Maker (come) when Bill called to him. *came*

B. Write each sentence. Use the past participle of the verb in parentheses ( ).

16. I have (ride) horses for a long time. *ridden*
17. I have (fall) off a few horses before. *fallen*
18. Widow Maker had (take) food from Bill's hand. *taken*
19. Widow Maker had (do) anything that Bill asked. *done*
20. This horse had never (wear) a saddle until Bill tamed him. *worn*
21. I have (go) to many rodeos. *gone*
22. I have (see) many fine horses. *seen*
23. No horse like Widow Maker has ever (run) in them. *run*

C. 24–33. Write two sentences for each verb below. In the first sentence for each verb, use the past form. In the second sentence, use the past participle. *Sentences will vary.*

fly   see   fall   ride   write

Apply ♦ Think and Write

An Imaginary Meeting ♦ Imagine that you are an animal—perhaps one with special powers. You the animal are seeing you the person for the first time. Write five sentences about this meeting. Use some of the irregular verbs listed on page 128.

✏ **Remember**
to check the past forms of any irregular verbs you use.

USAGE: Irregular Verbs **129**

◀▥▥ TEACHING OPTIONS ▥▥▶

RETEACHING

A Different Modality Help students make flash cards to practice irregular verbs. Have them write on one side of the card the present tense of the irregular verbs in their Student Textbooks and on the reverse side the past and past participle forms. Have them work together, showing a partner the present tense and having the partner give the past and past participle forms. Finally, have students use the words on the cards in oral sentences.

CLASS ENRICHMENT

A Cooperative Activity Divide the class into two teams. Write the headings *Present*, *Past*, and *Past Participle* on the chalkboard. Beside *Past Participle* write *has*, *have*, and *had*. Under *Present* write irregular verbs, such as *freeze*, *speak*, *draw*, *forget*, *hide*, *drive*, *choose*, and *tear*. Have team members take turns writing the past tense and the past participle of each verb. The team that first writes the verbs correctly wins.

CHALLENGE

An Independent Extension Have students find a newspaper article in which irregular verbs are used. Have them underline the verbs and write them on a separate sheet of paper. Then have them write the other tenses of those verbs as well as example sentences for each tense. You may wish to have them read aloud their sentences.

UNIT 3/LESSON 8

■ Easy ■ Average ■ Challenging

OBJECTIVES
To identify and use the past and past participle forms of irregular verbs
To recognize that some irregular verbs follow patterns

ASSIGNMENT GUIDE
BASIC   Practice A
⬇
ADVANCED   Practice B

All should do the Apply activity.

RESOURCES
■ Reteaching Master 27
■ Practice Master 27
■■■ Extra Practice, pp. 164, 172

TEACHING THE LESSON

1. Getting Started
Oral Language Focus attention on this oral activity, encouraging all to participate. You may wish to model sentences of your own before students begin, such as *I sing slow sad songs. I sang songs about early pioneer days. I have sung before small audiences.* Encourage them to use as many past forms of the verb *sing* as they can.

2. Developing the Lesson
Guide students through the explanation of using irregular verbs that follow a pattern, emphasizing the examples and the summary. You may wish to have students say aloud each past and past participle form of the verbs so that they are sure to recognize the spelling-sound patterns. Lead students through the **Guided Practice**. Identify those who would benefit from reteaching. Assign independent Practice A and B.

3. Closing the Lesson
After students complete the Apply activity, have volunteers read aloud their riddles for classmates to guess. Point out to students that knowing about the patterns of irregular verbs can help them proofread their written work to be sure their meaning will be clear to their readers.

130

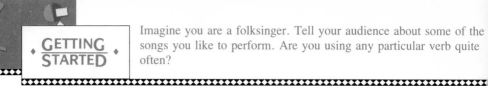

GETTING STARTED
Imagine you are a folksinger. Tell your audience about some of the songs you like to perform. Are you using any particular verb quite often?

8 Using Irregular Verbs

Some irregular verbs follow a pattern in forming the past and past participle. Three common patterns are shown below.

Some verbs have the same past and past participle.

Present	Past	Past Participle
bring	brought	(has, have, had) brought
catch	caught	(has, have, had) caught
find	found	(has, have, had) found
say	said	(has, have, had) said
think	thought	(has, have, had) thought

Some form the past participle by adding -n to the past.

Present	Past	Past Participle
break	broke	(has, have, had) broken
choose	chose	(has, have, had) chosen
freeze	froze	(has, have, had) frozen
speak	spoke	(has, have, had) spoken

Some change one vowel in the past and in the past participle.

Present	Past	Past Participle
drink	drank	(has, have, had) drunk
ring	rang	(has, have, had) rung
sing	sang	(has, have, had) sung
swim	swam	(has, have, had) swum

Summary ◆ Some irregular verbs follow a pattern in the way they are formed. When you write, use forms of irregular verbs carefully.

Guided Practice

Name the past and the past participle of each verb.
See the chart for answers.
1. sing   **2.** choose   **3.** break   **4.** say   **5.** swim

130   USAGE: Irregular Verbs

ESSENTIAL LANGUAGE SKILLS
This lesson provides opportunities to:

LISTENING ◆ listen for specific information ◆ follow the logical organization of an oral presentation ◆ participate in conversations and group discussions

SPEAKING ◆ speak before an audience to communicate specific information

READING ◆ understand content area vocabulary ◆ evaluate and make judgments ◆ use context to determine meaning ◆ follow a set of directions

WRITING ◆ write for a variety of purposes ◆ create language games, such as riddles, puns, etc.

LANGUAGE ◆ use correct forms of irregular verbs ◆ use language to imagine

Practice

A. Write each sentence. Use the past or the past participle of the verb in parentheses ( ).

6. People everywhere have (find) tall tales enjoyable. *found*

7. Some people say it got so cold in Michigan that the flames in lanterns (freeze). *froze*

8. Folks just (break) off the lantern flames to put them out. *broke*

9. People who have (choose) to live in cold places enjoy such tales. *chosen*

10. In some places, tales tell about people who have (catch) gigantic fish. *caught*

11. Anglers (bring) in fish that amazed everyone. *brought*

12. Some people (think) these ''fish stories'' were true. *thought*

13. Even so, such fish have (swim) only in imaginary rivers. *swum*

14. On Cape Cod they (sing) songs about the ''hoss-mackerel.'' *sang*

15. Bowleg Bill had almost (break) this huge fish by riding it like a wild horse. *broken*

16. I (choose) to believe this story. *chose*

17. In North Dakota the dinner bell once (ring) for Paul Bunyan's loggers. *rang*

18. The men (drink) a whole lake filled with pea soup. *drank*

19. People in Colorado (speak) of the slide-rock bolter. *spoke*

20. They have (say) this animal zoomed around scooping up tourists. *said*

21. In Oklahoma, storytellers have (speak) of giant grasshoppers eating cows. *spoken*

22. I had (think) such insects existed only in books. *thought*

B. How many past-tense forms of verbs from this lesson could you use to complete the sentence below? Write as many sentences as you can. Possible answers are *brought, caught, found, chose, froze.*

I _____ some fish this week.

Apply ♦ Think and Write

Active Animals ♦ Write a verb riddle about an animal. Use verbs from this lesson to tell what it did. Exchange riddles with a classmate. Try to guess each other's riddles.

✎ Remember
to check the past forms of any irregular verbs you use.
◆◆◆◆◆◆◆◆◆◆◆◆◆◆◆◆◆◆

USAGE: Irregular Verbs **131**

MASTERS ON FILE

RETEACHING 27

Using Irregular Verbs

Read the chart. Underline the past participles that are different from the past forms.

present	bring	break	sing
past	brought	broke	sang
past participle with has, have, had	brought	broken	sung

Some irregular verbs follow a pattern in the way they are formed. Some have the same past and past participle. Some form the past participle by adding -n to the past. Some change one vowel in the past and past participle.

A. Complete each sentence. Write the correct verb form in parentheses ( ).

EXAMPLE: We ___brought___ lunch that day. (bring, brought)

1. She has ___brought___ mittens. (bring, brought)
2. I had ___thought___ the day too warm. (think, thought)
3. I ___caught___ only one fish before. (catch, caught)
4. Jan had ___said___ that practice makes perfect. (say, said)
5. We have ___found___ that to be true. (find, found)

B. Complete each sentence. Write the correct past form in parentheses ( ).

EXAMPLE: The lake had ___frozen___ during the long, cold winter. (froze, frozen)

6. Pat ___broke___ a hole through the thick ice. (broke, broken)
7. He has ___chosen___ a good spot for fish. (chose, chosen)
8. Fritz has ___drunk___ hot cocoa all day. (drank, drunk)
9. We ___sang___ all the way home. (sang, sung)
10. I have ___spoken___ about that day many times. (spoke, spoken)
11. Wanda ___chose___ to go again last week. (chose, chosen)

PRACTICE 27

Using Irregular Verbs

Some irregular verbs follow a pattern in the way they are formed.

A. Complete the chart by writing in each missing verb form. The circled letters spell the answer to this question: Why is an irregular verb like a flat tire? Unscramble the letters and write the answer.

	Present	Past	Past Participle
1.	break	broke	b r o k e n
2.	drink	d r a n k	drunk
3.	c h o o s e	chose	chosen
4.	find	f o u n d	found
5.	say	said	s a i d
6.	s w i m	swam	swum
7.	c a t c h	caught	caught
8.	sing	s a n g	sung
9.	freeze	froze	f r o z e n

Answer: They both have to be ___changed___.

B. Complete each sentence. Write the past or past participle of a verb from the chart in Exercise A. Answers will vary. Possible answers follow.

10. Marvin had ___found___ a big stick during his walk in the woods.
11. Lina ___sang___ a song as she walked.
12. The lake had ___frozen___ under the snow.
13. Tony ___drank___ from an icy stream.
14. Everyone ___said___ a winter hike was great fun.

WRITE IT
On separate paper, write sentences describing sounds you might hear on a winter's walk. Use the past and past participles of irregular verbs. Answers will vary.

◀||| TEACHING OPTIONS |||▶

RETEACHING

A Different Modality Write these headings on the chalkboard: *Same form, Add -n to Past, Change One Vowel.* Write an example under each heading. Explain that some irregular verbs follow these patterns. Write on separate strips of paper the present, past, and past participle of other irregular verbs from the Student Textbook. Have volunteers read a strip and then on the chalkboard write the verb forms under the correct heading.

CLASS ENRICHMENT

A Cooperative Activity Divide the class into two teams. Have students go to the chalkboard, one team member at a time, and write the past tense or past participle of an irregular verb. Tell them that no verb may be repeated. Set a time limit. Tell them that their common goal is to have as many different verbs and verb forms as possible written on the chalkboard. When time is up, have the class review the lists for corrections and eliminate repetitions.

CHALLENGE

An Independent Extension Have students write three sentences, using a verb from the list below in each sentence. Then have them rewrite their sentences, changing the tense.

Example: Kim brought a dog to the picnic. Kim has brought a dog to the picnic.

1. brought
2. has chosen
3. found
4. sang
5. has swum
6. had broken
7. said
8. have rung
9. broke
10. had drunk
11. spoke
12. had thought

131

UNIT3/LESSON9

OBJECTIVES
To choose the correct verb form from pairs often confused

ASSIGNMENT GUIDE
BASIC   Practice A

ADVANCED   Practice B

All should do the Apply activity.

RESOURCES
■ Reteaching Master 28
■ Practice Master 28
■ ■ ■ Extra Practice, pp. 164, 173

TEACHING THE LESSON

1. Getting Started
Oral Language Focus attention on this oral activity, encouraging all to participate. You may wish to model a question and a response, such as *Mother, may I have a pet? Father, I can care for a pet.* Have students work with partners, one partner composing an oral question and the other partner offering an oral response.

2. Developing the Lesson
Guide students through the explanation of using troublesome verb pairs, emphasizing the examples and the summary. Lead students through the **Guided Practice.** Identify those who would benefit from reteaching. Assign independent Practice A and B.

3. Closing the Lesson
After students complete the Apply activity, have volunteers read their favorite question aloud and have classmates answer. Point out to students that correctly using the verbs *can, may, sit,* and *set* will help them avoid confusion in their written and spoken communications.

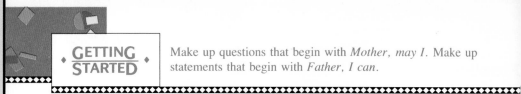
Make up questions that begin with *Mother, may I.* Make up statements that begin with *Father, I can.*

9 Using Troublesome Verb Pairs

Some pairs of verbs are often confused. You can avoid mistakes if you know the meanings of these verbs.

People often confuse the verbs *can* and *may*.

> <u>Can</u> you tell me about Paul Bunyan?
> <u>May</u> I borrow your collection of Paul Bunyan tales?

Use *can* when you mean "to be able." Use *may* when you ask or give permission.

People also confuse the verbs *sit* and *set*.

> <u>Sit</u> beside me and tell me about Davy Crockett.
> <u>Set</u> the book about Davy Crockett on the table.

Use *sit* when you mean "to rest." Use *set* when you mean "to put or place something."

> **Summary** ◆ Use the verb *can* when you mean "to be able to do something." Use the verb *may* when you ask or give permission. Use the verb *sit* when you mean "to rest." Use the verb *set* when you mean "to put or place something."

Guided Practice

Name the verb in parentheses ( ) that correctly completes each sentence.

1. I could (sit, set) for hours sharing tall tales.
2. (Can, <u>May</u>) I tell you about Annie Christmas now?
3. (Can, <u>May</u>) you describe her to me?
4. Did you (sit, set) the statue on Ms. Van's desk?
5. (Can, May) we read stories aloud now?

132   USAGE: Troublesome Verb Pairs

ESSENTIAL LANGUAGE SKILLS
This lesson provides opportunities to:

LISTENING ◆ respond appropriately to a speaker ◆ listen actively and attentively

SPEAKING ◆ speak clearly to a group

READING ◆ follow a set of directions ◆ use context to determine the appropriate form of a word

WRITING ◆ write for a variety of purposes ◆ apply conventions of punctuation and grammar

LANGUAGE ◆ use correct forms of irregular verbs ◆ use the fundamentals of grammar, spelling, and punctuation

Practice

A. Write each sentence. Use the correct verb in parentheses ( ).

6. (Can, May) we talk about the folk hero named Tomacito?

7. The hunters tell tiny Tomacito, "You (can, may) not go buffalo hunting with us."

8. Tomacito does not want to (sit, set) at home.

9. He thinks, "I (can, may) hunt buffalo as well as anyone."

10. When does Tomacito (sit, set) a plan in place to join the hunters?

11. Pat (can, may) tell how the buffalo swallows Tomacito.

12. Does Tomacito (sit, set) in the belly of the buffalo?

13. (Can, May) I tell how he escapes and returns to his village?

14. The other hunters cheer and (sit, set) Tomacito on their shoulders.

15. Afterwards, he is content to (sit, set) in his mother's kitchen.

B. Write the sentences. Use *can*, *may*, *sit*, or *set* to complete each sentence.

16. May the class have a tall-tale party?

17. We can dress up as our favorite characters.

18. We will sit in a circle and talk about heroines and heroes.

19. May Kristen come as Pocahontas, the Indian princess?

20. Sit with us, Kristen, and tell us about her.

21. I will set this book about Pocahontas on the desk.

22. I can say that Pocahontas was a real person.

23. May I tell you how Pocahontas saved Captain John Smith?

24. No historian can be certain that the story is true.

25. Set the painting of Pocahontas by the door.

Apply ◆ Think and Write

Posing Questions ◆ Write four questions, using the verbs *can*, *may*, *sit*, and *set*. Trade papers and then write sentences that answer your classmate's questions.

✎ **Remember**
to use the verbs *can*, *may*, *sit*, and *set* correctly, according to their meanings.

USAGE: Troublesome Pairs **133**

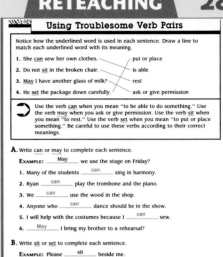

MASTERS ON FILE

RETEACHING **28**

Using Troublesome Verb Pairs

Notice how the underlined word is used in each sentence. Draw a line to match each underlined word with its meaning.

1. She can sew her own clothes. — put or place
2. Do not sit in the broken chair. — is able
3. May I have another glass of milk? — rest
4. He set the package down carefully. — ask or give permission

Use the verb *can* when you mean "to be able to do something." Use the verb *may* when you ask or give permission. Use the verb *sit* when you mean "to rest." Use the verb *set* when you mean "to put or place something." Be careful to use these verbs according to their correct meanings.

A. Write *can* or *may* to complete each sentence.

EXAMPLE: __May__ we use the stage on Friday?

1. Many of the students __can__ sing in harmony.
2. Ryan __can__ play the trombone and the piano.
3. We __can__ use the wood in the shop.
4. Anyone who __can__ dance should be in the show.
5. I will help with the costumes because I __can__ sew.
6. __May__ I bring my brother to a rehearsal?

B. Write *sit* or *set* to complete each sentence.

EXAMPLE: Please __sit__ beside me.

7. __Set__ the scenery on the marks on the floor.
8. __Sit__ on the stool until you hear a bell ring.
9. I must __sit__ and relax before the show.
10. Who __set__ that stack of papers on the desk near the stage?
11. The ushers __set__ a program on each auditorium seat.
12. __Set__ the box of costumes beside the stage door.

PRACTICE **28**

Using Troublesome Verb Pairs

Use the verb *can* when you mean "to be able to do something." Use the verb *may* when you ask or give permission. Use the verb *sit* when you mean "to rest." Use the verb *set* when you mean "to put or place something."

A. Complete each sentence. Write the correct verb in parentheses ( ).

1. Please __set__ that heavy package on the table. (sit, set)
2. I __can__ open it with this hammer and screwdriver. (can, may)
3. __Sit__ in that comfortable chair while you wait. (sit, set)
4. You __may__ read a magazine if you wish. (can, may)
5. __May__ I turn on the radio or play some records? (can, may)
6. __Set__ the records on the table. (sit, set)
7. That machine __can__ hold a stack of seven records. (can, may)
8. You __may__ raise or lower the volume of the music. (can, may)
9. I will __set__ out some refreshments for us to eat. (sit, set)
10. We will __sit__ and talk for a while. (sit, set)

B. Complete each sentence. Write *can*, *may*, *sit*, or *set*.

11. Teddy __can__ make a lump of clay into a statue.
12. __May__ I watch while he works on a project?
13. Please __sit__ quietly and do not disturb him.
14. You __may__ use that old stool near the counter.
15. Wipe it clean before you __set__ your camera on it.
16. Do not __sit__ too close to Teddy.
17. Teddy will __set__ his work on a tray to dry.

WRITE IT
Write some rules for a game you know well. Use the verbs *can*, *may*, *sit*, and *set* in your rules. Write on a separate sheet of paper. Answers will vary.

◀ⅢⅢ TEACHING OPTIONS ⅢⅢ▶

RETEACHING

A Different Modality After reviewing definitions with students, help them remember the difference between *sit* and *set* and *can* and *may* by working with them to make up sayings, such as the following:

Set the table with a special set of dishes. Don't sit down on your baby-sitter. You may pick my May flowers. Can I open the can? Write the sentences on the chalkboard and encourage students to add to the list.

CLASS ENRICHMENT

A Cooperative Activity Have partners work together to write sentences that include the verbs *can, may, sit,* and *set*. Encourage them to choose their own topics, such as presenting a case to a parent for a summer trip (e.g., *Mom, sit here with me. May we go to the Grand Canyon this summer? I will set the table every night for a whole year!*). Have partners read their paragraphs aloud while classmates check that verbs are used correctly.

CHALLENGE

An Independent Extension Have students write a list of rules for the world's quietest library. Have them make sure to use *may, can, sit,* and *set* correctly in their sentences. You may wish to have them proofread one another's work when they are finished and then combine the lists into one.

■ Easy ■ Average ■ Challenging

OBJECTIVES
To identify and use the prefixes
dis-, *mis-*, *un-*, *re-*, and *pre-*

ASSIGNMENT GUIDE
BASIC   Practice A
               Practice B
ADVANCED   Practice C

All should do the Language Corner.

RESOURCES
■ Reteaching Master 29
■ Practice Master 29

TEACHING
THE LESSON

1. Getting Started
Oral Language Focus attention on this oral activity, encouraging all to participate. You may wish to write students' responses on the chalkboard.

2. Developing the Lesson
Guide students through the explanation of prefixes, emphasizing the definition and the examples. You may wish to tell students that knowing the meanings of prefixes can help them determine the meanings of unknown words. Guide students through Building Your Vocabulary. Identify those who would benefit from reteaching. Assign independent Practice A–C.

3. Closing the Lesson
After students complete the Practice exercises, tell them to watch for words beginning with the prefixes they learned in this lesson in their reading for the rest of the day. Tell them to write the prefixed words and their definitions in their notebooks. Point out to students that knowing prefixes and their meanings can help them build their vocabulary.

Language Corner You may wish to have students discuss their ideas about how the changes occurred. You may wish to use the chalkboard to show students how the words changed and the articles *a* and *an* changed.

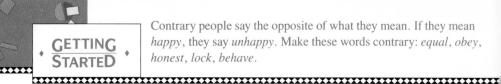

GETTING STARTED

Contrary people say the opposite of what they mean. If they mean *happy*, they say *unhappy*. Make these words contrary: *equal*, *obey*, *honest*, *lock*, *behave*.

VOCABULARY ◆
Prefixes

Many words have two parts—a base word and a prefix. A **base word** is the simplest form of a word. It has no letters added to its beginning or end. In the word *unwrap*, *wrap* is the base word.

The letters *un* in *unwrap* are a prefix. A **prefix** is a word part added to the beginning of a word. The prefix changes the meaning of the word.

Here are some examples of prefixes and their meanings.

Prefix	Meaning	Example
dis-	opposite of	disagree
mis-	wrong, wrongly	misjudge
pre-	before	prejudge
re-	again, back	rebuild
un-	not, opposite of	uncover

Building Your Vocabulary

In each sentence, find the word that starts with a prefix. Name the prefix.

1. Many tall tales were <u>retold</u> over the years. **re-**
2. Few people <u>dislike</u> these amusing, exaggerated stories. **dis-**
3. Paul Bunyan is a fictional character who grew to an <u>unbelievable</u> size. **un-**
4. Paul was a <u>misfit</u>, but everyone liked him. **mis-**
5. Paul had a blue ox named Babe, who was the size of a <u>prehistoric</u> dinosaur. **pre-**

134 VOCABULARY: Prefixes

ESSENTIAL LANGUAGE SKILLS
This lesson provides opportunities to:

LISTENING ◆ follow the logical organization of an oral presentation ◆ select from an oral presentation the information needed

SPEAKING ◆ use a variety of words to express feelings and ideas ◆ respond appropriately to questions from teachers and peers

READING ◆ understand content area vocabulary ◆ develop and expand word meanings through prefixes, suffixes, and root words ◆ evaluate and make judgments ◆ follow a set of directions ◆ use graphic sources for information, such as tables and lists, charts and graphs

WRITING ◆ write and compose for a variety of purposes ◆ apply conventions of capitalization and punctuation

LANGUAGE ◆ use the fundamentals of grammar, spelling, and punctuation

Practice

A. Add the prefix *dis-*, *mis-*, *pre-*, *re-*, or *un-* to the underlined base word in each sentence below. Notice how the meaning of the sentence changes when you add the prefix.

1. Denise and Dorothy <u>agreed</u> about which movie to see. *(disagreed)*
2. Miguel <u>understood</u> the teacher's instructions. *(misunderstood)*
3. Follow the recipe instructions and <u>heat</u> the oven. *(preheat, reheat)*
4. The hummingbird <u>appeared</u> each afternoon at three o'clock. *(disappeared, reappeared)*
5. Ernie was <u>able</u> to cut the wood with the dull saw. *(unable)*
6. Dinosaurs lived in <u>historic</u> times. *(prehistoric)*
7. Mary <u>read</u> the directions and turned left instead of right. *(misread, reread)*
8. Roger was told never to <u>use</u> his father's computer. *(misuse)*

B. Write a word for each definition. Use the prefixes and base words below to form the words.

PREFIXES: dis- mis- pre- un- re-
BASE WORDS: trust pay behave cover place think

9. to give money before *(prepay)*
10. to act badly *(misbehave)*
11. to lose *(misplace)*
12. to give money back *(repay)*
13. to take the top off something *(uncover)*
14. to put back in place *(replace)*
15. to lack confidence in *(mistrust, distrust)*
16. to go over again in one's mind *(rethink)*

C. Write the meaning of the underlined word in each sentence.

17. If *consider* means "to think about," <u>reconsider</u> means ___ . *(to think about again)*
18. If *guide* means "to steer," <u>misguide</u> means ___ . *(to steer wrongly)*
19. If *allow* means "to permit," <u>disallow</u> means ___ . *(not to permit)*
20. If *pleasant* means "enjoyable," <u>unpleasant</u> means ___ . *(not enjoyable)*
21. If *arrange* means "to make plans," <u>prearrange</u> means ___ . *(to make plans before)*

LANGUAGE CORNER ◆ Word History

Did you know that *an apron* was once *a napron*? Can you figure out what caused the change? Here are two clues: *an umpire* was once *a numpire* and *an adder* (a kind of snake) was once *a nadder*. **See Language Corner note.**

VOCABULARY: Prefixes **135**

MASTERS ON FILE

RETEACHING 29

Prefixes

A prefix is a letter or letters added to the beginning of a word. The prefix changes the meaning of the word.

Underline the prefix in each word.

1. unhappy
2. misspell
3. precook
4. disrepair
5. untie
6. disobey
7. rewrite
8. unfit
9. reapprove
10. retry
11. unbuckle
12. reopen
13. distrust
14. misfire
15. pretest

A. In each sentence, circle the word that has a prefix. Write the meaning for that word.

EXAMPLE: Mother was (displeased) that we did not clean the kitchen.
not pleased

1. Someone had (misplaced) her favorite pan. __put in the wrong place__
2. She was (unable) to find it anywhere in the kitchen. __not able__
3. We all hurried to (rearrange) the pots and pans. __arrange again__
4. We agreed to meet at a (prearranged) time. __arranged before__
5. I tried to pull the plug and (disconnect) the toaster. __not connect__
6. Jody (misread) the recipe. __read wrongly__
7. We will (reconsider) carefully before we cook again. __consider again__

B. Complete each sentence. Use the correct word in parentheses ( ).

EXAMPLE: We had to __reheat__ the cold food. (reheat, unheat)

8. The recipe said to __uncover__ the pot for five minutes. (discover, uncover)
9. Josh __reread__ the directions before mixing in the flour. (misread, reread)
10. The recipe was wrong. It had a __misprint__ . (reprint, misprint)

PRACTICE 29

Prefixes

A. Complete the puzzle by writing words that begin with the prefixes dis-, mis-, re-, pre-, and un-.

Across
1. opposite of buckle
4. opposite of please
5. pay before
8. connect again
9. opposite of approve
10. place wrongly

Down
2. not able
3. read wrongly
6. use again
7. judge before

[crossword puzzle: UNBUCKLE, DISPLEASE, PREPAY, RECONNECT, DISAPPROVE, MISPLACE]

B. Write a word to complete each sentence. Use a prefix and a base word from the chart below.

Prefixes	dis-	mis-	un-	re-	pre-
Base Words	pay	appear	assemble	load	

11. Dan will __repay__ the money he borrowed from you.
12. The box was empty after the magician made the rabbit __disappear__ .
13. Pat will __reassemble__ the old engine with new parts.
14. Joan had to __unload__ the used roll of film.

TEACHING OPTIONS

RETEACHING

A Different Modality Write on the chalkboard: *I packed my bag. When I arrived at the hotel, I unpacked it. When it was time to go back home, I repacked my bag.* Underline the verbs in each sentence and circle the prefixes *re-* and *un-*. Use the sentences to explain the meaning of *base word* and *prefix*. Help students see how the prefixes change the meaning of *packed*. Then have them write sentences with these three verbs: *glue, unglued, reglued.*

CLASS ENRICHMENT

A Cooperative Activity Have students work with partners. Give each pair a different prefix, such as *un-*, *re-*, *pre-*, *anti-*, or *mis-*. Have students work together to find in a dictionary as many words as possible that begin with their assigned prefix. Have them write the words and their definitions. Then have students work together to prepare a giant prefix chart for exhibition on the bulletin board.

CHALLENGE

An Independent Extension Explain to students that many prefixes come from Greek and Latin. Have students use a dictionary to write the meaning of the following words and their prefixes that come from Greek or Latin: *centimeter, telegram, triangle, tetrahedron, unicorn.*

Answers: hundred/hundredth of a meter; far/message; three/shape with three angles; four/a form with four sides; one/an animal with one horn

135

Grammar-Writing Connection

How to Revise Sentences with Verbs

Point out to students that they can use the grammar skills they learned in Unit 3 to help them develop good writing techniques. Explain that in this Grammar-Writing Connection, students will use what they know about action and linking verbs, main verbs and helping verbs, tenses of verbs, irregular verbs, and troublesome verb pairs to learn how to revise sentences with verbs.

You may wish to guide students through the explanation of how to make sentences clear and interesting by using verbs, stressing the examples. Then have students apply the information by completing the activity at the bottom of the first page. Students may work in small groups or with partners to choose exact verbs orally, or they may write exact verbs as an independent activity.

Help students to understand that using exact verbs is an effective way to improve writing by adding specific details that will help readers create clear pictures in their mind. Point out that using exact verbs can make their writing clearer and more interesting.

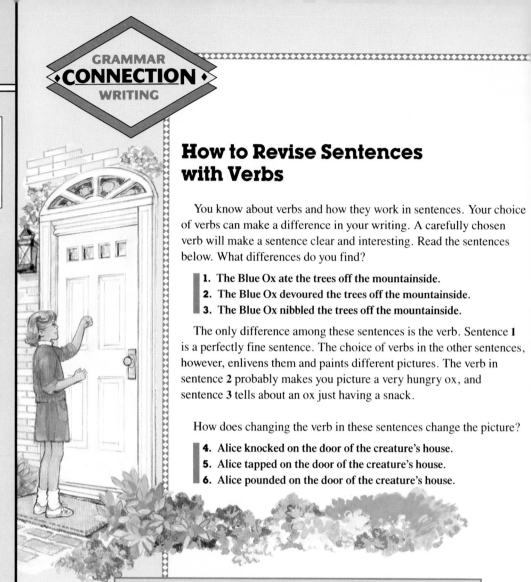

GRAMMAR
◆ CONNECTION ◆
WRITING

How to Revise Sentences with Verbs

You know about verbs and how they work in sentences. Your choice of verbs can make a difference in your writing. A carefully chosen verb will make a sentence clear and interesting. Read the sentences below. What differences do you find?

1. The Blue Ox ate the trees off the mountainside.
2. The Blue Ox devoured the trees off the mountainside.
3. The Blue Ox nibbled the trees off the mountainside.

The only difference among these sentences is the verb. Sentence **1** is a perfectly fine sentence. The choice of verbs in the other sentences, however, enlivens them and paints different pictures. The verb in sentence **2** probably makes you picture a very hungry ox, and sentence **3** tells about an ox just having a snack.

How does changing the verb in these sentences change the picture?

4. Alice knocked on the door of the creature's house.
5. Alice tapped on the door of the creature's house.
6. Alice pounded on the door of the creature's house.

The Grammar Game ◆ Check your verb power! Write exact verbs for each word below. Give yourself one point for each exact verb. Add a bonus point for every word with three or more exact verbs. **Answers will vary.**

| talk | throw | break | laugh | ask |
| cut | like | put | drink | |

◇ 136 ◇ COOPERATIVE LEARNING: Revising Sentences

136

Working Together

See how you can enliven your writing by using exact verbs. Work with your group on activities **A** and **B**.

In Your Group

♦ Contribute your ideas.

♦ Remind each other to listen carefully.

♦ Record the group's ideas.

♦ Show appreciation for people's ideas.

A. Take turns writing these sentences about imaginary creatures.
Replace each underlined verb with a more exact verb.

Answers will vary. Possible answers follow.

    shouted, telephoned

  1. The gowrow called from its dark cave.

    nibbled, gobbled   *slurped, gulped*

  2. The hoopajuba ate a mudworm and drank leaf juice.

           whines, sobs

  3. The unhappy squonk cries all the time.

    leap, bound   *snatch, find*

  4. Milamo birds jump into giant worm holes to get food.

B. Complete these newspaper headlines with exact verbs of the group's choice. Then, using different verbs, rewrite the headlines to change their meanings.

Answers will vary. Possible answers are shown.

  5. CITY COUNCIL _____ VOTES, ELECTED

  6. PRESIDENT _____ TO TEXAS FLIES, RETURNS

  7. FIREFIGHTERS _____ BLAZE BATTLE, CONTROL

  8. APRIL FOOL'S TRICK _____ SUCCEEDS, FAILS

  9. TIGERS _____ BIG GAME CARRY, DROP

  10. TEACHER _____ MILLIONS WINS, ADDRESSES

  11. HOSPITAL WORKERS _____ VOLUNTEER, STRIKE

  12. FLOOD _____ TOWN SWEEPS, MISSES

  13. GIRAFFE _____ ESCAPES, ARRIVES

  14. BANK TELLER _____ BOSS MARRIES, ARRESTS

WRITERS' CORNER ♦ Exact Meaning

Think about what you want to say when you choose your verbs. A little difference in the meaning of words can make a big difference in your writing.

VAGUE: Marty ran to the finish line and broke the school record. While going to the locker room, however, he hurt his ankle.

EXACT: Marty sprinted to the finish line and smashed the school record. While skipping to the locker room, however, he twisted his ankle.

Read what you wrote for the Writer's Warm-up. Could you improve your writing by choosing more exact verbs?

Working Together

The Working Together activities involve students in cooperative learning work groups. This is an opportunity to pair strong writers with students whose skills are weaker. Working together, they can all experience success.

Divide the class into small groups and have students read In Your Group. Encourage them to discuss why each task is important. Have them tell what might happen if the group does not follow through on each task. *(If we do not contribute our ideas, our classmates cannot benefit from them. If we do not listen carefully, we may miss important information. If we do not record ideas, we may forget some of them. If we do not show appreciation for others' ideas, they may no longer be willing to share them.)*

Before students begin activities A and B, you may wish to have groups appoint a timekeeper. Then set a limit of ten or fifteen minutes. After each activity is completed, have the groups compare the sentences and the headlines they wrote.

Writers' Corner

The Writers' Corner provides students with the opportunity to extend the Grammar-Writing Connection, helping them to develop the skills necessary to review and revise their own writing. Discuss the introductory sentences with students. Then have them work as a class or in pairs to discuss the two examples. Have students read aloud each example and identify the changes that were made. Have them tell how those changes made the improved example "sound better." Then have students apply the using exact verbs techniques from this Grammar-Writing Connection to the sentences they wrote about tall tales for the Writers' Warm-up. Encourage students to rewrite their sentences if necessary. Discuss with them how using exact verbs strengthened their sentences, enlivening them and improving the clarity of their ideas.

USING LANGUAGE TO IMAGINE

TWO-PART

flexibility

Unit 3 Overview

books

FOR EXTENDED READING

EASY

📖 **Paul Bunyan: A Tall Tale** by Steve Kellogg. Morrow. This tall tale about the legendary hero Paul Bunyan is illustrated with wacky, full-color drawings by the author.

AVERAGE

📖 **Ol' Paul: The Mighty Logger** by Glen Rounds. Holiday. This collection of humorous and far-fetched tales of Paul Bunyan tells how the giant lumberjack invented logging, straightened the Whistling River, and built the Rocky Mountains. **Lewis Carroll Shelf Award.**

CHALLENGING

📖 **Whoppers: Tall Tales and Other Lies** collected by Alvin Schwartz. Harper. This treasury of tall tales from American folklore includes long and short whoppers involving animals, the weather, human feats, and many other topics.

READ-ALOUD

📖 **Paul Bunyan** by Esther Shephard. Harcourt. This classic volume gathers more than twenty exploits of the legendary lumberjack and his blue ox, Babe.

UNIT
THREE

USING LANGUAGE
TO
IMAGINE

PART TWO

Literature "Sky-Bright Axe" by Adrien Stoutenburg

A Reason for Writing Imagining

CREATIVE
Writing

FINE ARTS ◆ John Henry is an American folk hero. He used just his hammer and his muscles to race a steam-driven hammer. John Henry became a hero because he was very strong and he worked hard. Imagine that you will become famous someday. What will make you famous? Write a speech accepting an award. Tell what award you have won and what you did to deserve it.

HIS HAMMER IN HIS HAND
painting by Palmer C. Hayden From the collection of the Museum of African American Art, Palmer C. Hayden Collection, Gift of Miriam A. Hayden.

start with
CREATIVE WRITING

Fine Arts gives your students a chance to express themselves creatively in writing. After students observe the illustration on page 138 for a moment or two, have a volunteer read aloud the Fine Arts paragraph on page 139. Have students write their reactions in their journals. Then encourage a discussion of their ideas.

VIEWING

See the **Fine Arts Transparencies with Viewing Booklet** and the **Video Library**.

THEN START WITH
part 2

A Reason for Writing: Imagining is the focus of Part 2. First students learn a thinking strategy for imagining. Then they read and respond to a selection of literature on which they may model their own writing. Developmental composition lessons, including "Exaggeration," a speaking and listening lesson, help students learn to use language to imagine. All the lessons reflect the literature. All culminate in the Writing Process lesson. The unit ends with the Curriculum Connection and Books to Enjoy, which help students discover how their new language skills apply to writing across the curriculum and to their own lives.

◆ If you began with grammar instruction, you may wish to remind students of the unit theme, Tall Tales. Tell them that the information they gathered through the thematic lessons helped them prepare for reading the literature, *Sky-Bright Axe* by Adrien Stoutenberg.

◆ If you are beginning with Part 2, use the lessons in Part 1 for remediation or instruction. For grammar, spelling, and mechanics instructional guidance, you may wish to refer to the end-of-text Glossary and Index, as well as to the *Spelling Connection* booklet; the full-color *Revising and Proofreading Transparencies;* and the Unit Pretest, Posttest, and Writing Samples.

				THEME BAR				
CATEGORIES	**Environments**	**Business/World of Work**	**Imagination**	**Communications/ Fine Arts**	**People**	**Science**	**Expressions**	**Social Studies**
THEMES	UNIT 1 Farm Life	UNIT 2 Handicrafts	UNIT 3 Tall Tales	UNIT 4 The Visual Arts	UNIT 5 Lasting Impressions	UNIT 6 Volcanoes	UNIT 7 Nature	UNIT 8 Animal Habitats
PACING	1 month	1 month	1 month	1 month	1 month	1 month	1 month	1 month

UNIT 3
Creative Thinking

■ Easy ■ Average ■ Challenging

OBJECTIVES
To use "what if?" questions as a strategy for imagining

TEACHING THE LESSON

1. Getting Started

Oral Language Introduce the thinking skill, supposing, by asking students to imagine that one day they woke up and found they were twenty feet tall. Ask: *What would you do? How would you feel?* Explain that asking and answering "what if" questions is a kind of thinking called *supposing*.

Metacognition Help students become aware of their own thinking (think metacognitively) by asking follow-up questions when they respond (e.g., *How did you figure out what might happen?* or *How did you think of your answer?*). Encourage students to be aware of their own and other students' thinking strategies and to appreciate that thinking strategies are as different as the people who use them. Explain that in this lesson they will learn about the strategy of asking and answering "what if" questions.

2. Developing the Lesson

Guide students through the introduction to imagining (the function of literature and writing they will deal with in this unit) and its connection to answering "what if" questions. Lead them through Learning the Strategy, emphasizing the model chart with "what if" and follow-up questions. Identify those who would benefit from reteaching. Assign Using the Strategy A and B.

3. Closing the Lesson

Metacognition Applying the Strategy is a metacognitive activity in which students consider *how* they think (question 1) and *when* they think (question 2).

Question 1: The ability to develop follow-up questions, to elaborate on the "what if" situation, is important. Encourage students to share how they arrived at their follow-up questions for Using the Strategy A or B and also to share any personal strategies they might prefer to use. For instance, some

CREATIVE THINKING ◆ A Strategy for Imagining

ANSWERING "WHAT IF?"

Imagining can be a way of pretending or making believe. One kind of imaginary tale is a tall tale. A tall tale is a story that stretches the truth. It sounds like a true story. Yet everything in it is bigger, or better, or just plain sillier than in real life. After this lesson, you will read the tall tale "Sky-Bright Axe." Later you will write your own tall tale.

The hero of "Sky-Bright Axe" is Paul Bunyan, a giant lumberjack. Now, what if Paul wanted pancakes for breakfast? How big would the pancake griddle have to be?

> Paul . . . decided that he had to do something about making a big enough griddle. He went down to the plow works . . . and said, "I want you fellows here to make me a griddle so big I won't be able to see across it on a foggy day."

Authors of tall tales often answer "what if" questions. The passage above is one of many possible answers to the question "What if Paul Bunyan wanted pancakes for breakfast?" Can you think of other answers?

 Learning the Strategy

Asking "what if" is a way of supposing or imagining a situation. When you answer a "what if" question, you imagine possible results. For example, what if you left your homework at home? What might be the consequences? What if you woke up and found that you were twenty feet tall? How would your life change? What if humans don't find a way to stop pollution? What might the earth's future be like? "What if" questions come up all the time. How can you think through possible answers?

◇ 140 ◇   CREATIVE THINKING: Supposing

ESSENTIAL LANGUAGE SKILLS
This lesson provides opportunities to:

LISTENING ◆ follow the logical organization of an oral presentation ◆ respond appropriately to orally presented directions

SPEAKING ◆ express ideas clearly and effectively ◆ use oral language for a variety of purposes

READING ◆ evaluate and make judgments ◆ follow a set of directions ◆ use graphic sources of information, such as tables and lists, charts and graphs

WRITING ◆ generate ideas using a variety of strategies, such as brainstorming, clustering, question and answer

LANGUAGE ◆ use language for imagining ◆ use the fundamentals of grammar, punctuation, and spelling

Sometimes a series of follow-up questions can help. For example, what if you left your homework at home? One follow-up question might be "What would I tell the teacher?" Another might be "What would the teacher do?" Can you think of others? The chart below shows some follow-up questions and answers to the question "What if I woke up and found that I was twenty feet tall?" What other follow-up questions and answers could there be?

What if I woke up and found that I was twenty feet tall?	
How would I feel?	surprised, confused
What would I do?	try to find out why I grew wonder if I was dreaming
What problems would I have?	clothes wouldn't fit furniture too small people would be afraid of me

Using the Strategy

A. Write "What if I traded places with my teacher?" Consider the "what if" question. Then write two or three good follow-up questions and answer them. You might like to ask your teacher what he or she thinks would happen!

B. What about that enormous pancake griddle Paul Bunyan orders? After it is made, can it be moved? Write "What if Paul Bunyan tries to move the giant pancake griddle?" Write some good follow-up questions and answer them. Then read "Sky-Bright Axe" to see if the author used any of your ideas.

Applying the Strategy

♦ How did you decide on follow-up questions for **A** or **B** above?
♦ When might you ask and answer "what if" questions in your daily life?

CREATIVE THINKING: Supposing 141

students may say they just like to visualize themselves in the "what if" situations and let their imagination take over. Reassure them that there are many strategies for supposing, that they should use what works for them.

Question 2: Encourage a variety of responses (e.g., *When I think about doing something new like going out for football I ask "What if I did it? What would happen?"*).

Looking Ahead
The thinking strategy introduced in this lesson, answering "what if," is used in Using the Strategy B as a prereading strategy to help students anticipate the literature, "Sky-Bright Axe." It will appear three more times in this unit and again in Unit 7.

ANSWERING "WHAT IF?"			
Strategy for Imagining	Writing to Learn	Prewriting	Writing Across the Curriculum
141	145	154	161

Strategy for Creating	Writing to Learn	Prewriting	Writing Across the Curriculum
355	359	370	376

Although the "what if" strategy is repeated in each presentation, the context in which it is used changes. Students will thus be given the opportunity to discover how the strategy can help them in reading, in writing across the curriculum, and in their daily lives.

◀▥▥ TEACHING OPTIONS ▥▥▶

RETEACHING

A Different Modality On the chalkboard write other follow-up questions to "What if you woke up and found that you were twenty feet tall?," such as *What would you wear? Where would you live? Who would be your friends?* Have volunteers choose a question and answer it. Write students' responses on the chalkboard. Encourage different responses to the same questions.

CLASS ENRICHMENT

A Cooperative Activity Have students work in small groups to compose a "what if?" question about waking up one day and finding they had become grown-ups overnight. Then have each group member write follow-up questions and answer them. Allow group members to share their follow-up questions and answers and then choose their favorites to present to the class.

CHALLENGE

An Independent Extension Have students write follow-up questions and answers to the question "What if you woke up and found that you were two inches tall?" Encourage students to use the information in their questions and answers as prewriting notes for writing a tall-tale paragraph. You may wish to have volunteers share their questions, answers, and tall tales with the class.

UNIT 3
Literature

VOCABULARY STRATEGIES

Developing Concepts and Teaching Vocabulary

Preteach the following words from the story. Use the Dictionary of Knowledge at the back of the book to provide definitions of base words and context sentences.

slurp, teamster, spraddle(d)

Discuss with students how using specific words in their writing can help readers imagine exactly what is happening or what something looks like. Have volunteers use the word pairs *eat* and *slurp, worker* and *teamster,* and *stand* and *spraddle* in sentences. Discuss with students how using the words *slurp, teamster,* and *spraddle* give the reader more specific information and make their sentences more colorful.

GUIDING COMPREHENSION

Building Background

The first half of this unit includes information especially chosen to build background for *Sky-Bright Axe.* If you started the unit with grammar instruction, you may wish to have a class discussion on the unit theme, **Tall Tales,** based on the information in those lessons.

If you started the unit with composition instruction, you may wish to build students' knowledge of tall tales by asking: *What tall tales have you read? What are the main characters in tall tales like? What do they do?* (Students may recall that the main characters in tall tales often are involved in "bigger-than-life" adventures, in which the characters do impossible things, such as make lakes with their footprints.) You may wish to share with students that many tall tales are unique to the United States and

LITERATURE

from
Sky-Bright Axe
by Adrien Stoutenburg

Some people say that Paul Bunyan, who was over fifty feet tall, could chop down a hundred trees just by swinging his sky-bright axe in a wide circle. In those days, a lot of trees had to be cut down and turned into lumber for building houses and ships. The work was called logging, and people say that Paul Bunyan was the best logger who ever lived.

Logging was lonely work for Paul, though, until he found Babe the Blue Ox. Babe was as long as Paul was tall. Together, they made a mighty logging team.

Paul and the Blue Ox logged all over the northern timber country, from Maine to Michigan, Wisconsin, and Minnesota. Paul hired many men to help him. These lumberjacks liked working for Paul Bunyan, because he was always good to them and made sure that they had plenty of food.

The lumber crews liked pancakes best, but they would gobble up and slurp down the pancakes so fast that the camp cooks couldn't keep up with them, even when the cooks got up twenty-six hours before daylight. The main problem was that the griddles the cooks used for frying the pancakes were too small.

The winter that Paul was logging on the Big Onion River in Michigan, he decided that he had to do something about making a big enough griddle. He went down to the plow works at Moline, Illinois, and said, "I want you fellows here to make me a griddle so big I won't be able to see across it on a foggy day."

The men set to work. When they were finished, they had

142 LITERATURE: Story

ESSENTIAL LANGUAGE SKILLS
This lesson provides opportunities to:

LISTENING ◆ listen for specific information ◆ select from an oral presentation the information needed

SPEAKING ◆ respond appropriately to questions from teachers and peers ◆ participate in storytelling and creative dramatics

READING ◆ identify an implied main idea of a longer selection ◆ summarize a selection ◆ understand cause-and-effect relationships ◆ predict probable future outcomes or actions ◆ evaluate and make judgments ◆ respond to various forms of literature

WRITING ◆ generate ideas using a variety of strategies, such as brainstorming, clustering, mapping, question and answer ◆ improve writing based on peer and/or teacher response ◆ identify audience and purpose

LANGUAGE ◆ recognize both the denotative and the connotative meanings of words ◆ use language to imagine

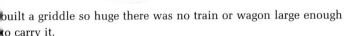

built a griddle so huge there was no train or wagon large enough to carry it.

"Let me think what to do," said Paul. "We'll have to turn the griddle up on end, like a silver dollar, and roll it up to Michigan." He hitched the Blue Ox to the upturned griddle, and away they went. It wasn't any job at all for Babe and Paul, though they had to hike a couple of hundred miles. A few mile from the Big Onion lumber camp, Paul unhitched Babe and let the griddle roll on by itself. When it stopped rolling, it started to spin as a penny does when it's ready to fall. It spun around and around and dug a deep hole in the ground before it flopped down like a cover over the hole.

The lumberjacks cheered and rushed off to haul a few acres of trees into the hole for a fire. The cook and a hundred and one helpers mixed tons of batter. When everything was ready, with the flames under the griddle blazing like a forest fire, Paul picked out a crew of men who could stand the heat better than others. He had them strap fat, juicy slabs of bacon on their feet.

"You men skate around on that griddle and that'll keep it well-greased," he told them.

The men skated until the griddle shone with bacon fat. White batter came pouring out onto the griddle and soon the smell of crisp, brown, steaming pancakes was drifting across the whole state. There were tons of pancakes—with plenty left over for Babe, who could eat a carload in one gulp.

There wasn't much Paul couldn't do, especially with Babe's help. But there was one job that seemed almost too hard even for him. That was in Wisconsin, on the St. Croix River. The logging road there was so crooked, it couldn't find its own way through the timber. It would start out in one direction, then turn around and go every which way until it grew so snarled up it didn't know its beginning from its end. The <u>teamsters</u> hauling logs over it would start home for camp and meet themselves coming back.

Maybe even Babe couldn't pull the kinks and curves out of a road as crooked as that one, Paul thought, but there was nothing to do but try.

LITERATURE Story ◇ 143

---

to express the writers' excitement about the richness and great size of our country.

Developing a Purpose for Reading

Option 1: Have students set their own purpose for reading. Then have them read the story introduction and study the illustrations. On the chalkboard write *I predict . . .* and ask students to complete the sentence with things they believe might happen in a tall tale. Remind students to recall what they know about tall tales before writing. When the sentences are written, have volunteers share their sentences with the class. Suggest that students read the story to discuss if any of their predictions are in the story.

Option 2: If you wish to set a reading purpose for everyone, have students pay special attention to what they find particularly appealing or humorous about these tales. Have them ask themselves: *What is funny in this tale?*

GUIDED READING

Please note that opportunities for students' personal responses to the selection are offered in the Reader's Response question and the Selection Follow-up at the end of this lesson.

Page 142 *Why were the camp cooks unable to make enough pancakes for the lumberjacks?* (The griddles they used for frying the pancakes were too small.) RECALL: CAUSE/EFFECT

Page 143 *What job was almost too difficult for Paul and Babe?* (straightening the logging road on the St. Croix River) RECALL: DETAILS

Page 144 *How did the description of the crookedness of the road contribute to the tallness of this tale?* (It included the impossible detail of teamsters starting home for camp and meeting themselves coming back.) ANALYZE: MAIN IDEA/DETAILS

SUMMARY

This selection, a tall tale about Paul Bunyan, describes such feats of the mighty lumberjack as making a pancake griddle so big you could not "see across it on a foggy day," and, with the help of his blue ox, Babe, pulling the kinks and curves out of a logging road "so crooked, it couldn't find its own way through the timber."

ABOUT THE AUTHOR

ADRIEN STOUTENBERG (1916–) was born in Darfur, Minnesota, and currently lives in Santa Fe, New Mexico. She has worked as a librarian, a reporter, and an editor in addition to her career as a writer and poet. She has written a number of juvenile books, including *American Tall Tales,* from which this selection was taken. She has also contributed poetry to anthologies, such as *This Land Is Mine: An Anthology of American Verse.*

Returning to the Reading Purpose

Option 1: Those students who have written "I predict" sentences may wish to review them to determine if any of their predictions actually happened in the tall tale.

Option 2: If you have established a common reading purpose, review it and ask students to tell what they found humorous or appealing about this tale.

READER'S RESPONSE

After reading about Paul Bunyan, do you think you would like to read more tall tales? Explain why or why not. (Suggest to students that they base their explanation on what they liked or did not like about this tale.)

STORY MAP

You may want to have students make a story map for this excerpt from *Sky-Bright Axe* similar to the one below.

Characters:	Paul Bunyon, Babe the Blue Ox
Setting:	the northern logging country of the United States long ago when North America was first being settled

↓

Problem: The camp cooks are not able to make enough pancakes to feed the loggers because the griddles are too small.

Event 1: Paul has a huge griddle made at the plow works in Moline, Illinois.

↓

Event 2: The griddle is so huge there is no train or wagon large enough to carry it.

↓

Event 3: Paul turns the griddle on its side and has Babe pull it to the camp.

Resolution: The cooks are able to make tons of pancakes to feed the men.

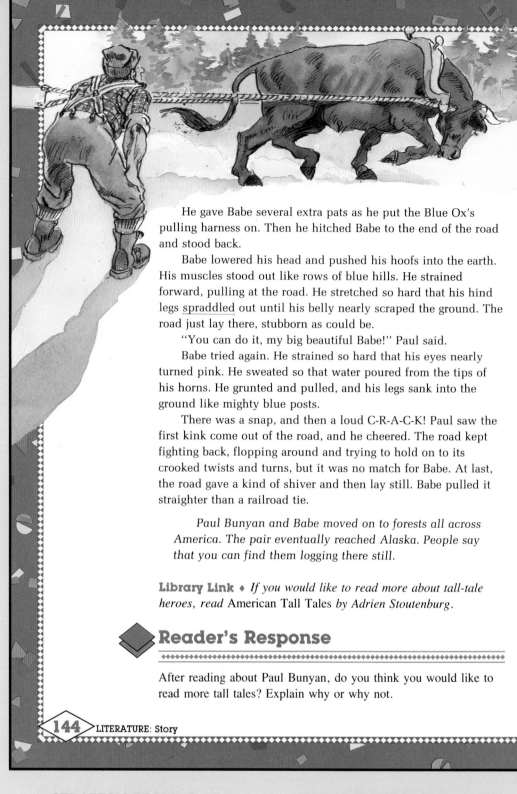

He gave Babe several extra pats as he put the Blue Ox's pulling harness on. Then he hitched Babe to the end of the road and stood back.

Babe lowered his head and pushed his hoofs into the earth. His muscles stood out like rows of blue hills. He strained forward, pulling at the road. He stretched so hard that his hind legs spraddled out until his belly nearly scraped the ground. The road just lay there, stubborn as could be.

"You can do it, my big beautiful Babe!" Paul said.

Babe tried again. He strained so hard that his eyes nearly turned pink. He sweated so that water poured from the tips of his horns. He grunted and pulled, and his legs sank into the ground like mighty blue posts.

There was a snap, and then a loud C-R-A-C-K! Paul saw the first kink come out of the road, and he cheered. The road kept fighting back, flopping around and trying to hold on to its crooked twists and turns, but it was no match for Babe. At last, the road gave a kind of shiver and then lay still. Babe pulled it straighter than a railroad tie.

Paul Bunyan and Babe moved on to forests all across America. The pair eventually reached Alaska. People say that you can find them logging there still.

Library Link ♦ *If you would like to read more about tall-tale heroes, read* American Tall Tales *by Adrien Stoutenburg.*

◆ Reader's Response

After reading about Paul Bunyan, do you think you would like to read more tall tales? Explain why or why not.

STRATEGIC READING

Page 144 Have students summarize what has happened in the story. (Paul's lumber crews have not had enough pancakes to eat. Paul went to Illinois to have a huge griddle made.) Have them write "what if" questions to predict what will happen next. Have students share "what if" questions with the class. (They will probably predict that the griddle will solve the problem.) METACOGNITION: SUMMARIZING AND PREDICTING

HIGHLIGHTING LITERATURE

Page 144 Tell students that exaggeration, or hyperbole, must be used to tell a tall tale. Point out examples of exaggeration in this tale, such as "a griddle so huge there was no train or wagon large enough to carry it." You may wish to have students point out other examples.

Sky-Bright Axe

Responding to Literature

1. Which part of the story made you smile the most? Why?

2. Spin a yarn. Tell a tale. Retell your favorite part of the story to a partner. Since it is now your tale, make it even more outlandish. Listen to your partner's tale. Try to outdo your partner. See who can spin the tallest tale. If you like, you may enlist others and act out your tale.

3. What are the characteristics of a tall tale? Write a definition with a partner. Then share your definition with another pair of partners. Work on your definition until all of you agree with what it says.

Writing to Learn

Think and Suppose ◆ Write a "what if" story about Babe the Blue Ox or Paul. Start by writing three "what if" questions. Then choose one question to explore with follow-up questions.

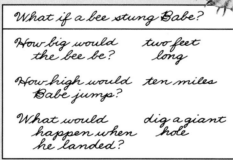

What if Babe began to drink the Mississippi?

What if a bee stung Babe?

What if Paul rode a bicycle?

What if a bee stung Babe?	
How big would the bee be?	two feet long
How high would Babe jump?	ten miles
What would happen when he landed?	dig a giant hole

What-if Chart

Write ◆ Write answers to your follow-up questions. Then take notes on what your new story will be.

LITERATURE: Story ⟨145⟩

SELECTION FOLLOW-UP

You may wish to incorporate any or all of the following discussion questions and activities in your follow-up to the literature selection, *Sky-Bright Axe.*

RESPONDING TO LITERATURE

Encourage students to use their personal experiences as well as what they learned from the selection to discuss these questions. The questions are designed to encourage students to think of and respond to the selection as a whole. Explain to students that although they may use details from the selection to support their opinions, the questions have no right or wrong answers. Encourage them to express a variety of points of view. You may wish to have students respond as a class, in groups, or with partners.

1. *Which part of the story made you smile the most? Why?* (You may wish to have students read aloud the parts of the story they found most amusing.)

2. *Spin a yarn. Tell a tale. Retell your favorite part of the story to a partner. Since it is now your tale, make it even more outlandish. Listen to your partner's tale and try to outdo each other. See who can spin the tallest tale. If you like, you may enlist others and act out your tale.* (You may wish to have a brainstorming session with the whole class on what might happen in a tall tale before having students work with a partner.)

3. *What are the characteristics of a tall tale? Write a definition with a partner. Then share your definition with another pair of partners. Work on your definition until all of you agree with what it says.* (Encourage students to include in their definition what they have learned through the discussion of *Sky-Bright Axe* and also how tall tales differ from folktales and fairy tales.)

WRITING TO LEARN

Have students apply the thinking strategy of writing "what if" and follow-up questions about Babe the Blue Ox or Paul. Encourage them to be imaginative in thinking of impossible situations for Paul or Babe to solve.

World of Language Audio Library

A recording of this selection is available in the **Audio Library.**

UNIT 3
Speaking/Listening

OBJECTIVES
To identify exaggeration in a tall tale
To use guidelines for telling and listening to a tall tale

ASSIGNMENT GUIDE
BASIC   Practice A

ADVANCED   Practice B

All should do the Apply activity.

RESOURCES
■ World of Language Video Library

TEACHING THE LESSON

1. Getting Started
Oral Language Focus attention on this oral activity, encouraging all to participate. To help them describe huge pancake griddles, you may wish to suggest that students complete the following: *It was as big as . . .* or *It was so big that . . .* Encourage imaginative responses, such as *It was so big that some people thought the pancakes were flying carpets when he flipped them.*

2. Developing the Lesson
Guide students through a discussion of the lesson, emphasizing the guidelines for telling a tall tale and being an active listener. Have them tell how each guideline for telling a tall tale would contribute to the success of the tale. Ask students what would happen if the listeners did not follow each guideline for active listening. Then lead students through the **Guided Practice**. Identify those who would benefit from reteaching. Assign independent Practice A and B.

3. Closing the Lesson
After students complete the Apply activity, call on individuals to read aloud their tall tales about Davy Crockett. Point out that learning how to recognize exaggeration in a tall tale may help students tell what is true and not true in other stories they hear.

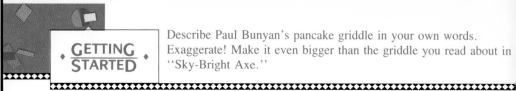

♦ GETTING STARTED ♦

Describe Paul Bunyan's pancake griddle in your own words. Exaggerate! Make it even bigger than the griddle you read about in "Sky-Bright Axe."

SPEAKING and LISTENING ♦
Exaggeration

Tall tales are an American tradition. From frontier times on, Americans have had fun swapping stories to see who could tell the tallest tale, the biggest whopper.

Here is how you can swap stories. First tell your tale with a straight face, as if it were absolutely true. Then your listener can try to top your tall tale with a taller one—also told with a straight face, of course. Since a tall tale is told as if it were true, you need to be alert for exaggeration, or the stretching of the truth. You will need to listen very carefully. Otherwise, you might miss the humor and the fun.

Whenever you are telling tall tales or listening to them, use the following guidelines. The guidelines will help you use and listen for exaggeration.

Telling a Tall Tale	1. Tell a tall tale with a straight face. Resist the urge to laugh or grin as you tell it. 2. Show emotion, however, if the story calls for it. Use your voice, face, and body for drama. 3. Speak clearly and distinctly. Having to repeat part of your tale detracts from its humor.
Being an Active Listener	1. Be ready to listen. Pay close attention. 2. Listen for exaggeration. Ask yourself, "Could this really happen? Could this be true?" 3. To enjoy its humor, picture the exaggerated situation in your mind.

Summary ♦ When telling a tall tale, be sure to use exaggeration. When listening to one, try to picture mentally the exaggerated details.

146   SPEAKING and LISTENING: Exaggeration

ESSENTIAL LANGUAGE SKILLS
This lesson provides opportunities to:

LISTENING ♦ follow oral directions ♦ follow the logical organization of an oral presentation ♦ respond appropriately to a speaker

SPEAKING ♦ retell a story ♦ speak expressively by varying volume, rate, and intonation ♦ speak before an audience to communicate information ♦ participate in storytelling and creative dramatics ♦ read aloud a variety of written materials

READING ♦ distinguish fantasy from reality ♦ recall specific facts and details that support a main idea

WRITING ♦ write short stories, plays, essays, or poems ♦ generate ideas using a variety of strategies ♦ apply conventions of punctuation and capitalization

LANGUAGE ♦ produce a variety of sentence patterns ♦ use the fundamentals of grammar, spelling, and punctuation ♦ use language for imagining

Guided Practice

Tell what is exaggerated in this selection from the Paul Bunyan tale. Then practice reading it aloud with expression.
the severity of the cold

> That same winter, men's words froze in front of their mouths and hung stiff in the air. Brimstone Bill, who was a great talker, was frozen in by a solid wall of words all turned to ice. Paul had to chip the ice from around Bill's shoulders, tie a rope to him, and have Babe pull him out.

Practice

A. With a partner, take turns reading these sentences aloud. Have your partner tell what the exaggeration is. Remember to read the sentences with feeling.

1. "I want you fellows here to make me a griddle so big I won't be able to see across it on a foggy day."
   size of griddle
2. When they were finished, they had built a griddle so huge there was no train or wagon large enough to carry it.
   size of griddle
3. There were tons of pancakes—with plenty left over for Babe, who could eat a carload in one gulp.
   amount of pancakes
4. The logging road there was so crooked, it couldn't find its own way through the timber.
   crookedness of road
5. The teamsters hauling logs over it would start home for camp and meet themselves coming back.
   crookedness of road

B. Have a tall-tale swapping contest. For each situation below, make up a tall tale by adding exaggeration. Then have a partner top your tale by adding more exaggeration. **Tall tales will vary.**

6. It is the seventh game of the World Series. The game is tied in the ninth inning. It is your turn at bat.
7. Four mountain climbers are trapped in a snowstorm near the peak of Mount Everest. Only you can save them.

Apply ◆ Think and Write

Dictionary of Knowledge ◆ Davy Crockett was a real hero who is now a folk hero as well. Read about him. Then write a tall tale about him by exaggerating what you read.

> ✎ **Remember** that exaggeration is what makes a tall tale humorous.

SPEAKING and LISTENING: Exaggeration **147**

World of Language Video Library

You may wish to refer to the *Video Library* to teach this lesson.

EVALUATION PROGRAM

See Evaluation and Testing Program, pp. C9–C11.

Speaking and Listening Checklist Masters

◀▥▥ TEACHING OPTIONS ▥▥▶

RETEACHING

A Different Modality Choose a brief tall tale to read aloud. Before you begin, ask students to summarize the lesson guidelines for being an active listener. Emphasize listening for and picturing exaggerations. Tell students that after you finish the tale they will draw one exaggerated scene as they pictured it. Have volunteers display and explain their drawings.

CLASS ENRICHMENT

A Cooperative Activity Have small groups of students work together. Have one person tell a tall tale and try to make the others laugh while the teller is trying to keep a perfectly straight face. Have group members take turns being the teller. Have each group decide which was the best tale and who was the best tale-teller and have their best teller present their best tale to the class.

CHALLENGE

An Independent Extension Have students choose a current celebrity such as a sports star, actor, or musician. Have them write a tall tale with that person as the main character who does extraordinary feats that are based on or are exaggerated versions of things that person really does. You may wish to have students share their tale without giving name of the celebrity and have classmates guess the identity.

UNIT 3
Writing

OBJECTIVES
To identify similes and metaphors
To recognize that similes and
metaphors express comparisons

ASSIGNMENT GUIDE
BASIC   Practice A
           Practice B
ADVANCED   Practice C

All should do the Apply activity.

RESOURCES
■ Reteaching Master 30
■ Practice Master 30

TEACHING THE LESSON

1. Getting Started
Oral Language Focus attention on
this oral activity, encouraging all to
participate. You may wish to write on
the chalkboard: *The old car* _____
like _____. *The ocean waves are*
_____. Then provide responses of
your own, such as *The old car sounds
like a freight train. It shakes like a
bucket of bolts. The ocean waves are
Neptune's fingers reaching for land.
They are cliffs of foam and salt.*

2. Developing the Lesson
Guide students through the explanation of similes and metaphors, emphasizing the examples and the summary.
You may wish to write examples of similes and metaphors on the chalkboard
and ask volunteers to circle the words
like and *as* in similes and forms of the
verb *be* in metaphors. Lead students
through the **Guided Practice.** Identify
those who would benefit from reteaching. Assign independent Practice A–C.

3. Closing the Lesson
After students complete the Apply activity, have volunteers read aloud and
discuss their similes and metaphors
with the class. Point out to students
that being able to recognize similes
and metaphors as comparisons can
help them make their own speaking
and writing vivid.

GETTING STARTED

Here are two comparisons: *The old car moved like a snail. The
ocean waves are hammers pounding the shore.* Create new
comparisons that begin with *The old car* and *The ocean waves.*

WRITING ◆
Similes and Metaphors

To compare one thing to another, writers often use short
comparisons called similes. A simile uses the word *like* or *as* to
make a comparison. Here are two examples. In each one the road
is compared to something else.

1. The crooked road twisted and turned <u>like</u> a pretzel.
2. Babe pulled it as straight <u>as</u> a railroad tie.

In sentence **1** the road is compared to a pretzel, and in **2** it is
compared to a railroad tie. Notice how those comparisons help us
picture what the writer wants us to "see."

Writers also use another kind of comparison, called a metaphor.
A metaphor makes a comparison without using the word *like* or *as.*
Instead a metaphor says that one thing <u>is</u> another.

1. The road <u>is</u> a pretzel, with its twists and turns.
2. Babe's legs <u>were</u> mighty blue posts.

Similes and metaphors can make your writing more vivid. The
key is to be creative. Avoid old, worn-out comparisons, such as
"sweet as sugar." Instead, try for unusual comparisons. Create
your own!

> **Summary** ◆ A **simile** uses the word *like* or *as* to compare
> two things. A **metaphor** compares two things by saying one
> thing *is* the other. Use similes and metaphors to make your
> writing vivid.

148   WRITING: Similes and Metaphors

ESSENTIAL LANGUAGE SKILLS
This lesson provides opportunities to:

LISTENING ◆ employ active listening in a variety
of situations

SPEAKING ◆ speak expressively by varying volume, rate, and intonation

READING ◆ use context to complete a sentence
with an appropriate word or words ◆ read and
follow printed directions ◆ understand figurative as
well as literal meanings of language

WRITING ◆ apply conventions of punctuation and
capitalization

LANGUAGE ◆ use language for personal expression

Guided Practice

Tell what is being compared in each sentence. Then tell whether the comparison is a simile or a metaphor.

1. Big trees fell like toothpicks when Paul Bunyan swung his axe. simile
2. Babe was a two-ton bundle of blue dynamite. metaphor
3. Babe's hoofbeats were thunder resounding through the hills. metaphor

Practice

A. Write what is being compared in each sentence. Then write *simile* or *metaphor* to identify the type of comparison.

4. The forest was as quiet as a falling leaf. simile
5. Paul's voice was a cannon breaking the silence. metaphor
6. His words were blocks of ice in the frigid air. metaphor
7. Frozen words shattered like glass. simile
8. Icy syllables splattered in the forest like hailstones. simile

B. Complete each sentence to make a simile.
Answers will vary.

9. Paul Bunyan was as strong as ____ .
10. Babe's iron shoes were like ____ .
11. Paul's laughter was as merry as ____ .
12. Paul's mind worked fast like ____ .
13. Babe was as blue as ____ .

C. Complete each sentence to make a metaphor.
Answers will vary.

14. Babe's blazing eyes were ____ .
15. When Paul made up his mind, he was ____ .
16. The sun was ____ over the deep woods.
17. To Paul, making a giant pancake was just ____ .
18. The wind whistling through the trees was ____ .

Apply ◆ Think and Write

Imagining Likenesses ◆ Write a simile and a metaphor about yourself. Choose something to compare yourself with, such as an animal or object. Think about ways in which you and the thing you chose are alike. Then write your simile and metaphor.

✎ **Remember**
to use similes and metaphors to make your writing vivid.

WRITING: Similes and Metaphors   **149**

◀◀▥▥ TEACHING OPTIONS ▥▥▶▶

RETEACHING

A Different Modality Explain that comparisons can help a reader "see" what a writer sees. On the chalkboard write: *Raindrops sparkle like diamonds.* Have volunteers identify the things being compared (*raindrops* and *diamonds*) and tell how they are alike (*they sparkle*). Circle *like* and explain that similes use *like* or *as* to compare. Write *Raindrops are diamonds,* circle *are,* and explain that metaphors compare by saying one thing *is* another.

CLASS ENRICHMENT

A Cooperative Activity Have students work in small groups to create similes and metaphors. Before they begin, have each group choose two favorite characters from sports, TV, or the movies to use in creating similes and metaphors. Have each member write at least one simile and one metaphor about each character. Have group members share and discuss their work and then choose two of the best similes and metaphors to share with the class.

CHALLENGE

An Independent Extension Have students write similes and metaphors that compare people to animals. For each comparison, have students underline the two things being compared and circle the word *like* or *as* or the form of the verb *be*.

Reading–Writing Connection

Focus on Tall Tales

Review the Unit 3 literature selection from *Sky-Bright Axe* with students and have them describe the exaggeration that makes this a tall tale. Discuss how the humor in the tall tale stems from the use of exaggeration and surprise. Then point out to students that they can use this selection to help them learn how to use exaggeration to write tall tales of their own.

You may wish to guide students through the introductory paragraphs, stressing the examples. Then have students read the example sentences on their own. Discuss the exaggeration in the sentences and have students explain how it adds to the humor of the story.

Next, have students apply the information in the Reading-Writing Connection by discussing the question at the bottom of the page. As students respond to the question, you may wish to list their responses on the chalkboard. Guide them to realize that the use of exaggeration in tall tales is usually so outrageous that it is easy to tell a tall tale from a true story.

READING ◆ **CONNECTION** ◆ WRITING

Focus on Tall Tales

A **tall tale** is pure fun. It tells of events that never happened and never could. It takes the truth and s–t–r–e–t–c–h–e–s it past all belief. Outlandish and chock-full of exaggeration, these tales are preposterous but never dull!

Tall tales have a hero — but not just any hero. He or she is usually a larger-than-life figure, such as Paul Bunyan. Bunyan, like other heroes of tall tales, is the biggest, strongest, roughest, toughest character around. His deeds are breath-taking. He will tackle any problem, no matter how large or difficult. (He will solve it, too!)

> The teamsters hauling logs over [the crooked road] would start home for camp and meet themselves coming back.
>   Maybe even Babe [Paul Bunyan's blue ox] couldn't pull the kinks out of a road as crooked as that one, Paul thought, but there was nothing to do but try.

The humor in a tall tale stems from both exaggeration and surprise. The storyteller starts slowly, as if in dead earnest. He or she seems to be trying to remember all the facts. The story sounds believable. Then suddenly — *surprise*! An outrageous exaggeration startles us. We realize that this is not just an ordinary tale, but a tall tale.

The Writer's Voice ◆ Some tall-tale heroes, such as John Henry, Davy Crockett, and Mike Fink, were real people. When you read about one of them, how can you tell whether you are reading a true account or a tall tale? A tall tale will be exaggerated and preposterous. A true account will be believable.

 150 COOPERATIVE LEARNING: Writer's Craft

Working Together

Use your imagination and your sense of humor as you work with your group on activities **A**, **B**, and **C**.

A. Create a tall-tale hero. Have your group decide on each of your hero's characteristics, using the list below. Choose someone from the group to record what you decide.   **Answers will vary.**

1. Your hero's name
2. Your hero's appearance and clothes
3. Your hero's larger-than-life abilities
4. Your hero's amazing deeds, even from childhood

B. Your group now has a hero (from activity **A**). What gigantic problems will he or she solve? What amazing feats will he or she accomplish? Brainstorm ideas with your group. You might choose a local lake, river, mountain, or other feature, and then explain how your hero created it.   **Answers will vary.**

C. Choose one of the tall-tale problems your group discussed in activity **B**. Work with your group to write a tall tale in which your hero solves the problem. Remember that a tall tale is outlandish!

THESAURUS CORNER • Word Choice

Look up the verb *do* in the Thesaurus. Then write three sentences telling what your group's tall-tale hero is able to do. Use a different synonym for *do* in each sentence. Be sure that each synonym fits the meaning of the sentence.

Answers will vary.

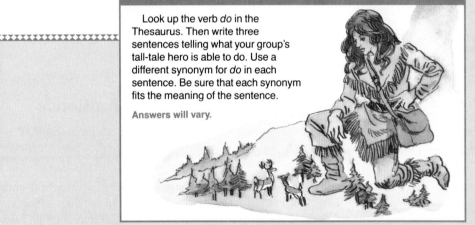

COOPERATIVE LEARNING: Writer's Craft 151

Working Together

The Working Together activities provide opportunities for students to work together in cooperative learning groups. You may wish to pair strong writers with students whose skills are weaker so that all students may experience success in writing.

Have small groups read In Your Group. Encourage them to discuss why each task is important. Have them tell what might happen if the group does not follow through on each task. *(If we do not encourage everyone to share ideas, we might miss important ideas from others. If we do not record the group's ideas, we might forget important points. If we do not listen carefully or we do not keep the group on the subject, we will not be able to complete the activities successfully.)*

You may wish to have each group appoint a recorder and a timekeeper. Then set a time limit. After students complete activity A, encourage groups to compare their tall-tale heroes and discuss the characteristics that are exaggerated. After activity B, encourage groups to compare the feats of their heroes and discuss ways to add exaggeration. After activity C, call on each group to read aloud their tall tale. Have the class listen to determine how exaggeration was used and to suggest more ways to add to the humor.

Thesaurus Corner

The Thesaurus Corner provides students with the opportunity to extend the Reading-Writing Connection by using the Thesaurus in the back of the textbook. If necessary, remind them how a thesaurus is used. After students have written their sentences, call on individuals to read them aloud. Encourage students to compare their sentences and tell why the synonyms they used convey an exaggerated impression needed for a tall-tale hero. Have students save their sentences for use later in the Writing Process lesson. Point out that learning about exaggeration and surprise can help students develop their ability to create imaginative stories, such as tall tales.

OBJECTIVES

To write a tall tale

To use five stages of the writing process: prewriting, writing, revising, proofreading, and publishing

RESOURCES

Writing Process Transparencies 9–12

Revising and Proofreading Transparencies

Spelling Connection

Writing Sample Tests, p. T553

INTRODUCTION

Connecting to Literature Have a volunteer read the lesson introduction aloud. Remind students of the literature selection, *Sky-Bright Axe*. Tell them it is a tall tale because it stretches the truth about characters, plot, and setting. Have students point out elements in the selection that show it is a tall tale. (Paul's size and strength are exaggerated. The size of the griddle and the way it is used also are exaggerated. In addition, Paul's ox, Babe, is larger than life. The truth is stretched when the story tells how Babe straightened a road by pulling on it.) Tell students that they will be writing a tall tale of their own.

Purpose and Audience Ask students to tell whether or not they enjoyed the selection *Sky-Bright Axe*. Have students give reasons for their answers, citing words from the story to support those reasons. Then ask students to tell why they might want to write a tall tale of their own. Encourage personal responses, but stress that tall tales are usually written to entertain others.

Have students consider the questions: *What is my purpose?* (To stretch the truth) *Who is my audience?* (My classmates) Have students discuss what they believe they need to consider when they write for other fifth-graders. Encourage a diversity of responses.

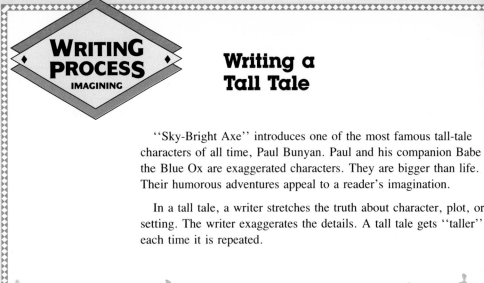

WRITING PROCESS
IMAGINING

Writing a Tall Tale

"Sky-Bright Axe" introduces one of the most famous tall-tale characters of all time, Paul Bunyan. Paul and his companion Babe the Blue Ox are exaggerated characters. They are bigger than life. Their humorous adventures appeal to a reader's imagination.

In a tall tale, a writer stretches the truth about character, plot, or setting. The writer exaggerates the details. A tall tale gets "taller" each time it is repeated.

What's **MY PURPOSE**

Who's **MY AUDIENCE**

Know Your Purpose and Audience

In this lesson you will write a tall tale. Your purpose will be to s-t-r-e-t-c-h the truth. Tell the biggest, funniest, strangest tall tale you can imagine.

Your audience will be your classmates. Try to make them smile. Later you and your classmates will share your tall tales during a folkfest. You can put them together in a "Tall Book of Tall Tales."

◇ 152 WRITING PROCESS: Tall Tale

ESSENTIAL LANGUAGE SKILLS
This lesson provides opportunities to:

LISTENING ◆ listen actively and attentively ◆ select from an oral presentation the information needed

SPEAKING ◆ read aloud a variety of written materials ◆ express ideas clearly and effectively ◆ make organized oral presentations ◆ participate in story-telling and creative dramatics

READING ◆ recall facts and details that support the main idea ◆ distinguish reality from fantasy ◆ draw conclusions ◆ follow a set of directions ◆ respond to various forms of literature

WRITING ◆ generate ideas using a variety of strategies, such as brainstorming, clustering, question and answer ◆ adapt information to accomplish a specific purpose with a particular audience ◆ improve writing based on peer and/or teacher response

LANGUAGE ◆ use language for narrating ◆ use clear and interesting words to express thoughts

1 Prewriting

Get ready to write. First choose a topic. Then gather details that will make your tall tale different and special.

Choose Your Topic ◆ Begin to think about stretching the truth. Start with one statement, then try to exaggerate that statement. Look at the ideas below for help.

Think About It

Recall tall tales that you know. Instead of being a large man, Paul Bunyan was as tall as the trees. Pecos Bill lassoed a tornado. What feat could you exaggerate to start your story? What if you were as tall as a tree? What could you do then?

Talk About It

With a partner, play a game of "I used to ____ but now ____." First make an ordinary statement and then finish it with an exaggeration. Look at the Topic Ideas box below for ideas. When your partner smiles, you have found your topic.

Topic Ideas

I used to collect fireflies to light the back porch, but now I collect stars and light the whole state.

I used to have a dog that lapped water from his dish, but now I have a dog that drinks the Pacific Ocean when he is thirsty.

WRITING PROCESS: Tall Tale ⟨153⟩

Pacing

A five-day pacing guide follows, but the writing process can stretch over a longer time, especially if students want to write several drafts.

Day 1—Prewriting   Day 3—Revising
Day 2—Writing   Day 4—Proofreading
        Day 5—Publishing

Evaluation

Process Check questions at the end of each stage of the writing process help you to keep track of students' progress.

Holistic Evaluation Guidelines may be found in the teaching notes on page 159. They offer criteria for average, above-average, and below-average compositions.

*Possible responses are overprinted on this reduced facsimile only. Use Writing Process Transparencies *to interact with your students on the ideas that interest them.*

---

1. PREWRITING

Guide students through the explanation of Prewriting, pointing out that Prewriting is the stage in which writers choose a topic and gather ideas and information to use in their writing.

MODELING THE WRITING PROCESS

If you feel students need instruction before they begin, you may wish to model this stage of the process. Tell students you want to find a topic for a tall tale. Have students help you work through the thinking process of finding a topic by having them exaggerate, or stretch the truth.

On the chalkboard or on *Writing Process Transparency 9*, write a list of statements that describe ordinary things that a fifth-grade student might do, such as ride a bike, build model cars, drink milk for lunch, read books, camp in the forest, and talk to a dog. Then let students hear how you exaggerate each statement. As you exaggerate, encourage students to help you. Record each exaggeration next to the truth. Then have students tell which exaggeration might make a good topic for a tall tale. Encourage personal responses. (Possible discussion: I like many of these topics, but the one I'd like to write about is growing a forest in my room. I think I could write a funny tall tale about that topic.)

Writing Process Transparency 9*

Stretching the Truth	
Truth	Exaggeration
I Used To:	But Now I:
1. ride my bike	fly with wings
2. build model cars	build mountains
3. drink milk for lunch	drink whole rivers
4. read many books	read ten books at once
5. grow a garden outside	grow a forest in my room
6. talk to my dog	listen to my dog talk

Choose Your Strategy Before inviting students to choose a prewriting strategy that will help them gather information for their tall tales, guide them through the explanations of both strategies. Then have students choose a strategy they feel will help them get started.

As a variation on the second strategy, answering "What If?," you may wish to suggest that the listeners write their follow-up questions and give them to the storytellers.

You may wish to remind students that they have learned about answering "What If?" as a strategy for supposing in the Creative Thinking lesson on pages 140–141.

I D E A   B A N K

Prewriting Ideas

Always encourage young writers to try new ways to discover ideas they want to write about. Reassure them, though, that it is appropriate to use the strategies that work best for them. You may wish to remind them of the prewriting ideas already introduced in their textbooks:

- A Conversation, p. 40
- An Observation Chart, p. 40
- An Order Circle, p. 96
- A Clock Graph, p. 96
- A Comic Strip, p. 154
- Answering "What If?," p. 154

Choose Your Strategy ◆ Here are two strategies that can help you gather details for your tall tale. Read both. Then decide which strategy you will use.

PREWRITING IDEAS

CHOICE ONE

A Comic Strip   Model

Plan the plot of your tall tale by drawing a comic strip. In each frame of the strip, sketch a different story event. Arrange the events in the order that they will occur in the story. Write a caption for each sketch.

I USED TO CATCH FIREFLIES TO LIGHT OUR PORCH.

MILLIONS OF STARS DANCED ABOVE ME.

I DECIDED I'D CAPTURE A STAR TO LIGHT THE PORCH.

IT LIT UP ALL OF TEXAS!

CHOICE TWO

Answering "What If?"   Model

Write a "what if" question about your topic. Then begin to tell your story to a partner. Have your partner ask you follow-up questions. List the questions. Then write your answers. Make your answers as imaginative as you can.

What if I decided to capture a star

How would you get there?
How would the star act when you tried to catch it?
What would happen when you got it?

In a rented rocket
Hard to catch as jumpy as a nervous bullfrog
It would light the state!

154   WRITING PROCESS: Tall Tale

PROCESS CHECK At the completion of the Prewriting stage, students should be able to answer *yes* to these questions:
- Do I have a topic I like for a tall tale?
- Do I have a comic strip or "What If?" questions and answers that give details for the plot of my tall tale?

Teacher to Teacher

If possible, write when your students write. By using the writing process, and letting students see you use it, you and they gain a deeper understanding of the process and of problems students may experience. Be an example. Express yourself when you encounter a problem. Then model retracing your steps in the process, making the necessary changes, and going on. You will gain students' trust, because your help and advice come from hands-on experience.

Writing

Look at your comic strip or your "what if" answers. Then begin to write your tall tale. You may want to begin with your "I used to ____ but now ____." statement. You might also begin with a question or an exclamation. Here are some example sentences.

- Do you want to know how I catch stars?
- Don't call the police! I'm off to steal a star.

As you write, tell story events in order. Include similes and metaphors that will make your readers smile.

Sample First Draft ◆

> *I used to catch fireflies to light my porch, but now I catch stars. One night I looked up. The sky sparkled like a sea full of dimonds. Millions of stars shone like tiny beautiful lanterns could one of those stars light my porch?*
>
> *The next day I made a big net. I rented a Rocket from the space center. When the first evening star twinkled, I went.*
>
> *Catching stars was hard. Finally I caught a brilliant star that lit up every porch in Texas! They jumped like nervous bullfrogs when I got close.*

WRITING PROCESS: Tall Tale ◁155▷

---

2. WRITING

Before students write their first drafts, guide them through the explanation of Writing, emphasizing that at this stage the most important task is to get all their ideas on paper.

Encourage students to use comparisons that will entertain their audience. Point out that the first sentence often sets the tone for the entire story.

MODELING THE WRITING PROCESS

If you feel students need instruction before they begin this stage of the process, you may wish to ask them to recall the topic from *Writing Process Transparency 9* that they liked best. Write that topic on the chalkboard or in the sentence at the top of *Writing Process Transparency 10*. Have students help you create sentences with exaggerated and humorous details that tell about that topic. Record those sentences, crossing them out or changing them as they accumulate. Tell students to try to create a tall tale with these sentences.

Then ask students to review the sentences and help you put them in a logical order. Number the sentences as students direct you.

Writing Process Transparency 10*

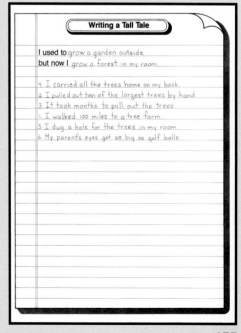

> **Writing a Tall Tale**
>
> I used to grow a garden outside
> but now I grow a forest in my room
>
> 4. I carried all the trees home on my back.
> 2. I pulled out ten of the largest trees by hand
> 3. It took months to pull out the trees
> 1. I walked 100 miles to a tree farm
> 5. I dug a hole for the trees in my room
> 6. My parent's eyes got as big as golf balls

PROCESS CHECK At the completion of the Writing stage, students should be able to answer *yes* to these questions:

- Do I have a complete first draft?
- Have I told story events in order?
- Have I exaggerated the truth to make my tall tale humorous?

*Possible responses are overprinted on this reduced facsimile only. Use Writing Process Transparencies *to interact with your students on the ideas that interest them.*

3. REVISING

Help students understand that during Revising writers are not to concern themselves with errors in spelling, capitalization, and punctuation; instead they should concentrate on the quality and effectiveness of their ideas.

I D E A   B A N K

Grammar Connection

You may wish to remind students of the Grammar Checks already introduced in their textbooks:
- Use a variety of sentence types, p. 43
- Use exact nouns, p. 99
- Use vivid verbs, p. 157

Option 1 ◆ If you wish to begin grammar instruction related to the Grammar Check in this lesson, then refer to Part 1 of this unit.

Option 2 ◆ If you wish to begin grammar instruction *not* related to the Grammar Check in this lesson, then refer to the end-of-book Glossary or Index.

First Read to Yourself You may wish to emphasize that students need not make actual changes during the first reading. Remind students to check to make sure that they have written a tale in which the truth is greatly exaggerated. Ask whether they have included lively and interesting words that will make their readers smile.

Then Share with a Partner Suggest that writers' partners offer three responses, at least one positive, and that they accompany any critical responses with suggestions for improvement. Be sure writers ask the Focus question: *Can I add any funny exaggerations?*

Emphasize that partners need to show their appreciation of the tall tale they read. Encourage students to smile or laugh out loud as they read their partner's story. When criticism is given, make sure that it is constructive.

Then explain to writers that they should use their partners' suggestions only if they feel the suggestions will help improve their writing.

---

3 Revising

Would you like to improve your tall tale? Here is one idea for revising that may help you.

REVISING IDEA

FIRST Read to Yourself

As you read, review your purpose and audience. Did you tell a tall tale? Will your audience understand it? Read your story from beginning to end. Mark unclear parts with a wavy line〰. Later go back and try to improve those parts.

Focus: A tall tale makes things bigger than life. A tall tale uses humor. Will your audience smile at your exaggerations?

THEN Share with a Partner

Ask your partner to read your tall tale aloud as you listen. Note any parts you would like to improve. Encourage your partner to make helpful comments. Here are some guidelines.

The Writer

Guidelines: Be the audience for your own story. Listen carefully as your partner reads to you.

Sample questions:
- Were any parts of my story hard to read?
- **Focus question:** Can I add any funny exaggerations?

The Writer's Partner

Guidelines: Read the writer's story aloud with humor and feeling. Help the writer enjoy his or her own story.

Sample responses:
- This part would read more smoothly if you _____.
- Maybe you could exaggerate this part by saying _____.

◁ **156** ▷ WRITING PROCESS: Tall Tale

Teacher to Teacher

Once students have begun writing, they will proceed at their individual paces. All students will not be in the same stage at the same time. Some writers will spend a long time on Prewriting. Others may move quickly to writing a first draft. They may then revise and do a new draft, moving back and forth between stages. Learning your students' different styles will enable you to help them move from stage to stage.

WRITING AS A RECURSIVE PROCESS

Connecting Grammar to the Writing Process

Writing is a recursive process. In other words, good writers will often go back and forth among steps. Depending on the individual styles of your students, some may choose to correct grammar at Step Three, Revising; others may prefer to fix grammar or usage errors at Step Four, Proofreading. Ideally, this should be a decision made by the writer. Remind students, however, that once they have completed their proofreading, all the grammar errors should be corrected.

Revising Model ◆ Look at this sample tall tale that is being revised. The marks show changes the writer wants to make.

Revising Marks

cross out ———

add ∧

move ⟿

I used to catch fireflies to light my porch, but now I catch stars. One night I looked up. The sky sparkled like a sea full of dimonds. Millions of stars

shone like tiny ~~beautiful~~ lanterns (add: dazzling)

could one of those stars light my porch?

The next day I made a big net. I (add: from a telephone pole and a fence.)

rented a Rocket from the space center.

When the first evening star twinkled,

I ~~went~~. (add: blasted off)

Catching stars was hard. Finally I caught a brilliant star that lit up every porch in Texas! They jumped like nervous bullfrogs when I got close.

Dazzling is a stronger adjective than *beautiful.*

The writer's partner suggested adding an exaggeration here.

Blasted off is more vivid than the verb *went.*

This simile was moved to make the comparison clearer.

Read the tall tale above the way the writer thinks it *should* be. Then revise your own tall tale.

Grammar Check ◆ Vivid verbs can make your writing more lively and interesting to read.

Word Choice ◆ Do you want a stronger word for a word like *beautiful*? A thesaurus can help you improve your word choice.

Revising Checklist

☐ **Purpose:** Did I write a tall tale?

☐ **Audience:** Will my classmates understand my tall tale?

☐ **Focus:** Did I use humorous exaggerations in my tall tale?

WRITING PROCESS: Tall Tale ◇157◇

Revising Model Guide students through the model, noting the reasons for changes and the revision marks. Point out to students that on the model the revising marks are in blue. Encourage the class to discuss the changes in the model. Ask them to consider whether or not the changes made the writing more vivid or more humorous to the reader.

MODELING THE WRITING PROCESS

If you feel students need instruction before they begin this stage of the process, you may wish to present *Writing Process Transparency 11*. Have students read the draft silently, or have a volunteer read it aloud. Then ask whether there is anything that needs to be changed. Work through the thinking process to help students give reasons for the changes. Then have them tell you how to mark the changes on the draft. (Students might use a more vivid verb such as *yanked* instead of *pulled*; substitute a stronger adjective for *big*, such as *enormous*; and improve the exaggeration and humor in the tale by adding outrageous or especially funny words and phrases.) Remind students that at this time, they are revising for meaning. They will correct spelling and punctuation when they proofread.

Writing Process Transparency 11*

The World's Biggest Forest

I used to grow a garden outside, but now I grow a forest in my room. Where did I get the trees for my
bedroom forest? I walked 100 miles to a tree Farm. I (add: in another State)
~~pulled~~ out ten of the largest trees by hand it took me (add: yanked)
~~because the roots were fifty miles long~~
months. Then I carried all the trees hom on my back.
When I got home, I dug a big hole in the floor of my (add: an enormous)
room for the trees. Their eyes got as big and round as
~~basketballs~~ golf balls! My Parents couldn't speek when they saw
what I had done.

PROCESS CHECK At the completion of the Revising stage, students should be able to answer *yes* to the following questions:
- Do I have a complete draft with revising marks that show changes I plan to make?
- Has my draft been reviewed by another writer?

Possible responses are overprinted on this reduced facsimile only. Use Writing Process Transparencies *to interact with your students on the ideas that interest them.*

4. PROOFREADING

Guide students through the explanation of proofreading and review the Proofreading Model. Point out to students that on the model the proofreading marks are in red. Tell them that proofreading helps to eliminate errors such as incorrect spelling or run-on sentences that may distract or confuse their readers.

Review the Proofreading Strategy, Proofreading Marks, and the Proofreading Checklist with students. Then invite students to use the checklist and proofread their own tall tales.

MODELING THE WRITING PROCESS

If you feel students need instruction before they begin this stage of the process, you may wish to use *Writing Process Transparency 12*. Have students work with partners. Have each pair go through the transparency word by word to identify words that they think are misspelled. Have students compare their findings in class.

Then have volunteers read each item on the Proofreading Checklist and answer the question or suggest a correction. Mark students' corrections on the transparency.

Writing Process Transparency 12*

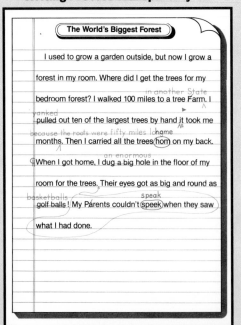

4 Proofreading

Proofreading can help you find and correct any errors.

Proofreading Model ♦ Here is the tall tale about star-catching. The new red marks are proofreading marks.

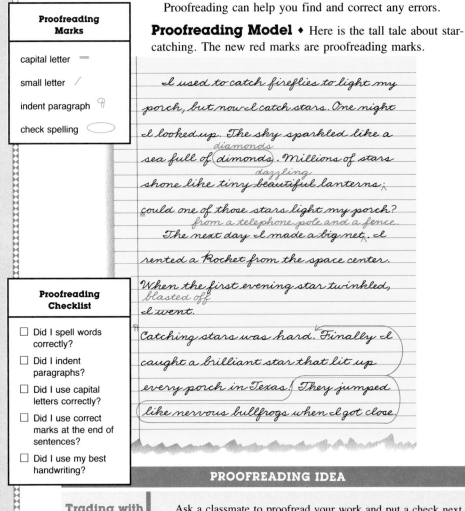

Proofreading Marks

capital letter ═
small letter /
indent paragraph ¶
check spelling ⬭

Proofreading Checklist

☐ Did I spell words correctly?
☐ Did I indent paragraphs?
☐ Did I use capital letters correctly?
☐ Did I use correct marks at the end of sentences?
☐ Did I use my best handwriting?

PROOFREADING IDEA

Trading with a Partner

Ask a classmate to proofread your work and put a check next to lines that contain a mistake. Then find and correct the errors in those lines. Help your partner in the same way.

After proofreading, add a title, and make a neat copy of your tall tale.

◆ 158 ◆ WRITING PROCESS: Tall Tale

PROCESS CHECK At the completion of the Proofreading stage, students should be able to answer *yes* to the following questions:
• Do I have a complete draft with proofreading marks that show changes I plan to make?
• Have I used the proofreading marks shown in the lesson?

Possible responses are overprinted on this reduced facsimile only. Use Writing Process Transparencies *to interact with your students on the ideas that interest them.*

EVALUATION PROGRAM

See Evaluation and Testing Program, pp. C1–C8

Masters are available for the following:
Self Evaluation Checklist
Personal Goals for Writing
Peer Response
Teacher Response

Holistic Evaluation Guides
Analytic Evaluation Guides

Publishing

To share your tall tale with an audience, try one of the ideas below.

Catching Stars

I used to catch fireflies to light my porch, but now I catch stars. One night I looked up. The sky sparkled like a sea full of diamonds. Millions of stars shone like tiny dazzling lanterns. Could one of those stars light my porch?

The next day I made a net from a telephone pole and a fence. I rented a rocket from the space center. When the first evening star twinkled, I blasted off.

Catching stars was hard. They jumped like nervous bullfrogs when I got close. Finally I caught a brilliant star that lit up every porch in Texas!

PUBLISHING IDEAS

Share Aloud	Share in Writing
Hold a class folkfest. Groups of listeners will sit in small circles. Wear a costume. You can dress like a character in your tale. Tell your tall tale. Ask each listener to tell you one exaggeration he or she heard in your story.	Illustrate and gather all the stories into a book with tall pages. Call it "The Tall Book of Tall Tales." Put it in the library. Ask readers to write their own "I used to _____ but now I _____." statements on blank pages at the back.

WRITING PROCESS: Tall Tale 〈159〉

Holistic Evaluation Guidelines

A tall tale of **average** quality will:
1. exaggerate the truth
2. present humorous characters

A tall tale of **above-average** quality also may:
1. use language that is rich in similes and metaphors
2. demonstrate unusual creativity and imagination in its plot

A tall tale of **below-average** quality may:
1. lack humor and exaggeration
2. be incomplete

PROCESS CHECK At the completion of the Publishing stage, students should be able to answer *yes* to these questions:
- Have I shared my writing with an audience?
- Have readers shared reactions with me?
- Have I thought about what I especially liked in this writing? Or about what was particularly difficult?
- Have I thought about what I would like to work on the next time I write?

Encourage students to keep a log or journal of their own and their readers' reactions.

IDEA BANK

Spelling and Mechanics Connection

You may wish to remind students of Proofreading ideas already introduced in their textbooks:
- Read through a window, p. 44
- Check for poorly formed letters, p. 100
- Trade with a partner, p. 158

Spelling ◆ If you wish to include spelling instruction with this lesson, then refer to the Spelling Guide on pages 490–492, the Index, or the *Spelling Connection* booklet.

Mechanics ◆ If you wish to include mechanics instruction with this lesson, then refer to the Glossary, the Index, or the *Revising and Proofreading Transparencies*.

5. PUBLISHING

Oral Sharing If students choose to share their writing orally in a class folkfest, set aside a day for this special event. Help students create costumes in class or suggest items that they may bring from home in order to create their costumes. You may wish to have parents or students from other classes join you at your folkfest. Invite discussion of each tall tale that is told.

Written Sharing If students choose to share their writing by displaying it, set aside a specific time when students may work together to create their tall book of tall tales. After the book has been displayed, have students take turns reading aloud the responses that their readers wrote at the back of the book.

CURRICULUM
CONNECTION

OBJECTIVES
To practice a thinking strategy for writing across the curriculum
To write a journal entry

Writing Across the Curriculum

Explain to students that one way writers get their ideas is by asking "what if" questions. Tell students that they will use a "what if" chart to help them find out and write a story about Babe the blue ox or Paul Bunyan.

You may wish to remind students that they have used a "what if" chart as a strategy for imagining in the Creative Thinking lesson, in their response to the literature selection, and in the Writing Process lesson.

Writing to Learn

To help students get started, have them suggest "what if" questions that would be interesting to find out about. Write the questions on the chalkboard.

> You may wish to have students with limited English proficiency describe actions that Paul Bunyan or Babe might take and provide the English equivalents.

Help students use collections of tall tales or books of humor from their classroom library to find examples of exaggeration and humor that might remind them of Paul Bunyan or Babe.

Writing in Your Journal

When they have finished writing, have students read their earlier journal entries. Encourage them to discuss what they have learned about the theme, and to observe how their writing has changed or improved.

Remind students that their journals have many purposes. Besides paragraphs and stories, they can write questions, story ideas, or thoughts and reflections on a subject. Suggest to them that entries in their journals may provide ideas for later writing.

Writing Across the Curriculum
Mathematics

In this unit you wrote a tall tale. Asking and answering some "what if" questions may have helped you plan your tale. Mathematicians also use the skill of asking and trying to answer "what if" questions.

Writing to Learn 72 days (Each number is 36 less than the pre

Think and Suppose ◆ Suppose that logs are floating slowly down a winding river. Paul Bunyan and Babe the Blue Ox decide to straighten the river. As they do so, the logs start to travel faster. What if the first shipment downstream takes 180 days, the second 144 days, and the third 108 days? How long will the next one take? (Hint: Look for a pattern in the numbers.)

What-if Chart

Write ◆ There is more than one way to solve this problem. Explain how *you* arrived at your answer. Then explain how you think Paul and Babe may have straightened out the river.

Writing in Your Journal

In the Writer's Warm-up you wrote about a familiar tall tale. Throughout this unit you learned about different characters in tall tales. Browse through the unit again. Choose the character you think was the cleverest. In your journal explain why you think so.

ESSENTIAL LANGUAGE SKILLS
This lesson provides opportunities to:

LISTENING ◆ listen actively and attentively ◆ respond appropriately to orally presented directions

SPEAKING ◆ use oral language for a variety of purposes ◆ participate in group discussions ◆ read aloud a variety of written materials

READING ◆ respond to various forms of literature ◆ become acquainted with a variety of selections, characters, and themes of our literary heritage ◆ select books for individual needs and interests ◆ explain and relate to the feelings and emotions of characters

WRITING ◆ select and narrow a topic for a specific purpose ◆ expand topics by collecting information from a variety of sources ◆ adapt information to accomplish a specific purpose with a particular audience ◆ keep journals, logs, or notebooks to express feelings and record ideas

LANGUAGE ◆ use language for personal expression ◆ recognize ways in which language can be used to influence others

BOOKS TO ENJOY

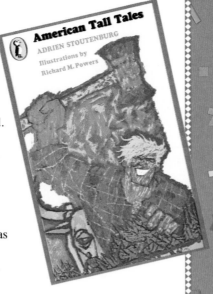

Read More About It

American Tall Tales *by Adrien Stoutenburg*
If you enjoyed ''Sky-Bright Axe,'' you'll enjoy
some of the other tall tales the author has collected.
Marvel at Mike Fink, the river roarer. Meet
Stormalong, the salty sailor. Each character in this
collection is an American folk hero.

John Henry, The Steel Driving Man
by C.J. Naden
John Henry was a steelworker. His greatest feat was
a race against a steam drill. His strength and
determination have made him an American legend.

Book Report Idea Book Collage

The next time you give a book
report, make a collage to recall
its main ideas, important
characters, or memorable scenes.

Create a Book Collage
Look through old magazines for
pictures that remind you of your
book. You won't find a picture
of the main character, but you
may find a picture of something
that character liked to do. Cut out
a variety of pictures and words.
Combine the words and pictures
in a collage. Be sure to give the
title and author.

Casey Jones was the legendary driver of the Cannonball
Express. He was smart, strong, brave, and proud to be
a railroad man.

Books to Enjoy 161

WORLD OF BOOKS
CLASSROOM LIBRARIES
is a collection of high-quality children's literature
available with this program.

OBJECTIVES
To appreciate a variety of
literature
To share a book through a creative
activity

Read More About It
Call students' attention to Read More
About It and discuss theme-related
books. Point out that the books listed
here contain tall tales, including more
tales about Paul Bunyan and his blue
ox Babe. Encourage students to
mention other titles that deal with
these topics. Encourage students to
examine pictures and jacket illustrations of books in the classroom to find
books they will enjoy reading.

Book Report Idea
You may wish to have students use the
book report form provided in the back
of their textbooks. Book Report Idea
presents a lively alternative way for
interested students to share books
they have read.

You may wish to share the reports
with the class or in small groups. Have
students hold up their book collages
for classmates to guess about characters and events. Then have students
share the title, author, and caption
before posting the collages in a book
review display.

Integrated Language Arts Project
The **Integrated Language Arts
Project** on pages T516–T517 may be
used with this unit.

REVIEW OR TEST
You may wish to use the Unit Review as
a review of the unit skills before administering the Unit Posttest, or you may
wish to use the Unit Review in lieu of
the Unit Posttest.

REVIEW PROCEDURES
The lesson pages that are reviewed are
listed beside the heading of each segment. You may wish to choose one of
the procedures listed below for using
the pages with the Unit Review
exercises.

Review/Evaluate Have students restudy the lesson pages before doing
the Unit Review exercises.

Open-Book Review Allow students
to refer to the lesson pages if they
need to while they are doing the Unit
Review exercises.

Evaluate/Review Have students do
the Unit Review exercises, then turn to
the lesson pages to restudy concepts
for which incorrect responses are
given.

ADDITIONAL REVIEW AND PRACTICE
For additional review and practice,
turn to the Extra Practice pages at the
end of the unit.

162

UNIT REVIEW

Unit 3

Verbs *pages 116–133*

A. Write the action verb from each
sentence.

1. The rabbit sniffed the carrot.
2. The black cat curled its tail.
3. The snake hissed.
4. The panther leaped to the ground.
5. This book discusses many animals.
6. I read it yesterday.
7. Darryl borrowed it from me.
8. We share books all the time.
9. Some books educate their readers.
10. Other books entertain us.

B. Write the verb from each sentence.
Then write whether it is an *action verb* or
a *linking verb*.

11. Janice returned the records to the
    library. *action*
12. You are almost ten minutes late. *linking*
13. Cecilia was the star of the play. *linking*
14. The dog growled at the new letter carrier. *action*
15. This orange tastes bitter. *linking*
16. The earthquake shook the ground. *action*
17. The horse galloped along the track. *action*
18. This jacket feels damp. *linking*
19. Betty won first prize. *action*
20. Mark seems especially happy today. *linking*
21. Yoni sampled her brother's cookies. *action*
22. They were delicious! *linking*

C. Write whether each underlined verb is
a *main verb* or a *helping verb*.

23. Susan is planning to visit her aunt's
    house. *helping*
24. Jenny will go with her. *main*
25. They have thought about this trip for
    many months. *main*
26. Aunt Margaret will take the girls on a
    tour of New York City. *main*
27. Jenny has lived in Florida all her life *helping*
28. She is buying a warm sweater for the
    trip. *main*
29. Susan has stayed in New York several
    times. *helping*
30. She has toured the Museum of
    Modern Art twice. *main*
31. The class was asking Susan about her
    most recent trip. *helping*
32. She will tell us about her next trip
    upon her return. *helping*

D. Write the direct object of each
sentence.

33. Jamie bought a new wristwatch.
34. Sally plays the piano beautifully.
35. I met Carl at the fair.
36. The squirrel gripped the nut between
    its paws.
37. Our class wrote a poem together.
38. John baked a tasty spinach pie.
39. Rosemary brought her tame skunk to
    school today.
40. Harold told Lynn about his new baby
    sister.
41. The cat guarded its kittens.
42. The small boy dragged the rusty old
    wagon up the hill.

162 Unit Review

E. Write the verb in each sentence. Then write *present*, *past*, or *future* to show what tense it is.

43. Ms. Ruiz will speak at the dinner. *future*
44. Liu gave her old toys to her baby brother. *past*
45. I talk to my best friend every day of the week. *present*
46. Our class learned about reptiles today. *past*
47. Mr. Ward shops at the supermarket around the corner. *present*
48. I never shall understand this problem! *future*
49. Yolanda jumped over the rope. *past*
50. The class will go to the science museum on Friday. *future*
51. The movers struggle with the large sofa. *present*
52. Carol stayed at our house last weekend. *past*

F. Write the correct present-tense form of the verb in parentheses ( ).

53. My friend Stu (live) next door. *lives*
54. My brother and I (visit) him often. *visit*
55. Stu (play) piano in a rock band. *plays*
56. He even (write) his own songs. *writes*
57. Everyone (enjoy) Stu's music. *enjoys*
58. We (attend) all of his concerts. *attend*

G. Write the past tense and past participle of each verb. Use the helping verb *has* with each past participle.

59. catch *caught, has caught*
60. say *said, has said*
61. bring *brought, has brought*
62. swim *swam, has swum*
63. choose *chose, has chosen*
64. eat *ate, has eaten*
65. speak *spoke, has spoken*
66. freeze *froze, has frozen*
67. ring *rang, has rung*
68. think *thought, has thought*

H. Write the verb in parentheses ( ) that correctly completes each sentence.

69. (Can, May) I read your newspaper this morning?
70. (Set, Sit) the candle on the table near the window.
71. I (can, may) see Venus in the sky!
72. Ron (sets, sits) down at the table.

Prefixes *pages 134–135*

I. Read each definition. Write a word that has the same meaning by adding the prefix *dis-*, *mis-*, *pre-*, *re-*, or *un-* to the underlined word.

73. opposite of lucky *unlucky*
74. to judge wrongly *misjudge*
75. to fail to agree *disagree*
76. to work again *rework*
77. to test before *pretest*
78. to build again *rebuild*
79. opposite of approval *disapproval*
80. opposite of happy *unhappy*
81. to place wrongly *misplace*
82. to view before *preview*

Proofreading

J. Proofread each sentence. Then write each sentence correctly.

83. Carl's mother asked him a question.
84. "Where are you going?" she asked.
85. "I'm going to the game," he replied.
86. Mr. Wu drove Carl to taylor park.
87. Jane, Fran, and, Alex came, too.
88. the soccer game was very exciting.
89. Fran scored the winning Goal.
90. "Did we win?" asked Fran?
91. "Carl answered, "We sure did!"

Unit Review **163**

OBJECTIVES
To solve language puzzles based on skills taught in the unit

ANSWERS

Hidden Verbs

hurry	dry
rely	cry
decide	hope
try	hop
empty	exchange

Puzzles will vary. The following words should be hidden.

trapped	mopped
trotted	attended
qualified	applied
worried	shopped
opened	used

Claim-to-fame Matchup
1. flew, Orville Wright
2. rang, Liberty Bell
3. grew, Paul Bunyan
4. brought, *Santa María*
5. wore, Florence Nightingale

LANGUAGE PUZZLERS   Unit 3 Challenge

Hidden Verbs

Look at how the past-tense forms of ten verbs are hidden in this puzzle. Write the present-tense form of each hidden verb.

Hide the past-tense form of each verb below in a similar puzzle. Ask a classmate to solve your puzzle.

d	e	i	r	r	u	h
e	e	a	d	b	c	o
g	d	c	e	e	f	p
n	a	t	r	i	e	d	p
a	g	d	l	d	h	e
h	o	p	e	d	e	d
c	i	c	r	i	e	d
x	j	k	l	m	r	n
e	m	p	t	i	e	d

trap	qualify	open	attend	shop
trot	worry	mop	apply	use

Claim-to-fame Matchup

Match each famous person or thing with the correct claim to fame. (Hint: The answer to what each did is the past tense of a verb in the list below.)

Santa María   Florence Nightingale   Orville Wright
Liberty Bell   Paul Bunyan

1. I ____ the first airplane. My name is ____.
2. I ____ in 1776 to announce the signing of the Declaration of Independence. I am the ____.
3. I ____ to be a giant. My name is ____.
4. I ____ Christopher Columbus to America. I am a ship called the ____.
5. I ____ the first nurse's uniform. My name is ____.

wear	grow	fly	bring	ring

164   Language Puzzlers

Unit 3 Extra Practice

1 Writing with Action Verbs   *p. 116*

A. Each sentence below contains an action verb. Write each sentence and underline the verb.

1. Two scientists traveled to Nepal.
2. They studied the habits of tigers in the wild.
3. They watched the tigers for months.
4. They learned many interesting facts.
5. Their article describes the life of a tiger.
6. The tigers make their home in a large valley.
7. Tall, thick grass covers much of the ground.
8. Rivers run through the valley.
9. In hot weather the tigers cool themselves in the water.
10. The tigers hunt various kinds of deer.
11. They hide in the tall grasses.
12. Tigers live alone, not in groups.
13. Young tigers learn from their mothers for two years.
14. Each tiger controls its own territory.
15. It roams long distances inside this area.

B. Write the sentences. Use an action verb to complete each sentence.

EXAMPLE: Angelo _____ a tiny kitten.
ANSWER: Angelo found a tiny kitten.

16. It _____ outside the front door in the rain.
17. Angelo _____ it with a towel.
18. He _____ the kitten to his mother.
19. Then they _____ it something to eat and drink.
20. The kitten _____ its paws carefully.
21. It _____ straight into Angelo's room.
22. With a loud "meow," it _____ onto the bed.
23. It _____ down right in the middle of the pillow.
24. Angelo _____ its sleek, soft head.
25. The kitten _____ happily before it fell asleep.
26. Angelo _____ his friends about his new pet.

Extra Practice **165**

Extra Practice
Unit 3

OBJECTIVES
To practice skills taught in the unit

ANSWERS
Writing with Action Verbs
A. 1. traveled
    2. studied
    3. watched
    4. learned
    5. describes
    6. make
    7. covers
    8. run
    9. cool
    10. hunt
    11. hide
    12. live
    13. learn
    14. controls
    15. roams

B. Answers will vary. The following are possible answers.
    16. It stood outside the front door in the rain.
    17. Angelo dried it with a towel.
    18. He showed the kitten to his mother.
    19. Then they gave it something to eat and drink.
    20. The kitten licked its paws carefully.
    21. It ran straight into Angelo's room.
    22. With a loud "meow," it jumped onto the bed.
    23. It settled down right in the middle of the pillow.
    24. Angelo patted its sleek, soft head.
    25. The kitten purred happily before it fell asleep.
    26. told

Extra Practice and Challenge

For those students who need additional grammar practice have them refer to these pages. **The practice exercises progress in difficulty from Easy to Average. Practice A is Easy. Practice B is Average.** Difficult concepts requiring more practice have additional Exercises C and D at the Average level.
We do not recommend these exercises for students who have mastered the skill in the basic lesson. Those students should do the **Challenge** word puzzles on page 164.

Extra Practice

Linking Verbs

A.
1. winters are mild
2. days seem endless
3. aunt is teacher
4. breeze feels delightful
5. Hawaii is warm
6. Surfing looks dangerous
7. Pineapples taste wonderful
8. coconut smells sweet
9. Orchids look fragile
10. Kim was surfer

B. Words to be connected by arrows are shown in parentheses.
11. was (December, cold)
12. seems (winter, longer)
13. was (Hawaii, destination)
14. feels (sun, warm)
15. taste (coconuts, creamy)
16. look (cabdrivers, happy)
17. is (Tanaka, fire-walker)
18. is (Honolulu, capital)
19. was (Liliuokalani, queen)
20. were (volcanoes, quiet)

C.
21. were
22. am
23. was
24. were
25. are
26. were
27. are
28. were
29. is
30. is

2 Linking Verbs
p. 118

A. Write the linking verb in each sentence. Write and underline the words in the subject and the predicate that the linking verb connects.

1. Hawaiian winters are mild.
2. Sunny days seem endless.
3. My aunt is a hula teacher.
4. The breeze feels delightful.
5. Hawaii is warm all year.
6. Surfing looks dangerou
7. Pineapples taste wonde
8. A coconut smells sweet
9. Orchids look fragile.
10. Kim was a fine surfer.

B. Write each sentence. Underline the linking verb. Use an arrow to connect the two words that the verb links.

EXAMPLE: Some waves are very large.
ANSWER: Some waves are very large.

11. December was too cold.
12. Every year the winter seems longer.
13. Hawaii was our destination.
14. The sun feels warm on our faces.
15. Fresh coconuts taste creamy.
16. Even the cabdrivers look happy.
17. Tanaka is a fire-walker.
18. Honolulu is the capital of Hawaii.
19. Liliuokalani was the last queen of Hawaii.
20. The volcanoes were quiet during our stay.

C. Write the sentences. Choose the correct form of *be* in parentheses ( ) to complete each sentence.

21. Palm trees _____ heavy with fruit. (was, were)
22. I _____ glad we spent our vacation there. (is, am)
23. Fresh pineapple _____ new to me. (was, were)
24. You _____ right about the beaches. (was, were)
25. Coral reefs _____ homes for many fish. (is, are)
26. Feather cloaks _____ the badges of royalty. (was, were)
27. They _____ still bright today. (is, are)
28. We _____ eager to try the outrigger canoes. (was, were)
29. Haleakala _____ a very large volcano. (is, are)
30. It _____ inactive today. (is, are)

3 Main Verbs and Helping Verbs *p. 120*

A. Write each sentence. Draw one line under the main verb.
Draw two lines under the helping verb.

1. Kay and Nick are practicing for a contest.
2. They have danced together for two years.
3. Someday they will become professional dancers.
4. This contest has attracted many talented people.
5. The winners will appear with a professional company.
6. Each dancer is performing twice.
7. They all have worked very hard for this chance.
8. They will exercise for two hours every morning.
9. Kay has stretched her leg muscles.
10. Nick was bending forward and backward.
11. The musicians had practiced, too.
12. Soon everyone will compete.

B. Write whether the underlined word in each sentence is a main
verb or a helping verb.

13. They will present the fourth annual ballet competition.
14. Dancers have arrived from all over the world.
15. The town was preparing to house and feed everyone.
16. The judges are arriving today.
17. This contest has provided much excitement.

C. Write the sentences. Use the helping verb *are*, *have*, or *will* to
complete each sentence.

18. Kay and Nick ____ performing today.
19. They ____ prepared two dances.
20. In one, Kay ____ wear special shoes.
21. In them she ____ stand on the tips of her toes.
22. The two young dancers ____ feeling very nervous.
23. The judges ____ watching carefully.
24. Both dancers ____ turned in circles around the stage.
25. They each ____ balanced on one foot, with their arms
gracefully and proudly raised.
26. Now they ____ bowing to the audience.
27. The judges ____ make their decision soon.

Main Verbs and Helping Verbs
A. 1. <u>are</u> practicing
 2. <u>have</u> danced
 3. <u>will</u> become
 4. <u>has</u> attracted
 5. <u>will</u> appear
 6. <u>is</u> performing
 7. <u>have</u> worked
 8. <u>will</u> exercise
 9. <u>has</u> stretched
 10. <u>was</u> bending
 11. <u>had</u> practiced
 12. <u>will</u> compete

B. 13. helping verb
 14. helping verb
 15. main verb
 16. helping verb
 17. main verb

C. 18. are
 19. have
 20. will
 21. will
 22. are
 23. are
 24. have
 25. have
 26. are
 27. will

Extra Practice and Challenge

For those students who need additional grammar practice have them refer to
these pages. **The practice exercises progress in difficulty from Easy to
Average. Practice A is Easy. Practice B is Average.** Difficult concepts requiring more practice have additional Exercises C and D at the Average level.
We do not recommend these exercises for students who have mastered the skill
in the basic lesson. Those students should do the **Challenge** word puzzles on
page 164.

Extra Practice

Verbs with Direct Objects

A. 1. absorb energy
    2. cause changes
    3. helps gardeners
    4. holds moisture
    5. shows direction
    6. measures speed
    7. measure pressure
    8. brings weather
    9. blow clouds

B. 10. take pictures
   11. seek shelter
   12. studies weather
   13. damaged coastline
   14. cause damage
   15. scares dog
   16. bring thunderstorms
   17. affect weather
   18. follows patterns

C. 19. snowstorm, what
   20. ground, what
   21. window, what
   22. motorists, whom
   23. drifts, what
   24. sister, whom
   25. blanket, what
   26. driveway, what
   27. schools, what
   28. friends, whom
   29. sleds, what

4 Verbs with Direct Objects

p. 122

A. Write the action verb and the direct object in each sentence.

   1. Clouds absorb much energy from the earth.
   2. Large air masses cause changes in the weather.
   3. Weather information helps gardeners.
   4. Air holds more moisture on a hot day.
   5. A weather vane shows the direction of the wind.
   6. An anemometer measures its speed.
   7. Barometers measure the pressure of the atmosphere.
   8. Low pressure usually brings rainy weather.
   9. High pressure systems blow clouds away.

B. Write each sentence. Draw one line under the action verb. Draw two lines under the direct object.

   10. Weather satellites take pictures of the clouds.
   11. During tornadoes, people seek shelter.
   12. A meteorologist studies weather.
   13. The hurricane damaged the coastline.
   14. Tornadoes cause the most damage of any storm.
   15. Sometimes a powerful thunderstorm scares my dog.
   16. Huge cumulonimbus clouds bring thunderstorms.
   17. Bodies of water affect the weather of the nearby land.
   18. Weather follows regular patterns in most cases.

C. Write the direct object of each sentence. Then write *what* or *whom* to show what question the direct object answers.

   19. The meteorologist predicted a huge snowstorm.
   20. The first flakes hit the ground at six o'clock.
   21. The snow almost covered my window by midnight.
   22. The mayor warned the motorists about the blizzard.
   23. High winds caused drifts four feet high.
   24. I called my sister over to my window.
   25. My sister Rita brought an extra blanket for warmth.
   26. Three feet of snow covered our driveway.
   27. The superintendent closed the schools.
   28. We invited our friends for lunch.
   29. Then we took our sleds to the park.

5 Tenses of Verbs

p. 124

A. The verbs in the sentences below are underlined. Write whether each verb is in the present, past, or future tense.

1. Noreen <u>wanted</u> a job as a fire fighter.
2. Next month the fire department <u>will offer</u> the test.
3. Noreen <u>asks</u> for an application at the station.
4. She <u>worked</u> hard before the test.
5. She <u>will study</u> at the fire academy for six weeks.

B. Write the verb in each sentence. Then write *present*, *past*, or *future* to show what tense it is in.

6. The men and women prepare for the test.
7. They jogged eight miles every day.
8. They carried sandbag dummies up and down the stairs.
9. Some of them also lift weights.
10. For strength, Noreen eats only healthful foods.
11. They will drag eighty pounds of hose.
12. They will climb a ladder to a second-story window.
13. They will run up five flights of stairs.
14. The test lasts just over four minutes.
15. Noreen finished it in less than three minutes.

C. Each underlined verb below is in the present tense. Write each sentence. Change the verb to the tense shown in parentheses ( ).

EXAMPLE: The fire fighters <u>wear</u> leather hats. (future)
ANSWER: The fire fighters will wear leather hats.

16. Day shifts <u>last</u> nine hours. (future)
17. Noreen <u>stays</u> at the firehouse all day. (past)
18. The fire alarm <u>interrupts</u> dinner. (past)
19. The engines <u>race</u> to the fire. (future)
20. The fire fighters <u>need</u> air masks. (future)
21. They <u>enter</u> the burning building. (past)
22. Noreen <u>pulls</u> the hose up the stairs. (past)
23. Gallons of water <u>pour</u> out of the hose. (past)
24. Noreen <u>struggles</u> with the heavy hose. (past)
25. After work the fire fighters <u>rest</u> at home. (future)
26. The fire fighters <u>protect</u> people's lives. (past)

Extra Practice

Tenses of Verbs

A.
1. past
2. future
3. present
4. past
5. future

B.
6. prepare, present
7. jogged, past
8. carried, past
9. lift, present
10. eats, present
11. will drag, future
12. will climb, future
13. will run, future
14. lasts, present
15. finished, past

C.
16. will last
17. stayed
18. interrupted
19. will race
20. will need
21. entered
22. pulled
23. poured
24. struggled
25. will rest
26. protected

Extra Practice and Challenge

For those students who need additional grammar practice have them refer to these pages. **The practice exercises progress in difficulty from Easy to Average. Practice A is Easy. Practice B is Average.** Difficult concepts requiring more practice have additional Exercises C and D at the Average level. We do not recommend these exercises for students who have mastered the skill in the basic lesson. Those students should do the **Challenge** word puzzles on page 164.

Extra Practice

Using the Present Tense

A. 1. works
2. studies
3. supplies
4. lay
5. eat
6. hunt
7. has
8. gets
9. fills
10. roar
11. like
12. sleeps
13. lies
14. show
15. lives
16. serve
17. swims
18. uses

B. 19. leaves
20. see
21. provide
22. play
23. cover
24. uses
25. feeds
26. keeps
27. help
28. dives
29. feed
30. jumps
31. ride
32. flies

6 Using the Present Tense
p. 126

A. Write each sentence. Use the correct form of the verb in parentheses ( ).

1. Maureen (work, works) as a marine biologist.
2. She (study, studies) sea life.
3. She (supply, supplies) facts about sea turtles.
4. Sea turtles (lay, lays) their eggs in the sand.
5. Shorebirds (eat, eats) the turtle eggs.
6. Humans also (hunt, hunts) turtles for food.
7. The narwhal (have, has) a tusk like a unicorn's horn.
8. The elephant seal (get, gets) its name from its large nose.
9. During the mating season its nose (fill, fills) with air.
10. The male seals (roar, roars) their readiness to fight.
11. They (like, likes) a diet of penguins and fish.
12. After eating, a leopard seal (sleep, sleeps) on land.
13. Often it (lie, lies) underwater.
14. Only its nostrils (show, shows) above the water.
15. The walrus (live, lives) in a small family group.
16. Its tusks (serve, serves) as a powerful weapon.
17. A walrus mother (swim, swims) with her infant on her back
18. It (use, uses) its bristly mustache for hunting fish.

B. Write each sentence. Use the correct present-tense form of the verb in parentheses ( ).

19. Our boat _____ in an hour. (leave)
20. I _____ an otter family over there. (see)
21. Sea urchins _____ a tasty meal for otters. (provide)
22. Like their land relatives, sea otters _____ a lot. (play)
23. While napping, they _____ their eyes with their paws. (cove
24. A sea otter _____ a rock to open shellfish. (use)
25. It _____ on squid and fish, too. (feed)
26. A thick coat _____ the otter warm. (keep)
27. Their webbed feet _____ them swim easily. (help)
28. The animal _____ to the ocean floor. (dive)
29. Humpback whales _____ playfully at the surface. (feed)
30. The Blue-fin Tuna also _____ out of the water. (jump)
31. Dolphins _____ the waves in pods of twenty or more. (ride)
32. A sea gull _____ close to the water. (fly)

7 Using Irregular Verbs

p. 128

A. Write each sentence. Use the past tense of the verb in parentheses ( ).

1. Hooray! Our tickets finally (come).
2. Our family (fly) to Cairo with a tour group.
3. Our group (see) the three pyramids at Giza.
4. We (do) a great deal of walking that day.
5. Ken (wear) out two pairs of sneakers on the trip.
6. We (take) a trip up the Nile on our way to Alexandria.
7. Cotton (grow) on the Nile banks in ancient times, too.
8. Rain (fall) unexpectedly when we were in Alexandria.
9. Marta (write) postcards from her high-rise hotel.
10. My parents (give) a farewell gift to our tour guide.

B. Write each sentence. Use the past participle of the verb in parentheses ( ).

11. Our passports had already (come).
12. Sami had (eat) Egyptian food many times.
13. I had (do) all the packing for the trip.
14. Jim had never (fall) off a camel before.
15. Ellie has (run) a mile at dawn every day.
16. She had (go) to the train with us.
17. Mom and Dad have (take) the last camels to the hotel.
18. I have (see) twenty souvenir stands in three days.
19. Dust, wind, and rain have (wear) away the temple steps.
20. The pilot has (fly) this route many times before.

C. Write the past tense or past participle of each verb in parentheses ( ).

21. The storm had (grow) worse by midnight.
22. Several inches of snow (fall) before morning.
23. I (take) the dog for a walk during the storm.
24. By noon, more than a foot of snow had (fall).
25. We had never (see) such a storm.
26. The mound of snow on the car (grow) huge.
27. Luckily, I had (take) my bicycle inside the house.
28. After the storm we (ride) our sleds on the big hill.

Extra Practice **171**

Using Irregular Verbs

A.
1. came
2. flew
3. saw
4. did
5. wore
6. took
7. grew
8. fell
9. wrote
10. gave

B.
11. come
12. eaten
13. done
14. fallen
15. run
16. gone
17. taken
18. seen
19. worn
20. flown

C.
21. grown
22. fell
23. took
24. fallen
25. seen
26. grew
27. taken
28. rode

Extra Practice and Challenge

For those students who need additional grammar practice have them refer to these pages. **The practice exercises progress in difficulty from Easy to Average. Practice A is Easy. Practice B is Average.** Difficult concepts requiring more practice have additional Exercises C and D at the Average level.
We do not recommend these exercises for students who have mastered the skill in the basic lesson. Those students should do the **Challenge** word puzzles on page 164.

D. 29. saw, has seen
30. rode, has ridden
31. gave, has given
32. wore, has worn
33. wrote, has written
34. grew, has grown
35. did, has done
36. went, has gone
37. ate, has eaten
38. fell, has fallen

Using Irregular Verbs
A. 1. found, has found
2. drank, has drunk
3. thought, has thought
4. brought, has brought
5. broke, has broken
6. swam, has swum
7. chose, has chosen
8. spoke, has spoken
9. sang, has sung
10. caught, has caught

B. 11. said
12. froze
13. spoken
14. thought
15. swum
16. frozen
17. caught
18. rang
19. brought
20. drank
21. broken
22. sang
23. chose
24. brought
25. said
26. chosen
27. sung
28. swam
29. found
30. spoke
31. thought
32. caught
33. rung
34. drunk

D. Write the past and past participle of each verb. Use the helping verb *has* with each past participle.

29. see **31.** give **33.** write **35.** do **37.** eat
30. ride **32.** wear **34.** grow **36.** go **38.** fall

8 Using Irregular Verbs   *p. 130*

A. Write the past tense and past participle of each verb.

1. find **3.** think **5.** break **7.** choose **9.** sing
2. drink **4.** bring **6.** swim **8.** speak **10.** catch

B. Write each sentence. Use the past or the past participle of the verb in parentheses ( ).

11. Ronnie (say) that he could hardly wait for summer.
12. The lake (freeze), but he dreamed of warm weather.
13. He had (speak) to Gary about the vacation program.
14. Everyone (think) it would be fun to do again.
15. They had (swim) every day at the community center.
16. Cheryl complained that she had (freeze) in the cold water.
17. No one had (catch) a cold, though.
18. A bell always (ring) to call the campers.
19. All the campers (bring) bag lunches with them.
20. They (drink) juice with their sandwiches.
21. After lunch they had (break) into different groups.
22. Some of the campers (sing) in a chorus.
23. Some (choose) colored glass for their crafts projects.
24. One day Gary had (bring) fishing poles for everyone.
25. He had (say) that they were going on a trip.
26. Darryl had (choose) the seat next to Leona.
27. Everyone had (sing) loudly during the bus ride.
28. At the park they (swim) in the lake.
29. Then they (find) a place to go fishing.
30. No one (speak) while they baited their hooks.
31. Suzanne had (think) she would be bored.
32. She was surprised when she (catch) so many fish.
33. At sundown Ronnie had (ring) the bell for taps.
34. After they had (drink) some cocoa, everyone went home.

9 Using Troublesome Verb Pairs   *p. 132*

A. Write each sentence. Use the correct verb in parentheses ( ).

1. Did you (sit, set) the paper plates on the table?
2. Is there anyone who (can, may) blow up these balloons?
3. Where will everyone (sit, set) during the show?
4. (Can, May) I taste the popcorn now?
5. In which room (can, may) Eva practice her juggling act?
6. Yes, you (can, may) bring a friend to the party.
7. The extra guests will (sit, set) on the floor.
8. (Can, May) we eat before the magic show begins?
9. Magic Marla (sit, set) a covered basket on the table.
10. A good magician (can, may) fool the audience every time.
11. Magic Marla asked Leroy to (sit, set) in the Chair of Invisibility.
12. How did she (sit, set) it down again?
13. (Can, May) you figure out how it's done?
14. A good juggler (can, may) juggle five objects at a time.
15. The juggler's dog likes to (sit, set) and beg.

B. Write the sentences. Use *can*, *may*, *sit*, or *set* to complete each sentence.

16. You ____ begin eating right after the show.
17. Where should we ____ for the refreshments?
18. Nicky, ____ you reach the jar of pickles?
19. Please don't ____ a place for me at that table.
20. Who ____ reach the pitcher of juice?
21. If you ____ it on the edge, it will fall off.
22. Jody and his mother ____ together at a table.
23. Nothing has been ____ on the table.
24. ____ we have some napkins?
25. Jody ____ some on the table.
26. ____ you reach those tomatoes?
27. Be careful when you ____ the bowl down.
28. You ____ leave the table when you're finished.
29. Let's ____ in the living room and tell jokes.
30. ____ I borrow that deck of cards for a card trick?
31. If you ____ here, you'll be able to see her better.
32. ____ you show us another card trick?

Extra Practice

Using Troublesome Verb Pairs

A.
1. set
2. can
3. sit
4. May
5. may
6. may
7. sit
8. May
9. set
10. can
11. sit
12. set
13. Can
14. can
15. sit

B.
16. may
17. sit
18. can
19. set
20. can
21. set
22. sit
23. set
24. May
25. sets
26. Can
27. set
28. may
29. sit
30. May
31. sit
32. can

Extra Practice and Challenge

For those students who need additional grammar practice have them refer to these pages. **The practice exercises progress in difficulty from Easy to Average. Practice A is Easy. Practice B is Average.** Difficult concepts requiring more practice have additional Exercises C and D at the Average level.
We do not recommend these exercises for students who have mastered the skill in the basic lesson. Those students should do the **Challenge** word puzzles on page 164.

UNIT 4

OVERVIEW

TWO-PART
flexibility

Unit 4 Overview

books
ON UNIT THEME

USING LANGUAGE TO PERSUADE

EASY

 **Lives of the Artists** by M. B. Goffstein. Farrar. Masters such as Rembrandt and Van Gogh are introduced through reproductions of their artwork and brief poetic text.

From the Mixed-Up Files of Mrs. Basil E. Frankweiler by E. L. Konigsburg. Atheneum. Claudia and her younger brother run away and live, for one glorious week, amid the treasures of the Metropolitan Museum of Art in New York City. **Newbery Medal.**

AVERAGE

Dorothy Lange: Life Through the Camera by Milton Meltzer. Viking. This well-written biography introduces the life and work of the famous photographer.

Onstage/Backstage by Caryn Huberman and JoAnne Wezel. Carolrhoda. This photo essay provides a backstage look at the Palo Alto Children's Theatre, as a ten-year-old girl wins a role in the production of Kipling's *Just So Stories*.

CHALLENGING

People at Work: Looking at Art by Patrick Conner. McElderry. Reproductions of famous artwork. and informative descriptions draw the reader into this introduction to art.

Burnish Me Bright by Julia Cunningham. Dell. In this story set in Paris, a retired pantomimist teaches an orphaned mute boy the art of mime.

READ-ALOUDS

I, Juan de Pareja by Elizabeth Borton de Trevino. Farrar. In this historical novel, the character of the artist Velázquez is revealed through the eyes of his slave, Juan de Pareja. **Newbery Medal.**

The Master Puppeteer by Katherine Paterson. Crowell. This historical novel, set inside the Hanaza puppet theater in eighteenth-century Osaka, Japan, features the experiences of Jiro, a young apprentice. **National Book Award.**

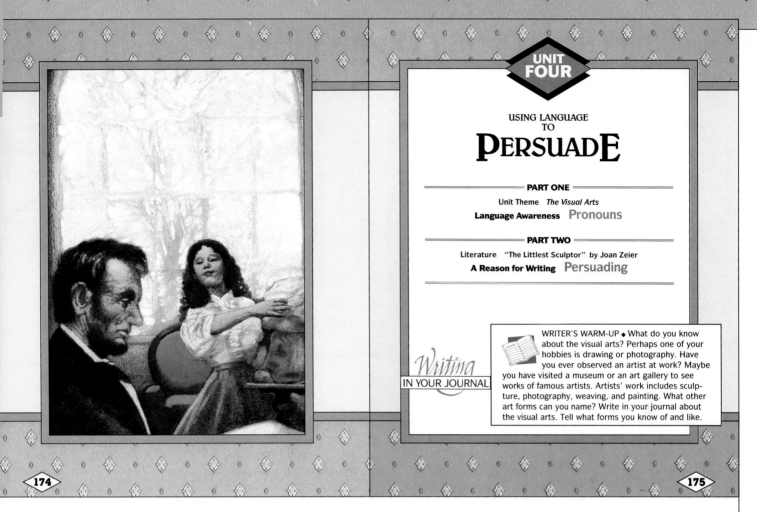

UNIT FOUR

USING LANGUAGE TO
PERSUADE

───── **PART ONE** ─────

Unit Theme *The Visual Arts*

Language Awareness Pronouns

───── **PART TWO** ─────

Literature "The Littlest Sculptor" by Joan Zeier

A Reason for Writing Persuading

Writing
IN YOUR JOURNAL

WRITER'S WARM-UP ♦ What do you know about the visual arts? Perhaps one of your hobbies is drawing or photography. Have you ever observed an artist at work? Maybe you have visited a museum or an art gallery to see works of famous artists. Artists' work includes sculpture, photography, weaving, and painting. What other art forms can you name? Write in your journal about the visual arts. Tell what forms you know of and like.

start with WRITING IN YOUR JOURNAL

Writers' Warm-up is designed to help students activate prior knowledge of the unit theme, "Handicrafts." Whether you begin instruction with Part 1 or Part 2, encourage students to focus attention on the illustration on page 174 of their textbooks. Encourage them to discuss what they see. Then have a volunteer read aloud the **Writers' Warm-up** on page 175. Have students write their thoughts in their journals. You may wish to tell them that they will refer to this writing in the first lesson of Part 1, in the Grammar-Writing Connection, and in the Curriculum Connection.

THEN START WITH *part 1*

Language Awareness: Pronouns Developmental lessons focus on the concept of pronouns. Each lesson is carefully constructed not only to help students learn the concept well but also to help build interest and background knowledge for the thinking, reading, and writing they will do in Part 2. The last lesson in Part 1 is a vocabulary lesson with which students learn how to use homophones. The Grammar-Writing Connection that follows serves as a bridge to Part 2, encouraging students to work together to apply their new language skills at the sentence level of writing.

...OR WITH *part 2*

A Reason for Writing: Persuading is the focus of Part 2. First, students learn a thinking strategy for persuading. Then they read and respond to a selection of nonfiction on which they may model their writing. Developmental composition lessons, including "Expressing Opinions," a speaking and listening lesson, all reflect the literature and culminate in the Writing Process lesson. There a "Grammar Check," a "Word Choice" hint, and proofreading strategies help you focus on single traits for remediation or instruction through the lessons in Part 1. The unit ends with Curriculum Connection and Books to Enjoy, which help students discover how their new skills apply to writing across the curriculum.

THEME BAR

CATEGORIES	Environments	Business/World of Work	Imagination	Communications/ Fine Arts	People	Science	Expressions	Social Studies
THEMES	UNIT 1 Farm Life	UNIT 2 Handicrafts	UNIT 3 Tall Tales	UNIT 4 The Visual Arts	UNIT 5 Lasting Impressions	UNIT 6 Volcanoes	UNIT 7 Nature	UNIT 8 Animal Habitats
PACING	1 month	1 month	1 month	1 month	1 month	1 month	1 month	1 month

Build background knowledge of the unit theme, "The Visual Arts," by reading aloud this selection to your class. At the same time you will be building your students' knowledge of our rich heritage of fine literature. You may wish to use the "Notes for Listening" on the following page before and after reading aloud.

THE GOOD OLD DAYS

from *Grandma Moses: My Life's History*

BY ANNA MARY ROBERTSON MOSES

Grandma Moses, America's best-loved primitive painter, was born Anna Mary Robertson in 1860, on a farm in upstate New York. She began to paint in her 70s, teaching herself by copying prints, illustrations in magazines, and greeting cards. She turned to painting farm scenes and landscapes "so that people will see how we used to live." People loved her brightly-colored scenes of rural life. Her enthusiasm never slowed—she painted twenty-five pictures in the year after her one-hundredth birthday. In the following excerpts from her autobiography, Grandma Moses talks about her art.

The First Large Picture

One time I was papering the parlor, and I ran short of paper for the fire board. So I took a piece of paper and pasted it over the board, and I painted it a solid color first, then I painted two large trees on each side of it, like butternut trees. And back in it I did a little scene of a lake and painted it a yellow color, really bright as though you were looking off into the sun light. In the front, to fill in that space, I brought in big bushes. I daubed it all on with the brush I painted the floor with. Dorothy's grandfather, when he saw it, he made a great to-do. "Oh, isn't that beautiful, that's the most wonderful thing I ever see, don't let anything happen to that!" he said. It run on three or four years, and we re-papered the parlor and papered over the picture. When we re-papered the room again a few years ago, Dorothy remembered the picture, and we took the paper off the fire board, but the colors had faded somewhat.

That was my first large picture.

Painting

As for myself, I started to paint in my old age, one might say, though I had painted a few pictures before.

My sister Celestia came down one day and saw my worsted pictures and said: "I think you could paint better and faster than you could do worsted pictures." So I did, and painted for pleasure, to keep busy and to pass the time away, but I thought of it no more than of doing fancy work.

When I had quite a few paintings on hand, someone suggested that I send them down to the old Thomas' drug store in Hoosick Falls, so I tried that. I also exhibited a few at the Cambridge Fair with some canned fruits and raspberry jam. I won a prize for my fruit and jam, but no pictures.

And then, one day, a Mr. Louis J. Caldor of New York City, an engineer and art collector, passing through the town of Hoosick Falls, saw and bought my paintings. He wanted to know who had painted them, and they told him it was an old woman that was living down on the Cambridge Road by the name of Anna Mary Moses. So when I came home that night, Dorothy said: "If you had been here, you could have sold all your paintings, there was a man here looking for them, and he will be back in the morning to see them. I told him how many you had." She thought I had about ten, something like that.

Well, I didn't sleep much that night, I tried to think where I had any paintings and what they were, I knew I didn't have many, they were mostly worsted, but I thought, towards morning, of a painting I had started on after house cleaning days, when I found an old canvas and frame, and I thought I had painted a picture on it of Virginia. It was quite large, and I thought if I could find frames in the morning I could cut that right in two and make two pictures, which I did, and by so doing I had the ten pictures for him when he came. I did it so it wouldn't get Dorothy in the dog house. But he didn't discover the one I had cut in two for about a year, then he wanted to know what made me cut my best picture in two. I told him, it's just Scotch thrift.

My Tip-up Table

Painting is a very pleasant hobby, if one does not have to hurry, I love to take my time and finish things up right.

I have an old tip-up table, on which I can paint. My aunt gave it to me thirty-five years ago, it was built for a log cabin. Back in the 18th century, Phinious Whiteside came and made his home in the township of Washington County, New York, taking up a tract of land, on which he made his home. He had a large family of girls and boys. When his oldest son became of age he gave him his portion, which was the custom in those days, a freedom suit, so many sheep, an ax and I think 200 acres of land, and said, now go and build a home for yourself. He went into the 200 acres of heavy timber which joined his father's, cut down trees and built himself a bed, and a trundlebed, then the tip-back table, so as when the trundlebed was run out, there would be room enough to move about. The table was made of pine planks, under the top between the standards there was a box in which they kept their pewter dishes, this had a plank cover so that it formed a chair. Long years after the new large brick house was built, the table was moved over into the cellar and used as a milk table for many more years. Then one day my aunt sent it to me for a flower stand; I have painted scenes on the standards and covered the top with postal cards, and now use it for my easel.

The Dream

If I didn't start painting, I would have raised chickens. I could still do it now. I would never sit back in a rocking chair, waiting for someone to help me. I have often said, before I would call for help from outsiders, I would rent a room in the city some place and give pancake suppers, just pancake and syrup, and they could have water, like a little breakfast. I never dreamed that the pictures would bring in so much, and as for all that publicity, and as for the fame which came to Grandma so late, that I am too old to care for now. Sometimes it makes me think of a dream that my father once told at the breakfast table one morning many years ago. He said, "I had a dream about you last night, Anna Mary." "Was it good or bad, Pa?" And he said, "That depends on the future, dreams cast their shadows before us." He dreamed, I was in a large hall and there were many people there, they were clapping their hands and shouting and he wondered what it was all about. "And looking I saw you, Anna Mary, coming my way, walking on the shoulders of men; you came right on stepping from one shoulder to another, waving to me." Of late years I have often thought of that dream, since all the publicity about me, and of my mother saying to my father, "Now, Russell, Anna Mary would look nice walking on men's shoulders!" She saw the folly of that dream. Or did that dream cast its shadows before? I often wonder. ◇

NOTES FOR
listening

Introducing the Selection

Relate to theme Tell students that the unit theme is "The Visual Arts." Encourage them to discuss their own experiences with painting.

Discuss word meanings Explain to students that in the excerpts from *Grandma Moses: My Life's History,* they will hear new words that they may not understand. Pronounce the words below and write them on the chalkboard. Give students the meaning of each word and tell them that knowing the words will help them to better understand the excerpts.

worsted a yarn spun from of wool
Scotch thrift being especially careful about money
trundlebed a bed with a low frame that can be rolled under another bed
folly foolishness

Listening to the Selection

Set a purpose Tell students they are going to listen to excerpts from *Grandma Moses: My Life's History* by Anna Mary Robertson Moses. Have students listen to discover what painting meant to Grandma Moses.

Starting with Literature

Discussing the Selection

Return to purpose After you have read the selection, discuss with students how Grandma Moses felt about her painting both before her fame and after. Then have students make a more general statement, such as: *Grandma Moses always felt that her painting was a pleasant hobby, not a way to become rich.*

UNIT 4 PLANNING AND PACING GUIDE

	LESSON TITLE	STUDENT TEXT				TEACHING RESOURCES		
		Student Lesson	Unit Review	Cumulative Review	Extra Practice	Reteaching Master	Practice Master	Testing Program
1 DAY	Unit Opener							
1 DAY	Writing with Pronouns	176–177	220	225, 331, 434	226, 227	31	31	
1 DAY	Subject Pronouns	178–179	220	225, 331, 434	226, 228	32	32	T538
1 DAY	Object Pronouns	180–181	220	225, 331, 434	226, 228	33	33	T538
1 DAY	Possessive Pronouns	182–183	220	225, 331, 434	226, 229	34	34	T538
1 DAY	Using Pronouns	184–185	220	225, 331, 434	226, 230	35	35	T538
1 DAY	Contractions	186–187	221	225, 331, 434	226, 231	36	36	T538
1 DAY	VOCABULARY ◆ Homophones	188–189	221			37	37	T538
1 DAY	GRAMMAR-WRITING CONNECTION ◆ How to Revise Sentences with Pronouns	190–191						
	▶ THINK							
1 DAY	CREATIVE THINKING ◆ A Strategy for Persuading	194–195	See also pages 199, 212, 218					
	▶ READ							
1 DAY	NONFICTION ◆ *The Littlest Sculptor* by Joan Zeier	196–199				Audio Library 2		
	▶ SPEAK/LISTEN							
1 DAY	SPEAKING AND LISTENING ◆ Expressing Opinions	200–201				Video Library		
	▶ WRITE							
1 DAY	WRITING ◆ Fact and Opinion	202–203	221			38	38	T538
1 DAY	WRITING ◆ A Persuasive Paragraph	204–205				39	39	
1 DAY	WRITING ◆ A Business Letter	206–207	221			40	40	T538
1 DAY	READING-WRITING CONNECTION ◆ Focus on Persuasive Words	208–209						
	▶ WRITING PROCESS ◆ Prewriting • Writing • Revising • Proofreading • Publishing							
4–5 DAYS	WRITING PROCESS ◆ Writing a Persuasive Letter	210–211				Spelling Connection Transparencies		T553
1 DAY	CURRICULUM CONNECTION ◆ Writing for Social Studies	218				Writing Across the Curriculum Guide		

PART 1 · PART 2

Teacher Resource File
Reteaching Masters 31–40
Practice Masters 31–40
Evaluation and Testing Program, including Unit Pretest, Posttest, and Picture Prompt Writing Samples
Parent Letters in English and Spanish
Classroom Theme Posters
Writing Across the Curriculum Teacher Guide
Integrated Language Arts Projects with Masters (see pages T511–T529)
Spelling Corner, Teacher Edition
Writing Process Transparencies
Audio Library 1: Read-Alouds and Sing-Alouds

Also available:
Achieving English Proficiency Guide and Activities
Spelling Connection, Pupil Edition
Student Resource Books
Student Writing Portfolios
Professional Handbook
WORLD OF BOOKS Classroom Library

Multi-Modal Materials
Audio Library 1: Read-Alouds and Sing-Alouds
Audio Library 2: Listening to Literature
Video Library
Revising and Proofreading Transparencies
Fine Arts Transparencies with Viewing Booklet
Writing Process Transparencies
Writing Process Computer Program

Unit 4 Planning and Pacing Guide

LANGUAGE
game

Pronoun Personalities

Objective: To use subject and object pronouns
Materials: Index cards, spinner
Write each of the following character names on an index card:

Helpful Henry	Mary Mermaid	Dawn Wakeup	Flora Dora	Will Willnot
Cheery Cleary	Travis Traveler	Hooray Ray	Lean Lou	Ana Artist
Lana Learner	Robert Reader	Grace Gracious	Chip Chipmunk	Owly Wise

Display lists of subject and object pronouns on the chalkboard. Explain that each player will get one index card bearing the name of an imaginary character. Players must draw a picture of the character on the card. When the pictures are drawn, one player will shuffle the cards. A spinner with two choices—*Subject Pronoun* or *Object Pronoun*—will be used. Players will choose a card, show it to the class, spin the spinner, and make up two sentences about the character. The character's name should be used in the first sentence. The type of pronoun indicated by the spinner should be used in the second.

Multi-Modal Activities

BULLETIN BOARD
idea

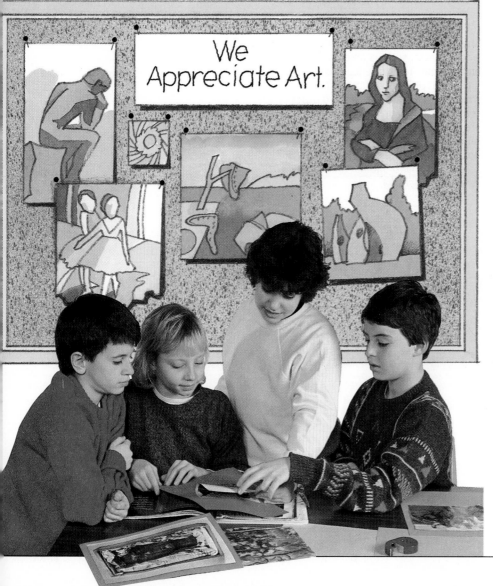

You may wish to use a bulletin board as a springboard for discussing the unit theme, or you may prefer to have students create a bulletin board as they move through the unit. Encourage students to look in newspapers and magazines for pictures of works of art in various forms—paintings, drawings, prints, sculpture, and so on. Have students paste each clipping on construction paper and then write information about the work of art on the other side. Under the heading *We Appreciate Art,* post the pictures along with a list of questions:

1. Who do you think created this art?
2. Why do you think someone created it?
3. What do you find interesting about it?
4. What do you think is a good title for it?

Have students evaluate the pictures and reach conclusions before checking the information about each one.

Students with different learning styles will all benefit from a natural approach to language learning, including frequent and varied use of oral language in the classroom.

Students "At Risk"

The following suggestions can help you help the students in your classroom who may be considered "at risk."

Create Learning Environments

Consider teaching skills through one or more of the Integrated Language Arts Projects at the back of your Teacher Edition. All students, especially those who are considered at risk, benefit from global, kinesthetic, high-interest activities that require interaction with others. The Projects have been created to meet that need. They engage students in group enterprises through which they practice essential language arts skills while they learn to work cooperatively. Reading, writing, speaking, and listening skills, together with thinking skills, are integrated naturally and meaningfully as students focus on accomplishing their tasks. A sense of excitement engendered by a common group goal helps to motivate all students to stretch beyond themselves—to wonder, imagine, invent, explore, trust, and learn.

Limited English Proficiency

Teachers whose classes contain students with limited English proficiency may find the following activities helpful in developing students' skills in grammar and composition.

Using Pronouns to Describe

On the chalkboard draw stick figures and simple illustrations, such as those below. Help students identify the pictures. Explain that the person they see in the mirror will be themselves, the double mirrors will reflect themselves and someone else, and the finger is pointing at you. Then encourage students to brainstorm all the pronouns they can think of that can be used to tell about each picture, such as boy—*he, him, his;* girl—*she, her, hers;* dog—*it, its;* children—*they, them, their, theirs;* reflection in mirror—*I, me, my, mine;* double reflection—*we, us, our, ours;* you—*you, your, yours.*

As students suggest pronouns, write them in clusters around each picture. Then encourage students to say all the pronouns in sentences about the pictures (He *has a cap on* his *head.* Look at him).

Pronoun Riddles

Show students ten to fifteen different small objects, such as an eraser, a pencil, and a comb. Tell students to decide to be one of the objects without telling anyone which one. Have them say two or three sentences to give clues about what they are in a pronoun riddle, such as *Teachers and schoolchildren pick me up. If they hold me the wrong way, I can make a screeching sound against the chalkboard. What am I?* (chalk)

After students have had a turn saying their riddles, write two or three of them on the chalkboard. Have students identify the pronouns used in place of the names of the objects.

You may wish to emphasize the use of pronouns to avoid repetition of nouns by writing one of the riddles repeating the object's name. For example: *Teachers and school children write with chalk. If teachers and school children hold the chalk the wrong way, the chalk can make a screeching sound.* Encourage discussion of how using pronouns can improve the flow of language.

Using Pronouns in Opinions

Write subject, object, and possessive pronouns on 3 by 5 index cards, one pronoun per card. Place the cards facedown in a pile. Have students take turns choosing a card and using the pronoun in a sentence expressing an opinion.

Gifted and Talented Students

To enable gifted and talented students to work at their own pace and to explore the content further, you may wish to use one or more of these activities.

Marketing a Product

Have students work with a partner or in small groups to create a product, name it, and market it. Remind students to keep the buyer in mind as they create advertisements to persuade others to buy their products. Encourage students to use as many pronouns as possible in their ads.

Have pairs or groups exchange ads and evaluate them for their persuasiveness and their use of pronouns. Encourage students to discuss which pronoun was used most frequently (probably the pronoun *you,* aimed at the buyer).

You may wish to have students share their ads by compiling a classified ad section for a class newspaper. Encourage students to explore the use of such graphic devices as bold print and different-size lettering to make their ads stand out.

Giving Opinions

Have students work in pairs or small groups to write at least five reasonable and five outlandish opinions on topics of current interest to students. Have students repeat nouns rather than use any pronouns. Then have pairs or groups exchange papers and rewrite each opinion using pronouns to avoid repeating nouns.

Have students share their work by reading their opinions aloud. Encourage discussion of which opinions are of greatest interest to students and which opinions are most outlandish. You may wish to have students post the rewritten opinions on a bulletin board display with two columns, one for realistic opinions and one for outlandish opinions.

As a more difficult task, you may wish to have students choose an opinion and write a persuasive paragraph about it. Encourage students to use as many pronouns as possible in the paragraph. You may wish to allow students to share their work by compiling a Letters to the Editor page for a class newspaper.

Replacing Nouns with Pronouns

Supply each student with a short article from a children's magazine. First, have students underline each noun in the article. Then have them write the pronoun that could replace each noun above it. When students have completed the activity, have them exchange papers and discuss the use of each pronoun.

You may wish to have students choose one paragraph to rewrite, replacing each noun with an appropriate pronoun. Have them exchange papers and discuss how the clarity of the passage was affected by the pronouns they used.

Suggest that students work in groups to develop rules for effective use of pronouns, including reminders for subject, object, and possessive cases.

Meeting Individual Needs

UNIT 4/LESSON 1

■ Easy ■ Average ■ Challenging

OBJECTIVES
To identify pronouns and the nouns they replace
To use pronouns in writing

ASSIGNMENT GUIDE
BASIC   Practice A
  ↓   Practice B
ADVANCED   Practice C

All should do the Apply activity.

RESOURCES
■ Reteaching Master 31
■ Practice Master 31
■■■ Extra Practice, pp. 226, 227
Unit 4 Pretest, p. T538

TEACHING THE LESSON

1. Getting Started
Oral Language Focus attention on this oral activity, encouraging all to participate. You may wish to divide the class into three groups and have the first name nouns that make the sentence humorous, the second group name nouns that make the sentence frightening, and so forth. Encourage volunteers to read the sentences with their nouns. You may wish to write the nouns on the chalkboard under the pronouns *it* and *them*.

2. Developing the Lesson
Guide students through the explanation of pronouns, emphasizing the examples and the summary. Lead students through the **Guided Practice**. Identify those who would benefit from reteaching. Assign independent Practice A–C.

3. Closing the Lesson
After students complete the Apply activity, have volunteers write their lists of pronouns on the chalkboard and tell what noun each replaces. Point out to students that knowing about and using pronouns in their compositions can help them avoid needlessly repeating the same nouns.

176

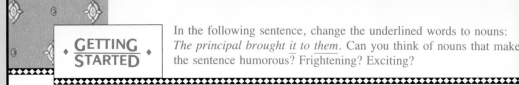

♦ GETTING STARTED ♦

In the following sentence, change the underlined words to nouns: *The principal brought it to them.* Can you think of nouns that make the sentence humorous? Frightening? Exciting?

1 Writing with Pronouns

When you speak and write, you can avoid repeating the same noun by using a pronoun instead. Look at the sentences below. The words in red are nouns. The words in blue are pronouns.

1. The book about art was helpful. It contained several chapters on sculpture.
2. The class enjoyed the photographs. Students used them for ideas.
3. Lisa borrowed Deven's book. She took his book home.

In sentence **1** the singular pronoun *it* replaces the noun *book*. In **2** the plural pronoun *them* replaces *photographs*. In **3** the singular pronoun *his* replaces *Deven's*.

The following chart shows the singular and plural pronouns.

Singular Pronouns	Plural Pronouns
I, me, my, mine	we, us, our, ours
you, your, yours	you, your, yours
she, he, it, her, him,	they, them, their, theirs
hers, his, its	

Summary ♦ A **pronoun** takes the place of a noun or nouns. When you write, use pronouns to avoid repeating the same nouns.

Guided Practice

Name the pronoun in each sentence below.

1. Deven told us about the history of sculpture.
2. Did you see the African sculpture at the museum?
3. The special masks held our attention for a long time.

176 GRAMMAR and WRITING: Pronouns

Practice

A. Write each sentence. Underline the pronoun.

4. Today I learned that sculpture is an ancient art.
5. It was practiced by the ancient Greeks.
6. Which pieces of sculpture on display are theirs?
7. Usually they carved statues from marble.
8. Sculpture has left us a record of human history.
9. Africans' wooden statues show their beliefs.
10. Later we saw Italian sculpture by Bernini.
11. His works are dramatic and realistic.
12. Is this book about Bernini yours?
13. That statue shows great detail in its facial features.

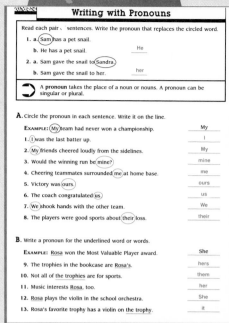

B. Rewrite each sentence using pronouns in place of the underlined words.

EXAMPLE: Peter is studying African sculpture.
ANSWER: He is studying African sculpture.

14. Several of Peter's ancestors were sculptors. *his*
15. In Africa, sculptors made statues of bronze. *they*
16. The large collection of statues was very impressive. *them*
17. Peter spent much of Peter's time in the museum. *his*
18. The museum contained exciting exhibits for Peter to see. *him*

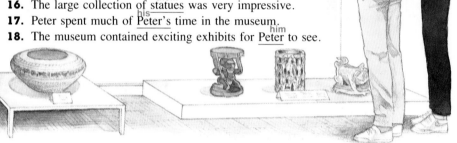

C. 19–23. Write five sentences of your own. Use these pronouns in your sentences: *she, him, mine, your,* and *their.*
Sentences will vary.

Apply ◆ Think and Write

From Your Writing ◆ Read what you wrote for the Writer's Warm-up. If necessary, replace some of the nouns with pronouns to avoid repetition.

✏️ **Remember**
to use pronouns to avoid repeating the same nouns.

GRAMMAR and WRITING: Pronouns **177**

◀▏▎▎ TEACHING OPTIONS ▎▎▏▶

RETEACHING

A Different Modality Remind students that they can avoid repeating nouns by using pronouns. Write on the chalkboard: *Juan built a cage for Juan's hamsters.* Have volunteers identify the repeated noun (Juan). Point out that the noun names a male person. Write *hers, his,* and *its* on the chalkboard and have students choose the pronoun that could replace *Juan's* (his). Repeat this process with additional sentences, using different pronouns.

CLASS ENRICHMENT

A Cooperative Activity Have students write with a partner. Have one partner write five singular and five plural nouns. Have the other partner write the pronouns that could replace the nouns, such as *museum—it, its; teachers—they, them, their, theirs.* To expand the activity, you may wish to have partners switch roles. Ask volunteers to share their lists with the class.

CHALLENGE

An Independent Extension. Have students clip a newspaper or magazine article. Tell them to circle the pronouns and underline the noun each pronoun replaces. Have students list the information in two columns —*Pronoun* and *Noun It Replaces.* Encourage them to write a paragraph about the article using the pronouns on their lists.

177

UNIT 4/LESSON 2

■ Easy ■ Average ■ Challenging

OBJECTIVES
To identify and use subject pronouns

ASSIGNMENT GUIDE
BASIC   Practice A
↓   Practice B
ADVANCED Practice C

All should do the Apply activity.

RESOURCES
■ Reteaching Master 32
■ Practice Master 32
■ ■ ■ Extra Practice, pp. 226, 228

TEACHING THE LESSON

1. Getting Started
Oral Language Focus attention on this oral activity, encouraging all to participate. You may wish to ring a bell each time a student uses a name instead of a pronoun. Allow students a few seconds to change the name to a pronoun.

2. Developing the Lesson
Guide students through the explanation of subject pronouns, emphasizing the examples and the summary. You may wish to point out to students that the antecedent of a pronoun must agree in number with the pronoun. Tell them that if the pronoun is singular, then its antecedent is singular; if the pronoun is plural, then its antecedent is plural as well. Lead students through the **Guided Practice.** Identify those who would benefit from reteaching. Assign independent Practice A–C.

3. Closing the Lesson
After students complete the Apply activity, encourage volunteers to read their sentences aloud. Point out that knowing when and how to use pronouns can help them avoid needless repetition of nouns and will help vary their speech and their written work.

178

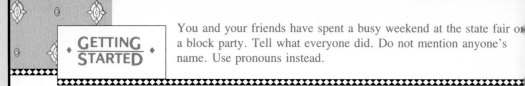

◆ GETTING STARTED ◆

You and your friends have spent a busy weekend at the state fair or a block party. Tell what everyone did. Do not mention anyone's name. Use pronouns instead.

2 Subject Pronouns

Certain pronouns can take the place of a noun used as the subject of a sentence. In the sentences below, the subjects are underlined. Each subject is a noun or a subject pronoun. In sentence **1b,** the pronoun *she* replaces the noun *Louise Nevelson.* In sentence **2b,** the pronoun *they* replaces the noun *sculptures.*

> **1.** a. <u>Louise Nevelson</u> is a well-known artist.
>   b. <u>She</u> is a famous sculptor.
> **2.** a. <u>The sculptures</u> created by Nevelson are often boxlike.
>   b. <u>They</u> are usually made out of wood.

The word or group of words that a pronoun replaces is called the antecedent. The name *Louise Nevelson* in sentence **1a** is the antecedent of the pronoun *she* in sentence **1b.**

The subject pronouns are below. *I* is always capitalized.

Subject Pronouns		
Singular	**Used for**	**Plural**
I	talking about yourself	we
you	talking to someone	you
she, he, it	talking about someone or something	they

> **Summary** ◆ The **subject pronouns** are *I, you, she, he, it, we,* and *they.* When you write, you can use these pronouns to replace nouns that are the subjects of your sentences.

Guided Practice

Name the subject pronoun in each sentence.

1. I once visited the Mount Rushmore National Memorial.
2. It is a huge piece of sculpture carved in a mountain.
3. Have you ever been there?

178   GRAMMAR: Subject Pronouns

ESSENTIAL LANGUAGE SKILLS
This lesson provides opportunities to:

LISTENING ◆ follow the logical organization of an oral presentation ◆ select from an oral presentation the information needed

SPEAKING ◆ use a variety of words to express feelings and ideas

READING ◆ use context to understand the meaning of words ◆ follow a set of directions

WRITING ◆ use ideas and information from sources other than personal experience for writing

LANGUAGE ◆ use correct agreement between pronouns and antecedents

Practice

A. Write the subject pronoun in each sentence.

4. I enjoyed the visit to Mount Rushmore.
5. It is in the Black Hills of South Dakota.
6. We saw carvings of the faces of four American presidents.
7. They are Washington, Jefferson, Lincoln, and T. Roosevelt.
8. While there, I watched a film about Gutzon Borglum.
9. He was the American sculptor of the memorial.
10. Did you know that workers carved with dynamite?
11. After fourteen years of work, they finished the memorial.

B. Write each sentence. Use a subject pronoun in place of the underlined word or words.

They
12. Tanya and Billy will visit Mount Rushmore in July.
She
13. Tanya is very excited about the trip.
he
14. Yesterday Harold gave Tanya a picture of Mount Rushmore.
It
15. The picture is magnificent.
They
16. Mountain goats can be seen walking near the faces.

C. Write each pair of sentences using the correct subject pronoun in each blank. Underline the word or words each pronoun replaces.

17. Tanya and Billy studied the life of Gutzon Borglum.
    They discovered some interesting facts.
18. Borglum spent several years in London and Paris.
    In 1901 *he* settled in New York City.
19. Auguste Rodin was a sculptor from France.
    He influenced the work of Borglum.
20. Tanya said something that was surprising.
    She said that Borglum's son Lincoln was also a sculptor.
21. In fact, Gutzon and Lincoln Borglum shared a big project.
    They carved the Mount Rushmore National Memorial.

Apply ◆ Think and Write

Creative Writing ◆ Pretend you are a sculptor. Tell what kind of sculpture you would make. Use a variety of subject pronouns in your sentences.

> ✏️ **Remember**
> that you can use subject pronouns to replace nouns in the subject of a sentence.

GRAMMAR: Subject Pronouns **179**

◀⫿⫿⫿ TEACHING OPTIONS ⫿⫿⫿▶

RETEACHING

A Different Modality Remind students that subject pronouns can replace nouns as the subjects of sentences. Pantomime an action. Have each student write the pronoun *you* in a sentence describing your action. (*You clapped your hands.*) Continue by having a boy, a girl, and then two students pantomime actions. Have students write appropriate pronouns in sentences describing the actions. You may wish to have students compare their sentences.

CLASS ENRICHMENT

A Cooperative Activity Have students choose a topic that interests them, such as "My Favorite Place" or "My Best Friend." Then have them write a paragraph about their topic using only nouns as subjects. Next have them exchange papers with a partner and rewrite the partner's paragraph, substituting pronoun subjects for noun subjects where appropriate. You may wish to have partners compare and contrast the two paragraphs.

CHALLENGE

An Independent Extension. Have students use subject pronouns—*I, you, she, he, it, we, they*—as the subjects of a list of sentences they write about students in the class. Have students write *singular* or *plural* to describe each subject pronoun.

Examples: You are a good batter. (singular)
          You are the best teammates of all. (plural)

179

UNIT 4/LESSON 3

■ Easy ■ Average ■ Challenging

OBJECTIVES
To identify and use object pronouns

ASSIGNMENT GUIDE
BASIC   Practice A
              Practice B
ADVANCED   Practice C

All should do the Apply activity.

RESOURCES
■ Reteaching Master 33
■ Practice Master 33
■■■ Extra Practice, pp. 226, 228

TEACHING THE LESSON

1. Getting Started
Oral Language Focus attention on this oral activity, encouraging all to participate. You may wish to have students create a collective class story. Use the example sentence in the text as the story starter. Have the first student provide the next sentence, another student add a new sentence, and so on. You may also wish to list the pronouns *me, you, him, her, it, us,* and *them* on the chalkboard to help them. Put a check beside each one as it is used.

2. Developing the Lesson
Guide students through the explanation of object pronouns, emphasizing the examples and the summary. You may wish to point out to students that the object pronoun *you* may be used as a singular pronoun or as a plural pronoun. Lead students through the **Guided Practice.** Identify those who would benefit from reteaching. Assign independent Practice A–C.

3. Closing the Lesson
After students complete the Apply activity, encourage volunteers to read their paragraphs aloud. Point out to students that using object pronouns to stand for nouns can help them write with clarity and variety.

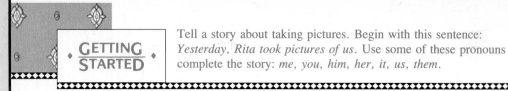

GETTING STARTED

Tell a story about taking pictures. Begin with this sentence: *Yesterday, Rita took pictures of us.* Use some of these pronouns to complete the story: *me, you, him, her, it, us, them.*

3 Object Pronouns

You have learned that certain pronouns can replace nouns used as the subject of a sentence. Other pronouns can replace nouns used as direct objects. Remember that a direct object follows an action verb. In the sentences below, the direct objects are underlined.

> 1. a. Marta received a camera for her birthday.
>   b. She took it out of the box.
> 2. a. Marta snapped pictures with the camera.
>   b. She will show them to us.

In sentence **1b** the pronoun *it* replaces the noun *camera.* In sentence **2b** the pronoun *them* replaces the noun *pictures.* Pronouns that replace nouns used as direct objects are called object pronouns. The following chart lists them.

Object Pronouns		
Singular	**Used for**	**Plural**
me	talking about yourself	us
you	talking to someone	you
him, her, it	talking about someone or something	them

> **Summary** ◆ The **object pronouns** are *me, you, him, her, it, us,* and *them.* When you write, you can use these pronouns to stand for nouns used as direct objects.

Guided Practice

Name the object pronoun in each sentence.

1. Marta surprised us with a new instant camera.
2. Bryan and Anthony carefully examined it.
3. Marta told them about the features of the camera.

ESSENTIAL LANGUAGE SKILLS
This lesson provides opportunities to:

LISTENING ◆ follow the logical organization of an oral presentation ◆ select from an oral presentation the information needed

SPEAKING ◆ use a variety of words to express feelings and ideas ◆ make organized oral presentations

READING ◆ use context to understand the meaning of words ◆ summarize a selection ◆ follow a set of directions

WRITING ◆ use ideas and information from sources other than personal experience for writing

LANGUAGE ◆ use correct agreement between pronouns and antecedents ◆ use all other parts of speech correctly

Practice

A. Write the second sentence of each pair. Underline the object pronoun.

    4. The first cameras were developed early in the nineteenth century. Today, many people use them.

    5. A camera captures a picture on film. After the film is developed, we see it.

    6. In 1888 George Eastman introduced a practical, inexpensive camera. This invention made him famous.

    7. Today professional photographers may work for a magazine. I admire them.

    8. Photographer Margaret Bourke-White worked for *Life* magazine. The magazine sent her to cover the events of World War II.

B. Write each sentence. Use an object pronoun in place of the underlined words.

    9. People everywhere admired Margaret Bourke-White. *(her)*

    10. She recorded events for future generations. *(them)*

    11. Wherever there was action, she captured the episode. *(it)*

    12. Soldiers, sailors, and air force pilots welcomed Margaret. *(her)*

    13. Margaret often accompanied a pilot on a dangerous mission. *(him)*

C. Write the sentences. Complete each sentence with the singular (S) or plural (P) object pronoun you use to talk about yourself.

    14. Tell ____(P) us____ more about Margaret Bourke-White.

    15. Let ____(S) me____ see her photographs.

    16. This photograph especially pleases ____(S) me____.

    17. Paco told ____(P) us____ that she also wrote books.

    18. Margaret Bourke-White's talents impress ____(S) me____.

Apply ◆ Think and Write

Dictionary of Knowledge ◆ Read about the life and work of photographer Ansel Adams. Write a paragraph about his life and artistic achievements. Use object pronouns in your sentences.

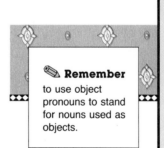

📝 **Remember**
to use object pronouns to stand for nouns used as objects.

GRAMMAR: Object Pronouns   **181**

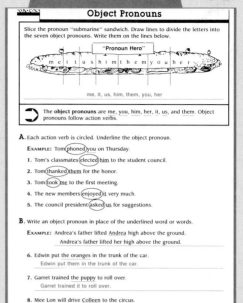

RETEACHING 33

Object Pronouns

Slice the pronoun "submarine" sandwich. Draw lines to divide the letters into the seven object pronouns. Write them on the lines below.

"Pronoun Hero"

m e i t u s h i m t h e m y o u h e r

me, it, us, him, them, you, her

The **object pronouns** are me, you, him, her, it, us, and them. Object pronouns follow action verbs.

A. Each action verb is circled. Underline the object pronoun.

  EXAMPLE: Tom phoned you on Thursday.

  1. Tom's classmates elected him to the student council.

  2. Tom thanked them for the honor.

  3. Tom took me to the first meeting.

  4. The new members enjoyed it very much.

  5. The council president asked us for suggestions.

B. Write an object pronoun in place of the underlined word or words.

  EXAMPLE: Andrea's father lifted Andrea high above the ground.
    Andrea's father lifted her high above the ground.

  6. Edwin put the oranges in the trunk of the car.
    Edwin put them in the trunk of the car.

  7. Garret trained the puppy to roll over.
    Garret trained it to roll over.

  8. Mee Lon will drive Colleen to the circus.
    Mee Lon will drive her to the circus.

PRACTICE 33

Object Pronouns

The **object pronouns** are me, you, him, her, it, us, and them.

A. Circle the object pronoun in the second sentence of each pair.

  1. I often read history books. History shows me the roles women have played.

  2. Emma Lazarus wrote an inspiring poem. An artist placed it on the Statue of Liberty.

  3. Rachel Carson wrote articles and books about the environment. She warned us about the harmful effects of chemicals.

  4. Nellie Bly was a newspaper reporter. The editor of the newspaper sent her to investigate many stories.

  5. Eleanor Roosevelt aided President Franklin Roosevelt. Eleanor represented him at public functions.

  6. Eleanor and Franklin Roosevelt worked hard for human rights. Such efforts made them worthy of honor.

B. Use the pronouns in the envelope to write the missing object pronouns. *Answers will vary. Possible answers follow.*

it   you   them
him   her   me   us

Thank ___you___ for the great book about American women. It made ___me___ happy. Elliot read ___it___, too. The story about Rachel Carson pleased ___him___ the most. The story about Harriet Tubman thrilled ___me___. The slaves followed ___her___ north. She led ___them___ to freedom. Please visit ___us___ soon.

Answers will vary.

◀▥▥ TEACHING OPTIONS ▥▥▶

RETEACHING	CLASS ENRICHMENT	CHALLENGE
A Different Modality Say *I use pens.* Ask students to replace *pens* with a pronoun *(them)*. Point out that an object pronoun follows an action verb. Write *The artist painted _____.* on the chalkboard. Distribute index cards with *me, you, him, her, it, us,* or *them* written on them. Have volunteers read aloud each new sentence they form with their pronoun. Then have students supply a noun to replace their pronoun.	**A Cooperative Activity** Have groups of students try to use as many object pronouns as possible while they devise directions for making a very simple paper object, such as a tube or a spiral. Tell each group to select a recorder, who is to write the directions on a sheet of chart paper. When they are finished, have each group share its directions with the class. Have the class try to follow them.	**An Independent Extension** Have students write ten sentences about a class trip or project. Have students use singular nouns as direct objects in five sentences and plural nouns as direct objects in the other five sentences. Then have students exchange sentences with a partner. Have partners write appropriate object pronouns about the nouns. You may wish to have volunteers read aloud their sentences with object pronouns.

UNIT 4/LESSON 4

■ Easy ■ Average ■ Challenging

OBJECTIVES
To identify and use possessive pronouns

ASSIGNMENT GUIDE

BASIC   Practice A
↓   Practice B
ADVANCED   Practice C

All should do the Apply activity.

RESOURCES
■ Reteaching Master 34
■ Practice Master 34
■ ■ ■ Extra Practice, pp. 226, 229

TEACHING THE LESSON

1. Getting Started
Oral Language Focus attention on this oral activity, encouraging all to participate. You may wish to begin by using pronouns in the pair of sentences, such as *The football is mine. It's my football.* You may also wish to have one student supply the first sentence and another student supply its companion sentence.

2. Developing the Lesson
Guide students through the explanation of possessive pronouns, emphasizing the examples and the summary. You may wish to point out to students that the possessive pronoun *its* is not written with an apostrophe. You also may wish to help them make the distinction between the possessive pronouns *their* and *theirs* and the homophones *there, they're* (they are), and *there's* (there is). Lead students through the **Guided Practice**. Identify those who would benefit from reteaching. Assign independent Practice A–C.

3. Closing the Lesson
After students complete the Apply activity, encourage them to share their letters with a grandparent or older relative. Point out to students that using possessive pronouns in their writing can help them show ownership clearly.

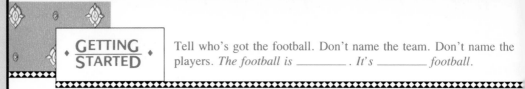

♦ GETTING STARTED ♦

Tell who's got the football. Don't name the team. Don't name the players. *The football is _____ . It's _____ football.*

4 Possessive Pronouns

You have learned that possessive nouns show ownership. Pronouns can show ownership, too. In the sentences below, the possessive words are underlined.

1. a. Ruth's father is a photographer.
   b. Her father is a photographer.
2. a. Mr. Irwin's darkroom is better equipped than Ruth's.
   b. His darkroom is better equipped than hers.

In sentence **1b** the pronoun *her* replaces the possessive noun *Ruth's*. In sentence **2b** the pronouns *his* and *hers* replace the possessive nouns *Mr. Irwin's* and *Ruth's*.

Pronouns that show ownership are called possessive pronouns. Some possessive pronouns are used before nouns: *Is that your camera?* Other possessive pronouns are used alone: *That camera is mine.* The possessive pronoun *his* can be used both ways.

Used Before Nouns	Used Alone
my, your, his, her its, our, their	mine, yours, his, hers ours, theirs

Summary ♦ A **possessive pronoun** shows ownership. You can use possessive pronouns to replace possessive nouns.

Guided Practice

Name the possessive pronoun in each sentence.

1. Ruth got her new camera last week.
2. She enjoys using its zoom lens.
3. The book of photographs is theirs.
4. Please bring your camera along.

182   GRAMMAR: Possessive Pronouns

ESSENTIAL LANGUAGE SKILLS
This lesson provides opportunities to:

LISTENING ♦ follow the logical organization of an oral presentation ♦ select from an oral presentation the information needed

READING ♦ use context to understand the meaning of words ♦ follow a set of directions

WRITING ♦ use ideas and information from sources other than personal experience for writing ♦ adapt information to accomplish a specific purpose with a particular audience ♦ use conventional formats (letters and other commonly used forms)

LANGUAGE ♦ use correct agreement between pronouns and antecedents ♦ use all other parts of speech correctly

Practice

A. Write each sentence. Use the pronoun in parentheses ( ) that correctly completes the sentence.

5. Photographers practice (their, <u>theirs</u>) art in different ways.
6. Is this photo album (you, <u>yours</u>)?
7. A photo essay uses pictures to tell (it, <u>its</u>) story.
8. Dorothea Lange is known for (<u>her</u>, hers) pictures of people.
9. This report about Lange is (my, <u>mine</u>).

B. Write the sentences. Use possessive pronouns in place of the underlined words.

10. Which photographs in this book are <u>Dorothea Lange's</u>? *hers*
11. This book has her picture on <u>the book's</u> cover. *its*
12. Has Leon written <u>Leon's</u> report about her yet? *his*
13. Is this collection of photos <u>Pat and Lee's</u>? *theirs*
14. I like <u>Olivia Parker's and Mitch Epstein's</u> photos. *their*
15. Have you ever seen pictures as interesting as <u>Parker's and Epstein's</u>? *theirs*
16. <u>Ernst Haas's</u> photographs have breathtaking colors. *His*
17. That deep blue picture of rippling water is <u>Haas's</u>. *his*
18. Portraits by Richard Avedon show <u>celebrities'</u> personalities. *their*
19. <u>Avedon's</u> photos show the latest fashions. *His*

C. 20–24. Write five sentences of your own. Use these pronouns in your sentences: *my, mine, our, ours, theirs*.

Apply • Think and Write

A Friendly Letter • Imagine you have explored your grandparents' attic. Write a brief letter to a friend telling about the things you found. Use possessive pronouns in your letter.

Gentle Ripples by Ernst Haas

photograph by Mitch Epstein

✏ **Remember**
that possessive pronouns show ownership.

GRAMMAR: Possessive Pronouns **183**

◀‖‖ **TEACHING OPTIONS** ‖‖▶

RETEACHING

A Different Modality Have a volunteer tell briefly about a favorite possession, pet, or friend. Write on the chalkboard each sentence that uses the word *my* or *mine*. Point out the use of these possessive pronouns before nouns and by themselves. Substitute names, such as *Tom's* and *Kay's*, for the pronouns in the sentences. Have students replace the names with possessive pronouns as they read aloud the new sentences on the chalkboard.

CLASS ENRICHMENT

A Cooperative Activity Have students compose a short description of their favorite character from history or fiction. Tell them to use possessive pronouns to help them write about the character's personality, friends, famous feats, discoveries, or adventures. When they are finished, have the class form small groups to share their descriptions orally and then tally the possessive pronouns they used.

CHALLENGE

An Independent Extension Distribute magazine or newspaper articles and have students find sentences with possessive pronouns. Have each student make a chart or graph to show the possessive pronouns found, the number of times each possessive pronoun was used, and how the possessive pronoun was used—either before a noun or by itself.

UNIT 4/LESSON 5

OBJECTIVES
To use subject and object pronouns correctly

ASSIGNMENT GUIDE
BASIC   Practice A
             Practice B
ADVANCED   Practice C

All should do the Apply activity.

RESOURCES
■ Reteaching Master 35
■ Practice Master 35
■■■ Extra Practice, pp. 226, 230

TEACHING THE LESSON

1. Getting Started
Oral Language Focus attention on this oral activity, encouraging all to participate. You may wish to write on the chalkboard sentences volunteers provide. Encourage creative responses by asking questions, such as *What might it be like if two artists were working on the same painting? How would they share the colors and brushes?*

2. Developing the Lesson
Guide students through the explanation of using pronouns correctly, emphasizing the examples and the summary. Lead students through the **Guided Practice.** Identify those who would benefit from reteaching. Assign independent Practice A–C.

3. Closing the Lesson
After students complete the Apply activity, have volunteers read their sentences aloud to the class. Point out to students that knowing how and when to use subject and object pronouns will help them express their thoughts clearly, when they speak as well as when they write.

184

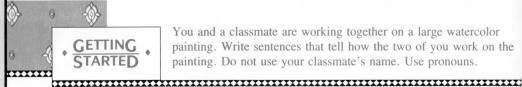

GETTING STARTED

You and a classmate are working together on a large watercolor painting. Write sentences that tell how the two of you work on the painting. Do not use your classmate's name. Use pronouns.

5 Using Pronouns

Read the following sentences.

1. My sister and I are inviting you to our house.
2. You can help Lita and me.
3. We have new watercolor paints.
4. She and I are painting animals.

The words in red are subject pronouns. They are the subjects of sentences. The words in blue are object pronouns. They are used after action verbs.

Notice that when you name yourself and someone else, you always name yourself last: *my sister and I, Lita and me,* and *she and I.*

> **Summary** ♦ Use a subject pronoun as the subject of a sentence. Use an object pronoun after an action verb.

Guided Practice

Name the pronoun in parentheses ( ) that correctly completes each sentence.

1. Kristen and (I, me) are learning to use watercolors.
2. Mr. Wong is teaching her and (I, me).
3. (He, Him) and Ms. Gomez teach proper technique.
4. You will see her and (we, us) at the art exhibit.
5. (She, Her) and other art teachers will show their paintings.

184   USAGE: Subject Pronouns and Object Pronouns

ESSENTIAL LANGUAGE SKILLS
This lesson provides opportunities to:

LISTENING ♦ follow the logical organization of an oral presentation ♦ select from an oral presentation the information needed

READING ♦ use context to understand the meaning of words ♦ follow a set of directions

WRITING ♦ use ideas and information from sources other than personal experience for writing ♦ use chronological and spatial order and order of importance

LANGUAGE ♦ use the fundamentals of grammar, punctuation, and spelling

Practice

A. Write each sentence. Use the word or words in parentheses ( )
that correctly complete each sentence.

   6. (Me and Kristen, Kristen and I) spend much time painting.

   7. Right now (she, her) and I like the same kinds of paintings.

   8. Mr. Wong, our art teacher, encourages (she and I,
       her and me).

   9. (He, Him) and the other art teachers are talented artists.

  10. Why don't you visit (he and I,
       him and me) in art class?

B. Write each sentence. Use the pronoun in
parentheses ( ) that correctly completes the
sentence. Then write whether the pronoun you
used is a subject or an object pronoun.

  11. Cindy and (she, her) went to the art class. _subj._

  12. Sue and (I, me) studied paintings by _subj._
       two artists.

  13. The works of Georgia O'Keeffe and Grant
       Wood impressed Sue and (I, me). _obj._

  14. You and (she, her) would enjoy O'Keeffe's _subj._
       paintings of flowers and rocks.

  15. Wood's painting titled *American Gothic*
       might surprise Pat and (she, her). _obj._

Oriental Poppies by Georgia O'Keeffe. University Art Museum,
University of Minnesota, Minneapolis

C. Write the sentence. Use *I* or *me* to complete each sentence.

  16. Velma and ___I___ are interested in modern art.

  17. Our parents took Velma and ___me___ to an art exhibit.

  18. The exhibit of Picasso's paintings thrilled her and ___me___ .

  19. She and ___I___ discovered Picasso's cubist paintings.

  20. The cubist style of painting puzzled Velma and ___me___ .

Apply ♦ Think and Write

A Newspaper Article ♦ Pretend you and your class have visited
an art museum. Write a school newspaper article about your class
trip. Use subject and object pronouns in your sentences.

> ✎ **Remember**
> to choose carefully
> the subject and
> object pronouns
> you use.

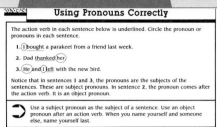

RETEACHING   35

Using Pronouns Correctly

The action verb in each sentence below is underlined. Circle the pronoun or
pronouns in each sentence.

  1. (I) bought a parakeet from a friend last week.

  2. Dad thanked (her)

  3. (He) and (I) left with the new bird.

Notice that in sentences 1 and 3, the pronouns are the subjects of the
sentences. These are subject pronouns. In sentence 2, the pronoun comes after
the action verb. It is an object pronoun.

> Use a subject pronoun as the subject of a sentence. Use an object
> pronoun after an action verb. When you name yourself and someone
> else, name yourself last.

A. Write each sentence with the correct word or words in parentheses ( ).

   EXAMPLE: Judy and (I, me) read books about birds.
       Judy and I read books about birds.

  1. Mom and Dad gave (me and Judy, Judy and me) some information.
     Mom and Dad gave Judy and me some information.

  2. Dad and (I, me) taught the bird how to talk.
     Dad and I taught the bird how to talk.

B. Write each sentence with the correct pronoun in parentheses ( ). Circle
subject if the pronoun is in the subject part. Circle object if the pronoun is in
the predicate part.

   EXAMPLE: Hilda and (her, she) own a parrot.
       Hilda and she own a parrot.   (subject) object

  3. Fernando and (I, me) are raising pigeons.
     Fernando and I are raising pigeons.   (subject) object

  4. Our parents help Fernando and (I, me).
     Our parents help Fernando and me.   subject (object)

PRACTICE   35

Using Pronouns Correctly

> Use a **subject pronoun** as the subject of a sentence. Use an **object**
> **pronoun** after an action verb.

A. Circle the pronouns in each sentence below. Write each pronoun under the
correct heading on the chart.

  1. Tena and (I) made that clay sculpture of a cat.

  2. (It) and the other sculptures are on the table.

  3. The art instructors helped (her) and (me).

  4. A famous artist once spoke to (us).

  5. (She) and (they) worked with the students.

  6. (We) and the other students learned a great deal.

  7. (You) and (he) should visit the art class sometime.

  8. Tena will show (you) two and (him) what to do.

Subject Pronouns		Object Pronouns	
I	It	her	me
She	they	us	you
We	You	him	
he			

B. Complete each sentence by writing a name from the name box and the
correct pronoun from the pronoun box. Answers will vary. Possible answers
follow.

Bill Emilio Kim Lucy	I me

  9. ___Lucy___ and ___I___ bought a book.

 10. The store owner led ___Kim___ and ___me___ to it.

 11. My father drove ___Emilio___ and ___me___ to the store.

WRITE IT
On a separate sheet of paper, write about a hobby or craft. Write sentences
telling how you and a friend would work together. Use subject and object
pronouns. Answers will vary.

◄‖‖ TEACHING OPTIONS ‖‖►

RETEACHING

A Different Modality List the subject
pronouns and the object pronouns in chart
form on the chalkboard. Then write a sentence, such as _____ *thanked* _____
for the gift. Have volunteers complete the
sentence orally, using as many different
pronouns as possible. Have them identify
the subject pronoun, action verb, and object pronoun.

CLASS ENRICHMENT

A Cooperative Activity Have students
write two sentences, one with a subject
pronoun and one with an object pronoun.
Distribute two index cards to each student.
Have students copy their sentences onto
the cards, omitting the pronouns. Have
them exchange cards with a partner to
complete the sentences. You may wish to
have partners read their completed sentences to the class.

CHALLENGE

An Independent Extension Have students write an original sentence for each
pair of pronouns listed below. Encourage
them to write sentences that tell a story.
Then have them exchange papers with a
partner to check for correct usage.

1. I, her   5. he, us
2. you, him   6. they, it
3. she, me   7. we, them
4. it, you   8. I, you

UNIT 4/LESSON 6

OBJECTIVES
To identify, form, and use pronoun contractions

ASSIGNMENT GUIDE
BASIC   Practice A
⬇   Practice B
ADVANCED   Practice C

All should do the Apply activity.

RESOURCES
■ Reteaching Master 36
■ Practice Master 36
■ ■ ■ Extra Practice, pp. 226, 231

TEACHING THE LESSON

1. Getting Started
Oral Language Focus attention on this oral activity, encouraging all to participate. You may wish to expand the activity by orally providing more sentences like the one in the text, such as *She is doing well. They are doing well. He has done well.*

2. Developing the Lesson
Guide students through the explanation of contractions, emphasizing the examples and the summary. You may wish to caution students not to confuse the contraction for *it is (it's)* with the possessive pronoun *its* and the contraction for *you are (you're)* with the possessive pronoun *your*. Lead students through the **Guided Practice**. Identify those who would benefit from reteaching. Assign independent Practice A–C.

3. Closing the Lesson
After students complete the Apply activity, encourage volunteers to use their sentences to begin a conversation with a partner. Point out to students that using contractions can help them make their writing seem more natural, as natural as a spoken conversation.

186

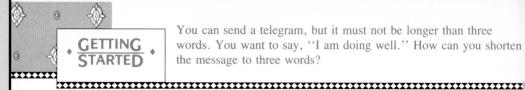

You can send a telegram, but it must not be longer than three words. You want to say, "I am doing well." How can you shorten the message to three words?

6 Contractions

You have learned that the subject pronouns are *I, you, she, he, it, we,* and *they*. These pronouns can be combined with the verbs *am, is, are, has, have, had, will, shall,* and *would*. The combined forms are called contractions. You can write *she will,* for example, as the contraction *she'll.*

In the following sentences, the contractions are underlined.

1. It's a fine day for painting.
2. I think I'll take my easel to the lake.
3. He'd like to come with me.
4. We're going to paint together.

Notice that in each contraction, an apostrophe (') shows where a letter or letters have been left out.

Pronoun + Verb	= Contraction
pronoun + am	= I'm
pronoun + are	= you're, we're, they're
pronoun + is or has	= he's, she's, it's
pronoun + have	= I've, we've, you've, they've
pronoun + had or would	= I'd, you'd, he'd, she'd, we'd, they'd
pronoun + shall or will	= I'll, we'll
pronoun + will	= you'll, he'll, she'll, they'll

Summary ◆ A **contraction** is a shortened form of two words. When you write a contraction, use an apostrophe to show where a letter or letters have been left out.

Guided Practice

Name the contraction for each pair of words.

    I'm   you've   it's   she'll   we're
1. I am   **2.** you have   **3.** it is   **4.** she will   **5.** we are

186   MECHANICS: Contractions

ESSENTIAL LANGUAGE SKILLS
This lesson provides opportunities to:

LISTENING ◆ follow the logical organization of an oral presentation ◆ select from an oral presentation the information needed

SPEAKING ◆ respond appropriately to questions from teachers and peers

READING ◆ use context to understand the meaning of words ◆ follow a set of directions

WRITING ◆ use ideas and information from sources other than personal experience for writing ◆ apply increasingly complex conventions of punctuation and capitalization

LANGUAGE ◆ use the fundamentals of grammar, punctuation, and spelling

---

Practice

A. Write the contraction for each pair of words.

6. you have *you've* 11. we have *we've* 16. he had *he'd*
7. they are *they're* 12. it would *it'd* 17. you will *you'll*
8. it has *it's* 13. they will *they'll* 18. she would *she'd*
9. we shall *we'll* 14. you are *you're* 19. I will *I'll*
10. I am *I'm* 15. she has *she's* 20. he is *he's*

B. Write the contraction in each sentence. Then write the words from which the contraction is formed.

21. *We are*
We're going to see an art show by great artists.
22. *We have*
We've already seen some of Romare Bearden's work.
23. *He is*
He's a well-known painter.
24. *You will*
You'll really enjoy Augusta Savage's sculptures.
25. *I would*
I'd like to see more murals by Aaron Douglas.
26. *I am*
I'm told he painted a portrait of Marian Anderson.
27. *you have*
Perhaps you've heard of the painter, Jacob Lawrence.
28. *I have*
I've seen several of his works.
29. *she has*
Becky says she's got a copy of a painting by Norma Morgan.
30. *you have*
Wait until you've seen the sculpture by Elizabeth Catlett.

C. For each pair of words below, first write its contraction. Then write a sentence using that contraction.

31. *I've* I have
32. *she'd* she would
33. *we're* we are
34. *it's* it is
35. *you'd* you had

Apply ◆ Think and Write

An Advertisement ◆ Pretend you own an art supply store and will have a one-day sale. Write an ad to persuade shoppers to come to the sale. Use some contractions in your ad.

The Old Waterworks, n.d. Aaron Douglas. Oil on canvas, 18″ × 15″. Hampton University Museum Collection.

✏ **Remember**
that you can use contractions to capture the way people talk.

MECHANICS: Contractions **187**

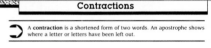
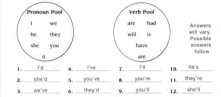
◀‖‖‖ **TEACHING OPTIONS** ‖‖‖▶

RETEACHING

A Different Modality Explain that a contraction is a shortened form of two words, such as *it's* for *it is,* with an apostrophe to show where a letter or letters have been left out. Write on index cards pronoun contractions and their meanings (e.g., *I am, I'm, we are, we're, he is, he's, they will, they'll, you have, you've*). Distribute a card to each student and have the students with cards that mean the same find each other and write the matching pairs.

CLASS ENRICHMENT

A Cooperative Activity Have partners compose a paragraph about their favorite cartoon superhero, using pronouns and verbs as contractions. If you wish, give the class a story starter, such as *Superman will leap across the widest river. He _____ .* When they are finished, have partners share their work orally with the class. Encourage them to ask the class to help them decide if they have used all their pronoun contractions correctly.

CHALLENGE

An Independent Extension Have students write a short conversation between two friends. Tell them to avoid using pronoun contractions. Whey they are finished, have them revise their work with these questions in mind: *Would I use the pronouns and verbs if I were speaking? Would I use a contraction instead?* Have them do a final copy. Encourage them to read aloud the original and the revised versions.

■ Easy ■ Average ■ Challenging

OBJECTIVES
To identify and use homophones

ASSIGNMENT GUIDE
BASIC   Practice A

ADVANCED   Practice B

All should do the Language Corner.

RESOURCES
■ Reteaching Master 37
■ Practice Master 37

TEACHING THE LESSON

1. Getting Started
Oral Language Focus attention on this oral activity, encouraging all to participate. To assist students in composing other sentences, you may wish to write the following word pairs on the chalkboard: *ate/eight, I/eye, be/bee, blew/blue, build/billed, sent/scent, male/mail.*

2. Developing the Lesson
Guide students through the explanation of homophones, emphasizing the definition and the examples. You may wish to tell students that in the example sentences, the words with apostrophes are all contractions of two words and the words without apostrophes are all possessive pronouns. Guide students through Building Your Vocabulary. Identify those who would benefit from reteaching. Assign independent Practice A and B.

3. Closing the Lesson
After students complete the Practice exercises, tell them to watch for some of the homophones from this lesson in their reading for the rest of the day. Have them write in their notebooks the words and their homophone pairs along with sentences showing each word's meaning. Point out to students that being aware of homophones and their spelling will help them avoid spelling errors in their writing.

Language Corner You may wish to have students discuss their methods of figuring out the portmanteau words.

188

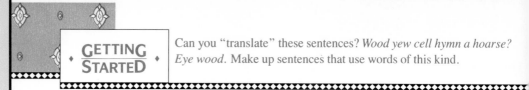

GETTING STARTED
Can you "translate" these sentences? *Wood yew cell hymn a hoarse? Eye wood.* Make up sentences that use words of this kind.

VOCABULARY ◆
Homophones

Study the following sentences.

> To me, two bears are two too many.
> The maid, a bore, made the boar sleepy.
> The bare bear buries his head in the berries.

The underlined words above are homophones. **Homophones** are words that sound alike but have different meanings and spellings.

English has many homophones. Sometimes these homophones cause trouble in writing. The pronouns *their*, *its*, and *your* are often confused with the contractions *they're*, *it's*, and *you're*. These homophones are underlined in the sentences below. Notice how they are used.

> They're walking their pet rabbit.
> It's strange to see its bushy tail on the sidewalk.
> You're funny with your whiskers and floppy ears, rabbit!

Building Your Vocabulary

Find the homophones below and tell their meanings.

1. Ned knew there were two new animals at the zoo; Nan did, too.
2. Nellie thinks that two gnus are good news.
3. Norma thinks they're funny with their big, oxlike heads.

Correct the homophone errors in the sentences below.

1. The truck driver saw that it was time to brake for lunch. *[break]*
2. Ducks like to fly in fowl weather. *[foul]*
3. *Lettuce Flea* is a book about an escape from a terrible storm. *[Let Us Flee]*
4. After he fell in the bucket of water, he looked very pail. *[pale]*

188   VOCABULARY: Homophones

ESSENTIAL LANGUAGE SKILLS
This lesson provides opportunities to:

LISTENING ◆ employ active listening in a variety of situations

SPEAKING ◆ use a variety of words to express feelings and ideas

READING ◆ use context to understand the meaning of words ◆ understand content area vocabulary ◆ identify an implied main idea of a longer selection ◆ evaluate and make judgments

LANGUAGE ◆ understand the conventions of usage and mechanics

Practice

A. Write the rhyme below. Use the correct form of all homophones.

The animals entered a bakery shop—
A dear *(deer)*, a bare *(bear)*, and a hoarse *(horse)*.
In order two *(to buy)* by the things that they liked,
They kneaded sum *(needed some)* cash, of coarse *(course)*.
The dear *(deer)* longed four *(for)* "doenuts *(doughnuts)*," at least to *(two or)* oar three;
The bare *(bear)* dreamed of buries *(berries)*, dipped in sweet honey.
The hoarse *(horse)* wished for oatmeal cookies with hey *(hay)*
(Witch *(Which)* the baker thought funny, serving cookies this weigh *(way)*).
They soon left, I'm sorry two *(to)* tell ewe *(you)*,
And the baker maid *(made)* nary a sail *(sale)*,
But he had a grate *(great)* laugh, and his wife, to *(too)*.
And that is the end of this tail *(tale)*.

B. Use the words below to complete the sentences.

their   they're   your   you're   its   it's

1. "_You're_ sure of _your_ answer?" Ted's teacher asked.
2. "_It's_ that nasty rabbit that always gets _its_ paws on our lettuce!" exclaimed the gardener.
3. Leave them alone, _they're_ having the time of _their_ lives.

LANGUAGE CORNER ‣ Portmanteau Words

A **portmanteau** word is made from two words that have been blended into one. For example, *flurry*, as in "snow flurry," is a blend of the words *flutter* and *hurry*.

What blends can you make out of these words?

breakfast + lunch = ? brunch
splash + surge = ? splurge
smoke + fog = ? smog
squirm + wiggle = ? squiggle

VOCABULARY: Homophones **189**

Homophones

Homophones are words that sound alike but have different meanings and spellings. The sentences below contain homophones. Circle the words in each sentence that sound alike.

1. We (ate) (eight) cookies for our afternoon snack.
2. Just one (rose) grew among the (rows) of flowers.

A. Complete each sentence with the correct homophone in parentheses ( ).

EXAMPLE: The fastest horse ___won___ the race. (one, won)

1. Kim was ___hoarse___ because of her cold. (horse, hoarse)
2. Kim's mother thought Kim looked very ___pale___. (pail, pale)
3. Her mother ___made___ her stay home from school. (maid, made)
4. The doctor said Kim was too ___weak___ to go out. (weak, week)
5. The doctor wanted to ___see___ Kim again in her office. (see, sea)
6. Each day her friend ___would___ call her up on the phone. (wood, would)
7. She ___knew___ that Kim was feeling lonely. (knew, new)
8. After a few days, Kim was very ___bored___ at home. (board, bored)

B. Find the pair of homophones in each sentence. Write the homophones in the blank.

EXAMPLE: It was too late to leave. _too, to_

9. We had to pay a fare to ride a bus to the fair.   fare, fair
10. We heard the noise made by the herd of cattle.   heard, herd
11. A boy in a blue uniform blew his horn.   blue, blew
12. It was so hard to sew all those costumes.   so, sew
13. We read the sign printed in red on the door.   read, red
14. While Dean rowed, his friends just rode along.   rowed, rode
15. Dean sighed when he reached the other side.   sighed, side

PRACTICE 37

Homophones

A. Complete each rhyme with a homophone.

1. She was wise and had good sense.
   She saved her dollars and counted her ___cents___.
2. The rabbit was old and had no hair.
   He truly was a hairless ___hare___.
3. The dog would scratch and try to flee,
   But never could he chase away the ___flea___.
4. The bug you see that you let be,
   Is one that stings just like a ___bee___.
5. We won! We won!
   We're number ___one___.
6. The baker's son was bred
   To know the value of good ___bread___.

B. Write the letter below. Use the correct homophone for each underlined word.

<u>Deer Rows</u>,
     <u>Wee</u> have been traveling <u>four</u> several <u>daze</u>. We have gone <u>threw</u> three states. <u>Won</u> time we took the wrong <u>rode</u> because we <u>maid</u> a <u>write</u> turn <u>two</u> soon. Later, the car broke down, and we had <u>too</u> <u>bee</u> <u>toad</u>. It has still been a <u>grate</u> trip, but I have <u>mist</u> <u>you</u> <u>sew</u> much. I can hardly <u>weight</u> to <u>sea</u> you again. When we <u>meat</u>, I will show you <u>hour</u> pictures.
     <u>You're</u> friend,

Dear Rose,
     We have been traveling for several days. We have gone through three
states. One time we took the wrong road because we made a right turn too
soon. Later, the car broke down, and we had to be towed. It has still been
a great trip, but I have missed you so much. I can hardly wait to see you
again. When we meet, I will show you our pictures.
                                             Your friend,

◀||| TEACHING OPTIONS |||▶

RETEACHING

A Different Modality Ask three volunteers to spell *there, their,* and *they're*. Explain that to know how to spell these words one must know the meanings. Write on the chalkboard three sentences, each containing *there, they're* or *their*. Explain that words that sound alike but are spelled differently and have different meanings are called *homophones*.

CLASS ENRICHMENT

A Cooperative Activity Have students work in pairs. Have students write a paragraph that uses four or five homophones incorrectly. Then have students exchange papers and write the correct words above the incorrect ones. Have students proofread the paragraphs together to be sure the corrections were made accurately.

CHALLENGE

An Independent Extension Have students research the history of these portmanteau words in a dictionary that contains etymologies: *chortle* (chuckle + snort), *clump* (chunk + lump), *flare* (flame + glare), *pixel* (picture + element), *splatter* (splash + spatter), and *telethon* (television + marathon). You may wish to have students write a paragraph using the portmanteau words.

Grammar-Writing Connection

OBJECTIVES
To apply grammar skills to writing
To work together to use pronouns in place of repeated nouns

How to Revise Sentences with Pronouns

Point out to students that they can use the grammar skills they learned in Unit 4 to help them develop good writing techniques. Explain that in this Grammar-Writing Connection, students will use what they know about subject, object, and possessive pronouns to learn how to revise sentences with pronouns.

You may wish to guide students through the explanation of how to use pronouns to avoid repeating the same nouns, stressing the examples. Then have students apply the information by completing the activity at the bottom of the first page. Students may work in small groups or with partners to replace nouns with pronouns orally, or they may replace nouns with pronouns in writing as an independent activity.

Help students to understand that using pronouns is an effective way to improve writing by avoiding repeating the same noun too often. Point out that pronouns can make their writing smoother to read and easier to understand.

GRAMMAR CONNECTION WRITING

How to Revise Sentences with Pronouns

In this unit you have been learning how to use pronouns in sentences. You know that pronouns are used to replace nouns. You can use pronouns instead of repeating the same noun too often. Would you expect to read or hear a sentence like the one below?

1. Mr. Craig says Mr. Craig met Mr. Craig's wife at an exhibit of Mr. Craig's and Mrs. Craig's favorite artist's work.

Sentence 1 is a very confusing and awkward sentence! The noun *Craig* is used five times in this sentence. Now read sentence 2 to see how pronouns can make an improvement.

2. Mr. Craig says he met his wife at an exhibit of their favorite artist's work.

The pronouns in sentence 2 make it much smoother to read and easier to understand. Look for chances to use pronouns to improve your writing.

The Grammar Game ◆ Check your pronoun progress! Replace the underlined words with subject, object, and possessive pronouns. Some of the words could be replaced by more than one pronoun. Give yourself one point for each pronoun. (A score of 20 is excellent!)

the poet's limericks — *his, her*
about the nurses — *them*
Joe's neighbors — *his*
when Nellie arrives — *she*
written by Ed and Todd — *them*
if the bricks are heavy — *they*
about the mayor — *him, her*
the girls' soccer team — *their, our*

for Sandy and me — *us*
as the storm raged — *it*
if Mike objects — *he*
to Peg's and my friend — *our*
Mrs. Karlan's house — *her*
laughed at the clown — *him, her, it*
after David and I talked — *we*
at the river's edge — *its*

190 COOPERATIVE LEARNING: Revising Sentences

ESSENTIAL LANGUAGE SKILLS
This lesson provides opportunities to:

LISTENING ◆ select from an oral presentation the information needed

SPEAKING ◆ use a variety of words to express feelings and ideas

READING ◆ understand cause-and-effect relationships ◆ draw logical conclusions ◆ evaluate and make judgments ◆ follow a set of directions

WRITING ◆ adapt information to accomplish a specific purpose with a particular audience ◆ participate in writing conferences

LANGUAGE ◆ use correct agreement between pronouns and antecedents ◆ use all other parts of speech correctly

Working Together

Work as a group on activities **A** and **B**, using pronouns instead of repeating the same nouns too often.

In Your Group

♦ Pay attention to each person's ideas.

♦ Don't interrupt each other.

♦ Encourage others to talk.

♦ Help the group reach agreement.

A. Write these familiar song lines, using pronouns to complete them. If you aren't sure of the correct pronoun, use one that makes sense. Can your group add more lines to this list?

1. Oh say, can __you__ see, by the dawn's early light?
2. __I__ come from Alabama with __my__ banjo on __my__ knee.
3. Merrily __we__ roll along, roll along, roll along.
4. Oh, give __me__ a home where the buffalo roam.
5. __I__ left __my__ heart in San Francisco.
6. Daisy, Daisy, give __me__ __your__ answer, do.
7. __She__'ll be coming 'round the mountain when __she__ comes.
8. __It__'s a small world after all; __it__'s a small, small world.

B. Write the paragraph below, using pronouns in place of nouns wherever possible. Be sure your group agrees that the new paragraph makes sense! **Answers will vary. Possible answers follow.**

Joan and Joan's brother have a business called Hands for Hire. (her) (They) Joan and Joan's brother work hard every summer. People hire Joan and Joan's brother to wash cars, pull weeds, and care for pets. (them) Joan says Joan's favorite job is gardening, because gardening is relaxing (her) (it) and Joan loves flowers. Joan's brother says Joan's brother's (she) (Her) (his) favorite job is walking dogs and playing with the dogs. Joan's (them) brother enjoys the exercise. (He)

WRITERS' CORNER · Fuzzy Sentences

Sometimes replacing too many nouns with pronouns can make your writing fuzzy. Can you tell *who* was excited in the fuzzy sentence below?

FUZZY: **Mark wrote Juan a letter. He was very excited.**
IMPROVED: **Mark wrote Juan a letter. Mark was very excited.**

Read what you wrote for the Writer's Warm-up. Did you write any fuzzy sentences? Can you improve them by replacing any pronouns?

COOPERATIVE LEARNING: Revising Sentences ⟨191⟩

Working Together

The Working Together activities involve students in cooperative learning work groups. This is an opportunity to pair strong writers with students whose skills are weaker. Working together, they can all experience success.

Divide the class into small groups and have students read In Your Group. Encourage them to discuss why each task is important. Have them tell what might happen if the group does not follow through on each task. *(If we do not pay attention to each other's ideas, we might miss some ideas that could be helpful. If we interrupt each other, no one will be able to present ideas effectively. If we do not encourage everyone to talk, we might miss out on important ideas. If we don't help the group reach agreement, we cannot complete the activities successfully.)*

Before students begin activities A and B, you may wish to have each group appoint a member to record their sentences. You also may wish to have groups appoint a timekeeper. Then set a limit of ten or fifteen minutes. After each activity is completed, have the groups compare the sentences and the headlines they wrote.

Writers' Corner

The Writers' Corner provides students with the opportunity to extend the Grammar-Writing Connection, helping them to develop the skills necessary to review and revise their own writing. Discuss the introductory sentences with students. Then have them work as a class or in pairs to discuss the two examples. Have students read aloud each example and identify the change that was made. Have them tell how that change made the improved example "better." Then have students apply the replacing repeated nouns with pronouns techniques from this Grammar-Writing Connection to the sentences they wrote about visual arts for the Writers' Warm-up. Encourage students to rewrite their sentences if necessary. Discuss with them how replacing repeated nouns with pronouns improved their sentences, helping them to avoid repetition of the same nouns.

TWO-PART
flexibility

USING LANGUAGE TO PERSUADE

Unit 4 Overview

books

FOR EXTENDED READING

EASY

📖 **The Story of the Statue of Liberty** by Betsy and Giulio Maestro. Lothrop. This beautifully illustrated history of the world's most famous statue covers all the years of its creation, from Bartholdi's first visit to the United States in 1871 to the final unveiling of the statue in 1886.

AVERAGE

📖 **I Carve Stone** by Joan Fine. Harper. In this photo essay, a sculptor tells how she creates a work of art from a three-hundred-pound marble block.

CHALLENGING

📖 **A Carrot for a Nose: The Form of Folk Sculpture on America's City Streets and Country Roads** by M. J. Gladstone. Scribner. Outdoor folk sculpture, from weather vanes and snowmen to trade signs and scarecrows, is described in lucid text and numerous photographs.

READ-ALOUD

📖 **The Mount Rushmore Story** by Judith St. George. Putnam. This in-depth look at sculpture on a grand scale discusses the monumental achievement of sculptor Gutzon Borglum, who devoted the last fourteen years of his life to carving four presidents on the face of Mount Rushmore.

FLAMINGO
stabile by Alexander Calder
at Federal Center, Chicago © ARS New York/ADAGP.

◆ UNIT FOUR

USING LANGUAGE
TO
PERSUADE

=== PART TWO ===

Literature   "The Littlest Sculptor" by Joan Zeier
A Reason for Writing Persuading

CREATIVE
Writing

FINE ARTS ◆ The giant sculpture by Alexander Calder is called "Flamingo." In what ways does the sculpture resemble a flamingo? Does the sculpture resemble any other bird? Write an arts review of the sculpture. Explain how the various shapes of the sculpture resemble a bird.

◆ 192

◆ 193

---

start with
CREATIVE WRITING

Fine Arts gives your students a chance to express themselves creatively in writing. After students observe the illustration on page 192 for a moment or two, have a volunteer read aloud the Fine Arts paragraph on page 193. Have students write their reactions in their journals. Then encourage a discussion of their ideas.

 VIEWING

See the **Fine Arts Transparencies with Viewing Booklet** and the **Video Library**.

THEN START WITH
part 2

A Reason for Writing: Persuading is the focus of Part 2. First students learn a thinking strategy for persuading. Then they read and respond to a selection of nonfiction on which they may model their own writing. Developmental composition lessons, including "Expressing Opinions," a speaking and listening lesson, help students learn to use language correctly to persuade. All the lessons reflect the literature. All culminate in the Writing Process Lesson. The unit ends with the Curriculum Connection and Books to Enjoy, which help students discover how their new language skills apply to writing across the curriculum and to their own lives.

◆ If you began with grammar instruction, you may wish to remind students of the unit theme, "The Visual Arts". Tell them that the information they gathered through the thematic lessons helped them prepare for reading the literature, *The Littlest Sculptor* by Joan Zeier.

◆ If you are beginning with Part 2, use the lessons in Part 1 for remediation or instruction. For grammar, spelling, and mechanics instructional guidance, you may wish to refer to the end-of-text Glossary and Index, as well as to the *Spelling Connection* booklet; the full-color *Revising and Proofreading Transparencies;* and the Unit Pretest, Posttest, and Writing Samples.

THEME BAR

CATEGORIES	Environments	Business/World of Work	Imagination	Communications/ Fine Arts	People	Science	Expressions	Social Studies
THEMES	UNIT 1 Farm Life	UNIT 2 Handicrafts	UNIT 3 Tall Tales	UNIT 4 The Visual Arts	UNIT 5 Lasting Impressions	UNIT 6 Volcanoes	UNIT 7 Nature	UNIT 8 Animal Habitats
PACING	1 month	1 month	1 month	1 month	1 month	1 month	1 month	1 month

UNIT 4
Creative Thinking

■ Easy ■ Average ■ Challenging

OBJECTIVES
To use a thought balloon as a strategy for persuading

TEACHING THE LESSON

1. Getting Started
Oral Language Introduce the thinking skill, point of view, by asking students to imagine that their best friend has a cold and must stay home for a week. Say: *You want to take a book to your friend. What kind of book might he or she like?*

Metacognition Help students become aware of their own thinking (think metacognitively) by asking follow-up questions when they respond (e.g., *How did you figure out what your friend might like?*) Many students will have tried to consider their friend's point of view, to guess how the friend would feel, to think about subjects the friend is interested in, or to use their own experience to help them imagine their friend's. Explain that being able to understand someone else's point of view is a valuable thinking skill and that in this lesson they will learn about one strategy for understanding another point of view.

2. Developing the Lesson
Guide students through the introduction to persuading (the kind of literature and writing they will deal with in this unit) and its connection to understanding a point of view. Lead them through Learning the Strategy, emphasizing the model thought balloon. Identify those who would benefit from reteaching. Assign Using the Strategy A and B.

3. Closing the Lesson
Metacognition Applying the Strategy is a metacognitive activity in which students consider *how* they think (question 1) and *when* they think (question 2).
Question 1: Encourage students to share how they arrived at their ideas about what the principal would think and also to share any personal strategies they might prefer to use instead of

194

CREATIVE THINKING ◆
A Strategy for Persuading

A THOUGHT BALLOON

Persuading means getting someone to believe or to do something. After this lesson, you will read part of "The Littlest Sculptor." It is about Vinnie Ream, who wanted to sculpt President Lincoln. It tells how she tried to persuade him to pose for her. Later you will write a persuasive letter.

President Lincoln did not want to pose for Vinnie. The passage below shows how she tried to change his mind.

> "Miss Ream," he sighed. "I would like to oblige you, but as you know, we are in the midst of a horrible war. How could I possibly take the time to pose for a sculpture now? . . ."
>
> "I work quickly," she said . . . . "If I were to bring my clay here and work for three hours every afternoon, I could complete most of the project while you are at your desk."

Vinnie listened carefully to the President's reasons. She put herself in his place. She tried to see things from his point of view. It was during the Civil War, and she understood how important his work was. She thought he might agree to pose if he did not have to stop working. Do you think he agreed?

Learning the Strategy

It is often helpful to understand another person's point of view. Suppose you meet someone who has moved to America from another country. Could you understand that person's feelings about being in a new land? How? Suppose you find a science fiction book for a friend with the chickenpox. Would that please your friend? How do you know? Suppose you are watching the Academy Awards on television. An actress wins. What is she thinking as she walks up to the stage? How can you guess?

⟨ **194** ⟩   CREATIVE THINKING: Point of View

One way to understand another person's point of view is to imagine what *you* might think. Have you ever received an award? Can you guess how you would feel if you did? Making a thought balloon is another way to help imagine someone else's point of view. Think of that actress on her way to the stage. The thought balloon below shows what she might be thinking. What ideas could you add to this thought balloon?

Could I be dreaming? I hope I don't trip! I'd better smile for the cameras. Who's that waving at me?

actress

Using the Strategy

A. Imagine that the principal of your school drops in for a visit right this minute. Look around the classroom. Try to see it through the principal's eyes. Then make a thought balloon for your principal.

B. Reread the passage from "The Littlest Sculptor" on page 194. What do you imagine President Lincoln thought after Vinnie spoke? Make a thought balloon for President Lincoln. As you read "The Littlest Sculptor," decide if President Lincoln felt the way you thought he would.

Applying the Strategy

♦ How did you decide what your principal would think?
♦ When might knowing someone else's point of view help you?

CREATIVE THINKING: Point of View ⬦195⬦

a thought balloon. For instance, some students may say they like to pretend they are the other person or that they are looking out through the other person's eyes. Some may just say to themselves: *If I were that other person I would . . .* Some may use their own prior knowledge, recalling how they themselves have felt in similar circumstances. Reassure them that a thought balloon is only one strategy they can use when they try to understand a point of view, and that they should use what works for them.

Question 2: Encourage a diversity of responses (e.g., *It would help me get along with my brother. It would help me understand when my parents ask me to do something*).

Looking Ahead
The thinking strategy introduced in this lesson, a thought balloon, is used in Using the Strategy B as a prereading strategy to help students anticipate the literature, "The Littlest Sculptor." It will appear three more times in this unit and again in Unit 5.

THOUGHT BALLOON			
Strategy for Persuading	Writing to Learn	Prewriting	Writing Across the Curriculum
195	199	212	218

Strategy for Describing	Writing to Learn	Prewriting	Writing Across the Curriculum
249	255	266	272

Although the thought balloon strategy is repeated in each presentation, the context in which it is used changes. Students will thus be given the opportunity to discover how the strategy can help them in reading, in writing across the curriculum, and in their daily lives.

⬅▥▥ **TEACHING OPTIONS** ▥▥➡

RETEACHING

A Different Modality Cut, or have students cut, pictures of people from newspapers and magazines. Have each student look at and think about the person in one picture. Then ask each student to hold the picture in front of the face like a mask and speak the thoughts he or she imagines for the person in the picture. Ask students to explain how they decided on their responses.

CLASS ENRICHMENT

A Cooperative Activity Have pairs of students work together. Say: *Pretend that school will now be open on Saturday. In Saturday school you can study any subject you want including cooking or sports.* Ask students to use what they know about their partners to write (1) how the partner feels about going to school on Saturday and (2) what subject the partner would enjoy studying most. Have them trade papers, then tell each other what they *really* think.

CHALLENGE

An Independent Extension Provide students with familiar cartoon strips in which the characters' words and thoughts are cut out. Have students study the cartoons and write thought balloons for the characters to explain what is happening. Remind students to write from each character's point of view as they work.

UNIT 4
Literature

VOCABULARY STRATEGIES

Developing Concepts and Teaching Vocabulary

Preteach the following words from the story. Use the Dictionary of Knowledge at the back of the book to provide definitions of base words and context sentences.

creditable, indignant(ly), mire(d), oblige

Write the vocabulary words on the chalkboard. Ask questions that involve the students with the words, such as: *Have you ever behaved indignantly? Describe that time. How did you feel? What did you say? Has your bicycle ever become mired in mud? What did you do about it?*

GUIDING COMPREHENSION

Building Background

The first half of this unit includes information especially chosen to build background for *The Littlest Sculptor.* If you started the unit with grammar instruction, you may wish to have a class discussion on the unit theme, **The Visual Arts,** based on the information in those lessons.

If you started the unit with composition instruction, you may wish to build students' knowledge of fine arts by asking: *What paintings and sculpture have you seen and enjoyed in museums or other places? What different kinds of materials have you learned to work with in art class? What do you know about the way artists learn their skills?* (Students may recall trips to museums and the works of art they enjoyed. They may be aware that many artists learn their skills by going to art schools or working with more experienced artists. In art classes students may have learned about different media.)

LITERATURE

from

The Littlest Sculptor
by Joan T. Zeier

"They tell me that you'd like to sculpt a statue of me—is that correct?"

The deep, gentle voice helped calm Vinnie's nerves. Asking a favor of the President of the United States was no casual matter, especially for a seventeen-year-old girl.

"Yes, sir," she replied, her dark eyes meeting his. "I wouldn't have dared to ask you, but my teacher, Mr. Mills, says I am ready. I plan to sculpt you in a creditable manner."

President Lincoln smiled. "Painters, sculptors—they've all

196 LITERATURE: Nonfiction

ESSENTIAL LANGUAGE SKILLS

This lesson provides opportunities to:

LISTENING ◆ employ active listening in a variety of situations

SPEAKING ◆ use a variety of words to express feelings and ideas

READING ◆ relate experiences with appropriate vocabulary in complete sentences ◆ summarize a selection ◆ understand cause-and-effect relationships ◆ predict probable future outcomes or actions ◆ evaluate and make judgments ◆ respond to various forms of literature ◆ explain and relate to the feelings and emotions of characters

WRITING ◆ use ideas and information from sources other than personal experiences for writing

LANGUAGE ◆ use the fundamentals of grammar, punctuation, and spelling

ried to make the best of this homely face, but I'm afraid there's not much hope. What did you have in mind, Miss Ream? A bust?"

Vinnie opened her mouth to say yes, but before she could speak, the President hurried on, a shade of apology in his voice. "Of course—I shouldn't have asked. A full-length pose would be much too strenuous a project for a young woman your size."

Vinnie flushed. She realized that she looked like a child, with her shoulder-length black ringlets and her tiny frame. "Small does not mean weak, sir," she replied indignantly. "I was born in the wilderness of Wisconsin. I've driven teams of horses and carried water. Many times I've put my shoulder to a wheel mired in mud. Molding a full-length clay figure would not tax my strength at all—and that is what I intend to do!"

The President's eyes twinkled at her show of spirit. "My apologies, madam. Had I known your background, I wouldn't have underestimated you. I, too, am from the West, so I understand the hardships of frontier life."

But his smile faded as he rubbed his beard with bony fingers, in thought. "Miss Ream," he sighed. "I would like to oblige you, but as you know, we are in the midst of a horrible war. How could I possibly take the time to pose for a sculpture now? I scarcely have a minute to myself."

Vinnie glanced around and noted the size of his office. "I work quickly," she said. Her voice was soft but confident as she pointed to the corner near the windows. "If I were to bring my clay here and work for three hours every afternoon, I could complete most of the project while you are at your desk."

The President seemed to consider her idea seriously. He got up, shook Vinnie's hand warmly, and looked down upon her from his great height. "I've heard from Mr. Clark Mills that you are a talented young woman, and I have found you charming and intelligent as well. I cannot make my decision immediately, but you will hear from me soon."

The very next day Vinnie received a note from the President.

LITERATURE: Nonfiction ◁197▷

Developing a Purpose for Reading

Option 1: Have students set their own purpose for reading. Then have them read the story introduction and study the illustrations. Explain that in this selection they will learn about Vinnie Ream, the young sculptor who created figures of Abraham Lincoln. Then have students write questions they think the selection might answer about Vinnie Ream and President Lincoln. Have students read the selection to see which of their questions are answered.

Option 2: If you wish to set a reading purpose for everyone, have students pay special attention to the description that shows Vinnie's character. Have them ask themselves: *How did Vinnie's character help her succeed even though she was young and inexperienced?*

GUIDED READING

Please note that opportunities for students' personal responses to the selection are offered in the Reader's Response question and the Selection Follow-up at the end of this lesson.

Page 196 *How were Vinnie and Lincoln different?* (Vinnie was a seventeen-year-old female sculptor; Lincoln was older, male, and president of the United States. She was short; he was tall.) ANALYZE: COMPARISONS

Page 197 *How were they the same?* (Both grew up on the western frontier, knew about the hardships of frontier life, and had the drive and determination to overcome hardships.) ANALYZE: COMPARISONS

SUMMARY

Vinnie Ream, the artist who created the full-size sculpture of Abraham Lincoln that stands in the rotunda of the Capitol, was just seventeen years old when she first met the president. In this selection she asks Lincoln to pose for a sculpture. Lincoln responds to her persuasive request with a formal invitation for Vinnie to begin work on modeling a bust.

ABOUT THE AUTHOR

JOAN T. ZEIER (1931–) is a Wisconsin native who loves to incorporate her state's history into poetry and fiction. Her story *Beyond the Iron Canvas*, about Georgia O'Keeffe, who, like Vinnie Ream, was born in Wisconsin, won a first place **Jade Ring Award** in 1984. Zeier's poetry has been published in many state and national magazines. She is at present writing a novel for children, as well as short stories, and assists young writers in the Yahara River Writing Project and Madison enrichment classes.

Returning to the Reading Purpose

Option 1: Those students who have written questions may wish to review them to determine whether their most important ones have been answered.

Option 2: If you have established a common reading purpose, review it and ask students to summarize what they learned about Vinnie Ream's character.

READER'S RESPONSE

If you had been President Lincoln, would you have honored Vinnie Ream's request? Why or why not? (Give students a framework for answering the question by asking them to describe what problems they might face as the president of a country at war.)

STORY MAP

You may want to have students make a story map for this excerpt from *The Littlest Sculptor* similar to the one below.

Characters:	Vinnie Ream, President Abraham Lincoln
Setting:	the President's office 1865

↓

Problem: Seventeen-year-old Vinnie Ream wants the opportunity to sculpt a statue of President Lincoln.

Event 1: Vinnie asks President Lincoln to pose for a sculpture.

↓

Event 2: The President says he would like to oblige but hardly has time since the country is in the midst of a war.

↓

Event 3: Vinnie tries to persuade him she could do her work without disturbing him.

↓

Event 4: The President promises to make a decision soon.

Resolution: President Lincoln invites Vinnie to begin modeling a bust of him.

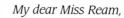

My dear Miss Ream,

I have considered your request and invite you to come to my office next Monday afternoon at two o'clock. You may bring whatever supplies are necessary to begin your work. However, owing to limitations of time and space, I can only agree to the modeling of a bust.

Yours,

A. Lincoln

Vinnie proudly showed the invitation to Mr. Mills, who was delighted with her success. "What luck! He's turned down some very famous artists, you know. Your enthusiasm must have won him over."

During the next few months, Vinnie Ream observed and sculpted President Lincoln in his office. She was just finishing her bust of President Lincoln when he was shot to death on April 14, 1865. Sadly, Vinnie left the completed bust of the President in the White House.

As the nation mourned President Lincoln, Congress voted to honor him by commissioning a full-length sculpture. There was a contest to select the artist, and Vinnie Ream won. In 1871 her magnificent marble statue of President Abraham Lincoln was placed in the Capitol rotunda. Vinnie Ream's personal memory of a great President still stands in the rotunda today.

Library Link ♦ *To learn more about Vinnie Ream, read "The Littlest Sculptor" in the February 1986 issue of* Cricket *magazine.*

 Reader's Response

If you had been President Lincoln, would you have honored Vinnie Ream's request? Why or why not?

198 LITERATURE: Nonfiction

STRATEGIC READING

Page 198 Have students predict how Vinnie might persuade the President to let her make a sculpture of him. Suggest that they use a thought balloon to help them understand what Vinnie is thinking. (Students may predict that Vinnie will try to understand the President's needs and find some way to do her work without disturbing him.) Have students read to see if their predictions are correct. METACOGNITION: PREDICTING

HIGHLIGHTING LITERATURE

Page 198 Explain to students that this selection is about two real figures from history: Abraham Lincoln and a young sculptor named Vinnie Ream. Point out that the story contains many facts. Then explain that a story that contains historical facts along with made-up thoughts, words, and actions is called *historical fiction*.

The Littlest Sculptor

 ## Responding to Literature

1. Mr. Mills thought Vinnie's enthusiasm must have won the argument for her. Why, do you think, did the President accept Vinnie's request? Was it her enthusiasm, her talent, or another quality that most impressed President Lincoln? Explain.

2. If you were to sculpt a bust of a famous person, whom would you choose? Why? What reasons would you give the person for wanting to do this?

3. Vinnie Ream has a place in history as a sculptor of Lincoln. What would you like to do to earn a place in history? Draw a picture of yourself achieving your dream. Then write a headline for your accomplishment. Add the headline to your picture.

 ## Writing to Learn

Think and Imagine ✦ Imagine the President's point of view when he heard Miss Vinnie Ream's request. Draw two thought balloons. In the first balloon, write the request that Vinnie made of the President. In the other balloon, write President Lincoln's thoughts.

Thought Balloon

Write ✦ Use the notes from the thought balloons to write a short conversation between the President and Vinnie.

LITERATURE: Nonfiction **199**

WRITING TO LEARN

Have students apply the thinking strategy of creating a thought balloon to show their understanding of the selection. Encourage them to put themselves in Vinnie Ream's and President Lincoln's places in order to understand their points of view.

 World of Language Audio Library

A recording of this selection is available in the **Audio Library.**

You may wish to incorporate any or all of the following discussion questions and activities in your follow-up to the literature selection, *The Littlest Sculptor.*

RESPONDING TO LITERATURE

Encourage students to use their personal experiences as well as what they learned from the selection to discuss these questions. The questions are designed to encourage students to think of and respond to the selection as a whole. Explain to students that although they may use details from the selection to support their opinions, the questions have no right or wrong answers. Encourage them to express a variety of points of view. You may wish to have students respond as a class, in groups, or with partners.

1. *Mr. Mills thought Vinnie's enthusiasm must have won the argument for her. Why, do you think, did the president accept Vinnie's request? Was it her enthusiasm, her talent, or another quality that most impressed President Lincoln? Explain.* (Students might suggest that a combination of Vinnie's qualities helped her to win her argument. Her enthusiasm may have been the first thing that impressed Lincoln. Then he probably considered her talent. Lincoln might have also considered Vinnie's honesty and dedication.)

2. *If you were to sculpt a bust of a famous person, whom would you choose? Why? What reasons would you give the person for wanting to do so?* (Have each student name a famous person and explain the reason for the choice. Students might suggest that they would tell that person how much they admire him or her, that they feel others would appreciate a sculpture of the person, or that they think the person's image should be preserved for future generations to enjoy.)

3. *Vinnie Ream has a place in history as a sculptor of Lincoln. What would you like to do to earn a place in history? Draw a picture of yourself achieving your dream. Then write a headline for your accomplishment. Add the headline to your picture.* (Encourage students to think about their interests, hobbies, and special talents.

199

UNIT 4
Speaking/Listening

■ Easy ■ Average ■ Challenging

OBJECTIVES
To express opinions respectfully
To use guidelines for expressing and listening to opinions

ASSIGNMENT GUIDE
BASIC   Practice A

⬇

ADVANCED   Practice B

All should do the Apply activity.

RESOURCES
■ World of Language Video Library

TEACHING THE LESSON

1. Getting Started
Oral Language Focus attention on this oral activity, encouraging all to participate. You may wish to have students who feel they can change a friend's opinion tell how they believe they might go about it. You may then wish to have the class discuss why they feel that student will or will not be successful.

2. Developing the Lesson
Guide students through a discussion of the lesson, emphasizing the guidelines for expressing opinions and for being a critical listener. Then lead students through the **Guided Practice.** Identify those who would benefit from reteaching. Assign independent Practice A and B.

3. Closing the Lesson
After students complete the Apply activity, call on individuals to read aloud the negative and positive statements they recorded on their charts. Then have students work in small groups or with partners to compare and discuss the statements they wrote. Encourage students to use the guidelines for expressing opinions and for being a critical listener as they work together. Point out that learning how to express opinions clearly and respectfully will help students share their own ideas and understand the ideas of others.

200

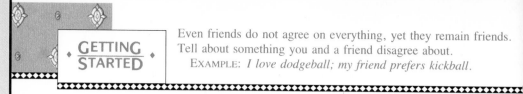

Even friends do not agree on everything, yet they remain friends. Tell about something you and a friend disagree about.
EXAMPLE: *I love dodgeball; my friend prefers kickball.*

SPEAKING and LISTENING ◆
Expressing Opinions

Melissa: This painting is exciting. I love the bold lines and wild splashes of color. It's wonderful!

James: Are you kidding? I can't even tell what it is. How could anyone like it? That's not art!

Melissa: Well, I like it, and it's great art. You have no taste. You're ignorant!

Melissa and James are allowing their difference of opinion to turn into a heated argument. How can they express their opinions without destroying their friendship? Here are some guidelines to help you share opinions.

Expressing Your Opinion	1. State your opinion clearly, but do not be a know-it-all. Use phrases such as *in my opinion* or *I believe*. 2. Give facts or reasons to support your opinion. 3. Respect the opinions of others. When you make fun of people's opinions, you insult them and make them angry. Then they will not listen to anything you say. 　**This:** Could you give me an example of what you mean? **Not this:** What a dumb idea! That's a stupid remark! 4. When you want to persuade others to agree with you, start by stating all the points on which you do agree. 　**This:** I like that artist's use of color, too. **Not this:** You like modern art; I hate it.
Being a Critical Listener	1. Listen for proof of the speaker's opinion. Does the speaker give facts or reasons to support it? 2. Evaluate the speaker. Does the speaker know the facts? 3. Try to keep an open mind if you disagree with the speaker.

> **Summary** ◆ Both speakers and listeners need to respect each other's opinions. Find points on which you both agree. Be courteous when you disagree.

200   SPEAKING and LISTENING: Opinions

ESSENTIAL LANGUAGE SKILLS
This lesson provides opportunities to:

LISTENING ◆ employ active listening in a variety of situations

SPEAKING ◆ use a variety of words to express feelings and ideas ◆ use a set of reasons to persuade a group

READING ◆ identify an implied main idea of a longer selection ◆ evaluate and make judgments ◆ follow a set of directions

WRITING ◆ adapt information to accomplish a specific purpose with a particular audience

LANGUAGE ◆ use the fundamentals of grammar, punctuation, and spelling

Guided Practice

Read each sentence. If it follows the guidelines for speaking and listening, say *yes*. If it does not, say *no*.

1. Anyone who likes modern art ought to have an eye exam! no
2. I feel that the camera can capture real life more accurately than an artist can. yes
3. In my opinion, modern art is not beautiful. yes

Practice

A. Take turns reading the sentences aloud with a partner. If a sentence follows the guidelines for speaking and listening, say *yes*. If it does not, say *no*.

4. It seems to me that today's artists should study the work of the nineteenth century masters. yes
5. Your ideas are old-fashioned; they belong in a museum! no
6. Others may disagree, but I think that a photograph can be more realistic than a painting. yes
7. How could you say such a thing and mean it? no
8. I may not agree, but you do have a good point. yes
9. You are right. Picasso was one of the world's greatest artists, but I prefer the Old Dutch masters. yes
10. You may be right. Could you give me an example? yes
11. I'll prove that I'm right and you're wrong! no

B. Practice sharing opinions with your classmates. Decide on a topic, such as whether homework is valuable for students. Use the guidelines in this lesson.

Apply ◆ Think and Write

Expressions Chart ◆ Make a chart like the one below.

Expressions to Avoid	Expressions to Use
Your idea is really dumb.	I'll consider what you just said.

On the left, list other expressions that cause people to quarrel, not discuss. On the right, list expressions that encourage people to discuss, not quarrel.

✎ **Remember** to show respect for the opinions of others.

SPEAKING and LISTENING: Opinions **201**

📺 **World of Language Video Library**

You may wish to use the *World of Language Video Library* to teach this lesson.

EVALUATION PROGRAM

See Evaluation and Testing Program, pp. C9–C11.

Speaking and Listening Checklist Masters

◀||||| TEACHING OPTIONS ||||▶

RETEACHING

A Different Modality Have students use the lesson guidelines to role-play the correct way to express opinions. Begin by writing two opinions on the chalkboard, such as: *Students should have two hours of homework every night. Students should not be given more than one hour of homework.* Then have a discussion in which you support one opinion and students support the other.

CLASS ENRICHMENT

A Cooperative Activity Have small groups work together to take polls of classroom opinions. Tell each group to think of a different question or issue on which students might have a strong opinion, such as: *Do you think young people watch too much television? Do you think our school needs a new playground (or ball field)?* Have groups record their classmates' opinions. Then have groups review, summarize, and present the information they gathered.

CHALLENGE

An Independent Extension Have students make opinion charts. Provide students with a copy of a newspaper editorial page and explain the page's function. Have students find examples of opinions on the page. Then have them copy the opinions onto a chart with two columns entitled *Opinions* and *Supporting Facts.* Have the class discuss whether or not each opinion is completely supported by persuasive facts or reasons.

UNIT 4
Writing

OBJECTIVES
To distinguish between fact and opinion
To write facts and opinions

ASSIGNMENT GUIDE
BASIC   Practice A
           Practice B
ADVANCED   Practice C

All should do the Apply activity.

RESOURCES
■ Reteaching Master 38
■ Practice Master 38

TEACHING THE LESSON

1. Getting Started
Oral Language Focus attention on this oral activity, encouraging all to participate. You may wish to show and read aloud some newspaper and magazine advertising slogans for students to discuss.

2. Developing the Lesson
Guide students through the explanation of fact and opinion, emphasizing the examples and the summary. You may wish to remind students of the phrases that signal opinions, such as *I believe, I think,* and *in my opinion.* Lead students through the **Guided Practice.** Identify those who would benefit from reteaching. Assign independent Practice A–C.

3. Closing the Lesson
After students complete the Apply activity, have them work in small groups to discuss how they might check or test the facts they wrote. (Students may respond that they can check facts in reference books and ask experts on the subject.) Point out to students that knowing how to provide facts that support their opinions can help them be more persuasive.

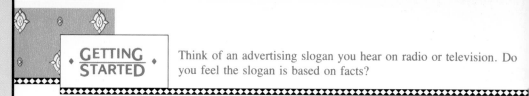

GETTING STARTED ◆ Think of an advertising slogan you hear on radio or television. Do you feel the slogan is based on facts?

WRITING ◆
Fact and Opinion

Every day you hear and read messages that try to persuade you. Advertisements and speeches try to persuade you to do something or think a certain way. How can you tell whether to believe them? To decide this, you must be able to tell facts from opinions.

Sometimes, on the other hand, *you* want to persuade others to share your opinion. You want to convince them. To do this, you need to back up your opinion with facts.

What is the difference between a fact and an opinion? A fact is true information. It can be checked or proved to be true. An opinion is what a person *thinks* about something. It is not always easy to tell from opinions. An opinion may be stated very positively. It may sound like a fact, even though it is just someone's opinion. Here are three ways to check a statement to see if it is really a fact.

Use what you already know ◆ Think, ''Do I know from my own knowledge or experience that the statement is true?''
Experiment ◆ Test the ''fact'' yourself to find out if it is true.
Investigate ◆ Read about the fact. Check the fact in reference books. an expert about it.

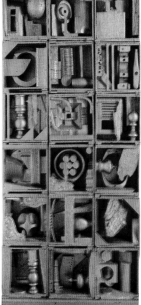

Royal Tide I by Louise Nevelson. Photograph courtesy of The Pace Gallery

Facts:	1.	Clay is a soft, moldable material.
	2.	Congress awarded Vinnie Ream $30,000 for a statue.
	3.	Louise Nevelson, the sculptor, was born in Russia.
Opinions:	1.	Louise Nevelson's walls are her best sculptures.
	2.	The finest statues are made of white marble.
	3.	No sculptor will ever surpass Michelangelo.

Summary ◆ A **fact** is true information that can be checked. An **opinion** is what someone *thinks* is true. When you want to persuade other people, use facts to show how you arrived at your opinion.

202   WRITING: Fact and Opinion

ESSENTIAL LANGUAGE SKILLS
This lesson provides opportunities to:

LISTENING ◆ employ active listening in a variety of situations

SPEAKING ◆ use a variety of words to express feelings and ideas

READING ◆ distinguish between fact and opinion ◆ evaluate and make judgments ◆ follow a set of directions

WRITING ◆ adapt information to accomplish a specific purpose with a particular audience

LANGUAGE ◆ use the fundamentals of grammar, punctuation, and spelling

Guided Practice

Tell whether each statement is a fact or an opinion.

1. You would have enjoyed meeting the sculptor, Vinnie Ream. opinion
2. Vinnie Ream's last sculpting session with Lincoln was on April 14, 1865. fact
3. On the evening of April 14, 1865, Lincoln was shot by John Wilkes Booth. fact

Practice

A. Write *fact* or *opinion* for each statement below.

4. Vinnie Ream was born in the wilderness of Wisconsin. fact
5. The wilderness is not the best home for an artist. opinion
6. Congress voted to have a sculpture made of Lincoln. fact
7. Every sculptor dreamed of being chosen to do the work. opinion
8. Vinnie Ream was selected to be the sculptor. fact
9. Ream's statue of Lincoln stands in the Capitol. fact

B. Decide how you could check each fact below. Write *already know it*, *test it*, or *read about it* for each statement.

10. Paris is a large city in France. already know it or read about it
11. Auguste Rodin was born in Paris, France. already know it or read about it
12. A bronze statue will sound hollow when you tap it. test it
13. The statue called "The Thinker" was sculpted by Rodin. already know it or read about it

C. Write two sentences for each word below. In the first sentence express an opinion. In the second sentence, state a fact.
Answers will vary.

14–15. photograph   16–17. city   18–19. wood

Apply ◆ Think and Write

An Art Review ◆ Here is your chance to be an art critic. Write your opinion of the sculpture shown on the opposite page. Remember to give reasons for your opinion.

✏️ **Remember**
to give facts or reasons to support your opinions.

WRITING: Fact and Opinion   **203**

RETEACHING   38

Fact and Opinion

Write <u>fact</u> beside each statement with true information you can check. Write <u>opinion</u> if you cannot check the information. Use the picture for information.

1. Roller skates have wheels, and ice skates have blades. ___fact___
2. Both roller skates and ice skates may have shoe parts. ___fact___
3. Roller skates fit more comfortably than ice skates. ___opinion___

A **fact** is true information that can be checked. Three ways to check a fact are to use your own knowledge, to experiment, or to investigate. An **opinion** is what someone <u>thinks</u> is true.

A. Write <u>fact</u> or <u>opinion</u> for each sentence.

EXAMPLE: Speed skating is not as difficult as figure skating. ___opinion___

1. Speed skates differ from figure skates. ___fact___
2. Skating indoors is more fun than skating outdoors. ___opinion___
3. Private ice-skating lessons can make anyone an expert. ___opinion___
4. Private ice-skating lessons are offered in town. ___fact___
5. The town rink charges too much to rent skates. ___opinion___
6. The town rink rents ice skates. ___fact___

B. Tell how you would check each statement to discover if it is a fact. Write use own knowledge, experiment, or investigate. Answers will vary. Possible answers follow.

EXAMPLE: People in the Netherlands skate on frozen canals. ___investigate___

7. The earliest ice skates were made of bone. ___investigate___
8. Skates with steel blades were first made in the 1850s. ___investigate___
9. A regular ice skate has a single blade. ___use own knowledge___

PRACTICE   38

Fact and Opinion

A **fact** is true information that can be checked. An **opinion** is what someone <u>thinks</u> is true.

A. Write <u>fact</u> or <u>opinion</u> for each statement below.

1. A glacier is a large, slow-moving mass of ice. ___fact___
2. A glacier looks like scenery for a science-fiction movie. ___opinion___
3. Heavy, moving glaciers scratch and polish rocks. ___fact___
4. Moving glaciers create valleys and lakes. ___fact___
5. We need more lakes for fishing, swimming, and boating. ___opinion___
6. No one wants to live near a glacier. ___opinion___
7. Melting glaciers leave piles of rocks and soil. ___fact___
8. Glaciers provide a thrilling spectacle for travelers. ___opinion___
9. Glaciers are great for winter sports. ___opinion___
10. Most glaciers get bigger in the winter. ___fact___

B. These statements are facts. Write how you could check each fact. Answers will vary. Possible answers follow.

11. Water freezes at zero degrees.
Experiment, or look in a science or other reference book.

12. Most rivers empty into the ocean.
Ask an expert, or look in a science or other reference book.

13. The Colorado River carries away tons of earth, rocks, and sand each day.
Ask an expert, or look in a science or other reference book.

14. In 1848 gold was discovered in a stream at Sutter's Mill in California.
Look in a reference book, or ask an expert on California's history.

WRITE IT
Write two facts and two opinions about something in nature. Write on a separate sheet of paper. Answers will vary.

◀|||| TEACHING OPTIONS ||||▶

RETEACHING	CLASS ENRICHMENT	CHALLENGE
A Different Modality Remind students that facts can be checked or tested. Explain that the following statement is an opinion. Read the statement and have volunteers explain why it is an opinion. *The Great Outdoors Store has the largest selection of sports equipment anywhere.* Then explain that the next statement is a fact. Have volunteers explain why. *The Great Outdoors Store sells downhill skis and ski boots.*	**A Cooperative Activity** Have students work in small groups to write an advertisement about an imaginary product. You may wish to have students look in newspapers and magazines to get ideas for their ads. Have students draw a picture of their product and write both facts and opinions about it in their ads. Have one member of each group show and read the ad to the class. Have volunteers identify the facts and opinions.	**An Independent Extension** Have students write two paragraphs that tell about something they know well, such as a pet, the building they live in, or a nearby park. In the first paragraph have them include only facts. In the second paragraph have them use only opinions. You may wish to give students the option of making their paragraphs serious or humorous.

UNIT 4
Writing

■ Easy ■ Average ■ Challenging

OBJECTIVES
To give reasons to support an opinion
To write a persuasive paragraph

ASSIGNMENT GUIDE
BASIC   Practice A

ADVANCED   Practice B

All should do the Apply activity.

RESOURCES
■ Reteaching Master 39
■ Practice Master 39

TEACHING THE LESSON

1. Getting Started
Oral Language Focus attention on this oral activity, encouraging all to participate. You may wish to add that students may use fantastic reasons to support fantastic opinions.

2. Developing the Lesson
Guide students through the explanation of a persuasive paragraph, emphasizing the example and the summary. You may wish to ask students if they believe the paragraph could persuade them to help clean up the park. Encourage open, whole-class discussions. Lead students through the **Guided Practice.** Identify those who would benefit from reteaching. Assign independent Practice A and B.

3. Closing the Lesson
After students complete the Apply activity, have volunteers read their scripts aloud. Have classmates identify the reasons that might persuade them to buy the product. Point out to students that supporting an opinion with reasons is important when trying to persuade a listener or reader.

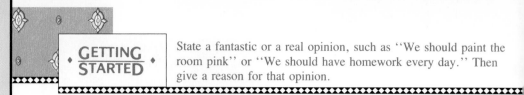

GETTING STARTED

State a fantastic or a real opinion, such as "We should paint the room pink" or "We should have homework every day." Then give a reason for that opinion.

WRITING ♦
A Persuasive Paragraph

How did Vinnie Ream persuade Abraham Lincoln to let her sculpt him? She gave him convincing reasons. When you want to persuade someone to agree with you, you need to do the same thing. You need to give reasons to prove you are right. You need to state them clearly. You need to focus on what matters to the people you are trying to persuade. What you need is a plan.

Read the paragraph below. It is a persuasive paragraph with a plan. Think about the reasons the writer presented. Notice, too, how the reasons are organized. Which reason is presented first?

the most important

Topic sentence gives opinion

Reasons, with most important reason first

Last sentence repeats opinion

> I think the students in Jefferson School should volunteer to help clean up the park. It is, after all, our park. Most of us live near it. We would play in the park if it were clean. But it is littered with bottles, cans, and old newspapers. The trash is not only dirty and ugly; it is dangerous. How would you like to run to catch a softball and trip on a broken bottle someone tossed aside? Imagine a clean park, a park without litter—a safe place to play. That could be our park. Let's volunteer to help make the park clean.

Notice that the writer states an opinion in the topic sentence of the paragraph. Then the writer, wanting to persuade the readers, gives reasons for the opinion. In this paragraph the most important reason is given first and other reasons follow. Sometimes a writer chooses to build up to the most important reason and gives it last. What does the writer do in the last sentence of this paragraph?

Summary ♦ A **persuasive paragraph** gives the writer's opinion and reasons to support it. Reasons are often listed in the order of importance.

204   WRITING: Persuasive Paragraph

ESSENTIAL LANGUAGE SKILLS
This lesson provides opportunities to:

LISTENING ♦ employ active listening in a variety of situations

SPEAKING ♦ use a variety of words to express feelings and ideas ♦ make organized oral presentations

READING ♦ distinguish between fact and opinion ♦ make valid inferences from a reading selection

WRITING ♦ adapt information to accomplish a specific purpose with a particular audience

LANGUAGE ♦ use the fundamentals of grammar, punctuation, and spelling

Guided Practice

State a topic sentence that gives an opinion about each of these questions. **Answers will vary.**

1. Should school be held in the summer?
2. What TV program is worth watching?
3. Is reading comic books a waste of time?

Practice

A. Write a topic sentence that gives an opinion about each of these questions. **Answers will vary.**

4. How much homework should students your age have?
5. Should students your age get an allowance?
6. How old should you be to deliver newspapers?
7. What time should students your age go to bed?
8. Is it better to be the oldest or the youngest child in a family?
9. What television program is boring?
10. What sport is the most interesting?
11. Which season is the most enjoyable?
12. Who is the best popular singer?
13. What is the greatest invention of all time?

B. Choose one of the topic sentences you wrote for **Practice A.** Write a persuasive paragraph to convince your classmates that you are right. Give at least four reasons that will convince them. Remember to give the most important reason first. **Paragraphs will vary.**

Apply ♦ Think and Write

Dictionary of Knowledge ♦ Sayings such as "Haste makes waste" are called proverbs. Read about proverbs in the Dictionary of Knowledge, and choose one to write about. Write a paragraph to persuade your reader that the saying is true, or that it is sometimes not true.

✎ **Remember**
to support an opinion with reasons that are important to your readers.

WRITING: Persuasive Paragraph **205**

RETEACHING 39

A Persuasive Paragraph

The reasons below support the following opinion: I think bicycle riders should be required to pass a driver's test. Number the your reasons in the order of most important to least important.

1	Too many accidents involve bicycle riders.
3	Many bicycle riders ignore walkers and cars.
4	Bicycle riders are often a danger to themselves.
2	Bicycle riders should know about bicycle riding safety.

Answers will vary. Possible answers follow.

↪ A **persuasive paragraph** gives the writer's opinion and reasons to support it. Reasons are often listed in the order of importance. The most important reason is usually first. The last sentence often repeats the writer's opinion.

A. Write a topic sentence that gives your opinion. Answers will vary. Possible answers follow.
EXAMPLE: Should music be played in the school cafeteria?
_____ I think music should be played in the school cafeteria.

1. Should animals be kept in zoos? _____ I think some animals should be kept in zoos.

2. Should students go to school twelve months a year? _____ I think that students should not go to school twelve months a year.

3. Should all movie tickets be free for students? _____ I think movie tickets should not be free for students.

B. Write four reasons to support this opinion: I think there should be a crossing guard on every corner on the way to school. Answers will vary. Possible answers follow.
EXAMPLE: Crossing guards make it safer for children to walk to school.

4. _____ It is fun to talk to the guards.
5. _____ Crossing guards help direct the cars.
6. _____ There are no traffic lights on many corners.
7. _____ Many children need help to cross the street.

PRACTICE 39

A Persuasive Paragraph

↪ A **persuasive paragraph** gives the writer's opinion and reasons to support it. Reasons are often listed in the order of importance. The most important reason is usually first.

A. Write a topic sentence that gives your opinion about two of these questions:
• Should parents limit the amount of time children watch television?
• Should the students in your school publish a weekly newspaper?
• What is the best exercise, sport, club, game, or after-school activity?

1. _____ Answers will vary.

2. _____

B. Write four reasons to support one of the opinions you wrote in Exercise A. Then write four reasons to support an opposing opinion. Number each set of reasons in the order of importance. Answers will vary.

For
_____
_____
_____
_____

Against
_____
_____
_____
_____

WRITE IT
Write a persuasive paragraph to convince a friend or a classmate to join a team or club. Write on a separate sheet of paper. Answers will vary.

◀▥▥ TEACHING OPTIONS ▥▥▶

RETEACHING

A Different Modality Write the following question on the chalkboard: *Should students have to go to school on their birthday?* Then write the headings *Yes* and *No* and write the reasons volunteers dictate for their opinions. Help students number the reasons under each heading from most important to least important. Then, writing on the chalkboard, work as a group to compose paragraphs of opinion for and against the idea.

CLASS ENRICHMENT

A Cooperative Activity Have students work with a partner to choose a topic, such as *Every town should have a bike path* or *More school time should be devoted to art* (or to another subject). Have one partner write a paragraph supporting the idea and the other write one arguing against it. You may wish to have partners read their paragraphs to the class and then conduct a secret ballot.

CHALLENGE

An Independent Extension Have students write a persuasive paragraph with this topic sentence: *I think _____ should be class president.* You may wish to have students write about a real or an imaginary person. Have students support their opinion with at least three reasons. You may wish to remind students to repeat their opinion in their last sentence.

OBJECTIVES
To identify the parts of a business letter
To write a business letter

ASSIGNMENT GUIDE
BASIC	Practice A
	Practice B
ADVANCED	Practice C

All should do the Apply activity.

RESOURCES
■ Reteaching Master 40
■ Practice Master 40

TEACHING THE LESSON

1. Getting Started
Oral Language Focus attention on this oral activity, encouraging all to participate. Before you begin you may wish to use *Business Letter* as the focus of a semantic map listing kinds of business letters, such as request, complaints, and thank-you wishes.

2. Developing the Lesson
Guide students through the explanation of a business letter, emphasizing the example and the summary. You may wish to have students compare and contrast the parts of a friendly letter and the parts of a business letter. Lead students through the **Guided Practice.** Identify those who would benefit from reteaching. Assign independent Practice A–C.

3. Closing the Lesson
After students complete the Apply activity, have volunteers read their business letters aloud. Have classmates identify the six parts of each letter. Point out to students that stating clearly their purpose for writing a business letter can help them achieve their goal.

♦ GETTING STARTED ♦

The abbreviations of state names are the answers to these challenging riddles. Which state abbreviation

says "hello"?	is never out?
has nothing in it?	means the same as *I*?

WRITING ♦
A Business Letter

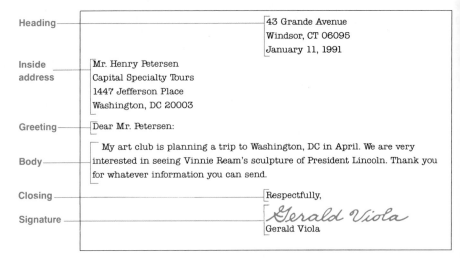

1. The **heading** shows the writer's address and the date. Use a comma between the city and state and between the date and year.
2. The **inside address** gives the name and address of the person and company to whom the letter is written.

Six Parts of a Business Letter

3. The **greeting** is formal. If you do not have a name, use a greeting such as *Dear Sir or Madam*. End the greeting with a colon.
4. The **body** states the purpose of the letter. It may be short.
5. The **closing** is formal. Another formal closing is *Sincerely*.
6. The **signature** gives the writer's name. If the letter is typed or word-processed, the name goes four lines below the closing.

See pages 487 and 489 for information about friendly letters and about addressing envelopes.

> **Summary** ♦ A **business letter** has six parts: the heading, inside address, greeting, body, closing, and signature.

206 WRITING and MECHANICS: Business Letter

ESSENTIAL LANGUAGE SKILLS
This lesson provides opportunities to:

LISTENING ♦ employ active listening in a variety of situations

SPEAKING ♦ use a variety of words to express feelings and ideas

READING ♦ understand content area vocabulary ♦ evaluate and make judgments ♦ follow a set of directions

WRITING ♦ use conventional formats (business letters and other commonly used forms)

LANGUAGE ♦ use the fundamentals of grammar, punctuation, and spelling

Guided Practice

Name the following parts of a business letter.

greeting
1. Dear Art Director:
signature
2. Deborah Wells
closing
3. Sincerely,

inside address
4. Public Art Society
   10 Madison Street
   Washington, DC 20203

Practice

A. Write the name of each part of a business letter.

5. I am interested in learning more about the programs offered by the museum. Please send me your latest brochure. *body*

6. Yours truly, *closing*

7. 312 Brook Lane *heading*
   Meredith, NH 03253
   November 8, 1991

B. Write the answers to these questions about a business letter.

heading
8. Which part gives the writer's address?
Dear Sir or Madam
9. What greeting could you use if you have no specific name?
colon
10. What punctuation ends the greeting?
comma
11. What punctuation ends the closing?

C. Write these items as if they were parts of business letters. Punctuate and capitalize them correctly.

12. 487 blue hills road ᴮ ᴴ ᴿ
13. hartford ct 06103 ᴴ ᶜᵀ
14. march 4 1991 ᴹ
15. silver inn ˢ ᴵ
16. 18 georgia avenue ᴳ ᴬ

17. silver spring md 20910 ˢ ˢ ᴹᴰ
18. dear manager : ᴰ
19. with best regards , ᵂ
20. april 2 1990 ᴬ
21. dear ms. taylor : ᴰ ᴹ ᵀ

Apply ◆ Think and Write

A Letter of Request ◆ Pretend your club was planning a trip to Washington, DC. What would you need to know? Think of some information that would be helpful. Write a business letter with a message that asks for facts or advice.

HAMPTON UNIVERSITY MUSEUM

THE UNIVERSITY MUSEUM is located on the Hampton University campus in Hampton, Virginia. The campus is easily reached via Interstate 64.

Hours: 8 a.m. to 5 p.m., Monday through Friday, Noon to 4 p.m., Saturday and Sunday (September-May).

HAMPTON UNIVERSITY MUSEUM
Hampton University
Hampton, Virginia 23668
(804) 727-5308

✏ **Remember**
that the purpose of a business letter should be clear and the message brief.

WRITING and MECHANICS: Business Letter **207**

A Business Letter

Read the list below. Match each label with the correct letter part. The first one is done for you.

151 Shepard Street
Ithaca, NY 14850
October 22 1991

1. Heading

Ed Howard
Bounce Sports Shoes
22 Park Avenue
Scottsdale, AZ 85254

2. Inside address

Dear Mr. Howard

3. Greeting

Please send me a list of your best running shoes
I want to win this year's local race

4. Body

Sincerely,
Lorraine Block

5. Closing

Lorraine Block

6. Signature

➥ A **business letter** has six parts: the heading, inside address, greeting, body, closing, and signature.

Label the parts of the business letter. Write heading, inside address, greeting, body, closing, signature.

EXAMPLE: *heading*
22 Wilson Avenue
Stamford, CT 06903
May 29, 1991

Mrs. Ellen Kiefer
Mountain Sports Equipment Company
83 Cornwall Street
Amherst, MA 01002
1. _____ *inside address*

Dear Mrs. Kiefer: 2. _____ *greeting*
Will you please send me your free booklet
"Hiking Safety Tips." My classmates and I hope 3. _____ *body*
to start a hiking club.

Sincerely, 4. _____ *closing*
Ron Evans 5. _____ *signature*
Ron Evans

PRACTICE 40

A Business Letter

➥ A **business letter** has six parts: the heading, inside address, greeting, body, closing, and signature.

A. Write two examples of a greeting and a closing. Use capital letters and punctuation marks correctly. Answers will vary. Possible answers follow.

1. Greeting _Dear Sir or Madam:_ 3. Closing _Sincerely,_

2. Closing _Yours truly,_ 4. Greeting _Dear Sir:_

B. Complete this business letter. Write each missing part in the correct place. Answers will vary. Possible answers follow.

135 New Road
Kent, WA 98032
November 15, 1991

Miss Gail Rogers
Flightways Freight Company
10 Foxdale Drive
Kent, WA 98032

Dear Ms. Rogers:

Will you please tell me _how much it would cost to have a bicycle_
sent from Kent to Orlando, Florida. Thank you for your help.

Sincerely,
Linda White
Linda White

WRITE IT
Write a short business letter to a company to say that you enjoyed a product you bought recently. Write on a separate sheet of paper. Answers will vary.

◀▥▥ TEACHING OPTIONS ▥▥▶

RETEACHING

A Different Modality Write on the chalkboard a business letter to an imaginary company that sends free magazines to schools, asking if it would put your school on its list. In a separate column list the names of the six parts of a business letter. As you read the letter aloud, ask students to identify each part from the list of letter parts on the chalkboard.

CLASS ENRICHMENT

A Cooperative Activity Have students work in small groups to choose a business they would all like to start. Have them name their business and then identify possible topics for business letters, such as ordering supplies and requesting prices. Have one student in each group serve as scribe as group members choose a topic and compose a business letter to another group. You may wish to have each group read aloud the letters they receive.

CHALLENGE

An Independent Extension Have students pretend they ordered a new watch that was guaranteed to last for ten years. Tell them that the watch stopped after one day, when they wore it in the shower. Tell them to request a replacement by writing to the XL Watch Company, 2 O'Clock Avenue, Timely, NY 00010.

Reading–Writing Connection

OBJECTIVES
To recognize words with positive connotations
To recognize words with negative connotations
To work together to use words with positive and negative connotations
To use the Thesaurus to improve word choice

Focus on Persuasive Words

Review the Unit 4 literature selection, *The Littlest Sculptor,* with students and have them describe the character of Vinnie. Students may say that even though Vinnie was young, she was able to use her power of persuasion to influence one of the most important men in history—Abraham Lincoln. Then point out to students that they can use the selection to help them learn how to use language with positive and negative connotations.

You may wish to guide students through the introductory paragraphs, stressing the first set of example sentences. Then have students read example sentences 1–4 on their own. Discuss how the wording in each pair of sentences differs. Note that these wording changes give the second sentence in each pair a negative feeling. Point out that the words Vinnie chose in sentences 1 and 3 convey the idea that she is an intelligent, confident person.

Next, have students apply the information in the Reading-Writing Connection by discussing the questions at the bottom of the page. As students talk about the questions, guide them to recognize that if Vinnie had used the words in sentences 2 and 4, President Lincoln probably would have had a very different impression of her. Because the words in sentences 2 and 4 are less descriptive and much less professional, Lincoln might have received a negative impression of Vinnie. This most likely would have led him to deny her permission to do a sculpture of him.

Focus on Persuasive Words

There will be times when you will want to persuade a person or a group of persons. When you want to persuade someone to agree with you, the words you choose are very important. Words that mean almost the same thing can cause quite different feelings in the listener or reader. Some words suggest pleasant feelings; other words suggest unpleasant feelings.

Here are some statements about "The Littlest Sculptor," which you read earlier in the unit. Compare the underlined words in each pair of sentences. These words mean basically the same thing in each sentence, but notice the different feelings they suggest.

1. Vinnie said that molding a <u>full-length</u> clay <u>figure</u> would not <u>tax</u> her <u>strength</u> at all.
2. Vinnie said that molding a <u>big</u> clay <u>dummy</u> would not <u>hurt</u> her <u>muscles</u> at all.
3. Although Lincoln would sometimes <u>smile</u> and <u>chuckle</u>, Vinnie wanted to portray his <u>sadness</u> and <u>concern</u>.
4. Although Lincoln would sometimes <u>smirk</u> and <u>chortle</u>, Vinnie wanted to portray his <u>misery</u> and <u>anxiety</u>.

You can see how the underlined words in sentences **2** and **4** affect meaning. A "big clay dummy" does not have the force and impressiveness of a "full-length clay figure." A man with a "smile and chuckle" tends to be likable, while a man with a "smirk and chortle" probably is not very likable.

The Writer's Voice ◆ Some words with basically the same meanings suggest different feelings. In each of the following groups of words, which word suggests the *best*, or *most favorable*, impression?

1. molder, carver, <u>sculptor</u>
2. boastful, <u>confident</u>, arrogant
3. smart, brainy, <u>intelligent</u>
4. <u>young</u>, childish, babyish

208 COOPERATIVE LEARNING: Writer's Craft

ESSENTIAL LANGUAGE SKILLS
This lesson provides opportunities to:

LISTENING ◆ employ active listening in a variety of situations

SPEAKING ◆ use a variety of words to express feelings and ideas ◆ use a set of reasons to persuade a group

READING ◆ understand content area vocabulary ◆ evaluate and make judgments ◆ follow a set of directions ◆ explain and relate to the feelings and emotions of characters

WRITING ◆ adapt information to accomplish a specific purpose with a particular audience ◆ participate in writing conferences

LANGUAGE ◆ use the fundamentals of grammar, punctuation, and spelling

Working Together

A writer needs to consider the effects of certain words on the reader when deciding which words to use. Keep this in mind as your group does activities **A** and **B**.

In Your Group

♦ Make sure group members understand the directions.

♦ Record the group's ideas.

♦ Show appreciation for others' ideas.

♦ Agree or disagree in a pleasant way.

A. Discuss these sentences about "The Littlest Sculptor." Pay special attention to the underlined words. Write each one on paper. Label the underlined word with a plus sign (+) if it suggests good feelings. Label it with a minus sign (−) if it does not.

1. Lincoln speaks in a deep, <u>gentle</u> voice that <u>calms</u> Vinnie.
2. His smile <u>fades</u> as he rubs his beard with <u>bony</u> fingers.
3. The war has <u>dragged</u> on for four years, with much <u>suffering</u>.
4. Lincoln, apparently <u>impressed</u>, shakes Vinnie's hand <u>warmly</u>.
5. The final days of the war were filled with <u>sorrow</u> and <u>turmoil</u>.

B. In "The Littlest Sculptor," Vinnie and President Lincoln get along well together. They use the right words with each other. Choose three or four of the direct quotations and suggest some different, *in*appropriate words that they might have used.

THESAURUS CORNER • Word Choice

The five words in dark type suggest the wrong feelings for the content of the paragraph. Rewrite the paragraph. Choose five words from the Thesaurus that are more appropriate. Use the Thesaurus Index when necessary. Change all *Vinnies* and *Lincolns* to pronouns after their first appearance.

Answers will vary.

Vinnie **interrogated** President Lincoln about doing a statue of Lincoln. Vinnie's teacher, Mr. Mills, had **exclaimed** that Vinnie was talented enough to **construct** a **pretty** statue. Although Vinnie was only seventeen, Vinnie **thought** that Vinnie could sculpt an excellent likeness of the President, one that would please Lincoln.

COOPERATIVE LEARNING: Writer's Craft **209**

Working Together

The Working Together activities provide opportunities for students to work together in cooperative learning groups. You may wish to pair strong writers with students whose skills are weaker so that all students may experience success in writing sentences with positive connotations.

Divide the class into small groups and have students read In Your Group. Encourage them to discuss why each task is important. Have them tell what might happen if the group does not follow through on each task. *(If we do not encourage everyone to contribute ideas, some members of the group may be reluctant to speak up. If we do not record ideas, we may forget important points that were discussed. If we argue and fail to reach an agreement, we will be unable to work together to complete the activity.)*

You may wish to have each group appoint a member to record the group's work. You also may wish to have students appoint a timekeeper. Then set a time limit. After students complete activity A, encourage groups to compare the lists they wrote and discuss why the words give a favorable or unfavorable impression. After activity B, call on a member of each group to read aloud the paragraph students created. Have the rest of the class listen to determine how the paragraph was changed.

Thesaurus Corner

The Thesaurus Corner provides students with the opportunity to extend the Reading-Writing Connection by using the Thesaurus in the back of the textbook. If necessary, remind them how a thesaurus is used. After students have written six sentences, call on individuals to read their sentences aloud. Encourage students to compare their sentences and tell why the synonyms convey a positive impression. Have students save their sentences for later use in the Writing Process lesson. Point out that learning about persuasive words can help students develop their ability to influence people in their writing and speaking.

UNIT 4

OBJECTIVES
To write a persuasive letter

To use five stages of the writing process: prewriting, writing, revising, proofreading, and publishing

RESOURCES
Writing Process Transparencies 13–16

Revising and Proofreading Transparencies

Spelling Connection

Writing Sample Tests, p. T553

INTRODUCTION

Connecting to Literature Have students read the lesson introduction, or ask a volunteer to read the introduction aloud. Explain that in the literature selection, *The Littlest Sculptor,* Vinnie Ream used persuasion to help her achieve her goals. Then have students tell what Vinnie did to persuade Lincoln to let her sculpt him. (She told him she would sculpt him in a creditable manner. She stressed her strength to show him she was able to do the job. She suggested a way she could sculpt the president while he worked.) Tell students they will be writing their own persuasive letter.

Purpose and Audience Ask students to tell about times they have used persuasion to achieve their goals. Have them tell about times they wrote in a persuasive way or spoke in a persuasive manner. (Point out that students speak in a persuasive way whenever they try to change the mind of someone else. They may have written persuasively in letters or in their journals.)

Have students consider the questions: *What is my purpose?* (To write persuasively on a topic I care about) *Who is my audience?* (The person to whom I choose to write) Have students discuss what they believe they need to consider when trying to persuade a person in writing. Encourage a diversity of responses.

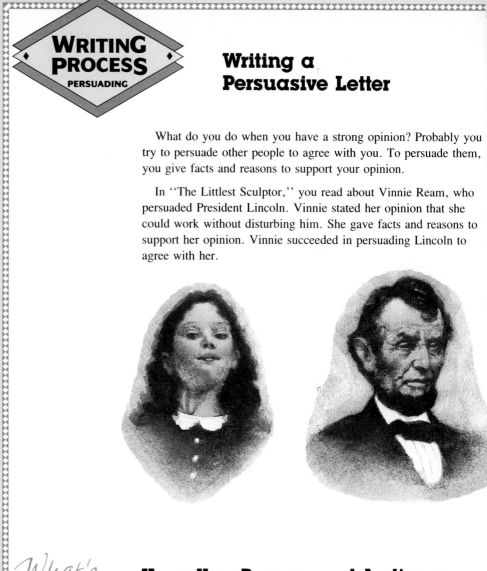

WRITING PROCESS
PERSUADING

Writing a Persuasive Letter

What do you do when you have a strong opinion? Probably you try to persuade other people to agree with you. To persuade them, you give facts and reasons to support your opinion.

In "The Littlest Sculptor," you read about Vinnie Ream, who persuaded President Lincoln. Vinnie stated her opinion that she could work without disturbing him. She gave facts and reasons to support her opinion. Vinnie succeeded in persuading Lincoln to agree with her.

What's
MY PURPOSE

Who's
MY AUDIENCE

Know Your Purpose and Audience

In this lesson you will write a letter. Your purpose will be to write persuasively on a topic that you care about.

Your audience will be the person you choose to write to. Later, you can mail or deliver your letter. You and your classmates might also produce a radio show to share your opinions.

210   WRITING PROCESS: Persuasive Letter

ESSENTIAL LANGUAGE SKILLS
This lesson provides opportunities to:

LISTENING ◆ listen for specific information ◆ follow the logical organization of an oral presentation ◆ employ active listening in a variety of situations

SPEAKING ◆ read aloud a variety of written materials ◆ participate in group discussions ◆ use a set of reasons to persuade a group

READING ◆ recall specific facts and ideas that support a main idea ◆ read for specific details or information ◆ draw logical conclusions ◆ follow a set of directions

WRITING ◆ select and narrow a topic for a specific purpose ◆ generate ideas using a variety of strategies, such as brainstorming, clustering, free writing ◆ identify audience and purpose ◆ improve writing based on peer and/or teacher response

LANGUAGE ◆ use language for persuading ◆ use correct agreement between pronouns and antecedents ◆ recognize ways in which language can be used to influence others

Prewriting

First you will need to choose a topic. Then you will want to gather ideas about your topic.

Choose Your Topic ♦ Perhaps you would like to have more books in the library. Maybe you feel your town needs a leash law for dogs. Make a list of topics, then circle your favorite.

Think About It	Talk About It
Look at your list. Which do you feel most strongly about? Which do you know most about? Cross out your least favorite, then pick one. Now decide whom you would like to persuade. It might be your principal or the mayor. Write that person's name.	Work with a small group of classmates. Discuss improvements that you think can be made in your school or community. Brainstorm a list of possible topics. You will get ideas from the class list.

Topic Ideas

we need more books in the library
~~we need a leash law~~
our park needs new flowers
people should not litter

WRITING PROCESS: Persuasive Letter ◆ 211 ◆

---

1. PREWRITING

Guide students through the explanation of Prewriting, pointing out that Prewriting is the stage in which writers gather ideas for writing.

MODELING THE WRITING PROCESS

If you feel students need instruction before they begin, you may wish to model this stage of the process. Tell students you want to find a topic for a persuasive letter. Have students help you work through the thinking process. Have them help you name a variety of things in school or in the community that need improvement. Write four or five suggestions on the chalkboard or use *Writing Process Transparency 13*. Then have students help you decide how each thing can be improved. Add the ideas for improvement to the transparency.

Let students hear how you might go about selecting the best topic to write about in a persuasive letter. As you speak, encourage students to help you choose. At the conclusion of the discussion, circle the topic that emerges as the favorite. (Possible discussion: I'm very interested in the band since I play in it. I think it is important to the school that the band look nice. The corner stop sign should be replaced, but the corner really isn't that dangerous. Maybe a stoplight isn't necessary.)

Writing Process Transparency 13*

Improving Our School and Our Community

Needs to Be Improved:	How to Improve It:
1. band uniforms	buy new band uniforms to replace old ones
2. corner stop sign	replace it with a stoplight
3. park	add a swimming pool for all to enjoy
4. school buses	add more buses, newer and better buses

Pacing

A five-day pacing guide follows, but the writing process can take longer if students want to spend several days on prewriting, revising, or preparing for publishing.

Day 1—Prewriting   Day 3—Revising
Day 2—Writing   Day 4—Proofreading
      Day 5—Publishing

Evaluation

Process Check questions at the end of each stage of the writing process help you to keep track of students' progress.

Holistic Evaluation Guidelines may be found in the teaching notes on page 217. They offer criteria for average, above-average, and below-average compositions.

Possible responses are overprinted on this reduced fac-simile only. Use Writing Process Transparencies *to inter-act with your students on the ideas that interest them.*

WRITING PROCESS

Choose Your Strategy Before inviting students to choose a prewriting strategy that will help them gather information for their persuasive letters, guide them through the explanations of both strategies. Then have students choose a strategy they feel will help them get started. Many students will benefit from using both strategies.

As a variation on the second strategy, you may wish to have students trade thought balloons with partners. Have partners think of ways to answer the concerns expressed in each other's thought balloons.

You may wish to remind students that they have learned about a Thought Balloon as a strategy for understanding point of view in the Creative Thinking lesson on pages 194–195.

IDEA BANK

Prewriting Ideas

Always encourage young writers to try new ways to discover ideas they want to write about. Reassure them, though, that it is appropriate to use the strategies that work best for them. You may wish to remind them of the prewriting ideas already introduced in their textbooks:

- A Conversation, p. 40
- An Observation Chart, p. 40
- An Order Circle, p. 96
- A Clock Graph, p. 96
- A Comic Strip, p. 156
- Answering "What If?," p. 156
- An Opinion Ladder, p. 212
- A Thought Balloon, p. 212

Choose Your Strategy ◆ Here are two strategies for gathering ideas. Read both. Then use the strategy you think will be more helpful in planning your letter.

PREWRITING IDEAS

CHOICE ONE

An Opinion Ladder

A good persuasive strategy is to save your most important fact or reason for last. Make an "opinion ladder." Write your opinion at the bottom. Write your supporting arguments in reverse order of importance. Put the least important at the bottom, the most important at the top.

Model

4. Unleashed dogs cause accidents.

3. Many dogs get hit by cars.

2. Too many dogs get lost.

1. Dogs can harm neighbors' lawns.

My opinion: We need a leash law.

CHOICE TWO

A Thought Balloon

In order to persuade someone, it helps if you understand his or her point of view. Make a thought balloon for the person you are writing to. In it, write what you believe that person thinks about your topic.

Then think of ways to answer these concerns. For example, "Three families on our block have complained about stray dogs." or "People would obey the leash law if they knew that the law can protect their dogs as well as themselves."

Model

Most dogs don't bother anyone. People would not obey a leash law.

Mayor Steiner

PROCESS CHECK At the completion of the Prewriting stage, students should be able to answer *yes* to these questions:
- Do I have a topic I like for a persuasive letter?
- Do I have an opinion ladder or a thought balloon that expresses my opinion about the topic?

Teacher to Teacher

Establish procedures that will help make the writing process comfortable and familiar to your students. Create regular writing times and make sure that students have the materials they need for writing, revising, proofreading, and publishing. Make preliminary mini-lessons a part of each session. Encourage students to use their journals to record writing topics, notes, and words they wish to learn. Keep individual folders for students' finished work.

Writing

Look over your opinion ladder or your thought balloon. Then begin to write your persuasive letter. Begin with a topic sentence that lets your reader know your opinion. Here are some ways to begin.

- I believe that _____.
- It is my opinion that _____.

Add facts and reasons that support your opinion. Include persuasive words and polite language. When you have finished the body, add the other parts of a business letter. Add a heading, an inside address, a greeting, a closing, and your signature. As you write, don't worry about errors. You can fix them later.

Sample First Draft ◆

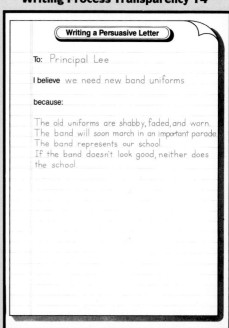

Dear Mayor Steiner:
Unleashed dogs often run away from their owners and get lost. Dogs dash into bisy streets. They get hit by cars. I believe our city should have a leash law. Some dogs scare bike riders and cause serious acidents. You have said that people would not obey a leash law. I believe they would.
Im sure youll agree that our City wants a leash law.

respectfully,

Roberto Gomez

---

2. WRITING

Before students write their first drafts, guide them through the explanation of Writing, emphasizing that at this stage the most important task is to get all their ideas on paper.

Help students use persuasive words to add valid facts and convincing reasons to support the opinions expressed in their letters.

MODELING THE WRITING PROCESS

If you feel students need instruction before they begin this stage of the process, you may wish to ask them to think about the topic that was circled on *Writing Process Transparency 13*. Write that topic on the chalkboard or on *Writing Process Transparency 14*. Help students cite reasons and facts to support what they believe about that topic. Record those suggestions. Then have students suggest a person to whom they might write about their topic. Add that person's name to the chart. Ask students to review the facts and reasons you recorded and decide which one is the most important. Mark it with an *X*.

Writing Process Transparency 14*

Writing a Persuasive Letter

To: Principal Lee

I believe we need new band uniforms

because:

The old uniforms are shabby, faded, and worn.
The band will soon march in an important parade.
The band represents our school.
If the band doesn't look good, neither does the school.

PROCESS CHECK At the completion of the Writing stage, students should be able to answer *yes* to these questions:
- Do I have a complete first draft?
- Is my draft written in the form of a business letter?
- Did I give facts and reasons for the opinions I expressed?

Possible responses are overprinted on this reduced fac-simile only. Use Writing Process Transparencies to inter-act with your students on the ideas that interest them.

3. REVISING

Help students understand that during Revising writers make their drafts communicate ideas more clearly and effectively to an audience.

I D E A   B A N K

Grammar Connection

You may wish to remind students of the Grammar Checks already introduced in their textbooks:
- Use a variety of sentence types, p. 43
- Use exact nouns, p. 99
- Use vivid verbs, p. 157
- Replace nouns with pronouns, p. 215

Option 1 ◆ If you wish to begin grammar instruction related to the Grammar Check in this lesson, then refer to Part 1 of this unit.

Option 2 ◆ If you wish to begin grammar instruction *not* related to the Grammar Check in this lesson, then refer to the end-of-book Glossary or Index.

First Read to Yourself Remind students to check to make sure that they have used the most persuasive words they can think of. Have them ask themselves: *Would this letter persuade me if I were the person who received it?*

Then Share with a Partner Suggest that writers' partners offer three responses, at least one positive, and that they accompany any critical responses with suggestions for improvement. Be sure writers ask the Focus question: *What is a more persuasive word for _____?*

Remind students to be considerate of their classmate's feelings when expressing criticism. Then explain to writers that they should use their partners' suggestions only if they feel the suggestions will help improve their writing.

---

3 Revising

Now that you have written your letter, you may want to improve it. Here is an idea for revising that may help you.

REVISING IDEA

FIRST   Read to Yourself

Review your purpose. Have you written a persuasive letter? Consider your audience. Will they understand your opinion and supporting arguments? Will they be persuaded to agree with you?

Focus: Have you used the most persuasive words you can think of? Circle any words you may want to change.

THEN   Share with a Partner

Ask a partner to pretend to be the person receiving your letter. Ask him or her to read the letter silently. How does your partner react to the letter? Below are some guidelines that may help you both.

The Writer

Guidelines: Listen to your partner's comments. Then make the changes you think are important.

Sample questions:
- Did I persuade you? Why or why not?
- Are there other facts or reasons I should include?
- **Focus question:** What is a more persuasive word for _____?

The Writer's Partner

Guidelines: Say what you really think, but say it politely.

Sample responses:
- I still don't agree that _____.
- Another argument may be _____.
- A persuasive word you might use is _____.

Teacher to Teacher

Take five minutes at the beginning of each writing session to present a quick mini-lesson on some aspect of the writing process. Topics for the mini-lessons may arise in the course of conferences or from reviewing students' finished work. Examples of topics are writing dialogue, using similes and metaphors, and correct end punctuation. Discuss just one concept in each mini-lesson. Mini-lessons allow you to address the needs of individuals and small groups, as well as general problems.

WRITING AS A RECURSIVE PROCESS

Connecting Grammar to the Writing Process

Writing is a recursive process. In other words, good writers will often go back and forth among steps. Depending on the individual styles of your students, some may choose to correct grammar at Step Three, Revising; others may prefer to fix grammar or usage errors at Step Four, Proofreading. Ideally, this should be a decision made by the writer. Remind students, however, that once they have completed their proofreading, all the grammar errors should be corrected.

Revising Model ♦ Here is a persuasive letter that is being revised. The revising marks show the writer's changes.

Revising Marks

cross out ——
add ∧
move ⟋

The pronoun *they* replaced the repeated noun *dogs*.

The writer wanted to put the topic sentence first.

The writer added this detail to answer the mayor's concern.

The writer's partner suggested that *needs* is a more persuasive word than *wants*.

Dear Mayor Steiner:

~Unleashed dogs often run away from their owners and get lost. ~~Dogs~~ *They* dash into bisy streets. They get hit by cars. (I believe our city should have a leash law.) Some dogs scare bike riders and cause serious acidents. You have said that people would not obey a leash law. I believe they would. *if they knew that the law would protect their dogs.*

Im sure youll agree that our ~~City~~ wants a *needs* leash law.

respectfully,

Roberto Gomez

Roberto Gomez

Read the letter above as the writer has decided it *should* be. Then revise your own persuasive letter.

Grammar Check ♦ Replacing some nouns with pronouns can make your writing less repetitive.

Word Choice ♦ Do you want a more persuasive word for a word like *wants*? A thesaurus can help you find these words.

Revising Checklist

☐ **Purpose:** Did I write a persuasive letter?

☐ **Audience:** Will my reasons persuade the person I wrote to?

☐ **Focus:** Did I use persuasive words?

Revising Model Guide students through the model, noting the reasons for changes and the revision marks. Point out to students that on the model the revising marks are in blue. Encourage the class to discuss the changes in the model. Ask them to consider whether or not the changes made the writing clearer and more persuasive.

MODELING THE WRITING PROCESS

If you feel students need instruction before they begin this stage of the process, you may wish to present *Writing Process Transparency 15*. Have students read the draft silently, or have a volunteer read it aloud. Then ask students whether there is anything that needs to be changed. Work through the thinking process to help students give reasons for the changes. Then have them tell you how to mark the changes on the draft. (Students might suggest putting the topic sentence first, adding words such as *want to consider* to make the letter more persuasive, using the pronoun *they* to make writing less repetitive, and adding facts and reasons to respond to the principal's concerns.) Remind students that at this time they are revising for meaning. They will correct spelling and punctuation later when they proofread.

Writing Process Transparency 15*

┌──────────────────────────────┐

A Better-Looking Band

dear Principal Lee:

They
~~The old uniforms~~ are shabby. The old uniforms are

faded and worn. (I believe we need new band uniforms.)

Soon the band will march in an improtant parade. You
I don't believe that is true.
say people won't care about the uniforms. The band

represents our school. If the Band doesn't look good,
want to consider
niether does the school. I'm sure you'll ~~probably think~~

about new uniforms for the band.

respecfully,

Marsha Riggs

└──────────────────────────────┘

PROCESS CHECK At the completion of the Revising stage, students should be able to answer *yes* to the following questions:
- Do I have a complete draft with revising marks that show changes I plan to make?
- Has my draft been reviewed by another writer?

Possible responses are overprinted on this reduced fac-simile only. Use Writing Process Transparencies *to interact with your students on the ideas that interest them.*

4. PROOFREADING

Guide students through the explanation of proofreading and review the Proofreading Model. Point out to students that on the model the proofreading marks are in red. Tell them that proofreading helps to eliminate errors such as incorrect spelling or run-on sentences that may distract or confuse their readers.

Review the Proofreading Strategy, Proofreading Marks, and the Proofreading Checklist with students. Then invite students to use the checklist and proofread their own persuasive letters.

MODELING THE WRITING PROCESS

If you feel students need instruction before they begin this stage of the process, you may wish to use *Writing Process Transparency 16*. Divide the class into two groups. Have one group go through the transparency to look for spelling errors. Have the other group look for errors in punctuation. Have students in each group discuss their findings in class.

Point out that in order for the letter to be correct, it must include a date, a return address, and the address to which the letter is being sent. On the transparency, copy the date and addresses shown below in red. Omit the commas. Have volunteers tell where commas should be placed.

Writing Process Transparency 16*

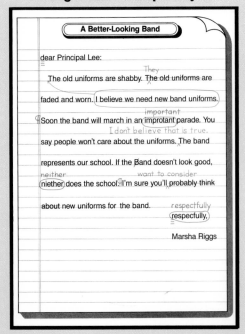

---

4 Proofreading

Proofread your letter to find spelling, capitalization, and punctuation errors. A correct letter will be more persuasive.

Proofreading Model ♦ Here is the sample letter to the mayor. Notice that red proofreading marks have now been added.

Proofreading Marks

capital letter	=
small letter	/
indent paragraph	¶
check spelling	⬭

Dear Mayor Steiner:

Unleashed dogs often run away from their owners and get lost. Dogs dash into busy streets. They get hit by cars. I believe our city should have a leash law. Some dogs scare bike riders and cause serious accidents. You have said that people would not obey a leash law. I believe they would. If they knew that the law would protect their dogs.

I'm sure you'll agree that our City needs a leash law.

respectfully,

Roberto Gomez

Roberto Gomez

Proofreading Checklist

☐ Did I spell words correctly?

☐ Did I indent paragraphs?

☐ Did I use capital letters correctly?

☐ Did I use correct marks at the end of sentences?

☐ Did I use my best handwriting?

PROOFREADING IDEA

One Thing at a Time

When you are looking for more than one kind of error, you may miss mistakes. Pay attention to just one thing at a time. Read your paper once for spelling errors. Read it again for capitalization and punctuation.

Now proofread your persuasive letter. Check the heading, greeting, closing, and signature. Be sure to put commas and capital letters in the right places. Then make a neat copy.

PROCESS CHECK At the completion of the Proofreading stage, students should be able to answer *yes* to the following questions:
- Do I have a complete draft with proofreading marks that show changes I plan to make?
- Have I used the proofreading marks shown in the lesson?

EVALUATION PROGRAM

See Evaluation and Testing Program, pp. C1–C8.

Masters are available for the following:
- **Self Evaluation Checklist**
- **Personal Goals for Writing**
- **Peer Response**
- **Teacher Response**

- **Holistic Evaluation Guides**
- **Analytic Evaluation Guides**

Possible responses are overprinted on this reduced facsimile only. Use Writing Process Transparencies to interact with your students on the ideas that interest them.

Publishing

Now it's time to share your persuasive letter. Try one of the ideas below.

26 Clearview Lane
Safety Harbor, FL 33572
June 23, 1991

ayor Mildred Steiner
) City Hall Plaza
afety Harbor, FL 33572

ear Mayor Steiner:
I believe our city should have a leash law.
nleashed dogs often run away from their
wners and get lost. They dash into busy
streets. They get hit by cars. Some dogs scare
ike riders and cause serious accidents.

You have said that people would not obey
a leash law. I believe they would if they knew
that the law would protect their dogs.

I'm sure you'll agree that our city needs a
leash law.

Respectfully,

Roberto Gomez

Roberto Gomez

PUBLISHING IDEAS

Share Aloud	Share in Writing
Produce a radio talk show. Take turns being the host. Have guests read their letters "over the air." Encourage listeners to "call in" to agree or disagree.	Mail or deliver your letter. Be sure to address the envelope correctly. Perhaps you will get a letter back!

WRITING PROCESS: Persuasive Letter 217

Holistic Evaluation Guidelines

A persuasive letter of **average** quality will:
1. present a topic persuasively, supported by facts and reasons
2. express the opinion(s) of the writer

A persuasive letter of **above-average** quality may:
1. use persuasive language skillfully
2. present an opinion in an unusual way

A persuasive letter of **below-average** quality may:
1. present opinions that are not supported by facts and reasons
2. depart from the form of a business letter

PROCESS CHECK At the completion of the Publishing stage, students should be able to answer *yes* to these questions:
• Have I shared my writing with an audience?
• Have readers shared reactions with me?
• Have I thought about what I especially liked in this writing? Or about what was particularly difficult?
• Have I thought about what I would like to work on the next time I write?

Encourage students to keep a log or journal of their own and their readers' reactions.

5. PUBLISHING

Oral Sharing If students choose to share their writing orally in a radio talk show format, invite class discussion after each "host" has presented two or three of the letters. Encourage listeners to "call in" constructive comments. You may wish to "poll" the students after all the letters have been read, awarding one letter the title of "most persuasive."

Written Sharing If some students choose to share their writing by mailing it, help them address an envelope to the recipient of their letter. Encourage students who plan to hand-deliver their letter also to address an envelope to the recipient. Then before the letters are mailed or delivered, provide time during class for students to read each other's letters and respond to them.

Curriculum Connection

OBJECTIVES
To practice a thinking strategy for writing across the curriculum
To write a journal entry

Writing Across the Curriculum

Explain to students that writers often make their story characters come alive by describing how a person thinks and feels. Tell students they will use thought balloons to help them imagine others' points of view and write a description of what it might feel like to emigrate to another country.

You may wish to remind students that they have used thought balloons as a strategy for persuading in the Creative Thinking lesson, in their response to the literature selection, and in the Writing Process lesson.

Writing to Learn

To help students get started, have them suggest some of the emigrants' thoughts and fears. Write them on the chalkboard.

You may wish to have students with limited English proficiency describe how they think emigrants feel and provide the English adjectives.

Help students use their social studies books or books from their classroom library to find information about emigrants and immigrants from and to this country.

Writing in Your Journal

When they have finished writing, have students read their earlier journal entries. Encourage them to discuss what they have learned about the theme and to observe how their writing has changed or improved.

Remind students that their journals have many purposes. Besides paragraphs and stories, they can write questions, story ideas, or thoughts and reflections on a subject. Suggest to them that entries in their journals may provide ideas for later writing.

218

Writing Across the Curriculum

Social Studies

During this unit you read about Vinnie Ream. Her sculpture of President Lincoln shows the sadness he felt for his war-torn country. The paintings and photographs in social studies texts can enrich your study of history. Look carefully. You can often imagine the thoughts and feelings of the people they show.

Writing to Learn

Think and Imagine ◆ Look at the picture below. It shows people who have left their homeland to come to America. Write a thought balloon for one of the people in the picture.

Thought Balloon

Write ◆ Think about the picture and your thought balloon. Write about what it might feel like to emigrate to another country.

Writing in Your Journal

In the Writer's Warm-up you wrote about the visual arts. Throughout the unit you saw how the arts can help us remember people. Someday, a photograph, portrait, or other form of art might help people remember *you*. In your journal describe how you would like to be remembered.

218 Curriculum Connection

ESSENTIAL LANGUAGE SKILLS
This lesson provides opportunities to:

LISTENING ◆ listen actively and attentively ◆ follow the logical organization of an oral presentation

SPEAKING ◆ participate in group discussions ◆ make organized oral presentations

READING ◆ respond to various forms of literature ◆ become acquainted with a variety of selections, characters, and themes of our literary heritage ◆ select books for individual needs and interests ◆ explain and relate to the feelings and emotions of characters

WRITING ◆ select and narrow a topic for a specific purpose ◆ expand topics by collecting information from a variety of sources ◆ adapt information to accomplish a specific purpose with a particular audience ◆ keep journals, logs, or notebooks to express feelings, record ideas, discover new knowledge, and free the imagination

LANGUAGE ◆ use language to imagine ◆ recognize ways in which language can be used to influence others

BOOKS TO ENJOY

Read More About It

Dorothea Lange: Life Through the Camera
by Milton Meltzer
Dorothea Lange (1895–1965) worked very hard to become a professional photographer. She used her camera to capture scenes of American life. Read this biography of a pioneering artist.

Snap! *by Miriam Cooper*
You can be a photographer, too. All you need to begin is a camera, some film, and the desire to take pictures. This book will help you understand how cameras work and how to plan good pictures.

Book Report Idea Model a Book

Visual book reports can persuade readers to try a new book. The next time you share a book, choose a character or object that represents the book you have read. Make a simple sculpture or model of it.

Create a Sculpture ◆ Use
clay, plaster, wire, papier-mâché, or any other sculpting material you like to use. Create a model or sculpture of a main character or important idea that represents your book. When your model is finished, write a brief book report on a card. Place the card next to your model for display.

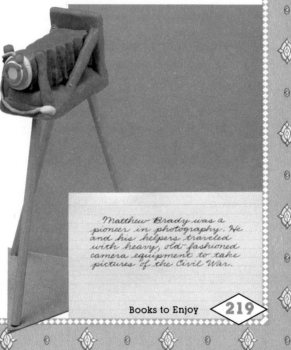

Matthew Brady was a pioneer in photography. He and his helpers traveled with heavy, old-fashioned camera equipment to take pictures of the Civil War.

Books to Enjoy ◄ 219

OBJECTIVES
To appreciate a variety of literature
To share a book through a creative activity

Read More About It

Call students' attention to Read More About It and discuss theme-related books. Point out that the books listed here contain stories about the visual arts and the use of fine arts to communicate. Encourage students to mention other titles that deal with these topics. Encourage students to examine pictures and jacket illustrations of books in the classroom to find books they will enjoy reading.

Book Report Idea

You may wish to have students use the book report form provided in the back of their textbooks. Book Report Idea presents a lively alternative way for interested students to share books they have read.

You may wish to share the reports with the class or in small groups. Have students display their sculptures for classmates to guess about characters and events before reading the index cards about each book. Display the sculptures and index cards in a book review corner.

Integrated Language Arts Project

The **Integrated Language Arts Project** on pages T518–T519 may be used with this unit.

REVIEW OR TEST
You may wish to use the Unit Review as
a review of the unit skills before administering the Unit Posttest, or you may
wish to use the Unit Review in lieu of
the Unit Posttest.

REVIEW PROCEDURES
The lesson pages that are reviewed are
listed beside the heading of each segment. You may wish to choose one of
the procedures listed below for using
the pages with the Unit Review
exercises.

Review/Evaluate Have students restudy the lesson pages before doing
the Unit Review exercises.

Open-Book Review Allow students
to refer to the lesson pages if they
need to while they are doing the Unit
Review exercises.

Evaluate/Review Have students do
the Unit Review exercises, then turn to
the lesson pages to restudy concepts
for which incorrect responses are
given.

ADDITIONAL REVIEW AND PRACTICE
For additional review and practice,
turn to the Extra Practice pages at the
end of the unit.

UNIT REVIEW

Unit 4

Pronouns *pages 176–185*

A. Write the pronoun in each sentence.
Then write whether it is a *subject pronoun*
or an *object pronoun*.

1. Sandy and I like Chinese food. *subject*
2. Bill told her about a new restaurant called Hunan Village. *object*
3. It is located on Mott Street. *subject*
4. We ate there last night. *subject*
5. They make a delicious dish of asparagus and beef. *subject*
6. The chef cooks it with seven spices. *object*
7. He prepares many terrific dishes. *subject*
8. Sandy wants to try them all! *object*
9. Andrea told us about a fine Indian restaurant. *object*
10. Last week we had dinner there. *subject*
11. You ought to try the restaurant. *subject*
12. Sandy spoke with the waiter and gave him a good tip. *object*
13. She recommends the restaurant. *subject*
14. Tell me about Mexican food. *object*
15. It uses many spices, right? *subject*
16. Connie gave me a recipe for Mexican-style chicken. *object*
17. Grandma cooked it with two different kinds of chili peppers. *object*
18. We enjoyed the delicious chicken. *subject*
19. I soon became very thirsty. *subject*
20. Connie would be happy to give you the recipe. *object*

B. Write each sentence. Use the pronoun
in parentheses ( ) that correctly completes
the sentence.

21. Will you lend me (your, yours) record album?
22. I accidently broke (my, mine).
23. (Her, Hers) is one of the best voices I have heard.
24. (My, Mine) sister likes many rock singers.
25. Come to (my, mine) house this afternoon.
26. We will play one of (her, hers) records.
27. That group blends (their, theirs) voices beautifully.
28. (Their, Theirs) is a difficult type of singing.
29. (They, Them) do it very well.
30. There is always music in (our, ours) home.
31. Few families are more musical than (our, ours).
32. (My, Mine) mother loves to sing.
33. We often sing along with (her, hers) after dinner.
34. (My, Mine) oldest brother plays in a jazz band.
35. He works hard at (him, his) music.
36. Will you tell me about (your, yours) musical talents?
37. What about that sister of (your, yours) who plays the trumpet?
38. Beth told me about (her, hers) uncle Stanley.
39. We saw (him, his) play a concert in our town.
40. (Him, His) dream is to appear at Carnegie Hall some day.

Unit 4

Contractions *pages 186–187*

C. Write the contraction for each pair of words.

41. we are — we're
42. I am — I'm
43. she is — she's
44. you will — you'll
45. they had — they'd
46. you are — you're
47. we will — we'll
48. it is — it's
49. I have — I've
50. they have — they've
51. he will — he'll
52. it has — it's
53. he would — he'd
54. she had — she'd
55. I will — I'll
56. we had — we'd
57. you have — you've
58. they are — they're

Homophones *pages 188–189*

D. Write the sentences. Use the homophones in parentheses ( ) that correctly complete the sentences.

59. (Its, <u>It's</u>) a beautiful day down by the (<u>sea</u>, see) today.
60. (<u>Would</u>, Wood) you like to (sale, <u>sail</u>) my boat with me?
61. (Meat, <u>Meet</u>) me on the dock at (ate, <u>eight</u>) o'clock.
62. You might (knot, <u>not</u>) have time (<u>to</u>, too) eat breakfast.
63. I have saved a delicious golden (pair, <u>pear</u>) (four, <u>for</u>) you.
64. I (<u>ate</u>, eight) (<u>two</u>, too) of these juicy fruits earlier.
65. (Their, <u>They're</u>) perfectly ripe, and I got them on (sail, <u>sale</u>)!
66. Did you (<u>know</u>, no) (hour, <u>our</u>) uncle Leonard?
67. He always (war, <u>wore</u>) a (blew, <u>blue</u>) fishing cap.
68. (Won, <u>One</u>) day it (<u>blew</u>, blue) away and landed on a fish's head!

Fact and Opinion *pages 202–203*

E. Write *fact* or *opinion* for each of the following statements.

69. John Adams was the second president of the United States. fact
70. John Quincy Adams was the son of John Adams. fact
71. John Quincy Adams was not as good a president as his father was. opinioin
72. The Declaration of Independence was written in 1776. fact
73. Mathematics is an easy subject. opinion
74. Jupiter is the largest planet in the solar system. fact
75. *Heidi* is a wonderful movie. opinion
76. My mother is certainly a brilliant lawyer. opinion
77. Not all snakes are poisonous. fact
78. That brand of soap isn't very good. opinion
79. Austin is the capital of Texas. fact

F. Write an opinion that goes with each fact below. Answers will vary.

80. Blueberries grow on bushes.
81. Nearly all birds can fly.
82. New York is a very large city.
83. A baseball field has four bases.

Business Letters *pages 206–207*

G. Write the following items as if they were parts of business letters. Capitalize and punctuate them correctly.

84. dear madam:
85. yours truly,
86. dear ms.coe :
87. sincerely,
88. sirs :
89. atlanta ga 30305
90. dear sir or madam:
91. 425 willow avenue
92. may 31,1990
93. fran's fruit mart

Cumulative Review

CUMULATIVE REVIEW
The Cumulative Review reviews basic skills from the first through the present unit. The lesson pages that are reviewed are listed beside the heading for each segment. You may wish to have students restudy the lesson pages listed before assigning the Cumulative Review exercises.

ADDITIONAL REVIEW AND PRACTICE
For additional review and practice of skills, you may wish to assign the appropriate Extra Practice pages found at the end of each unit.

CUMULATIVE REVIEW

UNIT 1: Sentences *page 6–15*

A. Write the declarative, interrogative, imperative, and exclamatory sentences. Begin each sentence correctly. Use correct punctuation at the end.

1. what a beautiful sunset!
2. a lone bird flew high in the sky.
3. can you see the distant mountains from here?
4. hand me the binoculars.
5. will you go with me to the museum?
6. the special showing of the film ends tomorrow.
7. how slow you are!
8. is your sister ready to go yet?
9. the sun sets early in January.
10. did Bobbie bring the picnic basket?
11. my mother's hobby is archery.
12. she has won many contests.
13. watch the wren feed its young.
14. how funny it is!
15. turn up the electric fan.
16. have you done your chores for today?
17. her cousin is my best friend.
18. come over here.
19. shall we join the others now?
20. his brother plays for a professional basketball team.
21. what a great story this is!
22. please set the table.
23. where did I leave my jacket?
24. look out below!
25. the lazy cat snoozed on the couch

B. Write each sentence. Underline the complete subject once. Underline the complete predicate twice.

26. I can do a triple somersault.
27. The timid kitten stayed close to its mother.
28. That blue ceramic bowl was made by my mother.
29. Thousands of tiny ants crawled on the sand.
30. The girl in the front seat of the car hummed a tune.
31. An owl in the huge oak tree hooted.
32. Ms. Ryan is a karate expert.
33. The White House is the home of our President.
34. My father's brother is my uncle.
35. A pile of dirty dishes was stacked in the sink.
36. We just missed the bus.
37. Sam is learning to speak Spanish.
38. The runners in the race grew tired.
39. Gloria plays the piano beautifully.
40. Ned's least favorite food is liver.

C. Write the simple subject of each sentence. Write (*You*) if the subject is understood.

41. Mary is my cousin.
42. Bring your record with you. (You)
43. The frightened squirrel fled.
44. Take a picture of our team. (You)
45. A huge blizzard is heading our way.
46. Lend me your field glasses. (You)
47. Send the package by express mail. (You)
48. The herd of elephants stampeded.
49. Watch my bike for me. (You)
50. The man in that car is my father.

222 CUMULATIVE REVIEW: Units 1–4

222

D. Write the simple predicate of each of the following sentences.

51. I <u>am writing</u> my essay for American history.
52. Mrs. Diaz <u>has returned</u> from her trip to Mexico.
53. The moon <u>hid</u> behind a cloud.
54. Roger <u>will sing</u> at the music festival.
55. The girls <u>have learned</u> their lines for the school play.
56. The wind <u>blew</u> through the trees.
57. The little man <u>was whistling</u> an old tune.
58. Two cats <u>are howling</u> outside my bedroom window.
59. The small black horse <u>had outrun</u> its rivals.
60. We <u>will harvest</u> the corn crop soon.

Unit 2: Nouns   *pages 60–65*

E. Write the plural form of each noun.

61. horse — horses
62. chicken — chickens
63. story — stories
64. turkey — turkeys
65. box — boxes
66. mouse — mice
67. moose — moose
68. bench — benches
69. shelf — shelves
70. radish — radishes

F. Write *common* or *proper* for each of the following nouns.

71. city — common
72. Dallas — proper
73. museum — common
74. Dr. Woods — proper
75. doctor — common
76. water buffalo — common
77. Broadway — proper
78. South Carolina — proper
79. spaceship — common
80. Amazon River — proper

Unit 2: Capital Letters and Periods   *pages 66–69*

G. Write each sentence. Capitalize the proper nouns.

81. My family visited relatives in new orleans, louisiana. (N O L R)
82. The mississippi river flows through this city. (M R)
83. We toured the site of the battle of new orleans. (B N O)
84. General andrew jackson defeated the british there in 1815. (A J B)
85. My mother and I visited the delgado museum of art. (D M A)
86. My aunt lives on tulane avenue. (T A)
87. We listened to a lively jazz band at preservation hall. (P H)

H. Write the sentences. Abbreviate the underlined words.

88. Will you meet me on Pelham <u>Avenue</u>? (Ave.)
89. That car belongs to <u>Doctor</u> Simpson. (Dr.)
90. It snowed on <u>Tuesday</u> morning. (Tues.)
91. Grand <u>Drive</u> is a one-way street. (Dr.)
92. Alan Thomas, <u>Senior</u>, is my father. (Sr.)

Unit 2: Apostrophes   *pages 70–71*

I. Write the possessive form of each noun.

93. tree — tree's
94. mice — mice's
95. Ms. Peters — Ms. Peters's
96. children — children's
97. schools — schools'
98. men — men's
99. citizens — citizens'
100. dragon — dragon's
101. princess — princess's
102. buses — buses'

Cumulative Review

UNIT 3: Verbs *pages 116–133*

J. Write the verb from each sentence. Then write whether it is an *action verb* or a *linking verb*.

103. Harold writes funny stories. *action*
104. Sheila is a tremendous athlete. *linking*
105. Snow covered the ground. *action*
106. The wind feels cold. *linking*
107. You look angry. *linking*
108. Mr. Larsen collects rare books. *action*
109. We examined some lovely pictures. *action*
110. This apple tastes sour. *linking*
111. Roger hops on one foot. *action*
112. The dog seemed frightened. *linking*
113. This milk smells bad. *linking*
114. Barbara sniffed the flowers. *action*

K. Write each sentence. Draw one line under the main verb. Draw two lines under the helping verb.

115. Valerie is studying insects.
116. The rain has stopped.
117. The plane will arrive late.
118. The puppies are playing.
119. Lewis had read the book already.
120. We shall go to the opera next Thursday.
121. Donald was visiting his uncle.
122. The actors have rehearsed all afternoon.
123. Mr. Brooks will announce the contest's outcome.
124. I am painting a portrait of my grandfather.
125. Claudia has lost her keys.
126. The boys were raking the leaves.
127. The leaves had fallen overnight.

L. Write the direct object of each sentence. Then write *what* or *whom* to show what question the direct object answers.

128. I invited Miguel to my house. *whom*
129. We ate a delicious dinner. *what*
130. The baby chicks made soft sounds. *what*
131. Tornados frighten me. *whom*
132. Suzy helps her sister with the housework. *whom*
133. Rico wraps the gift neatly. *what*
134. Ann saw Louise at the playground after lunch. *whom*
135. Tina bought a camera yesterday. *what*
136. I found a dollar in the park. *what*
137. The fine weather pleased the picnickers. *whom*
138. Dave will deliver the newspapers. *what*
139. This photograph shows my entire family. *whom*
140. Jeb threw the ball in the air. *what*

M. Write the verb in each sentence. Then write *present*, *past*, or *future* to show what tense it is.

141. Dorothy sings well. *present*
142. The ferocious lion growled loudly. *past*
143. Ms. Tanaka will present the award. *future*
144. Sean told us about his trip. *past*
145. I shall solve the mystery eventually. *future*
146. Marie has twin brothers. *present*
147. The duck waddled toward the pond. *past*
148. The rain will fall for hours. *future*
149. The doctor examines the patient. *present*
150. The student in the front row raised his hand. *past*
151. Jodi will train her new puppy. *future*
152. The kangaroo hops across a field. *present*

N. Write the past-tense form of each verb.

153. eat — ate
154. run — ran
155. go — went
156. grow — grew
157. do — did
158. fall — fell
159. try — tried
160. buy — bought
161. sing — sang
162. bake — baked

163. take — took
164. walk — walked
165. fly — flew
166. jump — jumped
167. see — saw
168. ride — rode
169. carry — carried
170. think — thought
171. meet — met
172. greet — greeted

O. Write the verb in parentheses ( ) that correctly completes each sentence.

173. (Can, May) you do a cartwheel?
174. You (can, may) go to the party.
175. Florence (sets, sits) next to me.
176. (Set, Sit) the books on the desk.

UNIT 4: Pronouns   *pages 176–185*

P. Write the pronoun in each sentence. Then write whether it is a *subject pronoun* or an *object pronoun*.

177. Ms. Reed told them the good news. — object
178. I eat fresh fruit for dessert. — subject
179. Hand me the chalkboard eraser. — object
180. It has fallen onto the floor. — subject
181. The zany clown entertained us. — object
182. Laura's uncle invited her to Ohio. — object
183. She is leaving home on Saturday. — subject
184. Adventure stories can take you to faraway places. — object
185. You would like Mr. Watie. — subject
186. He is a terrific teacher. — subject
187. We finally found the missing cat. — subject
188. Dan discovered it behind a bush. — object
189. Mr. and Mrs. Taylor thanked him. — object
190. They were worried about the cat. — object

Q. Write each sentence. Use the pronoun in parentheses ( ) that correctly completes the sentence.

191. (We, Us) are rehearsing the play.
192. The director has chosen Alan and (I, me) for the two main roles.
193. (Her, She) picked Alan for the part of the lion.
194. Alan thanked (her, she).
195. Imagine (he, him) in that role!
196. Alan and (me, I) have always wanted to act in a play.
197. The audience gave (us, we) a standing ovation.
198. (Them, They) must have enjoyed the play.

R. Write each sentence. Underline the possessive pronoun.

199. That kite is mine.
200. Your father called last night.
201. Their kitten is only six days old.
202. Al took his baby brother to the zoo.
203. The best model plane was ours.
204. The cat licked its fur.
205. My bicycle is starting to rust.
206. Hers is the newer bicycle.

UNIT 4: Contractions
pages 186–187

S. Write the contraction for each pair of words.

207. I shall — I'll
208. she is — she's
209. it has — it's
210. you will — you'll
211. he had — he'd
212. they are — they're

213. he would — he'd
214. you have — you've
215. I am — I'm
216. we are — we're
217. they will — they'll
218. she has — she's

Language Puzzlers

UNIT 4

OBJECTIVES
To solve language puzzles based on skills taught in the unit

ANSWERS

A Pronoun Acrostic
Acrostics will vary.

Pronoun Gymnastics
1. she
2. our
3. them
4. you
5. I
6. it

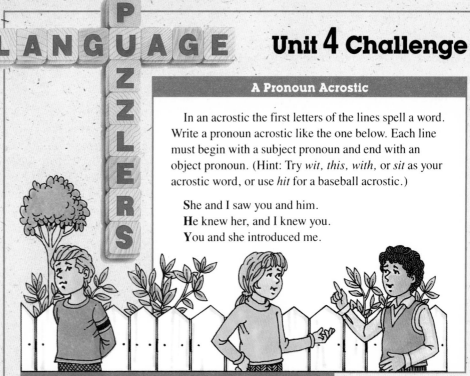

LANGUAGE PUZZLERS

Unit 4 Challenge

A Pronoun Acrostic

In an acrostic the first letters of the lines spell a word. Write a pronoun acrostic like the one below. Each line must begin with a subject pronoun and end with an object pronoun. (Hint: Try *wit*, *this*, *with*, or *sit* as your acrostic word, or use *hit* for a baseball acrostic.)

She and I saw you and him.
He knew her, and I knew you.
You and she introduced me.

Pronoun Gymnastics

Figure out the six pronouns from the clues below.

1. Take the monkey out of *shape* and add a vowel. You have a subject.
2. Drop the *h* from sixty minutes. You have a possessive.
3. Add a *t* to the bottom edge of a skirt to form this object.
4. Take an ear out of the twelve months and add two vowels. This one can be a subject or an object.
5. Drop the *m* from *gloom* and turn the rest into a house made of ice. Now remove the house's glue and this subject will stand alone.
6. Drop the first four letters from the small animal that hops. You have a subject or an object.

226 Language Puzzlers

226

Unit 4 Extra Practice

1 Writing with Pronouns
p. 176

A. Write each sentence. Underline the pronoun.

EXAMPLE: Vote for your favorite movie star.
ANSWER: Vote for <u>your</u> favorite movie star.

1. We watched a silent movie.
2. Michael had borrowed it from the library.
3. Mr. Oppenheim asked me to turn out the lights.
4. Could you see the screen easily?
5. Was Charlie Chaplin your first choice?
6. In this film a young woman helps him.
7. The Little Fellow becomes her friend.
8. They walk down the road together.
9. The Marx Brothers—Groucho, Harpo, Chico, and Zeppo—always make us laugh.
10. Their act is usually the same.
11. Chico and Harpo often get them into trouble.
12. Chico outsmarts his brother Groucho.
13. We love to hear Harpo play the harp.
14. Our favorite Marx Brothers film is *A Night at the Opera*.
15. Harold Lloyd films are my mother's favorites.

B. Write both sentences in each pair. Underline the pronoun in sentence **b**. Underline the noun or nouns in sentence **a** that the pronoun replaces.

16. **a.** Marla decided to make a movie.
    b. She would be the producer and director.
17. **a.** Carlos and Rana heard about the movie.
    b. Marla wanted them to be the stars.
18. **a.** Marla filmed Carlos's special stunts.
    b. His best stunt was tightrope walking.
19. **a.** Rana's scene also had a special effect.
    b. Her finest scene featured a disappearing act.
20. **a.** Marla showed the movie to her family.
    b. Marla's brother and sister enjoyed it very much.

Extra Practice **227**

Extra Practice

Unit **4**

OBJECTIVES
To practice skills taught in the unit

ANSWERS
Writing with Pronouns
A.
1. We
2. it
3. me
4. you
5. your
6. him
7. her
8. They
9. us
10. Their
11. them
12. his
13. We
14. Our
15. my

B.
16. Marla, She
17. Carlos and Rana, them
18. Carlos's, His
19. Rana's, Her
20. movie, it

Extra Practice and Challenge

For those students who need additional grammar practice have them refer to these pages. **The practice exercises progress in difficulty from Easy to Average. Practice A is Easy. Practice B is Average.** Difficult concepts requiring more practice have additional Exercises C and D at the Average level.
We do not recommend these exercises for students who have mastered the skill in the basic lesson. Those students should do the **Challenge** word puzzles on page 226.

Extra Practice

Subject Pronouns
A. 1. I
2. It
3. you
4. We
5. It
6. they
7. You
8. I
9. We
10. I
11. She

B. 12. She
13. they
14. It
15. They
16. He

C. 17. We
18. I
19. We
20. I

Object Pronouns
A. 1. us
2. her
3. them
4. me
5. it

2 Subject Pronouns
p. 178

A. Write each sentence. Underline the subject pronoun.

1. Yesterday I studied several maps of Canada.
2. It is the second largest country in the world.
3. Did you know that Canada has ten provinces?
4. We went to the province of Quebec.
5. It was settled by the French in the early 1600s.
6. Today they speak both French and English there.
7. You can see signs written in both languages.
8. I heard German and Italian spoken in Ontario.
9. We traveled 4,280 miles on the Trans-Canada Highway.
10. In Nova Scotia I talked to a Scottish Canadian dancer.
11. She danced a lively Highland fling.

B. Write each sentence. Use a subject pronoun in place of the underlined word or words.

12. Jeannette Clery speaks both French and English.
13. After the dance competition, Maureen and Patrick had tea.
14. Nova Scotia was a new home for many Scottish people.
15. The Scots and the Irish settled in eastern Canada.
16. James MacGregor Anderson played the bagpipes.

C. Write the sentences. Complete each sentence with the singular (S) or the plural (P) subject pronoun that you use to talk about yourself.

17. (P) liked Winnipeg.
18. (S) sailed to Halifax.
19. (P) skied in Montreal.
20. (S) saw a caribou.

3 Object Pronouns
p. 180

A. Write the object pronoun in each sentence.

1. Ramona told us about South America.
2. Sal asked her to talk about the countries there.
3. Ramona described them well.
4. Peru particularly interested me.
5. Ramona described it as mountainous.

228 Extra Practice

B. Write the second sentence of each pair. Underline the object pronoun.

6. Copper ore comes from Chile. Mining companies sell it around the world.
7. Many farmers in Ecuador grow bananas. Merchants buy them after the harvest.
8. Señora Torres exports coffee. Brazilian coffee growers supply her with coffee.
9. Manfred visited an oil well in Venezuela. A relative invited him there.
10. Sam worked on a cattle ranch in Argentina last year. Sam may take you along next year.

C. Write each sentence. Use an object pronoun in place of the underlined words.

11. Puerto Rico welcomed Christopher Columbus in 1493.
12. Columbus claimed the island for Spain.
13. Columbus's crew tasted the fruits and vegetables.
14. Later they told Queen Isabella about the strange foods.
15. The Spaniards did not like the corn.

D. Write the sentences. Complete each sentence with the singular (S) or the plural (P) object pronoun you use to talk about yourself.

16. A guide told (P).
17. Felipe invited (S).
18. Carlos helped (S).
19. The captain knew (P).
20. A friend asked (S).
21. Sonia saw (P).

4 Possessive Pronouns   *p. 182*

A. Write the possessive pronoun in each sentence.

1. Cleaning up is our job today.
2. My brother is washing the dishes.
3. The easiest chore is mine.
4. I will clean your room.
5. Yours is the neatest room.
6. Molly's room is messier than his room.

Extra Practice

B. 6. it
7. them
8. her
9. him
10. you

C. 11. him
12. it
13. them
14. her
15. it

D. 16. us
17. me
18. me
19. us
20. me
21. us

Possessive Pronouns
A. 1. our
2. My
3. mine
4. your
5. Yours
6. his

Extra Practice and Challenge

For those students who need additional grammar practice have them refer to these pages. **The practice exercises progress in difficulty from Easy to Average. Practice A is Easy. Practice B is Average.** Difficult concepts requiring more practice have additional Exercises C and D at the Average level.
We do not recommend these exercises for students who have mastered the skill in the basic lesson. Those students should do the **Challenge** word puzzles on page 226.

Extra Practice

B. 7. their
    8. her
    9. your
    10. Mine
    11. Our
    12. yours
    13. theirs
    14. my
    15. hers

C. 16. his
    17. their
    18. its (or her or his)
    19. hers
    20. her
    21. his
    22. its (or her or his)

Using Pronouns
A. 1. Dora and I
    2. her
    3. She
    4. they
    5. them
    6. me
    7. him
    8. He
    9. we
    10. us

B. Write each sentence. Use the pronoun in parentheses ( ) that correctly completes the sentence.

  7. Chim and Cam want to clean (their, theirs) bookcase.
  8. Ming Chin has offered (her, hers) help.
  9. Please bring (your, yours) ladder.
  10. (My, Mine) is too short to reach the top shelves.
  11. (Our, Ours) first step is to take everything out.
  12. The books about snakes are (your, yours).
  13. Which books are (their, theirs)?
  14. Where is (my, mine) car magazine?
  15. Cam says the mystery stories are (her, hers).

C. Write each sentence. Use a possessive pronoun in place of the underlined word or words.

  16. Eddie helped Eddie's sister bathe the dog.
  17. They put Eddie and Doris's dog in the tub.
  18. The dog has the dog's own shampoo.
  19. Doris decided to use Doris's instead.
  20. Doris said that drying the dog was Doris's job.
  21. The towel she used was Eddie's.
  22. Eddie trimmed the pet's nails.

5 Using Pronouns p. 184

A. Write each sentence. Use the word or words in parentheses ( ) that correctly complete the sentence.

  1. (I and Dora, Dora and I) would like to thank you for the tour of your bakery.
  2. You helped (she, her) and me with our project.
  3. (She, Her) and I enjoyed meeting your helpers.
  4. You and (they, them) explained everything so clearly.
  5. We especially liked watching you and (they, them).
  6. Dora's brother asked her and (I, me) about our report.
  7. I told (he, him) about your bakery.
  8. (He, Him) and Teresa tasted the rolls you made.
  9. Our friends and (we, us) would like to visit again.
  10. Would you show (we, us) how to make bread?

B. Write each sentence. Use the pronoun in parentheses ( ) that correctly completes the sentence. Then write whether the pronoun you used is a subject or an object pronoun.

11. Luis and (I, me) wrote to the Tiny Toy Company.
12. (He, Him) and I asked for some information.
13. The president of the company answered (he, him) and me.
14. She thanked Luis and (I, me) for our letter.
15. She told (we, us) about the company.
16. (She, Her) and the vice-president invited our parents and us to visit the company.
17. Our parents and (we, us) accepted the invitation.
18. The president showed (they, them) and us the factory.
19. We thanked (she, her) and the vice-president.
20. Then (they, them) and we said good-by.

6 Contractions   *p. 186*

A. Write the contraction for each pair of words.

1. we will	**5.** you are	**9.** I am	**13.** they have
2. it is	**6.** I will	**10.** it has	**14.** we are
3. I would	**7.** she has	**11.** I had	**15.** you would
4. we shall	**8.** you have	**12.** he is	**16.** they are

B. Write the contraction in each sentence. Then write the words from which the contraction is formed.

17. I'm going camping in a Tennessee mountain range.
18. It's called the Great Smoky Mountains.
19. The mountains look smoky because they're covered with a blue-gray haze.
20. After camping we'll go to Oak Ridge.
21. We've always wanted to visit the American Museum of Science and Energy in Oak Ridge.
22. We're also planning a trip to Memphis.
23. I'd like to visit Nashville, too.
24. They've named it the country-music capital of the world.
25. You've probably heard of the Grand Ole Opry House.
26. Uncle Sy said he'll take us there for a concert.

B. 11. I, subject
12. He, subject
13. him, object
14. me, object
15. us, object
16. She, subject
17. we, subject
18. them, object
19. her, object
20. they, subject

Contractions
A. **1.** we'll
2. it's
3. I'd
4. we'll
5. you're
6. I'll
7. she's
8. you've
9. I'm
10. it's
11. I'd
12. he's
13. they've
14. we're
15. you'd
16. they're

B. 17. I'm, I am
18. It's, It is
19. they're, they are
20. we'll, we will
21. We've, We have
22. We're, We are
23. I'd, I would
24. They've, They have
25. You've, You have
26. he'll, he will

Extra Practice and Challenge

For those students who need additional grammar practice have them refer to these pages. **The practice exercises progress in difficulty from Easy to Average. Practice A is Easy. Practice B is Average.** Difficult concepts requiring more practice have additional Exercises C and D at the Average level.
We do not recommend these exercises for students who have mastered the skill in the basic lesson. Those students should do the **Challenge** word puzzles on page 226.

TWO-PART
flexibility

**Unit 5
Overview**

books
ON UNIT THEME

USING LANGUAGE TO DESCRIBE

EASY

Charlotte's Web by E. B. White. Harper. Also available with Silver Burdett & Ginn's World of Books Classroom Library. The animals in the barnyard conspire to save the life of Wilbur the pig in this unforgettable modern classic. **Newbery Honor Book, Lewis Carroll Shelf Award.**

Nadia the Willful by Sue Alexander. Pantheon. A young girl is determined to keep alive the memory of her lost brother.

AVERAGE

Tuck Everlasting by Natalie Babbitt. Farrar. A young girl stumbles on a family that has discovered a spring that brings eternal life. **Christopher Award.**

In the Year of the Boar and Jackie Robinson by Bette Bao Lord. Harper. Also available with Silver Burdett & Ginn's World of Books Classroom Library. Shirley Temple Wong describes her first year in the United States. **American Library Association Notable Children's Book.**

CHALLENGING

Bridge to Terabithia by Katherine Paterson. Harper. Also available with Silver Burdett & Ginn's World of Books Classroom Library. This is a powerful novel about a friendship that is severed. **Newbery Medal.**

The Little Prince by Antoine de Saint-Exupéry. Harcourt. In this masterful tale a poet-aviator shares his vision of life through the adventures of a little prince.

READ-ALOUDS

The Incredible Journey by Sheila Burnford. Little. This memorable animal story vividly describes the journey of two dogs and a cat through the Canadian wilderness. **Young Reader's Choice Award.**

Banner in the Sky by James Ramsey Ullman. Harper. This is a story about a boy's attempt to climb the alp that took his father's life. **Newbery Honor Book.**

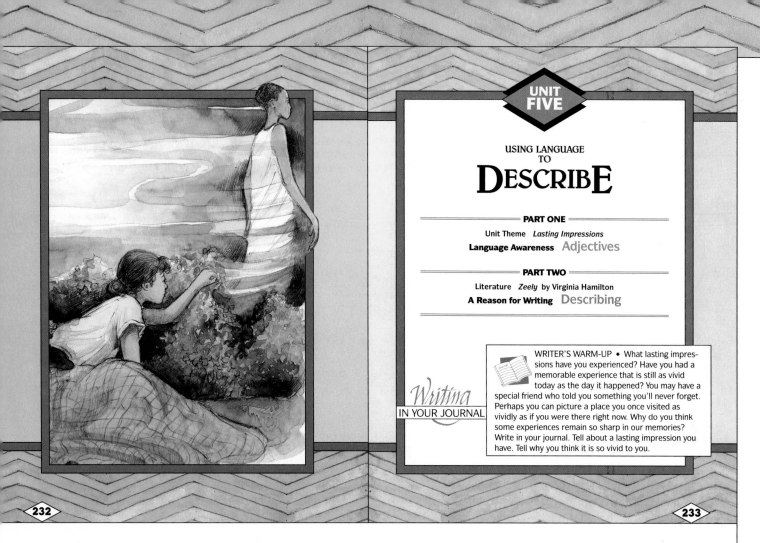

UNIT FIVE

USING LANGUAGE TO DESCRIBE

PART ONE

Unit Theme *Lasting Impressions*

Language Awareness Adjectives

PART TWO

Literature *Zeely* by Virginia Hamilton

A Reason for Writing Describing

Writing
IN YOUR JOURNAL

WRITER'S WARM-UP ◆ What lasting impressions have you experienced? Have you had a memorable experience that is still as vivid today as the day it happened? You may have a special friend who told you something you'll never forget. Perhaps you can picture a place you once visited as vividly as if you were there right now. Why do you think some experiences remain so sharp in our memories? Write in your journal. Tell about a lasting impression you have. Tell why you think it is so vivid to you.

start with WRITING IN YOUR JOURNAL

Writers' Warm-up is designed to help students activate prior knowledge of the unit theme, "Lasting Impressions." Whether you begin instruction with Part 1 or Part 2, encourage students to focus attention on the illustration on page 232 of their textbooks. Encourage them to discuss what they see. Then have a volunteer read aloud the **Writers' Warm-up** on page 233. Have students write their thoughts in their journals. You may wish to tell them that they will refer to this writing in the first lesson of Part 1, in the Grammar-Writing Connection, and in the Curriculum Connection.

THEN START WITH *part 1*

Language Awareness: Adjectives Developmental lessons focus on the concept of adjectives. Each lesson is carefully constructed not only to help students learn the concept well but also to help build interest and background knowledge for the thinking, reading, and writing they will do in Part 2. The last lesson in Part 1 is a vocabulary lesson with which students learn about adjective suffixes. The Grammar-Writing Connection that follows serves as a bridge to Part 2, encouraging students to work together to apply their new language skills at the sentence level of writing.

...OR WITH *part 2*

A Reason for Writing: Describing is the focus of Part 2. First students learn a thinking strategy for describing. Then they read and respond to a selection of literature on which they model their writing. Developmental composition lessons, including "Interviews," a speaking and listening lesson, all reflect the literature and culminate in the Writing Process lesson. There a "Grammar Check," a "Word Choice" hint, and proofreading strategies help you focus on single traits for remediation or instruction through the lessons in Part 1. The unit ends with Curriculum Connection and Books to Enjoy, which help students discover how their new skills apply to writing across the curriculum.

THEME BAR

CATEGORIES	Environments	Business/World of Work	Imagination	Communications/ Fine Arts	People	Science	Expressions	Social Studies
THEMES	UNIT 1 Farm Life	UNIT 2 Handicrafts	UNIT 3 Tall Tales	UNIT 4 The Visual Arts	UNIT 5 Lasting Impressions	UNIT 6 Volcanoes	UNIT 7 Nature	UNIT 8 Animal Habitats
PACING	1 month	1 month	1 month	1 month	1 month	1 month	1 month	1 month

Build background knowledge of the unit theme, "Lasting Impressions," by reading aloud this selection to your class. At the same time you will be building your students' knowledge of our rich heritage of fine literature. You may wish to use the "Notes for Listening" on the following page before and after reading aloud.

The Strangest House Anyone Ever Lived In

from *The Secret Garden*

BY FRANCES HODGSON BURNETT

It was the sweetest, most mysterious-looking place anyone could imagine. The high walls which shut it in were covered with the leafless stems of climbing roses, which were so thick that they were matted together. Mary Lennox knew they were roses because she had seen a great many roses in India. All the ground was covered with grass of a wintry brown, and out of it grew clumps of bushes which were surely rose-bushes if they were alive. There were numbers of standard roses which had so spread their branches that they were like little trees. There were other trees in the garden, and one of the things which made the place look strangest and loveliest was that climbing roses had run all over them and swung down long <u>tendrils</u> which made light swaying curtains, and here and there they had caught at each other or at a far-reaching branch and had crept from one tree to another and made lovely bridges of themselves. There were neither leaves nor roses on them now, and Mary did not know whether they were dead or alive, but their thin grey or brown branches and sprays looked like a sort of hazy <u>mantle</u> spreading over everything, walls, and trees, and even brown grass, where they had fallen from their fastenings and run along the ground. It was this hazy tangle from tree to tree which made it look so mysterious. Mary had thought it must be different from other gardens which had not been left all by themselves so long; and, indeed, it was different from any other place she had ever seen in her life.

'How still it is!' she whispered. 'How still!'

Then she waited a moment and listened at the stillness. The robin, who had flown to his tree-top, was still as all the rest. He did not even flutter his wings; he sat without stirring, and looked at Mary.

'No wonder it is still,' she whispered again. 'I am the first person who has spoken in here for ten years.'

She moved away from the door, stepping as softly as if she were afraid of awakening someone. She was glad that there was grass under her feet and that her steps made no sounds. She walked under one of the fairy-like arches between the trees and looked up at the sprays and tendrils which formed them.

'I wonder if they are all quite dead,' she said. 'Is it all a quite dead garden? I wish it wasn't.'

If she had been Ben Weatherstaff she could have told whether the wood was alive by looking at it, but she could only see that there were only grey or brown sprays and branches, and none showed any signs of even a tiny leaf-bud anywhere.

But she was *inside* the wonderful garden, and she could come through the door under the ivy any time, and she felt as if she had found a world all her own.

The sun was shining inside the four walls and the high arch of blue sky over this particular piece of Misselthwaite seemed even more brilliant and soft than it was over the moor The robin flew down from his tree-top and hopped about or flew after her from one bush to another. He chirped a good deal and had a very busy air, as if he were showing her things. Everything was strange and silent, and she seemed to be hundreds of miles away from anyone, but somehow she did not feel lonely at all. All that troubled her was her wish that she knew whether all the roses were dead, or if perhaps some of them had lived and might put out leaves and buds as the weather got warmer. She did not want it to be a quite dead garden. If it were a quite alive garden, how wonderful it would be, and what thousands of roses would grow on every side?

Her skipping-rope had hung over her arm when she came in, and after she had walked about for a while she thought she would skip round the whole garden, stopping when she wanted to look at things. There seemed to have been paths here and there, and in one or two corners there were <u>alcoves</u> of evergreen with stone seats or all moss-covered flower-urns in them.

As she came near the second of these alcoves she stopped skipping. There had once been a flower-bed in it, and she thought she saw something sticking out of the black earth—some sharp little pale green points. She remembered what Ben Weatherstaff had said, and she knelt down to look at them.

'Yes, they are tiny growing things and they *might* be crocuses or snowdrops or daffodils,' she whispered.

She bent very close to them and sniffed the fresh scent of the damp earth. She liked it very much.

'Perhaps there are some other ones coming up in other places,' she said. 'I will go all over the garden and look.'

She did not skip, but walked. She went slowly and kept her eyes on the ground. She looked in the old border-beds and among the grass, and after she had gone round, trying to miss nothing, she had found ever so many more sharp, pale green points, and she had become quite excited again.

'It isn't a quite dead garden,' she cried out softly to herself. 'Even if the roses are dead, there are other things alive.'

She did not know anything about gardening, but the grass seemed so thick in some of the places where the green points were pushing their way through that she thought they did not seem to have room enough to grow. She searched about until she found a rather sharp piece of wood and knelt down and dug and weeded out the weeds and grass until she made nice little clear places around them.

'Now they look as if they could breathe,' she said, after she had finished with the first ones. 'I am going to do ever so many more. I'll do all I can see. If I haven't time today I can come tomorrow.'

She went from place to place, and dug and weeded, and enjoyed herself so immensely that she was led on from bed to bed and into the grass under the trees. The exercise made her so warm that she first threw her coat off, and then her hat, and without knowing it she was smiling down on to the grass and the pale green points all the time.

The robin was tremendously busy. He was very much pleased to see gardening begun on his own estate. He had often wondered at Ben Weatherstaff. Where gardening is done all sorts of delightful things to eat are turned up with the soil. Now here was this new kind of creature who was not half Ben's size and yet had the sense to come into his garden and begin at once.

Mistress Mary worked in her garden until it was time to go to her midday dinner. In fact she was rather late in remembering, and when she put on her coat and hat and picked up her skipping-rope, she could not believe that she had been working two or three hours. She had been actually happy all the time; and dozens and dozens of the tiny, pale green points were to be seen in cleared places, looking twice as cheerful as they had looked before when the grass and weeds had been smothering them.

'I shall come back this afternoon,' she said, looking round at her new kingdom, and speaking to the trees and rose-bushes as if they heard her. ◇

	LESSON TITLE	STUDENT TEXT				TEACHING RESOURCES		
		Student Lesson	Unit Review	Cumulative Review	Extra Practice	Reteaching Master	Practice Master	Testing Program
1 DAY	Unit Opener							
1 DAY	Writing with Adjectives	234–235	274	331, 434	276, 277	41	41	T542
1 DAY	Adjectives After Linking Verbs	236–237	274	331, 434	276, 278	42	42	T542
1 DAY	Adjectives That Compare	238–239	274	331, 434	276, 279	43	43	T542
1 DAY	Using *more* and *most* with Adjectives	240–241	274	331, 434	276, 280	44	44	T542
1 DAY	VOCABULARY ◆ Adjective Suffixes	242–243	275			45	45	T542
1 DAY	GRAMMAR-WRITING CONNECTION ◆ How to Expand Sentences with Adjectives	244–245						
	▶ **THINK**							
1 DAY	CREATIVE THINKING ◆ A Strategy for Describing	248–249	See also pages 255, 266, 272					
	▶ **READ**							
1 DAY	LITERATURE ◆ *Zeely* by Virginia Hamilton	250–255				Audio Library 2		
	▶ **SPEAK/LISTEN**							
1 DAY	SPEAKING AND LISTENING ◆ Interviews	256–257				Video Library		
	▶ **WRITE**							
1 DAY	WRITING ◆ Organizing Descriptive Details	258–259				46	46	T542
1 DAY	WRITING ◆ A Descriptive Paragraph	260–261	275			47	47	
1 DAY	READING-WRITING CONNECTION ◆ Focus on Sensory Words	262–263						T542
	▶ **WRITING PROCESS** ◆ Prewriting • Writing • Revising • Proofreading • Publishing							
4–5 DAYS	WRITING PROCESS ◆ Writing a Character Sketch	264–271				Spelling Connection Transparencies		T554
1 DAY	CURRICULUM CONNECTION ◆ Writing for Health	272				Writing Across the Curriculum Guide		

(PART 1 spans the first group of lessons; PART 2 spans from THINK onward.)

Teacher Resource File
Reteaching Masters 41–47
Practice Masters 41–47
Evaluation and Testing Program, including Unit Pretest, Posttest, and Picture Prompt Writing Samples
Parent Letters in English and Spanish
Classroom Theme Posters
Writing Across the Curriculum Teacher Guide
Integrated Language Arts Projects with Masters (see pages T511–T529)
Spelling Connection, Teacher Edition
Writing Process Transparencies
Audio Library 1: Read-Alouds and Sing-Alouds

Also available:
Achieving English Proficiency Guide and Activities
Spelling Connection, Pupil Edition
Student Resource Books
Student Writing Portfolios
Professional Handbook
WORLD OF BOOKS Classroom Library

Multi-Modal Materials
Audio Library 1: Read-Alouds and Sing-Alouds
Audio Library 2: Listening to Literature
Video Library
Revising and Proofreading Transparencies
Fine Arts Transparencies with Viewing Booklet
Writing Process Transparencies
Writing Process Computer Program

Unit 5 Planning and Pacing Guide

LANGUAGE
game

Animal Adjectives

Objective: To use adjectives
Materials: Scrap paper, looseleaf paper

Write the word *Animal* on the chalkboard and have the class discuss different kinds of wild and tame animals. On scrap paper have students list a wild animal, a household pet, and a cartoon animal. Next to each animal they are to write three adjectives describing it. While the class is working, display an alphabet code ($A = 1$, $B = 2$, $C = 3$, and so on). Dividing a fresh sheet of looseleaf paper into three sections and labeling them *wild animal, household pet,* and *cartoon animal,* each student must clearly write *in code* three adjectives for each animal listed on the scrap paper. When this is complete, students will exchange papers, decipher the codes, and try to figure out which animal is being described.

Multi-Modal Activities

BULLETIN BOARD
idea

You may wish to use a bulletin board as a springboard for discussing the unit theme, or you may prefer to have students create a bulletin board as they move through the unit. Encourage students to discuss vanity license plates on automobiles and how people often use them to sum up themselves or their interests, such as *TOOTHDR* and *RUN4FUN* (tooth doctor, run for fun). Allow students to share various vanity plates they have seen or know about. Then have students design their own vanity plates, using no more than seven letters and/or numbers, to tell something about themselves or their interests. Post the vanity plates on the bulletin board under the heading *Guess Who?* You may wish to set aside time for students to guess who designed each plate.

Students with different learning styles will all benefit from a natural approach to language learning, including frequent and varied use of oral language in the classroom.

Students "At Risk"

The following suggestions can help you help the students in your classroom who may be considered "at risk."

Encourage Positive Attitudes

At-risk students often are characterized as having low self-esteem. These students especially need to see you model and project the positive attitude that all your students *can* learn. Avoid low expectations. Help them begin to perceive themselves as able. Set step-by-step goals for each learning objective. Make sure students know the goal they are working toward. As they accomplish each task, provide immediate feedback and sincere applause. Emphasize continuous progress and always show your genuine respect for goals met well.

Limited English Proficiency

Teachers whose classes contain students with limited English proficiency may find the following activities helpful in developing students' skills in grammar and composition.

Description Chart

On the chalkboard draw a description chart such as the one on this page.

Have students suggest nouns that name things. List the nouns they suggest in the first column on the chart. Remind students that adjectives are words that tell about, or describe, nouns. Then have students suggest adjectives that might be used to describe each noun listed on the chart (e.g., *dog—one, large, brown, hunting*).

When the chart is complete, have students use the adjectives and nouns to create complete sentences, such as *One large brown hunting dog raced across the field.*

Using Adjectives to Compare

Display about ten small objects, such as a marble, a ball, a paper clip, a rubber band. Spread them out on a table and have students take turns choosing two objects they think are alike in some way, such as a marble and a ball *(both are round)*. Have students use a complete sentence to tell how the objects they choose are alike *(A marble and a ball are both round)*. Encourage students to find as many similarities as possible among the objects. You may wish to record the adjectives students suggest on the chalkboard.

To emphasize the use of adjectives to compare, ask such questions as: *Which is smaller, the marble or the ball? What is the largest object on the table? Which is more useful, the marble or the comb?* Have students answer in complete sentences.

A Character Sketch

Help students brainstorm about different superheroes they know from books, movies, and television. Discuss what each hero is like. Then write questions such as the following and read them aloud.

1. How old is the hero?
2. What costume does the hero wear?
3. How does the hero's voice sound?
4. What does the hero like to do?
5. How does the hero move?

Have students think about each question. Then have them use the questions to help them tell about a character they know.

Description Chart

Noun	What Number?	What Size?	What Color?	What Kind?
dog	one	large	brown	hunting

Gifted and Talented Students

To enable gifted and talented students to work at their own pace and to explore the content further, you may wish to use one or more of these activities.

Using Language to Describe

Have students work in pairs to brainstorm adjectives that describe two characters —one they might like and one they might dislike. Have students make a list of positive character traits, such as *brave, adventurous, intelligent, kind,* and *thoughtful,* and negative character traits, such as *selfish, pushy, thoughtless, cruel,* and *greedy.* Have each student choose one list to use to write a descriptive paragraph about a hero or villain, friend or foe.

As a more challenging task, have pairs of students create a plot for their characters. Have pairs share their work by reading aloud. Encourage discussion of the plots of the stories. Have students tally the number of stories in which the hero/friend was victorious and the number in which the villain/foe was victorious.

Story Character Parade

Have students create a parade of favorite story characters to display around the classroom or in a reading corner. Have each student choose a favorite character (either animal or human) from a favorite book. Have students brainstorm descriptive words and phrases about the character and what he/she/it looks like,

such as *Paul Bunyan—towering, long beard, booming voice, wool cap, black leather belt, high boots, mighty as a mountain.* Besides the physical characteristics, encourage students to think about clothing and other items appropriate to the character, the place in which the character lives, and the time in which the character lives.

Have students write a brief descriptive paragraph about the character to paste on a construction-paper outline of the character. Have students share their work by reading aloud. Have students discuss the use of adjectives in each descriptive paragraph.

When all students have had a chance to share by reading aloud, have students display their outlines in a story character parade. As a more challenging task, you may wish to have students choose two of the characters and write a narrative about a meeting between them.

Creating a Menu

Have students imagine that they are the owner of a restaurant and have to create a menu for it. You may wish to have on hand as models two or three menus from a local diner or restaurant. Have students brainstorm foods they might serve and then choose at least five specialties to write descriptions about for their menu. Encourage students to make the foods sound wonderfully delicious.

Have volunteers share their favorite menu items by reading them aloud. Allow classmates to choose their favorite foods to add to a class menu. You may wish to write some of the descriptions on the chalkboard and have students identify the use of adjectives, as in the following: *Our thick, juicy* hamburgers smothered in *rich dark-brown* gravy are served with *crispy fried* onions and *piping-hot* biscuits.

Meeting Individual Needs

■ Easy ■ Average ■ Challenging

OBJECTIVES
To identify adjectives
To use adjectives in writing

ASSIGNMENT GUIDE
BASIC   Practice A
⬇   Practice B
ADVANCED   Practice C

All should do the Apply activity.

RESOURCES
■ Reteaching Master 41
■ Practice Master 41
■■■ Extra Practice, pp. 276, 277
Unit 5 Pretest, p. T542

TEACHING THE LESSON

1. Getting Started
Oral Language Focus attention on this oral activity, encouraging all to participate. You may wish to help students respond by asking them questions, such as *What shapes might you see? What colors might you see?* You also may wish to tell students that only one thing humans have made can be seen from space: the Great Wall of China.

2. Developing the Lesson
Guide students through the explanation of writing with adjectives, emphasizing the examples and the summary. You may wish to discuss the use of the articles *a* and *an*, pointing out to students that *an* is used before words that begin with the vowels *a, e, i, o,* and *u* and before the consonant *h* when it is silent, as in *an hour.* Lead students through the **Guided Practice.** Identify those who would benefit from reteaching. Assign independent Practice A–C.

3. Closing the Lesson
After students complete the Apply activity, have volunteers read aloud the changes they made in their writing and have them give their reasons for choosing the adjectives they did. Point out to students that using adjectives will make their writing more colorful and interesting.

GETTING STARTED Imagine that you are on a space flight orbiting the Earth. What words would you use to describe how the Earth looks from space?

1 Writing with Adjectives

When we write, we often need words that add important details. Such words are adjectives. An adjective tells something about a noun or a pronoun. An adjective often answers the question "What kind?" or "How many?"

Notice the difference between the following two sentences.

■ Astronauts put on helmets.
■ Five confident astronauts put on the strong and shiny helmets.

The second sentence is much more vivid than the first. The adjectives in the second sentence are underlined. They add interesting details. *Confident, strong*, and *shiny* help readers see the astronauts and the helmets. They tell *what kind.* The adjective *five* tells *how many.*

Notice that the word *the* is also underlined. *A, an,* and *the* are a special kind of adjective called an **article.** Use *a* before a word that begins with a consonant sound. Use *an* before a word that begins with a vowel sound.

■ a rocket   an immense rocket   an astronaut   a brave astronaut

> **Summary** ◆ An **adjective** describes a noun or a pronoun. Use adjectives to add details to your writing.

Guided Practice

Name the adjectives in these sentences. Include articles.

1. Sally Ride is a true pioneer.
2. She was the first woman from the United States to fly in space.
3. Sally Ride was a dedicated and exceptional student.
4. Sally's favorite subject in school was science.
5. She never dreamed she would become a famous astronaut.

234 GRAMMAR and WRITING: Adjectives

ESSENTIAL LANGUAGE SKILLS
This lesson provides opportunities to:

LISTENING ◆ follow the logical organization of an oral presentation ◆ select from an oral presentation the information needed

SPEAKING ◆ engage in creative dramatic activities and nonverbal communication

READING ◆ use context to understand the meaning of words ◆ follow a set of directions

WRITING ◆ use ideas and information from sources other than personal experience for writing

LANGUAGE ◆ use modifiers (adjectives and adverbs) correctly

Practice

A. The sentences below tell about Sally Ride's flight in the space shuttle *Challenger*. Write the adjectives in each sentence. Include articles.

6. At dawn on June 18, 1983, the gleaming *Challenger* waited.
7. Soon Sally Ride and four other astronauts would zoom into space.
8. The powerful shuttle roared into the clear sky above Florida.
9. A trail of bright hot flame followed the speedy *Challenger*.
10. The powerful force of gravity pressed on the five astronauts.
11. The uncomfortable feeling lasted for a few minutes.
12. When sufficient altitude was achieved, a smooth and peaceful ride followed.
13. Sally Ride enjoyed the new and startling feeling of weightlessness.
14. Cheerful astronauts floated about the cabin.
15. The astronauts performed many important experiments.

B. Write each group of words. Use the correct article.

16. (a, an) orbiting space shuttle
17. (a, an) spectacular view
18. (a, an) open cargo bay
19. (a, an) broken satellite
20. (a, an) successful mission

C. Write each sentence. Use an adjective to complete it.
Answers will vary. Possible answers follow.
21. The ___exciting___ space voyage neared its end.
22. The spacecraft glided toward the ___beautiful___ ground below.
23. The space shuttle made a ___perfect___ landing.
24. The astronauts walked across the ___long___ runway.
25. They took one final look at the ___magnificent___ space shuttle.

Apply ◆ Think and Write

From Your Writing ◆ Read what you wrote for the Writer's Warm-up. Try to make your writing more vivid by changing some of the adjectives.

✏ **Remember** to use adjectives to make your writing colorful and interesting.

GRAMMAR and WRITING: Adjectives **235**

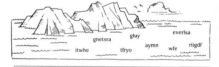

◀▥▥ TEACHING OPTIONS ▥▥▶

RETEACHING

A Different Modality Distribute index cards on which are written adjectives that tell *how many* (two, some) and *what kind* (brave, heavy). Place a circus poster or something similar on the chalkboard and have volunteers use their adjectives to describe something in the picture (e.g., *I see two acrobats. A lion is growling at the brave animal trainer*). Have students tell whether each adjective adds a detail that tells *how many* or *what kind*.

CLASS ENRICHMENT

A Cooperative Activity Have students write and describe lunchtime at school or at home. Encourage them to use adjectives to tell about what they see, hear, smell, and taste. You may wish to put some examples on the chalkboard, such as *sweet, spicy, loud, crowded*. Have students share their description with a partner. Have each partner identify the adjectives.

CHALLENGE

An Independent Extension Distribute movie and restaurant reviews you have cut from newspapers. Have students identify the adjectives in the articles. Encourage them to circle the adjectives that help give a particular slant to a review. (Adjectives such as *fresh, special,* and *delicious* would give a positive slant to a restaurant review.)

235

UNIT 5/LESSON 2

■ Easy ■ Average ■ Challenging

OBJECTIVES
To identify predicate adjectives and the words they describe

ASSIGNMENT GUIDE
BASIC   Practice A
⬇   Practice B
ADVANCED   Practice C

All should do the Apply activity.

RESOURCES
■ Reteaching Master 42
■ Practice Master 42
■■■ Extra Practice, pp. 276, 278

TEACHING THE LESSON

1. Getting Started
Oral Language Focus attention on this oral activity, encouraging all to participate. You may wish to begin with models of your own, such as *right/tight* (My *right* shoe feels *tight*); *funny/sunny* (The cat looks *funny*. It is lying in a *sunny* window); *sad/mad* (I am *sad* because you are *mad*). You may wish to write students' responses on the chalkboard.

2. Developing the Lesson
Guide students through the explanation of adjectives after linking verbs, emphasizing the examples and the summary. Lead students through the **Guided Practice**. Identify those who would benefit from reteaching. Assign independent Practice A–C.

3. Closing the Lesson
After students complete the Apply activity, have volunteers read aloud their sentences to the class. Have them ask the class to help them determine if they have used predicate adjectives correctly. Point out to students that using predicate adjectives can help them make their oral and written descriptions more vivid.

GETTING STARTED

Change one adjective to another by changing one letter in the word. Use both of the adjectives in sentences. For example: *The road was bumpy. The gravy was lumpy.*

2 Adjectives After Linking Verbs

Adjectives often come before the nouns they describe.

■ The <u>fascinating</u> **books** are by Laura Ingalls Wilder.

Adjectives can also follow the nouns or pronouns they describe.

The **characters** are <u>memorable</u>.

Charles Ingalls was <u>brave</u>.

He felt <u>secure</u> and <u>relaxed</u> in the wilderness.

In the sentences above, the adjectives *memorable*, *brave*, *secure*, and *relaxed* are predicate adjectives. A predicate adjective describes the subject of the sentence. Sometimes the subject is a noun like *characters*. Sometimes it is a pronoun like *he*.

A linking verb connects a predicate adjective with the subject. The most commonly used linking verbs are forms of the verb *be*: *am*, *is*, *are*, *was*, and *were*. Some other linking verbs are *seem*, *look*, *feel*, *taste*, *smell*, and *become*.

> **Summary** ◆ An adjective that follows a linking verb describes the subject of a sentence. Use predicate adjectives to add details to your writing.

Guided Practice

Name the predicate adjectives in the sentences. Tell which noun or pronoun in the subject each adjective describes.
Predicate adjectives are underlined once. Subjects are underlined twice.
1. The <u>Ingalls</u> were <u>comfortable</u> in their home in Wisconsin.
2. However, the <u>woods</u> became <u>crowded</u>.
3. <u>Charles Ingalls</u> was <u>anxious</u> and <u>restless</u>.

236   GRAMMAR: Predicate Adjectives

ESSENTIAL LANGUAGE SKILLS
This lesson provides opportunities to:

LISTENING ◆ follow the logical organization of an oral presentation ◆ select from an oral presentation the information needed

SPEAKING ◆ use a variety of words to express feelings and ideas ◆ use oral language for a variety of purposes

READING ◆ use context to understand the meaning of words ◆ follow a set of directions ◆ describe the time and setting of a story

WRITING ◆ use ideas and information from sources other than personal experiences for writing

LANGUAGE ◆ use modifiers (adjectives and adverbs) correctly

Practice

A. Write each sentence about Laura Ingalls Wilder's book, *Little House on the Prairie*. Draw one line under each predicate adjective. (Several sentences have more than one.) Draw two lines under the noun or pronoun it describes.

  EXAMPLE: Charles Ingalls was sensitive to his family's needs.

  ANSWER: Charles Ingalls was <u>sensitive</u> to his family's needs.

  4. The morning was cold and quiet for the Ingalls' departure.
  5. The sky was pale in the east.
  6. The frozen lake seemed empty and still.
  7. Laura felt better after spotting a little log house.
  8. The westward journey seemed endless.
  9. The land became black after sundown.
  10. The stars seemed close in the dark sky.
  11. The Ingalls' campfire looked tiny.
  12. Their new log cabin was solid and sturdy.
  13. Pa Ingalls was proud of his house on the prairie.

B. Write sentences for each pair of adjectives and nouns. Use a linking verb, and use the adjective as a predicate adjective.
Answers will vary. Possible answers follow.

  EXAMPLE: industrious Pa Ingalls

  ANSWER: Pa Ingalls was industrious.

The logs are long.	The supper tastes delicious.
14. long logs	**19.** delicious supper
The work seemed hard.	The wind becomes strong.
15. hard work	**20.** strong wind
The neighbor is helpful.	The sky seems vast.
16. helpful neighbor	**21.** vast sky
Our house is snug.	The moon is bright.
17. snug house	**22.** bright moon
The campfire felt warm.	The air smells fresh.
18. warm campfire	**23.** fresh air

C. 24–28. Use the model below to write five sentences of your own.
Sentences will vary. A possible sentence follows.
(Noun) (linking verb) (predicate adjective).
Pa Ingalls was courageous.

Apply ◆ Think and Write

Dictionary of Knowledge ◆ Read about the author Laura Ingalls Wilder and her life on the prairie. Write some sentences about her. Use predicate adjectives in each of your sentences.

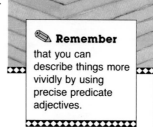

✏️ Remember
that you can describe things more vividly by using precise predicate adjectives.

GRAMMAR: Predicate Adjectives   **237**

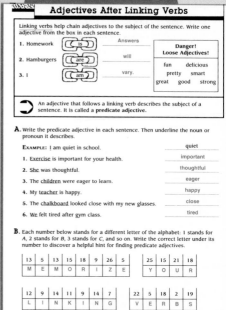

MASTERS ON **FILE**

RETEACHING   42

Adjectives After Linking Verbs

Linking verbs help chain adjectives to the subject of the sentence. Write one adjective from the box in each sentence.

		Answers		**Danger!** **Loose Adjectives!**
1. Homework	is			fun delicious
2. Hamburgers	are	will		pretty smart
3. I	am	vary.		great good strong

↪ An adjective that follows a linking verb describes the subject of a sentence. It is called a **predicate adjective**.

A. Write the predicate adjective in each sentence. Then underline the noun or pronoun it describes.

  EXAMPLE: I am quiet in school.   quiet

  1. Exercise is important for your health.   important
  2. She was thoughtful.   thoughtful
  3. The children were eager to learn.   eager
  4. My teacher is happy.   happy
  5. The chalkboard looked close with my new glasses.   close
  6. We felt tired after gym class.   tired

B. Each number below stands for a different letter of the alphabet: 1 stands for *A*, 2 stands for *B*, 3 stands for *C*, and so on. Write the correct letter under its number to discover a helpful hint for finding predicate adjectives.

13	5	13	15	18	9	26	5		25	15	21	18
M	E	M	O	R	I	Z	E		Y	O	U	R

12	9	14	11	9	14	7		22	5	18	2	19
L	I	N	K	I	N	G		V	E	R	B	S

PRACTICE   42

Adjectives After Linking Verbs

↪ An adjective that follows a linking verb describes the subject of a sentence. It is called a **predicate adjective**.

A. Circle the predicate adjective in each sentence. Draw an arrow pointing to the noun it describes. The first one is done for you.

  1. Teddy Roosevelt's father appeared stern as he spoke to his son.
  2. Teddy Roosevelt looked unhealthy.
  3. Teddy had been sickly as a boy.
  4. His muscles were weak.
  5. His body became strong through hard work and exercise.
  6. Teddy was curious about different animals.
  7. He was happy about his butterfly collection.
  8. Roosevelt seemed calm when he became President.
  9. Roosevelt was effective as President of the United States.

B. Complete each sentence by supplying a linking verb and a predicate adjective. The first one is done for you. Answers will vary.

  10. I was happy with the book about Teddy Roosevelt.
  11. My sister was eager to read it, too.
  12. She was lucky to find it in the library.
  13. I am glad to share the information.
  14. We are interested in learning about President Roosevelt.
  15. They are anxious to see the material as soon as possible.
  16. Teddy Roosevelt was strong as a President of this country.
  17. My father is proud of his picture of President Roosevelt.

WRITE IT
Theodore Roosevelt created national parks to protect our natural resources. Use predicate adjectives to write sentences that describe a park near you. Write on a separate sheet of paper. Answers will vary.

◀◀||| TEACHING OPTIONS |||▶▶

RETEACHING

A Different Modality Have students fill in the chart to form sentences. Then have students circle the words the predicate adjectives describe.

Subject	Linking Verb	Adjective
1. The puppy	was	_____.
2. My friend	is	_____.
3. _____	are	delicious.
4. _____		beautiful.
5. _____		_____.

CLASS ENRICHMENT

A Cooperative Activity Have students work in small groups to compose five sentences that use predicate adjectives to describe something in school (e.g., *The chalkboard is green*). Have one volunteer from each group write the group's favorite sentence on the chalkboard and then circle the word the predicate adjective describes.

CHALLENGE

An Independent Extension Have students write a sentence containing an adjective that describes a noun or pronoun, such as *She is wearing a colorful jacket.* Then have the student use the adjective and the noun it describes to form a sentence with a linking verb and a predicate adjective. (*The jacket is colorful.*) You may wish to have students work in pairs, taking turns writing sentences and forming new ones.

UNIT 5/LESSON 3

■ Easy ■ Average ■ Challenging

OBJECTIVES
To identify and use comparative and superlative forms of adjectives with -er and -est endings

ASSIGNMENT GUIDE
BASIC   Practice A
↓   Practice B
ADVANCED   Practice C

All should do the Apply activity.

RESOURCES
■ Reteaching Master 43
■ Practice Master 43
■■■ Extra Practice, pp. 276, 279

TEACHING THE LESSON

1. Getting Started
Oral Language Focus attention on this oral activity, encouraging all to participate. You may want students to work in pairs. Have one student suggest the two nouns and the other supply the comparing words with -er. Then you may want them to reverse their roles.

2. Developing the Lesson
Guide students through the explanation of using adjectives that compare, emphasizing the examples and the summary. You may wish to review the spelling changes that sometimes occur when -er or -est are added. You may also want to write a list of words and rules on the chalkboard and have students tell which spelling rule applies, such as *strange*—drop final *e; silly*—change final *y* to *i; fit*—double final consonant. Lead students through the Guided Practice. Identify those who would benefit from reteaching. Assign independent Practice A–C.

3. Closing the Lesson
After students complete the Apply activity, have volunteers take turns reading their sentences. Point out that using -er and -est words in their writing will help them to compare persons, places, or things clearly.

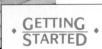

GETTING STARTED

Choose two persons, places, or things. Compare the nouns in each pair, using as many -er words as you can. For example: *Arizona is bigger (warmer, drier) than Vermont.*

3 Adjectives That Compare

Adjectives describe nouns. One way they describe is by comparing persons, places, or things. When you want to compare two nouns, use the -er form of the adjective. In the sentence below, two folk heroes are compared.

■ John Henry was <u>stronger</u> than Casey Jones.

When you want to compare three or more nouns, use the -est form of the adjective. In the sentence below, John Henry is compared with all the persons in a group.

■ John Henry was the <u>strongest</u> of all the railroad workers.

When you write, you sometimes have to change the spelling of an adjective to add -er or -est.

Drop final e:	brave	braver	bravest
Change final y to i:	heavy	heavier	heaviest
Double final consonant:	hot	hotter	hottest

> **Summary** ◆ When you speak and write, use the -er form of an adjective to compare two persons, places, or things. Use the -est form of an adjective to compare three or more persons, places, or things.

Guided Practice

Tell which word in parentheses ( ) correctly completes each sentence.

1. Digging a railroad tunnel is (harder, hardest) than other work.
2. John Henry was the (faster, fastest) worker on the railroad.
3. Casey Jones was the (braver, bravest) of all engineers.
4. Casey's Cannonball Express was (faster, fastest) than the local train.

238   GRAMMAR and USAGE: Comparison of Adjectives

ESSENTIAL LANGUAGE SKILLS
This lesson provides opportunities to:

LISTENING ◆ follow the logical organization of an oral presentation ◆ select from an oral presentation the information needed

SPEAKING ◆ use a variety of words to express feelings and ideas

READING ◆ use context to understand the meaning of words ◆ understand content area vocabulary ◆ follow a set of directions

WRITING ◆ adapt information to accomplish a specific purpose with a particular audience

LANGUAGE ◆ use modifiers (adjectives and adverbs) correctly ◆ use the fundamentals of grammar, punctuation, and spelling

Practice

A. Write each sentence. Use the form of the adjective shown in parentheses ( ).

5. Railroad steel drivers were (strong + -er) *stronger* than other workers.
6. Sheep-nose hammers were the (fine + -est) *finest* tools available.
7. The (heavy + -est) *heaviest* spikes were hammered in place.
8. Even the (long + -est) *longest* tunnels were drilled by hand.
9. Automatic steam drills were used in (late + -er) *later* times.
10. John Henry's two hammers were the (large + -est) *largest* of all.
11. His arms were (big + -er) *bigger* than tree trunks.
12. His (fierce + -est) *fiercest* duel was against the steam drill.
13. John Henry's hammers were (speedy + -er) *speedier* than the steam drill.
14. He dug (deep + -er) *deeper* holes than the steam drill but died doing it.

B. Write each sentence. Use the correct form of the adjective in parentheses ( ).

15. Casey Jones's Cannonball Express was the (swift) *swiftest* train of all.
16. A freight train that was (big) *bigger* than a monster blocked the track.
17. Casey's grip on the brakes was (firm) *firmer* than a wrench.
18. His locomotive slammed into the freight train with the (loud) *loudest* bang of all.
19. The death of Casey Jones may be the (sad) *saddest* tale I know.

C. 20–24. Write five pairs of sentences that use adjectives to compare. Use the model below for each pair.
Pairs of sentences will vary. A possible pair follows.
The (noun) is (adjective) than the (noun).
The (noun) is the (adjective) of all.
The car is bigger than the motorcycle. The truck is the biggest of all.

Apply ♦ Think and Write

Descriptive Comparisons ♦ Think of two characters you know through stories and songs. Write several sentences comparing the two characters.

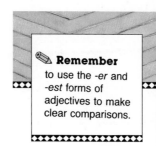

> **✎ Remember**
> to use the *-er* and *-est* forms of adjectives to make clear comparisons.

Using Adjectives That Compare

Victor   Fluffy   Taco
Underline the one adjective in each sentence.
1. Fluffy is small.
2. Taco is smaller than Fluffy.
3. Smallest of all is Victor.
Did you notice that the adjective smaller compared two things? Did you notice that the adjective smallest compared three things?

> Use the *-er* form of an adjective to compare two persons, places, or things. Use the *-est* form of an adjective to compare three or more persons, places, or things. The spelling of some adjectives changes when *-er* or *-est* is added.

A. Complete each sentence by writing the correct form of the adjective in parentheses ( ).
Example: My dog is friendlier than your dog. (friendlier, friendliest)
1. That is the ___funniest___ joke in the world. (funnier, funniest)
2. Kansas is ___flatter___ than Arizona. (flatter, flattest)
3. Jetliners are ___bigger___ than helicopters. (bigger, biggest)
4. Whales are the ___heaviest___ animals on earth. (heavier, heaviest)
5. Mercury is the ___hottest___ planet. (hotter, hottest)

B. Write the correct form of the adjective in parentheses ( ).
Example: Truth is sometimes ___ than fiction. (strange) *stranger*
6. A hurricane is ___ than a blizzard. (rare) *rarer*
7. June was the ___ month of the year. (hot) *hottest*
8. Mount Everest is the ___ mountain in the world. (tall) *tallest*
9. China is a ___ country than India. (large) *larger*
10. Mars is the ___ of all the other planets. (near) *nearest*

PRACTICE 43

Using Adjectives That Compare

> Use the *-er* form of an adjective to compare two persons, places, or things. Use the *-est* form of an adjective to compare three or more persons, places, or things.

A. Write the missing forms for each adjective below.

	Adjective	Comparing Two	Comparing Three or More
1.	fresh	fresher	freshest
2.	dry	drier	driest
3.	free	freer	freest
4.	fat	fatter	fattest
5.	keen	keener	keenest
6.	slim	slimmer	slimmest
7.	nice	nicer	nicest
8.	bald	balder	baldest

B. Use the word in parentheses ( ) to write an adjective with *-er* or *-est* that completes each comparison.
9. In many places our air is ___cleaner___ today than it was in the 1950s. (clean)
10. Scientists are working ___harder___ than ever before. (hard)
11. Power plants use the ___biggest___ air filters of all. (big)
12. The monorail is a ___newer___ form of transportation than the train. (new)
13. The ___strictest___ law to control air pollution is the Clean Air Act of 1970. (strict)

WRITE IT
On a separate sheet of paper, write why it is important to keep our air and water clean. Use the *-er* and *-est* form of adjectives in your sentences.
Answers will vary.

◀▥▥ TEACHING OPTIONS ▥▥▶

RETEACHING

A Different Modality Display pictures of two different kinds of birds, dogs, and cats. Say *The robin is small* and identify the predicate adjective. Then write on the chalkboard a model sentence that describes the first pair of pictures, such as *The robin is smaller than the bluebird.* Point out the adjective that compares the two birds. Continue with the other animal pairs. For comparison with *-est,* add a third picture to each group of animals.

CLASS ENRICHMENT

A Cooperative Activity Have students work in small groups to clip magazine or newspaper articles with adjectives that compare using *-er* and *-est* endings. Have each group work together to paste its findings in a chart with these headings: *Spellings Stay the Same, Final e Is Dropped, Final y Is Changed to* i, and *Final Consonant Is Doubled.* You may wish to have students present their charts aloud and exhibit them on a bulletin board.

CHALLENGE

An Independent Extension Provide magazine or newspaper ads as models. Have students write their own ads, using adjectives that compare. Then you may wish to have them discuss how these words help make the ads persuasive, such as pointing out that a product is *bigger* or *lighter* than its competitor.

UNIT 5/LESSON 4

■ Easy ■ Average ■ Challenging

OBJECTIVES
To identify and use comparative and superlative forms of adjectives with *more* and *most*

ASSIGNMENT GUIDE

BASIC   Practice A
⬇   Practice B
ADVANCED   Practice C

All should do the Apply activity.

RESOURCES
■ Reteaching Master 44
■ Practice Master 44
■ ■ ■ Extra Practice, pp. 276, 280

TEACHING THE LESSON

1. Getting Started
Oral Language Focus attention on this oral activity, encouraging all to participate. You may wish to write the example from the textbook on the chalkboard. Then have volunteers replace the adjective *serious* with other adjectives, such as *interesting, talented,* and *dignified.*

2. Developing the Lesson
Guide students through the explanation of using *more* and *most* with adjectives, emphasizing the examples and the summary. Lead students through the **Guided Practice.** Identify those who would benefit from reteaching. Assign independent Practice A–C.

3. Closing the Lesson
After students complete the Apply activity, have volunteers read their sentences and identify for the class the adjectives that use *more* or *most*. Point out to students that knowing when to use *-er, -est, more,* and *most* can help them make clear comparisons when they write and when they speak.

240

Think of some American heroes. Compare them with sentences using *more* and *most*. For example: *I think that John Henry was more inspiring than Casey Jones. I think that Molly Pitcher was the most inspiring of all.*

4 Using *more* and *most* with Adjectives

Some adjectives do not use the *-er* or *-est* form to compare.

One syllable: calm   calmer   calmest
Two or more syllables: inspiring   more inspiring   most inspiring

Many adjectives of two or more syllables use *more* or *most* to make comparisons. *More* is used with an adjective to compare two persons, places, or things. *Most* is used with an adjective to compare three or more persons, places, or things.

> Luisa is a <u>more powerful</u> speaker than you are.
> Dr. Martin Luther King, Jr., was the <u>most powerful</u> speaker of all.

Never use *more* before the *-er* form of an adjective.
> **Wrong:** Dr. King was more braver than I.
> **Right:** Dr. King was braver than I.

Never use *most* before the *-est* form of an adjective.
> **Wrong:** Dr. King was the most bravest person I know.
> **Right:** Dr. King was the bravest person I know.

Notice how the adjectives *good* and *bad* show comparison.

> a <u>good</u> speech   a <u>better</u> speech   the <u>best</u> speech
> a <u>bad</u> situation   a <u>worse</u> situation   the <u>worst</u> situation

Summary ◆ When you make comparisons, you must often use *more* and *most* with adjectives of two or more syllables.

Guided Practice

For each adjective below, name the two forms used to compare.

taller	more sincere	better	more admirable	more ser...
1. tall	**2.** sincere	**3.** good	**4.** admirable	**5.** serious
tallest	most sincere	best	most admirable	most ser...

240   GRAMMAR and USAGE: Comparison of Adjectives

ESSENTIAL LANGUAGE SKILLS
This lesson provides opportunities to:

LISTENING ◆ follow the logical organization of an oral presentation ◆ select from an oral presentation the information needed

SPEAKING ◆ use oral language for a variety of purposes ◆ make organized oral presentations

READING ◆ use context to understand the meaning of words ◆ follow a set of directions ◆ explain and relate to the feelings and emotions of characters

WRITING ◆ write and compose for a variety of purposes ◆ use ideas and information from sources other than personal experience for writing

LANGUAGE ◆ use modifiers (adjectives and adverbs) correctly

Practice

A. Write each sentence. Use the correct form of the adjective in parentheses ( ).

   6. Martin Luther King, Jr., was (smart) *smarter* than his classmates.
   7. His grades were the (impressive) *most impressive* of all.
   8. When he entered Morehouse College, he was (young) *younger* than most of his classmates.
   9. His decision to be a minister was the (wise) *wisest* one of all.
  10. Dr. King was the (courageous) *most courageous* leader in the struggle for equal rights.
  11. Dr. King's pleas for justice are some of the (great) *greatest* speeches of his time.
  12. His (memorable) *most memorable* speech proclaimed ''I have a dream.''
  13. His deeds were even (honorable) *more honorable* than his words.
  14. The Nobel Peace Prize was his (important) *most important* honor.
  15. Dr. Martin Luther King, Jr., was one of the (inspiring) *most inspiring* of all leaders.

B. Write the sentences about the essay contest on Dr. Martin Luther King, Jr. Use the correct form of *good* or *bad* to complete each sentence.

  16. This year's essays were (good) *better* than last year's.
  17. Liu's essay was the (good) *best* of all.
  18. Finishing second was the (bad) *worst* disappointment for me.
  19. It felt like nothing (bad) *worse* than that could ever happen.
  20. My next essay will be (good) *better* than this one.

C. Write four sentences that compare persons, places, or things. Use the following adjectives in your sentences.
Sentences will vary.
  21. sincere **22.** honest **23.** truthful **24.** brave

Apply ◆ Think and Write

Descriptive Comparisons ◆ Write sentences comparing two famous people of the twentieth century. One might be Dr. Martin Luther King, Jr. Use a variety of adjectives, including several that need *more* or *most*, to make comparisons.

✎ **Remember**
to use *more* and *most* with some adjectives to make clear comparisons.

GRAMMAR and USAGE: Comparison of Adjectives **241**

◀┃┃┃┃ TEACHING OPTIONS ┃┃┃┃▶

RETEACHING

A Different Modality Remind students that adjectives of two or more syllables usually use *more* and *most* in comparisons. Have students complete this chart.

Adjective	Compare Two	Compare Three or More
terrific	more terrific	most terrific
wonderful	_____	_____
beautiful	_____	_____

CLASS ENRICHMENT

A Cooperative Activity Have students create an adjective reference box for the class. Write on index cards adjectives of two or more syllables, such as *delicious, amazing,* and *magnificent.* Have small groups write the comparative form on each index card, with an example sentence and a note that says *compares two* or *compares three or more.* You may wish to have volunteers alphabetize the cards.

CHALLENGE

An Independent Extension Using *The Guinness Book of World Records* as a reference, have students write about two unusual record-breaking feats. Tell them to use adjectives that compare in their writing. You may wish to have them share their completed comparisons with the class.

■ Easy ■ Average ■ Challenging

OBJECTIVES
To identify and use the adjective suffixes *-able*, *-ful*, *-less*, and *-y*

ASSIGNMENT GUIDE
BASIC   Practice A
               Practice B
ADVANCED   Practice C

All should do the Language Corner.

RESOURCES
■ Reteaching Master 45
■ Practice Master 45

TEACHING THE LESSON

1. Getting Started
Oral Language Focus attention on this oral activity, encouraging all to participate. Begin by asking students if they know the meaning of each word with the suffix *-less*. Explain that *-less* means "without."

2. Developing the Lesson
Guide students through the explanation of adjective suffixes, emphasizing the definition and the examples. Guide students through Building Your Vocabulary. Identify those who would benefit from reteaching. Assign independent Practice A–C.

3. Closing the Lesson
After students complete the Practice exercises, tell them to listen and look for words with adjective suffixes. When they have gathered at least three, have them use a dictionary to check the spelling. Point out to students that knowing how to add suffixes to base words can help them increase their vocabulary and express their ideas effectively.

Language Corner You may wish to have students discuss and list acronyms with which they are familiar, such as *RADAR* (Radio detecting and ranging) and *UNICEF* (United Nations International Children's Emergency Fund), before having them create their own acronyms.

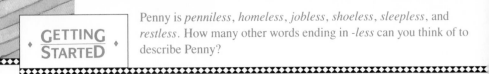

GETTING STARTED
Penny is *penniless*, *homeless*, *jobless*, *shoeless*, *sleepless*, and *restless*. How many other words ending in *-less* can you think of to describe Penny?

VOCABULARY ◆
Adjective Suffixes

You have already learned that a prefix—a word part added to the beginning of a word—changes a word's meaning. For example, *un-* can be added to *happy* to form *unhappy*.

A word part can also be added to the end of a word. For example, *-less* can be added to *luck* to form *luckless*. A word part added to the end of a word is called a **suffix**. A suffix also changes the meaning of a word.

Remember that a base word is the simplest form of a word. Many adjectives are formed by adding a suffix to a base word. Here are some common suffixes and their meanings.

Suffix	Meaning	Example
-able	worthy of, able to be	honorable, likable
-ful	full of, having qualities of	helpful, beautiful
-less	without	tasteless, colorless
-y	having, being like	funny, fuzzy

Notice how the spellings change when suffixes are added to base words like these: like, likable; beauty, beautiful; fun, funny.

Building Your Vocabulary

Your family is having a picnic. You are having a wonderful time. Suddenly, however, you notice a huge band of dark clouds quickly covering the sky. Tell more about your picnic. Use adjectives made from the words below. **Answers will vary.**

storm	wind	harm	power	rain
cloud	help	scare	enjoy	care

242   VOCABULARY: Adjective Suffixes

ESSENTIAL LANGUAGE SKILLS
This lesson provides opportunities to:

LISTENING ◆ select from an oral presentation the information needed

SPEAKING ◆ use a variety of words to express feelings and ideas ◆ make organized oral presentations

READING ◆ relate experiences with appropriate vocabulary in complete sentences ◆ use context to understand the meaning of words ◆ understand content area vocabulary ◆ follow a set of directions

WRITING ◆ spell increasingly complex words ◆ apply increasingly complex conventions of punctuation and capitalization ◆ write legible cursive letters

LANGUAGE ◆ use modifiers (adjectives) correctly ◆ use the fundamentals of grammar, punctuation, and spelling

Practice

A. Write each sentence. Add one of the suffixes below to the word in parentheses ( ) to complete the sentence.

-able   **-ful**   **-less**   **-y**

1. That shirt is too expensive; it is not (afford).
2. The cobblestone road was long and (bump).
3. Maria was well liked because she was very (thought).
4. The ride by wagon was quite (uncomfort).
5. It was a (cloud) and (star) night.
6. Steven bakes (wonder) chocolate chip cookies.
7. The cat crouched (motion) under the bush.
8. The young soldier was (fear) in the face of danger.

B. *Joyful* means "full of joy." *Joyless* means "without joy." Use *-ful* and *-less* to form adjectives from the words in parentheses.

9. Thad was (help) to the (help) bird with the broken wing.
10. A (power) bear grabbed the (power) salmon.
11. Airline mechanics must do (care), not (care), work.
12. The garter snake is (harm), but the rattlesnake is (harm).

C. Write a word for each definition. Use the suffixes below.

-able   **-ful**   **-less**   **-y**

13. without life
14. full of peace
15. being like a mouse
16. having scales
17. able to break
18. without worth

LANGUAGE CORNER • Acronyms

Have you ever been scuba diving? *Scuba* is an **acronym**, a word made from the first letters of *self-contained underwater breathing apparatus*. *Soth* might be an acronym for *students opposed to homework*. Make some acronyms of your own.

Self
Contained
Underwater
Breathing
Apparatus

VOCABULARY: Adjective Suffixes   **243**

MASTERS ON FILE

RETEACHING   **45**

Adjective Suffixes

An adjective suffix is a word part added to the end of a base word to form an adjective. Each word below has an adjective suffix. Draw a line between each base word and its adjective suffix.

1. comfort|able   3. care|less   5. power|ful
2. play|ful   4. cloud|y   6. manage|able

A. Write each sentence. Add a suffix from the box to the word in parentheses ( ).

| -able | -ful | -less | -y |

EXAMPLE: The pioneers made (remark) journeys.
The pioneers made remarkable journeys.

1. The trip west seemed (end).
The trip west seemed endless.

2. (Rain) weather often caused floods.
Rainy weather often caused floods.

3. It was hard for the pioneers to remain (cheer).
It was hard for the pioneers to remain cheerful.

B. In each column draw lines to match each word with its definition.

EXAMPLE: washable — having qualities of beauty
beautiful — able to be washed

4. joyful	having fuzz / having no fuzz	9. enjoyable	without care / full of care
5. fuzzy	having worth / without worth	10. careful	without leaves / having leaves
6. worthless	full of joy / being like joy	11. readable	full of joy / able to be enjoyed
7. cloudless	having rain / without rain	12. harmless	without being read / able to be read
8. rainy	without clouds / full of clouds	13. leafy	without harm / full of harm

PRACTICE   **45**

Adjective Suffixes

A. Underline the word with the adjective suffix in each sentence. Then write the base word.

1. Some spiders have hairy bodies.   hair
2. These creepy insects scare me.   creep
3. Most spiders are harmless.   harm
4. They really are quite useful.   use
5. They eat harmful bugs.   harm
6. The web of a spider is remarkable.   remark
7. Their webs are strong but breakable.   break
8. Spiders are skillful in spinning their webs.   skill
9. The strands of the web are smooth and silky.   silk
10. Spiders spin careful patterns and designs in their webs.   care

B. Write a word for each meaning. Use the underlined word as the base word. Then add one of these suffixes: -able, -ful, -less, -y.

11. without sleep	sleepless	23. without care	careless
12. worthy of honor	honorable	24. full of grace	graceful
13. full of joy	joyful	25. without harm	harmless
14. having lumps	lumpy	26. worthy of notice	noticeable
15. full of color	colorful	27. being like a fox	foxy
16. full of wonder	wonderful	28. able to be depended on	dependable
17. having a hill	hilly	29. being like fluff	fluffy
18. worthy of respect	respectable	30. having good luck	lucky
19. full of peace	peaceful	31. without motion	motionless
20. full of truth	truthful	32. being like water	watery
21. able to be read	readable	33. without fear	fearless
22. full of shame	shameful	34. without blame	blameless

◀|||| TEACHING OPTIONS ||||▶

RETEACHING

A Different Modality Emphasize that an adjective suffix can change the meaning of a word. Distribute cards with a base word written on one side and the same base word with an adjective suffix on the other. Include words such as *break/breakable*, *use/useful*, *fear/fearless*, and *fuzz/fuzzy*. Encourage students to find and discuss the definitions of both the base word and the suffixed word.

CLASS ENRICHMENT

A Cooperative Activity Have students work in pairs to create a written suffix test for their classmates. Have them include at least fifteen items similar to the following:

1. depend + _?_ = dependable
2. _?_ + -ful = cheerful
3. harm + -less = _?_ .

CHALLENGE

An Independent Extension Have students create their own acronyms on paper strips that fold out to reveal the words the acronym stands for. You may wish to suggest that they use sports, TV shows, music, or hobbies to get their ideas. You may also wish students to create a bulletin board using their fold-out acronyms.

243

Grammar-Writing Connection

OBJECTIVES
To apply grammar skills to writing
To work together to use adjectives to add detail to writing

How to Expand Sentences with Adjectives

Point out to students that they can use the grammar skills they learned in Unit 5 to help them develop good writing techniques. Explain that in this Grammar-Writing Connection, students will use what they know about adjectives, predicate adjectives, comparative and superlative forms of adjectives, and adjective suffixes to learn how to expand sentences with adjectives.

You may wish to guide students through the explanation of how to expand sentences with adjectives, stressing the examples. Then have students apply the information by completing the activity at the bottom of the first page. Students may work in small groups or with partners to choose adjectives for each noun orally, or they may add adjectives in writing as an independent activity.

Help students to understand that using adjectives is an effective way to improve writing by adding details that will help readers create clear pictures in their minds. Point out that using adjectives can make their writing more descriptive and interesting.

GRAMMAR CONNECTION WRITING

How to Expand Sentences with Adjectives

You have been using adjectives to write more colorful and interesting sentences. Adjectives can make a difference in your writing. The ones you choose can add details that will help readers create clear pictures in their minds. Which sentence below gives you a better description of what Dale delivers?

- **1.** Dale delivers dinners and desserts.
- **2.** Dale delivers delicious dinners and delightful desserts.

Both sentences tell us what Dale delivers, but sentence **2** gives us much more than the facts. Sentence **2** includes adjectives that describe the nouns *dinners* and *desserts*. The adjectives *delicious* and *delightful* make Dale's meals sound very inviting.

Different adjectives could give an entirely different picture. Would you order a meal from Dale if he served the food described in sentence **3**?

- **3.** Dale delivers dreadful dinners and drab desserts.

> **The Grammar Game** ◆ Get active with adjectives! Choose a noun and write three adjectives that describe it. Try to include adjectives that appeal to different senses. Then choose another noun and start again. Can you write adjectives for all of the nouns below?
> Answers will vary.
>
> | | | | | |
> |---|---|---|---|---|
> | tiger | dream | machine | explorer | castle |
> | idea | skateboard | mountain | fire | flag |
> | dancer | sweater | tower | planet | elephant |
> | ocean | house | boots | winter | bridge |

◆ **244** ◆ COOPERATIVE LEARNING: Expanding Sentences

ESSENTIAL LANGUAGE SKILLS
This lesson provides opportunities to:

LISTENING ◆ select from an oral presentation the information needed

SPEAKING ◆ use a variety of words to express feelings and ideas ◆ participate in group problem-solving activities

READING ◆ evaluate and make judgments ◆ follow a set of directions

WRITING ◆ adapt information to accomplish a specific purpose with a particular audience

LANGUAGE ◆ use modifiers (adjectives) correctly

Working Together

As you do activities **A** and **B** with your group, use adjectives to add interesting details to your writing.

A. Use two adjectives of the group's choice to describe each noun below. Then have the group choose a person, place, or thing that fits the description. **Answers will vary. Possible answers follow.**

EXAMPLE: athlete

ANSWER: outstanding female athlete — Wilma Rudolph

1. _____ guitarist
   talented young
2. _____ story
   exciting mystery
3. _____ hamburger
   thick juicy
4. _____ town
   quaint old
5. _____ rabbit
   unusual talking
6. _____ lake
   clear blue
7. _____ movie
   long boring
8. _____ building
   red brick
9. _____ song
   lively popular
10. _____ beach
    crowded sandy
11. _____ hair
    black curly
12. _____ fruit
    tangy exotic

B. Expand each sentence by adding at least one adjective of the group's choice. The adjective must begin with the same sound as the noun it describes. Then make up more tongue twisters. **Answers will vary. Possible answers are shown.**

EXAMPLE: Tailors took tacks to Toytown.

ANSWER: Ten tall tailors took tiny tacks to tough Toytown.

13. Bruce brought back bread from the bakery.
    Brilliant burned bumbling
14. Nora's niece nibbles noodles.
    Nosy nimble ninety
15. Oliver owns an owl and oysters.
    Old ornery orange
16. Parrots polished pails of pineapples at the park.
    Purple painted prickly people's
17. A ram read riddles and rules on Roger's roof.
    royal ridiculous racing rusty

In Your Group

♦ Use people's names during discussion.

♦ Help keep everyone on the topic.

♦ Record all ideas and suggestions.

♦ Agree or disagree in a pleasant way.

WRITERS' CORNER • Overused Adjectives

Using the same adjectives too many times can make your writing dull and boring. Avoid using words like *great* and *good* too often.

OVERUSED: The movie was good because the acting was good and the ending was especially good.

IMPROVED: The movie was delightful because the acting was superb and the ending was especially clever.

Read what you wrote for the Writer's Warm-up. Did you overuse any adjectives? Could you replace any overused adjective with a different descriptive word?

COOPERATIVE LEARNING: Expanding Sentences ◇ **245** ◇

Working Together

The Working Together activities involve students in cooperative learning work groups. This is an opportunity to pair strong writers with students whose skills are weaker. Working together, they can all experience success.

Divide the class into small groups and have students read In Your Group. Encourage them to discuss why each task is important. Have them tell what might happen if the group does not follow through on each task. *(If we do not use people's names during discussion, we might not know who shared important ideas or whose turn is next. If we do not keep everyone on the topic, we might not complete the tasks. If we do not record all ideas and suggestions, we might miss some ideas that could be helpful. If we do not agree or disagree in a pleasant way, it will be difficult to work together.)*

Before students begin activities A and B, you may wish to have each group appoint a member to record the adjective-noun combinations and the expanded sentences. After each activity is completed, have the groups discuss how the adjectives added details that created clear pictures.

Writers' Corner

The Writers' Corner provides students with the opportunity to extend the Grammar-Writing Connection, helping them to develop the skills necessary to review and revise their own writing. Discuss the introductory sentences with students. Then have them work as a class or in pairs to discuss the two examples. Have students read aloud each example and identify the changes that were made. Have them tell how those changes made the improved example "better." Then have students apply the expanding sentences with adjectives techniques from this Grammar-Writing Connection to the sentences they wrote about lasting impressions for the Writers' Warm-up. Encourage students to rewrite their sentences if necessary. Discuss with them how using adjectives added details that improved their sentences, making their ideas more interesting and colorful.

UNIT 5

OVERVIEW

TWO-PART

flexibility

Unit 5 Overview

USING LANGUAGE TO DESCRIBE

books

FOR EXTENDED READING

EASY

 **The Best Town in the World** by Byrd Baylor. Scribner. The narrator takes a nostalgic look at a small Texas town where the blackberries seemed tastier, the dogs seemed smarter, and the creek water seemed clearer and colder.

AVERAGE

The Gift by Joan Lowery Nixon. Macmillan. The author deftly weaves reality and fantasy together in this story about a boy who is visiting his family in rural Ireland. Students will be as caught up as young Brian in the stories of leprechauns and other enchanted creatures his great-grandfather tells and will come away with a feel for Ireland and its lore.

CHALLENGING

The House of Dies Drear by Virginia Hamilton. Macmillan. The family in this absorbing mystery moves into a house that was once part of the Underground Railroad. The house has tunnels and secret passageways, and, possibly, a ghost. **Edgar Allan Poe Award, American Library Association Notable Children's Book.**

READ-ALOUD

Beyond the Divide by Kathryn Lasky. Macmillan. In this novel about life on a wagon train in the late 1840s, views of prairies, mountains, people, and events are seen through the eyes of a fourteen-year-old Amish girl. **New York Times Outstanding Book Award.**

SPACIOUS SKIES *quilt by Charlotte Warr-Andersen, Kearns, Utah. Collection of the Museum of American Folk Art; Museum of American Folk Art: The Scotchgard Collection of Contemporary Quilts.*

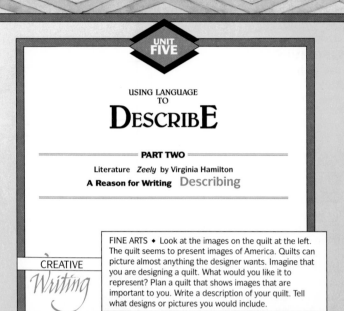

UNIT FIVE

USING LANGUAGE
TO
DESCRIBE

PART TWO

Literature *Zeely* by Virginia Hamilton
A Reason for Writing Describing

CREATIVE *Writing*

FINE ARTS ◆ Look at the images on the quilt at the left. The quilt seems to present images of America. Quilts can picture almost anything the designer wants. Imagine that you are designing a quilt. What would you like it to represent? Plan a quilt that shows images that are important to you. Write a description of your quilt. Tell what designs or pictures you would include.

start with CREATIVE WRITING

Fine Arts gives your students a chance to express themselves creatively in writing. After students observe the illustration on page 246 for a moment or two, have a volunteer read aloud the Fine Arts paragraph on page 247. Have students write their reactions in their journals. Then encourage a discussion of their ideas.

VIEWING

See the **Fine Arts Transparencies with Viewing Booklet** and the **Video Library.**

THEN START WITH *part 2*

A Reason for Writing: Describing is the focus of Part 2. First students learn a thinking strategy for describing. Then they read and respond to a selection of literature on which they may model their own writing. Developmental composition lessons, including "Interviews," a speaking and listening lesson, help students learn to use language correctly to describe. All the lessons reflect the literature. All culminate in the Writing Process lesson. The unit ends with the Curriculum Connection and Books to Enjoy, which help students discover how their new language skills apply to writing across the curriculum and to their own lives.

◆ If you began with grammar instruction, you may wish to remind students of the unit theme, "Lasting Impressions." Tell them that the information they gathered through the thematic lessons helped them prepare for reading the literature, *Zeely* by Virginia Hamilton.

◆ If you are beginning with Part 2, use the lessons in Part 1 for remediation or instruction. For grammar, spelling, and mechanics instructional guidance, you may wish to refer to the end-of-text Glossary and Index, as well as to the *Spelling Connection* booklet; the full-color *Revising and Proofreading Transparencies;* and the Unit Pretest, Posttest, and Writing Samples.

THEME BAR

CATEGORIES	Environments	Business/World of Work	Imagination	Communications/ Fine Arts	People	Science	Expressions	Social Studies
THEMES	UNIT 1 Farm Life	UNIT 2 Handicrafts	UNIT 3 Tall Tales	UNIT 4 The Visual Arts	UNIT 5 Lasting Impressions	UNIT 6 Volcanoes	UNIT 7 Nature	UNIT 8 Animal Habitats
PACING	1 month	1 month	1 month	1 month	1 month	1 month	1 month	1 month

■ Easy ■ Average ■ Challenging

OBJECTIVES
To use a thought balloon as a
strategy for describing

TEACHING THE LESSON

1. Getting Started
Oral Language Introduce the thinking skill, point of view, by asking students to imagine that they are in a store and are in a hurry to pay and leave. Say: *An elderly person in front of you is taking a lot of time. Are you patient and polite or impatient and rude? Why?* If no one mentions it, suggest the possibility of considering the elderly person's feelings.

Metacognition Help students become aware of their own thinking (think metacognitively) by asking follow-up questions *(e.g., How can you know or guess what another person might think or feel?)*. Encourage a variety of responses *(e.g., I tried to imagine how I would feel. I've heard my grandmother talking about situations like this).* Explain that being able to understand other points of view is a valuable thinking skill and that in this lesson they will learn about one strategy for understanding points of view.

2. Developing the Lesson
Guide students through the introduction to describing (the kind of literature and writing they will deal with in this unit) and its connection to point of view. Lead them through Learning the Strategy, emphasizing the model thought balloon. Identify those who would benefit from reteaching. Assign Using the Strategy A and B.

3. Closing the Lesson
Metacognition Applying the Strategy is a metacognitive activity in which students consider *how* they think (question 1) and *when* they think (question 2).

Question 1: Encourage students to share how making a thought balloon might have helped them imagine a point of view *(e.g., It made me slow down and gave me time to think it through. Having to write words for the*

CREATIVE THINKING ◆
A Strategy for Describing

A THOUGHT BALLOON

Describing is using details to paint word pictures. Authors use descriptive writing to make story characters come alive. After this lesson, you will read part of *Zeely* by Virginia Hamilton. It is a story with many interesting and well-described characters. Later you will describe someone when you write a character sketch.

What is a character description? It may be about the outside, how a person looks or acts. It may also be about the inside, how a person thinks and feels. In *Zeely*, Virginia Hamilton puts the reader right inside a young girl's mind. In this passage the girl, Geeder, is spending the night outdoors.

She had closed her eyes again when she heard a rustling sound on Leadback Road. . . . Night travellers! She dove under the covers. But something's happening! she told herself, poking her head out again. It took all her courage to crawl out of the covers and the few feet over the wet grass up to the hedge. She trembled with fear but peeked through the hedge in spite of it. . . . Something tall and white was moving down the road. It didn't quite touch the ground.

How does Geeder feel when she hears strange sounds at night? Can you understand her point of view? How would *you* feel? Can you see how getting inside a character's mind can make a story interesting and exciting?

◆ Learning the Strategy

Understanding someone else's point of view is often useful. How can you do it? You can put yourself in that person's place. You can imagine how you would feel in the same situation. For

248   CREATIVE THINKING: Point of View

ESSENTIAL LANGUAGE SKILLS
This lesson provides opportunities to:

LISTENING ◆ employ active listening in a variety of situations

SPEAKING ◆ use a variety of words to express feelings and ideas ◆ use a set of reasons to persuade a group

READING ◆ draw logical conclusions ◆ evaluate and make judgments ◆ follow a set of directions ◆ use graphic sources for information, such as pictures and diagrams ◆ make valid inferences about a reading selection

WRITING ◆ adapt information to accomplish a specific purpose with a particular audience

LANGUAGE ◆ use the fundamentals of grammar, punctuation, and spelling

example, suppose you have a younger cousin who is afraid to swim. Are you sympathetic? Why? Imagine that you are checking out of a store. You are in a hurry. An elderly person in front of you is moving slowly. Why might you be patient and polite even though you are in a hurry?

Making a thought balloon is one way to help imagine someone's point of view. Consider that cousin who is afraid to swim. The thought balloon below shows what that child might be thinking. What else might your cousin be thinking? What ideas can you add?

I won't be able to float. I'll sink. I'll get too tired.

cousin

Using the Strategy

A. Who is your favorite character from books, movies, or television? Imagine that that character has come to visit your community. How might he or she (or it!) feel about the place? What might that character want to do there? Make a thought balloon for that character about your community. You might want to use the balloon as the basis for a story.

B. Reread the passage from *Zeely* on page 248. What is the white shape coming down the road? Make a thought balloon for Geeder. Write what you think *she* thinks it is. Then read *Zeely* and decide if you—and Geeder—were right!

Applying the Strategy

♦ How does making a thought balloon help you imagine someone's point of view?
♦ When have you recently thought about someone else's point of view—and why?

CREATIVE THINKING: Point of View ◁249▷

other person made me think more deeply about that person's thoughts). Also encourage students to share any personal strategies they might prefer to use. For instance, some students may say they draw pictures of the person or list observations about the person or visualize themselves looking out from the person's eyes. Reassure them that a thought balloon is only one strategy for understanding a point of view, and that they should use what works for them.

Question 2: Encourage a diversity of responses (e.g., *My friend got mad at me and I tried to see it her way so we could be friends again. I wanted to persuade my mother to let me join a club, so I tried to think of reasons that would appeal to her).*

Looking Ahead

The thinking strategy introduced in this lesson, a thought balloon, is used in Using the Strategy B as a prereading strategy to help students anticipate the literature, *Zeely.* It will appear three more times in this unit and again in Unit 4.

THOUGHT BALLOON			
Strategy for Persuading	Writing to Learn	Prewriting	Writing Across the Curriculum
195	199	212	218

Strategy for Describing	Writing to Learn	Prewriting	Writing Across the Curriculum
249	255	266	272

Although the thought balloon strategy is repeated in each presentation, the context in which it is used changes. Students will thus be given the opportunity to discover how the strategy can help them in reading, in writing across the curriculum, and in their daily lives.

◀║║║ TEACHING OPTIONS ║║║▶

RETEACHING

A Different Modality Pass around a photograph of a person with an interesting facial expression or in an interesting situation (e.g., a homeless person, a circus highwire performer). Post the photograph. Have students write thought balloons, cut them out, and post them all around the photograph. Discuss how students thought of their responses and foster appreciation of the diversity of insights and responses.

CLASS ENRICHMENT

A Cooperative Activity Give an assignment such as a math problem or a social studies chapter to read. Have partners do the assignment and also observe each other doing it. When the assignment is finished, ask students to write thought balloons for their partners telling what they believe the partner was thinking as he or she heard the assignment and carried it out. Let the partners discuss how accurate they were.

CHALLENGE

An Independent Extension Assign students to watch the evening news broadcasts on television and to choose one person in the news (e.g., the President, a flood victim, the winning quarterback in a football game) and to write a thought balloon or balloons for that person. Have the students use their thought balloons as a prewriting strategy for a story in which the person they chose is the main character.

UNIT 5
Literature

VOCABULARY STRATEGIES

Developing Concepts and Teaching Vocabulary

Preteach the following words from the story. Use the Dictionary of Knowledge at the back of the book to provide definitions of base words and context sentences.

ominous(ly), ebony, oblong

Show students something made of dark wood and ask them to describe its color. Introduce the word *ebony*, explaining that it is the black or very dark brown wood of certain tropical trees. Ask volunteers to name shapes they have seen. Then have volunteers name objects that are *oblong*. (tables, bulletin boards, notebooks) Have a volunteer glare at the class *ominously*. Then have students tell how the volunteer looked and how the expression made them feel. (alarmed, frightened)

GUIDING COMPREHENSION

Building Background

The first half of this unit includes information especially chosen to build background for *Zeely*. If you started the unit with grammar instruction, you may wish to have a class discussion of the unit theme, **Lasting Impressions**, based on the information in those lessons.

    If you started the unit with composition instruction, you may wish to build students' knowledge of memorable people by asking: *What people in your life have made lasting impressions? What was it about those people that made them so memorable?* (Students may mention famous people who have done great, exciting, or admirable things. They also may mention people who have influenced them personally to strive harder and achieve in school or other areas of their lives.)

250

LITERATURE

AWARD WINNING AUTHOR

from

Zeely

by Virginia Hamilton

◇ **250** ◇ LITERATURE: Story

ESSENTIAL LANGUAGE SKILLS

This lesson provides opportunities to:

LISTENING ◆ employ active listening in a variety of situations

SPEAKING ◆ engage in creative dramatic activities and nonverbal communication ◆ use a variety of words to express feelings and ideas

READING ◆ relate experiences with appropriate vocabulary in complete sentences ◆ summarize a selection ◆ understand cause-and-effect relationships ◆ predict probable future outcomes ◆ evaluate and make judgments ◆ respond to various forms of literature ◆ explain and relate to the feelings and emotions of characters

WRITING ◆ use ideas and information from sources other than personal experience for writing ◆ write and compose for a variety of purposes

LANGUAGE ◆ use the fundamentals of grammar, punctuation, and spelling

Elizabeth Perry was determined to make this a special summer on Uncle Ross's farm. She began by giving herself and her younger brother the new summer names of Geeder and Toeboy. During her first day on the farm, Geeder also made up names for the town and the road, but not for the huge razorback hogs that Mr. Nat Tayber and his daughter kept on Uncle Ross's land. That evening Geeder made up a story about night travellers.

Geeder told the frightening story as she and Toeboy were sleeping out behind the lilac bush on the farm's front lawn. Geeder could almost see these ghostly creatures, who walk along dark roads at night and scare anyone who dares to watch them. The thought of night travellers going by on Leadback Road kept Geeder and Toeboy awake for a long time. Then they finally fell asleep, hidden safely behind the hedge.

A long time passed. Geeder dozed and awoke with a start. The grass behind the tip of her toes was wet with dew. She pulled the blankets more tightly around her, tucking her feet safely inside. She had closed her eyes again when she heard a rustling sound on Leadback Road.

Some old animal, she thought. The sound grew louder and she could not think what it was. Suddenly, what she had told Toeboy flashed through her mind.

Night travellers! She dove under the covers.

But something's happening! she told herself, poking her head out again.

It took all her courage to crawl out of the covers and the few feet over the wet grass up to the hedge. She trembled with fear but peeked through the hedge in spite of it. What she saw made her bend low, hugging the ground for protection. Truthfully, she wasn't sure what she saw. The branches of the hedge didn't allow much of a view.

Something tall and white was moving down the road. It didn't quite touch the ground. Geeder could hear no

LITERATURE: Story 〈251〉

Developing a Purpose for Reading

Option 1: Have students set their own purpose for reading. Then have them read the story introduction and study the illustrations. Explain that in this story Geeder is a girl who lives on Uncle Ross's farm and that she and her little brother are sleeping outside one night. On the chalkboard write: *I think a person who is _____, _____, and _____ might impress Geeder.* Have volunteers complete the sentence. Remind them to use what they know about themselves, the introduction, and the story illustrations for information on which to base their predictions. You may wish to record students' predictions for later use.

Option 2: If you wish to set a reading purpose for everyone, have students pay special attention to the selection's descriptions. Have them ask themselves: *What about Zeely is so memorable? What is she like?*

GUIDED READING

Please note that opportunities for students' personal responses to the selection are offered in the Reader's Response question and the Selection Follow-up at the end of this lesson.

Page 251 *What did the sound Geeder heard remind her of?* (night travelers) RECALL: DETAILS

SUMMARY

One night when Geeder and her brother Toeboy are camping out under the stars, Geeder sees a mysterious figure moving down the road. She does not know what to make of the spooky "night traveler," but the next day she learns the identity of her vision. It is Miss Zeely Tayber, the daughter of a man who is renting land on Uncle Ross's farm. Geeder is spellbound by the sight of Zeely, who is very tall, very thin, and very beautiful.

ABOUT THE AUTHOR

VIRGINIA HAMILTON (1936–1988) was born in Yellow Springs, Ohio, and studied at Antioch College and Ohio University. In 1967 she began her distinguished literary career with the publication of *Zeely,* the book from which this selection was taken. The author's achievements include *M. C. Higgins, the Great,* which won both the **Newbery Medal** and the **National Book Award** in 1975, and two **Newbery Honor Books**—*The Planet of Junior Brown* and *Sweet Whispers, Brother Rush.*

sound of footsteps. She couldn't see its head or arms. Beside it and moving with it was something that squeaked ominously. The white, very long figure made a rustling sound when she held her breath. It passed by toward town.

Geeder watched, moving her head ever so slowly until she could no longer see it. After waiting for what seemed hours, quaking at each sound and murmur of the night, she crept back to bed, pulling the covers over her eyes. She lay, cold and scared, unable to think and afraid even to clear her dry throat. This way, she fell asleep. She awoke in the morning, refreshed but stiff in every muscle.

Geeder lay for a moment, watching mist rise from the pink, sweet clover that sprinkled the lawn. The air smelled clean and fresh and was not yet hot from the sun.

"I've got to decide," she whispered. In the stillness, the sound of her own voice startled her. She turned carefully around to see if Toeboy had stirred. The tangled bedding deep in the lilac bush did not move.

"If I tell Toeboy about the night traveller," she whispered, "he might not want to sleep outside any more. Just think of it! Not more than a few hours ago, an awful, spooky thing walked by here!"

Geeder wasn't at all sure she wanted to sleep outside again, herself.

"Goodness knows what a night traveller will do if it sees you watching! Maybe I'd better tell Uncle Ross . . . . Maybe I shouldn't."

Geeder knew it would take her a while to figure out what course to take. Almost any minute now, the people Uncle Ross rented land to would come down the road. Uncle Ross had said they came every morning as soon as the sun was well up in the sky. It was just about time, and watching them would be something to do.

When her dew-soaked blankets grew warm from the sun, Geeder whistled for Toeboy as softly as she could. Turning around, she saw one eye peek out from the lilac bush.

"Wake up, Toeboy!" she whispered loudly. "I think I hear them coming!"

Toeboy leaped up before he looked where he was going

and hit his head against a branch.
Leaves spilled dew all over him.
He was wet and still half asleep
when Geeder yanked him to the
ground before they could be seen.

They knelt low by the hedge. Trying
not to move or blink an eye, they
watched Mr. Tayber and his daughter
come into view along Leadback Road.
What they saw was no ordinary sight.
They watched, spellbound, for nothing
in the world could have prepared them
for the sight of Miss Zeely Tayber.

Zeely Tayber was more than six and
a half feet tall, thin and deeply dark as a
pole of Ceylon ebony. She wore a long
smock that reached to her ankles. Her
arms, hands and feet were bare, and her

LITERATURE: Story

Page 252 *Why do you think Geeder wanted to be able to observe Mr. Tayber and his daughter without them seeing her?* (Students may feel that Geeder is a child with an active imagination who likes mysteries. Watching Mr. Tayber and his daughter without being seen herself and without talking to them would allow Geeder to imagine what she wants to about the strangers.) INFER: FEELING/ATTITUDES

GUIDED READING

Page 254 *Why do you believe Geeder was so stunned at seeing Zeely Tayber?* (Zeely was very tall and unusual looking. Also, Geeder may have partly realized that this was not the first time she had seen Zeely and that Zeely was, in fact, the ''night traveler'' she saw in the middle of the night.) INFER: CAUSE/EFFECT

Returning to the Reading Purpose

Option 1: Those students who have written words to describe a person who might impress Geeder may wish to review them to see if their first thoughts were correct.

Option 2: If you have established a common reading purpose, review it and ask students to summarize what is so memorable about Zeely Tayber.

Who was your favorite character in the story? Why? (You may wish to suggest to students that they cite passages from the story to help them explain why they chose a particular character.)

STORY MAP

You may want to have students make a story map for this excerpt from *Zeely* similar to the one below.

Characters:	Geeder; her younger brother, Toeboy; Mr. Tayber; Mr. Tayber's daughter, Zeely
Setting:	the front lawn at Uncle Ross's farm late one night and the following morning

Problem: Geeder doesn't know what to make of a mysterious figure she sees while camping out on the lawn one night.

Event 1: During the night, Geeder is frightened when she sees a tall, white figure moving down the road and hears a mysterious squeaking sound.

Event 2: In the morning Geeder and her brother see the people their uncle rents land to walking down the road.

Event 3: Geeder is impressed by Zeely, who is very tall and beautiful and is wearing a long smock.

Event 4: Zeely and her father are carrying feed pails that make a grating sound.

Resolution: Geeder realizes the mysterious night traveler was actually Zeely.

---

thin, <u>oblong</u> head didn't seem to fit quite right on her shoulders.

She had very high cheekbones and her eyes seemed to turn inward on themselves. Geeder couldn't say what expression she saw on Zeely's face. She knew only that it was calm, that it had pride in it, and that the face was the most beautiful she had ever seen.

Zeely's long fingers looked exactly like bean pods left a long time in the sun.

Geeder wanted to make sure Toeboy noticed Zeely's hands but the Taybers were too close, and she was afraid they would hear her.

Mr. Tayber and Zeely carried feed pails, which made a grating sound. It was the only sound on the road besides that of Mr. Tayber's heavy footsteps. Zeely made no sound at all.

You would think she would, thought Geeder, she was so long and tall.

Geeder and Toeboy stayed quiet as the Taybers passed, and the Taybers gave no sign that they saw them hiding there. Uncle Ross had said that they were not known to speak much, even to one another. They had not lived in Crystal always, as Uncle Ross had.

Geeder and Toeboy watched the Taybers until they went out of sight. It was then that Toeboy said, "Let's go watch them in the field."

"No," said Geeder quietly, "no, Toeboy." She could not possibly have made him understand how stunned she had been at seeing Miss Zeely Tayber for the first time. Never in her life had she seen anyone quite like her.

Library Link ◆ *If you would like to read more about Geeder, Toeboy, and Zeely, read* Zeely *by Virginia Hamilton.*

 ## Reader's Response

Who was your favorite character in the story? Why?

STRATEGIC READING

Page 254 Have students predict whether or not Geeder will tell Toeboy about the night traveler and whether or not Toeboy will sleep outside again. Suggest that they use a thought balloon to help them understand what Geeder is thinking. (Students may predict that Geeder will tell Toeboy because it is hard to keep so big a secret and that they both will decide to sleep outside again to find out who or what the night traveler is.)
METACOGNITION: SUMMARIZING AND PREDICTING

HIGHLIGHTING LITERATURE

Page 254 Point out that the author compares Zeely to a pole of Ceylon ebony and her fingers to bean pods left a long time in the sun. Have students identify color and shape as two things Zeely and the pole of ebony have in common, pointing out that writers and poets often compare people to things in order to create clearer pictures of the people they are describing. Ask students how this comparison and the one about Zeely's fingers make them feel about Zeely.

Zeely

Responding to Literature

1. Have you ever been as amazed by your first sight of someone as Geeder was by her first sight of Zeely? Explain.

2. Mr. Tayber and Zeely seem to be mysterious people. What makes a person "mysterious"?

3. Virginia Hamilton paints a word picture of Zeely. Draw a picture of how you think Zeely looks. Show details that make her a special person unlike any other. Underneath the picture write a sentence to tell classmates who or what Zeely reminds you of.

Writing to Learn

Think and Imagine ◆ One way to learn about someone is to imagine what that person is thinking. In a thought balloon write words and phrases Geeder might have been thinking as Zeely and Mr. Tayber walked by her.

Thought Balloon

Write ◆ Write the entry that Geeder might have written in her journal that day.

LITERATURE: Story 255

SELECTION FOLLOW-UP

You may wish to incorporate any or all of the following discussion questions and activities in your follow-up to the literature selection, *Zeely.*

RESPONDING TO LITERATURE

Encourage students to use their personal experiences as well as what they learned from the selection to discuss these questions. The questions are designed to encourage students to think of and respond to the selection as a whole. Explain to students that although they may use details from the selection to support their opinions, the questions have no right or wrong answers. Encourage them to express a variety of points of view. You may wish to have students respond as a class, in groups, or with partners.

1. *Have you ever been as amazed by your first sight of someone as Geeder was when she first saw Zeely?* (Give students a point of view for answering the question by asking them to describe Geeder's reaction to Zeely.)

2. *Mr. Tayber and Zeely seem to be mysterious people. What makes a person "mysterious"?* (You may wish to have students discuss mysteries and what, in general, they think of as mysterious before having them tell what makes a specific person mysterious.)

3. *Virginia Hamilton paints a word portrait of Zeely. Draw a picture of how you think Zeely looks. Show details that make her a special person unlike any other. Underneath the picture write a sentence to tell classmates who or what Zeely reminds you of.* (If students have trouble visualizing Zeely, suggest that they reread the description of her in the story. They may want to decide what she reminds them of before they begin to draw. Or they may want to decide what she reminds them of after their drawing is finished.)

World of Language Audio Library

A recording of this selection is available in the **Audio Library.**

WRITING TO LEARN

Have students apply the thinking strategy of creating a thought balloon to show their understanding of the selection. Encourage them to put themselves in Geeder's place in order to understand what she was thinking. Then have them complete the sketch and the thought balloons as described in Think and Imagine. Students might write sentences such as: *I've never seen anyone like her. How beautiful she is! I wonder where she comes from.* Then have students complete the Write activity by using the sentences from their thought balloons to create a journal entry.

■ Easy ■ Average ■ Challenging

OBJECTIVES
To formulate questions for an interview

To use guidelines for conducting and responding to an interview

ASSIGNMENT GUIDE
BASIC   Practice A

           Practice B

ADVANCED   Practice C

All should do the Apply activity.

RESOURCES
■ World of Language Video Library

TEACHING THE LESSON

1. Getting Started
Oral Language Focus attention on this oral activity, encouraging all to participate. Before having students tell what questions they would ask, you may wish to develop with them a list of intriguing story characters and write the list on the chalkboard.

2. Developing the Lesson
Guide students through a discussion of the lesson, emphasizing the guidelines for asking interview questions and being an active listener. You may wish to discuss with students the idea that being an active listener will help them to be better interviewers. Lead students through the **Guided Practice.** Identify those who would benefit from reteaching. Assign independent Practice A–C.

To allow students to practice their speaking and listening skills, you may wish to provide as much class time as possible for oral discussion throughout this lesson.

3. Closing the Lesson
After students complete the Apply activity, call on individuals to read aloud their interview questions. Point out to students that knowing good interview techniques will help them learn more about people, which will in turn help them write more interesting papers and stories.

GETTING STARTED

Choose an intriguing story character, such as Zeely. What questions would you like to ask that person?

SPEAKING and LISTENING ◆
Interviews

Are you interested in people? Do you enjoy talking to people? Do you like to find out what people do, and why? Most of us find people fascinating. That is why people make such good subjects for writers.

One of the best ways for a writer to collect accurate and lively details about a person is to conduct an interview. Before you begin an interview, it is important to prepare for it. Decide what main things you would like to find out about the person. Then develop a list of questions to use while you are interviewing. Write the questions on cards. They are easy to handle. Here are some guidelines to help you conduct an interview.

Asking Interview Questions	1. Avoid questions that can be answered by *yes* or *no*. They are conversation stoppers. 2. Ask questions that encourage your subject to talk—questions that begin with *who, what, when, where, why,* and *how.* 3. Keep the interview focused. 4. Take notes or ask permission to use a tape recorder. 5. Thank the person for the interview.
Being an Active Listener	1. *Really* listen, instead of thinking "What will I ask next?" 2. If the person makes a surprising remark, follow up on it. Be willing to leave your prepared list of questions. 3. Watch the person's body language. Watch for a raised eyebrow, a sudden grin, a frown, a glance at the clock. What does it show about the person's feelings? 4. Listen for good quotes and write them down. Later, have the person approve your written quotations.

Summary ◆ Writers interview people to observe and collect details about them. Before you interview someone, prepare a list of questions that focus on your main topics.

ESSENTIAL LANGUAGE SKILLS
This lesson provides opportunities to:

LISTENING ◆ employ active listening in a variety of situations

SPEAKING ◆ use oral language for a variety of purposes

READING ◆ identify an implied main idea of a longer selection ◆ relate experiences with appropriate vocabulary in complete sentences ◆ evaluate and make judgments ◆ follow a set of directions

WRITING ◆ adapt information to accomplish a specific purpose with a particular audience

LANGUAGE ◆ use the fundamentals of grammar, punctuation, and spelling

Guided Practice

Make up questions you might ask when interviewing each of the people below. Be sure to ask *who*, *what*, *when*, *why*, *where*, and *how* questions. Answers will vary.

1. a popular TV star
2. the governor of your state
3. a computer programmer
4. a trapeze artist

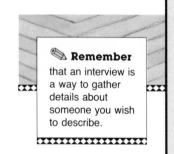

Practice

A. Work with a partner. Take turns making up questions that you might ask when interviewing each of the people below. Ask questions that begin with *who*, *what*, *when*, *why*, *where*, and *how*. Answers will vary.

  5. a forest ranger
  6. an airline pilot
  7. the owner of a movie theater
  8. an Olympic gymnast

B. Work with a partner. Take turns asking and answering questions you could use when interviewing each person below. Answers will vary.
  9. the inventor of the vacuum cleaner
  10. the student who won a national science award

C. Prepare to interview your partner. Make a list of questions you will ask. Then follow the guidelines in this lesson as you interview each other in turn. Answers will vary.

Apply ◆ Think and Write

Dictionary of Knowledge ◆ Read about Virginia Hamilton, author of *Zeely* and other award-winning books for young people. What else would you like to know about her? Write five questions you would ask if you could interview this author.

> ✎ **Remember**
> that an interview is a way to gather details about someone you wish to describe.

SPEAKING and LISTENING: Interviews **257**

World of Language Video Library

You may wish to use the *Video Library* to teach this lesson.

EVALUATION PROGRAM

See Evaluation and Testing Program, pp. C9–C11.

Speaking and Listening Masters

◀▥ TEACHING OPTIONS ▥▶

RETEACHING

A Different Modality Emphasize listening. Have a volunteer ask you a question (e.g., *Where were you born?*). Ask students to listen to your answer and write a follow-up question (e.g., *What was your home town like?*). Have the group listen to and evaluate the follow-up questions by two criteria: 1. Did they really follow up on the answer? 2. Which ones would elicit the most additional information and why?

CLASS ENRICHMENT

A Cooperative Activity Have small groups do round-robin interviews. Have each group choose one member to be the interviewee. Have the group decide on a topic for the interview (e.g., the person's hobbies or experiences in moving from another place). Have group members take turns asking questions to elicit information on the topic. Have each group report to the class what they learned about their subject.

CHALLENGE

An Independent Extension Have students watch or listen to a television or radio interview on a news program or talk show. Have them take notes on the interview and note how well the interviewer followed each of the lesson guidelines. You may wish to have them report their findings to the class. If equipment is available, some students may enjoy making a videotape of the interview to show as part of their report.

UNIT 5
Writing

OBJECTIVES
To arrange details in a paragraph by space order and order of importance

ASSIGNMENT GUIDE
BASIC   Practice A
         ↓   Practice B
ADVANCED Practice C

All should do the Apply activity.

RESOURCES
■ Reteaching Master 46
■ Practice Master 46

TEACHING THE LESSON

1. Getting Started
Oral Language Focus attention on this oral activity, encouraging all to participate. You may wish to expand the activity by having students tell three details about famous figures from history, movie stars, or characters from books. After each set of details, you may wish to have volunteers guess who the person is.

2. Developing the Lesson
Guide students through the explanation of organizing details, emphasizing the examples and the summary. Lead students through the **Guided Practice.** Identify those who would benefit from reteaching. Assign independent Practice A–C.

3. Closing the Lesson
After students complete the Apply activity, encourage volunteers to share their descriptions with the class. Point out to students that when details are organized well, their descriptions will be clearer and easier to understand.

GETTING STARTED

Choose one of your good friends. Tell three details you would include if you were describing your friend to a stranger. If the class knows your friend, see if they can guess who it is.

WRITING ◆
Organizing Descriptive Details

How could these details be organized into a description of a girl?

well-worn sneakers	space between front teeth	brown eyes
laughs a lot	mischievous eyes	new braces
writing on high tops	great sense of humor	large feet

Alissa's mischievous brown eyes sparkle when she laughs. She laughs a lot, because she has a great sense of humor. She wears shiny new braces to correct the space between her front teeth. The metal glistens when she grins. The writing on her well-worn high tops distracts anyone who might notice her very large feet.

The details in this descriptive paragraph are organized in space order. Space order is the order in which objects are arranged in space. You can, for example, describe a person from top to bottom, as this writer did. You can also organize details in space order from front to back, left to right, near to far, or bottom to top.

Another way to organize details is by arranging them in their order of importance. You either state the most important detail first, or you build up to it last. For example, read the paragraph below that describes Zeely. (It is also on page 254.) Notice how the author leads up to the proud, serene beauty that Geeder sees in Zeely.

She had very high cheekbones and her eyes seemed to turn inward on themselves. Geeder couldn't say what expression she saw on Zeely's face. She knew only that it was calm, that it had pride in it, and that the face was the most beautiful she had ever seen.

Summary ◆ **Space order** and **order of importance** are two ways to organize details in a paragraph. They are especially useful ways to organize descriptive writing.

258   WRITING: Organizing Details

Guided Practice

Tell in what order you would arrange details to describe each item below. Choose *top to bottom*, *bottom to top*, *left to right*, *near to far*, or *front to back*. Answers may vary. Possible answers follow.

    left to right
1. clothes on a rack
   top to bottom or bottom to top
2. the Statue of Liberty

    front to back
3. shoppers in a checkout line
   near to far
4. your front door to the curb

Practice

A. Tell in what order you would arrange details to describe each item below. Choose *top to bottom*, *bottom to top*, *left to right*, *near to far*, or *front to back*. Answers may vary. Possible answers follow.

    front to back
5. the cars in a train
   top to bottom or bottom to top
6. a ski slope

    left to right
7. trophies on a shelf
   near to far
8. a highway stretching ahead

B. Write the topic sentence below. Under it, write the five details in correct space order. The correct sentence order is 10, 12, 9, 13, 11.

Topic Sentence: Five cars were parked in the driveway.

9. The station wagon was parked behind the taxicab.

10. The red convertible was parked at the head of the driveway.

11. The black limousine was parked at the end of the driveway.

12. In back of the convertible was the yellow taxicab.

13. The antique sedan was sandwiched between the station wagon and the black limousine.

C. Write the sentences below in the order of their importance. Put the most important detail first. The best sentence order is 16, 15, 14, 17.
Some students may say 16, 14, 15, 17.

14. Sparks of color flashed from the fabric as she moved.

15. Threads of gold, red, and blue glimmered in the sun.

16. The robe was of shimmering, multicolored silk.

17. The fabric fell in graceful folds to her ankles.

Apply ◆ Think and Write

Organizing a Description ◆ Describe your favorite outfit—a sports uniform, party clothes, or something you wear to school. Use space order or order of importance to organize your description.

> ✏️ **Remember**
> to organize details to help the reader picture what you describe.

WRITING: Organizing Details **259**

◀—— TEACHING OPTIONS ——▶

RETEACHING	CLASS ENRICHMENT	CHALLENGE
A Different Modality Have students place three objects on their desks. Then ask volunteers to describe in complete sentences what is on their desks. Have other students listen for the order in which the objects are mentioned, such as from left to right or from nearest to farthest. Point out that this is space order. Have students shift the position of the objects and describe them again.	**A Cooperative Activity** Have groups of students brainstorm the details for a description of their classroom. Suggest that in organizing these details, space order or order of importance might be used. Have the group decide which order to use and then have individuals in each group write a paragraph describing the classroom, using that kind of order. You may wish to have volunteers read their paragraphs aloud to compare and contrast their results.	**An Independent Extension** Have students write two paragraphs about an important person in their lives. Have them use space order in the first paragraph to tell what the person looks like and order of importance in the second paragraph to describe the person's character or personality. You may wish to have students write at the bottom of their page one sentence that tells which way of organizing details they prefer.

■ Easy ■ Average ■ Challenging

OBJECTIVES
To write a paragraph that
describes

ASSIGNMENT GUIDE
BASIC   Practice A
↓   Practice B
ADVANCED Practice C

All should do the Apply activity.

RESOURCES
■ Reteaching Master 47
■ Practice Master 47

TEACHING THE LESSON

1. Getting Started
Oral Language Focus attention on this oral activity, encouraging all to participate. You may wish to encourage students to tell one sentence about a character who other students know. You may wish to extend the activity by having students say sentences about figures from history. After each sentence have another student guess the identity of the character.

2. Developing the Lesson
Guide students through the explanation of a descriptive paragraph, emphasizing the examples and the summary. You may wish to discuss with students the topic sentence, *Judd's manner is overwhelmingly serious,* and review why certain details support the topic and other details do not support the topic. Lead students through the **Guided Practice.** Identify those who would benefit from reteaching. Assign independent Practice A–C.

3. Closing the Lesson
After students complete the Apply activity, encourage volunteers to read their descriptions to the class. Have the class decide to which photographs the descriptions refer. Point out to students that knowing how to write a descriptive paragraph will help them choose details that create the strongest, most desirable impression.

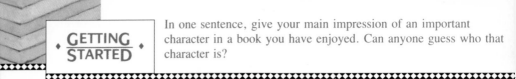

In one sentence, give your main impression of an important character in a book you have enjoyed. Can anyone guess who that character is?

WRITING ♦
A Descriptive Paragraph

Description starts with observation. You notice details that make your subject unique. You observe what a person looks like. You listen to the person's voice and the words he or she uses. When you have finished observing, you will have noticed many details. You will want to use some in your writing and discard others.

How will you decide which details to use and which to discard? You know that a paragraph focuses on one main idea, or topic. Often that topic is stated in a topic sentence. The other sentences give details that support the topic sentence. Details that do not support the topic sentence should be discarded.

How will you begin? Decide what impression you want to create. When you describe a person, think of one adjective that captures your main impression. Use that adjective in a topic sentence.

■ **Judd's manner is overwhelmingly <u>serious</u>.**

Then organize the details. Decide which support the topic and which do not. Decide which support the impression you want to create.

Support the Topic		Do Not Support the Topic	
gentle smile	solemn eyes	nervous laugh	not very tall
moves slowly	listens intently	taps feet	always late

Finally, decide on the best order for arranging the details. In this case, it might be order of importance. When your paragraph is written, the result should be a clearly organized description that creates the impression you want.

> **Summary** ♦ A **descriptive paragraph** has a main idea and descriptive details. Choosing the appropriate details helps you create the desired impression.

260   WRITING: Descriptive Paragraph

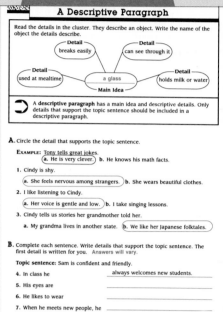

Guided Practice

Give a detail that supports each of these topic sentences.
Answers will vary.

1. Brad looks unhappy today.
2. Anthony looks friendly.
3. Janine is very dignified.
4. Suzanne was really surprised.

Practice

Write a detail sentence for each topic sentence below.
Answers will vary.

5. Kristen is dressed like a rock star.
6. Tyrone looks calm and cool.
7. Brenda appears to be annoyed.
8. Mark's haircut suits his personality.
9. Josh definitely looks angry.

Read the topic sentence below. Then read sentences 10–14. Write *yes* if the sentence gives a detail that supports the topic sentence. Write *no* if it does not.

TOPIC SENTENCE: Anna is bold and outgoing.

10. When she meets you, she flashes a dazzling smile. *yes*
11. She sits in pale silver moonlight, reading poetry. *no*
12. Her eyes sparkle as she talks "a mile a minute." *yes*
13. Her favorite outfit is fire-engine red. *yes*
14. Her voice is soft and soothing, a mere whisper. *no*

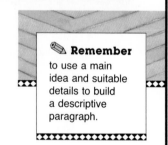

Write a paragraph describing one thing about someone you know well.
Paragraphs will vary.

Apply ♦ Think and Write

Descriptive Paragraph ♦ Look at the people in the photographs on these two pages. Choose one person to describe. As you study the person, ask yourself, "What is my main impression?" Then write a paragraph that describes the person. Remember to choose details that support your main idea.

> ✎ **Remember**
> to use a main idea and suitable details to build a descriptive paragraph.

WRITING: Descriptive Paragraph **261**

A Descriptive Paragraph

Read the details in the cluster. They describe an object. Write the name of the object the details describe.

- **Detail** breaks easily
- **Detail** can see through it
- **Detail** used at mealtime
- a glass — **Main Idea**
- **Detail** holds milk or water

A descriptive paragraph has a main idea and descriptive details. Only details that support the topic sentence should be included in a descriptive paragraph.

A. Circle the detail that supports the topic sentence.

EXAMPLE: Tony tells great jokes.
(a. He is very clever.) b. He knows his math facts.

1. Cindy is shy.
(a. She feels nervous among strangers.) b. She wears beautiful clothes.

2. I like listening to Cindy.
(a. Her voice is gentle and low.) b. I take singing lessons.

3. Cindy tells us stories her grandmother told her.
a. My grandma lives in another state. (b. We like her Japanese folktales.)

B. Complete each sentence. Write details that support the topic sentence. The first detail is written for you. Answers will vary.

Topic sentence: Sam is confident and friendly.

4. In class he ___ always welcomes new students.
5. His eyes are ___
6. He likes to wear ___
7. When he meets new people, he ___

PRACTICE 47

A Descriptive Paragraph

A descriptive paragraph has a main idea and descriptive details.

A. Write detail sentence for each topic sentence. Answers will vary.

1. The garden looked neglected.
2. Gina's favorite possession is the patchwork quilt from her grandmother.
3. The comedian seemed nervous.
4. Todd dressed carefully for the party.
5. The librarian was very helpful.

B. Circle yes if a sentence gives a detail that supports the topic sentence. Circle no if a sentence does not.

Topic sentence: The house looked haunted.

6. A large iron gate surrounded the property. (yes) no
7. Bright yellow daisies grew in the garden. yes (no)
8. Heavy wooden shutters covered all the windows. (yes) no
9. Boards were nailed across the cracked glass in the front door. (yes) no
10. Occasionally a low moaning sound came from inside. (yes) no
11. Even mice scampered quickly by the house. yes (no)

WRITE IT
On a separate sheet of paper, write a paragraph that describes your hands. Include as many details as you can. Answers will vary.

◀|||| TEACHING OPTIONS ||||▶

RETEACHING

A Different Modality Draw two pictures on the chalkboard, one of a tree in full bloom with birds flying around it and the other of a tree with bare branches and no birds in sight. As you record their ideas, have students tell what each picture is and say which details are missing in the second picture. Then have students use the main idea and details in a written descriptive paragraph about each picture.

CLASS ENRICHMENT

A Cooperative Activity Have partners find descriptive paragraphs in their student Textbooks. Tell them to copy on one sheet of paper the best paragraph they find, omitting the sentence that tells the main idea. Tell them to copy the main idea on another sheet of paper. Then have partners gather in groups of six, mix their paper strips, and work together to match each main idea to the correct detail sentences.

CHALLENGE

An Independent Extension Give each student a colorful picture, poster, or photograph. Have them decide what main impression the picture gives them and write a topic sentence based on that main impression. Have them write a paragraph describing the picture.

Reading–Writing Connection

262

OBJECTIVES

To identify sensory words
To work together to use sensory words
To use the Thesaurus to improve word choice

Focus on Sensory Words

Review the Unit 5 literature selection, *Zeely,* with students and have them recall the sensory words Virginia Hamilton uses that let the reader feel, see, hear, smell, or taste what is happening in the story. Then point out to students that they can use the selection to help them learn how to use sensory words that will let their readers see, hear, feel, smell, or taste what they are writing about.

You may wish to guide students through the introductory paragraphs, stressing the examples of details and sensory words. Explain that the details give a specific picture of what was happening, and that the sensory words let the reader feel, see, and hear what was going on.

Next, have students apply the information in the Reading-Writing Connection by discussing the activities at the bottom of the page. As students supply details from the story, guide them to recognize that the details tell about what is happening. As students supply sensory words from the story, have them identify the sense or senses the words appeal to. Emphasize that details give exact bits of information and that sensory words appeal to the senses.

Focus on Sensory Words

A writer writes a description hoping that you, the reader, will picture just what he or she had in mind. To do this, the writer uses details. Details are exact bits of information. They are like the focus of a camera, giving a clear image.

In addition, the writer uses **sensory words**. Those are words that appeal to the senses. Sensory words help the reader *see, hear, feel* — and sometimes even *smell* or *taste* — what is being described.

Virginia Hamilton uses both details and sensory words in *Zeely.* You read part of the book earlier in the unit.

DETAILS: "awoke with a start"; "hit his head against a branch"; "carried feed pails"

SENSORY WORDS: "dew-soaked blankets"; "warm from the sun"; "thin and deeply dark"; "made a grating sound"

The details give a specific picture of what was happening —Geeder waking suddenly, Toeboy hitting his head against a branch, Mr. Tayber and Zeely carrying feed pails. The sensory words let you feel the dew-soaked blankets and warmth of the sun. They let you see the appearance of Zeely and hear the sound made by the feed pails.

The Writer's Voice ◆ Look back at the passage from *Zeely.* Find at least five details (in addition to the ones above) that show you what is happening in the story.

Find at least five sensory words in *Zeely* (in addition to the ones above). These words help readers see, hear, feel, smell, or taste.

 262 COOPERATIVE LEARNING: Writer's Craft

ESSENTIAL LANGUAGE SKILLS

This lesson provides opportunities to:

LISTENING ◆ follow the logical organization of an oral presentation

SPEAKING ◆ make organized oral presentations

READING ◆ relate experiences with appropriate vocabulary in complete sentences ◆ use context clues for word identification ◆ recall specific facts and details that support the main idea and/or conclusion ◆ follow a set of directions ◆ use the dictionary and the encyclopedia to locate information

◆ adjust the method and rate of reading to the purpose and type of material ◆ respond to various forms of literature ◆ describe the time and setting of a story ◆ explain and relate to the feelings and emotions of characters

WRITING ◆ adapt information to accomplish a specific purpose with a particular audience

LANGUAGE ◆ use modifiers (adjectives) correctly

Working Together

Well-chosen details and sensory words help a reader picture what is being described. Use details and sensory words to create clear descriptions as your group does activities **A** and **B**.

In Your Group

♦ Contribute ideas.

♦ Keep the group on the subject.

♦ Help the group reach agreement.

♦ Record the group's ideas.

A. What sensory words would help create vivid and accurate pictures in the following sentences? Your group may wish to suggest two or three words for each sentence.
Answers may vary.   Possible answers follow.

1. After ten minutes in the rain, my wool suit felt _____ . soggy, sodden, leaden
2. The tall grass made a _____ sound in the gentle wind. whispering, rustling, rippling
3. Through the trees we saw an abandoned house; its windows were _____ . cobwebbed, bearded, grimy
4. Church bells _____ cheerily in the small New England town. chimed, pealed, rang
5. The chili tasted almost _____ after the blazing hot salsa. cool, mild, bland

B. With your group, write five sentences like those in activity **A**. Each sentence should focus on a different sense. Leave blanks for the sensory words. Then choose the sensory word that your group feels is best for each blank. Answers will vary.

THESAURUS CORNER • Word Choice

Each of the adjectives in dark type is a main entry in the Thesaurus. Replace it with a good synonym. After each sentence, write the name of the sense to which it appeals. Answers will vary.

1. The hot soup had become **warm** before the girls returned.
2. On her finger was a **beautiful** and expensive diamond ring.
3. The cake is so **light** that it will barely support twelve candles.
4. The **exciting** odor of bacon frying awakened us in the morning.
5. Across the valley came the **clear** notes of a Swiss yodeler.

COOPERATIVE LEARNING: Writer's Craft ◄ 263 ►

Working Together

The Working Together activities provide opportunities for students to work together in cooperative learning groups. You may wish to pair strong writers with students whose skills are weaker so that all students may experience success in writing.

Divide the class into small groups and have students read In Your Group. Encourage them to discuss why each task is important. (If we do not encourage everyone to contribute ideas, some members of the group may be afraid to speak up. If we do not keep on the subject, we will be unable to work together to complete the activity. If we cannot reach agreement, we will be unable to complete the activity. If we do not record ideas, we may forget important points that are discussed.)

You may wish to have each group appoint a timekeeper and a recorder. Then set a time limit. After students complete activity A, encourage groups to compare the sensory words they added to the sentences and discuss which senses the words appeal to. After activity B, call on a member of each group to read aloud the sentences students created. Have the class listen to determine how sensory words are used to let you see, hear, feel, smell, or taste what is being described.

Thesaurus Corner

The Thesaurus Corner provides students with the opportunity to extend the Reading-Writing Connection by using the Thesaurus in the back of the textbook. If necessary, remind them how a thesaurus is used. After students have replaced words with synonyms, call on individuals to read their sentences aloud. Encourage classmates to name the sense or senses to which each synonym appeals. Have students save their sentences for use later in the Writing Process lesson. Point out that learning about sensory words can help students develop their ability to create clear and interesting descriptions.

OBJECTIVES

To write a character sketch

To use five stages of the writing process: prewriting, writing, revising, proofreading, and publishing

RESOURCES

Writing Process Transparencies 17–20

Revising and Proofreading Transparencies

Spelling Connection

Writing Sample Tests, p. T554

INTRODUCTION

Connecting to Literature Have students read the lesson introduction, or ask a volunteer to read the introduction aloud. Remind students that one of the most memorable aspects of the literature selection, *Zeely,* is the character sketch of Zeely Tayber that the author gives. Have students add to the description of Zeely that is given in the introduction to this lesson. (Possible responses: She had high cheekbones; her eyes seemed to turn inward on themselves; she had long fingers and a thin oblong head; her face expressed calm, pride, and beauty.) Tell students that they will be writing a character sketch.

Purpose and Audience Ask students to give their own definition of a character sketch. (A vivid description of how someone looks, acts, and feels) Then have them tell about times they gave a description of someone they liked. (Students have probably described friends, family members, or classmates to other people. They may have written descriptions of others in letters or in their journals.)

Have students consider the questions: *What is my purpose?* (To write a vivid description of someone I know or admire) *Who is my audience?* (My classmates). Have students discuss what they believe they need to consider when trying to describe someone to another fifth-grader. Encourage a diversity of responses.

WRITING PROCESS
DESCRIBING

Writing a Character Sketch

"Zeely Tayber was more than six and a half feet tall, thin and deeply dark as a pole of Ceylon ebony." These words introduce the main character of the book *Zeely.* Geeder thinks Zeely looks like an African princess. Zeely, however, does not understand how special she is. She only feels different and shy. In the book, the

author Virginia Hamilton tells a great deal more about Geeder and Zeely. She tells her readers not only how her characters look, but also how they act and how they feel.

Know Your Purpose and Audience

In this lesson you will write a character sketch. Your purpose will be to write a vivid description of someone you know and admi

Your audience will be your classmates. Later you can have a Who's Who Day to share character sketches. You might also make a gift card for the person you described.

What's
MY PURPOSE

Who's
MY AUDIENCE

264   WRITING PROCESS: Character Sketch

ESSENTIAL LANGUAGE SKILLS

This lesson provides opportunities to:

LISTENING ◆ listen for specific information ◆ select from an oral presentation the information needed

SPEAKING ◆ read aloud a variety of written materials ◆ contribute to small group discussions ◆ respond appropriately to questions from teachers and peers

READING ◆ draw logical conclusions ◆ evaluate and make judgments ◆ follow a set of directions ◆ explain and relate to the feelings and emotions of characters

WRITING ◆ expand topics by collecting information from a variety of sources ◆ generate ideas using a variety of strategies, such as brainstorming, clustering, mapping, question and answer ◆ write biographical or autobiographical sketches ◆ use the thesaurus as a means to expand vocabulary ◆ improve writing based on peer and/or teacher response

LANGUAGE ◆ use language for describing ◆ use the fundamentals of grammar, spelling, and punctuation

Prewriting

First choose your topic—the person you will describe. Then use a strategy to gather details for your character sketch.

Choose Your Topic ♦ Start by listing the names of people who come to mind easily. Add to your list by giving it deeper thought. Then consider your list. Circle your best choice.

Think About It	Talk About It
How will you narrow your list? Cross out the name of any person about whom you do not know many details. Visualize each name remaining. Whom can you see most clearly in your mind? Whose personality would be most interesting to describe? Circle that name.	Talk with a partner about people who are special to you. Is there someone that you know well or admire? Do you have a relative who is special to you? Tell your partner details about the characteristics and personality of each person.

Topic Ideas

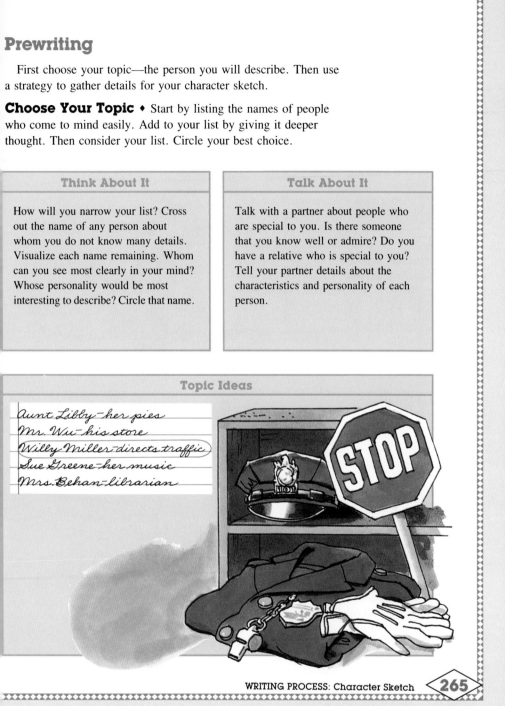

Aunt Libby—her pies
Mr. Wu—his store
Willy Miller—directs traffic
Sue Greene—her music
Mrs. Behan—librarian

WRITING PROCESS: Character Sketch ◆265◆

---

1. PREWRITING

Guide students through the explanation of Prewriting, pointing out that Prewriting is the stage in which writers choose a topic and gather ideas and information to use in their writing.

MODELING THE WRITING PROCESS

If you feel students need instruction before they begin, you may wish to model this stage of the process. Tell students you want to choose a person to describe in a character sketch. Have students help you work through the thinking process. Work with them to name people whom they admire, such as public figures, teachers, or family members. Emphasize that these individuals should be people who would be interesting to describe. Write four or five names on the chalkboard or use *Writing Process Transparency 17*.

Let students hear how you might go about selecting the best person to describe in a character sketch. As you speak, encourage students to help you. Record the responses. Then circle the person who all agree is the best candidate for a character sketch. (Possible discussion: Everyone admires the president, but I don't know many personal details about him. I really admire Mrs. Kenton. She's liked by everyone and she loves her job.

Writing Process Transparency 17*

Special People I Admire		
Person:	**+**	**—**
1. President of the United States	admire him very much, but don't know many details	
2. Mrs. Kenton, librarian	very helpful, liked by everyone, loves her job	
3. My brother	admire him, know him well,	may not interest audience
4. Mr. Largo, Mayor		don't know him well, can't visualize him well

---

Pacing

Children write better, just as adults do, if they have time to think—to let ideas and fresh insights develop between prewriting and writing, writing and revising. A five-day pacing guide follows, but the writing process may take longer.

Day 1—Prewriting   Day 3—Revising
Day 2—Writing   Day 4—Proofreading
         Day 5—Publishing

Evaluation

Process Check questions at the end of each stage of the writing process help you to keep track of students' progress.

Holistic Evaluation Guidelines may be found in the teaching notes on page 271. They offer criteria for average, above-average, and below-average compositions.

*Possible responses are overprinted on this reduced facsimile only. Use Writing Process Transparencies *to interact with your students on the ideas that interest them.*

WRITING PROCESS

Choose Your Strategy Before inviting students to choose a prewriting strategy that will help them gather information for their character sketches, guide them through the explanations of both strategies. Then have students choose a strategy they feel will help them get started.

As a variation on the first strategy, a Character Map, you may wish to have students share their character maps with partners. Have partners look at the maps and tell what else they would like to know about the person who is the subject of the map.

You may wish to remind students that they have learned about a Thought Balloon as a strategy for understanding point of view in the Creative Thinking lesson on pages 248–249.

I D E A   B A N K

Prewriting Ideas

Always encourage young writers to try new ways to discover ideas they want to write about. Reassure them, though, that it is appropriate to use the strategies that work best for them. You may wish to remind them of the prewriting ideas already introduced in their textbooks:
- A Conversation, p. 40
- An Observation Chart, p. 40
- An Order Circle, p. 96
- A Clock Graph, p. 96
- A Comic Strip, p. 154
- Answering "What If?," p. 154
- An Opinion Ladder, p. 212
- A Thought Balloon, p. 212, 266
- A Character Map, page 266

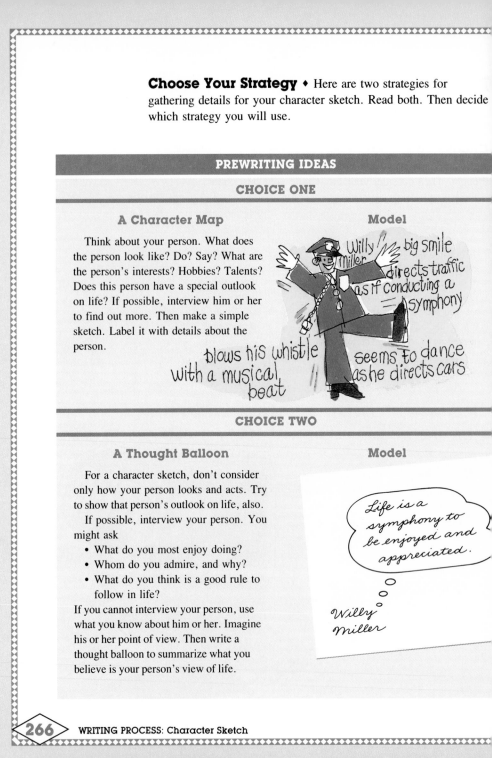

Choose Your Strategy ♦ Here are two strategies for gathering details for your character sketch. Read both. Then decide which strategy you will use.

PREWRITING IDEAS

CHOICE ONE

A Character Map   **Model**

Think about your person. What does the person look like? Do? Say? What are the person's interests? Hobbies? Talents? Does this person have a special outlook on life? If possible, interview him or her to find out more. Then make a simple sketch. Label it with details about the person.

CHOICE TWO

A Thought Balloon   **Model**

For a character sketch, don't consider only how your person looks and acts. Try to show that person's outlook on life, also.

If possible, interview your person. You might ask
- What do you most enjoy doing?
- Whom do you admire, and why?
- What do you think is a good rule to follow in life?

If you cannot interview your person, use what you know about him or her. Imagine his or her point of view. Then write a thought balloon to summarize what you believe is your person's view of life.

266   WRITING PROCESS: Character Sketch

PROCESS CHECK At the completion of the Prewriting stage, students should be able to answer *yes* to these questions:
- Do I know whom I will write about in my character sketch?
- Do I have a character map or a thought balloon that tells details about that person?

Teacher to Teacher

Circulate around the classroom and stop to confer with individual students. To help students develop their content, ask questions about the subject. "What else can you tell about . . . (a topic)?" "Tell me about . . . What happened when. . .? Get children to talk. Then have them write just what they said. By starting with what students say and helping them to elaborate, you give them confidence that they have something significant to write.

Writing

How can you begin your character sketch? You might begin with an interesting fact. You might quote your person. You might tell why you chose that person. Here are some examples.

- Mr. Lopez was only eight years old the first time he ____.
- The first thing Lisa said when we met was, "____."
- Would you like to meet a person who is the best ____?

Use your interview notes, character map, or thought balloon to help you continue. End by summing up why this person is so special.

Sample First Draft •

> Willy Miller loves his job. Willy thinks all of life should be enjoyed. He told me, "Life is a symphony." He conducks his with style and spirit. That's just what Willy does when he works. He seems to dance as he directs traffic when I watch, I can almost hear the music. Willy has been a Police officer for ten years, directing traffic all that time. Willy is a lejund in our city. People go out of their way to drive through his intersection. They want to see his smile and join his symphony.

WRITING PROCESS

2. WRITING

Before students write their first drafts, guide them through the explanation of Writing, emphasizing that at this stage the most important task is to get all their ideas on paper.

Help students include sensory details about the people in their character sketches.

MODELING THE WRITING PROCESS

If you feel students need instruction before they begin this stage of the process, you may wish to ask them to think about the person whose name was circled on *Writing Process Transparency 17*. Then work with students to recall and organize details about that person. Write the details on the chalkboard or on *Writing Process Transparency 18*. For example, you might recall how the person looks or sounds, the person's jobs or interests, and the outlook on life that the person follows. Then have students work with you to suggest an opening sentence for a character sketch about that person. Suggest that the opening sentence quote the person, (e.g., *The first thing _____ said when we met was _____.*)

Writing Process Transparency 18*

> **Writing a Character Sketch**
>
> 1. What is the person's name? Mrs. Kenton
> 2. What does the person look like? Sound like? sometimes stern, talks with excitement, eyes sparkle when she is enjoying something
> 3. What does the person do? Job? Interests? has job as librarian, interested in books and in making library a special place
> 4. What rules for life does this person follow? believes everyone should appreciate books, says books can bring wonder to our lives

---

PROCESS CHECK At the completion of the Writing stage, students should be able to answer *yes* to these questions:

- Do I have a complete first draft
- Does my draft give a vivid picture of the person about whom I am writing?
- Did I use sensory details and organize them well?

Possible responses are overprinted on this reduced facsimile only. Use Writing Process Transparencies *to interact with your students on the ideas that interest them.*

3. REVISING

Help students understand that during Revising writers make their drafts communicate ideas more clearly and effectively to an audience. During Revising writers are not to concern themselves with errors in spelling, capitalization, and punctuation; instead they should concentrate on the quality and effectiveness of their ideas.

IDEA BANK

Grammar Connection

You may wish to remind students of the Grammar Checks already introduced in their textbooks:

- Use a variety of sentence types, p. 43
- Use exact nouns, p. 99
- Use vivid verbs, p. 157
- Replace nouns with pronouns, p. 215
- Add adjectives for specific detail, p. 269

Option 1 ◆ If you wish to begin grammar instruction related to the Grammar Check in this lesson, then refer to Part 1 of this unit.

Option 2 ◆ If you wish to begin grammar instruction *not* related to the Grammar Check in this lesson, then refer to the end-of-book Glossary or Index.

First Read to Yourself You may wish to emphasize that students need not make actual changes during the first reading. This is a time to think about whether their writing is clear and says what they mean it to say.

Remind students to check to make sure that they have added sensory and other details when describing the person in their character sketch.

Then Share with a Partner Suggest that writers' partners offer three responses, at least one positive, and that they accompany any critical responses with suggestions for improvement. Be sure writers ask the Focus question: *Do I need to add any details to show what this person is like?*

3 Revising

Now you have written your character sketch. Can you make it even better? This idea for revising may help you.

REVISING IDEA

FIRST   Read to Yourself

As you read, review your purpose. Did you write a vivid description of someone you know or admire? Consider your audience. Will your classmates enjoy your description?

Focus: Have you included sensory and other details to show what your person is like? Put a caret (ˆ) to mark any places where you'd like to add a detail.

THEN   Share with a Partner

Ask a partner to be your first audience. These guidelines may help you work together on your character sketch.

The Writer

Guidelines: Ask your partner to read your character sketch silently, then respond.

Sample questions:
- Should I change the order of any details?
- **Focus question:** Do I need to add any details to show what this person is like?

The Writer's Partner

Guidelines: Be honest. Don't be afraid to give your opinion, but do it politely.

Sample responses:
- I think _____ is the most important detail. Maybe you should put it first.
- I could picture this person even better if you told _____.

268   WRITING PROCESS: Character Sketch

Teacher to Teacher

Often young writers omit something crucial in the story they are telling. Use content conferences to help a student clarify a point. You may wish to say, for example, "You've told a very funny story about how your sister taught you to ski. But what is a *slalom*?" As students begin to explain say, "Why not add that detail when you revise that part on your paper?" By asking specific questions, you can help students to focus on their audience.

WRITING AS A RECURSIVE PROCESS

Connecting Grammar to the Writing Process

Writing is a recursive process. In other words, good writers will often go back and forth among steps. Depending on the individual styles of your students, some may choose to correct grammar at Step Three, Revising; others may prefer to fix grammar or usage errors at Step Four, Proofreading. Ideally, this should be a decision made by the writer. Remind students, however, that once they have completed their proofreading, all the grammar errors should be corrected.

Revising Model ◆ Here is a character sketch that is being revised. The marks show changes the writer wants to make.

Willy Miller loves his job. Willy thinks all of life should be enjoyed. He told me, "Life is a symphony." He conducks his with style and spirit. ^zest^

That's just what Willy does when he works. ^He raises his hands above his head, blows his whistle, and begins to move.^ *He seems to dance as he directs traffic when I watch, I can almost hear the music.* ⟨*Willy has been a Police officer for ten years, directing traffic all that time.*⟩ *Willy is a lejund in our city. People go out of their way to drive through his intersection. They want to see his* ^big^ *smile and join his* ^grand^ *symphony.*

st is a more precise word for this sentence in *spirit.*

The writer's partner suggested adding these sensory details.

The writer decided these details belong at the beginning.

These adjectives add descriptive details.

Read the character sketch above with the writer's changes. Then revise your own character sketch.

> **Grammar Check** ◆ Adjectives add specific details to your writing.
>
> **Word Choice** ◆ Do you want a more precise word for a word like *spirit*? A thesaurus is a good source of synonyms.

Revising Checklist

☐ **Purpose:** Did I write a vivid description of the person?

☐ **Audience:** Will my classmates enjoy my character sketch?

☐ **Focus:** Did I include details to show what this person is like?

Revising Model Guide students through the model, noting the reasons for changes and the revision marks. Point out to students that on the model the revising marks are in blue. Encourage the class to discuss the changes in the model. Ask them to consider whether or not the changes made the writing more precise as well as more colorful and descriptive.

MODELING THE WRITING PROCESS

If you feel students need instruction before they begin this stage of the process, you may wish to present *Writing Process Transparency 19*. Have students read the draft silently, or have a volunteer read it aloud. Then ask whether there is anything that needs to be changed. Work through the thinking process to help students give reasons for the changes. Then have them tell you how to mark the changes on the draft. (Students might suggest adding adjectives such as *great* and *stern* for descriptive detail, adding a sentence or a phrase for sensory detail, substituting the more precise word *excitement* for *gladness,* and moving a sentence to the opening paragraph.) Remind students that at this time they are revising for meaning. They will correct spelling and punctuation when they proofread.

PROCESS CHECK At the completion of the Revising stage, students should be able to answer *yes* to the following questions:

- Do I have a complete draft with revising marks that show changes I plan to make?
- Has my draft been reviewed by another writer?

Writing Process Transparency 19*

Mrs. Kenton

The first thing Mrs. Kenton said when we met was, "Who is your favorite Author?" She shares her ^great^ love of books with everone she meets.

As you watch Mrs. Kenton, you can see how much ~~Her eyes sparkle when she reads.~~ ^excitement^ she enjoys her job. Her voice is full of gladness as she talks about new books ^stern^ even her reminders to talk quietly show how much she cares. Mrs. Kenton has been the school librarian for eight years. Mrs. Kenton is the hart of ^a room full of books^ our library. She has turned it into a world of wonder and enjoyment.

Possible responses are overprinted on this reduced facsimile only. Use Writing Process Transparencies *to interact with your students on the ideas that interest them.*

WRITING PROCESS

4. PROOFREADING

Guide students through the explanation of proofreading and review the Proofreading Model. Point out to students that on the model the proofreading marks are in red. Tell them that proofreading helps to eliminate errors such as incorrect spelling or run-on sentences that may distract or confuse their readers.

Review the Proofreading Strategy, Proofreading Marks, and the Proofreading Checklist with students. Then invite students to use the checklist and proofread their own character sketches.

MODELING THE WRITING PROCESS

If you feel students need instruction before they begin this stage of the process, you may wish to use *Writing Process Transparency 20.* Have a volunteer read the draft backward, from the end to the beginning. Tell students to follow along and look for spelling, punctuation, and other errors that are listed on the Proofreading Checklist. Mark students' corrections on the transparency.

Writing Process Transparency 20*

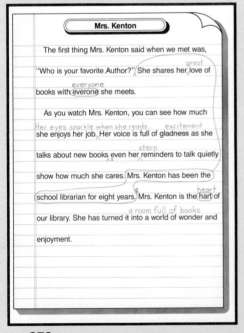

270

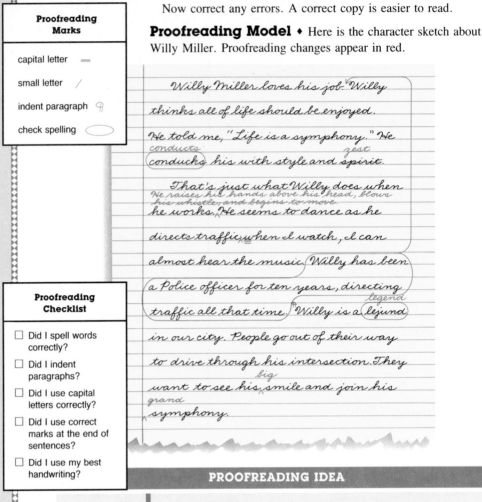

4 Proofreading

Now correct any errors. A correct copy is easier to read.

Proofreading Model ◆ Here is the character sketch about Willy Miller. Proofreading changes appear in red.

PROOFREADING IDEA

Punctuation Check

To catch spelling, punctuation, and other errors, read backwards from the end to the beginning. When you block out meaning, you can concentrate on finding mistakes.

Now proofread your character sketch, add a title, and make a neat copy.

270   WRITING PROCESS: Character Sketch

PROCESS CHECK At the completion of the Proofreading stage, students should be able to answer *yes* to the following questions:
- Do I have a complete draft with proofreading marks that show changes I plan to make?
- Have I used the proofreading marks shown in the lesson?

EVALUATION PROGRAM

See Evaluation and Testing Program, pp. C1–C8.

Masters are available for the following:
Self Evaluation Checklist
Personal Goals for Writing
Peer Response
Teacher Response

Holistic Evaluation Guides
Analytic Evaluation Guides

Possible responses are overprinted on this reduced facsimile only. Use Writing Process Transparencies to interact with your students on the ideas that interest them.

270

Publishing

Try one of these ideas for sharing your character sketch.

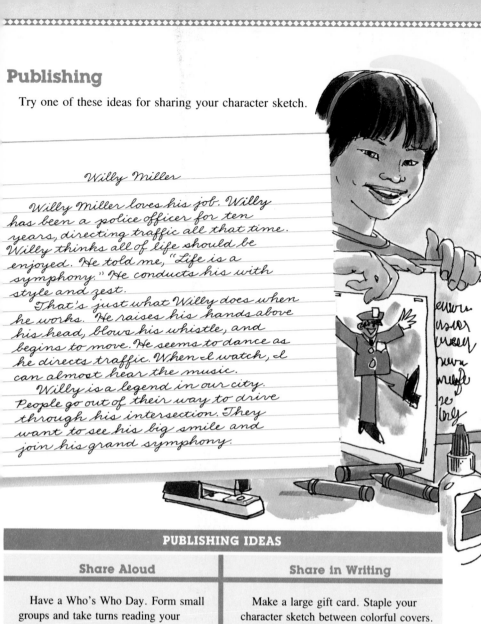

Willy Miller

Willy Miller loves his job. Willy has been a police officer for ten years, directing traffic all that time. Willy thinks all of life should be enjoyed. He told me, "Life is a symphony." He conducts his with style and zest.

That's just what Willy does when he works. He raises his hands above his head, blows his whistle, and begins to move. He seems to dance as he directs traffic. When I watch, I can almost hear the music.

Willy is a legend in our city. People go out of their way to drive through his intersection. They want to see his big smile and join his grand symphony.

PUBLISHING IDEAS

Share Aloud	Share in Writing
Have a Who's Who Day. Form small groups and take turns reading your character sketches aloud. Ask each listener to tell what he or she found most admirable about your person.	Make a large gift card. Staple your character sketch between colorful covers. Illustrate the top cover. Sign the card and give it to the person you wrote about. Perhaps that person will respond in person or in writing.

WRITING PROCESS: Character Sketch ◁271▷

Holistic Evaluation Guidelines

A character sketch of **average** quality will:
1. describe a person the writer knows or admires
2. include descriptive details

A character sketch of **above-average** quality may:
1. use details that are more vivid or precise
2. begin or end in an unusual way
3. make a person come to life

A character sketch of **below-average** quality may:
1. lack details and proper organization
2. be incomplete

PROCESS CHECK At the completion of the Publishing stage, students should be able to answer *yes* to these questions:
- Have I shared my writing with an audience?
- Have readers shared reactions with me?
- Have I thought about what I especially liked in this writing? Or about what was particularly difficult?
- Have I thought about what I would like to work on the next time I write?

Encourage students to keep a log or journal of their own and their readers' reactions.

I D E A   B A N K

Spelling and Mechanics Connection

You may wish to remind students of Proofreading ideas already introduced in their textbooks:
- Read through a window, p. 44
- Check for poorly formed letters, p. 100
- Trade with a partner, p. 158
- Check one thing at a time, p. 216
- Read backwards, p. 270

Spelling ◆ If you wish to include spelling instruction with this lesson, then refer to the Spelling Guide on pages 490–492, the Index, or the *Spelling Connection* booklet.

Mechanics ◆ If you wish to include mechanics instruction with this lesson, then refer to the Glossary, the Index, or the *Revising and Proofreading Transparencies*.

5. PUBLISHING

Oral Sharing If students choose to share their writing orally during a Who's Who Day, set aside a specific time during class for this special event. Encourage listeners to make constructive comments and explain why they feel as they do about the character sketches they heard. As an alternative to forming small groups, you may wish to have the entire class participate together as one large group.

Written Sharing If students choose to share their writing by displaying it, provide them with construction paper to use for making covers for their character sketches. Before students give their cards to the people about whom they wrote, you may wish to display the cards in the classroom.

Curriculum Connection

Writing Across the Curriculum

Explain to students that writers often use story characters to get across their own point of view. Tell students they will use thought balloons to help them project what someone else might be thinking or feeling.

You may wish to remind students that they have used thought balloons as a strategy for describing in the Creative Thinking lesson, in their response to the literature selection, and in the Writing Process lesson.

Writing to Learn

To help students get started, have them name some of their favorite athletes and the sports they are involved with. Write the responses on the chalkboard.

You may wish to have students with limited English proficiency describe sports that interest them and provide the sports' English names.

Help students use their health books, biographies, autobiographies, and sports magazines to find information about health and the athletes of their choice.

Writing in Your Journal

When they have finished writing, have students read their earlier journal entries. Encourage them to discuss what they have learned about the theme, and to observe how their writing has changed or improved.

Remind students that their journals have many purposes. Besides paragraphs and stories, they can write questions, story ideas, or thoughts and reflections on a subject. Suggest to them that entries in their journals may provide ideas for later writing.

Writing Across the Curriculum   Health

In this unit you wrote a character sketch that gave your point of view about a person you admired. Many people admire the performance of athletes. To perform well in a sport, an athlete must exercise regularly and eat good foods.

Writing to Learn

Think and Imagine ♦ Picture your favorite athlete making a commercial about good health practices. Make a thought balloon showing what he or she might say.

Thought Balloon

Write ♦ What should you do to be healthy? Review your thought balloon. Then share your *own* point of view on the subject.

Writing in Your Journal

In the Writer's Warm-up you wrote about qualities that make lasting impressions on people. Throughout this unit you learned about people who have made lasting impressions. Browse through the unit again. Choose one person. In your journal tell why many people admire this person. Then explain why you either agree or disagree with them.

ESSENTIAL LANGUAGE SKILLS

This lesson provides opportunities to:

LISTENING ♦ listen actively and attentively ♦ follow the logical organization of an oral presentation

SPEAKING ♦ participate in group discussions ♦ make organized oral presentations ♦ participate in storytelling and creative dramatics

READING ♦ respond to various forms of literature ♦ become acquainted with a variety of selections, characters, and themes of our literary heritage ♦ select books for individual needs and interests ♦ explain and relate to the feelings and emotions of characters

WRITING ♦ select and narrow a topic for a specific purpose ♦ adapt information to accomplish a specific purpose with a particular audience ♦ keep journals, logs, or notebooks to express feelings, record ideas, discover new knowledge, and free the imagination

LANGUAGE ♦ use language to imagine ♦ recognize ways in which language can be used to influence others

BOOKS TO ENJOY

◆ Read More About It

To Space and Back
by Sally Ride with Susan Okie
Sally Ride, the first American woman astronaut, writes about spaceflight. You will find out how astronauts manage some daily space chores, such as making a sandwich or brushing their teeth.

Ellis Island: Gateway to the New World
by Leonard Everett Fisher
Between 1890 and 1954, Ellis Island was the first stop in America for millions of arriving immigrants. Ellis Island is located in New York Harbor. Hopes and dreams got a start in the immigration buildings here.

◆ Book Report Idea   Character Interview

Next time you share a book, interview a character.

Make Up a Character
Interview ◆ Work alone or with a partner. Choose a main character in the book. Write some questions an interviewer might ask the character to learn more about his or her life. Use a tape recorder. Ask questions; then answer them as you think the character would. Change your voice so listeners can tell the interviewer from the character. If you work with a partner, be the character as your partner asks the questions you prepared.

WORLD OF BOOKS
CLASSROOM LIBRARIES
is a collection of high-quality children's literature available with this program.

OBJECTIVES
To appreciate a variety of literature
To share a book through a creative activity

Read More About It
Call students' attention to Read More About It and discuss theme-related books. Point out that the books listed here contain stories about people, places and times that made lasting impressions. Encourage students to mention other titles that deal with these topics. Encourage students to examine pictures and jacket illustrations of books in the classroom to find books they will enjoy reading.

Book Report Idea
You may wish to have students use the book report form provided in the back of their textbooks. Book Report Idea presents a lively alternative way for interested students to share books they have read.

You may wish to share the reports with the class or in small groups. Have students discuss what they learned about the main character of each book from listening to the interviews they tape-recorded. Encourage discussion of whether or not listeners learned enough about each character to want to learn more by reading the book.

Integrated Language Arts Project
The **Integrated Language Arts Project** on pages T520–T521 may be used with this unit.

Unit 5
Review

REVIEW OR TEST
You may wish to use the Unit Review as a review of the unit skills before administering the Unit Posttest, or you may wish to use the Unit Review in lieu of the Unit Posttest.

REVIEW PROCEDURES
The lesson pages that are reviewed are listed beside the heading of each segment. You may wish to choose one of the procedures listed below for using the pages with the Unit Review exercises.

Review/Evaluate Have students restudy the lesson pages before doing the Unit Review exercises.

Open-Book Review Allow students to refer to the lesson pages if they need to while they are doing the Unit Review exercises.

Evaluate/Review Have students do the Unit Review exercises, then turn to the lesson pages to restudy concepts for which incorrect responses are given.

ADDITIONAL REVIEW AND PRACTICE
For additional review and practice, turn to the Extra Practice pages at the end of the unit.

274

Unit 5

Adjectives *pages 234–241*

A. Write each of the following sentences. Underline each adjective. Include articles.

1. The smiling tourists admired the beautiful sunset.
2. In early America families made homespun clothes.
3. The tallest building in town stands next to a vacant lot.
4. A small dog crept along the crooked path.
5. Clever people welcome a difficult challenge.
6. The shimmering green light suddenly vanished.
7. The weird creature from Planet X made strange hooting noises.
8. A little old man entered the haunted house.
9. I like sweet, ripe strawberries.
10. The beautiful painting stood in the dark hall.
11. The shy kitten hid behind the giant, flowery bush.
12. The cheerful guests danced and sang joyous songs.
13. Ms. Sanders is a dedicated and understanding teacher.
14. A lonely leaf fell to the cold ground.
15. A strong, bitter wind swooped down from the tall mountain.

B. Write each sentence. Underline the predicate adjective once. Underline twice the noun or pronoun it describes.

16. You look tired today.
17. Tony doesn't seem happy.
18. Robert E. Lee was brave in battle.
19. Martha is witty.
20. That giant yellow flower smells beautiful.
21. We are delighted to welcome you to our home.
22. The tacos tasted delicious.
23. Florence Nightingale was heroic.
24. The mother bear seemed angry.
25. The teenager looked impressed with himself.

C. Write each sentence. Use the correct form of the adjective in parentheses ( ).

26. My piece of spinach pie is (small) *smaller* than yours.
27. Leon is the (tiny) *tiniest* member of our family.
28. Randy is the (intelligent) *most intelligent* person I know.
29. No one is (brave) *braver* than Tanya.
30. You seem (cheerful) *more cheerful* than I am.
31. This stamp is (valuable) *more valuable* than any other one in my collection.
32. Is your cat (swift) *swifter* than my German shepherd?
33. That book is the (helpful) *most helpful* guide to woodcraft I have found.
34. Tom is the (bashful) *most bashful* person I know.
35. That is the (beautiful) *most beautiful* painting in the entire museum.
36. Jill arrived (early) *earlier* than Beverly.
37. Sam came (early) *earliest* of all.

Suffixes *pages 242–243*

D. Read each definition. Then write a word that has the same meaning by adding the suffix *-able, -ful, -less,* or *-y* to the underlined word.

38. being full of <u>mist</u> misty
39. with <u>skill</u> skillful
40. having <u>honor</u> honorable
41. without <u>speech</u> speechless
42. full of <u>fear</u> fearful
43. able to be <u>refilled</u> refillable
44. without <u>harm</u> harmless
45. worthy of <u>notice</u> noticeable

Organizing Details
pages 258–259

E. Read the topic sentence below. Then write the four details in bottom-to-top space order.

TOPIC SENTENCE: Chef Leo had created a beautiful salad.

46. Tasty leaves of romaine lettuce lay underneath the other vegetables. 1
47. Sprigs of parsley and strips of red pepper topped the salad. 4
48. Artichoke hearts and asparagus spears covered the cheese. 3
49. Fine cheese sat upon the lettuce. 2

F. Write the sentences below in the order of their importance. Put the most important detail first.

50. When Ed smiles, his face lights up. 1
51. His eyebrows arch a little. 4 or 3
52. His normally harsh features soften. 2
53. His cheeks dimple quite noticeably. 3 or 4

Describing *pages 260–261*

G. Read the following paragraph. Then write answers to the questions.

Try as they might, Maria and Jared could not recall so cold a day. They were bundled from head to toe in heavy woolen caps, fluffy earmuffs, thick scarves, bulky coats, and fur-lined boots. Even so, the biting cold penetrated their clothing. Their legs were numb and felt almost frozen. Each leg seemed to weigh a ton. The crisp snow crackled under their feet as they trudged home. Their unprotected faces stung with the pain of the cold.

54. Which words and details indicate how cold it was? could not recall so cold a day; biting cold penetrated their clothing
55. Which words and details help you see how Maria and Jared looked? bundled from head to toe in heavy woolen caps, fluffy earmuffs, thick scarves, bulky coats, and fur-lined boots
56. Which words and details describe how Maria and Jared felt? legs were numb and felt almost frozen; unprotected faces stung
57. Which word describes the snow? crisp
58. Which word indicates the sound they made as they walked? crackled

H. Read the topic sentence below. Then read sentences 59–62. Write *yes* if a sentence gives a detail that supports the topic sentence. Write *no* if it does not.

It was an extremely hot summer day in the big city.

59. The bank sign said ninety degrees. yes
60. I wore a hat to keep my ears warm. no
61. A street vendor was selling cups of ice-cold lemonade. yes
62. The pond was bustling with numerous skaters. no

Unit Review **275**

Language Puzzlers

Unit 5

ANSWERS

Impossible Possibility Rhymes
Rhymes will vary.

Arty Adjectives
1. forty
2. broken
3. most underhanded
4. beautiful
5. mysterious
6. crisscross
7. circular
8. splitting
9. exciting
10. easy
11. most overrated
12. comfortable

LANGUAGE PUZZLERS

Unit 5 Challenge

Impossible Possibility Rhymes

Write two-line Impossible Possibility rhymes like the ones below. The first line should contain a linking verb and a predicate adjective. The second line should contain an action verb.

The sweet rolls tasted sour.
I made the dough without flour.

The snow was hot in the sixth month of May
And sunshine was raining all night and all day.

The sun in the sky always is flat
When the bareheaded girl wears her top hat.

Arty Adjectives

Find the adjective in each box. You may check spellings in a dictionary.

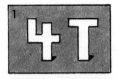 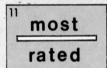 

   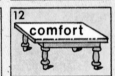

Use an adjective to make a puzzle like the ones above. Ask a classmate to solve your puzzle.

Unit 5 Extra Practice

1 Writing with Adjectives
p. 234

A. Write the adjectives in each sentence. Include articles.

1. Many people visit the historic sites in North Carolina.
2. The tourists enjoy the old mansions and villages.
3. One village is in an old section of Winston-Salem.
4. The colonial buildings and early clothing attract sightseers.
5. Some buildings are from 1766 and have interesting styles.
6. A popular event in North Carolina is a historical play.
7. It is staged at an old fort where early colonists lived.
8. The play shows the hard life the colonial settlers led.
9. The story tells about a lost colony and a strange word.
10. The colony was founded on an island called Roanoke thirty-three years before the Pilgrims landed.
11. Three years later all the colonists had vanished.
12. Some people searched for the lost colonists.
13. One word, *Croatoan*, was carved on a big post.
14. The mysterious disappearance has never been explained.

B. Write each sentence. Use *a* or *an* to complete it.

15. Pamela made _____ visit to Tryon Palace in New Bern.
16. It is _____ old North Carolina mansion.
17. The mansion was built by _____ colonial governor.
18. In 1774 _____ American revolutionary group met there.
19. The patriots made _____ pact against the British there.

C. Write each sentence. Underline the adjectives that tell *what kind* once. Underline the adjectives that tell *how many* twice. Do not include articles.

20. North Carolina's lovely capital, Raleigh, is an old city.
21. The original capitol was the big palace in New Bern.
22. The state flag has three colors and two dates.
23. Both dates stand for early declarations of independence.
24. It is a large state with a hundred counties.
25. We spent one vacation on the sandy beaches.

Extra Practice
Unit 5

OBJECTIVES
To practice skills taught in the unit

ANSWERS
Writing with Adjectives
A.
1. Many, the historic
2. The, the old
3. One, an old
4. The colonial, early
5. Some, interesting
6. A popular, a historical
7. an old, early
8. The, the hard, the colonial
9. The, a lost, a strange
10. The, an, thirty-three, the
11. Three, all the
12. Some, the lost
13. One, a big
14. The mysterious

B.
15. a visit
16. an old
17. a colonial
18. an American
19. a pact

C.
20. lovely, old
21. original, big
22. state, three, two
23. Both, early
24. large, hundred
25. one, sandy

Extra Practice and Challenge
For those students who need additional grammar practice have them refer to these pages. **The practice exercises progress in difficulty from Easy to Average. Practice A is Easy. Practice B is Average.** Difficult concepts requiring more practice have additional Exercises C and D at the Average level.
We do not recommend these exercises for students who have mastered the skill in the basic lesson. Those students should do the **Challenge** word puzzles on page 276.

D. 26. a southern, fertile, thick, a long, many
27. Two
28. The, wooden, many, the
29. Textile, an, important
30. all, textile

Adjectives After Linking Verbs

A. 1. famous Washington
2. secure people
3. wise They
4. successful George Washington
5. loyal he
6. harsh Great Britain
7. unavoidable war
8. ready colonies
9. prepared They

B. 10. George Washington is famous
11. he was careless
12. George was guilty
13. father looked angry
14. Washington was honest
15. George Washington was brave
16. he seemed fearless
17. He was sensitive
18. They were ready
19. Washington was effective

D. Write the adjectives in these sentences. Include articles.

26. North Carolina is a southern state with fertile farms, thick forests, a long coastline, and many industries.
27. Two products are furniture and cloth.
28. The wooden furniture in many homes in the United States is from North Carolina.
29. Textile production is an important industry, too.
30. North Carolina leads all states in textile manufacturing.

2 Adjectives After Linking Verbs   *p. 236*

A. Write the predicate adjective in each sentence. Tell which noun or pronoun in the subject each adjective describes.

1. Washington was famous before the American Revolution.
2. The people felt secure with him as the President.
3. They were wise in their choice of a leader.
4. George Washington was successful at farming.
5. For a long while he was loyal to Great Britain.
6. Great Britain was harsh toward its colonies.
7. Then war seemed unavoidable.
8. The colonies were ready to fight for freedom.
9. They felt prepared for war.

B. Write each sentence. Underline the predicate adjective once. Underline twice the noun or pronoun it describes.

EXAMPLE: That cherry pie smells wonderful!
ANSWER: That cherry pie smells wonderful!

10. George Washington is famous for his honesty.
11. According to legend, he was careless cutting trees.
12. Young George was guilty of ruining the cherry tree.
13. His father probably looked angry.
14. However, Washington was honest about his mistake.
15. George Washington was brave, too.
16. During the long winters of the war, he seemed fearless.
17. He was sensitive to the hardships of the soldiers.
18. They were ready to follow him anywhere.
19. Later, Washington was also effective as President.

C. Write sentences using each of the following pairs of adjectives and nouns. Use a linking verb, and use the adjective as a predicate adjective.

EXAMPLE: brave soldiers
ANSWER: The soldiers were brave.

20. brilliant Thomas Jefferson
21. industrious John Adams
22. angry taxpayers
23. endless war
24. short supplies
25. weary colonists
26. delicious food
27. acceptable peace
28. independent country
29. happy people

D. Write the sentence. Underline the predicate adjective once and the noun or pronoun it describes twice.

30. Mexico is famous as the home of the Mayas.
31. These Indians were powerful a thousand years ago.
32. The Mayan cities are ancient.
33. Scientists were excited by their discovery.
34. Even today, the cities seem new.
35. Their condition is excellent.
36. The buildings are beautiful.
37. The Mayas were unknown to the outside world.
38. The land was rich and supplied all their needs.
39. They felt safe in their villages.
40. Astronomy was important to the Mayas.
41. The planets were special to them.
42. Mathematics seemed easy to these people.
43. The people were happy when it rained.

3 Adjectives That Compare

p. 238

A. Write the word in parentheses ( ) that correctly completes each sentence.

1. A duck egg is (smaller, smallest) than an ostrich egg.
2. A hummingbird egg is the (smaller, smallest) of all.
3. A giraffe is the (taller, tallest) animal in the world.
4. It is even (taller, tallest) than an elephant.
5. Is that the (bigger, biggest) animal you can think of?

C. Answers will vary. The following are possible answers.
20. Thomas Jefferson was brilliant.
21. John Adams was industrious.
22. The taxpayers were angry.
23. The war seemed endless.
24. Supplies were short.
25. The colonists looked weary.
26. The food tasted delicious.
27. Peace was acceptable.
28. The country was independent.
29. The people felt happy.

D. 30. <u>Mexico</u> is <u>famous</u>
31. <u>Indians</u> were <u>powerful</u>
32. <u>cities</u> are <u>ancient</u>
33. <u>Scientists</u> were <u>excited</u>
34. <u>cities</u> seem <u>new</u>
35. <u>condition</u> is <u>excellent</u>
36. <u>buildings</u> are <u>beautiful</u>
37. <u>Mayas</u> were <u>unknown</u>
38. <u>land</u> was <u>rich</u>
39. <u>They</u> felt <u>safe</u>
40. <u>Astronomy</u> was <u>important</u>
41. <u>planets</u> were <u>special</u>
42. <u>Mathematics</u> seemed <u>easy</u>
43. <u>people</u> were <u>happy</u>

Adjectives That Compare
A. 1. smaller
2. smallest
3. tallest
4. taller
5. biggest

Extra Practice and Challenge

For those students who need additional grammar practice have them refer to these pages. **The practice exercises progress in difficulty from Easy to Average. Practice A is Easy. Practice B is Average.** Difficult concepts requiring more practice have additional Exercises C and D at the Average level.
We do not recommend these exercises for students who have mastered the skill in the basic lesson. Those students should do the **Challenge** word puzzles on page 276.

B. 6. earliest
    7. Later
    8. Flatter
    9. wetter
   10. wider
   11. heavier
   12. largest
   13. busiest
   14. earlier
   15. latest

C. 16. shorter
   17. shortest
   18. biggest
   19. smaller
   20. longest
   21. longer
   22. fastest
   23. faster
   24. higher
   25. highest
   26. longer
   27. longest
   28. heavier
   29. heavier
   30. biggest

Using *more* and *most* with Adjectives
A. 1. longer, longest
    2. more admirable, most admirable
    3. worse, worst
    4. more serious, most serious
    5. more polite, most polite

B. Write each sentence. Use the form of the adjective shown in parentheses ( ).

   6. The (early + -est) bridges were fallen trees.
   7. (Late + -er) bridges were copies of this design.
   8. (Flat + -er) pieces of wood were laid across streams.
   9. In the (wet + -er) weather they were washed away.
  10. People looked for ways to cross (wide + -er) rivers.
  11. Bridge builders started using (heavy + -er) materials.
  12. A special design was used for the (large + -est) bridge.
  13. A bridge crosses Australia's (busy + -est) harbor.
  14. Some modern bridges look like (early + -er) designs.
  15. The (late + -est) idea is to make bridges of concrete.

C. Write each sentence. Use the correct form of the adjective in parentheses ( ).

  16. Díaz is a (short) name than Fernández.
  17. O is the (short) name in the world.
  18. This tiger is the (big) cat in the zoo.
  19. This leopard is (small) than that tiger.
  20. The (long) worm of all is the bootlace worm.
  21. It is (long) than 150 feet.
  22. The cheetah is the (fast) animal on land.
  23. The sailfish is even (fast) than the cheetah.
  24. Is Mount Everest (high) than Mount McKinley?
  25. Yes, it is the (high) mountain in the world.
  26. Which is (long), the Mississippi or the Nile?
  27. The Nile is the (long) river in the world.
  28. Which is (heavy), an ounce or a gram?
  29. An ounce is much (heavy) than a gram.
  30. The world's (big) pizza was more than eight feet across.

4 Using *more* and *most* with Adjectives
p. 240

A. For each adjective below, write the two forms used to compare persons, places, or things.

   1. long   **2.** admirable   **3.** bad   **4.** serious   **5.** polite

B. Write each sentence. Use the correct form of the adjective in parentheses.

6. These track shoes are (comfortable) than those.
7. The bar on the high jump is (low) now than it was before.
8. Rosa is the (dependable) runner we have.
9. I'm (breathless) after running than after swimming.
10. Jim is a (careful) runner than Manuel.
11. Nikki gave the (impressive) performance of her career.
12. That high jumper was (nervous) than Nikki was.
13. Pole vaulting is the (hard) event of the whole meet.
14. Our team looked (cheerful) than their team.
15. Tripping was the (awkward) way to start.
16. Ours was the (high) score of the entire season.
17. The high jump was the (difficult) event of all.
18. The floor here is (slippery) than in our gym.
19. A good warm-up is the (helpful) way to prepare.
20. The coach's advice is (sensible) than Joe's.
21. The Olympic Games are the (famous) of all sports events.
22. To the ancient Greeks, nothing was (important) than the Games.
23. They chose the (beautiful) spot in Greece for the Games.
24. Only the (serious) athletes of all could take part in the events.
25. They underwent (demanding) training than today's athletes.
26. Winners received even (great) honors than war heroes.
27. The Olympics still feature the (good) athletes of all.
28. Some Olympic events are (recent) than others.
29. Wrestling is an (old) event than volleyball.

C. Write the sentences. Use the correct form of *good* or *bad* to complete each sentence.

30. Jim Thorpe was the (good) all-around Olympic athlete.
31. His record was far (good) than anyone else's.
32. This is the (good) score Howin ever had.
33. Last season was (bad) than this one for us.
34. This year we have done (good) than Hill School.
35. Our (bad) event is the broad jump.
36. Next year we plan to have an even (good) team than we have this year.
37. Our (good) event is the 100-meter dash.

Extra Practice

B. 6. more comfortable
7. lower
8. most dependable
9. more breathless
10. more careful
11. most impressive
12. more nervous
13. hardest
14. more cheerful
15. most awkward
16. highest
17. most difficult
18. more slippery or slipperier
19. most helpful
20. more sensible
21. most famous
22. more important
23. most beautiful
24. most serious
25. more demanding
26. greater
27. best
28. more recent
29. older

C. 30. best
31. better
32. best
33. worse
34. better
35. worst
36. better
37. best

Extra Practice and Challenge

For those students who need additional grammar practice have them refer to these pages. **The practice exercises progress in difficulty from Easy to Average. Practice A is Easy. Practice B is Average.** Difficult concepts requiring more practice have additional Exercises C and D at the Average level. We do not recommend these exercises for students who have mastered the skill in the basic lesson. Those students should do the **Challenge** word puzzles on page 276.

OVERVIEW

TWO-PART

flexibility

Unit 6
Overview

books

ON UNIT THEME

USING LANGUAGE TO RESEARCH

EASY

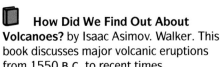 **Volcanoes** by Franklyn Branley. Harper. This explanation of how volcanoes are born and grow makes a complex subject accessible to all students.

Volcanoes and Earthquakes by Martyn Bramwell. Watts. The clear, well-organized text, supported by color photographs and diagrams, explains two powerful forces in nature.

How Did We Find Out About Volcanoes? by Isaac Asimov. Walker. This book discusses major volcanic eruptions from 1550 B.C. to recent times.

Volcanoes: The Fiery Mountains by Margaret Poynter. Messner. Illustrated text describes the causes and effects of volcanoes and presents popular beliefs and legends surrounding them.

CHALLENGING

The Twenty-One Balloons by William Pene du Bois. Viking. A retired schoolteacher balloons across the Pacific in 1883 and learns about a unique way of life on the island of Krakatoa. **Newbery Medal.**

Pompeii: Exploring a Roman Ghost Town by Ron and Nancy Goor. Crowell. This book explores the ancient Roman city, which was buried, but also preserved, by the eruption of Mt. Vesuvius in A.D. 79.

The Firelings by Carol Kendall. Atheneum. In this fantasy the Firelings must find a way to safety before the volcano on which they live erupts.

A Journey to the Center of the Earth by Jules Verne. Dutton. First published in 1864, this science-fiction classic tells how three people descend into the crater of an inactive volcano.

USING LANGUAGE
TO
RESEARCH

=== PART ONE ===

Unit Theme *Volcanoes*

Language Awareness Adverbs

=== PART TWO ===

Literature *Volcano* by Patricia Lauber

A Reason for Writing Researching

Writing
IN YOUR JOURNAL

WRITER'S WARM-UP ◆ What do you know about volcanoes? You may have heard of some famous volcanic eruptions of the past, such as the eruption of Mount Vesuvius. Have you ever built a model of a volcano in science class? Why is a volcano dangerous? What happens when a volcano erupts? Find out what you know by writing in your journal. Start by writing the word *volcano*, then just write whatever you know about volcanoes.

start with WRITING IN YOUR JOURNAL

Writers' Warm-up is designed to help students activate prior knowledge of the unit theme, "Volcanoes." Whether you begin instruction with Part 1 or Part 2, encourage students to focus attention on the illustration on page 282 of their textbooks. Encourage them to discuss what they see. Then have a volunteer read aloud the **Writers' Warm-up** on page 283. Have students write their thoughts in their journals. You may wish to tell them that they will refer to this writing in the first lesson of Part 1, in the Grammar-Writing Connection, and in the Curriculum Connection.

THEN START WITH *part 1*

Language Awareness: Adverbs Developmental lessons focus on the concept of adverbs. Each lesson is carefully constructed not only to help students learn the concept well but also to help build interest and background knowledge for the thinking, reading, and writing they will do in Part 2. The last lesson in Part 1 is a vocabulary lesson with which students learn about compounds. The Grammar-Writing Connection that follows serves as a bridge to Part 2, encouraging students to work together to apply their new language skills at the sentence level of writing.

...OR WITH *part 2*

A Reason for Writing: Researching is the focus of Part 2. First, students learn a thinking strategy for researching. Then they read and respond to a selection of literature on which they may model their writing. Developmental composition lessons, including "An Oral Report," a speaking and listening lesson, all reflect the literature and culminate in the Writing Process lesson. There a "Grammar Check," a "Word Choice" hint, and proofreading strategies help you focus on single traits for remediation or instruction through the lessons in Part 1. The unit ends with Curriculum Connection and Books to Enjoy, which help students discover how their new skills apply to writing across the curriculum.

THEME BAR

CATEGORIES	Environments	Business/World of Work	Imagination	Communications/ Fine Arts	People	Science	Expressions	Social Studies
THEMES	UNIT 1 Farm Life	UNIT 2 Handicrafts	UNIT 3 Tall Tales	UNIT 4 The Visual Arts	UNIT 5 Lasting Impressions	UNIT 6 Volcanoes	UNIT 7 Nature	UNIT 8 Animal Habitats
PACING	1 month	1 month	1 month	1 month	1 month	1 month	1 month	1 month

Build background knowledge of the unit theme, "Volcanoes," by reading aloud this selection to your class. You may wish to use the "Notes for Listening" on the following page before and after reading aloud.

What Goes Up Must Come Down

from *The Twenty-One Balloons*

BY WILLIAM PÈNE DU BOIS

Mr. F. waited until all of the tables had been cleared by the D. family, then placed a chair on one of the tables. He silenced the crowd, introduced me as the speaker in a most informal and nice way, looked at me, and pointed to the chair. I climbed up on the table, sat down, and after the twenty families were all comfortably settled began my talk. The response to it was amazing and most gratifying. Each time I mentioned a new name, at least one face in the audience would light up. There would be much nudging of elbows, smiles, and faraway homesick looks. Giving this simple talk which seemed to bring so much genuine pleasure to these people was a tremendous joy to me. While I was talking all eyes were attentively fixed on me and I was looking around the room catching the reactions to each new name I mentioned and thinking up incidents to talk about next. Looking out of the window, I noticed that the ground seemed a little more active than usual. Being a new citizen of the Island I didn't know whether there was anything unusual about this at first. I went on with my talk. As I recall it, before being most rudely interrupted by a singularly sinister event, I had talked over three hours. I noticed that the earth was moving with increasing violence. I looked at my watch. The movement of the earth's surface usually subsided completely for a few minutes out of each hour, but that afternoon it had been getting increasingly violent over a period of two hours. This was quite alarming. I called this to the attention of the other people. They all turned and looked out of the windows. Some of them didn't seem at all alarmed but others looked quite frightened. I was far from feeling at ease. Mr. M. walked over to the window and looked out. After a few minutes he said, "I don't think it's anything to get much alarmed over. After all, most of our houses were knocked down in '77."

"But they were simple huts," said Mr. T.

"I know, but they had diamond foundations too. This house hasn't shown any signs of the slightest vibration. Please go on with your talk, Professor Sherman."

This seemed to reassure everyone considerably though I can't say my heart was in my speech as much as before. I noticed that my audience was rather restless too. *Suddenly*—and this was a sight which is as vivid to me now as it was when I first saw it—the wall opposite me slowly and almost noiselessly opened up in a crack large enough to allow the sun to shine through. It was the most terrifying and sinister sight I have ever seen. A considerable amount of powdered plaster dropped on the heads of the families in the room and the windows near the cracked wall broke open. The windows had all been closed so that the usual noise of the mountain wouldn't interfere with my talk. Now, through the crack in the wall and through the broken windows, the rumblings of the mountain thundered in full force.

Mr. M. rushed to the table where I was sitting, leaped onto it, and immediately started shouting instructions. "I want all of the women and little children to run to the platform at once and start taking the covers off the balloons! I want all of the men to run quickly to their houses and grab their family parachutes (hearing the word 'parachute' at that moment came to me like a blow on the head) and dash to the balloon platform! I want the six boys who are fifteen years old to take whatever food Mrs. D. has prepared for tonight and rush it to the platform!" He clapped his hands loudly and the room was emptied at once. He turned to me and said, "We've rehearsed this a thousand times; don't be alarmed, Professor Sherman, I am confident that everything will turn out all right. We'll be off in less than fifteen minutes. Now," he said, "you're the only man with no particular job at this time. We all have pretty large amounts of diamonds sewn into a pouch attached to our family parachutes. Why don't you take a bucket and see if you can get to the mines and grab some diamonds? A few big ones will take care of you quite nicely. *But don't go near the mines if it's too dan-*

gerous, please, Sherman, don't go near the mines if. . . ."
He was shouting after me, for I was off for the mines like a madman as soon as I got the gist of his suggestion. Unfortunately for me this was a waste of time. It was impossible to approach the mountain. I knew I had just a little over ten minutes time, the time needed to fill the balloons. I tried running—the action of the earth's surface threw me to the ground. I tried walking—I doddered, staggered, floundered, and tumbled. I tried crawling, but the earth's rumblings and heavings kept rolling me over on my side. I looked up at the mountain ahead and saw at once that it would be impossible to reach in the short time allotted me. I threw away my bucket, turned, and ran through the village for the platform, reeling, buckling, and falling every few feet of the way. I was the last to see the Village of Krakatoa from the ground. When I arrived at the balloon platform, it was straining at the hoses ready to leap. There were many hands extended my way. I reached up and my arms were grabbed just as the balloon platform tore itself away. I was lifted onto the platform. I remember twenty pops like champagne corks in rapid succession as the rubber ball-and-socket connections were broken, and the eighty-one Krakatoans swiftly bounded off into the air.

Here, we were greeted by a roaring swift upward blast of hot air which catapulted us far up into the sky. When we were about a half mile up, we were comparatively still. There might have been a little wind, but it wasn't strong enough to blow us off this hot sulphurous airshaft.

We spent seventeen hours over the volcano, from five o'clock in the afternoon of the 26th until ten o'clock the following morning. At that time the shaft of hot air seemed to have lost its strength. We were lowered to an altitude of about one hundred feet above the mountain, or roughly fifteen hundred feet above sea level; and there a wind cleared us of that dreadful crater. The boys busied themselves keeping the platform level again, and the men and women of Krakatoa gave longing looks at their Island believing that the eruptions had ceased and that they had been foolish to leave. I cannot say that I shared this feeling at all. There wasn't a house left standing and I had no desire to return to this now desolate and fearful place even if the diamond mines were intact.

We flew until we were a mile over Java when, with stunning suddenness, the Island of Krakatoa in seven rapid ear-splitting explosions blew up straight into the air for as far as we could see. Our flying platform was rocked back and forth at thirty-degree angles by the concussions. Those of us who were near the balustrade hung on for life. A few of those who were in the middle of the platform were tossed about like flapjacks in a skillet. We were twenty-seven miles away from the Island when it happened, which was just about far enough away for safety. Any closer and we would have been dumped right off the platform into the Sunda Strait. We couldn't see what was left of Krakatoa because it was wrapped in a thick huge tremendously tall black cloud of pumice, ashes, smoke, lava, dirt, with I suppose a few billion dollars worth of diamonds thrown in. We were fortunate in that the explosion was followed by a strong air current, produced in the same manner as waves on the surface of a lake when a stone is thrown in. We were swiftly being taken away from the scene of the eruption.

The wind generated by the explosion was tremendous and for the entire duration of this extraordinary journey we were hurtling through space at a fabulous speed. ◇

NOTES FOR
listening

Introducing the Selection

Relate to theme Tell students that the unit theme is "Volcanoes." Encourage them to discuss what they know about volcanoes, such as what happens when a volcano becomes active.

Discuss word meanings Explain to students that in "What Goes Up Must Come Down," they will hear new words that they may not understand. Pronounce the words below and write them on the chalkboard. Give students the meaning of each word and tell them that knowing the words will help them to better understand "What Goes Up Must Come Down."

sinister threatening or suggesting evil
catapulted hurled; shot out
balustrade handrail

Listening to the Selection

Set a purpose Tell students they are going to listen to an excerpt from *The Twenty-One Balloons* by William Pène du Bois. Have students listen to discover what happens when a volcano becomes active.

Starting with Literature

Discussing the Selection

Return to purpose After you have read the selection, discuss with students what was realistic and what was fantastic about the narrative. Have students tell about the realistic volcanic eruption and the fantastic actions of the people, and then make a more general statement, such as: *The people found an unusual way to escape from a terrible, real volcanic eruption.*

		LESSON TITLE	STUDENT TEXT				TEACHING RESOURCES		
			Student Lesson	Unit Review	Cumulative Review	Extra Practice	Reteaching Master	Practice Master	Testing Program
	1 DAY	Unit Opener							
PART 1	1 DAY	Writing with Adverbs	284–285	328	331, 434	332, 333	48	48	T544
	1 DAY	Adverbs That Compare	286–287	328	331, 434	332, 334	49	49	T544
	1 DAY	Adverbs Before Adjectives and Other Adverbs	288–289	328	331, 434	332, 335	50	50	T544
	1 DAY	Using Adverbs and Adjectives	290–291	328	331, 434	332, 336	51	51	T544
	1 DAY	Using Negative Words	292–293	329	331, 434	332, 337	52	52	T544
	1 DAY	VOCABULARY ◆ Compounds	294–295	329			53	53	T544
	1 DAY	GRAMMAR-WRITING CONNECTION ◆ How to Expand Sentences with Adverbs	296–297						
PART 2		▶THINK							
	1 DAY	CRITICAL THINKING ◆ A Strategy for Researching	300–301	See also pages 307, 320, 326					
		▶READ							
	1 DAY	LITERATURE ◆ *Volcano* by Patricia Lauber	302–307				Audio Library 2		
		▶SPEAK/LISTEN							
	1 DAY	SPEAKING AND LISTENING ◆ An Oral Report	308–309				Video Library		
		▶WRITE							
	1 DAY	STUDY SKILLS ◆ Using an Encyclopedia	310–311	329			54	54	T544
	1 DAY	WRITING ◆ Taking Notes in Your Own Words	312–313				55	55	
	1 DAY	WRITING ◆ An Outline	314–315	329			56	56	
	1 DAY	READING-WRITING CONNECTION ◆ Focus on Topic Choice	316–317						T544
		▶WRITING PROCESS ◆ Prewriting • Writing • Revising • Proofreading • Publishing							
	4–5 DAYS	WRITING PROCESS ◆ Writing a Research Report	318–325				Spelling Connection Transparencies		T554
	1 DAY	CURRICULUM CONNECTION ◆ Writing for Social Studies	326				Writing Across the Curriculum Guide		

Teacher Resource File

Reteaching Masters 48–56
Practice Masters 48–56
Evaluation and Testing Program, including Unit Pretest, Posttest, and Picture Prompt Writing Samples
Parent Letters in English and Spanish
Classroom Theme Posters
Writing Across the Curriculum Teacher Guide
Integrated Language Arts Projects with Masters (see pages T511–T529)
Spelling Connection, Teacher Edition
Writing Process Transparencies
Audio Library 1: Read-Alouds and Sing-Alouds

Also available:

Achieving English Proficiency Guide and Activities
Spelling Connection, Pupil Edition
Student Resource Books
Student Writing Portfolios
Professional Handbook
WORLD OF BOOKS Classroom Library

Multi-Modal Materials

Audio Library 1: Read-Alouds and Sing-Alouds
Audio Library 2: Listening to Literature
Video Library
Revising and Proofreading Transparencies
Fine Arts Transparencies with Viewing Booklet
Writing Process Transparencies
Writing Process Computer Program

Unit 6 Planning and Pacing Guide

LANGUAGE *game*

Adjective or Adverb?

Objective: To distinguish between adjectives and adverbs
Materials: Index cards or slips of paper

Write each of the following words on an index card or slip of paper:

surely	carefully	kind	roughly	cleverly	intelligent
quickly	careless	gladly	strong	bravely	intensely
powerful	bold	noisily	badly	certain	incorrect

Divide the class into two teams. Players will choose a word, use it in a sentence, then tell if the word is an adverb or an adjective. Allow one minute for completion of tasks at first, then decrease time allowed. Points are given for correct use and correct identification.

Multi-Modal Activities

BULLETIN BOARD *idea*

You may wish to use a bulletin board as a springboard for discussing the unit theme, or you may prefer to have students create a bulletin board as they move through the unit. Encourage students to use their five senses to discuss what pictures and ideas come to mind when they think of volcanoes. For example, they may think of sounds, such as the sizzle of hot lava, the hiss of rising steam, and the rumble of a live volcano. Mount a picture of a volcano and have students list their impressions around it under the headings *Sight, Sound, Smell, Taste,* and *Touch*. Label the display *Volcanoes*. Have students continue to add their impressions to the display as they learn more about volcanoes.

Students with different learning styles will all benefit from a natural approach to language learning, including frequent and varied use of oral language in the classroom.

Students "At Risk"

The following suggestions can help you help the students in your classroom who may be considered "at risk."

Offer Tools for Learning

Students who may be considered at risk often have difficulty focusing and organizing their thought for learning effectively and efficiently. Help them take advantage of the graphic organizers, or thinking strategies, introduced in the Critical Thinking or Creative Thinking lesson in each unit. Be sure each time the same graphic organizer appears (four times per unit, two units per book), students "try it on" and explore its potential as a powerful tool for generating, focusing, organizing, and managing their ideas.

Limited English Proficiency

Teachers whose classes contain students with limited English proficiency may find the following activities helpful in developing students' skills in grammar and composition.

Telling How, When, and Where

Have students quickly suggest several sentences that contain a simple subject and an action verb. You may wish to say one sentence as an example, such as *A horse gallops.* Record students' suggestions on a chart on the chalkboard. Then have students complete the chart by telling *how, when,* and *where* for each sentence. The beginning of the chart may look like the one on this page.

When the chart is complete, have students use the information on it to compose complete sentences. Remind students to place adverbs carefully. Explain that *The clock never chimed* makes more sense than *The clock chimed never.*

Simon Says

Have students play a game of Simon Says, using an adverb in each command. Remind students that they are to follow a command only if it includes the words *Simon says.* Then give such commands as: *Simon says clap softly. Wave quickly.* After all the students have become familiar with the game, you may wish to have volunteers take turns being the leader. At the conclusion of the game you may wish to have students list on the chalkboard the adverbs they heard in the commands.

Acting Out How

On 3 by 5 cards write action verb-adverb combinations. Have students take turns choosing a card to act out. Allow time for students to prepare their actions. As classmates identify the actions being portrayed, write their responses on the chalkboard, such as *Kim spins quickly. Jeff stretched high.* When the list is complete, have students identify each adverb.

You may wish to use these action verb–adverb combinations:

waved excitedly   hummed softly
walked quickly   bends low
tapped gently   claps loudly
smiles happily   skips slowly

You may wish to continue the activity by having students see how many different adverbs they can combine with each verb.

Using Negatives

Have students brainstorm science topics about which they would like to know more, such as *Why does a volcano become active?* List students' suggestions on the chalkboard. Then help students turn each question into a negative statement, such as *I do not know why a volcano becomes active.* After all the questions have been turned into negative statements, encourage discussion of how students might go about finding the answer to each question.

How, When, and Where Chart

Sentence	How	When	Where
A horse gallops	quickly	often	outside
The clock chimed	loudly	never	nearby

Gifted and Talented Students

To enable gifted and talented students to work at their own pace and to explore the content further, you may wish to use one or more of these activities.

Science Facts

Have students write at least ten science facts, such as *A magnet attracts iron filings.* Then have students exchange papers with a partner and try to add an appropriate adverb to each sentence, such as *A magnet quickly attracts iron filings. A magnet easily attracts iron filings.* Encourage partners to discuss the appropriateness of each adverb.

You may wish to have students choose the best science facts to be illustrated and posted in a science corner or on a science bulletin board display. You may wish to have students work in small groups to research and collect science facts that identify the *biggest, smallest, fastest, slowest, hottest, hardest, softest, heaviest, lightest, oldest, coldest, farthest,* and *tallest* objects in nature. Then have them use their information to create a set of rules, a playing board, and cards for a game called "Top-It."

You also may wish to have students collect facts about a specific category such as plants, the solar system, natural phenomena, or land animals. Encourage students to present their findings with charts, tables, and graphs. You may wish to have students combine their facts to create a group book such as a *Book of Records* or *The Best/Worst of Nature,* which can be displayed in a science corner.

Negatives

Have students work in groups of three. Have one student write a negative sentence such as *I haven't any research topics.* The other two group members should rephrase the sentence, using negatives in a different way, as in *I don't have any research topic. I have no research topic.* Have each group member take a turn writing the first sentence. Encourage group members to compose at least ten negative sentence sets.

Have groups exchange papers and evaluate the use of negatives. After papers have been returned, you may wish to have groups share their work by posting correct sentence sets on a bulletin board display entitled *Negatives.*

Tom Swifties

Encourage students to write at least ten Tom Swifties. Explain that Tom Swifties are sentences that use adverbs creatively to tell how Tom spoke. You may wish to use the following as models or suggest Tom Swifties of your own.

"The light is burned out," he said darkly. "I always agree," he said positively. "I turned on all the lights," he said brightly.

You may wish to have students share their work by illustrating their sentences and posting them on a bulletin board with the heading *How?*

Meeting Individual Needs

■ Easy ■ Average ■ Challenging

OBJECTIVES
To identify adverbs that modify verbs
To recognize the *-ly* suffix
To use adverbs in writing

ASSIGNMENT GUIDE
BASIC   Practice A
⬇   Practice B
ADVANCED   Practice C

All should do the Apply activity.

RESOURCES
■ Reteaching Master 48
■ Practice Master 48
■ ■ ■ Extra Practice, pp. 332, 333
Unit 6 Pretest, p. T544

TEACHING THE LESSON

1. Getting Started
Oral Language Focus attention on this oral activity, encouraging all to participate. You may wish to extend the activity by asking questions, such as *When does the lightning flash?* (sometimes) *Where does the thunder rumble?* (everywhere) Be sure to remind students to provide one-word responses.

2. Developing the Lesson
Guide students through the explanation of writing with adverbs, emphasizing the examples and the summary. You may wish to point out to students that an adverb may appear in a sentence before a verb or after a verb. Lead students through the **Guided Practice.** Identify those who would benefit from reteaching. Assign independent Practice A–C.

3. Closing the Lesson
After students complete the Apply activity, have volunteers share their lists of adverbs. Point out that knowing what adverbs are and how they can be used will add interesting details and strength to their writing and speaking.

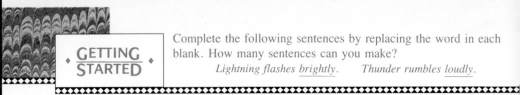

GETTING STARTED

Complete the following sentences by replacing the word in each blank. How many sentences can you make?

Lightning flashes brightly.   *Thunder rumbles loudly.*

1 Writing with Adverbs

You have learned that every sentence contains a verb and that many verbs express action. When you write, you can use adverbs with verbs to make the action seem more real.

Read the sentences below. The underlined words in the sentences are adverbs. Each adverb describes a verb by telling *how*, *when*, or *where*.

> Rita eagerly reads books about volcanoes. (reads how?)
>
> She reported about volcanoes today. (reported when?)
>
> A volcano erupted somewhere. (erupted where?)

Here are some common adverbs. Notice that many adverbs end in *-ly*, especially adverbs that tell *how*.

How?   gladly, slowly, suddenly, quietly, well, badly, fast
When?   always, often, lately, never, usually, now, today
Where?   everywhere, here, there, forward, outside, nearby

> **Summary** ◆ A word that describes a verb is an **adverb**. Use adverbs to add details to your writing.

Guided Practice

In the sentences below, the verbs are underlined. Name the adverbs that describe them.

1. Rita told us today about the eruption of Mount St. Helens.
2. She spoke excitedly about the burning lava.
3. The hot lava flowed everywhere.
4. I gave my report yesterday.
5. The class listened attentively.

ESSENTIAL LANGUAGE SKILLS
This lesson provides opportunities to:

LISTENING ◆ follow the logical organization of an oral presentation ◆ select from an oral presentation the information needed

SPEAKING ◆ use a variety of words to express feelings and ideas

READING ◆ use context clues for word identification ◆ follow a set of directions

WRITING ◆ keep journals, logs, or notebooks to express feelings, record ideas, discover new knowledge, and free the imagination

LANGUAGE ◆ use modifiers (adverbs) correctly

Practice

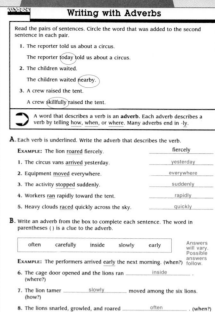

A. In the sentences below, the verbs are underlined. Find the adverb in each sentence and write it.

6. Tourists frequently visited Mount St. Helens in Washington.
7. They gladly camped near this beautiful mountain.
8. Herds of elk and deer lived nearby.
9. Volcanoes often erupt after many years of stillness.
10. In the nineteenth century, Mount St. Helens erupted occasionally.
11. For over a hundred years, this volcano slept quietly.
12. In 1975, scientists correctly predicted another eruption.
13. On March 20, 1980, the mountain suddenly shook.
14. People fearfully awaited the volcano's eruption.
15. Some quickly left the area.

B. Write each sentence and underline the adverb. Write *how*; *when*, or *where* to show what the adverb tells about the verb.

ow 16. On March 27, 1980, Mount St. Helens exploded violently.
ere 17. Steam and ash flew skyward.
hen 18. Smaller explosions frequently occurred through early May.
hen 19. Ash soon covered the mountain peak.
ere 20. Scientists traveled there to study this volcano.

C. Write each sentence. Use an adverb to complete it.
Adverbs will vary. Possible answers follow.
21. The herd of deer _fearfully_ fled the mountain.
22. The ash _quickly_ covered the ground.
23. Scientists _carefully_ studied the effects of the eruption.
24. They tried to determine if another eruption would _soon_ follow.
25. Clearly, Mount St. Helens had _violently_ awakened.

Apply ◆ Think and Write

From Your Writing ◆ Read what you wrote for the Writer's Warm-up. List the adverbs you used under these columns: *how*, *when*, *where*.

✎ **Remember**
that you can use adverbs to add strength to your images of action.

GRAMMAR and WRITING: Adverbs **285**

RETEACHING 48

Writing with Adverbs

Read the pairs of sentences. Circle the word that was added to the second sentence in each pair.

1. The reporter told us about a circus.
   The reporter (today) told us about a circus.
2. The children waited.
   The children waited (nearby.)
3. A crew raised the tent.
   A crew (skillfully) raised the tent.

➥ A word that describes a verb is an **adverb**. Each adverb describes a verb by telling how, when, or where. Many adverbs end in -ly.

A. Each verb is underlined. Write the adverb that describes the verb.

EXAMPLE: The lion roared fiercely. _fiercely_
1. The circus vans arrived yesterday. _yesterday_
2. Equipment moved everywhere. _everywhere_
3. The activity stopped suddenly. _suddenly_
4. Workers ran rapidly toward the tent. _rapidly_
5. Heavy clouds raced quickly across the sky. _quickly_

B. Write an adverb from the box to complete each sentence. The word in parentheses ( ) is a clue to the adverb.

| often | carefully | inside | slowly | early |

Answers will vary. Possible answers follow.

EXAMPLE: The performers arrived early the next morning. (when?)
6. The cage door opened and the lions ran _inside_ (where?)
7. The lion tamer _slowly_ moved among the six lions. (how?)
8. The lions snarled, growled, and roared _often_ . (when?)

PRACTICE 48

Writing with Adverbs

➥ A word that describes a verb is an **adverb**.

A. Circle the adverb that describes the underlined verb.

1. The large white and orange kite flew (gracefully.)
2. The family members (carefully) constructed the kite.
3. Kite builders (often) enter various contests.
4. Many curious and enthusiastic spectators come (here.)
5. The gentle breeze (soon) became a strong wind.

B. Write under the correct heading each adverb you circled in Exercise A.

Adverbs		
How?	When?	Where?
6. gracefully	8. often	10. here
7. carefully	9. soon	

C. Complete each sentence with an adverb. Use an adverb from the box or use your own word.

| beautifully | here | today |
| carefully | patiently | wildly |

Answers will vary. Possible answers follow.

11. Our new kite with the long tail flew _beautifully_ through the sky.
12. We built the delicate kite _carefully_ .
13. Two large kites crashed _here_ in this pond.
14. The spectators at the event applauded _wildly_ .

WRITE IT
On a separate sheet of paper, write about a hobby you enjoy or would like to try. Use adverbs to describe the verbs in your sentences. Answers will vary.

◀▦▦▦ TEACHING OPTIONS ▦▦▦▶

RETEACHING

A Different Modality Write the headings *How? When?* and *Where?* on the chalkboard. Help students brainstorm adverbs that can be written under each heading. Then write *I walked* _____ on the chalkboard. Have volunteers use adverbs from the list to tell how, when, and where they walked. Encourage as many different responses as possible.

CLASS ENRICHMENT

A Cooperative Activity Have groups of five students brainstorm ten activities they saw, read, or heard about recently. Then have them write sentences using adverbs to describe the various actions, such as *The drum corps proudly led the parade.* Have a member of each group write on the chalkboard three of the group's sentences. Then have them ask the class to help decide under which heading—*How, When,* or *Where*—each adverb belongs.

CHALLENGE

An Independent Extension Have students write the following sentences and underline each verb once and each adverb twice. Have them write *how, when,* or *where* above each adverb to show which question the word answers. Then have students rewrite each sentence, replacing the adverb with one that answers a different question.
1. Groups marched quickly to the music.
2. The bands often played Sousa marches.

OBJECTIVES
To identify and use comparative
and superlative forms of adverbs

ASSIGNMENT GUIDE

BASIC   Practice A
             Practice B
ADVANCED   Practice C

All should do the Apply activity.

RESOURCES
■ Reteaching Master 49
■ Practice Master 49
■ ■ ■ Extra Practice, pp. 332, 334

TEACHING THE LESSON

1. Getting Started
Oral Language Focus attention on
this oral activity, encouraging all to
participate. Before the class begins the
comparisons, you may wish to have
students brainstorm adverbs that
could describe falling rain, such as *gently, rarely, heavily, blindingly.* Write
their responses on the chalkboard.

2. Developing the Lesson
Guide students through the explanation of using adverbs that compare,
emphasizing the examples and the
summary. Lead students through the
Guided Practice. Identify those who
would benefit from reteaching. Assign
independent Practice A–C.

3. Closing the Lesson
After students complete the Apply activity, have volunteers read and discuss
their comparison sentences. Point out
to students that recognizing and using
adverbs that compare can help them
read about, listen to, and write comparisons more accurately.

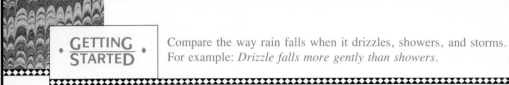

GETTING STARTED Compare the way rain falls when it drizzles, showers, and storms. For example: *Drizzle falls more gently than showers.*

2 Adverbs That Compare

Adverbs can describe by making comparisons, just the way
adjectives can. The *-er* form of an adverb is used to compare two
actions. The *-est* form is used to compare three or more actions.

| Lava travels <u>fast</u>.
| Mud travels <u>faster</u> than lava.
| Water travels the <u>fastest</u> of all.

Many adverbs use *more* and *most* to show comparison.

| Linda watched <u>excitedly</u> as she neared the volcano.
| Linda watched <u>more</u> excitedly when hot steam hissed.
| Linda watched <u>most</u> excitedly when red lava gushed upward.

More and *most* are often used with adverbs that end in *-ly* and
adverbs that have two or more syllables. Be careful not to use
more with the *-er* form or *most* with the *-est* form of an adverb.

The adverbs *well* and *badly* use these forms for comparison.

| Huckleberries grow <u>well</u>.   The trees fared <u>badly</u>.
| Trillium plants grow <u>better</u>   The lake fared <u>worse</u> than
| than that.   the trees.
| Fireweed grows <u>best</u> of   The bridges fared <u>worst</u>
| all.   of all.

> **Summary** ◆ Adverbs have forms that are used to compare
> actions. When you write comparisons with adverbs, use the
> *-er* and *-est* forms, or *more* and *most*, to compare actions.

Guided Practice

For each adverb, give the form that is used to compare two
actions. Then give the form used to compare three or more actions.

	earlier		more slowly		more neatly		worse		more quic
1. early		**2.** slowly		**3.** neatly		**4.** badly		**5.** quickly
	earliest		most slowly		most neatly		worst		most qui

ESSENTIAL LANGUAGE SKILLS
This lesson provides opportunities to:

LISTENING ◆ respond appropriately to orally presented directions

SPEAKING ◆ use a variety of words to express
feelings and ideas ◆ make organized oral presentations

READING ◆ understand content area vocabulary
◆ evaluate and make judgments ◆ follow a set of
directions

WRITING ◆ organize information related to a single topic

LANGUAGE ◆ use modifiers (adverbs) correctly ◆
use the fundamentals of grammar, punctuation,
and spelling

Practice

A. Write the sentences about Mount St. Helens. For each adverb in parentheses ( ), add *more* or use the *-er* form.

     more thoroughly
6. Scientists study volcanoes (thoroughly) than other people do.
    earlier
7. Some scientists arrived at Mount St. Helens (early) than others.
    faster
8. After the eruptions, life on the mountain reappeared (fast) than expected.
    more easily
9. Some burrowing animals, especially those living under the ground, survived (easily) than others.
    more quickly
10. Chipmunks appeared (quickly) than deer and elk.

B. Write each sentence. For each adverb in parentheses ( ), add *most* or use the *-est* form.

    soonest
11. Plants that were buried under snow appeared (soon) of all.
    most hardily
12. Ants and other tiny forms of life survived (hardily) of all.
    most densely
13. The tiny plants grew the (densely) of all the plants.
    most commonly
14. Fungi are the plants we found (commonly) of all.
    fastest
15. They also grow the (fast) of all plants.

C. Write the sentences. Use the correct form of *well* or *badly* to complete each sentence.

    better
16. Rita read her report on Mount St. Helens (well) than I read mine on Krakatoa.
    worse
17. I think the people near Krakatoa suffered (badly) than the people near Mount St. Helens.
    best
18. Rita gathered facts the (well) of all the students.
    better
19. Next time, I am determined to do (well) than this time.
    worst
20. My report will not be prepared the (badly) of all.

Apply ♦ Think and Write

Dictionary of Knowledge ♦ Mount St. Helens is one of many famous volcanoes. Read about volcanoes in the Dictionary of Knowledge. Write some sentences comparing Mauna Loa, Mount Etna, and Cotopaxi. Use adverbs in your comparisons.

✏️ **Remember**
to use the correct forms of adverbs to compare actions.

GRAMMAR and USAGE: Comparison of Adverbs **287**

TEACHING OPTIONS

RETEACHING

A Different Modality Have three students walk at different rates of speed. Use *quickly* to compare how the students walked. Write comparisons on the chalkboard, such as *Kim walked quickly. Hal walked more quickly than Kim. Anna walked most quickly of all.* Have students describe orally other actions they observe, such as *speaking softly* and *spelling well.* Encourage volunteers to write the comparisons on the chalkboard.

CLASS ENRICHMENT

A Cooperative Activity Have students work in small groups to compose a paragraph telling about a real or an imaginary science project they are working on. Encourage students to use as many adverbs as possible to compare actions. You may wish to have one member of each group read aloud the paragraph, having classmates identify each adverb that compares and tell whether it compares two actions or three or more actions.

CHALLENGE

An Independent Extension Write the following list on the chalkboard. Have students use the comparison forms of each adverb in sentences of their own.

Example: A train travels faster than a bus.
A jet plane travels fastest of all.

1. fast
2. early
3. badly
4. cheerfully
5. slowly
6. cleverly
7. well
8. gladly

287

UNIT 6/LESSON 3

■ Easy ■ Average ■ Challenging

OBJECTIVES
To identify adverbs that modify adjectives and other adverbs
To recognize commonly used adverbs

ASSIGNMENT GUIDE
BASIC   Practice A
↓   Practice B
ADVANCED   Practice C

All should do the Apply activity.

RESOURCES
■ Reteaching Master 50
■ Practice Master 50
■■■ Extra Practice, pp. 332, 335

TEACHING THE LESSON

1. Getting Started
Oral Language Focus attention on this oral activity, encouraging all to participate. You may wish to provide a sentence in which the descriptive words may be inserted, such as *He is a _____ _____ person. It is a _____ _____ place.* Encourage creative responses, such as *extremely eager, early, earnest, eerie, enjoyable; slightly serious, slimy, slippery, special, strange; completely calm, clever, comfortable, cozy, curly; terribly terrific, thirsty, tidy, timid, tricky.*

2. Developing the Lesson
Guide students through the explanation of adverbs before adjectives and other adverbs, emphasizing the examples and the summary. You may wish to review the definitions: an adjective describes a noun or a pronoun and tells *what kind* or *how many*; an adverb describes a verb, an adjective, or another adverb and tells *how, when, where,* or *to what extent.* Lead students through the **Guided Practice.** Identify those who would benefit from reteaching. Assign independent Practice A–C.

3. Closing the Lesson
After students complete the Apply activity, you may have volunteers identify each adverb that describes an adjective or another adverb. Point out to students that knowing about commonly used adverbs can help make their writing and speaking more exact.

288

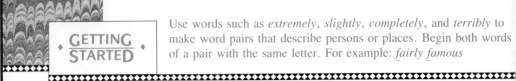

GETTING STARTED

Use words such as *extremely, slightly, completely,* and *terribly* to make word pairs that describe persons or places. Begin both words of a pair with the same letter. For example: *fairly famous*

3 Adverbs Before Adjectives and Other Adverbs

You have used adverbs to describe verbs.

■ Mount Fuji, an inactive volcano, rises <u>majestically</u> above the land.

Adverbs can also describe adjectives or other adverbs by telling *to what extent.*

1. A volcanic eruption is a <u>fairly</u> <u>rare</u> event.
2. The lava flowed <u>so</u> <u>fast</u> that people had no time to escape.

Notice that in sentence **1** the adverb *fairly* describes the adjective *rare.* In sentence **2** the adverb *so* describes the adverb *fast.*

Here are some adverbs you can use to describe adjectives and other adverbs.

rather	fairly	unusually	almost
certainly	slightly	quite	totally
incredibly	considerably	unbelievably	too
justly	very	terribly	so

> **Summary** ◆ An adverb may describe a verb, an adjective, or another adverb. Use adverbs in your writing to make adjectives and other adverbs more exact.

Guided Practice

Name the adverb that describes each underlined adjective or adverb in the sentences below.

1. Mount Fuji is <u>incredibly</u> <u>beautiful</u>.
2. A volcanic eruption can occur <u>quite</u> <u>suddenly</u>.
3. People living near a volcano cannot be <u>too</u> <u>careful</u>.
4. I am <u>rather</u> <u>afraid</u> of volcanoes.
5. I wouldn't live <u>very</u> <u>close</u> to one.

288   GRAMMAR: Adverbs

ESSENTIAL LANGUAGE SKILLS
This lesson provides opportunities to:

LISTENING ◆ follow the logical organization of an oral presentation ◆ select from an oral presentation the information needed

SPEAKING ◆ use oral language for a variety of purposes ◆ make organized oral presentations

READING ◆ use context clues for word identification ◆ follow a set of directions

WRITING ◆ adapt information to accomplish a specific purpose with a particular audience

LANGUAGE ◆ use modifiers (adjectives and adverbs) correctly

Practice

A. Write each sentence. Then write the adverb that describes the underlined adjective or adverb.

6. A volcanic eruption is an <u>unusually</u> <u>interesting</u> phenomenon.
7. Magma, or melted rock, forms because the earth's interior is <u>so</u> <u>hot</u>.
8. The magma is <u>considerably</u> <u>lighter</u> than the rock around it.
9. Magma can rise <u>terribly</u> <u>quickly</u> to the top of a volcano.
10. The rising magma <u>very</u> <u>gradually</u> forms a magma chamber.
11. Magma that is <u>completely</u> <u>outside</u> is called lava.
12. <u>Highly</u> <u>fluid</u> lava flows down the sides of the mountain.
13. This lava forms <u>extremely</u> <u>smooth</u> sheets of rock.
14. Other <u>fairly</u> <u>thick</u> lava forms rough sheets of rock.
15. Flowing lava can be <u>quite</u> <u>destructive</u>.

B. Write each sentence. Use these adverbs to complete the sentences. Use each adverb only once. Answers may vary. Possible answers follow.

extremely	incredibly	too	significantly	very

16. ___Too___ much gas can make sticky magma blast into fragments.
17. The rock fragments differ ___very___ much in size.
18. Volcanic dust consists of ___incredibly___ tiny particles.
19. ___Extremely___ large fragments are called volcanic bombs.
20. Volcanic bombs may be ___significantly___ larger than basketballs.

C. 21–25. Write five sentences that use adverbs to modify adjectives and other adverbs. Choose five of the adverbs below to use in your sentences. Sentences will vary.

extremely	too	very	rather
unusually	slightly	fairly	almost

Apply • Think and Write

Riddle Paragraph • Write a paragraph describing a common object that is behaving in a very strange way, but do not name the object. How about a vacuum cleaner that gobbles up carpets? Use adverbs that describe adjectives and other adverbs. Exchange papers with a classmate. Try to guess each other's object.

> ✎ **Remember**
> that you can use adverbs to make adjectives and other adverbs more precise.

GRAMMAR: Adverbs **289**

◀|||| **TEACHING OPTIONS** ||||▶

RETEACHING

A Different Modality Write the adverbs *quite, rather, too, unusually,* and *very* on the chalkboard. Also write *The speaker seemed _____ nervous.* Have volunteers insert each adverb into the sentence. Point out that *nervous* is an adjective and that adverbs can make adjectives more exact. Write *We learned _____ quickly* on the chalkboard. Have volunteers use the adverbs to describe *quickly* and explain how each one makes *quickly* more exact.

CLASS ENRICHMENT

A Cooperative Activity Have students work in small groups to write a descriptive paragraph about an animal with an unusual feature, such as an elephant with its odd trunk or an anteater with its long snout and tongue. Have each group member supply at least one adverb that describes an adjective and one adverb that describes an adverb. You may wish to have a volunteer from each group read the paragraph to the class.

CHALLENGE

An Independent Extension Have students rewrite the following sentences, replacing each adverb.

1. Some machines use very little electricity.
2. Is solar energy very practical?
3. It heats water extremely well.
4. Cooking with solar energy is rather easy.
5. These hot dogs taste quite good.

Possible responses: 1. so 2. totally 3. unusually 4. fairly 5. incredibly

289

UNIT 6/LESSON 4

OBJECTIVES
To distinguish between adjectives and adverbs and to use them correctly

ASSIGNMENT GUIDE
BASIC — Practice A
Practice B
ADVANCED — Practice C

All should do the Apply activity.

RESOURCES
■ Reteaching Master 51
■ Practice Master 51
■ ■ ■ Extra Practice, pp. 332, 336

TEACHING THE LESSON

1. Getting Started
Oral Language Focus attention on this oral activity, encouraging all to participate. You may wish to write on the chalkboard the headings *Adjectives* and *Adverbs*. List under each heading each student's adjective and adverb responses.

2. Developing the Lesson
Guide students through the explanation of using adverbs and adjectives, emphasizing the examples and the summary. You may wish to emphasize the use of *well* as an adjective meaning "healthy" and as an adverb telling "how," as in *If you feel well, you can do well in the contest.* Lead students through the **Guided Practice.** Identify those who would benefit from reteaching. Assign independent Practice A–C.

3. Closing the Lesson
After students complete the Apply activity, have volunteers read their sentences aloud. You may wish to invite students to list on the chalkboard each use of *good, well, bad,* and *badly* as an adjective or an adverb. Help students understand that using adverbs and adjectives correctly can add important details to their speech and their writing.

290

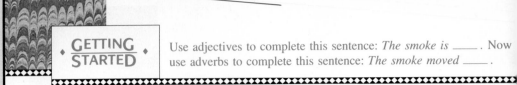

GETTING STARTED
Use adjectives to complete this sentence: *The smoke is ___ .* Now use adverbs to complete this sentence: *The smoke moved ___ .*

4 Using Adverbs and Adjectives

In the sentences below, one underlined adjective describes a noun, and another describes a pronoun. The adjective *enormous* describes the noun *plume. Impressive* describes the pronoun *it.*

■ The volcano's smoky plume seems <u>enormous</u>. It is <u>impressive</u>.

While adjectives are used to describe nouns and pronouns, adverbs are used to describe verbs, adjectives, and other adverbs. In the sentences below, *violently* describes the verb *erupted. Unusually* describes the adjective *exciting. Very* describes the adverb *quickly.*

The volcano erupted <u>violently</u>.   It was <u>unusually</u> exciting.
The lava flowed <u>very</u> quickly.

The words *good, bad,* and *well* may be used as adjectives. *Well* is an adjective when it means "healthy." The adjective *well* usually follows a linking verb such as *is, seem, feel,* or *look.*

The tourists at Pompeii had a <u>good</u> time. The hotel food was <u>bad</u>
After a day of rest, the tourists were <u>well</u> again.

Well and *badly* are often used as adverbs that tell *how.*

The youngest tourist behaved <u>well</u>.
The child acted <u>badly</u> in the restaurant.

> **Summary** ◆ Use adjectives to describe nouns and pronouns. Use adverbs to describe verbs, adjectives, and other adverbs.

Guided Practice

Tell which word correctly completes each sentence.

1. Vesuvius in Italy looks (beautiful, beautifully).
2. Centuries ago, it (sudden, suddenly) erupted.
3. Scientists have studied this volcano (thorough, thoroughly).

290   GRAMMAR and USAGE: Adverbs and Adjectives

ESSENTIAL LANGUAGE SKILLS
This lesson provides opportunities to:

LISTENING ◆ respond appropriately to orally presented directions ◆ select from an oral presentation the information needed

SPEAKING ◆ use a variety of words to express feelings and ideas

READING ◆ use context to understand the meaning of words ◆ follow a set of directions

WRITING ◆ write and compose for a variety of purposes

LANGUAGE ◆ use modifiers (adjectives and adverbs) correctly

Practice

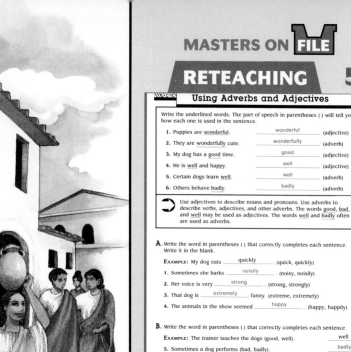

A. Write the word in parentheses ( ) that correctly completes each sentence about the volcano Vesuvius.

4. Vesuvius appears (<u>high</u>, highly) over the Bay of Naples.
5. The soil around Vesuvius is (unusual, <u>unusually</u>) fertile.
6. Its most (<u>famous</u>, famously) eruption occurred in A.D. 79.
7. The volcano exploded (unexpected, <u>unexpectedly</u>).
8. The city of Pompeii was (complete, <u>completely</u>) buried.
9. Pompeii was not a (<u>great</u>, greatly) city.
10. Today, however, this tourist spot is (<u>popular</u>, popularly).
11. People (eager, <u>eagerly</u>) come to see how ancient Romans lived.
12. Romans used Pompeii (main, <u>mainly</u>) as a vacation place.
13. They built (<u>large</u>, largely) homes near the Mediterranean Sea.
14. The people of Pompeii carried on a (<u>rich</u>, richly) trade in oil.
15. The eruption (sudden, <u>suddenly</u>) changed all that.

B. Choose the word in parentheses ( ) that correctly completes each sentence. Write the sentence. Then write whether *good*, *well*, *bad*, or *badly* is an adjective or an adverb in the sentence.

EXAMPLE: The ancient city of Pompeii is (well, good) preserved.
ANSWER: The ancient city of Pompeii is well preserved. (adverb)

adv. 16. The eruption of Vesuvius damaged Pompeii (bad, <u>badly</u>).
adv. 17. Early excavations of the city were not done (good, <u>well</u>).
adj. 18. A (<u>good</u>, well) method of digging began after 1860.
adj. 19. Uncovered city blocks were not in (<u>bad</u>, badly) condition.
adv. 20. Ancient buildings of Pompeii are (good, <u>well</u>) kept.

Answers will vary. Possible answers follow.
C. Use adjectives and adverbs to complete the sentences.

21. The <u>frightened</u> townspeople fled <u>rapidly</u> from the eruption.
22. Today the volcano seems <u>calm</u>.
23. It might <u>suddenly</u> erupt at any time.

Apply ♦ Think and Write

Travel Sentences ♦ Write sentences about a place you have visited or want to visit. Use the words *good*, *well*, *bad*, and *badly*.

GRAMMAR and USAGE: Adverbs and Adjectives **291**

✏️ **Remember**
to use adjectives and adverbs correctly to add important details.

◀|||| TEACHING OPTIONS ||||▶

RETEACHING

A Different Modality Write on the chalkboard: *We took an* easy *test. The problem was solved easily.* Point out that *easy* is an adjective that describes the noun *test; easily* is an adverb that describes the verb *solved.* Explain that adjectives describe nouns and pronouns and adverbs describe verbs, adjectives, and other adverbs. Write additional pairs of sentences and have students circle adjectives and underline adverbs.

CLASS ENRICHMENT

A Cooperative Activity Have students work with partners to list at least ten adjective-adverb pairs, such as *safe–safely.* Then have partners use both words in sentences, such as *A safe driver wears a seat belt; Drive safely.* After partners have checked their sentences for correct adjective/adverb usage, you may wish to have them share their favorite sentence pairs with classmates.

CHALLENGE

An Independent Extension Have students complete the paragraph below, using *good* or *well.* Then have them write a paragraph of their own using *good* and *well.*

The Aztecs were _____ builders. Montezuma, the Aztec emperor, was a _____ ruler. He behaved _____ toward the Spanish explorers. They, however, didn't want to become _____ friends with the Aztecs. The Aztecs fought _____, but the Spaniards won.

UNIT 6/LESSON 5

OBJECTIVES
To avoid using double negatives
To identify, form, and use negative contractions

ASSIGNMENT GUIDE
BASIC   Practice A
             Practice B
ADVANCED   Practice C

All should do the Apply activity.

RESOURCES
■ Reteaching Master 52
■ Practice Master 52
■ ■ ■ Extra Practice, pp. 332, 337

TEACHING THE LESSON

1. Getting Started
Oral Language Focus attention on this oral activity, encouraging all to participate. To extend this activity, you may wish to ask volunteers to create positive and negative statements, such as *I do speak English. I don't speak Italian. I will be on time. I won't be late.*

2. Developing the Lesson
Guide students through the explanation of using negative words, emphasizing the examples and the summary. Lead students through the **Guided Practice.** Identify those who would benefit from reteaching. Assign independent Practice A–C.

3. Closing the Lesson
After students complete the Apply activity, have volunteers read aloud the sentences they wrote. Encourage a discussion of how people use negatives in everyday speech. Point out to students that avoiding the use of two negative words in the same sentence will help them speak and write clearly and correctly.

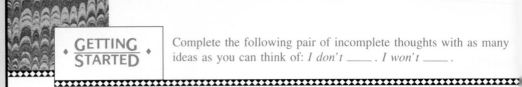

GETTING STARTED Complete the following pair of incomplete thoughts with as many ideas as you can think of: *I don't _____. I won't _____.*

5 Using Negative Words

You use negative words to say or write *no.* Look at the following sentences. The underlined words are negative words.

Lien is <u>not</u> interested in volcanoes. She <u>never</u> reads about them.
"I <u>don't</u> feel that way," said Anita, "but I <u>won't</u> argue about it."

Here is a list of some other common negative words.

no   nobody   nothing   no one   nowhere   none

Often you express ''no'' by writing a contraction—a shortened form of two words. The contractions below are negatives. Each is formed from a verb and the adverb *not*.

isn't = is not	don't = do not	couldn't = could not
wasn't = was not	hasn't = has not	wouldn't = would not
doesn't = does not	haven't = have not	won't = will not

You need to use only one word to make a sentence negative. Avoid double negatives—two negatives in a sentence.

Wrong: Anita doesn't never stop talking about volcanoes.
Right: Anita never stops talking about volcanoes.
Right: Anita doesn't ever stop talking about volcanoes.

> **Summary** ◆ Negative words mean ''no.'' Avoid using two negative words in the same sentence.

Guided Practice

Name the negative word in each sentence. Tell which are contractions.

1. <u>No one</u> in class knows more about volcanoes than Maria.
2. She <u>can't</u> hide her enthusiasm. contraction
3. <u>Isn't</u> a volcanic eruption an incredible event? contraction

ESSENTIAL LANGUAGE SKILLS
This lesson provides opportunities to:

LISTENING ◆ employ active listening in a variety of ways ◆ follow the logical organization of an oral presentation ◆ select from an oral presentation the information needed

SPEAKING ◆ use oral language for a variety of purposes

READING ◆ use context to understand the meaning of words ◆ follow a set of directions

WRITING ◆ keep journals, logs, or notebooks to express feelings, record ideas, discover new knowledge, and free the imagination

LANGUAGE ◆ use the fundamentals of grammar, punctuation, and spelling

Practice

A. Write the sentences. Underline the negative words.

4. <u>No one</u> knows when the first volcanic eruptions happened.
5. Scientists <u>can't</u> tell when a volcano near Crete exploded.
6. They <u>aren't</u> certain it happened in 1500 B.C.
7. The mountain on the island of Thera was <u>not</u> ordinary.
8. People on the island <u>couldn't</u> escape the flowing lava.
9. <u>Nobody</u> expected the volcano to erupt.
10. <u>Nowhere</u> on the island did people survive the blast.
11. Some ancient people thought an eruption occurred because a god <u>wasn't</u> happy.
12. Others <u>didn't</u> accept this idea.
13. <u>None</u> were sure of the facts.

B. Write the word in parentheses ( ) that correctly completes each sentence. Avoid double negatives.

14. Perhaps ancient people didn't (<u>ever</u>, never) realize how dangerous a volcano could be.
15. The volcanic area (<u>was</u>, wasn't) no place for a home.
16. There really (was, <u>wasn't</u>) any hope for survival.
17. Probably nothing (<u>could</u>, couldn't) have saved the people.
18. I wouldn't live (nowhere, <u>anywhere</u>) near a volcano.

C. Rewrite the following sentences. Correct each double negative.
Answers may vary. Possible answers follow.
EXAMPLE: Anita won't never lose interest in volcanoes.
ANSWER: Anita will never lose interest in volcanoes. *or*
        Anita won't ever lose interest in volcanoes.

I haven't any interest in volcanoes.
19. I haven't no interest in volcanoes.
They don't ever bore Mary Ellen.
20. They don't never bore Mary Ellen.
Doesn't anything about volcanoes ever interest Michael?
21. Doesn't nothing about volcanoes never interest Michael?
Nancy will never stop talking about them.
22. Nancy won't never stop talking about them.
No one here has ever seen a volcano.
23. No one here hasn't never seen a volcano.

Apply ◆ Think and Write

Negative Sentences ◆ Listen to what people around you say. Write five sentences you hear that contain negatives.

✎ **Remember**
not to use two negative words in the same sentence.

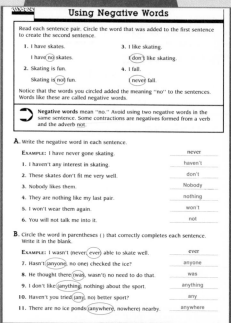

Using Negative Words

Read each sentence pair. Circle the word that was added to the first sentence to create the second sentence.

1. I have skates.
   I have (no) skates.
2. Skating is fun.
   Skating is (not) fun.
3. I like skating.
   I (don't) like skating.
4. I fall.
   I (never) fall.

Notice that the words you circled added the meaning "no" to the sentences. Words like these are called negative words.

◔ **Negative words** mean "no." Avoid using two negative words in the same sentence. Some contractions are negatives formed from a verb and the adverb *not*.

A. Write the negative word in each sentence.

EXAMPLE: I have never gone skating. — never
1. I haven't any interest in skating. — haven't
2. These skates don't fit me very well. — don't
3. Nobody likes them. — Nobody
4. They are nothing like my last pair. — nothing
5. I won't wear them again. — won't
6. You will not talk me into it. — not

B. Circle the word in parentheses ( ) that correctly completes each sentence. Write it in the blank.

EXAMPLE: I wasn't (never, (ever)) able to skate well. — ever
7. Hasn't ((anyone), no one) checked the ice? — anyone
8. He thought there ((was), wasn't) no need to do that. — was
9. I don't like ((anything), nothing) about the sport. — anything
10. Haven't you tried ((any), no) better sport? — any
11. There are no ice ponds ((anywhere), nowhere) nearby. — anywhere

PRACTICE 52

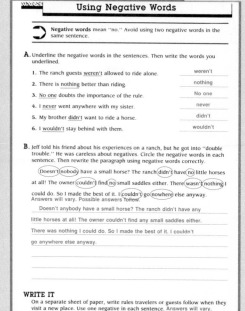

Using Negative Words

◔ **Negative words** mean "no." Avoid using two negative words in the same sentence.

A. Underline the negative words in the sentences. Then write the words you underlined.
1. The ranch guests <u>weren't</u> allowed to ride alone. — weren't
2. There is <u>nothing</u> better than riding. — nothing
3. <u>No one</u> doubts the importance of the rule. — No one
4. I <u>never</u> went anywhere with my sister. — never
5. My brother <u>didn't</u> want to ride a horse. — didn't
6. I <u>wouldn't</u> stay behind with them. — wouldn't

B. Jeff told his friend about his experiences on a ranch, but he got into "double trouble." He was careless about negatives. Circle the negative words in each sentence. Then rewrite the paragraph using negative words correctly.

(Doesn't) (nobody) have a small horse? The ranch (didn't) have (no) little horses at all! The owner (couldn't) find (no) small saddles either. There (wasn't) (nothing) I could do. So I made the best of it. I (couldn't) go (nowhere) else anyway.
Answers will vary. Possible answers follow.

Doesn't anybody have a small horse? The ranch didn't have any
little horses at all! The owner couldn't find any small saddles either.
There was nothing I could do. So I made the best of it. I couldn't
go anywhere else anyway.

WRITE IT
On a separate sheet of paper, write rules travelers or guests follow when they visit a new place. Use one negative in each sentence. Answers will vary.

◀━ TEACHING OPTIONS ━▶

RETEACHING	CLASS ENRICHMENT	CHALLENGE
A Different Modality Write negative words such as *can't, don't, nowhere, none, no,* and *never* on index cards and distribute them. Remind students that only one negative word belongs in a sentence. Then have volunteers use their negative word in an original sentence. Have classmates listen to see if the sentence uses the negative word correctly.	**A Cooperative Activity** Divide the class into two teams to play a game of opposites. Have the first player on Team 1 say something positive, such as *I like chess.* Have the first player on Team 2 turn the sentence into a negative statement, such as *I don't like chess.* Continue until all players have supplied either a positive or a negative statement. You may wish to reverse the procedure, asking the first player to supply a negative statement.	**An Independent Extension** Write the incorrect sentences below on the chalkboard. Then have students rewrite each sentence in two different ways that do not use double negatives. Example: I can't play any musical instrument. I can play no musical instrument. 1. I can't play no musical instrument. 2. I haven't never taken lessons. 3. Can't no one teach me? 4. I won't never complain about practicing.

UNIT 6
Vocabulary

OBJECTIVES
To identify one-word, two-word, and hyphenated compounds
To write compounds correctly

ASSIGNMENT GUIDE
BASIC   Practice A
           Practice B
ADVANCED   Practice C

All should do the Language Corner.

RESOURCES
■ Reteaching Master 53
■ Practice Master 53

TEACHING THE LESSON

1. Getting Started
Oral Language Focus attention on this oral activity, encouraging all to participate. You may wish to begin by demonstrating how to test for compound words by joining the first word *up* with each of the other words to reach the conclusion that only *upside down, uproar,* and *upstair(s)* can be formed with *up*.

2. Developing the Lesson
Guide students through the explanation of compounds, emphasizing the definition and the examples. You may wish to tell students that one of the best ways to be sure a compound is spelled correctly is to use a dictionary. Guide students through Building Your Vocabulary. Identify those who would benefit from reteaching. Assign independent Practice A–C.

3. Closing the Lesson
After students complete the Practice exercises, tell them to listen and watch for compounds during the rest of the day. Have them list each one they hear or see. At the end of the day, have students use a dictionary to check if the words they wrote are compounds and if they are spelled correctly. Point out to students that knowing how to form compounds can help them increase their vocabulary.

Language Corner You may wish to have students discuss and compare their methods of coining words.

294

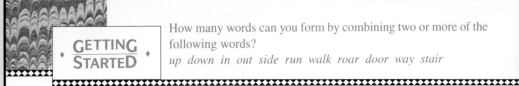
♦ GETTING ♦ STARTED

How many words can you form by combining two or more of the following words?
up down in out side run walk roar door way stair

VOCABULARY ♦
Compounds

James is a big <u>baseball</u> fan. He likes to watch the pitcher's <u>windup</u> and to see the batter hit a <u>grand slam</u>. He enjoys eating <u>hot dogs</u> and <u>watermelon</u>. He wants to play <u>big-league</u> ball <u>someday</u>.

The underlined words above are called compounds. A **compound** is a word formed from two or more words. Many words in English are compounds.

Notice that compounds can be written in different ways. Some compounds, such as *baseball* and *watermelon*, are written as a single word. Some, such as *hot dog* and *grand slam*, are written as separate words. Other compounds, such as *big-league*, are written with a hyphen (-). More examples of these three kinds of compounds are shown below.

Ways to Form Compounds
One word: birthday, handbag, fireplace, cupcake, rowboat
Separate words: air conditioner, comic strip, ice cream, alley cat
With hyphens: good-by, merry-go-round, cross-eyed, high-rise

Building Your Vocabulary

Find the compounds in these sentences.

1. We found <u>driftwood</u> on the beach near the <u>Coast Guard</u> station.
2. The sailor watched the <u>half-moon</u> from the <u>crow's nest</u>.
3. Sally sold <u>seashells</u> by the <u>seashore</u> <u>sometimes</u>.
4. Dan made a <u>flying saucer</u> with a paper plate and a <u>flashlight</u>.
5. Her <u>baby-sitter</u> goes to <u>high school</u>.

294   VOCABULARY: Compounds

ESSENTIAL LANGUAGE SKILLS
This lesson provides opportunities to:

LISTENING ♦ select from an oral presentation the information needed

SPEAKING ♦ use a variety of words to express feelings and ideas ♦ make organized oral presentations

READING ♦ use context clues for word identification ♦ develop and expand word meanings through prefixes, suffixes and root words, compound words, and multiple meanings ♦ draw logical conclusions ♦ follow a set of directions

WRITING ♦ generate ideas using graphic organizers ♦ adapt information to accomplish a specific purpose with a particular audience ♦ spell increasingly complex words

LANGUAGE ♦ use the fundamentals of grammar, punctuation, and spelling ♦ use clear and interesting words to express thoughts

Practice

Later in this unit, you will read about Mount St. Helens. This volcano in Washington State erupted in 1980. Join words in column **A** with words in column **B** to form single-word compounds from the story. Then use the compounds in sentences.

	A	**B**		**A**	**B**
	earthquake			_uprooted_	
1.	earth	blasted	**6.**	up	shoe
	sideways			_mountaintop_	
2.	side	heated	**7.**	mountain	land
	superheated			_horseshoe_	
3.	super	side	**8.**	horse	rooted
	sandblasted			_landscape_	
4.	sand	quake	**9.**	land	top
	countryside			_wasteland_	
5.	country	ways	**10.**	waste	scape

Compounds sometimes make funny pictures if you look at the meaning of each word they are made from. A "nosedive" might look like this.

Write a compound for each picture below.

pillow fight   **fishbowl**   **sawhorse**

11.   13.   15.

12.   14.   16.

shoebox   **boardwalk**   **armchair**

Draw pictures of other compounds to share with your classmates.

LANGUAGE CORNER · Coining Words

One way to coin, or invent, a new word is to combine two old words. For example, a fish that swims belly-up could be called a *bellyfish*. What would you call a bull that looks like a dog? Coin some new compounds of your own.

a dogbull

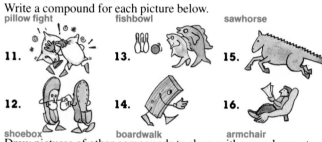

VOCABULARY: Compounds   **295**

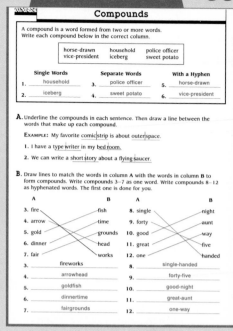

Compounds

A compound is a word formed from two or more words. Write each compound below in the correct column.

horse-drawn	household	police officer
vice-president	iceberg	sweet potato

Single Words	**Separate Words**	**With a Hyphen**
1. household	3. police officer	5. horse-drawn
2. iceberg	4. sweet potato	6. vice-president

A. Underline the compounds in each sentence. Then draw a line between the words that make up each compound.

EXAMPLE: My favorite comic strip is about outer space.

1. I have a type writer in my bed room.

2. We can write a short story about a flying saucer.

B. Draw lines to match the words in column A with the words in column B to form compounds. Write compounds 3–7 as one word. Write compounds 8–12 as hyphenated words. The first one is done for you.

	A	**B**		**A**	**B**
3.	fire	fish	8.	single	night
4.	arrow	time	9.	forty	aunt
5.	gold	grounds	10.	good	way
6.	dinner	head	11.	great	five
7.	fair	works	12.	one	handed

3.	fireworks	8.	single-handed	
4.	arrowhead	9.	forty-five	
5.	goldfish	10.	good-night	
6.	dinnertime	11.	great-aunt	
7.	fairgrounds	12.	one-way	

PRACTICE   **53**

Compounds

A. Underline each compound in the paragraph. Then write each compound in the correct column.

The high school fair was last weekend. My entire class was there. I went with my girlfriend Jill. We ate popcorn, hot dogs, and ice cream. We rode on the old-fashioned merry-go-round and the tilt-a-whirl. Some small children rode a fire truck with their babysitters. I wanted to stay longer, but it was late. We had to say good-bye.

Single Words	**Separate Words**	**With a Hyphen**
1. weekend	5. high school	9. old-fashioned
2. girlfriend	6. hot dogs	10. merry-go-round
3. popcorn	7. ice cream	11. tilt-a-whirl
4. babysitters	8. fire truck	12. good-bye

B. Solve each puzzle. Use a dictionary to check the spelling of each compound.

13. + = basketball

14. + = cupcake

15. + = horseshoe

16. + = sunlight

17. + = cloudburst

18. + = doghouse

◀▐▐▐ TEACHING OPTIONS ▐▐▐▶

RETEACHING

A Different Modality Emphasize that a compound is a word formed from two or more words. Review with students the three ways to form compounds. Distribute cards with a single word written on one side and the compound to which it belongs on the other. Include words such as *dishpan*, *right-handed*, and *peanut butter*. Have students discuss the meanings of both the single and the compound words.

CLASS ENRICHMENT

A Cooperative Activity Write these categories on the chalkboard: *First Names, Relatives, Community Workers*. You may wish to add other categories of people suggested by the class. Then have students work in small groups to list compounds that fit each category, such as *Mary Jo, grandma,* and *firefighter*. Encourage group members to check the spelling of each compound. You may wish to have groups share their favorite compound in each category.

CHALLENGE

An Independent Extension Have students coin several new compounds and then make rebus puzzles of them for each other to solve. You may wish to model an example by drawing an ocean wave holding up a boat as if in the palm of a hand. Ask students what they might call an ocean wave that lifts up a boat (possible answer: *a boatlifter*). Encourage students to create a file of rebus puzzles of coined words for classmates to use during free time.

295

Grammar-Writing Connection

How to Expand Sentences with Adverbs

Point out to students that they can use the grammar skills they learned in Unit 6 to help them develop good writing techniques. Explain that in this Grammar-Writing Connection, students will use what they know about adverbs and their forms, how to distinguish between adjectives and adverbs, and how to avoid double negatives to learn how to expand sentences with adverbs.

You may wish to guide students through the explanation of how to expand sentences with adverbs, stressing the examples. Then have students apply the information by completing the activity at the bottom of the first page. Students may work in small groups or with partners to choose verbs and write adverbs to describe them, or they may combine verbs and adverbs orally.

Help students to understand that expanding sentences with adverbs is an effective way to improve writing, and that it can make their writing more descriptive, clearer, and more interesting.

How to Expand Sentences with Adverbs

You know that adverbs are used to describe verbs, adjectives, and other adverbs. Verbs alone don't always give sentences as much detail as a writer would like. Adding adverbs can supply details and add information to your writing. Read the two sentences below. Which one gives you more detail? Which one seems to describe a more dangerous volcanic eruption?

■ **1. A volcano erupted in Hawaii.**

■ **2. A volcano erupted violently in Hawaii.**

Sentence **1** is a perfectly fine sentence. However, adding the adverb *violently* in sentence **2** gives more detail. The adverb tells you *how* the volcano erupted. Now read sentence **3** to see how adding another adverb can add even more detail to the sentence.

■ **3. Yesterday a volcano erupted violently in Hawaii.**

Like adjectives, different adverbs can paint different pictures in a reader's mind. Read sentence **4** to see how changing one adverb can turn the picture of a destructive volcano into a less dangerous one.

■ **4. Yesterday a volcano erupted quietly in Hawaii.**

The Grammar Game ◆ Concentrate on adverbs! Choose six verbs from the list below. Quickly write as many adverbs as you can to describe each one.   Answers will vary.

draw	drive	snore	end
jump	leave	cheer	discuss
tiptoe	chew	play	touch

Now that you're warmed up, do the same with the rest of the verbs. How many adverbs did you write in all?

◆ 296 ◆   COOPERATIVE LEARNING: Expanding Sentences

ESSENTIAL LANGUAGE SKILLS

This lesson provides opportunities to:

LISTENING ◆ select from an oral presentation the information needed ◆ listen actively and attentively

SPEAKING ◆ participate in group discussions ◆ use a variety of words to express feelings and ideas

READING ◆ accurately comprehend the details in a reading selection ◆ evaluate and make judgments ◆ follow a set of directions

WRITING ◆ adapt information to accomplish a specific purpose with a particular audience ◆ improve writing based on peer and/or teacher response

LANGUAGE ◆ use modifiers (adverbs) correctly

Working Together

As your group works on activities **A** and **B**, use adverbs to give detail and information to your writing.

In Your Group

♦ Help everyone understand the directions.

♦ Give everyone a chance to share ideas.

♦ Look at others when they are talking.

♦ Show appreciation for different opinions.

A. Each group member should add an adverb to expand each sentence below. Choose the most exact word possible to tell *how, when,* or *where.* Then mix up the papers and try as a group to guess who's who. Answers will vary. Possible answers follow.

1. I dance. seldom
2. I sing. loudly
3. I laugh. often
4. I run. sweetly
5. I frown. sometimes
6. I rest. quietly
7. I work. today
8. I read. silently
9. I talk. softly
10. I play. easily
11. I wait. quickly
12. I travel. far
13. I study. always
14. I draw. constantly
15. I argue. never
16. I smile. here
17. I eat. rarely
18. I walk. slowly

B. Find the verbs in the paragraph below. Write the paragraph, adding adverbs of the group's choice to describe each verb. Then write the paragraph again, using different adverbs to change the story of the baseball game. Answers will vary. Possible answers are shown.

The baseball game begins at noon. The players arrive and form teams. Aunt Sally walks toward home plate. She chooses a bat and holds it in place. She looks at little Tommy, the pitcher. We all smile. Tommy throws the first ball and Aunt Sally swings. The game gets underway. Aunt Sally hits a fly ball to center field. The center fielder catches the ball for the first out.

(adverb annotations above the paragraph: usually, promptly; early, late; quickly, slowly; hesitantly, confidently; carefully, eagerly; firmly, gingerly; cautiously, boldly; wisely, secretly; gracefully, happily; finally, now; powerfully, gently; barely, easily)

WRITERS' CORNER • Precise Adverbs

Be sure that your adverbs are actually describing the words you want them to describe. Read the sample sentence below. Think about it. Can a letter be "full of hope"? Can it *arrive hopefully*?

EXAMPLE: **Hopefully the letter will arrive.**
IMPROVED: **I waited hopefully for the letter to arrive.**

Read what you wrote for the Writer's Warm-up. Did you use adverbs in your writing? Do they describe verbs correctly? If they do not, can you improve the sentences?

COOPERATIVE LEARNING: Expanding Sentences 297

Working Together

The Working Together activities involve students in cooperative learning work groups. This is an opportunity to pair strong writers with students whose skills are weaker. Working together, they can all experience success.

Divide the class into small groups and have students read In Your Group. Encourage them to discuss why each task is important. Have them tell what might happen if the group does not follow through on each task. *(If we do not all understand the directions, we cannot complete the tasks successfully. If we do not give everyone a chance to share ideas, we might miss some ideas that could be helpful. If we do not look at others when they are talking, we might misunderstand what they are saying. If we do not show appreciation for different opinions, others may be reluctant to share their opinions.)*

Before students begin activities A and B, you may wish to have each group appoint a member to record their adverbs and sentences. You also may wish to have groups appoint a timekeeper. Then set a limit of ten or fifteen minutes. After each activity is completed, have the groups discuss how using adverbs added important descriptive details to their writing.

Writers' Corner

The Writers' Corner provides students with the opportunity to extend the Grammar-Writing Connection, helping them to develop the skills necessary to review and revise their own writing. Discuss the introductory sentences with students. Then have them work as a class or in pairs to discuss the two examples. Have students read aloud each example and identify the changes that were made. Have them tell how those changes made the improved example "better." Then have students apply the expanding sentences with adverbs techniques from this Grammar-Writing Connection to the sentences they wrote about volcanoes for the Writers' Warm-up. Encourage students to rewrite their sentences if necessary. Discuss with them how using adverbs added interesting details that improved their writing.

OVERVIEW

TWO-PART
flexibility

USING LANGUAGE TO RESEARCH

Unit 6 Overview

books

FOR EXTENDED READING

EASY

📖 **Hawaii Volcanoes National Park** by Ruth Radlauer. Children. Vivid photographs and a well-organized text provide an introduction to volcanoes and highlight what visitors can see and do at one of America's most fascinating national parks.

AVERAGE

📖 **Dinosaurs Walked Here and Other Stories Fossils Tell** by Patricia Lauber. Bradbury. The author of *Volcanoes* investigates how fossils are used to tell us about life in ancient times.

CHALLENGING

📖 **The Mount St. Helens Disaster** by Thomas G. Aylesworth and Virginia L. Aylesworth. Watts. This book recounts the eruption of Mount St. Helens and the damage it caused and explains how close scientific monitoring of the area has added to our knowledge of volcanoes.

READ-ALOUD

📖 **Historical Catastrophes: Volcanoes** by Walter R. Brown and Norman D. Anderson. Addison. This history of volcanoes from early times to the present is made especially interesting through the use of anectodes.

ERUPTION OF VESUVIUS
painting by Volaire
Virginia Museum of Fine Arts, Richmond, Virginia
Giraudon/Art Resource.

USING LANGUAGE
TO
RESEARCH

PART TWO

Literature *Volcano* by Patricia Lauber
A Reason for Writing Researching

CREATIVE
Writing

FINE ARTS ◆ At the left you can see a painting of a volcano erupting. Can you imagine what would happen if a volcano were to erupt near your town? What news bulletins would you hear? What would they advise you to do? Write a radio news bulletin. Warn your friends and neighbors about the volcano.

start with CREATIVE WRITING

Fine Arts gives your students a chance to express themselves creatively in writing. After students observe the illustration on page 298 for a moment or two, have a volunteer read aloud the Fine Arts paragraph on page 299. Have students write their reactions in their journals. Then encourage a discussion of their ideas.

 VIEWING

See the **Fine Arts Transparencies with Viewing Booklet** and the **Video Library**.

THEN START WITH *part 2*

A Reason for Writing: Researching is the focus of Part 2. First students learn a thinking strategy for researching. Then they read and respond to a selection of literature on which they may model their own writing. Developmental composition lessons, including "An Oral Report," a speaking and listening lesson, help students learn to use language correctly to research. All the lessons reflect the literature. All culminate in the Writing Process lesson. The unit ends with the Curriculum Connection and Books to enjoy, which help students discover how their new language skills apply to writing across the curriculum and to their own lives.

◆ If you began with grammar instruction, you may wish to remind students of the unit theme, "Volcanoes". Tell them that the information they gathered through the thematic lessons helped them prepare for reading the literature, *Volcano* by Patricia Lauber.

◆ If you are beginning with Part 2, use the lessons in Part 1 for remediation or instruction. For grammar, spelling, and mechanics instructional guidance, you may wish to refer to the end-of-text Glossary and Index, as well as to the *Spelling Connection* booklet; the full-color *Revising and Proofreading Transparencies;* and the Unit Pretest, Posttest, and Writing Samples.

THEME BAR							
CATEGORIES	Environments	Business/World of Work	Imagination	Communications/ Fine Arts	People	Science	Expressions	Social Studies
THEMES	UNIT 1 Farm Life	UNIT 2 Handicrafts	UNIT 3 Tall Tales	UNIT 4 The Visual Arts	UNIT 5 Lasting Impressions	UNIT 6 Volcanoes	UNIT 7 Nature	UNIT 8 Animal Habitats
PACING	1 month	1 month	1 month	1 month	1 month	1 month	1 month	1 month

UNIT 6
Critical Thinking

OBJECTIVES
To use an order circle as a strategy for researching

TEACHING THE LESSON

1. Getting Started
Oral Language Introduce the thinking skill, sequencing, by asking students to imagine that they have a busy weekend coming up. Say: *You have chores to do and places to go. You've been invited to your cousin's birthday party and you haven't bought a gift yet. A "Things to Do" list would help you. In what order would you set it up?* Encourage a variety of responses (e.g., *I'd put the most important things first. I'd list "Things to do Saturday morning," "Things to do Saturday afternoon.")*. Explain that putting things in order is called *sequencing*.

Metacognition Help students become aware of their own thinking (think metacognitively) by asking follow-up questions when they respond (e.g., *How did you figure out your answer?*). Encourage students to appreciate that thinking strategies are as different as the people who use them. Explain that in this lesson they will learn about one possible strategy for putting things in order.

2. Developing the Lesson
Guide students through the introduction to researching (the kind of literature and writing they will deal with in this unit) and its connection to sequencing or putting things in order. Lead them through Learning the Strategy, emphasizing the model order circle. Identify those who would benefit from reteaching. Assign Using the Strategy A and B.

3. Closing the Lesson
Metacognition Applying the Strategy is a metacognitive activity in which students consider *how* they think (question 1) and *when* they think (question 2).

Question 1: Possible answers: *time, space, size, color, importance, interest, alphabetical, numerical.* Encourage students to think of original ways of

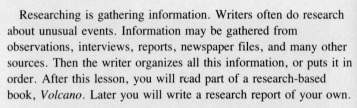

CRITICAL THINKING ◆
A Strategy for Researching

AN ORDER CIRCLE

Researching is gathering information. Writers often do research about unusual events. Information may be gathered from observations, interviews, reports, newspaper files, and many other sources. Then the writer organizes all this information, or puts it in order. After this lesson, you will read part of a research-based book, *Volcano*. Later you will write a research report of your own.

Here is a passage from *Volcano*. How has the author organized her material? In what order does she present the facts?

> Meanwhile the avalanche had hit a ridge and split. One part of it poured into Spirit Lake, adding a 180-foot layer of rock and dirt to the bottom of the lake. . . . The main part of the avalanche swept down the valley of the North Fork of the Toutle River. There, in the valley, most of the avalanche slowed and stopped.

In this passage, the author uses space order. She gives information in an order that shows the path of the avalanche. Information that is given in order is easier to understand.

 ## Learning the Strategy

You can put things in order in many different ways. Suppose you are listing what you want to do this weekend. You might list those things in order of importance, most important first. In what other kind of order might you write your list? Suppose you are following a recipe for pizza. In what order would the steps be listed? Would any other order work as well? Imagine you are writing a letter describing your cousin's birthday. In what order would you tell what happened? In what order would you tell the

⟨ 300 ⟩   CRITICAL THINKING: Sequencing

ESSENTIAL LANGUAGE SKILLS
This lesson provides opportunities to:

LISTENING ◆ employ active listening in a variety of situations ◆ select from an oral presentation the information needed

SPEAKING ◆ use oral language for a variety of purposes

READING ◆ draw logical conclusions ◆ evaluate and make judgments ◆ follow a set of directions ◆ use graphic sources for information, such as charts and graphs, timelines, pictures and diagrams

WRITING ◆ generate ideas using a variety of strategies, such as brainstorming, clustering, mapping, question and answer

LANGUAGE ◆ use language for personal expression

etails about the party decorations? Imagine you are making a book
f your friends' names and phone numbers. In what order would
ou arrange the names?

An order circle can help you put things in order. Inside the circle
rite what you want to put in order. On the arrows write some
inds of order. Decide which kind of order works best for what
ou plan to organize.

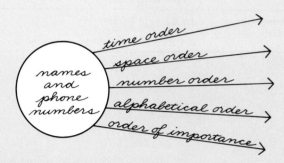

Using the Strategy

A. Suppose you have been chosen to keep track of the birthdays in
your family. In what kind of order should you list them? Write
family birthdays inside an order circle. Write some kinds of
order on the arrows. Make a birthday list for your family in the
kind of order you decide is best.

B. *Volcano* is about the eruption of a famous volcano. Write the
title inside an order circle. Write some kinds of order on the
arrows. In what kind of order do you think most of the
information in *Volcano* will be given? As you read *Volcano*,
decide if you were right.

Applying the Strategy

♦ What kinds of ordering do you have to or like to do most
often?

♦ When might you find it helpful to use an order circle?

CRITICAL THINKING: Sequencing 301

ordering things (e.g. *seasonal*—all the
spring chores together, *shape*—all the
round things together, or *noisiness*—
loud instruments in the back, soft instruments in the front). Point out that
the key is to think of what needs to be
put in order, then decide the best,
clearest, or most useful order to suit a
purpose.

Question 2: Possible answers: *time
order to organize the school day, order
of importance to be sure most important chores get done.* Point out that
learning to choose kinds of order can
help students be more organized, efficient, and effective.

Looking Ahead
The thinking strategy introduced in this
lesson, an order circle, is used in Using
the Strategy B as a prereading strategy to help students anticipate the literature, *Volcano*. It will appear three
more times in this unit and again in
Unit 2.

ORDER CIRCLE			
Strategy for Informing	Writing to Learn	Prewriting	Writing Across the Curriculum
79	83	96	102

Strategy for Researching	Writing to Learn	Prewriting	Writing Across the Curriculum
301	307	320	326

Although the order circle strategy is
repeated in each presentation, the
context in which it is used changes.
Students will thus be given the opportunity to discover how the strategy can
help them in reading, in writing across
the curriculum, and in their daily lives.

VOCABULARY STRATEGIES

Developing Concepts and Teaching Vocabulary

Preteach the following words from the story. Use the Dictionary of Knowledge at the back of the book to provide definitions of base words and context sentences.

magma, geologist, sandblast(ed), pumice, colonizer(s)

Write the vocabulary words on the chalkboard and call on a volunteer to pronounce them. Ask students if they have ever used or seen *pumice* stone. Have them tell what it looks like and what it can be used for in the home. (smooth stone; It can smooth away rough skin) Have students relate any experiences they may have had with the things named by the other vocabulary words.

GUIDING COMPREHENSION

Building Background

The first half of this unit includes information especially chosen to build background for *Volcano*. If you started the unit with grammar instruction, you may wish to have a class discussion on the unit theme, **Volcanoes,** based on the information in those lessons.

If you started the unit with composition instruction, you may wish to build students' knowledge of volcanoes by asking: *What do you know about volcanoes? What volcano erupted in 1980 in the United States?* (Students may recall that volcanoes are openings in the earth's surface through which molten rock from inside the earth is emitted. These openings often form cone-shaped mountains, which also are called volcanoes.)

NEWBERY HONOR 1987

LITERATURE

from

VOLCANO

The Eruption and Healing of Mount St. Helens

"The Big Blast"

by Patricia Lauber

302   LITERATURE: Nonfiction

ESSENTIAL LANGUAGE SKILLS

This lesson provides opportunities to:

LISTENING ◆ employ active listening in a variety of situations

SPEAKING ◆ respond appropriately to questions from teachers and peers ◆ use creative devices such as figurative language

READING ◆ understand content area vocabulary ◆ arrange events in sequential order when sequence is not stated ◆ understand cause-and-effect relationships ◆ draw logical conclusions ◆ evaluate and make judgments ◆ respond to various forms of literature

WRITING ◆ write and compose for a variety of purposes ◆ generate ideas using graphic organizers

LANGUAGE ◆ use language for informing

For many years, Mount St. Helens in southern Washington seemed to be only a big, beautiful mountain. It was thought to be one of the most beautiful mountains in the Cascade Range. Yet Mount St. Helens was really a still, sleeping volcano. At any time, it could have awakened and erupted with hot melted rock from inside the earth.

Mount St. Helens had erupted many times over thousands of years. Each time, the volcano had grown bigger. It had grown by being built up from the materials of its own eruptions—melted rock called lava, bits of rock called ash, and gas-filled rock called pumice. Together, the lava, ash, and pumice had built Mount St. Helens into a mountain more than nine thousand feet high.

On March 20, 1980, a strong earthquake shook Mount St. Helens. The earthquake was a sign that the volcano was waking after a long sleep of 123 years. On March 27, the volcano exploded, with smaller explosions coming in April and May. But the big blast, the most destructive one of all, came on May 18. Here is the true account, just as it happened.

The May 18 eruption began with an earthquake that triggered an avalanche. At 8:32 A.M. instruments that were miles away registered a strong earthquake. The pilot and passengers of a small plane saw the north side of the mountain rippling and churning. Shaken by the quake, the bulge was tearing loose. It began to slide, in a huge avalanche that carried along rock ripped from deep inside Mount St. Helens.

The avalanche tore open the mountain. A scalding blast shot sideways out of the opening. It was a blast of steam, from water heated by rising magma.

Normally water cannot be heated beyond its boiling point, which is 212 degrees Fahrenheit at sea level. At boiling point, water turns to a gas, which we call steam. But if water is kept under pressure, it can be heated far beyond its boiling point and still stay liquid. (That is how a pressure cooker works.) If the pressure is removed, this superheated water suddenly turns, or flashes, to steam. As steam it

LITERATURE: Nonfiction ◁ 303 ▷

Developing a Purpose for Reading

Option 1: Have students set their own purpose for reading. Then have them read the story introduction and study the illustrations. Explain that this selection is a factual article that tells about the eruption of Mount St. Helens. Have students list several questions they feel the article might answer. Remind students to recall what they know about volcanoes before writing. When the lists are completed, have volunteers share their questions with the class. Suggest that students set their own reading purpose by reviewing their lists and underlining the most important information they would like to learn from the article.

Option 2: If you wish to set a reading purpose for everyone, have students pay special attention to the descriptions of the damage done to the countryside by the volcano. Have them ask themselves: *How did the eruption of the volcano affect the surrouding area?*

GUIDED READING

Please note that opportunities for students' personal responses to the selection are offered in the Reader's Response question and the Selection Follow-up at the end of this lesson.

Page 303 *How had the eruptions before 1980 shaped Mount St. Helens?* (The mountain had grown taller by being built up with lava, ash, and pumice until it was more than 9,000 feet high.) RECALL: DETAILS

Page 303 *What was the first sign that Mount St. Helens was about to wake from its 123-year sleep?* (A strong earthquake on March 20, 1980, was the first sign.) RECALL: DETAILS

SUMMARY	ABOUT THE AUTHOR
This selection is an account of the volcanic eruption of Mount St. Helens on May 18, 1980, the most destructive in the history of the United States. It explains the causes of the earthquake that triggered an avalanche that tore open the mountain. It also describes the vast destruction it caused to the mountain itself and to a huge area surrounding it.	PATRICIA LAUBER lives in Weston, Connecticut. Her many award-winning books include *Journey to the Planets*, an **American Library Association Notable Children's Book.** The book from which this selection was taken, *Volcano: The Eruption and Healing of Mount St. Helens*, was chosen as a **Newbery Honor Book** in 1987. Ms. Lauber received the **Washington Post/Children's Book Guild Nonfiction Award** in 1983 for her informational books for young readers.

Page 304 *What was Mount St. Helens like before it erupted on May 18, 1980?* (It was like a giant pressure cooker that held superheated water.) RECALL: DETAILS

Page 304 *What caused the explosion?* (The superheated water turned to steam.) RECALL: CAUSE/EFFECT

Page 304 *What was the "stone wind"?* (The "stone wind" was a 200-mile-an-hour wind that carried rocks ranging in size from grains of sand to pieces as big as cars.) RECALL: DETAILS

takes up much more room—it expands. The sudden change to steam can cause an explosion.

Before the eruption Mount St. Helens was like a giant pressure cooker. The rock inside it held superheated water. The water stayed liquid because it was under great pressure, sealed in the mountain. When the mountain was torn open, the pressure was suddenly relieved. The superheated water flashed to steam. Expanding violently, it shattered rock inside the mountain and exploded out the opening, traveling at speeds of up to 200 miles an hour.

The blast flattened whole forests of 180-foot-high firs. It snapped off or uprooted the trees, scattering the trunks as if they were straws. At first, this damage was puzzling. A wind of 200 miles an hour is not strong enough to level forests of giant trees. The explanation, geologists later discovered, was that the wind carried rocks ranging in size from grains of sand to blocks as big as cars. As the blast roared out of the volcano, it swept up and carried along the rock it had shattered.

The result was what one geologist described as "a stone wind." It was a wind of steam and rocks, traveling at high speed. The rocks gave the blast its great force. Before it, trees snapped and fell. Their stumps looked as if they had been sandblasted. The wind of stone rushed on. It stripped bark and branches from trees and uprooted them, leveling 150 square miles of countryside. At the edge of this area other trees were left standing, but the heat of the blast scorched and killed them.

The stone wind was traveling so fast that it overtook and passed the avalanche. On its path was Spirit Lake, one of the most beautiful lakes in the Cascades. The blast stripped the trees from the slopes surrounding the lake and moved on.

Meanwhile the avalanche had hit a ridge and split. One part of it poured into Spirit Lake, adding a 180-foot layer of rock and dirt to the bottom of the lake. The slide of avalanche into the lake forced the water out. The water sloshed up the slopes, then fell back into the lake. With it came thousands of trees felled by the blast.

The main part of the avalanche swept down the valley of the North Fork of the Toutle River. There, in the valley, most of the

304   LITERATURE: Nonfiction

HIGHLIGHTING LITERATURE

Pages 302–304 When students have read to the end of page 304, have them suggest questions that might be used to test understanding of volcanoes. If students have difficulty answering the questions, you may wish to suggest they reread the material, paying special attention to what happens first, next, and so forth. Explain that putting details in order in one's mind can be an aid to understanding. METACOGNITION: SUMMARIZING AND DETAILS

avalanche slowed and stopped. It covered 24 square miles and averaged 150 feet thick.

The blast itself continued for 10 to 15 minutes, then stopped. Minutes later Mount St. Helens began to erupt upwards. A dark column of ash and ground-up rock rose miles into the sky. Winds blew the ash eastward. Lightning flashed in the ash cloud and started forest fires. In Yakima, Washington, some 80 miles away, the sky turned so dark that street lights went on at noon. Ash fell like snow that would not melt. This eruption continued for nine hours.

Shortly after noon the color of the ash column changed. It became lighter, a sign that the volcano was now throwing out mostly new magma. Until then much of the ash had been made of old rock.

At the same time the volcano began giving off huge flows of pumice and ash. The material was very hot, with temperatures of about 1,000 degrees Fahrenheit, and it traveled down the mountain at speeds of 100 miles an hour. The flows went on until 5:30 in the afternoon. They formed a wedge-shaped plain of pumice on the side of the mountain. Two weeks later temperatures in the pumice were still 780 degrees.

Finally, there were the mudflows, which started when heat from the blast melted ice and snow on the mountaintop. The water mixed with ash, pumice, ground-up rock, and dirt and rocks of the avalanche. The result was a thick mixture that was like wet concrete, a mudflow. The mudflows traveled fast, scouring the landscape and sweeping down the slopes into river valleys. Together their speed and thickness did great damage.

The largest mudflow was made of avalanche material from the valley of the North Fork of the Toutle River. It churned down the river valley, tearing out steel bridges, ripping houses apart, picking up boulders and trucks and carrying them along. Miles away it choked the Cowlitz River and blocked shipping channels in the Columbia River.

When the sun rose on May 19, it showed a greatly changed St. Helens. The mountain was 1,200 feet shorter than it had been the morning before. Most of the old top had slid down the mountain in the avalanche. The rest had erupted out as shattered rock. Geologists

LITERATURE: Nonfiction ◁ 305 ▷

GUIDED READING

Page 305 *Why did the street lights in Yakima, Washington, 80 miles from the mountain, go on at noon?* (A huge cloud of ash turned the sky dark and the darkness caused the automatic timers to turn on. INFER: CAUSE/EFFECT

Page 305 *How did mudflows form?* (Heat from the blast melted ice and snow on the mountaintop. The water mixed with ash, pumice, and dirt, and the result was a mudflow.) RECALL: CAUSE/EFFECT

Page 306 *How did the May 18 eruption change the shape of the mountain?* (The mountain was 1,200 feet shorter, and its north side had changed from a green and lovely slope to a fan-shaped wasteland.) RECALL: CAUSE/EFFECT

Page 306 *What are some of the things scientists will learn from studying Mount St. Helens?* (Responses will vary. The article mentions being able to predict future eruptions. Students also may mention learning about how life re-establishes itself, such as which plants and animals return to life first.) ANALYZE: CONCLUSIONS

Returning to the Reading Purpose

Option 1: Those students who have written lists of questions may wish to review them to determine whether the most important ones have been answered.

Option 2: If you have established a common reading purpose, review it and ask students to summarize what they learned about the effects of the eruption of the volcano.

Do you think Mount St. Helens will ever recover from the devastation? Why or why not? (Encourage students to share what they know about other volcanoes, active and extinct, before they answer the questions.)

later figured that the volcano had lost three quarters of a cubic mile of old rock.

The north side of the mountain had changed from a green and lovely slope to a fan-shaped wasteland.

At the top of Mount St. Helens was a big, new crater with the shape of a horseshoe. Inside the crater was the vent, the opening through which rock and gases erupted from time to time over the next few years.

In 1980 St. Helens erupted six more times. Most of these eruptions were explosive—ash soared into the air, pumice swept down the north side of the mountain. In the eruptions of June and August, thick pasty lava oozed out of the vent and built a dome. But both domes were destroyed by the next eruptions. In October the pattern changed. The explosions stopped, and thick lava built a dome that was not destroyed. Later eruptions added to the dome, making it bigger and bigger.

During this time, geologists were learning to read the clues found before eruptions. They learned to predict what St. Helens was going to do. The predictions helped to protect people who were on and near the mountain.

Among these people were many natural scientists. They had come to look for survivors, for plants and animals that had lived through the eruption. They had come to look for <u>colonizers,</u> for plants and animals that would move in. Mount St. Helens had erupted many times before. Each time life had returned. Now scientists would have a chance to see how it did. They would see how nature healed itself.

Library Link ♦ *If you would like to learn more about Mount St. Helens, read* Volcano *by Patricia Lauber.*

 Reader's Response

Do you think Mount St. Helens will ever recover from the devastation? Why or why not?

306 LITERATURE: Nonfiction

HIGHLIGHTING LITERATURE

Page 306 Point out that the article students have just read is essentially about one eruption of Mount St. Helens. There were a number of different things that the author wanted to describe that were all happening at the same time or in a relatively short space of time. The author uses words such as *meanwhile, at the same time, minutes later,* and *finally* to tell the reader about the order of events.

VOLCANO

Responding to Literature

1. You are high above Mount St. Helens. It is 8:32 A.M. on the morning of May 18, 1980. You are watching the explosion bursting beneath you. What are you thinking? What are you feeling? Write a page in your journal about the experience.

2. Scientists help us understand new information by making comparisons with things we do know. Patricia Lauber wrote that "Ash fell like snow that would not melt." What part of *Volcano* interested you? Write a comparison that you would use to explain that part to a younger person.

3. Scientists discovered that nature tried to heal itself after the Mount St. Helens blast. Will nature always be able to heal itself? Why or why not?

Writing to Learn

Think and Order ◆ A scientist may tell how something happens by presenting information in a certain order. Prepare information for one paragraph about the Mount St. Helens eruption. How can you best arrange your information? Draw an order circle like the one below.

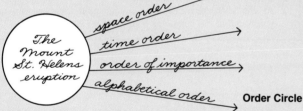

Order Circle

Write ◆ Use the order you chose to write a one-paragraph summary about the eruption at Mount St. Helens.

LITERATURE: Nonfiction ◇ 307

You may wish to incorporate any or all of the following discussion questions and activities in your follow-up to the literature selection, *Volcano*.

RESPONDING TO LITERATURE

Encourage students to use their personal experience as well as what they learned from the selection to discuss these questions. The questions are designed to encourage students to think of and respond to the selection as a whole. Explain to students that although they may use details from the selection to support their opinions, the questions have no right or wrong answers. Encourage them to express a variety of points of view. You may wish to have students respond as a class, in groups, or with partners.

1. *You are high above Mount St. Helens. It is 8:32 A.M. on the morning of May 18. You are watching the explosion bursting beneath you. What are you thinking? What are you feeling? Write a page in your journal about the experience.* (You may wish to have students share some of their thoughts and feelings with the class before they write their journal entries.)

2. *Scientists help us understand new information by making comparisons with things we do know. Patricia Lauber wrote that "Ash fell like snow that would not melt." What part of* Volcano *interested you the most? Write a comparison that you would use to explain that part to a younger person.* (Before students write their comparisons, you may wish to discuss other comparisons Patricia Lauber makes, such as comparing Mount St. Helens to a giant pressure cooker or the mudflows to wet concrete.)

3. *Scientists discovered that nature tried to heal itself after the Mount St. Helens blast. Will nature always be able to heal itself? Why or why not?* (Encourage students to share what they know about other situations in which nature was destroyed and what happened after the destruction.)

 World of Language Audio Library

A recording of this selection is available in the **Audio Library**.

WRITING TO LEARN

Have students apply the thinking strategy of creating an order circle to show their understanding of the selection. Have them draw and shade the wheel as described in Think and Imagine. Then have students complete the Write activity by using the order they chose to write a one-paragraph summary of the eruption of Mount St. Helens. Call on volunteers to read aloud their paragraphs.

UNIT 6
Speaking/Listening

OBJECTIVES
To identify interesting facts that can be used for opening sentences in an oral report
To use guidelines for giving and listening to an oral report

ASSIGNMENT GUIDE
BASIC   Practice A
      ↓   Practice B
ADVANCED   Practice C

All should do the Apply activity.

RESOURCES
■ World of Language Video Library

TEACHING THE LESSON

1. Getting Started
Oral Language Focus attention on this oral activity, encouraging all to participate. You may wish to have students share all the interesting facts they remember about volcanoes before encouraging them to share interesting facts about other natural phenomena.

2. Developing the Lesson
Guide students through a discussion of the lesson, emphasizing the guidelines for giving and listening to an oral report. You may wish to have volunteers share with the class some of the ways they deal with their feelings of nervousness when speaking to an audience. Lead students through the **Guided Practice.** Identify those who would benefit from reteaching. Assign independent Practice A–C.

3. Closing the Lesson
After students complete the Apply activity, call on individuals to read aloud their opening sentences, first identifying the topic of their oral report. Point out to them that knowing how to form strong opening sentences will help them capture and hold their listeners' attention when giving oral reports.

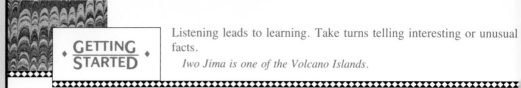

♦ GETTING STARTED ♦

Listening leads to learning. Take turns telling interesting or unusual facts.

Iwo Jima is one of the Volcano Islands.

SPEAKING and LISTENING ♦
An Oral Report

Oral reports are different from written reports in one important way. When you give an oral report, you face your audience directly. You must capture and hold their attention. You often start a written report with a topic sentence, but that kind of opening may not work with a "live" audience. You need to get the members of your audience interested in what you have to say. That is why speakers often start with an amusing statement or a fact that is startling or unusual.

Since you want to look at your audience as you speak, you do not want to read your report. Therefore, do not write it out word for word. Outline it on note cards to prompt yourself. Use only key words and phrases as reminders of what you want to say. Your listeners will expect you to be very familiar with your topic and the main ideas of your report. Use the guidelines below to give your report and to listen to the reports of others.

Giving a Report	1. Practice in front of a mirror. Know in advance what to say. 2. Relax. Take a deep breath before you speak. 3. Speak clearly and look at your audience. 4. Use charts and illustrations if you wish.
Being a Critical Listener	1. Give the speaker your attention. Look at the speaker. 2. Listen for main points and details. 3. As you listen, form questions in your mind. Later ask any questions you had that the speaker's report did not answer.

Summary ♦ An effective speaker prepares an oral report in advance. An effective listener pays attention to the main points and supporting ideas.

308   SPEAKING and LISTENING: Oral Reports

ESSENTIAL LANGUAGE SKILLS
This lesson provides opportunities to:

LISTENING ♦ listen for specific information ♦ respond appropriately to a speaker

SPEAKING ♦ speak before an audience to communicate specific information ♦ express ideas clearly and effectively

READING ♦ identify an implied main idea of a longer selection ♦ evaluate and make judgments ♦ follow a set of directions

WRITING ♦ adapt information to accomplish a specific purpose with a particular audience ♦ select topics of personal interest

LANGUAGE ♦ use language for personal expression

Guided Practice

Turn each of these facts into an interesting opening sentence for an oral report. Try different kinds of sentences, such as statements, exclamations, and questions. Answers will vary.

1. Mount St. Helens has erupted several times since 1980.
2. Many caverns are filled with oddly shaped rock formations.
3. Some of the highest waterfalls in North America are in Yosemite National Park.
4. Tokyo is the busiest and most populated city in Japan.
5. Tornado winds are first seen as a rotating funnel cloud.

Practice

A. Turn each fact below into an interesting opening sentence for an oral report. Try different kinds of sentences, such as statements, exclamations, and questions. Write your sentences. Answers will vary.

6. Drifting icebergs in the ocean are dangerous to ships.
7. Some plants can survive the eruption of a volcano.
8. Insects are found all over the earth.
9. The production of iron has become essential to modern life.
10. Mount Rainier and Mount Hood are both inactive volcanoes.

B. Read the sentences you wrote for **Practice A.** Choose the one you like best. Read it aloud to your classmates. When it is your turn to listen, tell your classmates what you like about their opening sentences. Then offer any suggestions that you have.

C. Think of something you have recently learned in school. What would you like to tell about it? Make notes of key words and phrases you will use. Using the guidelines in this lesson, practice giving an oral report to a partner. When you are the listener, ask the speaker any questions that come to mind about what you hear.

Apply ◆ Think and Write

Strong Opening Sentences ◆ Write an opening sentence for an oral report on a subject that you would like to talk about.

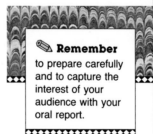

✎ **Remember**
to prepare carefully and to capture the interest of your audience with your oral report.

SPEAKING and LISTENING: Oral Reports **309**

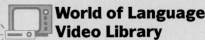
World of Language Video Library

You may wish to use the *Video Library* to teach this lesson.

EVALUATION PROGRAM
See Evaluation and Testing Program, pp. C9–C11.
Speaking and Listening Checklist Masters

◀▥▥ TEACHING OPTIONS ▥▥▶

RETEACHING

A Different Modality Have students choose one topic from Guided Practice, consider the interesting opening sentences that were suggested, and name further information the oral report might include. Then have students make a chart or illustration they might use as a visual aid with an oral report on that topic. Allow them to use made-up details if necessary.

CLASS ENRICHMENT

A Cooperative Activity Have students present group oral reports on school trivia. Have each group choose a topic to research (e.g., *What games are played most often during recess?*). Let the group decide how to divide the tasks of research, outlining the report, and making visual aids. Require that each group find a way for all its members to participate in the oral presentation.

CHALLENGE

An Independent Extension Point out to students that television news anchors and reporters usually begin their reports with attention-grabbing sentences. Have students watch television news programs and transcribe three catchy news story openings they hear. Have them report on each interesting opening, including a brief description of what each story was about.

309

UNIT 6
Study Skills

OBJECTIVES
To locate information in an encyclopedia, using key words, alphabetical order, volume numbers, guide words, and the index volume

ASSIGNMENT GUIDE
BASIC   Practice A
⬇   Practice B
ADVANCED Practice C

All should do the Apply activity.

RESOURCES
■ Reteaching Master 54
■ Practice Master 54

TEACHING THE LESSON

1. Getting Started
Oral Language Focus attention on this oral activity, encouraging all to participate. You may wish to model example responses, such as *skateboarding, kite flying, computers (subjects); Joann Frank, Mañuel Vega (students' names).*

2. Developing the Lesson
Guide students through the explanation of using an encyclopedia, emphasizing the example and the summary. You may wish to have volumes of an encyclopedia on hand for students to refer to as you discuss finding the key parts. Lead students through the **Guided Practice.** Identify those who would benefit from reteaching. Assign independent Practice A–C.

3. Closing the Lesson
After students complete the Apply activity, have volunteers read aloud one question and identify the key word. You may wish to have students work with a partner to discuss the key words in the other questions. Point out to students that knowing how to find the key word in a question will help them select the appropriate encyclopedia volume to get the information they want.

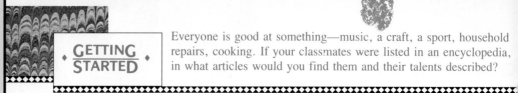

♦ GETTING STARTED ♦

Everyone is good at something—music, a craft, a sport, household repairs, cooking. If your classmates were listed in an encyclopedia, in what articles would you find them and their talents described?

STUDY SKILLS ♦
Using an Encyclopedia

Jason wondered, "What makes a volcano erupt?" He decided to look in an encyclopedia for the answer.

An encyclopedia is a set of reference books with many volumes. Each volume contains articles about people, places, things, and ideas. Articles appear in alphabetical order. In an article about a person, of course, the last name is listed first.

To find information, Jason first identified the key word in his question. He decided to look up *volcano*. Then he found the volume that contains the key word. Jason saw that Volume 18 has articles for the letters *U* and *V*. The guide words at the top of each page helped him find the exact page of the article.

Jason could have found the key word in the index, Volume 20. The index alphabetically lists all the topics in the encyclopedia. It tells the volume and page number for each topic.

> **Summary** ♦ Articles in an encyclopedia are arranged in alphabetical order.

Guided Practice

Name the key word in each of the following research questions.

1. What is a <u>geologist</u>?
2. What does the word *Fahrenheit* mean?
3. In what state is <u>Mount St. Helens</u> located?
4. How tall do <u>fir</u> trees usually grow?

310   STUDY SKILLS: Encyclopedia

ESSENTIAL LANGUAGE SKILLS
This lesson provides opportunities to:

LISTENING ♦ select from an oral presentation the information needed

SPEAKING ♦ use a variety of words to express feelings and ideas

READING ♦ understand content area vocabulary ♦ evaluate and make judgments ♦ follow a set of directions ♦ use the dictionary and the encyclopedia to locate information

WRITING ♦ adapt information to accomplish a specific purpose with a particular audience

LANGUAGE ♦ use the fundamentals of grammar, punctuation, and spelling

Practice

Write the key word in each of these questions.

5. How does an <u>avalanche</u> cause damage?
6. What are the highest peaks in the <u>Cascade Mountains</u>?
7. How deep is <u>Crater Lake</u>?
8. What is special about <u>Mount Rainier</u>?
9. Where is <u>magma</u> found?

Write the key word in each question. Then write the volume number of the encyclopedia that has the article. Use the illustration on page 310 to find the number.

10. What are some uses for <u>pumice</u>? 13
11. How hot can <u>steam</u> get? 16
12. How do scientists predict an <u>earthquake</u>? 5
13. What different shapes can a <u>crater</u> have? 3   11
14. How many times has <u>Mount St. Helens</u> erupted?
15. What other <u>volcanoes</u> are in the United States?   18
16. Are there different kinds of <u>lava</u>? 10   15
17. What can scientists learn from a <u>seismograph</u>?
18. Where is <u>igneous rock</u> found? 9

The questions below have two key words. Write both key words. Then give both volume numbers in which articles would appear.

19. How are <u>earthquakes</u> and <u>volcanoes</u> related? 5, 18
20. What does the <u>Richter</u> scale tell about <u>earthquakes</u>? 14, 5
21. Which state has the bigger fishing industry, <u>Alaska</u> or <u>Oregon</u>? 1, 12
22. Why did <u>George Vancouver</u> pick the name Mount St. Helens? 18, 11
23. Do the <u>Yakima Indians</u> live in the state of <u>Washington</u>? 19, 19

Apply ◆ Think and Write

Key Words in Questions ◆ Write three questions that you would like to know the answers to. Underline the key word in each question. If you can, use an encyclopedia to find the answer to one question.

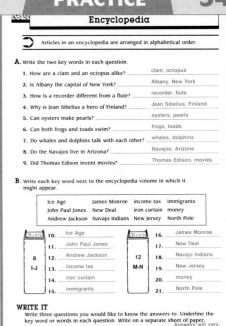

✏ **Remember** to use the key word in a question to select the correct encyclopedia volume.

STUDY SKILLS: Encyclopedia   311

RETEACHING 54

Encyclopedia

Complete the paragraph with words from the box. The first one is done for you.

| alphabetically | Letters | encyclopedia | volumes | articles |

An ___encyclopedia___ is a set of books, or ___volumes___ . Each volume is a collection of ___articles___ about people, places, things, and ideas. The articles are arranged ___alphabetically___ . ___Letters___ and numbers on the spine of each volume help you find the book you want.

↻ To find information in an encyclopedia, first decide on the key word in the topic you are interested in. Articles in an encyclopedia are arranged in alphabetical order.

A. Write the key word in each question.

EXAMPLE: What is a plain? ___plain___

1. Who were the Mayas? ___Mayas___
2. Who was Sir Francis Drake? ___Drake, Sir Francis___
3. What happened at Yorktown? ___Yorktown___

B. Write the number of the volume in which you would look up each key word. Use the picture of the volumes to help you.

| 1 A | 2 B | 3 C | 4 D | 5 E-F | 6 G | 7 H | 8 I-J | 9 K | 10 L | 11 M | 12 N | 13 O-P |

EXAMPLE: Mississippi River ___11___

4. alligator ___1___   7. grizzly ___6___   10. Port Royal ___13___
5. Oklahoma City ___13___   8. firefly ___5___   11. Jane Addams ___1___
6. Annie Oakley ___13___   9. Oregon Trail ___13___   12. Cape Canaveral ___3___

PRACTICE 54

Encyclopedia

↻ Articles in an encyclopedia are arranged in alphabetical order.

A. Write the two key words in each question.

1. How are a clam and an octopus alike? ___clam, octopus___
2. Is Albany the capital of New York? ___Albany, New York___
3. How is a recorder different from a flute? ___recorder, flute___
4. Why is Jean Sibelius a hero of Finland? ___Jean Sibelius, Finland___
5. Can oysters make pearls? ___oysters, pearls___
6. Can both frogs and toads swim? ___frogs, toads___
7. Do whales and dolphins talk with each other? ___whales, dolphins___
8. Do the Navajos live in Arizona? ___Navajos, Arizona___
9. Did Thomas Edison invent movies? ___Thomas Edison, movies___

B. Write each key word next to the encyclopedia volume in which it might appear.

Ice Age	James Monroe	income tax	immigrants
John Paul Jones	New Deal	iron curtain	money
Andrew Jackson	Navajo Indians	New Jersey	North Pole

(Volume 8 I-J)
10. ___Ice Age___
11. ___John Paul Jones___
12. ___Andrew Jackson___
13. ___income tax___
14. ___iron curtain___
15. ___immigrants___

(Volume 12 M-N)
16. ___James Monroe___
17. ___New Deal___
18. ___Navajo Indians___
19. ___New Jersey___
20. ___money___
21. ___North Pole___

WRITE IT
Write three questions you would like to know the answers to. Underline the key word or words in each question. Write on a separate sheet of paper. Answers will vary.

◀▥▥ TEACHING OPTIONS ▥▥▶

RETEACHING

A Different Modality Explain that articles in an encyclopedia are arranged in alphabetical order. Add that for names of people, the alphabetical order is by last name. List the following topics on the chalkboard and help students identify each key word.

1. Alexander Hamilton
2. Fort Sumter
3. Thomas Jefferson
4. Eleanor Roosevelt
5. Continental Congress
6. John Adams

CLASS ENRICHMENT

A Cooperative Activity Have students work in small groups. Have group members write three questions they would like to know the answer to. Have group members exchange questions and underline the key word or words in their partner's questions. Have students check each other's work before asking volunteers to share their questions and key words with the class.

CHALLENGE

An Independent Extension Have students go to the library and find the set of encyclopedias with the most recent publication date. Have students list the following information: the title, date of publication, number of volumes, and volume containing the index. Have students write a brief explanation of the advantages of using an encyclopedia with a recent publication date.

UNIT 6
Writing

■ Easy ■ Average ■ Challenging

OBJECTIVES
To take notes in one's own words by summarizing key ideas in written material

ASSIGNMENT GUIDE
BASIC   Practice A

ADVANCED   Practice B

All should do the Apply activity.

RESOURCES
■ Reteaching Master 55
■ Practice Master 55

TEACHING THE LESSON

1. Getting Started
Oral Language Focus attention on this oral activity, encouraging all to participate. You may wish to have copies of newspapers on hand to use as models as students create their own headlines.

2. Developing the Lesson
Guide students through the explanation of taking notes in their own words, emphasizing the example and the summary. You may wish to list on the chalkboard each sentence from the sample paragraph and then have volunteers list Derek's matching notes alongside the paragraph. Lead students through the **Guided Practice.** Identify those who would benefit from reteaching. Assign independent Practice A–B.

3. Closing the Lesson
After students complete the Apply activity, have volunteers tell what they have learned about geysers and volcanoes while classmates take notes. Have students compare their own notes with the notes of each student giving the talk. Point out to students that taking notes with meaningful words will help them remember important information.

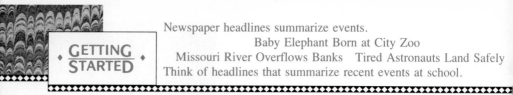

Newspaper headlines summarize events.
Baby Elephant Born at City Zoo
Missouri River Overflows Banks   Tired Astronauts Land Safely
Think of headlines that summarize recent events at school.

WRITING ◆
Taking Notes in Your Own Words

Taking notes helps you recall what you have read by summarizing the most important facts and ideas. Notes can remind you of main ideas and supporting details for a report. Take notes in your own words. You don't have to use full sentences.

Derek read the following paragraph about volcanoes. He took notes on an index card. He wrote the main idea at the top. Supporting ideas were listed under it. Derek used his own words.

> *Early Roman myth explains volcanoes.*
> *– Vulcan, god of fire and metals*
> *– had great underground workshop*
> *– sounds escaped through mountains*
> *– Vulcan's name–volcano*

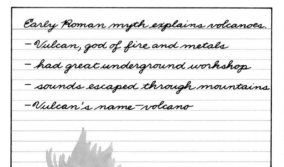

Throughout history, people have wondered about volcanoes. The early Romans had a myth to explain the smoke and rumbling that came from the earth. They believed in Vulcan, the god of fire and metals. The Romans said that Vulcan lived below the earth. There he had a great blacksmith shop. Mountains were his giant chimneys. Noises from underground were Vulcan's hammer banging the anvil. Sparks proved his enormous power. Our word *volcano* is from Vulcan's name.

Summary ◆ Use your own words to take notes on what you read.

Guided Practice
Answers will vary. Possible answers follow.
Summarize each idea in your own words.

Volcanoes—source of wonder
1. Throughout history, people have wondered about volcanoes.
Romans said Vulcan lived underground.
2. The Romans said that Vulcan lived below the earth.
Sparks evidence of Vulcan's strength
3. Sparks proved his enormous power.
Vulcan gave us word *volcano*
4. Our word *volcano* is from Vulcan's name.

312 WRITING and STUDY SKILLS: Taking Notes and Paraphrasing

ESSENTIAL LANGUAGE SKILLS
This lesson provides opportunities to:

LISTENING ◆ employ active listening in a variety of situations

SPEAKING ◆ use oral language for a variety of purposes

READING ◆ understand content area vocabulary ◆ summarize a selection ◆ evaluate and make judgments ◆ follow a set of directions ◆ use the dictionary and the encyclopedia to locate information

WRITING ◆ use a variety of resources to research a topic ◆ write and compose for a variety of purposes

LANGUAGE ◆ use language for informing

Practice

Answers will vary. Possible answers follow.

A. Write these statements in your own words.

Long ago, people knew the earth held heat.
5. Centuries ago, people realized there was heat inside the earth.

People saw the results of volcanic eruptions.
6. They observed the terrible destruction a volcano could cause.

A volcano is a special mountain.
7. A volcano is a particular kind of mountain.

A volcano can build up during an eruption.
8. Some volcanic mountains build themselves as they erupt.

Some eruptions break the mountain apart.
9. Some volcanic eruptions destroy the mountain.

Volcanoes have openings called vents.
10. A volcano has a vent, or opening, from the inner earth.

Vents run vertically.
11. A vent is like a vertical pipe, or tube.

Pressure can cause the explosion of a vent.
12. If enough pressure builds, the vent explodes.

Erupting lava is very hot.
13. When lava comes to the surface, it is red hot.

Hard lava can clog a vent.
14. Sometimes vents get blocked by hardened lava.

B. Read the paragraph below about Crater Lake in Oregon. Take notes, beginning with a main idea. Then add the supporting ideas. Notes will vary. A possible answer follows.

Crater Lake, Oregon, formed by volcano. Mt. Mazama erupted long ago; top collapsed. Deep crater left behind, filled with rainwater. Now Crater Lake. At first no fish; now stocked yearly.

Oregon's Crater Lake exists because of a violent volcanic eruption that occurred long ago. Mount Mazama was a volcano nearly twelve thousand feet high. A powerful eruption thousands of years ago caused its top to collapse. The cave-in formed a crater a half-mile deep. Rainwater eventually filled it, forming Crater Lake. At first there were no fish in Crater Lake. Eventually the lake was stocked with trout, and now fish are added every year.

Apply ♦ Think and Write

Dictionary of Knowledge ♦ How is a geyser like a volcano? Look up *geyser* to find out. Using your own words, take notes on what you read. Tell someone else what you have learned, using your notes for reference.

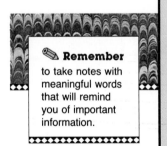

✎ **Remember**
to take notes with meaningful words that will remind you of important information.

WRITING and STUDY SKILLS: Taking Notes and Paraphrasing **313**

◀▥▥ **TEACHING OPTIONS** ▥▥▶

RETEACHING

A Different Modality Explain that it is important to use one's own words when taking notes. Play a game in which you give information and then have volunteers say the same thing in as many different ways as possible. Possible information: *Boston is one of the oldest cities in our country.* Possible response: *Boston is a very old city. Boston is older than most of the cities in the United States.*

CLASS ENRICHMENT

A Cooperative Activity Have students take notes in their own words on a topic of their choice, such as *snails, flutes, Casey Jones,* and *the Dust Bowl.* Have students use encyclopedias or content-area textbooks to find the information. Have partners take turns using the notes to tell one another about their topics.

CHALLENGE

An Independent Extension Have students take notes in their own words from a television or radio news program, or from a newspaper article on a story of national interest. Have students list the main idea (the most important fact) and then the subtopics or details. Tell students to write their notes on index cards. You may wish to have students use their notes to write a paragraph about their news story.

OBJECTIVES
To write an outline, organizing information by main ideas and supporting ideas

ASSIGNMENT GUIDE
BASIC   Practice A

          Practice B

ADVANCED   Practice C

All should do the Apply activity.

RESOURCES
■ Reteaching Master 56
■ Practice Master 56

TEACHING THE LESSON

1. Getting Started
Oral Language Focus attention on this oral activity, encouraging all to participate. You may wish to write students' responses on the chalkboard in the form of a semantic map.

2. Developing the Lesson
Guide students through the explanation of an outline, emphasizing the example and the summary. You may wish to write on the chalkboard a skeleton outline, pointing out the use of Roman numerals and periods for main ideas and capital letters and periods for supporting details. Lead students through the **Guided Practice**. Identify those who would benefit from reteaching. Assign independent Practice A–C.

3. Closing the Lesson
After students complete the Apply activity, have volunteers read their paragraphs aloud, having classmates identify each main topic and its subtopics. Point out to students that organizing information in an outline can help them to give information clearly and completely when speaking and writing.

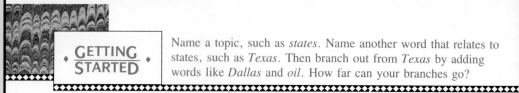

◆ GETTING STARTED ◆ Name a topic, such as *states*. Name another word that relates to states, such as *Texas*. Then branch out from *Texas* by adding words like *Dallas* and *oil*. How far can your branches go?

WRITING ◆
An Outline

An outline is a written plan. It can help you organize a report by showing how information goes together. Your outline can tell you if you have enough details for each main idea. The outline below has an explanation beside it. The outline gives information for a report about a famous volcano.

The Paricutín Volcano

I. Description of location
   A. Small Mexican village
   B. 200 miles west of Mexico City
II. Farmer witnesses first blast
   A. Dionisio Pulido, corn farmer
   B. Notices unusual ground heat
   C. Hears strange noises
   D. Suddenly sees ground cave in
III. Mountain grows overnight
   A. Explosion breaks land open
   B. Steam, ash, rock, lava fly
   C. Forms hill 120 feet high

An outline begins with a title, centered at the top, which can become your report title. Each main idea becomes a main topic. Main topics are listed in logical order. Each is labeled with a Roman numeral with a period.

Details become subtopics. They are grouped under the proper main topic. Subtopics are indented, and each is labeled with a capital letter followed by a period.

Notice that the first word on each line is capitalized.

> **Summary** ◆ An **outline** organizes information into main ideas and supporting details.

Guided Practice

Use the outline above to answer the questions.

1. What is the title of the outline? The Paricutín Volcano
2. How many main topics does the outline have? three
3. How many subtopics support the first main idea? two

314   WRITING: Outlines

ESSENTIAL LANGUAGE SKILLS
This lesson provides opportunities to:

LISTENING ◆ employ active listening in a variety of ways

SPEAKING ◆ use a variety of words to express feelings and ideas

READING ◆ understand content area vocabulary ◆ identify an implied main idea of a longer selection ◆ recall specific facts and details that support the main idea and/or conclusion ◆ summarize a selection ◆ evaluate and make judgments

WRITING ◆ use a variety of resources to research a topic ◆ use chronological and spatial order and order of importance

LANGUAGE ◆ use the fundamentals of grammar, punctuation, and spelling

Practice

A. 4–13. Copy the outline below about a new island. Beside each line, write *title, main topic,* or *subtopic.*

title
An Island Is Born
main topic
  I. Surtsey becomes an island
    subtopic
    A. In Atlantic Ocean near Iceland
    subtopic
    B. Underwater volcano erupted
    subtopic
    C. Lava reached surface, May 14, 1963
main topic
 II. Surtsey continues to grow
    subtopic
    A. Eruption went on for two years
    subtopic
    B. Island grew 568 feet high
    subtopic
    C. Area of one-and-a-half square miles
    subtopic
    D. Now considered part of Iceland

B. Use the topics below to form an outline titled "After Mount St. Helens." Identify the two main topics. Then group the subtopics under them. Remember Roman numerals and capital letters. *Order of main topics and subtopics may vary.*

Problems for fish	I.
Water lacked oxygen	I.A.
Trees damaged	II.A.
Nesting areas lost	II.B.
Plants and berries destroyed	II.C.
Birds also suffer	II.
Rivers clogged with mud	I.B.
Ash-coated wings	II.D.

C. Prepare an outline from the Dictionary of Knowledge entry on geysers. Identify one main topic from each paragraph in the entry. Add as many subtopics as you need. Don't forget to give your outline a title.
Outlines will vary, but should follow lesson guidelines.

Apply ♦ Think and Write

An Informational Paragraph ♦ Write a paragraph using information from the outline you wrote for **Practice C.** Choose one of the main topics and its subtopics as the basis of your paragraph.

✎ **Remember** that an outline is a good way to organize information.

WRITING: Outlines   **315**

◀◀◀▐▐▐ TEACHING OPTIONS ▐▐▐▶▶▶

RETEACHING

A Different Modality Explain that an outline is a way to organize information into main ideas and supporting ideas. On the chalkboard list the following: *Guitars, Accompanying instruments, Tambourine, Drum.* Write a skeleton outline with Roman numeral I and capital letters *A, B,* and *C* below the items. Help students identify the main idea and the supporting ideas and have volunteers fill in the skeleton outline.

CLASS ENRICHMENT

A Cooperative Activity You may wish to have students use a short selection in a textbook or an encyclopedia to prepare an outline with at least one main topic and three subtopics. Then have students rewrite their outlines in scrambled order on another sheet of paper. Have students exchange papers with a partner and rearrange the outlines correctly. Have partners compare and discuss their outlines.

CHALLENGE

An Independent Extension Have students make an outline titled "The Boston Tea Party" with the information below. Tell them there are two main topics and two subtopics included in the list.

1. When and where it was held
2. To protest British laws
3. December 16, 1773
4. To protest taxes placed on goods
5. Why it was held
6. Griffin's Wharf in Boston harbor

Reading–Writing Connection

READING
◆CONNECTION◆
WRITING

Focus on Topic Choice

Review the Unit 6 literature selection from *Volcano* with students and have them describe how the broad topic of the book was narrowed to the topic of the chapter. Then point out to students that they can use the selection to help them learn how to choose a topic that is narrow enough to cover in a report.

You may wish to guide students through the introductory paragraphs, stressing the example. Discuss how the broad topic "Volcanoes of the World" is gradually narrowed to a workable topic for a report.

Next, have students apply the information in the Reading-Writing Connection by discussing the questions at the bottom of the page. As students talk about the questions, guide them to recognize that one eruption of Mount St. Helens is a narrow subject and that complete information about volcanoes could not be covered well in a few paragraphs.

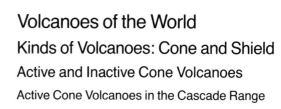

Focus on Topic Choice

To write a good report, you must choose the right topic. That means, first of all, choosing a topic that interests you and is likely to interest your readers. It also means choosing a topic that is narrow enough to cover in your report. A topic like "Volcanoes of the World," for example, is too broad to cover in a short report. It could easily be the subject of a whole book.

But suppose you want to write a short report about volcanoes. Can you do it? Yes, you can do it by narrowing the broad topic of volcanoes to one of a workable size. Look at the five topics below. Notice the steps by which the broad topic "Volcanoes of the World" becomes the narrowed topic of "Eruption of Mount St. Helens: May 18, 1980."

Volcanoes of the World
Kinds of Volcanoes: Cone and Shield
Active and Inactive Cone Volcanoes
Active Cone Volcanoes in the Cascade Range
Eruption of Mount St. Helens: May 18, 1980

The Writer's Voice • "Eruption of Mount St. Helens: May 18, 1980" is a suitable topic for a short report. Would it also make a good subject for a whole book? Explain.

Could the broad topic "Volcanoes" possibly be covered in a few paragraphs? Explain.

 316 COOPERATIVE LEARNING: Writer's Craft

ESSENTIAL LANGUAGE SKILLS
This lesson provides opportunities to:

LISTENING ◆ follow the logical organization of an oral presentation ◆ select from an oral presentation the information needed ◆ employ active listening in a variety of situations

SPEAKING ◆ participate in group discussions ◆ use a set of reasons to persuade a group

READING ◆ relate experiences with appropriate vocabulary in complete sentences ◆ understand content area vocabulary ◆ evaluate and make judgments ◆ follow a set of directions

WRITING ◆ select and narrow a topic for a specific purpose ◆ adapt information to accomplish a specific purpose with a particular audience

LANGUAGE ◆ use modifiers (adjectives and adverbs) correctly ◆ use all other parts of speech correctly

Working Together

When you write a short report, you should begin by choosing a topic that interests you. Then narrow the topic so that it can be covered well in a limited number of paragraphs or pages. With your group, complete activities **A** and **B**.

In Your Group
◆ Contribute ideas.
◆ Be sure everyone understands what to do.
◆ Help the group reach agreement.
◆ Record the group's ideas.

A. All the topics below are too broad for a short report. With your group, narrow each one until it is suitable for a short report. Compare your narrowed topics with those of other groups.
Answers will vary.

1. Birds of North America
2. Heroes of the American Revolution
3. Volcanoes (not the Mount St. Helens eruption)
4. Tall Buildings of the World
5. Professional Sports

B. Choose a broad subject area, such as *science, health, geography, history, entertainment.* With your group, try to decide on five good topics for short reports within that one subject area. You might want to work individually at first. Then, when everyone has finished, the group can decide on the five most appealing topics. Finally, each group can share its list with the rest of the class.
Answers will vary.

THESAURUS CORNER ◆ Word Choice

Two of the main entry words in the Thesaurus are adverbs: *fast* and *well*. Write two original sentences about volcanoes. Use *fast* (or a synonym) as an adverb in one sentence. Use *well* (or a synonym) as an adverb in the other. Then write three more original sentences about volcanoes, using any of the words listed in the Thesaurus. The noun *energy* and the adjective *large* are possible choices. Underline the words you have chosen.
Answers will vary.

COOPERATIVE LEARNING: Writer's Craft ◆ 317

Working Together

The Working Together activities provide opportunities for students to work together in cooperative learning groups. You may wish to pair strong writers with students whose skills are weaker so that all students may experience success in writing.

Divide the class into small groups and have students read In Your Group. Have them tell what might happen if the group does not follow through on each task. *(If we do not encourage everyone to contribute ideas, some members of the group may be afraid to speak up. If some group members do not understand what to do, they cannot help complete the activity. If we cannot reach agreement, we will be unable to work together to complete the activity. If we do not record ideas, we may forget important points that are discussed.)*

You may wish to have each group appoint a recorder and a timekeeper. Then set a time limit. After students complete activity A, encourage groups to compare the lists of narrowed topics they wrote and discuss why the topics are or are not suitable for a short report. After activity B, call on a member of each group to read aloud the group's list of five good topics for short reports. Have the class listen to determine whether or not each topic is suitable for a short report.

Thesaurus Corner

The Thesaurus Corner provides students with the opportunity to extend the Reading-Writing Connection by using the Thesaurus in the back of the textbook. If necessary, remind them how a thesaurus is used. After students have written five sentences, call on individuals to read their sentences aloud. Encourage students to compare their sentences and tell how the words they chose convey the information they wish to share. Have students save their sentences for use later in the Writing Process lesson. Point out that learning about word choice can help students develop their ability to give information accurately and clearly in their writing and speaking.

OBJECTIVES
To write a research report
To use five stages of the writing process: prewriting, writing, revising, proofreading, and publishing

RESOURCES
Writing Process Transparencies 21–24
Revising and Proofreading Transparencies
Spelling Connection
Writing Sample Tests, p. T554

INTRODUCTION

Connecting to Literature Have a volunteer read the introduction aloud. Emphasize that the literature selection, *Volcano,* is based on research that its author, Patricia Lauber, did. Remind students that the author may have interviewed witnesses, read newspapers, and studied scientific information in order to do her research. Have students tell what else the author could have done to research material for this article. (She could have studied pictures of the Mount St. Helens area. She could have listened to radio or television reports about the eruption. She might have even gone to the area near the volcano to study what happened.) Tell students they will write a report of their own based on their research.

Purpose and Audience Ask students to give their own definition of a research report. (An account or description that is based on a careful study of facts) Then have volunteers tell about times they have done research in order to learn more about something or someone. (Students may have done research for school reports. They may have done research outside school on subjects that interest them.)

Have students consider the questions: *What is my purpose?* (To write about an unusual natural event) *Who is my audience?* (My classmates) Have students discuss what they believe they need to consider when writing a research report that will appeal to another fifth-grader.

Writing a Research Report

Volcano is a fascinating report of the eruption of Mount St. Helens. We do not know what kind of research its author, Patricia Lauber, did. We can imagine, however, that she might have interviewed witnesses. She might have read newspaper reports and studied scientific information about volcanoes. She probably gathered information from many sources.

Patricia Lauber arranged her facts in a logical order. She used time order to explain when the main events happened. She used space order to describe the scene of the volcano blast.

What's MY PURPOSE

Who's MY AUDIENCE

Know Your Purpose and Audience

In this lesson you will write your own research report. Your purpose will be to write about an unusual natural event.

Your audience will be your classmates. Later you can give an oral report based on your research. You can also help to create a collection of "Amazing But True" reports.

◆ 318 ◆

ESSENTIAL LANGUAGE SKILLS
This lesson provides opportunities to:

LISTENING ◆ listen for specific information ◆ select from an oral presentation the information needed

SPEAKING ◆ read aloud a variety of written materials ◆ speak before an audience to communicate specific information ◆ make organized oral presentations ◆ adapt content and formality of oral language to fit purpose and audience

READING ◆ recall facts and details that support the main idea ◆ arrange events in sequential order when sequence is not stated ◆ locate and utilize

desired information in reference sources ◆ draw conclusions ◆ follow a set of directions

WRITING ◆ expand topics by collecting information from a variety of sources ◆ identify audience and purpose ◆ write summaries and reports of events and situations ◆ organize information related to a single topic ◆ improve writing based on peer and teacher response

LANGUAGE ◆ use language for informing ◆ select a usage level appropriate for a given audience or purpose

Prewriting

Before you write, you need to choose and narrow a topic. Then you need to find and organize information on your topic.

Choose Your Topic ◆ Browse through the library, looking for ideas. Look at science books, encyclopedias, and science magazines. Write down every topic that sounds interesting. Find out a little about each.

Think About It	Talk About It
Make a list of possible topics. Which topic makes you most curious? Circle the topic you want to research. If your topic is too broad to write about, narrow it. Instead of writing about hurricanes, for example, write about one hurricane.	Find out what topics your classmates are choosing. Ask them how they made their choices. You could work with a partner to look through library books for topic ideas. Working with a partner often helps ideas come to you more easily.

Topic Ideas

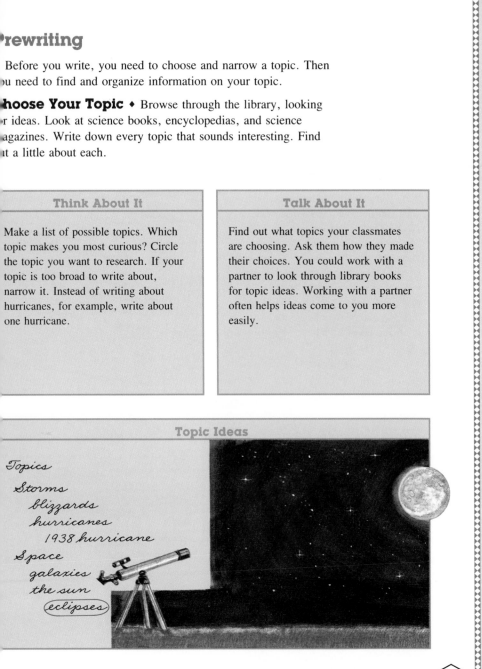

Topics
Storms
  blizzards
  hurricanes
    1938 hurricane
Space
  galaxies
  the sun
  (eclipses)

WRITING PROCESS: Research Report ◁319▷

---

1. PREWRITING

Guide students through the explanation of Prewriting, pointing out that Prewriting is the stage in which writers choose a topic and gather ideas and information to use in their writing.

MODELING THE WRITING PROCESS

If you feel students need instruction before they begin, you may wish to model this stage of the process. Tell students you want to choose a topic for a research report. Have students help you work through the thinking process. Work with them to name interesting topics from nature, such as change of seasons, natural disasters, or unusual events in the sky or at sea. Write four or five topics on the chalkboard or use *Writing Process Transparency 21.* Have students help you narrow each topic so that it tells about a specific event. Record the responses.

Let students hear how you might go about selecting the best topic to use in a research report. As you speak, encourage students to help you. (Possible discussion: Autumn is not really an unusual event. Writing about how the leaves change probably would not interest my audience. Earthquakes have always fascinated me. A report about their cause and their effects would probably interest my classmates.

Writing Process Transparency 21*

Unusual Natural Events	
Topic of Interest	Narrowing Topic
1. autumn	how it affects trees
	how leaves change color
2. natural disasters	earthquakes
	cause/effects of earthquakes
3. unusual sights in sky	northern lights
	location
4. unusual events at sea	whirlpools
	how whirlpools are formed

Pacing

A five-day pacing guide follows, but the writing process can stretch over a longer time, especially if students want to write several drafts.

Day 1—Prewriting Day 3—Revising
Day 2—Writing Day 4—Proofreading
     Day 5—Publishing

Evaluation

Process Check questions at the end of each stage of the writing process help you to keep track of students' progress.

Holistic Evaluation Guidelines may be found in the teaching notes on page 325. They offer criteria for average, above-average, and below-average compositions.

Possible responses are overprinted on this reduced facsimile only. Use Writing Process Transparencies *to interact with your students on the ideas that interest them.*

Choose Your Strategy Before inviting students to choose a prewriting strategy that will help them gather information for their research reports, guide them through the explanations of both strategies. Then have students choose a strategy they feel will help them get started. Students may benefit from using both strategies.

You may wish to remind students that they have learned about an Order Circle as a strategy for sequencing in the Critical Thinking lesson on pages 300–301.

I D E A   B A N K

Prewriting Ideas

Always encourage young writers to try new ways to discover ideas they want to write about. Reassure them, though, that it is appropriate to use the strategies that work best for them. You may wish to remind them of the prewriting ideas already introduced in their textbooks:

- A Conversation, p. 40
- An Observation Chart, p. 40
- An Order Circle, pp. 96, 320
- A Clock Graph, p. 96
- A Comic Strip, p. 154
- Answering "What If?," p. 154
- An Opinion Ladder, p. 212
- A Thought Balloon, pp. 212, 266
- A Character Map, p. 266
- Taking Notes, p. 320

Choose Your Strategy ◆ Here are two fact-gathering strategies. Read both. Then use the strategy you think will help you more to prepare to write.

PREWRITING IDEAS

CHOICE ONE

Taking Notes

As you do your research, take notes on what you discover. Make a separate group of note cards for each main idea. The cards should contain supporting ideas. Be sure the notes are in your own words. Make source cards, too. Follow the examples shown for a book, a magazine, and an encyclopedia. Then make an outline to organize the information you found.

Model

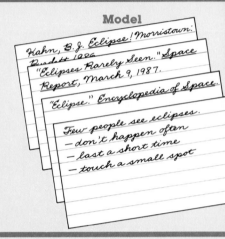

CHOICE TWO

An Order Circle

Write your topic inside an order circle. Write some kinds of order on arrows. How will you arrange your facts? Look at your order circle and decide which kind of order will work best.

You might try one of these kinds of order. Time order tells what happened first, next, last. Space order tells what happened in one place, then another. Size order starts or ends with the biggest or longest. Order of interest tells the most interesting fact first or last.

Model

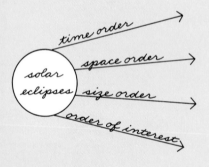

PROCESS CHECK At the completion of the Prewriting stage, students should be able to answer *yes* to these questions:
- Do I know what I will research and write about in my research report?
- Do I have notes or an order circle with facts and details about my topic?

Teacher to Teacher

The purpose of a conference is to help the writer react to their writing. Through a conference writers can get feedback on how well they are communicating. Conferences can be with the teacher, with a peer, or with oneself. To plan a conference, think about the writer. Remember to listen. Give feedback on what you heard, and respond to content rather than form. Discuss one thing at a time. Your responses will stimulate the writer to clarify and solve problems.

Writing

Arrange your prewriting notes in the order you plan to use. Then begin to write. Be sure to state your topic in your first paragraph. You might begin with a dramatic, attention-getting fact. Here are two ideas.

- All hurricanes are bad, but some are worse than others. One of the worst was the hurricane of 1938.
- Solar eclipses do not happen very often. In an eclipse the moon moves between the sun and the earth.

Then keep writing in the order you chose. Include details that help the reader understand the event. End with a summary paragraph that includes a prediction for the future. Your prediction should be based on facts in your report.

Sample First Draft ◆

Few people ever see a total eclipse of the sun. An eclipse happens when the moon gets between the sun and the earth. When the moon hides the sun completly, the eclipse is total. Eclipses of the moon also happen. When an eclipse starts, an edge of the sun dissappears. It looks like a bite out of the sun that keeps growing. When the eclipse is Total, the sky is dark you can even see the stars. Minutes later, the sun starts to reapear. It soon grows to its full size again. An eclipse is total for only a few minutes.

You probably won't never see a total eclipse. Such an event is very rare. also, it lasts a short time.

2. WRITING

Before students write their first drafts, guide them through the explanation of Writing, emphasizing that at this stage the most important task is to get all their ideas on paper.

Help students organize their facts and notes about their topic in an orderly manner. Make sure students state the topic in the first paragraph of their report.

MODELING THE WRITING PROCESS

If you feel students need instruction before they begin this stage of the process, you may wish to ask them to think about how they might organize a research report about the cause and effects of earthquakes. Display *Writing Process Transparency 22,* or write the information from that transparency on the chalkboard. Point out the main ideas labeled *A* and *B* and the details below those headings. Have students work through the thinking process with you to tell which details belong under each heading. Then have students organize the details for heading *A* according to time order. Ask them also to create an opening sentence for this report, such as: *Can you imagine the earth moving beneath your feet?*

Writing Process Transparency 22*

Writing a Research Report
A. Cause of an Earthquake
B. Effects of an Earthquake

A	earth has plates of rock beneath surface	1
B	earth moves, land slides, ground opens up	
A	plates move and slide past each other	2
B	fires often occur	
B	floods and huge waves often follow earthquake	
A	grating or shift in plates causes earthquake	3

PROCESS CHECK At the completion of the Writing stage, students should be able to answer *yes* to these questions:

- Do I have a complete first draft?
- Are my facts arranged in an order that is logical?
- Did I end my report with a prediction about the future?

Possible responses are overprinted on this reduced facsimile only. Use Writing Process Transparencies *to interact with your students on the ideas that interest them.*

3. REVISING

Help students understand that during Revising writers make their drafts communicate ideas more clearly and effectively to an audience. During Revising writers are not to concern themselves with errors in spelling, capitalization, and punctuation; instead they should concentrate on the quality and effectiveness of their ideas.

IDEA BANK

Grammar Connection

You may wish to remind students of the Grammar Checks already introduced in their textbooks:
- Use a variety of sentence types, p. 43
- Use exact nouns, p. 99
- Use vivid verbs, p. 157
- Replace nouns with pronouns, p. 215
- Add adjectives for specific detail, p. 269
- Avoid double negatives, p. 323

Option 1 ◆ If you wish to begin grammar instruction related to the Grammar Check in this lesson, then refer to Part 1 of this unit.

Option 2 ◆ If you wish to begin grammar instruction *not* related to the Grammar Check in this lesson, then refer to the end-of-book Glossary or Index.

First Read to Yourself You may wish to emphasize that students need not make actual changes during the first reading. This is a time to think about whether their writing is clear and says what they mean it to say.

Remind students to check to make sure that they have narrowed their topic enough so that it can be covered sufficiently in their report.

Then Share with a Partner Suggest that writers' partners offer three responses, at least one positive, and that they accompany any critical responses with suggestions for improvement. Be sure writers ask the Focus questions: *Is my topic narrow enough? Should I take anything out?*

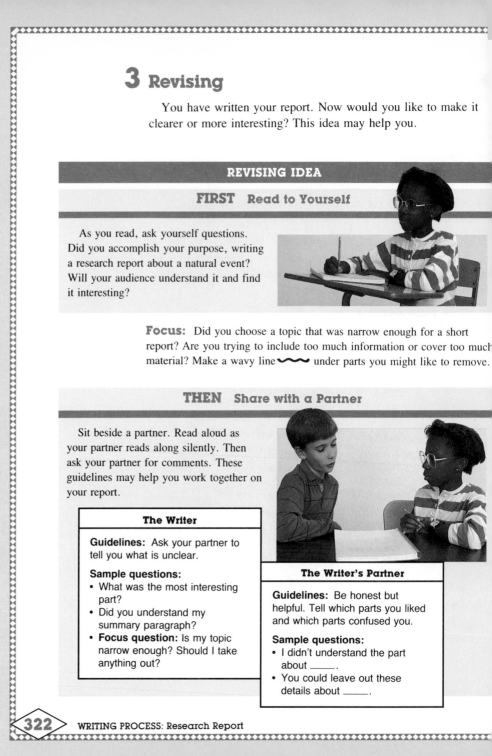

3 Revising

You have written your report. Now would you like to make it clearer or more interesting? This idea may help you.

REVISING IDEA

FIRST   Read to Yourself

As you read, ask yourself questions. Did you accomplish your purpose, writing a research report about a natural event? Will your audience understand it and find it interesting?

Focus: Did you choose a topic that was narrow enough for a short report? Are you trying to include too much information or cover too much material? Make a wavy line ∿ under parts you might like to remove.

THEN   Share with a Partner

Sit beside a partner. Read aloud as your partner reads along silently. Then ask your partner for comments. These guidelines may help you work together on your report.

The Writer

Guidelines: Ask your partner to tell you what is unclear.

Sample questions:
- What was the most interesting part?
- Did you understand my summary paragraph?
- **Focus question:** Is my topic narrow enough? Should I take anything out?

The Writer's Partner

Guidelines: Be honest but helpful. Tell which parts you liked and which parts confused you.

Sample questions:
- I didn't understand the part about _____.
- You could leave out these details about _____.

322   WRITING PROCESS: Research Report

Teacher to Teacher

The following are some questions you might ask in a content conference:
- What is the most important thing you want your audience to know?
- What else do you know about this topic?
- Have you used descriptive language in your writing?
- Is all the information you have given necessary?

WRITING AS A RECURSIVE PROCESS

Connecting Grammar to the Writing Process

Writing is a recursive process. In other words, good writers will often go back and forth among steps. Depending on the individual styles of your students, some may choose to correct grammar at Step Three, Revising; others may prefer to fix grammar or usage errors at Step Four, Proofreading. Ideally, this should be a decision made by the writer. Remind students, however, that once they have completed their proofreading, all the grammar errors should be corrected.

Revising Model ◆ This research report is being revised. The blue revising marks show changes the writer is making.

Revising Marks	
cross out	——
add	∧
move	⟳

See is overused. *Witness* is more interesting.

The writer decided this was really about a broader topic.

This detail would make the summary paragraph stronger.

The writer's partner heard the double negative.

witness
Few people ever see a total eclipse of the sun. An eclipse happens when the moon gets between the sun and the earth. When the moon hides the sun completly, the eclipse is total. Eclipses of the moon also happen. When an eclipse starts, an edge of the sun dissappears. It looks like a bite out of the sun that keeps growing. When the eclipse is Total, the sky is dark you can even see the stars. Minutes later, the sun starts to reapear. It soon grows to its full size again. An eclipse is total for only a few minutes.
will
You probably won't never see a total eclipse. Such an event is very rare. also, it
only
lasts a short time.

Read the above report the way the writer has decided it *should* be. Then revise your own research report.

Grammar Check ◆ Double negatives can make meaning unclear.

Word Choice ◆ Have you overused any words like *see* in your writing? A thesaurus can help you find more interesting words.

Revising Checklist
☐ **Purpose:** Did I write a research report about an unusual natural event?
☐ **Audience:** Will my classmates find my report understandable and interesting?
☐ **Focus:** Is my topic narrow enough to be covered well in a short report?

WRITING PROCESS: Research Report ⟨**323**⟩

PROCESS CHECK At the completion of the Revising stage, students should be able to answer *yes* to the following questions:
• Do I have a complete draft with revising marks that show changes I plan to make?
• Has my draft been reviewed by another writer?

Possible responses are overprinted on this reduced fac-simile only. Use Writing Process Transparencies *to interact with your students on the ideas that interest them.*

WRITING PROCESS

Revising Model Guide students through the model, noting the reasons for changes and the revision marks. Point out to students that on the model the revising marks are in blue. Encourage the class to discuss the changes in the model. Ask them to consider whether or not the changes made the writing clearer and easier to understand.

MODELING THE WRITING PROCESS

If you feel students need instruction before they begin this stage of the process, you may wish to present *Writing Process Transparency 23.* Have students read the draft silently, or have a volunteer read it aloud. Then ask whether there is anything that needs to be changed. Work through the thinking process to help students give reasons for the changes. Have them tell you how to mark the changes on the draft. (Students might suggest substituting words for the overused word *moving,* deleting a sentence that is too broad for the topic, moving a sentence to make the summary stronger, and correcting the double negative.) Remind students that at this time they are revising for meaning. They will correct spelling and punctuation when they proofread.

Writing Process Transparency 23*

Nature's Power
shaking and sliding
Can you imagine the earth moving beneath your feet?

That is what happens during an earthquake earthquakes

occur when plates of rock beneath the earth's surface

shift or grate together. A strong earthquake can bring

about tremendus destruction. It can cause fire, floods,

and even huge ocean waves. Volcanos also start fires.

Earthquakes will always remain as proof of nature's

power.

Today scientist are working to predickt earthquakes,
will
but earthquakes won't never be tamed.

4. PROOFREADING

Guide students through the explanation of proofreading and review the Proofreading Model. Point out to students that on the model the proofreading marks are in red. Tell them that proofreading helps to eliminate errors such as incorrect spelling or run-on sentences that may distract or confuse their readers.

Review the Proofreading Strategy, Proofreading Marks, and the Proofreading Checklist with students. Then invite students to use the checklist and proofread their own research reports.

MODELING THE WRITING PROCESS

If you feel students need instruction before they begin this stage of the process, you may wish to use *Writing Process Transparency 24*. Read through the copy on the transparency, using a ruler as suggested on textbook page 324. Go through the draft word by word, having students use their Proofreading Checklist to help you check for errors. Mark students' corrections on the transparency.

Writing Process Transparency 24*

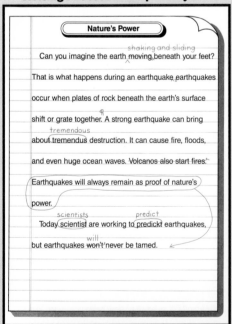

Nature's Power

shaking and sliding
Can you imagine the earth moving beneath your feet?

That is what happens during an earthquake. earthquakes

occur when plates of rock beneath the earth's surface

shift or grate together. A strong earthquake can bring
tremendous
about tremendus destruction. It can cause fire, floods,

and even huge ocean waves. Volcanos also start fires.

Earthquakes will always remain as proof of nature's

power.
scientists   predict
Today scientist are working to predickt earthquakes,
will
but earthquakes won't never be tamed.

324

---

4 Proofreading

Be courteous to those who will read your writing. Now is the time to make sure that your report is neat and correct.

Proofreading Model ◆ Here is a draft of the report on solar eclipses. Proofreading changes in red have been added.

Proofreading Marks

capital letter   —

small letter   /

indent paragraph   ¶

check spelling   ⬭

Proofreading Checklist

☐ Did I spell words correctly?

☐ Did I indent paragraphs?

☐ Did I use capital letters correctly?

☐ Did I use correct marks at the end of sentences?

☐ Did I use my best handwriting?

---

                    witness
Few people ever see a total eclipse of the sun. An eclipse happens when the moon gets between the sun and the earth. When the
              completely
moon hides the sun completly, the eclipse is total. Eclipses of the moon also happen. When an eclipse starts, an edge of the sun
 disappears
dissappears. It looks like a bite out of the sun that keeps growing. When the eclipse is Total, the sky is dark. you can even see the stars.
                        reappear
Minutes later, the sun starts to reapear. It soon grows to its full size again. An eclipse is total for only a few minutes.
           will
You probably won't never see a total
       only
eclipse. Such an event is very rare. also, it lasts a short time.

PROOFREADING IDEA

Using a Ruler

A ruler can help you proofread. Place the ruler under the first line. Proofread that line carefully. Then do the same on each of the following lines. Reading one line at a time makes it easier to find mistakes.

Now proofread your research report, add a title, and make a neat copy.

324 WRITING PROCESS: Research Report

PROCESS CHECK At the completion of the Proofreading stage, students should be able to answer *yes* to the following questions:
- Do I have a complete draft with proofreading marks that show changes I plan to make?
- Have I used the proofreading marks shown in the lesson?

EVALUATION PROGRAM

See Evaluation and Testing Program, pp. C1–C8.

Masters are available for the following:
Self Evaluation Checklist
Personal Goals for Writing
Peer Response
Teacher Response

Holistic Evaluation Guides
Analytic Evaluation Guides

Possible responses are overprinted on this reduced facsimile only. Use Writing Process Transparencies to interact with your students on the ideas that interest them.

Publishing

Make a bibliography for your report. In it, list all your sources in alphabetical order. Write authors' last names first. Then look at the ideas for sharing your report.

Bibliography
1. "Eclipse." Encyclopedia of Space.
2. "Eclipses Rarely Seen." Space Report, March 9, 1987.
3. Kahn, B.J. Eclipse! Morristown: Burdett, 1986.

A Total Eclipse

Few people ever witness a total eclipse of the sun. An eclipse happens when the moon gets between the sun and the earth. When the moon hides the sun completely, the eclipse is total.

When an eclipse starts, an edge of the sun disappears. It looks like a bite out of the sun that keeps growing. When the eclipse is total, the sky is dark. You can even see the stars. Minutes later, the sun starts to reappear. It soon grows to its full size again.

You will probably never see a total eclipse. Such an event is very rare. It lasts only a short time. An eclipse is total for only a few minutes.

PUBLISHING IDEAS

Share Aloud	Share in Writing
Read your report aloud to your classmates. Ask them to note facts about your topic. Later ask your audience to tell you which facts they found most interesting.	Help to make a file of "Amazing But True" reports. Place each report in its own folder and file alphabetically by title. The file should include a sheet titled "Readers' Comments."

WRITING PROCESS: Research Report 〈325〉

Holistic Evaluation Guidelines

A research report of **average** quality will:
1. use research information to describe an unusual natural event
2. arrange facts and details in an orderly way

A research report of **above-average** quality may:
1. begin in an unusual way or end with a particularly strong summary
2. include vivid details

A research report of **below-average** quality may:
1. lack logical organization or correct facts
2. attempt to cover too broad a topic

PROCESS CHECK At the completion of the Publishing stage, students should be able to answer *yes* to these questions:
- Have I shared my writing with an audience?
- Have readers shared reactions with me?
- Have I thought about what I especially liked in this writing? Or about what was particularly difficult?
- Have I thought about what I would like to work on the next time I write?

Encourage students to keep a log or journal of their own and their readers' reactions.

IDEA BANK

Spelling and Mechanics Connection

You may wish to remind students of proofreading ideas already introduced in their textbooks:
- Read through a window, p. 44
- Check for poorly formed letters, p. 100
- Trade with a partner, p. 158
- Check one thing at a time, p. 216
- Read backwards, p. 270
- Use a ruler, p. 324

Spelling ◆ If you wish to include spelling instruction with this lesson, then refer to the Spelling Guide on pages 490–492, the Index, or the *Spelling Connection* booklet.

Mechanics ◆ If you wish to include mechanics instruction with this lesson, then refer to the Glossary, the Index, or the *Revising and Proofreading Transparencies*.

5. PUBLISHING

Before students share their work with others, you may wish to have them make a bibliography for their reports.

Oral Sharing If students choose to share their writing orally, invite class discussion after each sharing. Encourage students to give polite feedback and to explain why they feel as they do. You may wish to have students read their reports aloud to a small group or to the entire class.

Written Sharing If students choose to share their writing by displaying it, help them prepare an "Amazing but True" file. Set aside a specific time during class when students may go to the file, choose a report, and read it. Encourage students to respond to the reports that they read by recording their reactions on the "Readers' Comments" sheets.

325

Curriculum Connection

Writing Across the Curriculum

Explain to students that scientists plan their research in an organized way. Tell students they will use an order circle to help them sort their ideas about what is important to learn about volcanoes.

You may wish to remind students that they have used an order circle as a strategy for researching in the Critical Thinking lesson, in their response to the literature selection, and in the Writing Process lesson.

Writing to Learn

To help students get started, have them suggest important things to learn about volcanoes. Write their responses on the chalkboard.

You may wish to have students with limited English proficiency point to a cutaway diagram of a volcano as you provide the English names for the various parts of the volcano.

Help students use their science books or books from their classroom library to find information about volcanoes.

Writing in Your Journal

When they have finished writing, have students read their earlier journal entries. Encourage them to discuss what they have learned about the theme, and to observe how their writing has changed or improved.

Remind students that their journals have many purposes. Besides paragraphs and stories, they can write questions, story ideas, or thoughts and reflections on a subject. Suggest to them that entries in their journals may provide ideas for later writing.

 ## Writing Across the Curriculum
Social Studies

Recently you wrote a research report about an unusual natural event. You may have used an order circle to help organize the information. You can also put in order the facts you learn in social studies. For example, you can arrange facts to show time order or order of importance.

Writing to Learn

Think and Decide ◆ Many books have been written about volcanic eruptions. Some people spend their lives studying volcanoes. What do you think are the most important things we can learn about volcanoes? Use an order circle to help sort your ideas.

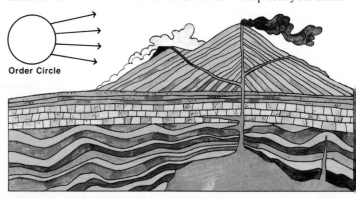

Order Circle

Write ◆ Make a list of important things to learn about volcanoes. Tell which you think is most important and why.

 ## Writing in Your Journal

In the Writer's Warm-up you wrote about volcanoes. Throughout this unit you learned much about volcanic eruptions. Browse through the pages. What is the most startling thing you learned? Write about it in your journal.

326   Curriculum Connection

ESSENTIAL LANGUAGE SKILLS
This lesson provides opportunities to:

LISTENING ◆ listen actively and attentively ◆ follow the logical organization of an oral presentation

SPEAKING ◆ participate in group discussions ◆ make organized oral presentations

READING ◆ recall specific facts and details that support the main idea and/or conclusion ◆ use graphic sources for information, such as charts ◆ respond to various forms of literature ◆ select books for individual needs and interests

WRITING ◆ select and narrow a topic for a specific purpose ◆ expand topics by collecting information from a variety of sources ◆ adapt information to accomplish a specific purpose with a particular audience ◆ keep journals, logs, or notebooks to express feelings, record ideas, discover new knowledge, and free the imagination

LANGUAGE ◆ use language to imagine ◆ recognize ways in which language can be used to influence others

BOOKS TO ENJOY

Read More About It

How Did We Find Out About Volcanoes?

by Isaac Asimov

You can learn about volcanoes because scientists share information. Isaac Asimov explains some of the mysteries of volcano study.

Pompeii: Exploring a Roman Ghost Town

by Ron and Nancy Goor

When Mount Vesuvius erupted in 79 A.D., lava and mudslides buried Pompeii. This book explains how scientists have pieced together a story of life in Pompeii before the terrible eruption.

Geology *by Dougal Dixon*

Geology is the study of the physical features of the earth. Geologists want to learn about what lies deep inside the earth. They examine ores, rocks, and minerals. Volcanoes give geologists a kind of window to the inner earth.

Book Report Idea   Scientist's Log Report

When scientists do experiments, they write down the steps they follow and what they find. For your next book report, try giving facts and details in the form of a scientist's report.

Create a Scientist's Log

Make up a form similar to the one shown here. Fill in information about your book. Give facts and details in a clear, exact way.

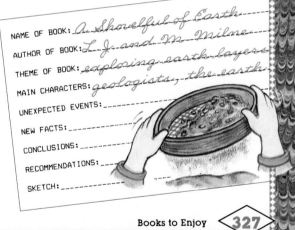

NAME OF BOOK: *A Shovelful of Earth*
AUTHOR OF BOOK: *L. J. and M. Milne*
THEME OF BOOK: *exploring earth layers*
MAIN CHARACTERS: *geologists, the earth*
UNEXPECTED EVENTS: _____
NEW FACTS: _____
CONCLUSIONS: _____
RECOMMENDATIONS: _____
SKETCH: _____

Books to Enjoy ◁ 327 ▷

Books to Enjoy

OBJECTIVES
To appreciate a variety of literature
To share a book through a creative activity

Read More About It

Call students' attention to Read More About It and discuss theme-related books. Point out that the books listed here contain stories about volcanoes and about geologists' interest in them. Encourage students to mention other titles that deal with these topics. Encourage students to examine pictures and jacket illustrations of books in the classroom to find books they will enjoy reading.

Book Report Idea

You may wish to have students use the book report form provided in the back of their textbooks. Book Report Idea presents a lively alternative way for interested students to share books they have read.

You may wish to share the reports with the class or in small groups. Have students compare the information in the log reports and decide which logs contain the clearest, most complete facts and details. Students may wish to post their log reports in a science corner or a book review corner.

Integrated Language Arts Project

The **Integrated Language Arts Project** on pages T522–T523 may be used with this unit.

Unit 6
Review

REVIEW OR TEST

You may wish to use the Unit Review as a review of the unit skills before administering the Unit Posttest, or you may wish to use the Unit Review in lieu of the Unit Posttest.

REVIEW PROCEDURES

The lesson pages that are reviewed are listed beside the heading of each segment. You may wish to choose one of the procedures listed below for using the pages with the Unit Review exercises.

Review/Evaluate Have students restudy the lesson pages before doing the Unit Review exercises.

Open-Book Review Allow students to refer to the lesson pages if they need to while they are doing the Unit Review exercises.

Evaluate/Review Have students do the Unit Review exercises, then turn to the lesson pages to restudy concepts for which incorrect responses are given.

ADDITIONAL REVIEW AND PRACTICE

For additional review and practice, turn to the Extra Practice pages at the end of the unit.

328

Unit 6

Adverbs and Adjectives
pages 284–291

A. Write each sentence. Underline the adverb.

1. The carpenter worked <u>carefully</u>.
2. She <u>accurately</u> measured everything.
3. She <u>easily</u> finished sawing the wood.
4. She <u>accidentally</u> hit her thumb with the hammer.
5. She groaned <u>loudly</u>.
6. She went back to work <u>immediately</u>.
7. <u>Soon</u> the cabinet was completed.
8. She smiled <u>contentedly</u> at her work.
9. Then she rested <u>happily</u> in a chair.

B. Write the correct form of the adverb in parentheses ( ).

10. Ron's essay is (neatly) *more neatly* written than Judy's.
11. Maggie rises (early) *earlier* than Fran.
12. My box is the (densely) *most densely* packed of all.
13. Terri runs (fast) *faster* than Charles.
14. Andrew chopped the vegetables (quickly) *more quickly* than Steven.
15. The (hard) *harder* I work, the more I learn.
16. I go to the library (often) *more often* on Thursday than on any other day.
17. Jeanne trains (energetically) *more energetically* than any other team member.
18. Pablo rides the (skillfully) *most skillfully* of all the cowboys.

C. Write the adverb that describes each underlined adjective or adverb.

19. This is a <u>rather</u> difficult problem.
20. <u>Quite</u> suddenly the rain stopped.
21. That is an <u>incredible</u> hard riddle.
22. Helga is <u>unbelievably</u> brilliant.
23. I am <u>totally</u> amazed by your reply.
24. It is an <u>unusually</u> cool evening.
25. Mr. Otis drives <u>fairly</u> skillfully.
26. The reward was <u>justly</u> deserved.
27. The band played <u>extremely</u> loudly.
28. The door was <u>partially</u> open.
29. A <u>very</u> tiny mouse darted by us.
30. We chased <u>quite</u> frantically after it.

D. Write each sentence. Choose the word in parentheses ( ) that correctly completes the sentence.

31. I whistle (bad, <u>badly</u>).
32. I feel (<u>bad</u>, badly) about my lack of skill.
33. Jenna whistles (good, <u>well</u>).
34. She has always been a (<u>good</u>, well) whistler.
35. She (proud, <u>proudly</u>) shows her skill.
36. I make a (<u>terrible</u>, terribly) noise when I try.
37. I know I sound (<u>awful</u>, awfully).
38. When my dog hears me, it howls (mournful, <u>mournfully</u>).
39. It (complete, <u>completely</u>) covers its ears with its paws.
40. I feel (<u>terrible</u>, terribly) about the whole thing.
41. My brother (thoughtful, <u>thoughtfully</u>) tries to console me.
42. I am (<u>fortunate</u>, fortunately) to have a brother who understands.

328 Unit Review

Negative Words *pages 292–293*

E. Write each sentence. Choose the word in parentheses ( ) that correctly completes the sentence.

43. Marc and Tammy don't have (no, <u>any</u>) homework to do.

44. No one can (<u>ever</u>, never) surpass Tina's skills on the diving board.

45. Doesn't (<u>anybody</u>, nobody) know the answer?

46. There (was, <u>wasn't</u>) no one at the park when I arrived.

47. I (won't, <u>will</u>) never go back to that place again.

48. None of your solutions (<u>are</u>, aren't) correct.

49. Sue hasn't done (<u>any</u>, none) of her homework.

50. There (<u>is</u>, isn't) nowhere Ms. Townsend hasn't visited.

51. Can't (<u>anybody</u>, nobody) help me?

52. I don't (<u>ever</u>, never) want to go through that again!

Compounds *pages 294–295*

F. Write the following sentences. Underline the compounds.

53. My uncle is a <u>police officer</u>.

54. His <u>sister-in-law</u> is a doctor.

55. The next bus goes <u>downtown</u>.

56. The <u>afternoon</u> sun made us squint.

57. The children were playing <u>outdoors</u>.

58. That noise is giving me a <u>headache</u>.

59. Have you seen the new <u>high school</u>?

60. I love my new <u>beanbag</u> chair.

61. The other car has the <u>right-of-way</u>.

62. This <u>tablecloth</u> is easy to clean.

Using an Encyclopedia *pages 310–311*

G. Write the key word in each question. Then write the number of the encyclopedia that has the article. Use the illustration on page 310 to find the number.

63. What are some uses for <u>sand</u>? 15

64. Who invented the game of <u>baseball</u>? 2

65. What causes a <u>tornado</u>? 17

66. How many automobiles and trucks are there in <u>Iceland</u>? 9

67. What state is the leading producer of <u>peaches</u>? 13

68. Are there different kinds of <u>algae</u>? 1

69. What is the nickname for <u>Wichita</u>, Kansas? 18

70. How many bones are there in an adult <u>human</u> body? 8

71. Where was the final battle of the <u>Revolutionary War</u> fought? 14

72. What famous musical piece did Johann <u>Strauss</u>, Jr., write? 16

Outlining *pages 314–315*

H. Copy the outline below about yeast bread. Beside each line, write *title, main topic,* or *subtopic*.

73.   Yeast Bread title

74. I. Kinds of yeast bread main topic

75.   A. Pan bread subtopic

76.   B. Hearth bread subtopic

77. II. How yeast bread is made main topic

78.   A. Commercial bakeries subtopic

79.   B. Home bakeries subtopic

80.   C. Conventional bread making subtopic

81.   D. Continuous bread making subtopic

Unit Review **329**

Cumulative Review

OBJECTIVES
To review skills taught in Units 1 through 6

CUMULATIVE REVIEW
The Cumulative Review reviews basic skills from the first through the present unit. The lesson pages that are reviewed are listed beside the heading for each segment. You may wish to have students restudy the lesson pages listed before assigning the Cumulative Review exercises.

ADDITIONAL REVIEW AND PRACTICE
For additional review and practice of skills, you may wish to assign the appropriate Extra Practice pages found at the end of each unit.

CUMULATIVE REVIEW

UNIT 1: Sentences *pages 6–15*

A. Write the complete subject of each sentence. Underline the simple subject. Write *(You)* if the simple subject is understood. The complete subject is underlined once, the simple subject twice.

1. The circus came to town yesterday.
2. Tell me all about it!(You)
3. A group of elephants marched in the parade.
4. A baby elephant was very appealing.
5. Look at those fantastic acrobats!(You)
6. The clowns in tramp costumes did funny tricks.
7. Let me have the souvenir booklet.(You)
8. I will always remember this wonderful circus!
9. (You) Come to the show with me next year.

B. Write the complete predicate of each of the following sentences. Underline the simple predicate. The complete predicate is underlined once, the simple predicate twice.

10. Helene is training for the swimming and diving meet.
11. She swims for two hours every day.
12. She is doing the backstroke now.
13. My friend Gary has practiced a daring new dive.
14. He performs it from a high platform.
15. He will perform at the sports meet next week.
16. All his friends will attend.
17. Many fine divers will compete.
18. Donna competed in last year's meet.

UNIT 2: Capital Letters and Periods *pages 66–69*

C. Write the sentences. Capitalize the proper nouns. Write the abbreviations correctly.

19. Take Wilson ave. to rte. 56 and then turn left.
20. Our family is going to Orono, maine, on aug. 15.
21. I read a newspaper article by phil cole, jr., my uncle harry's friend.
22. The committee will meet again on tues. at 6 p.m. sharp.
23. I am going to a lecture by prof. eric broudy.
24. My uncle's family will arrive from new mexico on fri. aug. 2.
25. My mother and mrs. fay linden often play tennis together.
26. The traffic on thompson blvd. during rush hour has gotten worse.

UNIT 2: Commas *pages 90–91*

D. Write the sentences. Add commas where they are needed.

27. Jason, please hand me the camera.
28. Yes, I am the one who wrote the letter.
29. Peter, Mary, and Steve went to the softball game.
30. We are grateful, Dennis, for your assistance.
31. The library card catalog lists the author's name as McKenzie, Ellen.
32. This Korean dish includes meat, vegetables, noodles, and spices.
33. No, we are not going to the game.
34. Well, Jim, you certainly made a mess!

330 CUMULATIVE REVIEW: Units 1–6

UNIT 3: Verbs   *pages 116–133*

E. Write each sentence. Choose the verb in parentheses ( ) that correctly completes the sentence.

35. Mr. Sherman (work, <u>works</u>) in the new office building.
36. The dog has (<u>come</u>, came) home.
37. We (<u>did</u>, done) our chores.
38. Tara and Lori (practices, <u>practice</u>) their duets every day.
39. I have (grew, <u>grown</u>) an inch since last summer.
40. Who (<u>wrote</u>, written) this note?
41. Sally has (wore, <u>worn</u>) this dress before.
42. I shall (<u>give</u>, gives) the letter to my sister.
43. John will (<u>take</u>, took) a seat in the back row.

UNIT 4: Pronouns   *pages 176–185*

F. Write each sentence. Choose the pronoun in parentheses ( ) that correctly completes the sentences.

44. Will (<u>they</u>, them) follow directions carefully?
45. Denise and (<u>I</u>, me) like salads.
46. Ms. Greene asked (they, <u>them</u>) to be quiet.
47. Will Jackie and Mike bring (<u>their</u>, theirs) parents?
48. The victory is (their, <u>theirs</u>).
49. Alison told (we, <u>us</u>) a funny story.
50. (<u>We</u>, Us) couldn't stop laughing.
51. Give the paintbrush to (I, <u>me</u>).
52. Richard and (<u>she</u>, her) tied for first place.

UNITS 5 and 6: Adjectives and Adverbs   *pages 234–241, 284–291*

G. Write each sentence. Choose the word in parentheses ( ) that correctly completes the sentence. Then write whether the word is an adjective or an adverb.

53. Mr. Chao is a (<u>proud</u>, proudly) man. *adj.*
54. This is a (real, <u>really</u>) good song. *adv*
55. Davy Crockett was a (<u>real</u>, really) person. *adj*
56. Sam ate his (<u>usual</u>, usually) lunch. *adj.*
57. Martha (usual, <u>usually</u>) does her homework before dinner. *adv*
58. The (<u>energetic</u>, energetically) child cleaned the bicycle. *adj.*
59. The child behaved (bad, <u>badly</u>). *adv*
60. I have a (<u>bad</u>, badly) headache. *adj*

UNIT 6: Negative Words   *pages 292–293*

H. Write each sentence. Use the correct word in parentheses.

61. No person has (<u>ever</u>, never) run a mile in less than three minutes.
62. Can't (<u>anyone</u>, no one) help me carry this box upstairs?
63. There (<u>is</u>, isn't) no reason to be afraid.
64. Nothing (<u>will</u>, won't) happen unless you make it happen.
65. I couldn't find my pet rabbit (<u>anywhere</u>, nowhere).
66. None of this has (<u>anything</u>, nothing) to do with the subject.
67. We (<u>have</u>, haven't) no reason to doubt his word.
68. You (won't, <u>will</u>) never finish your homework by watching television.

CUMULATIVE REVIEW: Units 1–6   **331**

Language Puzzlers

Unit 6

ANSWERS

Tom Swifties
Tom Swifties will vary.

Pig-Latin Puzzler

Susan:	We went to the movies yesterday.
Joanne:	What did you see?
Susan:	We saw *Bambi* again, for the third time.
Joanne:	How was it?
Susan:	Wonderful! I cried quietly at the sad parts and laughed so loudly at the funny ones.

Unit 6 Challenge

Tom Swifties

Tom Swifties are puns that are based on adverbs. Using different adverbs, write some Tom Swifties like the following.

1. "It hasn't rained in a month," said Tom dryly.
2. "You're late. It's already ten after ten," said Tom tensely.
3. "I think I have chickenpox," said Tom infectiously.
4. "May I have a spaniel for my birthday?" asked Tom doggedly.
5. "I didn't mean to break the window," said Tom fragilely.

Pig-Latin Puzzler

Pig Latin is a secret way of talking. In pig Latin the first consonant sound of each word is moved to the end and *-ay* is added. Figure out these messages. Then write your own message in pig Latin. Use some adverbs in your message.

Susan: E-way ent-way o-tay the ovies-may esterday-yay.

Joanne: At-whay id-day ou-yay ee-say?

Susan: E-way aw-say *ambi-Bay* again, or-fay the ird-thay ime-tay.

Joanne: Ow-hay as-way it?

Susan: Onderful-way! I ied-cray ietly-quay at the ad-say arts-pay and aughed-lay o-say oudly-lay at the unny-fay ones.

Unit 6 Extra Practice

1 Writing with Adverbs
p. 284

A. In the sentences below, the verbs are underlined. Find the adverb in each sentence and write it.

1. The group accidentally found a cave.
2. They searched inside.
3. The explorers quietly admired the cavern.
4. The tunnel sloped downward.
5. Tourists frequently visit Carlsbad Caverns.
6. Three children approached the cave cautiously.
7. Caves sometimes contain lakes.
8. Cave explorers test their equipment carefully.
9. Swarms of bats flew overhead.
10. Explorers ordinarily carry flashlight batteries.
11. She marked her trail clearly.
12. We started our journey early.
13. Water continually follows cracks in the rocks.
14. The water slowly carves the rock.
15. The cave's size always amazes tourists.
16. Beautiful rock formations rise upward.

B. Write each sentence and underline the adverb. Write *how*, *when*, or *where* to show what the adverb tells about the verb.

EXAMPLE: We never found the mysterious crystal cave.

ANSWER: We never found the mysterious crystal cave. (when)

17. Miki often brings a compass.
18. Ali studied the map closely.
19. The underground river flowed nearby.
20. Our voices echoed strangely.
21. Cave explorers usually wear sturdy boots.
22. The walls of the cave plunged downward.
23. They gladly gave her a hand.
24. My favorite rock formation will appear soon.
25. We finally reached the end of the tunnel.
26. Our friends were waiting for us outside.

Extra Practice **333**

Extra Practice

Unit 6

ANSWERS
Writing with Adverbs
A. 1. accidentally
    2. inside
    3. quietly
    4. downward
    5. frequently
    6. cautiously
    7. sometimes
    8. carefully
    9. overhead
  10. ordinarily
  11. clearly
  12. early
  13. continually
  14. slowly
  15. always
  16. upward

B. 17. often, when
  18. closely, how
  19. nearby, where
  20. strangely, how
  21. usually, when
  22. downward, where
  23. gladly, how
  24. soon, when
  25. finally, when
  26. outside, where

Extra Practice and Challenge

For those students who need additional grammar practice have them refer to these pages. **The practice exercises progress in difficulty from Easy to Average. Practice A is Easy. Practice B is Average.** Difficult concepts requiring more practice have additional Exercises C and D at the Average level.
We do not recommend these exercises for students who have mastered the skill in the basic lesson. Those students should do the **Challenge** word puzzles on page 332.

Extra Practice

334

Adverbs That Compare

A.
1. more often, most often
2. better, best
3. more densely, most densely
4. harder, hardest
5. more neatly, most neatly

B.
6. more gently
7. wider
8. more thickly
9. more frequently
10. sooner
11. drier

C.
12. earliest
13. fastest
14. highest
15. highest
16. most gradually
17. lowest
18. most commonly
19. most pleasantly

D.
20. better
21. worst
22. worse
23. better
24. better
25. best
26. worse
27. best

2 Adverbs That Compare

p. 28(

A. For each adverb below, write the form that is used to compare two actions. Then write the form that is used to compare three or more actions.

    1. often   **2.** well   **3.** densely   **4.** hard   **5.** neatly

B. Write the sentences. For each adverb in parentheses ( ), add *more* or use the *-er* form.

  6. The Sacramento River flows (gently) in late spring.
  7. The river valley opens (wide) between the Coast Ranges.
  8. Flowers grow (thickly) during the rainy season.
  9. The river overflows (frequently) in that season than now.
 10. The valley turns green (soon) than the mountaintop.
 11. Moist chinook winds over the Sierra Nevada mountains blow (dry) on the eastern slopes.

C. Write each sentence. For each adverb in parentheses ( ), add *most* or use the *-est* form.

 12. Trappers arrived (early) of all the explorers.
 13. That area grew (fast) because gold was discovered there.
 14. Which peak rises (high) in this range?
 15. Mount Shasta rises (high) in the Cascade Range.
 16. The mountains slope the (gradually) on the east side.
 17. The elevation drops (low) at Death Valley.
 18. These are the (commonly) grown flowers in warm weathe
 19. The breeze blows (pleasantly) on the mountain slopes.

D. Write the sentences. Use the correct form of *well* or *badly* to complete each sentence.

 20. This guide followed the trail (well) than that one.
 21. Our party rode the (badly) of the three groups.
 22. The horses managed (badly) than the mules on this trail.
 23. We understood the map (well) than the scout did.
 24. Ramon enjoyed hiking even (well) than riding.
 25. Who remembers this trip the (well) of all?
 26. Last year's vacation ended (badly) than this year's.
 27. Could next year's be the (well) of all?

Adverbs Before Adjectives and Other Adverbs

p. 288

A. Write each sentence. Then write the adverb that describes the underlined adjective or adverb.

1. The Rockies are incredibly <u>beautiful</u> mountains.
2. The temperature feels slightly <u>cooler</u> as you climb higher.
3. Even in early summer, snowstorms occur quite <u>suddenly</u>.
4. Unusually <u>cold</u> weather can be dangerous.
5. You can't be too <u>careful</u> in the mountains.
6. The Rocky Mountains rise so <u>dramatically</u> above the plain.
7. The bighorn sheep is a very <u>rare</u> animal.
8. The sheep jumps so <u>fast</u> it is hard to see.
9. Idaho is justly <u>famous</u> for its sheep ranches.
10. Sheep are very <u>hardy</u> animals.
11. They can survive remarkably <u>cold</u> weather.
12. In summer the shepherds move their flocks rather <u>quickly</u>.
13. Fairly <u>often</u> they go from hot valleys to cool mountains.
14. These herders almost <u>always</u> use horses to move the sheep.
15. Cattle also graze in the unusually <u>lush</u> meadows.
16. Potato farms are certainly <u>common</u> in southern Idaho.
17. An incredibly <u>small</u> amount of the crop is eaten fresh.
18. Quite <u>often</u> the potatoes become frozen french fries.
19. Totally <u>vacant</u> towns dot the state's mining country.
20. Silver City was unbelievably <u>wealthy</u> at one time.
21. Now wind blows through the completely <u>empty</u> streets.
22. Skiing attracts a considerably <u>large</u> number of tourists.
23. Idahoans like their extremely <u>varied</u> way of life.

B. Write each sentence. Use the adverbs below to complete the sentences.

quite   so   extremely   too   incredibly   wildly

24. Good weather is ____ important to a potato farmer.
25. ____ much rain in early spring can ruin the crop.
26. Tourism has become ____ successful in Idaho.
27. Rafting trips on the Snake River can be ____ exciting.
28. Stretches of ____ rolling white water are scary and fun.
29. Mountain climbing is hard work but ____ rewarding.

Extra Practice

Adverbs Before Adjectives and Other Adverbs

A.
1. incredibly
2. slightly
3. quite
4. Unusually
5. too
6. so
7. very
8. so
9. justly
10. very
11. remarkably
12. rather
13. Fairly
14. almost
15. unusually
16. certainly
17. incredibly
18. Quite
19. Totally
20. unbelievably
21. completely
22. considerably
23. extremely

B. Answers will vary. The following are possible answers.
24. so
25. Too
26. quite
27. incredibly
28. wildly
29. extremely

Extra Practice and Challenge

For those students who need additional grammar practice have them refer to these pages. **The practice exercises progress in difficulty from Easy to Average. Practice A is Easy. Practice B is Average.** Difficult concepts requiring more practice have additional Exercises C and D at the Average level.

We do not recommend these exercises for students who have mastered the skill in the basic lesson. Those students should do the **Challenge** word puzzles on page 332.

Extra Practice

Using Adverbs and Adjectives

A.
1. remarkably
2. extremely
3. gradually
4. commonly
5. badly
6. well
7. quickly
8. smart
9. occasionally
10. playful
11. angrily
12. fairly
13. slightly
14. usually
15. real
16. terribly
17. thick
18. carefully
19. happily
20. proud
21. fine

B.
22. well, adjective
23. good, adjective
24. badly, adverb
25. well, adverb
26. bad, adjective

4 Using Adverbs and Adjectives *p. 290*

A. Write the word in parentheses ( ) that correctly completes each sentence.

1. Koko is a (remarkable, remarkably) clever gorilla.
2. Koko's teacher is (extreme, extremely) patient.
3. Koko (gradual, gradually) learns the Ameslan language.
4. Ameslan, or American Sign Language, is the hand speech (common, commonly) used by about 200,000 deaf Ameri...
5. At first Koko made the signs (bad, badly).
6. Now she uses her fingers (good, well).
7. Koko's fingers move (quick, quickly) to make the signs.
8. She is extremely (smart, smartly).
9. She (occasional, occasionally) signs two words at once.
10. Koko often is (playful, playfully).
11. Sometimes she gestures (angry, angrily).
12. She is distracted (fair, fairly) easily.
13. She cleans things with a (slight, slightly) damp sponge.
14. Afterwards she (usual, usually) rips up the sponge.
15. Koko has never seen a (real, really) alligator.
16. But toy alligators frighten her (terrible, terribly).
17. Koko likes sandwiches that are (thick, thickly).
18. She brushes her teeth (careful, carefully).
19. She often smiles (happy, happily) in the mirror.
20. The teacher is (proud, proudly) of Koko's success.
21. Koko refers to herself as a (fine, finely) gorilla.

B. Choose the word in parentheses ( ) that correctly completes each sentence. Write the sentence. Then write whether *good*, *well*, *bad*, or *badly* is an adjective or an adverb in the sentence.

EXAMPLE: Koko needs a (good, well) night's sleep.
ANSWER: Koko needs a good night's sleep. (adjective)

22. Koko stays (good, well) by getting plenty of sleep.
23. A substitute teacher does a (good, well) job.
24. Unfortunately Koko performs (bad, badly) for him.
25. They do not work (good, well) together.
26. The substitute teacher feels (bad, badly).

5 **Using Negative Words**

p. 292

Write the negative word in each sentence. Tell which negatives are contractions.

1. In science, Mandy never gets lower than an A.
2. Mandy will not delay her science experiment.
3. "No extra equipment is needed," she said.
4. Didn't anyone know what to do first?
5. Nobody answered Mandy's question.
6. She put salt in the water till no more dissolved.
7. Now she doesn't know where to put the container.
8. Nothing will happen unless she heats it up.

Write the sentences. Underline the negative words.

9. Couldn't anyone guess what would happen next?
10. We haven't seen anything in the glass.
11. Perhaps none of the water has evaporated.
12. Actually I have never seen crystals form.
13. You surely need no help with this!
14. Nobody could understand the directions.
15. Doesn't anyone know how to solve the problem?
16. No one can fold a piece of paper in this shape.
17. Hasn't anybody tried yet?
18. I could find nothing to use as a funnel.

Write the word in parentheses ( ) that correctly completes each sentence. Avoid double negatives.

19. There is no tubing (nowhere, anywhere).
20. No one will (never, ever) be able to put this together.
21. There (was, wasn't) no place to work on my project.
22. Nothing (won't, will) happen if you change the water in the fish bowl.
23. Hasn't (no one, anyone) fed the fish yet?
24. None of this (isn't, is) visible without a microscope.
25. Couldn't (anyone, no one) see the blood vessels?
26. We haven't written down (any, none) of the steps.
27. We (won't, will) never be able to do this again.
28. There (was, wasn't) no need to check the results.

Using Negative Words

A.
1. never
2. not
3. No
4. Didn't, contraction
5. Nobody
6. no
7. doesn't, contraction
8. Nothing

B.
9. Couldn't
10. haven't
11. none
12. never
13. no
14. Nobody
15. Doesn't
16. No
17. Hasn't
18. nothing

C.
19. anywhere
20. ever
21. was
22. will
23. anyone
24. is
25. anyone
26. any
27. will
28. was

Extra Practice and Challenge

For those students who need additional grammar practice have them refer to these pages. **The practice exercises progress in difficulty from Easy to Average. Practice A is Easy. Practice B is Average.** Difficult concepts requiring more practice have additional Exercises C and D at the Average level.
We do not recommend these exercises for students who have mastered the skill in the basic lesson. Those students should do the **Challenge** word puzzles on page 332.

TWO-PART

flexibility

Unit 7 Overview

books

ON UNIT THEME

USING LANGUAGE TO CREATE

EASY

Fly with the Wind, Flow with the Water by Ann Atwood. Scribner. This collection of haiku, illustrated with spectacular color photographs, depicts movement in nature: whirling leaves, curling waves, and swooping birds.

Sam's Place: Poems from the Country by Lilian Moore. Atheneum. These free verse poems, told from the Allegheny Mountains, reflect the beauty of the natural world through the changing seasons.

AVERAGE

One Day in the Prairie by Jean Craighead George. Crowell. The author gives a lyrical description of a day on a prairie wildlife refuge when its inhabitants sense an approaching tornado and seek protection from it.

The Forgetful Wishing Well by X. J. Kennedy. Atheneum. Seventy humorous poems tell about growing up, city life, animals, the seasons, and interesting people. **American Library Association Notable Children's Book.**

CHALLENGING

Drawing from Nature by Jim Arnosky. Lothrop. This book shows how to draw subjects from nature in the categories of water, land, plants, and animals. **Christopher Award.**

Room for Me and a Mountain Lion: Poetry of Open Space selected by Nancy Larrick. Evans. This is a collection of nature poems arranged under such headings as *Woods* and *Mountains*.

READ-ALOUDS

Born Free: A Lioness of Two Worlds by Joy Adamson. Random. In this classic a natural scientist describes how she raises a lioness and then retrains her for release back into the wilds of Kenya.

The Daywatchers by Peter Parnall. Macmillan. An award-winning artist vividly describes, in text and drawings, his experiences observing American birds of prey.

UNIT SEVEN

USING LANGUAGE TO CREATE

——— PART ONE ———

Unit Theme *Nature*

Language Awareness Prepositions

——— PART TWO ———

Literature *Poetry*

A Reason for Writing Creating

Writing IN YOUR JOURNAL

WRITER'S WARM-UP ♦ How has nature inspired you? Have you ever tried to describe an unusual rock, leaf, or flower you saw? Do billowy clouds sometimes take on shapes before your eyes? Maybe you have seen a rock formation that reminded you of an old sailor's wrinkled, leathery face. Perhaps a vivid shadow of a tree startled you once. Think about all the aspects of nature that puzzle you. Then write in your journal. Write about nature and what it means to you.

start with WRITING IN YOUR JOURNAL

Writers' Warm-up is designed to help students activate prior knowledge of the unit theme, "Nature." Whether you begin instruction with Part 1 or Part 2, encourage students to focus attention on the illustration on page 338 of their textbooks. Encourage them to discuss what they see. Then have a volunteer read aloud the **Writers' Warm-up** on page 339. Have students write their thoughts in their journals. You may wish to tell them that they will refer to this writing in the first lesson of Part 1, in the Grammar-Writing Connection, and in the Curriculum Connection.

THEN START WITH part 1

Language Awareness: Prepositions
Developmental lessons focus on the concept of prepositions. Each lesson is carefully constructed not only to help students learn the concept well but also to help build interest and background knowledge for the thinking, reading, and writing they will do in Part 2. The last lesson in Part 1 is a vocabulary lesson with which students learn about synonyms and antonyms. The Grammar-Writing Connection that follows serves as a bridge to Part 2, encouraging students to work together to apply their new language skills at the sentence level of writing.

...OR WITH part 2

A Reason for Writing: Creating is the focus of Part 2. First, students learn a thinking strategy for creating. Then they read and respond to a selection of poetry on which they may model their writing. Developmental composition lessons, including "Reading Poetry Aloud," a speaking and listening lesson, all reflect the selections and culminate in the Writing Process lesson. There a "Grammar Check," a "Word Choice" hint, and proofreading strategies help you focus on single traits for remediation or instruction through the lessons in Part 1. The unit ends with Curriculum Connection and Books to Enjoy, which help students discover how their new skills apply to writing across the curriculum.

THEME BAR

CATEGORIES	Environments	Business/World of Work	Imagination	Communications/ Fine Arts	People	Science	Expressions	Social Studies
THEMES	UNIT 1 Farm Life	UNIT 2 Handicrafts	UNIT 3 Tall Tales	UNIT 4 The Visual Arts	UNIT 5 Lasting Impressions	UNIT 6 Volcanoes	UNIT 7 Nature	UNIT 8 Animal Habitats
PACING	1 month	1 month	1 month	1 month	1 month	1 month	1 month	1 month

Build background knowledge of the unit theme, "Nature," by reading aloud these poems to your class. At the same time you will be building your students' knowledge of our rich heritage of fine literature. You may wish to use the "Notes for Listening" on the following page before and after reading aloud.

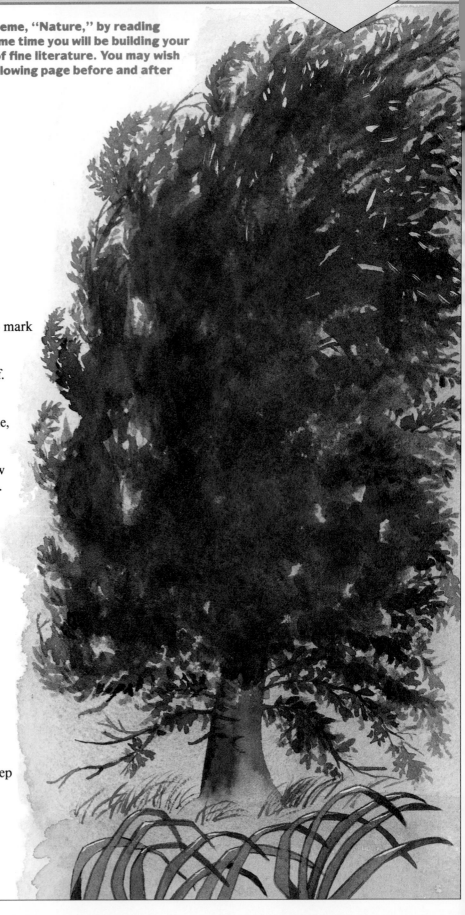

Beech

BY DAVID McCORD

I like the circling proud old family beech,
The carefully tailored cut of his grey bark;
His lower branches glad enough to reach
Straight out and touch the earth and leave no mark
Against the sky; the way his twigs turn up,
Like fingers of the hand, each barbel cup
Of gold from which will come the bronzy leaf.
His sails and topsails set without a <u>reef</u>,
All summer now he sways across the lawn;
And when from other trees the leaves are gone,
He <u>furls</u> the faded paper his became.
Some flutter dryly mentioning his name.
If you should find them there when only snow
Is on the ground where most leaves had to go.

Silver

BY WALTER DE LA MARE

Slowly, silently, now the moon
Walks the night in her silver <u>shoon</u>;
This way, and that, she peers, and sees
Silver fruit upon silver trees;
One by one the <u>casements</u> catch
Her beams beneath the silvery thatch;
Couched in his kennel, like a log,
With paws of silver sleeps the dog;
From their shadowy <u>cote</u> the white breasts peep
Of doves in a silver-feathered sleep;
A harvest mouse goes scampering by,
With silver claws, and silver eye;
And moveless fish in the water gleam,
By silver reeds in a silver stream.

The Wind

BY PADRAIC COLUM

I saw the wind to-day;
I saw it in the pane
Of glass upon the wall;
A moving thing—'twas like
No bird with widening wing,
No mouse that runs along
The meal-bag under the beam.

I think it like a horse,
All black, with frightening mane,
That springs out of the earth,
And tramples on his way.
I saw it in the glass,
The shaking of a mane
A horse that no one rides.

NOTES FOR listening

Introducing the Selection

Relate to theme Tell students that the unit is "Nature." Encourage them to discuss what they picture in their mind's eye when they hear the word *nature*.

Discuss word meanings Explain to students that in the poetry, they will hear new words that they may not understand. Pronounce the words below and write them on the chalk-board. Give students the meaning of each word and tell them that knowing the words will help them to better understand the poetry.

reef the part of a sail that can be taken in or let out
furls rolls up
shoon an old-fashioned word for *shoes*
casements windows hung on hinges
cote a shelter for birds

Listening to the Selection

Set a purpose Tell students they are going to listen to three poems— "Beech" by David McCord, "Silver" by Walter de la Mare, and "The Wind" by Padraic Colum. Have students listen to discover how the poets see things in nature.

Starting with Literature

Discussing the Selection

Return to purpose After you have read the poems, discuss with students the way each poet sees something in nature. Have students tell what each poet is describing and how they think each poet feels about what is being described. Then have students make a more general statement, such as: *The poets help us see things in nature in a different way.*

UNIT 7 PLANNING AND PACING GUIDE

	LESSON TITLE	STUDENT TEXT				TEACHING RESOURCES		
1 DAY	Unit Opener	Student Lesson	Unit Review	Cumulative Review	Extra Practice	Reteaching Master	Practice Master	Testing Program
1 DAY	Writing with Prepositions	340–341	378	435	380, 381	57	57	T546
1 DAY	Prepositional Phrases	342–343	378	435	380, 382	58	58	T546
1 DAY	Prepositions and Adverbs	344–345	378	435	380, 384	59	59	T546
1 DAY	Using Prepositional Phrases	346–347	378	435	380, 385	60	60	T546
1 DAY	VOCABULARY ◆ Synonyms and Antonyms	348–349	379			61	61	T546
1 DAY	GRAMMAR-WRITING CONNECTION ◆ How to Expand Sentences with Prepositions	350–351						
	▶ THINK							
1 DAY	CREATIVE THINKING ◆ A Strategy for Creating	354–355	See also pages 359, 370, 376					
	▶ READ							
1 DAY	LITERATURE ◆ Poetry	356–359				Audio Library 2		
	▶ SPEAK/LISTEN							
1 DAY	SPEAKING AND LISTENING ◆ Reading Poetry Aloud	360–361				Video Library		
	▶ WRITE							
1 DAY	WRITING ◆ Repetition in Poetry	362–363				62	62	
1 DAY	WRITING ◆ Haiku	364–365				63	63	
1 DAY	READING-WRITING CONNECTION ◆ Focus on the Poet's Voice	366–367						
	▶ WRITING PROCESS ◆ Prewriting • Writing • Revising • Proofreading • Publishing							
4–5 DAYS	WRITING PROCESS ◆ Writing a Poem	368–375				Spelling Connection Transparencies		T555
1 DAY	CURRICULUM CONNECTION ◆ Writing for Music	376				Writing Across the Curriculum Guide		

Unit 7 Planning and Pacing Guide

Teacher Resource File
Reteaching Masters 57–63
Practice Masters 57–63
Evaluation and Testing Program, including Unit Pretest, Posttest, and Picture Prompt Writing Samples
Parent Letters in English and Spanish
Classroom Theme Posters
Writing Across the Curriculum Teacher Guide
Integrated Language Arts Projects with Masters (see pages T511–T529)
Spelling Corner, Teacher Edition
Writing Process Transparencies
Audio Library 1: Read-Alouds and Sing-Alouds

Also available:
Achieving English Proficiency Guide and Activities
Spelling Connection, Pupil Edition
Student Resource Books
Student Writing Portfolios
Professional Handbook
WORLD OF BOOKS Classroom Library

Multi-Modal Materials
Audio Library 1: Read-Alouds and Sing-Alouds
Audio Library 2: Listening to Literature
Video Library
Revising and Proofreading Transparencies
Fine Arts Transparencies with Viewing Booklet
Writing Process Transparencies
Writing Process Computer Program

LANGUAGE
game

Preposition Treasure Hunt

Objective: To use prepositions correctly
Materials: Construction paper
Write the following prepositions on the chalkboard:

about	at	beside	from	on	to
above	before	by	inside	out	under
across	behind	down	near	outside	up
after	below	during	of	over	with
around	beneath	for	off	through	without

Students are to imagine a setting for a treasure hunt. They may want to set their treasure hunt in an abandoned mine, in a mountain cave, or on a tiny island. Each student should imagine a place in the setting to hide a treasure. Then, using as many prepositions from the list as possible, students should write instructions for a treasure hunt. You may wish to have students draw pictures of some part of their treasure hunt and read their directions to the class.

Multi-Modal Activities

BULLETIN BOARD
idea

You may wish to use a bulletin board as a springboard for discussing the unit theme, or you may prefer to have students create a bulletin board as they move through the unit. Encourage students to explore the many interesting designs in nature. If possible make a class trip outdoors to find small items in nature, such as fallen leaves, acorns, pebbles, blades of grass, or wildflowers, or have students bring small nature items to class. Have students mount the items on construction paper and label them. Then have students draw on separate paper one part of the design they see in each item, such as a petal on a flower, the vein on a leaf, or the cap on an acorn. Mount the labeled pictures with the unlabeled designs in random order below them. Have students try to connect each design with the item it is based on. You may wish to label the display *Designs in Nature*.

Students with different learning styles will all benefit from a natural approach to language learning, including frequent and varied use of oral language in the classroom.

Students "At Risk"

The following suggestions can help you help the students in your classroom who may be considered "at risk."

Focus on Meaning

Students who may be considered at risk often are poor readers. They seem to focus on words rather than meaning. Help students make meaning of the materials they are required to learn. First, identify for them the basic concept of the lesson and then pursue it at *all* levels of comprehension. Try to use questioning strategies that engage students' minds in ways that help them bring their own knowledge, perceptions, and experiences into the learning process. At the end of the lesson, restate the objective and help students understand it in terms of real-life applications.

Limited English Proficiency

Teachers whose classes contain students with limited English proficiency may find the following activities helpful in developing students' skills in grammar and composition.

Where Is It?

On the chalkboard or posterboard draw a scene such as the one on this page.

Move a small object such as a piece of chalk or an eraser to various places in the scene and have students identify where the chalk is. Students' responses may include: *The chalk is in the tree. The chalk is on the rock. The chalk is by the tent.* Write students' responses on the chalkboard and have students identify each preposition and the nouns or pronouns it relates.

Once students are familiar with the activity, you may wish to have volunteers place the object on the scene.

Adverb or Preposition?

Write the following words on 3 by 5 cards: *along, around, below, down, in, inside, near, off, out, outside, under, up.* On the chalkboard write the headings *Prepositional Phrase* and *Adverb Phrase.* Have students choose a word and turn it into both a prepositional phrase and an adverb phrase, such as *along—along the river, move along.* Write students' responses on the chalkboard and have students discuss the differences between the prepositions and the adverbs. *(A preposition begins a phrase and has an object. An adverb describes a verb and has no object.)*

To continue the activity you may wish to have students use each prepositional phrase and adverb phrase in a complete sentence.

Prepositional Verse

Help students brainstorm a variety of prepositional phrases. Write students' responses on the chalkboard. When you have ten to fifteen phrases, have students decide which phrases might fit together in a short preposition verse. Model an example such as:

Up the tree trunk
Into a hole
Ran a squirrel.

Have students choose two or three prepositional phrases from the list on the chalkboard or compose their own phrases and add words to them to make their verses complete.

You may wish to hold a reading session in which volunteers read their verses aloud. Have classmates identify the prepositional phrases in each one.

Gifted and Talented Students

To enable gifted and talented students to work at their own pace and to explore the content further, you may wish to use one or more of these activities.

Shape Poems

Have students create their shape poems using prepositional phrases. Encourage students to let their imaginations and feelings about a subject suggest the shape of their poems. Have them experiment with shapes, word placement, and the words themselves until they have an expressive arrangement of words and images.

You may wish to have students share their work by compiling an anthology of shape poems to be kept in a reading corner.

Story Starters

Have students work individually or in small groups to brainstorm a list of ten prepositional phrases, such as *behind the closed door, inside the box,* and *at last.* Then have students choose one prepositional phrase to use as a story starter. Have students use their imaginations to create characters, setting, and plot by asking themselves such questions as: *Where was the closed door? What might be behind the closed door? Who might have closed the door? Who might open it? When was it closed and why?* Remind students to write a beginning, a middle and an ending for their stories. You may wish to suggest that they use their story starter as a title.

You may wish to have students share their work by reading their stories aloud and then compiling them in an anthology to be kept in a reading corner.

Interviews

Have students work individually or in small groups to brainstorm a list of important events of their lifetime such as a presidential election, a summit meeting, or a break-

through in science. Then have them recall where they were when the event took place or when they first heard about the event. You may wish to have students interview friends, relatives, and other students to ask: *Where were you on the day that _____ happened?* Have students write a report about their findings to share with classmates. Encourage students to use as many prepositional phrases as possible in their reports.

You may wish to have students share their work by reading aloud or by posting their reports on a bulletin board display with the heading *Where Were You When . . . ?*

Meeting Individual Needs

UNIT 7/LESSON 1

■ Easy ■ Average ■ Challenging

OBJECTIVES
To identify prepositions
To identify objects of prepositions
To use prepositions in writing

ASSIGNMENT GUIDE
BASIC   Practice A
               Practice B
ADVANCED   Practice C

All should do the Apply activity.

RESOURCES
■ Reteaching Master 57
■ Practice Master 57
■ ■ ■ Extra Practice, pp. 380, 381
Unit 7 Pretest, p. T548

TEACHING THE LESSON

1. Getting Started
Oral Language Focus attention on this oral activity, encouraging all to participate. You may wish to have students identify a real park nearby, or you may wish to have them imagine a park. Have each student in turn add directions for winding around and overcoming large and small, realistic and fantastic obstacles. Encourage them to make their directions as detailed as possible.

2. Developing the Lesson
Guide students through the explanation of writing with prepositions, emphasizing the examples and the summary. Lead students through the **Guided Practice**. Identify those who would benefit from reteaching. Assign independent Practice A–C.

3. Closing the Lesson
After students complete the Apply activity, you may wish to have volunteers read two of their sentences that contain prepositions and objects. Then have other volunteers read two sentences that do not contain prepositions. Have them work with the class to add prepositions and objects. Point out to students that being able to identify and use prepositions and objects of prepositions can help them make their writing more complete and interesting to read.

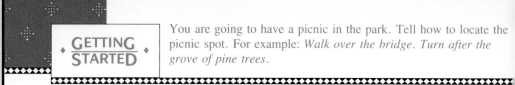

GETTING STARTED

You are going to have a picnic in the park. Tell how to locate the picnic spot. For example: *Walk over the bridge. Turn after the grove of pine trees.*

1 Writing with Prepositions

In the following sentences the underlined words are prepositions.

■ The sun was <u>near</u> the horizon.
■ Fiery flares shot <u>between</u> the clouds.

When you speak or write, you often use prepositions. A **preposition** relates the noun or pronoun that follows it to another word in the sentence. The noun or pronoun that follows the preposition is called the **object of the preposition**. In the sentence below, for example, the preposition *with* relates *gold* to *blazed*. *Gold* is the object of the preposition.

■ Soon the trees blazed <u>with</u> gold.

Thirty Common Prepositions					
about	at	by	in	on	to
above	before	down	inside	out	under
across	behind	during	near	outside	up
after	below	for	of	over	with
around	beside	from	off	through	without

Summary ◆ A **preposition** relates a noun or a pronoun to another word in the sentence.

Guided Practice

Name the preposition in each sentence. The object of the preposition is underlined.

1. Poets see beauty in the <u>world</u>.
2. They write about many <u>subjects</u>.
3. Of all <u>subjects</u>, nature is a favorite.
4. Below a clear <u>sky</u>, the writer begins a poem.
5. A poem can come from a gentle <u>breeze</u>.

340   GRAMMAR and WRITING: Prepositions

ESSENTIAL LANGUAGE SKILLS
This lesson provides opportunities to:

LISTENING ◆ follow the logical organization of an oral presentation ◆ select from an oral presentation the information needed

SPEAKING ◆ use a variety of words to express feelings and ideas ◆ make organized oral presentations

READING ◆ use context to understand the meaning of words ◆ follow a set of directions

WRITING ◆ participate in writing conferences

LANGUAGE ◆ produce a variety of sentence patterns ◆ use the fundamentals of grammar, spelling, and punctuation

Practice

A. Write each sentence. Underline the preposition.

6. Poets are inspired <u>by</u> nature.
7. The splendor <u>of</u> a blue sky thrills many.
8. A poet may write a poem <u>beside</u> a rushing brook.
9. She may write <u>about</u> a fragrant rose.
10. Poets see much beauty <u>around</u> them.
11. Some poets live <u>near</u> beautiful lakes.
12. Others see colorful flowers <u>under</u> their windows.
13. Poets search <u>for</u> beauty.
14. The search is often satisfied <u>by</u> a glorious sunset.
15. Other poets might gaze <u>at</u> the starry heavens.

B. Write each sentence. Underline the preposition once. Underline the object of the preposition twice.

EXAMPLE: Taro wrote a poem about nature's beauty.

ANSWER: Taro wrote a poem <u>about</u> <u>nature's beauty</u>.

16. He described the flowers <u>in</u> the <u>garden</u>.
17. He read the poem <u>to</u> the <u>class</u>.
18. <u>After</u> <u>class</u> the students discussed the poem.
19. Eve said that Taro's poem filled her <u>with</u> <u>pleasure</u>.
20. Later, Taro gave the poem <u>to</u> <u>her</u>.

C. Write a sentence for each of the following prepositions.
Sentences will vary.
21. above   23. behind   25. over
22. across   24. from   26. inside.

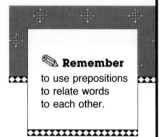

Apply ♦ Think and Write

From Your Writing ♦ Read what you wrote for the Writer's Warm-up. Did you use any prepositions? Try to add some prepositions and objects to your sentences to make your writing more complete.

🖉 **Remember**
to use prepositions to relate words to each other.

GRAMMAR and WRITING: Prepositions **341**

◀▥▥▥ TEACHING OPTIONS ▥▥▥▶

RETEACHING	CLASS ENRICHMENT	CHALLENGE
A Different Modality Write a sentence such as *I turned the key in the lock* on the chalkboard. Circle the preposition and show students that it connects *key* with *lock*. Then have individuals follow simple directions, such as *Put your book under your desk. Write your name on the paper.* As you give a direction, write it on the chalkboard. Underline the prepositions and show students that each preposition connects a noun or pronoun to another word.	**A Cooperative Activity** Have students work in pairs. Have each student write five sentences, each one containing one of the thirty common prepositions listed in their textbooks. Tell students to exchange papers and circle the prepositions in their partner's sentences. Encourage volunteers to share their sentences with the class.	**An Independent Activity** Have students write sentences about topics they like and know about, such as their last visit to a grandparent's home, an after-school activity, and so on. Tell them to use as many prepositions as they can from the thirty common prepositions chart in their textbooks. Remind them to write an object for each preposition. When they are finished, have them circle all the prepositions they used.

■ Easy ■ Average ■ Challenging

OBJECTIVES
To identify prepositional phrases

ASSIGNMENT GUIDE
BASIC   Practice A
↓   Practice B
ADVANCED   Practice C

All should do the Apply activity.

RESOURCES
■ Reteaching Master 58
■ Practice Master 58
■ ■ ■ Extra Practice, pp. 380, 382

TEACHING THE LESSON

1. Getting Started
Oral Language Focus attention on this oral activity, encouraging all to participate. You may wish to have one student supply the question, the next supply the answer, and so on. You may wish to begin by modeling questions of your own, such as *Where can you find a roof? Where can you find the title of a book? Where can you find a pencil?* Write on the chalkboard the prepositions *on, in, above, under, inside,* and *over* to help students respond.

2. Developing the Lesson
Guide students through the explanation of prepositional phrases, emphasizing the examples and the summary. You may wish to reemphasize that in a prepositional phrase there may be no words or many words between the preposition and its object. You may also wish to point out that a prepositional phrase must include a preposition. Lead students through the **Guided Practice.** Identify those who would benefit from reteaching. Assign independent Practice A–C.

3. Closing the Lesson
After students complete the Apply activity, encourage them to make a final copy and publish their poems by arranging them with illustrations on a bulletin board. Point out to students that knowing how to identify and use prepositional phrases in their writing can help them make their descriptions clear and complete.

♦ GETTING STARTED ♦

Play "Where Can You Find It?" Ask questions such as "Where can you find a swing?" The answer must contain one of these words: *on, in, above, under, inside,* or *over.* For example: *I can find a swing in the park.*

2 Prepositional Phrases

Read the sentences below. Then read just the words in the boxes. Remember that the noun or pronoun that follows a preposition is the object of that preposition.

Many poets write `about the seasons.`
Each season `of the year` has its own special charm.
`With every passing day` nature shows its beauty.

Every prepositional phrase starts with a preposition and ends with its object. The phrase also includes any words that come between. The chart below gives examples from the sentences above.

Prepositional Phrases		
Prepositions	**Words Between**	**Objects**
about	the	seasons
of	the	year
with	every passing	day

Summary ♦ A **prepositional phrase** includes the preposition, the object, and any words that come between them.

Guided Practice

Name each prepositional phrase. The prepositions are underlined.

1. Summer is a wonderful time <u>of</u> the year.
2. The flowers are alive <u>with</u> color.
3. <u>Inside</u> the deep woods the birds chatter happily.
4. Winter displays other wonders <u>from</u> nature.
5. The snow drifts <u>across</u> the frozen meadows.

342   GRAMMAR: Prepositional Phrases

ESSENTIAL LANGUAGE SKILLS
This lesson provides opportunities to:

LISTENING ♦ follow the logical organization of an oral presentation ♦ select from an oral presentation the information needed

SPEAKING ♦ use a variety of words to express feelings and ideas ♦ speak in complete sentences

READING ♦ use context to understand the meaning of words ♦ follow a set of directions

WRITING ♦ use conventional formats (business letters and other commonly used forms) ♦ write short stories, plays, essays, or poems

LANGUAGE ♦ use language for creating

Practice

Write each sentence. Underline the prepositional phrase.

6. The seasons show the continuing cycle of nature.
7. During each year we have spring, summer, fall, and winter.
8. We wonder about the seasonal changes.
9. Poets are inspired by them.
10. Winter often arrives with heavy snow.
11. Icicles, like spears, hang from frozen rooftops.
12. In other areas, winters are quite mild.
13. Warm winters have appeal for the poet.
14. A breeze through the palm trees whispers softly.
15. Nature's magic is outside your own window.

Write the prepositional phrase in each sentence. Underline the preposition once. Underline the object of the preposition twice.

EXAMPLE: I read a poem built around the twelve months.

ANSWER: around the twelve months

16. The poem was written by Christina Rossetti.
17. It describes each of the twelve months.
18. Rossetti describes January with icy words.
19. The lines about May are my favorites.
20. She mentions the birds singing to the lovely flowers.

Write a sentence for each prepositional phrase below.
Sentences will vary.

21. after the fierce storm
22. below the dark clouds
23. over the rainbow
24. before the sunset
25. at sunset
26. during the day

Apply • Think and Write

Creating a Verse • Write a Prepositional Phrase Verse. Try using a verse pattern. Study the example at the right. Then write your own verse.

In the frozen forest,
Near the icy creek,
On soft, new snow,
A startled deer leaps.

Remember
to use prepositional phrases to add details to your sentences.

GRAMMAR: Prepositional Phrases   **343**

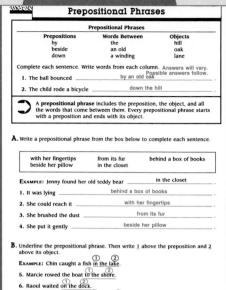

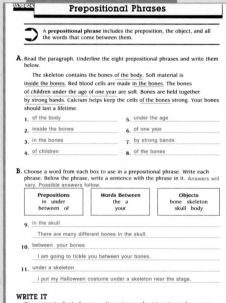

◀ TEACHING OPTIONS ▶

RETEACHING

A Different Modality Explain that a prepositional phrase includes the preposition, the object of the preposition, and all the words that come between them. Write several sentences with prepositional phrases on the chalkboard. Identify the preposition, the object, and the words between. Have students read aloud each sentence and then come to the chalkboard and write the appropriate words under the headings *Prepositions, Words Between,* and *Objects.*

CLASS ENRICHMENT

A Cooperative Activity Have small groups compose an imperative sentence that includes one prepositional phrase, such as *Put the chalk on the window sill.* Have each group write a group name on their papers and then exchange sentences. Tell group members to work together to pantomime their new sentence for the class. Have the class—all but the sentence authors—identify the action and the prepositional phrase.

CHALLENGE

An Independent Activity Have students write a paragraph about something they can do really well, such as hit a ball, prepare a meal, run with their dog, or make a puppet. Tell them to include prepositional phrases in their sentences and, when they are finished, underline each one. Encourage them to make a copy of their paragraph to give to a partner, who is to check that all prepositional phrases have been correctly identified.

343

UNIT 7/LESSON 3

OBJECTIVES
To distinguish between prepositions and adverbs

ASSIGNMENT GUIDE
BASIC   Practice A
     ↓   Practice B
ADVANCED   Practice C

All should do the Apply activity.

RESOURCES
■ Reteaching Master 59
■ Practice Master 59
■■■ Extra Practice, pp. 380, 384

TEACHING THE LESSON

1. Getting Started
Oral Language Focus attention on this oral activity, encouraging all to participate. You may wish to have groups of students work together to give the directions. Encourage imaginative responses, such as *Run up the path until you are out of breath.* Remind students to use *up, down,* and *around* in their directions.

2. Developing the Lesson
Guide students through the explanation of prepositions and adverbs, emphasizing the examples and the summary. Lead students through the **Guided Practice**. Identify those who would benefit from reteaching. Assign independent Practice A–C.

3. Closing the Lesson
After students complete the Apply activity, have volunteers read aloud their descriptions of the praying mantis. Have the class listen carefully and identify those sentences that contain prepositional phrases and those that contain adverbs. Point out to students that using prepositions and adverbs can help them add variety and interest to their writing.

344

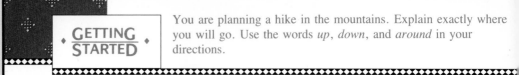

GETTING STARTED

You are planning a hike in the mountains. Explain exactly where you will go. Use the words *up*, *down*, and *around* in your directions.

3 Prepositions and Adverbs

When you speak or write, you can use some words, such as *inside* and *up*, as either prepositions or adverbs. There is an easy way to tell how you are using such words. You are using the word as a preposition if it begins a prepositional phrase and has an object. You are using the word as an adverb if it describes a verb and stands alone, without an object.

Prepositions	Adverbs
We went <u>inside</u> the cavern.	We went <u>inside</u>.
John climbed <u>up</u> the steps.	John climbed <u>up</u>.

There are many words that can be used as prepositions or as adverbs. Here are twelve common ones.

along	below	in	near	out	under
around	down	inside	off	outside	up

Summary ♦ Some words can be either prepositions or adverbs.

Guided Practice

For each sentence below, tell whether the underlined word is a preposition or an adverb.

1. When we hiked, my friend came <u>along</u>. *(adv.)*
2. We walked <u>along</u> a babbling brook. *(prep.)*
3. Two noisy chipmunks came <u>near</u>. *(adv.)*
4. Soon we stood <u>near</u> a stately oak tree. *(prep.)*

344   GRAMMAR: Prepositions and Adverbs

ESSENTIAL LANGUAGE SKILLS
This lesson provides opportunities to:

LISTENING ♦ respond appropriately to orally presented directions

SPEAKING ♦ make organized oral presentations

READING ♦ use context to understand the meaning of words ♦ understand content area vocabulary ♦ follow a set of directions

WRITING ♦ use a variety of resources to research a topic ♦ adapt information to accomplish a specific purpose with a particular audience

LANGUAGE ♦ use language for informing ♦ use the fundamentals of grammar, punctuation, and spelling

---

Practice

Write each sentence. Then write whether the underlined word is a preposition or an adverb.

prep.
5. In the summertime nature's beauty surrounds us.

adv.
6. Flowers are blooming outside.

ep. **7.** Butterflies are fluttering in the gentle breeze.

prep.
8. I watch as one quietly flies near me.

prep.
9. I walk up the steep hill.

adv.
10. Beside a giant tree I sit down.

p.**11.** Colorful flowers are all around me.

adv.
12. They are so beautiful that I will not go inside.

prep.
13. I stay under the tree and open my notebook.

adv.
14. My thoughts pour out as I write.

Write each sentence. If the underlined part is an adverb, change it to a prepositional phrase. If it is a prepositional phrase, change it to an adverb.
Answers will vary. Possible answers follow.

EXAMPLE: After writing my poem, I go inside the house.

ANSWER: After writing my poem, I go inside.

15. I walk up the stairs. up

16. I put the poem inside. inside my desk

17. Then I go out the door again. out

18. I stroll around the garden. around

19. I wander along. along the garden path

20–29. Write two sentences for each word. Use the word once as a preposition and once as an adverb.
Sentences will vary.

EXAMPLE: out

ANSWER: The bird flew out of the nest. The bird flew out.

along   below   inside   outside   off

Apply • Think and Write

Dictionary of Knowledge • Read about the praying mantis in the Dictionary of Knowledge. Using prepositions and adverbs, write about what makes this insect interesting.

✎ **Remember** to choose prepositions and adverbs carefully to make your meaning clear.

GRAMMAR: Prepositions and Adverbs   345

RETEACHING 59

Prepositions and Adverbs

Write the word outside to complete each sentence.

1. March winds blew _____ outside _____ .

2. I watched the snow fall _____ outside _____ the window.

In sentence 1, the word outside is used as an adverb. In sentence 2, the word outside is used as a prepositional phrase.

↺ Some words can be either prepositions or adverbs. A word is a preposition if it begins a prepositional phrase and has an object. A word is an adverb if it describes a verb and stands alone, without an object.

A. Write adverb or preposition to tell how each underlined word is used.

EXAMPLE: Jeremy ate breakfast outside. _____ adverb
         Julia strolled down the lane. _____ preposition

1. Jeremy saw the window washers high above. _____ adverb

2. They did not stop during the rain. _____ preposition

3. The workers did not see Jeremy below. _____ adverb

4. Julia saw a house near a small stream. _____ preposition

5. She saw a light inside. _____ adverb

6. A young girl stepped outside the door. _____ preposition

B. Complete each sentence with a prepositional phrase or an adverb. Answers will vary. Possible answers follow.

EXAMPLE: Sunflowers grew _____ along the road _____ . (prepositional phrase)

7. Their heavy heads pointed _____ up _____ . (adverb)

8. A lazy white cloud drifted _____ across the sky _____ . (prepositional phrase)

9. Three small mice ran _____ by _____ . (adverb)

10. A family of deer stood _____ in the field _____ . (prepositional phrase)

11. A pair of young rabbits hopped _____ along _____ . (adverb)

12. Several ducks swam _____ in the lake _____ . (prepositional phrase)

PRACTICE 59

Prepositions and Adverbs

↺ Some words can be either prepositions or adverbs.

A. Underline each prepositional phrase and adverb. Then write each one in the correct column below.

1. Megan and Maria walked up the stairs.

2. Megan's mother waited inside the house.

3. Maria and Megan sat down.

4. The sky darkened above.

5. Maria pointed her telescope up.

6. The comets shot across the sky.

Prepositional Phrase	Adverb
up the stairs	down
inside the house	above
across the sky	up

B. Write four sentences. Use each word in the box twice—once as an adverb and once as a preposition. Answers will vary. Possible answers follow.

> around   out

7. The small plane flew around.

8. The plane flew around the airport.

9. The brave skydiver jumped out.

10. The brave skydiver jumped out the door.

WRITE IT
On a separate sheet of paper, describe the night sky. Use prepositional phrases and adverbs to add variety to your sentences. Answers will vary.

◁|||| TEACHING OPTIONS ||||▷

RETEACHING

A Different Modality Explain that some words are used as both adverbs and prepositions and that a preposition has an object. Write on the chalkboard: *1. Climb inside the _____. 2. Climb inside.* Point out that Sentence 1 is missing an object and, therefore, *inside* is being used as a preposition. Have a volunteer dictate an object. Point out that Sentence 2 has no object; therefore, *inside* is being used as an adverb. Repeat with similar examples.

CLASS ENRICHMENT

A Cooperative Activity Tell groups of five students that they are either an "adverb group" or a "preposition group." Have each group work together to construct five sentences about a topic that interests them, using their part of speech. When they are finished, have the groups exchange papers. Have them take turns reading aloud a sentence, identifying the adverb or preposition, and then changing it to their group's part of speech.

CHALLENGE

An Independent Extension Have students write about their favorite place, such as a tree house, a neighborhood shop, or a playground. Tell them to write sentences that use the words *along, around, below, down, in,* and *up* as adverbs and then as prepositions. You may wish to encourage them to rewrite their sentences with blanks for a partner to complete with an adverb or preposition.

345

UNIT 7/LESSON 4

■ Easy ■ Average ■ Challenging

OBJECTIVES
To use object pronouns as objects of prepositions correctly
To use *between* and *among* correctly

ASSIGNMENT GUIDE
BASIC   Practice A
             Practice B
ADVANCED   Practice C

All should do the Apply activity.

RESOURCES
■ Reteaching Master 60
■ Practice Master 60
■■■ Extra Practice, pp. 380, 385

TEACHING THE LESSON

1. Getting Started
Oral Language Focus attention on this oral activity, encouraging all to participate. You may wish to begin by having the class brainstorm groups of three related nouns, such as *lakes, streams, rivers,* or *daisies, roses, lilacs,* and so on. Then have students take turns saying their sentences. For example, have one student choose three nouns and say *Among those three, my favorite is rivers.* Have the next student name two nouns from the same group and say *Between those two, I prefer lakes.*

2. Developing the Lesson
Guide students through the explanation of using prepositional phrases, emphasizing the examples and the summary. You may wish to reemphasize that a preposition may have one object or several and that the objects may be nouns, pronouns, or a combination of both. Write on the chalkboard the example sentences from the textbook. Lead students through the **Guided Practice.** Identify those who would benefit from reteaching. Assign independent Practice A–C.

3. Closing the Lesson
After students complete the Apply activity, have volunteers read aloud their phrases. Have students explain why some phrases use *among* and some use *between.* Point out that using prepositional phrases correctly will make their speech and writing clear.

346

♦ GETTING STARTED ♦

Think of three things associated with nature, such as mountains, forests, and oceans. Say, ''Among those three, my favorite is ____.'' Then narrow the group to two items. Say, ''Between those two, I prefer ____.''

4 Using Prepositional Phrases

When the object of a preposition is a pronoun, you need to use an object pronoun. The following are the object pronouns.

me	you	him	her	it	us	them

In these sentences, the prepositional phrases are underlined.

1. Show the book to me.
2. Will you share the poems with us?
3. With Luisa and her I read the nature poems.

In sentence **3**, the preposition has two objects, a noun and a pronoun.

The prepositions *between* and *among* are sometimes confused. In the sentences below, these prepositions are underlined.

The poetry books are between the two dictionaries.
Divide the poetry books among Carlos, Rachel, and Dave.

Use the preposition *between* when you refer to two persons, places, or things. Use the preposition *among* when you refer to three or more persons, places, or things.

> **Summary** ♦ When you speak or write, use object pronouns in prepositional phrases. Use the prepositions *between* and *among* correctly.

Guided Practice

Name the word that correctly completes each sentence.

1. Mr. Albeniz brought a book of poems with (he, **him**).
2. He read the first poem aloud to Pat and (I, **me**).
3. It told of ten geese flying (**between**, among) two mountains.
4. (Between, **Among**) the ten geese, one was the leader.
5. That poem was special to the students and (he, **him**).

346   GRAMMAR and USAGE: Prepositions and Prepositional Phrases

---

ESSENTIAL LANGUAGE SKILLS

This lesson provides opportunities to:

LISTENING ♦ follow the logical organization of an oral presentation ♦ select from an oral presentation the information needed

SPEAKING ♦ make organized oral presentations ♦ use oral language for a variety of purposes

READING ♦ draw logical conclusions ♦ follow a set of directions

WRITING ♦ generate ideas using a variety of strategies, such as brainstorming, clustering, mapping, question and answer

LANGUAGE ♦ use language for creating

Practice

A. Write each sentence. Choose the pronoun in parentheses ( ) that correctly completes the sentence.

6. Mr. Albeniz often read nature poems with (we, us).
7. Many of the poems enjoyed by Jason and (me, I) were written by Christina Rossetti.
8. To children and (she, her) some clouds look like sheep.
9. I found clouds like animals with my cousin and (he, him).
10. For (me, I) Rossetti's poem about colors was fun.
11. To (she, her) only an orange is orange.
12. To Kim and (I, me) many flowers are orange.
13. Rossetti loves cherry trees with blossoms on (they, them).
14. Such sights are a treat for Maria and (me, I).
15. Petals fall like pink snow near (we, us) and (they, them).

B. Write each sentence. Complete the sentence correctly with *among* or *between*.

16. Have you heard the wind blow (between, among) many leafy trees?
17. Have you felt the wind blow (between, among) two houses?
18. (Between, Among) you and me have you ever seen the wind?
19. A Rossetti poem asks who, (between, among) all people, has seen the wind.
20. Yet when the wind passes (between, among) two trees, we see them bow their heads.

C. Complete each prepositional phrase with an object pronoun. Then write a sentence for each phrase.
Object pronouns and sentences will vary.

21. to Ana and _____   23. by them and _____
22. for _____ and me   24. from Lou and _____

Apply ◆ Think and Write

Creating Phrases ◆ The poet Robert Frost wrote about stopping to rest ''between the woods and frozen lake.'' Make a list of phrases beginning with *between* and *among* that you might use in a poem.

> ✎ **Remember**
> to use object pronouns in prepositional phrases.

GRAMMAR and USAGE: Prepositions and Prepositional Phrases   **347**

◀◁▏▏▏▏ TEACHING OPTIONS ▏▏▏▏▷▶

RETEACHING

A Different Modality Write the following in two columns on the chalkboard: *Use between when you refer to two persons, places, or things. Use among when you refer to three or more persons, places, or things.* Write a sentence that uses *between* in the first column and one that uses *among* in the second column. Have students dictate additional sentences correctly using *between* or *among*. Write the sentences in the appropriate columns.

CLASS ENRICHMENT

A Cooperative Activity Have students pretend they are sports announcers. Have them write a brief play-by-play for their favorite sport. Encourage them to make the play-by-play exciting and to use prepositional phrases, object pronouns, and *between* and *among*. Then have them trade papers with a partner. Have the partners underline each object pronoun and check for correct usage of *between* and *among*.

CHALLENGE

An Independent Extension Have students write a brief paragraph describing the position of their desks in the classroom and the contents of the desk. Have them use object pronouns and *between* and *among* correctly in their descriptions, such as *My desk is between you and him. My books are in it.* Have students underline the prepositional phrases and circle the object pronouns. Encourage them to check for the correct use of *between* and *among*.

347

UNIT 7
Vocabulary

OBJECTIVES
To identify synonyms and antonyms

ASSIGNMENT GUIDE

BASIC	Practice A
↓	Practice B and C
ADVANCED	Practice D

All should do the Language Corner.

RESOURCES
■ Reteaching Master 61
■ Practice Master 61

TEACHING THE LESSON

1. Getting Started
Oral Language Focus attention on this oral activity, encouraging all to participate. You may wish to begin by asking volunteers to define the word *furious*. Tell students to listen carefully for the important words in the definitions that tell what *furious* means, such as *angry, mad, upset,* and *fierce*.

2. Developing the Lesson
Guide students through the explanation of synonyms and antonyms, emphasizing the definition and the examples. You may wish to tell students that some dictionaries give synonyms and antonyms for many words. Guide students through Building Your Vocabulary. Identify those who would benefit from reteaching. Assign independent Practice A–D.

3. Closing the Lesson
After students complete the Practice exercises, tell them to listen for often-repeated words in a conversation. Have them list the words and then see if they can find synonyms for them. Point out to students that using synonyms and antonyms when they speak and write can help them express their ideas effectively and colorfully.

Language Corner You may wish to have students discuss and describe the appropriateness of their echo words.

How many different words can you think of to replace *furious* in this sentence? *The double-crossed wolf was furious.*

VOCABULARY ♦
Synonyms and Antonyms

Synonyms are words with similar meanings. **Antonyms** are words with opposite meanings. *Fast* and *quick* are synonyms. *Fast* and *slow* are antonyms.

Knowing synonyms and antonyms of words or knowing where to find them is helpful in making your writing more interesting. A thesaurus is one important tool that can help you.

Building Your Vocabulary
Answers will vary. Possible answers follow.
Replace the underlined words in the paragraph below with synonyms.

Tom talked on the phone for nearly an hour. He discussed an
[spoke]   [almost]
assortment of topics—current events, the fair weather, and the
[a variety]   [news]   [clear]
latest trends in fashion. As he chatted, Tom kept active. He wiped
[directions]   [talked]   [moving]   [cleaned]
the counter, put away the plates and mugs, and shined the spigot.
[dishes]   [cups]   [brightened]   [faucet]

Antonyms give opposite meanings to sentences. Make the sentences below opposite in meaning by replacing each underlined word with an antonym. Answers may vary. Possible answers follow.

1. Brad bought his bike for thirty dollars.
   [sold]
2. Tammy shouted something in Elma's ear.
   [whispered]
3. Susie likes swimming in cool water.
   [dislikes]   [warm]

348   VOCABULARY: Synonyms and Antonyms

ESSENTIAL LANGUAGE SKILLS
This lesson provides opportunities to:

LISTENING ♦ select from an oral presentation the information needed ♦ listen to appreciate the sound device of onomatopoeia

SPEAKING ♦ use oral language for a variety of purposes ♦ use creative devices, such as figurative language, jingles, coined words, and anecdotes

READING ♦ explain processes ♦ evaluate and make judgments ♦ follow a set of directions

WRITING ♦ adapt information to accomplish a specific purpose with a particular audience ♦ spell increasingly complex words

LANGUAGE ♦ use clear and interesting words to express thoughts ♦ use language for creating

Practice

A. Write each pair of words below. Then write *S* after each pair of synonyms. Write *A* after each pair of antonyms.

1. accident, mishap S
2. find, discover S
3. exciting, dull A
4. courage, daring S
5. rare, unusual S
6. joy, delight S
7. ask, answer A
8. arrive, depart A

B. Find synonyms in the Thesaurus to replace the underlined words in the sentences below. **Answers will vary. Possible answers follow.**

9. Niagara Falls has an exciting view. *breathtaking*
10. "What a beautiful day for a picnic," Pepita declared. *lovely*
11. Thelma often thinks about visiting the Grand Canyon. *dreams*
12. Ian wants roasted almonds; they are his favorite snack. *craves*
13. Nelda always keeps her bedroom neat. *tidy*

C. Find antonyms in the Thesaurus to replace the underlined words in the sentences below.

14. We searched all day but only found some rare rocks. *common*
15. The night sky was clear, so we couldn't see any stars. *cloudy*
16. You will find your watch if you leave it lying around. *lose*
17. The large insect could only be seen under a microscope. *tiny*

D. Use *un-* or *dis-* to make antonyms of the words below.

18. afraid *unafraid*
19. bend *unbend*
20. please *displease*
21. likely *unlikely*
22. honest *dishonest*
23. trust *distrust*
24. comfortable *uncomfortable*
25. friendly *unfriendly*

LANGUAGE CORNER • Echo Words

Some words "echo" the sound of the thing that they name. For example, *buzz* echoes the sound that bees make. *Zoom* echoes the sound that something passing by quickly makes.

Make up your own echo words. Explain the sound that each word stands for.

MASTERS ON FILE

RETEACHING 61

Synonyms and Antonyms

Synonyms are words with similar meanings. Antonyms are words with opposite meanings. Identify each pair below. Write synonym or antonym.

1. glad, happy — synonym
2. lost, found — antonym
3. modern, old-fashioned — antonym
4. crawl, creep — synonym

A. Read the underlined words in each sentence. Write s if the words are synonyms and a if the words are antonyms.

EXAMPLE: Read the music from left to right. — a

1. Play the recording softly, not loudly. — a
2. Tap lightly and gently in time to the music. — s
3. Shall I play a lengthy song or a short song? — a
4. Play some song with a strong, forceful beat. — s
5. That unusual desk is a rare antique. — s
6. The starchy collar was stiff and uncomfortable. — s
7. The sad clown had a tearful face. — s
8. Give me the correct answer, not the wrong one. — a

B. Read each sentence. Choose the word in parentheses ( ) that is a synonym for the underlined word. Write it in the blank.

EXAMPLE: What a big rabbit! (large, pretty) — large

9. What a beautiful day for the school fair! (lovely, ugly) — lovely
10. We are all happy to be here. (pretty, glad) — glad
11. Get in line quickly for that game. (neatly, fast) — fast

C. Read each sentence. Choose the word in parentheses ( ) that is an antonym for the underlined word. Write it in the blank.

12. The trip was short and exciting. (long, quick) — long
13. It is a nice, sunny day. (cloudy, bright) — cloudy
14. We really like this school event. (love, hate) — hate

PRACTICE 61

Synonyms and Antonyms

A. Write a synonym and an antonym for each word. Answers will vary. Possible answers follow.

	Synonyms	Antonyms
1. start	begin	end
2. fascinating	interesting	dull
3. rapid	swift	slow
4. smooth	even	rough
5. soft	gentle	hard or loud
6. wise	smart	ignorant
7. bold	confident	afraid
8. sad	unhappy	glad
9. unique	unusual	common
10. large	huge	tiny

B. Rewrite each sentence twice. First replace each underlined word with a synonym. Then replace each underlined word with an antonym. Answers will vary. Possible answers follow.

11. Today's crossword puzzle is easy to solve.
    a. Today's crossword puzzle is simple to solve.
    b. Today's crossword puzzle is difficult to solve.

12. My answers are always accurate.
    a. My answers are always correct.
    b. My answers are always wrong.

13. I recall many of my favorites.
    a. I remember many of my favorites.
    b. I forget many of my favorites.

14. I seldom leave a blank space in a puzzle.
    a. I rarely leave a blank space in a puzzle.
    b. I often leave a blank space in a puzzle.

◀▥ TEACHING OPTIONS ▥▶

RETEACHING

A Different Modality Emphasize that synonyms are words with similar meanings and antonyms are words with opposite meanings. Distribute cards with a synonym pair or an antonym pair on one side and the appropriate label on the other side. Include such synonym pairs as *fast—quick, big—large,* and *calm—quiet* and such antonym pairs as *fast—slow, big—small* and *calm—excited.* Encourage students to use the words in each pair in sentences.

CLASS ENRICHMENT

A Cooperative Activity Have partners each list five synonym pairs in scrambled order. Partners should then exchange lists and identify the correct synonym pairs. Then have them repeat the activity with antonym pairs. You may wish to have partners share with the class any pairs that puzzled them.

CHALLENGE

An Independent Extension Have students create at least five synonym pairs of echo words. For example, *crankle* and *skroosh* might be synonyms for the sound of eating popcorn. Have students write one of their synonym pairs on one side of an index card and an explanation of the sound the echo words stand for on the other side. Encourage students to create a file of echo word synonym pairs for classmates to decipher during free time.

Grammar-Writing Connection

How to Expand Sentences with Prepositions

Point out to students that they can use the grammar skills they learned in Unit 7 to help them develop good writing techniques. Explain that in this Grammar-Writing Connection, students will use what they know about prepositions, prepositional phrases, distinguishing between prepositions and adverbs, and using object pronouns as objects of prepositions correctly to learn how to expand sentences with prepositions.

You may wish to guide students through the explanation of how to expand sentences with prepositions, stressing the examples. Then have students apply the information by completing the activity at the bottom of the first page. Students may work in small groups or with partners to unscramble the prepositional phrase puzzles orally, or they may solve the puzzles in writing as an independent activity.

Help students to understand that expanding sentences with prepositions is an effective way to improve writing, and that it can make their writing clearer and more interesting.

How to Expand Sentences with Prepositions

In this unit you have been learning about prepositions and how to use them in sentences. Prepositions can add a great deal of information to your writing. Do you know, though, how important it is to choose your prepositions carefully? Read the following sentences to discover the difference prepositions can make.

1. Joe found the hidden treasure.
2. Joe found the hidden treasure inside the oak tree.
3. Joe found the hidden treasure behind the oak tree.

Sentence **1** gives us information. Sentence **2** tells us even more because it tells *where* the treasure was found. In sentence **3**, however, a single preposition completely changes the information.

Choose prepositions carefully when you write. Prepositions can make the information in your sentences exact.

The Grammar Game ◆ Focus on phrases! Unscramble the puzzles below to form prepositional phrases. Choose a piece from puzzle **A**. Then match the preposition with a piece from puzzle **B** to form a phrase. Write as many prepositional phrases as possible in three minutes. Answers will vary.

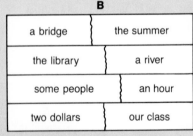

A		
under	for	on
by	above	near
about	over	to
in	across	from

B	
a bridge	the summer
the library	a river
some people	an hour
two dollars	our class

Now trade lists with a classmate. Write sentences using your partner's prepositional phrases. Your sentences must make sense!

350   COOPERATIVE LEARNING: Expanding Sentences

ESSENTIAL LANGUAGE SKILLS

This lesson provides opportunities to:

LISTENING ◆ select from an oral presentation the information needed ◆ participate in conversations and group discussions

SPEAKING ◆ express ideas clearly and effectively ◆ contribute to class and small group discussions

READING ◆ draw logical conclusions ◆ evaluate and make judgments ◆ follow a set of directions

WRITING ◆ gain an understanding of complete sentence structure

LANGUAGE ◆ recognize and use options for word order

Working Together

Using exact prepositions will add specific information to your writing. Use them to complete activities **A** and **B** with your group.

A. Do the song lyrics below sound familiar? Write them, adding the missing prepositions. If you aren't sure of the correct word, use a preposition that makes sense. Can your group add other lyrics that include prepositional phrases?

1. Row, row, row your boat, gently <u>down</u> the stream.
2. <u>On</u> top <u>of</u> old Smokey, all covered <u>with</u> snow...
3. <u>Over</u> the river and <u>through</u> the woods <u>to</u> Grandmother's house we go.
4. Oh beautiful, <u>for</u> spacious skies, <u>for</u> amber waves <u>of</u> grain, <u>for</u> purple mountain majesties, <u>above</u> the fruited plain...

B. Write a set of detailed directions that explains how to get from your classroom to another place in your school. Include at least ten prepositions or prepositional phrases. Some common prepositions are supplied here, but use any prepositions that the group agrees are necessary. **Answers will vary.**

around	behind	into	against	after
before	past	upon	without	down
along	toward	through	over	during

When your group is finished, exchange the written directions with those of another group. Try to follow the directions. Can your group get to the right place?

WRITERS' CORNER ♦ Positioning Phrases

Be sure your prepositional phrases are correctly placed, or your sentences may sound confusing or silly. Can you explain what is wrong with the example sentence below?

EXAMPLE: I hummed a tune about elephants in the shower.
IMPROVED: In the shower I hummed a tune about elephants.

Read what you wrote for the Writer's Warm-up. Look carefully at the prepositional phrases you used. Are they correctly placed?

COOPERATIVE LEARNING: Expanding Sentences ◁ **351** ▷

Working Together

The Working Together activities involve students in cooperative learning work groups. This is an opportunity to pair strong writers with students whose skills are weaker. Working together, they can all experience success.

Divide the class into small groups and have students read In Your Group. Encourage them to discuss why each task is important. Have them tell what might happen if the group does not follow through on each task. *(If we do not pay attention to each other's ideas, we might miss some ideas that could be helpful. If we do not encourage everyone to participate, we are not being fair. If we do not take turns recording information, the work will not be shared equally. If we do not help the group finish on time, our work will possibly be late.)*

Before students begin activities A and B, you may wish to have each group appoint a member to record the missing prepositions and the detailed directions. You also may wish to have groups appoint a timekeeper. Then set a limit of ten or fifteen minutes. After each activity is completed, have the groups compare their work.

Writers' Corner

The Writers' Corner provides students with the opportunity to extend the Grammar-Writing Connection, helping them to develop the skills necessary to review and revise their own writing. Discuss the introductory sentences with students. Then have them work as a class or in pairs to discuss the two examples. Have students read aloud each example and identify the changes that were made. Have them tell how those changes made the improved example "better." Then have students apply the expanding sentences with prepositions techniques from this Grammar-Writing Connection to the sentences they wrote about nature for the Writers' Warm-up.

Encourage students to rewrite their sentences if necessary. Discuss with them how using prepositions in prepositional phrases added important details to their sentences, strengthening them and improving the flow of their writing and the clarity of their ideas.

TWO-PART

flexibility

Unit 7
Overview

USING LANGUAGE TO CREATE

books

FOR EXTENDED READING

EASY

A Song in Stone: City Poems selected by Lee Bennett Hopkins. Crowell. These poems celebrate the city with unique images. There are headlights that stare, umbrellas opening like flowers in the rain, and subway ''dragons'' roaring in underground caves. **American Library Association Notable Children's Book.**

AVERAGE

Cold Stars and Fireflies: Poems of the Four Seasons by Barbara Juster Esbensen. Crowell. The poems in this collection about nature and the changing seasons sparkle with striking images and personification.

CHALLENGING

The Sidewalk Racer and Other Poems of Sports and Motion by Lillian Morrison. Lothrop. These rhythmic poems about sports, ranging from baseball and biking to sailing and surfing, express the joy of movement.

READ-ALOUD

Rainbows Are Made: Poems by Carl Sandburg by Carl Sandburg. Harcourt. This collection of seventy poems by the great American poet includes sections on people, wordplay, nature, the sea, and night. **New York Times Best Illustrated Children's Book, American Library Association Notable Children's Book.**

THE PARC MONCEAU
painting by Claude Oscar Monet
© The Metropolitan Museum of Art,
Bequest of Loula D. Lasker, New York City, 1961. (59.206).

UNIT SEVEN

USING LANGUAGE
TO
CREATE

—————— **PART TWO** ——————

Literature *Poetry*

A Reason for Writing Creating

CREATIVE
Writing

FINE ARTS ◆ Poems, stories, songs, and legends have been created about trees. Look at the painting at the left. Monet painted this lovely scene of a park in France. The trees will be preserved forever in his painting. What is your favorite tree? Is it the tree you swing from in your backyard? Is it the tree in front of the town hall that was planted by early settlers? Picture your favorite tree. Then write either a poem, a song, a story, or a legend about your tree.

start with CREATIVE WRITING

Fine Arts gives your students a chance to express themselves creatively in writing. After students observe the illustration on page 352 for a moment or two, have a volunteer read aloud the Fine Arts paragraph on page 353. Have students write their reactions in their journals. Then encourage a discussion of their ideas.

 VIEWING

See the **Fine Arts Transparencies with Viewing Booklet** and the **Video Library**.

THEN START WITH *part 2*

A Reason for Writing: Creating is the focus of Part 2. First students learn a thinking strategy for creating. Then they read and respond to a selection of poetry on which they may model their own writing. Developmental composition lessons, including "Reading Poetry Aloud," a speaking and listening lesson, help students learn to use language to create poetry selections. All the lessons reflect the literature. All culminate in the Writing Process lesson. The unit ends with the Curriculum Connection and Books to Enjoy, which help students discover how their new language skills apply to writing across the curriculum and to their own lives.

◆ If you began with grammar instruction, you may wish to remind students of the unit theme, "Nature." Tell them that the information they gathered through the thematic lessons helped them prepare for reading poetry.

◆ If you are beginning with Part 2, use the lessons in Part 1 for remediation or instruction. For grammar, spelling, and mechanics instructional guidance, you may wish to refer to the end-of-text Glossary and Index, as well as to the *Spelling Connection* booklet; the full-color *Revising and Proofreading Transparencies;* and the Unit Pretest, Posttest, and Writing Samples.

THEME BAR

CATEGORIES	Environments	Business/World of Work	Imagination	Communications/ Fine Arts	People	Science	Expressions	Social Studies
THEMES	UNIT 1 Farm Life	UNIT 2 Handicrafts	UNIT 3 Tall Tales	UNIT 4 The Visual Arts	UNIT 5 Lasting Impressions	UNIT 6 Volcanoes	UNIT 7 Nature	UNIT 8 Animal Habitats
PACING	1 month	1 month	1 month	1 month	1 month	1 month	1 month	1 month

UNIT 7
Creative Thinking

■ Easy ■ Average ■ Challenging

OBJECTIVES
To use "what if?" questions as a strategy for creating

TEACHING THE LESSON

1. Getting Started

Oral Language Introduce the thinking skill, supposing, by asking students to imagine that they are sketching a horse. Ask: *What if the horse suddenly comes to life? What might it do? How would you react?* Explain that asking and answering "what if" questions is a kind of thinking called *supposing*.

Metacognition Help students become aware of their own thinking (think metacognitively) by asking follow-up questions when they respond (e.g., *How did you think of your answer?*). Encourage students to appreciate that thinking strategies are as different as the people who use them. Explain that in this lesson they will learn about the strategy of asking and answering "what if" questions.

2. Developing the Lesson

Guide students through the introduction to poetry (the kind of literature and writing they will deal with in this unit) and its connection to supposing. Lead them through Learning the Strategy, emphasizing the model chart with "what if" and follow-up questions. Identify those who would benefit from reteaching. Assign Using the Strategy A and B.

3. Closing the Lesson

Metacognition Applying the Strategy is a metacognitive activity in which students consider *how* they think (question 1) and *when* they think (question 2). Encourage a diversity of oral responses.

Question 1: Encourage students to share ideas about why it is important to think of follow-up questions (e.g., *They help you think of where the "what if" situation leads. They help you think of more ideas*). Encourage them also to share any personal strategies they might prefer to use. For instance, some students may say they like to draw pictures of the "what if" situation as a

CREATIVE THINKING ♦
A Strategy for Creating

ANSWERING "WHAT IF?"

Creating is making up or expressing something new. Poetry is one kind of creative writing. Poets often see things in new, fresh ways. For example, sometimes a poet will describe a thing as if it were a person. This is called personification. After this lesson, you will read some poems that use personification. Later you will use personification to write a poem.

For example, suppose *night* were a person. Read these lines from the poem "Four Glimpses of Night" by Frank Marshall Davis.

> Peddling
> From door to door
> Night sells
> Black bags of peppermint stars. . . .

How do poets think of ideas like this? One way is to ask "what if" questions. You could ask, "What if night were a person? What kind of person would it be? What would it do?" How does Frank Marshall Davis's poem answer those questions?

◆ Learning the Strategy

Asking "what if" is a way of supposing or imagining. When you answer a "what if" question, you can imagine many possibilities. For example, what if a storm knocked out electrical power in your school? What might happen? What if America built a space colony on Mars? What do you think life there might be like?

Sometimes "what if" questions can be about a make-believe situation. What if a horse you were drawing came to life? What answers might you give to that question? How would you think of your answers?

354 CREATIVE THINKING: Supposing

ESSENTIAL LANGUAGE SKILLS
This lesson provides opportunities to:

LISTENING ◆ listen actively and attentively

SPEAKING ◆ respond appropriately to questions from teachers and peers

READING ◆ draw logical conclusions ◆ evaluate and make judgments ◆ follow a set of directions ◆ use graphic sources for information, such as charts and graphs, timelines, pictures and diagrams

WRITING ◆ generate ideas using a variety of strategies, such as brainstorming, clustering, mapping, question and answer

LANGUAGE ◆ use language for creating

How can you think up possibilities in answer to a "what if" question? One way is to think of follow-up questions to your original "what if" question. Asking and answering these questions can help you develop your ideas. For example, think of that storm that might knock out electrical power. Here is a chart with a "what if" question and follow-up questions. What follow-up questions could you add? What answers could you add?

> *What if a storm knocked out electrical power in the school?*
>
> | | |
> |---|---|
> | *What would the teachers do?* | *Try to keep teaching.* |
> | *What would the kids do?* | *Start giggling.* |
> | *What physical things would happen?* | *Clocks would stop.* |

Using the Strategy

A. Write "What if I won a trip to anywhere I wanted to go?" Consider the question. Then write two or three good follow-up questions and answer them. Find out what your classmates wrote. Find out what your teacher would write!

B. Later you will read some poems. They are about school, fog, night, the sun, the moon, clouds, tomatoes, and the wind. In each poem the poet writes about the thing as if it were a person. Before you read the poems, choose one of the things. Write "What if (the thing you chose) were a person? What would it do?" Then read to see what ideas the poets had.

Applying the Strategy

♦ Why were the follow-up questions important for **A** and **B**?
♦ What "what if" questions might you ask and answer about one of your school subjects?

CREATIVE THINKING: Supposing **355**

---

way to stimulate their imaginations. Reassure them that there are many strategies for supposing, that they should use what works for them.

Question 2: Encourage students to think of how they might use "what if" questions in several different subject areas. For example in math *(I could think "What if I tried to solve this problem a different way?")* or in social studies *(I could ask "What if the Declaration of Independence had not been written?")* or in art *(I could look at this painting upside down or from a different position).* Point out that asking "what if" questions can help them look at and understand things in fresh ways.

Looking Ahead

The thinking strategy introduced in this lesson, answering "what if," is used in Using the Strategy B as a prereading strategy to help students anticipate the poetry. It will appear three more times in this unit and again in Unit 3.

ANSWERING "WHAT IF?"			
Strategy for Imagining	Writing to Learn	Prewriting	Writing Across the Curriculum
141	145	154	161

Strategy for Creating	Writing to Learn	Prewriting	Writing Across the Curriculum
355	359	370	376

Although the "what if" strategy is repeated in each presentation, the context in which it is used changes. Students will thus be given the opportunity to discover how the strategy can help them in reading, in writing across the curriculum, and in their daily lives.

◀━━▥▥▥ **TEACHING OPTIONS** ▥▥▥━━▶

RETEACHING

A Different Modality On the chalkboard write follow-up questions to "What if you woke up and found you had exchanged places with your pet," such as *What would you eat? How would you let your owner know what you wanted? What would you do for fun?* Have volunteers choose a question and answer it. Then encourage students to act out their answers or the role of a pet.

CLASS ENRICHMENT

A Cooperative Activity Give groups of students the following "what if?" question: *What if your school building could talk?* Have each group member write a follow-up question and hand it to the next group member to write an answer. Encourage imaginative and original follow-up questions and answers. Allow group members to choose their favorites to present to the class. Encourage the class to suggest additional answers to each question.

CHALLENGE

An Independent Extension Have students write follow-up questions and answers to the question *What if you woke up and found that you were a spider?* You may wish to have students use the information in their chart to write a poem or story.

UNIT 7
Literature

OBJECTIVES
To appreciate poetry
To read and respond to personification
To use a thinking strategy

VOCABULARY STRATEGIES

Developing Concepts and Teaching Vocabulary

Preteach the following words from the story. Use the Dictionary of Knowledge at the back of the book to provide definitions of base words and context sentences.

hide, pulse, ware(s), sideboards, salt-cellar(s), radiance

Write the vocabulary words on the chalkboard. Ask students if they have ever used a salt-cellar. Have volunteers describe the one they used and how they worked it. Then have students relate any experiences they may have had with the objects named by the other vocabulary words.

GUIDING COMPREHENSION

Building Background

The first half of this unit includes information especially chosen to build background for reading poetry about nature. If you started the unit with grammar instruction, you may wish to have a class discussion on the unit theme, **Nature,** based on the information in those lessons.

If you started the unit with composition instruction, you may wish to build students' knowledge of nature by asking: *What poems about nature have you enjoyed?* You may also want to introduce the term *personification*. Explain that when poets and other writers write as though a thing or a part of nature or even an idea has the qualities of a person, they are using personification. Give students examples, such as "the stubborn boulder" or "the tree sneezed, and leaves fluttered to the ground." Ask volunteers to give examples of their own personifying things in nature.

LITERATURE

Like many of us, poets often look at the world and imagine it differently. Sometimes they imagine that ordinary objects can come to life and act like people. A school, clouds, the sun, and the moon once came to life in these poets' imaginations. Read the poets' stories about each one.

What They Say

"Hooray, ray, ray"
  says the sun at noon

"It's been so lovely"
  says the setting sun

"If only, my darling"
  says the rising moon

"Don't lose hope"
  say the white clouds floating by.
                                        — Lillian Morrison

Definitions

Fog: a cloud
That no matter how hard it tried
Couldn't get off the ground.

Cloud: a fog
That finally got tired
Lying around, a lot of useless weather.

So now it walks the sky
Trying to bunch a rain-bouquet together.
                                        — X. J. Kennedy

ESSENTIAL LANGUAGE SKILLS

This lesson provides opportunities to:

LISTENING ◆ employ active listening in a variety of situations ◆ listen to appreciate sound devices of rhythm, rhyme, alliteration, and onomatopoeia

SPEAKING ◆ make organized oral presentations ◆ use a variety of words to express feelings and ideas

READING ◆ understand cause-and-effect relationships ◆ draw logical conclusions ◆ evaluate and make judgments ◆ respond to various forms of literature

WRITING ◆ generate ideas using a variety of strategies, such as brainstorming, clustering, mapping, question and answer

LANGUAGE ◆ use language for creating

Four Glimpses of Night

III.

Peddling
From door to door
Night sells
Black bags of peppermint stars
Heaping cones of vanilla moon
Until
His <u>wares</u> are gone
Then shuffles homeward
Jingling the gray coins
Of daybreak.

— *Frank Marshall Davis*

Again and again,
The wind wipes away the clouds
And shines up the moon.

— *Kazue Mizumura*

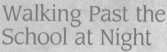

Walking Past the School at Night

It lies
solid   stretched out
eyes blank   a blind
beast
dozing in the glare
of moonlight.

Under the dusty <u>hide</u>
heartbeats echo
in the hollow chest   <u>pulse</u>
has slowed to
nothing   the clanging bell
around its neck
is still.

We hurry past   staring at
each other   something
is moving!   A shadow?
Did you see an eye
blink?
A hot wind blows—breath of
the mammoth!
Run!

— *Barbara Juster Esbensen*

LITERATURE: Poetry **357**

SUMMARY

In the poems on pages 356–358, the use of personification, giving human or lifelike qualities to nonhuman things, is the unifying theme. For example, Barbara Juster Esbensen describes a school at night as "a blind beast dozing in the glare of the moonlight." Frank Marshall Davis describes night as a door-to-door peddler selling "black bags of peppermint stars." Lillian Morrison gives the power of speech to the sun, the moon, and the clouds. Pablo Neruda writes about a tomato that "invades kitchens, takes over lunches."

Developing a Purpose for Reading

Option 1: Have students read the introduction to the poems and study the illustrations. Explain that these poems all give human qualities to nonhuman things. On the chalkboard write *If I were a poet . . .* and have students complete the sentence with things they might want to give human qualities in a poem. You may wish to record students' sentences for later use. Suggest that students read to find whether the poets had any of the same ideas they did.

Option 2: If you wish to set a reading purpose for everyone, have students pay special attention to how the poets use words to make things come alive. Have them ask themselves: *What is being compared in these poems?*

GUIDED READING

Please note that opportunities for students' personal responses to the selection are offered in the Reader's Response question and the Selection Follow-up at the end of this lesson.

Page 356 "Walking Past the School at Night" *In this poem the school building is compared to a mammoth. How are a school building and a mammoth alike?* (Answers will vary, but students may suggest that a school at night is empty, quiet, and mysterious, as mysterious and frightening as an ancient mammoth.) ANALYZE: COMPARISONS

Page 357 "Definitions" *Imagine a friendly cloud. What words would you use to describe it?* (Answers will vary. Encourage imaginative responses by having students tell what the cloud might do to show its friendliness. For example, the cloud might follow them to school, bouncing along in the sky.) ANALYZE: COMPARISONS

Page 357 "Again and again" *In this poem the wind is compared to a friendly being that "shines up the moon." Imagine the wind in different situations, such as during a storm or cooling you on a hot day. What other human traits might you give the wind?* (Answers will vary, but the tone should reflect the different situations. A wind during a storm might scratch or tear. A cool wind on a hot day might be compared to a person fanning you.) SYNTHESIZE: COMPARISONS

Page 358 "Ode to the Tomato" *In this poem the tomato is described as something that cuts loose, invades, and takes over. Recall a food that you like or have strong feelings about. How would you describe that food as though it were human?* (Answers will vary. Remind students to use their feelings in describing the food. Students might describe a food that they like, such as ice cream, as soothing or calming them, and a food they dislike, such as certain vegetables, as trying to choke them.) SYNTHESIZE: COMPARISONS

Returning to the Reading Purpose

Option 1: Those students who have written "If I were the poet" sentences may wish to review them to see if they and the poet shared any of the same ideas about what to give human qualities.

Option 2: If you have established a common reading purpose, review it and ask students to tell what is being compared in each poem.

READER'S RESPONSE

Which poem was your favorite? What did you like about it? (Give students the opportunity to read aloud the poems that were their favorites.)

from

Ode to the Tomato

. . .

In December
the tomato
cuts loose,
invades
kitchens,
takes over lunches,
settles
at rest
on sideboards,
with the glasses,
butter dishes,
blue salt-cellars.
It has
its own radiance,
a goodly majesty. . . .
— *Pablo Neruda*

◆ **Reader's Response**

Which poem was your favorite? What did you like about it?

◆ **358** ▷ LITERATURE: Poetry

STRATEGIC READING

Page 358 Ask students to visualize, or make a mental picture, as you read aloud "Walking Past the School at Night." You may wish to have students recall what a school is like during the day—busy people, noisy halls, ringing bells. Then allow students to describe the mental picture the poem gave them. Explain that visualizing is one way for students to check their understanding of what they read. METACOGNITION: FEELINGS/ATTITUDES AND DETAILS

HIGHLIGHTING LITERATURE

Page 358 Discuss with students how each poem looks on the page. Point out how the position and space between words in "Walking Past the School at Night" affects how those words are said or read. You may wish to have students write out in sentence form "Walking Past the School at Night," "Four Glimpses of Night," and "Ode to the Tomato." Ask students to compare the feelings the sentence forms give them with the feelings the poems as they appear in their books give them.

Poetry

Responding to Literature

1. X. J. Kennedy defined fog and a cloud. He gave them personalities. What aspect of weather puzzles you? Work with a partner to choose and define one aspect of weather. Start by listing types of weather, and then choose one to define. Discuss whether it might be sad or joyful. Then show that personality through your definition. Share your definition with the class.

2. Barbara Juster Esbensen passes a school at night and it becomes a mammoth. Look through a poet's eyes. Imagine one other thing that a school at night could be.

3. The tomato in Pablo Neruda's poem invades the kitchen. What would a potato, an onion, an ear of corn, or a squash do? Draw a picture that shows your vegetable at work.

Writing to Learn

Think and Create ◆ Use a "what if" question to help you create. Look at the questions below. Then create three of your own.

What if stars were eyes?
What if clouds had arms?
What if trees were soldiers?

What if clouds had arms?	
How many arms would they have?	*ten each*
Would they have hands?	*feet instead of hands*
How would they use their arms?	*to throw rainbows*

What-if Chart

Write ◆ Choose your favorite question. Build on your "what if" idea, and answer the question that it asks.

LITERATURE: Poetry ⟨359⟩

WRITING TO LEARN

Have students apply the thinking strategy. They may choose to ask questions about nature, using the material in this unit for background knowlege, or they may ask questions about other things of interest to them. Remind them to use personification as they create questions. Have them write their "what if" questions as described in Think and Create. Then have students complete the Write activity by answering their favorite question. Call on volunteers to read their questions and answers aloud.

SELECTION FOLLOW-UP

You may wish to incorporate any or all of the following discussion questions and activities in your follow-up to the poetry.

RESPONDING TO LITERATURE

Encourage students to use their personal experiences as well as what they learned from the selection to discuss these questions. The questions are designed to encourage students to think of and respond to the selection as a whole. Explain to students that although they may use details from the selection to support their opinions, the questions have no right or wrong answers. Encourage them to express a variety of points of view. You may wish to have students respond as a class, in groups, or with partners.

1. *X. J. Kennedy defined fog and a cloud. He gave them personalities. What aspect of weather puzzles you? Work with a partner to choose and define one aspect of the weather. Start by listing types of weather, and then choose one to define. Discuss whether it might be angry or sad or joyful. Then show that personality through your definition. Share your definition with the class.* (You may wish to provide class time for students to discuss different kinds of weather and different emotions before they work with partners.)

2. *Barbara Juster Ebensen passes a school at night and it becomes a mammoth. Look through a poet's eyes. Imagine one other thing that a school at night could be.* (To give students a point of view for answering, discuss with them what a school is like during the day and what it is like at night. You may wish to have students recall what feelings they associate with school.)

3. *The tomato in Pablo Neruda's poem invades the kitchen. What would a potato, an onion, an ear of corn, or a squash do? Draw a picture that shows your vegetable at work.* (The pictures students draw will depend on the feelings or ideas they associate with the vegetable they choose. They might, for instance, draw an onion telling a very sad story.)

 World of Language Audio Library

A recording of this selection is available in the **Audio Library**.

■ Easy ■ Average ■ Challenging

OBJECTIVES
To listen to poetry for enjoyment
To recognize that sound, rhythm, and expression in poetry can enhance meaning
To use guidelines for reading and listening to poetry

ASSIGNMENT GUIDE
BASIC   Practice A
 ⬇   Practice B
ADVANCED   Practice C

All should do the Apply activity.

RESOURCES
■ World of Language Video Library

TEACHING THE LESSON

1. Getting Started
Oral Language Focus attention on this oral activity, encouraging all to participate. To vary the activity you may wish to have some students say another tongue twister, such as: *How much wood could a woodchuck chuck, if a woodchuck could chuck wood?*

2. Developing the Lesson
Guide students through a discussion of the lesson, emphasizing the guidelines for reading a poem aloud and being an active listener. You may wish to demonstrate the sound, rhythm, and expression in poetry by reading one or more poems aloud to the class. Lead students through the **Guided Practice.** Identify those who would benefit from reteaching. Assign independent Practice A–C.

3. Closing the Lesson
After students complete the Apply activity, call on individuals to read aloud the poem in the article. Point out to them that knowing how to read poetry aloud can increase their own and other people's enjoyment of poetry.

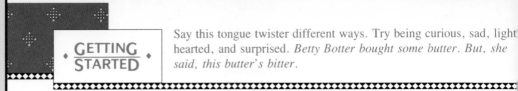

♦ GETTING STARTED ♦

Say this tongue twister different ways. Try being curious, sad, light hearted, and surprised. *Betty Botter bought some butter. But, she said, this butter's bitter.*

SPEAKING and LISTENING ♦
Reading Poetry Aloud

Every poem ever written was meant for reading aloud. Poems have sounds and rhythms that are meant to be heard. Hearing poetry also helps people imagine their own pictures as they listen. Reading poetry aloud engages our imaginations as well as our ears.

With a little practice and some imagination, you can learn to read poetry aloud and to be an active listener. Here are some guides to help you.

Reading a Poem Aloud	1. Choose a poem you like and would enjoy reading for others. 2. Practice reading it aloud until you are comfortable with the words and rhythms. 3. Notice the poet's clues to understanding the poem. Look for complete thoughts and brief pauses, like the spaces between verses. The poem's shape and the length of its lines are also visual clues. Be alert to them all. 4. Think about how you can read the poem with expression. Make your own copy of the poem to mark for reading. You might underline words to emphasize, add a brief pause or two, or note where to lower your voice. 5. Imagine your own pictures for the poem as you say it. 6. Speak clearly in a natural, but expressive, voice.
Being an Active Listener	1. Use your imagination to create pictures for the poem. 2. Listen for repeated words, rhymes, and other clues that will help you remember what you heard.

Summary ♦ Choose a poem you like and practice reading it. Pay attention to the poet's clues to sound, rhythm, and meaning. Speak clearly, with expression.

360   SPEAKING and LISTENING: Poetry

ESSENTIAL LANGUAGE SKILLS
This lesson provides opportunities to:

LISTENING ♦ listen to appreciate sound devices of rhythm, rhyme, alliteration, and onomatopoeia ♦ listen actively and attentively

SPEAKING ♦ participate in storytelling and creative dramatics ♦ speak expressively by varying volume, rate, or intonation

READING ♦ accurately comprehend the details in a reading selection ♦ evaluate and make judgments ♦ follow a set of directions

WRITING ♦ write and compose for a variety of purposes ♦ stimulate creative activities through drawing

LANGUAGE ♦ recognize ways in which language can be used to influence others

Guided Practice

Read aloud these sentences, expressing a feeling of mystery and mounting suspense. Notice the end marks, the words that are underlined, and the spaces between words that indicate pauses.

1. Something is coming!   **3.** Don't   come   any   <u>closer</u>!
2. Who is it? Who's <u>there</u>?   **4.** <u>Where</u> could they be?

Practice

A. Make your own copy of the last verse of the poem "Walking Past the School at Night," on page 357. On your copy, add notes and marks that will prepare you for reading this verse aloud.

- ♦ Note complete thoughts and pauses. How will you mark them?
- ♦ Are there words that you would like to emphasize by underlining?
- ♦ Look at the word *blink*. Why do you think it is on a line all by itself? How will you say it?
- ♦ Look at the word *Run!* at the end of the verse. Why is it printed in italic, or slanted, type? How will you say it?
- ♦ What mood or feeling does this poem have?

B. With a partner, take turns reading "Walking Past the School at Night." Sketch the pictures you imagine as you listen.

C. With a small group, prepare a choral reading of "What They Say," on page 356. Decide which lines could be said by solo, or single, voices and which ones could be said by everyone.

Apply ♦ Think and Write

Dictionary of Knowledge ♦ Read about the poet X. J. Kennedy in the Dictionary of Knowledge. Read the poem in the article to a friend or relative.

> ✏ **Remember**
> to look for clues in a poem that will help you read it aloud.

SPEAKING and LISTENING: Poetry **361**

🖥 **World of Language Video Library**

You may wish to use the *Video Library* to teach this lesson.

EVALUATION PROGRAM

See Evaluation and Testing Program, pp. C9–C11.

Speaking and Listening Check-list Masters

◀▥▥ TEACHING OPTIONS ▥▥▶

RETEACHING

A Different Modality Have the group listen to a poem that is easy to visualize. You may wish to play a recording of the poem, invite someone special such as the principal or the librarian to read the poem to the class, or ask a student who reads poetry well to present the poem. Ask students to make mental pictures as they listen, then make drawings or paintings to illustrate the poem.

CLASS ENRICHMENT

A Cooperative Activity Have small groups tape record choral readings, such as readings they prepared for exercise C in the lesson. Have the groups practice with the tape recorder until they are satisfied that each line, whether read as a solo or by the group, can be clearly understood. Have each group play its tape for the class.

CHALLENGE

An Independent Extension Have students collect poems they would like to read aloud. You may wish to have them categorize the poems for different audiences, such as *Poems for First Graders* and *Poems for Fifth Graders*. You also may wish to have them organize a poetry program and read some of the poems aloud to the target groups. Encourage students to illustrate their collections.

UNIT 7
Writing

■ Easy ■ Average ■ Challenging

OBJECTIVES
To listen to poetry for enjoyment
To identify repetition in poetry
To use repetition in writing

ASSIGNMENT GUIDE
BASIC   Responding to Poetry
⬇
ADVANCED

All should do the Apply activity.

RESOURCES
■ Reteaching Master 62
■ Practice Master 62

TEACHING
THE LESSON

1. Getting Started
Oral Language Focus attention on this oral activity, encouraging all to participate. You may wish to record on the chalkboard the words to "Row, Row, Row Your Boat" as students sing the song. Then you may wish to have volunteers underline the repeated words or phrases, such as *row* and *merrily*. Other familiar songs with repeated words include "Happy Birthday" and "Skip to My Lou."

2. Developing the Lesson
Guide students through the explanation of repetition in poetry, emphasizing the examples and the summary. Identify those who would benefit from reteaching. Assign Responding to Poetry.

3. Closing the Lesson
After students complete the Apply activity, you may wish to have volunteers share the words or phrases they have chosen to repeat in a poem. Encourage discussion of how the words or phrases might bring a sound pattern to poems about different subjects. Point out to students that knowing how to use repetition can help them create a sound pattern in their poetry.

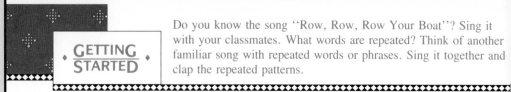

GETTING STARTED

Do you know the song "Row, Row, Row Your Boat"? Sing it with your classmates. What words are repeated? Think of another familiar song with repeated words or phrases. Sing it together and clap the repeated patterns.

WRITING ◆
Repetition in Poetry

Sound is one of the ways in which poetry appeals to our senses. Many poets use rhyme or rhythm to produce pleasing sound patterns. Other poets create sound patterns by using repetition, the repeating of a word or phrase. Listen to the repetition in these two poems. What beginning words do these poets repeat?

Direction

I was directed by my grandfather   To the, so I might
To the East,
     so I might have the power of the bear;
To the South,
     so I might have the courage of the eagle;
To the West,
     so I might have the wisdom of the owl;
To the North,
     so I might have the craftiness of the fox;
To the Earth,
     so I might receive her fruit;
To the Sky,
     so I might lead a life of innocence.
                 —*Alonzo Lopez*

Night
—from *The Windy City*

Night gathers itself into a ball of dark yarn,   Night
Night loosens the ball and it spreads.
The lookouts from the shores of Lake Michigan
     find the night follows day,
       and ping! ping! across the sheet gray
       the boat lights put their signals.
Night lets the dark yarn unravel,
Night speaks and the yarns change
     to fog and blue strands.
                 —*Carl Sandburg*

362   WRITING: Repetition in Poetry

ESSENTIAL LANGUAGE SKILLS
This lesson provides opportunities to:

LISTENING ◆ employ active listening in a variety of situations ◆ listen to appreciate sound devices of rhythm, rhyme, alliteration, and onomatopoeia

SPEAKING ◆ engage in creative dramatic activities and nonverbal communication ◆ use creative devices, such as figurative language, jingles, coined words, and anecdotes

READING ◆ use context to understand the meaning of words ◆ evaluate and make judgments ◆ follow a set of directions ◆ respond to various forms of literature ◆ recognize literary forms and explain how they differ

WRITING ◆ generate ideas using a variety of strategies, such as brainstorming, clustering, free writing

LANGUAGE ◆ recognize ways in which language can be used to influence others ◆ use language for imagining

Alonzo Lopez repeats the phrase *so I might* six times in "Direction." What words does Carl Sandburg repeat in "Night"? How does he use repetition to describe a particular sound? night, ball, dark yarn; ping! ping!

In "River," Locke repeats beginning words and phrases to add to the sound pattern. How many kinds of repetition can you find? The river is repeated six times. The phrases *The river moans* and *The river sings* each occur twice.

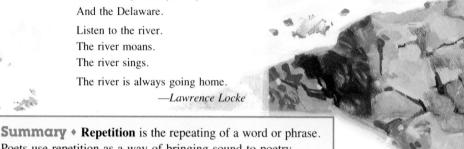

River

The river moans.

The river sings.

Listen to the Fox, the Menominee,
The Susquehanna, Colorado, Platte,
The Ottawa, Snake, Bear,
And the Delaware.

Listen to the river.
The river moans.
The river sings.

The river is always going home.

—*Lawrence Locke*

Summary ◆ **Repetition** is the repeating of a word or phrase. Poets use repetition as a way of bringing sound to poetry.

Responding to Poetry

To poet Lawrence Locke, the river moans and sings. What else have you heard in nature that seems to be crying or singing?

Lopez's grandfather wanted the poet to be like many animals. What are the characteristics you would most like to have?

Carl Sandburg uses the words *ping! ping!* to describe the signals sent by boat lights. Make a list of some repetitive words or phrases that *you* often use to describe things.

Apply ◆ Think and Write

Creative Writing ◆ Choose a subject you might like to write a poem about. Make a list of words and phrases you might like to use. Then underline two words or phrases you would like to repeat.

✏️ **Remember** to listen for rhyme or repetition in poetry.

WRITING: Repetition in Poetry **363**

Repetition in Poetry

Read the poem. Underline the words that repeat.

Happily, with abundant showers, may I walk.
Happily, with abundant plants, may I walk.
Happily, on the trail of pollen, may I walk.
Happily may I walk.

—Navajo

Repetition is the repeating of a word or phrase. Repetition in poetry can add meaning to a poet's words. Poets use repetition as a way of bringing sound to poetry.

A. Use the poem above to answer each question.

1. Which words are repeated?
   happily, with, abundant, may, I, walk

2. Why do you think repetition is used in this poem? Answers will vary.
   Possible answer includes: The repetition helps to show how much
   the poet enjoys walking.

B. Read the poem. Look at the underlined words. Then answer the questions.

Long Trip
The sea is a wilderness of waves,
A desert of water.
We dip and dive,
Rise and roll,
Hide and are hidden

On the sea,
Day, night,
Night, day,
The sea is a desert of waves,
A wilderness of water.
—Langston Hughes

3. Which words in the poem are repeated? Sea, wilderness, waves, desert, water, day, night

4. How many times is the word wilderness repeated? two

5. How many times is the word desert repeated? two

6. How many times are the words day and night repeated? two

7. How many times is the word sea repeated? two

PRACTICE 62

Repetition in Poetry

Repetition is the repeating of a word or phrase. Poets use repetition as a way of bringing sound to poetry.

A. As you read, notice how the poet uses repetition. Then answer each question below.

How Gray the Rain
How gray the rain
And gray the world
And gray the rain clouds overhead,
When suddenly
Some cloud is furled
And there is gleaming sun instead!

The raindrops drip
Prismatic light,
And trees and meadows burn in green,
And arched in air
Serene and bright
The rainbow all at once is seen.
—Elisabeth Coatsworth

1. Which words are repeated in "How Gray the Rain"?
   gray, rain

2. Why do you think the poet repeats these words? How do you think the repetitions affect the meaning of the poem?
   Answers will vary. Possible answers include: The poet wants to emphasize
   how gray the world looks on a rainy day. The repetitions help
   contrast the dreariness of a rainy day with the brightness of a
   sunny day.

3. Elisabeth Coatsworth expresses the grayness of a rainy day. How does a rainy day make you feel?
   Answers will vary. Possible answers include: A rainy day makes me
   feel sad. I feel like being quiet on a rainy day.

WRITE IT
Write words you might repeat in a poem about rain when rain makes you feel sad. Then write words you might repeat in a poem about rain when rain makes you feel happy. Write on a separate sheet of paper. Answers will vary.

◀||| TEACHING OPTIONS |||▶

RETEACHING

A Different Modality Have students recall words and phrases they hear over and over again, such as *Have a nice day* and *No problem,* and phrases in advertising slogans and jingles. List students' responses on the chalkboard. Encourage discussion of the reasons why people often repeat words and phrases (e.g., to remember things, for emphasis, to enjoy rhyme or rhythm in songs and games).

CLASS ENRICHMENT

A Cooperative Activity Have students work in small groups and have each group choose a subject of general interest, such as kite flying or summertime. Then have students list words or phrases that might be used to describe the subject. Have group members choose two words or phrases they might like to repeat to create a sound pattern. You may wish to have one member of each group share the words or phrases with the class.

CHALLENGE

An Independent Extension Have students write an original poem using repetition. Before students write, have them make a list of words or phrases describing their subject. Then have students underline two words or phrases they might want to repeat in their poem. You may wish to have students illustrate their poems and then collect their work in an anthology.

UNIT 7
Writing

■ Easy ■ Average ■ Challenging

OBJECTIVES
To listen to poetry for enjoyment
To understand the rules of the haiku form
To appreciate haiku

ASSIGNMENT GUIDE
BASIC   Responding to Poetry
↓
ADVANCED

All should do the Apply activity.

RESOURCES
■ Reteaching Master 63
■ Practice Master 63

TEACHING THE LESSON

1. Getting Started
Oral Language Focus attention on this oral activity, encouraging all to participate. You may wish to model an example response, emphasizing that you are speaking in the present tense: *The school bus stops, and I look out the window. I see two people riding bright blue bicycles in and out of the dark trees in the park.*

2. Developing the Lesson
Guide students through the explanation of haiku, emphasizing the examples and the summary. When discussing the haiku by Meisetsu, you may wish to ask students for specific images, such as *The river runs over a waterfall and disappears from sight.* When discussing the haiku by Boncho, you may wish to mention that the haiku has three lines with 17 syllables, it has the nature words *cloud* and *moon,* and it is about one thing described in the present tense. Then identify students who would benefit from reteaching. Assign Responding to Poetry.

3. Closing the Lesson
After students complete the Apply activity, you may wish to have them share their ideas for haiku. Point out to students that they can write a haiku to present an image of one thing as if it were happening now.

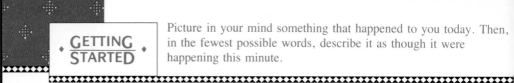

◆ GETTING STARTED ◆ Picture in your mind something that happened to you today. Then, in the fewest possible words, describe it as though it were happening this minute.

WRITING ◆
Haiku

The haiku is a Japanese verse form that presents a picture to its readers. Long ago, the haiku was the beginning part of a longer poem. So the word *haiku* literally means ''beginning phrase.'' Today, the haiku is still very much like the beginning of a story, but its readers must continue the story for themselves. Here is a haiku by the poet Meisetsu.

> A river leaping,
> tumbling over rocks roars on . . .
> as the mountain smiles.
> —*Meisetsu*

Meisetsu's haiku gives us a picture of a leaping river. Close your eyes and imagine that you, too, are watching the river tumble and roar over rocks. Can you add something to this image? Can you picture how far the river goes?

Haiku has many strict rules that give this form its special character. A haiku is usually written in three lines and seventeen syllables. The first and third lines each have five syllables. The second line has seven. In addition, a haiku should always contain a nature or a season word, or use words that suggest a particular season. A haiku should be about only one thing, just as Meisetsu's haiku is about a leaping river. Every haiku should picture what is happening in the present tense, as if it is happening now.

Boncho's haiku follows many rules of the haiku form. Read this haiku. How does it follow the rules you have learned?

> 1 2 3   4 5
> The ragged phantom
> 1 2 3   4 5 6 7
> of a cloud ambles after
> 1 2   3   4   5
> a slim dancing moon.

3 lines, 17 syllables; nature words *cloud* and *moon*;   —*Boncho*
about night sky; in present tense

364   WRITING: Haiku

ESSENTIAL LANGUAGE SKILLS
This lesson provides opportunities to:

LISTENING ◆ respond appropriately to orally presented directions ◆ employ active listening in a variety of situations

SPEAKING ◆ use creative devices such as figurative language, jingles, coined words, and anecdotes ◆ read aloud a variety of written materials

READING ◆ accurately comprehend the details in a reading selection ◆ make valid inferences about a reading selection ◆ use context to understand the meaning of words ◆ evaluate and make judgments ◆ follow a set of directions ◆ recognize literary forms and explain how they differ

WRITING ◆ stimulate creative activities through drawing ◆ generate ideas using a variety of strategies, such as brainstorming, clustering, free writing

LANGUAGE ◆ use language for imagining ◆ recognize and understand the meaning of figurative language ◆ use language for creating

These two haiku about the rain seem to suggest two different seasons. What season does each haiku seem to picture? What words that suggest a season helped you answer the question?

> All day in gray rain
> hollyhocks follow the sun's
> invisible road.
> —Basho
>
> summer

> Slanting, windy rain . . .
> umbrella, raincoat, and rain
> talking together . . .
> —Buson
>
> spring (autumn or winter)

Because a haiku is so brief, each word must be carefully chosen. Haiku poets seldom use repetition unless it is necessary. Haiku poets never use rhyme. Instead, they give us an image of a moment. The best haiku give us an image that leads us to make our own pictures to carry away in our minds.

Summary ◆ Haiku is a Japanese verse form that presents a picture to which we add our own thoughts and images.

Responding to Poetry

A. All the haiku on these two pages use personification. Human qualities and movement are given to such nonhuman things as a river, a mountain, a cloud, hollyhocks, rain, an umbrella, and a raincoat. What other things around you might leap, or amble, or talk together? Answers will vary.

B. In Basho's haiku, *hollyhocks* and *sun's* are season words for summer. What other season words could you use for summer? Make lists of season words for spring, autumn, and winter. Answers will vary.

C. Choose one haiku that you have read. What else do you see that is not pictured by the words? Draw a picture showing how you would complete this haiku image. Pictures will vary.

Apply ◆ Think and Write

Creative Writing ◆ Think of something you have seen happening that might make a good haiku. Write down the subject for your haiku. Then note the important words you might use in your poem.

📝 **Remember**
that poets write haiku to present one image as if it were happening now.

WRITING: Haiku **365**

Haiku

Read the poem. It is haiku. Haiku contains a nature word. It uses the present tense. It contains 17 syllables in three lines. Write the number of syllables (/) in each line. The first line is done for you.

> I must go begging ——— Line 1. _5_
> for water . . . morning glories ——— Line 2. _7_
> have captured my well. ——— Line 3. _5_
> —Chiyo ——— TOTAL: _17_

↻ **Haiku** is a Japanese verse form that presents a picture to which we add our own thoughts and images. Haiku has strict rules that give this form its special character.

A. Read the haiku. Then answer each question. Answers may vary.

> How cool hay smells
> when carried through the farm gate
> as the sun comes up.
> —Boncho

1. What does the poem tell about? _the smell of cut hay on a farm_
2. What is the time of day in the poem? _the morning_
3. What words tell about the time of day? _the sun comes up_
4. List the words in the poem that tell you about something in nature.
   cool cut hay; sun comes up
5. Does the verb <u>smells</u> tell about the past, the present, or the future?
   the present

B. Choose three topics in nature that might make a good haiku. Then write two important words to describe each topic.

EXAMPLE: _thunder_   _loud, frightening_
6. _Answers will vary._
7. _____
8. _____

PRACTICE 63

Haiku

↻ **Haiku** is a Japanese verse form that presents a picture to which we add our own thoughts and images.

A. Answer each question about the haiku.

> A mountain village
> deep in snow . . . under the drifts
> a sound of water.
> —Shiki

1. How can you tell this poem is haiku? Use all the facts you know about haiku to support your answer.
   Answers will vary. Possible answers: The poem contains 5-7-5
   syllables per line. It is about something in nature. It is written in
   the present tense. It is about one thing.

2. What sounds in nature do you think might be good subjects for a haiku? Write three ideas.
   Answers will vary.

B. Choose two of the sounds you listed above. Write some important words about the sounds. Answers will vary.
3. _____
4. _____

WRITE IT
In the middle of a separate sheet of paper, write the name of an animal. Then write related words around the animal's name. Underline words you might use in a haiku about the animal. Answers will vary.

◀▦ TEACHING OPTIONS ▦▶

RETEACHING

A Different Modality Have students take turns describing something in nature in complete sentences, such as a butterfly. List students' responses on the chalkboard. Then have students underline the most important words in each sentence. Have volunteers retell the description as vividly as possible, trying to use only the underlined words. Discuss the idea that a haiku is a nature poem that follows strict rules and presents a clear picture.

CLASS ENRICHMENT

A Cooperative Activity Have students work in small groups to write ideas for haiku about a seasonal activity, such as picnicking. Have each group choose a different topic and a recorder to list important words that describe the activity and the time of the year. Then have group members choose among the words to create a phrase that might be used in haiku. You may wish to have one member of each group share the phrase with the class.

CHALLENGE

An Independent Extension Have students write about an experience using the haiku form. You may wish to have them use personification. If so, tell them that Meisetsu's or Boncho's haiku in the lesson can serve as a model.

Reading–Writing Connection

OBJECTIVES
To identify personification in poetry
To work together to pantomime an action in a poem
To work together to write sentences using personification
To use the Thesaurus to improve word choice

Focus on the Poet's Voice

Review the Unit 7 poetry selections with students and have them describe how the poets used personification to give life to inanimate objects. Then point out to students that they can use the selections to help them learn how to use personification.

You may wish to guide students through the introductory paragraphs, stressing the examples. Then have students read the poems on their own. Discuss how in the poems balloons and clouds seem to act like animals or people. Point out the words and phrases that make balloons seem like animals, such as *bumps and butts its head on the cage walls, bellow, strain at their string leashes.* Have students tell how clouds act like humans. *(They weave.)* Ask volunteers to tell how the sky is made to seem human. *(It puts on a shawl in bad weather.)*

Next, have students apply the information in the Reading-Writing Connection by discussing the questions at the bottom of the page. As students talk about the questions, guide them to recognize how balloons and clouds are made to seem like animals or people.

Focus on the Poet's Voice

A poet may show something that is not human behaving in a human or lifelike way. If so, the poet is using **personification**. Poets often use personification to give life to what they see around them. Notice in these poems how balloons and clouds seem to act like animals or people.

Balloons

A balloon
is a wild
space animal,
restless pet
who bumps and butts
its head
on the cage walls
of a room —
bursts
with a bellow,
or escapes slowly
with sighs
leaving a limp skin

Balloons
on the street
fidget
in fresh air
strain
at their string
leashes.
If you loose
a balloon,
it bolts home
for the moon.
— *Judith Thurman*

Garment

The clouds weave a shawl
Of downy plaid
For the sky to put on
When the weather's bad.
— *Langston Hughes*

The Writer's Voice ◆ What actions do balloons and clouds have in common with animals or people?

What different personalities do the poets give to balloons and clouds? How well do these personalities fit? Why?

ESSENTIAL LANGUAGE SKILLS
This lesson provides opportunities to:

LISTENING ◆ select from an oral presentation the information needed ◆ listen actively and attentively

SPEAKING ◆ engage in creative dramatic activities and nonverbal communication ◆ contribute to class and small group discussions ◆ use a set of reasons to persuade a group ◆ present stories, puns, riddles, anecdotes or plays for entertainment

READING ◆ recall specific facts and details that support the main idea and/or conclusion ◆ evaluate and make judgments ◆ follow a set of directions ◆ respond to various forms of literature

WRITING ◆ use the thesaurus as a means to expand vocabulary ◆ write and compose for a variety of purposes

LANGUAGE ◆ recognize and understand the meaning of figurative language

Working Together

Give human or lifelike qualities to things that are not alive as your group works on activities **A** and **B**.

A. Volunteers in the group read aloud the poems containing personification, on pages 356–358. Choose one of the poems to act out with pantomime, or body movement. Different people may act out different parts. Decide who will do each part. Then plan the actions and work together practicing them. Finally, present the pantomime to the rest of the class. Have the audience try to guess what is being portrayed. *Answers will vary.*

B. Choose three things to personify from the following list of objects. Discuss what each object has in common with people. For example, a pencil sharpener *moves* its *arm* and *teeth* to *eat* the pencils put in its *mouth*. Decide which object can be most successfully presented as a human being. With your group, write three original sentences personifying the object.
Answers will vary.

1. Venetian blinds
2. airplane
3. wastebasket
4. windmill
5. bulldozer
6. weathervane

In Your Group

◆ Encourage everyone to share ideas.

◆ Record the group's ideas.

◆ Remind group members to listen carefully.

◆ Help the group reach agreement.

THESAURUS CORNER • Word Choice

Look up these five words in the Thesaurus. For each word, choose a synonym that will help you personify a kite. Use each synonym in a sentence that brings the kite to life.
Answers will vary.

Working Together

The Working Together activities provide opportunities for students to work together in cooperative learning groups. You may wish to pair strong writers with students whose skills are weaker so that all students may experience success in writing.

Divide the class into small groups and have students read In Your Group. Encourage them to discuss why each task is important. Have them tell what might happen if the group does not follow through on each task. *(If we do not encourage everyone to share ideas, some members of the group may be afraid to speak up. If we do not record ideas, we may forget important points that are discussed. If we do not listen carefully, we may miss important ideas. If we do not reach agreement, we will be unable to work together to complete the activity.)*

You may wish to have each group appoint a recorder and a timekeeper. Then set a time limit of ten or fifteen minutes for each activity. After each group pantomimes a poem, have the class identify what was portrayed. After activity B, call on a member of each group to read aloud the three sentences using personification. Have the class listen carefully to determine the human characteristics given to each object.

Thesaurus Corner

The Thesaurus Corner provides students with the opportunity to extend the Reading-Writing Connection by using the Thesaurus in the back of the textbook. If necessary, remind them how a thesaurus is used. Then have them complete the Thesaurus Corner activity. After students have written five sentences, call on individuals to read their sentences aloud. Encourage students to compare their sentences and tell how the synonyms help personify a kite. Have students save their sentences for use later in the Writing Process lesson. Point out that learning how to use synonyms that bring life to inanimate objects can help students develop their ability to use personification in poetry and in other writing.

OBJECTIVES

To write a poem

To use five stages of the writing process: prewriting, writing, revising, proofreading, and publishing

RESOURCES

Writing Process Transparencies 25–28

Revising and Proofreading Transparencies

Spelling Connection

Writing Sample Tests, p. T555

INTRODUCTION

Connecting to Literature Have students read the introduction to themselves, or ask a volunteer to read the introduction aloud. Emphasize that the poetry selections students read in this unit all show examples of personification. Have students point out examples of personification in those poems. If necessary, go back to the poems and help students find the words the poets use to tell about things as if they were people. Encourage responses that cite the poets' words. Then tell students that they will soon write a poem of their own.

Purpose and Audience Ask volunteers to name other poems or rhymes that they have enjoyed. Have them discuss those poems and the personification in the poems. Then ask students to tell when they have used personification in their own speech or writing. Encourage personal responses.

Have students consider the questions: *What is my purpose?* (To express a fresh image or idea through personification) *Who is my audience?* (A friend) Have students discuss what they believe they need to consider when writing a poem for a friend. Guide students to give a diversity of responses.

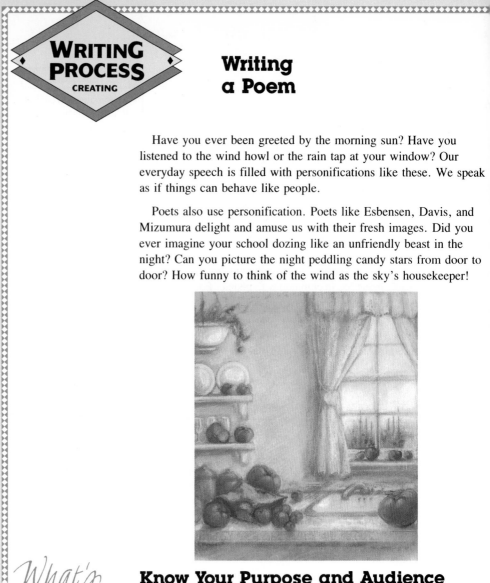

WRITING PROCESS
CREATING

Writing a Poem

Have you ever been greeted by the morning sun? Have you listened to the wind howl or the rain tap at your window? Our everyday speech is filled with personifications like these. We speak as if things can behave like people.

Poets also use personification. Poets like Esbensen, Davis, and Mizumura delight and amuse us with their fresh images. Did you ever imagine your school dozing like an unfriendly beast in the night? Can you picture the night peddling candy stars from door to door? How funny to think of the wind as the sky's housekeeper!

Know Your Purpose and Audience

In this lesson you will write a poem. Your purpose will be to express a fresh image or idea through personification.

Your audience will be a friend you choose. The friend can be older, younger, or your own age. Later you can create a poetry gift card for your friend. You can also take part in a poetry festival.

 *What's*
MY PURPOSE

Who's
MY AUDIENCE

 368 WRITING PROCESS: Poem

ESSENTIAL LANGUAGE SKILLS
This lesson provides opportunities to:

LISTENING ◆ listen for specific information ◆ select from an oral presentation the information needed

SPEAKING ◆ respond appropriately to questions from teachers and peers ◆ participate in storytelling and creative dramatics ◆ contribute to class and small group discussions

READING ◆ follow a set of directions ◆ recognize that simile and metaphor involve comparison ◆ respond to various forms of literature

WRITING ◆ generate ideas using a variety of strategies, such as brainstorming, clustering, mapping, question and answer ◆ expand topics by collecting information from a variety of sources ◆ improve writing based on peer and/or teacher response ◆ write short stories, essays, plays or poems

LANGUAGE ◆ use language for imagining and creating ◆ use the fundamentals of grammar, punctuation, and spelling

Prewriting

First choose a topic for your poem. Then gather ideas.

Choose Your Topic ◆ Start by making a list of possible topics for a personification poem. Look at your list carefully, then circle your favorite topic.

Think About It	Talk About It
Your are surrounded by possible topics for a personification poem. Look around your classroom and out the window. Maybe you notice a dancing curtain or a sleeping pair of shoes. Which item would be the most fun to write about? Circle your choice.	Discuss your topic ideas with a partner. Try to name two things each object could do if it were a person. You might give your object a name and then describe its personality. You might try talking to your object. Call it by name. What answers would it give?

Topic Ideas

tree   bus
(flower)   apple
cloud   wind
moon   highway
desk   taxi

WRITING PROCESS: Poem   **369**

WRITING PROCESS

1. PREWRITING

Guide students through the explanation of Prewriting, pointing out that Prewriting is the stage in which writers gather ideas for writing.

MODELING THE WRITING PROCESS

If you feel students need instruction before they begin, you may wish to model this stage of the process. Tell students you want to choose a topic for a personification poem. Have students help you work through the thinking process. Work with them to make a list of objects that might be used as the topic of a personification poem, such as a tree, a clock, a radio, or a rowboat. Put the objects into categories such as *Objects from Nature, Objects in the Classroom, Objects at Home,* and *Objects Far Away.* Record the lists on the chalkboard or use *Writing Process Transparency 25.*

Let students hear how you might go about selecting the best topic to use for a personification poem. As you speak, encourage students to help you. Circle the name of the object that students consider to be the best topic. Encourage personal responses. (Possible discussion: It would be fun to write about the clock in school or the old rowboat at the lake, but my favorite topic is the sea. I love being by the sea in the summer, and I could write about the sea as if it were my friend.)

Writing Process Transparency 25*

Pretend It's a Person	
Objects from Nature	Objects in the Classroom
a tree	my desk
snow	the clock
the sea	the computer
Objects at Home	Objects Far Away
the stove	Grandpa's house
my radio	rowboat at the lake
the television	cab in the city

Pacing

A five-day pacing guide follows, but the writing process can take longer if students want to spend several days on prewriting, revising, or preparing for publishing.

Day 1—Prewriting   Day 3—Revising
Day 2—Writing   Day 4—Proofreading
        Day 5—Publishing

Evaluation

Process Check questions at the end of each stage of the writing process help you to keep track of students' progress.

Holistic Evaluation Guidelines may be found in the teaching notes on page 375. They offer criteria for average, above-average, and below-average compositions.

Possible responses are overprinted on this reduced facsimile only. Use Writing Process Transparencies *to interact with your students on the ideas that interest them.*

WRITING PROCESS

Choose Your Strategy Before inviting students to choose a prewriting strategy that will help them gather information for their personification poems, guide them through the explanations of both strategies. Then have students choose a strategy they feel will help them get started. Students may benefit from using both strategies.

As a variation on the first strategy, Playing a Role, you may wish to have students act out each other's objects. Tell students to take notes about the way their partner acts and speaks as the object that they have chosen.

You may wish to remind students that they have learned about answering "What If?" as a strategy for supposing in the Creative Thinking lesson on pages 354–355.

IDEA BANK

Prewriting Ideas
Always encourage young writers to try new ways to discover ideas they want to write about. Reassure them, though, that it is appropriate to use the strategies that work best for them. You may wish to remind them of the prewriting ideas already introduced in their textbooks:
- A Conversation, p. 40
- An Observation Chart, p. 40
- An Order Circle, pp. 96, 320
- A Clock Graph, p. 96
- A Comic Strip, p. 154
- Answering "What If?," pp. 154, 370
- An Opinion Ladder, p. 212
- A Thought Balloon, pp. 212, 266
- A Character Map, p. 266
- Taking Notes, p. 320
- Playing a Role, p. 370

Choose Your Strategy ♦ Here are two idea-gathering strategies. Read both. Use the one that appeals to you more.

PREWRITING IDEAS

CHOICE ONE

Playing a Role

Work with a partner. Act the part of the object you have chosen. Move around. Talk. Tell your partner what you are doing. Tell what you are thinking. Then ask your partner to help you make notes about what your object did and said. Use these as ideas for your poem.

Model

CHOICE TWO

Answering "What If?"

Write "What if ____ were a person?" Then write some follow-up questions, such as "What would it do?" Think of as many follow-up questions as you can. Write as many answers as you can to each question. Use your questions and answers as ideas for your poem.

Model

What if a daffodil were a person?
What would it do? — smile, curtsy, wave
What would it say? — good morning
What would it wear? — a yellow sunbonnet
How would it feel? — cheerful but shy

PROCESS CHECK At the completion of the Prewriting stage, students should be able to answer *yes* to these questions:
- Do I have a topic for a personification poem?
- Do I have notes or questions and answers that give ideas for my poem?

Teacher to Teacher

Train students to be effective in peer conferences by writing simple guidelines on the chalkboard and modeling a peer conference with the whole class. Have a confident writer read a draft to the class. Encourage students to ask questions to clarify their understanding and to respond to the content of the draft. Responses should be appreciations of the quality and content of the draft or specific suggestions for making the piece better.

Writing

Look over your role-playing notes or your "what if" answers. Recall the first idea you had about your object acting like a person. Did you imagine it bowing to you? Was it whispering in the wind? Was it just thinking about something? Your first idea might be the one you could use to begin your poem. Use other ideas from your prewriting notes or answers to help you develop your poem. Here are some sample beginnings.

- The daffodil wears a yellow sunbonnet.
- The cloud runs around the sky.
- The wind whistles a friendly tune.

As you write, try repeating a line or a word. This can help give your poem a special sound and meaning. You may wish to rhyme your poem, but it is not necessary. Look back at the poems in this unit for ideas.

Sample First Draft ◆

> The young daffodil
> wears a yellow sunbonnet.
> Shyly she razes her head
> to say good morning
> her voice is just a whisper
> just a whisper in the garden.
> Cheerfully the daffodil smiles
> at the warm Summer breezes
> that play at her feet.
> Her green stem makes a gentle curtsy
> to the wind, a gentle curtsy.

WRITING PROCESS: Poem ◁371▷

2. WRITING

Before students write their first drafts, guide them through the explanation of Writing, emphasizing that at this stage the most important task is to get all their ideas on paper.

Help students give special sound and meaning to their poem by reminding them to try to repeat words or phrases as they write.

MODELING THE WRITING PROCESS

If you feel students need instruction before they begin this stage of the process, you may wish to ask them to recall the object from *Writing Process Transparency 25* that they felt would make the best topic for a personification poem. Write the name of that object on the chalkboard or in the first line of *Writing Process Transparency 26*. Then have students work through the thinking process with you to determine what that object might do, say, and feel if it were a person. Record the responses. Have students indicate the words or ideas that are the most poetic. Then have them write the first line for a poem about that object.

Writing Process Transparency 26*

> **Writing a Poem**
>
> If the sea were a person:
>
> What would it do? sing, call to me, breathe with salty breath
> What would it say? "Come to me" "Listen to my secret song" "Walk on my beaches."
> How would it feel? It would feel it was my friend It would want to see me.
> Begin the Poem: The sea sings its secret song to me.

PROCESS CHECK At the completion of the Writing stage, students should be able to answer *yes* to these questions:
- Do I have a complete first draft?
- Does my poem tell about an object that acts like a person?
- Have I repeated words and phrases to give my poem a special sound?

Possible responses are overprinted on this reduced fac-simile only. Use Writing Process Transparencies *to interact with your students on the ideas that interest them.*

WRITING PROCESS

3. REVISING

Help students understand that during Revising writers make their drafts communicate ideas more clearly and effectively to an audience.

I D E A   B A N K

Grammar Connection
You may wish to remind students of the Grammar Checks already introduced in their textbooks:
- Use a variety of sentence types, p. 43
- Use exact nouns, p. 99
- Use vivid verbs, p. 157
- Replace nouns with pronouns, p. 215
- Add adjectives for specific detail, p. 269
- Avoid double negatives, p. 323
- Use prepositions or prepositional phrases to clarify relationships, p. 373

Option 1 ◆ If you wish to begin grammar instruction related to the Grammar Check in this lesson, then refer to Part 1 of this unit.

Option 2 ◆ If you wish to begin grammar instruction *not* related to the Grammar Check in this lesson, then refer to the end-of-book Glossary or Index.

First Read to Yourself   You may wish to emphasize that students need not make actual changes during the first reading. This is a time to think about whether their writing is clear and says what they mean it to say.

Remind students to check to make sure that they showed their object behaving like a person. Have them check to see if they repeated words or lines.

Then Share with a Partner   Suggest that writers' partners offer three responses, at least one positive, and that they accompany any critical responses with suggestions for improvement. Be sure writers ask the Focus question: *How else could this object behave like a person?*

3 Revising

Now you have finished writing your poem. Would you like to make it even better? This idea for revising may help you.

REVISING IDEA

FIRST   Read to Yourself

As you read, think of your purpose. Did you write a poem that expresses a fresh image or idea? Consider your audience, the friend you are writing this poem for. Will your friend enjoy it? Decide what part *you* like best, and why.

Focus: Did you use personification? Did you show your object behaving like a person?

THEN   Share with a Partner

Ask a partner to be your first audience. Read your poem aloud. Then ask for suggestions. These guidelines may help.

The Writer

Guidelines: Read slowly and with expression. Welcome your partner's ideas, but make only the changes *you* want to make.

Sample questions:
- Are there any words or lines I might repeat?
- **Focus question:** How else could this object behave like a person?

The Writer's Partner

Guidelines: Listen carefully. Help the writer think how the object can be like a person.

Sample responses:
- Why don't you try repeating the words _____?
- You've really made this object seem alive. Maybe you can add a personification by saying _____.

372   WRITING PROCESS: Poem

Teacher to Teacher

Guidelines for Peer Conferences
- The writer reads out loud.
- Listeners ask questions and respond.
- Respect the writer's work.
- Ask questions about things you do not understand.
- Tell what you like in the writing, as well as problems that you see.
- Give a reason for any change you suggest.

WRITING AS A RECURSIVE PROCESS

Connecting Grammar to the Writing Process

Writing is a recursive process. In other words, good writers will often go back and forth among steps. Depending on the individual styles of your students, some may choose to correct grammar at Step Three, Revising; others may prefer to fix grammar or usage errors at Step Four, Proofreading. Ideally, this should be a decision made by the writer. Remind students, however, that once they have completed their proofreading, all the grammar errors should be corrected.

Revising Model ◆ This poem is being revised. Notice how the writer's changes are marked in blue.

The writer decided that *budding* is more poetic than *young*.

The prepositional phrase makes the image clearer.

The repeated words were moved for a different poetic effect.

The writer's partner suggested adding this personification.

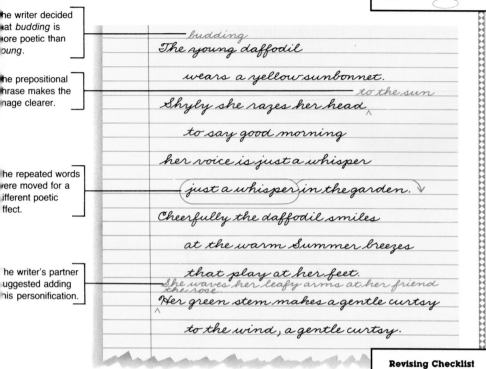

budding
The young daffodil
wears a yellow sunbonnet.
                                    to the sun
Shyly she razes her head ∧
to say good morning
her voice is just a whisper
~~just a whisper~~ in the garden. ↓
Cheerfully the daffodil smiles
at the warm Summer breezes
that play at her feet.
~~She waves her leafy arms at her friend the rose.~~
∧ Her green stem makes a gentle curtsy
to the wind, a gentle curtsy.

Read the poem above the way the writer has decided it *should be*. Then revise your own poem.

> **Grammar Check** ◆ A preposition or prepositional phrase can clarify the relationship between one thing and another.
>
> **Word Choice** ◆ Are you searching for a poetic word? A thesaurus is a good place to look.

Revising Checklist

- [ ] **Purpose:** Did I write a poem that expresses a fresh image or idea?

- [ ] **Audience:** Will my friend enjoy the poem I wrote for him or her?

- [ ] **Focus:** Did I use personification? Did I show my object behaving like a person?

WRITING PROCESS: Poem **373**

Revising Model Guide students through the model, noting the reasons for changes and the revision marks. Point out to students that on the model the revising marks are in blue. Encourage the class to discuss the changes in the model. Ask them to consider whether or not the changes helped the writer express feelings and ideas in a way that was fresh and clear.

MODELING THE WRITING PROCESS
If you feel students need instruction before they begin this stage of the process, you may wish to present *Writing Process Transparency 27*. Have students read the draft silently, or have a volunteer read it aloud. Then ask whether there is anything that needs to be changed. Work through the thinking process to help students give reasons for the changes. Then have them tell you how to mark the changes on the draft. (Students might suggest adding prepositional phrases to make the images clearer, using a more poetic word than *beach*, adding another personification, and moving the repeated words for a different poetic effect.) Remind students that at this time they are revising for meaning. They will correct spelling and punctuation later when they proofread.

Writing Process Transparency 27*

> **Song of the Sea**
>
>   *to me*
> The sea sings its secret song.
>
> "Hear my whisper, hear my roar," says the sea,
>
> and I listen
>
>   *sandy shore*
> "Walk upon my ~~beach~~," says the sea,
>
> and I listen
>
> ~~I can feel the heartbeat of its waves.~~
> I can feel its salty breth upon my face.
>
>   *to me*
> The sea opens its arms and calls.
>
> the sea is like a Friend
>
> that knows me well (a Friend.)

PROCESS CHECK At the completion of the Revising stage, students should be able to answer *yes* to the following questions:
- Do I have a complete draft with revising marks that show changes I plan to make?
- Has my draft been reviewed by another writer?

Possible responses are overprinted on this reduced facsimile only. Use Writing Process Transparencies to interact with your students on the ideas that interest them.

4. PROOFREADING

Guide students through the explanation of proofreading and review the Proofreading Model. Point out to students that on the model the proofreading marks are in red. Tell them that proofreading helps to eliminate errors such as incorrect spelling or run-on sentences that may distract or confuse their readers.

Review the Proofreading Strategy, Proofreading Marks, and the Proofreading Checklist with students. Then invite students to use the checklist and proofread their own poems.

MODELING THE WRITING PROCESS

If you feel students need instruction before they begin this stage of the process, you may wish to use *Writing Process Transparency 28*. Before students proofread the poem on the transparency, remind them that poets do not always follow normal indenting, punctuation, and capitalization rules. Tell students to use their own good judgment as well as the Proofreading Checklist as they check the poem. Then have students proofread the poem for spelling mistakes on the transparency by reading every other word as suggested on page 374 in the textbook. Mark students' corrections on the transparency.

Writing Process Transparency 28*

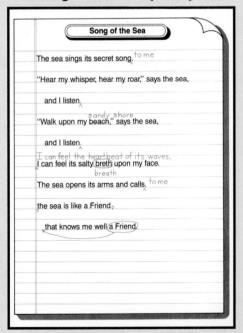

4 Proofreading

Poets do not always follow normal indenting, punctuation, and capitalization rules. Use the poems in this book as models. Check your poem for correct spelling and readable handwriting.

Proofreading Model ◆ Here is the poem about the daffodil. The writer has made proofreading changes in red.

Proofreading Marks	
capital letter	—
small letter	/
check spelling	⬭

The poem as shown with handwritten corrections:

budding
The young daffodil

wears a yellow sunbonnet.

raises   to the sun
Shyly she razes her head

to say good morning.

her voice is just a whisper

just a whisper in the garden,

Cheerfully the daffodil smiles

at the warm Summer breezes

that play at her feet.
She waves her leafy arms at her friend
the rose.
Her green stem makes a gentle curtsy

to the wind, a gentle curtsy.

Proofreading Checklist

☐ Did I spell words correctly?

☐ Did I use capital letters correctly?

☐ Did I use correct marks at the end of sentences?

☐ Did I use my best handwriting?

PROOFREADING IDEA

Spelling Check

Here is a trick for finding spelling mistakes. Check every other word the first time you read. Check the other words on your second reading. This way you will forget about meaning and concentrate on spelling.

Now proofread your poem, add a title, and make a neat copy.

374 WRITING PROCESS: Poem

PROCESS CHECK At the completion of the Proofreading stage, students should be able to answer *yes* to the following questions:
- Do I have a complete draft with proofreading marks that show changes I plan to make?
- Have I used the proofreading marks shown in the lesson?

EVALUATION PROGRAM

See Evaluation and Testing Program, pp. C1–C8.

Masters are available for the following:
Self Evaluation Checklist
Personal Goals for Writing
Peer Response
Teacher Response

Holistic Evaluation Guides
Analytic Evaluation Guides

Possible responses are overprinted on this reduced facsimile only. Use Writing Process Transparencies *to interact with your students on the ideas that interest them.*

Publishing

Try these ways of sharing your poem with others.

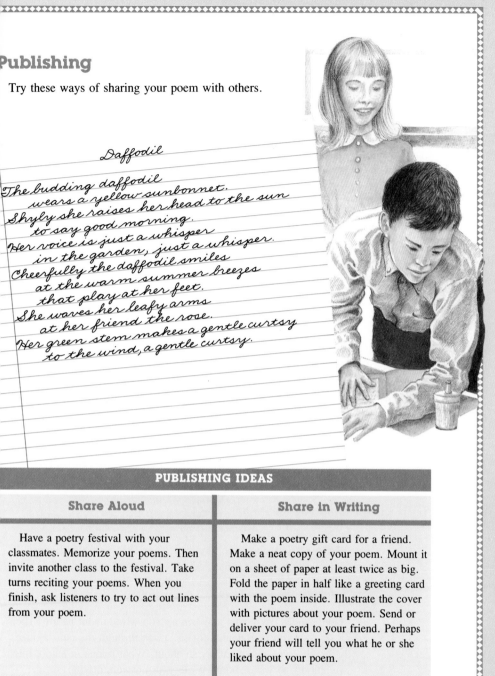

Daffodil

The budding daffodil
  wears a yellow sunbonnet.
Shyly she raises her head to the sun
  to say good morning.
Her voice is just a whisper,
  in the garden, just a whisper.
Cheerfully the daffodil smiles
  at the warm summer breezes
  that play at her feet.
She waves her leafy arms
  at her friend the rose.
Her green stem makes a gentle curtsy
  to the wind, a gentle curtsy.

PUBLISHING IDEAS

Share Aloud	Share in Writing
Have a poetry festival with your classmates. Memorize your poems. Then invite another class to the festival. Take turns reciting your poems. When you finish, ask listeners to try to act out lines from your poem.	Make a poetry gift card for a friend. Make a neat copy of your poem. Mount it on a sheet of paper at least twice as big. Fold the paper in half like a greeting card with the poem inside. Illustrate the cover with pictures about your poem. Send or deliver your card to your friend. Perhaps your friend will tell you what he or she liked about your poem.

WRITING PROCESS: Poem 375

Holistic Evaluation Guidelines

A poem of **average** quality will:
1. present an object or a thing as a person
2. include repeated words or lines

A poem of **above-average** quality may:
1. use words or phrases that are very poetic
2. present a strong image in a fresh way

A poem of **below-average** quality may:
1. lack poetic words or images
2. be unorganized or incomplete

PROCESS CHECK At the completion of the Publishing stage, students should be able to answer *yes* to these questions:
- Have I shared my writing with an audience?
- Have readers shared reactions with me?
- Have I thought about what I especially like in this writing? Or about what was particularly difficult?
- Have I thought about what I would like to work on the next time I write?

Encourage students to keep a log or journal of their own and their readers' reactions.

I D E A   B A N K

5. PUBLISHING

Oral Sharing If students choose to share their writing orally by having a poetry festival, set aside a day for this special event. Provide an opportunity for students to practice reciting their poems aloud. Then have students present their poems to another class. You also may wish to ask parents to attend the students' poetry festival.

Written Sharing If students choose to share their writing by displaying it, provide them with a large sheet of paper to use for their poetry gift cards. After the cards have been created, you may wish to display them in the classroom before students send or deliver their cards to their friends.

Curriculum Connection

Writing Across the Curriculum

Remind students that one way writers get their ideas is to ask "what if" questions. Tell students they will use a "what if" chart to help them write a new verse to add to our national anthem.

You may wish to remind students that they have used a "what if" chart as a strategy for creating in the Creative Thinking lesson, in their response to the literature selection, and in the Writing Process lesson.

Writing to Learn

To help students get started, have them suggest what our flag means to them today. Write their responses on the chalkboard.

You may wish to have students with limited English proficiency describe their feelings about the flag and provide the English adjectives.

Help students use their history books and books of poetry from their classroom library to find information about our flag and poems about patriotism to use as models.

You may wish to model making a "what if" chart for your verse. Have students contribute "what if" questions, and write each question on the chart.

Writing in Your Journal

When they have finished writing, have students read their earlier journal entries. Encourage them to discuss what they have learned about the theme and to observe how their writing has changed or improved.

Remind students that their journals have many purposes. Suggest to them that entries in their journals may provide ideas for later writing.

Writing Across the Curriculum   Music

During this unit you wrote a poem about something in nature. Poems are often set to music and become the words of a song.

Writing to Learn

Think and Suppose ♦ In 1814 America was at war with Britain. During a battle Francis Scott Key watched the American flag waving over Fort McHenry. He saw it by the light of exploding bombs during the night. In the morning it was still there. His poem about it became the words to our national anthem.

What if you were asked to write one new verse for "The Star-Spangled Banner"? You would not write about the flag in 1814. You would write about what the flag means today. Read the verse below and think about what *you* would write.

What-if Chart

And the rockets' red glare,
the bombs bursting in air,
Gave proof through the night
that our flag was still there.
Oh, say does that star-spangled
banner yet wave
O'er the land of the free
and the home of the brave?

Write ♦ Think about the words to "The Star-Spangled Banner." Then write a new verse to add to our national anthem.

Writing in Your Journal

In the Writer's Warm-up you wrote about nature. Then you read nature poems. Look through the unit. Notice what the poets wrote about. What things in nature might *you* choose to write about? Write your answers in your journal.

ESSENTIAL LANGUAGE SKILLS
This lesson provides opportunities to:

LISTENING ♦ listen actively and attentively ♦ follow the logical organization of an oral presentation

SPEAKING ♦ participate in group discussions ♦ make organized oral presentations

READING ♦ respond to various forms of literature ♦ become acquainted with a variety of selections, characters, and themes of our literary heritage ♦ select books for individual needs and interests ♦ explain and relate to the feelings and emotions of characters

WRITING ♦ select and narrow a topic for a specific purpose ♦ expand topics by collecting information from a variety of sources ♦ adapt information to accomplish a specific purpose with a particular audience ♦ keep journals, logs, or notebooks to express feelings, record ideas, discover new knowledge, and free the imagination

LANGUAGE ♦ use language to create ♦ recognize ways in which language can be used to influence others

Read More About It

A Visit to William Blake's Inn
by Nancy Willard
William Blake was a poet who lived long ago.
Nancy Willard was inspired by his poems to write
this book. Each poem here tells about one of
Blake's poetic characters.   **Newbery Award**
Caldecott Honor Book

River Winding *by Charlotte Zolotow*
Mrs. Zolotow is inspired by nature and the seasons.
Each poem gives a glimpse of an image in nature.

Book Report Idea   Book Jacket

A hardback book often has a
paper cover called a book jacket.
The book jacket may contain
information about the story or
author. It may give impressions
of the book written by book
reviewers. The next time you
share a book, create an original
book jacket for it.

Create a Book Jacket ◆ Look
at some real book jackets for
ideas about design and content.
Use construction paper. Fold it
like a real book jacket. Create a
cover illustration that suits your
book. Give the title and the
names of the author and
illustrator. On the back, give a
brief summary of the book, but
don't give away the ending.

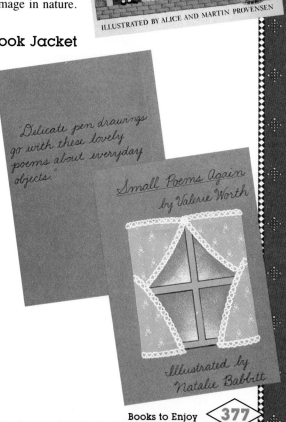

Books to Enjoy 377

Books to Enjoy

Read More About It

Call students' attention to Read More
About It and discuss theme-related
books. Point out that the books listed
here contain nature poems. Encourage
students to mention other titles that
deal with these topics. Encourage
students to examine pictures and
jacket illustrations of books in the
classroom to find books they will enjoy
reading.

Book Report Idea

You may wish to have students use the
book report form provided in the back
of their textbooks. Book Report Idea
presents a lively alternative way for
interested students to share books
they have read.

You may wish to share the reports
with the class or in small groups. Have
students display their book jackets for
classmates to guess about characters
and events before reading the
summaries on the backs of the jackets.
Post the book jackets in a book review
corner.

Integrated Language
Arts Project

The **Integrated Language Arts
Project** on pages T524–T525 may be
used with this unit.

WORLD OF BOOKS
CLASSROOM LIBRARIES
is a collection of high-quality children's literature
available with this program.

Unit 7 Review

REVIEW OR TEST
You may wish to use the Unit Review as a review of the unit skills before administering the Unit Posttest, or you may wish to use the Unit Review in lieu of the Unit Posttest.

REVIEW PROCEDURES
The lesson pages that are reviewed are listed beside the heading of each segment. You may wish to choose one of the procedures listed below for using the pages with the Unit Review exercises.

Review/Evaluate Have students re-study the lesson pages before doing the Unit Review exercises.

Open-Book Review Allow students to refer to the lesson pages if they need to while they are doing the Unit Review exercises.

Evaluate/Review Have students do the Unit Review exercises, then turn to the lesson pages to restudy concepts for which incorrect responses are given.

ADDITIONAL REVIEW AND PRACTICE
For additional review and practice, turn to the Extra Practice pages at the end of the unit.

378

UNIT REVIEW

Unit 7

Prepositions   *pages 340–347*

A. Write each sentence. Underline the preposition once. Underline the object of the preposition twice.

1. The kitten with the black paws is mine.
2. He stood in the doorway.
3. Ian clambered onto the platform.
4. Joe received the news from Anna.
5. The wastebasket is near the desk.
6. During the evening we discuss the day's work.
7. The runners raced around the track.
8. Everyone was passed by Jill.
9. The thrill of victory was hers!
10. Philip hid behind the tree.
11. The policeman on the corner blew his whistle.
12. The little plane flew over the airport.
13. The black cap above the green coat is Roger's.
14. The salesperson from the store is here.
15. Ricky gave Jan his box of old toys.
16. The road to town is being repaired.
17. A small creek flows under the road.
18. That story was written by my aunt.
19. Yesterday afternoon we had a picnic in the park.
20. An enormous grasshopper appeared beside us.

378   Unit Review

B. Write each sentence. Underline the prepositional phrases.

21. Peggy and Aaron will work with the group.
22. This novel was written by Louisa May Alcott.
23. The ball soared through the air.
24. Behind the little boy stood a tall woman.
25. Yesterday we went to our grandparents' house.
26. The Knights of the Roundtable had many exciting adventures.
27. This poem by Marianne Moore delights me.
28. The horse with the brown spots jumped.
29. A huge tree swayed above the little log cabin.
30. We sat beside the cool, rippling stream.
31. Can I have one of your blueberry muffins?

C. Write *adverb* if the underlined word is an adverb. Write *preposition* if it is a preposition.

32. Mr. Austin went down [prep.] the stairs.
33. Let's go inside [adv.].
34. Quiet down [adv.], please!
35. The worm crept along [prep.] the roadside.
36. Debra stood under [prep.] the big clock.
37. Put the coin in [prep.] the collection box.
38. The fly buzzed around [prep.] the room.
39. The mail carrier is outside [adv.].
40. Ms. Hayes got off [prep.] the train.
41. Summer vacation is getting near [adv.].
42. Greg waited outside [prep.] the store.

D. Write each sentence. Choose the word in parentheses ( ) that correctly completes the sentence.

43. Below (us, we), the waves dashed against the rocks.

44. The gifts are from Tom and (I, me).

45. Lee borrowed a book from (he, him).

46. Did you see the photo of (them, they)?

47. The scenery for our play was designed by Ms. Lee and (she, her).

48. Come with Kim and (me, I).

E. Write each sentence. Complete the sentence correctly with *among* or *between*.

49. (Between, Among) the three of us, she's the tallest.

50. A yellow line runs (between, among) the two sides of the road.

51. (Between, Among) you and me, I can't stand this heat!

52. How can anybody choose (between, among) all these flavors?

Synonyms and Antonyms

pages 348–349

F. Write the sentences. Find synonyms in the Thesaurus on pages 466–485 to replace the underlined words.

53. Belinda came before any of the other guests did.
   arrived

54. Find the mouse in this picture.
   Locate

55. I leaned against the large boulder.
   enormous, great, huge, immense, massive

56. The trip to Mexico was exciting.
   breathtaking, thrilling

57. The sculptor made a bronze statue.
   created

58. Please cut me a piece of turkey.
   carve, slice

59. She gave me a definite answer.
   explicit, unequivocal

G. Write the sentences. Find antonyms in the Thesaurus on page 466–485 to replace the underlined words.

60. "What a beautiful dress!" exclaimed Helga.
   ugly, unattractive

61. This kind of metal is extremely rare.
   common

62. The student gave the wrong answer.
   right, correct

63. Bill will come tomorrow.
   go, depart, leave

64. This large piece of wood feels quite rough.
   smooth

65. It's especially fun on a warm day.
   cool

66. My brother's room is very neat.
   messy, sloppy, untidy, cluttered

Proofreading

H. Proofread each sentence. Then write each sentence correctly.

67. Did you visit seattle?
   S

68. "Wait for me," said Jennifer.

69. My uncle's house is nearby.

70. I don't want to be late for school.

71. This is the clearer sky that I have ever seen.
   clearest

72. The choice is between Susan, Jill, and Debbie.
   among

73. Oaks, maples, and pines grow in this area.

74. Mr. Buford's classroom is on the second floor.

75. How many countrys are in North America?
   countries

76. Let's walk to the Bus terminal.
   b

77. That building is immense?.

78. Tommys' bicycle has red reflectors.

79. There is a fountain among the two buildings.
   between

80. The bus stoped at the corner.
   stopped

81. Lisa said, "You can do it."

Unit Review **379**

379

Language Puzzlers

Unit 7 Challenge

OBJECTIVES
To solve language puzzles based on skills taught in the unit

ANSWERS

An Animal Twister
1. on an April afternoon
2. across an ancient archway
3. Above an abandoned ark
4. of aluminum
5. of the awkward animal
6. on the ark
7. about anteaters

A Preposition Crossword

Across	Down
1. above	2. between
4. at	3. down
5. within	6. to
8. on	7. inside
9. in	
10. beside	

An Animal Twister

Find the seven prepositional phrases in the following tongue twister.

An aging African aardvark
Ate an apple on an April afternoon
As it ambled across an ancient archway
Above an abandoned ark of aluminum.

Asked an ant of the awkward animal
"Are any ant-eating ant bears on the ark?"
"Approach and ask again about anteaters,"
Anxiously answered the ant-eating aardvark.

Write a third part for the tongue twister. In it tell how the ant escaped or was saved. Include as many prepositional phrases as you can.

Choose another letter of the alphabet, and write a tongue twister on another topic. Include as many prepositional phrases as possible.

Preposition Crossword

Draw the crossword graph on a sheet of paper. Then complete the puzzle. (Hint: The answers are all prepositions.)

Across
1. on top of; over
4. *cat* without a *c*
5. opposite of *without*
8. opposite of *off*
9. *mine* without *me*
10. next to

Down
2. in the middle
3. opposite of *up*
6. sounds like *two*
7. not outside

Unit 7 Extra Practice

Writing with Prepositions
p. 340

A. Write each sentence. Underline the preposition.

1. April Fool's Day falls on April 1.
2. This was once the date of New Year's Day.
3. The date changed, but some people forgot about it.
4. Each April 1 they still exchanged gifts with their friends.
5. Only now they gave joke gifts placed in pretty boxes.
6. April Fool's Day is celebrated in many countries.
7. Many tricks are played on this day.
8. Three hundred years ago it began in France.
9. The holiday soon spread across Europe.
10. The French call it "The Day of the Fish."
11. Children surprise each other with paper fish.
12. "April fish" is the French name for an April fool.
13. Friends learn each other's tricks over the years.
14. Most pranks are planned before April 1.
15. Few people can spend the whole day without a smile.

B. Write each sentence. Underline the preposition once. Underline the object of the preposition twice.

EXAMPLE: She plays jokes on her friends.

ANSWER: She plays jokes <u>on</u> <u>her friends</u>.

16. People play practical jokes during this day.
17. You might find a dollar by a tree.
18. Someone is hiding behind a bush.
19. He holds a long thread in his hand.
20. The other end is attached to the dollar.
21. He pulls on the thread.
22. The dollar disappears when you reach for it.
23. Don't be angry about the joke.
24. Get back at him.
25. Tell him a spider is crawling up his back.
26. Keep your practical jokes in the spirit of fun.
27. No one should be harmed by any practical joke.

Practice ◆ Practice ◆ Practice ◆ Practice ◆ Practice ◆ Practice ◆ Practice ◆ Practice ◆ Practice

Extra Practice

Unit 7

OBJECTIVES
To practice skills taught in the unit

ANSWERS
Writing with Prepositions

A.
1. on
2. of
3. about
4. with
5. in
6. in
7. on
8. in
9. across
10. of
11. with
12. for
13. over
14. before
15. without

B.
16. during this <u>day</u>
17. by a <u>tree</u>
18. behind a <u>bush</u>
19. in his <u>hand</u>
20. to the <u>dollar</u>
21. on the <u>thread</u>
22. for <u>it</u>
23. about the <u>joke</u>
24. at <u>him</u>
25. up his <u>back</u>
26. in the <u>spirit</u>, of <u>fun</u>
27. by any practical <u>fun</u>

Extra Practice and Challenge

For those students who need additional grammar practice have them refer to these pages. **The practice exercises progress in difficulty from Easy to Average. Practice A is Easy. Practice B is Average.** Difficult concepts requiring more practice have additional Exercises C and D at the Average level.
We do not recommend these exercises for students who have mastered the skill in the basic lesson. Those students should do the **Challenge** word puzzles on page 380.

Extra Practice

Practice ◆ Practice ◆ Practice ◆ Practice ◆ Practice ◆ Practice ◆ Practice

C. 28. <u>of</u> <u><u>power</u></u>
29. <u>around</u> <u><u>the world</u></u>
30. <u>on</u> <u>Roman</u> <u><u>coins</u></u>
31. <u>of</u> <u>the</u> <u><u>emperors</u></u>
32. <u>to</u> <u>certain</u> <u><u>countries</u></u>
33. <u>for</u> <u>national</u> <u><u>symbols</u></u>
34. <u>on</u> <u><u>it</u></u>
35. <u>before</u> <u>the</u> <u><u>revolution</u></u>
36. <u>for</u> <u>the</u> <u><u>country</u></u>
37. <u>about</u> <u><u>it</u></u>
38. <u>over</u> <u><u>America</u></u>
39. <u>across</u> <u>this</u> <u><u>country</u></u>
40. <u>to</u> <u>the</u> <u><u>problem</u></u>
41. <u>Without</u> <u>special</u> <u><u>protection</u></u>
42. <u>from</u> <u><u>hunters</u></u>
43. <u>in</u> <u><u>streams</u></u>
44. <u>At</u> <u>one</u> <u><u>time</u></u>
45. <u>of</u> <u><u>eagles</u></u>

Prepositional Phrases

A. 1. about some humorous poets
2. by the famous Edward Lear
3. at the public library
4. to her friend Gerald
5. on their faces
6. by Edward Lear
7. in a special form
8. from Ireland
9. after an Irish city
10. about silly subjects
11. with wonderful nonsense
12. of humor
13. at other poets
14. through the night

C. Write the sentence. Underline each preposition once. Underline the object of the preposition twice.

28. The eagle has long been a symbol of power.
29. This symbol has been used around the world.
30. It was stamped on Roman coins.
31. Eagles decorated the palaces of the emperors.
32. The eagle means certain things to certain countries.
33. Some countries have used eagles for national symbols.
34. The Austrian flag has an eagle on it.
35. Russian rulers' uniforms had them before the revolution.
36. Our founding fathers needed a symbol for the country.
37. People had many different ideas about it.
38. Once these great birds flew over America.
39. Now not even 3,000 eagles remain across this country.
40. Lately people have been paying more attention to the pro
41. Without special protection all eagles could die.
42. Now laws protect eagles from hunters.
43. DDT in streams no longer poisons the eagles' food suppl
44. At one time many feared that eagles would die out comp
45. The number of eagles is now increasing.

2 Prepositional Phrases

p. 342

A. Write each sentence. Underline the prepositional phrase.

1. Kate was reading about some humorous poets.
2. She found some poems by the famous Edward Lear.
3. Kate read his poems at the public library.
4. She showed them to her friend Gerald.
5. Gerald and Kate had smiles on their faces.
6. They were both reading a poem by Edward Lear.
7. It was a limerick, a poem in a special form.
8. The name *limerick* comes from Ireland.
9. Supposedly it is named after an Irish city.
10. Lear wrote poems about silly subjects.
11. His poems are filled with wonderful nonsense.
12. People enjoyed his sense of humor.
13. Sometimes his writing poked fun at other poets.
14. Friends sometimes recited his poems through the night.

. Write the prepositional phrase in each sentence. Underline the preposition once. Underline the object of the preposition twice.

EXAMPLE: We read poems from a large book.
ANSWER: from a large book

15. Kate and Gerald read Lear's nonsense poems for fun.
16. There is often a serious message behind the nonsense.
17. He loved writing about people's habits.
18. One book had funny drawings above the limericks.
19. Gerald paused after his favorite poems.
20. He copied these poems in his notebook.
21. Kate kept a poetry collection beside her bed.
22. Sometimes she memorized a poem at bedtime.
23. Their teacher read some limericks before lunch.
24. Their favorite began, "We went to the animal fair."

. Write the prepositional phrase in each sentence. Then underline the preposition once and the object of the preposition twice.

EXAMPLE: The sleds are put into the garage.
ANSWER: into the garage

25. The dew is heavy on the grass.
26. The rays of the sun are still strong.
27. There are more hours of daylight every day.
28. The air and the ground are being warmed by the sun.
29. Buds are forming on the trees.
30. Soon they will open into leaves.
31. Dandelions sprout in the lawn.
32. Bulbs begin poking their heads through the warming earth.
33. Soon they will delight us with their beautiful flowers.
34. Birds are gathering twigs and vines for their nests.
35. Bikes, skates, and wagons are taken to the street again.
36. Sweaters take the place of parkas.
37. Rakes and brooms clear away the last of the dead leaves.
38. A hose washes the winter's dirt from the porch.
39. People begin working in their gardens.
40. They set tiny seedlings carefully in the ground.
41. Spring is a time for new beginnings.
42. It is a welcome relief from the long winter.

Extra Practice **383**

Extra Practice

B. 15. for fun
16. behind the nonsense
17. about people's habits
18. above the limericks
19. after his favorite poems
20. in his notebook
21. beside her bed
22. at bedtime
23. before lunch
24. to the animal fair

C. 25. on the grass
26. of the sun
27. of daylight
28. by the sun
29. on the trees
30. into leaves
31. in the lawn
32. through the warming earth
33. with their beautiful flowers
34. for their nests
35. to the street
36. of parkas
37. of the dead leaves
38. from the porch
39. in their gardens
40. in the ground
41. for new beginnings
42. from the long winter

Extra Practice and Challenge

For those students who need additional grammar practice have them refer to these pages. **The practice exercises progress in difficulty from Easy to Average. Practice A is Easy. Practice B is Average.** Difficult concepts requiring more practice have additional Exercises C and D at the Average level. We do not recommend these exercises for students who have mastered the skill in the basic lesson. Those students should do the **Challenge** word puzzles on page 380.

Extra Practice

Prepositions and Adverbs

A.
1. preposition
2. preposition
3. adverb
4. adverb
5. preposition
6. preposition
7. preposition
8. adverb
9. adverb
10. preposition
11. preposition
12. adverb
13. preposition
14. preposition
15. adverb
16. preposition
17. preposition
18. adverb
19. adverb

B. Answers will vary. The following are possible answers.
20. They took their coats off.
21. A guard gave them directions as she came near them.
22. To see the Eskimo masks, go up.
23. Let's go down the stairs now.
24. Rachel looked around.
25. She waited for me inside the shop.
26. Are you ready to go outside the shop?

---

3 Prepositions and Adverbs

A. Write each sentence. Then write whether the underlined word is a preposition or an adverb.

1. We are <u>near</u> the Museum of Natural History.
2. Rachel was <u>in</u> the subway car.
3. Leo was still standing <u>outside</u>.
4. Just before the door closed, he stepped <u>in</u>.
5. It was their first ride <u>below</u> the ground.
6. Rachel looked <u>down</u> the subway tunnel.
7. No one seemed to mind being so far <u>under</u> the city.
8. The train seemed to fly <u>along</u>.
9. At Seventy-seventh Street, they got <u>out</u>.
10. They saw that the museum was just <u>outside</u> the subway.
11. The doors were opening as they hurried <u>up</u> the walk.
12. Let's walk <u>around</u>.
13. The animals <u>in</u> these displays are so lifelike!
14. Which is the way <u>to</u> the cafeteria?
15. Let's go <u>in</u>.
16. Are the dinosaur skeletons <u>in</u> that room?
17. Observe the dinosaurs and walk <u>around</u> them.
18. Shall we see the marine life <u>next</u>?
19. To see the blue whale, look <u>up</u>.

B. Write each sentence. If the underlined part is an adverb, change it to a prepositional phrase. If it is a prepositional phrase, change it to an adverb.

EXAMPLE: Their friends were waiting <u>inside</u>.
ANSWER: Their friends were waiting inside the door.

EXAMPLE: Please put a donation <u>in the box</u>.
ANSWER: Please put a donation in.

20. They took their coats <u>off the bench</u>.
21. A guard gave them directions as she came <u>near</u>.
22. To see the Eskimo masks, go <u>up one floor</u>.
23. Let's go <u>down</u> now.
24. Rachel looked <u>around the gift shop</u>.
25. She waited for me <u>inside</u>.
26. Are you ready to go <u>outside</u>?

Using Prepositional Phrases   *p. 346*

Choose the word in parentheses ( ) that correctly completes each sentence. Write the sentence.

1. Cassie showed the garden book to (they, them).
2. The community garden was started by Alice and (him, he).
3. I divided my time (among, between) digging and planting.
4. Delsin planted six kinds of fruit for Pam and (she, her).
5. The tools were shared (between, among) Pat, Mona, and Ed.
6. Carla went to the garden center with (we, us).
7. Joan dug a strawberry bed beside Todd and (I, me).
8. Ms. Florio gave some seedlings to (she, her).
9. We planted sweet corn for Jesse and (her, she).
10. I borrowed tools from the Carons and (they, them).
11. The wheelbarrow and hose belong to Carrie and (me, I).
12. Leave a space in the garden for Robbie and (he, him).
13. Did you share the parsley plants with Leo and (she, her)?
14. Will the biggest tomatoes be grown by Gerry or (us, we)?
15. This area was donated by the Florios and (they, them).
16. Give the rake and hoe to Alonzo and (he, him).
17. The weeding was done by Martha and (I, me).
18. Shira put in a fence with the Florios and (we, us).
19. We fertilized an area for (them, they).
20. Carrie sprayed water at Luana and (he, him).

Write the sentences. Complete each sentence correctly with *among* or *between*.

21. Walk carefully (among, between) the two rows of lettuce.
22. I must decide (between, among) melon and squash.
23. Divide the fruits (among, between) Pam, Chen, and Jo.
24. Choose your favorite vegetable (between, among) carrots, peas, string beans, and broccoli.
25. (Among, Between) Arlo and Edith, who works harder?
26. At the fair, judges decided (between, among) the prize vegetables.
27. Second prize was shared (among, between) four farmers.
28. Then the decision was (between, among) their melon and our tomato.
29. (Among, Between) the two, the judges chose our tomato.

Using Prepositional Phrases
A.
1. them
2. him
3. between
4. her
5. among
6. us
7. me
8. her
9. her
10. them
11. me
12. him
13. her
14. us
15. them
16. him
17. me
18. us
19. them
20. him

B.
21. between
22. between
23. among
24. among
25. Between
26. among
27. among
28. between
29. Between

Extra Practice and Challenge

For those students who need additional grammar practice have them refer to these pages. **The practice exercises progress in difficulty from Easy to Average. Practice A is Easy. Practice B is Average.** Difficult concepts requiring more practice have additional Exercises C and D at the Average level.
We do not recommend these exercises for students who have mastered the skill in the basic lesson. Those students should do the **Challenge** word puzzles on page 380.

TWO-PART
flexibility

Unit 8 Overview

books
ON UNIT THEME

USING LANGUAGE TO CLASSIFY

EASY

📖   **Zoos Without Cages** by Judith E. Rinard. National Geographic. This book describes the work being done at zoos to make homes for animals that simulate their natural habitats. Beautiful color photographs accompany the text.

📖   **Tasmania: A Wildlife Journey** by Joyce Powzyk. Lothrop. Based on the author's experiences, this book describes the wildlife and habitats found on Tasmania, an island off the coast of southern Australia.

AVERAGE

📖   **Tundra: The Arctic Land** by Bruce Hiscock. Atheneum. This book describes the treeless terrain of the Arctic tundra and the ways various plants and animals, including caribou, wolves, polar bears, and giant mosquitoes, have adapted to living there.

📖   **Secrets of a Wildlife Watcher** by Jim Arnosky. Lothrop. The author-illustrator shares his advice and secrets on how to find and observe such wildlife as owls, deer, squirrels, and rabbits.

CHALLENGING

📖   **In Search of a Sandhill Crane** by Keith Robertson. Viking. Link Keller is on an assignment to get photographs of sandhill cranes.

📖   **From Cage to Freedom: A New Beginning for Laboratory Chimpanzees** by Linda Koebner. Dutton. The author describes her experiences in returning a group of laboratory chimpanzees to freedom in an animal preserve in Florida.

READ-ALOUDS

📖   **Gentle Ben** by Walt Morey. Dutton. An Alaskan brown bear is tamed by a boy who eventually rescues him from imprisonment. **American Library Association Notable Children's Book.**

📖   **Julie of the Wolves** by Jean Craighead George. Harper. A thirteen-year-old Eskimo girl survives the Arctic wilderness with the help of wolves. **Newbery Medal.**

UNIT EIGHT

USING LANGUAGE TO CLASSIFY

PART ONE
Unit Theme *Animal Habitats*
Language Awareness Sentences

PART TWO
Literature "Two of a Kind" by Ron Hirschi
A Reason for Writing Classifying

Writing
IN YOUR JOURNAL

WRITER'S WARM-UP ◆ Did you know that a habitat is a place where an animal naturally lives? You know that different kinds of animals are suited to live under different conditions. You may have seen exhibits at a natural history museum that explain how camels can survive in the desert or how polar bears manage in the frozen north. What special characteristics allow animals to live in places where survival is difficult? What do you know about special habitats for animals? Write about them in your journal.

start with WRITING IN YOUR JOURNAL

Writers' Warm-up is designed to help students activate prior knowledge of the unit theme, "Animal Habitats." Whether you begin instruction with Part 1 or Part 2, encourage students to focus attention on the illustration on page 386 of their textbooks. Encourage them to discuss what they see. Then have a volunteer read aloud the **Writers' Warm-up** on page 387. Have students write their thoughts in their journals. You may wish to tell them that they will refer to this writing in the first lesson of Part 1, in the Grammar-Writing Connection, and in the Curriculum Connection.

THEN START WITH part 1

Language Awareness: Sentences
Developmental lessons focus on the concept of sentences. Each lesson is carefully constructed not only to help students learn the concept well but also to help build interest and background knowledge for the thinking, reading, and writing they will do in Part 2. The last lesson in Part 1 is a vocabulary lesson with which students learn about homographs. The Grammar-Writing Connection that follows serves as a bridge to Part 2, encouraging students to work together to apply their new language skills at the sentence level of writing.

...OR WITH part 2

A Reason for Writing: Classifying is the focus of Part 2. First, students learn a thinking strategy for classifying. Then they read and respond to a selection of literature on which they may model their writing. Developmental composition lessons, including "Group Discussions," a speaking and listening lesson, all reflect the literature and culminate in the Writing Process lesson. There a "Grammar Check," a "Word Choice" hint, and proofreading strategies help you focus on single traits for remediation or instruction through the lessons in Part 1. The unit ends with Curriculum Connection and Books to Enjoy, which help students discover how their new skills apply to writing across the curriculum.

THEME BAR

CATEGORIES	Environments	Business/World of Work	Imagination	Communications/ Fine Arts	People	Science	Expressions	Social Studies
THEMES	UNIT 1 Farm Life	UNIT 2 Handicrafts	UNIT 3 Tall Tales	UNIT 4 The Visual Arts	UNIT 5 Lasting Impressions	UNIT 6 Volcanoes	UNIT 7 Nature	UNIT 8 Animal Habitats
PACING	1 month	1 month	1 month	1 month	1 month	1 month	1 month	1 month

Build background knowledge of the unit theme, "Animal Habitats," by reading aloud this selection to your class. At the same time you will be building your students' knowledge of our rich heritage of fine literature. You may wish to use the "Notes for Listening" on the following page before and after reading aloud.

The Beavers Build A Home

from Beaver Valley

BY WALTER D. EDMONDS

Every evening when he came home, Skeet had something new to tell about the beaver. To Samantha and Loopey none of it seemed to amount to much because the pond was not yet visible from the spruce <u>knoll</u> where they played, and they preferred their games to making the roundabout trip Skeet took daily to the site of the dam. Even when one morning the water backed up past the nearest bushes in the <u>swale</u>, they saw no point in going because they could see the pond from home anyway.

Skeet's mother was always busy and did not pay much attention to what he had to say. Grandfather Overdare listened, but he hardly ever offered a comment until the day the water showed from the knoll. Then he said it would be all right if the pond were to stay the way it was.

"But it won't," he went on grimly. "Beaver always want things bigger and better than they've got."

Skeet could not imagine what else the beaver would want to do, but he was surprised next morning when he saw that the level of the pond had risen again. It now touched the spruce knoll itself, backing up the brook to the very point he had been standing on when he first saw the beaver. The still water came right between the knoll and the steep bank opposite and the brook entered it with a little bubbling curl of froth. For the first time Skeet had an uneasy feeling that the <u>forebodings</u> of his grandfather might just possibly be right. But next day when he saw that the still water had risen no farther, these doubts began to leave him.

For the next two weeks the water stayed at the same level and when he went down to the site of the dam he saw that the beaver were occupied on a new job. Out in the middle of the pond, beside the deeper channel of the brook, they had begun to build a house.

It was quite a while before Skeet understood what it was, and then only because a muskrat who had come to inspect the pond told him.

"*We* build houses, too," he said, in a not very pleasant voice. "But we don't feel we have to put up a palace."

It was hardly a palace once the beavers had got through building its base below water. For several days they were constantly diving, taking down sod and mud and also clay, which they had found at the foot of the high bank opposite the spruce knoll. They worked at it night and day without letup until a flat island of mud and clay had risen six or seven inches above the level of the pond. It was roughly round in shape and twelve feet across, and it did not look much like a house to Skeet, who thought of houses in terms of nests and holes in the ground.

Actually this was only the foundation. The next step was to put down flooring. This the beaver did by laying straight narrow sticks side by side and treading them partway into the mud. Only then, with Seemore superintending, did they start on the house itself.

He had the rest of the beaver bring brush and mud to the platform, and with it he made a block about two feet thick and two feet high in the center of the floor. Then he laid long sticks in a circle, with their tips on the block and butt ends about two feet in from the edge of the round platform. Once these had been laid the other beaver helped pile sticks and brush and mud on them, until they had a rounded covering nearly two feet thick. They daubed it all over with clay except for the very top. Here they left just sticks and brush so that the air could pass through.

It looked rough and clumsy, but it was completely weatherproof and its inside arrangements were something Skeet was completely unaware of. Only the beaver themselves knew, though an otter or muskrat could find out. For as soon as the roof was done and no one could see into the house, not even a hawk flying over, the beaver had dug three different places in the floor. Next they took away the center block of brush and mud on which the roofing poles had originally rested. The poles, with their tips interlocking and the rest of them interwoven with brush and packed with clay, now supported the roof by themselves, and the beaver had an open domed room in which to spend the winter.

That evening, though no one heard them, they had the first of their sings. They felt very pleased with the house they had built, but during the night old Seemore began to think about plans for getting in their winter food supply. ◇

NOTES FOR
listening

Introducing the Selection

Relate to theme Tell students that the unit theme is "Animal Habitats." Encourage them to discuss what they know of how animals build their shelters.

Discuss word meanings Explain to students that in "The Beavers Build a Home" they will hear new words that they may not understand. Pronounce the words below and write them on the chalkboard. Give students the meaning of each word and tell them that knowing the words will help them to better understand "The Beavers Build a Home."

knoll a small, round hill
swale a low place in a tract of land, usually wet
forebodings senses of something bad about to happen

Listening to the Selection

Set a purpose Tell students they are going to listen to an excerpt from *Beaver Valley* by Walter D. Edmonds. Have students listen to discover how beavers build their shelter.

Starting with Literature

Discussing the Selection

Return to purpose After you have read the selection, discuss with students the way beavers build their shelter. Have students share what they learned and then make a more general statement, such as: *Beavers work hard to build their shelters.*

UNIT 8 PLANNING AND PACING GUIDE

	LESSON TITLE	STUDENT TEXT				TEACHING RESOURCES		
1 DAY	**Unit Opener**	Student Lesson	Unit Review	Cumulative Review	Extra Practice	Reteaching Master	Practice Master	Testing Program
1 DAY	Reviewing the Parts of Speech	388–389	430	432	436, 437	64	64	T548
1 DAY	Compound Subjects	390–391	430	432	436, 438	65	65	T548
1 DAY	Using Subjects and Verbs That Agree	392–393	430	432	436, 438, 439	66	66	T548
1 DAY	Compound Predicates	394–395	430	432	436, 439, 440	67	67	T548
1 DAY	Compound Sentences	396–397	430	432	436, 440, 441	68	68	T548
1 DAY	Avoiding Run-on Sentences	398–399	430	432	436, 441	69	69	T548
1 DAY	VOCABULARY ◆ Homographs	400–401	431			70	70	T548
1 DAY	GRAMMAR-WRITING CONNECTION ◆ How to Combine Sentences	402–403						
	▶ **THINK**							
1 DAY	CRITICAL THINKING ◆ A Strategy for Classifying	406–407	See also pages 411, 422, 428					
	▶ **READ**							
1 DAY	LITERATURE ◆ *Two of a Kind* by Ron Hirschi	408–411				Audio Library 2		
	▶ **SPEAK/LISTEN**							
1 DAY	SPEAKING AND LISTENING ◆ Group Discussions	412–413				Video Library		
	▶ **WRITE**							
1 DAY	WRITING ◆ A Paragraph That Compares	414–415	431			71	71	
1 DAY	WRITING ◆ A Paragraph That Contrasts	416–417	431			72	72	
1 DAY	READING-WRITING CONNECTION ◆ Focus on Likenesses and Differences	418–419						T548
	▶ **WRITING PROCESS** ◆ Prewriting • Writing • Revising • Proofreading • Publishing							
4–5 DAYS	WRITING PROCESS ◆ Writing an Article That Compares	420–427				Spelling Connection Transparencies		T555
1 DAY	CURRICULUM CONNECTION ◆ Writing for Science	428				Writing Across the Curriculum Guide		

(Left margin labels: PART 1, PART 2)

Teacher Resource File
Reteaching Masters 64–72
Practice Masters 64–72
Evaluation and Testing Program, including
 Unit Pretest, Posttest, and Picture Prompt
 Writing Samples
Parent Letters in English and Spanish
Classroom Theme Posters
Writing Across the Curriculum Teacher Guide
Integrated Language Arts Projects with
 Masters (see pages T511–T529)
Spelling Corner, Teacher Edition
Writing Process Transparencies
Audio Library 1: Read-Alouds and
 Sing-Alouds

Also available:
Achieving English Proficiency Guide and
 Activities
Spelling Connection, Pupil Edition
Student Resource Books
Student Writing Portfolios
Professional Handbook
WORLD OF BOOKS Classroom Library

Multi-Modal Materials
Audio Library 1: Read-Alouds and Sing-Alouds
Audio Library 2: Listening to Literature
Video Library
Revising and Proofreading Transparencies
Fine Arts Transparencies with Viewing Booklet
Writing Process Transparencies
Writing Process Computer Program

Unit 8 Planning and Pacing Guide

LANGUAGE
game

Sentence Builders

Objective: To review the parts of speech
Materials: Index cards

Divide the class into rows. Explain that each row must try to create a logical sentence from the parts of speech you will dictate. The first person in the row will write a word on the index card for the part of speech you dictate. The index card is then passed along the row. Other parts of speech are dictated and each person writes a word. The last person in the row writes a word and a period. Each sentence is read aloud, and the class decides if the correct parts of speech were used.

1. Noun/verb/preposition/adjective/adjective/noun
2. Adjective/noun/preposition/noun/verb/adverb
3. Noun/verb/adverb/preposition/pronoun/noun
4. Pronoun/verb/adverb/preposition/pronoun/noun
5. Verb/adverb/preposition/adjective/adjective/noun

Multi-Modal Activities

BULLETIN BOARD
idea

You may wish to use a bulletin board as a springboard for discussing the unit theme, or you may prefer to have students create a bulletin board as they move through the unit. Encourage students to think about animal habitats by having them create want ads for animals' homes. Write the following sample or one of your own on the chalkboard for students to use as a model.

WANTED: A large cave on a quiet mountainside away from people. It should be near running water, berry bushes, and beehives. Contact Mr. and Mrs. Bear.

Have students add to or revise their ads as they learn more about animal habitats during the unit. You may wish to label the display *Home Sweet Home*.

Students with different learning styles will all benefit from a natural approach to language learning, including frequent and varied use of oral language in the classroom.

Students "At Risk"

The following suggestions can help you help the students in your classroom who may be considered "at risk."

Model Thinking Behaviors

Students who feel they are the only ones who "don't get it," may not even attempt to meet a goal or complete an assignment. Help them by modeling *your* thinking. Demonstrate how you might approach and complete a task. Have students help you. Encourage them to suggest possibilities and predict outcomes at each step. This modeling activity can serve as a rehearsal before students proceed on their own, and it can help you discover where in a task difficulties may arise or extra help may be needed. When students do not meet their own or your expectations, help them revisit their thinking. Be sure to reward the positive aspects.

Limited English Proficiency

Teachers whose classes contain students with limited English proficiency may find the following activities helpful in developing students' skills in grammar and composition.

Composing Sentences

Review with students the definitions of the parts of speech. Then help students complete the part of speech chart below as follows.

Have students brainstorm a list of words for each part of speech. Then help them use the words to compose complete sentences. Encourage students to try to fit at least one word for each part of speech in their sentences.

You may wish to have students write their sentences on oaktag strips, then cut the strips apart, shuffle the parts, and put the sentences back together again. After students have had practice putting their own sentences back together, you may wish to have them exchange sentences with a partner or partners.

Sentence Strips

On oaktag strips write a sentence for each student. Try to include at least one noun, pronoun, verb, adjective, adverb, and preposition in each sentence. As you describe a part of speech, have students find a word fitting that description on their strip. Have students find the following:

1. a noun, which names a person, place, or thing
2. a pronoun, which takes the place of a noun or pronoun
3. a verb, which shows action or being
4. an adjective, which describes a noun or pronoun
5. an adverb, which describes a verb, an adjective, or another adverb
6. a preposition, which relates a noun or pronoun to another word

Have students identify in turn each word on their strip for each part of speech. Encourage students to discuss why each word does or does not fit the description you give. You may wish to use these sentences:

1. The large dog raced excitedly toward its owner.
2. The noisy jays flew over the tree.
3. A tiny fawn lay quietly near its mother.
4. A flock of gulls swooped gracefully toward the small boat below them.

Part of Speech Chart

Noun	Pronoun	Verb	Adjective	Adverb	Preposition
dog	*it*	*raced*	*large*	*excitedly*	*toward*

Gifted and Talented Students

To enable gifted and talented students to work at their own pace and to explore the content further, you may wish to use one or more of these activities.

Part-of-Speech Puzzles

Have students work individually or in small groups to write six related sentences. Have students blank out one word in each sentence for each part of speech and include the blanked-out words in a jumbled list to the right of the sentences. Have students or groups exchange sentence sets to complete the sentence puzzles.

As a more challenging task, you may wish to have students eliminate the word list. Have students select their own words to complete the sentences and then compare their word choices with the original words.

You may wish to have students share their work by compiling a part-of-speech puzzle book for students to enjoy.

Combining Subjects, Predicates, and Sentences

Have students work in small groups to brainstorm similarities between animals and then use the similarities to compose sentences with compound subjects, compound predicates, or compound sentences. For example, students may use the fact that penguins are flightless birds and ostriches are flightless birds to write a sentence with a compound subject—*Penguins and ostriches are flightless birds.*

You may wish to give students an assignment, or have them decide what the requirements are (for example, three sentences with a compound subject, three with a compound predicate, and three compound sentences). Have groups exchange papers and identify whether each sentence has a compound subject, a compound predicate, or is a compound sentence. You may wish to have groups classify the sentences by writing them on the chalkboard under the headings *Compound Subject, Compound Predicate,* and *Compound Sentence.*

Animal Combinations

Have students work in pairs or in small groups to brainstorm a list of attributes of common animals. Have them use the list to combine attributes to create sentences describing imaginary animals. Encourage students to use compound subjects, compound predicates, or compound sentences when describing their creatures.

Have students write a brief paragraph explaining where this imaginary creature might be found and how this creature compares to other animals in terms of appearance, movement, and eating habits.

You may wish to have students create wire sculptures to accompany their paragraphs and to arrange these in a classroom zoo.

Meeting Individual Needs

■ Easy ■ Average ■ Challenging

OBJECTIVES
To review the parts of speech
To identify predicate nouns and the words they rename

ASSIGNMENT GUIDE
BASIC   Practice A
   ⬇   Practice B
ADVANCED   Practice C

All should do the Apply activity.

RESOURCES
■
■ Reteaching Master 64
■ ■ ■ Practice Master 64
Extra Practice, pp. 436, 437
Unit 8 Pretest, p. T548

TEACHING THE LESSON

1. Getting Started
Oral Language Focus attention on this oral activity, encouraging all to participate. You may wish to ask volunteers to make up sentence pairs based on their daily activities, such as *Tomorrow I will walk to school. My friend and I are going for a walk.* Encourage creative responses, such as *Bat* the ball. A *bat* eats insects. *Bear* a burden. See the grizzly *bear. Bill* the customer. Look at the bird's *bill.* He *bows* courteously. The ship has a *bow.* Prepare a *bowl* of rice. I can *bowl.* I will *box* for the title. Eggs are in a *box.* I *can* do it. The peas are in a *can.* A rooster *crows.* I see several black *crows.*

2. Developing the Lesson
Guide students through the explanation of the parts of speech, emphasizing the examples and the summary. You may wish to emphasize that how a word is used in a sentence determines its part of speech. Lead students through the **Guided Practice.** Identify those who would benefit from reteaching. Assign independent Practice A–C.

3. Closing the Lesson
After students complete the Apply activity, have volunteers write words from each of their six categories for the class on a chalkboard chart. Point out to students that using a variety of parts of speech can add interest to their speaking and writing.

They *race* to the finish line.   Lou came in one *second* later.
Pat won the *race.*   Lou took *second* place.

Make up other pairs of sentences in which the same word is used as two different parts of speech.

1 Reviewing the Parts of Speech

The following chart reviews six parts of speech.

	Definition	Example
noun	A **noun** names a person, place, thing, or idea.	Prancer is a reindeer.
pronoun	A **pronoun** takes the place of a noun or nouns.	It lives in the Arctic.
verb	An **action verb** shows action. A **linking verb** shows being.	It eats plants. A reindeer is a strong animal.
adjective	An **adjective** describes a noun or a pronoun.	It thrives in cold climates. Its coat looks smooth.
adverb	An **adverb** describes a verb, an adjective, or another adverb.	A reindeer is very quick. It runs extremely fast.
preposition	A **preposition** relates a noun or pronoun to another word.	A reindeer is related to other hoofed animals.

A noun can follow a linking verb: *A fawn is a young reindeer.* A noun that follows a linking verb renames or identifies the subject.

> **Summary** ◆ A **part of speech** tells how a word is used.

Guided Practice

Tell whether each underlined word is a noun, a pronoun, a verb, an adjective, an adverb, or a preposition.

1. Reindeer have thick coats.   *(adj.)*
2. Reindeer usually travel in herds.   *(adv.)*
3. They roam across the tun—   *(pron.) (prep.)*
4. The tundra has no trees.   *(v.) (n.)*

ESSENTIAL LANGUAGE SKILLS
This lesson provides opportunities to:

LISTENING ◆ follow the logical organization of an oral presentation ◆ select from an oral presentation the information needed

SPEAKING ◆ respond appropriately to questions from teachers and peers ◆ use a variety of words to express feelings and ideas

READING ◆ use context to understand the meaning of words ◆ evaluate and make judgments ◆ follow a set of directions

WRITING ◆ classify ideas and information ◆ generate ideas using graphic organizers

LANGUAGE ◆ use parts of speech correctly ◆ understand the conventions of usage and mechanics

Practice

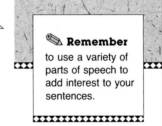

A. Write each sentence. Draw a line under the noun that follows the linking verb. Draw two lines under the subject that the noun renames or identifies.

EXAMPLE: A caribou is a reindeer.

ANSWER: A caribou is a reindeer.

5. Reindeer are mammals.
6. They are sturdy animals.
7. These animals are strong swimmers.

B. Write each underlined word. After the word, write *noun*, *pronoun*, *verb*, *adjective*, *adverb*, or *preposition*.

8. The reindeer has some long, hollow hairs. adj. adj. n.
9. They serve as a kind of life jacket for the animal. pron. v. prep.
10. Reindeer have very large feet. adv. adj.
11. The feet act as snowshoes. v. n.
12. Reindeer move gracefully. v. adv.
13. In the summer, reindeer are uncomfortable creatures. prep. v. adj.
14. Mosquitoes and blackflies bite them constantly. n. pron. adv.
15. The reindeer run into cold streams. prep. adj.
16. These animals are well adapted for survival in the cold parts of North America. n. prep. n.
17. They feed on small plants under the snow. pron. adj. prep.
18. Their speed enables them to outrun wolves. pron. n. n.
19. Their antlers also protect them. n. v.

C. Study the sentence triangle on the right. Identify the part of speech of each word. Then write your own triangle.

Reindeer
Reindeer sprint.
Speedy reindeer sprint.
Speedy reindeer often sprint.
Speedy reindeer often sprint in snow.

adj. n. adv. v. prep. n.

Apply ♦ Think and Write

From Your Writing ♦ List the words you used in the Writer's Warm-up. Use these six categories: nouns, pronouns, verbs, adjectives, adverbs, and prepositions.

✎ **Remember**
to use a variety of parts of speech to add interest to your sentences.

GRAMMAR: Parts of Speech **389**

◀▥▥ TEACHING OPTIONS ▥▥▶

RETEACHING

A Different Modality On the chalkboard write one line at a time of the pyramid below. As you write *n.*, tell students that a noun names a person, place, idea, or thing. Have students name a noun, and begin writing a word pyramid with the given noun. Complete both pyramids.

n.	Robins
n. v.	Robins fly.
adj. n. v. adv.	Hungry robins are near.
pron. v. prep. n.	They peck for worms.

CLASS ENRICHMENT

A Cooperative Activity Have students work together in small groups to compose simple sentences, each one clearly illustrating the use of one part of speech. When they have chosen their best five sentences, have recorders copy them with a fill-in blank and the part of speech label at the end of the sentence. Have groups exchange papers to complete the sentences.

CHALLENGE

An Independent Extension Have students write sentences using each word as indicated. Encourage them to use a dictionary for word meanings.

1. down (noun, adverb)
2. fan (noun, verb)
3. fleet (noun, adjective)
4. hail (noun, verb)

1. down (feathers, direction) 2. fan (admirer, to stir air) 3. fleet (ships, rapid) 4. hail (icy rain, to shout welcome)

UNIT 8/LESSON 2

OBJECTIVES
To identify conjunctions
To identify compound subjects

ASSIGNMENT GUIDE
BASIC   Practice A
             Practice B
ADVANCED   Practice C

All should do the Apply activity.

RESOURCES
■ Reteaching Master 65
■ Practice Master 65
■ ■ ■ Extra Practice, pp. 436, 438

TEACHING THE LESSON

1. Getting Started
Oral Language Focus attention on this oral activity, encouraging all to participate. You may wish to have volunteers compose sentences based on their observations of people in the classroom, such as *Susie and Bob are wearing red sweaters.*

2. Developing the Lesson
Guide students through the explanation of compound subjects, emphasizing the examples and the summary. You may wish to point out to students the use of commas illustrated in the lesson. Tell them that when three or more simple subjects are joined by a conjunction, a comma is to follow each simple subject that precedes the conjunction. Lead students through the **Guided Practice.** Identify those who would benefit from reteaching. Assign independent Practice A–C.

3. Closing the Lesson
After students complete the Apply activity, have the class discuss what they learned about moose. Point out to students that using compound subjects can help them avoid repeating the same idea in different sentences.

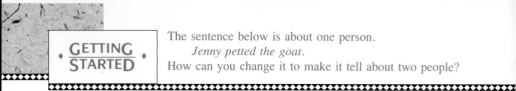

The sentence below is about one person.
Jenny petted the goat.
How can you change it to make it tell about two people?

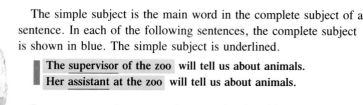

2 Compound Subjects

The simple subject is the main word in the complete subject of a sentence. In each of the following sentences, the complete subject is shown in blue. The simple subject is underlined.

> The <u>supervisor</u> of the zoo will tell us about animals.
> Her <u>assistant</u> at the zoo will tell us about animals.

Some sentences have more than one simple subject. In the following sentences, notice how the two simple subjects are combined to avoid repeating the predicate.

> The <u>supervisor</u> and her <u>assistant</u> will tell us about animals.
> <u>Ms. Juarez</u> and <u>Mr. Clayton</u> will tell us about animals.

Two or more simple subjects that have the same predicate are called a compound subject. Here are some more sentences that have compound subjects.

> <u>Forests</u>, <u>mountains</u>, and <u>deserts</u> are animal habitats.
> <u>Leon</u> and <u>I</u> will enjoy the talk.

Notice that the simple subjects are joined by the conjunction *and* or *or*. A **conjunction** joins words.

> **Summary** ◆ A **compound subject** is two or more simple subjects that have the same predicate. Using compound subjects can make your writing less repetitious.

Guided Practice

Each sentence below has a compound subject. Name the simple subjects in each compound subject.

1. <u>Sheep</u>, <u>deer</u>, and <u>goats</u> are animals with hoofs.
2. <u>Camels</u> and <u>antelopes</u> eat only plants.
3. Many <u>children</u> and <u>adults</u> enjoy the petting zoo.

390   GRAMMAR: Compound Subjects

ESSENTIAL LANGUAGE SKILLS
This lesson provides opportunities to:

LISTENING ◆ follow the logical organization of an oral presentation ◆ select from an oral presentation the information needed

SPEAKING ◆ use oral language for a variety of purposes

READING ◆ use context to understand the meaning of words ◆ evaluate and make judgments ◆ follow a set of directions

WRITING ◆ organize information related to a single topic ◆ adapt information to accomplish a specific purpose for a particular audience

LANGUAGE ◆ produce a variety of sentence patterns ◆ use language for informing

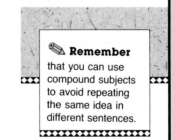

Practice

A. Write the complete subject of each sentence. If the subject is compound, write *compound*.

4. Animals with hoofs are important.
5. They provide food for people in many parts of the world.
6. Mr. Clayton looks after the hoofed animals in the zoo. comp.
7. Ms. Juarez and he studied them in native habitats. comp.
8. Asia, Europe, and South America have many kinds of deer.
9. Caribou and reindeer can run faster than their enemies. comp.
10. The powerful hippopotamus is not as swift.
11. Many creatures run faster than the hippopotamus. comp.
12. Buffalo and antelopes band together in herds.
13. The herds move to different areas to find food.

B. Write each sentence. Underline the compound subject.

EXAMPLE: Lou and another student are reading about animals.
ANSWER: Lou and another student are reading about animals.

14. Hoofed animals and other creatures depend upon their habitats for survival.
15. Berries and leaves provide a diet for the gazelle.
16. Amy and Lou showed us pictures of antelopes.
17. Gazelles and impalas are antelopes that run fast.
18. Ellen and I admire the impala's gracefulness.

C. 19–23. Write five sentences of your own that have compound subjects. You may want to write about animals and their habitats. Sentences will vary.

Apply ◆ Think and Write

Dictionary of Knowledge ◆ Read about the moose in the Dictionary of Knowledge. Write a paragraph about these animals using compound subjects in several sentences.

> ✏ **Remember**
> that you can use compound subjects to avoid repeating the same idea in different sentences.

RETEACHING 65

Compound Subjects

Underline the simple subject in each sentence.
1. <u>Mary</u> carried the picnic basket.   2. <u>Lin</u> carried the picnic basket.

The same simple subjects from above are in the next sentence. They form a compound subject. Circle the two simple subjects.
3. Ⓜary and Ⓛin carried the picnic basket.

> A **compound subject** is two or more simple subjects that have the same predicate. Simple subjects may be joined by the conjunction *and* or *or*.

A. The simple subjects are underlined. If the subject is compound, circle *Yes*. If the subject is not compound, circle *No*.

EXAMPLE: <u>Keith</u> and <u>Chen</u> wore sunglasses. (Yes) No
1. <u>Boys</u> and <u>girls</u> climbed aboard the bus. (Yes) No
2. A bus <u>driver</u> closed the doors behind us. Yes (No)
3. The <u>driver</u> and a <u>teacher</u> explained the rules. (Yes) No
4. The happy <u>children</u> sang many songs together. Yes (No)
5. One park <u>attendant</u> and her <u>helper</u> welcomed the class. (Yes) No
6. The <u>teachers</u> and <u>parents</u> arranged picnic tables. (Yes) No

B. Write a word from the box to complete each compound subject. Some answers may vary. Possible answers follow.

children	I	attendant	fruit	Luis

EXAMPLE: My friends and ___I___ raced toward a shady table.
7. Tina and ___Luis___ passed out cartons of milk.
8. Sandwiches and ___fruit___ were already on the tables.
9. A park ranger and an ___attendant___ spoke to our group after lunch.
10. Adults and ___children___ cleaned up the picnic area afterward.
11. My classmates and ___I___ had a wonderful day at the park.

PRACTICE 65

Compound Subjects

> A **compound subject** is two or more simple subjects that have the same predicate.

A. Write the complete subject of each sentence. If the subject is compound, write *compound*. If the subject is not compound, write *not compound*.

1. My friends and I disagree on salad ingredients.
   My friends and I — compound
2. They sometimes add fish and fruit to salads.
   They — not compound
3. My family and I like only crunchy vegetables in salads.
   My family and I — compound
4. Many people mix salads long before a meal.
   Many people — not compound
5. Oil and other salad dressings can make vegetables soggy.
   Oil and other salad dressings — compound

B. Combine the sentence pairs. Write one sentence with a compound subject.
6. Fruits are part of a good diet. Vegetables are part of a good diet.
   Fruits and vegetables are part of a good diet.
7. Healthy muscles need a proper diet, exercise, and rest. Bones need a proper diet, exercise, and rest.
   Healthy muscles and bones need a proper diet, exercise, and rest.
8. Vitamins make bones hard. Minerals make bones hard.
   Vitamins and minerals make bones hard.
9. Breads provide energy. Cereals provide energy.
   Breads and cereals provide energy.

WRITE IT
Write the foods that you would include in a proper diet for one day. Give reasons for your choices. **Write sentences with compound subjects.** Write on a separate sheet of paper. Answers will vary.

◀⫿⫿⫿ TEACHING OPTIONS ⫿⫿⫿▶

RETEACHING

A Different Modality Prepare a classification activity. Write on paper strips pairs of simple subjects and related predicates as below. Have students find the two subjects that match each predicate, manipulating the strips to form and then write sentences.

and	birds	
	planes	have wings

CLASS ENRICHMENT

A Cooperative Activity Have small groups of students write five sentences, each with a compound subject, about planning a party or designing a science project. Have groups exchange sentences and underline the compound subjects. Have each group choose one member to write one sentence on the chalkboard without underlining and have the class identify the compound subject and conjunctions.

CHALLENGE

An Independent Extension Have students unscramble the sentences. Then have them underline the complete subject and identify it as simple or compound.

Example: <u>Frogs and toads</u> have moist bodies.
(compound)

1. frogs, have, bodies, moist, and, toads
2. dry, snakes, have, bodies, lizards, and
3. are, with, birds, covered, feathers
4. birds, eggs, reptiles, and, lay
5. reptiles, lay, eggs, land, on

■ Easy ■ Average ■ Challenging

OBJECTIVES
To use compound subjects joined by *and* correctly

ASSIGNMENT GUIDE
BASIC   Practice A
             Practice B
ADVANCED   Practice C

All should do the Apply activity.

RESOURCES
■ Reteaching Master 66
■ Practice Master 66
■ ■ ■ Extra Practice, pp. 436, 438

TEACHING THE LESSON

1. Getting Started
Oral Language Focus attention on this oral activity, encouraging all to participate. You may wish to model responses, such as *Casey and Judie train the cats. Judie and Muffin work on special tricks.*

2. Developing the Lesson
Guide students through the explanation of using subjects and verbs that agree, emphasizing the examples and the summary. Lead students through the **Guided Practice**. Identify those who would benefit from reteaching. Assign independent Practice A–C.

3. Closing the Lesson
After students complete the Apply activity, have volunteers read their sentences with compound subjects. Have the class decide whether or not verb forms agree with the subjects. Point out to students that making subjects and verbs agree can help them make their writing clear.

♦ GETTING STARTED ♦

Think of sentences that tell about Puff and Muffin, cats that do tricks. What does Puff, a large Persian cat, do? What does the small calico cat, Muffin, do? What tricks do they perform together? What do their owners, Casey and Judie, do?

3 Using Subjects and Verbs That Agree

The correct verb form must be used in a sentence in order for the subject and verb to agree. The singular form of a verb is used with a singular subject. The plural form of a verb is used with a plural subject. Study the chart below.

	Singular	Plural
action verbs	Danny raises goats.	They raise goats.
linking verbs	I am busy. He is a farmer.	They are busy. The goats are tame.

You know that a compound subject is two or more simple subjects that have the same verb. When the parts of a compound subject are joined by *and*, the verb is plural.

> Fran and Louise live on a farm.
> Their cows and their goat win prizes at the county fair.
> The Moffetts and the Garcias raise cattle.
> Cattle, goats, and sheep are domestic animals.

Summary ♦ Compound subjects joined by *and* use the form of a verb that is used with a plural noun. When a sentence has a compound subject, use the correct verb form.

Guided Practice

Name the verb in parentheses ( ) that completes each sentence.

1. Bill, Nancy, and Liu (visit, visits) Fran's farm.
2. Fran and her friend (watches, watch) the pigs.
3. Cows and goats (give, gives) milk.

392   USAGE: Subject-Verb Agreement

ESSENTIAL LANGUAGE SKILLS
This lesson provides opportunities to:

LISTENING ♦ follow the logical organization of an oral presentation ♦ select from an oral presentation the information needed

SPEAKING ♦ express ideas clearly and effectively ♦ respond appropriately to questions from teachers and peers

READING ♦ use context to understand the meaning of words ♦ evaluate and make judgments ♦ follow a set of directions

WRITING ♦ identify audience and purpose ♦ use conventional formats (business letters, essays, and other commonly used forms)

LANGUAGE ♦ use language for imagining ♦ use the fundamentals of grammar, punctuation, and spelling

Practice

A. Write the verb in parentheses ( ) that correctly completes each sentence.

4. The domestic hog and the wild boar (<u>are</u>, is) cousins.
5. Asia and Africa (<u>have</u>, has) wild boar habitats.
6. Roots and grain (<u>serve</u>, serves) as food for the animal.
7. Chinese and Americans (raises, <u>raise</u>) hogs.
8. Hogs and cattle (<u>thrive</u>, thrives) on farms.
9. The hog and the steer (provides, <u>provide</u>) meat.
10. Cow's milk and goat's milk (<u>are</u>, is) sources of cheese.
11. Wild goats and wild sheep (lives, <u>live</u>) on mountains.
12. Sheep and goats (<u>resemble</u>, resembles) each other.

B. Read the sentences below. If the subject and verb of a sentence agree, write *correct*. If the subject and verb do not agree, rewrite the sentence so that it is correct.

13. Mountains and plateaus ~~was~~ the first homes of wild sheep. *were*
14. The ibex and the markhor are kinds of wild goats. *correct*
15. Juan and his parents ~~has~~ domestic goats on their farm. *have*
16. Scots and Australians raise domestic sheep. *correct*
17. Both fine-wooled sheep and long-wooled sheep ~~produces~~ excellent wool. *produce*

C. Complete each sentence below. Remember that the form of the verb you use needs to agree with the subject of the sentence.
Answers will vary.

18. Farmers and ranchers _____ .
19. Sheep and goats _____ .
20. Horses and cattle _____ .
21. The cowhands and clowns at the rodeo _____ .
22. From the bleachers my friends and I _____ .

Apply • Think and Write

A Friendly Letter • Imagine that you are visiting a farm or ranch. Write a letter telling a friend about the animals you see. Use compound subjects in some of your sentences.

> ✎ **Remember**
> to use the plural form of a verb with a compound subject.

USAGE: Subject-Verb Agreement **393**

◀╫ TEACHING OPTIONS ╫▶

RETEACHING

A Different Modality Write simple subjects, compound subjects, and present-tense action verbs on card strips. Write *simple = one* or *compound = two or more* on the reverse of each subject. Write *singular* or *plural* on the reverse of each verb. Place the subjects and verbs in separate piles. Have students take turns matching subjects and verbs. Have them check the labels on the reverse side to make sure the subjects and verbs agree.

CLASS ENRICHMENT

A Cooperative Activity Divide the class into small groups. Have each group write several singular subjects on separate index cards. Then have groups exchange cards. Have each group member choose two index cards, form a compound subject by using the word *and*, and then use the compound subject in a sentence. Have group members check the subject-verb agreement of each sentence.

CHALLENGE

An Independent Extension Have students use five verbs in sentences with compound subjects. Encourage them to use a dictionary for word meaning.
Example: Roses and lilies wilt without water.

1. wilt　5. assure　9. falter
2. gnaw　6. bestow　10. pursue
3. adapt　7. devour　11. chortle
4. amble　8. endure　12. console

393

UNIT 8/LESSON 4

OBJECTIVES
To identify compound predicates

ASSIGNMENT GUIDE
BASIC   Practice A
↓   Practice B
ADVANCED   Practice C

All should do the Apply activity.

RESOURCES
■ Reteaching Master 67
■ Practice Master 67
■ ■ ■ Extra Practice, pp. 436, 439

TEACHING THE LESSON

1. Getting Started
Oral Language Focus attention on this oral activity, encouraging all to participate. Encourage creative responses that follow a story line, such as *The pitcher dropped the ball. She kicked it by accident to the shortstop. The shortstop threw himself on the ball. He tossed it to the teammate on second base. The second baseman leaped into the air. He fell backward.*

2. Developing the Lesson
Guide students through the explanation of compound predicates, emphasizing the examples and the summary. You may wish to explain the use of commas when three or more verbs have the same subject. Lead students through the **Guided Practice.** Identify those who would benefit from reteaching. Assign independent Practice A–C.

3. Closing the Lesson
After students complete the Apply activity, have volunteers read aloud their favorite sentence. Encourage them to engage the class in a discussion of using vivid, active verbs. Point out to students that being able to identify and use compound predicates can help them add variety and color to their writing.

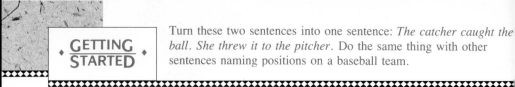

♦ GETTING STARTED ♦

Turn these two sentences into one sentence: *The catcher caught the ball. She threw it to the pitcher.* Do the same thing with other sentences naming positions on a baseball team.

4 Compound Predicates

The simple predicate is the main word in the complete predicate of a sentence. It is the verb. In the following examples the words in green are the complete predicate of each sentence. The underlined word is the simple predicate, or verb.

■ Carla opened the book.   Carla read the book.

Some sentences contain two or more verbs in the complete predicate.

■ Carla opened and read the book.

Notice that *Carla* is the subject of both *opened* and *read*. The ideas of the sentences are combined, and the two verbs are joined by *and*.

A predicate with two or more verbs that have the same subject is called a compound predicate. Here are two more sentences with compound predicates.

| She searched the index and found the word *llama*.
| She smiled, stretched, and turned the pages.

Summary ♦ A **compound predicate** is two or more verbs that have the same subject. You can use sentences with two or more verbs to add variety to your writing.

Guided Practice

Name the verbs in the complete predicate of each sentence.

1. We went to the zoo and watched the llamas.
2. One llama stared at us and walked by.
3. Another bared its teeth and tossed its head.
4. Carla sat nearby and opened her book.

394   GRAMMAR: Compound Predicates

ESSENTIAL LANGUAGE SKILLS
This lesson provides opportunities to:

LISTENING ♦ follow the logical organization of an oral presentation ♦ select from an oral presentation the information needed

SPEAKING ♦ express ideas clearly and effectively ♦ speak in complete sentences

READING ♦ use context to understand the meaning of words ♦ evaluate and make judgments ♦ follow a set of directions

LANGUAGE ♦ produce a variety of sentence patterns ♦ use language to narrate

Practice

A. Write the complete predicate of each sentence.
If the predicate is compound, write *compound*.

5. Llamas <u>live in the Andes Mountains of</u>
   <u>South America</u>.
6. Llamas <u>belong to the camel family</u>.
7. A llama <u>resembles a camel and has an</u>
   <u>unusual expression</u>. comp.
8. Its large teeth <u>bite and chew tough grasses</u>. comp.
9. An angry llama <u>glares and sometimes bites</u>. comp.
10. This animal <u>adapted to the high altitudes</u>
    <u>of the Andes</u>.
11. It <u>endures cold and survives long dry periods</u>. comp.
12. Its fleece <u>protects it and provides warmth</u>. comp.
13. Llamas <u>rarely descend below eight thousand feet</u>.
14. Their unusual behavior <u>interests, amuses, and delights me</u>. comp.

B. Write each sentence. Underline the compound predicate.

EXAMPLE: Llamas carry heavy loads and travel many miles.
ANSWER: Llamas <u>carry</u> heavy loads and <u>travel</u> many miles.

15. The Indians of Bolivia <u>raise</u> llamas and <u>use</u> them as
    pack animals.
16. Pack llamas <u>transport</u> grain and <u>work</u> at high altitudes.
17. They <u>graze</u> during the day and <u>sleep</u> at night.
18. A llama caravan <u>moves</u> slowly and <u>stops</u> often for food.
19. The first llama <u>wears</u> a bell and <u>walks</u> ahead of the others.
20. The driver <u>talks</u> to the llamas and <u>encourages</u> them.

C. 21-25. Write five sentences of your own that have compound
predicates. You may want to write about unusual animals.
Sentences will vary.

Apply ◆ Think and Write

A Story ◆ Write a story about a herd of animals that is pursued by
an enemy. Tell how the herd escapes danger. Use compound
predicates in your story.

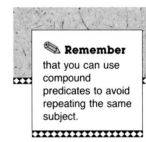

> 🖉 **Remember**
> that you can use
> compound
> predicates to avoid
> repeating the same
> subject.

RETEACHING 67

Compound Predicates

Sometimes the predicate part of a sentence has more than one verb. The complete predicate is underlined in each sentence below. Circle each verb.
1. Albert (measures) and (cuts) the pattern.   2. They (run) and (kick) the ball.

> A **compound predicate** is two or more verbs that have the same subject. The verbs in a compound predicate are joined by a conjunction.

A. The complete predicate in each sentence is underlined. If the predicate has more than one verb, circle *compound*. If the predicate has one verb, circle *not compound*.

EXAMPLE: Helpers collected books and put them on shelves.   (compound)   not compound

1. One helper dusted the tops of the books.   compound   (not compound)
2. The librarian got a projector and set it up.   (compound)   not compound
3. We entered the room and sat near the screen.   (compound)   not compound
4. The teacher shut the door and started the film.   (compound)   not compound
5. The film entertained us for over an hour.   compound   (not compound)
6. Students clapped and cheered at the end.   (compound)   not compound
7. Then our teacher started the lesson.   compound   (not compound)

B. Write the two verbs in each compound predicate.

EXAMPLE: The teacher draws and writes on the chalkboard.   draws   writes

8. Students read and study the worksheets.   read   study
9. Alonzo raises his hand and asks a question.   raises   asks
10. The teacher listens and then answers.   listens   answers
11. The teacher marks the papers and writes some comments.   marks   writes

PRACTICE 67

Compound Predicates

> A **compound predicate** is two or more verbs that have the same subject.

A. Write the complete predicate of each sentence. If the predicate is compound, write *compound*. If the predicate is not compound, write *not compound*. The first one is done for you.

1. Workers measured long boards and cut them to size.
   measured long boards and cut them to size   compound
2. Work progressed quickly because of power tools.
   progressed quickly because of power tools   not compound
3. The architect watched and offered suggestions.
   watched and offered suggestions   compound
4. Happy workers stood back and admired their completed project.
   stood back and admired their completed project   compound
5. Children rushed toward the new playground equipment.
   rushed toward the new playground equipment   not compound

B. Create a story by writing verbs to complete each compound predicate. Answers will vary.
One day Henry decided to build a clubhouse and ___asked___ his
friends for help. They ___dragged___ and ___carried___ boards
to Henry's backyard. Henry and his friends ___sawed___ and
___stacked___ the wood. They ___built___ a frame and then
___nailed___ boards to it. Finally, they ___painted___ the wood,
and then ___waited___ for the paint to dry. The next day they
___held___ their first club meeting.

WRITE IT
Write sentences that describe something you would like to build or make. Use compound predicates. Write on a separate sheet of paper. Answers will vary.

◀▥▥ TEACHING OPTIONS ▥▥▶

RETEACHING

A Different Modality Help students visualize the concept with high-contrast verbs. Write verb pairs on the chalkboard, such as *lost and found, opened and closed, pushed and pulled,* and *gives and takes.* Have students dictate a sentence for each pair (e.g., I lost my sock and found it under the bed). Write their sentences and have them underline the verbs and conjunction they used.

CLASS ENRICHMENT

A Cooperative Activity Divide the class into two groups. Have each student in one group write a complete subject on the chalkboard, such as *The little children.* Have each student in the other group write a complete compound predicate on the chalkboard, such as *stood at attention and saluted the general.* Have volunteers in each group take turns combining sentence parts and reading the sentences aloud.

CHALLENGE

An Independent Extension Have students write for each noun a sentence with a compound predicate.
Example: The train raced along the track and rounded the bend.

1. train   4. desert   7. trap
2. scientist 5. pasture   8. farm
3. cage   6. river   9. tree

UNIT 8/LESSON 5

■ Easy ■ Average ■ Challenging

OBJECTIVES
To identify compound sentences

ASSIGNMENT GUIDE
BASIC   Practice A
↓   Practice B
ADVANCED Practice C

All should do the Apply activity.

RESOURCES
■ Reteaching Master 68
■ Practice Master 68
■ ■ ■ Extra Practice, pp. 436, 440

TEACHING THE LESSON

1. Getting Started
Oral Language Focus attention on this oral activity, encouraging all to participate. You may wish to have pairs of students work together, with each partner providing half of the compound sentence.

2. Developing the Lesson
Guide students through the explanation of compound sentences, emphasizing the examples and the summary. You may wish to tell students that the simple sentences making up a compound sentence may have compound subjects and/or compound predicates. Point out the role of the comma in compound sentences. Lead students through the **Guided Practice.** Identify those who would benefit from reteaching. Assign independent Practice A–C.

3. Closing the Lesson
After students complete the Apply activity, have volunteers read aloud their compound sentences. You may wish to write some of the sentences on the chalkboard and draw a circle around each simple sentence in the compound sentence. Point out to students that using compound sentences can help them express related thoughts in an interesting, easy-to-read manner.

GETTING STARTED

Imagine that you have two pets, a dragon and a dinosaur. You have taught each one a special trick. Take turns making up sentences that tell the special tricks that both pets do. For example: *The dragon can roll over, and the dinosaur can shake hands.*

5 Compound Sentences

A simple sentence expresses one complete thought. It has one complete subject and one complete predicate.

> Llamas lived in the Andes.
> The Indians tamed the llamas.

A compound sentence contains two or more simple sentences. The simple sentences are joined by *and*, *or*, or *but*.

> Llamas lived in the Andes, and the Indians tamed the llamas.
> Cynthia likes camels, but I prefer llamas.
> We will go to the zoo, or Ms. Shaw will take us on a hike.

Notice that a compound sentence has at least two complete subjects and two complete predicates. It is not the same as a simple sentence that has a compound subject or a compound predicate.

Compound Sentence: Llamas are tame, but guanacos are wild.

Compound Subject: Llamas and guanacos live in South America.

Compound Predicate: Guanacos live in bands and are social animals.

> **Summary** ◆ A **compound sentence** contains two or more simple sentences joined by a conjunction. When you write, you can use compound sentences to combine related ideas.

Guided Practice

Tell whether each sentence is simple or compound.

1. A guanaco is a kind of llama. simp.
2. A band acts as a family, and it stays together. comp.
3. A guanaco band has about ten members. simp.
4. The male in the band leads it and assures its safety. simp.
5. Guanacos are found in Peru, and camels live in Arabia. comp.

396   GRAMMAR: Simple Sentences and Compound Sentences

ESSENTIAL LANGUAGE SKILLS
This lesson provides opportunities to:

LISTENING ◆ listen actively and attentively ◆ respond appropriately to orally presented directions

SPEAKING ◆ participate in storytelling and creative dramatics ◆ use oral language for a variety of purposes

READING ◆ use context to understand the meaning of words ◆ evaluate and make judgments ◆ follow a set of directions

WRITING ◆ write and compose for a variety of purposes ◆ organize information related to a single topic ◆ use chronological and spatial order and order of importance

LANGUAGE ◆ use language for imagining ◆ produce a variety of sentence patterns ◆ use language for narrating

Practice

A. Write *simple* or *compound* for each sentence.

6. The Arabian camel has one hump, and the Bactrian camel has two humps. comp.

7. The Arabian camel and the Bactrian camel are the chief kinds of camels. simp.

8. The dromedary is a special camel and is bred for racing. simp.

9. Once camels were wild, but today most of them are tame. comp.

10. Several hundred wild camels still live in Mongolia. simp.

11. I have never been on a camel, but Cynthia rode one once. comp.

12. The camel was friendly and gave her a smooth ride. simp.

B. Write the sentences below. Then underline the two simple sentences in each.

13. Camels once lived in North America, but they disappeared.

14. Camels carry a large load, and they are called "ships of the desert."

15. The camel's long hair provides wool, and the skin provides leather.

16. Its hump stores fat, and its hair gives protection against hot weather.

17. A camel can go without water for days, but its food provides some moisture.

18. The animal can live without any water in winter, and some camels have refused offers of water.

19. Llamas are well adapted to the mountains, and camels are suited to the desert.

20. A camel can be pleasant, or it can be hostile.

C. 21–25. Write five compound sentences of your own. You may want to write about animals that people can ride. Sentences will vary.

Apply • Think and Write

Creative Writing • Imagine that you took a trip across a vast desert. Write some compound sentences telling what happened on your trip.

> ✎ **Remember**
> that compound sentences express two or more connected thoughts.

GRAMMAR: Simple Sentences and Compound Sentences **397**

◀|||| TEACHING OPTIONS ||||▶

RETEACHING

A Different Modality Have students compare and contrast three sentences. Write on the chalkboard: *1. Jo and Ana waited. 2. They paced and stomped around the room. 3. Pat finally came, and they hugged him gratefully.* Have students circle all the simple subjects and compare their results. Repeat with verbs. Offer definitions, then ask which of the three is a compound sentence.

CLASS ENRICHMENT

A Cooperative Activity Have students find compound sentences in clipped newspaper or magazine articles. Have them copy two on index cards and then exchange cards with a partner. Have students underline the simple sentences that form the compound sentences and circle the conjunctions that join them. Have partners check each other's work before asking volunteers to share their sentences with the class.

CHALLENGE

An Independent Extension Have students create compound sentences by adding another related simple sentence.
Example: Lightning flashed across the sky, and large raindrops began to fall.

1. Lightning flashed across the sky.
2. The wind blew hard.
3. Hilda's umbrella blew inside out.
4. Some people ran toward shelter.
5. My jacket was drenched.
6. The rain came down harder.

■ **Easy** ■ **Average** ■ **Challenging**

OBJECTIVES
To punctuate compound sentences correctly
To identify and correct run-on sentences

ASSIGNMENT GUIDE
BASIC   Practice A
⬇   Practice B
ADVANCED   Practice C

All should do the Apply activity.

RESOURCES
■ Reteaching Master 69
■ Practice Master 69
■ ■ ■ Extra Practice, pp. 436, 441

TEACHING THE LESSON

1. Getting Started
Oral Language Focus attention on this oral activity, encouraging all to participate. You may wish to have class members raise their hands when they believe a sentence is complete.

2. Developing the Lesson
Guide students through the explanation of run-on sentences, emphasizing the examples and the summary. Lead students through the **Guided Practice.** Identify those who would benefit from reteaching. Assign independent Practice A–C.

3. Closing the Lesson
After students complete the Apply activity, have volunteers read their work to the class. Point out to students that knowing how to identify run-on sentences will help them proofread their writing to be sure every sentence expresses their ideas precisely and successfully.

♦ **GETTING STARTED** ♦

Play "One Word at a Time" with your classmates. One person says the first word of a sentence. Others in turn add a word to build a sentence. The player who adds the word that completes the sentence may suggest a word to begin a new sentence.

6 Avoiding Run-on Sentences

Remember that a compound sentence consists of two or more simple sentences joined by a conjunction. The conjunction can be *and*, *but*, or *or*. Notice that a comma is used before the conjunction in the following sentence.

> Hoofed animals live in many different places, and these places have different climates.

A run-on sentence strings sentences together incorrectly. The following is a run-on sentence.

> ■ Reindeer live in the Arctic camels live in the desert.

You can correct a run-on sentence in two ways. You can make two simple sentences. You can also make a compound sentence by adding a comma and a conjunction.

> Reindeer live in the Arctic. Camels live in the desert.
> Reindeer live in the Arctic, and camels live in the desert.

> **Summary** ♦ A **run-on sentence** is two or more sentences not separated by correct punctuation or connecting words. Avoid run-on sentences in your writing.

Guided Practice

Tell whether each is a compound sentence or a run-on sentence.
1. Some hoofed animals live in flat country, but others prefer mountains. _comp._
2. The chital deer avoids steep slopes the guanaco prefers them. _run-on_
3. The camel flourishes in dry country, and the hippopotamus spends much of its time in water. _comp._
4. Chevrotains also live close to water they feed on soft plants. _run-on_
5. Most antelopes live in Africa some are found in Asia. _run-on_

398   GRAMMAR and MECHANICS: Sentence Structure

ESSENTIAL LANGUAGE SKILLS
This lesson provides opportunities to:

LISTENING ♦ follow the logical organization of an oral presentation ♦ select from an oral presentation the information needed

SPEAKING ♦ contribute to class and small group discussions ♦ speak clearly to a group

READING ♦ use context clues for word identification ♦ evaluate and make judgments ♦ follow a set of directions

WRITING ♦ write and compose for a variety of purposes ♦ write summaries and reports of events and situations

LANGUAGE ♦ use the fundamentals of grammar, punctuation, and spelling ♦ use language to inform

Practice

Write each sentence. Add a comma before the conjunction.

6. The dik-dik is the smallest kind of antelope, and the eland is the largest.
7. Antelopes live on grassy plains, but the plains are dangerous.
8. A leopard might catch an antelope, or the antelope might outrun the cat.
9. Antelopes are known for their speed, and the adults can run up to fifty miles per hour.
10. They are extremely graceful animals, and a herd of racing antelopes is a thrilling sight.

Correct these run-on sentences. Write each as a compound sentence by adding a comma and a conjunction.

11. The giraffe is the tallest animal, *and* an adult can be eighteen feet tall.
12. Giraffes live in Africa, *and* they inhabit grasslands called savannas.
13. A giraffe's coat has brownish markings, *and* this color pattern protects the animal.
14. The giraffe's long neck helps it reach food in treetops, *and (or but)* its long legs help it outrun enemies.
15. Lions attack giraffes, *but (or and)* the giraffes defend themselves by kicking.
16. The giraffe can lie down, *but* it usually sleeps standing up.

Write compound sentences based on each idea below. Use the word in parentheses ( ). **Sentences will vary.**

17. an animal you like and an animal you dislike (but)
18. what you know and want to know about animals (and)
19. a wild animal and a tame animal (but)
20. an animal that either sits still or runs (or)

Apply • Think and Write

Observing Animals • Observe the behavior of an animal. Write compound sentences telling how the animal behaves.

> ✏️ **Remember**
> to express your ideas clearly and to avoid run-on sentences.

GRAMMAR and MECHANICS: Sentence Structure **399**

RETEACHING 69
Avoiding Run-on Sentences

Read the run-on sentence. Then read the corrections of the run-on sentence.

Run-on Sentence	Corrected Sentences
Our team won the race we were happy.	1. Our team won the race. We were happy.
	2. Our team won the race, and we were happy.

Circle the correction that is a compound sentence. Underline the correction that is made of two simple sentences.

> A **run-on sentence** is two or more sentences not separated by correct punctuation or connecting words. A run-on sentence strings sentences together incorrectly.

A. Underline the conjunction in each compound sentence. Add a comma before each conjunction.
EXAMPLE: Daniel may drive us, or we may take the bus.

1. I looked at the picture, but she looked out the window.
2. Linda delivered her newspapers, but Ginger waited.
3. Jana read the news about the race, but Mike listened to the radio.
4. Judy filled cups with water, and John set them out.

B. Correct each run-on sentence. Write a compound sentence by adding a comma and the conjunction and, but, or or. Answers will vary.
EXAMPLE: The race started on time I did not hear the signal.
The race started on time, but I did not hear the signal.

5. Duke ran his first race last week Ed started running years ago.
Duke ran his first race last week, but Ed started running years ago.
6. Lee's running shoes are badly worn mine are new.
Lee's running shoes are badly worn, but mine are new.
7. Len sipped water after the race Martha wanted lemonade.
Len sipped water after the race, and Martha wanted lemonade.

PRACTICE 69
Avoiding Run-on Sentences

> A **run-on sentence** is two or more sentences not separated by correct punctuation or connecting words.

A. Underline the conjunction, and place a comma in each compound sentence.

1. Warm air rises, but cool air descends.
2. Cold fronts move quickly, and warm fronts move slowly.
3. Cool air produces thunderstorms in the summer, but forms blizzards in the winter.
4. Warm fronts bring rain in the summer, but they cause snow in the winter.
5. Satellites carry television cameras, and they take pictures of clouds.

B. Rewrite each run-on sentence as a compound sentence. The first one is done for you. Conjunctions will vary.

6. Clouds are signs of rain fog is a low cloud.
Clouds are signs of rain, and fog is a low cloud.
7. Weather experts use weather maps they can use satellite photographs.
Weather experts use weather maps, or they can use satellite photographs.
8. Some clouds are made of water drops others have ice crystals.
Some clouds are made of water drops, but others have ice crystals.
9. A rainbow formed after the shower it disappeared quickly.
A rainbow formed after the shower, but it disappeared quickly.
10. The pond froze the stream did not.
The pond froze, but the stream did not.
11. The clouds blew away the sun came out.
The clouds blew away, and the sun came out.

WRITE IT
On a separate sheet of paper, write about a day when the weather changed your plans. Use compound sentences in your writing. Answers will vary.

◀ TEACHING OPTIONS ▶

RETEACHING

A Different Modality Write a run-on sentence such as the following the chalkboard: *Jan met her friend at the park they played together.* Point out that the example is confusing because it was written without the correct punctuation or connecting words. Show students how to eliminate the confusion by writing two separate sentences and by writing a compound sentence with a connecting word.

CLASS ENRICHMENT

A Cooperative Activity Have partners use their textbooks to select and copy a paragraph as one long run-on sentence. At the bottom of their papers, have them identify the paragraph with the title of the book and the page number. Have small groups choose papers from a pile and work together to correct the run-on. When they are finished, have them compare their revision with the in-book paragraph.

CHALLENGE

An Independent Extension Have students correct each run-on sentence by writing two simple sentences and then by writing a compound sentence.

1. Texas is big/it is wide across. 2. Cattle roam far/oil wells are common. 3. El Paso lies on the Rio Grande/bridges connect the city to Mexico. 4. We visited Texas/it was an interesting trip. 5. Laredo is near the river/the water was warm.

UNIT 8
Vocabulary

OBJECTIVES
To identify and use homographs

ASSIGNMENT GUIDE
BASIC   Practice A

ADVANCED   Practice B

All should do the Language Corner.

RESOURCES
■ Reteaching Master 70
■ Practice Master 70

TEACHING THE LESSON

1. Getting Started
Oral Language Focus attention on this oral activity, encouraging all to participate. You may wish to give hints if students have difficulty solving the riddles. To elicit the first answer—*because it had two banks*—ask students where money is usually kept. To elicit the second answer—*because it was a bass*—ask students to think of the names for the range of the human voice.

2. Developing the Lesson
Guide students through the explanation of homographs, emphasizing the definition and the examples. You may wish to tell students to use a dictionary to be sure of the meaning of a homograph. Guide students through Building Your Vocabulary. Identify those who would benefit from reteaching. Assign independent Practice A and B.

3. Closing the Lesson
After students complete the Practice exercises, tell them to look for homographs in their reading during the rest of the day. Have them list at least five homographs and then use a dictionary to write all of each word's meanings. Point out to students that knowing the different meanings of a word can help them better understand what they read and hear.

Language Corner You may wish to have students discuss and compare their methods of finding other meanings for the word *loaf*.

Can you answer these riddles: Why was the river rich? Why did the fish have a low voice?

VOCABULARY ◆
Homographs

Have you seen a *bow bow*? Can a *shed shed*? These nonsense sentences illustrate special kinds of words called homographs. **Homographs** are words that are spelled the same but have different meanings and origins.

Homograph comes from Greek and means "written alike." Some homographs, such as the ones below, look and sound alike but have different meanings.

■ Donna <u>rose</u> early in the morning.   She went to pick a <u>rose</u>.

Other homographs look alike but have different pronunciations as well as different meanings. Notice the different ways that *close* is pronounced in the sentences below.

■ The great bicycle race was very <u>close</u>. (klōs)

■ We asked him to <u>close</u> the door. (klōz)

Building Your Vocabulary

Homographs have separate entries in the dictionary because they are truly different words, with different meanings and origins. *Rear* appears twice in the dictionary, with these meanings.

Rhonda sat in the <u>rear</u> (the back) of the room.
Animals <u>rear</u> (raise) their young.

Find the homographs *hide* and *quiver* in the Dictionary of Knowledge. Use each word in two sentences to show the two different meanings.
Sentences will vary.

The words below are familiar homographs. Make up two sentences for each word to show the two different meanings.
Sentences will vary.
light   lean   lead   wind   bow

Which of these words have different pronunciations for each different meaning?

ESSENTIAL LANGUAGE SKILLS
This lesson provides opportunities to:

LISTENING ◆ select from an oral presentation the information needed

SPEAKING ◆ respond appropriately to questions from teachers and peers ◆ use oral language for a variety of purposes

READING ◆ use context clues for word identification ◆ draw logical conclusions ◆ evaluate and make judgments ◆ follow a set of directions

WRITING ◆ use a variety of resources to research a topic

LANGUAGE ◆ use and be aware of words with multiple meanings ◆ understand word origins

Practice

A. Choose homographs from the list below to complete the sentences.

bill	lead	sow	row
live	dove	light	tear

1. The __sow__ sat in the mud as the farmer began to __sow__ the seed.
2. The __dove__ __dove__ off the branch and into the air.
3. The vet gave us a __bill__ for fixing our bird's __bill__ .
4. A __tear__ in my shirt caused a __tear__ on my face.
5. John and I had a big __row__ over who should __row__ the boat.
6. I __live__ in the country and catch __live__ lightning bugs.
7. The __lead__ bullet was the only __lead__ the detectives had.
8. "This __light__ is not very __light__ ," I complained as I carried it up the stairs.

B. Write each underlined homograph. Then use your own words to write its meaning. **Answers will vary. Possible answers follow.**

EXAMPLE: The tools were kept in the shed.

ANSWER: a building used for storage

9. The bear tried to hide in its cave. **to keep out of sight**
10. Its hide is thick and furry. **an animal's skin**
11. His pen was made of gold and wrote in purple ink. **a tool for writing**
12. The sheep were kept in a small, fenced-in pen. **a place for animals**
13. The mother bird would not desert its nest. **to leave**
14. The iguana lizard lives in the desert **a very dry region**

LANGUAGE CORNER ◆ Word Histories

Loaf is a homograph with an interesting history. Long ago, you might have asked for a "bread of loaf"! *Loaf* originally was used to name what we now call *bread*, and *bread* meant "a piece of something."

What is another meaning of "loaf"? **to waste time, to do nothing**

VOCABULARY: Homographs **401**

◀║║ TEACHING OPTIONS ║║▶

RETEACHING

A Different Modality To emphasize that a word may have more than one meaning, write on the chalkboard: *Shed your dirty coat in the shed.* Have students use the dictionary to define *shed* as it is used in the sentence (*to take off; a small, low building*). Encourage students to use *shed* in two sentences that show the word's different meanings.

CLASS ENRICHMENT

A Cooperative Activity Have students work in pairs to discuss two meanings for each of these words: *duck, bark, ship, mold, pen.* Have each partner write an example sentence that explains one meaning as the other partner writes an example sentence that explains the other meaning. You may wish to have volunteers read their favorite sentence pairs to the class.

CHALLENGE

An Independent Extension Have students look up the origins of homographs such as the following: *arms* (body part; weapons), *bat* (club; flying animal; wink), *bridge* (card/game; structure that goes over), *hail* (welcome; pieces of ice), and *seal* (animal; mark). Have them write a homograph and its meanings on one side of an index card and a brief history of the word on the other side. You may wish to have students create a word origin file.

401

Grammar-Writing Connection

OBJECTIVES
To apply grammar skills to writing
To work together to combine sentences using a comma and the word *and, but,* or *or*
To use different kinds of sentences to improve writing

How to Combine Sentences

Point out to students that they can use the grammar skills they learned in Unit 8 to help them develop good writing techniques. Explain that in this Grammar-Writing Connection, students will use what they know about the parts of speech, conjunctions, compound subjects, compound predicates, compound sentences, and run-on sentences to learn how to combine sentences.

You may wish to guide students through the explanation of how to combine sentences, stressing the examples. Then have students apply the information by completing the activity at the bottom of the first page. Students may work with partners to create compound sentences orally, or they may create compound sentences in writing as an independent activity.

Help students to understand that combining sentences is an effective way to add variety to their writing, and that it can make their writing less repetitious and more interesting.

GRAMMAR
CONNECTION
WRITING

How to Combine Sentences

You can combine two short sentences with ideas that go together to form one compound sentence. Combining sentences can add variety to your writing and show relationships between ideas. For example, what two facts about Jesse's class are expressed in example **1** below?

1. **Jesse's class is studying sea animals. On Friday the students will visit the aquarium.**
2. **Jesse's class is studying sea animals, and on Friday the students will visit the aquarium.**

Both examples tell us the same facts, but example **2** uses a comma and the word *and* to combine the facts in both sentences into one strong compound sentence.

Some short sentences can go together in a different way. Sometimes two sentences are about the same idea, but the second sentence gives an unexpected fact that contrasts, or goes against, the fact in the first sentence. The contrasting sentence can be joined with the first sentence by using a comma and the word *but*.

3. **Ann had a cold. She went on the trip anyway.**
4. **Ann had a cold, but she went on the trip anyway.**

Sometimes two sentences give two possible choices. These sentences can be combined with a comma and the word *or*.

5. **Will you bring a lunch? Are you planning to buy a sandwich?**
6. **Will you bring a lunch, or are you planning to buy a sandwich?**

> **The Grammar Game** ◆ Create your own sentence examples! Write at least three pairs of sentences that can be combined with commas and the words *and*, *but*, or *or*. Then exchange papers with a classmate and combine each other's sentences. Answers will vary.

402 COOPERATIVE LEARNING: Combining Sentences

ESSENTIAL LANGUAGE SKILLS
This lesson provides opportunities to:

LISTENING ◆ select from an oral presentation the information needed

SPEAKING ◆ respond appropriately to questions from teachers and peers ◆ contribute to class and small group discussions

READING ◆ read and follow printed directions ◆ evaluate and make judgments

WRITING ◆ write and compose for a variety of purposes ◆ apply increasingly complex conventions of punctuation and capitalization

LANGUAGE ◆ produce a variety of sentence patterns ◆ use the fundamentals of grammar, spelling, and punctuation

Working Together

As your group works on activities **A** and **B**, combine sentences to add variety and strength to your writing.

In Your Group

♦ Ask questions to encourage discussion.

♦ Listen carefully to each other.

♦ Build on other people's ideas.

♦ Agree or disagree in a pleasant way.

A. Complete the pairs of sentences with words of the group's choice. Then combine each pair, using a comma and the word *and*, *but*, or *or*. Compare your results with those of other groups.

Answers will vary. Possible answers follow.

1. We looked in the ____ Your ____ wasn't there.
   We looked in the locker, but your wallet wasn't there.
2. Did Gail's team win the ____? Was it a tie?
   Did Gail's team win the medal, or was it a tie?
3. We ____ for a long time. We didn't find the ____.
   We painted for a long time, but we didn't finish the cupboards.
4. Mark cooked delicious ____ . Karen made some ____ .
   Mark cooked delicious omelets, and Karen made some muffins.
5. I really must study tonight. I will ____ the ____ test.
   I really must study tonight, or I will fail the final exam.

B. Find at least one pair of sentences to combine in the paragraph below. Think about how ideas in the sentences could go together. Can you write the paragraph again, combining four pairs of sentences?

Six of my friends and I play in a jazz band. We call ourselves "Sound System." Ellen is the best piano player. Joe also plays keyboards. We try to practice every Saturday afternoon. Sometimes we get together in the morning. Come to hear us practice this week. Drop in on any Saturday.

band, and we
player, and Joe
afternoon, but sometimes
week, or drop

WRITERS' CORNER ♦ Sentence Variety

Mixing kinds of sentences and varying sentence length can change a boring paragraph into an interesting one. Can you identify the kinds of sentences in the paragraph below? Can you find any combined sentences?

Give me your attention, pet owners. *exclamatory* Are you taking a vacation this summer, or do you have to stay home with your pet? *interrogative* You can hire a Pet Pal, and your troubles will be over. *imperative* *declarative* Our motto is "We sit when you split." *imperative* Call us, and ask for a caring pet. Pet Pals is the purr-fect solution for you. *declarative*

Read what you wrote for the Writer's Warm-up. Did you vary the kinds of sentences you wrote? Did you use any combined sentences?

Working Together

The Working Together activities involve students in cooperative learning work groups. This is an opportunity to pair strong writers with students whose skills are weaker. Working together, they can all experience success.

Divide the class into small groups and have students read In Your Group. Encourage them to discuss why each task is important. Have them tell what might happen if the group does not follow through on each of the tasks. *(If we do not ask questions to encourage discussion, the discussion might end. If we do not listen carefully to each other, we might miss helpful ideas. If we do not build on other people's ideas, we cannot learn from them. If we do not agree or disagree in a pleasant way, it will be difficult to work together.)*

Before students begin activities A and B, you may wish to have each group appoint a member to record their sentences. You also may wish to have groups appoint a timekeeper. Then set a limit of ten or fifteen minutes. After each activity is completed, have the groups compare the sentences they wrote.

Writers' Corner

The Writers' Corner provides students with the opportunity to extend the Grammar-Writing Connection, helping them to develop the skills necessary to review and revise their own writing. Discuss the introductory sentences with students. Then have them work as a class or in pairs to discuss the sentences in the paragraph. Have students read aloud each sentence and identify the kind of sentence and its length. Have them tell why the sentences fit well together. Then have students apply the sentence combining techniques from this Grammar-Writing Connection to the sentences they wrote about animal habitats for the Writers' Warm-up. Encourage students to rewrite their sentences if necessary. Discuss with them how combining short sentences added variety to their writing and helped them to show the relationships among their ideas.

TWO-PART
flexibility

USING LANGUAGE TO CLASSIFY

Unit 8 Overview

books
FOR EXTENDED READING

EASY

📙 **Rocky Mountain Bighorns** by Kay McDearmon. Dodd. This introduction to these fascinating animals describes their habitat, behavior, and feeding habits and the care and protection of their young.

AVERAGE

📙 **The World of the White-Tailed Deer** by Leonard Lee Rue. Harper. A year in the life of a white-tailed deer is told through photographs and text.

CHALLENGING

📙 **Bambi: A Life in the Woods** by Felix Salten. Grossett. Against the vivid backdrop of the forest world, this classic animal story describes the growing to maturity of an Austrian roe deer.

READ-ALOUD

📙 **The Yearling** by Marjorie Kinnan Rawlings. Scribner. Jody's love of animals and his fight to save the yearling have made this story set in the backwoods of Florida a modern classic. **Pulitzer Prize.**

PRAIRIE DOG VILLAGE
painting by W.J. Hays
Courtesy of Kennedy Galleries, Inc. New York.

UNIT
EIGHT

USING LANGUAGE
TO
CLASSIFY

PART TWO

Literature "Two of a Kind" by Ron Hirschi
A Reason for Writing Classifying

CREATIVE
Writing

FINE ARTS ♦ Look at the painting, "Prairie Dog Village," at the left. The prairie dogs all seem to be watching for something. What are they expecting? What will they do when it arrives? What sounds will they make? Will they run to the newcomer or run away? Write a story about this scene. Tell what the animals are waiting for and what will happen.

start with CREATIVE WRITING

Fine Arts gives your students a chance to express themselves creatively in writing. After students observe the illustration on page 404 for a moment or two, have a volunteer read aloud the Fine Arts paragraph on page 405. Have students write their reactions in their journals. Then encourage a discussion of their ideas.

VIEWING

See the **Fine Arts Transparencies with Viewing Booklet** and the **Video Library**.

THEN START WITH *part 2*

A Reason for Writing: Classifying is the focus of Part 2. First students learn a thinking strategy for classifying. Then they read and respond to a selection of literature on which they may model their own writing. Developmental composition lessons, including "Group Discussions," a speaking and listening lesson, help students learn to use language correctly to classify. All the lessons reflect the literature. All culminate in the Writing Process lesson. The unit ends with the Curriculum Connection and Books to Enjoy, which help students discover how their new language skills apply to writing across the curriculum and to their own lives.

♦ If you began with grammar instruction, you may wish to remind students of the unit theme, "Animal Habitats." Tell them that the information they gathered through the thematic lessons helped them prepare for reading the literature, "Two of a Kind" by Ron Hirschi.

♦ If you are beginning with Part 2, use the lessons in Part 1 for remediation or instruction. For grammar, spelling, and mechanics instructional guidance, you may wish to refer to the end-of-text Glossary and Index, as well as to the *Spelling Connection* booklet; the full-color *Revising and Proofreading Transparencies;* and the Unit Pretest, Posttest, and Writing Samples.

THEME BAR

CATEGORIES	Environments	Business/World of Work	Imagination	Communications/ Fine Arts	People	Science	Expressions	Social Studies
THEMES	UNIT 1 Farm Life	UNIT 2 Handicrafts	UNIT 3 Tall Tales	UNIT 4 The Visual Arts	UNIT 5 Lasting Impressions	UNIT 6 Volcanoes	UNIT 7 Nature	UNIT 8 Animal Habitats
PACING	1 month	1 month	1 month	1 month	1 month	1 month	1 month	1 month

■ Easy ■ Average ■ Challenging

OBJECTIVES
To use an observation chart as a strategy for classifying

TEACHING THE LESSON

1. Getting Started

Oral Language Introduce the thinking skill, observing, by asking students to imagine that they want to buy a bike to use on a paper route. Say: *In the bike shop you see two bikes you like. How can you decide which one to buy?* As students respond you may want to record their observations on the chalkboard under headings, such as *Color, Weight, Gears, Price,* and *Size.* Explain that noticing details is an important thinking skill called *observing.*

Metacognition Help students become aware of their own thinking (think metacognitively) by asking follow-up questions when they respond *(e.g., How did you figure out what to look for in a bike?).* Encourage students to be aware of their own and other students' thinking strategies and to appreciate that thinking strategies are as different as the people who use them. Explain that in this lesson they will learn about one possible strategy for observing.

2. Developing the Lesson

Guide students through the introduction to classifying (the function of literature and writing they will deal with in this unit) and its connection to observing. Lead them through Learning the Strategy, emphasizing the model observation chart. Identify those who would benefit from reteaching. Assign Using the Strategy A and B.

3. Closing the Lesson

Metacognition Applying the Strategy is a metacognitive activity in which students consider *how* they think (question 1) and *when* they think (question 2). Encourage a diversity of oral responses.

Question 1: Encourage students to share how they thought up the headings and details for the charts they made during Using the Strategy A and B. Also encourage them to share any

406

CRITICAL THINKING ◆
A Strategy for Classifying

AN OBSERVATION CHART

Classifying means sorting things into groups. It means putting together things that belong together. One way to classify is to compare, or notice how things are alike. Another way is to contrast, or notice how things are different. After this lesson, you will read part of "Two of a Kind." It is an article that compares and contrasts kinds of deer. Later you will write some comparisons and contrasts.

In this paragraph from "Two of a Kind," the author contrasts headgear. What is headgear? Read to find out.

> . . . did you know there are two species of deer native to North America? Headgear shape is one good way to tell one from the other. The mule deer's antlers rise abruptly, treelike. Each time a branch is formed, the branches fork in pairs. This is much different from the white-tailed buck's antlers. The single, main beams of his antlers arch forward. . . . Branches rise from the main beam, but they don't fork like those of the mule deer.

How does the author know so much about deer? He has observed them carefully. When you observe, you pay attention to details.

◆ Learning the Strategy

Observations are often useful. Suppose you are at the beach with your family. You want to go swimming. How would observation help you find your way back through the crowds? Imagine you have to decide which bike to buy to use on your paper route. How could observing help you choose? Suppose you are writing to a friend about your new cat. How could observations make your letter interesting?

406 CRITICAL THINKING: Observing

ESSENTIAL LANGUAGE SKILLS
This lesson provides opportunities to:

LISTENING ◆ employ active listening in a variety of situations ◆ listen and respond to orally presented language for the purpose of gathering information and making judgments

SPEAKING ◆ respond appropriately to questions from teachers and peers ◆ express ideas clearly and effectively

READING ◆ use context to understand the meaning of words ◆ evaluate and make judgments ◆ follow a set of directions ◆ use graphic sources of information, such as tables and lists, charts and graphs, timelines, pictures and diagrams

WRITING ◆ adapt information to accomplish a specific purpose with a particular audience ◆ write and compose for a variety of purposes

LANGUAGE ◆ use language for personal expression

How can you remember details you observe? One way is to make an observation chart. A chart about a cat might look like this.

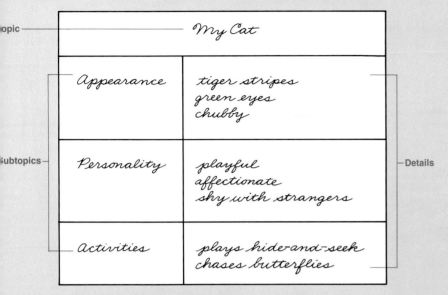

Topic — My Cat

Subtopics —

Appearance	tiger stripes green eyes chubby
Personality	playful affectionate shy with strangers
Activities	plays hide-and-seek chases butterflies

— Details

Using the Strategy

1. Observe your classroom and make an observation chart. Write "My Classroom" as the topic. Write several subtopics, such as "What I See." Record details for each heading. If you like, write an article contrasting your classroom on a weekday and on Saturday.

2. "Two of a Kind" tells about headgear. What do you already know about antlers? Make an observation chart. Decide on headings for your chart. Record the facts you know. Then read "Two of a Kind" and see what more you can find out.

Applying the Strategy

♦ Did you choose the same headings and details for your charts as your classmates? Why might your choices differ?
♦ When might you need to observe something carefully?

CRITICAL THINKING: Observing 407

personal strategies they might like to use for observing. For instance, some students may say they like to jot notes in a notebook or make labeled drawings of what they are observing. Reassure them that an observation chart is only one possible strategy they can use when they observe, and that they should use what works for them.

Question 2: Possible answers to "When might you need to observe carefully?": *When you move to a new neighborhood, to find your way around. To figure out what my pet's behavior means. When I'm trying to draw something.* Encourage a variety of responses.

Looking Ahead
The thinking strategy introduced in this lesson, an observation chart, is used in Using the Strategy B as a prereading strategy to help students anticipate the literature, "Two of a Kind." It will appear three more times in this unit and again in Unit 1.

OBSERVATION CHART			
Strategy for Narrating	Writing to Learn	Prewriting	Writing Across the Curriculum
23	29	40	46

Strategy for Classifying	Writing to Learn	Prewriting	Writing Across the Curriculum
407	411	422	428

Although the observation chart strategy is repeated in each presentation, the context in which it is used changes. Students will thus be given the opportunity to discover how the strategy can help them in reading, in writing across the curriculum, and in their daily lives.

◀▥▥ TEACHING OPTIONS ▥▥▶

RETEACHING

A Different Modality Ask for a volunteer who will pose as a model to be drawn by the other students. Have the volunteer pose, for example seated on a chair with arms crossed and feet flat on the floor. On the chalkboard, have students (including the model) suggest headings (e.g., *Hair, Clothes, Position*) and details for an observation chart. When the chart is completed, have students draw the model. Then discuss how the chart helped their drawing.

CLASS ENRICHMENT

A Cooperative Activity Have each student choose a partner. Then give each pair two related topics, such as *Snakes* and *Toads*. Have each partner make and complete an observation chart for the assigned topic. Then have them compare their work and together write a paragraph that explains how the two topics are alike and different. You may wish to have volunteers share their paragraphs with the class.

CHALLENGE

An Independent Extension Have students make and complete an observation chart using *The School Playground* as the topic. Then have them compare the information with that on the chart they made about their classroom for Using the Strategy A. Finally, you may wish to have them write a paragraph explaining how their classroom and the school playground are alike and different.

UNIT 8
Literature

VOCABULARY STRATEGIES

Developing Concepts and Teaching Vocabulary

Preteach the following words from the story. Use the Dictionary of Knowledge at the back of the book to provide definitions of base words and context sentences.

camouflage, predator, secrete, repellent, namesake

Write the vocabulary words on the chalkboard and have students pronounce them. Ask students to name the words with which they are familiar. Ask students if they have ever used insect *repellent* and have them tell what it did. Then have them give examples of other words that end with the suffix -ent (absorbent, confident). Explain that the verb *secrete* comes from a longer word, the noun *secretion*. Have students divide *namesake* into its two parts, *name* and *sake*.

GUIDING COMPREHENSION

Building Background

The first half of this unit includes information especially chosen to build background for *Two of a Kind*. If you started the unit with grammar instruction, you may wish to have a class discussion on the unit theme, **Animal Habitats**, based on the information in those lessons.

If you started the unit with composition instruction, you may wish to build students' knowledge of animal habitats by asking: *What do you know about how animals adapt to the environment? For example, how do different animals' coats protect them?* (Students may recall that animals that live in cold environments may have thick, furry coats that keep them warm. Animals that live in the Arctic may have

LITERATURE
TWO of a KIND
from Headgear
by Ron Hirschi

408 LITERATURE: Nonfiction

ESSENTIAL LANGUAGE SKILLS
This lesson provides opportunities to:

LISTENING ◆ listen for specific information ◆ participate in conversations and group discussions

SPEAKING ◆ use oral language for a variety of purposes ◆ respond appropriately to questions from teachers and peers

READING ◆ determine the main idea of a reading selection ◆ understand cause-and-effect relationships ◆ draw logical conclusions ◆ evaluate and make judgments ◆ respond to various forms of literature

WRITING ◆ generate ideas using graphic organizers ◆ adapt information to accomplish a specific purpose with a particular audience

LANGUAGE ◆ use language for describing ◆ use the fundamentals of grammar, punctuation, and spelling

The fragrant scent of ponderosa pine drifts on a gentle breeze. The light wind stirs overhead branches, bends golden stems of grass, and sets the tapered tips of shrubs in motion. But some of the branches tucked behind the shrubs do not move. These "branches" are attached to a deer.

The deer's branched antlers, spread behind the shrubs, help camouflage the buck. He naps in the late afternoon, chewing his cud as he keeps a watchful eye on the open hillside. Should the scent of a predator mingle with the odor of pine, he will be ready.

Like elk and moose, only male deer wear headgear. Their antlers are covered with velvet while growing and secrete an oily substance thought to act as sunburn protection or insect repellent. The antlers harden in the fall and drop each winter.

Perhaps the most familiar of all animals that wear headgear, deer are widespread in North America. You could probably describe a deer or draw its picture without looking at photographs. You may have even seen a deer bounding through the woods.

But did you know there are two species of deer native to North America? Headgear shape is one good way to tell one from the other.

The mule deer's antlers rise abruptly, treelike. Each time a branch is formed, the branches fork in pairs.

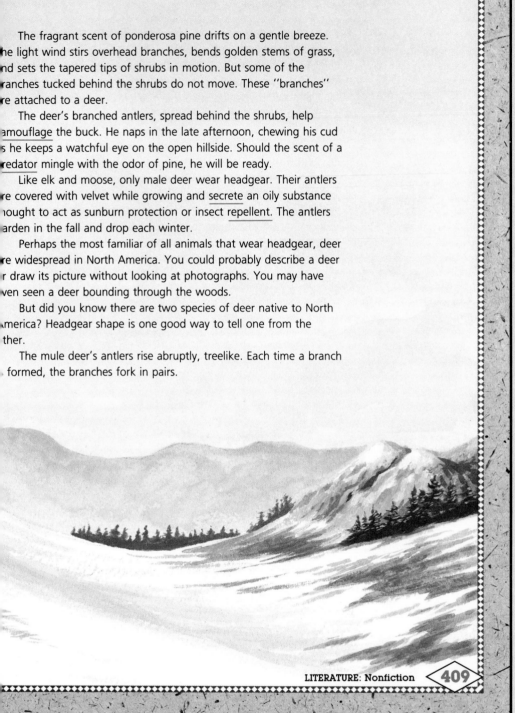

LITERATURE: Nonfiction ◁409▷

SUMMARY

This nonfiction selection compares and contrasts two North American deer—the mule deer and the white-tailed deer. It explains how you can tell one from the other from the antlers, or headgear, of the males, and other ways, such as the differences in their ears and tails.

ABOUT THE AUTHOR

RON HIRSCHI grew up in the Pacific Northwest and today lives in Poulsbo, Washington. He graduated from the University of Washington with a degree in Wildlife Ecology and worked as a biologist for the Washington Game Department. *Headgear,* the book about horned and antlered animals from which this selection was taken, was his first children's book.

white coats that make them difficult to see against the snow. A leopard's spotted coat will help it blend into the various colors of the jungle.)

Developing a Purpose for Reading

Option 1: Have students set their own purpose for reading. Then have them read the story introduction and study the illustrations. Explain that this selection is a factual article that tells about the two kinds of deer native to North America. Have students list several questions they think the article might answer about the similarities and differences between these two kinds of deer. Remind students to recall what they know about animal habitats before writing. When the lists are completed, have volunteers share their questions with the class. Suggest that students set their own reading purpose by reviewing their lists and underlining the most important information they would like to learn from the article.

Option 2: If you wish to set a reading purpose for everyone, have students look for the similarities and differences between the whitetail and mule deer.

GUIDED READING

Please note that opportunities for students' personal responses to the selection are offered in the Reader's Response question and the Selection Follow-up at the end of this lesson.

Page 408 *How do the deer's antlers help it to hide?* (When the deer sits behind shrubs, the antlers look like branches.) RECALL: CAUSE/EFFECT

Page 408 *Why do the deer's antlers give off an oily substance?* (Perhaps the oil on the antlers acts as sunburn protection or keeps insects away.) RECALL: CAUSE/EFFECT

Page 409 *How do the mule deer's antlers differ from the white-tailed deer's?* (The mule deer's antlers go straight up, while the white-tailed deer's arch forward. Also the branches on the mule deer's antlers fork, while the white-tailed deer's do not.) ANALYZE: COMPARISONS

GUIDED READING

Page 409 *In what other ways do the white-tailed deer and mule deer differ?* (The mule deer have larger ears. The white-tailed deers have longer, bushier tails with white edges and markings. The mule deer's tail is black-tipped.) ANALYZE: COMPARISONS

Returning to the Reading Purpose

Option 1: Those students who have written lists of questions may wish to review them to determine whether their most important ones have been answered.

Option 2: If you have established a common reading purpose, review it and have volunteers tell the similarities and differences between the mule deer and the white-tailed deer.

READER'S RESPONSE

Have you ever seen a deer in its natural surroundings? How did you feel? What did you think? (To give the students a point of view for answering the question, have them think about where they were, what time of year it was, and who they were with when they saw the deer. You may wish to have students who have not seen a deer in its natural setting recall how they felt and what they thought when they saw some other animal in its natural setting.)

This is much different from the white-tailed buck's antlers. The single, main beams of his antlers arch forward as though bent by a constant breeze. Branches rise from the main beam, but they don't fork like those of the mule deer.

Mule deer can be distinguished from whitetails in many other ways. Like their <u>namesakes,</u> mule deer generally have large ears. White-tailed deer have longer, bushier tails with white edges and underparts. The mule deer's black-tipped tails led some North American Indians to call them black-tailed deer. This name persists in the Pacific Northwest where a darker and somewhat smaller mule deer inhabits wet, coastal forests.

Watch closely the next time you see a deer. Its tail will be one clue to its identity. If a buck, its headgear will point to the answer. But remember that no two deer are ever the same. Like people and other animals, each mule deer and each white-tailed deer is an individual. Try as you might, you will never find two alike.

Library Link ◆ *If you would like to learn more about animals with antlers, read* Headgear *by Ron Hirschi.*

Reader's Response

Have you ever seen a deer in its natural surroundings? How did you feel? What did you think?

410   LITERATURE: Nonfiction

STRATEGIC READING

Page 410 When students have read to the end of page 410, have students work in pairs to ask and answer questions about what they have read. You may wish to suggest that they make an observation chart on what they have learned about deer. Explain that forming and answering questions is one way to check on their understanding. METACOGNITION: SUMMARIZING

HIGHLIGHTING LITERATURE

Page 410 Discuss with students how the author describes the scene in the first paragraph of the selection, giving a setting for what is to follow in much the same way as the writer of a fictional story would. Ask students: Do you feel you would have been as interested in the facts in the article if the author had begun by simply saying that there are two species of deer native to North America?

TWO of a KIND

Responding to Literature

1. Of all the facts that you have learned about deer, which piece of information was the most interesting? Why?

2. Make a survey of the wild animals that your classmates have seen in natural habitats. Show the information on a chart.

3. "Two of a Kind" compared two kinds of deer. With a partner, compare two species of dogs or other animal. Then in one sentence, tell the most striking likeness and the most noticeable difference.

4. People think deer are beautiful animals. What animal do you think is beautiful? Draw a picture of your animal. Tell why you think it is beautiful.

Writing to Learn

Think and Observe ◆ Make an observation chart like this one. Note differences between the mule deer and the whitetail deer.

Differences:	mule deer	whitetail deer
ears:		
tails:		
headgear:		

Observation Chart

Write ◆ Write a paragraph. Tell how the two deer are different.

LITERATURE: Nonfiction 411

You may wish to incorporate any or all of the following discussion questions and activities in your follow-up to the literature selection, *Two of a Kind*.

RESPONDING TO LITERATURE

Encourage students to use their personal experiences as well as what they learned from the selection to discuss these questions. Explain to students that although they may use details from the selection to support their opinions, the questions have no right or wrong answers. Encourage them to express a variety of points of view.

1. *Of all the facts that you have learned about deer, which piece of information was the most interesting? Why?* (You may wish to begin by having students tell what they knew about deer before they read the article.)

2. *Make a survey of the wild animals that your classmates have seen in natural habitats. Show the information on a chart.* (You may wish to have students work with partners or in small groups to complete the charts.)

3. Two of a Kind *compared two kinds of deer. With a partner, compare two species of dogs or some other animal. Then in one sentence, tell the most striking likeness and the most noticeable difference.* (You may wish to provide students with time to research their chosen animals in an encyclopedia.)

4. *People think deer are beautiful animals. What animal do you think is beautiful? Draw a picture of your animal. Tell why you think it is beautiful.* (You may wish to give the class time to exchage ideas on what animals they find beautiful before they draw their pictures.)

WRITING TO LEARN

Have students make an observation chart to show their understanding of the selection. (They may note in their charts that mule deer have bigger ears than white-tailed deer, white-tailed deer have longer, bushier tails than mule deer, and mule deer antlers rise treelike and branch and white-tailed deer antlers arch forward and don't branch.) Then have students complete the Write activity, telling how the two deer are different. Encourage volunteers to read aloud their paragraphs.

 World of Language Audio Library

A recording of this selection is available in the **Audio Library**.

UNIT 8
Speaking/Listening

OBJECTIVES
To participate in group discussions
To use guidelines for speaking and listening to a discussion

ASSIGNMENT GUIDE
BASIC   Practice A

ADVANCED   Practice B

All should do the Apply activity.

RESOURCES
■ World of Language Video Library

TEACHING THE LESSON

1. Getting Started
Oral Language Focus attention on this oral activity, encouraging all to participate. You may wish to remind students of the guidelines for expressing opinions (Unit 4) before beginning the discussion.

2. Developing the Lesson
Guide students through a discussion of the lesson, emphasizing the guidelines for speaking and being an active listener in a discussion. You may wish to point out to students the importance of listening to everyone's ideas as the discussion progresses. Lead students through the **Guided Practice.** Identify those who would benefit from reteaching. Assign independent Practice A and B.

3. Closing the Lesson
After students complete the Apply activity, call on volunteers to read aloud their topics. You may wish to have the class discuss which topics they like the best, choose one, and then prepare for a discussion on that topic. Point out to students that learning how to participate effectively in group discussions will be useful in class discussions and in discussions outside the classroom.

◆ GETTING STARTED ◆

Do you think it is important to protect all wild animals from extinction? State your opinion and the reasons for it. Ask others to state their opinions, too.

SPEAKING and LISTENING ◆
Group Discussions

What is the difference between ordinary conversation and a discussion? A discussion has a purpose. The purpose may be to solve a problem or to exchange ideas or information. Here are some possible topics for a classroom discussion.

> What should we do for the assembly program on conservation?
> What kinds of plants in our area are food for wildlife?
> Should we take a class trip to a conservation center?
> Are wildlife preserves a good idea?

As you can see, discussions enable us to share ideas and information and to solve problems. Here are guidelines to help you hold good discussions.

Speaking in a Discussion	1. Prepare for the discussion if possible. Find out the facts about a topic. 2. Contribute to the discussion. Your ideas count! 3. Use gestures, body movements, and facial expressions to emphasize what you say. 4. If you disagree with someone, politely explain why. 5. Stick to the topic of the discussion.
Being an Active Listener	1. Let others speak, and listen carefully to their ideas. 2. Do not interrupt the speaker. 3. While you listen, prepare to support or disagree with ideas that you hear. 4. If you do not understand something, prepare to ask questions.

Summary ◆ A **discussion** provides an opportunity to share ideas and information and to solve problems.

412   SPEAKING and LISTENING: Group Discussions

ESSENTIAL LANGUAGE SKILLS
This lesson provides opportunities to:

LISTENING ◆ listen actively and attentively ◆ select from an oral presentation the information needed

SPEAKING ◆ speak before an audience to communicate specific information ◆ use a set of reasons to persuade a group ◆ use questions to draw others into a conversation

READING ◆ determine the main idea of a reading selection ◆ evaluate and make judgments ◆ follow a set of directions

WRITING ◆ select and narrow a topic for a specific purpose

LANGUAGE ◆ use language for personal expression

Guided Practice

Tell whether or not each of the examples agrees with the discussion guidelines. Explain why or why not.
Students' answers should reflect the discussion guidelines.

1. Jan, what do you mean by "endangered species"? yes
2. Ralph: The deer in our area . . .
   Fran: If you want to see deer, just go to Bowman's Hill. no
3. You're wrong, Steve. That's a terrible idea. no
4. I disagree with you on that point. Let me explain why. yes
5. Speaking of wildlife conservation, did I ever tell you about the time I went on a camping trip to the Rockies? no

Practice

A. Decide if each example agrees with the discussion guidelines. Write *agrees* or *disagrees*. Then write a sentence explaining your answer.
Sentences should reflect the guidelines.   agrees

6. We must protect our wildlife heritage. Once an endangered species is lost, it is gone forever.
7. Your idea is ridiculous! How could anyone believe something like that? disagrees
8. Yes, we should help wildlife survive. By the way, did anyone see that movie last night about racing car drivers? disagrees
9. Wildlife preserves are important, but I disagree with one point you made. agrees
10. Beth: I would like to say two things about wildlife conservation. First . . .
    Michael: I know what you're going to say. disagrees

B. With three or four of your classmates, hold a group discussion about a topic that interests you. Follow the discussion guidelines given in this lesson.

Apply ◆ Think and Write

Discussion Topics ◆ Write three topics that you think would be interesting to discuss as a class.

> ✏ **Remember**
> that in a discussion you can exchange ideas and information or solve a problem.

SPEAKING and LISTENING: Group Discussions **413**

World of Language Video Library

You may wish to use the *Video Library* to teach this lesson.

EVALUATION PROGRAM

See Evaluation and Testing Program, pp. C9–C11.

Speaking and Listening Checklist Masters

◀║║║ TEACHING OPTIONS ║║║▶

RETEACHING

A Different Modality Present a topic such as *Where to Go on a Field Trip.* Give volunteers slips with statements such as *Stare out window and do not participate. Disagree rudely. Interrupt. Wander off the topic.* Have them play these roles as others try to follow the guidelines. Have students guess what the volunteers are doing. Then continue with all following the guidelines.

CLASS ENRICHMENT

A Cooperative Activity Assign a discussion topic such as *How We Can Improve Our Classroom Behavior.* Form small groups to discuss the topic. Have three monitors circulate, observe all the groups, and report on these questions: (1) Was anyone not talking enough? (2) Was anyone talking too much? (3) Was anyone being impolite? Alert all groups to what the monitors are watching for.

CHALLENGE

An Independent Extension Have students listen to a discussion on television, such as one presented on a news program or interview show. Have them decide whether the discussion guidelines were or were not followed and how that contributed to their understanding of the topic being discussed. You may wish to have them report their findings to the class.

UNIT 8
Writing

OBJECTIVES
To write a paragraph that
compares

ASSIGNMENT GUIDE
BASIC   Practice A

ADVANCED   Practice B

All should do the Apply activity.

RESOURCES
■ Reteaching Master 71
■ Practice Master 71

TEACHING THE LESSON

1. Getting Started
Oral Language Focus attention on this oral activity, encouraging all to participate. You may wish to list students' responses in chart form on the chalkboard.

2. Developing the Lesson
Guide students through the explanation of a paragraph that compares, emphasizing the example and the summary. You may wish to review the definition of a paragraph and discuss with students that in a paragraph of comparison you show how things are alike. Lead students through the **Guided Practice.** Identify those who would benefit from reteaching. Assign independent Practice A and B.

3. Closing the Lesson
After students complete the Apply activity, have volunteers read their lists aloud. Encourage discussion of the physical characteristics and personality traits that people might have in common. Point out to students that showing how things are alike can help them give clear descriptions in their speaking and writing.

414

♦ GETTING ♦
STARTED

Compare a butterfly and a kite. Tell how they are alike. How ma
likenesses can you discover?

WRITING ♦
A Paragraph That Compares

Scientists often compare things and describe how they are *alike*
That is how scientists classify plants and animals. Writers also us
comparisons to describe or explain how things are alike. For
example, a writer might compare
an anthill with a small city or
note that a cloud looks like a
castle in the sky.

Here is a paragraph that compares a deer's antlers with a tree.
Notice how the paragraph is organized.

Topic Sentence

Details That Give Likenesses

> The male deer's antlers are much like a growing tree. First of all, they look like a tree, with their forked branches. In fact, the antlers look so much like a tree that they help to camouflage the buck. Like the branches of a tree, the deer's antlers grow. Also, somewhat like the leaves that are shed by a tree, the antlers are shed by the buck each winter.

Summary ♦ A **paragraph of comparison** tells how one thing is *like* another. It begins with a topic sentence that tells what things are being compared.

414   WRITING: Comparison Paragraph

ESSENTIAL LANGUAGE SKILLS
This lesson provides opportunities to:

LISTENING ♦ follow the logical organization of an oral presentation ♦ respond appropriately to orally presented directions

SPEAKING ♦ make organized oral presentations ♦ express ideas clearly and effectively

READING ♦ determine the main idea of a reading selection ♦ draw logical conclusions ♦ evaluate and make judgments ♦ use graphic sources for information, such as tables and lists, charts and graphs, pictures and diagrams

WRITING ♦ adapt information to accomplish a specific purpose with a particular audience

LANGUAGE ♦ use language for informing ♦ use the fundamentals of grammar, punctuation, and spelling

Guided Practice

How are these two things alike? Think of as many likenesses as you can. Make a list of them.
Answers will vary.

Practice

. Write two ways in which each pair of things is alike.
Answers will vary.

1. a deer and a moose
2. a bear and a football player
3. a student your age and a puppy
4. a rabbit and an indoor TV antenna
5. a spider and a weaver

. Write a paragraph of comparison. Compare any two things you choose. Choose an idea from **Practice A**, for example, or compare yourself with something else. You might choose an animal, a flower, a car, or a famous person to compare with yourself. **Paragraphs will vary.**

Apply ◆ Think and Write

Listing Likenesses ◆ Think of a pair of twins or brothers or sisters that you know well. How are they alike? Write a list of the ways in which they are like one another.

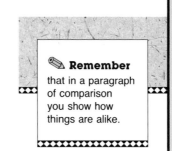

✎ **Remember**
that in a paragraph of comparison you show how things are alike.

WRITING: Comparison Paragraph   **415**

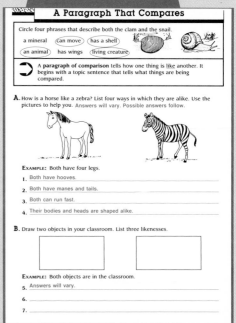

A Paragraph That Compares

Circle four phrases that describe both the clam and the snail.

a mineral   (can move)   (has a shell)
(an animal)   has wings   (living creature)

A **paragraph of comparison** tells how one thing is like another. It begins with a topic sentence that tells what things are being compared.

A. How is a horse like a zebra? List four ways in which they are alike. Use the pictures to help you. Answers will vary. Possible answers follow.

EXAMPLE: Both have four legs.
1. Both have hooves.
2. Both have manes and tails.
3. Both can run fast.
4. Their bodies and heads are shaped alike.

B. Draw two objects in your classroom. List three likenesses.

EXAMPLE: Both objects are in the classroom.
5. Answers will vary.
6.
7.

PRACTICE 71

A Paragraph That Compares

A **paragraph of comparison** tells how one thing is like another. It begins with a topic sentence that tells what things are being compared.

A. How are a globe and a map alike? List four likenesses.
Answers will vary. Possible answers follow.

1. Both show information about the earth.
2. Both show where places are.
3. Both show names of places.
4. Both can be found in schools.

B. Write a paragraph of comparison that tells how a globe is like a map. Use the notes you wrote in Exercise A to help you.   Answers will vary. Possible answers follow.
A globe is much like a map. Both show where places are.
Both show names of places. Globes and maps are often found in schools because of their useful information.

WRITE IT
Compare two places you have visited or read about. Write a paragraph that tells the ways in which two places are alike. Write on a separate sheet of paper.
Answers will vary.

◀||| TEACHING OPTIONS |||▶

RETEACHING	CLASS ENRICHMENT	CHALLENGE
A Different Modality In small envelopes place two objects or pictures of two objects that have clear similarities, such as a coin and a button. Have volunteers take turns choosing an envelope, taking out the objects, and telling how the objects are alike (e.g., *both are small, round, flat, hard, and can spin on their edges*).	**A Cooperative Activity** Have students work in small groups to choose and compare two objects in the classroom. Have one member of each group act as recorder as other group members suggest as many similarities as they can name between the objects. You may wish to have a volunteer read the list of similarities to the class.	**An Independent Extension** Have students compare two animals, sports, hobbies, or something else familiar to them. Have students draw pictures of the objects or things and then list the similarities. You may wish to have students write similes or metaphors using their comparisons (e.g., *The sweater buttons looked like a row of dimes*).

UNIT 8
Writing

■ Easy ■ Average ■ Challenging

OBJECTIVES
To write a paragraph that
contrasts

ASSIGNMENT GUIDE
BASIC   Practice A

ADVANCED   Practice B

All should do the Apply activity.

RESOURCES
■ Reteaching Master 72
■ Practice Master 72

TEACHING THE LESSON

1. Getting Started

Oral Language Focus attention on this oral activity, encouraging all to participate. You may wish to list students' responses in chart form on the chalkboard so that students can see a side-by-side contrast between the two pets. You may wish to start them with an example such as *A kitten can climb, but a puppy cannot.*

2. Developing the Lesson

Guide students through the explanation of a paragraph that contrasts, emphasizing the example and the summary. You may wish to discuss with students the difference between a paragraph that compares and a paragraph that contrasts. (*A paragraph of comparison tells how one thing is like another. A paragraph of contrast tells about differences between two similar things.*) Lead students through the **Guided Practice.** Identify those who would benefit from reteaching. Assign independent Practice A and B.

3. Closing the Lesson

After students complete the Apply activity, have volunteers read their contrasts aloud. You may wish to have volunteers suggest similarities as well. Point out to students that knowing ways to show how things are different can help them observe things more accurately.

♦ GETTING STARTED ♦

A classmate cannot decide whether he wants a kitten or a puppy as a pet. To help him decide, tell as many differences between the two pets as you can.

WRITING ♦
A Paragraph That Contrasts

In the preceding lesson you made comparisons. You compared two things to find out how they were alike. Now you will make contrasts. You will take two similar things and find out how they are *different*. Differences are important. They are what make each and every thing unique.

In the following paragraph from "Two of a Kind," the author contrasts two kinds of deer, mule deer and white-tailed deer. They are very similar. When you need to tell one from the other, however, the differences are what count. Notice how the author organizes this paragraph of contrast.

Topic Sentence →

Details That Give Differences →

Mule deer can be distinguished from whitetails in many other ways. Like their namesakes, mule deer generally have large ears. White-tailed deer have longer, bushier tails with white edges and underparts. The mule deer's black-tipped tails led some North American Indians to call them black-tailed deer. This name persists in the Pacific Northwest where a darker and somewhat smaller mule deer inhabits wet, coastal forests.

Summary ♦ A **paragraph of contrast** tells about *differences* between two similar things. It often begins with a topic sentence that tells what things are being contrasted.

416   WRITING: Contrast Paragraph

ESSENTIAL LANGUAGE SKILLS
This lesson provides opportunities to:

LISTENING ♦ listen actively and attentively ♦ select from an oral presentation the information needed

SPEAKING ♦ respond appropriately to questions from teachers and peers

READING ♦ read for specific details or information ♦ determine the main idea of a reading selection ♦ evaluate and make judgments ♦ use graphic sources for information, such as tables and lists, charts and graphs, timelines, pictures and diagrams

WRITING ♦ adapt information to accomplish a specific purpose with a particular audience

LANGUAGE ♦ use language for informing ♦ use the fundamentals of grammar, punctuation, and spelling

Guided Practice

Study these photographs of two similar animals, a hamster (left) and a gerbil (right). How are they different? Contrast them. Make a list of their differences.

Answers will vary.

Practice

. Take any two books that you have. Place them side by side. Examine them carefully to contrast them. Then copy this chart. Fill in the information. **Answers will vary.**

	Book 1	Book 2
1. Title		
2. Size		
3. Appearance of cover		
4. Number of pages		
5. Kinds of illustrations		
6. Subject		

. Write a paragraph of contrast. Choose a pair of similar things to contrast. Here are some ideas: two pets, two movies, two sports, two kinds of music, two kinds of storms. Begin your paragraph with a topic sentence. Then give detail sentences that tell how the two things are different.
Paragraphs will vary.

Apply ◆ Think and Write

Dictionary of Knowledge ◆ Look up the entry for Lewis and Clark. Then contrast the two explorers. Tell in what ways they were different.

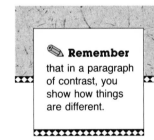

> ✏️ **Remember**
> that in a paragraph of contrast, you show how things are different.

WRITING: Contrast Paragraph **417**

◀▥▥ TEACHING OPTIONS ▥▥▶

RETEACHING

A Different Modality Review with students how a coin and a button are alike. (*Both are small, round, flat, hard, and can spin on edge.*). Help students list the differences by asking such questions as *What is each made of?* and *What is each used for?* You may wish to use a chart similar to the one in the lesson as a model.

CLASS ENRICHMENT

A Cooperative Activity Have students work in pairs to contrast two similar things they see in the classroom. Have partners complete a chart with side-by-side contrasts, each partner contributing details about one of the things. You may wish to write on chart paper a chart similar to the one in the lesson for partners to use as a model.

CHALLENGE

An Independent Extension Have students use an encyclopedia to complete contrast charts on the following pairs: ant/spider; star/planet; maple/oak; clover/mushroom. You may wish to have them add drawings to their charts to illustrate the contrasts.

417

Reading–Writing Connection

OBJECTIVES

To recognize comparisons and contrasts

To work together to write a paragraph that compares and contrasts

To use the Thesaurus to improve word choice

Focus on Likenesses and Differences

Review the Unit 5 literature selection, *Two of a Kind,* with students and have them describe the likenesses and differences between the antlers of white-tailed deer and those of mule deer. You may wish to record students' responses in chart form on the chalkboard. Then point out to students that they can use this selection to help them learn how to write an article on another topic that compares and contrasts.

You may wish to guide students through the introductory paragraphs, stressing the examples. Point out that the word *both* is often a signal that likenesses will follow. You may wish to have students discuss whether there are more likenesses or differences between the two species of deer.

Next, have students apply the information in the Reading-Writing Connection by discussing the activity at the bottom of the page. As students talk about the likenesses and differences of two shoes, guide them to recognize that the features of shoes, such as size, color, material, are compared and contrasted, just as the author of *Two of a Kind* compared and contrasted the antlers, ears, and tails of deer. As students listen to the lists of likenesses and differences, have them study the features of their classmates' shoes.

Focus on Likenesses and Differences

People classify, or organize, information according to likenesses and differences. That is why teachers so often ask you to find likenesses and differences when you study science, social studies, or even literature.

Finding and pointing out likenesses and differences is also important when you write. It is an excellent way to organize certain information. It helps the reader understand what you are saying.

The author of "Two of a Kind," which you read earlier, makes effective use of this organizing method.

LIKENESSES: Both white-tailed deer and mule deer have antlers. The antlers of both species are grown by male deer only. The antlers are covered with velvet while growing and secrete an oily substance.

DIFFERENCES: The mule deer's antlers rise abruptly and fork in pairs. The white-tailed deer's antlers arch forward and don't fork. Mule deer have larger ears than white-tailed deer. White-tailed deer have longer, bushier tails, which are white. Mule deer have black-tipped tails.

The Writer's Voice ◆ You have seen an author use likenesses and differences to explain the "headgear" of deer. Now try the same thing for human "footgear." In your mind, select one shoe from two different students. Do not tell whose shoes you are choosing. List the likenesses and differences of the shoes. Then read your lists aloud and see who can identify the two students whose shoes you have described.

Answers will vary.

418 COOPERATIVE LEARNING: Writer's Craft

ESSENTIAL LANGUAGE SKILLS

This lesson provides opportunities to:

LISTENING ◆ employ active listening in a variety of situations ◆ select from an oral presentation the information needed

SPEAKING ◆ contribute to class and small group discussions ◆ speak clearly to a group

READING ◆ determine the main idea of a reading selection ◆ recall specific facts and details that support the main idea and/or conclusion ◆ evaluate and make judgments ◆ follow a set of directions ◆ respond to various forms of literature

WRITING ◆ generate ideas by using a variety of strategies, such as brainstorming, clustering, mapping, question and answer ◆ adapt information to accomplish a specific purpose with a particular audience

LANGUAGE ◆ use language to inform ◆ use fundamentals of grammar, punctuation, and spelling

Working Together

Pay close attention to likenesses and differences and point them out as your group works on activities **A** and **B**.

- Discuss what you see in the picture below of an old-time classroom. Compare it with your own classroom. What are the likenesses? What are the differences? Make a list of each. **Answers will vary.**

- With your group, write a paragraph comparing the old schoolroom with your classroom. Begin with a topic sentence. Use your lists from activity **A** to tell how the rooms are alike and different. When you have finished, share your paragraph with other groups. Compare your observations with theirs. **Answers will vary.**

THESAURUS CORNER • Word Choice

Look up the entry for *same* in the Thesaurus. Choose five of the synonyms given for *same* and write a sentence for each one. In each sentence, compare two similar things. Underline the synonym. Be sure that each synonym fits the meaning of the sentence. **Answers will vary.**

COOPERATIVE LEARNING: Writer's Craft ◁ 419 ▷

Working Together

The Working Together activities provide opportunities for students to work together in cooperative learning groups. You may wish to pair strong writers with students whose skills are weaker so that all students may experience success in writing.

Divide the class into small groups and have students read In Your Group. Encourage them to discuss why each task is important. Have them tell what might happen if the group does not follow through on each task. *(If we do not encourage everyone to contribute ideas, some members of the group may be afraid to speak up. If we do not encourage others to share ideas, we will not benefit from others' knowledge. If we do not keep on the subject, we may not be able to complete the activity on time. If we do not record ideas, we may forget important points that are discussed.)*

You may wish to have each group appoint a recorder and a timekeeper. Then set a time limit for each activity. After students complete activity A, encourage the groups to compare the lists they wrote and discuss their completeness and accuracy. After activity B, call on a member of each group to read aloud the paragraph students created. Have the class listen to compare the groups' observations.

Thesaurus Corner

The Thesaurus Corner provides students with the opportunity to extend the Reading-Writing Connection by using the Thesaurus in the back of the textbook. If necessary, remind them how a thesaurus is used. After students have written five sentences, call on individuals to read their sentences aloud. Encourage students to compare their sentences and tell how each synonym fits the meaning of the sentence. Have students save their sentences for use later in the Writing Process lesson. Point out that learning about likenesses and differences can help students develop their ability to organize certain kinds of information when writing and speaking.

UNIT 8

OBJECTIVES

To write an article that compares

To use five stages of the writing process: prewriting, writing, revising, proofreading, and publishing

RESOURCES

Writing Process Transparencies 29–32

Revising and Proofreading Transparencies

Spelling Connection

Writing Sample Tests, p. T555

INTRODUCTION

Connecting to Literature Have a volunteer read aloud the introduction to the lesson. Emphasize the definitions of *classifying*, *comparing*, and *contrasting*. Then have students point out the way the author of the literature selection, *Two of a Kind*, used comparison and contrast. (To compare two kinds of deer, the mule deer and the white-tailed deer, the author pointed out how they are alike in appearance. To contrast the deer, he wrote about differences in their antlers, ears, and tails.) Explain to students that they will soon be writing an article in which they compare two things.

Purpose and Audience Ask students to give their own definitions of an article that compares. (A nonfiction work that tells how two things are alike) Then have volunteers tell about times they have compared things in writing or when speaking. (Students probably have compared many things when speaking to each other, such as athletes, clothes, or TV shows. They may have written comparisons in poems, in reports, in letters, or in their journals.) Encourage personal responses.

Have students consider the questions: *What is my purpose?* (To describe how two things are alike) *Who is my audience?* (My classmates) Have students discuss what they believe they need to consider when they write for other fifth-graders. Encourage them to tell what they think might interest other students.

420   ◀

WRITING PROCESS
CLASSIFYING

Writing an Article That Compares

When we classify, we group items that belong together. The items share similar qualities. For example, apples and oranges can both be classified as fruit. Like all fruit, they both contain seeds. Both also have a skin. Both grow on trees.

To tell how two things are alike is to compare them. To tell how they are different is to contrast them. In ''Two of a Kind,'' the author compares and contrasts two kinds of deer.

What's
MY PURPOSE

Who's
MY AUDIENCE

Know Your Purpose and Audience

In this lesson you will write an article that compares. Your purpose will be to describe how two things are alike.

Your audience will be your classmates. Later, you can have a team read-around or help to create a bulletin board display.

420   WRITING PROCESS: Article That Compares

ESSENTIAL LANGUAGE SKILLS
This lesson provides opportunities to:

LISTENING ◆ listen for specific information ◆ select from an oral presentation the information needed ◆ respond appropriately to orally presented directions

SPEAKING ◆ read aloud a variety of written materials ◆ contribute to class and small group discussions ◆ respond appropriately to questions from teachers and peers

READING ◆ classify ideas and information ◆ draw conclusions ◆ follow multistep directions ◆ use graphic sources for information

WRITING ◆ identify audience and purpose ◆ generate ideas using a variety of strategies, such as brainstorming, clustering, free writing ◆ expand topics by collecting information from a variety of sources ◆ improve writing based on peer and/or teacher response

LANGUAGE ◆ use language for creating ◆ recognize ways in which language can be used to influence others

Prewriting

First you need to choose a pair of topics, two things to compare. Then you will need to gather details about them.

Choose Your Topic ◆ Think creatively. What two things are alike in some ways? You might compare a red rose and a brilliant red ruby. Make a list of topics, and circle your first choice.

<table>
<tr><td>Think About It</td><td>Talk About It</td></tr>
<tr><td>Think creatively. You might make a list of single topics, then go back and give each a mate. When you have your topic list, narrow your choice to one. You might choose the pair you know the most about. Which comparison would be most interesting?</td><td>With your classmates brainstorm possible pairs of topics to compare. Listen as others offer topics. For each one, think of something that would make an interesting comparison for it.</td></tr>
</table>

Topic Ideas

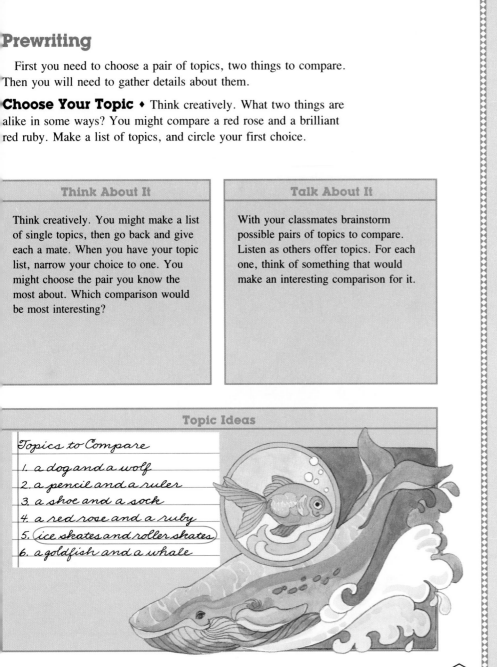

Topics to Compare

1. a dog and a wolf
2. a pencil and a ruler
3. a shoe and a sock
4. a red rose and a ruby
5. (ice skates and roller skates)
6. a goldfish and a whale

WRITING PROCESS: Article That Compares **421**

---

1. PREWRITING

Guide students through the explanation of Prewriting, pointing out that Prewriting is the stage in which writers gather ideas for writing.

MODELING THE WRITING PROCESS

You may wish to model this stage of the process. Tell students you want to choose a topic for an article that compares. Have them help you make a list of pairs of items that can be compared. Begin by recording single items, such as book, computer, road, school lunchroom, radio, soccer ball, and raindrop, on the chalkboard or on *Writing Process Transparency 29*. Emphasize that each item should be something with which students are familiar. Then have them help you find something that can be compared to each item on the list.

Next, let students hear how you might go about selecting the best pair of items to use as a topic for an article that compares. As you speak, guide students to help you. Circle the topic that students feel is best. (Possible discussion: The topic I like best is number 3. It might be fun to compare a road to a river. It would make an unusual comparison.)

Writing Process Transparency 29*

Pairs to Compare	
Compare This:	**To This:**
1. book	painting
2. computer	person's brain
3. road	river
4. school cafeteria	restaurant
5. radio	television
6. soccer ball	football
7. raindrop	diamond

Pacing

Children write better, just as adults do, if they have time to think—to let ideas and fresh insights develop between prewriting and writing, writing and revising. A five-day pacing guide follows, but the writing process may take longer.

Day 1—Prewriting   Day 3—Revising
Day 2—Writing   Day 4—Proofreading
       Day 5—Publishing

Evaluation

Process Check questions at the end of each stage of the writing process help you to keep track of students' progress.

Holistic Evaluation Guidelines may be found in the teaching notes on page 427. They offer criteria for average, above-average, and below-average compositions.

*Possible responses are overprinted on this reduced facsimile only. Use Writing Process Transparencies to interact with your students on the ideas that interest them.

Choose Your Strategy Before inviting students to choose a prewriting strategy that will help them gather information for their article that compares, guide them through the explanations of both strategies. Then have students choose a strategy they feel will help them get started.

As a variation on either strategy, you may wish to have students show their sketch or chart to a partner and discuss the two items that are described. Have the partners suggest additional ways the two items are alike.

You may wish to remind students that they have learned about using an Observation Chart as a strategy for observing in the Critical Thinking lesson on pages 406–407.

I D E A   B A N K

Prewriting Ideas

Always encourage young writers to try new ways to discover ideas they want to write about. Reassure them, though, that it is appropriate to use the strategies that work best for them. You may wish to remind them of the Prewriting ideas already introduced in their textbooks:

- A Conversation, p. 40
- An Observation Chart, pp. 40, 422
- An Order Circle, pp. 96, 320
- A Clock Graph, p. 96
- A Comic Strip, p. 154
- Answering ''What If?,'' pp. 154, 370
- An Opinion Ladder, p. 212
- A Thought Balloon, pp. 212, 266
- A Character Map, p. 266
- Taking Notes, p. 320
- Playing a Role, p. 370
- Sketch and Label, p. 422

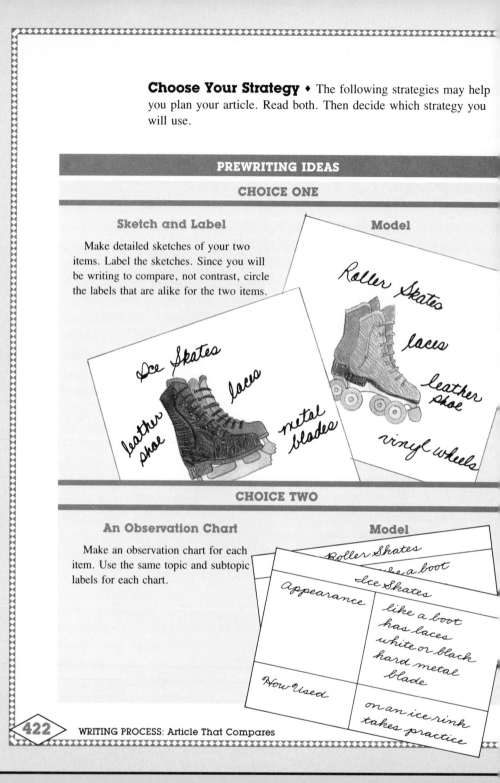

Choose Your Strategy ♦ The following strategies may help you plan your article. Read both. Then decide which strategy you will use.

PREWRITING IDEAS

CHOICE ONE

Sketch and Label

Make detailed sketches of your two items. Label the sketches. Since you will be writing to compare, not contrast, circle the labels that are alike for the two items.

Model

Roller Skates
laces
leather shoe
vinyl wheels

Ice Skates
laces
leather shoe
metal blades

CHOICE TWO

An Observation Chart

Make an observation chart for each item. Use the same topic and subtopic labels for each chart.

Model

Roller Skates — like a boot
Ice Skates

Appearance	like a boot
	has laces
	white or black
	hard metal blade
How Used	on an ice rink
	takes practice

422   WRITING PROCESS: Article That Compares

PROCESS CHECK At the completion of the Prewriting stage, students should be able to answer *yes* to these questions:
- Do I have a topic for an article that compares?
- Do I have a sketch or an observation chart that includes details that tell how the two items are alike?

Teacher to Teacher

Stress the recursive nature of the writing process with your students. The five stages are a guide, but a writer may circle back and forth between stages. If a student feels unable to proceed, you may wish to suggest a return to a prior stage. For example, you might say, ''Try going back to Prewriting to find a stronger image.'' Your positive attitude will give students ''permission'' to use and reuse the steps in the writing process as vital flexible tools for good writing.

Writing

Follow the diagram to write a four-paragraph article. Begin by introducing your topics and comparing them. For example:

• Gerbils and hamsters are very similar animals.
• Roses and rubies are different but surprisingly alike.

Write a paragraph telling how the items are alike on one point, such as appearance. Then write a paragraph telling how they are alike on another point. In the last paragraph, sum up the likenesses.

Sample First Draft •

Look carefully at ice skates and roller skates. They seem different, but they are realy a lot alike.

For one thing, they look very similar. Many roller skates have lace-up boots, just like ice skates also both ice skates and roller skates are usually white or black. One has blades and the other has wheels.

Ice skates and roller skates is used similarly, too. Both carry you fast over a hard surface. Once you lace on skates and step onto the Rink, you can really zoom! The trick is to stay on your feet.

Introduction Name the items. Say they are alike.
Paragraph 1 Compare the items on one point, such as appearance.
Paragraph 2 Compare the items on another point, such as uses.
Conclusion Sum up the likenesses.

WRITING PROCESS: Article That Compares ⟨423⟩

---

2. WRITING

Before students write their first drafts, guide them through the explanation of Writing, emphasizing that at this stage the most important task is to get all their ideas on paper.

Help students to include in their writing descriptions of how the two items are alike in appearance and use.

MODELING THE WRITING PROCESS

If you feel students need instruction before they begin this stage of the process, you may wish to ask them to recall the items from *Writing Process Transparency 29* that they felt would make the best topic for an article that compares. Write the name of the two items on the chalkboard or in the first line of *Writing Process Transparency 30*. Have students work through the thinking process with you to determine how those items are alike in appearance and use. Record the responses and then help students sum up the likenesses.

Writing Process Transparency 30*

Writing an Article That Compares
A road and a river are a lot alike.
1. Alike in Appearance: long, winding, cut through cities and country, have traffic
2. Alike in Use: used to get from one place to another, used to move goods
3. Sum Up Likenesses: Both are important features of our country. Without them travel would not be the same.

PROCESS CHECK At the completion of the Writing stage, students should be able to answer *yes* to these questions:
• Do I have a complete first draft?
• Does my article tell how two items are alike?
• Have I written an article that is four paragraphs in length?

*Possible responses are overprinted on this reduced facsimile only. Use Writing Process Transparencies *to interact with your students on the ideas that interest them.*

423

3. REVISING

Help students understand that during Revising writers make their drafts communicate ideas more clearly and effectively to an audience.

I D E A   B A N K

Grammar Connection

You may wish to remind students of the Grammar Checks already introduced in their textbooks:

- Use a variety of sentence types, p. 43
- Use exact nouns, p. 99
- Use vivid verbs, p. 157
- Replace nouns with pronouns, p. 215
- Add adjectives for specific detail, p. 269
- Avoid double negatives, p. 323
- Use prepositions or prepositional phrases to clarify relationships, p. 373
- Be sure subjects and verbs agree, p. 425

Option 1 ◆ If you wish to begin grammar instruction related to the Grammar Check in this lesson, then refer to Part 1 of this unit.

Option 2 ◆ If you wish to begin grammar instruction *not* related to the Grammar Check in this lesson, then refer to the end-of-book Glossary or Index.

First Read to Yourself Remind students to check to make sure that they clearly described how the two items are alike. Suggest that they consider taking out any sentences or phrases that tell how the items are different.

Then Share with a Partner Suggest that writers' partners offer three responses, at least one positive, and that they accompany any critical responses with suggestions for improvement. Be sure writers ask the Focus question: *Can you think of other ways these items are alike?*

---

3 Revising

Now that you have written your comparison article, would you like to improve it? Here is an idea that may help you.

REVISING IDEA

FIRST   Read to Yourself

As you read, think about your purpose. Have you written an article that compares two things? Think about your audience. Will your classmates understand your article? Circle any unclear parts that you would like to go back and improve.

Focus: Have you clearly described the likenesses of two items? Have you omitted details about their differences?

THEN   Share with a Partner

Sit next to a partner. Ask your partner to read along silently as you read aloud. Then discuss your article. These guidelines may help you work together.

The Writer

Guidelines: Read aloud slowly and clearly. Listen to your partner's suggestions. Make the changes *you* want to make.

Sample questions:
- Are there any details that don't belong?
- **Focus question:** Can you think of other ways these items are alike?

The Writer's Partner

Guidelines: Read along with the writer. Make comments that are honest but polite.

Sample responses:
- You might take out this detail about differences.
- Another way they are alike is ____.

424   WRITING PROCESS: Article That Compares

Teacher to Teacher

Publishing should be a happy occasion in which authors share their work and classmates give constructive responses. Set clear rules for Publishing sessions. For oral sharing the author may have a special chair from which he or she reads the work. Classmates should listen attentively and save their questions and responses for the end of the reading. You may also wish for students to share silently by reading each other's work.

WRITING AS A RECURSIVE PROCESS

Connecting Grammar to the Writing Process

Writing is a recursive process. In other words, good writers will often go back and forth among steps. Depending on the individual styles of your students, some may choose to correct grammar at Step Three, Revising; others may prefer to fix grammar or usage errors at Step Four, Proofreading. Ideally, this should be a decision made by the writer. Remind students, however, that once they have completed their proofreading, all the grammar errors should be corrected.

Revising Model ◆ The comparison article below is being revised. The revising marks show the writer's changes.

Look carefully at ice skates and roller skates. They seem different, but they are realy a lot alike.

For one thing, they look very similar. Many roller skates have lace-up *leather* boots, just like ice skates ~~also both ice skates and roller skates are usually white or black.~~ One has blades and the other has wheels.

Ice skates and roller skates *are* ~~is~~ used similarly, too. Both carry you fast over a hard surface. *swiftly* Once you lace on skates and step onto the Rink, you can really zoom! The trick is to stay on your feet.

The writer's partner suggested adding this likeness.

Details about differences do not belong in a comparison.

This verb did not agree with its compound subject.

Swiftly is a more vivid word than fast.

Read the comparison article above with the writer's changes. Then revise your own comparison article.

Revising Checklist

☐ **Purpose:** Did I write an article that compares two things?

☐ **Audience:** Will my classmates understand my article?

☐ **Focus:** Did I clearly describe likenesses?

Grammar Check ◆ Writing is clearer when subjects and verbs agree.

Word Choice ◆ Do you want a more vivid word for a word like *fast*? A thesaurus is a good source of vivid words.

WRITING PROCESS: Article That Compares ◆425◆

WRITING PROCESS

Revising Model Guide students through the model, noting the reasons for changes and the revision marks. Point out to students that on the model the revising marks are in blue. Encourage the class to discuss the changes in the model. Ask them to consider whether or not the changes helped to make the comparison stronger and clearer.

MODELING THE WRITING PROCESS

If you feel students need instruction before they begin this stage of the process, you may wish to present *Writing Process Transparency 31*. Have students read the draft silently, or have a volunteer read it aloud. Then ask whether anything needs to be changed. Work through the thinking process to help students give reasons for changes. Then have them tell you how to mark the changes on the draft. (Students might suggest moving a sentence to the conclusion, adding additional likenesses, deleting the sentence that states differences, adding a more vivid verb, and changing the last sentence to make subject and verb agree.) Remind students that at this time they are revising for meaning. They will correct spelling and punctuation later when they proofread.

Writing Process Transparency 31*

Roads and Rivers

Think about roads and rivers. Have you ever considered that they are a lot alike? Without them, travell would not be the same.

A road looks like a river in many ways. A road can be long *and winding* like a river. Both a road and a river have traffick. ~~Also, both run through cities as well as the country.~~ One has cars, the other has boats.

Roads and rivers are even used alike you can use a road or a river to get from one place to another or to *transport* ~~move goods.~~ Roads and rivers *are* is important features of our Country.

PROCESS CHECK At the completion of the Revising stage, students should be able to answer *yes* to the following questions:

- Do I have a complete draft with revising marks that show changes I plan to make?
- Has my draft been reviewed by another writer?

Possible responses are overprinted on this reduced facsimile only. Use Writing Process Transparencies to interact with your students on the ideas that interest them.

4. PROOFREADING

Guide students through the explanation of proofreading and review the Proofreading Model. Point out to students that on the model the proofreading marks are in red. Tell them that proofreading helps to eliminate errors such as incorrect spelling or run-on sentences that may distract or confuse their readers.

Review the Proofreading Strategy, Proofreading Marks, and the Proofreading Checklist with students. Then invite students to use the checklist and proofread their own articles that compare.

MODELING THE WRITING PROCESS

If you feel students need instruction before they begin this stage of the process, you may wish to use *Writing Process Transparency 32.* Have students check for crowded words or letters that are hard to read. Point out to students that leaving adequate space for each word and letter will make their article easier to read. Then have volunteers read each item on the Proofreading Checklist. Mark students' corrections on the transparency.

Writing Process Transparency 32*

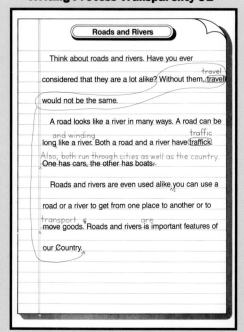

4 Proofreading

Be courteous to your readers by correcting your errors.

Proofreading Model ◆ Here is the article comparing ice skates and roller skates. Red proofreading marks have been added.

Proofreading Marks	
capital letter	=
small letter	/
indent paragraph	¶
check spelling	⬭

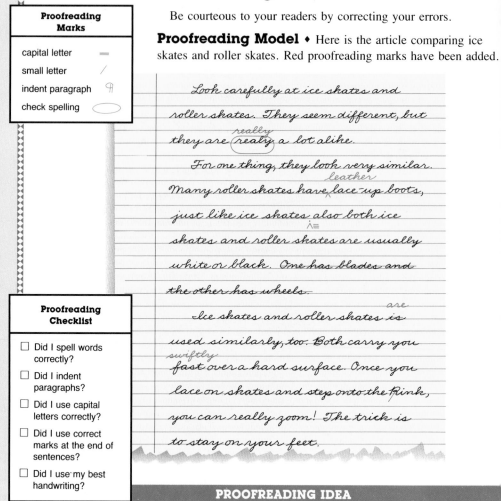

Proofreading Checklist

- ☐ Did I spell words correctly?
- ☐ Did I indent paragraphs?
- ☐ Did I use capital letters correctly?
- ☐ Did I use correct marks at the end of sentences?
- ☐ Did I use my best handwriting?

PROOFREADING IDEA

Handwriting Check

Check for crowded words that are hard to read. Then check for crowded letters.

Proofread your comparison article, add a title, and make a neat copy.

426   WRITING PROCESS: Article That Compares

PROCESS CHECK At the completion of the Proofreading stage, students should be able to answer *yes* to the following questions:
- Do I have a complete draft with proofreading marks that show changes I plan to make?
- Have I used the proofreading marks shown in the lesson?

EVALUATION PROGRAM

See Evaluation and Testing Program, pp. C1–C8.

Masters are available for the following:
**Self Evaluation Checklist
Personal Goals for Writing
Peer Response
Teacher Response**

**Holistic Evaluation Guides
Analytic Evaluation Guides**

Possible responses are overprinted on this reduced facsimile only. Use Writing Process Transparencies *to interact with your students on the ideas that interest them.*

Publishing

You have written and polished your comparison article. Now it's
time to share it. Here are two ideas you can try.

Ice Skates and Roller Skates

Look carefully at ice skates and roller skates. They seem different, but they are really a lot alike.

For one thing, they look very similar. Many roller skates have leather lace-up boots, just like ice skates. Also, both ice skates and roller skates are usually white or black.

Ice skates and roller skates are used similarly, too. Both carry you swiftly over a hard surface.

Once you lace on skates and step onto the rink, you can really zoom! The trick is to stay on your feet.

PUBLISHING IDEAS

Share Aloud	Share in Writing
Have a team read-around. Form small groups. Take turns reading your articles aloud. Have each writer challenge teammates to name one more likeness. If they do, score a point for that person!	Illustrate a cover for your article. Include the names of your two items. Display the articles with your classmates' articles. Look at each cover and try to guess how the items are alike. Then read the article to find out if you and the writer had the same ideas.

WRITING PROCESS: Article That Compares 427

Spelling and Mechanics Connection

You may wish to remind students of Proofreading ideas already introduced in their textbooks:

- Read through a window, p. 44
- Check for poorly formed letters, pp 100, 426
- Trade with a partner, p. 158
- Check one thing at a time, p. 216
- Read backwards, p. 270
- Use a ruler, p. 324
- Check every other word, p. 374
- Check for crowded words, p. 426

Spelling ◆ If you wish to include spelling instruction with this lesson, then refer to the Spelling Guide on pages 490–492, the Index, or the *Spelling Connection* booklet.

Mechanics ◆ If you wish to include mechanics instruction with this lesson, then refer to the Glossary, the Index, or the *Revising and Proofreading Transparencies*.

5. PUBLISHING

Oral Sharing If students choose to share their writing orally, provide a specific time during class for a team read-around. As an alternative to the team read-around activity, you may wish to perform the activity as a class read-around. Have students keep track of their own individual scores.

Written Sharing If students choose to share their writing by displaying it, set aside a specific time during the day when students may read each other's covers and articles. You may also wish to provide a special place in the classroom to store the articles for future reference.

Holistic Evaluation Guidelines

An article that compares of **average** quality will:
1. tell how two items are alike
2. present ideas in four organized paragraphs

An article that compares of **above-average** quality may:
1. use vivid words and unusual comparisons
2. begin or end in an unusual way

An article that compares of **below-average** quality may:
1. include details about differences
2. be unorganized or incomplete

PROCESS CHECK At the completion of the Publishing stage, students should be able to answer *yes* to these questions:

- Have I shared my writing with an audience?
- Have readers shared reactions with me?
- Have I thought about what I especially liked in this writing? Or about what was particularly difficult?
- Have I thought about what I would like to work on the next time I write?

Encourage students to keep a log or journal of their own and their readers' reactions.

Curriculum Connection

OBJECTIVES
To practice a thinking strategy for writing across the curriculum
To write a journal entry

Writing Across the Curriculum

Remind students that scientists observe and then record in an organized way what they learn. Tell students they will use observation charts to help them compare a domesticated and a wild animal.

You may wish to remind students that they have used an observation chart as a strategy for classifying in the Critical Thinking lesson, in their response to the literature selection, and in the Writing Process lesson.

Writing to Learn

To help students get started, have them name some domesticated and wild animals that would be interesting to find out about. Write the names on the chalkboard.

You may wish to have students with limited English proficiency describe tame and wild animals that interest them and provide the animals' English names.

Help students use their science books or books from their classroom library to find information about the animals of their choice.

Writing in Your Journal

When they have finished writing, have students read their earlier journal entries. Encourage them to discuss what they have learned about the theme, and to observe how their writing has changed or improved.

Remind students that their journals have many purposes. Besides paragraphs and stories, they can write questions, story ideas, or thoughts and reflections on a subject. Suggest to them that entries in their journals may provide ideas for later writing.

Writing Across the Curriculum   Science

In this unit you wrote an article describing how two things were alike. You used an observation chart to gather information and help you make comparisons. Scientists, too, gather information on observation charts. They make careful observations about the world around us.

Writing to Learn

Think and Observe ◆ What would the world be like if there were no domesticated animals? Make an observation chart for a domesticated animal, such as a chicken, cow, or dog. Show where the animal lives, how it gets food, and how it is useful to us. Then make another observation chart for a wild animal, such as a wild goose, deer, or wolf.

Observation Chart

Write ◆ Compare your two charts and list the differences between a domesticated and a wild animal. You may wish to discuss how life would be different if there were no domesticated animals.

Writing in Your Journal

In the Writer's Warm-up you wrote about animals and their habitats. Throughout this unit you learned how and where different animals live. Did any facts or passages puzzle you? In your journal write about an animal habitat that you would like to learn more about.

ESSENTIAL LANGUAGE SKILLS
This lesson provides opportunities to:

LISTENING ◆ listen actively and attentively ◆ follow the logical organization of an oral presentation

SPEAKING ◆ participate in group discussions ◆ make organized oral presentations

READING ◆ use graphic sources for information, such as charts and graphs ◆ respond to various forms of literature ◆ become acquainted with a variety of selections, characters, and themes of our literary heritage ◆ select books for individual needs and interests

WRITING ◆ select and narrow a topic for a specific purpose ◆ expand topics by collecting information from a variety of sources ◆ adapt information to accomplish a specific purpose with a particular audience ◆ keep journals, logs, or notebooks to express feelings, record ideas, discover new knowledge, and free the imagination

LANGUAGE ◆ use language to describe ◆ recognize ways in which language can be used to influence others

BOOKS TO ENJOY

Read More About It

Do Animals Dream? *by Joyce Pope*
This fascinating book answers 85 questions children most often ask at natural history museums. Perhaps you, too, have wondered if crocodiles really cry. How do animals find their way? The answers to these questions are waiting for you to read.

DO ANIMALS DREAM?
Children's questions about animals most often asked of the Natural History Museum answered by Joyce Pope

Misty of Chincoteague
by Marguerite Henry
Chincoteague Island is part of Virginia. Wild ponies have roamed there for many years. This is a classic story of a wild pony and the children who love her.

Book Report Idea Mask

Share your next book by making a mask to represent an animal, character, or theme.

Make a mask ◆ You can use a variety of materials to make masks. You might try papier-mâché, fabric, cardboard, or large brown paper shopping bags. Be creative! Make your mask colorful, dramatic, funny, or scary, depending on your book. Hang your completed mask on a bulletin board. Make a written report to go with the mask. In it, explain how the mask relates to the book. Describe in writing the details that the mask cannot convey.

Books to Enjoy ◀ 429

Read More About It

Call students' attention to Read More About It and discuss theme-related books. Point out that the books listed here contain stories about animals, particularly their habitats. Encourage students to mention other titles that deal with these topics. Encourage students to examine pictures and jacket illustrations of books in the classroom to find books they will enjoy reading.

Book Report Idea

You may wish to have students use the book report form provided in the back of their textbooks. Book Report Idea presents a lively alternative way for interested students to share books they have read.

You may wish to share the reports with the class or in small groups. Have students hang their masks for classmates to guess whether they represent an animal, character, or theme before finding out more about each book from the student who wrote the report and created the mask.

Integrated Language Arts Project

The **Integrated Language Arts Project** on pages T526–T527 may be used with this unit.

ANSWERS TO WRITING TO LEARN

A DOMESTICATED ANIMAL—COW

Where it lives	near people	barns, fields
How it gets food	people provide it	pastures, grain
Usefulness	food, clothing	meat, milk, leather

A WILD ANIMAL—DEER

Where it lives	away from people	forests
How it gets food	foraging	grasses, shrubs
Usefulness	food, clothing	meat, leather

WORLD OF BOOKS CLASSROOM LIBRARIES is a collection of high-quality children's literature available with this program.

Unit 8
Review

REVIEW OR TEST
You may wish to use the Unit Review as
a review of the unit skills before administering the Unit Posttest, or you may
wish to use the Unit Review in lieu of
the Unit Posttest.

REVIEW PROCEDURES
The lesson pages that are reviewed are
listed beside the heading of each segment. You may wish to choose one of
the procedures listed below for using
the pages with the Unit Review
exercises.

Review/Evaluate Have students restudy the lesson pages before doing
the Unit Review exercises.

Open-Book Review Allow students
to refer to the lesson pages if they
need to while they are doing the Unit
Review exercises.

Evaluate/Review Have students do
the Unit Review exercises, then turn to
the lesson pages to restudy concepts
for which incorrect responses are
given.

ADDITIONAL REVIEW AND
PRACTICE
For additional review and practice,
turn to the Extra Practice pages at the
end of the unit.

UNIT REVIEW

Unit 8

Sentences   *pages 388–399*

A. Write each underlined word or words
below. After the word or words write
noun, pronoun, verb, adjective, adverb,
or *preposition.*

1. Darryl **walks** to school every day. *(verb)*
2. **Ms. Payne** teaches mathematics. *(noun)*
3. Trudy ran **quickly** to the library. *(adverb)*
4. The cat sat quietly **in** the corner. *(preposition)*
5. The **ferocious** lion growled. *(adjective)*
6. Tell **me** what happened. *(pronoun)*
7. Sid gave **them** clear directions. *(pronoun)*
8. You are **very** intelligent. *(adverb)*
9. The committee **will meet** again soon. *(verb)*
10. I never watch television **on** Monday. *(preposition)*
11. **Tall** oaks grow from small acorns. *(adjective)*
12. The blacksmith **whistled** loudly. *(verb)*
13. The meeting was **unusually** brief. *(adverb)*
14. Jacob **had risen** early that morning. *(verb)*
15. The chores were finished **surprisingly**
    quickly. *(adverb)*
16. The lion's **cub** is adorable. *(noun)*
17. This orange juice tastes **sour**. *(adjective)*
18. She works **from** sunrise to sundown. *(preposition)*
19. I **shall study** harder. *(verb)*
20. The leopard sprung **suddenly**. *(adverb)*
21. **It** chased after the wild antelope. *(pronoun)*
22. The **frightened** antelope fled. *(adjective)*
23. The animals ran **across** the plain. *(preposition)*
24. A tour group observed the **chase**. *(adjective)*
25. A **photographer** filmed the event. *(noun)*

B. Write each sentence below. Underline
the compound subject or the compound
predicate.

26. The <u>woman</u> and her <u>son</u> enjoyed a
    good laugh.
27. The two spaniels <u>barked</u> and
    <u>growled</u>.
28. <u>Bob</u>, <u>Sally</u>, and <u>Marjorie</u> are very
    close friends.
29. The hikers <u>walked</u>, <u>rested</u>, and
    <u>walked</u> again.
30. The <u>supermarket</u> and the <u>department
    store</u> are having sales this week.
31. <u>Mr. Rosen</u> and <u>Dr. Orontes</u> have
    offices next to each other.
32. <u>Danielle</u> or <u>Megan</u> will play the lead
    in the play.
33. The audience <u>became</u> bored and
    <u>walked</u> out.
34. <u>Mr. Davis</u> and <u>Mrs. Perry</u> are writing
    a cookbook together.
35. New <u>hats</u> and <u>dresses</u> were displayed
    in the shop window.

C. Write each sentence. Choose the verb
in parentheses ( ) that correctly completes
the sentence.

36. Bob and I (is, <u>are</u>) in the same class.
37. Jill and Rodney (<u>make</u>, makes) the
    party decorations.
38. Lisa and her mother (is training, <u>are
    training</u>) for the race.
39. The muffins and the rolls (was baked,
    <u>were baked</u>) by Mr. Semple.
40. The soup and the salad (<u>taste</u>, tastes)
    delicious.
41. The Clausens (lives, <u>live</u>) in the
    yellow house across the street.

. Write each sentence. Underline the
two simple sentences in each.

2. Some people prefer to play golf, but some prefer tennis.

3. Will you wrap the party favors, or will Dorothy do it?

4. Jim pitched the ball, and Betty batted it over the fence.

5. The sun rises, and the day begins.

46. Troy has learned to ice skate, but he can't do a figure eight yet.

47. The Tigers might win the game, or they might lose it.

48. The guinea pig almost got away, but Ms. Weng caught it.

49. The fox crept up on the chickens, but the farmer chased it away.

50. A strong wind gusted, and the pine trees swayed.

. Write *compound* or *run-on* for each
sentence.

1. I like Ann she is pleasant company. _{run-on}

52. The train may arrive on time, or it may be late. _{compound}

53. Molly Pitcher was a hero her real name was Mary Ludwig Hays. _{run-on}

54. Steve is afraid of raccoons, and he doesn't like skunks either. _{compound}

55. The owl hooted the coyote howled. _{run-on}

56. Mrs. Bates teaches science her husband teaches history. _{run-on}

57. E. B. White is my favorite writer, and I have read many of his books. _{compound}

58. Yesterday was cold and rainy, but the day before that was pleasant. _{compound}

59. Jennie Cartwright is a fine singer her mother also sings. _{run-on}

Homographs *pages 400–401*

F. Write each pair of sentences. Underline
the two homographs.

60. Turn on the light. This package is very light.

61. Some snakes shed their skins. The shed stands next to the old house.

62. Help me wind this toy. A cold wind is coming from the north.

63. The fleet deer jumped over the fence. A fleet of ships set sail.

64. Will you lead us out of here? The lead in this pencil is almost gone.

65. The sink dripped all night. We watched the sun sink in the west.

66. The desert is covered with sand dunes. Please do not desert us!

67. The actors took a deep bow. Suzie put a yellow bow in her hair.

68. The ink in this pen is gone. The squealing pigs wrestled in the pen.

**Comparison and
Contrast** *pages 414–417*

G. Write two ways in which each of the
following are alike.
Answers will vary.

69. two friends of yours

70. an automobile and an airplane

71. a gerbil and a rabbit

72. a tennis ball and a basketball

H. Write two ways in which each of the
following are different.
Answers will vary.

73. a dog and a cat

74. two relatives of yours

75. swimming and jogging

76. a microscope and a telescope

Unit Review **431**

CUMULATIVE REVIEW

The Cumulative Review reviews basic skills from the first through the present unit. The lesson pages that are reviewed are listed beside the heading for each segment. You may wish to have students restudy the lesson pages listed before assigning the Cumulative Review exercises.

ADDITIONAL REVIEW AND PRACTICE

For additional review and practice of skills, you may wish to assign the appropriate Extra Practice pages found at the end of each unit.

◆ CUMULATIVE ◆ REVIEW

UNITS 1 and 8: Sentences
pages 6–15, 388–399

A. Write the complete subject of each sentence. Underline the simple subject. Write *(You)* if the subject is understood.

Complete subject underlined once, simple subject twice.

1. My mother has gone back to college.
2. Come with me to Stacy's party next Saturday. (You)
3. The hawk flew over the plain.
4. The running shoes with the yellow stripes are mine.
5. Close your books now. (You)
6. Put down your pencils. (You)
7. Ms. Matsu is a fine sculptor.
8. Kenny's dog is very frisky today.
9. Take this note to Annette. (You)
10. The man in the sports car waved.

Complete predicate is underlined once, simple predicate twice.

B. Write the complete predicate of each sentence. Underline the simple predicate.

11. My sister is writing a new story.
12. She gets her inspiration from everyday events.
13. Many reviewers have praised her work.
14. I shall ask her about her stories.
15. She also composes beautiful songs.
16. Many singers have performed them.
17. She will appear on a television program next Monday night.
18. My parents take great pride in her.
19. I have spoken about her often.
20. She is a very talented person.

C. Write each sentence. Underline the compound subject or the compound predicate.

21. Sam and Tina play on our team.
22. Tina bats and pitches well.
23. The shortstop and the catcher are members of the same family.
24. Coach Buckner has trained us and improved our batting averages.
25. He played professional baseball for ten years and then retired.
26. My collie and Tina's doberman like to watch us practice.
27. Coach Buckner pats them and gives them dog biscuits.
28. Ms. Cohen and Mrs. Soroba are the team's sponsors.
29. They attend our games and cheer.

D. Choose the verb in parentheses ( ) that correctly completes each sentence.

30. Rabbits and hamsters (makes, make) good pets.
31. Thunder and lightning (frightens, frighten) our cats.
32. Sandy and Sue (play, plays) tennis.
33. Tourists and sightseers rarely (travel, travels) this route.
34. Hamburgers and chili (is, are) my favorite foods.
35. Joe, Frank, and Beverly (practices, practice) their juggling act daily.
36. The Hayes brothers and Phil (performs, perform) jazz music.
37. Mr. Lee and Ms. Lang (manage, manages) our theater group.
38. Two deer and one rabbit (has come, have come) this way.

F. Write *simple* or *compound* for each sentence.

39. The mechanic took off the old tire and put on a new one. ^{simple}
simple

40. Brian smiled, and Cheryl took his picture. compound

41. Charles likes spinach, but I hate that vegetable! compound

42. Marie, Sam, and George told stories around the campfire. simple

43. We might go to the shoe store today, or we might go Tuesday. compound

44. We finished our homework and went to a movie. simple

45. You can argue with Alice, but you cannot convince her. compound

46. Steve and Harry came home completely soaked. simple

Unit 2: Capital Letters and Periods *pages 66–69*

E. Write the sentence. Capitalize the proper nouns. Write the abbreviations correctly.

47. You can find dr. cooper's office on kamen st. near rte. 85.

48. Nathan shaw, jr. will give a piano recital on tues., apr. 17.

49. Next mon., ms. flores will become chairperson of our committee.

50. Meet me on jan. 29 at 2 p m promptly.

51. Author j c pierce, sr. will speak about his new book.

52. The new store on madison ave. is always crowded.

53. Last sept. our family went to new hampshire.

Unit 2: Commas *pages 90–91*

G. Write the sentences. Add the commas where they are needed.

54. Jeff, Elise, and their parents have moved into a new house.

55. No, Donald, you may not have another dollar!

56. Shari, don't go outdoors without your overcoat.

57. You know perfectly well, Brad, that you are not allowed in that room.

58. The eagle swooped down, fed its young, and flew away.

59. These cups, saucers, and plates are beautiful.

60. Well, I'm fairly sure I know the answer.

61. Please tell us a story, Denise.

62. Michael, where have you been?

Unit 3: Verbs *pages 116–133*

H. Write each sentence. Underline the verb. Then write whether it is an action verb or a linking verb.

63. This apple tastes sour. linking

64. The squirrel scooped the nut off the ground. action

65. I gave the book to David. action

66. This weather is delightful. linking

67. That towel feels rather damp. linking

68. The tour group followed the guide. action

69. Maria tells scary ghost stories. action

70. Ned seems frightened by the tales. linking

71. Those two girls are best friends. linking

72. The robin flew around Paula's head. action

73. Paula watched the bird carefully. action

74. The movie was long and boring. linking

CUMULATIVE REVIEW: Units 1–8 **433**

Cumulative Review

I. Write each sentence. Draw one line under the main verb. Draw two lines under the helping verb.

75. The bird <u>is</u> <u><u>making</u></u> a nest for its young.
76. Jeff <u>will</u> <u><u>visit</u></u> some interesting places this summer.
77. Carol <u>has</u> <u><u>written</u></u> a lovely poem.
78. Penny and Sam <u>have</u> <u><u>sung</u></u> together often.
79. Marcia and Luis <u>had</u> <u><u>read</u></u> that story before.
80. Our band <u>is</u> <u><u>practicing</u></u> for the concert.
81. Now the Smiths <u>are</u> <u><u>waving</u></u> goodbye to us.
82. I <u>shall</u> <u><u>remember</u></u> your kind words always.

J. Write the past-tense form of each verb.

83. cry — cried
84. do — did
85. go — went
86. see — saw
87. eat — ate
88. fall — fell
89. run — ran
90. wear — wore
91. like — liked
92. hop — hopped
93. ride — rode
94. give — gave
95. take — took
96. worry — worried
97. sip — sipped
98. think — thought

Unit 4: Pronouns *pages 176–185*

K. Write whether each pronoun is a subject pronoun or an object pronoun.

99. I — subject
100. him — object
101. us — object
102. they — subject
103. me — object
104. we — subject
105. her — object
106. he — subject
107. them — object
108. she — subject

L. Write each sentence below. Choose the correct pronoun in parentheses ( ).

109. Give me (<u>my</u>, mine) pencil.
110. (Their, <u>Theirs</u>) is the fifth house on the block.
111. Florence practiced (<u>her</u>, hers) scales.
112. Is that painting above the dresser (your, <u>yours</u>)?
113. We went to (<u>our</u>, ours) history class together.
114. (<u>My</u>, Mine) brother walks with me to school.
115. Kathy and Norman saw (<u>their</u>, theirs) cousin at the mall.
116. That outfit of (her, <u>hers</u>) is certainly colorful!

Units 5 and 6: Adjectives and Adverbs *pages 234–241, 284–291*

M. Write each sentence. Underline the predicate adjective once. Underline twice the noun or pronoun it describes.

117. Georgia O'Keeffe's <u><u>paintings</u></u> are <u>famous</u>.
118. This <u><u>ladder</u></u> seems <u>shaky</u>.
119. The <u><u>work</u></u> was <u>difficult</u>.
120. The <u><u>popcorn</u></u> tasted <u>salty</u>.
121. The <u><u>bull</u></u> looked <u>angry</u> as it paced across the corral.
122. <u><u>I</u></u> feel <u>comfortable</u> in your company.
123. <u><u>We</u></u> were <u>exhausted</u> after the very long race.
124. The <u><u>woman</u></u> seems <u>restless</u> as she waits in line.
125. <u><u>Herman</u></u> was <u>ready</u> for anything!
126. The little <u><u>boy</u></u> felt <u>pleased</u> by the compliment.

For each adjective write the two forms
ed to compare persons, places, or
ngs.

ighter, brightest		more special, most special
7. bright	134.	special
ppier, happiest		stronger, strongest
8. happy	135.	strong
tter, best		more serious, most serious
9. good	136.	serious
nger, longest		worse, worst
0. long	137.	bad
icker, quickest		bigger, biggest
1. quick	138.	big
urdier, sturdiest		more helpful, most helpful
2. sturdy	139.	helpful
aver, bravest		more comfortable,
3. brave	140.	comfortable
		most comfortable

For each adverb write the form used to
mpare two actions. Then write the form
ed to compare three or more actions.

rlier, earliest		better, best
1. early	146.	well
re often, most often		harder, hardest
2. often	147.	hard
quickly, most quickly		more slowly, most slowly
3. quickly	148.	slowly
ster, fastest		more badly, most badly
4. fast	149.	badly
ore gently,		more remarkably,
5. gently	150.	remarkably
st gently		most remarkably

Write each sentence. Use the correct
ord in parentheses ( ).

51. The rehearsal went (fair, fairly)
quickly.

52. Ms. Perelli is certainly a (fair,
fairly) person.

53. Earl has been (extreme, extremely)
patient with his new puppy.

54. Most of the time, you write very
(good, well).

55. This is a very (good, well) book.

6. Mr. Stein has a very (low, lowly)
singing voice.

57. The bear (careful, carefully) walked
around the trap.

58. Carol raised her hand (impatient,
impatiently).

UNIT 7: Prepositions
pages 340–347

Q. Write each sentence. Then write
whether the underlined word is a
preposition or an adverb.

159. When the train stopped, Laurie got
off. *adverb*

160. Get off the couch, please. *preposition*

161. I shall be waiting outside. *adverb*

162. Janie lives near the subway. *preposition*

163. Step inside this cave. *preposition*

164. As the door slowly opened, we went
inside. *adverb*

165. To see our fancy ceiling, look up. *adverb*

166. I see my uncle coming up the walk. *preposition*

167. Wearing a suit, he is coming near. *adverb*

168. He shops at a store near us. *preposition*

R. Write each sentence. Underline the
preposition once. Underline the object of
the preposition twice.

169. Old clothes were piled in one
corner.

170. After a rainstorm the air smells
fresh.

171. She comes from a distant land.

172. The dog with the floppy ears hung
its head.

173. The train raced across the bridge.

174. I am pleased with my report.

175. Jake told Glen about the test.

176. Rosie accepted the bouquet from
Herbert.

177. She handed him a glass of juice.

178. They sat together on the porch.

179. Between them was a plump cat
named Irving.

180. Herbert handed a toy to Irving.

Language Puzzlers

OBJECTIVES
To solve language puzzles based on skills taught in the unit

ANSWERS

Presidential Pairings
1. Our first president has a state named for him.
2. Theodore and Franklin D. have the same last name.
3. Thomas Jefferson wrote the Declaration of Independence.
4. President Lincoln's face appears on a five-dollar bill.
5. Franklin D. Roosevelt's face is on a dime.
6. President Johnson and President Kennedy have space centers named for them.
7. The White House and Camp David are places where presidents stay.
8. The Oval Office is where the President works.

Coded Communication
Dear Ellen,
  You and Emily are invited for tea tomorrow. After tea we can play tennis or go to a movie. Jay and I wrote this in code to tease you. We wrote one for Kay too and sent it to her. Be a friend and come to our party. We will play any games you like and have a great time!

             Your friend,
             Katie Ellis

LANGUAGE PUZZLERS
Unit 8 Challenge

Presidential Pairings

Play this game about United States presidents. Match a subject in **Column A** with the correct predicate in **Column B**. Write each sentence.

Column A
1. Our first president
2. Theodore and Franklin D.
3. Thomas Jefferson
4. President Lincoln's face
5. Franklin D. Roosevelt's face
6. President Johnson and President Kennedy
7. The White House and Camp David
8. The Oval Office

Column B
appears on a five-dollar bill.
have space centers named for them.
have the same last name.
wrote the Declaration of Independence.
has a state named for him.
are places where presidents stay.
is where the President works.
is on a dime.

Coded Communication

Figure out the following message. (Hint: Each sentence contains either a compound subject or a compound predicate.)

Dear LN,
  U N MLE R Nvited 40 2morrO. After T we can plA 10S or go 2 a moV. J N I wrote this in code TT U. We wrote 1 4 K 2 N ¢ it 2 her. B a friend N come 2 R parT. We will plA NE games U like N have a gr8 time!
             Your friend,
             KT LS

Write a coded message like the one above for a classmate. Include some compound subjects and compound predicates.

Unit 8 Extra Practice

Reviewing the Parts of Speech

p. 388

Write whether each underlined word is a noun, a pronoun, a verb, an adjective, an adverb, or a preposition.

1. The <u>Romans</u> picked flowers.
2. They made <u>lovely</u> bouquets.
3. The flowers were <u>for</u> Flora.
4. <u>They</u> decorated her statue.
5. Everyone danced <u>merrily</u>.
6. It <u>was</u> her holiday.

Write each sentence. Draw a line under the noun that follows a linking verb. Draw two lines under the subject that it renames or identifies.

EXAMPLE: On May Day in Sweden, actors are warriors.
ANSWER: On May Day in Sweden, <u>actors</u> are <u>warriors</u>.

7. One fighter is Summer.
8. The other is Winter.
9. Of course, Summer is always the winner.

Write each underlined word. After the word, write *noun*, *pronoun*, *verb*, *adjective*, *adverb*, or *preposition*.

10. The <u>ancient</u> Celts <u>believed</u> in a sun god.
11. During the <u>winter</u> the sun god <u>disappeared</u>.
12. <u>They</u> <u>thought</u> he was a prisoner.
13. <u>Evil</u> spirits had captured <u>him</u>.
14. They lit <u>fires</u> to chase the spirits <u>away</u>.
15. Some <u>ancient</u> peoples <u>were</u> believers in tree gods.
16. The people got up <u>early</u> <u>on</u> May Day.
17. They went <u>into</u> the <u>woods</u> to cut tree branches.
18. The <u>branches</u> were supposed to bring <u>good</u> luck.
19. In <u>England</u>, May Day <u>became</u> a big holiday.
20. People were always glad to see <u>warm</u> days <u>again</u>.
21. <u>They</u> cut down a <u>tall</u> tree.
22. <u>Then</u> they decorated <u>it</u> to make a Maypole.
23. Everyone <u>danced</u> <u>around</u> the Maypole.
24. <u>Colorful</u> <u>Maypoles</u> can still be seen on this holiday.

OBJECTIVES
To practice skills taught in the unit

ANSWERS

Reviewing the Parts of Speech

A.
1. noun
2. adjective
3. preposition
4. pronoun
5. adverb
6. verb

B.
7. <u>fighter</u> is <u>Summer</u>
8. <u>other</u> is <u>Winter</u>
9. <u>Summer</u> is <u>winner</u>

C.
10. ancient, adjective; believed, verb
11. winter, noun; disappeared, verb
12. They, pronoun; thought, verb
13. Evil, adjective; him, pronoun
14. fires, noun; away, adverb
15. ancient, adjective; were, verb
16. early, adverb; on, preposition
17. into, preposition; woods, noun
18. branches, noun; good, adjective
19. England, noun; became, verb
20. warm, adjective, again, adverb
21. They, pronoun; tall, adjective
22. Then, adverb; it, pronoun
23. danced, verb; around, preposition
24. Colorful, adjective; Maypoles, noun

Extra Practice and Challenge

For those students who need additional grammar practice have them refer to these pages. **The practice exercises progress in difficulty from Easy to Average. Practice A is Easy. Practice B is Average.** Difficult concepts requiring more practice have additional Exercises C and D at the Average level.

We do not recommend these exercises for students who have mastered the skill in the basic lesson. Those students should do the **Challenge** word puzzles on page 436.

Extra Practice

Compound Subjects
A. 1. The principal and our teacher (compound)
2. Mrs. Colucci or my father (compound)
3. Our school and the newspaper (compound)
4. The police and fire fighters (compound)
5. Sidewalks and steps (compound)
6. You and Jonathan (compound)
7. One of the cleanest streets in our town
8. A cousin of mine
9. Her family and my family (compound)
10. We
11. Lew, Ira, or I (compound)
12. Davis Avenue
13. Sonja and I (compound)
14. Mrs. Colucci and my father (compound)

B. 15. mayor and governor
16. Antonia and she
17. Carl or you
18. drugstore and supermarket
19. Friday and Saturday

Using Subjects and Verbs That Agree
A. 1. make
2. were
3. sell
4. like

2 Compound Subjects
p. 3

A. Write the complete subject of each sentence. If the subject is compound, write *compound*.

1. The principal and our teacher announced a cleanup con
2. Mrs. Colucci or my father will be our block captain.
3. Our school and the newspaper will print advertisements
4. The police and fire fighters will help us.
5. Sidewalks and steps will be swept clean.
6. You and Jonathan can collect the fallen branches.
7. One of the cleanest streets in our town is Davis Avenue
8. A cousin of mine lives there.
9. Her family and my family planted trees there last spring
10. We put up fences to protect the young trees.
11. Lew, Ira, or I will care for the trees.
12. Davis Avenue doesn't need a contest to look neat.
13. Sonja and I hope our street will look as nice.
14. Mrs. Colucci and my father made a work plan.

B. Write each sentence. Underline the compound subject.

EXAMPLE: Asheville and our town tied for the award.
ANSWER: Asheville and our town tied for the award.

15. The mayor and the governor will award the prizes.
16. Antonia and she have painted their front door.
17. Carl or you should win a special award.
18. The drugstore and the supermarket displayed posters.
19. Friday and Saturday were the busiest cleanup days.

3 Using Subjects and Verbs That Agree
p. 39

A. Write the verb in parentheses ( ) that correctly completes each sentence.

1. Nancy and Oliver (make, makes) posters.
2. The races and the games (was, were) fun last year.
3. The students, parents, and teachers (sell, sells) tickets.
4. The adults and the children (like, likes) fairs.

Write the verb in parentheses ( ) that correctly completes each sentence.

5. Juice and peanuts (is, are) popular snacks at the fair.
6. Mr. Ching and his daughter (cook, cooks) the chicken.
7. The Boy Scouts and Girl Scouts (serve, serves) the food.
8. The corn, fruit, and potatoes (taste, tastes) great.
9. Coleslaw and salads (completes, complete) the meal.
10. After lunch the blue team and the gold team (plays, play) tug-of-war.
11. Masao and Serena (are, is) captains of their teams.
12. Parents and teachers (cheers, cheer) both sides.
13. Serena and her team (pull, pulls) Masao over the line.
14. The winning team and the losing team (looks, look) tired.

Write each sentence. Use the correct form of the verb in parentheses ( ).

15. Boris and Heather (make, makes) kites for the fair.
16. Two students and Boris (plans, plan) a kite contest.
17. The kite contest and the soccer game (begin, begins).
18. The Blues and the Golds (play, plays) for the soccer cup.
19. All the soccer players and kite fliers (run, runs) onto the field.
20. Boris and the Blues (crash, crashes) into each other.
21. The Golds and Heather (are, is) a tangle of string.
22. The principal and the coaches (come, comes) to help.
23. Other students and parents (helps, help), too.
24. Boris, Heather, and the soccer players (laughs, laugh) at themselves.

Compound Predicates

p. 394

Write the verbs in the complete predicate of each sentence.

1. The class planned and wrote a class newspaper.
2. The students chose and edited the articles.
3. Ms. Doyle read and approved each story.
4. Mr. Cortes typed and proofread everything.
5. Sandra photocopied, sorted, and stapled the pages.

B. 5. are
6. cook
7. serve
8. taste
9. complete
10. play
11. are
12. cheer
13. pull
14. look

C. 15. make
16. plan
17. begin
18. play
19. run
20. crash
21. are
22. come
23. help
24. laugh

Compound Predicates
A. 1. planned, wrote
2. chose, edited
3. read, approved
4. typed, proofread
5. photocopied, sorted, stapled

Extra Practice and Challenge

For those students who need additional grammar practice have them refer to these pages. **The practice exercises progress in difficulty from Easy to Average. Practice A is Easy. Practice B is Average.** Difficult concepts requiring more practice have additional Exercises C and D at the Average level.
We do not recommend these exercises for students who have mastered the skill in the basic lesson. Those students should do the **Challenge** word puzzles on page 436.

B.
6. helped with the newspaper
7. sat and thought of ideas (compound)
8. revised and corrected articles (compound)
9. stayed after school every day
10. explained things and answered questions (compound)
11. planned and designed the front page (compound)
12. arranged all the articles and pictures
13. pasted everything into place
14. surprised and pleased the other classes (compound)
15. read and enjoyed it (compound)

C.
16. <u>stopped</u>, <u>rested</u>, and <u>talked</u>
17. <u>sparkled</u> and <u>shone</u>
18. <u>opened</u> and <u>closed</u>
19. <u>danced</u> and <u>sang</u>
20. <u>cheered</u> and <u>clapped</u>

Compound Sentences

A.
1. <u>We see stars and planets at night</u>, and <u>we see other bright lights</u>, too.
2. <u>Some lights are comets</u>, and <u>some are meteors</u>.
3. <u>Meteors are often seen</u>, but <u>comets are rare</u>.
4. <u>Comets are balls of frozen gas</u>, and <u>they orbit the sun</u>.
5. <u>Meteors are called shooting stars</u>, and <u>they travel fast</u>.
6. <u>Meteors burn up in space</u>, or <u>they fall to Earth as meteorites</u>.
7. <u>Sometimes very large meteorites hit Earth</u>, and <u>they make big holes in the ground</u>.
8. <u>The largest meteorite was found in Africa</u>, and <u>the second largest was found in Greenland</u>.
9. <u>People sometimes find meteorite holes</u>, but <u>the meteorites are usually gone</u>.

B. Write the complete predicate of each sentence. If the predicate is compound, write *compound*.

6. Everyone helped with the newspaper.
7. Juan sat and thought of ideas.
8. Elena revised and corrected articles.
9. Ms. Doyle stayed after school every day.
10. She explained things and answered questions.
11. Matt planned and designed the front page.
12. He arranged all the articles and pictures.
13. He pasted everything into place.
14. The newspaper surprised and pleased the other classes.
15. Everyone read and enjoyed it.

C. Write each sentence. Underline the compound predicate.

16. We stopped, rested, and talked.
17. The auditorium sparkled and shone.
18. The curtain opened and closed.
19. We danced and sang.
20. The audience cheered and clapped.

5 Compound Sentences
p. 39(

A. Write the sentences below. Then underline the two simple sentences in each.

1. We see stars and planets at night, and we see other bright lights, too.
2. Some lights are comets, and some are meteors.
3. Meteors are often seen, but comets are rare.
4. Comets are balls of frozen gas, and they orbit the sun.
5. Meteors are called shooting stars, and they travel fast.
6. Meteors burn up in space, or they fall to Earth as meteorites.
7. Sometimes very large meteorites hit Earth, and they make big holes in the ground.
8. The largest meteorite was found in Africa, and the second largest was found in Greenland.
9. People sometimes find meteorite holes, but the meteorites are usually gone.

Write *simple* or *compound* for each sentence.

10. Mercury is a small planet, and Jupiter is a large planet.
11. Jupiter is very far away, but you can often see it.
12. Mercury is nearest the sun, and Venus is second closest.
13. Each planet moves around the sun.
14. Mercury's year lasts 88 days, but Mars's year is 687 days.
15. The sun is a star, and it supplies heat for Earth.
16. Our sun and the other stars are giant balls of gas.
17. The sun is very bright, but it has some dark spots.
18. Scientists call these areas sunspots and study them closely.

Avoiding Run-on Sentences   *p. 398*

Write each sentence. Add a comma before the conjunction.

1. Flag Day was first officially celebrated in 1877 and it became a national holiday in 1916.
2. Before the Revolution colonists flew the British flag but later they had their own flag.
3. It was called the Grand Union and it had thirteen stripes with the British flag in the corner.
4. The Grand Union flag flew over Boston and it could be seen for miles.
5. After July 4, 1776, the colonists needed a new flag but they had trouble deciding on one.
6. Each colony had its own flag and each thought its flag was best.
7. Virginia's flag had a rattlesnake and it had the words "Don't Tread on Me."

Correct these run-on sentences. Write each as a compound sentence by adding a comma and a conjunction.

8. A flag was chosen on June 14, 1777 it was soon flown.
9. In 1814, Francis Scott Key wrote a poem about the flag he called it "The Star-Spangled Banner."
10. He saw a flag with fifteen stars it had fifteen stripes.
11. Stripes were added for new states the flag got too large.
12. Today's flag has fifty stars it has only thirteen stripes.

Extra Practice **441**

B. 10. compound
11. compound
12. compound
13. simple
14. compound
15. compound
16. simple
17. compound
18. simple

Avoiding Run-on Sentences
A. 1. . . . in 1877, and it . . .
2. . . . flag, but later . . .
3. . . . Grand Union, and it . . .
4. . . . over Boston, and it . . .
5. . . . new flag, but they . . .
6. . . . flag, and each . . .
7. . . . rattlesnake, and it . . .

B. 8. A flag was chosen on June 14, 1777, and it was soon flown.
9. In 1814, Francis Scott Key wrote a poem about the flag, and he called it "The Star-Spangled Banner."
10. He saw a flag with fifteen stars, and it had fifteen stripes.
11. Stripes were added for new states, and (or but) the flag got too large.
12. Today's flag has fifty stars, and (or but) it has only thirteen stripes.

Extra Practice and Challenge
For those students who need additional grammar practice have them refer to these pages. **The practice exercises progress in difficulty from Easy to Average. Practice A is Easy. Practice B is Average.** Difficult concepts requiring more practice have additional Exercises C and D at the Average level.
We do not recommend these exercises for students who have mastered the skill in the basic lesson. Those students should do the **Challenge** word puzzles on page 436.

Acknowledgments   continued from page ii.

Permissions: We wish to thank the following authors, publishers, agents, corporations, and individuals for their permission to reprint copyrighted materials. Page 24: Excerpt from *The Midnight Fox* by Betsy Byars. Copyright © 1968 by Betsy Byars. All rights reserved. Reprinted by permission of Viking Penguin, Inc., NY, NY, and Faber & Faber, Ltd., London. Page 80: Excerpt from ''Handicrafts'' by Patricia Fent Ross from *Mexico* © 1982 Courtesy of Gateway Press, Inc. Page 142: Excerpt from ''Paul Bunyan'' from *American Tall Tales* by Adrien Stoutenburg. Copyright © 1966 by Adrien Stoutenburg. Reprinted by permission of the publisher Viking Penguin, Inc., and Curtis Brown, Ltd. All rights reserved. Page 196: "The Littlest Sculptor" Copyright © 1986 Joan T. Zeier. Used with permission. Page 250: Excerpt from *Zeely* by Virginia Hamilton. Copyright © 1971 by Virginia Hamilton. Reprinted with permission of Macmillan Publishing Co. and McIntosh & Otis, Inc. Page 302: "The Big Blast" by Patricia Lauber. Reprinted by permission of Bradbury Press, an affiliate of Macmillan, Inc., from *Volcano, The Eruption and Healing of Mount St. Helens* by Patricia Lauber. Copyright © 1986 by Patricia Lauber. Page 356: "Definitions" from *The Forgetful Wishing Well* by X.J. Kennedy. Reprinted with permission of Margaret K. McElderry Books, an imprint of Macmillan Publishing Co. Copyright © 1985 by X.J. Kennedy. "What They Say" from *Who Would Marry a Mineral?* by Lillian Morrison. Copyright © 1978 by Lillian Morrison. Used by permission. Page 357: "Again and Again" plus illustration from *Flower, Moon, Snow* by Kazue Mizimura (Thomas Y. Crowell). Text copyright © 1977 by Kazue Mizimura. Reprinted by permission of Harper & Row, Publishers, Inc. The poem "Walking Past the School at Night" from *Cold Stars and Fireflies* by Barbara Juster Esbensen (Thomas Y. Crowell). Copyright © 1984 by Barbara Juster Esbensen. Page 358: "Ode to the Tomato" by Pablo Neruda. From *Selected Poems*. © 1972 by Dell Publishing Co. Used by permission of Delacorte Press/Seymour Lawrence. Page 362: "Direction" Alonzo Lopez from *The Whispering Wind* edited by Terry Alle Copyright © 1972 by the Institute of American Indian Ar Reprinted by permission of Doubleday, a division of Banta Doubleday, Dell Publishing Group, Inc. "Night," nine lir from "The Windy City" in *Slabs of the Sunburnt West* by C Sandburg. Copyright 1922 by Harcourt Brace Jovanovich, Ir Renewed 1950 by Carl Sandburg. Reprinted by permission Harcourt Brace Jovanovich, Inc. "River" by Lawrence Locke. 1981 by Lawrence Locke. Reprinted by permission of the a thor. Page 364: "The ragged phantom..." by Boncho. Fro *More Cricket Songs* Japanese haiku translated by Harry Beh Copyright © 1971 by Harry Behn. All rights reserved. Reprint by permission of Marian Reiner. "A river leaping..." Meisetsu. From *Cricket Songs* Japanese haiku translated Harry Behn. © 1964 by Harry Behn. All rights reserved. R printed by permission of Marian Reiner. Page 365: "All day gray rain..." From *Cricket Songs* Japanese haiku translated Harry Behn. © 1964 by Harry Behn. All rights reserved. R printed by permission of Marian Reiner. "Slanting, win rain..." by Buson. From *More Cricket Songs* Japanese hai translated by Harry Behn. Copyright © 1971 by Harry Behn. / rights reserved. Reprinted by permission of Marian Reiner. Pa 366: "Balloons!" From *Flashlight and Other Poems* by Jud Thurman. Copyright © 1976 by Judith Thurman. All rig reserved. Reprinted by permission of Marian Reiner for t author. "Garment" by Langston Hughes. © 1941 Harper & Bro Reprinted by permission of Harold Ober Associates. Page 40 "Two of a Kind" from *Headgear* by Ron Hirschi. Reprinted permission of The Putnam & Grosset Group. Text copyright 1986 by Ron Hirschi. Every effort has been made to locate t authors. If any errors have occurred, the publisher can be notifi and corrections will be made.

442

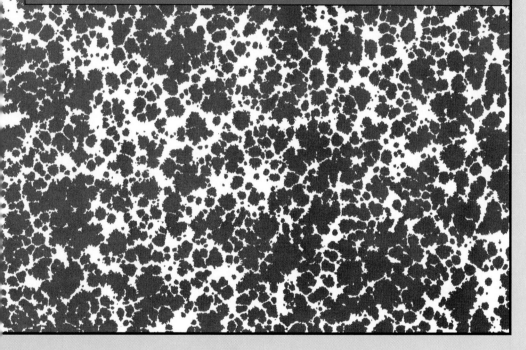

WRITER'S REFERENCE BOOK

Study Skills Lessons

Study Skills Lessons

Study Habits

1. **Listen in class.** Make sure that you understand exactly what your teacher wants you to do for homework. Write each homework assignment in a notebook.

2. **Have your homework materials ready.** You will need such items as textbooks, pens, pencils, erasers, rulers, and your notebook.

3. **Study in the same place every day.** Try to find a quiet and comfortable place where other people will not interrupt you. There should be good lighting, a comfortable chair, and a desk or table. Do not have the television or radio on while you are studying. The fewer distractions you have, the better you will study.

4. **Plan your study time.** Develop a daily study schedule. First decide on the best time of the day for studying. Then plan exactly when you will study each of your subjects. Also plan time for chores, or household tasks, and recreation. Use the study schedule below as a guide.

Study Schedule
3:30 to 4:00 P.M. — chores
4:00 to 5:00 P.M. — sports, play
5:00 to 5:30 P.M. — study science
5:30 to 6:00 P.M. — study math
6:00 to 7:00 P.M. — dinner and free time
7:00 to 7:30 P.M. — study English
7:30 to 9:00 P.M. — hobbies, reading, TV

5. **Set a goal or purpose each time you study.** Keep that goal in mind while you study. If you do, you will concentrate better.

Practice

Answer the following questions about study habits.
Answers will vary.

1. Which of the study tips above would most help you improve your study habits? Why?
2. Write a study schedule that would help you use your time wisely.

Study Skills Lessons

OBJECTIVES
To develop and practice good study habits

ASSIGNMENT GUIDE
BASIC   Practice A
          Practice B
ADVANCED   Practice C

TEACHING OPTIONS

Getting Started
Oral Language Have students review the suggestions given in the lesson. Then invite them to share their own experiences. Students may describe how good study habits make a difference in their concentration and in their being disciplined about studying. Some students may indicate that radio or television can be distracting.

Class Enrichment
A Cooperative Activity Have students work in pairs to create personalized study schedules using the one shown here as a model. Ask students to write their schedules in duplicate, in order to make a file of class study schedules. You may wish to encourage students to write special study tips on the back of their index cards.

Challenge
An Independent Extension Have students prepare an interview with someone whose work habits they admire, such as a relative, a neighbor, or a teacher. Ask students to think about what they could ask this person and write several questions that relate to study habits. Encourage students to list ideas for follow-up questions as well. You may wish to have students conduct the interviews and share important anecdotal information with the class.

Test-Taking Tips

1. **Be prepared.** Have several sharp pencils and an eraser.

2. **Read or listen to the directions carefully.** Be sure you know what you are to do and where and how you are to mark your answers.

3. **Answer the easy questions first.** Quickly read all the questions on the page. Then go back to the beginning and answer the questions you are sure you know.

4. **Next, try to answer the questions you are not sure you know.** You may have a choice of answers. If so, narrow your choice. First eliminate all the answers you know are wrong. Try to narrow your selection to two answers. Then mark the answer you think is right.

5. **Answer the hardest questions last.** If you can't answer a question at all, don't waste time worrying about it. Skip the question and go on to the next.

6. **Think about analogy questions.** Some tests you take may include analogy questions. An analogy is a way of showing relationships between things. To complete an analogy question, figure out the relationship betwen the first two items. Then complete the analogy so that the second pair has the same relationship.

   EXAMPLE: cat : kitten :: bear : cub

7. **Plan your time.** Don't spend too much time on just one question. Check your watch or a clock from time to time as you take the test.

8. **Check your answers when you have finished.** Make sure you have marked your answers correctly. Unless you're sure you made a mistake, you probably should not change an answer.

Practice

1. How can you best prepare for a test?
   Answers will vary.
2. In what order should you answer the questions on a test?
   Easy questions first, hardest questions last.
3. What should you do when you have answered all the questions?
   Check your answers.

STUDY SKILLS: Taking Test   **445**

Study Skills Lessons

OBJECTIVES
To develop and use test-taking skills

ASSIGNMENT GUIDE
BASIC   Practice A
⬇   Practice B
ADVANCED   Practice C

All should do the Apply activity.

TEACHING OPTIONS

Getting Started
Oral Language   Have students share how they feel before taking a test. Most students will mention feeling somewhat nervous. Invite students to describe what they feel is a good remedy for the testing jitters. They may mention that being well prepared for a test is the best remedy. You may wish to add that practice in taking tests and using special formats helps too.

Class Enrichment
A Cooperative Activity Have students work in small groups to create a series of cartoons or comic strips showing how to and how not to prepare for and take a test. Encourage them to be humorous. When students finished, post the cartoons on the bulletin board for the class to enjoy.

Challenge
An Independent Extension Have students prepare a brief test of at least ten analogies. Invite students to include examples of as many different relationships as they can. You may wish to list a few on the chalkboard, such as whole:part, part:whole; user:tool; parent:child; class membership (genus:species); and location (top:bottom). You may also wish to have students exchange papers with a partner to check each analogy for correctness.

Study Skills Lessons

OBJECTIVES
To become familiar with the use and format of the title page, copyright page, table of contents, and index of a book

ASSIGNMENT GUIDE
BASIC   Practice A
             Practice B
ADVANCED Practice C

TEACHING OPTIONS

Getting Started
Oral Language Ask students to tell on which page Unit Six begins in this book. Ask how the page number was found. If a student answers that he or she turned pages to find out, ask if there is an easier way (refer to the table of contents). Ask where they would look to find all the pages on which adjectives are explained *(the index)*.

Class Enrichment
A Cooperative Activity Write the following form on the chalkboard. Have students work with a partner to copy and complete it using any of their textbooks.
Title:
Author:
Publisher:
Date of Publication:
Organization of Book (Units?, Lessons?):
Number of Units, Lessons:
Number of pages in index:
Special features (glossary, etc.):

Challenge
An Independent Extension Have students create a test on using the parts of a book. Tell them to use this textbook to find questions a partner must answer. Suggest that they write the correct answers on a separate sheet of paper.

446

Parts of a Book

Certain parts of a book give important information about the book. These parts have special names.

In the front of the book is the **title page**. It shows the title, author, and publisher of the book. The **copyright page** is on the back of the title page. It tells the year in which the book was published. The copyright date can help to tell you how up-to-date the facts in the book are.

The **table of contents** usually comes next. It shows the major divisions of the book and lists each chapter. Use the table of contents to find out what broad topics a book covers.

Nonfiction books often have an **index** at the back. It alphabetically lists the topics covered in the book. Use the index to see if a book has the specific information you need.

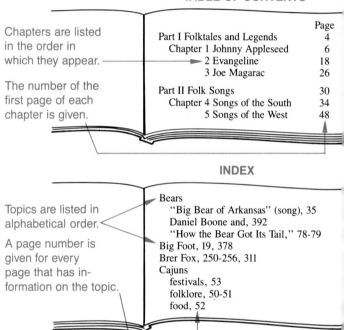

TABLE OF CONTENTS

Chapters are listed in the order in which they appear.

The number of the first page of each chapter is given.

	Page
Part I Folktales and Legends	4
Chapter 1 Johnny Appleseed	6
2 Evangeline	18
3 Joe Magarac	26
Part II Folk Songs	30
Chapter 4 Songs of the South	34
5 Songs of the West	48

INDEX

Topics are listed in alphabetical order.

A page number is given for every page that has information on the topic.

Bears
  "Big Bear of Arkansas" (song), 35
  Daniel Boone and, 392
  "How the Bear Got Its Tail," 78-79
Big Foot, 19, 378
Brer Fox, 250-256, 311
Cajuns
  festivals, 53
  folklore, 50-51
  food, 52

Study Skills Lessons

Practice

. Tell whether you would use the title page, copyright page, table of contents, or index to answer each of these questions about a book. Write each answer.

   1. Who is the author?   title page

   2. Does the book have any information on the folklore of Georgia?   index or table of contents

   3. On what page does Chapter 2 begin?   table of contents

   4. How up-to-date is the information in the book? copyright page

   5. Which pages tell about Barbara Frietchie?   index

. Use the sample table of contents and index on the opposite page to answer the following questions.

   6. How is the book organized? divided into parts; chapters in each part

   7. In which chapter would you expect to find cowboy songs?   Chapter 5

   8. Which pages tell about the folklore of the Cajuns?   pages 50–51

   9. Which page tells about Daniel Boone and bears? page 392

  10. On which pages would you look to find out who wrote tales about Brer Fox? pages 250–256, 311

. Use the copyright page, table of contents, and index of this book to answer the following questions.

  11. When was this book published? 1990

  12. On what page does the Dictionary of Knowledge begin? page 456

  13. In which unit will you learn about prepositions? unit 7

  14. On which pages will you find information on prefixes? pages 134–135

  15. On which pages will you find information about using an encyclopedia?

STUDY SKILLS: Parts of a Book   **447**

OBJECTIVES

To become familiar with library catalog cards: title, author, and subject

To recognize shelving arrangements for books of fiction and nonfiction

ASSIGNMENT GUIDE

BASIC   Practice A

              Practice B

ADVANCED   Practice C

TEACHING OPTIONS

Getting Started

Oral Language Ask students how they would go about finding a book in the library on making kites. Accept *ask the librarian* as an answer, but then ask if there is a way they could find a listing of books on kites. Try to elicit *by looking in the card catalog.*

Class Enrichment

A Cooperative Activity Bring to class nine library books on different subjects. Divide the class into three groups. Have each group prepare title, author, and subject cards for three of the books. Suggest that they use the sample catalog cards in the lesson as models. Tell students that the call number can be found on the spine of the book or on the book pocket in the front or back of the book. Have volunteers from each group write the information on the chalkboard.

Challenge

An Independent Extension Have each student identify a subject area they are interested in, such as *dinosaurs*. Tell them to use a library card catalog or computer listing to find three nonfiction titles on their subject. Have them copy the information they find for a class subject and title reference box.

Using the Library

Once you have chosen a topic for a report, where can you find information about it? For information on most topics, the first place to look is in the library. In the library, books are divided into two main categories; fiction and nonfiction. Fiction books contain made-up stories. They are arranged alphabetically by the author's last name. Nonfiction books are books that give facts. They are arranged numerically. Each nonfiction book has a number printed on its spine. This is the **call number** of the book. The books are numbered in such a way that books about the same subject are grouped together.

When you want to find a book in the library, check the card catalog or computer listing. These sources list every book in the library by its title, its author, and its subject. Catalog cards are arranged in alphabetical order. Study the information given on each kind of card.

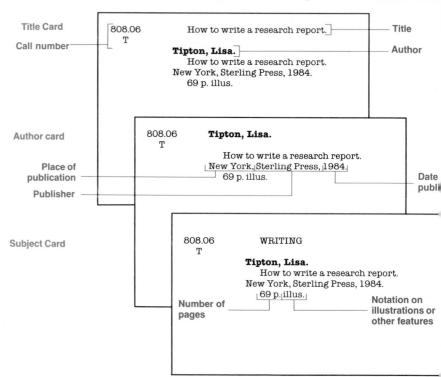

Practice

. Use the catalog cards on the opposite page to answer these questions.

1. What is the title of the book listed?   How to Write a Research Report

2. Who is the author?   Lisa Tipton

3. Where and when was the book published? New York, 1984

4. Is this book illustrated?   Yes

5. What is the book's call number?   808.06 T

. Write the word or words you would look up in the card catalog or computer listing to find the following items.

6. a book by Margery Sharp   Sharp, Margery

7. the call number of the book *Westward by Canal*   Westward by Canal

8. the title of a book about eating good foods   foods, or diet, or nutrition

9. the call numbers of books about volcanoes Volcanoes

10. the title of a book by P.L. Travers   Travers, P.L.

. Write *title, author,* or *subject* to tell what kind of catalog card you would use to answer each of these questions.

11. Who wrote *Kingdom of the Sun*?   title

12. What children's book did Ian Fleming write?   author

13. Does the library have any books about termites?   subject

14. Did Isaac Asimov write any novels?   author

15. Did the same author write *This is the Texas Panhandle* and *A Tree Grows in Brooklyn*?   title

STUDY SKILLS: Using the Library   **449**

Study Skills Lessons

TEACHING OPTIONS

Getting Started

Oral Language Arrange a small display of reference materials—an atlas, an almanac, and several periodicals, including at least one magazine and one newspaper. Then name three facts about your state, such as the capital, the population, and a recent event. Encourage volunteers to name the sources in which these facts could be found. Accept any reasonable answer. you may wish to suggest that students examine each of the reference materials.

Class Enrichment

A Cooperative Activity Have each student write one question they can find an answer to in an atlas, an almanac, or a recent periodical. Have students exchange slips with a partner and then write the answers to the questions on the slip, along with the title of the reference book and the page on which the answer was found. Have students share the questions and answers with the whole class.

Challenge

An Independent Extension Have students work together to create a set of questions about their state, such as *What is the state flower? How far is my home town from the capital city?* Have them decide for each question what reference they must use to find the information: an atlas, an almanac, or a periodical. Then you may wish to have them each take a question and research the answer.

450

Using Reference Materials

Libraries contain many kinds of reference materials besides encyclopedias. By using different kinds of reference materials, you can gather a wide variety of information on a topic.

Atlas   An **atlas** is a book of maps. A **key**, or **legend**, tells us what the symbols mean. A **physical map** gives facts about the natural surface of the earth. It shows rivers, mountains, and seas. A **political map** shows such items as cities and boundaries between countries. The map of Alaska below has both physical and political features. Notice in the map key, labeled *ALASKA*, that different colors stand for different elevations, or heights above sea level.

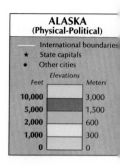

ALASKA
(Physical-Political)

— International boundaries
★ State capitals
• Other cities

Elevations

Feet		Meters
10,000		3,000
5,000		1,500
2,000		600
1,000		300
0		0

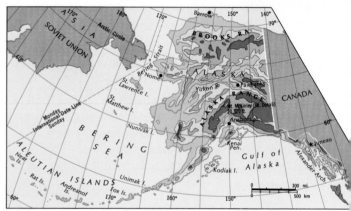

Practice

A. Use the map of Alaska above to answer the following question.

1. What is the capital of Alaska? Juneau
2. What country borders Alaska on the east? Canada
3. At about what elevation are most of the Aleutian Islands? 0–30 meters or 0–1000 feet
4. What is the name of the river that is shown on this map of Alaska? Yukon River
5. What is the highest peak in the Alaska Range? Mount McKinley

450   STUDY SKILLS: Atlas, Almanac, and Other Reference Materials

Almanac

An almanac specializes in up-to-date information and is usually published every year. The information in an almanac is often given in the form of a chart or table. An almanac does not devote as much space to background information as an encyclopedia does.

High Peaks in United States, Canada, Mexico

Name	Place	Feet	Name	Place	Feet
McKinley	Alas	20,320	South Buttress	Alas	15,885
Logan	Can	19,850	Wood	Can	15,885
Citlaltepec (Orizaba)	Mexico	18,700	Vancouver	Alas-Can	15,700
St. Elias	Alas-Can	18,008	Churchill	Alas	15,638
Popocatepetl	Mexico	17,400	Fairweather	Alas-Can	15,300
Foraker	Alas	17,400	Zinantecatl (Toluca)	Mexico	15,016
Iztacchuatl	Mexico	17,343	Hubbard	Alas-Can	15,015
Lucania	Can	17,147	Bear	Alas	14,831
King	Can	16,971	Walsh	Can	14,780
Steele	Can	16,644	East Buttress	Alas	14,730
Bona	Alas	16,550	Matlalcueyetl	Mexico	14,636
Blackburn	Alas	16,390	Hunter	Alas	14,573
Kennedy	Alas	16,286	Alverstone	Alas-Can	14,565
Sanford	Alas	16,237	Browne Tower	Alas	14,530

Other Reference Materials

Newspapers and magazines are periodicals. You can find them in libraries. Many libraries also have records, films, and videotapes.

Practice

B. Use the almanac entry above to answer these questions.

6. In what state is Mount Kennedy located? *Alaska*

7. What is the highest peak in the United States? *Mount McKinley*

8. Which mountain is higher—Mount Blackburn or Mount Steele? *Mount Steele*

C. Decide where you would look for answers to the questions below. Write *atlas, almanac,* or *periodical* for each.

9. Where is Lake Tahoe? *atlas*

10. What cities were hit by last month's hurricane? *periodical*

11. Is Switzerland a coastal country? *atlas*

12. Who won gold medals in the most recent Olympic Games? *almanac*

13. What is the tallest building in the United States? *almanac*

STUDY SKILLS: Atlas, Almanac, and Other Reference Materials **451**

TEACHING OPTIONS

Getting Started
Oral Language Ask students why words are sometimes put in alphabetical order. (It makes them easier to find.) Remind them that words in the dictionary are organized this way. Introduce the term *guide words*. Write this example on the chalkboard: *car—catch.* Have students name some words that would appear between these two in a dictionary (e.g., *care, carry, case*).

Class Enrichment
A Cooperative Activity Have students work in groups. Have one student act as the leader, and find a word in a dictionary that is unfamiliar to the rest of the group. Have the leader pronounce and spell the word. Then have everyone in the group write a definition, including the leader, who writes the correct one. Ask the leader to collect the definitions and read any that are correct. Encourage students who guess the correct definition to choose another unfamiliar word.

Challenge
An Independent Extension Have students use a dictionary to find answers to these questions.

1. How many means are there for *familiar?* **Answers will vary.**
2. How many syllables does *familiar* have? **3**
3. What are the example sentences for *familiar?* **Answers will vary.**
4. What part of speech is *familiar?* **adjective**

452

Using a Dictionary

A dictionary contains thousands of words in alphabetical order. Each word that is defined is called an **entry word**. How can you find the word you want? Luckily, there are some shortcuts to help you.

The first shortcut is to think of the dictionary in three parts: the front, *a–g;* the middle, *h–p;* and the back, *q–z.*

> Front: a, b, c, d, e, f, g
> Middle: h, i, j, k, l, m, n, o, p
> Back: q, r, s, t, u, v, w, x, y, z

When you need to look up a word, decide in which part of the dictionary it appears. Then open to that part, trying to open to the first letter of the word you want.

The second shortcut is to use the guide words. The **guide words** show the first and last entry words on the page. All the other entry words on the page fall between the guide words in alphabetical order.

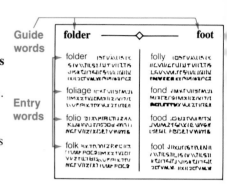

Practice

A. Write each word. Then write *front, middle,* or *back* to show in which part of a dictionary it appears.

1. tradition **back**
2. ballot **front**
3. fantasy **front**
4. rhyme **back**
5. hive **middle**
6. mole **middle**
7. suburb **back**
8. ancient **front**
9. primitive
10. culture
11. villain
12. hero

B. Follow the directions below. Write the words you choose in alphabetical order.   Answers will vary.

> **Hint:** Remember that words are put into alphabetical order by the first letter that is different.
>
> **game, sport**   **rate, rent**
> **chin, chunk**   **blue, blush**

13. Write five words that name animals.
14. Write the first names of five classmates.
15. Write five words that name articles of clothing.

C. Guide words for imaginary dictionary pages 218–221 are shown at the right. Write words **16–27**. Then write the page number for each entry word.

bunt	**218**	burro		burrow	**219**	butterfly
buttermilk	**220**	cabbage		cabin	**221**	calcium

16. bushel 219   **20.** buttercup 219   **24.** burnt 218
17. bygone 220   **21.** cafeteria 221   **25.** cabbage 220
18. cactus 221   **22.** cadet 221   **26.** caboose 221
19. burlap 218   **23.** buzzard 220   **27.** burr 218

D. Write each set of guide words below. After each set, write three words that could be entry words on that page. You may use a dictionary if you wish.   Answers will vary.

28. guide words: chant—clash
29. guide words: plum—point
30. guide words: royal—sack

E. Write five words from the Dictionary of Knowledge, which begins on page 456. Scramble the alphabetical order of the words. Then exchange papers with a classmate. See how quickly you can find each other's words. Repeat this activity with other words, and try to improve your time.   Answers will vary.

Study Skills Lessons

The answers to all the questions at the right can be found in one book, the dictionary. Of all reference books, the dictionary is probably the most useful. To find out why, study the entry below. It is from the Dictionary of Knowledge.

How is chasm pronounced?

Do you write on stationary or stationery?

Did I spell yield right?

What does leonine mea[n]

Pronunciation · Part of Speech

Entry word — **cam•ou•flage** (kam′ə fläzh) *n.* **1.** the act of hiding soldiers and things from an enemy by making them blend in with the landscape. *The soldiers used a camouflage of twigs and leaves in the jungle.* **2.** a disguise of this kind in nature, as the green color of insects that live on leaves. —*v.* **camouflaged, camouflaging.** to hide by blending in. *The insect's green color camouflages it from enemies.* [from Italian *camuffare* to disguise] — *Syn.* **disguise.**

— Meanings

Example sentence

— Verb forms

— Etymology
— Synonym

Entry word   This shows how to spell the word. The dots between syllables show how to divide it at the end of a line of writing.

Pronunciation   This tells how to say the word. It is given in symbols that stand for certain sounds. For example, the symbol ä stands for the vowel sound heard in *father* and *march*. The Pronunciation Key on page 456 tells the sound for each symbol.

Part of speech   This label is abbreviated, such as *v.* for *verb*.

Meaning   The different meanings of the word are numbered.

Example sentence   This helps to make a meaning clear.

Verb forms or plural forms   These are shown when the spelling of the base word changes.

Etymology   This is a word history, and it appears in brackets.

Synonym   This is a word that has a meaning similar to that of the entry word. Its label is abbreviated *Syn.*

Practice

. Write the answer to each question. Use the dictionary entry on page 454.

31. How many syllables does the entry word contain? 3
32. How many meanings are given for *camouflage* as a noun? 2
33. How many meanings are given for *camouflage* as a verb? 1
34. How many example sentences are included in the entry? 2

. Use the dictionary entries below for questions **35–38**.

buoy (bo͞i) *n.* **1.** a floating object kept in a certain place on the water to show safe areas or dangerous areas. **2.** a life buoy; something used to keep a person afloat in the water.

leg•end (lej′ ənd) *n.* **1.** a story handed down through the years, which many people have believed. **2.** such stories as a group. **3.** what is written on a coin or medal. *The legend on a dime is "IN GOD WE TRUST."* **4.** a remarkable person, much talked about while still alive.

35. What is the number of the meaning that *buoy* has in the following sentence? *Throw a buoy to the weakest swimmer.* 2
36. For which meaning of *legend* could the following be an example sentence? *Hank Aaron is a baseball legend.* 4
37. Which entry word rhymes with *annoy*? buoy
38. What part of speech is each entry word? noun

H. Use the Dictionary of Knowledge to answer the questions below.

39. What does a geologist study? the earth's crust
40. Which word is spelled incorrectly, and how should it be spelled: *creditable, ebony, laquer, repellent*? laquer; lacquer
41. What is pumice used for? polishing, smoothing, or cleaning
42. What does the word *quiver* mean in the following sentence? *Is the quiver made of leather*? a case for holding arrows

. Use the Dictionary of Knowledge to write a word quiz for your classmates. Write three questions like those in **Practice H**. Then see who can answer the questions in the shortest time. Answers will vary.

STUDY SKILLS: Dictionary **455**

Dictionary of Knowledge

This Dictionary of Knowledge has two kinds of entries, **word entries** and **encyclopedic entries.** Many of the word entries in this dictionary are taken from the literature pieces found throughout this book. You might use these entries to help you understand the meanings of words. You will use the encyclopedic entries in two ''Apply'' sections in each unit.

Word Entries ✦ These entries are just like the ones found in the ordinary dictionaries you are familiar with. Each entry includes such elements as pronunciation respellings, definitions, and example sentences.

Encyclopedic Entries ✦ These entries resemble encyclopedia articles. Each entry provides interesting information about a particular topic or person.

Abbreviations Used in this Dictionary			
adj.	adjective	pl.	plural
adv.	adverb	prep.	preposition
Ant.	Antonym	pron.	pronoun
conj.	conjunction	Syn.	Synonym
n.	noun	v.	verb

Full pronunciation key* The pronunciation of each word is shown just after the word, in this way:
abbreviate (ə brē′ vē āt).

The letters and signs used are pronounced as in the words below.

The mark ′ is placed after a syllable with a primary or heavy accent as in the example above.

The mark ′ after a syllable shows a secondary or lighter accent, as in **abbreviation** (ə brē′vē ā′shən).

SYMBOL	KEY WORDS	SYMBOL	KEY WORDS	SYMBOL	KEY WORDS	SYMBOL	KEY WORDS
a	ask, fat	͞oo	look, pull	b	bed, dub	v	vat, have
ā	ape, date	͞o͞o	ooze, tool	d	did, had	w	will, always
ä	car, father	yoo	unite, cure	f	fall, off	y	yet, yard
		yo͞o	cute, few	g	get, dog	z	zebra, haze
e	elf, ten	ou	out, crowd	h	he, ahead		
er	berry, care			j	joy, jump	ch	chin, arch
ē	even, meet	u	up, cut	k	kill, bake	ṅg	ring, singer
		ʉr	fur, fern	l	let, ball	sh	she, dash
i	is, hit			m	met, trim	th	thin, truth
ir	mirror, here	ə	a in ago	n	not, ton	*th*	then, father
ī	ice, fire		e in agent	p	put, tap	zh	s in pleasure
			e in father	r	red, dear		
o	lot, pond		i in unity	s	sell, pass	′	as in (ā′b'l)
ō	open, go		o in collect	t	top, hat		
ô	law, horn		u in focus				
oi	oil, point						

*Pronunciation key adapted from *Webster's New World Dictionary; Basic School Edition.*
Copyright © 1983 by Simon & Schuster, Inc. Reprinted by permission.

——————— A ———————

Ad·ams, An·sel (ad′əmz, an′səl) 1902–1984

Ansel Adams was an American photographer. He took pictures of the wilderness areas of the West. He loved nature, and he was an active conservationist.

Adams believed in a straight style of photography. His photographs are simple and direct. Some photographers believe in a misty, out-of-focus style. Adams took detailed, sharply focused photographs.

Most of Adams's photographs are of landscapes. His pictures feature rivers, mountains, and forests. The pictures are quite beautiful.

Adams helped establish the Department of Photography at New York's Museum of Modern Art. He also founded a photography department at the California School of Fine Arts. It was the first such department of study at any college in the United States. Adams also wrote several books on photography.

——————— B ———————

Boone, Dan·iel (bo͞on, dan′yəl) 1734–1820

Daniel Boone was a real-life American hero. He explored unknown regions of Kentucky. He marked trails and led settlers there. He blazed the Wilderness Road, which became the main roadway for families moving west. Boone was the most famous pioneer of the Colonial period.

Boone was captured by Native Americans several times. The Shawnee developed such respect for him that they adopted him into their tribe. Boone was made a full-fledged Shawnee brave. He pretended to love his life with the Shawnee. He finally escaped to warn his friends in Boonesborough that the Shawnee were about to attack them. By the time of his death, Daniel Boone had become one of the most famous and well-respected men in American history.

——————— C ———————

cam·ou·flage (kam′ə fläzh) *n.* **1.** the act of hiding soldiers and things from an enemy by making them blend in with the landscape. *The soldiers used a camouflage of twigs and leaves in the jungle.* **2.** a disguise of this kind in nature, as the green color of insects that live on leaves. — *v.* **camouflaged, camouflaging.** to hide by blending in. *The insect's green color camouflages it from enemies.* [from Italian *camuffare* to disguise] — *Syn.* **disguise.**

a fat	**er** care	**ī** bite, fire	**oi** oil	**u** up	**th** thin	ə = a *in* ago
ā ape	**ē** even	**o** lot	**o͝o** look	**ur** fur	***th*** then	e *in* agent
ä car, father	**i** hit	**ō** go	**o͞o** tool	**ch** chin	**zh** leisure	i *in* unity
e ten	**ir** here	**ô** law, horn	**ou** out	**sh** she	**ng̍** ring	o *in* collect
						u *in* focus

Car•ver, George Wash•ing•ton   (kär′vər, jôrj wôsh′iñg tən *or* wosh′iñg tən) 1864–1943

George Washington Carver was an American scientist who developed products from different plants, such as sweet potatoes and pecans. He is best known for his work with peanuts. Carver produced more than three hundred products, including soap and ink, from this one crop. Carver was born in Missouri of slave parents. As a youngster, he always showed interest in plants. He graduated from Iowa State College in 1894 and became an assistant botanist there. In 1896, Carver became an instructor at Tuskegee

Portrait of George Washington Carver, Mary Randolph Witmer. 1935 National Portrait Gallery, Smithsonian Institution. Washington, D.C.

Institute in Alabama. He spent the rest of his life there, later becoming the head of the agricultural department. Carver did a lot of research on soil conservation and on ways to grow bigger and better crops. He wrote much helpful material for farmers. Carver received many awards for his valuable contributions to science.

col•o•niz•er   (kol′ə nīz ′ər) *n.* **1.** a person or group of persons that settles in a distant land and establishes a colony or settlement. *The English were colonizers of America.* **2.** a group of animals or plants that begins to live or grow in an area. *Tiny flowers were colonizers of the mountain slope.*

cred•it•a•ble   (kred′it ə b′l) *adj.* deserving praise or credit for something. *Sam did a creditable job on his report.*—*syn.* **honorable.**—**creditably** *adv.*

Crock•ett, Da•vy   (krok′it, dā′vē) 1786–1836

Few frontiersmen in America were ever as famous as Davy Crockett. He was an expert marksman, a member of Congress, a scout, a humorist, and a real hero.

Crockett started school at age thirteen. His education lasted only four days. He got into a

fight with another student and ran away for thre years to avoid punishment.

As a humorist, Crockett told many tall tales about himself. Writers exaggerated Crockett's stories even more. Because of this, Crockett became a famous folk hero during his lifetime. He settled in a wild area of Tennessee where he claimed to have killed 105 bears in seven months. Later he became a Tennessee congressman.

Davy Crockett is best known for trying to defend the Alamo against Mexican troops in 1836, during the war for Texas independence. All of the defenders of the San Antonio missior including Crockett, were killed during that famous battle. The name Davy Crockett remain one of the first names in American folklore.

Portrait of David Crockett, William Henry Huddle (painted 1889) State Preservation Board, Texas State Capitol. Photo courtesy of

———— D ————

de•mol•ish   (di mol′ish) *v.* to tear down; to smash or ruin. *The wrecking crew demolished the old building.* [from Latin *de-* down + *moliri* to build, to construct] — *Syn.* **destroy.** — *Ant.* **construct.**

———— E ————

eb•on•y   (eb′ə nē) *n.* the black, hard wood of certain tropical trees. — *adj.* **1.** made of ebony. **2.** black or dark. *The ebony statue gleamed in the display case.*

Dictionary of Knowledge

—————— **G** ——————

e·ol·o·gist (jē ol′ə jist) *n.* one who studies the earth's crust and the ways in which its layers were formed. *The geologist gave a speech about rocks and fossils.*

ey·ser (gī′zər)
A geyser is a spring that shoots hot water with great force. Among the most famous geysers is Old Faithful, in Yellowstone National Park.

Geysers are formed deep below the earth's surface. Cold water seeps into a channel until it reaches very hot rocks. The water is heated by the rocks. It cannot boil, however, because of the weight of other water on it. The heat at the bottom of the channel continues to rise, and steam begins to form. A small amount of water bubbles over the earth's surface, leaving more room for deep water to turn into steam. Suddenly the water at the bottom expands and forces out the rest of the steam in an explosion.

In some ways, geysers are similar to volcanoes. They both shoot forth with explosive force. Volcanoes, however, shoot molten rock; geysers shoot water with mineral matter in it. Volcanoes and geysers both usually erupt at irregular time periods. Old Faithful is an exception to this. It erupts about once in every sixty-five minutes.

gourd (gôrd *or* goord) *n.* **1.** a vine with large fruit containing many seeds. *Gourds and pumpkins belong to the same family of plants.* **2.** the fruit of this vine, not fit for eating but often dried and used for cups, bowls, and decorations. *The basket filled with gourds makes a charming decoration.*

—————— **H** ——————

Ham·il·ton, Vir·gin·ia (ham′ əl t′n, vər jin′yə) 1936–
Virginia Hamilton is an American writer of children's books. The subjects of her books reflect the dignity of the black American heritage.

Hamilton has won several important awards in children's literature. She won the Newbery Medal and the National Book Award for the book *M.C. Higgins, the Great,* published in 1974. This is a story about a mountain family.
Hamilton was born in Yellow Springs, Ohio. Some of her other books are *Zeely, The House of Dies Drear, The Time-Ago Tales of Jahdu,* and *The Planet of Junior Brown.*

hide¹ (hīd) *v.* **hid, hidden** or **hid, hiding. 1.** to keep or put out of sight. **2.** to keep others from knowing about. *He tried to hide the birthday present in the closet.* — *Syn.* **conceal.**

hide² (hīd) *n.* the skin of an animal, either raw or tanned. *Some belts and shoes are made from the hides of animals.*

							ə = a *in* ago
a fat	**er** care	**ī** bite, fire	**oi** oil	**u** up	**th** thin		e *in* agent
ā ape	**ē** even	**o** lot	**oo** look	**ur** fur	**th** then		i *in* unity
ä car, father	**i** hit	**ō** go	**oo** tool	**ch** chin	**zh** leisure		o *in* collect
e ten	**ir** here	**ô** law, horn	**ou** out	**sh** she	**ŋ** ring		u *in* focus

---
I
---

in•dig•nant   (in dig′ nənt) *adj.* angry about something that seems unfair or mean. *She was indignant when he criticized her work.* [from Latin *in-* not + *dignari* to deem worthy]—*Syn.* **angry. —indignantly** *adv.*

K

Ken•ne•dy, X.J.   (ken′ə dē, eks jā) 1929–
   X.J. Kennedy is a poet and writer. Many of his works were written for children. Kennedy has won several awards for his writing. He has also taught English at numerous colleges and universities.

   Kennedy was born in Dover, New Jersey. His real name is Joseph Charles Kennedy. He chose the initial *X* so he would not be confused with other well-known Kennedys.
   Kennedy became seriously interested in writing during childhood. He has not stopped writing since then. Among his publications for children are a collection of poetry called *The Phantom Ice Cream Man* and a novel named *The Owlstone Crown.* Here is one of his poems.

Exploding Gravy
My mother's big green gravy boat
Once thought he was a navy boat.

I poured him over my mashed potatoes
And out swam seven swift torpedoes.

Torpedoes whizzed and whirred, and—WHAM!
One bumped smack into my hunk of ham

And blew up with an awful roar,
Flinging my carrots on the floor.

Exploding gravy! That's so silly!
Now all I ever eat is chili.

L
---

lac•quer   (lak′ər) *n.* a varnish made of shellac and other substances. **2.** a natural varnish obtained from certain trees in Asia. — *v.* to coat with lacquer. *We lacquered the table to give it a waterproof finish.*

Lew•is, Mer•i•weth•er   (loo′ is, mer′ē we*th*′ər) 1774–1809 **and Clark, Wil•liam**   (klärk, wil′yəm) 1770–1838
   Together, Meriwether Lewis and William Clark explored the northwestern wilderness of America during the early nineteenth century. The most important result of their work was that the United States was able to claim the Oregon region for itself.
   Lewis was a private secretary to President Thomas Jefferson, who commissioned him to lead the expedition. Lewis had been an army captain and seemed a good choice for the hard job. The expedition, which included about forty-five persons, was filled with many great adventures. Lewis spent a lot of time talking with Native Americans and learning about their lives. On the return journey, Lewis took part of the group down the Marias River. Clark took the other part down the Yellowstone River. Later on, Lewis became governor of the Louisiana Territory.

Lewis and Clark at Three Forks (Detail), E.S. Paxson, Completed 1912 Courtesy of the Montana Historical Society

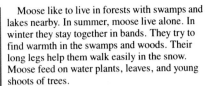

Before the expedition, Clark had been a retired soldier. He rejoined the army to go west with Lewis, as the second in command. Clark trained men for the dangerous journey. He was a fine mapmaker and drew routes for the expedition. He also drew the animals he saw along the way. After the expedition, Clark became superintendent of Indian affairs and governor of the Missouri Territory.

─────────── **M** ───────────

mag•ma (mag′mə) *n.* **1.** molten rock deep in the earth from which igneous rock is formed. *The magma inside a volcano is extremely hot.* **2.** a pasty mixture of mineral or organic matter.

mire (mīr) *n.* **1.** an area of wet, soft ground; a bog. **2.** deep mud. *The rock sank in the mire.* —*v.* **mired, miring.** to sink or get sunk in mire. *The animal was mired in the swamp.*—*Syn.* **swamp.**

moose (mo͞os)

The moose is the largest member of the deer family. The animal lives in most of the northern parts of the world. The moose has long legs and high, humplike shoulders. It also has an unusual hair-covered growth, called a bell, under its throat. It has heavy, flat antlers. Each year the moose sheds its antlers and grows new ones. It polishes these great weapons against trees.

Moose like to live in forests with swamps and lakes nearby. In summer, moose live alone. In winter they stay together in bands. They try to find warmth in the swamps and woods. Their long legs help them walk easily in the snow. Moose feed on water plants, leaves, and young shoots of trees.

At one time, hunters almost destroyed the entire moose population of our country. Today, moose are protected by law.

─────────── **N** ───────────

name•sake (nām′sāk) *n.* one that has the same name as another; especially, one named after another. *Jeff is my uncle's namesake.*

─────────── **O** ───────────

o•blige (ə blīj′) *v.* **obliged, obliging.** **1.** to force to do something because the law, conscience, or something else demands it. **2.** to make feel as if something is owed because of a favor or kindness received. *I am obliged to return the favor.* **3.** to do a favor for. *I'll oblige you and rake the leaves.* [from Latin *obligare* to bind] —*Syn.* **force.**

ob•long (ob′lông) *adj.* different from a square or circular form through elongation. *That long, rounded swimming pool is oblong in shape.* —*n.* an oblong figure.

om•i•nous (om′ə nəs) *adj.* threatening, like a bad sign or omen. *There were ominous clouds overhead.* [from Latin *ominiosus*] — **ominously** *adv.*

─────────── **P** ───────────

pot•ter•y (pot′ər ē)

Pottery is a kind of ware made from baked clay. Some pottery is very valuable and unique. Some of it is inexpensive. Pottery can be made in a factory or by a potter at home.

There are three main kinds of pottery. One kind, earthenware, is made mostly from mixed

a fat	er care	ī bite, fire	oi oil	u up	th thin	ə = a *in* ago
ā ape	ē even	o lot	o͝o look	ur fur	th then	e *in* agent
ä car, father	i hit	ō go	o͞o tool	ch chin	zh leisure	i *in* unity
e ten	ir here	ô law, horn	ou out	sh she	ŋ ring	o *in* collect
						u *in* focus

earthenware clays. It usually has colorful glazes, but it breaks more easily than other kinds of pottery. Earthenware is fired at a low temperature.

Stoneware, a second kind of pottery, is hard and heavy. It is made from a mixture of stoneware clays and is fired at a very high temperature. It often becomes shiny when fired, so many potters don't glaze it. Stoneware is stronger and heavier than earthenware.

Porcelain is the most delicate kind of pottery. Porcelain can be fired at high or low temperatures. Light can shine through a thin piece of porcelain.

The four steps in making pottery are preparing the clay, shaping the clay, decorating and glazing the clay, and firing it.

Potters prepare clay by pressing it with their hands. This softens the clay.

There are many methods of shaping the clay. One method makes use of a potter's wheel. This device consists of a flat, round surface that turns while the potter shapes clay on it.

Potters decorate pottery by scratching lines into it. A colorful glaze is often brushed on.

Firing makes pottery strong. Pottery is fired in an oven called a kiln.

poul•tice (pōl′ tis) *n.* a soft, hot, wet mixture, as of flour or mustard and water, put on a sore or inflamed part of the body.

pov•er•ty (pov′ ər tē) *n.* **1.** the condition of being poor, or not having enough to live on. **2.** the condition of being poor in quality or lacking in something. *The poverty of this writer's imagination is disgraceful.*

praise•wor•thy (prāz′wʉr′ *th*ē) *adj.* deserving praise; that should be admired.

pray•ing man•tis (prā′ing man′tis)

This insect got its name because it often lifts its front legs as if it were praying. It takes this position when hunting. Praying mantises, or mantids, are among the greediest of all insects. They feed on other kinds of insects and on their own kind as well. They usually eat their prey alive.

The praying mantis is an example of nature's camouflage. In shape and color, it looks very much like the plants on which it stays.

The forelegs of a praying mantis look like arms. They have sharp hooks that hold the victims. Human beings benefit from the praying mantis because it eats harmful insects.

pred•a•tor (pred′ə tər) *n.* an animal that lives by killing and eating other animals. *The shark is a predator of the sea.*

prov•erb (prov′ərb)

A proverb is a saying that tells something useful or wise. Only sayings that have been used for a long time and are fairly well known are proverbs.

Proverbs exist in all languages. In fact, the same proverb can often be found in several different languages.

Some frequently used proverbs are
● A bird in the hand is worth two in the bush.
● Don't put off till tomorrow what you can do today.

- Smile, and the world smiles with you. Weep, and you weep alone.
- A place for everything, and everything in its place.

Many proverbs can be found in Benjamin Franklin's *Poor Richard's Almanac.*

pulse   (puls) *n.* **1.** the regular beating in the arteries, caused by the movements of the heart in pumping the blood. *A person's pulse can be felt in the wrist.* **2.** any regular beat. *I can hear the pulse of the drum.* [from Latin *pulsus* beating]

pum•ice   (pum'is) *n.* a light, spongy rock sometimes formed when lava from a volcano hardens. It is often used for polishing, smoothing, or cleaning. *This piece of pumice is as light as a feather.*

——————— **Q** ———————

quiv•er[1]   (kwiv'ər) *v.* to shake with little, trembling movements. *The delicate flowers quivered in the gentle breeze.* — *Syn.* **shake.**

quiv•er[2]   (kwiv'ər) *n.* a case for holding arrows. *How many arrows are in that quiver?*

——————— **R** ———————

ra•di•ance   (rā'dē əns) *n.* **1.** bright shininess. **2.** an appearance of joy or good health.

Radiance shone in her sparkling eyes and her cheery smile.

re•pel•lent   (ri pel'ənt) *adj.* that drives back in various ways. *The spoiled milk had a repellent smell.* — *n.* something that repels, or makes stay away. *I hope that the insect repellent will keep the mosquitoes away.* — *Ant.* **attractive.**

——————— **S** ———————

salt•cel•lar   (sôlt'sel'ər) *n.* a small dish for salt at the table; a saltshaker. *All of the saltcellars need refilling.* [from Latin *sal* salt]

sand•blast   (sand'blast) *n.* a strong stream of air carrying sand, used to etch glass or clean the surface of stone. — *v.* to etch or clean with a sandblast. *The workers sandblasted the walls of the building in two days.*

se•crete   (si krēt') *v.* **secreted, secreting. 1.** to put in a secret place; to hide. **2.** to make in or give off into or out of the body. *Our salivary glands secrete a substance that helps us digest food.*

side•board   (sīd'bôrd) *n.* a piece of furniture with drawers and shelves for holding dishes, silverware, linen, and other things. *Please get more dishes from the sideboard.*

slurp   (slʉrp) *v.* to drink or eat in a noisy way. *It is not polite to slurp food.* — *n.* a loud sucking or sipping sound.

speech-making technique
(spēch' māk'iñg tek něk')
    There are many opportunities both in school and outside of school to make speeches. A good speech-maker considers the following points: the subject of the speech, the audience, him- or herself as the speaker, and the occasion.
    Speakers must know their subjects well. It is best to have firsthand information about a subject. There are usually three kinds of subjects to choose from: those that persuade, those that inform, and those that entertain.
    Speakers must know their audience. They should determine what the audience already

						ə = a *in* ago
a fat	**er** care	**ī** bite, fire	**oi** oil	**u** up	**th** thin	e *in* agent
ā ape	**ē** even	**o** lot	**oo** look	**ʉr** fur	**th** then	i *in* unity
ä car, father	**i** hit	**ō** go	**ōo** tool	**ch** chin	**zh** leisure	o *in* collect
e ten	**ir** here	**ô** law, horn	**ou** out	**sh** she	**ñg** ring	u *in* focus

knows about the subject of the speech and, if possible, what their opinions are. If a speaker knows that the audience is already against something, then he or she will have to use strong or charming techniques to win the audience over.

A speaker's best tool is his or her personality. Speakers should look at themselves carefully to discover their own strengths and weaknesses.

When a speaker is a natural storyteller, he or she should include an anecdote — a brief amusing story — in a speech. A speaker should always stand straight and speak loudly and slowly enough to be heard by everyone.

A speaker should understand the occasion at which a speech is to be given. Is the subject of the speech appropriate? A speech about great baseball players might not impress the local gardening club.

A speech should always have an interesting introduction, a clear main idea, a lot of supporting material, and a strong conclusion.

sprad•dle (sprad''l) *v.* **spraddled, spraddling.** to stand or sit with legs spread apart as on a horse. *The child spraddled the log fence.* [a blend of the words *spread* and *straddle*]

sta•tion•ar•y (stā′shə ner′ē) *adj.* **1.** not to be moved; fixed. *That stationary bicycle is attached to the floor.* **2.** not changing in condition or value. *How long has the price of fuel remained stationary?*

sta•tion•er•y (stā′shə ner′ē) *n.* paper and envelopes for writing letters. *My stationery has a small picture of a flower on it.*

T

team•ster (tēm′stər) *n.* a person whose work is hauling goods with a team or truck. *He works a a teamster hauling paper products in his truck.*

U

Ur•sa Ma•jor (ur′ sə mā′jər)

Ursa Major is the constellation, or group of stars, known as the Great Bear. This constellation includes the Big Dipper. The two stars in the front of the dipper's cup point to the North Star. The dipper's cup marks the hindquarters of the bear. The handle shows the bear's tail. Other stars make up the head and legs.

On winter evenings the handle of the Big Dipper points down. On summer evenings its handle points up. By morning, the Big Dipper's position changes because of the rotation of the earth.

To find Ursa Major, simply look for the Big Dipper. Then use your knowledge and imagination.

V

vol•ca•no (vol kā′nō)

A volcano is an opening in the earth's surface through which lava, hot gases, and rock fragments are ejected from the earth's interior. Most volcanoes are atop cone-shaped mountains. In fact, the mountains themselves are also called volcanoes. Erupting volcanoes can be quite beautiful, but many have caused a great deal of death and destruction.

Perhaps the most famous volcano is Vesuvius, located in Italy. In A.D. 79 a huge eruption of this volcano destroyed three towns and many thousands of lives.

Mauna Loa, in Hawaii, is the world's largest volcano. It rises almost 30,000 feet from the ocean floor and has a 60-mile-wide base.

In 1912, Mount Katmai, in Alaska, created a glowing flood of hot ash. The ash traveled 15 miles, forming the Valley of Ten Thousand Smokes.

Cotopaxi, in Ecuador, is 19,347 feet above sea level. It erupted in 1877, producing a mudflow that traveled 150 miles. About one thousand people were killed.

At 22,831 feet above sea level, Aconcagua, in Argentina, is the highest mountain in the Western Hemisphere. Its volcano is now extinct.

Mount Etna, in Italy, is 11,122 feet above sea level. In 1669 its eruption killed about twenty thousand people.

--- **W** ---

ware (wer) *n.* **1.** a thing or things for sale. *The store sells unusual wares such as corn cob holders.* **2.** pottery or earthenware.—*Syn.* **goods.**

Wil•der, Lau•ra In•galls (wīl′ dər, lôr′ə ing′ gəlz) 1867–1957

Laura Ingalls Wilder was an American author of children's books. She is best known for her *Little House* books. The books were based on her childhood in the pioneer Midwest. They tell about the hardships of prairie life and the importance of a close family. The books are filled with warmth and the spirit of the American frontier.

Imagine what it would be like to travel to a rugged, unpopulated place and to establish a home there. This is the experience Wilder lived through.

Today the Laura Ingalls Wilder award is given every three years to an outstanding author of children's literature. Wilder herself received the first award in 1954. During the 1970s, a successful television series based on the *Little House* books was created.

a fat	**er** care	**ī** bite, fire	**oi** oil	**u** up	**th** thin	ə = a *in* ago
ā ape	**ē** even	**o** lot	**oo** look	**ur** fur	**th** then	e *in* agent
ä car, father	**i** hit	**ō** go	**ōō** tool	**ch** chin	**zh** leisure	i *in* unity
e ten	**ir** here	**ô** law, horn	**ou** out	**sh** she	**ṅg** ring	o *in* collect
						u *in* focus

Dictionary of Knowledge **465**

THESAURUS

A thesaurus contains lists of synonyms and antonyms. You will use this Thesaurus for the thesaurus lesson in Unit 1 and for the Thesaurus Corner in each Reading-Writing Connection in this book. You can also use the Thesaurus to find synonyms to make your writing more interesting.

Sample Entry

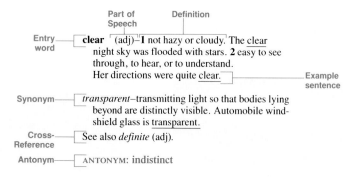

How to Use the Thesaurus Index

To find a word, use the Thesaurus Index on pages 467–471. All entry words, synonyms, and antonyms are listed alphabetically in the index. Words in dark type are entry words, words in italic type are synonyms, and words in blue type are antonyms. A cross-reference (marked "See also") lists an entry that gives additional synonyms, related words, and antonyms. The page numbers tell you where to find the word you are looking for.

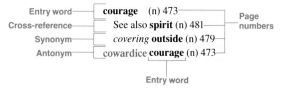

THESAURUS INDEX
A list of all the words in this thesaurus

Thesaurus

ve (v) 475
ve **want** (v) 484
zy **clear** (adj) 472
art **courage** (n) 473
avy light (adj) 477
roism **courage** (n) 473
arity **joy** (n) 476
story **story** (n) 482
nest **good** (adj) 476
ver **fly** (v) 475
ge **large** (adj) 475
ge **little** (adj) 477
mble **famous** (adj) 474
nger **want** (v) 484

entical **same** (adj) 480
nore (v) 481
ustrious **famous** (adj) 474
agine **think** (v) 482
mature **young** (adj) 485
mense **large** (adj) 476
mense **little** (adj) 477
perfectly **well** (adv) 485
portant **little** (adj) 477
consistent **same** (adj) 480
correct **wrong** (adj) 485
definite **definite** (adj) 473
distinct **clear** (adj) 472
distinguishable **same** (adj) 480
ertia **energy** (n) 474
flammatory **exciting** (adj) 474
form **tell** (v) 482
frequent **many** (adj) 478
frequent **rare** (adj) 480
herit **get** (v) 475
itial (adj) **last** (adj) 476
quire **ask** (v) 472
securely **fast** (adv) 475
sert **put** (v) 479
side **outside** (adj) 479
significant **little** (adj) 477
stall **put** (v) 479
struct **tell** (v) 482
tensity **vigor** (n) 483
terior outside (n) 479
terrogate **ask** (v) 472
the face of **before** (prep) 472
the presence of **before** (prep) 472
troductory **last** (adj) 476
regular **rough** (adj) 480

J

jagged **rough** (adj) 480
jet **fly** (v) 475
joy (n) 476
judge **think** (v) 482
junior **young** (adj) 485
just **good** (adj) 476

K

kind **warm** (adj) 484

L

lack (v) **have** (v) 476
lack **want** (v) 484
large (adj) 476
large **little** (adj) 477
lasso **trap** (v) 482
last (adj) 476
leave (v) **come** (v) 473
leave (v) **wait** (v) 484
legend **story** (n) 482
lethargy **vigor** (n) 483
level (adj) **rough** (adj) 480
lifelessness **spirit** (n) 481
light (adj) 477
linger **wait** (v) 484
listen **tell** (v) 482
little (adj) 477
little **large** (adj) 476
liveliness **energy** (n) 474
liveliness **spirit** (n) 481
locale **place** (n) 479
locate **find** (v) 475
loosely **fast** (adv) 475
lose **find** (v) 475
lose **get** (v) 475
lovely **beautiful** (adj) 472
loyal **true** (adj) 482
lucid **clear** (adj) 472
lure **trap** (v) 482

M

make (v) 477
 See also **do** (v) 474
manufacture **do** (v) 474
many (adj) 478

massive **large** (adj) 476
mature (adj) **young** (adj) 485
mention **say** (v) 481
messy **neat** (adj) 478
microscopic **little** (adj) 477
mild **warm** (adj) 484
minor **little** (adj) 477
minute (adj) **large** (adj) 476
minute **little** (adj) 477
misadventure **accident** (n) 472
miserable **nice** (adj) 479
misery **joy** (n) 476
misfortune **accident** (n) 472
mishap **accident** (n) 472
mislay **find** (v) 475
misplace **find** (v) 475
miss (v) **find** (v) 475
monotonous **exciting** (adj) 474
monotonous **same** (adj) 480
much **many** (adj) 478
must **need** (n) 478
myth **story** (n) 482

N

narrate **tell** (v) 482
narrative **story** (n) 482
near **come** (v) 473
nearest **next** (adj) 478
neat (adj) 478
necessity **need** (n) 478
need (n) 478
need (adj) **have** (v) 476
need **want** (v) 484
neighboring **next** (adj) 478
net **trap** (v) 482
new **young** (adj) 485
next (adj) 478
nice (adj) 479
notable **famous** (adj) 474
notorious **famous** (adj) 474
numerous **many** (adj) 478

O

obscure **clear** (adj) 472
obscure **famous** (adj) 474
observe **see** (v) 481
obtain **get** (v) 475
old (adj) **young** (adj) 485

Thesaurus

Thesaurus

A

accident (n)–An unfortunate event that happens by chance and that results in loss, injury, or death. There is an automobile accident almost every month at that dangerous intersection.

calamity–an extremely grave event or misfortune marked by great loss and lasting distress; a disaster. The fire was a calamity to the family whose home was destroyed.

catastrophe–a sudden or widespread tragic event or disaster; a great calamity. The earthquake that devastated most of the city is a catastrophe that will not be easily forgotten.

disaster–a sudden event that causes much damage, suffering, or loss. The train wreck was a disaster that fortunately took no lives.

misadventure–an unfortunate accident; a piece of bad luck. I knew that our vacation trip was a misadventure when it began to rain on the very first day.

misfortune–bad luck; adverse fortune. By misfortune I arrived on the island just ahead of the typhoon.

mishap–an unfortunate accident. Falling from her bicycle was a mishap that left Kim badly bruised.

ask (v)–**1** to question; to call on to answer. I asked my brother questions about geography. **2** to make a request for something. I asked the waiter for more water.

inquire–to ask about someone or something. Have you inquired about the time that the game will be played?

interrogate–to question systematically. The police officer interrogated the woman who saw the accident.

question–to ask for the purpose of finding out. Mark questioned me about my science project.

quiz–to question carefully. Our teacher quizzed us on yesterday's homework assignment.

request–to ask for. I requested extra help in math after school.

ANTONYMS: **answer (v), reply (v), respond**

B

beautiful (adj)–very pleasing to see or hear; delighting the mind or the senses. That is a beautiful painting.

attractive–pleasing; winning attention and liking. You are wearing an attractive sweater.

dazzling–brilliantly shining; splendid. Dazzling gems sparkled in the jewelry store display case

glorious–having great beauty; splendid; magnificent. This crisp and clear autumn day is truly glorious.

handsome–pleasing or impressive in appearance. That limousine is certainly a handsome automobile.

lovely–beautiful in mind, appearance, or characte delightful. Having dinner at that new restauran sounds like a lovely idea.

pretty–pleasing by delicacy or grace. Look at this pretty bouquet of daisies.

ANTONYMS: **ugly, unattractive**

before (prep)–**1** preceding in time; earlier than. Does Memorial Day come before Flag Day? **2** the sight or presence of. Bill was standing befo the principal. **3** in front of. There is a curtain before the window.

ahead of–in front of. I saw Berta ahead of me in line.

in advance of–prior to. The thunderstorms along the cold front should arrive in advance of the cooler air.

in the face of–in the presence of; confronting. In the face of danger, Susan remained calm and d not panic.

in the presence of–in front of; before. Was she eve in the presence of royalty?

prior to–earlier than. We had breakfast prior to our departure.

ANTONYMS: **after (prep), behind (prep)**

C

clear (adj)–**1** not hazy or cloudy. The clear night sky was flooded with stars. **2** easy to see through, to hear, or to understand. Her directions were quite clear.

audible–loud enough to be heard. The volume control is turned down so low that the sound is barely audible.

cloudless–free from clouds; clear. The full moon shone brilliantly in the cloudless winter sky.

distinct–easily heard, seen, or understood; plain. Cara drew the distinct outline of a jet airplane.

ar *(continued)*   **definite**

licit–clearly expressed or distinctly stated.
The auto manual had explicit instructions.

id–easy to understand or follow. He gave a lucid
explanation of his whereabouts.

nsparent–transmitting light so that bodies lying
beyond are distinctly visible. Automobile wind-
shield glass is transparent.

e also *definite* (adj).

NTONYMS: cloudy, hazy, indistinct, obscure,
unclear, vague

me   (v)–**1** to move toward or approach. Come
here as soon as you can. **2** to arrive at a certain
place, end, or conclusion. We came to this town
five years ago.

vance–to move forward. The long freight train
is steadily advancing toward the tunnel.

proach–to come nearer to. Emilio approached
the busy intersection with caution.

rive–to reach the end or destination of a journey; to come to a place. The plane will arrive in
Dallas at four o'clock.

ain–to arrive at or reach by living or by developing. That department store has attained a reputation for quality.

ar–to come close to; to approach. When you
begin to see skyscrapers in the distance, you will
be nearing New York City.

ach–to arrive at; to get to. The mountain
climbers reached the summit of Mt. Rainier on
Wednesday.

NTONYMS: depart, go, leave (v), retreat (v),
withdraw

urage   (n)–the strength of mind or will to face
danger. Fire fighters showed courage in battling
the blaze.

ldness–show of scorn for danger; daring. The
boldness of the plan surprised us.

avery–fearlessness in the face of danger or difficulty; courage. The bravery of the hostages was
astounding.

art–enthusiastic courage. It takes heart to
persist.

roism–willingness to take risks to help others;
valor. Davy Crockett's heroism is admired.

lor–willingness to take risks to help others; heroism. Knights of old showed valor in battle.

e also *spirit* (n).

NTONYMS: cowardice, fear (n), timidity

---

cut   (v)–**1** to separate, divide, or remove with a
knife or any tool that has a sharp edge. Cut the
paper in two pieces with scissors. **2** to make by
or as if by cutting. The sculptor will cut a human
figure from that block of wood.

carve–**1** to cut into pieces or slices. When will you
carve the Thanksgiving Day turkey? **2** to make
by cutting. Which Presidents are carved on Mt.
Rushmore?

cleave–to cut, split open, or divide. The construction crew will cleave those giant rocks by using
jackhammers.

engrave–to form by cutting; to carve in an artistic
manner. The jeweler will engrave your initials
on the back of the ring.

prune–to cut undesirable twigs or branches from a
bush, a tree, or a vine. I must prune some of the
older branches from the forsythia bushes.

score–to cut, scratch, or line. Before baking the
ham, score it by cutting shallow grooves into it
with a knife.

slice–to cut into flat, broad pieces. Slice the roast
beef very thin, please.

D

definite   (adj)–**1** exact or clear; precise; not
vague. The dark clouds and strong winds are
definite signs that a thunderstorm is approaching. **2** having certain limits; restricted. There
are definite procedures to follow in case of an
emergency.

certain–without any doubt; sure. I am certain that
the concert is at seven o'clock.

defined–having settled limits or boundaries. This
fence forms a clearly defined property boundary
between the two lots.

explicit–clearly expressed or distinctly stated.
Carol's explicit remarks about the basketball
game could hardly be misinterpreted.

specific–definite; particular; precise. Every pair of
shoes has a specific size.

unequivocal–having no doubt or ambiguity;
straightforward; blunt and plain. Toshio's unequivocal refusal to attend the meeting was a surprise to everyone.

unmistakable–not capable of being misunderstood
or mistaken; clear. A 747 aircraft has an unmistakable shape.

See also *clear* (adj).

definite *(continued)*

Thesaurus

ANTONYMS: ambiguous, equivocal, imprecise, indefinite, undefined, vague

do (v)–**1** to carry through to the end any action or piece of work; to perform; to complete. Juan did a report on conservation. **2** to produce or make. He does beautiful landscapes in watercolors.
construct–to make by combining parts; to put together: to build. The workers have already constructed a new bridge over the river.
execute–to carry out fully; to do. A plan of action is useless unless it is properly executed.
manufacture–to make by hand or by machinery; to make something that is useful. That corporation manufactures paper towels.
perform–to do or to carry out; to go through and finish; to accomplish. Since you must perform that difficult task, be sure to ask questions about what you do not understand.
practice–**1** to do something again and again to learn to do it well. Great violinists practice several hours a day. **2** to work at a profession or occupation. He has practiced law for over ten years.
produce–to bring into existence by labor; to create; to make from various materials; to manufacture. How many automobiles does that company produce in one year?
See also *make* (v).

E

energy (n)–the ability for forceful action; the capacity for doing work. Toby had enough energy to run five miles.
liveliness–high spirits; the quality of being full of life and spirit. The liveliness of the kittens was evident in their spirited play.
power–force or strength; might; the ability to act or do. Does that railroad locomotive have enough power to pull one hundred freight cars?
stamina–power to resist that which weakens; endurance; staying power. Derrick has the stamina to run long distances.
strength–the condition or quality of being strong; force; power; vigor. I do not have the strength to move that heavy table.
vigor–strength or force; flourishing physical condition; intensity of action. Pam does push-ups and sit-ups with vigor.

vitality–vital force; the power to live and develop. My little sister is a happy and healthy young gir who is filled with vitality.
See also *vigor* (n).
ANTONYMS: fatigue, inertia, powerlessness, sluggishness, tiredness, weakness

exciting (adj)–producing excitement or a feelin of agitation; arousing; stirring. Traveling by air plane is always an exciting and enjoyable exper ence for me.
breathtaking–thrilling; exciting. The view from th scenic overlook just off the interstate highway i breathtaking.
inflammatory–tending to arouse or excite; tending to excite anger or disorder. The manager of the baseball team made several inflammatory remarks regarding the umpires.
stimulating–rousing to action; inspiring; stirring. Cold, stimulating mornings in winter wake me up in a hurry.
stirring–exciting; rousing; inspiring. The mayor's stirring speech left everyone applauding and cheering.
suspenseful–characterized by or full of suspense; causing the condition of being mentally uncertain, especially such a condition induced by craft in order to hold the attention of an audienc or reader. Alfred Hitchcock directed some of th most suspenseful and terrifying movies ever made.
thrilling–characterized by excitement, or causing sudden sharp feeling of excitement. Riding a roller coaster is a thrilling experience for most people.
ANTONYMS: dull, monotonous, tedious, uneventful, unexciting.

F

famous (adj)–well-known; much talked about or written about; celebrated; noted. The famous singer gladly signed autographs after the concert.
celebrated–well-known; much talked about. The celebrated ballet dancer will perform tomorrow evening.
eminent–above most or all others; outstanding; famous. The eminent scientist made a profound discovery that left most of her peers in awe.
illustrious–brilliantly outstanding because of

achievements or actions. His <u>illustrious</u> motion-picture career included several award-winning performances.

otable–remarkable; worth noticing; striking; important. Winning a gold medal in the Olympic Games is certainly a <u>notable</u> achievement.

otorious–generally known and talked about because of something bad; having a bad reputation. The <u>notorious</u> gang robbed many banks a long time ago.

opular–liked by most people; liked by associates or acquaintances. That toy is so <u>popular</u> that most stores do not have any left to sell.

NTONYMS: humble, inconspicuous, obscure, undistinguished, unknown

st (adv)–**1** in a rapid manner; quickly; swiftly. I walked <u>fast</u> in order to get to the bus stop in time. **2** in a fixed or firm manner, tightly. The window frame is stuck <u>fast</u>.

rmly–solidly or securely. Make sure that the handle on that pan is <u>firmly</u> attached.

astily–in a hurried manner; in a rash or careless manner. It was obvious by the numerous errors in spelling and punctuation that the letter was written <u>hastily</u>.

uickly–with haste; rapidly; very soon. Go <u>quickly</u> to your room.

apidly–in a manner marked by a high rate of motion, succession, or occurrence. The seasons seem to be <u>rapidly</u> flying by.

ecurely–firmly or solidly. The steel railing is bolted <u>securely</u> to the bridge.

wiftly–in a fast or speedy manner. A deer ran <u>swiftly</u> across the road.

NTONYMS: insecurely, loosely, slow (adv), slowly

nd (v)–to come upon by chance; to discover by searching. We could not <u>find</u> the glove that Lori had misplaced.

atch–to hold or capture, especially after a chase. After several days of detective work, the police finally <u>caught</u> the thief.

etect–to discover the presence, existence, or fact of. I <u>detect</u> the odor of gas near the kitchen stove.

iscover–to see or learn of for the first time; to find out. Astronomers continually <u>discover</u> new stars in the universe.

ncounter–to meet or come upon unexpectedly.

Tourists driving on narrow mountain roads often <u>encounter</u> dangerous hairpin turns.

locate–to seek out the exact position of. The forest rangers <u>located</u> the hungry deer and gave them food.

trace–to follow by means of tracks, signs, or other evidence. Scientists easily <u>traced</u> the source of the town's air pollution.

ANTONYMS: lose, mislay, misplace, miss (v)

fly (v)–to move through the air with wings; to travel in an airplane or a spacecraft; to wave or float in the air. We will <u>fly</u> to Chicago next week.

flutter–to wave back and forth lightly and quickly. The flag in front of our school <u>fluttered</u> in the breeze.

glide–to move along effortlessly, smoothly, and evenly. The bird calmly <u>glided</u> in a circular pattern high above the treetops.

hover–to remain in or near one place in the air; to hang suspended or fluttering in the air. The helicopter <u>hovered</u> above the traffic jam.

jet–to fly by jet airplane. You can <u>jet</u> across the country in a relatively short time.

soar–to fly in the air, often at a great height; to fly upward. The rocket <u>soared</u> into the sky and soon disappeared from view.

G

get (v)–to come to have; to gain possession of; to obtain. Allen will <u>get</u> a new pair of glasses tomorrow.

acquire–to get by one's own efforts; to come to have. Through years of work he <u>acquired</u> a large fortune.

contract–to get, usually without choice. Ellen <u>contracted</u> the flu last week.

earn–to get in return for service or work. I <u>earned</u> extra money by delivering newspapers.

inherit–to receive after someone dies. The Benson family <u>inherited</u> their beautiful house many years ago.

obtain–to get through effort or diligence; to come to have. Sharon <u>obtained</u> two tickets to the basketball game.

receive–to take into one's hands; to be given. I <u>received</u> a wonderful birthday present from my parents.

ANTONYMS: give, lose, relinquish

Thesaurus

good (adj)–**1** having high quality; superior. A good rocking chair lasts a long time. **2** as it ought to be; right; proper; agreeable. Doing what is good sometimes takes courage. **3** clever; skillful. He always tells a good joke.

beneficial–producing good; helpful. Proper exercise is beneficial to good health.

excellent–very good; better than others. The food in this restaurant is excellent.

honest–not lying, stealing, or cheating; truthful. An honest person does not cheat others.

just–fair; right; impartial. The judge made a just decision.

pleasant–giving pleasure; agreeable. A person with a pleasant disposition usually has a warm smile.

proficient–well advanced in an art, science, or subject; skilled. A proficient carpenter can do excellent work quickly.

ANTONYMS: awful, bad, disagreeable, dishonest, incompetent, worthless

H

have (v)–**1** to hold in one's possession or in one's keeping. Do you have a pencil I could borrow? **2** to experience. Henry has a terrible toothache.

command–to have power over; to be in authority over; to control by position. The fortress commands the harbor entrance.

endure–to put up with; to tolerate; to experience. I endured a terrible sore throat for about three days.

experience–to feel; to live through. That famous actress experienced many thrilling moments.

own–to have or hold as property; to possess. They own two automobiles.

possess–to have as a knowledge, an attribute, or a skill; to have as property. Gan possesses exceptional artistic ability.

undergo–to go through; to experience. The library will undergo a major renovation during the next couple of years.

ANTONYMS: lack (v), need (v)

J

joy (n)–a glad feeling; a strong feeling of pleasure; happiness. On a morning this beautiful, Marta felt joy at being alive.

bliss–great happiness or joy. Walking in the park on a warm morning in spring is sheer bliss.

delight–great pleasure or joy. The little boy ate hi ice-cream cone with delight.

ecstasy–a feeling of very great joy; strong feeling that thrills or delights. The older man was fille with ecstasy when he saw his brother for the fi time in many years.

glee–great delight or lively joy; merriment. We laughed with glee as we watched the monkeys at the zoo.

happiness–a state of contentment and well-being joy; gladness. Sometimes happiness can be found in the simplest things.

hilarity–great mirth or enjoyment; boisterous or noisy merriment. My friends and I talked and laughed with hilarity at the party.

ANTONYMS: despair (n), grief, misery, sadness, sorrow (n), unhappiness.

L

large (adj)–of more than the usual amount, size or number; big. The large tray was filled with delicious sandwiches.

considerable–in large quantity; much. A conside able number of people will take part in the Fourth of July parade.

enormous–extremely large; huge. That enormou tree must be over one hundred years old.

great–large in amount, extent, number, or size; big. Many great boulders line the shoulder of the road.

huge–very large; unusually large in bulk, dimensions, or size. A huge stalled tractor blocked th entrance to the freeway.

immense–very big; vast; huge. The state of Alask covers an immense area.

massive–large and solid: big and heavy; huge. Th massive wall was over four feet thick.

ANTONYMS: little, minute (adj), slight (adj), small, tiny

last (adj)–coming after all others; being at the end; final; conclusive. I know someone who likes to read the last page of a novel before read ing the rest of it.

closing–being the final portion or last stage of an item. The closing chapter of the book was by f. the most exciting.

nclusive–convincing; decisive; final. Those X rays gave <u>conclusive</u> proof that the tennis player had fractured her wrist.

rewell–parting; last; final. The <u>farewell</u> address of our retiring principal was truly inspiring.

rthest–most distant in time or space. Are satellites now exploring the <u>farthest</u> reaches of outer space?

al–being the last; at the end. The <u>final</u> game of the season takes place tomorrow afternoon at two o'clock.

imate–most remote in time or space; farthest; last in a series of steps; extreme. Her <u>ultimate</u> goal is to win a gold medal in the Oympics.

NTONYMS: beginning (adj), first (adj), inconclusive, initial (adj), introductory, opening (adj)

ght   (adj)–**1** not heavy; having little weight. Those suitcases are surprisingly <u>light</u> when empty. **2** easy to do or bear. Ted has to do some <u>light</u> chores. **3** of little importance. Sheila enjoys <u>light</u> reading just before bedtime.

fortless–showing or requiring little use of energy; easy. The gymnast performed with seemingly <u>effortless</u> skill and grace.

athery–light and delicate; almost weightless. With a <u>feathery</u> touch the pianist produced delicate tones that could hardly be heard.

mple–easy to do, understand, or solve. Assembling that model airplane was <u>simple.</u>

perficial–of or on the surface; lying on or affecting only the surface. Although she tripped on the step, she received only a <u>superficial</u> scratch on her knee.

ivial–not important; insignificant. We talked about <u>trivial</u> things like the weather.

eightless–having little or no weight. Astronauts experience <u>weightless</u> conditions when they travel in space.

NTONYMS: burdensome, cumbersome, difficult, heavy (adj), profound, strenuous

ttle   (adj)–**1** not big or great; small. The diamond stylus on a stereo phonograph is <u>little.</u> **2** small in amount, number, or importance. There is <u>little</u> time remaining before the end of this class.

insignificant–having little influence or importance; too small to be important. An <u>insignificant</u> amount of snow fell last night, so we were able to get to school easily.

microscopic–unable to be seen without using a microscope; extremely small; minute; tiny. Those <u>microscopic</u> dots on the leaves of the plant are actually tiny insects.

minor–inferior in importance, size, or degree; smaller. Get the job done without worrying about <u>minor</u> details.

minute–very small. That restaurant served <u>minute</u> portions of food.

slight–lacking in strength or importance; having a slim build. The movie has a <u>slight</u> plot, but, after all, it is a comedy.

small–not large; little in size; not large in comparison with other things of the same kind. Be sure to buy only a <u>small</u> loaf of bread and a quart of milk.

ANTONYMS: big (adj), great (adj), huge, immense, important, large (adj)

M

make   (v)–**1** to bring into being; to build, form, put together, or shape. I can <u>make</u> a bowl from this modeling clay. **2** to cause to; to force to. Will you <u>make</u> us run three laps around the entire track?

assemble–to put or fit together. Brian <u>assembled</u> that model airplane in less than five days.

build–to make by putting materials together; to construct. Did you <u>build</u> the shelves in this closet?

compel–to urge or drive with force; to force. The high-wind warnings <u>compelled</u> us to keep the boat close to the shore.

create–to make something which has not been made before; to bring into being. The florist <u>created</u> a beautiful floral centerpiece for the dinner party.

force–to make someone act against his or her will. My sister <u>forced</u> me to wash all the dishes.

form–to make in a certain shape; to give shape to. Take the three strips of cardboard and <u>form</u> a triangle.

See also *do* (v).

ANTONYMS: destroy, wreck (v)

Thesaurus

many (adj)–consisting of a large number; numerous. There are <u>many</u> new office buildings in this part of town.

abundant–more than enough; amply supplied. There was an <u>abundant</u> harvest of wheat this year.

frequent–happening often or every little while. We have <u>frequent</u> bus service to and from the city.

much–in great degree or amount. Try not to eat too <u>much</u> food at the picnic.

numerous–very many; consisting of great numbers of individuals or units. I have swum in that lake on <u>numerous</u> occasions.

plentiful–more than enough; ample. We are fortunate to live where food is <u>plentiful</u>.

several–more than two, but fewer than many. Michele was late for school <u>several</u> times last month.

ANTONYMS: few (adj), infrequent, rare, scant (adj), sole (adj)

has to be; a requirement; a necessity. The reaso for the <u>need</u> for quiet when working in a librar is obvious.

absence–the state of being without; a lack. The <u>absence</u> of rainfall has geatly diminished the water supply in the reservoir.

deficiency–an absence or lack of something needed; incompleteness. Because of a <u>deficiency</u> of funds, a new municipal building cou not be built.

must–something that is necessary; an obligation. Seeing that exciting new movie is a <u>must</u>.

necessity–that which cannot be done without; a needed thing. Good lighting is a <u>necessity</u> whe you are reading.

requirement–something needed; a necessity. One <u>requirement</u> for that job is the completion of a special training course to handle medical emergencies.

shortage–too small an amount; a deficiency; a lack. During the water <u>shortage</u> the watering o lawns was prohibited.

ANTONYMS: abundance, adequacy, excess (n)

N

neat (adj)–clean and in order; marked by tasteful simplicity. Diego keeps his room <u>neat</u>.

orderly–in order; with regular system, arrangement, or method. When the alarm sounds for the fire drill, proceed to the exits in an <u>orderly</u> fashion.

organized–arranged in some order or pattern; put into working order. He has the most <u>organized</u> loose-leaf binder in our class.

tidy–neat and in order; trim; orderly. He keeps the inside of his car as <u>tidy</u> as his home.

trim–in good order or condition; tidy; neat. Their <u>trim</u> apartment is obviously well taken care of.

uncluttered–not littered; in order; neat. This <u>uncluttered</u> living room appears very spacious.

well-groomed–well dressed and very neat; neat and trim. Even on extremely hot days, Kai always wears a tie and maintains a <u>well-groomed</u> appearance.

ANTONYMS: cluttered (adj), disorderly, disorganized (adj), messy, sloppy, untidy

need (n)–**1** the lack of a desired or useful thing; a want. There is a desperate <u>need</u> for more room in the overcrowded hospital. **2** something that

next (adj)–**1** nearest. The <u>next</u> town is Pleasantville. **2** immediately following. The <u>next</u> train will arrive at this station in about fifteen minutes.

adjacent–lying close or near, or touching; adjoining or neighboring. Do <u>adjacent</u> apartments usually have soundproof walls between them?

adjoining–being next to or in contact; adjacent; bordering. Those two <u>adjoining</u> buildings are connected to each other by a glass-enclosed pedestrian mall.

following–that immediately follows; next after. the <u>following</u> day huge waves pounded the already-battered rocky shore as the storm grew even more fierce.

nearest–closest; least distant. The <u>nearest</u> service station must be at least ten or twelve miles fror here.

neighboring–being or living near; adjacent; bordering. The <u>neighboring</u> county is almost entirely made up of rolling acres of rich producti farmland.

succeeding–following in time, place, or order. T mystery story will be continued in the next thr <u>succeeding</u> issues of the magazine.

e (adj)–pleasing or satisfying. It will be a nice fternoon if the sun comes out.

eeable–suiting one's pleasure. We will do everything possible to be sure our guests have an agreeable stay.

sful–full of great happiness or joy. The child pent a blissful afternoon playing with the new oy.

ightful–enjoyable and very pleasing. Most of he movie was delightful, but the ending made ne cry.

–excellent; very good. The new community enter has fine facilities, including an indoor ce-skating rink.

eshing–pleasantly different or unusual. After ou spend all day in the house, a long walk can be a refreshing activity.

endid–grand; wonderful. Everyone is still talking about this year's splendid school carnival.

TONYMS: awful (adj), disagreeable, dreadful, miserable, terrible, unpleasant

---

tside (n)–the outer part of something. I would ike to try on the jacket that has pockets on the outside.

ting–the layer that covers a surface. The table and chairs come in different colors of plastic coatings.

ering–the outer part of something, which projects or hides what is inside. It is difficult to tell what is in that package with the plain, paper covering.

erior–the outside. They live in the new apartment building with the brick exterior.

e–the front, top, or outer side of something. The face of her watch has many dials that glow in the dark.

ll–a hard outer covering. I cannot crack the shell of this walnut with my fingers.

face–the outer part of something solid; the top level of a liquid. I would use the paper with the shiny surface for the bulletin-board display.

TONYMS: center (n), core (n), inside (n), interior (n)

---

ce (n)–a part of a whole. Be careful not to step on a piece of glass from the broken window.

---

allotment–a person's share of the whole. Each band member was given an allotment of tickets to sell.

chunk–a short, thick piece. Would you like a chunk of cheese with your lunch?

fragment–a piece broken off something. They found a fragment from an antique pot near the ruins.

portion–a part that is divided or separated from the whole. Each person may take a small portion of mashed potatoes.

share–the part belonging to one person. Carolyn did more than her share of work on the project.

shred–a small strip that is torn or cut off. Maybe there is a shred of paper caught in the copying machine.

ANTONYMS: all (n), entirety, whole (n)

---

place (n)–the space occupied by or intended for a person or thing. The cross-country skiers looked for a place to stop and rest.

area–an open space used for a special purpose. There is a large area for parking behind the shopping center.

dwelling–a place where someone lives. This museum was originally a family dwelling.

habitat–the place where an animal or plant grows or lives. The photographer traveled to India to observe the animals in their natural habitat.

locale–the scene of an event or some action. Several reporters dashed to the locale of the blazing fire.

site–a particular place where something is, was or will be located. The site chosen for the monument is near the river.

territory–a section of land. The settlers claimed the undeveloped territory for farmland.

---

put (v)–to lay or cause to be in some place or position. At the end of the day, the librarian always puts the books back on the shelves.

arrange–to put in a proper or desirable order. Marcus arranged the name cards in alphabetical order.

deposit–to set down. We deposited items for the garage sale on a long table.

insert–to put into something. I'll try, but I don't think I can insert this bent key into the lock.

put (continued)

install–to put in position and fix for use. Someone from the store will <u>install</u> our new washing machine tomorrow.

position–to put in a particular place. Sandy carefully <u>positioned</u> the clock on the mantel.

rest–to place something to prevent it from falling. Michelle <u>rested</u> her bicycle against a tree while she waited for her friend.

ANTONYMS: displace, remove, withdraw

R

rare (adj)–**1** uncommonly found or happening. A snowstorm in April is <u>rare</u> here. **2** unusual in quality, often valuable. The <u>rare</u> gem is priceless.

exceptional–not like it usually is; not like others. The choir director was impressed by Christopher's <u>exceptional</u> voice.

infrequent–not occurring often. Our trips to the beach have been <u>infrequent</u> because of the poor weather.

uncustomary–not the usual way of acting or doing something. It is <u>uncustomary</u> for her to go to bed this early.

unique–being the only one of its kind. Katie's aunt made her a <u>unique</u> wooden jewelry box.

unusual–out of the ordinary; different. We tasted many <u>unusual</u> foods at the international bazaar. See also *unusual* (adj).

ANTONYMS: common (adj), everyday (adj), ordinary (adj), regular (adj), routine (adj), usual (adj)

report (n)–a written or spoken account of something. Before Steve wrote his <u>report</u>, he researched his topic carefully.

address–a formal speech. In his <u>address</u>, the senator said he would support the housing bill.

announcement–a report that is given to bring something to the public's attention. The principal sent out a newsletter to make several <u>announcements</u> about the new school year.

bulletin–a brief report of the latest news. The television program was interrupted to present an important news <u>bulletin</u>.

chronicle–a record of events in time sequence. The speaker showed slides to go with the <u>chronicle</u> she had written about her worldwide journey.

critique–a review of something in which person judgment is expressed. The judges gave a <u>critique</u> of each drawing entered in the contes

rumor–a story or report that is told to others, bu has not been proven to be true. Did you hear t <u>rumor</u> that Joshua is moving to another state?

rough (adj)–not smooth, even, or level; bump This floor is too <u>rough</u> to roller-skate on.

bristly–having a texture like that of short, stiff, coarse hairs. You will need strong soap and a <u>bristly</u> sponge to scrub those mud-caked tires.

coarse–rough in appearance or texture. The tent made of a <u>coarse</u> material.

harsh–rough or unpleasant to the touch or other sense. The stiff towel felt <u>harsh</u> against my fac

irregular–uneven. The ceiling is <u>irregular</u> becau some of the tiles have come loose.

jagged–having sharp points sticking out. Adam his foot on a piece of <u>jagged</u> glass.

rugged–having an irregular, broken surface. The northern part of the state has a cold climate an a <u>rugged</u> terrain.

ANTONYMS: even (adj), flat (adj), level (adj), silky, smooth (adj), soft

S

same (adj)–being alike or unchanged; not diff ent. My brother and I listen to the <u>same</u> kind c music.

consistent–without changing one's way of thinki or acting. She believes in <u>consistent</u> exercise a good eating habits.

identical–exactly alike in every way. Pat and Kir laughed when they realized they were wearing <u>identical</u> coats.

indistinguishable–not able to be recognized by d ferences. The street signs are <u>indistinguishabl</u> in this thick fog.

monotonous–not varying or changing; boring. D we have to play that <u>monotonous</u> game again?

stable–not likely to change or move; steady. Bar bara would like to have a <u>stable</u> job after she completes the training program.

uniform–like all others; all the same. The garder planted the bushes so they would be a <u>uniform</u> height.

ANTONYMS: contrasting (adj), different, dissimilar, distinct, inconsistent, variable (adj

480 Thesaurus

Thesaurus

ave (v)–**1** to keep or make free from harm or danger. Lona <u>saved</u> the baby bird from falling out of its nest. **2** to lay aside; to have or hold on to. Should we <u>save</u> the empty cartons or throw them away?

onserve–to keep from being used up. You can <u>conserve</u> electricity by turning off the light when you leave a room.

conomize–to keep from waste. The office workers are <u>economizing</u> their supplies so they do not run out before the end of the year.

reserve–to keep from change; to keep safe from harm. Matina <u>preserves</u> her favorite photographs in a picture album.

eserve–to hold back, usually for a brief period of time. The librarian said he would <u>reserve</u> the book for me until tomorrow.

alvage–to save from being ruined or wrecked. The citrus growers <u>salvaged</u> a part of the orange crop from the severe frost.

tore–to put away for later use. We <u>store</u> old clothes and toys in the attic.

ANTONYMS: consume, discard (v), endanger, risk (v), spend, waste (v)

ay (v)–to speak; to put into words. Carlotta did not <u>say</u> where she was going.

omment–to make a brief statement, giving a personal judgment about something. Many people <u>commented</u> on the colorful decorations we made for the party.

declare–to make known by publicly announcing. In the broadcast, the city official <u>declared</u> her acceptance of the job.

xclaim–to speak with force, usually when surprised or angry. "I can't believe that I really won!" <u>exclaimed</u> the tennis champion.

xpound–to explain in detail in order to make something clear or understood. The famous doctor <u>expounded</u> the results of his latest research study.

nention–to speak about or refer to briefly. Did anyone <u>mention</u> what time the next train will be arriving?

reveal–to say what was not known before. At the next meeting, the club president will <u>reveal</u> her plans for a charity event.
See also *tell* (v).

see (v)–**1** to perceive by use of the eyes; to look at. Can you <u>see</u> that beautiful little bird in the dogwood tree? **2** to form a picture in the mind. I can still <u>see</u> the castle we visited two years ago.

glimpse–to catch a quick or brief view of. We <u>glimpsed</u> the express train as it sped through the station.

observe–to see and note; to notice; to carefully examine; to watch; to study. Peter <u>observed</u> the cooking demonstration with great interest.

picture–to form an image of in the mind. I <u>pictured</u> the hotel to be much larger than it actually is.

view–to look at; to see. As her mother drove the car, Teena <u>viewed</u> the majestic countryside of Montana.

visualize–to form a mental picture of. Try to <u>visualize</u> the store as it was the last time you were there.

witness–to observe; to see for oneself. Jonathan <u>witnessed</u> a landing of the space shuttle.

ANTONYMS: disregard (v), ignore

spirit (n)–liveliness; courage; vigor; enthusiasm. Her cheery smile shows that she has <u>spirit</u>.

enthusiasm–eager interest; zeal; strong excitement of feeling. The fans cheering loudly at the game were filled with <u>enthusiasm</u>.

fervor–intense enthusiasm, emotion, or earnestness. After she received some encouragement and helpful advice from her teacher, Patty continued working on her science project with renewed <u>fervor</u>.

grit–courage; endurance; pluck. Showing true <u>grit</u>, she finished running the marathon even though she was on the verge of total collapse.

liveliness–the quality or condition of being full of life and spirit; vigor. The <u>liveliness</u> of kittens at play is a joy to behold.

vitality–life force; the power to live. The bustling city has a <u>vitality</u> of its own.

zest–keen enjoyment; an exciting or pleasant quality. With a <u>zest</u> for the beauty of nature, he watched the sun slowly disappear beneath the motionless pines.
See also *courage* (n).

ANTONYMS: dullness, lifelessness, spiritlessness, timidity

story (n)–an account of a happening or group of happenings. Do you enjoy reading adventure stories as much as I do?

biography–a written story of a person's life. Jeff has just read a biography of Abraham Lincoln.

history–a record or story of important events, usually including an explanation of their causes. Every day I learn more of the history of the United States.

legend–a story coming down from the past, especially one that many people have thought of as true. The stories about King Arthur are legends.

myth–a story or legend, usually one that tries to explain something in nature. Is there a myth that explains the causes of thunder and lighting?

narrative–an account or story; a tale. Who was the author of the funny narrative that our teacher read to us?

tale–a story of an incident or event, especially a fictional story. I just read an exciting tale about pirates.

T

tell (v)–to express in words; to say; to give an account of; to relate. Tell me what you think of it.

advise–to give advice to; to counsel; to offer an opinion to. Would you advise me about what to get my mother for a birthday present?

communicate–to give news or information by speaking or writing; to telephone; to write. Have you communicated recently with your sister in New Mexico?

inform–to supply with facts, knowledge, or news; to tell. I was not informed of the change in plans until today.

instruct–to teach; to train; to give knowledge to; to give orders or directions to. I was instructed to hand out the drawing materials.

narrate–to tell the story of; to relate. He will narrate the well-known story, which has been set to music.

report–to tell of something seen, done, heard, or read; to state or announce. Allison reported the results of her science experiment to us.

See also *say* (v).

ANTONYMS: listen

think (v)–**1** to exercise the powers of the mind; to have an idea or thought in mind. I think about many different things all of the time. **2** to have an opinion. I think the librarian is a very nice person.

believe–to think something is real or true. I believe that the rocky cliffs along the coastline are being slowly worn away by the pounding surf.

conclude–to reach certain decisions or opinions by reasoning; to infer. The jury concluded that the defendant was not guilty of the crime for which he was being tried.

dream–to think, see, hear, or feel while sleeping. Did you ever dream that you were trying to run but could not move?

imagine–to form a picture of something in the mind. Juan imagined that he was an astronaut floating in space.

judge–to make up one's mind about; to conclude; to think. Can you judge the distance from this side of the lake to the other?

suppose–to consider as possible; to assume; to consider as probably true. Do you suppose we could all fit in that little car?

trap (v)–to catch; to entrap. The police trapped the crafty criminal.

capture–to take captive; to take by force, skill, or trickery. The troops captured the enemy headquarters.

catch–to take and hold; to capture; to seize. The shortstop caught the hard-hit ground ball.

entrap–to catch in a trap; to bring into danger. The small boat was entrapped by the huge ice floes in the river.

lasso–to catch with a long rope that has a running noose at one end. The rancher lassoed the stray steer.

lure–to attract or tempt, as with a bait. When fishing, people often lure fish by using worms.

net–to catch in a net. Many fish were netted by the trawlers that day.

ANTONYMS: discharge (v), extricate, free (v), release (v), remove

true (adj)–**1** agreeing with fact; not false. The story about the adventures of the explorer was true. **2** genuine, real. The miners found true gold. **3** loyal, faithful. He was true to his word and returned as he had promised.

authentic–coming from the stated source; not copied; real; genuine. The signature on the document is authentic.

actual–concerned with something known to be true. The factual account of the admiral's visit to the South Pole was fascinating.

genuine–actually being what it seems or is claimed to be; true. How can you tell if that gemstone is a genuine diamond?

loyal–faithful and true to duty, promise, love, or other obligations. A loyal fan roots for the same team whether it wins or loses.

real–existing as a fact; not made up or imagined; true; actual; not artificial; genuine. The mountain scene depicted on the stage was so well made that the mountains looked real.

steadfast–loyal; firm of purpose; not changing; unwavering. Clarita remained steadfast in her desire to finish the fifty-mile hike.

ANTONYMS: artificial, counterfeit (adj), false, fictitious, untrue, untrustworthy

urn   (v)–**1** to move around as a wheel does; to revolve; to move partway around in this manner. Please turn the handle counterclockwise. **2** to take the opposite direction or a new direction. After about two miles the road turns westward.

bend–to curve out of a straight position. The branches of white birch trees usually bend under the weight of heavy snow or ice.

circle–to move in or as if in a circle; to form a circle. The seagull circled above the fishing boat.

curve–to bend in a line that has no straight part; to move in the course of such a line. The rising tiers of seats curve gracefully around the center of the arena.

revolve–to move in a curve around a point; to move in a circle. The planets of the solar system revolve around the sun.

spin–to revolve or turn around rapidly. The pinwheel spins whenever a strong breeze blows.

twist–to turn around; to have a winding course or shape; to curve or wind. The steep trail twisted through the rugged terrain.

nusual   (adj)–out of the ordinary; different; not commonly seen, used, or happening; uncommon. That unusual plant grows in the tropical areas of the world.

rare–uncommonly found or happening; unusual. Some species of birds are rare.

singular–unusual; extraordinary; strange. With singular devotion to duty, the soldier carried out the difficult assignment.

uncommon–unusual or rare; exceptional or remarkable. He had many uncommon minerals in his rock collection.

unexpected–not expected; not anticipated; unforeseen. The unexpected major snowfall caught everyone by surprise.

unfamiliar–not well-known; strange; unusual. While traveling in Europe, we sampled many unfamiliar foods.

unique–being the only one of its kind. This unique painting was done nearly a century ago.

See also *rare* (adj).

ANTONYMS: common (adj), commonplace (adj), customary, familiar, routine (adj), usual (adj)

use   (v)–**1** to put into action or service; to utilize; to practice or employ actively; to exercise. Whenever I use tools, I keep safety in mind. **2** to consume or take regularly. That old automobile uses too much gasoline.

consume–to use up; to spend; to destroy. The forest fire consumed hundreds of acres of trees.

employ–to use; to use the services of. Chris employed a pair of tweezers to remove that tiny wire from the model.

exercise–to actively use to cause improvement or to give practice and training. If you exercise every day, you may actually begin to feel healthier.

exhaust–to empty completely; to drain. The campers exhausted their food supply within a week.

operate–to keep at work; to run or drive. May I operate the model train set?

utilize–to make use of; to put to a practical use. A good student utilizes his or her time wisely when studying.

ANTONYMS: conserve (v), preserve (v), save (v)

V

vigor   (n)–strength or force; flourishing physical conditions; intensity of action. Lien begins each day with surprising vigor.

vigor *(continued)*

vigor *(continued)*

war

drive–initiative, energy, vigor. Being a person with drive, she pushed herself beyond the normal limits of endurance.

energy–the ability for forceful action; the capacity for doing work. Mowing the lawn takes a great deal of energy.

fervor–great warmth of feeling; intense earnestness, enthusiasm, or emotion. With fervor in his eyes, the artist gazed at his masterpiece.

intensity–vigorous activity or strong feeling; great strength. My parents said they never saw anyone play tennis with more intensity than Jimmy Connors.

vim–energy, force, vigor. The joggers began their daily run with vim.

vitality–vital force; the power to live and develop. I never saw anyone with as much vitality as that actress.

See also *energy* (n).

ANTONYMS: apathy, feebleness, lethargy, slowness, sluggishness, weakness

W

wait (v)–to stop doing something or to stay until something happens or someone comes. Please wait here until I return.

dawdle–to waste time; to be idle; to dally. If you dawdle over your homework, you will never finish it.

delay–to put off until a later time. Severe thunderstorms delayed the departure of our plane for over an hour.

linger–to be slow in quitting something or in parting, as if unwilling to leave. Some of the guests lingered for quite some time after the wedding reception had ended.

remain–to continue in a place; to stay. We remained indoors through much of the sub-freezing weather.

stay–to continue in a place or condition; to remain. We will stay here until it is time to board the train.

tarry–to delay leaving; to stay, to remain. If you tarry any longer, you will not get to school on time.

ANTONYMS: depart, go, leave (v)

want (v)–**1** to feel that one needs or would like to have; to wish for; to desire. I want to visit Hawaii someday. **2** to fail to possess, especially in the required or customary amount; to be without. The ballet dancer's performance was good, but at times it wanted gracefulness.

crave–to desire very much; to long for. The new student craved friendship.

desire–to long or to hope for; to wish earnestly for. Above all else he desired happiness.

hunger–to feel uncomfortable because of not having eaten; to be hungry. At about the same time every evening, Gene hungers for a snack.

lack–to be without; to not have enough; to need. Although she plays basketball well, she lacks the desire to become an outstanding player.

need–to be in want of; to be unable to do without; to require. This houseplant needs water right now.

wish–to have a desire for; to want. I wish I could go swimming today.

See also *wish* (v).

ANTONYMS: decline (v), have, own (v), possess, refuse (v), reject (v)

warm (adj)–**1** more hot than cold; having or giving off heat to a moderate or adequate degree; having some heat. Is it warm outside today? **2** marked by or showing affection, gratitude, or sympathy. Being a warm person, he is always considerate of other people's feelings.

affectionate–having or showing fondness or tenderness. The new mother gave her baby an affectionate kiss.

compassionate–wishing to help those that suffer; sympathetic; pitying. The compassionate doctor comforted the seriously ill patient.

kind–doing good rather than harm; sympathetic; friendly; gentle. The kind woman gave her sweater to the shivering child.

mild–calm; warm; moderate; not severe or harsh. We had a mild winter with less snow than usual.

temperate–neither very hot nor very cold; moderate. Places with a temperate climate generally have summers that are not too hot and winters that are not too cold.

tepid–slightly or moderately warm; lukewarm. My hot tea had become tepid before I had a chance to drink it.

ANTONYMS: coldhearted, cool (adj), cruel, uncaring, unfriendly, unsympathetic

ell (adv)–in a satisfactory, good, or proper manner; all right. She did her work well.

pably–in a competent manner; with ability; ably. During the captain's illness, the next officer in rank capably commanded the ship.

ficiently–ably producing the effect wanted without waste of energy or time. Working efficiently, I was able to finish my homework in much less time than it usually takes me.

ccellent–in a manner better than others; very well; superiorly. Kim's teacher said that her composition was excellently done.

pertly–in a skillful or knowledgeable manner, adroitly. That diagram was expertly drawn.

geniously–in an inventive, resourceful, original, or clever manner. She solved that difficult puzzle ingeniously.

illfully–with expert ability; expertly. The technician skillfully adjusted the equipment.

NTONYMS: badly, imperfectly, improperly, poorly, unsatisfactorily

ish (v)–**1** to have a desire for; to express or feel a desire for; to desire something for someone. I wish we were going to the zoo today. **2** to command or request a person to do something. Mark wishes you to attend his birthday party.

sk–to make a request for something. He asked the movers to be careful with the large couch.

rave–to desire very much; to long for. The lonely child craved affection.

emand–to ask or call for, either as a right or with authority. My parents demand my respect.

esire–to long or hope for; to wish earnestly for. Francis desired to play on the team.

equest–to ask for. Terry requested a map for the city.

ant–to feel that one would like to have; to wish for; to desire. Tom wants a new bicycle for his birthday.

ee also want (v).

rong (adj)–**1** not right; unjust, bad. Cheating on a test is wrong. **2** not correct; not according to truth or facts; inaccurate. You gave a wrong answer to the question. **3** not proper or right according to a code or standard. A sweat suit is the wrong thing to wear to a wedding.

mproper–not in accordance with accepted standards; not suitable; wrong. It is improper for

spectators to shout when a tennis player is about to serve.

inappropriate–not right for an occasion; not suitable; not fitting. A tuxedo is inappropriate clothing for a camping trip.

incorrect–not correct; containing mistakes or errors; faulty; wrong. That clock keeps incorrect time.

unjust–characterized by the absence of justice; not fair. It is unjust to force one person to do the work of many.

unlawful–against the law; contrary to law; prohibited by law; illegal. It is unlawful to drive faster than the speed limit.

untrue–not true to the facts; incorrect; false. That story you heard about me is untrue.

ANTONYMS: correct (adj), fair (adj), proper, right (adj), suitable, true

Y

young (adj)–in the early part of life, growth, or development; not old; of, belonging to, or having to do with youth; having the vigor, freshness, looks, or other qualities of youth. That young woman graduated from college last year.

budding–being in an early stage of development; in the process of emergence. The budding astronomer made her visit to the planetarium.

fresh–newly arrived, gathered, or made; recent; looking young or heathly. I enjoy eating peaches that are fresh and not yet mushy.

immature–not full-grown; not completely developed; not ripe. These immature seedlings must be protected from extreme cold.

junior–**1** the younger (used chiefly to distinguish a son with the same given name as his father). William Dobbs, Junior, is on the phone. **2** of or for younger people; youthful. Do you sing in the junior chorus?

new–never having been before; now first made, heard of, or discovered; not old. Noriko is moving into a new house.

youthful–young; suitable for young people; having the qualities or looks of youth; vigorous; fresh. My grandfather, who jogs every morning, is a youthful person.

ANTONYMS: adult (adj), ancient (adj), mature (adj), old (adj), ripe, senior (adj)

Reports, Letters, Notes

Book Reports

A **book report** tells what a book is about and gives an opinion of the book. Read Jaime's book report. What does it tell about the book?

> *True Tall Tales of Stormalong*
> *by Harold W. Felton*
>
> This book tells the story of Alfred Bulltop Stormalong. It begins with his birth in the middle of a hurricane. Even as a baby, Stormalong was meant to be a sailor. His cradle was a whaleboat!
>
> When Stormy and his friend Jonathan sailed over a peninsula, I learned what a good sailor Stormy was. He had an answer for every problem. He solved each one with his imagination and strength. Stormy sailed the oceans all over the world.
>
> The story has exaggeration, suspense, and humor. I liked this exciting, fun-filled book.

Notice these things about the book report.

1. The title and author are named. The title of the book is underlined. In a book title the first word, the last word, and all important words are capitalized.
2. The report describes the book's characters, setting, and plot, but it does not tell the whole story.
3. The report gives an opinion about the book.

Practice

Write answers to these questions about the book report.

1. What is the title and author of the book?
   True Tall Tales of Stormalong, Harold Felton
2. What words are used to describe Stormalong?
   Good sailor, had an answer for every problem, imagination, strength
3. Why does Jaime like the book?
   The book has exaggeration, suspense, and humor.

Friendly Letters

A **friendly letter** has five parts: the heading, the greeting, the body, the closing, and the signature.

The **heading** shows the address of the writer and the date. Proper nouns are capitalized. A comma is used between the city and the state and between the day and the year.

The first word of the **greeting**, as well as the proper noun, is capitalized. The greeting is followed by a comma.

The **closing** is followed by a comma. Only the first word in the closing is capitalized.

The **signature** tells who wrote the letter.

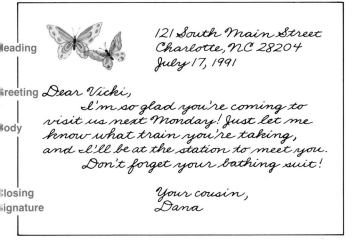

Heading
121 South Main Street
Charlotte, NC 28204
July 17, 1991

Greeting
Dear Vicki,

Body
I'm so glad you're coming to visit us next Monday! Just let me know what train you're taking, and I'll be at the station to meet you. Don't forget your bathing suit!

Closing
Your cousin,

Signature
Dana

Practice

Using the form shown above, write a friendly letter to a friend or relative. Give that person some news about yourself. Tell what you have been doing lately. Use the form shown on page 489 to address the envelope correctly.

WRITING: Friendly Letters **487**

Thank-You Notes and Invitations

♦ A **thank-you note** is a short letter of thanks for a gift or favor. It follows the form of a friendly letter.

> 23 King Street
> Richmond, VA 23222
> June 4, 1991
>
> Dear Aunt Sara,
>   I really enjoyed the book you sent me for my birthday, *The Case of the Curious Computer*. It was fascinating, and it taught me a lot about computers, too!
>
>   Love,
>   Todd

♦ An **invitation** is a note or letter that invites someone to an event. It should name the event, tell where and when it is being held, and tell who sent the invitation.

> **You are invited to** *my Halloween party*
> **Place:** *423 Lincoln Avenue*
> **Date and Time:** *October 31, 2:00–4:00 P.M.*
> **Held by:** *Scott Park*
>   *Wear a costume!*

Practice

A. Write an invitation to a party or other special event.
B. Write a thank-you note to a real person or someone you make up.

ddressing Envelopes

When you address an envelope, you write the return address and the receiver's address.

Write your name and address in the upper left-hand corner. This is the **return address**. It shows where to return the letter if it cannot be delivered.

In the center of the envelope, write the **receiver's address**. This is the name of the person who will receive the letter. For business letters, the receiver's address is an exact copy of the inside address.

You may use an abbreviation for the name of a state. There is an official two-letter abbreviation for each state name. You can get a list of the abbreviations from our local post office.

Return address

Elena Sanchez
6 Sunset St.
El Paso, TX 77910

Receiver's address
State abbreviation

Dr. Joyce Chang
11 South Street
Muncie, IN 47302

actice

Using a ruler, draw three envelopes like the sample above. Then address each one, using the information given below.

Return address: Robert Gula   418 Monroe St.   Oxford, CT 06483
Receiver's address: Ms. Theresa Kwon   4 Lake Rd.   Aztec, NM 87410

Return address: Jesse A. Stanton   31 Wayne Ave.   Lodi, NJ 07644
Receiver's address: Mrs. Ann Tully   28 Reed Rd.   Cody, WY 82414

Return address: Vincent Ricci   8 Budd Ave.   Barre, VT 05641
Receiver's address: Mr. Scott Macey   27 Cedar Dr.   Bristol, TN 37620

A Guide to Spelling

Some useful spelling rules are listed below. Learning them will help you to spell words easily. Remember to use these rules when you write.

1. The suffix *-s* can be added to most nouns and verbs. If the word ends in *s*, *ss*, *sh*, *ch*, *x*, or *zz*, add *-es*.

Nouns		**Verbs**	
gas	gases	hiss	hisses
bush	bushes	match	matches
fox	foxes	buzz	buzzes

2. If a word ends in a consonant and *y*, change the *y* to *i* when you add a suffix, unless the suffix begins with *i*.

Nouns		**Verbs**		
cherry	cherries	study	studies	studied
baby	babies	try	trying	

Adjectives		
muddy	muddier	muddiest

3. If a word ends in a vowel and *y*, keep the *y* when you add a suffix.

Nouns		**Verbs**	
turkey	turkeys	stay	stayed

4. If a one-syllable word ends in one vowel and one consonant, double the last consonant when you add a suffix that begins with a vowel.

Nouns		**Verbs**	
swim	swimmer	stop	stopping

Adjectives		
big	bigger	biggest

5. When you choose between *ie* and *ei*, use *ie* except after *c* or for the long *a* sound.
(Exceptions: *leisure, neither, seize, weird*)

Nouns	**Verbs**
field	shriek
neighbors	receive

6. If a word ends in a single *f* or *fe*, usually change the *f* to *v* when you add *-s* or *-es*.

Nouns calf   calves   knife   knives

7. If a word ends in *e*, drop the *e* when you add a suffix that begins with a vowel. Keep the *e* when you add a suffix that begins with a consonant.

Verbs drive   driving   **Adverbs** sure   surely

8. Add an apostrophe and *s* (**'s**) to a singular noun to show possession, but do not add them to a pronoun. Special pronouns show possession.

doctor   doctor's   Mary   Mary's
his   hers   its   ours   yours   theirs

9. The letter *q* is always followed by the letter *u* in English words. The letter *v* is always followed by another letter; it is never the last letter in a word.

question   give

10. Use an apostrophe (**'**) to show where a letter or letters have been left out in a contraction.

is not   isn't   we are   we're   you will   you'll

Another way to help improve your spelling is to keep a notebook of special words. Collect words you think are interesting or hard to spell. Write them carefully in your spelling notebook. You may wish to add a short meaning next to each word.

Your notebook should have a page for each letter of the alphabet. Keeping these words in alphabetical order will make your personal words easy to find when you need them. If you use a looseleaf binder, you can add pages as your spelling notebook grows.

Words Often Written

The words in the list below came from compositions that were written by students your age. They are the words the students used most often. Are they the words *you* use most often, too?

1. also	26. next
2. apple	27. night
3. around	28. no
4. asked	29. off
5. boy	30. old
6. dad	31. once
7. didn't	32. other
8. find	33. put
9. first	34. ran
10. found	35. really
11. friends	36. summer
12. girl	37. take
13. has	38. teacher
14. how	39. their
15. I'd	40. thing
16. I'm	41. think
17. it's	42. thought
18. looked	43. told
19. make	44. took
20. man	45. two
21. more	46. way
22. morning	47. well
23. name	48. where
24. named	49. who
25. never	50. why

Diagraming Guide

Subjects, Verbs, and Direct Objects

Whenever you assemble a model airplane, you use a diagram to see how the parts fit together. In the same way, a sentence diagram can help you see how all the words of a sentence fit together.

To begin a sentence diagram, draw a horizontal line. On this line, write the subject and the verb of the sentence you wish to diagram. Then draw a vertical line to separate the subject and the verb. This shows how you do it.

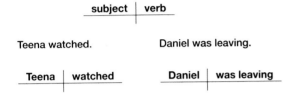

subject	verb

Teena watched.   Daniel was leaving.

Teena	watched

Daniel	was leaving

The subject of an imperative sentence is usually understood to be *you*. In a diagram, write *you* in parentheses in the subject place, like this.

Walk.   Do continue.

(you)	Walk

(you)	Do continue.

A direct object receives the action of a verb. (See pages 122–123.) To diagram a direct object, write it on the horizontal line after the verb. Separate the direct object from the verb by drawing a vertical line that does not cut through the horizontal line. These diagrams show you how.

Susan repairs bicycles.

subject	verb	direct object

Susan	repairs	bicycles

Notice that a sentence diagram shows the capital letters of a sentence. Punctuation marks, however, are not shown.

Diagraming **493**

Diagraming Guide

Answers for Practice A, page 494:

1. Children | sing
2. (you) | Listen
3. Sharon | is talking
4. I | was drawing
5. Linda | will try
6. They | forgot
7. Mark | was smiling
8. (you) | Stand
9. They | understand
10. Frank | laughed

Answers for Practice B, page 494:

11. Joe | carried | boxes
12. We | moved | them
13. Juan | is drinking | milk
14. Mr. Harrison | opened | windows
15. They | ate | supper
16. Ted | cooked | chicken
17. Ann | has planted | flowers
18. Judy | is taking | pictures
19. Michelle | told | jokes
20. I | will make | shelves

Practice

A. Identify the subject and the verb in each sentence. Then diagram each sentence. Answers are in margin.

1. Children sing.
2. Listen.
3. Sharon is talking.
4. I was drawing.
5. Linda will try.
6. They forgot.
7. Mark was smiling.
8. Stand.
9. They understand.
10. Frank laughed.

B. Identify the subject, the verb, and the direct object of each sentence. Then diagram each sentence. Answers are in margin.

11. Joe carried boxes.
12. We moved them.
13. Juan is drinking milk.
14. Mr. Harrison opened windows.
15. They ate supper.
16. Ted cooked chicken.
17. Ann has planted flowers.
18. Judy is taking pictures.
19. Michelle told jokes.
20. I will make shelves.

C. Diagram each of the following sentences. Answers are in margin.

21. Amy is playing ball.
22. Stop.
23. Cindy was running.
24. We picked tomatoes.
25. Wait.
26. Jill shouted.
27. I bought bread.
28. She has seen Bill.
29. Michael is waving.
30. They sang songs.
31. We were working.
32. Julie painted pictures.
33. I enjoy movies.
34. Arnold is attaching streamers.

Every sentence part can be shown in a sentence diagram. An
[adj]ective is written on a slanting line connected to the noun or
[pro]noun it describes. The articles *a, an*, and *the* are also diagramed
[in t]his way.

The big truck carries new cars.

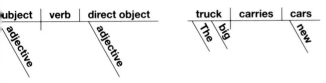

[A] predicate adjective follows a linking verb and describes the
[sub]ject. (See pages 236–237.) Diagram a predicate adjective by
[pla]cing it on the horizontal line after the verb. A line that slants
[ba]ckward separates the predicate adjective from the verb. This
[sla]nting line does not cross the horizontal line.

Pat seems happy.

Adverbs are diagramed on slanting lines. An adverb that describes a
[ve]rb appears directly under the verb.

Trees were swaying slowly.

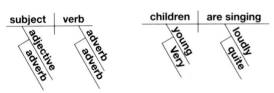

Diagram an adverb that modifies an adjective or another adverb by
[wr]iting it on a slanting line connected to the word it describes.

Very young children are singing quite loudly.

| subject | verb | | children | are singing |

Answers for Practice C, page 494:

21.	Amy	is playing	ball
22.	(you)	Stop	
23.	Cindy	was running	
24.	We	picked	tomatoes
25.	(you)	Wait	
26.	Jill	shouted	
27.	I	bought	bread
28.	She	has seen	Bill
29.	Michael	is waving	
30.	They	sang	songs
31.	We	were working	
32.	Julie	painted	pictures
33.	I	enjoy	movies
34.	Arnold	is attaching	streamers

Answers for Practice A, page 496:

1.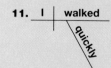
kitten | played
The / tiny

2. He | appeared \ confident

3. Pam | threw | ball
the \ red

4. Bob | is \ tall

5. We | picked | flowers
colorful

6. highways | cross | America
Many

7. You | are \ ready

8. Jill | borrowed | book
an \ interesting

9. Mountains | are \ majestic

10. Doris | wore | sweater
a \ pretty \ blue

Practice

A. Diagram each sentence. Notice the adjectives and the predicate adjectives.   Answers are in margin.

1. The tiny kitten played.
2. He appeared confident.
3. Pam threw the red ball.
4. Bob is tall.
5. We picked colorful flowers.
6. Many highways cross America.
7. You are ready.
8. Jill borrowed an interesting book.
9. Mountains are majestic.
10. Doris wore a pretty blue sweater.

B. Diagram each sentence. Notice the adverbs.   Answers are in margin

11. I walked quickly.
12. The very large elephant came near.
13. The noisy crowd watched excitedly.
14. Very warm weather continued.
15. The bird flew quite swiftly.
16. Heather slept soundly.
17. The powerful storm moved closer.
18. The extremely hungry birds ate noisily.
19. The overdue train finally arrived.
20. A very bright light blinked rapidly.

C. Diagram each of the following sentences.   Answers are in margin

21. The green grass is beautiful.
22. A very colorful butterfly fluttered silently.
23. The gate slowly closed.
24. The little dog barked quite noisily.
25. A new theater opened yesterday.
26. The temperature was falling quite rapidly.
27. Very dark clouds suddenly appeared.
28. The very tall boy bought a newspaper.
29. The little birds chirped softly.
30. Two young girls carefully planted a very small tree.

496 Diagraming

Answers for Practice B, page 496:

11. I | walked
quickly

12.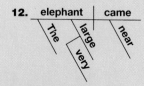
elephant | came
The \ large \ very \ near

13.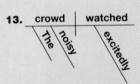
crowd | watched
The \ noisy \ excitedly

14.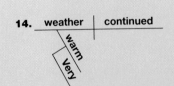
weather | continued
warm \ Very

15.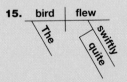
bird | flew
The \ swiftly \ quite

16.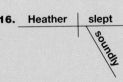
Heather | slept
soundly

Glossary of Terms

‚reviation An abbreviation is a shortened ‚rm of a word. Many abbreviations begin with ‚ capital letter and end with a period. *page 68.*

ion verb An action verb shows action. *age 116.*

ective An adjective describes a noun or a ‚ronoun. *page 234.*

erb An adverb describes a verb, an ‚djective, or another adverb. *pages 284, 288.*

ecdote An anecdote is a short, interesting ‚ory about someone. *page 30.*

onyms Antonyms are words with opposite ‚eanings. *page 348.*

‚strophe An apostrophe (') shows where a ‚tter or letters have been left out. *page 186.*

e word A base word is the simplest form of a ‚ord. *page 134.*

‚iness letter A business letter has six parts: ‚e heading, inside address, greeting, body, ‚losing, and signature. *page 206.*

‚aracter A character is a person, an animal, or ‚n imaginary creature in a story. *page 32.*

‚mmon noun A common noun is the general ‚ame for a person, place, or thing. *page 64.*

‚nplete predicate The complete predicate is ‚ll the words in the predicate part of a sentence. ‚he predicate part tells what the subject is or ‚oes. *page 8.*

‚nplete subject The complete subject is all ‚e words in the subject part of a sentence. The ‚ubject part names someone or something. *page 8.*

‚npound A compound is a word formed from ‚vo or more words. *page 294.*

‚npound predicate A compound predicate is ‚vo or more verbs that have the same subject. *‚age 394.*

‚npound sentence A compound sentence ‚ontains two or more simple sentences joined by ‚ conjunction. *page 396.*

‚npound subject A compound subject is two ‚r more simple subjects that have the same ‚redicate. *page 390.*

Conjunction A word such as *and* or *or* that joins other words is a conjunction. *page 390.*

Context clue A clue that helps a reader find the meaning of an unknown word is a context clue. *page 72.*

Contraction A contraction is a shortened form of two words. *page 186.*

Declarative sentence A declarative sentence makes a statement. It ends with a period. *page 6.*

Direct object A direct object receives the action of the verb. *page 122.*

Encyclopedia An encyclopedia is a set of reference books with articles about people, places, things, and ideas. The articles are arranged in alphabetical order. *page 310.*

Exaggeration Exaggeration is the stretching of the truth. *page 146.*

Exclamatory sentence An exclamatory sentence expresses strong feeling. It ends with an exclamation mark. *page 6.*

Fact A fact is true information that can be checked. *page 202.*

Future tense The future tense of a verb shows action that will happen in the future. *page 124.*

Haiku Haiku is a Japanese verse form that presents a picture to which we add our own thoughts and images. *page 365.*

Helping verb A helping verb works with the main verb. *page 120.*

Homographs Homographs are words that are spelled the same but have different meanings and origins. *page 400.*

Homophones Homophones are words that sound alike but have different meanings and spellings. *page 188.*

Answers for Practice C, page 496:

21.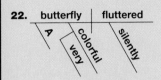
22.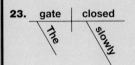
23.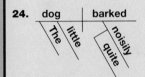
24.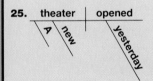
25.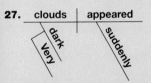
26.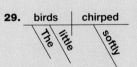
27.
28.
29.
30.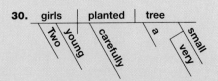

17–20.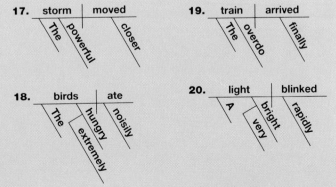

Glossary

Imperative sentence   An imperative sentence gives a command or makes a request. It ends with a period. *page 6.*

Initial   An initial is the first letter of a name. It is written with a capital letter and followed by a period. *page 68.*

Interjection   An interjection is a word that expresses feeling or emotion. It is usually followed by an exclamation mark. *page 34.*

Interrogative sentence   An interrogative sentence asks a question. It ends with a question mark. *page 6.*

Irregular verb   An irregular verb does not form the past or past participle by adding *-ed*. *page 128.*

Linking verb   A linking verb shows being. It connects the subject of a sentence with a word or words in the predicate. *page 118.*

Main verb   The main verb is the most important verb in the predicate of a sentence. *page 120.*

Metaphor   A metaphor compares two things by saying one thing *is* the other. *page 148.*

Noun   A noun names a person, a place, a thing, or an idea. *page 60.*

Object of the preposition   An object of the preposition is the noun or pronoun that follows a preposition. *page 340.*

Object pronoun   The pronouns *me*, *you*, *him*, *her*, *it*, *us*, and *them* are object pronouns. *page 184.*

Opinion   An opinion is what someone *thinks* is true. *page 202.*

Order of importance   Order of importance is a way of organizing details, either by stating the most important first, or by building up to it last. *page 258.*

Outline   An outline organizes information into main ideas and supporting details. *page 314.*

Paragraph   A paragraph is a group of sentences that tell about one main idea. The first word of a paragraph is indented. *page 86.*

Paragraph of comparison   A paragraph of comparison tells how one thing is *like* another. *page 414.*

Paragraph of contrast   A paragraph of contrast tells about differences between two similar things. *page 416.*

Part of speech   A part of speech tells how a word is used in a sentence. *page 388.*

Past tense   The past tense of a verb shows action that already happened. *page 124.*

Persuasive paragraph   A persuasive paragraph gives the writer's opinion and reasons to support it. Reasons are often listed in the order of importance. *page 204.*

Plot   A plot is the series of events in a story in the order in which they happen. *page 32.*

Plural noun   A plural noun names more than one person, place, thing, or idea. *page 62.*

Possessive noun   A possessive noun shows ownership. *page 70.*

Possessive pronoun   The pronouns *my*, *your*, *his*, *her*, *its*, *our*, and *their* are possessive pronouns. They show ownership and replace possessive nouns. *page 182.*

Predicate adjective   A predicate adjective follows a linking verb and describes the subject of a sentence. *page 236.*

Prefix   A prefix is a word part added to the beginning of a word. It changes the meaning of the word. *page 134.*

Preposition   A preposition relates a noun or a pronoun to another word in the sentence. *page 340.*

Prepositional phrase   A prepositional phrase includes the preposition, its object, and any words that come between them. *page 346.*

Present tense   The present tense of a verb shows action that happens now. *page 124.*

Prewriting   Prewriting is the stage in which writers gather ideas and get ready to write. *page Introduction 4.*

Pronoun   A pronoun takes the place of a noun or nouns. *page 176.*

Proofreading   Proofreading is the stage in which writers look for and correct errors in their writing. *page Introduction 7.*

Proper noun   A proper noun names a particular person, place, or thing. Each important word in a proper noun is capitalized. *page 64.*

Publishing   Publishing is the stage in which writers share their writing with others. *page Introduction 7.*

▪tation marks Quotation marks (" ") show ▪e exact words of a speaker. *page 34.*

▪etition Repetition is the repeating of a word ▪r phrase as a way of bringing sound to poetry. *▪ge 363.*

▪ising Revising is the stage in which writers ▪ake changes to improve their writing. *page ▪troduction 6.*

▪-on sentence A run-on sentence is two or ▪ore sentences not separated by correct ▪unctuation or connecting words. *page 398.*

▪tence A sentence is a group of words that ▪xpresses a complete thought. *page 4.*

▪ting A setting is the time and the place of a ▪ory. *page 32.*

▪ile A simile uses the word *like* or *as* to ▪ompare two things. *page 148.*

▪ple predicate The simple predicate is the ▪ain word or words in the complete predicate of ▪ sentence. *page 12.*

▪ple subject The simple subject is the main ▪ord in the complete subject of a sentence. *▪age 10.*

▪gular noun A singular noun names one ▪erson, place, thing, or idea. *page 62.*

▪ce order Space order is the way things are ▪rranged in space. *page 258.*

Subject pronoun The pronouns *I, you, she, he, it, we,* and *they* are subject pronouns. They replace nouns that are the subjects of sentences. *page 178.*

Suffix A suffix is a word part added to the end of a word. It changes the meaning of the word. *page 242.*

Supporting sentence A supporting sentence develops the main idea of a paragraph. *page 88.*

Synonyms Synonyms are words with similar meanings. *page 348.*

Tense The tense of a verb shows the time of the action. *page 124.*

Thesaurus A thesaurus is a book that lists entries in alphabetical order. It gives synonyms, or words with similar meanings, for each entry. Antonyms, or words with opposite meanings, are listed for many entries. *page 16.*

Topic sentence The topic sentence states the main idea of a paragraph. *page 88.*

Verb A word that shows action or being is a verb. *pages 116, 118.*

Writing Writing is the stage in which writers put their ideas on paper. *page Introduction 5.*

Index

A, an, the, 234–235
Abbreviations, 68–69, 105, 112–113, 489
Acronyms, 243
Action verbs, 116–117, 136–137, 162, 392–393
   definition of, 116–117, 165, 388, 433
Addresses
   in business letters, 206–207
   capitalization in, 487, 488, 489
   on envelopes, 489
   in friendly letters, 487
   state abbreviations in, 489
Adjectives
   and adverbs, 288–289, 290–291, 328, 331, 336
   articles (*a*, *an*, *the*), 234–235
   comparison of, with -*er* and -*est*, 238–239, 279–280
   comparison of, with *more* and *most*, 240–241, 280–281
   definition of, 234–235, 388–389
   identifying, 234–235, 274, 388–389
   predicate, 236–237, 278–279
   sentence combining with, 244–245
   suffixes added to, 238–239, 242–243, 275
   that tell how many, 234–235
   that tell what kind, 234–235
   writing with, 234–235, 237, 239, 241, 245, 277–278, 291
Adverbs
   and adjectives, 288–289, 290–291, 331, 336
   comparison of, with -*er* and -*est*, 286–287, 334
   comparison of, with *more* and *most*, 286–287, 334
   definition of, 284–285, 388–389
   identifying, 378–379, 388–389
   and prepositions, 344–345, 378, 384, 435
   sentence combining with, 296–297
   that describe adjectives, 288–291, 335, 388–389
   that describe other adverbs, 288–289, 290–291, 335, 388–389
   that describe verbs, 284–285, 286–287, 288–289, 290–291, 388–389
   that tell how, when, or where, 284–285
   well and *badly*, 286–287, 290–291
   with -*ly*, 284–285
   writing with, 284–285, 287, 289, 291, 296–297, 333
Agreement of subject and predicate
   noun and verb, 118–119, 126–127, 392–393, 425
   pronoun and verb, 118–119, 126–127, 392–393
Alliteration, 73
Almanac, 450–451
Alphabetical order
   in a dictionary, 452–453, 454–455
   in an encyclopedia, 310–311
   in an index, 310–311, 446–447
   in a thesaurus, 16–17
Anecdote, 30–31
Antonyms. *See also* Thesaurus
   definition of, 348–349
   in a thesaurus, 16–17, 379
Apostrophes
   in contractions, 186–187
   in possessive nouns, 70–71, 105, 107, 223

Articles (*a*, *an*, *the*), 234–235
Atlas, 450–451
Audience for writing, Introduction 4, 38, 94, 152, 210, 264, 318, 368, 420

Base Words, 134–135, 242–243
Be
   agreement with subject, 118–119, 126–127, 392–393
   forms of, 118–119
   past and present tenses of, 118–119, 126–127
   See also Helping verbs; Linking verbs.
Bibliographies, 47, 103, 161, 219, 273, 327, 377, 429
Bodies of letters, 206–207, 487, 488
Book reports, 47, 103, 161, 219, 273, 327, 377, 429, 4
Books
   bibliographies, 47, 103, 161, 219, 273, 327, 377, 429
   parts of, 446–447
   titles of, 486
Books to Enjoy, 47, 103, 161, 219, 273, 327, 377, 429
Business letters, 206–207, 221, 489

Calendar words
   capitalization of, 66–67
   abbreviation of, 68–69
Call numbers of library books, 448–449
Capitalization
   of abbreviations, 68–69, 104, 107, 489
   in addresses, 489
   of book titles, 486
   of calendar words, 66–67
   in dates, 487, 488, 489
   of first word of sentences, 6–7
   of initials, 68–69
   in letters, 206–207, 487, 488, 489
   in outlines, 314–315
   of names of people or pets, 66–67, 104
   of place names, 66–67, 104, 487, 488, 489
   of pronoun *I*, 178–179
   proofreading mark for, 44, 100, 158, 216, 270, 324, 374
   of proper nouns, 66–67, 104, 107, 111–112, 223, 330, 4 487, 488, 489
   in quotations, 34–35, 49
   in report titles, 314–315
   in story title, 486
   of titles for people, 68–69
Characters
   definition of, 32–33, 49
   in book reports, 486
Choosing and Narrowing Topics, Strategies for
   browsing through the library, 319
   listing animals you've seen recently, 39
   listing things you could be, 369
   listing things that can be compared, 421
   listing things your town might need, 211
   listing things you do well, 95
   listing things that interest you, 316–317
   looking around the room, 369
   practice exaggerating, 153

Index

Index

Index

505

Index

Index

TABLE OF CONTENTS

INTEGRATED LANGUAGE ARTS PROJECTS

Enhancing Textbook Lessons
Integrated Language Arts Projects are designed to involve students in a meaningful group activity that is multi-modal and integrates language arts with the content and skills from other curriculum areas. Suggested use for each Project is noted.

Integrating the Language Arts
Each Project creates a real-life situation in which students, brought together by a common goal, naturally use their language arts skills. This integration of reading, writing, speaking, listening, and thinking skills reflects the way language is learned and applied in everyday life. New skills will be learned and previously learned skills will be applied to accomplish tasks and solve problems.

Connecting with Other Curriculum Areas
The Integrated Language Arts Projects extend into all areas of the curriculum, integrating the subject matter and skills of social studies, science, math, art, music, and health education with language arts experiences.

Incorporating Literature and Whole Language
Literature plays a significant role in the Projects. A bibliography of ten appropriate books is provided as a suggested library for each one. In some Projects the books are the core from which the activity grows, supporting a whole-language approach. In other Projects the books are research resources or enrichment to enhance the activities.

Fostering Cooperative Learning
The Integrated Language Arts Project activities foster the cooperative and collaborative skills students will need in group situations throughout their lives. Students will develop and use these valuable group skills as they participate in generating ideas, sharing tasks, editing each others' work, solving problems, and making decisions.

Meeting the Needs of Students at Risk
At-risk students are in need of motivation and of language and social skills. The Integrated Language Arts Projects provide special support for such students in a regular classroom setting.

TABLE OF CONTENTS

The real-life situations created by the Projects are especially important as motivation for at-risk students. The integrated use of language arts skills fosters natural learning of language for students with limited proficiency. The use of literature promotes personal identification and involvement with the content.

Cooperative learning not only develops life skills but also provides powerful support and stimulation for students at all ability levels.

Supplementing the Projects
Eight black-line masters augment the Integrated Language Arts Projects at each grade level. Since this kind of support is not equally required with all Projects, the black-line masters have been distributed among the Projects as needed. The black-line masters are shown in reduced size on pages T528–T529 and are available separately.

Choosing the Projects
A typical school year may not accommodate the use of all the Integrated Language Arts Projects. If you cannot or do not wish to use all the Projects, choose the ones that will work best with your class.

Using the Projects
Each Integrated Language Arts Project offers suggestions for motivating students and for executing the Projects successfully. The Project plans are not meant to be detailed lesson plans or substitutes for the textbook lessons. Here are some ways to coordinate the Projects with the lessons in each unit.

◆ Start a Project after completing the suggested unit. Students will apply the skills they have learned and practiced.

◆ Use the Project immediately before a suggested unit as a natural way to motivate students to learn the skills of a textbook unit, integrating the textbook lesson into the Project activities.

◆ During the teaching of a suggested unit, alternate the activities of a Project with the textbook lessons. As students master each skill, they experience immediate, real-life application.

Use the Project at any time during the year when students' natural curiosity lends itself to an ongoing group project. You may wish to modify the Integrated Language Arts Projects to fit your class and your personal teaching style. Project activities may spark your own ideas for related or alternative activities. Be adventurous and trust yourself and your students to use feeling, thought, and imagination as you proceed.

Making History Come Alive

PROJECT PREVIEW

The Integrated Language Arts Project described on these pages centers on **narrating**, the reason for writing in Unit 1. Use the Project before, during, or after the skills study in that unit. As students work in groups to create a fictionalized account of history, they can incorporate skills presented in Unit 1: writing different types of sentences; writing character, setting, and plot for a narrative; writing quotations; and using the writing process.

After analyzing accounts of historical events in both fiction and nonfiction, groups will plan the characters, setting, and plot for historical fiction and then work together to create historical fiction. Skills of reading, writing, speaking, listening, thinking, and cooperating will be integrated as students focus on their common goals.

Skills Objectives

Reading—To read about events in history, to read story plans for historical fiction

Writing—To write the characters, setting, and plot for historical fiction; to combine the elements of historical fiction into a narrative

Speaking and Listening—To participate in discussions, to read aloud accounts of historical events, to share knowledge of historical events

Thinking—To analyze and generalize the characters, setting, and plot of historical fiction; to elaborate on ideas; to create imaginary characters, setting, and plot; to order events

Cooperating—To brainstorm in order to develop a list of characters, the setting, and plot for historical fiction; to share in the creative process; to participate in peer conferencing and editing; to contribute to a class library

Materials

paper, pencils, pens, a black-line master, drawing paper, crayons and/or colored markers, social studies textbooks, encyclopedias

BOOK LIST

The following books may serve as the beginning of a classroom library for this Integrated Language Arts Project. Use them as springboards for the activities in this Project.

- *An Album of the Civil War* by William L. Katz. Watts.
- *By the Great Horn Spoon!* by Sid Fleischman. (Orphan Jack and Praiseworthy the butler team up in the California gold rush.) Little.
- *Caddie Woodlawn* by Carol Ryrie Brink. Macmillan.
- *Children of the Wild West* by Russell Freedman. Houghton.
- *Make Way for Sam Houston* by Jean Fritz. Putnam.
- *Me and Willie and Pa: The Story of Abraham Lincoln and His Son Tad* by F. N. Monjo. Simon.
- *Model Buildings and How to Make Them* by Harvey Weiss. Crowell.
- *Mr. Revere and I* by Robert Lawson. Little.
- *Queenie Peavy* by Robert Burch. (A young girl grows up in Georgia during the Depression.) Viking.
- *Touchmark* by Mildred Lawrence. (A young girl involves herself in the patriot activities of revolutionary Boston.) Harcourt.

PROJECT PLAN

1. Discussing the Nature of Historical Fiction

Have students read a variety of historical fiction stories plus accounts of historical events in their social studies textbooks and encyclopedias. Then have students meet in small groups to share what they have learned by discussing the characters, setting, and action of the historical events they have read about. Help students gain insight into the task of the historical fiction author, who creates fictional characters and plots in the context of real settings and events.

2. Choosing Events in History

Ask students in which historic events they would like to have participated. Choices will most likely be events they have been reading about in social studies textbooks or in historical fiction books. Have the class form four or five groups, each choosing one event.

3. Cooperating to Describe Characters, Setting, and Plot in History

Discuss the fact that an author of historical fiction must learn about the lives of the people in a particular place and time. Have groups generate lists of topics to research about the people, time, and place of their chosen event. Have group members present their findings orally and then cooperate to complete "Story Plan for Historical Fiction," a black-line master, to compile characters, setting, and action and events for their historic event.

4. Breathing Life Into History

Have groups meet to discuss how to turn the characters, setting, and action of their event into a fictionalized story. Have students use their five senses to add vivid details to their story plan. Encourage students to write conversations that bring their characters to life. Provide time for group members to edit and revise their story plan and conversations to make the characters, setting, and action seem as real as possible.

5. Writing About an Event in History

Have group members work together to turn their story plan into a lively account of an event in history. Have students hold editing sessions for suggestions and revisions. Have one student in each group make a final copy of the revised story, complete with appropriate title.

6. Sharing Historical Fiction

Hold storytelling sessions in which group members act out the parts of their characters to tell classmates about their historic event. Encourage students to turn story conversations into play dialogue. If you wish, have students make simple props and/or costumes to enhance their presentations. Finally, have group members make covers for their stories and place them in the class library.

Producing a Television News Program

PROJECT PREVIEW

The Integrated Language Arts Project described on these pages centers on **informing,** the reason for writing in Unit 2. Use the Project before, during, or after the skills study in that unit. As students work in groups to produce simulated television newscasts, they can incorporate skills presented in Unit 2: writing with nouns; giving and following directions; writing a paragraph with a topic sentence and supporting sentences; using commas correctly; and using the writing process.

After analyzing TV news stories and newscasts, groups will plan, write, and present the material for newscasts, including on-the-scene reports and interviews. Skills of reading, writing, speaking, listening, thinking, and cooperating will be integrated as students focus on their common goals.

Skills Objectives

Reading—To read newspaper news stories and books

Writing—To write newscast guidelines, news stories, and interview questions; to complete forms

Speaking and Listening—To participate in discussions, to listen to news programs, to read news stories aloud, to conduct interviews

Thinking—To compare a newspaper news story with a television news story, to analyze the presentation of a news program, to identify the basis of good newswriting, to establish and follow criteria, to create imaginary news events (optional), to evaluate peers' newscasts

Cooperating—To collaborate in developing guidelines, to plan newscasts, to participate in peer editing, to coordinate group presentations, to respond to student presentations

Materials

copies of a news story; paper; pencils; pens; a black-line master; timer; miscellaneous props: optional television set, videotape equipment, videotape of a news story

BOOK LIST

The following books may serve as the beginning of a classroom library for this Integrated Language Arts Project. Use them as springboards for the activities in this Project.

- *Alvin Fernald, TV Anchorman* by Clifford B. Hicks. Holt.
- *Behind the Television Scene* by Don and Barb Fenten. Childrens.
- *A Billion for Boris* by Mary Rodgers. Harper.
- *Broadcasting Careers for You* by William F. Hallstead. Lodestar.
- *Confessions of a Prime Time Kid* by Mark J. Harris. Lothrop.
- *A Day in the Life of a Television News Reporter* by William Jaspersohn. Little.
- *Get Rich Mitch!* by Marjorie Weinman Sharmat. (Mitch is interviewed on several TV talk shows.) Morrow.
- *Mister Rogers: Good Neighbor to America's Children* by Anthony Mario Di Franco. Dillon.
- *News Media* by Ruth and Mike Wolverton. Watts.
- *See Inside a TV Studio* by George Beal. Watts.

PROJECT PLAN

1. Comparing Newspaper and TV News Stories

Plan a presentation of an important news story of current interest. Use photocopies of a newspaper article about the subject and, if possible, a videotape of a TV news presentation of the same story. Have students read the article and discuss the facts of the story, using the questions *Who? When? What? Where? Why?* and *How?* Next present the TV version of the same story or have students watch the story on a TV newscast at home. Have students compare the two versions of the news story, noting similarities and differences. The most obvious difference will be the brevity and lack of detail in the TV version. However, the advantage of the visual effect and the immediacy of on-the-scene reporting in the TV version also should be noted. Conclude that the basis of good newswriting is the same in either medium, but that the presentations have important differences because one is seen and heard and the other is read.

2. Cooperating to Analyze a TV Newscast

Have students form groups to produce simulated TV news programs to learn about writing and presenting news stories for television. Play a videotape of an entire news program or have students watch TV news programs at home. Have them record their observations, using "Analyzing a Television News Program," a black-line master. Groups should meet to discuss these observations. Using the program as a model and books about TV news, each group should develop and record guidelines for presenting a newscast.

3. Cooperating to Develop Newscast Guidelines

Have the recorders from the groups pool their guidelines into a master set of guidelines. These should probably include the following:

- Know your job and plan it carefully.
- Present the most important news first.
- Present on-the-scene reports.
- Keep a good pace to hold interest.
- Address each person by name.
- Plan and write each story carefully.
- Plan the program to fit an agreed-on time period (about fifteen minutes).
- Plan the beginning and end of the program and the connections between stories.

4. Planning the Newscasts

Have groups meet to assign jobs (anchorperson, on-the-scene reporter, sports reporter, weather forecaster, interviewer, and person interviewed) and to plan the news stories and their sequence in the program. You may choose to have all students present real news, researching a newspaper and the community for their stories. As an alternative, you may allow groups to create their own news by writing original stories about imaginary people, places, and events.

5. Writing the News Stories

Individuals should write their own news stories, and the interviewer should plan questions to use. Direct students to read their stories aloud in their groups, discussing revisions and improvements in delivery. Caution students to time everything carefully. Suggest that they type or print their reports, leaving space between lines for easy reading.

6. Rehearsing and Performing the News Stories

Have groups rehearse several times, following the guidelines developed in Activity 3. Encourage students to be creative in their presentations of interviews and on-the-scene reports. Allow time for comments from the viewers after each presentation.

Sharing a Gallery of Tall-Tale Heroes

PROJECT PREVIEW

The Integrated Language Arts Project described on these pages centers on **imagining,** the reason for writing in Unit 3. Use the Project before, during, or after the skills study in that unit. As they create and share a gallery of tall-tale heroes, students can incorporate most of the specific language arts skills presented in Unit 3: writing with action verbs; reading and responding to a tall tale; listening for exaggeration; writing similes and metaphors; and using the writing process to write a tall tale.

Students will create original tall-tale heroes and will display descriptions and pictures of them in a classroom gallery. Each student will then write and publish a tall tale using two of the characters from the gallery. Skills of reading, writing, speaking, listening, thinking, and cooperating will be integrated as students focus on their common goals.

Skills Objectives

Reading—To read tall tales; to read student character descriptions, story plans, and tall tales

Writing—To write character descriptions, story plans, tall tales, and promotional copy

Speaking and Listening—To share character descriptions from tall tales, to participate in discussions, to tell stories

Thinking—To analyze and generalize the characteristics of tall-tale heroes, to elaborate on ideas, to imagine characters, to imagine situations, to predict outcomes, to order events

Cooperating—To brainstorm in order to develop a list of characters, to identify with regional pride, to share in the creative process, to participate in peer conferencing and editing, to contribute to a class library

Materials

paper, pencils, pens, drawing paper, construction paper, staples or other fasteners, crayons and /or colored markers

BOOK LIST

The following books may serve as the beginning of a classroom library for this Integrated Language Arts Project. Use them as springboards for the activities in this Project.

- *Altogether, One at a Time* by E. L. Konigsburg. (short stories) Atheneum.
- *American Tall Tales* by Adrien Stoutenburg. Viking.
- *Courage to Adventure: Stories of Boys and Girls Growing Up with America* by the Child Study Association of America. Crowell.
- *Dear Mr. Henshaw* by Beverly Cleary. (A young boy who wants to be a writer writes letters to his favorite author.) Morrow.
- *A Furl of Fairy Wind* by Mollie Hunter. (short stories) Harper.
- *The Hundredth Dove and Other Tales* by Jane Yolen. Crowell.
- *The Jack Tales* by Richard Chase. Houghton.
- *Louisa May Alcott, Young Writer* by Laurence Santrey. Troll.
- *Self Portrait* by Margot Zemach. Harper.
- *Writing for Kids* by Carol Lee Benjamin. Crowell.

PROJECT PLAN

1. Discussing the Nature of the Tall-Tale Hero

Let students have fun reading many tall tales about several different heroes, both male and female. Have students generalize about the characteristics of the heroes, such as the exaggeration of size, strength, or ability. Provide time for students to share their favorite descriptions by reading them aloud. Lead students to understand the techniques used by the writers of these descriptions. Have students identify the regional setting of each hero and let them speculate about the reasons for such regional focus. Discuss the interest and pride that people have in the geography and occupations of their own regions.

2. Brainstorming to Develop a List of Characters

Stimulate the class's interest in creating new tall-tale heroes who will demonstrate students' pride in their particular region of the country. Have students brainstorm to develop a list of possible kinds of characters and activities. The list may include farmer, mountain climber, miner, builder, firefighter, and so on.

3. Creating Original Tall-Tale Heroes

Have each student choose one of the characters from the list developed in Activity 2. Encourage a diversity of choices. Then have students develop a cluster of exaggerated traits for their character. Small-group sharing sessions may help to stimulate students' creative imaginations during this planning process and to encourage students to make each character unique. Students will write descriptions of their characters and meet in groups for editing and revising.

4. Creating a Gallery of Tall-Tale Heroes

Completed character descriptions, along with pictures illustrating the heroes, should be placed in a special bulletin board display. Provide time for students to enjoy their gallery and to become familiar with each character.

5. Sharing Heroes for Writing New Tall Tales

Pose this question: *What would happen if two of the heroes met?* Ask each student to write a story to answer this question. Tell students to use their own character along with another displayed in the gallery. You may wish to have students choose their second characters or draw them randomly from cards with the names written on them. The chance joining of two characters should make for some fascinating story ideas. Next have students plan their plots. Have students meet in small groups during the writing process to review story plans and to help one another in revising and editing stories.

6. Sharing the New Tall Tales

Have students make covers and illustrations for their stories and place the books where others may read them. To stimulate interest in reading the stories, have students add promotional material to the gallery displays, announcing the titles of the stories in which each hero appears. Students may enjoy writing and sharing more tall tales using one or more of the original characters. You may vary the presentations from time to time by having storytelling sessions in which students imitate the oral tradition of passing on tales to others.

Compiling a Welcome Kit for New Students

PROJECT PREVIEW

The Integrated Language Arts Project described on these pages centers on **persuading**, the reason for writing in Unit 4. Use the Project before, during, or after the skills study in that unit. As the class prepares a welcome kit for students new to the school and community, students can incorporate the language arts skills presented in Unit 4: writing with pronouns; expressing opinions orally and listening to opinions of others; using facts and opinions to write a persuasive paragraph; writing business letters; and using the writing process.

Groups will cooperate to gather, create, and assemble materials that will give new students the factual information they need and that will encourage them to become involved in various school and community organizations and activities. Skills of reading, writing, speaking, listening, thinking, and cooperating will be integrated as students focus on their common goals.

Skills Objectives

Reading—To read books and stories, to read information and promotional brochures

Writing—To write letters, persuasive paragraphs, and informative brochures; to make signs and posters

Speaking and Listening—To participate in discussions, to make telephone calls

Thinking—To analyze experiences and feelings, to compose questions, to identify needs, to generate ideas, to formulate opinions, to support opinions, to design promotional materials

Cooperating—To brainstorm, to formulate a hospitality program, to collaborate in collecting and preparing materials, to participate in peer editing

Materials

brochures from school and community organizations, a black-line master, paper, pencils, pens, construction paper, crayons and/or colored markers, poster-board, large envelopes

BOOK LIST

The following books may serve as the beginning of a classroom library for this Integrated Language Arts Project. Use them as springboards for the activities in this Project.

- *Amy Moves In* by Marilyn Sachs. Scholastic.
- *Anastasia Again!* by Lois Lowry. (Anastasia survives moving to the suburbs.) Houghton.
- *Bridge to Terabithia* by Katherine Paterson. Crowell.
- *Careers with the City* by Christopher Benson. Lerner
- *In the Year of the Boar and Jackie Robinson* by Bette Bao Lord. (Shirley Temple Wong adjusts to Brooklyn and her first year in public school.) Harper.
- *Mapmaking* by Karin N. Mango. Messner.
- *Nothing's Fair in Fifth Grade* by Barthe DeClements. Viking.
- *One of Us* by Nikki Amdur. Dial.
- *Things to Know Before You Move* by Lisa A. Marsoli. Silver.
- Tony and Me by Alfred Slote (The baseball team in Bill's new town is terrible except for Tony.) Lippincott.

PROJECT PLAN

1. Identifying Concerns of New Students

Have students read and discuss books about the experiences of young people moving into new communities. Allow students time to discuss any personal experiences with moving and their feelings as they had to adjust to new people and places. Ask students to consider the concerns of new students in their particular community. Have students brainstorm to develop a list of questions a new student might ask. Among the questions might be the following:

- What kinds of clubs are there? How can I join?
- What sports programs are offered? How do I get involved?
- Where is the park? Are there any bike paths?
- Where is the library, the theater, the Y?

2. Planning a New-Student Welcome Kit

Stimulate interest among students in helping new students feel at home and welcome in their school and community. Encourage attitudes of friendliness and acceptance. Suggest than an information kit containing answers to the questions listed in Activity 1 could facilitate the adjustment of students to their new surroundings. Stress that the kit would also communicate to newcomers that they have come to a special place with friendly and helpful people. Have students brainstorm to develop a list of items they could include in the kit. Here are some items they may want to include:

- a school map
- a calendar of school events
- information about school clubs and programs
- a town or city map
- information about community organizations
- important addresses and phone numbers (library, museum, theater, recreation department)
- application forms (library card, student discount card, Y membership)

3. Exploring Community Resources

Have students explore community organizations for appropriate materials. Students can write to or call the chamber of commerce and other groups, explaining their project and requesting a supply of printed materials appropriate for new students. Help all students to participate in these activities.

4. Creating Additional Materials

Have students form groups to prepare materials that promote school programs of interest to them (sports, drama, newspaper, and various clubs). Each student will write about one club, activity, or aspect of school life, using "Persuasive Writing Plan," a black-line master, to organize the writing. Then hold peer editing sessions for suggestions and revisions. As materials arrive from community groups, have the class reevaluate the contents of the kit and decide on additional materials to prepare. They may, for example, want to add a letter to new students welcoming them and explaining the welcome kit and its contents. The quality of the materials will depend on the interests, talents, and creativity of the students. In all cases, however, remind them that the kit will reflect their hospitality and encourage them to produce attractive and thoughtful materials.

5. Compiling the Kits

Have students decide on the number of kits to make, complete any necessary copying, put the materials in order, and place the materials in large envelopes.

6. Creating and Promoting a Welcoming Center

Decide on a place for the welcoming center, such as the principal's office or library. Have students make a sign identifying the center and create posters announcing this new resource. Have volunteers check the display periodically to replenish the materials.

Creating a City of the Future

PROJECT PREVIEW

The Integrated Language Arts Project described on these pages centers on **describing,** the reason for writing in Unit 5. Use the Project before, during, or after the skills study in that unit. As students project themselves into the future to picture and design an imaginary future city, they can incorporate skills in Unit 5: writing with adjectives; reading descriptions; choosing and organizing descriptive details; writing a descriptive paragraph; focusing on sensory words; and using the writing process.

Students will work together to create a mural depicting a city of the future and to write descriptions of its components. Skills of reading, writing, speaking, listening, thinking, and cooperating will be integrated as students focus on their common goals.

Skills Objectives

Reading—To read science fiction, other books about the future, and descriptive paragraphs

Writing—To write descriptions of places or things, to write letters

Speaking and Listening—To participate in discussions, to interview classmates

Thinking—To observe details, to imagine living in the future, to invent a city of the future, to design a mural, to generate ideas, to make comparisons, to order details

Cooperating—To brainstorm, to contribute to a group project, to participate in peer editing, to write letters

Materials

butcher paper, drawing paper, ruled paper, pencils, pens, crayons and/or colored markers, a black-line master

BOOK LIST

The following books may serve as the beginning of a classroom library for this Integrated Language Arts Project. Use them as springboards for the activities in this Project.

- *C.L.U.T.Z.* by Marilyn Z. Wilkes. Dial.
- *The Drought on Ziax II* by John Morressy. Walker.
- *Fact or Fantasy?* by Neil Ardley. Watts.
- *Fat Men from Space* by Daniel Manus Pinkwater. Dell.
- *The First Travel Guide to the Moon* by Rhoda Blumberg. Scholastic.
- *The Kids' Whole Future Catalog* by Paula Taylor. Random.
- *Matthew Looney in the Outback* by Jerome Beatty, Jr. Avon.
- *My Trip to Alpha 1* by Alfred Slote. Lippincott.
- *Old Cities and New Towns: The Changing Face of the Nation* by Alvin Schwartz. Dutton.
- *The Seeds of Tomorrow* by Ben Bova. McKay.

PROJECT PLAN

1. Imagining a City of the Future

Have students read and discuss science-fiction stories and other books describing life in the future. Have them notice in particular the descriptive language used by authors to build mental pictures. Call attention to descriptive details and comparisons appealing to the senses. Ask students to imagine a city of the future. Have them develop a list of things they might see there. Here are some examples:

- robot cars
- a spaceport
- helicopter buses
- an electronic library
- hologram theaters
- a city dome for weather and pollution control
- underground shopping malls
- robot repair shops
- moving sidewalks

Students may include in their list ideas about architectural styles and materials as well as other projections of their imaginations.

2. Planning and Designing a Future City

Have students plan a mural depicting their ideas of a futuristic city. List all the components they want to include and assign groups and individuals to draw particular components and complexes. Have one group plan the overall layout, designating space for each component on a long piece of butcher paper. Have students practice their drawings and share them in groups for suggestions and revisions. After all the drawings have been completed on the mural, have students add details such as trees, fountains, and outdoor sculptures to enhance and connect the different components.

3. Describing the Components of the City

Have individual students be responsible for writing a paragraph describing the part of the city they helped to design for the mural, using "Planning a Description," a black-line master, as a guide. Have groups of students meet for sharing and revising their writing. Post the descriptions around the mural or on a nearby bulletin board. Key each description by number to the part of the mural it describes.

4. Sightseeing in the City

Provide time for students to read the descriptions and enjoy the illustrations of their city. Have students choose special places other than their own to "visit." Suggest that they find out more about each place by interviewing the classmate or classmates who designed it.

5. Writing Letters About the Visit to the Future

Have students write letters to people in the present describing the special places they visited in this city of the future. Encourage students to create vivid, clear word pictures by using details and comparisons appealing to the senses. These letters may be keyed by number to the mural and become part of the display.

Creating an Exhibit of Unusual Inventions

PROJECT PREVIEW

The Integrated Language Arts Project described on these pages centers on **researching,** the reason for writing in Unit 6. Use the Project before, during, or after the skills study in that Unit. As students collaborate to create an exhibit of unusual inventions, they can incorporate skills presented in Unit 6: writing with adverbs; giving and listening to oral reports; using an encyclopedia and other reference materials; taking notes; outlining; and using the writing process to write a research report.

Students will explore books and references to locate inventions, write reports about them, and create models or illustrations of them. Individual inventions will be keyed to a world map to show where they originated. In addition, students will make tape recordings of their reports so that classmates and visitors can learn about each invention. As they focus on their common goals, students will integrate skills of reading, writing, speaking, listening, thinking, and cooperating.

Skills Objectives

Reading—To read accounts of inventions, to use reference materials
Writing—To take notes on a topic, to outline and write a two-paragraph report, to make labels and signs
Speaking and Listening—To listen to accounts about inventions, to participate in discussions, to give oral reports, to listen to reports
Thinking—To investigate by researching, to plan an exhibit, to identify main ideas, to select relevant details, to order details, to classify information, to design models and illustrations, to evaluate information, to generate ideas, to imagine new inventions
Cooperating—To make suggestions, to respond to suggestions, to contribute to a classroom exhibit, to participate in peer editing

Materials

encyclopedia, atlas, index cards, paper, pencils, pens, a black-line master, drawing paper, model-making supplies, construction paper, crayons and/or colored markers, tape recorders

BOOK LIST

The following books may serve as the beginning of a classroom library for this Integrated Language Arts Project. Use them as springboards for the activities in this Project.

- *Danny Dunn and the Universal Blue* by Jay Williams and Raymond Abrashkin. McGraw.
- *Fun with Next to Nothing: Handicraft Projects for Boys and Girls* by Wesley F. Arnold and Wayne C. Cardy. Harper.
- *Guess Again: More Weird and Wacky Inventions* by Jim Murphy. Bradbury.
- *How to Be an Inventor* by Harvey Weiss. Crowell.
- *Marv* by Marilyn Sachs. (He invents useless objects.) Doubleday.
- *The Phantom Tollbooth* by Norton Juster. Random.
- *Steven Caney's Invention Book* by Steven Caney. Workman.
- *The Unconventional Invention Book* by Bob Stanish. Good Apple.
- *The Wacky World of Alvin Fernald* by Clifford B. Hicks. Holt.
- *Wild Inventions* ed. by Isaac Asimov. Raintree.

PROJECT PLAN

1. Thinking About Unusual Inventions

Locate information about an unusual invention or a little-known story about the invention of a common item. Share the information with the class to stimulate an interest in finding other stories of unusual inventions. Give students a few days to explore books in the classroom and the library to see how many unusual inventions they are able to find out about.

2. Planning the Research

Hold a class meeting to discuss what students have found and to plan an exhibit of unusual inventions. List the inventions on the chalkboard and lead the class to decide how the topics should be assigned for research. This will depend on the kind of information students have found. One or two students may be assigned to work on one invention or a group of students may research one category of inventions. If more than one student is working on a topic, help pairs or groups divide the work, being sure that everyone has a significant role.

3. Researching Topics and Writing Reports

Have students research their topics, using encyclopedias and other references as well as the kinds of books listed for this Project. Encourage further research in the library, having students practice using the card catalog and requesting the aid of a reference librarian. Students will take notes on their topics and make outlines, using "Outlining Information," a black-line master. Finally, students will write reports of more than one paragraph. Remind them to include in their notes the titles and page numbers of their reference materials. Be sure to provide time for peer editing sessions before final copies of the reports are written.

4. Creating Models and Completing the Exhibit

Be sure all students have a role in completing the exhibit. For example, several students may work on making a model; or if one student completes a model or drawing, others may draw diagrams showing how the invention works. Other students may take part by making labels for the exhibit or making suggestions for improving it. Designate a place for each model or drawing to be displayed. Next to each you may have the written report posted or you may have some students bind the reports into a guidebook for the exhibit. Have some students make a world map to place at the center of the exhibit. Students responsible for specific inventions can mark on the map the place where each originated, keying the location by number to the inventions displayed.

5. Making Oral Presentations

When the exhibit is ready, have students present their inventions in an oral report. These reports may be taped so that classmates and visitors can listen to the recordings as they view the exhibit. Provide time for students to ask questions and to make comments about the displays and the reports.

6. Imagining New Inventions

As a follow-up to this Project, have students think of things that still need to be invented to make their lives easier or more interesting. Students can have fun meeting in groups to discuss their ideas. This activity may prove to be a springboard for an entirely new Project in which some or all students create an exhibit of their own concepts for new inventions.

Creating Four Seasonal Books of Haiku

PROJECT PREVIEW

The Integrated Language Arts Project described on these pages centers on **creating,** the reason for writing in Unit 7. Use the Project before, during, or after the skills study in that unit. As students collaborate to create a collection of haiku, they can incorporate skills presented in Unit 7: writing with prepositions and prepositional phrases; recognizing personification; repetition; and the haiku form; reading poetry aloud; writing haiku; and using the writing process to compose a poem.

Four groups will attempt to capture in books of haiku the essence of specific seasons of the year. Authors will illustrate each haiku with an appropriate drawing or painting. Finally, students as co-creators will write responses to various haiku that appeal to them. Skills of reading, writing, speaking, listening, thinking, and cooperating will be integrated as students focus on their common goals.

Skills Objectives

Reading—To read haiku, diagrams, and responses to poetry
Writing—To write personifications, other poetic comparisons, and haiku
Speaking and Listening—To participate in discussions, to read poetry aloud, to listen to poetry
Thinking—To observe a particular poetic form, to analyze poetry, to draw conclusions, to generate ideas, to reason by analogy, to compare, to compose poems, to design drawings or paintings, to make inferences
Cooperating—To brainstorm, to make suggestions, to respond to suggestions, to participate in peer editing, to expand on another's creative work, to publish a book

Materials

paper, pencils, two black-line masters, drawing paper, construction paper, art pens and black ink, paints and brushes, art paper, yarn, hole punch

BOOK LIST

The following books may serve as the beginning of a classroom library for this Integrated Language Arts Project. Use them as springboards for the activities in this Project.

- *Butterflies and Moths Around the World* by Eveline Jourdan. Lerner.
- *The Fall of Freddie the Leaf* by Leo Buscaglia (Freddie experiences the changing of seasons.) Holt.
- *Flower, Moon, Snow: A Book of Haiku* by Kazue Mizumura. Crowell.
- *Haiku: The Mood of the Earth* by Ann Atwood. Scribner.
- *Knock at a Star: A Child's Introduction to Poetry* by X. J. Kennedy and Dorothy M. Kennedy. Little.
- *The Missing Piece* by Shel Silverstein (A circle hunts for its missing part.) Harper.
- *Mushrooms* by Sylvia A. Johnson (features stunning color photography). Lerner.
- *My Side of the Mountain* by Jean C. George. Dutton.
- *Out in the Dark and Daylight* by Aileen Fisher. Harper.
- *Something New Begins* by Lilian Moore (new and selected poems). Atheneum.

PROJECT PLAN

1. Reading and Discussing Haiku

Have small groups of students read aloud and enjoy several haiku. Help students to discover the nature of haiku by choosing poems with representative characteristics. You might approach this activity as a puzzle, challenging the groups to unlock the characteristics of form and content. With guidance they should be able to discover the usual form of seventeen syllables occurring in three lines and following the pattern of five syllables, seven syllables, five syllables. They may also discover that each haiku is a little word picture written in the present tense about one event in a specific season of the year. Help the class appreciate the poetic comparisons, personifications, and the appeal to the reader's senses in each small poem. Call attention also to the elements of surprise and humor created in these poems. Because of the short, unique form, you will find that reading haiku is an excellent way to help students begin to appreciate poetic language.

2. Forming Groups and Brainstorming Subjects

Have students form four groups, each to focus on one season of the year. Tell them that each group will produce an illustrated book of haiku for one particular season. Have the groups brainstorm to list a multitude of details that they can use as subjects of haiku about their seasons.

3. Generating Poetic Comparisons

Using the lists of subjects generated in Activity 2, have students explore the possibilities of personifying various objects. For this activity students may use "Personification Possibilities," a blackline master. Show students how the diagram can help them make imaginative inferences to generate three ways an object or force of nature may be personified. Students may develop other poetic comparisons by using the cluster approach, generating many ideas from one single detail of nature. Provide time for members of each group to share the results of these prewriting activities. They can help one another choose their best comparisons and spark more ideas.

4. Writing Haiku

Individual students should work on writing several haiku, incorporating personifications and other poetic comparisons developed during Activity 3. Encourage students to follow the haiku form and to choose each word carefully in order to create vivid word pictures that appeal to the senses. Have groups hold peer editing sessions for corrections and revisions.

5. Cooperating to Publish a Book of Haiku

Groups should decide how to publish their seasonal books. Suggest that each page be devoted to one haiku, along with a painting or line drawing to illustrate it. You may want to encourage the use of a Japanese art style, engaging the help of an art teacher if possible. Have the authors carefully print their haiku in the center or in one corner of their pictures, signing their names under their poems. Have one student in each group create a cover with the name of the season as the title. You may wish to have groups punch holes in the pages and tie them together with yarn.

6. Responding to Haiku

Provide time for each student to enjoy the haiku books and to respond as a co-creator to one or more of the poems. Traditionally a response to haiku should expand on the haiku in some personal way. You may suggest that the responses be in the form of another haiku, a story, a letter to the author, or a piece of art. Students may use "Responses to Haiku," a black-line master, for this activity.

Conducting a Job Awareness Program

PROJECT PREVIEW

The Integrated Language Arts Project described on these pages centers on **classifying,** the reason for writing in Unit 8. Use the Project before, during, or after the skills study in that unit. As they work together to become more aware of jobs and possible job preferences, students can incorporate skills presented in Unit 8: speaking and listening in group discussions; analyzing and composing a paragraph that compares and one that contrasts; focusing on likenesses and differences; and using the writing process.

Students will cooperate to complete a chart that classifies jobs by qualities or conditions that describe them. This chart will serve as a center for comparison as students investigate the world of work and analyze their preferences. Skills of reading, writing, speaking, listening, thinking, and cooperating will be integrated as students focus on their goals.

Skills Objectives

Reading—To read fiction books, lists of job qualities, reference books, job descriptions; to scan information on a chart
Writing—To write names and job titles in appropriate chart columns, to write job descriptions and comparisons, to write letters (optional)
Speaking and Listening—To participate in discussions, to listen to directions
Thinking—To identify cause and effect, to make choices, to analyze preferences, to investigate jobs, to classify jobs by qualities or conditions, to make inferences, to compare jobs
Cooperating—To brainstorm, to share information, to participate in peer editing, to counsel peers

Materials

a black-line master, posterboard, crayons and/or colored markers, paper, pencils, pens

BOOK LIST

The following books may serve as the beginning of a classroom library for this Integrated Language Arts Project. Use them as springboards for the activities in this Project.

- *Careers in a Supermarket* by Joy Schaleben-Lewis. Raintree.
- *Careers in Animal Care* by Christopher Benson. Lerner.
- *Careers in Sports* by Bob and Marquita McGonagle. Lothrop.
- *Chimney Sweeps* by James C. Giblin. Crowell.
- *First Things First* by Kristi D. Holl. (Shelley has her own business buying and selling at garage sales.) Atheneum.
- *Joel: Growing Up a Farm Man* by Patricia Demuth. Dodd.
- *Kid Power* by Susan Beth Pfeffer. Watts.
- *So You Want to Be a Dancer* by William E.Thomas. Messner.
- *To Space and Back* by Sally Ride. Lothrop.
- *What to Be* by Steve Berman and Vivian Weiss. Prentice.

PROJECT PLAN

1. Thinking About People and Work

Have students read books about young people having firsthand experiences with the world of work through part-time or summer jobs. Discuss the characters' satisfaction or dissatisfaction and have students analyze the reasons for the reactions. Discuss students' own experiences with working, helping them connect chores and hobbies with future job choices.

2. Taking a Preference Test

Have students complete "Job Quality Preferences," a black-line master. Though not a scientific instrument, the inventory should prove helpful as students begin the process of analyzing their preferences and relating them to the world of work. Have students meet in groups to compare the items they marked, noting likenesses and differences among members of the group.

3. Making a Chart of Job Qualities

Help students make a wall chart composed of thirty columns. Use each job quality from the black-line master as a column head. Have students take turns writing their names under the qualities they checked as preferences in Activity 2. Add to the chart any quality that at least three students would like to add. Ask students to think of a good title for the chart, such as "Job Quality Classifications."

4. Brainstorming to Develop a List of Jobs

Ask students to suggest jobs they are interested in investigating. Encourage them to think of a wide variety of jobs, including skilled and professional jobs and jobs in many kinds of settings.

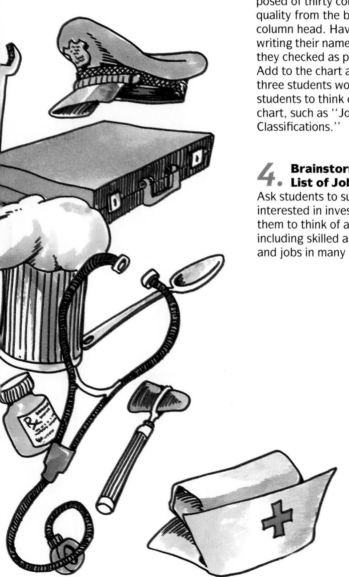

5. Investigating Jobs and Writing Job Descriptions

Have students form groups based on job categories, such as sales, food service, beauty and fashion, medicine, law, government, community, education, agriculture, religion, music, art, business, and skilled trades. Then have each student choose one job to investigate in a group's category. Groups should meet to share sources and to help one another locate materials from the library and identify people to interview. Each student will write a paragraph describing a job, adding a list of job qualities that go with it. Finally, groups should meet for peer editing sessions, using dictionary and thesaurus skills. The job descriptions should be put in separate folders and placed in the classroom library.

6. Classifying Jobs by Their Qualities

Have students classify their jobs by writing their job titles beneath their names in appropriate columns of the chart. Provide time for all to study the chart to see which jobs match their individual preferences. Be sure students understand that the chart provides only an indication of their preferences at the present time. Choosing a career will finally be based on their abilities as well as their interests and on a series of decisions that will go on for many years.

7. Comparing Jobs That Fit Student Preferences

Have each student locate on the chart two job titles that most often appear under his or her job quality preferences. Using the student-written job descriptions and the job quality chart, each student will write a paragraph comparing the two jobs.

8. Connecting People and Jobs (Optional)

Have each student locate on the chart the name of a classmate that appears most often in the columns with the job he or she has studied. Have each student write a letter to that classmate, explaining why he or she might enjoy the job.

for Project, page T512

NAME _____

Story Plan for Historical Fiction

Title of story _____

Setting (Time and Place)	Details
_____	_____
_____	_____
_____	_____
_____	_____

Characters	Details
_____	_____
_____	_____
_____	_____
_____	_____

Plot (Action and Events)	Details
_____	_____
_____	_____
_____	_____

Conversations

_____
_____
_____
_____
_____
_____

Directions: After reading about a historical event, list the characters, setting, events, and details in the appropriate columns. Then write conversations among the characters.

INTEGRATED LANGUAGE ARTS PROJECT MASTERS, Grade 5   1

---

for Project, page T514

NAME _____

Analyzing a Television News Program

News Stories

1. List the subject of each news story in the order presented.

_____ _____
_____ _____

2. Before each subject above, write L for local, N for national, and W for world news.

3. What do you notice about the order of the news stories? _____
_____

Jobs on a Newscast

4. Describe the different jobs of the people who present the news. _____
_____
_____
_____

Presenting the News

5. Write the words used by newscasters at the special times listed below.

Beginning of program _____

Introducing a reporter _____

At the "wrap up," or end, of an on-the-scene story _____

At the end of the program _____

6. Write anything else you think is important about the newscast.

_____

Directions: Watch a newscast and analyze it by completing this form. Use the information when you plan your TV news program.

2   INTEGRATED LANGUAGE ARTS PROJECT MASTERS, Grade 5

---

for Project, page T516

NAME _____

Persuasive Writing Plan

1. What is your topic?
_____

2. What will you try to persuade someone to do or to believe? _____
_____

3. Organize your supporting details. Make a cluster about your topic, with the key word or phrase in the center.

4. Write your topic sentence. _____
_____

Directions: Use this page to plan your writing report.

INTEGRATED LANGUAGE ARTS PROJECT MASTERS, Grade 5   3

---

for Project, page T518

NAME _____

Planning a Description

1. What part of the city are you going to describe?
_____

2. Study the completed picture on the mural. List the details you will describe. Next to each detail, write a description by using your senses and comparisons.
_____
_____
_____
_____
_____
_____

3. Write a topic sentence. If you can, compare the place to something in your world today.
_____

4. Now write the rest of your paragraph. Use some of the details you wrote above, organizing them with space-order words. Try to create a mental picture for your readers.
_____
_____
_____
_____
_____
_____

Directions: Use this page to plan and write a description. Share it with other students and revise it. Then write the completed paragraph on another piece of paper.

4   INTEGRATED LANGUAGE ARTS PROJECT MASTERS, Grade 5

for Project, page T520

NAME _____

Outlining Information

Invention _____

Inventor _____

Date of Invention _____

Site of Invention _____

Outline the information for your report. Be sure the facts help to show why the invention is unusual.

_____
_____
_____
_____
_____
_____
_____
_____
_____
_____
_____
_____
_____
_____
_____
_____
_____
_____

Directions: Use this page to plan and outline the information for your report about an unusual invention. Then write your report on another piece of paper.

INTEGRATED LANGUAGE ARTS PROJECT MASTERS, Grade 5

5

for Project, page T522

NAME _____

Personification Possibilities

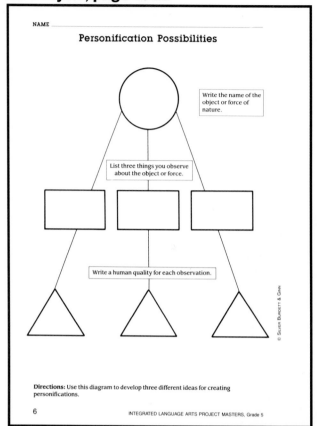

Write the name of the object or force of nature.

List three things you observe about the object or force.

Write a human quality for each observation.

Directions: Use this diagram to develop three different ideas for creating personifications.

6

INTEGRATED LANGUAGE ARTS PROJECT MASTERS, Grade 5

for Project, page T524

NAME _____

Response to Haiku

I am writing this response to the following haiku by _____ .

(author's name)

_____
_____
_____

This is my response.

_____
_____
_____
_____
_____
_____
_____
_____
_____
_____
_____
_____
_____

_____
(your signature)

Directions: Copy one haiku you would like to respond to. Write your response in the form of a letter, another haiku, a story, or an explanation. If you choose to make a painting, tape it over the lines above. Let the author of the haiku be the first to see your response. Then share it with the class.

INTEGRATED LANGUAGE ARTS PROJECT MASTERS, Grade 5

7

for Project, page T526

NAME _____

Job Quality Preferences

I would like to work _____

☐ 1. in a city
☐ 2. in a rural area
☐ 3. in a small town
☐ 4. indoors
☐ 5. outdoors
☐ 6. both indoors and outdoors
☐ 7. with people most of the time
☐ 8. with people some of the time
☐ 9. alone most of the time
☐ 10. having the same hours daily
☐ 11. having different hours daily
☐ 12. traveling away from home
☐ 13. staying mostly in one place
☐ 14. in a noisy place
☐ 15. in a quiet place

☐ 16. with moderate noise
☐ 17. with no control by a boss
☐ 18. with some control by a boss
☐ 19. with close control by a boss
☐ 20. with plenty of thinking
☐ 21. with plenty of action
☐ 22. with machines
☐ 23. directing other people
☐ 24. following another's directions
☐ 25. persuading other people
☐ 26. solving problems alone
☐ 27. solving problems with others
☐ 28. letting others solve problems
☐ 29. creating original ideas
☐ 30. knowing exactly what is expected

Write about the preference that is most important to you.

_____
_____
_____
_____
_____

Directions: Put a ✔ in the box before each job quality you think you would prefer. There are no right or wrong answers.

8

INTEGRATED LANGUAGE ARTS PROJECT MASTERS, Grade 5

For your convenience, the Evaluation and Testing Program is provided here in reduced form. It is also available separately in black-line, spirit master, and consumable form, as well as in a computer-managed instruction system, the MicroManager.

WHERE TO FIND THE TESTS AND ANSWER KEYS

In the back of the Teacher Edition, the following test-related items can be found:

◆ **Unit Pretests, Unit Posttests, Midyear Test, and End-of-Year Test** in reduced form with answers shown

◆ **Picture Prompt Writing Samples** in reduced form

In the Teacher Resource File, the following test-related items can be found:

◆ **All tests** as a separate set of black-line masters, including a Sample Test that can be used to familiarize students with these multiple-choice tests or to reinforce students' test-taking skills

◆ **A Teacher's Section for the Tests** containing scoring guides, class and individual record charts for the tests and writing samples, and evaluation guides and response forms for writing, and evaluation checklists for speaking and listening skills. Also included is information on evaluating writing, using the Picture Prompt Writing Samples, preparing students for proficiency testing, and examples of student writing.

DESCRIPTION OF TESTS

Silver Burdett & Ginn WORLD OF LANGUAGE provides four types of tests: Unit Tests, a Midyear Test, an End-of-Year Test, and two Picture Prompt Writing Samples for each unit. Each test measures skills taught in the Student Textbook. Below are descriptions of the tests, accompanied by recommendations for their use.

Unit Tests   Each unit has a four-page Pretest and a four-page Posttest. Both tests measure the same skills with multiple-choice items. Although intended to be administered before and after instruction of each unit, the Pretest and Posttest may also be used to test and retest students, or as a two-part posttest.

Midyear and End-of-Year Tests   These cumulative multiple-choice tests are designed to be administered after Unit 4 and Unit 8 respectively.

Picture Prompt Writing Samples   The Picture Prompt Writing Samples are an optional final section of the Pretest and Posttest. They may be used as a writing assignment or as a writing test. The kind of writing tested is the same as that taught in the Writing Process lesson of that unit. The students may list prewriting ideas on a separate sheet of paper, then write on the Answer Sheet provided in the test booklet. Although state-mandated writing tests do not allow extra time for revising, encourage students to proofread their work before handing it in.

ADMINISTERING THE TESTS

◆ Have students write their name on each sheet that will be scored (answer sheet or test sheets and lined paper).

◆ Read the directions with students. Be specific about whether they are to mark answers on the test or on the separate answer sheet.

◆ Remind students to read directions for each test section carefully. For unit tests, explain that the last section is a writing exercise for which answers will written on lined paper.

TIME

The following suggested times allow about one minute per multiple-choice item:

Unit Pretest/Posttest	Writing Sample	Midyear/ End-of-Year Test
30 minutes	20-30 minutes	60 minutes

SCORING THE TESTS

Score each correctly answered multiple choice item as 1. To convert the total score to a percentage, use this formula: 100 x (number of correct responses) ÷ (total number of responses) = %. A 0=4 holistic scoring scale is recommended for the Writing Sample.

Unit 1 Pretest

Name _____ Unit 1 ♦ Pretest

501P

Fill in the circle for each correct answer.

A. Choose whether each sentence is *declarative, interrogative, imperative,* or *exclamatory.*

1. Finish your report on magnets.
   - (a) declarative
   - (b) interrogative
   - (c) imperative ●
   - (d) exclamatory

2. Mr. Romano speaks three languages.
   - (a) declarative ●
   - (b) interrogative
   - (c) imperative
   - (d) exclamatory

3. What a beautiful sunset that is!
   - (a) declarative
   - (b) interrogative
   - (c) imperative
   - (d) exclamatory ●

4. How far away is the moon?
   - (a) declarative
   - (b) interrogative ●
   - (c) imperative
   - (d) exclamatory

B. Choose the sentence that is written correctly.

5.
   - (a) do you have your baseball?
   - (b) What a great catch?
   - (c) Sarah loves her new bicycle. ●
   - (d) Have you finished your homework!

6.
   - (a) Did you get your allowance? ●
   - (b) that car is silver and black.
   - (c) Ask your Mom?
   - (d) How much does it cost?

7.
   - (a) I like to travel?
   - (b) they are going home.
   - (c) Pass me my book. ●
   - (d) Why do birds sing!

8.
   - (a) Jupiter and Saturn are planets? ●
   - (b) Can you keep a secret.
   - (c) those apples are too expensive.
   - (d) How strange the old house looks!

C. Choose whether the underlined part of each sentence is the *complete subject, complete predicate, simple subject,* or *simple predicate.*

9. Aaron <u>studied</u> the solar system.
   - (a) complete subject
   - (b) complete predicate
   - (c) simple subject
   - (d) simple predicate ●

10. <u>The house painters</u> finished early.
   - (a) complete subject ●
   - (b) complete predicate
   - (c) simple subject
   - (d) simple predicate

11. The loud <u>noise</u> startled us.
   - (a) complete subject
   - (b) complete predicate
   - (c) simple subject ●
   - (d) simple predicate

12. The plumbers <u>worked on the sink.</u>
   - (a) complete subject
   - (b) complete predicate ●
   - (c) simple subject
   - (d) simple predicate

Please go to the next page.

World of Language ♦ Grade 5 ♦ UNIT 1 PRETEST   1

Name _____ Unit 1 ♦ Pretest

501P

Fill in the circle for each correct answer.

D. Choose the simple subject in each sentence. Choose *You* if the subject is understood.

13. The new governor signed the bill into law.
   - (a) You
   - (b) new
   - (c) governor ●
   - (d) bill

14. Get the yellow bucket out from under the sink.
   - (a) You ●
   - (b) bucket
   - (c) yellow
   - (d) sink

15. Dad put the papers in his briefcase and left for work.
   - (a) You
   - (b) Dad ●
   - (c) work
   - (d) briefcase

16. All the players on the football team took the same bus.
   - (a) You
   - (b) bus
   - (c) team
   - (d) players ●

17. Give Laura directions to the baseball card store in Greenfield.
   - (a) You ●
   - (b) Laura
   - (c) store
   - (d) baseball

E. Choose the quotation that is written correctly.

18.
   - (a) "Did you hear that noise"? Rafael asked.
   - (b) "Yes" said Yvonne "I wonder what it could be?"
   - (c) "It's probably just the wind," David said calmly. ●
   - (d) "Look! Joan cried, it's Maureen's cat."

19.
   - (a) "Someone took my baseball glove! Scott wailed." ●
   - (b) "Are you sure someone took it"? his mother wondered.
   - (c) "Yes," said Scott, "I put it in the garage after the game last night."
   - (d) "Then why did I find it on the kitchen table? his mother asked."

20.
   - (a) "Do you think it will rain today"? asked Maria.
   - (b) "No," said her father, "there isn't a cloud in the sky." ●
   - (c) "Can we go the beach? Maria asked."
   - (d) "Yes, said her father, but first we must finish our chores."

21.
   - (a) "Let's go!" Samantha shouted. "We're going to be late!" ●
   - (b) "Don't worry, said Juanita. They won't leave without us."
   - (c) "Mr. Davis told us to be there at nine o'clock sharp, said Samantha."
   - (d) "Well," said Juanita, "that means we have more than half an hour."

Please go to the next page.

World of Language ♦ Grade 5 ♦ UNIT 1 PRETEST   2

Name _____ Unit 1 ♦ Pretest

501P

Fill in the circle for each correct answer.

F. Read the thesaurus entries. Then choose the correct answer to each question.

> **build** (v) — to construct; form. They are going to
> <u>build</u> a new house.
> *erect* — to put up.
> *create* — to bring into existence.
> ANTONYMS: destroy, wreck

22. What part of speech is *build* and its synonyms?
   - (a) noun
   - (b) adjective
   - (c) verb ●
   - (d) adverb

23. Which of the following words is an antonym for *build*?
   - (a) erect
   - (b) construct
   - (c) create
   - (d) destroy ●

> **courage** (n) — bravery; valor. He faced the danger
> with great <u>courage.</u>
> *boldness* — fearlessness; daring.
> *resolution* — determination; firmness.
> *confidence* — assurance.
> ANTONYMS: fear, alarm

24. What part of speech is *courage* and its synonyms?
   - (a) verb
   - (b) adverb
   - (c) adjective
   - (d) noun ●

25. Which of the following words is an antonym for *courage*?
   - (a) boldness
   - (b) valor
   - (c) alarm ●
   - (d) confidence

26. Which synonym for *courage* means "determination"?
   - (a) resolution ●
   - (b) confidence
   - (c) daring
   - (d) bravery

Please go to the next page.

World of Language ♦ Grade 5 ♦ UNIT 1 PRETEST   3

Name _____ Unit 1 ♦ Pretest

501P

Fill in the circle for each correct answer.

G. Read the story below. Then choose the correct answer to each question.

> Leah loved to play the piano. She played very well, too, as long
> as no one else was around. Audiences scared her, and she would make
> mistakes. One day Leah's brother Josh walked by the living room
> when Leah was practicing. He tried to play a duet with her, but they
> made mistakes.
> "Maybe if I just sang along we would sound good," said Josh.
> Soon they were singing and playing and having a good time. Then
> Leah noticed there were other voices. She looked up and saw her
> friends standing in the doorway smiling and singing. She'd had an
> audience the whole time.

27. What is the story's setting?
   - (a) a school
   - (b) the backyard
   - (c) the living room ●
   - (d) an auditorium

28. Who is the main character?
   - (a) the audience
   - (b) Leah ●
   - (c) Josh
   - (d) Leah's piano teacher

29. What is the most important event in the story?
   - (a) Leah plays the piano well.
   - (b) Josh likes to play duets.
   - (c) Leah learns to play with people around. ●
   - (d) Josh and Leah always sing songs together.

Read the story below. Then choose the correct answer to each question.

> Mike was having trouble sleeping. His family had rented a cabin
> in the state forest for two weeks. Every night Mike heard scuffling
> and murmuring outside his window. His parents talked about a bandit
> and capturing a sneaky thief. As far as Mike could tell, though, all
> that had been stolen were several nights of sleep. Then, four nights
> before their vacation was over, Mike heard his father shout, "Got
> him!" Mike looked out his window. He saw Dad and a forest ranger
> standing by a cage. Inside the cage was the masked criminal, a fat
> raccoon eating an orange.

30. What is the story's setting?
   - (a) a city
   - (b) a state forest ●
   - (c) a foreign country
   - (d) a lake

31. Who is the main character?
   - (a) Mike ●
   - (b) the forest ranger
   - (c) Mike's father
   - (d) the raccoon

World of Language ♦ Grade 5 ♦ UNIT 1 PRETEST   **STOP**   4

Unit 1 Posttest

Fill in the circle for each correct answer.

A. Choose whether each sentence is *declarative*, *interrogative*, *imperative*, or *exclamatory*.

1. Paco has a baby brother.
   - (a) declarative
   - (c) imperative
   - (b) interrogative
   - (d) exclamatory

2. Where did you put the hammer?
   - (a) declarative
   - (c) imperative
   - (b) interrogative
   - (d) exclamatory

3. How different she looks today!
   - (a) declarative
   - (c) imperative
   - (b) interrogative
   - (d) exclamatory

4. Please get your bathing suit.
   - (a) declarative
   - (c) imperative
   - (b) interrogative
   - (d) exclamatory

B. Choose the sentence that is written correctly.

5.
   - (a) That chair is uncomfortable.
   - (b) go find your brother.
   - (c) Do you want to go to the beach!
   - (d) Chocolate is my favorite flavor?

6.
   - (a) it is too hot to sleep.
   - (b) I like open fields?
   - (c) Where are your pajamas?
   - (d) the hills are covered with snow.

7.
   - (a) How long will it rain.
   - (b) Kathy and I went to the park?
   - (c) What a fancy cake that is!
   - (d) Can you play the piano.

8.
   - (a) Andy, please close the door.
   - (b) Bricks are made from clay!
   - (c) How did you know the answer.
   - (d) Please pass the potatoes.

C. Choose whether the underlined part of each sentence is the *complete subject*, *complete predicate*, *simple subject*, or *simple predicate*.

9. <u>The dining room table</u> is new.
   - (a) complete subject
   - (b) complete predicate
   - (c) simple subject
   - (d) simple predicate

10. <u>His magazine</u> came in the mail.
   - (a) complete subject
   - (b) complete predicate
   - (c) simple subject
   - (d) simple predicate

11. Mitsuri <u>painted her first picture</u>.
   - (a) complete subject
   - (b) complete predicate
   - (c) simple subject
   - (d) simple predicate

12. The umpire <u>called</u> the runner out.
   - (a) complete subject
   - (b) complete predicate
   - (c) simple subject
   - (d) simple predicate

Please go to the next page.

© Silver, Burdett & Ginn Inc.

Fill in the circle for each correct answer.

D. Choose the simple subject in each sentence. Choose *You* if the subject is understood.

13. Put the vase in a box before it falls on the floor.
   - (a) You
   - (b) vase
   - (c) floor
   - (d) box

14. The children played in the park after lunch.
   - (a) You
   - (b) park
   - (c) children
   - (d) lunch

15. Aunt Margaret baked Nathan her special apple pie.
   - (a) You
   - (b) pie
   - (c) Nathan
   - (d) Aunt Margaret

16. Attach the wings and tail before you put on the wheels.
   - (a) You
   - (b) wings
   - (c) tail
   - (d) wheels

17. Lightning lit up the black clouds above the lake.
   - (a) You
   - (b) lake
   - (c) Lightning
   - (d) clouds

E. Choose the quotation that is written correctly.

18.
   - (a) "Where did Alice go?" Melinda wondered.
   - (b) "I think she went home", said David.
   - (c) "No" Gary said "I just saw her by the swings."
   - (d) "Let's join her! said Melinda. I love the swings."

19.
   - (a) "Wow!" Max cried. "That's the tallest building I've ever seen!"
   - (b) "It must be a mile high! said Theresa."
   - (c) "Well" said Mr. Ito "I don't think it is quite that tall."
   - (d) "Is there any building taller"? Francine asked.

20.
   - (a) "That was a wonderful movie"! said Martha.
   - (b) "Yes," Pablo agreed, "it had terrific special effects."
   - (c) "I especially liked the flight to Mars" said Erica.
   - (d) "I liked that part, too, added Pablo. It seemed so real!"

21.
   - (a) "Remember the last time we went camping"? Abe asked.
   - (b) "How could I forget?" Bob replied. "I didn't sleep all night."
   - (c) "You were so sure there was a bear outside the tent." laughed Abe.
   - (d) "Well, said Bob, how was I supposed to know it was just a cow?"

Please go to the next page.

© Silver, Burdett & Ginn Inc.

Fill in the circle for each correct answer.

F. Read the thesaurus entries. Then choose the correct answer to each question.

> **leisure** (n) — spare time. Summer vacation gave him the <u>leisure</u> to learn how to swim.
> *freedom* — ability to do what you want.
> *idleness* — lack of anything to do.
> *ease* — rest; relaxation.
> ANTONYMS: work, duty.

22. What part of speech is *leisure* and its synonyms?
   - (a) verb
   - (b) adverb
   - (c) adjective
   - (d) noun

23. Which of the following words is an antonym for *leisure*?
   - (a) duty
   - (b) freedom
   - (c) ease
   - (d) idleness

> **shrill** (adj) — loud, high-pitched. She yelled at him in a <u>shrill</u> voice.
> *piercing* — sharp; ear-splitting.
> *penetrating* — harsh; intense.
> ANTONYMS: soft, gentle.

24. What part of speech is *shrill* and its synonyms?
   - (a) verb
   - (b) adjective
   - (c) adverb
   - (d) noun

25. Which of the following words is an antonym for *shrill*?
   - (a) sharp
   - (b) penetrating
   - (c) noisy
   - (d) soft

26. Which synonym for *shrill* means "intense"?
   - (a) piercing
   - (b) loud
   - (c) high-pitched
   - (d) penetrating

Please go to the next page.

© Silver, Burdett & Ginn Inc.

Fill in the circle for each correct answer.

G. Read the story below. Then choose the correct answer to each question.

> Shara watched the sun slowly rise over the ocean. The early morning waves rolled gently onto the sand. The cold salt water tickled as it ran between Shara's toes.
> Shara had never been to the seashore. She was visiting her friend Bea at Bea's grandmother's house. The house sat on the edge of the beach. The house was old and smelled salty, like the sea. Shara and Bea explored the house, swam in the sea, and built castles in the sand. Most of all, though, Shara liked watching the sea at dawn.

27. What is the story's setting?
   - (a) the seashore
   - (b) a town
   - (c) a boat
   - (d) the waves

28. Who is the main character?
   - (a) Bea
   - (b) the grandmother
   - (c) the beach
   - (d) Shara

Read the story below. Then choose the correct answer to each question.

> Cal walked down Main Street, looking in all the shop windows. Cal wanted to get something special for his older sister Jenna. She was a wonderful dancer, and now she was going to be the main dancer in the school dance recital.
> Cal wanted Jenna to have something for her performance that was just from him. Cal winked at a teddy bear in the toy store window but shook his head. Then he noticed the ribbons in the window of the fabric shop. A bright, flowing ribbon, he thought, would be perfect. He would give Jenna a rose-colored satin ribbon to tie in her hair. Smiling, Cal went into the shop.

29. What is the story's setting?
   - (a) a toy store
   - (b) a street
   - (c) a library
   - (d) a playground

30. Who is the main character?
   - (a) Jenna
   - (b) the teddy bear
   - (c) Cal
   - (d) the store owner

31. What is the most important event in this story?
   - (a) Cal decides what would be the perfect gift for Jenna.
   - (b) Jenna is going to be the main dancer in the recital.
   - (c) Cal sees the teddy bear in the store window.
   - (d) Cal walks down Main Street looking in shop windows.

© Silver, Burdett & Ginn Inc.

Unit 2 Pretest

Fill in the circle for each correct answer.

A. Choose the plural noun in each group of words.

1. (a) desk   (b) class   (c) eraser   (d) books
2. (a) problem   (b) test   (c) sums   (d) answer
3. (a) daughter   (b) woman   (c) ladies   (d) mother
4. (a) stick   (b) steps   (c) skate   (d) slice
5. (a) brother   (b) uncle   (c) father   (d) cousins

B. Choose the correct plural form of each underlined noun.

6. party
   (a) partys   (c) parites
   (b) partyes   (d) parties
7. child
   (a) childs   (c) childrens
   (b) children   (d) childes
8. guess
   (a) guesses   (c) gueses
   (b) guess   (d) guessess
9. blanket
   (a) blanket   (b) blankets
   (b) blanketss   (d) blanketies
10. calf
    (a) calfs   (c) calfes
    (b) calves   (d) calvies

C. Choose the word that should be capitalized in each sentence.

11. Nathan will visit his brother in new Haven tomorrow.
    (a) brother   (b) new   (c) visit   (d) tomorrow
12. Julius took his sister alice to the baseball game.
    (a) sister   (b) alice   (c) baseball   (d) game
13. Billy's mother and father drove from Washington to texas.
    (a) mother   (b) father   (c) drove   (d) texas
14. I told mrs. Jefferson to take the bus into the city.
    (a) mrs.   (b) told   (c) bus   (d) city
15. The leader of our club says we will camp tonight at daisy Pond.
    (a) leader   (b) camp   (c) tonight   (d) daisy

Please go to the next page.

Fill in the circle for each correct answer.

D. Choose the correct abbreviation of each underlined word.

16. Road
    (a) Roa.   (c) Rd.
    (b) R.   (d) Ro.
17. Thursday
    (a) Thurdy.   (c) Trd.
    (b) Thurs.   (d) Thrd.
18. 3:30 in the afternoon
    (a) 3:30 a.m.   (c) 3:30 p.m.
    (b) 3:30 A.M.   (d) 3:30 P.M.
19. November
    (a) Nber.   (c) Nov.
    (b) Nvb.   (d) Nemb.

E. Choose the correct possessive form of each underlined noun.

20. Betty
    (a) Bettys'   (c) Bettys
    (b) Betty's   (d) Betties'
21. stadium
    (a) stadium's   (c) stadiums's
    (b) stadiums'   (d) stadiums
22. women
    (a) womens   (c) women's
    (b) womens'   (d) womens's
23. lions
    (a) lion's   (c) lions
    (b) lions'   (d) lions's

F. Choose the correct meaning of the underlined word in each sentence.

24. The cheers of the crowd made Tara even prouder of her accomplishment.
    (a) book   (b) success   (c) outfit   (d) mistake
25. Let's stack the dishes. That's the most efficient use of limited space.
    (a) orderly   (b) busy   (c) difficult   (d) extra
26. Sheri smiled as she looked at the gently serene and pretty countryside.
    (a) dark   (b) crowded   (c) stormy   (d) peaceful
27. The use of oil is vital to keeping a car engine in good shape.
    (a) necessary   (b) electrical   (c) heavy   (d) strange
28. Tommy will persist in his demands until he finally gets what he wants.
    (a) delay   (b) forget   (c) continue   (d) relax

Please go to the next page.

Fill in the circle for each correct answer.

G. Read the directions below. Then choose the correct answer to each question.

> Planting your own tomato garden is easier than you might think. Start out by choosing a plot of ground that gets plenty of sunlight. Rake and weed the soil thoroughly, then loosen it with a shovel. After that go to a garden shop and buy ten or fifteen young tomato plants. Dig holes about five inches deep and two feet apart. Carefully place each plant in a hole. Fill the hole with soil so that the roots and lower stem are covered. Finish by watering your new tomato garden.

29. What do the directions tell you to do first?
    (a) Place a plant in each hole.
    (b) Choose a sunny plot of ground.
    (c) Fill each hole with soil.
    (d) Dig holes five inches deep.
30. What do you do just before you fill each hole with soil?
    (a) Water your tomato garden.
    (b) Rake and weed the garden soil.
    (c) Place a plant in each hole.
    (d) Buy young tomato plants.
31. What do you do right after you rake and weed your garden thoroughly?
    (a) Loosen the soil with a shovel.
    (b) Water your new tomato garden.
    (c) Fill each hole with soil.
    (d) Place a plant in each hole.
32. What do the directions tell you to do last?
    (a) Fill each hole with soil.
    (b) Buy young tomato plants.
    (c) Dig a hole for each plant.
    (d) Water your new tomato garden.

H. Choose the sentence in which commas are used correctly.

33. (a) Jane can dance, sing and, act.
    (b) He wore a scarf, hat, and, coat.
    (c) Al used a fork knife, and spoon.
    (d) Dad scrapes, sands, and paints.
34. (a) Will you be in the parade, Alex?
    (b) No Ed, I'll be out of town.
    (c) Well I can march, for you.
    (d) I think that's, a good idea, Ed.
35. (a) I baked, cut and served the pie.
    (b) You can chop, dice, or, peel it.
    (c) It comes in pink, blue and, red.
    (d) The air was clear, dry, and hot.
36. (a) Are you feeling, all right Meg?
    (b) Yes, but my leg is still sore.
    (c) Well you should go, home.
    (d) No the doctor said, to exercise.

Please go to the next page.

Fill in the circle for each correct answer.

I. Choose the sentence that supports the topic sentence.

37. TOPIC SENTENCE: Soccer is a very popular and exciting sport.
    (a) Thousands saw the thrilling world soccer finals in Mexico City.
    (b) Baseball and basketball are also popular sports.
    (c) A famous soccer player named Pele is from Brazil.
    (d) In England soccer is called football.
38. TOPIC SENTENCE: Mark Twain wrote many books that are still read today.
    (a) Mark Twain's real name was Samuel Clemens.
    (b) Twain once was a boatman on the Mississippi River.
    (c) People of all ages enjoy reading Twain's *The Adventures of Tom Sawyer*.
    (d) Mark Twain grew up in Hannibal, Missouri.
39. TOPIC SENTENCE: There are many unusual animals in a tropical rain forest.
    (a) Tropical rain forests have more kinds of trees than dry forests.
    (b) Squirrel monkeys, parrots, sunbirds, and giant cats live in rain forests.
    (c) The Amazon rain forest covers nearly one third of South America.
    (d) All tropical rain forests are similar, and all are always green.
40. TOPIC SENTENCE: The night sky of the far north glows with strange lights.
    (a) These glowing northern lights are called the Aurora Borealis.
    (b) The Arctic Circle covers the northern top of the world.
    (c) In the summer the sun never sets in the Arctic Circle.
    (d) What we call the Morning Star is actually the planet Venus.

STOP

Unit 2 Posttest

Fill in the circle for each correct answer.

A. Choose the plural noun in each group of words.

1. (a) trap   ⓑ maps   (c) floss   (d) kiss
2. (a) cheeses   (b) breeze   (c) disease   (d) goose
3. (a) graphs   (b) grass   (c) jar   (d) glass
4. ⓐ salespeople   (b) firefighter   (c) officer   (d) chairperson
5. (a) grizzly   (b) zebra   ⓒ turkeys   (d) giraffe

B. Choose the correct plural form of each underlined noun.

6. brush
   (a) brushs   (c) brushess
   ⓑ brushes   (d) brush
7. belief
   (a) believes   ⓒ beliefs
   (b) beliefes   (d) believs
8. leaf
   (a) leafs   (c) leafes
   ⓑ leaves   (d) leves
9. deer
   ⓐ deer   (c) deeres
   (b) deers   (d) deerys
10. city
    (a) city   (c) cityes
    (b) citys   ⓓ cities

C. Choose the word that should be capitalized in each sentence.

11. Grandma went with jeffrey to the doctor's office.
    (a) went   ⓑ jeffrey   (c) doctor's   (d) office
12. Mercury and pluto are the smallest planets in the solar system.
    ⓐ pluto   (b) planets   (c) solar   (d) system
13. We took a class trip to the Ohio river to watch the boat race.
    (a) class   (b) trip   ⓒ river   (d) race
14. I told lucy and her little sister to call the boys to dinner.
    ⓐ lucy   (b) sister   (c) boys   (d) dinner
15. The letter from africa was covered with blue stamps.
    (a) letter   ⓑ africa   (c) blue   (d) stamps

Please go to the next page.

Fill in the circle for each correct answer.

D. Choose the correct abbreviation of each underlined word.

16. Junior
    (a) Jnr.   (c) Jun.
    ⓑ Jr.   (d) Junr.
17. before noon
    (a) B.N.   (c) P.M.
    ⓑ A.M.   (d) Bn.
18. October
    ⓐ Oct.   (c) Otb.
    (b) Ocr.   (d) Octb.
19. Wednesday
    (a) Wdy.   (c) Wnd.
    ⓑ Wed.   (d) Wday.

E. Choose the correct possessive form of each underlined noun.

20. zoo
    (a) zoo'   (c) zoos
    ⓑ zoo's   (d) zoos's
21. Jones
    ⓐ Jones's   (c) Jone's
    (b) Jones'   (d) Joness
22. couple
    (a) couples   ⓒ couple's
    (b) couples'   (d) couples's
23. river
    (a) river'   (c) rivers's
    (b) rivers   ⓓ river's

F. Choose the correct meaning of the underlined word in each sentence.

24. That mountain path is too treacherous. We should take this safer one.
    (a) ridiculous   (b) easy   ⓒ dangerous   (d) overgrown
25. The scouts solemnly pledged always to tell the truth.
    (a) laughed   (b) forgot   (c) bragged   ⓓ promised
26. Dad always prohibits us from swimming before the lifeguard arrives.
    ⓐ forbids   (b) allows   (c) helps   (d) shows
27. The tree branches became so rigid from the cold that they wouldn't bend.
    ⓐ stiff   (b) leafy   (c) bare   (d) crooked
28. The bird's nervous chatter annoyed Tom while he was trying to work.
    (a) cheered   ⓑ bothered   (c) found   (d) calmed

Please go to the next page.

Fill in the circle for each correct answer.

G. Read the directions below. Then answer the questions that follow.

> You can help with dinner by learning to make a tossed salad. All you need is a head of lettuce, two tomatoes, a pepper, an onion, a carrot, and salad dressing. Start by washing the vegetables in water. Then break the lettuce into pieces with your hands. Next cut up the tomatoes, onion, and pepper. Follow by slicing the carrot into strips. Now place your prepared vegetables into a big bowl. Finish by adding your favorite dressing and tossing the salad with two wooden forks.

29. What do the directions tell you to do first?
    (a) Add your favorite dressing.
    (b) Place the vegetables in a bowl.
    ⓒ Wash the vegetables in water.
    (d) Learn to help with dinner.
30. What do you do right after you wash the vegetables?
    ⓐ Break the lettuce into pieces.
    (b) Cut up the tomatoes.
    (c) Slice the carrot into strips.
    (d) Toss the vegetables with a fork.
31. What do you do right before you place the vegetables in a bowl?
    (a) Cut up the onion and pepper.
    ⓑ Slice the carrot into strips.
    (c) Add your favorite dressing.
    (d) Wash the vegetables in water.
32. What do the directions tell you to do last?
    (a) Break the lettuce into pieces.
    (b) Slice the carrot into strips.
    ⓒ Toss the vegetables with forks.
    (d) Place the vegetables in a bowl.

H. Choose the sentence in which commas are used correctly.

33. (a) Well that, was a fine play.
    ⓑ Who directed it this year, Ted?
    (c) My friend Al, directed it.
    (d) Yes I heard, he likes theater.
34. (a) Farmers plant, harvest and sell.
    (b) Leaves turn red gold, and brown.
    ⓒ Jill wore a cape, hat, and mask.
    (d) Juan can pitch, hit, and, throw.
35. (a) Where is the, bookstore Amy?
    (b) Well I think, it's on Pine St.
    ⓒ No, I heard it moved from there.
    (d) Are you sure, about that, Jo?
36. ⓐ Ed likes peas, corn, and beans.
    (b) Will, he turn eight nine or ten?
    (c) Do you want, water juice or tea?
    (d) The hat is red, blue and, green.

Please go to the next page.

Fill in the circle for each correct answer.

I. Choose the sentence that supports the topic sentence.

37. TOPIC SENTENCE: The white Lippizaner horses are famous around the world.
    ⓐ Some Lippizaners are trained at the Spanish Riding School of Vienna.
    (b) Arabian horses also have strong, short legs and arched necks.
    ⓒ These beautiful show horses exhibit their skills at shows in many lands.
    (d) At the school the horses are taught graceful jumping and dancing acts.
38. TOPIC SENTENCE: Rock-and-roll music is a blend of many styles of music.
    ⓐ Elements of jazz, folk, and blues can be heard in some rock music.
    (b) The Beatles were the most popular rock musicians of all time.
    (c) The electric guitar is the basic instrument for rock-and-roll music.
    (d) "Rock Around the Clock" was the first international rock hit.
39. TOPIC SENTENCE: Egypt's pyramids are one of the seven ancient world wonders.
    (a) The ancient Greeks and Romans made lists of things travelers should see.
    ⓑ The three pyramids at Giza are the most famous of the pyramids.
    (c) The Suez Canal is one of the seven wonders of the modern world.
    (d) Many of the ancient wonders of the world no longer exist.
40. TOPIC SENTENCE: Whales are the largest mammals in the world.
    (a) Whales are warm-blooded, but fish are cold-blooded.
    (b) Whales are sea animals that look like big fish.
    (c) The sperm whale can hold its breath for over an hour.
    ⓓ Blue whales can grow to a length of 100 feet and weigh over 90 tons.

STOP

T535

Unit 3 Pretest

503P

Fill in the circle for each correct answer.

A. Choose the correct answer to each question.

1. In which sentence is an action verb underlined?
   - (a) Builders draw plans for houses.
   - (b) These are called blueprints.
   - (c) Blueprints are like maps.
   - (d) They have many details.

2. In which sentence is a linking verb underlined?
   - (a) I am going to Grandma's house.
   - (b) Grandma makes treats for me.
   - (c) She baked an apple pie yesterday.
   - (d) Apple pie is my favorite treat.

3. In which sentence is the main verb underlined?
   - (a) Eddie has waited all day.
   - (b) He is playing baseball tonight.
   - (c) He has practiced every day.
   - (d) His parents will watch him.

4. In which sentence is the helping verb underlined?
   - (a) Roger is collecting empty cans.
   - (b) We will bring them to the store.
   - (c) He already has fifty cans.
   - (d) Tom and Kathy have helped him.

5. In which sentence is a linking verb underlined?
   - (a) Winter winds are so cold.
   - (b) The snow falls so quietly.
   - (c) Mitch has built a hockey pond.
   - (d) He plays there often.

B. Choose the direct object of the underlined verb in each sentence.

6. We saw a moose across the lake.
   - (a) lake
   - (b) moose
   - (c) across
   - (d) the

7. I visited Jake at his aunt's house.
   - (a) aunt's
   - (b) his
   - (c) house
   - (d) Jake

8. Strong winds blew the trees over.
   - (a) Strong
   - (b) over
   - (c) trees
   - (d) winds

9. Maria put her books on the table.
   - (a) Maria
   - (b) her
   - (c) books
   - (d) table

10. We moved the chest into the attic.
    - (a) We
    - (b) chest
    - (c) into
    - (d) attic

Please go to the next page.

World of Language ♦ Grade 5 ♦ UNIT 3 PRETEST   17

503P

Fill in the circle for each correct answer.

C. Choose the correct answer to each question.

11. Which verb is in the present tense?
    - (a) dreams
    - (b) dreamed
    - (c) will dream
    - (d) has dreamed

12. Which verb is in the past tense?
    - (a) climb
    - (b) climbed
    - (c) climbs
    - (d) will climb

13. Which verb is in the future tense?
    - (a) describe
    - (b) describes
    - (c) described
    - (d) will describe

14. Which verb is in the past tense?
    - (a) sip
    - (b) sips
    - (c) will sip
    - (d) sipped

15. Which verb is in the present tense?
    - (a) measure
    - (b) measured
    - (c) will measure
    - (d) has measured

D. Choose the correct present-tense form of the verb for each sentence.

16. Every Monday Patrick _____ soccer.
    - (a) playes
    - (b) playss
    - (c) plays
    - (d) play

17. Amy _____ to sing funny songs.
    - (a) like
    - (b) likes
    - (c) likeses
    - (d) likkes

18. Hector always _____ the ball.
    - (a) throw
    - (b) thros
    - (c) throwes
    - (d) throws

19. Mark _____ things faster than I do.
    - (a) decideses
    - (b) decides
    - (c) decide
    - (d) decidses

20. Two deer _____ through the forest.
    - (a) races
    - (b) race
    - (c) racess
    - (d) raceses

E. Choose the form of the verb that correctly completes each sentence.

21. Kenny _____ his own vegetables.
    - (a) grow
    - (b) grew
    - (c) growed
    - (d) growing

22. Mother _____ her new dress today.
    - (a) wear
    - (b) worn
    - (c) wore
    - (d) wearing

23. Jed has _____ too many apples.
    - (a) eaten
    - (b) eats
    - (c) ate
    - (d) eating

24. All the leaves have _____ down.
    - (a) falls
    - (b) falled
    - (c) fell
    - (d) fallen

25. Louise _____ on a pony yesterday.
    - (a) rode
    - (b) ridden
    - (c) ride
    - (d) rided

Please go to the next page.

World of Language ♦ Grade 5 ♦ UNIT 3 PRETEST   18

503P

Fill in the circle for each correct answer.

F. Choose the correct answer to each question.

26. In which sentence should you use set and not sit?
    - (a) I like to _____ next to Jimmy.
    - (b) Ben will _____ in his chair.
    - (c) You must _____ on the ground.
    - (d) Please _____ the glasses there.

27. In which sentence should you use can and not may?
    - (a) Jamie _____ do a back flip.
    - (b) You _____ play ball after lunch.
    - (c) Now _____ I play with Margaret?
    - (d) Mom, _____ I ask Tess to dinner?

28. In which sentence should you use sit and not set?
    - (a) You can _____ the box here.
    - (b) _____ your boots on the mat.
    - (c) Let's go _____ on that rock.
    - (d) Dick _____ down the tools.

29. In which sentence should you use may and not can?
    - (a) Pat, _____ you make lunch now?
    - (b) I _____ figure out that answer.
    - (c) Yes, you _____ use the phone.
    - (d) I _____ run faster than anyone.

30. In which sentence should you use set and not sit?
    - (a) I want to _____ in the balcony.
    - (b) Why did Sam _____ the bag there?
    - (c) _____ on the picnic blanket.
    - (d) Now there's nowhere to _____.

G. Choose the correct meaning of each underlined word.

31. reexamined
    - (a) examined before
    - (b) not examined
    - (c) examined again
    - (d) examined wrongly

32. disagree
    - (a) to agree before
    - (b) to agree wrongly
    - (c) to agree again
    - (d) opposite of agree

33. misjudged
    - (a) judged again
    - (b) judged wrongly
    - (c) judged before
    - (d) not judged

34. preheat
    - (a) not to heat
    - (b) to heat before
    - (c) to heat again
    - (d) to heat wrongly

35. unfold
    - (a) to fold again
    - (b) opposite of fold
    - (c) to fold before
    - (d) to fold wrongly

Please go to the next page.

World of Language ♦ Grade 5 ♦ UNIT 3 PRETEST   19

503P

Fill in the circle for each correct answer.

H. Proofread the sentences. Each sentence contains a mistake. Choose the part of each sentence that has the mistake.

36. Lizas mother asked Liza to go to Murphy's Market for some things.
    a   b   c   d

    Which is the mistake in the sentence above?
    - (a) Lizas
    - (b) asked
    - (c) Market
    - (d) things.

37. She told Liza to get milk, bread, and, eggs for tomorrow's breakfast.
    a   b   c   d

    Which is the mistake in the sentence above?
    - (a) She
    - (b) get
    - (c) and,
    - (d) tomorrow's

38. When she got to the corner, Liza saw a Girl sitting next to a cardboard box.
    a   b   c   d

    Which is the mistake in the sentence above?
    - (a) When
    - (b) Girl
    - (c) next
    - (d) box.

39. "Oh, what a cute little kitten! cried Liza as she peered into the box.
    a   b   c   d

    Which is the mistake in the sentence above?
    - (a) "Oh,
    - (b) cute
    - (c) kitten!
    - (d) into

40. "It needs a nice home," said the girl as she handed the kitty to Liza?
    a   b   c   d

    Which is the mistake in the sentence above?
    - (a) "It
    - (b) home,"
    - (c) handed
    - (d) Liza?

STOP

World of Language ♦ Grade 5 ♦ UNIT 3 PRETEST   20

T536

Unit 3 Posttest

Fill in the circle for each correct answer.

A. Choose the correct answer to each question.

1. In which sentence is an action verb underlined?
   - (a) Kate is an expert hiker.
   - (b) She has climbed every weekend.
   - (c) She photographs birds and trees.
   - (d) She has collected many pictures.

2. In which sentence is a linking verb underlined?
   - (a) I travel by bus.
   - (b) Buses tour around the country.
   - (c) Airplanes are much faster.
   - (d) On buses you see more.

3. In which sentence is the main verb underlined?
   - (a) Joe is working at the theatre.
   - (b) He has worked there often.
   - (c) He likes being around actors.
   - (d) They have told him many stories.

4. In which sentence is the helping verb underlined?
   - (a) Clark and I are trading marbles.
   - (b) He sorted my moonstones.
   - (c) Clark has already organized his.
   - (d) Monday we will buy new marbles.

5. In which sentence is a linking verb underlined?
   - (a) My mother is very clever.
   - (b) She looked at Tom's car.
   - (c) She told him what was wrong.
   - (d) Now he will fix the spark plug.

B. Choose the direct object of the underlined verb in each sentence.

6. Morris put his hand on the mirror.
   - (a) Morris
   - (b) his
   - (c) hand
   - (d) mirror

7. The whole family watched the dog.
   - (a) The
   - (b) whole
   - (c) family
   - (d) dog

8. Joel mowed the lawn this morning.
   - (a) Joel
   - (b) lawn
   - (c) this
   - (d) morning

9. I caught the butterfly with my net.
   - (a) with
   - (b) my
   - (c) net
   - (d) butterfly

10. The clown wore six different hats.
   - (a) hats
   - (b) six
   - (c) different
   - (d) clown

Please go to the next page.

Fill in the circle for each correct answer.

C. Choose the correct answer to each question.

11. Which verb is in the present tense?
   - (a) jogged
   - (b) jogs
   - (c) will jog
   - (d) has jogged

12. Which verb is in the past tense?
   - (a) agrees
   - (b) agree
   - (c) agreed
   - (d) will agree

13. Which verb is in the future tense?
   - (a) considers
   - (b) considered
   - (c) will consider
   - (d) consider

14. Which verb is in the past tense?
   - (a) will shout
   - (b) shouts
   - (c) shout
   - (d) shouted

15. Which verb is in the present tense?
   - (a) zip
   - (b) zipped
   - (c) has zipped
   - (d) will zip

D. Choose the correct present-tense form of the verb for each sentence.

16. Jackie _____ everything Dick says.
   - (a) forget
   - (b) forgetts
   - (c) forgets
   - (d) forgetes

17. This train _____ at every station.
   - (a) stopes
   - (b) stops
   - (c) stop
   - (d) stopss

18. Andy always _____ a backpack.
   - (a) carries
   - (b) carrys
   - (c) carry
   - (d) carryes

19. Photos _____ in humid weather.
   - (a) curles
   - (b) curl
   - (c) curls
   - (d) curels

20. Tina _____ the beach ball with Mom.
   - (a) bounces
   - (b) bouncies
   - (c) bounce
   - (d) bouncess

E. Choose the form of the verb that correctly completes each sentence.

21. Stacey has _____ home already.
   - (a) going
   - (b) goes
   - (c) gone
   - (d) went

22. Dad _____ letters to the President.
   - (a) write
   - (b) written
   - (c) wrote
   - (d) wrotted

23. George _____ all of the peanuts.
   - (a) taken
   - (b) took
   - (c) tooks
   - (d) taking

24. Dan has _____ the picture to Sue.
   - (a) gave
   - (b) give
   - (c) gived
   - (d) given

25. Lindbergh _____ across the ocean.
   - (a) flew
   - (b) fly
   - (c) flown
   - (d) flying

Please go to the next page.

Fill in the circle for each correct answer.

F. Choose the correct answer to each question.

26. In which sentence should you use set and not sit?
   - (a) The tall boy must _____ in back.
   - (b) Don't worry, we can _____ here.
   - (c) Just _____ them on the shelf.
   - (d) Look where Ron wants to _____.

27. In which sentence should you use can and not may?
   - (a) No, Sam, you _____ not watch TV.
   - (b) Kim _____ swim six laps easily.
   - (c) When _____ I see the pictures?
   - (d) You _____ want to change that.

28. In which sentence should you use sit and not set?
   - (a) If I don't _____ down I'll drop!
   - (b) _____ the boxes on the floor.
   - (c) Dad has to _____ the table.
   - (d) Where did Julio _____ the book?

29. In which sentence should you use may and not can?
   - (a) Hans _____ lift over 50 pounds.
   - (b) I think I _____ finish by noon.
   - (c) Janice _____ get us tickets.
   - (d) Yes, you _____ go fishing today.

30. In which sentence should you use set and not sit?
   - (a) If I _____ down I won't get up!
   - (b) Don, _____ the eggs over there.
   - (c) May we _____ in the first row?
   - (d) When can Rita _____ with us?

G. Choose the correct meaning of each underlined word.

31. resupply
   - (a) to supply before
   - (b) not supply
   - (c) to supply again
   - (d) to supply wrongly

32. disallow
   - (a) to allow before
   - (b) to allow wrongly
   - (c) to allow again
   - (d) opposite of allow

33. misfire
   - (a) fired again
   - (b) fired wrongly
   - (c) fired before
   - (d) not fired

34. prepay
   - (a) opposite of pay
   - (b) to pay again
   - (c) to pay before
   - (d) not to pay

35. unpack
   - (a) to pack again
   - (b) opposite of pack
   - (c) to pack before
   - (d) to pack wrongly

Please go to the next page.

Fill in the circle for each correct answer.

H. Proofread the sentences. Each sentence contains a mistake. Choose the part of each sentence that has the mistake.

36. Sid looked up the Mountain path and sighed because Mike was walking too fast.
    a   b   c   d

   Which is the mistake in the above sentence?
   - (a) Sid
   - (b) Mountain
   - (c) sighed
   - (d) fast.

37. "How does he do it?" Sid wondered? as he struggled to keep his legs moving.
          a   b   c   d

   Which is the mistake in the above sentence?
   - (a) does
   - (b) it?"
   - (c) wondered?
   - (d) struggled

38. Just then Mike turned around and shouted "Don't stop or you'll cramp."
        a   b   c   d

   Which is the mistake in the above sentence?
   - (a) then
   - (b) turned
   - (c) shouted
   - (d) stop

39. The hike was hard work, but Sid groaned and followed his friends lead.
                        a   b   c   d

   Which is the mistake in the above sentence?
   - (a) work,
   - (b) groaned
   - (c) followed
   - (d) friends

40. "just take it slow," said Mike, "and you will be there in no time."
      a   b   c   d

   Which is the mistake in the above sentence?
   - (a) "just
   - (b) Mike,
   - (c) will
   - (d) time."

(STOP)

T537

Unit 4 Pretest

Fill in the circle for each correct answer.

A. Choose the pronoun that takes the place of the underlined word or words.

1. Bob's sports shop has everything from bowling balls to batons.
   (a) Their   (b) His ●   (c) He   (d) Our

2. The park ranger showed Dick and me which trail was the most challenging.
   (a) her   (b) we   (c) us ●   (d) our

3. The storm left three feet of snow on the ground.
   (a) It ●   (b) She   (c) He   (d) Its

4. Aunt Emma always makes us wash up before dinner.
   (a) Hers   (b) She ●   (c) They   (d) Her

5. Stephanie forgot to tell Mr. Osgood that she would be late.
   (a) him ●   (b) he   (c) us   (d) his

6. This huge horse ranch is Jim and Ray's.
   (a) them   (b) their   (c) theirs ●   (d) they

7. Dustin gave Tom and his brother directions to the football stadium.
   (a) we   (b) they   (c) him   (d) them ●

8. When will Jamilla's picture be in the newspaper?
   (a) my   (b) their   (c) hers   (d) her ●

B. Choose the pronoun that correctly completes each sentence.

9. Will you show _____ how to use your telescope?
   (a) I   (b) me ●   (c) he   (d) she

10. _____ and Paul are going to camp together this summer.
    (a) Me   (b) Them   (c) Him   (d) He ●

11. Dad wants _____ to wash the car before we go downtown.
    (a) we   (b) us ●   (c) I   (d) he

12. Rene and _____ spent the afternoon listening to records.
    (a) me   (b) her   (c) I ●   (d) us

© Silver, Burdett & Ginn Inc.

Please go to the next page.

World of Language ♦ Grade 5 ♦ UNIT 4 PRETEST   25

Fill in the circle for each correct answer.

B. Choose the pronoun that correctly completes each sentence.

13. I can't believe _____ left our sandals at the beach.
    (a) we ●   (b) her   (c) us   (d) them

14. Mr. and Mrs. Washington took _____ dog to the vet.
    (a) their ●   (b) its   (c) they   (d) us

15. Luther keeps _____ allowance in a big glass jar.
    (a) they   (b) he   (c) she   (d) his ●

C. Choose the correct contraction for each pair of underlined words.

16. I would
    (a) I'wd   (b) I'd ●   (c) I'ld   (d) I'ed

17. we are
    (a) were'   (b) w'ere   (c) we're ●   (d) wer'e

18. she will
    (a) she'ill   (b) shel'l   (c) she'il   (d) she'll ●

19. they are
    (a) they're ●   (b) the're   (c) th'eyre   (d) th'are

20. you would
    (a) you'wd   (b) you'd ●   (c) you'ld   (d) yo'ud

D. Choose the homophone for each underlined word.

21. I can hear the train coming.
    (a) rain   (b) listen   (c) here ●   (d) dear

22. Alan worked on the squeaky stair.
    (a) stare ●   (b) leaky   (c) hair   (d) railing

23. The sleeping dog wags its tail.
    (a) pail   (b) tale ●   (c) nose   (d) head

24. Greg jumped off the diving board.
    (a) soared   (b) splash   (c) beam   (d) bored ●

25. The sale will only last one day.
    (a) buy   (b) sail ●   (c) bargain   (d) gale

© Silver, Burdett & Ginn Inc.

Please go to the next page.

World of Language ♦ Grade 5 ♦ UNIT 4 PRETEST   26

Fill in the circle for each correct answer.

E. Choose the correct answer to each question.

26. Which sentence is a fact rather than an opinion?
    (a) Camp Sequoia is the best summer camp in the county.
    (b) Campers can stay either in tents or in cabins. ●
    (c) The food is delicious and the activities are fun.
    (d) Everyone always has a wonderful time at Camp Sequoia.

27. Which sentence is an opinion rather than a fact?
    (a) John Tyler was the tenth president of the United States.
    (b) He served as president from 1841 to 1845.
    (c) He signed the first American trade treaty with China.
    (d) He was a very patient and courageous man. ●

28. Which sentence is a fact rather than an opinion?
    (a) Whiparound is the fastest jump rope ever made.
    (b) Whiparound lets you jump faster than you ever imagined.
    (c) A Whiparound jump rope costs between $5.00 and $6.00. ●
    (d) You'll be the star of the playground with Whiparound.

29. Which sentence is an opinion rather than a fact?
    (a) Tubas are fascinating musical instruments. ●
    (b) They are the largest brass instruments.
    (c) High school bands often have tubas.
    (d) Tubas make a low bass sound.

30. Which sentence is a fact rather than an opinion?
    (a) A Tiger's Tale is the best book ever written.
    (b) The story tells about a tiger's life in the jungle. ●
    (c) The tiger's adventures are exciting and sometimes scary.
    (d) Tigers are the most interesting of all the big cats.

© Silver, Burdett & Ginn Inc.

Please go to the next page.

World of Language ♦ Grade 5 ♦ UNIT 4 PRETEST   27

Fill in the circle for each correct answer.

F. Choose the correct name for each part of a business letter.

31. Sincerely yours,
    (a) closing ●   (b) signature   (c) body   (d) greeting

32. Dear Dr. Savalas:
    (a) body   (b) greeting ●   (c) signature   (d) inside address

33. Horatio X. Mins, Editor
    Nautical News
    Leagueton, CA 94400
    (a) heading   (b) body   (c) inside address ●   (d) closing

34. 144 Main Street
    Lefferts, NY 10203
    August 30, 1991
    (a) body   (b) heading ●   (c) closing   (d) inside address

35. Please run the drama club ad in Monday's paper. This year's play is a musical, *Wonderful Town*.
    (a) body ●   (b) closing   (c) greeting   (d) heading

© Silver, Burdett & Ginn Inc.

STOP

World of Language ♦ Grade 5 ♦ UNIT 4 PRETEST   28

Unit 4 Posttest

Fill in the circle for each correct answer.

A. Choose the pronoun that takes the place of the underlined word or words.

1. Mr. Albertini plays the trumpet in the town band.
   ⓐ Him   ⓑ Them   ⓒ He   ⓓ His

2. The lifeguard at the pool taught Susan and me how to do a swan dive.
   ⓐ us   ⓑ her   ⓒ I   ⓓ we

3. Bernice left the package in the car by mistake.
   ⓐ its   ⓑ them   ⓒ it   ⓓ him

4. Please don't lose Charlie's baseball glove!
   ⓐ him   ⓑ their   ⓒ he   ⓓ his

5. The two police officers brought Alan home safely.
   ⓐ Their   ⓑ They   ⓒ Theirs   ⓓ She

6. The blue loafers with the little tassels are Jody's.
   ⓐ its   ⓑ hers   ⓒ she   ⓓ her

7. Uncle David promised to take Aaron and Nathaniel fishing.
   ⓐ them   ⓑ him   ⓒ us   ⓓ they

8. Mr. and Mrs. Jackson's baby has dark brown hair.
   ⓐ Our   ⓑ His   ⓒ Theirs   ⓓ Their

B. Choose the pronoun that correctly completes each sentence.

9. Billy told _____ about the water slide at the amusement park.
   ⓐ I   ⓑ they   ⓒ him   ⓓ he

10. _____ and Sophia sold lemonade to the neighbors.
    ⓐ Me   ⓑ Them   ⓒ Her   ⓓ She

11. Mom asked _____ to leave our muddy shoes in the hall.
    ⓐ we   ⓑ us   ⓒ I   ⓓ he

12. _____ want them to finish painting the stairs.
    ⓐ I   ⓑ Me   ⓒ He   ⓓ Us

Please go to the next page.

Fill in the circle for each correct answer.

B. Choose the pronoun that correctly completes each sentence.

13. Suzanne and I bought _____ skirts at the new department store.
    ⓐ them   ⓑ we   ⓒ our   ⓓ us

14. Tell Ms. Gutierrez how you put _____ kite together.
    ⓐ him   ⓑ you   ⓒ they   ⓓ your

15. Tamara told me that the history book was _____.
    ⓐ her   ⓑ she's   ⓒ hers   ⓓ its

C. Choose the correct contraction for each pair of underlined words.

16. we have
    ⓐ w'eve   ⓒ we've
    ⓑ wev'e   ⓓ we'ave

17. they will
    ⓐ they'll   ⓒ they'wl
    ⓑ the'll   ⓓ th'll

18. he is
    ⓐ h'es   ⓒ h's
    ⓑ he's   ⓓ hes'

19. you will
    ⓐ yo'll   ⓒ you'll
    ⓑ youl'   ⓓ y'wl

20. I have
    ⓐ I'ave   ⓒ Ive'
    ⓑ I've   ⓓ I'hv

D. Choose the homophone for each underlined word.

21. Where are your new shoes?
    ⓐ boots   ⓒ fair
    ⓑ wear   ⓓ news

22. Eliza had to wait at the bus stop.
    ⓐ late   ⓒ weight
    ⓑ rust   ⓓ go

23. Give your arm time to heal.
    ⓐ heel   ⓒ deal
    ⓑ rhyme   ⓓ farm

24. Put the pail back in the garage.
    ⓐ sack   ⓒ bucket
    ⓑ nail   ⓓ pale

25. The sun burned his bare skin.
    ⓐ shin   ⓒ learned
    ⓑ bear   ⓓ care

Please go to the next page.

Fill in the circle for each correct answer.

E. Choose the correct answer to each question.

26. Which sentence is an opinion rather than a fact?
    ⓐ Join the Pep Society for the most fun you'll have in school.
    ⓑ Pep members go to all the school games for free.
    ⓒ Members lead the other students in the school cheers.
    ⓓ Pep sweaters are red with thin green stripes.

27. Which sentence is an opinion rather than a fact?
    ⓐ Sometimes after a storm a rainbow will appear in the sky.
    ⓑ A rainbow is a wonderfully beautiful sight.
    ⓒ The colors of a rainbow are caused by reflected sunlight.
    ⓓ There are usually seven colors in a rainbow.

28. Which sentence is a fact rather than an opinion?
    ⓐ The computer is the world's greatest invention.
    ⓑ A computer makes anything possible.
    ⓒ You can use a computer to play games or write a book.
    ⓓ Learning to use a computer is simple and fun.

29. Which sentence is a fact rather than an opinion?
    ⓐ Everyone loves to travel to faraway places.
    ⓑ World Trips can plan your next vacation for you.
    ⓒ World Trips is the best travel company in the state.
    ⓓ No one is ever disappointed with World Trips.

30. Which sentence is an opinion rather than a fact?
    ⓐ All people have had dreams about flying to the moon.
    ⓑ Moon flights did not begin until the 1960s.
    ⓒ The people who make such trips are called astronauts.
    ⓓ Twelve astronauts have walked on the moon.

Please go to the next page.

Fill in the circle for each correct answer.

F. Choose the correct name for each part of a business letter.

31. Ms. Juanita Corso, President
    Regional Books, Inc.
    Tolbern, MI 58392
    ⓐ greeting   ⓒ inside address
    ⓑ body   ⓓ closing

32. Yours truly,
    ⓐ closing   ⓒ greeting
    ⓑ signature   ⓓ heading

33. Dear Mr. Verveen:
    ⓐ heading   ⓒ closing
    ⓑ greeting   ⓓ inside address

34.   Thank you for your letter. I will try to
    send the books to you by next Thursday.
    ⓐ closing   ⓒ body
    ⓑ heading   ⓓ greeting

35. 4 Fountain Avenue
    Edmay, NJ 02191
    October 7, 1991
    ⓐ greeting   ⓒ inside address
    ⓑ body   ⓓ heading

STOP

Midyear Test

Fill in the circle for each correct answer.

A. Choose whether each sentence is *declarative*, *interrogative*, *imperative*, or *exclamatory*.

1. Take a seat at the back.
   - (a) declarative
   - (b) interrogative
   - (c) imperative
   - (d) exclamatory

2. How impressive that painting is!
   - (a) declarative
   - (b) interrogative
   - (c) imperative
   - (d) exclamatory

3. Can you pitch a tent?
   - (a) declarative
   - (b) interrogative
   - (c) imperative
   - (d) exclamatory

4. The town square is crowded.
   - (a) declarative
   - (b) interrogative
   - (c) imperative
   - (d) exclamatory

B. Choose whether the underlined part of each sentence is the *complete subject*, *complete predicate*, *simple subject*, or *simple predicate*.

5. We saw a turtle on the road.
   - (a) complete subject
   - (b) complete predicate
   - (c) simple subject
   - (d) simple predicate

6. Three geese flew by.
   - (a) complete subject
   - (b) complete predicate
   - (c) simple subject
   - (d) simple predicate

7. Steve drives a red jeep.
   - (a) complete subject
   - (b) complete predicate
   - (c) simple subject
   - (d) simple predicate

8. The sports car is out of gas.
   - (a) complete subject
   - (b) complete predicate
   - (c) simple subject
   - (d) simple predicate

C. Choose the simple subject in each sentence. Choose *You* if the subject is understood.

9. The writer's new play will open at the experimental theater.
   - (a) You
   - (b) writer's
   - (c) play
   - (d) theater

10. Put the big cushions back on the blue couch.
   - (a) You
   - (b) cushions
   - (c) back
   - (d) couch

11. Ella's favorite painting hangs over the brick fireplace.
   - (a) You
   - (b) Ella's
   - (c) favorite
   - (d) painting

12. Get the brown sugar in the top kitchen cabinet.
   - (a) You
   - (b) brown
   - (c) sugar
   - (d) cabinet

Please go to the next page.

Fill in the circle for each correct answer.

D. Read the thesaurus entry. Then choose the correct answer to each question.

> **form** (v)—to give a certain shape to.
> The artist *formed* the wet clay into a small statue.
> *compose*—to make by combining.
> *create*—to make for the first time.
> *develop*—to grow or expand.
> ANTONYMS: break, destroy, undo

13. What part of speech is *form* and its synonyms?
   - (a) noun
   - (b) adverb
   - (c) verb
   - (d) adjective

14. Which synonym for *form* means "to make for the first time"?
   - (a) compose
   - (b) expand
   - (c) shape
   - (d) create

E. Choose the correct plural form of each underlined noun.

15. sheep
   - (a) sheepes
   - (b) sheep
   - (c) sheepies
   - (d) sheeps

16. ability
   - (a) abilities
   - (b) abilityes
   - (c) abilitys
   - (d) abilitis

17. curb
   - (a) curbes
   - (b) curbses
   - (c) curbs
   - (d) curbies

18. lock
   - (a) locks
   - (b) lockeses
   - (c) lock
   - (d) lockes

F. Choose the word that should be capitalized in each sentence.

19. The passenger ship is headed toward great Britain.
   - (a) passenger
   - (b) ship
   - (c) headed
   - (d) great

20. Paula's family toured the Statue of liberty last summer.
   - (a) family
   - (b) toured
   - (c) liberty
   - (d) summer

21. Did you ever visit the sandy beaches of puerto Rico?
   - (a) you
   - (b) sandy
   - (c) beaches
   - (d) puerto

22. Liz's mother met many famous americans on her trip.
   - (a) mother
   - (b) famous
   - (c) americans
   - (d) trip

Please go to the next page.

Fill in the circle for each correct answer.

G. Choose the correct possessive of each underlined noun.

23. actors
   - (a) actors's
   - (b) actor's
   - (c) actors'
   - (d) actorses'

24. babies
   - (a) babies'
   - (b) babies'es
   - (c) babies's
   - (d) baby's

25. rock
   - (a) rocke's
   - (b) rock's
   - (c) rock'es
   - (d) rock'

26. party
   - (a) party's
   - (b) party'
   - (c) party'es
   - (d) partyes

H. Choose the correct answer to each question.

27. In which sentence is the main verb underlined?
   - (a) Gretchen has danced all night.
   - (b) She will go home with her aunt.
   - (c) Her aunt is waiting outside.
   - (d) They have enjoyed the evening.

28. In which sentence is a helping verb underlined?
   - (a) Ed has scraped the old paint.
   - (b) The paint was peeling off.
   - (c) Ed will paint the fence white.
   - (d) He has done this work before.

29. In which sentence is a linking verb underlined?
   - (a) Owen and Al swim in the pool.
   - (b) Owen's arms look very strong.
   - (c) Al must practice his swimming.
   - (d) The boys enjoy the cool water.

30. In which sentence is an action verb underlined?
   - (a) Deb will hike the long trail.
   - (b) She has seen this trail before.
   - (c) The trail was built in 1955.
   - (d) Her uncle had helped work on it.

I. Choose the direct object of the underlined verb in each sentence.

31. Mary planted a garden in her yard.
   - (a) garden
   - (b) yard
   - (c) her
   - (d) in

32. He climbed the tall fence twice.
   - (a) tall
   - (b) the
   - (c) fence
   - (d) twice

33. Daryl baked a cake for his mother.
   - (a) Daryl
   - (b) mother
   - (c) for
   - (d) cake

34. Max painted the wall with a brush.
   - (a) the
   - (b) with
   - (c) wall
   - (d) brush

Please go to the next page.

Fill in the circle for each correct answer.

J. Choose the correct answer to each question.

35. Which verb is in the present tense?
   - (a) chased
   - (b) will chase
   - (c) has chased
   - (d) chases

36. Which verb is in the future tense?
   - (a) looked
   - (b) will look
   - (c) looks
   - (d) look

37. Which verb is in the past tense?
   - (a) travel
   - (b) will travel
   - (c) traveled
   - (d) travels

38. Which verb is in the future tense?
   - (a) directs
   - (b) directed
   - (c) direct
   - (d) will direct

K. Choose the correct answer to each question.

39. In which sentence should you use *sit* and not *set*?
   - (a) Let's _____ the table.
   - (b) _____ the bottle there.
   - (c) _____ on that stool.
   - (d) Can you _____ it there?

40. In which sentence should you use *may* and not *can*?
   - (a) Michael, _____ you come?
   - (b) Dad, _____ I go?
   - (c) Ginger _____ draw well.
   - (d) Jill, _____ you try it?

L. Choose the pronoun that takes the place of the underlined word or words.

41. Sam and Nick biked to the city park for the outdoor concert.
   - (a) Them
   - (b) We
   - (c) They
   - (d) Us

42. LuAnn reached the finish line before her classmates did.
   - (a) it
   - (b) them
   - (c) her
   - (d) they

43. The model airplane hanging in the corner is Scott's.
   - (a) him
   - (b) his
   - (c) mine
   - (d) theirs

44. Philippa wanted Arthur and Evan to play a game of darts.
   - (a) they
   - (b) us
   - (c) we
   - (d) them

45. On Thursday Rene takes his sister to her dancing class.
   - (a) she
   - (b) her
   - (c) hers
   - (d) them

Please go to the next page.

T540

Midyear Test (continued)

Fill in the circle for each correct answer.

M. Choose the pronoun that correctly completes each sentence.

46. Sue drove Jesse, Odessa, and ____ home after the soccer tryouts.
   ⓐ they   ⬤ me   ⓒ I   ⓓ we

47. Ms. Tinker and ____ visited the aquarium.
   ⬤ I   ⓑ me   ⓒ us   ⓓ them

48. Corey met Luis and ____ at the subway stop.
   ⬤ I   ⓑ me   ⓒ mine   ⓓ we

49. Mr. Grant went flying with ____ in a hot air balloon.
   ⓐ they   ⬤ us   ⓒ we   ⓓ their

N. Choose the correct contraction for each pair of underlined words.

50. he will
   ⓐ he'l   ⬤ he'll
   ⓑ he'd   ⓓ hel'd

51. we have
   ⓐ w'ave   ⓒ weha'e
   ⓑ we'e   ⬤ we've

52. they are
   ⓐ they'e   ⓒ the'ye
   ⬤ they're   ⓓ thy'r

53. she would
   ⬤ she'd   ⓒ she'wd
   ⓑ she'ud   ⓓ sh'ld

O. Choose the pair of words that are homophones.

54. ⓐ serious, fun   ⓒ smooth, rough
   ⬤ rode, road   ⓓ funny, comical

55. ⓐ lie, lay   ⓒ through, threw
   ⓑ jump, clump   ⓓ my, may

56. ⓐ loud, noisy   ⬤ seen, scene
   ⓑ up, down   ⓓ tonight, today

57. ⓐ wire, tire   ⓒ soft, rough
   ⬤ ate, eight   ⓓ rely, relay

Please go to the next page.

World of Language ♦ Grade 5 ♦ MIDYEAR TEST   37

Name _____ ♦ Midyear Test
5MID

Fill in the circle for each correct answer.

P. Choose the correct meaning of each underlined word.

58. misbehave
   ⓐ to behave again
   ⬤ to behave wrongly
   ⓒ the opposite of behave
   ⓓ to behave before

59. retell
   ⓐ to tell before
   ⓑ not to tell
   ⬤ to tell again
   ⓓ to tell the opposite

60. prearrange
   ⓐ to arrange again
   ⬤ to arrange before
   ⓒ opposite of arrange
   ⓓ to arrange incorrectly

61. distrust
   ⓐ to trust again
   ⓑ before trust
   ⬤ opposite of trust
   ⓓ to trust wrongly

Q. Proofread the sentences. Each sentence contains a mistake. Choose the part of each sentence that has the mistake.

62. Last Tuesday Mrs Burrows made an announcement to her fifth grade class.
   a   b   c   d
   Which is the mistake in the above sentence?
   ⓐ Last   ⬤ Mrs   ⓒ her   ⓓ class.

63. "The mayors office will sponsor a drawing contest this fall," she said.
        a   b   c   d
   Which is the mistake in the above sentence?
   ⬤ mayors   ⓑ drawing   ⓒ this   ⓓ said.

64. "The theme of the contest will be national symbols." added Mrs. Burrows.
   a   b   c   d
   Which is the mistake in the above sentence?
   ⓐ "The   ⓑ contest   ⬤ symbols."   ⓓ Burrows.

65. "Your entrys should reflect some part of America that makes you proud."
          a   b   c   d
   Which is the mistake in the above sentence?
   ⬤ entrys   ⓑ reflect   ⓒ America   ⓓ makes

66. "Three students will win a trip to Washington, D C ," she added with a smile.
              a   b   c   d
   Which is the mistake in the above sentence?
   ⓐ students   ⓑ trip   ⬤ D C   ⓓ smile.

World of Language ♦ Grade 5 ♦ MIDYEAR TEST   🛑 STOP   38

T541

Unit 5 Pretest

Name _____ Unit 5 ♦ Pretest
505P

Fill in the circle for each correct answer.

A. Choose all the adjectives in each sentence. Include articles.

1. Many talented musicians performed in the variety show.
   - (a) musicians, show
   - (b) talented, performed, the
   - (c) Many, talented, the, show
   - (d) Many, talented, the, variety

2. A red flower grew in the sandy desert.
   - (a) flower, sandy
   - (b) A, red, the, sandy
   - (c) the, sandy, desert
   - (d) A, flower, desert

3. The two boys sat by the cool, rippling stream.
   - (a) The, cool, rippling
   - (b) The, two, the, cool, rippling
   - (c) The, two, down, the, cool
   - (d) two, down, cool, rippling

4. Amanda's favorite dress is made of soft cotton.
   - (a) favorite, dress, made
   - (b) favorite, soft
   - (c) favorite, made, cotton
   - (d) dress, cotton

5. Many different fish live in the small pond.
   - (a) Many, different, fish, small
   - (b) Many, different, the, small
   - (c) Many, different, live, the, small
   - (d) different, the, small

B. Choose the predicate adjective in each sentence.

6. The swimmer seemed confident before the race.
   - (a) confident (b) before (c) swimmer (d) race

7. The guitar's strings felt cold to Nancy's fingers.
   - (a) fingers (b) guitar's (c) cold (d) strings

8. Ramona looked unhappy after she read the short letter.
   - (a) read (b) short (c) unhappy (d) after

9. Uncle Peter becomes upset when his dog barks loudly.
   - (a) upset (b) when (c) his (d) loudly

10. The oak chair in the corner of the room is very sturdy.
   - (a) oak (b) corner (c) very (d) sturdy

Please go to the next page.

World of Language ♦ Grade 5 ♦ UNIT 5 PRETEST   39

Name _____ Unit 5 ♦ Pretest
505P

Fill in the circle for each correct answer.

C. Choose the correct form of the adjective to complete each sentence.

11. That is the ____ story I have ever heard.
   - (a) strange (b) stranger (c) more strange (d) strangest

12. Who has the ____ hair in the class?
   - (a) most curly (b) curlier (c) curliest (d) more curly

13. Some newspapers have ____ articles than others.
   - (a) most long (b) longest (c) more long (d) longer

14. Alex is the ____ boy in school.
   - (a) more solemn (b) solemner (c) most solemn (d) solemnest

15. Perry was amazed to learn that diamonds are ____ than steel.
   - (a) hardest (b) more hard (c) harder (d) most hard

D. Choose the correct meaning of each underlined word.

16. painless
   - (a) worthy of pain
   - (b) having pain
   - (c) full of pain
   - (d) without pain

17. thoughtful
   - (a) full of thought
   - (b) having thought
   - (c) without thought
   - (d) worthy of thought

18. dusty
   - (a) worthy of dust
   - (b) having dust
   - (c) full of dust
   - (d) without dust

19. respectable
   - (a) full of respect
   - (b) without respect
   - (c) able to be respected
   - (d) being like respect

20. cloudless
   - (a) full of clouds
   - (b) without clouds
   - (c) having clouds
   - (d) worthy of clouds

Please go to the next page.

World of Language ♦ Grade 5 ♦ UNIT 5 PRETEST   40

Name _____ Unit 5 ♦ Pretest
505P

Fill in the circle for each correct answer.

E. Read each topic sentence. Then choose the detail sentence that should be written first.

21. TOPIC SENTENCE: There are nine planets in our solar system.
   - (a) After Mercury comes Venus.
   - (b) Mercury is the planet closest to the sun.
   - (c) Earth is the third planet from the sun.
   - (d) Beyond Earth lies Mars.

22. TOPIC SENTENCE: Every day at noon we line up outside the school cafeteria.
   - (a) Jack sometimes lines up right behind us.
   - (b) Behind Elaine is her best friend, Anita.
   - (c) Marco and I often stand behind Elaine and Anita.
   - (d) Elaine is usually at the head of the line.

23. TOPIC SENTENCE: We stood on the corner and watched the parade pass by.
   - (a) Next came a large float filled with flowers.
   - (b) Behind the drum major came the high school marching band.
   - (c) The high school drum major led the parade.
   - (d) A group of men and women on horseback escorted the float.

24. TOPIC SENTENCE: There are many interesting shops along Main Street.
   - (a) Next to the pottery shop is a camera shop.
   - (b) The first shop you will see is a pottery shop.
   - (c) Across the street from the jewelry store is an antique shop.
   - (d) Just beyond the camera shop there is a jewelry store.

25. TOPIC SENTENCE: The old house has a beautiful dining room.
   - (a) Around the table are six chairs with high backs.
   - (b) The table and chairs rest on a colorful oval rug.
   - (c) In the center of the dining room is a long oak table.
   - (d) A high archway stands at the entrance to the room.

Please go to the next page.

World of Language ♦ Grade 5 ♦ UNIT 5 PRETEST   41

Name _____ Unit 5 ♦ Pretest
505P

Fill in the circle for each correct answer.

F. Choose the correct answer to each question.

26. Which sentence describes the sound of a fire engine?
   - (a) The bright red truck bolted out of the station.
   - (b) The siren wailed as it raced toward the burning building.
   - (c) Columns of water poured from the hoses.
   - (d) Thick clouds of black smoke drifted across the city.

27. Which sentence describes the feel of glass?
   - (a) Nancy looked out her window and watched the storm pass by.
   - (b) A few large raindrops spattered against the pane.
   - (c) She pressed her hand against the cool, smooth surface.
   - (d) The faint outline of a rainbow cut across the sky.

28. Which sentence describes the taste of a lemon?
   - (a) The farm stand had dozens of bright yellow lemons.
   - (b) Ingrid could see that they had been freshly picked.
   - (c) She squeezed a few, and some juice trickled out.
   - (d) She made a face as she sampled the sour juice.

29. Which sentence describes the smell of the ocean?
   - (a) Andy ran quickly over the hot, dry sand.
   - (b) The fresh, salty air filled him with energy.
   - (c) Bright arrows of sunlight darted across the water.
   - (d) The water along the shore felt cool on his feet.

30. Which sentence describes the sight of a summer night?
   - (a) Nina went outside to escape the thick heat.
   - (b) A soft, warm breeze brushed across her face.
   - (c) The laughter of children rang in the distance.
   - (d) The stars sparkled like diamonds against the sky.

STOP

World of Language ♦ Grade 5 ♦ UNIT 5 PRETEST   42

T542

Unit 5 Posttest

Fill in the circle for each correct answer.

A. Choose all the adjectives in each sentence. Include articles.

1. The old boat was tied to the sturdy dock.
   - (a) The, tied, dock
   - (b) The, old, the, sturdy
   - (c) old, boat, sturdy
   - (d) tied, the, dock

2. There was a large pile of newspapers on the front porch.
   - (a) A, large, pile, the, front
   - (b) A, the, front
   - (c) A, large, the, front
   - (d) large, pile, front

3. Myra wrote an interesting song for the play.
   - (a) song, the, play
   - (b) an, the, play
   - (c) wrote, an, song
   - (d) an, interesting, the

4. The funny clown held a bunch of colorful balloons.
   - (a) a, clown, bunch
   - (b) The, held, a, of
   - (c) The, funny, a, colorful
   - (d) The, bunch, balloons

5. A beautiful bird landed in the middle of the field.
   - (a) A, beautiful, middle, the
   - (b) A, the, middle, the
   - (c) A, beautiful, the, the
   - (d) A, beautiful, the, field

B. Choose the predicate adjective in each sentence.

6. Amanda's eyes felt sore after she swam in the pool.
   - (a) Amanda's
   - (b) eyes
   - (c) sore
   - (d) after

7. Late in the autumn the leaves on the trees become brown.
   - (a) Late
   - (b) leaves
   - (c) become
   - (d) brown

8. All the piano music in the talent show is original.
   - (a) original
   - (b) music
   - (c) piano
   - (d) talent

9. The strawberries we picked yesterday tasted delicious.
   - (a) The
   - (b) strawberries
   - (c) yesterday
   - (d) delicious

10. Louis looked sad when the school soccer team lost.
    - (a) sad
    - (b) school
    - (c) soccer
    - (d) lost

Please go to the next page.

© Silver, Burdett & Ginn Inc.

Fill in the circle for each correct answer.

C. Choose the correct form of the adjective to complete each sentence.

11. Last Monday was the ____ day of the year.
    - (a) hotter
    - (b) hottest
    - (c) more hot
    - (d) most hot

12. Old Phoenix Road is ____ than the new highway.
    - (a) bumpy
    - (b) bumpier
    - (c) more bumpy
    - (d) most bumpy

13. Mount Rainier is the ____ mountain I've ever seen.
    - (a) more high
    - (b) highest
    - (c) most high
    - (d) higher

14. Is this watch ____ than that one?
    - (a) expensive
    - (b) expensiver
    - (c) more expensive
    - (d) most expensive

15. Of the three children, Milo is the ____.
    - (a) quiet
    - (b) quieter
    - (c) quietest
    - (d) most quiet

D. Choose the correct meaning of each underlined word.

16. joyful
    - (a) worthy of joy
    - (b) without joy
    - (c) being like joy
    - (d) full of joy

17. noticeable
    - (a) without notice
    - (b) being like notice
    - (c) full of notice
    - (d) worthy of notice

18. noiseless
    - (a) without noise
    - (b) worthy of noise
    - (c) having noise
    - (d) being like noise

19. doubtful
    - (a) without doubt
    - (b) worthy of doubt
    - (c) able to doubt
    - (d) full of doubt

20. crusty
    - (a) being like crust
    - (b) without crust
    - (c) full of crust
    - (d) worthy of crust

Please go to the next page.

© Silver, Burdett & Ginn Inc.

Fill in the circle for each correct answer.

E. Read each topic sentence. Then choose the detail sentence that should be written first.

21. TOPIC SENTENCE: Ariel decided to organize the books on her bookshelf.
    - (a) Above the large books she put her science and nature books.
    - (b) Stories of every kind were arranged by size above the science books.
    - (c) She began by putting her largest books on the bottom shelf.
    - (d) Last she put her favorite book of poems on the top shelf.

22. TOPIC SENTENCE: Yesterday the school photographer took our class picture.
    - (a) Molly and Lasalle were in the third row behind Beth and Arnold.
    - (b) Our teacher, Mr. O'Neill, also sat in the third row, next to Lasalle.
    - (c) My best friend and I sat in the front row.
    - (d) Beth and Arnold stood right behind us.

23. TOPIC SENTENCE: From the top of the hill Emilio could see for miles.
    - (a) Beyond the pond he could see an open meadow filled with cows.
    - (b) Next to the farmhouse was a huge red barn.
    - (c) At the edge of the meadow was a white farmhouse.
    - (d) A beautiful pond was the first thing he noticed.

24. TOPIC SENTENCE: Linda looked at the photo in Grandma's wedding album.
    - (a) Grandpa, wearing a black suit and a hat, stood next to her.
    - (b) Behind the bride and groom were Uncle Stefan and Aunt Marge.
    - (c) In the middle of the picture stood Grandma, wearing a white dress.
    - (d) Beside Uncle Stefan were two people Linda did not recognize.

25. TOPIC SENTENCE: There was a lovely flower arrangement on the hall table.
    - (a) In the center of the vase were two large peonies.
    - (b) The purple irises were taller than the other flowers.
    - (c) Around the peonies were several irises.
    - (d) A bunch of tulips surrounded the irises.

Please go to the next page.

© Silver, Burdett & Ginn Inc.

Fill in the circle for each correct answer.

F. Choose the correct answer to each question.

26. Which sentence describes the sound of a concert?
    - (a) A large crowd of students filled the auditorium.
    - (b) The stage glowed under the bright white lights.
    - (c) The musicians looked nervous as they took their seats.
    - (d) The steady beat of the drums echoed off the walls.

27. Which sentence describes the sight of a mountain?
    - (a) The peak glistened in the sun as we began our hike.
    - (b) The air grew cool and thin as we climbed upward.
    - (c) The wind whistled softly down the slope.
    - (d) By late afternoon my leg muscles had begun to ache.

28. Which sentence describes the taste of a watermelon?
    - (a) The watermelons John grew this year were enormous.
    - (b) One melon weighed more than twenty pounds.
    - (c) Yesterday we ate one of his melons for dessert.
    - (d) The ripe fruit was cool and sweet.

29. Which sentence describes the smell of a bakery shop?
    - (a) On Saturday we stopped at the new bakery shop on Elm Street.
    - (b) The scent of freshly baked bread filled the air.
    - (c) The cookies in the display case made my mouth water.
    - (d) The doorbell jingled as we left the shop.

30. Which sentence describes the feel of a cactus plant?
    - (a) Many different kinds of cactus plants grow in the desert.
    - (b) Some are tall and straight, and others are short and round.
    - (c) The prickly needles of a cactus can scratch unprotected skin.
    - (d) Cactus plants need very little water to survive and grow.

STOP

© Silver, Burdett & Ginn Inc.

Unit 6 Pretest

Name _____ Unit 6 ◆ Pretest
506P

Fill in the circle for each correct answer.

A. Choose the adverb in each sentence.

1. Everyone in the auditorium clapped loudly at the end of the recital.
   (a) everyone   (b) loudly ●   (c) end   (d) recital

2. Sarah usually finishes her reading assignments in the library.
   (a) usually ●   (b) finishes   (c) reading   (d) library

3. The lead actress in the play moved slowly across the stage.
   (a) lead   (b) actress   (c) slowly ●   (d) stage

4. Yesterday Mrs. Clark told everyone about the new puppet show.
   (a) yesterday ●   (b) told   (c) about   (d) new

5. Brenda never forgets the names of authors or the titles of books.
   (a) never ●   (b) titles   (c) books   (d) names

B. Choose the correct form of the adverb to complete each sentence.

6. Wild flowers grow _____ along this path than poison ivy.
   (a) more commonly ●   (b) most commonly   (c) commonly   (d) more commoner

7. Chicken bakes _____ of all the dishes we could have for supper.
   (a) quicker   (b) more quickly   (c) quickest ●   (d) quickly

8. Angelina keeps her room _____ arranged than her sister does.
   (a) neatly   (b) neater   (c) most neat   (d) more neatly ●

9. Jason works _____ than all the other newspaper carriers.
   (a) hardly   (b) more harder   (c) hardest   (d) harder ●

10. Of all the students in Mr. Teng's piano class, Hoa practices _____.
    (a) most often ●   (b) oftener   (c) oftenest   (d) more often

Please go to the next page.

World of Language ◆ Grade 5 ◆ UNIT 6 PRETEST   47

Name _____ Unit 6 ◆ Pretest
506P

Fill in the circle for each correct answer.

C. Choose the adverb that describes each underlined adverb or adjective.

11. The baseball game was especially slow in the late innings.
    (a) baseball   (b) game   (c) especially ●   (d) innings

12. The weather in San Francisco is very pleasant at this time of year.
    (a) weather   (b) very ●   (c) time   (d) this

13. Jeremiah learned to speak a second language quite easily.
    (a) quite ●   (b) speak   (c) second   (d) language

14. Rebecca was slightly puzzled by the rules of the new card game.
    (a) was   (b) rules   (c) slightly ●   (d) card

15. When Michelle first moved to the city, she felt extremely lonesome.
    (a) when   (b) city   (c) felt   (d) extremely ●

D. Choose the correct answer to each question.

16. In which sentence should you use carefully and not careful?
    (a) Wyatt is a _____ dresser.   (c) He chooses his clothes _____. ●
    (b) He is _____ in matching colors.   (d) He is _____ to hang his clothes up.

17. In which sentence should you use wonderfully and not wonderful?
    (a) Tyrone's band plays _____. ●   (c) We have a _____ time at concerts.
    (b) It's _____ to hear a good band.   (d) Each performance is _____.

18. In which sentence should you use good and not well?
    (a) Christina is doing _____ in music.   (c) Jim is doing a _____ job, too. ●
    (b) Cora always speaks _____ of him.   (d) Adele also wants to play _____.

19. In which sentence should you use quickly and not quick?
    (a) That goalie made a _____ move.   (c) The first period passed _____. ●
    (b) Do you want to get a _____ snack?   (d) You were _____ to respond!

20. In which sentence should you use really and not real?
    (a) That was a _____ adventure.   (c) Do you know her _____ name?
    (b) Are you _____ leaving? ●   (d) It doesn't seem _____ to me.

Please go to the next page.

World of Language ◆ Grade 5 ◆ UNIT 6 PRETEST   48

Name _____ Unit 6 ◆ Pretest
506P

Fill in the circle for each correct answer.

E. Choose the sentence that is written correctly.

21. (a) We haven't seen nothing here.
    (b) No one wants to go on the trip. ●
    (c) Nobody can never know all that.
    (d) She never wants none.

22. (a) She never goes nowhere.
    (b) No one has none of those.
    (c) He never has any food. ●
    (d) Nothing is never free.

23. (a) Paul won't move nothing.
    (b) He isn't nowhere to be found.
    (c) No one has any books. ●
    (d) Nobody knows nothing to do.

24. (a) Steve haven't done his work.
    (b) Elise haven't arrived yet.
    (c) They isn't very comfortable.
    (d) I don't have any paper. ●

25. (a) They wouldn't choose that movie. ●
    (b) I isn't attending the concert.
    (c) Miri don't like to sing.
    (d) He haven't played the drums.

F. Choose the compound in each group of words.

26. (a) behavior   (b) train station   (c) carriage   (d) define

27. (a) newspaper ●   (b) melon   (c) artistic   (d) general

28. (a) insect   (b) afternoon   (c) saddle   (d) foster

29. (a) forward   (b) silence   (c) sidewalk ●   (d) blizzard

30. (a) two-sided ●   (b) carpet   (c) describe   (d) sandal

Please go to the next page.

World of Language ◆ Grade 5 ◆ UNIT 6 PRETEST   49

Name _____ Unit 6 ◆ Pretest
506P

Fill in the circle for each correct answer.

G. Choose the correct answer to each question.

31. In which volume of the encyclopedia would you find information on submarines?
    (a) Sa-Sn ●   (b) So-Sz   (c) Ta-Uz   (d) Va-Wy

32. What is the key word in the question When did Vermont enter the Union?
    (a) Union   (b) enter   (c) when   (d) Vermont ●

33. In which volume of the encyclopedia would you find information on former President Jimmy Carter?
    (a) Aa-Al   (b) Ca-De ●   (c) Ef-Ez   (d) Ga-Gh

34. What is the key word in the question In what year was Thomas Edison born?
    (a) Edison ●   (b) year   (c) Thomas   (d) born

35. In which volume of the encyclopedia would you find information on Mars?
    (a) Ja-Kh   (b) Lo-Me ●   (c) Ni-Nz   (d) Sa-Sn

H. Choose the correct answer to each question.

36. Which topic is the narrowest?
    (a) caterpillars   (c) flying insects
    (b) monarch butterflies ●   (d) the study of bugs

37. Which topic is the narrowest?
    (a) Robert Frost ●   (c) American poets
    (b) writers   (d) poetry

38. Which choice is the narrowest for the topic Trees?
    (a) forestry   (c) oaks ●
    (b) tropical rain forests   (d) lumber industry

39. Which choice is the narrowest for the topic Space?
    (a) solar systems   (c) planets
    (b) astronomy   (d) moon landings ●

40. Which topic is the narrowest?
    (a) The Old West   (c) horses
    (b) cowboys   (d) The Oregon Trail ●

STOP

World of Language ◆ Grade 5 ◆ UNIT 6 PRETEST   50

T544

Unit 6 Posttest

Name _____ Unit 6 ♦ Posttest
506T

Fill in the circle for each correct answer.

A. Choose the adverb in each sentence.

1. Kevin and his brother always take the bus to school.
   (a) brother   (b) always   (c) take   (d) bus

2. The astronomer gazed intently at the distant star.
   (a) astronomer   (b) gazed   (c) intently   (d) distant

3. Jennifer performed all the difficult dance exercises gracefully.
   (a) performed   (b) difficult   (c) exercises   (d) gracefully

4. Kyu listened carefully to each of the teacher's instructions.
   (a) carefully   (b) each   (c) teacher's   (d) instructions

5. The tall boy in the back of the room stepped forward.
   (a) tall   (b) back   (c) room   (d) forward

B. Choose the correct form of the adverb to complete each sentence.

6. Rosalita dances _____ in a group than by herself.
   (a) more well   (b) well   (c) better   (d) best

7. Of the various mountain streams, this little one flows _____.
   (a) swiftly   (b) most swiftly   (c) swiftlier   (d) more swiftly

8. We finished this project _____ than the last one.
   (a) easiest   (b) most easily   (c) more easily   (d) easier

9. The gray fox moves _____ than the raccoon does.
   (a) more quietly   (b) quietest   (c) most quiet   (d) quieter

10. Of all the players, Alan threw his horseshoe _____ to the post.
    (a) nearer   (b) nearest   (c) more near   (d) most near

Please go to the next page.

Name _____ Unit 6 ♦ Posttest
506T

Fill in the circle for each correct answer.

C. Choose the adverb that describes each underlined adverb or adjective.

11. Stuart recited the poem so perfectly that we all applauded.
    (a) recited   (b) poem   (c) so   (d) that

12. Nanci was seriously disappointed by the team's score.
    (a) seriously   (b) by   (c) team's   (d) score

13. The weather looks fairly promising for today's picnic.
    (a) weather   (b) looks   (c) fairly   (d) picnic

14. Tim's decision to run in the race was certainly unexpected.
    (a) decision   (b) run   (c) race   (d) certainly

15. The book was unusually long, so Emma did not finish reading it.
    (a) book   (b) unusually   (c) finish   (d) reading

D. Choose the correct answer to each question.

16. In which sentence should you use badly and not bad?
    (a) This milk tastes _____.   (c) We made a _____ choice.
    (b) That was _____ planned.   (d) I gave a _____ example.

17. In which sentence should you use calmly and not calm?
    (a) The wind is quite _____ today.   (c) She reacted _____.
    (b) The _____ day was welcome.   (d) I am _____ about that.

18. In which sentence should you use thickly and not thick?
    (a) This is a _____ sandwich.   (c) That garden is _____ with weeds.
    (b) The village is _____ settled.   (d) What a _____ book!

19. In which sentence should you use playfully and not playful?
    (a) Ann was unusually _____ today.   (c) The cat is _____.
    (b) He has a _____ nature.   (d) He joked _____ with her.

20. In which sentence should you use warmly and not warm?
    (a) Dress _____ for the cold.   (c) It's _____ in this house.
    (b) You have a _____ coat.   (d) A _____ day is predicted.

Please go to the next page.

Name _____ Unit 6 ♦ Posttest
506T

Fill in the circle for each correct answer.

E. Choose the sentence that is written correctly.

21. (a) Phil won't get any.
    (b) Elaine won't go nowhere.
    (c) Nobody wasn't there.
    (d) She can't say nothing.

22. (a) Kathy won't attend no play.
    (b) Nobody gained any advantage.
    (c) She won't do nothing.
    (d) No one couldn't reach the top.

23. (a) He never saw no one.
    (b) He couldn't find nobody.
    (c) She hasn't bought none.
    (d) No one is at home.

24. (a) Gina haven't received a note.
    (b) The book isn't finished.
    (c) Adrienne don't want to go.
    (d) They hasn't seen it before.

25. (a) Carol hasn't gone anywhere.
    (b) They doesn't like soup.
    (c) Paul weren't at the show.
    (d) Emma don't play too well.

F. Choose the compound in each group of words.

26. (a) cheerleader   (b) total   (c) message   (d) ladder

27. (a) rancher   (b) infant   (c) seashore   (d) homely

28. (a) saucer   (b) garage   (c) kite-flying   (d) harbor

29. (a) tornado   (b) dragonfly   (c) daughter   (d) chocolate

30. (a) poultry   (b) blossom   (c) annual   (d) tape measure

Please go to the next page.

Name _____ Unit 6 ♦ Posttest
506T

Fill in the circle for each correct answer.

G. Choose the correct answer to each question.

31. In which volume of the encyclopedia would you find information on zebras?
    (a) Ta-Th   (b) Ti-Tz   (c) Ua-Ul   (d) Ya-Z

32. What is the key word in the question What is the population of the state of Arizona?
    (a) population   (b) Arizona   (c) state   (d) what

33. In which volume of the encyclopedia would you find information on Africa?
    (a) Aa-Al   (b) Am-Az   (c) Em-Ez   (d) Gh-Gz

34. What is the key word in the question Who invented the game of basketball?
    (a) game   (b) invented   (c) basketball   (d) who

35. In which volume of the encyclopedia would you find information on Poland?
    (a) Ih-Iz   (b) Na-Nh   (c) Pa-Ph   (d) Pi-Pz

H. Choose the correct answer to each question.

36. Which topic is the narrowest?
    (a) Italian foods   (c) lasagna
    (b) recipes   (d) Italy

37. Which choice is the narrowest for the topic Flight?
    (a) first gas balloon   (c) astronauts
    (b) inventors   (d) sound barrier

38. Which topic is the narrowest?
    (a) lakes and rivers   (c) bodies of water
    (b) African continent   (d) Victoria Falls

39. Which choice is the narrowest for the topic History?
    (a) South America   (c) Portuguese explorers
    (b) Brazil   (d) Western Hemisphere

40. Which topic is the narrowest?
    (a) animals of the desert   (c) Gila monster
    (b) Southwestern States   (d) lizards

(STOP)

Unit 7 Pretest

Name _____ Unit 7 ♦ Pretest
507P

Fill in the circle for each correct answer.

A. Choose whether the underlined part of each sentence is a *preposition*, *prepositional phrase*, *object of the preposition*, or *adverb*.

1. Allison and Janet went <u>outside</u>.
   - (a) preposition
   - (b) prepositional phrase
   - (c) object of the preposition
   - (d) adverb

2. A tree <u>near</u> the bridge blew over.
   - (a) preposition
   - (b) prepositional phrase
   - (c) object of the preposition
   - (d) adverb

3. Don't walk <u>through that door</u>.
   - (a) preposition
   - (b) prepositional phrase
   - (c) object of the preposition
   - (d) adverb

4. The pigs escaped under the <u>fence</u>.
   - (a) preposition
   - (b) prepositional phrase
   - (c) object of the preposition
   - (d) adverb

5. Our team marched <u>in the parade</u>.
   - (a) preposition
   - (b) prepositional phrase
   - (c) object of the preposition
   - (d) adverb

6. The two squirrels jumped <u>down</u>.
   - (a) preposition
   - (b) prepositional phrase
   - (c) object of the preposition
   - (d) adverb

7. Did you look <u>inside</u> the box?
   - (a) preposition
   - (b) prepositional phrase
   - (c) object of the preposition
   - (d) adverb

8. He walked across the <u>street</u>.
   - (a) preposition
   - (b) prepositional phrase
   - (c) object of the preposition
   - (d) adverb

9. Would you like to come <u>along</u>?
   - (a) preposition
   - (b) prepositional phrase
   - (c) object of the preposition
   - (d) adverb

10. Did you look <u>under the rug</u>?
   - (a) preposition
   - (b) prepositional phrase
   - (c) object of the preposition
   - (d) adverb

Please go to the next page.

© Silver, Burdett & Ginn Inc.

World of Language ♦ Grade 5 ♦ UNIT 7 PRETEST   55

Name _____ Unit 7 ♦ Pretest
507P

Fill in the circle for each correct answer.

B. Choose the correct answer to each question.

11. In which sentence should you use <u>him</u> and not <u>he</u>?
   - (a) _____ and I liked the movie.
   - (b) Usually _____ knows the way.
   - (c) The dog ran behind _____.
   - (d) Tonight _____ plays in the show.

12. In which sentence should you use <u>among</u> and not <u>between</u>?
   - (a) The marker is _____ chapters four and five.
   - (b) The ball was _____ the other toys.
   - (c) Let's split the work _____ you and me.
   - (d) Buses travel _____ here and Charleston.

13. In which sentence would you use <u>us</u> and not <u>we</u>?
   - (a) Without a watch, how will _____ know the time?
   - (b) Next week _____ will go hiking.
   - (c) Jenna arrived before _____ did.
   - (d) My friends and I admired the flowers around _____.

14. In which sentence should you use <u>between</u> and not <u>among</u>?
   - (a) Many weeds are growing _____ the flowers.
   - (b) Choose the best ones _____ them.
   - (c) I saw crows _____ the cornstalks.
   - (d) The elevator stopped _____ the second and third floors.

15. In which sentence should you use <u>them</u> and not <u>they</u>?
   - (a) Yesterday I wrote a letter to _____.
   - (b) After _____ sang, we danced.
   - (c) Did _____ remember to send Terry a card?
   - (d) During the winter _____ go sledding.

Please go to the next page.

© Silver, Burdett & Ginn Inc.

World of Language ♦ Grade 5 ♦ UNIT 7 PRETEST   56

Name _____ Unit 7 ♦ Pretest
507P

Fill in the circle for each correct answer.

C. Choose the correct answer to each question.

16. Which word is an antonym for *despair*?
   - (a) sadness
   - (b) hope
   - (c) decay
   - (d) freedom

17. What is a synonym for *rely*?
   - (a) direct
   - (b) cure
   - (c) depend
   - (d) provide

18. Which word is a synonym for *hesitate*?
   - (a) promise
   - (b) keep
   - (c) manage
   - (d) pause

19. Which word is an antonym for *repair*?
   - (a) finish
   - (b) protect
   - (c) break
   - (d) guide

20. Which word is a synonym for *lecture*?
   - (a) silence
   - (b) cycle
   - (c) leader
   - (d) speech

Please go to the next page.

© Silver, Burdett & Ginn Inc.

World of Language ♦ Grade 5 ♦ UNIT 7 PRETEST   57

Name _____ Unit 7 ♦ Pretest
507P

Fill in the circle for each correct answer.

D. Proofread the sentences below. Choose the mistake in each sentence.

21. <u>Laurie</u> was happy when her grandfather <u>invited</u> her to <u>visit</u> him in <u>fairfield</u>.
      a   b   c   d

   Which is the mistake in the sentence above?
   - (a) Laurie
   - (b) invited
   - (c) visit
   - (d) fairfield.

22. <u>She</u> was excited because she <u>had'nt</u> taken a <u>train</u> since she was six years <u>old</u>.
    a   b   c   d

   Which is the mistake in the sentence above?
   - (a) She
   - (b) had'nt
   - (c) train
   - (d) old.

23. <u>She</u> <u>remembered</u> that the train <u>traveled among</u> two beautiful <u>mountains</u>.
        a   b   c   d

   Which is the mistake in the sentence above?
   - (a) remembered
   - (b) traveled
   - (c) among
   - (d) mountains.

24. Grandfather <u>said</u> that <u>those</u> mountains were <u>oldest</u> than the <u>Rocky</u> Mountains.
               a   b   c   d

   Which is the mistake in the sentence above?
   - (a) said
   - (b) those
   - (c) oldest
   - (d) Rocky

25. Laurie <u>couldn't</u> wait to <u>meet</u> her grandfather at the <u>old</u> brick train <u>station</u>.
           a   b   c   d

   Which is the mistake in the sentence above?
   - (a) couldn't
   - (b) meet
   - (c) old
   - (d) station

STOP

© Silver, Burdett & Ginn Inc.

World of Language ♦ Grade 5 ♦ UNIT 7 PRETEST   58

Unit 7 Posttest

Fill in the circle for each correct answer.

A. Choose whether the underlined part of each sentence is a *preposition, prepositional phrase, object of the preposition,* or *adverb.*

1. The boat sailed up the <u>river</u>.
   - ⓐ preposition
   - ⓑ prepositional phrase
   - ⓒ object of the preposition
   - ⓓ adverb

2. Lights went out <u>during the storm</u>.
   - ⓐ preposition
   - ⓑ prepositional phrase
   - ⓒ object of the preposition
   - ⓓ adverb

3. Don't leave <u>without</u> your coat.
   - ⓐ preposition
   - ⓑ prepositional phrase
   - ⓒ object of the preposition
   - ⓓ adverb

4. Peg had to stay <u>inside</u>.
   - ⓐ preposition
   - ⓑ prepositional phrase
   - ⓒ object of the preposition
   - ⓓ adverb

5. Mom told us not to run <u>around</u>.
   - ⓐ preposition
   - ⓑ prepositional phrase
   - ⓒ object of the preposition
   - ⓓ adverb

6. They passed <u>through</u> the open gate.
   - ⓐ preposition
   - ⓑ prepositional phrase
   - ⓒ object of the preposition
   - ⓓ adverb

7. The river flowed over the <u>rocks</u>.
   - ⓐ preposition
   - ⓑ prepositional phrase
   - ⓒ object of the preposition
   - ⓓ adverb

8. We walked <u>under</u> the tall bridge.
   - ⓐ preposition
   - ⓑ prepositional phrase
   - ⓒ object of the preposition
   - ⓓ adverb

9. The baby crawled <u>near the table</u>.
   - ⓐ preposition
   - ⓑ prepositional phrase
   - ⓒ object of the preposition
   - ⓓ adverb

10. Some animals live below the <u>earth</u>.
    - ⓐ preposition
    - ⓑ prepositional phrase
    - ⓒ object of the preposition
    - ⓓ adverb

Please go to the next page.

Fill in the circle for each correct answer.

B. Choose the correct answer to each question.

11. In which sentence should you use *me* and not *I*?
    - ⓐ Dave and ____ went for a walk.
    - ⓑ The letter was signed by ____.
    - ⓒ Can ____ give the key to you?
    - ⓓ Yesterday ____ visited my cousins.

12. In which sentence should you use *us* and not *we*?
    - ⓐ Will sprayed water on ____.
    - ⓑ Patsy knows when ____ will leave.
    - ⓒ Somehow ____ missed each other.
    - ⓓ Do ____ have the right books?

13. In which sentence should you use *among* and not *between*?
    - ⓐ Phil stood ____ Rob and Leo.
    - ⓑ The kite was caught ____ two branches.
    - ⓒ One white duck swam ____ the geese.
    - ⓓ It's a secret ____ you and me.

14. In which sentence should you use *her* and not *she*?
    - ⓐ The answer ____ gave was very clever.
    - ⓑ Will ____ be there, too?
    - ⓒ ____ and Renee are going skating.
    - ⓓ The news from ____ is good.

15. In which sentence should you use *between* and not *among*?
    - ⓐ This story is the best ____ several good ones.
    - ⓑ Hang this picture ____ the others.
    - ⓒ The moon looked huge shining ____ the stars.
    - ⓓ The cat ran ____ two buildings.

Please go to the next page.

Fill in the circle for each correct answer.

C. Choose the correct answer to each question.

16. What is an antonym for <u>unique</u>?
    - ⓐ common
    - ⓑ dainty
    - ⓒ valuable
    - ⓓ odd

17. What is a synonym for <u>feeble</u>?
    - ⓐ strong
    - ⓑ seldom
    - ⓒ weak
    - ⓓ awake

18. What is a synonym for <u>dense</u>?
    - ⓐ smooth
    - ⓑ flat
    - ⓒ high
    - ⓓ solid

19. What is an antonym for <u>praise</u>?
    - ⓐ regret
    - ⓑ scorn
    - ⓒ terrify
    - ⓓ compliment

20. What is an antonym for <u>remove</u>?
    - ⓐ replace
    - ⓑ resume
    - ⓒ subtract
    - ⓓ install

Please go to the next page.

Fill in the circle for each correct answer.

D. Proofread the sentences below. Choose the mistake in each sentence.

21. Emily Miles is the <u>more</u> experienced <u>actress</u> in Baker Elementary <u>School</u>.
    a   b   c   d

    Which is the mistake in the sentence above?
    - ⓐ Emily
    - ⓑ more
    - ⓒ actress
    - ⓓ School.

22. <u>That</u> is why she was <u>picked</u> for the lead part in this <u>years'</u> school <u>play</u>.
    a   b   c   d

    Which is the mistake in the sentence above?
    - ⓐ That
    - ⓑ picked
    - ⓒ years'
    - ⓓ play.

23. <u>Mr.</u> Wright had to choose <u>between</u> Emily, <u>Anita</u>, Dawn, and <u>Rachel</u>.
    a   b   c   d

    Which is the mistake in the sentence above?
    - ⓐ Mr.
    - ⓑ between
    - ⓒ Anita
    - ⓓ Rachel.

24. No one was <u>happiest</u> for Emily <u>than</u> her <u>best</u> friend, Linda <u>Williamson</u>.
    a   b   c   d

    Which is the mistake in the sentence above?
    - ⓐ happiest
    - ⓑ than
    - ⓒ best
    - ⓓ Williamson.

25. <u>Linda</u> <u>didn't</u> try out for the school play because she <u>prefers</u> to play <u>Music</u>.
    a   b   c   d

    Which is the mistake in the sentence above?
    - ⓐ Linda
    - ⓑ didn't
    - ⓒ prefers
    - ⓓ Music.

(STOP)

Unit 8 Pretest

Fill in the circle for each correct answer.

A. Choose the part of speech that is underlined in each sentence.

1. I like singing with my friends.
   (a) noun   (c) preposition
   (b) adjective (d) pronoun

2. Pang kicked the soccer ball into the net.
   (a) verb   (c) noun
   (b) pronoun (d) adverb

3. Patty painted her sculpture red.
   (a) adverb   (c) preposition
   (b) adjective (d) verb

4. The house was warm and cozy.
   (a) preposition (c) pronoun
   (b) noun   (d) adverb

B. Choose the noun in each sentence that renames the subject.

5. Reggie was the captain of the kickball team.
   (a) Reggie   (c) kickball
   (b) captain (d) team

6. Kim is a student at Russell School.
   (a) Russell (c) student
   (b) School   (d) Kim

7. The tall farmer in that field is Mr. Chang.
   (a) Mr. Chang (c) farmer
   (b) field   (d) tall

8. Mr. Ríos is the manager of a store in Willton.
   (a) manager (c) Mr. Ríos
   (b) Willton (d) store

C. Choose the correct answer to each question.

9. Which sentence has a compound subject?
   (a) Healthy teeth and bones need proper amounts of calcium.
   (b) People can get calcium by eating dairy products.
   (c) Green vegetables are also a good source of calcium.
   (d) It is important to supply your body with enough calcium each day.

10. Which sentence has a compound predicate?
   (a) My class went to visit Old Sturbridge Village last week.
   (b) There was a variety of things planned for us to do.
   (c) In the morning, we toured the village and took part in the workshops.
   (d) In the afternoon, we helped some village people with their chores.

Please go to the next page.

Fill in the circle for each correct answer.

C. Choose the correct answer to each question.

11. Which of the following is a compound sentence?
   (a) Are you looking for an interesting way to pass the time?
   (b) A good book can be entertaining, and it can challenge the mind.
   (c) A library is a great place to find just the right book.
   (d) You may be surprised at how much enjoyment you can get from a book.

12. Which of the following is a run-on sentence?
   (a) Not everyone was prepared for the big science test last Tuesday.
   (b) Only one person in the whole class got a perfect score.
   (c) Roland studied hard for the test, he wondered if he did well on it.
   (d) He smiled when the teacher handed him the test with the perfect score.

D. Choose the sentence that is written correctly.

13. (a) Lola and Rudy, helped Mrs. Fischer weed the lawn.
   (b) My grandfather, and I, are going to see a play.
   (c) Seth, and Michael, will have to set the table.
   (d) Lynnette raised her hand, and she asked a question.

14. (a) My running suit is warm, and it is comfortable.
   (b) Let's go to the circus or the fair Thursday, and Saturday.
   (c) Eli, Stephen, and Tammy like, to play basketball at the park.
   (d) Once a month Sergio and his father clean the basement, and the garage.

15. (a) I like to go to the zoo I like watching the animals.
   (b) The police officer, and her husband know my teacher.
   (c) Tara and Chris played on the beach, and later they went swimming.
   (d) Jacy, please go, to the store, and buy some milk.

16. (a) Our school library is small, and cozy and very quiet.
   (b) The food at the party was healthy, and it was delicious, too.
   (c) Lionel, and Tim, couldn't find the buried treasure.
   (d) Tao and her mother like, to paint, with watercolors.

Please go to the next page.

Fill in the circle for each correct answer.

E. Read the homographs below. Then choose the correct answer to each question.

> fast: 1. quick, speedy 2. eat little or no food
> fine: 1. of high quality 2. a sum of money paid as a result of breaking a rule
> fit: 1. suitable 2. a sudden, sharp attack

17. Which sentence uses meaning 2 of the word fine?
   (a) Koby said that he felt just fine.
   (b) It was a fine day for a picnic.
   (c) Annie had to pay a 25¢ fine.
   (d) Gordon is a fine singer.

18. Which sentence uses meaning 1 of the word fit?
   (a) Ocean water is not fit for drinking.
   (b) Sue was in a fit of anger.
   (c) Paco had a terrible coughing fit.
   (d) The boys had a fit of laughter.

19. Which sentence uses meaning 2 of the word fast?
   (a) Kimi's bike didn't go fast.
   (b) The school year seems to go by fast.
   (c) Duane's watch is fast.
   (d) We were hungry after our fast.

> rear: 1. the back part or place 2. to help grow up
> refuse: 1. say no to 2. rubbish or trash

20. Which sentence uses meaning 2 of the word refuse?
   (a) Such a feast was hard to refuse.
   (b) I refuse to talk about it any longer.
   (c) Only Jill would refuse an offer like that.
   (d) We were told to dispose of our refuse properly.

21. Which sentence uses meaning 2 of the word rear?
   (a) I stood at the rear of the line.
   (b) The rear entrance is locked.
   (c) My parents say it is both fun and tiring to rear children.
   (d) We can avoid the crowd by staying to the rear.

Please go to the next page.

Fill in the circle for each correct answer.

F. Choose the correct answer for each question.

22. Which sentence shows a likeness?
   (a) Janet says that raking the lawn is her favorite job.
   (b) Mr. Benson's house looks like Mrs. Moore's house.
   (c) Doing math homework is different from practicing the piano.
   (d) Ike felt angry when he lost his new ball in the woods.

23. Which sentence shows a difference?
   (a) Riding on a bike is different from riding in a car.
   (b) The wind grew stronger just before the big storm hit.
   (c) No one felt like playing checkers with Uncle Arthur.
   (d) Peter's new pillow is filled with soft goosedown feathers.

24. Which sentence shows a likeness?
   (a) Learning to play guitar is different from learning to play piano.
   (b) If the snow continues to fall, we'll be stuck inside for days.
   (c) Both the moon and the planet Mercury have large craters and no atmosphere.
   (d) John's new house in Springfield is unlike his old house in Warwick.

25. Which sentence shows a difference?
   (a) When the wind blows, Jackie imagines how it would feel to fly.
   (b) Mrs. Howard says that her flower garden has won many prizes.
   (c) Mr. Jacobson's tent reminded Dave of last summer's camping trip.
   (d) Jenny's opinion about the play was different from Hal's.

26. Which sentence shows a likeness?
   (a) Henry's neighborhood is similar to Cynthia's neighborhood.
   (b) The wind blew gently through the leaves in the oak tree.
   (c) We agreed that Joni's poem was unlike those she'd written before.
   (d) The boys felt like laughing when the clown slipped off the chair.

STOP

T548

Unit 8 Posttest

Fill in the circle for each correct answer.

A. Choose the part of speech that is underlined in each sentence.

1. Mrs. Akona needed some more flour.
   - (a) adverb
   - (c) verb
   - (b) noun
   - (d) preposition

2. Jean gave her bike to Tommy.
   - (a) pronoun
   - (c) adjective
   - (b) preposition
   - (d) noun

3. We tried to avoid walking on the road.
   - (a) adjective
   - (c) pronoun
   - (b) preposition
   - (d) adverb

4. Carl quickly left the room.
   - (a) verb
   - (c) noun
   - (b) adjective
   - (d) adverb

B. Choose the noun in each sentence that renames the subject.

5. Gerry became a pilot last year.
   - (a) pilot
   - (c) Gerry
   - (b) last
   - (d) year

6. Marla was the president of our class.
   - (a) our
   - (c) Marla
   - (b) class
   - (d) president

7. Whitney Houston is my favorite singer.
   - (a) favorite
   - (c) my
   - (b) singer
   - (d) Whitney Houston

8. We became friends over summer vacation.
   - (a) friends
   - (c) We
   - (b) vacation
   - (d) summer

C. Choose the correct answer to each question.

9. Which sentence has a compound subject?
   - (a) Area scouts will be conducting a paper drive on Saturday.
   - (b) Newspapers and magazines will be picked up at 8 A.M. sharp.
   - (c) You can stack them by the curb.
   - (d) Tie your papers into bundles so that they are easy to carry.

10. Which sentence has a compound predicate?
    - (a) We were happy when Aunt Joanie came to visit.
    - (b) She is always very nice to us.
    - (c) Today Aunt Joanie promised we would have a fun time.
    - (d) She took us shopping and bought us lunch.

© Silver, Burdett & Ginn Inc.

Please go to the next page.

Fill in the circle for each correct answer.

C. Choose the correct answer to each question.

11. Which of the following is a compound sentence?
    - (a) Cory's new model car was difficult to build, and it was also very fragile.
    - (b) It took him several hours just to assemble the pieces.
    - (c) It took him weeks to glue them all together.
    - (d) Cory was very pleased when he finished.

12. Which of the following is a run-on sentence?
    - (a) My brother and I got a kitten last spring.
    - (b) At first, we couldn't agree on a name for our new pet.
    - (c) We decided to ask every member of our family for advice.
    - (d) We found choosing a name to be fun, the whole family can get involved.

D. Choose the sentence that is written correctly.

13.
    - (a) Jackson, and Fred were playing tennis, but they lost the ball.
    - (b) Beth went to the mall, and did some shopping.
    - (c) A female horse is called a mare, and a baby horse is called a foal.
    - (d) Ana, Perry and Luke, will be there, and so will I.

14.
    - (a) Mindy, and I, are planning to enter the spelling bee or the debate.
    - (b) The children went to the lake, and they dove right in.
    - (c) We'd like to go, to Elaine's farm or to Lisa's bike shop.
    - (d) Ricardo is in my math class, but we have, different assignments.

15.
    - (a) As he ran to home plate, Erich fell but he was safe anyway.
    - (b) Robin and Trevor raked the lawn, this morning, and did a great job!
    - (c) Lio's brother Sid and I went bowling, but Lio stayed home.
    - (d) We can have a salad, a sandwich and, a bowl, of hot soup.

16.
    - (a) Byron smiled, and then he passed the butter to his mother.
    - (b) Darby, and Sam, are walking to the park and, Don is joining them.
    - (c) The mother duck, and all her babies waddled into the pond.
    - (d) Ben's sister, and I are going to the festival.

© Silver, Burdett & Ginn Inc.

Please go to the next page.

Fill in the circle for each correct answer.

E. Read the homographs below. Then choose the correct answer to each question.

> rash: 1. too quick, or risky 2. a breaking out of red spots
> reel: 1. a frame or spool used for winding things 2. to pull in 3. a lively dance

17. Which sentence uses meaning 1 of the word *rash*?
    - (a) Eating cherries gives me a rash.
    - (b) Pete made a rash decision and ended up going the wrong way.
    - (c) Sam's mother told him not to scratch his rash.
    - (d) Chicken pox looks like a rash.

18. Which sentence uses meaning 3 of the word *reel*?
    - (a) That is a large reel of film.
    - (b) Hilda had to reel in the fish.
    - (c) The Virginia reel has some fancy footwork.
    - (d) Stan connected the rope to the reel.

> shed: 1. a small building 2. to take something off
> sink: 1. to go beneath the surface of water 2. a basin
> slip: 1. to slide or fall by accident 2. small piece of paper

19. Which sentence uses meaning 2 of the word *shed*?
    - (a) We shed our shoes and socks and waded in the stream.
    - (b) Leave your dirty boots in the shed.
    - (c) A tool shed can be big or small.
    - (d) That shed is in need of repair.

20. Which sentence uses meaning 1 of the word *sink*?
    - (a) Mom soaks her sweaters in the sink.
    - (b) The sink is filled with dishes.
    - (c) Turn off the water or the sink will overflow.
    - (d) My model ships always sink.

21. Which sentence uses meaning 2 of the word *slip*?
    - (a) Marge handed the slip with the message to Andy.
    - (b) Don't slip on the ice.
    - (c) The waxed floor makes the cats slip when they run.
    - (d) You will slip if you are not careful.

© Silver, Burdett & Ginn Inc.

Please go to the next page.

Fill in the circle for each correct answer.

F. Choose the correct answer to each question.

22. Which sentence shows a difference?
    - (a) He says the weather in Spain is likely to be rainy next month.
    - (b) Theresa's freshly picked apples taste sweet and juicy.
    - (c) Everyone knows that this year's team is different from last year's.
    - (d) John felt like a hero as he walked up front to receive the award.

23. Which sentence shows a likeness?
    - (a) Henry and his brother Richard are both tall and thin.
    - (b) Mexico was unlike any country Pat had ever seen before.
    - (c) The man at the bus stop acted as if he'd lost something.
    - (d) The new road winds through the mountains and down to the valley.

24. Which sentence shows a difference?
    - (a) Just before her speech Pam felt like hiding under a table.
    - (b) Both Jerry and Angela usually ride their bikes to school.
    - (c) Tony was afraid to slide down the hill because it was too steep.
    - (d) Stewart's heavy winter coat is unlike his light summer jacket.

25. Which sentence shows a likeness?
    - (a) The bumpy dirt road is different from the smooth highway.
    - (b) The snow fell gently to the ground and covered the town.
    - (c) Like ostriches and other birds, turtles build nests and lay eggs.
    - (d) Everyone felt like crying at the end of the sad movie.

26. Which sentence shows a difference?
    - (a) The ice covering the lake is unlike the hot sand at the beach.
    - (b) Karen feels like singing when she hears that song on the radio.
    - (c) The man who moved the furniture was careful and patient.
    - (d) When Jan comes home to visit, people's faces light up with joy.

© Silver, Burdett & Ginn Inc.

(STOP)

T549

End-of-Year Test

Page 71

Name _____ ♦ End-of-Year Test
5END

Fill in the circle for each correct answer.

A. Choose whether each sentence is *declarative, interrogative, imperative,* or *exclamatory.*

1. What a sunny day it is!
   - (a) declarative
   - (c) imperative
   - (b) interrogative
   - (d) exclamatory ●

2. Finish cleaning your room.
   - (a) declarative
   - (c) imperative ●
   - (b) interrogative
   - (d) exclamatory

3. How do you spell that word?
   - (a) declarative
   - (c) imperative
   - (b) interrogative ●
   - (d) exclamatory

4. The air is warmer today.
   - (a) declarative ●
   - (c) imperative
   - (b) interrogative
   - (d) exclamatory

B. Choose the correct answer to each question.

5. Which abbreviation is written correctly?
   - (a) Ave. ●
   - (c) feb.
   - (b) Mr
   - (d) PM

6. Which proper noun is written correctly?
   - (a) Memorial day
   - (c) denver
   - (b) Thomas edison
   - (d) Liberty Bell ●

7. Which possessive noun is written correctly?
   - (a) partie's
   - (c) workers'es
   - (b) cats's
   - (d) children's ●

8. Which plural noun is written correctly?
   - (a) porchs
   - (c) mices
   - (b) tables ●
   - (d) giftes

C. Choose the correct answer to each question.

9. In which sentence is a linking verb underlined?
   - (a) Dan found a book in the attic.
   - (b) The book was very old. ●
   - (c) Dan read the story last night.
   - (d) Then he loaned the book to Ann.

10. In which sentence is the main verb underlined?
    - (a) Pam has bought some new yarn.
    - (b) She will make a sweater with it.
    - (c) Pam can knit many things. ●
    - (d) Her work is improving each year.

11. In which sentence is a helping verb underlined?
    - (a) Juan is practicing the piano. ●
    - (b) He has played piano for years.
    - (c) Juan will join a band someday.
    - (d) Many bands are forming in town.

12. In which sentence is the action verb underlined?
    - (a) Hal was arguing with Ralph.
    - (b) Ralph had broken Hal's model.
    - (c) Hal's aunt stopped the argument. ●
    - (d) The two boys were separated.

Please go to the next page.

World of Language ♦ Grade 5 ♦ END-OF-YEAR TEST 71

Page 72

Name _____ ♦ End-of-Year Test
5END

Fill in the circle for each correct answer.

D. Choose the correct answer to each question.

13. Which verb is in the present tense?
    - (a) baked
    - (c) will bake
    - (b) bakes ●
    - (d) has baked

14. Which verb is in the past tense?
    - (a) fixed ●
    - (c) fixing
    - (b) fixes
    - (d) will fix

15. Which verb is in the future tense?
    - (a) watches
    - (c) will watch ●
    - (b) watched
    - (d) watching

16. Which verb is in the present tense?
    - (a) will open
    - (c) had opened
    - (b) opened
    - (d) opens ●

E. Choose the form of the verb that correctly completes each sentence.

17. Rosa told the police officer that she had ____ the car before.
    - (a) saw
    - (b) see
    - (c) sees
    - (d) seen ●

18. Penny's brown puppy ____ six inches in only three months.
    - (a) grew ●
    - (b) grow
    - (c) growed
    - (d) grown

19. Rita always ____ across the playground with her friend Marcia.
    - (a) skip
    - (b) skipses
    - (c) skips ●
    - (d) skipes

20. Emily walked to the corner and mailed the letter she had ____.
    - (a) write
    - (b) written ●
    - (c) wrote
    - (d) writed

21. Amanda admitted that she ____ the last piece of pie out of the freezer.
    - (a) take
    - (b) taked
    - (c) tooked
    - (d) took ●

22. Theodore ____ to his favorite radio station after school.
    - (a) listens ●
    - (b) listen
    - (c) listenes
    - (d) listenses

23. Everyone was excited to have ____ in a big hot air balloon.
    - (a) flied
    - (b) flew
    - (c) fly
    - (d) flown ●

24. Aunt Rachel and Uncle Henry ____ to our house for dinner last Wednesday.
    - (a) come
    - (b) came ●
    - (c) comes
    - (d) coming

Please go to the next page.

World of Language ♦ Grade 5 ♦ END-OF-YEAR TEST 72

Page 73

Name _____ ♦ End-of-Year Test
5END

Fill in the circle for each correct answer.

F. Choose the pronoun that correctly completes each sentence.

25. ____ like to play catch.
    - (a) Us
    - (c) We ●
    - (b) Our
    - (d) Them

26. This red rose is ____.
    - (a) her
    - (c) me
    - (b) mine ●
    - (d) him

27. I read ____ book report.
    - (a) her ●
    - (c) them
    - (b) me
    - (d) we

28. Sandy gave ____ the key.
    - (a) they
    - (c) he
    - (b) ours
    - (d) us ●

29. Owen painted ____ fence.
    - (a) their ●
    - (c) them
    - (b) they
    - (d) mine

G. Choose the correct contraction for the underlined words.

30. I will
    - (a) Ill'
    - (c) Il'l
    - (b) I'll ●
    - (d) 'Ill

31. they are
    - (a) they'e
    - (c) the'yre
    - (b) theyre'
    - (d) they're ●

32. she would
    - (a) shed'
    - (c) she'd ●
    - (b) sh'ed
    - (d) s'hed

33. you have
    - (a) yo'uve
    - (c) youve'
    - (b) you've ●
    - (d) youv'e

34. they would
    - (a) they'd ●
    - (c) the'yd
    - (b) the'yd
    - (d) theyd'

H. Choose the predicate adjective in each sentence.

35. The roses in Aunt Pat's flower garden smell lovely.
    - (a) roses
    - (b) flower
    - (c) garden
    - (d) lovely ●

36. The teacher was proud of the students' performance on the math test.
    - (a) teacher
    - (b) proud ●
    - (c) students'
    - (d) math

37. Marta felt better after taking a swim in the lake.
    - (a) better ●
    - (b) after
    - (c) swim
    - (d) lake

38. The last inning of the baseball game seemed endless.
    - (a) last
    - (b) baseball
    - (c) game
    - (d) endless ●

Please go to the next page.

World of Language ♦ Grade 5 ♦ END-OF-YEAR TEST 73

Page 74

Name _____ ♦ End-of-Year Test
5END

Fill in the circle for each correct answer.

I. Choose the correct form of the adjective or adverb to complete each sentence.

39. Father's fresh tomatoes are ____ than Mother's canned tomatoes.
    - (a) sweet
    - (b) sweeter ●
    - (c) sweetest
    - (d) more sweet

40. The ocean waves pounded ____ against the big gray rocks.
    - (a) furious
    - (b) more furious
    - (c) furiously ●
    - (d) most furious

41. Theresa's bicycle is the ____ in the entire neighborhood.
    - (a) faster
    - (b) fastest ●
    - (c) more fast
    - (d) most fast

42. Sarah can solve math problems ____ than her brother Ronny can.
    - (a) quick
    - (b) quickly
    - (c) more quickly ●
    - (d) most quickly

43. The sun is ____ today than it was yesterday.
    - (a) brighter ●
    - (b) more bright
    - (c) brightest
    - (d) bright

J. Choose the adverb that describes each underlined adverb or adjective.

44. The weather is definitely hotter this summer than it was last summer.
    - (a) weather
    - (b) definitely ●
    - (c) than
    - (d) last

45. The pretty painting was very carefully done by my older brother.
    - (a) pretty
    - (b) very ●
    - (c) my
    - (d) older

46. The tired farmer steers her plow through the fields quite slowly.
    - (a) tired
    - (b) her
    - (c) through
    - (d) quite ●

47. Ruth is extremely bored with the new project she started last month.
    - (a) extremely ●
    - (b) new
    - (c) started
    - (d) last

48. Maple sugar farms are certainly common in parts of northern New England.
    - (a) Maple
    - (b) certainly ●
    - (c) parts
    - (d) northern

Please go to the next page.

World of Language ♦ Grade 5 ♦ END-OF-YEAR TEST 74

End-of-Year Test *(continued)*

Fill in the circle for each correct answer.

K. Choose the correct answer to each question.

49. In which sentence should you use <u>loud</u> and not <u>loudly</u>?
   - ⓐ They heard a ____ noise.
   - ⓑ The young man speaks ____.
   - ⓒ The angry dog barked ____.
   - ⓓ The bell rings ____ at noon.

52. In which sentence should you use <u>proudly</u> and not <u>proud</u>?
   - ⓐ The band marches ____.
   - ⓑ They were ____ of the award.
   - ⓒ The ____ parents looked on.
   - ⓓ We are all ____ of you.

50. In which sentence should you use <u>good</u> and not <u>well</u>?
   - ⓐ She catches the ball ____.
   - ⓑ Alan had a ____ vacation.
   - ⓒ How ____ did you do?
   - ⓓ We work ____ together.

53. In which sentence should you use <u>terrible</u> and not <u>terribly</u>?
   - ⓐ She had a ____ time.
   - ⓑ The story ended ____.
   - ⓒ The musician plays ____.
   - ⓓ Peter cooks food ____.

51. In which sentence should you use <u>slightly</u> and not <u>slight</u>?
   - ⓐ I have a ____ cold.
   - ⓑ A ____ breeze blew that day.
   - ⓒ The towel is ____ wet.
   - ⓓ The road has a ____ curve in it.

L. Choose whether the underlined part of each sentence is a *preposition*, *prepositional phrase*, *object of the preposition*, or *adverb*.

54. Flowers bloom in the <u>spring</u>.
   - ⓐ preposition
   - ⓑ prepositional phrase
   - ⓒ object of the preposition
   - ⓓ adverb

56. The ball is <u>in</u> the closet.
   - ⓐ preposition
   - ⓑ prepositional phrase
   - ⓒ object of the preposition
   - ⓓ adverb

55. The young twins ran <u>inside</u>.
   - ⓐ preposition
   - ⓑ prepositional phrase
   - ⓒ object of the preposition
   - ⓓ adverb

57. Mel took a picture <u>of the team</u>.
   - ⓐ preposition
   - ⓑ prepositional phrase
   - ⓒ object of the preposition
   - ⓓ adverb

Please go to the next page.

Fill in the circle for each correct answer.

M. Choose the correct answer to each question.

58. Which sentence has a compound subject?
   - ⓐ Josh and his friends like to go swimming in the lake.
   - ⓑ The children ate their lunch in the treehouse.
   - ⓒ Ali's house is being repaired and completely painted.
   - ⓓ We like to go camping and hiking in the summer.

59. Which of the following is a run-on sentence?
   - ⓐ When I go fishing with Zack, we always talk about trout and bait.
   - ⓑ Toshi draws animals and plants very well.
   - ⓒ Since it was raining we sat on the porch the storm was fun.
   - ⓓ Maria and Tony are going to the movies tonight.

60. Which sentence has a compound predicate?
   - ⓐ Walter likes theaters much better than museums.
   - ⓑ Billy and Linda collected all the money for our class picnic.
   - ⓒ The hot sand and the bright sun added to a perfect summer day.
   - ⓓ Sarah Cheever wrote and arranged all the songs on the record.

61. Which of the following is a compound sentence?
   - ⓐ How many elephants and giraffes are in the zoo?
   - ⓑ I like to sing and play the guitar.
   - ⓒ Ben and Helen played tennis, and then they went home.
   - ⓓ Let's go to the store and buy more fruit.

62. Which of the following is a run-on sentence?
   - ⓐ The campers began their hike along the shores of Lake Arnold.
   - ⓑ Patty went to the beach the water was chilly and the sky was blue.
   - ⓒ Everyone agrees that Paul's baby brother has a cute smile.
   - ⓓ Jane doesn't like camping or hiking because she's afraid of snakes.

Please go to the next page.

Fill in the circle for each correct answer.

N. Read the dictionary entries. Then choose the correct answer to each question.

> **vol ume** (väl´yoom) *n.* **1.** A book. **2.** One of the books in a set of books. **3.** The amount of space inside something. **4.** Loudness of sound.
>
> **vol un tar y** (väl´ən ter´ē) *adj.* **1.** Done or given of one's own free will; by choice. **2.** Controlled by one's mind or will.

63. What part of speech is the word *voluntary*?
   - ⓐ noun
   - ⓑ adjective
   - ⓒ adverb
   - ⓓ verb

65. Which definition of the word *volume* is used in this sentence?

   Turn down the volume on your radio.
   - ⓐ part of a set of books
   - ⓑ given freely
   - ⓒ loudness of sound
   - ⓓ space inside something

64. What is one definition of the word *volume*?
   - ⓐ a book
   - ⓑ choice
   - ⓒ will
   - ⓓ mind

> **a void** (ə void´) *v.* **1.** To keep away from; get out of the way of. **2.** To keep from happening.
>
> **a wait** (ə wāt´) *v.* **1.** To wait for; expect. **2.** To be ready for; be in store for.

66. What part of speech is the word *await*?
   - ⓐ noun
   - ⓑ adverb
   - ⓒ adjective
   - ⓓ verb

67. What is one definition of the word *avoid*?
   - ⓐ to wait for
   - ⓑ to expect
   - ⓒ to be ready
   - ⓓ to keep away from

Please go to the next page.

Fill in the circle for each correct answer.

O. Proofread the sentences. Each sentence contains a mistake. Choose the part of each sentence that has the mistake.

68. <u>juan</u> learned a lot about <u>turtles</u> while <u>working</u> on his science <u>report</u>.
    a   b   c   d

   Which is the mistake in the above sentence?
   - ⓐ juan
   - ⓑ turtles
   - ⓒ working
   - ⓓ report

69. <u>He</u> discovered that <u>some</u> turtles have <u>flipperes</u> to help them swim in <u>water</u>.
    a   b   c   d

   Which is the mistake in the above sentence?
   - ⓐ He
   - ⓑ some
   - ⓒ flipperes
   - ⓓ water.

70. <u>Desert</u> tortoises use <u>they</u> short legs to <u>walk</u> across dry, rough <u>ground</u>.
    a   b   c   d

   Which is the mistake in the above sentence?
   - ⓐ Desert
   - ⓑ they
   - ⓒ walk
   - ⓓ ground.

71. The <u>larger</u> turtle in the <u>world</u> can <u>grow</u> up to eight feet <u>long</u>.
    a   b   c   d

   Which is the mistake in the above sentence?
   - ⓐ larger
   - ⓑ world
   - ⓒ grow
   - ⓓ long.

72. <u>Green</u> turtles <u>feed</u> mainly on <u>plants,</u> and map turtles eat small <u>fish</u>
    a   b   c   d

   Which is the mistake in the above sentence?
   - ⓐ Green
   - ⓑ feed
   - ⓒ plants,
   - ⓓ fish

T551

Unit 1 Picture Prompt Writing Samples

Name _____

Unit 1
Writing Sample 1

The picture below shows a girl on a fishing trip with her grandfather. Think about something you enjoyed doing with one of your parents or grandparents. Write a story about what you did. Tell where you were and what happened.

WRITING HINTS

• Write a clear beginning and ending.
• Tell the events in order.
• Combine sentences to avoid repeating words.

World of Language ♦ Grade 5 ♦ UNIT 1 WRITING SAMPLE   81

Name _____

Unit 1
Writing Sample 2

The picture below shows a ship returning from a long journey. The sailors on deck are tired but happy. Pretend you are one of the sailors. Write a story about what happened on your journey.

WRITING HINTS

• Write a clear beginning and ending.
• Tell the events in order.
• Combine sentences to avoid repeating words.

World of Language ♦ Grade 5 ♦ UNIT 1 WRITING SAMPLE   82

Unit 2 Picture Prompt Writing Samples

Name _____

Unit 2
Writing Sample 1

The picture below shows a girl helping her brother learn to ride a bike. Think of a time when you taught someone how to do something. Explain what you taught. What did you tell the person to do? What steps did you teach?

WRITING HINTS

• Imagine yourself doing each step.
• Describe each step clearly and fully.
• Put each step in the proper order.

World of Language ♦ Grade 5 ♦ UNIT 2 WRITING SAMPLE   83

Name _____

Unit 2
Writing Sample 2

The picture below shows a boy and a girl. They are building a model plane from a kit. Write a paragraph telling about something that you have made or built yourself. What steps were involved? Explain what you made and how you made it.

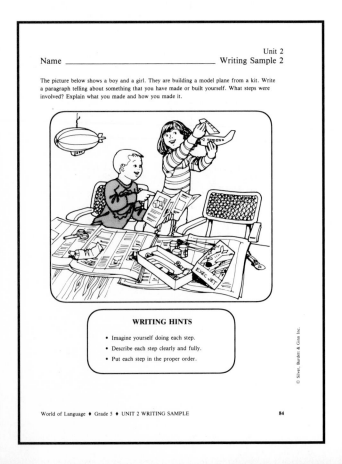

WRITING HINTS

• Imagine yourself doing each step.
• Describe each step clearly and fully.
• Put each step in the proper order.

World of Language ♦ Grade 5 ♦ UNIT 2 WRITING SAMPLE   84

Unit 3 Picture Prompt Writing Samples

Name _____

Unit 3
Writing Sample 1

The picture below shows the old man who lives in the Great Smoky Mountains. His breath makes the mists and clouds that drift over the mountains. His smile makes the sun shine, and his tears make the rain. Make up a story about the Smoky Mountain Man. What unusual and funny things can he do that no one else can?

WRITING HINTS

* Write a clear beginning and ending.
* Exaggerate the details.
* Use your imagination.

© Silver, Burdett & Ginn Inc.

Name _____

Unit 3
Writing Sample 2

The picture below shows Windlass, the daughter of the North Wind. She is collecting stars from the night sky. Tell a tall tale about Windlass. Tell why she collects the stars and what she does with them.

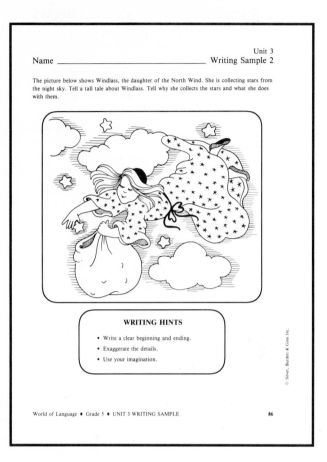

WRITING HINTS

* Write a clear beginning and ending.
* Exaggerate the details.
* Use your imagination.

© Silver, Burdett & Ginn Inc.

Unit 4 Picture Prompt Writing Samples

Name _____

Unit 4
Writing Sample 1

The picture below shows two children discussing a movie they have just seen. One liked the movie very much, but the other did not. What is the best movie you have ever seen? Write a paragraph explaining why that movie is your favorite.

WRITING HINTS

* Write a topic sentence.
* Give reasons for your opinion.
* Explain each reason clearly.

© Silver, Burdett & Ginn Inc.

Name _____

Unit 4
Writing Sample 2

Do you agree or disagree that exploring outer space is important? Write a paragraph persuading your classmates to agree with your opinion. Explain the reasons for your opinion.

WRITING HINTS

* Write a topic sentence.
* Give reasons for your opinion.
* Explain each reason clearly.

© Silver, Burdett & Ginn Inc.

Unit 5 Picture Prompt Writing Samples

The picture below shows two best friends watching a basketball game. Write a paragraph describing your best friend. What does your friend look like? Is your friend shy or funny or smart? How long have you known each other? Tell what makes your friend a special person.

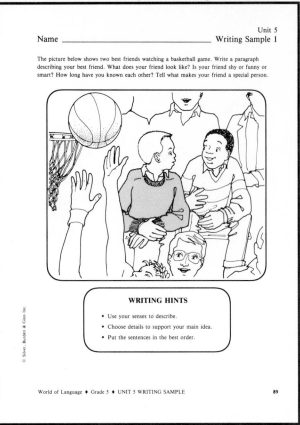

WRITING HINTS

- Use your senses to describe.
- Choose details to support your main idea.
- Put the sentences in the best order.

© Silver, Burdett & Ginn Inc.

The picture below shows a girl talking to the town librarian. Write a paragraph describing someone you have met. Do you remember your first impression of this person? What do you like about this person? Tell how he or she looks and talks.

WRITING HINTS

- Use your senses to describe.
- Choose details to support your main idea.
- Put the sentences in the best order.

© Silver, Burdett & Ginn Inc.

Unit 6 Picture Prompt Writing Samples

Read the outline below and examine the picture next to it. Write a two-paragraph report about the walrus based on the outline and picture.

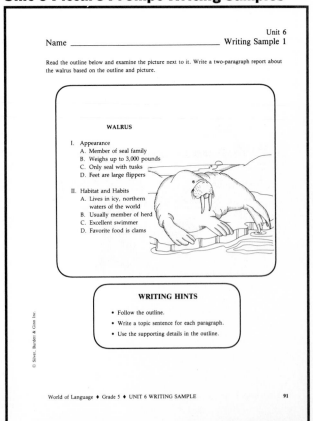

WALRUS

I. Appearance
  A. Member of seal family
  B. Weighs up to 3,000 pounds
  C. Only seal with tusks
  D. Feet are large flippers

II. Habitat and Habits
  A. Lives in icy, northern waters of the world
  B. Usually member of herd
  C. Excellent swimmer
  D. Favorite food is clams

WRITING HINTS

- Follow the outline.
- Write a topic sentence for each paragraph.
- Use the supporting details in the outline.

© Silver, Burdett & Ginn Inc.

Read the outline below and examine the picture next to it. Write a two-paragraph report about the Viking long ship based on the outline and picture.

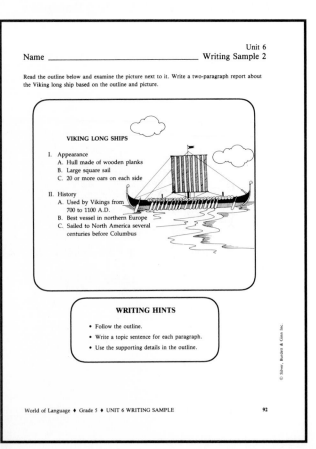

VIKING LONG SHIPS

I. Appearance
  A. Hull made of wooden planks
  B. Large square sail
  C. 20 or more oars on each side

II. History
  A. Used by Vikings from 700 to 1100 A.D.
  B. Best vessel in northern Europe
  C. Sailed to North America several centuries before Columbus

WRITING HINTS

- Follow the outline.
- Write a topic sentence for each paragraph.
- Use the supporting details in the outline.

© Silver, Burdett & Ginn Inc.

T554

Unit 7 Picture Prompt Writing Samples

Name _____
Unit 7
Writing Sample 1

The picture below shows a neighborhood. Every neighborhood has its own sounds. What are the sounds in your neighborhood? Write a poem about your neighborhood's sounds. Give lifelike qualities to things that are not alive. Your poem does not have to rhyme.

WRITING HINTS

- Think about what you want to say.
- Try to use repetition in your poem.
- Arrange the lines in order.

Name _____
Unit 7
Writing Sample 2

The picture below shows a spring day in a city park. Every season has its own special sounds. What are the sounds of spring that you particularly notice? Write a poem about the sounds of spring. Give lifelike qualities to things that are not alive. Your poem does not have to rhyme.

WRITING HINTS

- Think about what you want to say.
- Try to use repetition in your poem.
- Arrange the lines in order.

Unit 8 Picture Prompt Writing Samples

Name _____
Unit 8
Writing Sample 1

The picture below shows two birds. In which ways are they alike? Is there anything similar that you notice about them? Write a paragraph that compares the two birds.

WRITING HINTS

- Begin with a topic sentence.
- Point out likenesses.
- Use your powers of observation.

Name _____
Unit 8
Writing Sample 2

The pictures below show two bodies of water, an ocean and a lake. In which ways are they alike? Do you notice anything similar about them? Write a paragraph that compares oceans and lakes.

WRITING HINTS

- Begin with a topic sentence.
- Point out likenesses.
- Use your powers of observation.

ISBN 0–382–10674–1

B C D E F G H I J—VH—96 95 94 93 92 91 **90 89**